# Nineteenth-Century Literature Criticism

# Guide to Gale Literary Criticism Series

**When you need to review criticism of literary works, these are the Gale series to use:**

| If the author's death date is: | You should turn to: |
| --- | --- |
| After Dec. 31, 1959 (or author is still living) | **CONTEMPORARY LITERARY CRITICISM**<br>for example: Jorge Luis Borges, Anthony Burgess, William Faulkner, Mary Gordon, Ernest Hemingway, Iris Murdoch |
| 1900 through 1959 | **TWENTIETH-CENTURY LITERARY CRITICISM**<br>for example: Willa Cather, F. Scott Fitzgerald, Henry James, Mark Twain, Virginia Woolf |
| 1800 through 1899 | **NINETEENTH-CENTURY LITERATURE CRITICISM**<br>for example: Fedor Dostoevski, George Sand, Gerard Manley Hopkins, Emily Dickinson |
| 1400 through 1799 | **LITERATURE CRITICISM FROM 1400 TO 1800**<br>**(excluding Shakespeare)**<br>for example: Anne Bradstreet, Pierre Corneille, Daniel Defoe, Alexander Pope, Jonathan Swift, Phillis Wheatley |
| | **SHAKESPEAREAN CRITICISM**<br>Shakespeare plays and poetry |

---

**Gale also publishes related criticism series:**

**CONTEMPORARY ISSUES CRITICISM**

Presents criticism on contemporary authors writing on current issues. Topics covered include the social sciences, philosophy, economics, natural science, law, and related areas.

**CHILDREN'S LITERATURE REVIEW**

Covers authors of all eras. Presents criticism on authors and author/illustrators who write for the preschool to junior-high audience.

Volume 5

# Nineteenth-Century Literature Criticism

Excerpts from Criticism of the
Works of Novelists, Poets, Playwrights,
Short Story Writers, and Other Creative Writers
Who Died between 1800 and 1900,
from the First Published Critical
Appraisals to Current Evaluations

Laurie Lanzen Harris
Sheila Fitzgerald
Editors

Emily Wade Barrett
Associate Editor

 *Gale Research Inc.* • DETROIT • LONDON

# STAFF

Laurie Lanzen Harris, *Senior Editor*

Sheila Fitzgerald, *Editor*

Emily Wade Barrett, *Associate Editor*

Cherie D. Abbey, Jelena Obradovic Kronick, Patricia Askie Mackmiller,
Janet S. Mullane, Gail Ann Schulte, *Assistant Editors*

Sharon K. Hall and Anna C. Wallbillich, *Contributing Editors*

Robert J. Elster, *Production Supervisor*

Lizbeth A. Purdy, *Production Coordinator*

Denise Michlewicz, *Assistant Production Coordinator*

Eric F. Berger, Michael S. Corey, Paula J. DiSante, Maureen Duffy,
Amy Marcaccio, Yvonne Huette Robinson, *Editorial Assistants*

Karen Rae Forsyth, *Research Coordinator*

Jeannine Schiffman Davidson, *Assistant Research Coordinator*

Victoria B. Cariappa, Robert J. Hill, James A. MacEachern,
Leslie Kyle Schell, Valerie J. Webster, *Research Assistants*

Linda Marcella Pugliese, *Manuscript Coordinator*

Donna D. Craft, *Assistant Manuscript Coordinator*

Colleen M. Crane, Maureen A. Puhl, Rosetta Irene Simms Carr, *Manuscript Assistants*

L. Elizabeth Hardin, *Permissions Supervisor*
Filomena Sgambati, *Permissions Coordinator*
Janice M. Mach, *Assistant Permissions Coordinator*
Patricia A. Seefelt, *Assistant Permissions Coordinator, Illustrations*
Susan D. Nobles, *Senior Permissions Assistant*
Margaret A. Chamberlain, *Permissions Assistant*
Virgie T. Leavens, *Permissions Clerk*
Margaret Mary Missar, Audrey B. Wharton, *Photo Research*

The paper used in this publication meets the minimum requirements
of American National Standard for Information Sciences—Permanence
Paper for Printed Library Materials, ANSI Z39.48-1984. ∞™

10 9 8 7 6 5 4

Copyright © 1984 by Gale Research Company

Library of Congress Catalog Card Number 81-6943
ISBN 0-8103-5805-0
ISSN 0732-1864

Printed in the United States of America.
Published simultaneously in the United Kingdom
by Gale Research International Limited
(An affiliated company of Gale Research Inc.)

# CONTENTS

# PREFACE

The nineteenth century was a time of tremendous growth in human endeavor: in science, in social history, and particularly in literature. The era saw the development of the novel, witnessed radical changes from classicism to romanticism to realism, and contained intellectual and artistic ideas that continue to inspire authors of our own century. The importance of the writers of the nineteenth century is twofold, for they provide insight into their own time as well as into the universal nature of human experience.

The literary criticism of an era can also give us insight into the moral and intellectual atmosphere of the past, for the criteria by which a work of art is judged reflect current philosophical and social attitudes. Literary criticism takes many forms: the traditional essay, the book or play review, even the parodic poem. Criticism can also be of several kinds: normative, descriptive, interpretive, textual, appreciative, generic. Collectively, the range of critical response helps us to understand a work of art, an author, an era.

## The Scope of the Work

The success of Gale's two current literary series, *Contemporary Literary Criticism (CLC)* and *Twentieth-Century Literary Criticism (TCLC)*, which excerpt criticism of creative writing from the twentieth century, suggested an equivalent need among students and teachers of literature of the nineteenth century. Moreover, since the critical analysis of this literature spans almost two hundred years, a vast amount of critical material confronts the student.

*Nineteenth-Century Literature Criticism (NCLC)* presents significant passages from published criticism on authors who died between 1800 and 1900. The author list for each volume of *NCLC* is carefully compiled to represent a variety of genres and nationalities and to cover authors who are currently regarded as the most important writers of an era as well as those whose contribution to literature and literary history is significant. The truly great writers are rare, and in the intervals between them lesser but genuine artists, as well as writers who enjoyed immense popularity in their own time and in their own countries, are important to the study of nineteenth-century literature. The length of each author's entry is intended to represent the author's critical reception in English. Articles and books that have not been translated into English are excluded. Each author entry represents a historical overview of the critical response to the author's work: early criticism is presented to indicate initial responses, later selections represent any rise or decline in the author's literary reputation. We have also attempted to identify and include excerpts from the seminal essays on each author, and to include recent critical comment providing modern perspectives on the writer. Thus, *NCLC* is designed to serve as an introduction for the student of nineteenth-century literature to the authors of that period and to the most significant commentators on these authors.

*NCLC* entries are intended to be definitive overviews. Approximately 20 authors are included in each 600-page volume, compared with about 75 authors in a *CLC* volume of similar size. Because of the great quantity of critical material available on many authors, and because of the resurgence of criticism generated by events such as an author's centennial or anniversary celebration, the republication of an author's works, or publication of a newly translated work or volume of letters, an author may appear more than once.

## The Organization of the Book

An author section consists of the following elements: author heading, biocritical introduction, principal works, excerpts of criticism (each followed by a citation), and an annotated bibliography of additional reading.

- The *author heading* consists of the author's full name, followed by birth and death dates. The unbracketed portion of the name denotes the form under which the author most commonly wrote. If an author wrote consistently under a pseudonym, the pseudonym will be listed in the author heading and the real name given in parentheses on the first line of the biocritical introduction. Also located at the beginning of the biocritical introduction are any name variations under which an author wrote, including transliterated forms for authors whose languages use nonroman alphabets. Uncertainty as to a birth or death date is indicated by a question mark.

- The *biocritical introduction* contains biographical and other background information that elucidates the author's creative output.

- The list of *principal works* is chronological by date of first book publication and identifies genres. In those instances where the first publication was in other than the English language, the title and date of the first English-language edition is given in brackets. Unless otherwise indicated, dramas are dated by the first performance, rather than first publication.

- *Criticism* is arranged chronologically in each author section to provide a perspective on any changes in critical evaluation over the years. In the text of each author entry, titles by the author are printed in boldface type. This allows the reader to ascertain without difficulty the works discussed. For purposes of easier identification, the critic's name and the publication date of the essay are given at the beginning of each piece of criticism. Unsigned criticism is preceded by the title of the journal in which it appeared. For an anonymous essay later attributed to a critic, the critic's name appears in brackets in the heading and in the citation.

- Beginning with Volume 4, important critical essays will be prefaced with *explanatory notes* as an additional aid to students using *NCLC*. The explanatory notes will provide several types of useful information, including: the reputation of the critic, the importance of a work of criticism, the specific approach of the critic (biographical, psychoanalytic, structuralist, etc.), and the growth of critical controversy or changes in critical trends regarding an author's work. In many cases, these notes will include a cross-reference to related criticism in the author's entry.

- A complete *bibliographical citation* designed to facilitate the location of the original essay or book follows each piece of criticism. An asterisk (*) at the end of the citation indicates that the essay is on more than one author.

- The *annotated bibliography* appearing at the end of each author section suggests further reading on the author. In some cases it includes essays for which the editors could not obtain reprint rights. An asterisk (*) at the end of a citation indicates that the essay is on more than one author.

Each volume of *NCLC* includes a cumulative index to critics. Under each critic's name are listed the authors on whom the critic has written and the volume and page where the criticism appears. *NCLC* also includes a cumulative index to authors with the volume number in which the author appears, as well as a cumulative nationality index to authors. Authors are listed alphabetically by nationality, followed by the volume number in which they appear.

An appendix is included which lists the sources from which material in the volume is reprinted. It does not, however, list every book or periodical consulted for the volume.

### Acknowledgments

No work of this scope can be accomplished without the cooperation of many people. The editors especially wish to thank the copyright holders of the excerpts included in this volume, the permissions managers of the book and magazine publishing companies for assisting us in securing reprint rights, and the staffs of the Detroit Public Library, University of Michigan Library, and Wayne State University Library for making their resources available to us. We are also grateful to Jeri Yaryan for her assistance with copyright research and Norma J. Merry for her editorial assistance.

### Suggestions Are Welcome

The editors welcome the comments and suggestions of readers to expand the coverage and enhance the usefulness of the series.

# Authors to Appear in Future Volumes

About, Edmond François 1828-1885
Ainsworth, William Harrison 1805-1882
Aksakov, Konstantin 1817-1860
Alcott, Louisa May 1832-1888
Aleardi, Aleadro 1812-1878
Alecsandri, Vasile 1821-1890
Alencar, José 1829-1877
Alfieri, Vittorio 1749-1803
Alger, Horatio 1834-1899
Almquist, Carl Jonas Love 1793-1866
Alsop, Richard 1761-1815
Altimirano, Ignacio Manuel 1834-1893
Alvarenga, Manuel Inâcio da Silva
  1749-1814
Alvares de Azevedo, Manuel Antoniô
  1831-1852
Andersen, Hans Christian 1805-1875
Arany, János 1817-1882
Arène, Paul 1843-1893
Arjona de Cubas, Manuel Mariá de
  1771-1820
Arnim, Bettina von 1785-1859
Arnold, Matthew 1822-1888
Ascasubi, Hilario 1807-1875
Atterbom, Per Daniel Amadeus
  1790-1855
Auerbach, Berthold 1812-1882
Augier, Guillaume V.E. 1820-1889
Azevedo, Guilherme de 1839-1882
Bakin (pseud. of Takizawa Okikani)
  1767-1848
Banville, Théodore de 1823-1891
Barnes, William 1801-1886
Baudelaire, Charles Pierre 1821-1867
Beattie, James 1735-1803
Beckford, William 1760-1844
Bécquer, Gustavo Adolfo 1836-1870
Bentham, Jeremy 1748-1832
Béranger, Jean-Pierre de 1780-1857
Berchet, Giovanni 1783-1851
Black, William 1841-1898
Blair, Hugh 1718-1800
Blake, William 1757-1827
Blicher, Steen Steensen 1782-1848
Bocage, Manuel Maria Barbosa du
  1765-1805
Boratynsky, Yevgeny 1800-1844
Borel, Pétrus 1809-1859
Boreman, Yokutiel 1825-1890
Borrow, George 1803-1881
Botev, Hristo 1778-1842
Brackenridge, Hugh Henry 1748-1816
Bremer, Fredrika 1801-1865
Brinckman, John 1814-1870
Brontë, Emily 1812-1848
Brown, Charles Brockden 1777-1810
Browning, Robert 1812-1889
Bryant, William Cullen 1794-1878
Büchner, Georg 1813-1837
Burney, Fanny 1752-1840

Campbell, James Edwin 1867-1895
Campbell, Thomas 1777-1844
Carlyle, Thomas 1795-1881
Castelo Branco, Camilo 1825-1890
Channing, William Ellery 1780-1842
Clare, John 1793-1864
Claudius, Matthais 1740-1815
Clough, Arthur Hugh 1819-1861
Cobbett, William 1762-1835
Colenso, John William 1814-1883
Coleridge, Hartley 1796-1849
Coleridge, Samuel T. 1772-1834
Collett, Camilla 1813-1895
Conrad, Robert T. 1810-1858
Conscience, Hendrik 1812-1883
Constant, Benjamin 1767-1830
Corbière, Edouard 1845-1875
Cowper, William 1731-1800
Crabbe, George 1754-1832
Crawford, Isabella Valancy 1850-1886
Deschamps, Emile 1791-1871
Dickinson, Emily 1830-1886
Dinsmoor, Robert 1757-1836
Dumas, Alexandre (père) 1802-1870
Dumas, Alexandre (fils) 1824-1895
Du Maurier, George 1834-1896
Dwight, Timothy 1752-1817
Echeverria, Esteban 1805-1851
Eichendorff, Joseph von 1788-1857
Eminescy, Mihai 1850-1889
Espronceda, José 1808-1842
Ettinger, Solomon 1799-1855
Euchel, Issac 1756-1804
Ferguson, Samuel 1810-1886
Fernandez de Lizardi, José Joaquín
  1776-1827
Fernandez de Moratin, Leandro
  1760-1828
Fet, Afanasy 1820-1892
Feuillet, Octave 1821-1890
Fitzgerald, Edward 1809-1883
Fontane, Theodor 1819-1898
Forster, John 1812-1876
Foscolo, Ugo 1778-1827
Frederic, Harold 1856-1898
Freytag, Gustav 1816-1895
Ganivet, Angel 1865-1898
Garrett, Almeida 1799-1854
Garshin, Vsevolod Mikhaylovich
  1855-1888
Gezelle, Guido 1830-1899
Ghálib, Asadullah Khan 1797-1869
Godwin, William 1756-1836
Goldschmidt, Meir Aron 1819-1887
Gonçalves Dias, Antonio 1823-1864
Goncourt, Edmond 1822-1896
Goncourt, Jules 1830-1870
Griboyedov, Aleksander Sergeyevich
  1795-1829

Grigor'yev, Appolon Aleksandrovich
  1822-1864
Groth, Klaus 1819-1899
Grün, Anastasius (pseud. of Anton
  Alexander Graf von Auersperg)
  1806-1876
Guerrazzi, Francesco Domenico
  1804-1873
Ha-Kohen, Shalom 1772-1845
Halleck, Fitz-Greene 1790-1867
Harris, George Washington 1814-1869
Hayne, Paul Hamilton 1830-1886
Hazlitt, William 1778-1830
Hebbel, Christian Friedrich 1813-1863
Hebel, Johann Peter 1760-1826
Hegel, Georg Wilhelm Friedrich
  1770-1831
Herculano, Alexandre 1810-1866
Herder, Johann Gottfried 1744-1803
Hernandez, José 1834-1886
Hertz, Henrik 1798-1870
Herzen, Alexander Ivanovich 1812-1870
Hoffman, Charles Fenno 1806-1884
Hölderlin, Friedrich 1770-1843
Holmes, Oliver Wendell 1809-1894
Hood, Thomas 1799-1845
Hopkins, Gerard Manley 1844-1889
Hughes, Thomas 1822-1896
Imlay, Gilbert 1754?-1828?
Irwin, Thomas Caulfield 1823-1892
Issacs, Jorge 1837-1895
Jacobsen, Jens Peter 1847-1885
Jean Paul (pseud. of Johann
  Paul Friedrich Richter) 1763-1825
Jippensha, Ikku 1765-1831
Keats, John 1795-1821
Keble, John 1792-1866
Kierkegaard, Søren 1813-1855
Kinglake, Alexander W. 1809-1891
Kingsley, Charles 1819-1875
Kivi, Alexis 1834-1872
Klopstock, Friedrich Gottlieb 1724-1803
Kotzebue, August von 1761-1819
Krasicki, Ignacy 1735-1801
Kraszewski, Josef Ignacy 1812-1887
Kreutzwald, Friedrich Reinhold
  1803-1882
Lamartine, Alphonse 1790-1869
Lamb, Charles 1775-1834
Lampman, Archibald 1861-1899
Landon, Letitia Elizabeth 1802-1838
Landor, Walter Savage 1775-1864
Lanier, Sidney 1842-1881
Lautréamont (pseud. of Isodore Ducasse)
  1846-1870
Lebensohn, Micah Joseph 1828-1852
Leconte de Lisle, Charles-Marie-René
  1818-1894
Le Fanu, Joseph Sheridan 1814-1873
Lenau, Nikolaus 1802-1850

Leontyev, Konstantin 1831-1891
Leopardi, Giacoma 1798-1837
Leskov, Nikolai 1831-1895
Lever, Charles James 1806-1872
Lewes, George Henry 1817-1878
Lewis, Matthew Gregory 1775-1810
Leyden, John 1775-1811
Longstreet, Augustus Baldwin 1790-1870
Lover, Samuel 1797-1868
Macedo, Joaquim Manuel de 1820-1882
Mácha, Karel Hynek 1810-1836
Mackenzie, Henry 1745-1831
Mangan, James Clarence 1803-1849
Marii, José 1853-1895
Markovic, Sv. 1846-1875
Martinez de La Rosa, Francisco 1787-1862
Mathews, Cornelius 1817-1889
Maturin, Charles Robert 1780-1824
McCulloch, Thomas 1776-1843
Merimée, Prosper 1803-1870
Merriman, Brian 1747-1805
Meyer, Conrad Ferdinand 1825-1898
Montagu, Elizabeth 1720-1800
Montgomery, James 1771-1854
Moodie, Susanna 1803-1885
Moore, Thomas 1779-1852
Mörike, Eduard 1804-1875
Morton, Sarah Wentworth 1759-1846
Müller, Friedrich 1749-1825
Murger, Henri 1822-1861
Musset, Alfred de 1810-1857
Nekrasov, Nikolai 1821-1877
Neruda, Jan 1834-1891
Nestroy, Johann 1801-1862
Newman, John Henry 1801-1890
Niccolini, Giambattista 1782-1861
Nievo, Ippolito 1831-1861
Nodier, Charles 1780-1844
Novalis (pseud. of Friedrich von Hardenberg) 1772-1801
Obradovíc, Dositej 1742-1811
Oehlenschläger, Adam 1779-1850
Oliphant, Margaret 1828-1897
O'Neddy, Philothée (pseud. of Théophile Dondey) 1811-1875
O'Shaughnessy, Arthur William Edgar 1844-1881

Ostrovsky, Alexander 1823-1886
Paine, Thomas 1737-1809
Parkman, Francis 1823-1893
Pater, Walter 1839-1894
Patmore, Coventry Kersey Dighton 1823-1896
Peacock, Thomas Love 1785-1866
Perk, Jacques 1859-1881
Pisemsky, Alexey F. 1820-1881
Pompéia, Raul D'Avila 1863-1895
Popovíc, Jovan Sterija 1806-1856
Praed, Winthrop Mackworth 1802-1839
Prati, Giovanni 1814-1884
Preseren, France 1800-1849
Pringle, Thomas 1789-1834
Pye, Henry James 1745-1813
Quental, Antero Tarquínio de 1842-1891
Quintana, Manuel José 1772-1857
Radcliffe, Ann 1764-1823
Radishchev, Aleksander 1749-1802
Raftery, Anthony 1784-1835
Raimund, Ferdinand 1790-1836
Reid, Mayne 1818-1883
Renan, Ernest 1823-1892
Reuter, Fritz 1810-1874
Rogers, Samuel 1763-1855
Rückert, Friedrich 1788-1866
Runeberg, Johan 1804-1877
Rydberg, Viktor 1828-1895
Saavedra y Ramirez de Boquedano, Angel de 1791-1865
Saltykov-Shchedrin, Mikhail 1826-1892
Satanov, Isaac 1732-1805
Schiller, Friedrich 1759-1805
Schlegel, August 1767-1845
Schlegel, Karl 1772-1829
Scott, Sir Walter 1771-1832
Scribe, Augustin Eugene 1791-1861
Senoa, August 1838-1881
Shelley, Mary W. 1797-1851
Shelley, Percy Bysshe 1792-1822
Shulman, Kalman 1819-1899
Silva, José Asunción 1865-1896
Slaveykov, Petko 1828-1895
Słowacki, Juliusz 1809-1848
Smith, Richard Penn 1799-1854
Smolenskin, Peretz 1842-1885
Southey, Robert 1774-1843

Stagnelius, Erik Johan 1793-1823
Staring, Antonie Christiaan Wynand 1767-1840
Stendhal (pseud. of Henri Beyle) 1783-1842
Stifter, Adalbert 1805-1868
Stone, John Augustus 1801-1834
Taunay, Alfredo d'Ecragnole 1843-1899
Taylor, Bayard 1825-1878
Tennyson, Alfred, Lord 1809-1892
Terry, Lucy (Lucy Terry Prince) 1730-1821
Thompson, Daniel Pierce 1795-1868
Thompson, Samuel 1766-1816
Thomson, James 1834-1882
Thoreau, Henry David 1817-1862
Tiedge, Christoph August 1752-1841
Timrod, Henry 1828-1867
Tommaseo, Nicolo 1802-1874
Tompa, Mihály 1817-1888
Topelius, Zachris 1818-1898
Trollope, Anthony 1815-1882
Turgenev, Ivan 1818-1883
Tyutchev, Fedor I. 1803-1873
Uhland, Ludvig 1787-1862
Valaoritis, Aristotelis 1824-1879
Vallès, Jules 1832-1885
Verde, Cesário 1855-1886
Very, Jones 1813-1880
Vigny, Alfred Victor de 1797-1863
Villaverde, Cirilio 1812-1894
Vinje, Aasmund Olavsson 1818-1870
Vörosmarty, Mihaly 1800-1855
Wagner, Richard 1813-1883
Warren, Mercy Otis 1728-1814
Weisse, Christian Felix 1726-1804
Welhaven, Johan S. 1807-1873
Werner, Zacharius 1768-1823
Wescott, Edward Noyes 1846-1898
Wessely, Nattali Herz 1725-1805
Whitman, Sarah Helen 1803-1878
Whittier, John Greenleaf 1807-1892
Wieland, Christoph Martin 1733-1813
Woolson, Constance Fenimore 1840-1894
Wordsworth, William 1770-1850
Zhukovsky, Vasily 1783-1852
Zorrilla y Moral, José 1817-1893

# Achim von Arnim
# (Ludwig Joachim von Arnim)
## 1781-1831

German novella and short story writer, poet, novelist, dramatist, essayist, and critic.

An influential though minor figure in the German Romantic movement, Arnim inspired among his contemporaries a renewed interest in their national literature and culture. His unfinished novel, *Die Kronenwächter,* was Germany's first historical novel, and is considered important to the development of that genre in German literature. He is best known, however, for his collection of folktales and lyrics, *Des Knaben Wunderhorn,* which he compiled with Clemens Brentano, and which prompted a significant revival of interest in German folklore.

A descendant of Prussian nobility, Arnim was born in Berlin and raised there by his maternal grandmother. He attended the University of Halle where he pursued studies in the sciences, particularly experimental physics. While attending Halle, Arnim published several articles in scientific journals. In 1800, he entered the University of Göttingen, where he met Brentano, his later collaborator and lifelong friend. Brentano encouraged Arnim to abandon his scientific studies and concentrate his talents on writing.

While traveling through Western Europe and England between 1801 and 1804, Arnim published his first novel, *Hollins Liebeleben.* Modeled closely after Johann Wolfgang von Goethe's *The Sorrows of Young Werther,* the novel received little critical attention. Arnim eventually settled in Heidelberg, where he organized and became a leader of the Heidelberg Romantics. Here he published *Des Knaben Wunderhorn* which brought him the recognition he sought. Goethe, especially, encouraged his literary efforts, and Arnim looked to him as a mentor. Although Goethe approved of Arnim's style, he could not support the younger man's preoccupation with German medievalism, and the relationship deteriorated. Arnim's literary concerns were shared, however, by such figures as Brentano, the brothers Jakob and Wilhelm Grimm, and Joseph Görres, and together the group edited the short-lived journal *Zeitschrift für Einsiedler,* which encouraged the study of German folklore. It was discontinued after five months, but was published in book form as *Tröst-Einsamkeit.* Stirred by the wars of liberation against Napoleon, the Heidelberg Romantics then concentrated on more realistic and historical depictions of Germany, composing patriotic war songs and producing nationalistic propaganda.

In 1809, Arnim returned to Prussia where he developed the mature writing style characteristic of his later work, particularly his novellas. *Isabella von Ägypten, Kaiser Karl des Fünften erste Jugendliebe (Isabella of Egypt), Der tolle Invalide auf dem Fort Ratonneau,* and *Die Majoratsherren* are regarded as three of his finest efforts, and were quite popular in nineteenth-century Germany. In these novellas, Arnim successfully blends a historical picture of Germany with elements of the fantastic and grotesque. *Der tolle Invalide* is considered by many to be his most accomplished work. In addition to skillfully combining the realistic and the fantastic in this novella, Arnim also

conveys a psychological awareness and moral insight not found in any of his other compositions.

Arnim's novels, *Die Kronenwächter* and *Armuth, Reichtum, Schuld und Busse der Gräfin Dolores: Eine wahre Geschichte zur lehrreichen Unterhaltung armer Fräulein aufgeschrieben,* are often faulted for their lack of cohesiveness. Many observe that in these works Arnim failed to achieve the unity of style and subject that he attained in *Der tolle Invalide.* Although regarded as Germany's first historical novel, and valued for its colorful and vivid portrayal of the German Middle Ages, *Die Kronenwächter* is often criticized for its structural weaknesses and disjointedness. *Gräfin Dolores,* however, has gained distinction for its ethical focus, particularly in its treatment of the conflict between passionate love and marriage. It is also the only work in which Arnim depicts his own era and its problems rather than those of the Middle Ages.

Arnim's dramas have generally elicited negative comment. Unpopular and never performed, they are considered confusing and ineffectual. Of those that continue to be studied, *Halle und Jerusalem: Studentspiel und Pilgerabentheuer* is cited as the only one of Arnim's dramas that displays any dramatic form. Although *Halle und Jerusalem* is the most widely read of Arnim's dramas, critics note that it, too, lacks effective characterization and clarity.

Arnim's criticism is considered undistinguished, the product of inspiration rather than erudition. Lacking a sense of order and organization, his commentaries never included discussions of style, form, or content, but concentrated solely on the "Geist," or spirit of the work. His reviews were often emotional and reactionary; he alienated many of his old friends, particularly Jakob Grimm and Görres, with his denunciations of their work. His last years were spent as a gentleman farmer in Wiepersdorf, Brandenburg, Germany, where he wrote only sporadically.

Although Arnim is generally given a minor position in the German Romantic movement, he is valued for his part in inspiring a renewed interest in German folklore. Recent commentators agree that his most successful creative works are his novellas. In this shorter form, critics observe, Arnim overcame his predilection for extraneous detail and tendency toward diffuseness which mar his longer works.

## PRINCIPAL WORKS

*Hollins Liebeleben* (novel) 1802
*Des Knaben Wunderhorn.* 3 vols. [with Clemens Brentano] (folktales and lyrics) 1806-08
*Der Wintergarten* (novellas) 1809
*Armuth, Reichtum, Schuld und Busse der Gräfin Dolores: Eine wahre Geschichte zur lehrreichen Unterhaltung armer Fräulein aufgeschrieben* (novel) 1810
*Halle und Jerusalem: Studentspiel und Pilgerabentheuer* [first publication] (drama) 1811
*Isabella von Ägypten, Kaiser Karl des Fünften erste Jugendliebe* (novella) 1812
   [*Isabella of Egypt* (abridged edition) published in *Fiction and Fantasy of German Romance,* 1927]
*Die Kronenwächter* (unfinished novel) 1817
*Der tolle Invalide auf dem Fort Ratonneau* (novella) 1818
*Die Majoratsherren* (novella) 1820
*Landhausleben* (short stories) 1826
*Ludwig Achim's von Arnim sämmtliche Werke.* 22 vols. (novels, poetry, and novellas) 1839-57

---

**GEORGE BRANDES** (essay date 1873)

[*Des Knaben Wunderhorn*] was not only of the greatest historical interest, but was epoch-making in German lyric poetry and German literature generally. It struck that natural note which for many years gave freshness and sonority to both the Romantic and the ante-Romantic lyric poetry. . . . The superiority of German to French lyric poetry in this century possibly lies chiefly in that absence of everything rhetorical which it owes to the influence of *Des Knaben Wunderhorn.* (p. 230)

[Whereas] Brentano's strength lies in his naïveté and his childlike fancies, Arnim is profoundly serious even in his wildest flights. With all his love for the popular, with all his eagerness to open the eyes of the cultured to the beauty of the simple and childlike, he remained the dignified aristocrat in his own writings; he never let himself go as Brentano did. When his

muse has a paroxysm of madness, it is cold, almost severe insanity. . . . (pp. 231-32)

His power of plastic representation was great, but quickly exhausted. It shows to advantage in some of his short stories, and in some still shorter fragments of his long novels; but along with descriptions and figures which evince real talent, we are presented with a mass of padding—diffuse digressions from the subject, interpolated tales which have little or no connection with the tale proper, fantastic, impossible episodes, against which even the reader with the most undeveloped sense of realism must protest. Sometimes he lays the whole stock of popular superstitions under contribution, treating them with the utmost seriousness—clay figures are magically endowed with life; a mandrake develops into Field-Marshal Cornelius Nepos. At other times he has recourse to the stock-in-trade of the old-fashioned romances—fabulous parentage, recovery of long-lost children, disguises, strange meetings after the lapse of many years. He is also given to introducing ballads and songs, generally under the rather flimsy pretext that they are the composition of one or other of his characters: fluent, but not melodious, they interrupt the course of the action, momentarily attract the attention of the reader, and are immediately forgotten.

Arnim's principal novel with a modern plot, **Armuth, Reichthum, Schuld und Busse der Gräfin Dolores: Eine wahre Geschichte zur lehrreichen Unterhaltung armer Fräulein aufgeschrieben** ("Poverty, Wealth, Sin, and Penance of Countess Dolores: A True Story, Recorded for the Instruction and Amusement of Poor Young Ladies"), is, taken as a whole, quite as tedious as its title. This novel is another of *Wilhelm Meister's* progeny. . . . But there is a smooth, pious strain throughout the whole which is altogether unlike *Wilhelm Meister.*

The story opens with a description of a castle which has fallen almost into ruins because of its owner's poverty. This description is striking and good. . . . We are made to feel all the melancholy associated with the idea of former grandeur and present decay. The somewhat frivolous and selfish character of the penniless young Countess Dolores is also drawn with a masterly hand. . . . In the character of Count Karl, Arnim has succeeded in doing what had perhaps never been done in German literature before, namely, depicting what the English call *a perfect gentleman,* a conception for which other nations have no corresponding expression. A *gentleman* is a man of honour, manly, serious, born to command; he is, moreover, a good Christian, conscientious, unselfish, the protector of those around him, not only good by natural disposition, but moral on principle. In this character Arnim seems to have embodied much of what was best in his own nature. Unfortunately he did not succeed in imparting to it sufficient life; a kind of dream-haze surrounds this man of fine feelings, who is always writing verses and who talks a language inspired by the spirit of romance. (pp. 232-33)

It would almost seem as though it had been Arnim's intention to describe with the aid of [his] fictitious characters, the mystic-sensual debaucheries of one of his fellow Romanticists, a Werner or a Brentano. (p. 234)

But it is not only the excesses peculiar to the Romanticists which Arnim reprehends; he also sharply and wittily castigates the anti-Romanticist, Jens Baggesen. . . . It was, however, undoubtedly less Baggesen's verses than his extraordinary instability of character which provoked Arnim's satire. The life of this enemy of Romanticism was more planless and capricious than the life of any one of the Romanticists; and Arnim, for whom everything strange and improbable had an attraction, could not fail to be interested in such a singular personality. In *Dolores* he caricatures him wittily and mercilessly in the person of the poet "Waller." But though, in this instance, the weaknesses of a special individual are caricatured, Arnim's general purpose unmistakably is to throw into salient relief characteristics which exemplify the lawlessness and levity of the emotional life of a whole generation.

His unfinished historical novel, *Die Kronenwächter* (**"The Guardians of the Crown"**) . . . , presents us, like *Dolores,* with several well-conceived and ably elaborated characters along with a mass of undigested mystic and lyric material. In the background of this tale looms a huge, mysterious, enchanted castle. . . . But it is not this mystical background which is of importance. What one really remembers are one or two characters portrayed with such virile force as probably no German author has exhibited since, unless it be Gottfried Keller, in his historical novels. (pp. 235-36)

Mystic incidents are, of course, not lacking. If Arnim could not forego them in his modern novel, in which we read of a priest who, with one look, imparted to childless wives the power of conception, they were certain to occur much more frequently, and to be of an even more surprising nature, in a tale of times long past. . . . *Die Kronenwächter,* like all Arnim's longer productions, is a piece of patchwork, though it must be allowed that the patchwork does not lack poetic value.

It was only in his short tales that he succeeded in producing the effect of unity. *Philander* is a clever and pleasing imitation of the style of Moscherosch, a writer who lived in the days of the Thirty Years' War. In *Fürst Ganzgott und Sänger Halbgott,* we have a humorous variation of the favourite Romantic "Doppelgänger" theme, based upon an extraordinary likeness between two half-brothers who do not know each other; the story is at the same time a travesty of the stiffness and burdensome conventions of small courts. But Arnim's best and most characteristic work is the short tale, *Der tolle Invalide auf dem Fort Ratonneau.* In it we have all his quaint extravagance, without any breach of the laws of possibility; and the central idea is touchingly human. (p. 237)

The effect of this little work is rather weakened by the introduction of supernatural agencies; the whole calamity, namely, is explained to be the result of a stepmother's foolish curse; still, the story in its simplicity is a glorification of that strong, beautiful love which has power to drive out even the devil himself.

And in this, as in several of his other tales, Arnim evinces a humane sympathy with the lower classes which becomes the aristocratic Romanticist well. It is the same feeling of affection for those who are simple of heart as that which led him to collect and publish the popular songs and ballads, and which finds expression in *Dolores*. . . . (pp. 238-39)

> *George Brandes, "Arnim and Brentano," in his* Main Currents in Nineteenth Century Literature: The Romantic School in Germany, Vol. II, *translated by Diana White and Mary Morison (originally published as* Hovedstrømninger i det 19de aarhundredes litteratur: Den romantiske Skole i Tydakland, 1873), William Heinemann Ltd., 1902 (and reprinted by Boni & Liveright, 1923, pp. 230-52).*

**E. K. BENNETT** (essay date 1934)

Arnim is a story-teller who is moved by no such profound motives as Kleist or Hoffmann, and has no such individual view of life to express in his stories of magic, mystery or marvel: it is the delight in the many coloured wealth of incident which stimulates his imagination. . . . (p. 68)

In the poetical genius of Arnim there is a lack of unity, a failure to persevere in a single definite direction. He was at the same time a skilled resuscitator of the past, particularly of the past of Germany at the time of the Renaissance and the Reformation; an exploiter of the world of magic and fantastic dreams, and a writer concerned with ethical problems and the criticism of society. All these various interests and pre-occupations conflict and result in a confusion of effect, so that even in his best work, as for instance in *Isabella von Aegypten,* no single striking impression is produced. In this Novelle as in his unfinished novel *Die Kronenwächter,* he reveals the power of recreating the historic past not so much in the presentation of important events as in the detailed vision of ordinary life. . . . In *Die Majoratsherren* he conjures up a world of magic and imagination akin to that of Hoffmann, but one in which the intrusion of ethical problems only acts as a disturbing factor in the basic impression. He believes, like Hoffmann, in another world which is in some sense more real and intense than the world which is revealed by the senses. But the two worlds are not identified to the same extent as they are with Hoffmann. For Arnim they remain distinct; only the imagination is the mediator between the two, and can bring messages from the one for the solace or delectation of the other. In some of his Novellen, as in *Mistress Lee* and in his novel *Gräfin Dolores,* he is entirely concerned with ethical problems, pre-eminently the conflict between marriage and the freedom of passionate love. The action of his stories is laid almost exclusively in the past—a past which for him possessed a greater variety and wealth of forms before the French Revolution reduced everything to a drab unity. (pp. 68-9)

Both [*Isabella von Aegypten* and *Der tolle Invalide auf dem Fort Ratonneau*] are stories of fantastic happenings, the former enriched by episodic folk-lore incidents: mandrake, Golem and Bärenhäuter, and having seemingly no justification beyond its own power to charm and hold the attention by its sheer fantasy. In *Der tolle Invalide,* however, the incidents serve as an illustration to the idea which is then expressed in words explicitly at the end of the story: 'Liebe treibt den Teufel aus' [Love drives out the devil]. (p. 70)

Arnim's Novellen . . . have not the same power to hold the interest of readers to-day as those of Hoffmann, for they have not the same intensity of emotional experience informing them. Nor does Arnim's prose style contribute to make them popular: it is hurried, breathless and without repose, so that the reader is quickly wearied. With the exception of *Isabella von Aegypten* and *Der tolle Invalide* they are little known. Arnim's contribution to the form of the Novelle can hardly be regarded as individual but merely partakes of the general characteristics of the Romantic Novelle. . . . His most individual trait lies in his tendency to embroider the strict narrative with a wealth of arabesque tracery. (pp. 70-1)

> *E. K. Bennett, "The Romantic Novelle," in his* A History of The German "Novelle," *Cambridge at the University Press, 1934, pp. 47-76.*

**HERBERT R. LIEDKE** (essay date 1937)

[*Liedke's* Literary Criticism and Romantic Theory in the Work of Achim von Arnim *is the only book-length study in English of*

*Arnim's life and work. In it, Liedke examines the Romantics' view of literary criticism, Arnim's relationship with the Heidelberg Circle, and the influences of German classicism, nationalism, and realism on his work. Liedke also explores the effects of Arnim's family ties, travels, and early fascination with science on the development of his literary ideals. In the conclusion, excerpted here, Liedke speculates on Arnim's position in the history of German literary criticism.*]

Literary critics may be divided into two groups. The members of one of these, through their vast range of information in the historical field, their clear and logical reasoning, and their brilliant style, have been able to guide contemporary poets and prose writers into new paths and to make important contributions to the theory of literary genres and the methodology of criticism. . . . [The second group of critics] includes many writers whose chief importance was in the creative rather than the judicial office. Such critics are idealists and their attitude is an outgrowth of genius ruled by emotion. Their opinions on literature have their greatest value as interpretations of the writers' personalities and of their contributions in other fields of production. As idealists they project their view of life into their discussions of literature, thus making a fuller revelation of themselves and of the struggles and aspirations of the generation to which they belong.

Goethe and Herder were outstanding representatives of this type of critic and it is to this group that Achim von Arnim must be assigned. His impulsive, idealistic *Weltanschauung,* which found expression in a long series of productions in the field of romantic poetry and fiction, could not adapt itself to processes of analytical reasoning and logical categorizing which are necessary for the establishment of theories of general validity. Arnim was first and foremost a *Dichter* [creative writer] and his judgment of literary sources and achievements flowed from the same fountain of intuitive genius as his *Dichtung* [fiction and poetry]. His critical style, even in the later, more realistic years, bears everywhere the stamp of romantic imagination. This makes his work at times difficult to understand, and it may be added, none too easy to translate into English. Often his meaning must be *felt,* and certainly a part of the importance of his contribution lies in the enthusiastic and fanciful manner in which his ideas are presented.

Nevertheless, Arnim has a significant place in the history of German criticism. (pp. 174-75)

In his early critical writing Arnim shows himself a progressive. This appears first in his essays on physical science, where [he is] a protagonist of a dynamic, monistic view of nature's processes. Later, it reveals itself in his attitude toward art. Here he supports the Schlegel brothers and Tieck in the fight against the wretched state of contemporary criticism, the same struggle against cliquish narrowness, pedantry, and shallow gossip that has been waged a little earlier by Schiller and Goethe in their *Xenienkampf.* Arnim's concepts of art, then, developed . . . under the influence of the political events of the first decade of the new century. His national feeling was fanned into flame when Prussia's glory was annihilated at Jena and Germany lay prostrate under Napoleon's heel.

This enthusiasm becomes outspoken with the establishment of the *Zeitung für Einsiedler* in 1808. Here he voices emphatically the idea that art must be an expression of the creative genius of a people, for only that literature is truly great which is imbued with a national, popular spirit. Arnim is now firmly convinced that literary schools, such as classicism and romanticism, have outlived their day and that the need now arises

for a literature that voices a unified German spirit. . . . Arnim now assigns to literary criticism the task of making the reader acquainted with the best creations of this popular spirit, of unearthing and making known the treasures of a mighty past, of re-creating the "remote and unknown." Only when the critics shall have fulfilled this great mission can Germans expect a great national literature.

This is the doctrine that underlies the critical work of Arnim in the years that followed. While these ideas were in the main those of the younger generation of romanticists, Arnim has nevertheless a peculiar and striking position. . . . Arnim's criticism is programmatic, but for him the "program" is not an exact system or a set of dogmatic rules. It is rather an enthusiasm and a hopeful vision of an ideal artistic future.

This serves Arnim as a basis for a highly emotional approach. He scarcely ever analyzes single traits and features, but reacts to the work as a whole. His programmatic spirit prefers to select for consideration works which are in conformity with its conception of the purpose of literature and makes these constructive for the world of art as the critic envisions it. Thus, it is noteworthy that Arnim rarely writes about works that do not interest him personally. The writings of the physicist Ritter, the poems and dramas of the Schlegels, and other productions of romantic spirits, formed . . . welcome material for the exposition of his own ideas on nature and art. (pp. 175-77)

[Many] of the most interesting views of Arnim respecting poetry found expression in his correspondence with friends like Brentano, Goethe, and the Grimms. Here he is intensely serious in pressing his point, and although informal in style, his remarks are put in a form that is worthy of the dignified subject-matter. His reviews and critical essays, published and unpublished, are very uneven in quality. As is the case with his stories and plays, brilliant productions are at times succeeded by those that are hasty and superficial. (p. 177)

Judged by quality of content and vigor of style, the contributions to the *Berliner Abendblätter* and the *Preussischer Correspondent* rate lowest among [Arnim's criticism]. . . . Of highest rank are the reviews in the *Heidelbergische Jahrbücher.* Here we see Arnim, the critic, at his very best. He was writing primarily for two groups—the romantic sympathizers, for whom his ideas, as he hoped, would become a stimulus and a program for the development of national poetry; and his opponents, such as Johann Heinrich Voss, to whom he and his romantic associates were anathema and who, he felt, must now recognize the strength and beauty of the new literary garb which was to replace the outworn garment of dry classicism. After 1815 . . . [there is] a change in Arnim's critical style. The drift toward realism brings an increasing clarity of ideas and a more careful and finished form.

Finally, it must be stressed again that the literary-critical writings of Arnim are the expression of a thoroughly poetic soul. . . . His literary criticism, even more than his correspondence, reveals the noble idealist. (pp. 177-78)

*Herbert R. Liedke, in his* Literary Criticism and Romantic Theory in the Work of Achim Von Arnim *(copyright 1937, copyright renewed © 1965, by Columbia University Press; reprinted by permission of the publisher), Columbia University Press, 1937, 187 p.*

**WALTER SILZ** (essay date 1954)

The knightly figure of Achim von Arnim does not stand in the first rank of German writers. Romantic enthusiast and Prussian patriot richly endowed with poetic sensibility and fantasy, he was not equally gifted with self-criticism; and his healthy, harmonious nature lacked that passionate bias and intensity which distinguish the outright genius from the highly gifted amateur. Nevertheless, a few of Arnim's works have lived, chief among these the briefest [*Der tolle Invalide auf dem Fort Ratonneau*], the story of a crazed French soldier who for three days and nights held a harbor fort single-handed and terrorized a city, but was saved from death and restored to sanity by the fearless love of his German wife.

This bare summary suggests at once some of the recognized characteristics of a Novelle: an extraordinary event that has actually occurred (Goethe's definition) and a story that can be condensed into a short sentence. And other earmarks of the Novelle are not lacking: the general brevity (in this case, less than twenty printed pages) and economy of structure, with everything built around the central "Ereignis" or conflict to which the action leads up and from which it falls away to its final resolution. Dispensing with a [typical Novelle] "frame," the author limits himself to a few crucial scenes which he presents vividly with a minimum of description, using a flexible combination of direct speech and indirect subjunctive discourse. There are in the center two chief characters, Francoeur and Rosalie, both mature and "fertig;" farther out, a few minor figures, more or less types: the old commandant, the man-servant, the priest; on the periphery, two or three individuals (the mother, the Leipzig pastor, the child—all three nameless) and the Marseilles populace. The action sets in, with dramatic emphasis, shortly before the catastrophe; then the past is revealed by means of a report which at the same time characterizes the two main persons. The time-span is short, the locale restricted and well defined. The only really dispensable elements are the brief pseudo-comical episode of the ignited wooden leg at the beginning, the touches of the supernatural connected with the mother, and the "tag" of two verses at the end, in which the author sums up for us in abstract, moralizing terms the theme and substance of his tale. . . . (p. 29)

There are a number of leitmotifs: that of the Devil, that of the mother's curse, and others. The word "Teufel," in a variety of modulations, occurs about thirty times in this brief tale, the word and concept "Fluch" a dozen times. The color black recurs with a sinister suggestion of evil and supernatural forces. . . . The motif of "Feuerwerk" is prominent also. . . . A lily-motif is connected with the heroine, whose maiden name was Lilie. . . .

The use of these unifying motifs is consistent with the close-knit structure of the story as a whole. The action advances steadily and cogently, without gaps or pauses, with a certain military precision, and every step is adequately motivated. Arnim for once avoids all digressions and unnecessary embroidery and keeps to his main line. (p. 30)

The rise and fall [of the action] is distinctly dramatic, and indeed there is a dramatic quality in the movement and gestures of the persons throughout. . . . Individual scenes, like that between Francoeur and the bungling Basset, with its contrasting human types and speech and mounting excitement . . . , are full of dramatic life. As a writer, Arnim was marked, like so many "Novellisten," by a combination of narrative and dramatic powers.

The language is correspondingly terse and vigorous. Sentences of a Kleistian compression and tension occur. . . . In moments of supreme emotion, the expression attains a deeply moving

simplicity, as when Rosalie states her brave resolve to face her husband's rage. . . . (p. 31)

In this Novelle . . . , we can observe a blending of Romantic traditions with a new realism and an interest in abnormal psychology. The miraculousness and diabolism that lurk in the background still belong to Romanticism, but they are not allowed, except as psychological factors, to affect developments. The consistent and logical working-out of the physiological-psychological problem in the hero, culminating in the sober surgical explanation and procedure at the end . . . , belongs to the new realism. (pp. 31-2)

At times Arnim overworks the miraculous element. It would have sufficed to let Francoeur's blood and tears extinguish his fuse, but in addition a gust of wind must blow the powder from the vents of his cannon and the devil-flag from the tower. . . . The doves that come to the child are explained as household pets; putting green leaves into their beaks makes them too obvious a symbol. . . . The repentant mother's release by death on the very day of Rosalie's saving deed . . . is again too much of a "romantisches Wunder."

On the other hand the local color is authentic and quite in the spirit of Poetic Realism. . . . [Arnim's] story abounds in realistic detail which has functional value. . . . At every stage of Francoeur's "rebellion," which proceeds with the methodicalness characteristic of the man, we are shown with sharp realness the persons and also the things involved.

It is astounding what a wealth of characterization Arnim is able to compress within the limits of his brief Novelle. Francoeur, the hero, is to a large extent a type. (pp. 32-3)

[The] valet Basset, Francoeur's old friend, is deftly drawn. With his talkativeness and curiosity, his anxiety about his job, his well-intentioned meddling, his embarrassed voice "thin as a violin" . . . , his timidity and consternation, he is a real individual and a sort of foil to the hero. (p. 33)

The most impressive figure in the story, however, and the chief bearer of its ethical import, is Rosalie. It is significant that when she is first mentioned, she is engaged in an act of helpfulness. . . . She personifies "charity" in its full complement of meanings. She belongs in the line of Genoveva and the maid in Hartmann's *Der arme Heinrich* and Gretchen and some of Wagner's heroines—the line of German women whose self-forgetful love has saved men's souls. (pp. 33-4)

The two chief figures have a national representative value and afford an effective contrast: Francoeur with his French excitability and martial spirit and dash, triumphantly acclaimed by "a people who always prize boldness more than goodness;" Rosalie with her German faithfulness and self-subordination and "Fraulichkeit." They supplement each other excellently . . . , embodying in their way a like preachment of international understanding and cooperation which is the more striking as coming from so thorough a Prussian as Arnim and so soon after the great war with France.

The brevity and trained-down "leanness" of Arnim's story bring it close to the line of the "Anekdote." On the other hand the depth of character-drawing here, the scope of the action, and its general human significance, keep it well within the range of the true Novelle. In contrast, Kleist's *Bettelweib von Locarno*, which is commonly considered a Novelle, is by strict definition an anecdote, for it lacks just that depth of motivation and that correspondence of character with fate, which distinguish Arnim's story. Arnim, however, learned much from Kleist

. . . , and his masterpiece, **Der tolle Invalide,** bears unmistakably the stamp of that great forerunner of 19th-century realism and novellistic art. (pp. 34-5)

> *Walter Silz, "Arnim, 'Der tolle Invalide'," in his* Realism and Reality: Studies in the German Novelle of Poetic Realism *(copyright 1954 The University of North Carolina Press; copyright renewed © 1982 by Walter Silz), University of North Carolina Press, 1954, pp. 29-35.*

### RALPH TYMMS   (essay date 1955)

[*Tymms's is one of the most thorough studies of Arnim and his works available in English. He finds* Die Kronenwächter *"confused and multi-farious," and considers Arnim's dramas, especially* Halle und Jerusalem *"futile." Tymms cites* Isabella von Ägypten, Der tolle Invalide, *and* Fürst Ganzgott und Sänger Halbgott *as Arnim's best works and concludes that it is primarily Arnim's "detachment which effectively disqualifies him from the status of a truly great writer, though he can be an excellent story teller."*]

Although [Arnim] lacked Brentano's personal eccentricity, there is a great deal of violence and the grotesque in his work, and when this amiable young man let his imagination run wild he could produce literary situations of the most extravagant grisliness—never, however, with Brentano's artless and spontaneous verve. But he had to compensate for this prolific, if deliberate, imaginative power by poverty of sensibility: he was without Brentano's range and elasticity of feeling—his capacity for exquisite refinements of both joy and anguish, and his abrupt revulsions from exultation to remorse. To Arnim these extremes of temperament appear as remote, as imaginary, as the magic and horrors he could evoke with such facility, so that he describes passions without pain or concern, as he might speak of a change in the weather, or as if they were known to him only from hearsay; it is principally this detachment which effectively disqualifies him from the status of a truly great writer, though he can be an excellent story-teller. He is a curious phenomenon then, this Brandenburg Junker who could separate his ordered life so sharply from his literary extravagances that they do not seem to communicate or to nourish each other. . . . Arnim's excesses are literary only—his depiction of passion and mood is almost wholly culled from books; his view of life gives the impression of being observed and felt at second-hand, impersonally and bookishly. . . . The detachment with which the author stages his literary marvels and violent paroxysms of feeling is all too evident: sooner or later the reader becomes convinced of at least one thing—that the author does not really believe in the authenticity, the artistic inevitability, of his own creation.

That is why there is so much inferior writing uncritically mixed up with his good work, and why the absence of aesthetic urgency, or compulsion, is replaced by frequent diffuseness and excessive attention to irrelevant detail, why subsidiary themes may become more prominent than the main action. This happens most often when he strays from the modest dimensions of the *Novelle* and lets his predilection for quantity, length and detail overwhelm quality and economy. But the beginnings of even his longer works are often good, before this trend towards diffuseness and the commonplace suffocates the good qualities of his imaginative writing; consequently his best writing is to be found in a few *Novellen* and in the opening chapters of his two novels: his worst—or shall we say his habitually cumbersome and mediocre writing—is in the main body of the two novels and in his inflated, shapeless dramas (a genre which

most evidently requires a sense of timing and a selective instinct, if a successful exposition is to be achieved). The novels are **Die Kronenwächter (The Guardians of the Crown)** and the pretentiously named **Armut, Reichtum, Schuld und Busse der Gräfin Dolores (Poverty, Riches, Guilt and Penance of Countess Dolores).** The reader who is well-advised enough to read only the beginnings of the novels, and is fortunate in his choice of a few *Novellen,* may well form a more favourable impression of Arnim's accomplishments as a writer than his average achievement justifies.

It amounts to this: that Arnim, even more than Brentano, failed to make the most of his gifts, and dissipated them instead. (pp. 265-66)

His approach to the past is in keeping with [his] paradoxically stolid obsession with marvels, [his] strange combination of a taste for the bizarre and for factual delineation: both alike uncoloured by a real sense of immediacy or of deeper sympathy. No doubt the initial motive of his medievalism was escapism. . . . [Arnim] seemed to find in the Middle Ages an alternative sort of reality, as solid and substantial as the present, even though marvels and evidence of the supernatural were more clearly immanent then than now. . . . [It] is easy to see that for Arnim the historical framework of [*Die Kronenwächter*] did not exclude sprightly additions from his own imagination and from legend, to merge more or less unobtrusively with a reality which might itself be strange and seemingly magical. His conception of the past is elastic. . . . (p. 267)

The first of Arnim's two novels, **Armut, Reichtum, Schuld und Busse der Gräfin Dolores,** sub-titled: **Eine wahre Geschichte zur lehr-reichen Unterhaltung armer Fräulein (A true story for the Instruction and Entertainment of poor Young Ladies, . . . ),** is roughly contemporary in setting: the Revolution seems to occur early on in the course of the story, so that one looks in vain for the mystery and magical strangeness which Arnim finds principally in the past. Instead, he means to present a picture of his own age and its problems—a 'Zeitroman'. The absence of mystery and magic (which he can evoke so adeptly) is the first cause of the general dullness of the tale, another is the sanctimonious tone, and the insipidity and priggishness of the hero. The dullness comes as a disappointment after the excellent opening chapters. . . . Lacking the richness and colour which Arnim ascribed to the past, the novel equally lacks two other main sources of Arnim's best literary effects—he introduces neither farcical nor grisly-grotesque situations. In the absence of these agreeably strange or 'horrid' features the work becomes (or appears to become, to the restive reader) progressively deliberate and monotonous in pace, and drab in presentation, in spite of the occasionally sensational events depicted. Some of the things which happen to the Countess Dolores and her sister Klelia are indeed remarkable enough . . . , yet even these improbable incidents are told in an uninteresting way, and with little more spirit or emphasis than the quite trivial factual details with which the novel is principally crammed almost from beginning to end. (pp. 269-70)

[In] this novel Arnim . . . is at his least romantic, and therefore at his dullest, and he austerely renounces the enchantments of the supernatural, the magic of passions which make men their playthings. This is doubly unfortunate, because he has little of value to offer in place of supernaturalism, which he handles so well, and this novel—ostensibly one concerned with passion—is narrated with insensibility, as if the author had no first-hand knowledge of human emotions, and did not wish to have, either. His idiosyncrasy of singling out subordinate themes for particular attention is particularly displeasing here, too, since it stands in such unfavourable contrast to Goethe's care in introducing no detail which does not contribute to the purpose of the whole work and its central theme. Worse still, not only are digressions and irrelevancies emphasized in *Gräfin Dolores,* but the situations which either mark a climax in the affairs of the principal characters, or ought to do so, are as often as not dismissed hurriedly or with an embarrassed word of excuse: it is left to the reader to supply the missing description, motivation or subsequent analysis of the emotional impasse. . . . One might suspect that Arnim is trying to behave with what he supposes is a Goethean Olympian detachment in writing thus, if one did not know from his other works that the detachment is his own, and of a very different sort—the result, not of deliberate suppression of emotional features and over-tones, but of inherent inadequacy and temperamental coolness, preventing him from interpreting the inner motivation of human action: instead, precisely at this juncture, he launches out into long digressions. (pp. 271-72)

In his second novel, *Die Kronenwächter,* Arnim could allow more scope to his imagination, in the semi-mythical, semi-historical background of the age of Dürer and Luther, which was equally the age of the chap-books and of the Faustus-legend. . . . *Die Kronenwächter* belongs to the considerable number of major romantic works which were planned on a grandiose scale, but were never completed. (p. 273)

In this novel the simultaneous fidelity to factual realism and to imagination is not happy: each tends to spoil the effect of the other, and not to throw it into relief. . . . Arnim himself describes his procedure in the introduction to the novel: 'The endeavour to get to know this period in all the truth of history, from sources, developed this story, which in no way sets itself up to be historical truth, but to be an intuitive filling-in of the gaps in history, a picture in the framework of history.' This intuitive filling-in of gaps gives the historical, or semi-historical, writer of Arnim's own stamp a higher significance (in his own eyes), for by this wondrous, poetic insight he senses in the past the mysteries which are not revealed by orthodox history-books, and were not apparent, or clear, even to contemporaries in the historical past. This seems to justify, to Arnim's satisfaction at least, his incongruous blending of factual realism, and imaginative reconstruction or even pure invention: it is a subjective attitude to history analogous to his attitude to the folk-songs handed down from the past, which he edits, not with rigorous fidelity to the forms in which they reach him, but with what he fancies is an inspired, intuitive perception of their inner poetic mysteries.

His readers will realize that this is an unduly optimistic account of his procedure: Arnim does not in fact unearth the hidden mysteries and truly significant undercurrents of the past by intuitive, magically poetical insight, but what he does do is to impose on the framework of historical fact a vast amount of arbitrarily devised and often fantastic invention. Nor is there any sign that he, as the originator of all this intuitive, inventive, 'romanticization' of history, had true sympathy with the hidden mysteries, with the ultimate genius of the age he depicts with this combination of plodding detail and frisking invention. There is no genuine reinterpretation of the marvels in which people believed in the medieval age of faith—and credulity!—for he describes them as prosaically as the material concerns of everyday life. Arnim's detachment, his 'distance' from the passions he describes, applies to his marvels—they are equally exercises in his powers of invention, and not the result of an

inherent affinity with the marvellous, of an impelling desire to believe in the supernatural. (pp. 275-76)

At the close of *Die Kronenwächter,* this confused and multifarious work, the reader may feel that, taken all in all, the best thing in the whole book was—characteristically—on the first page, when Arnim's unsophisticated sense of fun produces the absurd jest about the new keeper of the city gate-tower who marries his predecessor's widow because she is too fat to get down the narrow spiral staircase!

This is the sort of happy invention—but absurd and grotesque—which comes into its own in a few of Arnim's *Novellen*—a genre of relative brevity, in which the main theme is less likely to be choked by the sheer mass of factual material and diffuse irrelevancies: the main theme is itself, in the best of these *Novellen,* a bizarre one, and may be made up in turn of minor *bizarreries*; or supported by their ivy-like parasitic growth. Probably the best is *Isabella von Ägypten, Kaiser Karl des Fünften erste Jugendliebe (Isabella of Egypt, the First Love of the Emperor Charles the Fifth's Youth* . . . , though it is a hybrid, comprising narrative on three distinct planes, and the effect is indecisive, as if the story were threatening to disintegrate into its various components. There are (a) the fairy-tale component, which has also its place in *Die Kronenwächter* (especially the second volume), (b) the historical narrative (the setting is of the same period as that of *Die Kronenwächter,* in the early sixteenth century), and (c) the ethical-cum-social critique—as in *Gräfin Dolores,* though in *Isabella* it is not the problem of adultery which comes in for attention, but the conflict between love and self-interest, the ethical problem posed by the problem of mésalliance between the heir to the Empire and the gipsy princess. This diversity of narrative purpose is further complicated by the introduction of strange figures drawn from the realm of folk-lore and legend: yet the central theme does keep moving, through the jungle of detail and fantastic imaginative devices—without ever reaching a proper conclusion, or ultimate solution; instead the story closes mainly, it appears, from inanition, stifled by sheer excess of irrelevant subject-matter. (pp. 277-78)

Of [the] strange beings the mandrake is described in an ingeniously elaborated version of the conventional folk-lore concept as a little monster endowed with animate life, a homuncule, after his previous root-existence under the gallows: he has a useful gift for smelling out hidden treasure. Unlike the sinister golem, the mandrake gives the author the chance of displaying his grotesque sense of fun: he is a ridiculous little caricature of mankind, vain and quarrelsome. (pp. 278-79)

The golem . . . is also—like the mandrake—essentially irrelevant and episodic, as she appears in this tale, in spite of her superficial appearance of playing an important part. The golem's symbolism is more unambiguous than that of Bella's love for the mandrake, and amounts simply to the idea that man in his frailty chooses the false instead of the true. (p. 279)

[The] fantastic themes, with their half-sardonic moralizing implications in the folk-tale convention, are not simply unassimilated folk-lore data weighing down the narrative as, say, Brentano's *Die Gründung Prags* is weighed down by the dead-weight of Slavonic mythology, or as many of Arnim's stories are crushed beneath the mass of uninspired and usually fruitless detail; for here Arnim's farcical humour comes into play and flickers magically round his strange gallery of freaks and monsters.

Arnim's narrative style, even when he deals with such marvels as these, in a farcical mood, is oddly factual: he relies on a visual effect, achieved by deliberately pieced-together documentation, and quite without the appeal of rich and evocative sounds. . . . For Arnim, the finer subtleties of literary style are a closed book: his narrative progresses unambitiously, soberly, without variation in speed or mood, and without relevance to what he is describing—gay or grave, fantastic or factual: all is told with apparent impassivity, in the primitive form of a mere succession of episodes. There is never a real climax, or, if there is, it is presented so unemphatically that it might pass unnoticed. So, in this story, to finish off the whole thing (as he is forced to, finally!) he abruptly interrupts the hitherto indeterminate catalogue of anecdotal incidents, and in the last pages tries to embed the fairy-tale extravagances more firmly into the historical framework. (p. 280)

The tale of *Isabella* is then an extraordinary mixture of magical elements from *Märchen* [fairy tales] or other forms of folklore tradition, a pseudo-historical framework of factual setting, and (finally) platitudinous ethical implications of the conflict between selfless love and selfish motives such as greed, ambition, sensuality and so on. By some miracle the story does not entirely disintegrate into these three components: perhaps it is the miracle of Bella herself—without doubt one of Arnim's most attractive, and in some ways a credible, female character (though not of the stature of Anna in *Die Kronenwächter*) even though she is only a *Märchen*-heroine.

Two further excellent *Novellen* by Arnim exist—excellent because, in the first case there are comical elements and a gripping, horrific main theme, and in the second case the wholly comic plot is given more 'body' by only semi-serious ethical and social satire which, for once in Arnim's writings, is not tedious, though it is superficial. They are *Der tolle Invalide auf dem Fort Ratonneau* . . . and *Fürst Ganzgott und Sänger Halbgott*. . . . Neither is effectively historical, for though *Fürst Ganzgott* may be supposed from one half-jesting passage to be set in the seventeenth century, the atmosphere is much more like that of the author's own time and contains many references to the amenities of Karlsbad, for instance, in the eighteenth or nineteenth century; *Der tolle Invalide* belongs to that pre-Revolutionary era which already seemed semi-mythical to Arnim; the time is that of the Seven Years War (1756-63) or soon afterwards, and the main subject of the tale is based on an actual happening recorded from that period.

*Der tolle Invalide* is an admirable tale, written with a narrative technique which does not allow the richness of invention to be outstripped by exhausting length and proliferation of incidents: for once Arnim does not obscure the main theme with digressions but develops it instead with economy and emphasis. It is almost as if he had learned in this one instance from some master of concise *Novelle*-writing. . . . The fairy-tale effect in this present instance of *Der tolle Invalide* is that of diabolical possession, or an obsessive apprehension of it: it is a theme which runs through romantic fiction as a heritage from Tieck's basic assumption (for the purposes of his *Märchen* at least) that man is exposed to the aggression of fiendish supernatural forces, right down to Hoffman's *Die Elixiere des Teufels (The Devil's Elixirs)* . . . and, later still, to the works of Hauff and Heine. In Arnim's tale this supernatural tyranny, and its overthrow, are explained in two alternative ways, one of which is obstinately realistic, the other symbolical. . . . *Der tolle Invalide* handles a potentially grisly theme with a combination of pathos and farcical fun: the second *Novelle*, *Fürst Ganzgott und Sänger Halbgott* has a main theme which is inherently comical, and is merely tempered by gentle implied social and

ethical satire; as a whole, the story is a festival, a carnival, of Arnim's cheerful inventiveness, and is unclouded by the sombre implications of *Der tolle Invalide*, with its catalogue of horrors. . . . (pp. 281-84)

[However, the] reader must turn back to Arnim's habitual dullness in such a tale as *Mistris [sic] Lee*, in which the author unwisely disdains the resources of either comical, grotesque, or historical effects—nor is there even a good beginning to this story. But the most serious omission—and a characteristic one—is that the author disdains the distinction which exists between the extraordinary and the ordinary, the principal and the subordinate theme, the significant and the commonplace circumstance, the logically evolving action and the paltry, unrelated anecdote: this is an omission which is doubly evident here because of the other omissions, the absence of the saving comical and grotesque touches. The result is that the narrative is flat and static, clogged with superfluous details and lacking in variation of speed and narration, and animation: nor is there convincing characterization to enliven the heavy-handed account of events. As usual Arnim jerks his personages about as if they were puppets, as if there were in fact no particular reason or impelling motive for their actions, for they lack even Tieck's off hand (and isolated) touches of psychological plausibility.

Apart from the absence of the farcical and grotesque, *Mistris Lee* is almost wholly dull because for once Arnim is niggardly too with his invention, and the solitary theme is distended, and flakes away into nearly disconnected incidents: but it remains one theme none the less, and it is so ineffective in itself (or is told so badly?) that the whole story seems pointless. This is certainly not the case with another of Arnim's serious *Novellen*—*Angelika, die Genueserin und Cosmus, der Seilspringer* . . . —which suffers from Arnim's more usual weakness of proliferation of incident. The beginning is characteristically good, and the reader settles down to enjoy the rest: undoubtedly he will be disappointed, as usual. (pp. 285-86)

In *Die Majoratsherren (The Heirs in Tail,* . . . ), on the other hand, though it too is a serious *Novelle* in tone, Arnim returns to his more successful concern with the grotesque and supernatural: both in their distinctively grim and weird aspects—culminating in the supposed duel between the old cousin of the hero and the ghost of his previous victim, a man he had killed in an actual duel. . . . Death and the angel of death, ghosts and the unhappy heritage of old deceptions and cold-blooded brutalities, fill the air with fluttering spectres of horror. It is all very effective, in spite of the author's habitual detachment . . . ; and if *Der tolle Invalide* approaches Heinrich von Kleist's economy in developing the story (a conscious attempt at emulation, perhaps?) so this *Novelle* of the *Majoratsherren* most nearly suggests the atmosphere of Hoffmann's masterpieces, and in some respects even suggests his more fluent style of writing; but unfortunately there is little trace of either Hoffmann's purposefulness or his carefully defined form. . . . [The plot] is all to little purpose: the various isolated incidents, situations and characters—almost all, this time, of an inherently bizarre quality (with a Jewish ghetto-background in place of the gipsy setting of *Isabella von Ägypten*)—do not really hang together; one thing does not lead to another, and instead the author drifts aimlessly from this to that, from one succession of disconnected episodes to others equally disconnected. As usual, he is prodigal with his extraordinary accumulations of grotesque touches of imagination. . . . (pp. 287-89)

With the same careless prodigality of ideas and motifs Arnim amassed the almost interminable succession of incidents in his elephantine 'double-drama' *Halle und Jerusalem*. . . . No doubt the component plays of *Halle* and *Jerusalem* are deemed to be comedies not only because they contain comic features but because, by the intervention of divine grace, their outcome is a conciliatory one; the whole work is probably called a tragedy partly because of its serious implications, and partly because Arnim used the word '*Trauerspiel*' [tragedy] in an elastic way, sometimes in the general sense of a play ('*Schauspiel*'). . . . [The] situation and most of the supporting motifs Arnim quite openly borrowed for *Halle* from the baroque tragedy by 'the old German poet' (as he called him) Andreas Gryphius: *Cardenio und Celinde oder Unglücklich Verlibete* (1647); it is hard to see what advantage he thought there might be in paraphrasing the original play in this manner. . . . Needless to say, Arnim had no strong objection to . . . redundancy: he increases it rather than diminishes it, smudging the clearly defined (though repetitive) outline of his baroque model. And, as is usual in his longer works—and not only in them—he delivers up himself and his readers (it is a book-drama, which it would be pointless to stage) to really exasperating diffuseness, irrelevancies, quasi-operatic effects, and general aimlessness of construction; on the credit side are occasional good comic lines and stage directions, and parodistic passages. Possibly too the phenomenal bustle and variety of the whole production offer some measure of compensation for the excessive (and in some scenes almost uninterrupted) inanity and flatness. It is again characteristic of his writing that there is no convincing characterization worth speaking of, except for what he inherits from Gryphius. He interprets and elaborates in his own way. . . . Most serious perhaps is the lack of significant dramatic form or organic evolution of situation; though the first component play *Halle: Ein Studentenspiel in drei Aufzügen (A Student Play in three Acts)* does at least have three clearly marked acts, in spite of its flamboyant profusion of scenes, but the second, *Jerusalem: Ein Pilgerabenteuer (A Pilgrim Adventure)* seems to have no form whatever—it is little more than a succession of charade-like scenes of an often allegorical, and usually pseudo-religious description which dimly echo the sumptuous and lively spectacles of Zacharias Werner's 'religious' plays: there are also a great many Tieckian jingling verse-interpolations. Nor, since the play is presumably practically contemporary in setting, is there interesting historical stage property from the age of chivalry, or from Dürer's era, though there is, it is true, some exoticism in the comic *turquerie*. In short, this is a futile drama, since it contains not a single instance of a situation, or a personage, or an idea being treated in such a way as to justify its existence by any sort of æsthetic urgency, plausibility or convincing emphasis. The work of the great artist seems inevitable: not so Arnim's, especially in this 'magnificent' freak of a play: there is nothing inevitable here, and the result is that we are offered neither indubitable realism nor adept artifice, neither life nor art. But it is a riot of imaginative extravagance: for sheer over-profuseness of invention nothing, surely, can beat it; and a genuine feeling of apprehension may seize the reader as he steels himself for the next daylight-firework display of fancy, particularly in the second component play, *Jerusalem*. . . . [Since] *Jerusalem* opens with a brief representation of Christ's crucifixion, one can hardly suppose that the remaining scenes are meant to be merely an example of Arnim's bizarre and often cruel sense of fun—an elaborate hoax—as they appear to be: rather do they give the impression of being the product of a sincere attempt to bring medieval piety up to date by means of a kaleidoscopic masquerade; the author—a

man with a taste for historical authenticity, like his fellow-Protestant Sir Walter Scott, who was equally a protagonist of the cult of Catholic medievalism—is apparently trying to recapture the exuberant crusading spirit of medieval Christendom. Is it an exaggeration to say that the result is as painful as that of any of the savage conflicts of colours in a mid-nineteenth-century neo-Gothic church-window, in which the romantic literary tradition is belatedly translated, in a debased form, into visual terms? For Arnim, whose capacity for describing realistically the material setting of the past was only exceeded by Scott, chooses to make this curious pilgrimage to the Holy Grave a chaotic pageant, however reverent his initial purpose may have been. From this point of view *Halle und Jerusalem* is in the direct lineal descent from Tieck's 'sacred' *Grossdramen*—particularly *Octavianus*. . . . (pp. 290-94)

Others of Arnim's book-dramas—*Novellen* in dialogue is the better expression—show the same good qualities and (overriding) faults. *Der Auerhahn (The Heath-cock)* is described on the title-page as 'A story in four Acts' and this is an accurate description, for, as before, the component themes are anecdotal; yet, by electing for dialogue (partly in the hybrid prose-verse which was also used in *Halle und Jerusalem*) Arnim wilfully sacrifices the only opportunity he could have to show his powers as a story-teller—by patiently amassing detailed description; without this diffuse narrative he cannot bring the action to life, nor yet, for that matter, the characters. . . . [There] are the usual supporting themes—premonitory dreams, miracles, pilgrims, and also a Rosalind-like disguise, in the tradition of *As You Like It* . . . , and a great many other disguises; and finally there is a secret society—in fact, many of the usual stage-properties of a romantic charade-like book-drama. But the prose dialogue-narrative is usually lively in style, in spite of the triviality with which its contents are treated, and its inherent inadequacy to take the place of Arnim's descriptive narrative; but one misses the grotesque and humorous touches which show him at his best in other works. The historical atmosphere is indeterminate, but contrasts favourably even so with Tieck's puppet-play *Ritterdramen* and *Märchen*-medievalism—as in *Karl von Berneck*, for instance.

Yet Arnim uses this very word 'puppet-play' to describe another of his episodic tales in prose dialogue: *Die Appelmänner (The Appelmann Family, . . .)*: disarmingly sub-titled '*Ein Puppenspiel*', though it is distinctly less puppet-like than, say, *Halle und Jerusalem*. The setting is, as often, in the sixteenth century, and there is a patriotic tendency; as in *Der Auerhahn*, and indeed any of Arnim's dialogue-*Novellen*, the absence of descriptive narrative deprives the author of his sole means of conveying a visual impression, but the dialogue in itself is brisk, if nothing more, and does come nearer than usual to bringing out some sort of progression in the principal theme. (pp. 294-95)

[Arnim holds] a relatively minor position in the romantic hierarchy as an artist, even though he contributed so much to romantic poetry as co-editor of *Des Knaben Wunderhorn*, and looked the part so admirably as a tribune of Heidelberg romanticism. One constantly regrets that one cannot admire his writing more, that he so consistently frustrates the full effect of his fertile imagination and also his awareness of reality by the sterility of his character-interpretation and inadequacy in constructing a story or play with reasonable economy of effort. If he must be regarded as a dilettante rather than a truly great author of compelling urgency, then it must equally be admitted that he was a dilettante of great talent—almost genius. . . .

Arnim's relegation to the second rank of the leading romantics is not of course merely a matter of being overshadowed by better, or more popular, writers who were his contemporaries: his final epitaph might be perhaps that a powerful imagination is not sufficient in itself to make a great writer. (pp. 296-97)

*Ralph Tymms, "Achim von Arnim," in his* German Romantic Literature *(reprinted by permission of Methuen & Co. Ltd.), Methuen, 1955, pp. 265-97.*

## WOLFGANG KAYSER   (essay date 1957)

In Arnim's novellas, . . . one often feels close to the grotesque without ever admitting its presence. In *Isabella von Ägypten,* for instance, a gypsy woman, a witch, a sluggard (*Bärenhäuter*), a golem, and a mandrake disguised as a field marshal travel in one coach. . . . [The] relaxed, almost liesurely way in which Arnim narrates his story indicates that here . . . the world is far from abysmal. Arnim has a special liking for folkloristic figures preformed in literature. These he embellishes and occasionally endows with new, fantastic traits, always regarding them as ''symbols'' of a spiritual essence hidden below the surface, as allusions to an ''eternal union'' and prefigurations of a higher world which he considers his special task to keep alive. Arnim's *Kronenwächter (Guardians of the Crown),* too, contains a number of grotesque elements. (p. 82)

One of Arnim's novellas, however, *Die Majoratsherren (The Owners of the Entail)* ranks as one of the greatest grotesques in German fiction. The narrative point of view in itself is rather striking; for the circumspection and equanimity which prevail in the opening portion of the story vanish as soon as we reach the action proper—which extends over a period of four days and nights—and its protagonist. At this point, the narrator turns into a mere reporter, who knows little more than the characters themselves and who, over long stretches, adopts the protagonist's point of view or directly quotes the other figures. . . . [The] protagonist does not see the higher world beyond reality by means of his imagination; the deeper meaning of men, objects, and events is constantly revealed to him as one who possesses the gift of second sight. . . . What he sees in his visions is by no means always lucid and exalted but usually possesses an evil, nocturnal and, occasionally, infernal aspect. What seems to be the coach of the physician on his way to one of his patients, with a lean driver on the box and surrounded by sparrows and a pack of barking dogs, appears to him in the following manner: ''Death sits on the box, hunger and pain between the horses; one-armed and one-legged ghosts hover about the carriage and demand that the cruel man, who stares at them with cannibalistic gusto, return their severed limbs. His accusers run shouting after him; they are the souls he prematurely tore away from this world. . . .'' A strange feeling invades him in the room of the lady-in-waiting: ''The squeaking tree frog on his little ladder seemed to exhale an evil spirit; the flowers in their pots looked all but innocent, since he thought he saw a dozen retired diplomats peering out of the bouquet. But he was especially bothered by the black poodle, although the latter seemed to be afraid of him; he took the dog to be an incarnation of the devil. . . .'' These are truly Goya-esque pictures, and no contemporary artist seems to have been more congenial to the Spanish master than Arnim where he is really grotesque. The pictures which Arnim produces, however, do not stem from the age of the post-Revolutionary wars but refer to the rotten, corrupt, and depraved world of the pre-Revolutionary era. (pp. 83-4)

[One] of the narrator's special concerns within the framework of the novella is to interpret the curious appearance of a hidden decadence and criminality as indicative of the rotten state of a world ready for the French Revolution. . . . But even in this way no unequivocal meaning based on an ethical scheme of guilt and punishment emerges. The narrator wants neither to celebrate nor to defend the Revolution; he does not even want to explain it. The changes which it brings about are not improvements in his eyes; to him, such improvements are apparently impossible within the earthly sphere. (p. 85)

*Die Majoratsherren,* Arnim's great ''Nocturnal story,'' remains unique among his narratives. In his other stories, he rarely abandons the circumspection and conviction of the credulous narrator, in whose presence the grotesque is unable to unfold. Things are essentially different in the drama, which lacks the mediating narrator whose calm voice keeps the uncanny elements in check and robs the grotesque of its ominous overtones. The fact that subsequently the gold background erupts with an ever increasing luminescence allows Arnim to paint these worlds in the beginning in darker and more desolate tones, a contrast which often prompts his fantastic imagination to create purely grotesque scenes. This is especially true of the first part of the double drama *Halle und Jerusalem,* namely up to the moment in which the message from the higher sphere is understood and the world transformed into lucidity. (pp. 85-6)

Unique as Arnim's plays may be in relation to their own time, they fit well into the context of literary history. They are peculiar only insofar as they depart from a common ground. . . . [In *Halle und Jerusalem*] Arnim's mistake in using the private characters Cardenio, Lysander, Olympia, and Celinde, rather than legendary figures, as the protagonists of the mythical action enabled him to create his fantastic grotesques. It is into this world that he felt entitled to insert the puppet-like figures of Wagner, Nathan, Dienemann, and the virginal chimera with her stork. Though one can well understand his motives, it is impossible to suppress one's doubts as to the success of his undertaking. There is little coherence in what he did; and the change of style effected between the first, more realistic and the second, more fantastic part of the drama is suspicious, especially since the latter is written from an increasingly epic point of view. Arnim's play is an erratic block in the history of the German drama. (p. 88)

*Wolfgang Kayser, "The Grotesque in the Age of Romanticism," in his* The Grotesque in Art and Literature, *translated by Ulrich Weisstein (translation copyright © 1963 by Indiana University Press; originally published as* Das Groteske, seine Gestaltung in Malerei und Dichtung, *Gerhard Stalling Verlag, 1957), Indiana University Press, 1963 (and reprinted by McGraw-Hill Book Company, 1966), pp. 48-99.**

## BRIAN ROWLEY   (essay date 1970)

Arnim, certainly, is difficult to characterize: not exactly a writer without character, but one whose creative character is heavily overlaid. . . . [Both he and Clemens Brentano] were too well-read for their own good: their work in collecting and editing folk-literature made them familiar with a storehouse of motifs, and this is reflected in the derivative nature of much of the material in Arnim's collection *Der Wintergarten* ('**The Winter-Garden**' . . .). Again, both writers were affected by the tradition of improvisation in folk-literature, and found it hard to resist the entertaining aside or decorative arabesque, locally delightful but damaging to the economy of the whole. And thirdly, both writers had a strong moral, not to say religious concern, and this sometimes comes out too explicitly in their creative writing: the pill of principle with a coating of verbal sugar is not a good prescription for longevity.

In Arnim's *Novellen,* then, which are the earliest in the Romantic movement, the reader is aware of an almost bewildering variety of bold attempts and near misses. Some of his stories are little more than anecdotes resting on coincidence; like *Die Einquartierung im Pfarrhause* (**'The Billetin [in] the Parsonage'** . . .), in which an infantry colonel happens to be billeted on a country parson whose wife turns out to be the daughter whom he deserted, with her mother, many years before. These anecdotes lack the resonance of Kleist's or Hebel's. At the opposite extreme, other stories try to encompass too much material. *Isabella von Ägypten, Kaiser Karl des Fünften erste Jugendliebe* (**'Isabella of Egypt, the first youthful love of the Emperor Charles the Fifth'** . . .) tries to marry a historical study of Charles V shortly before his accession with a story of how Isabella, Princess of the Gypsies, came to bear him a son; at the same time, historical fact and the most curious fairy-tale figures are juxtaposed. This attempt to link the worlds of the *Novelle* and the *Märchen* is found elsewhere in Arnim; but whereas Hoffmann or Chamisso evoke a sense of imminent (and immanent) horror from the intrusion of the supernatural into the everyday, the two realms in Arnim obstinately refuse to coalesce: the effect is one of cardboard figures standing about in a landscape. His stories, then, unlike Hoffmann's, do illustrate the dictum . . . from Goethe's *Conversations of German Refugees,* that the juxtaposition of reality and fancy is merely grotesque.

Arnim is at his best in those stories in which he is able to explore the psychology of human inadequacy. There are seeds of this theme lying dormant in many of his stories, but only rarely do they grow up into the light. They do so in *Mistris Lee* . . . , an interesting if somewhat unfocused early study of the anti-hero, centring on the abduction by two brothers of a wife living apart from her husband; none of the characters seem to know what they want, and this is the occasion of much ironic observation. A much better story—if a less subtle subject—is *Der tolle Invalide auf dem Fort Ratonneau* (**"The Mad Convalescent at Fort Ratonneau'** . . .), the only *Novelle* by which Arnim is now remembered, in which a strong story, irony, humour, psychological awareness and moral insight are combined. Arnim's tragedy, we may feel, is that he was born too soon to exploit the vein of psychological analysis he had hit upon. Or was it simply that he lacked the genius to exploit that vein? (pp. 141-43)

> *Brian Rowley, ''The 'Novelle','' in* The Romantic Period in Germany, *edited by Siegbert Prawer (© 1970 by the London University Institute of Germanic Studies), Weidenfeld and Nicolson, 1970, pp. 121-46.**

## ROGER PAULIN (essay date 1970)

Achim von Arnim saw the theatre as a salutary national institution which would instil patriotic values. . . . Not all of Arnim's wide output of dramas can be examined from this national point of view, but certainly older, well-tried German stage traditions and past history or legend influenced his choice of theme and presentation.

Arnim's dramas deserve more attention than is normally given to them, despite the fact that even his most sympathetic critics

reach the conclusion that he possessed little genuine dramatic talent. Indeed, Arnim is often made the scapegoat for all the dramatic sins of the Romantics. For this certain features of his work are normally held responsible. Inclusion of dramatic sections in works of other genres is considered evidence of his imprecise and confused use of the dramatic genre. An example is the novel *Gräfin Dolores.* The fact that he rejected the stage is held to reflect his inability to construct dramatically. In his actual dramatic exposition, supernatural forces seem always at hand to round off the action, especially in the long, loosely-built religious dramas. To this might be added his failure, itself a result of the common Romantic misunderstanding of Shakespearean form, to integrate scenes, which are sometimes successful, into a disciplined dramatic whole. . . . Certainly Arnim's longer, and more ambitious, religious and historical dramas were not written with the stage in mind, and they cannot escape many of these accusations. In fairness to Arnim it must however be rejoined that his shorter patriotic dramas and puppet-comedies are quite suitable for the stage, and that circumstances in Berlin in the years 1812-15, not dramatic ineptness, prevented their performance. (pp. 196-97)

The longer religious dramas gain little if they are subjected to close formal analysis. Any interest lies more in their content than in their form. Little excuse can be made for the formal indiscipline of Arnim's first full-scale drama, *Halle und Jerusalem* . . . , yet it is an important document of Romantic restorative concern in the religious and social fields. This drama continues the message of religious renewal proclaimed in the novel *Gräfin Dolores,* for both works were occasioned by Arnim's conviction that spiritual and political values had been lost in the confused events following the French Revolution. . . . It must be stressed that Arnim, in keeping with his practice in the prose works, deliberately alters and extends literary tradition, popular myth, and historical fact, in order to bring out what is for him the intrinsic religious truth [in *Halle und Jerusalem*]. The relatively realistic first part, mainly a depiction of dissolute student life, is Arnim's attempt at Shakespearean colour and movement. *Jerusalem,* with its symbolical pilgrimage to forgiveness and grace, owes more to Calderón.

Once Arnim returns to the Middle Ages to take up the theme of religious renunciation and divine providence, he loses immediacy and becomes pretentious. This is the case in the long prose drama *Der Auerhahn* (**'The Heathcock'**) . . . and in the six-act verse drama *Die Gleichen.* . . . *Der echte und der falsche Waldemar* (**'The True and the False Waldemar'** . . .) shows that Arnim, never averse to a parody of his most serious themes, can turn a medieval historical drama of renunciation, into a broad farce.

The last drama published in Arnim's life-time, *Marino Caboga* . . . , attempts to re-create the concise, rounded form of the short historical plays, but treats historical incident as an example of a wider religious problem. Arnim's unease is evident in the weak motivation of the play. The posthumously published historical tragedy *Markgraf Carl Philipp von Brandenburg* . . . is another well-constructed drama of performable length. This blank-verse drama draws on the story of the unhappy love of the youngest son of the Great Elector, but the more universal theme of love and duty in conflict, which transcends the purely historical action, is also feebly motivated. Arnim was far happier when limiting himself in dramatic presentation to the historical anecdotal sketch, and this must be considered his real contribution to Romantic drama. (pp. 197-99)

Roger Paulin, "The Drama," in The Romantic Period in Germany, *edited by Siegbert Prawer (© 1970 by the London University Institute of Germanic Studies), Weidenfeld and Nicolson, 1970, pp. 173-203.*

## ELISABETH STOPP  (essay date 1975)

[*Owen Tudor*] is a story with a medieval background set within a framework contemporary to Arnim. . . . In the romantic manner [Arnim] has successfully blended history and Märchen, fact and fiction, satirical wit and good humoured laughter, and has achieved a work that offers not only a good story in a light vein but much that is of structural interest. The same could not be said of some of the other curiously diverse tales inspired by Arnim's English journey; nevertheless they all reflect Arnim's poetic concerns and attitudes at that early stage of his career and form a telling contrast to *Owen Tudor* itself. (pp. 155-56)

Although *Owen Tudor* . . . has an element of history about it, as well as something of a moral lesson by laughter, Arnim's treatment of his sources is too fantastic and too idiosyncratic to conform to the general rather more sober pattern of the *Wintergarden*. . . . It must be admitted that in [*Die Ehenschmiede*, a posthumously published story,] and in the one on Charles Stuart, Arnim's depiction of the contemporary social scene in Scotland and particularly his sympathy for the Highlanders, is more overtly realistic than the vague glimpses of Wales afforded by *Owen Tudor*. And yet, in this fantasy, perhaps precisely because it is a fantasy, a medium really suited to Arnim, he has caught the essential spirit of the country more accurately than that of Scotland in the burlesque miscellany of scientific and amatory intrigue of *Die Ehenschmiede*. *Owen Tudor* also has greater artistic merit, having a unified central theme and a tautly designed structure: a double strand of narrative is held together by landscape and atmosphere where past and present coalesce in an effective and variegated symbol of the Welsh artistic consciousness—the symbol of the dance.

The story begins and ends with the theme of dancing and it reaches both its romantic and its grotesque climax in this same idea. For his framework narrative Arnim uses the fiction of a night coach journey from London to Holyhead. . . . The framework gives a vivid, impressionistic outline picture of the travellers and their fortunes, focusing at every point on the [Welsh] girl, who, it turns out, is shielding the good name of a friend . . . , and is being pursued by constables on horseback. She is helped by all the others who bury their differences so that she can reach Holyhead safely and there join her lover, Mallwyd. . . . Her narrative, Arnim's invention based on a printed source and embellished with his own Märchen and legend themes, keeps pace with, and is interrupted by, the adventures of the coach journey, both perspectives skilfully counterpointed all the time. It is this complex intermingling of perspectives, together with the speed and vivid simplicity of the actual narrative, that constitutes the chief artistic merit of Arnim's story. (pp. 158-59)

The love story, as related by the Welsh girl in the London carriage travelling through the night, proceeds . . . in Arnim's characteristic fusion of seriousness and laughter, with the laughter steadily gaining ground and winning in the end. (p. 163)

The fusion of past and present in a new artistic whole might perhaps be called Arnim's main structural preoccupation as a writer. . . . Arnim's method of putting this feeling [of past and present] across to the reader was direct in that he actually fused two or even more stories of different epochs, as here and so often elsewhere, most notably in the dramatic medium in *Halle und Jerusalem*; and indirect in that he welded past and present, history and Märchen within a system of usually quite inconspicuous signs and symbols. (pp. 163-64)

Elisabeth Stopp, "Arnim's 'Owen Tudor' and Its Background," in German Life & Letters, n.s. Vol. XXIX, No. 1, October, 1975, pp. 155-65.

## F. LÖSEL  (essay date 1977)

Arnim's [*Der tolle Invalide auf dem Fort Ratonneau*] has been assigned a place somewhere between Romanticism and Realism. It can also, however, be viewed rather differently if its 'realistic' features are understood as a continuation of the Romantic movement. In this light, Arnim's story becomes an attempt to develop further the objective attitudes of Late Romanticism into a moral stance without, however, sanctioning existing conditions in any way. He discards necessity and compulsion, putting the responsibility instead on the free individual personality. This makes it impossible to employ such Romantic devices as fatal objects and family curses. (p. 75)

For the presentation of psychological, religious and mythical features, Arnim mostly employs a conventional, unemotional, almost rationalistic language. His brittle prose reveals very few musical qualities, and where these actually occur, they appear to depend on a conscious device, as is the case in his other tales. . . . Arnim's associative story-telling has given way to a restrained tone in this novella, which excludes arabesque complexity and has a clearly recognizable plot. The 'madness' indicated in the title must not be sought in a background concatenation of complications, but is transposed into the foreground. Rosalie, passive in the beginning, is forced to act. In spite of the title, she carries more of the action than the 'Invalide', since it is from her character that development and solution spring. In contrast to other tales by Arnim, the cast is small, accentuating their isolation as individuals. Their character can only be assessed indirectly, they have little physical reality, and appear instead only as carriers of meaning. Their real everyday existence is hardly seen, and the life of the soldiers likewise is viewed exclusively from the outside. Their impulses and motives are not investigated by the narrator. No one acts in an underhand fashion. Even of Francoeur it would be wrong to claim that in his soul a drama, a struggle between the forces of light and darkness, is going on. Francoeur is seized by external forces and thereby appears to become an instrument of evil. . . . Unlike in the case of the other characters, we are never given a glimpse of his thoughts, apart from his aversion to clergymen. His behaviour is psychologically consistent, but there is no presentation of an inner development. . . . He is then literally and metaphorically speaking 'sprunghaft', erratic. Francoeur is a stranger in his own country and it is striking that his origins and family background are never mentioned. (pp. 77-8)

Accompanying . . . psychological and sociological themes, which make their way into Arnim's novella, is a strong religious, supernatural and mythological undercurrent. (p. 82)

[Even though] the incalculable power of evil is introduced as a theme, Arnim does not deny the existence of moral responsibility. To him the presence of the negative cannot be explained by reason alone, as some error in the Socratic sense . . . , but has to be accepted as a fact. The activity of evil in this world appears in a dualistic, almost manicheistic sense. (p. 83)

As the title of the novella stresses, everything ultimately converges on the 'Fort', a context in which the mountain has a potential for both good and evil, a centre of power or as a scene of supernatural revelation. Biblical parallels which come to mind are Mount Sinai, Tabor, Horeb or Zion or the mountain where Christ's temptation took place. At first it seems as if the mountain is the place for Francoeur to regain his health and his former self. His wife is also deceived. . . . [However,] the mountain becomes the place of temptation by the devil, symbolizing the lure of sacrilegious elevation, rebellion and pride in the biblical sense, where the rebel cuts himself off from the rest of his fellow men. But the mountain is also the site of the Passion and a place of salvation. Here as elsewhere symbols have an ambivalent function. (pp. 84-5)

Less convincing in the artistic sphere and bordering on the embarrassing in the religious, is the scene with the doves at the end. The pair of doves . . . might conceivably fit into a secular context (the dove of peace) as well as a religious one, but the religious associations rapidly become all too obvious, embracing both the Old Testament message of the doves with olive branches in the Noah's Ark story . . . and the New Testament concept of the Paraclete or Comforter in the image of the dove. (p. 85)

Arnim's style of writing has been rightly called syncretic, hence underneath the fabric of biblical references pointers to ancient mythology also become visible. The mountain as a place of power and temptation seems to be connected with the rebellion and punishment of Prometheus. . . . Arnim took only one specific strand of the Prometheus legend (creating human beings from clay) and developed it in a scurrilous and grotesque fashion. In the context of the novella, rebellious defiance against the gods and the theft of fire would have been more rewarding features, but these were not particularly developed in Arnim's fragment, although they may have been in his mind during the composition of *Der tolle Invalide*. (p. 86)

In the story as we have it there is no direct physical confrontation between the human and the infernal world. Nevertheless we are early made aware of the presence of the negative principle. The adversary remains hidden. Evil is present, but it is not allowed direct access by the narrator. Only through Rosalie's decision to leave her world and go beyond her previously accepted limits, does she fulfil her destiny and only then does the path become clear for grace to take effect. This convergence of the two components reminds one of the theological concept of synergism, in which the readiness of human action and the effect of divine intercession combine. (pp. 86-7)

Surveying the tale as a whole, it emerges that Arnim follows his customary technique, a fact apparently not previously recognized in *Der tolle Invalide*. He conflates and welds together a variety of strands in one story, a procedure which makes for difficult reading in his other writings. In this instance, he has concentrated on a single source but the novella is not as uniform as it appears at first sight; closer inspection reveals a number of undercurrents. Arnim unconsciously projects diverse images into one single plot and achieves here a synthesis which he is always seeking in his other works. (p. 88)

> F. Lösel, "Psychology, Religion and Myth in Arnim's 'Der tolle Invalide auf dem Fort Ratonneau'," in New German Studies (copyright © 1977 by The Editors, New German Studies), Vol. 5, No. 2, Summer, 1977, pp. 75-90.

**GLYN TEGAI HUGHES**  (essay date 1979)

It is now widely accepted that Arnim is the most unjustly neglected of the Romantic writers. . . . His novels and dramas, and most of the Novellen, have long been damned by praise of the intention and condemnation of its formless execution. (p. 89)

***Armut, Reichtum, Schuld und Buße der Gräfin Dolores*** takes the marriage of Graf Karl and Dolores and makes of it an image of society's sickness and the possibilities of therapy. (p. 90)

Arnim's contemporaries thought the novel characteristically chaotic. . . . *Gräfin Dolores* has some twenty interpolated anecdotes, retold legends or folktales, dramatic pieces, even a novel; and then there are sixty or more poems. It is all distinctly unpromising.

Yet this confusion is not purposeless; the meaning of the novel cannot be divorced from the sum of its richness and variety, even if we grant readily enough that not all interpolated scenes are judiciously fitted and balanced and that sheer exuberance is sometimes the uncomplicated progenitor. The form is not that of a patchwork quilt, still less the mosaic that some have called it; the principle is accretion. Arnim himself justifies his departure from a straight narrative path with the claim that what is important in a story is contact with everything, 'so that every event becomes our own, and lives on in us, a perpetual witness to the fact that all life stems from the one and returns to the one'. . . . (p. 91)

Arnim's concern is to introduce [the higher spiritual] world into the stream of history and he attempts to do this by reaching back to a primitive past for universal, unifying models. His purpose is no less than to give meaning to the present. The interaction of the old and new has been shattered by the French Revolution, a reenactment of the Fall. Yet, as he writes of Dolores, 'every sinner carries within himself a lost paradise'; so also do society and history. The poet, as he draws into one net the rich variety of things, begins to restore paradisal integrity. . . .

***Die Kronenwächter***, unfinished though it is, is [Arnim's] most ambitious attempt at using the past; its very ambition may indeed be the reason why it was never finished. (p. 92)

The interpenetration of myth and medieval reality is intended to release for us the spiritual forces of the past, though the symbolism may well not succeed in all cases and the coincidences can startle and irritate. One may also have reservations about his re-creation of the psychological motivation of medieval or Renaissance characters, as distinct from the surface atmosphere of the late fifteenth or early sixteenth centuries. The mythologizing inventiveness does, however, produce potent images of the mysterious unity underlying all being, images of increasing resonance. (p. 93)

[***Die Majoratsherren***] is of all Arnim's Novellen the one that owes most to mesmerism, clairvoyance, somnambulism and similar twilight states seen even more clearly in E.T.A. Hoffmann. In a closely plotted story, almost classical in its disciplined structure, he sets fevered states of mind against a background of the recent past, with the rise of materialism and the decay of the old order and the old families as prominent elements. Images from Jewish legend jostle with those from contemporary history and thought: Adam and Eve, Lilith, the Angel of Death, but also Kantian philosophers, Napoleon's Continental System, or a sal-ammoniac factory. (p. 95)

[*Der tolle Invalide auf dem Fort Ratonneau*] is the most accessible of Arnim's works, and the one constructed with most fidelity to the form of the Novelle. Its powerful polarities are reminiscent of Kleist; the daemonic is, however, viewed ironically if not grotesquely. The motifs flicker from the elemental to the comic, from the threat of consuming fire through fireworks to the burning of a wooden leg, from the devil as metaphysical despair to his function as a common swearword. Events and persons have a double meaning here too, but the ambivalence is securely carried by the strong characterization and the firm narrative lines.

The ingredients of Arnim's dramas are very similar to those of the novels and tales, but the gap between intention and achievement is greater. . . .

His most ambitious play is **Halle und Jerusalem** . . . , which was originally intended as little more than an adaptation of Gryphius's *Cardenio und Celinde* (1657) but which grew into a two-part work set in his own day. (p. 96)

A Shakespearian profusion of events and characters, without the inner discipline to organize them, marks the **Halle** play. In **Jerusalem** there is superimposed on this a clear debt to Calderón's religiously didactic mythological plays. Arnim mingles the real and fantastic, dream sequences and battle scenes, pilgrim songs and life in a harem, visions and temptations in the wilderness, Jesus on the Cross and an idealized Sir William Sidney Smith, defender of Acre against Napoleon in 1799. The scenes, often of considerable power, are unrelated, except in a very general way by the theme of redemption. The mood changes from exaltation to criticism of contemporary event, from mystic visions to obscure literary satirizing. It is all of a piece with his attempt to redeem his own time by infusing it with poetic and supernatural ideals incorporated in mythical and historical event. He is constantly importing symbols into inadequately realized, though richly described worlds. Yet the grandiose conception has an effect even in its final failure.

Wilhelm Grimm said of Arnim's works that they were like pictures framed on three sides but still being painted on the fourth, so that eventually the outlines of heaven and earth can no longer be told apart; from this there arose a painful uncertainty for the reader. The criticism is not unjust, but the openness of form now also conveys for us an openness to the world that attracts and excites. (p. 97)

> *Glyn Tegai Hughes, "The Legacy of Myth: The Grimms, Brentano and Arnim," in his* Romantic German Literature *(© Glyn Tegai Hughes 1979; reprinted by permission of Holmes & Meier Publishers, Inc., New York; in Canada by Edward Arnold (Publishers) Ltd), Holmes & Meier, 1979, Arnold, 1979, pp. 79-97.\**

## ADDITIONAL BIBLIOGRAPHY

Butler, Colin. "Psychology and Faith in Arnim's *Der tolle Invalide*." *Studies in Romanticism* 17, No. 2 (Spring 1978): 149-62.
> An extensive plot analysis of *Der tolle Invalide*. Butler maintains that in this novella Arnim achieved a perfect blend of religious and psychological themes and illustrated "the possibility of faith from the character of human experience."

Casey, Paul F. "Images of Birds in Arnim's *Majoratsherren*." *German Life and Letters* XXXIII, No. 3 (April 1980): 190-98.
> A discussion of the bird imagery in *Majoratsherren*. Casey concludes that the characterizations, motivations, and interrelationships of the four main characters are all dependent on this imagery, which lends "an intricate coherence to the story."

Duncan, Bruce. "Fate and Coincidence in Arnim's *Seltsames Begegnen und Wiedersehen*." *Seminar* XV, No. 3 (September 1979): 181-89.
> An in-depth analysis of the novella *Seltsames Begegnen und Wiedersehen*. Duncan argues that the coincidences in the novella, while seemingly contrived, "invite the reader to speculate on the causal relationships at work in the historical world and thus to gain insight into the higher reality that ultimately determines our destinies."

Hoermann, Roland. "Symbolism and Mediation in Arnim's View of Romantic Phantasy." *Monatshefte für deutschen Unterricht, deutsche Sprache und Literatur* LIV, No. 4 (April-May 1962): 201-05.
> Explores the influence of Romantic fantasy on Arnim's perception of reality through a detailed structural and textual analysis of his major works.

Mornin, J. Edward W. "National Subjects in the Works of Achim von Arnim." *German Life and Letters* XXIV, No. 4 (July 1971): 316-27.
> Considers the influence of German nationalism on Arnim's works. Mornin discusses the Germany of Arnim's day, and the author's important role in reviving interest in German folklore.

Riley, Helene M. "Scientist, Sorcerer, or Servant of Humanity: The Many Faces of Faust in the Work of Achim von Arnim." *Seminar* XIII, No. 1 (February 1977): 1-12.
> An analysis of three Faustian characters from *Gräfin Dolores*, *Isabella von Ägypten*, and *Die Kronenwächter*. Riley examines Arnim's view of the occult and the Romantics' view of illness and healing.

Washington, Lawrence M., and Washington, Ida H. "The Several Aspects of Fire in Achim von Arnim's *Der tolle Invalide*." *The German Quarterly* XXXVII, No. 4 (November 1964): 498-505.
> A discussion of the fire imagery in *Der tolle Invalide*. The critics conclude that the "various aspects of fire are so intimately connected with the events and characters of the story that they reflect the basic structure of the Novelle."

Weiss, Hermann F. "The Use of the Leitmotif in Achim von Arnim's Stories." *The German Quarterly* XLII, No. 3 (May 1969): 343-51.
> Discusses the leitmotif as a unifying device in several of Arnim's tales. Weiss demonstrates that Arnim was one of the earliest authors to employ a theme-related motif.

Wellek, René. "The Younger German Romantics: Arnim and Kleist." In his *A History of Modern Criticism, 1750-1950: The Romantic Age*, pp. 288-90. New Haven: Yale University Press, 1955.\*
> Explores Arnim's role in the revitalization of the German folk song. Wellek also elaborates on the accomplishments of all the Young Romantics.

# Honoré de Balzac

## 1799-1850

(Born Honoré Balzac; also wrote under the pseudonyms Lord R'hoone and Horace de Saint-Aubin) French novelist, short story and novella writer, dramatist, essayist, and editor.

Balzac is generally considered to be the greatest nineteenth-century French novelist. His importance rests on his vast work *La comédie humaine*, which consists of more than ninety novels and stories. Critics generally concur that his genius lies in his accurate use of observation and detail, his inexhaustible imagination, and his authentic portraits of men, women, and their physical environments. Considered an early exponent of realism, Balzac is praised for providing a comprehensive portrait of the French society of his day.

Balzac had a solitary childhood and received little attention from his parents. He lived with a wet nurse until the age of three, and at eight was sent to board at the Oratorian College at Vendôme. In 1884 his family moved from Tours to Paris, where Balzac completed his studies. He received his law degree in 1819; however, to his parents' disappointment, he announced that he intended to become a writer. From 1819 to 1825 Balzac experimented with literary forms, including verse tragedy and, later, sensational novels and stories, which he wrote under various pseudonyms. He considered these works to be stylistic exercises; they were conscious efforts to learn his craft, as well as his only means of support. At one point in his career he abandoned writing to become involved in a series of unsuccessful business ventures. Later, he returned to writing, but despite eventual renown, money problems continued to haunt him throughout his life.

*Le dernier Chouan; ou, La Bretagne en 1800 (The Chouans)* was Balzac's first critically successful work and the first to appear under his own name, to which he added, in 1831, the aristocratic particle *de*. The novel *Physiologie du mariage; ou, Méditations de philosophie éclectique sur le bonheur et le malheur conjugal (The Physiology of Marriage)* and the collection of short stories *Scènes de la vie privée*, both published in 1830, further enhanced his reputation. These works also enhanced his appeal to female readers, who valued his realistic and sympathetic portraits of women as vital members of society. In 1832, Balzac received a letter from one of his female admirers signed *l'Étrangère* (the Stranger). The writer expressed her admiration for *Scènes de la vie privée* and chided Balzac for the ironic tone in his newest work, *La peau de chagrin*. Later she revealed her identity as Madame Hanska, the wife of a wealthy Polish count. Balzac and Madame Hanska carried on an extended liaison through letters and infrequent visits. For nine years after her husband's death in 1841 she refused to remarry; her marriage to Balzac just five months before his death came too late to ease his financial troubles.

Commentators on Balzac rarely fail to note his flamboyant lifestyle and working habits. He never completed a work before sending it to the printer; instead, he sent a brief outline and scrupulously composed the entire work on successive galley proofs. To be free of distractions, he began working at midnight and continued, with only brief interruptions, until midday, fueled by tremendous quantities of strong black coffee.

After several months of this solitary, exhausting routine he would cease working and plunge into a frenzy of social activity, hoping to be admitted to the milieu of Parisian aristocracy. Balzac's ostentatious dress, extensive collection of antiques, outlandish printer's bills, and unsuccessful business schemes kept him perenially short of money. Many critics believe that the pressure of mounting debts pushed him to write faster and thus contributed to the creation of *La comédie humaine*.

*La comédie humaine*, written between 1830 and 1850, is considered to be his finest achievement. His preface to the 1842 collection outlines the goal of his writings. He refers to himself as "secretary to French society," and expresses his desire to describe and interpret his era. Balzac considered it possible to classify social species as the naturalists had classified zoological species. By organizing his stories into groups that depict the varied classes and their milieu, his work reveals his belief that environment determines an individual's development. *La comédie humaine* includes three main sections: the *Études analytiques*, *Études philosophiques*, and the bulk of his work, the *Études de moeurs*, which he further divided into the *Scènes de la vie de province*, *Scènes de la vie parisienne*, *Scènes de la vie politique*, *Scènes de la vie militaire*, *Scènes de la vie de campagne*, and *Scènes de la vie privée*, a title he had previously used for a collection of short stories. Balzac attempted to portray all levels of contemporary French society, but he did not live to complete the task.

Despite the great length and ambitious scope of *La comédie humaine*, most critics agree that the work should be approached as a whole. Many praise Balzac's technique of repeating characters in several novels, depicting them at different stages in their lives. For some critics, this strengthens the versimilitude of Balzac's fictional world and enabled Balzac to explore the psychology of individual characters more fully than is possible in single novels. Henry James considered Balzac's portraits of people to be his greatest talent. His best-known characters are monomaniacs, victims of a consuming passion, such as Goriot's obsessive love for his daughters in *Le père Goriot: Histoire parisienne (Old Goriot)*, and the miser Grandet's love for money in *Eugénie Grandet (Eugenia Grandet; or, The Miser's Daughter: A Tale of Everyday Life in the Nineteenth Century)*. In each of his memorable portraits, the essential characteristics of an individual are distilled into an embodiment and a reflection of an entire class. Balzac's accurate rendering of detail is generally attributed to his acute powers of observation; however, many critics, notably Charles Baudelaire and George Saintsbury, have emphasized other aspects of his work. They note that while he observed and recorded a wide variety of social milieus with objectivity and accuracy, his work also reveals a profound creative and imaginative power. Modern critics concur, finding Balzac's work to be a blend of acute observation and personal vision.

The morality of Balzac's works has long been debated. According to Ferdinand Brunetière, "Balzac brought about a revolution in the novel . . . by doing artistic work with elements reputed unworthy of art." In his effort to achieve a complete representation of society, Balzac included in his world not only virtue, faithfulness, and happiness, but also squalor, misery, chicanery, sexual perfidy, and greed. Many nineteenth-century readers and critics found his work to be depressing, and, more frequently, they considered his representation of life immoral. Others contended that Balzac was a realist and merely depicted society as he saw it.

Modern critical interest in Balzac attests to his enduring importance. His influence on the development of the novel in France is unsurpassed. Many critics contend that his use of the genre as social commentary steered the novel toward realism, and Balzac is now considered one of the world's greatest novelists. His ability to blend realistic detail, acute observation, and visionary imagination is considered his greatest artistic gift. His immense popularity continues unabated, as successive generations look to his novels for a universal as well as personal view of human life.

## PRINCIPAL WORKS

*Le dernier Chouan; ou, La Bretagne en 1800*   (novel) 1829; also published as *Les Chouans; ou, La Bretagne en 1799*, 1834
   [*The Chouans*, 1890]
*Physiologie du mariage; ou, Méditations de philosophie éclectique sur le bonheur et le malheur conjugal* (novel) 1830
   [*The Physiology of Marriage*, 1904]
*Scènes de la vie privée*   (short stories) 1830; also published as *Scènes de la vie privée* [enlarged edition] (novella and short stories) 1832

*La peau de chagrin*   (novel) 1831
   [*The Wild Ass's Skin*, 1895-98]
*Romans et contes philosophiques*   (novel and short stories) 1831
*\*Les célibataires*   (novella) 1832; published in *Scènes de la vie privée* [enlarged edition]; also published as *Le curé de Tours* in *Les célibataires*, 1858
   [*The Abbé Birotteau (Le Curé de Tours)*, 1895-98]
*Les cent contes drôlatiques: Colligez ès abbaïes de Touraine et mis en lumière par le sieur de Balzac, pour l'esbattement des Pantagruelistes et non aultres, premier dixain*   (short stories) 1832; *deuxième dixain*, 1833; *troisième dixain*, 1837
*Notice biographique sur Louis Lambert*   (novel) 1832; published in *Les nouveaux contes philosophiques;* also published in revised form as *Histoire intellectuel de Louis Lambert* in *Le livre mystique*, 1835
   [*Louis Lambert*, 1889]
*Les nouveaux contes philosophiques*   (novel and short stories) 1832
*Le medecin de campagne*   (novel) 1833
   [*The Country Doctor*, 1887]
*Études de moeurs au XIXe siècle. 12 vols.*   (novels, novellas, and short stories) 1834-37
*Histoire des treize*   (novellas) 1834-35; published in *Études de moeurs au XIXe siècle*
   [*The Thirteen*, 1895-98]
*La recherche de l'absolu*   (novel) 1834; published in *Études de moeurs au XIXe siècle;* also published as *Balthazar Claës; ou, La recherche de l'absolu*, 1839
   [*Balthazar; or, Science and Love*, 1859; also published as *The Quest of the Absolute*, 1888]
*Le livre mystique*   (novels and short stories) 1835
*Le père Goriot: Histoire parisienne*   (novel) 1835
   [*Daddy Goriot; or, Unrequited Affection*, 1860; also published as *Old Goriot*, 1895-98]
*Séraphita*   (novel) 1835; published in *Le livre mystique*
   [*Séraphita*, 1889]
*Le lys dans la vallée*   (novel) 1836
   [*The Lily of the Valley*, 1891]
*\*\*Les deux poètes*   (novella) 1837; published in *Études de moeurs au XIXe siècle*
*Eugénie Grandet*   (novel) 1837?; published in *Études de moeurs au XIXe siècle*
   [*Eugenia Grandet; or, The Miser's Daughter: A Tale of Everyday Life in the Nineteenth Century*, 1843]
*La vielle fille*   (novel) 1837; published in *Études de moeurs au XIXe siècle*
*Histoire de la grandeur et de la décadence de César Birotteau, parfumeur*   (novel) 1838
   [*History of the Grandeur and Downfall of César Birotteau*, 1860; also published as *The Rise and Fall of César Birotteau*, 1912]
*Béatrix; ou, Les amours forcés*   (novel) 1839
   [*Béatrix*, 1895-98]
*\*\*Un grand homme de province à Paris*   (novella) 1839
   [*A Great Man of the Provinces in Paris*, 1893]
*La femme de trente ans*   (novel) 1842; published in *Oeuvres complètes de M. de Balzac: La comédie humaine*
   [*A Woman of Thirty*, 1895-98]

*Illusions perdues* (novel) 1842-48; published in *Oeuvres complètes de M. de Balzac: La comédie humaine* [*Lost Illusions*, 1895-98]

*Oeuvres complètes de M. de Balzac: La comédie humaine.* 17 vols. (novels, novellas, and short stories) 1842-48

*Ursule Mirouët* (novel) 1842 [*Ursula*, 1891]

**Ève et David* (novella) 1843; published in *Oeuvres complètes de M. de Balzac: La comédie humaine;* also published as *Les souffrances de l'inventeur* in *Oeuvres complètes de H. de Balzac: Édition définitive*, 1879

*Honorine* (novella) 1844 [*Honorine*, 1895-98]

*Les trois amoureux* (novel) 1844; also published as *Modeste Mignon; ou, Les trois amoureux*, 1844 [*Modeste Mignon*, 1888]

****Histoire des parens* [sic] *pauvres: La cousine Bette et Les deux musiciens* (novels) 1847; also published as *Les parents pauvres.* 12 vols. 1847-48 [*Poor Relations*, 1880]

*Théâtre* [first publication] (dramas) 1853

*Oevures complètes de H. de Balzac.* 20 vols. (novels, novellas, short stories, and dramas) 1855-63

*Les célibataires* (novellas) 1858

*Pierrette* (novella) 1858; published in *Les célibataires* [*Pierrette*, 1895-98]

*La Rabouilleuse* (novella) 1858; published in *Les célibataires* [*A Bachelor's Establishment*, 1895-98]

*Les paysans* [completed by Madame Hanska] (novel) 1863; published in *Oeuvres complètes de H. de Balzac* [*The Peasantry*, 1895-98]

*Oeuvres complètes de H. de Balzac: Édition définitive.* 26 vols. (novels, novellas, short stories, dramas, letters, and essays) 1869-1906

*Balzac's Contes Drôlatiques: Droll Stories Collected from the Abbeys of Touraine* (short stories) 1874

*Correspondance de H. de Balzac, 1819-1850* (letters) 1876 [*The Correspondence of Honoré de Balzac*, 1878]

*Splendeurs et misères des courtisanes* (novel) 1879; published in *Oeuvres complètes de H. de Balzac: Édition définitive* [*A Harlot's Progress*, 1895-98; also published as *Splendors and Miseries of a Courtesan* (date unknown)]

*Comédie humaine.* 40 vols. (novels, novellas, and short stories) 1895-98

*Lettres à l'étrangère.* 4 vols. (letters) 1899-1950

*Honoré de Balzac: Letters to Madame Hanska, Born Countess Rzewuska, Afterwards Madame Honoré de Balzac, 1833-1846* (letters) 1900

*The Dramatic Works of Honoré de Balzac* (dramas) 1901

*The Love Letters of Honoré de Balzac: 1833-1842* (letters) 1901

*Oeuvres complètes de Honoré de Balzac.* 40 vols. (novels, novellas, short stories, dramas, letters, and essays) 1912-40

*\*Les célibataires*, the title of Balzac's 1832 novella, is also the title of his collection of novellas published in 1858. The novella appeared in the collection under the title *Le curé de Tours*.

**\*\*These works were collectively published as *Illusion perdues* in *Oevures complètes: La comédie humaine*, 1842-48.

\*\*\*This work includes the novels *La cousine Bette* and *Le cousin Pons*.

---

### L'ÉTRANGÈRE [PSEUDONYM OF MADAME HANSKA] (letter date 1832)

[*The following is Madame Hanska's second letter to Balzac. In her first letter, she had praised his works, as did Balzac's other female admirers; however, she resolved to remain anonymous. The personal and romantic allusions in the following excerpt indicate the direction their relationship later took. Their intimate correspondence eventually led to marriage. Only two of Madame Hanska's letters to Balzac have survived; she requested that the rest be destroyed.*]

I feel that I must write you and express to you, with all the enthusiasm I am capable of, the great admiration which your works have called forth in me.

Your soul seems to have been in existence for centuries, sir; your philosophical conceptions can only be the result of years of long study; and yet I am told that you are still young. . . .

Your exterior personality does not, I feel certain, indicate how vivid is your imagination; it is necessary to arouse you to awaken in you the sacred fire of genius which then enables one to see you as you really are; and you are what I feel you to be: a man with a superior knowledge of the human heart!

A thrill went through me as I read your books; you elevate woman to her proper position; love with her is a heavenly virtue, a divine production; I admire in you that admirable sensibility of soul which has made you understand this. . . .

Your career is a brilliant one, strewn with sweet and perfumed flowers; you must be happy and will ever be so.

At the time when I was reading your works I became identified with you, with your genius; your soul appeared to me to be full of light. I followed you step by step, proud of the praise which was lavished on you, or overcome with sorrow when bitter criticism poured its poisoned gall upon you. Several criticisms, nevertheless, seemed to me to be just, and notwithstanding my predilection for you I trembled. (p. 485)

Your genius appears to me to be sublime, but it must become divine; truth alone must make you attain this end; I see you as one soul does another; that is my only merit! Your genius is capable of everything; pure, colossal, its source is divine, its outpourings sacred. I should like to wrap you up in it, that you might live without succumbing to any of the numerous temptations which must surround your person, your talents and your genius!

For you I am l'Étrangère'' and will remain so all my life; you will never know me! . . .

As for myself, I think I understand your soul, which, with all its celestial emanations, may be discerned in your works. You know what love is and describe it with an angel's spirit. Oh! if you closely study the sacred enthusiasm which animates you, then most certainly will you produce works which will be handed down to posterity, and will throw great light upon the highest sum of real happiness attainable by man! . . .

Your writings have filled me with a feeling of deep enthusiasm; you are a luminous meteor which is destined to give direction and life to a new sense, but beware of reefs! . . . They surround you, I feel it! . . . I have neither talent nor genius, but a profound longing for truth permeates me. I would like to be an angel of light and protect you from all danger; the fire of your intelligence animates me; I can neither depict nor describe it, like you, with burning touches, but my entire being breathes it, and wishes to see you attain, without blemish, the end of a career which appears to me to be more closely connected with God than with other men.

In other words, you have possession of all my being; I admire your talent. I render homage to your soul; I would like to be your sister! . . .

I might show you some errors in your works, but never any untruth; I am whole-souled, and have but one virtue: to love, and I love for eternity! . . . How often have I wished myself near you when you have been wrapped up in those profound thoughts which you describe so well, when alone in silence with your powerful personality, alone with your brilliant imagination, when your every thought is a marvel of moral force, of almost supernatural forethought, and which, nevertheless, makes us feel so well that man's power of comprehension is almost without limit. Every night you thus give birth to some new idea; when everything around you is asleep your genius remains awake to bring us a superabundance of power, of harmony and of love! (p. 486)

> *L'Étrangère [pseudonym of Madame Hanska], in a letter to Balzac on November 7, 1832, translated by Bradford Colt de Wolf, in* The Bookman, *New York (copyright, 1902, by Dodd, Mead and Company, Inc.), Vol. XIV, No. 5, January, 1902, pp. 485-86.*

## HONORÉ DE BALZAC   (letter date 1834)

[*Balzac's letters to Madame Hanska, which were often devoted to a discussion of his recent work, reflect his preoccupation with his fictional world. In the following he outlines his plan for* La comédie humaine.]

The "**Études de Moeurs**" will represent all social effects, without a single situation in life, physiognomy, character of man or woman, manner of living, profession, social zone, French region, or anything whatever of childhood, maturity, old age, politics, justice, or war, having been forgotten.

That done, the history of the human heart traced thread by thread, the social history given in all its parts, there is *the base*. The facts will not be imaginary; they will be what is happening everywhere.

Then, the second structure is the "**Études Philosophiques;**" for after the *effects* will come the *causes*. I shall have painted in the "**Études de Moeurs**" sentiments and their action, life and its deportment. In the "**Études Philosophiques**" I shall tell *why* the sentiments, *on what* the life; what is the line, what are the conditions beyond which neither society nor man exist; and, after having surveyed society in order to describe it, I shall survey it again in order to judge it. So, in the "**Études de Moeurs**" *individualities* are typified; in the "**Études Philosophiques**" *types* are individualized. Thus I shall have given life everywhere: to the type by individualizing it, to the individual by typifying him. I shall have given thought to the fragment; I shall have given to thought the life of the individual.

Then, after *effects* and *causes*, will come the "**Études Analytiques,**" of which the "**Physiologie du Mariage**" is a part; for after *effects* and *causes* we must search for *principles*.

*Manners* and *morals* [*moeurs*] are the play; *causes* are the *coulisses* and the *machinery*. *Principles* are the *maker*. But in proportion as the work winds spirally up to the heights of thought, it draws itself in and condenses. Though twenty-four volumes are required for the "**Études de Moeurs,**" only fifteen are needed for the "**Études Philosophiques,**" and only nine for the "**Études Analytiques.**" Thus man, society, humanity will be described, judged, analyzed, without repetitions, and in a work which will be like an "Arabian Nights" of the West.

When all is done, my Madeleine scraped, my pediment carved, my last touches given, I shall have been *right,* or I shall have been *wrong.* But, after having made the poesy, the demonstration of a whole system, I shall make the science of it in an "**Essay on Human Forces**" ["**Essai sur les Forces Humaines**"]. And, on the cellar-walls of this palace I, child and jester, shall have drawn the immense arabesque of the "**Contes Drolatiques.**" (pp. 217-19)

> *Honoré de Balzac, in a letter to Madame Hanska on October 6, 1834, in his* Letters of Honoré de Balzac to Madame Hanska: 1833-1846, *translated by Katherine Prescott Wormeley (translation copyright 1900, by Hardy, Pratt and Co.; originally published in part as* Lettres à l'étrangère: 1833-1842, *Vol. I by Honoré de Balzac, Calmann Lévy, 1899), Hardy, Pratt and Co., 1900 (and reprinted by Little, Brown, and Company, 1911), pp. 211-19.*

## [J. W. CROKER]   (essay date 1836)

If we were considering the *literary merit* of his works, we should have much to say in praise and at least as much in censure of M. de Balsac. He has considerable powers of local description, but he considerably abuses them by idle and wearisome minutiae. He occasionally excites great interest, but quite as often destroys all interest by the improbability and incongruity of his incidents. He is often eloquent, and sometimes pathetic; but, in his efforts after these qualities, frequently deviates into whining and bombast. But it is only as evidence of the state of *moral* feeling and *social* life in France that we have at present to deal with M. de Balsac; and in this view his evidence is indeed most important, not only on account of his acknowledged talents, but because he claims—and because the public voice has assented to his claim—to be, *par excellence,* the most accurate painter of private life and existing society. The titles of his principal works—*Scenes of Private Life, Scenes of Parisian Life, Scenes of Provincial Life*—sufficiently attest this pretension. In the preface to the *Scenes of Private Life,* he sets out with a declaration which reveals an honest and noble ambition;—

> That his works are of such a tendency, that he hopes that well-educated mothers, who unite in their own persons feminine graces to manly good sense, will not hesitate to *place his works in the hands of their daughters.*

And he has found a panegyrist—in the writer of a rather elaborate essay, originally, it seems, published in some French review, but now affixed to the fourth volume of the *Scenes of Parisian Life*—who not only extols him as one of the greatest literary geniuses that ever lived, but as the most faithful painter of manners, and, above all, as one of the *purest moralists* of the age. This critic goes so far, indeed, as to endeavour, by a formal classification and commentary, to prove that these "*splendid works,*" instead of being, as they may appear to the common reader, a series of unconnected tales of the vulgarest and most licentious character, are, in fact, a profound and well-digested course of moral philosophy, written with one great design, and deserving to be distinguished by the loftier title of *Etudes sur les Moeurs!* (p. 81)

M. de Balsac, as his panegyrist tells us, has consigned to oblivion all his works published prior to 1830. . . . We were, at first sight, at a loss to account for this unconditional surrender of so much fame—for we really thought such of those repudiated works as we have looked at to be as good as, and some of them better than, his later productions. . . . (p. 82)

We wish we could believe that M. de Balsac's repudiation of these errors of his youth arose from good feeling, or even from good taste, but [subsequent works] will show that these could not have been his motives, and that he only regrets them because they are too *tame.*

The first separate work of the era by which M. de Balsac wishes to be judged is *La Peau de Chagrin,* of which—as the ground-work is supernatural, and therefore out of our present scope—we shall say little. . . . [The] story does not want a certain degree of interest; but it is awkwardly and inconsistently managed, and is only worth mentioning for its evidence—as far as it goes—of the general demoralization of the society it describes; but such a *romance,* we are aware, can be no satisfactory evidence, except of the bad taste which admires it. (p. 83)

We must here pause to observe that his French critic thinks it one of the greatest merits of M. de Balsac, that he re-produces the same personages—in different periods and circumstances of their lives—in his different works—'by which means,' says this panegyrist, 'he gives his novels a kind of historical connexion with each other, and spreads a greater air of reality over the whole.' The fact is indisputable, but we do not altogether believe in the assigned motive. It seems to us that M. de Balsac, writing with great haste and to produce sudden and powerful effects—both on the public and his *paymaster* the publisher—finds it more rapid and convenient to *jump,* as it were, from scene to scene, than to spend time and trouble in weaving a connected narrative. He may also think that the obscurity which these intervals leave tends to create a mysterious interest. It may be so; but it also produces inconsistencies and confusion, and we are often . . . not quite satisfied, nor does his French critic seem to be, as to the degree of connexion which the author means to establish between them. (p. 89)

The first volume of the *Scènes de la Vie de Province* [*Scenes of Provincial Life*] has five tales. Of three of them the heroines are adulteresses; in two the heroes died shocking deaths. Another is only the adventures of a *commis marchand,* or *bagman,* which are meant to be droll; but even M. de Balsac's admirers admit that the drollery is *feeble*—we should call it vulgar stuff. The fifth, called *Les Célibataires,* is the story of the rivalry of two priests of the cathedral of Tours: in this there is no indecency, and the intrigues and *tracassaries* of a country town are cleverly sketched; but the details exhibit a painful and discreditable state of society.

The second volume is occupied altogether by the story of *Eugénie Grandet,* one which, amongst M. de Balsac's countless tales, has the almost singular merit, that it may be read by a man without indignation, and by a woman without a blush. It is, as it were, *a Dutch picture of an interior*—of the family and society of the penurious merchant of a country town. The details are painted with vivid accuracy, and the characters are

worked up with equal originality and truth—but as usual with M. de Balsac, he too often pushes the minuteness of his local descriptions to tediousness, and the peculiarities of his personages to improbabilities. The character of Eugénie Grandet herself, combining the gentleness of her submissive mother with something of the shrewdness and firmness of her avaricious father, is ably conceived and happily executed; and if this work were separated from its corrupted companions, it might be read as a favourable and interesting specimen of M. de Balsac's powers. (p. 91)

[In] *Scenes of Parisian Life* many of the characters with whom we have become acquainted in the [earlier novel], *Père Goriot,* are reproduced, but with deeper immorality and exaggerated improbabilities. They for the most part hinge on an association of conspirators called *The Thirteen.* This association is formed of villains of *all ranks,* from the *stigmatized felon* to the *titled dandy,* who, by their union, secrecy, and desperate fidelity to their chief and to each other, are represented as *all-powerful*—to save or to destroy life—to confer or to ruin fortunes: the highest society and the lowest are equally at their mercy; money, office, rank, consideration, are all at their disposal; and from poison and poniard up to naval and military armaments, no instrument of power is beyond their reach. And this is the monstrous stuff—and only not ridiculous and contemptible because it is monstrous—which forms the ground-work of M. de Balsac's most applauded scenes of Parisian life; and we can assure our readers, that of about thirty tales which these twelve or fourteen volumes contain, there are not above four or five which are not tainted, impregnated, *saturated* with every kind of crime, every kind of filth, every kind of meanness, and, we must add, every kind of absurdity and improbability.

Besides his novels, or, as they are called, *Etudes sur les Moeurs,* M. de Balsac has published some other works, which, in concurrence with his panegyrists, he is now pleased to designate as *Etudes Philosophiques.* They seem to us to be nothing else but demoralizing maxims exemplified by licentious examples;—the design was infamous, but fortunately the *Studies* are in execution so stupid and so obscure, that even the curiosity of vice must be blunted at their aspect. M. Balsac never had any taste—and the shallow vein of his talents appears to be nearly worked out. (pp. 93-4)

> [*J. W. Croker*], *"French Novels,"* in The Quarterly Review, *Vol. LVI, No. CXI, April, 1836, pp. 65-131.**

## HONORÉ DE BALZAC (essay date 1842)

> [*The following is Balzac's often-quoted "Avant-propos" (preface) to the first collection of his works published under the title* La comédie humaine. *In this essay Balzac defines the scope, theory, and purpose of his vast work. He posits that there are different social species comparable to the different zoological species. He intended* La comédie humaine *to be a thorough, scientific portrayal of all elements of society. Yet, Balzac here reveals a larger goal than mere scientific portrayal: to present a "history of manners" of contemporary society. His division of* La comédie humaine *into the* Études de moeurs, Études philosophiques, *and* Études analytiques *reflects his understanding of society. Balzac concludes the essay with an explanation of the meaning of and the relationship between these divisions.*]

In giving the general title of *The Human Comedy* to a work begun nearly thirteen years since, it is necessary to explain its motive, to relate its origin, and briefly sketch its plan, while endeavoring to speak of these matters as though I had no personal interest in them. (p. li)

The idea of *The Human Comedy* was at first as a dream to me, one of those impossible projects which we caress and then let fly; a chimera that gives us a glimpse of its smiling woman's face, and forthwith spreads its wings and returns to a heavenly realm of phantasy. But this chimera, like many another, has become a reality; has its behests, its tyranny, which must be obeyed.

The idea originated in a comparison between Humanity and Animality.

It is a mistake to suppose that the great dispute which has lately made a stir, between Cuvier and Geoffroi Saint-Hilaire, arose from a scientific innovation. Unity of structure, under other names, had occupied the greatest minds during the two previous centuries. As we read the extraordinary writings of the mystics who studied the sciences in their relation to infinity, such as Swedenborg, Saint-Martin, and others, and the works of the greatest authors on Natural History—Leibnitz, Buffon, Charles Bonnet, etc., we detect in the *monads* of Leibnitz, in the *organic molecules* of Buffon, in the *vegetative force* of Needham, in the correlation of similar organs of Charles Bonnet—who in 1760 was so bold as to write, "Animals vegetate as plants do"—we detect, I say, the rudiments of the great law of Self for Self, which lies at the root of *Unity of Plan*. There is but one Animal. The Creator works on a single model for every organized being. "The Animal" is elementary, and takes its external form, or, to be accurate, the differences in its form, from the environment in which it is obliged to develop. (pp. li-lii)

I, for my part, convinced of this scheme of nature long before the discussion to which it has given rise, perceived that in this respect society resembled nature. For does not society modify Man, according to the conditions in which he lives and acts, into men as manifold as the species in Zoölogy! The differences between a soldier, an artisan, a man of business, a lawyer, an idler, a student, a statesman, a merchant, a sailor, a poet, a beggar, a priest, are as great, though not so easy to define, as those between the wolf, the lion, the ass, the crow, the shark, the seal, the sheep, etc. Thus social species have always existed, and will always exist, just as there are zoölogical species. If Buffon could produce a magnificent work by attempting to represent in a book the whole realm of zoölogy, was there not room for a work of the same kind on society? But the limits set by nature to the variations of animals have no existence in society. When Buffon describes the lion, he dismisses the lioness with a few phrases; but in society a wife is not always the female of the male. There may be two perfectly dissimilar beings in one household. The wife of a shopkeeper is sometimes worthy of a prince, and the wife of a prince is often worthless compared with the wife of an artisan. The social state has freaks which Nature does not allow herself; it is nature *plus* society. The description of social species would thus be at least double that of animal species, merely in view of the two sexes. Then, among animals the drama is limited; there is scarcely any confusion; they turn and rend each other—that is all. Men, too, rend each other; but their greater or less intelligence makes the struggle far more complicated. . . . Buffon found that life was extremely simple among animals. Animals have little property, and neither arts nor sciences; while man, by a law that has yet to be sought, has a tendency to express his culture, his thoughts, and his life in everything he appropriates to his use. Though Leuwenhoek, Swammerdam,

Spallanzani, Réaumur, Charles Bonnet, Müller, Haller and other patient investigators have shown us how interesting are the habits of animals, those of each kind are, at least to our eyes, always and in every age alike; whereas the dress, the manners, the speech, the dwelling of a prince, a banker, an artist, a citizen, a priest, and a pauper are absolutely unlike, and change with every phase of civilization.

Hence the work to be written needed a threefold form—men, women, and things; that is to say, persons and the material expression of their minds; man, in short, and life. (pp. lii-liv)

But how could such a drama, with the four or five thousand persons which a society offers, be made interesting? How, at the same time, please the poet, the philosopher, and the masses who want both poetry and philosophy under striking imagery? Though I could conceive of the importance and of the poetry of such a history of the human heart, I saw no way of writing it; for hitherto the most famous story-tellers had spent their talent in creating two or three typical actors, in depicting one aspect of life. It was with this idea that I read the works of Walter Scott. Walter Scott, the modern troubadour, or finder (*trouvère—trouveur*), had just then given an aspect of grandeur to a class of composition unjustly regarded as of the second rank. . . . Walter Scott raised to the dignity of the philosophy of History the literature which, from age to age, sets perennial gems in the poetic crown of every nation where letters are cultivated. He vivified it with the spirit of the past; he combined drama, dialogue, portrait, scenery, and description; he fused the marvelous with truth—the two elements of the times; and he brought poetry into close contact with the familiarity of the humblest speech. But as he had not so much devised a system as hit upon a manner in the ardor of his work, or as its logical outcome, he never thought of connecting his compositions in such a way as to form a complete history of which each chapter was a novel, and each novel the picture of a period.

It was by discerning this lack of unity, which in no way detracts from the Scottish writer's greatness, that I perceived at once the scheme which would favor the execution of my purpose, and the possibility of executing it. Though dazzled, so to speak, by Walter Scott's amazing fertility, always himself and always original, I did not despair, for I found the source of his genius in the infinite variety of human nature. Chance is the greatest romancer in the world; we have only to study it. French society would be the real author; I should only be the secretary. By drawing up an inventory of vices and virtues, by collecting the chief facts of the passions, by depicting characters, by choosing the principal incidents of social life, by composing types out of a combination of homogeneous characteristics, I might perhaps succeed in writing the history which so many historians have neglected: that of Manners. By patience and perseverance I might produce for France in the nineteenth century the book which we must all regret that Rome, Athens, Tyre, Memphis, Persia, and India have not bequeathed to us; [a] history of their social life. . . . (pp. liv-lvi)

The work, so far, was nothing. By adhering to the strict lines of a reproduction a writer might be a more or less faithful, and more or less successful painter of types of humanity, a narrator of the dramas of private life, an archaeologist of social furniture, a cataloguer of professions, a registrar of good and evil; but to deserve the praise of which every artist must be ambitious, must I not also investigate the reasons or the cause of these social effects, detect the hidden sense of this vast assembly of figures, passions, and incidents? And finally, having sought—I will not say having found—this reason, this motive power, must I not reflect on first principles, and discover in what particulars societies approach or deviate from the eternal law of truth and beauty? In spite of the wide scope of the preliminaries, which might of themselves constitute a book, the work, to be complete, would need a conclusion. Thus depicted, society ought to bear in itself the reason of its working. (pp. lvi-lvii)

As to the intimate purpose, the soul of this work, these are the principles on which it is based.

Man is neither good nor bad; he is born with instincts and capabilities; society, far from depraving him, as Rousseau asserts, improves him, makes him better; but self-interest also develops his evil tendencies. Christianity, above all, Catholicism, being—as I have pointed out in the **Country Doctor (Le Médecin de Campagne)**—a complete system for the repression of the depraved tendencies of man, is the most powerful element of social order.

In reading attentively the presentment of society cast, as it were, from the life, with all that is good and all that is bad in it, we learn this lesson—if thought, or if passion, which combines thought and feeling, is the vital social element, it is also its destructive element. In this respect social life is like the life of man. Nations live long only by moderating their vital energy. Teaching, or rather education, by religious bodies is the grand principle of life for nations, the only means of diminishing the sum of evil and increasing the sum of good in all society. Thought, the living principle of good and ill, can only be trained, quelled, and guided by religion. The only possible religion is Christianity. . . . Christianity created modern nationalities, and it will preserve them. Hence, no doubt, the necessity for the monarchical principle. Catholicism and Royalty are twin principles. (pp. lvii-lviii)

I write under the light of two eternal truths—Religion and Monarchy; two necessities, as they are shown to be by contemporary events, towards which every writer of sound sense ought to try to guide the country back. (p. lix)

Some persons may, perhaps, think that this declaration is somewhat autocratic and self-assertive. They will quarrel with the novelist for wanting to be an historian, and will call him to account for writing politics. I am simply fulfilling an obligation—that is my reply. The work I have undertaken will be as long as a history; I was compelled to explain the logic of it, hitherto unrevealed, and its principles and moral purposes. (p. lix)

Now every one who, in the domain of ideas, brings his stone by pointing out an abuse, or setting a mark on some evil that it may be removed—every such man is stigmatized as immoral. The accusation of immorality, which has never failed to be cast at the courageous writer, is, after all, the last that can be brought when nothing else remains to be said to a romancer. If you are truthful in your pictures; if by dint of daily and nightly toil you succeed in writing the most difficult language in the world, the word *immoral* is flung in your teeth. Socrates was immoral; Jesus Christ was immoral; they both were persecuted in the name of the society they overset or reformed. When a man is to be killed he is taxed with immorality. . . .

When depicting all society, sketching it in the immensity of its turmoil, it happened—it could not but happen—that the picture displayed more of evil than of good; that some part of the fresco represented a guilty couple; and the critics at once raised the cry of immorality, without pointing out the morality

of another portion intended to be a perfect contrast. . . . [The] time for an impartial verdict is not yet come for me. (p. lx)

Some persons, seeing me collect such a mass of facts and paint them as they are, with passion for their motive power, have supposed, but wrongly, that I must belong to the school of Sensualism and Materialism—two aspects of the same thing—Pantheism. But their misapprehension was perhaps justified—or inevitable. I do not share the belief in indefinite progress for society as a whole; I believe in man's improvement in himself. (p. lxii)

A sure grasp of the purport of this work will make it clear that I attach to common, daily facts, hidden or patent to the eye, to the acts of individual lives, and to their causes and principles, the importance which historians have hitherto ascribed to the events of public national life. The unknown struggle which goes on in a valley of the Indre between Mme. de Mortsauf and her passion is perhaps as great as the most famous of battles (**Le Lys dans la Vallée**). In one the glory of the victor is at stake; in the other it is heaven. The misfortunes of the two Birotteaus, the priest and the perfumer, to me are those of mankind (**Le Curé de Tours** and **Histoire de la Grandeur et de la Décadence de César Birotteau, Parfumeur**). La Fosseuse (**Médecin de Campagne**) and Mme. Graslin (**Curé de Village**) are almost the sum-total of woman. We all suffer thus every day. (pp. lxiii-lxiv)

It was no small task to depict the two or three thousand conspicuous types of a period; for this is, in fact, the number presented to us by each generation, and which **The Human Comedy** will require. This crowd of actors, this multitude of lives, needed a setting—if I may be pardoned the expression, a gallery. Hence the very natural division, as already known, into **Scenes of Private Life,** of **Provincial Life,** of **Parisian, Political, Military,** and **Country Life.** Under these six heads are classified all the studies of manners which form the history of society at large, of all its *faits et gestes,* as our ancestors would have said. These six classes correspond, indeed, to familiar conceptions. Each has its own sense and meaning, and answers to an epoch in the life of man. . . . After being informed of my plan, [the young writer Felix Davin] said that the **Scenes of Private Life** represented childhood and youth and their errors, as the **Scenes of Provincial Life** represented the age of passion, scheming, self-interest, and ambition. Then the **Scenes of Parisian Life** give a picture of the tastes and vice and unbridled powers which conduce to the habits peculiar to great cities, where the extremes of good and evil meet. Each of these divisions has its local color—Paris and the Provinces—a great social antithesis which held for me immense resources.

And not man alone, but the principal events of life, fall into classes by types. There are situations which occur in every life, typical phases, and this is one of the details I most sought after. I have tried to give an idea of the different districts of our fine country. My work has its geography, as it has its genealogy and its families, its places and things, its persons and their deeds; as it has its heraldry, its nobles and commonalty, its artisans and peasants, its politicians and dandies, its army—in short, a whole world of its own.

After describing social life in these three portions, I had to delineate certain exceptional lives, which comprehend the interests of many people, or or everybody, and are in a degree outside the general law. Hence we have **Scenes of Political Life.** This vast picture of society being finished and complete, was it not needful to display it in its most violent phase, beside itself, as it were, either in self-defence or for the sake of conquest? Hence the **Scenes of Military Life,** as yet the most incomplete portion of my work, but for which room will be allowed in this edition, that it may form part of it when done. Finally, the **Scenes of Country Life** are, in a way, the evening of this long day, if I may so call the social drama. In that part are to be found the purest natures, and the application of the great principles of order, politics, and morality.

Such is the foundation, full of actors, full of comedies and tragedies, on which are raised the **Philosophical Studies**—the second part of my work, in which the social instrument of all these effects is displayed, and the ravages of the mind are painted, feeling after feeling; the first of this series, **The Magic Skin,** to some extent forms a link between the **Philosophical Studies** and Studies of Manners, by a work of almost Oriental fancy, in which life itself is shown in a mortal struggle with the very element of all passion.

Besides these, there will be a series of **Analytical Studies,** of which I will say nothing, for one only is published as yet—**The Physiology of Marriage.**

In the course of time I purpose writing two more works of this class. First, the Pathology of Social Life, then an Anatomy of Educational Bodies, and a Monograph on Virtue. In looking forward to what remains to be done, my readers will perhaps echo what my publishers say, ''Please God to spare you!'' I only ask to be less tormented by men and things than I have hitherto been since I began this terrific labor. (pp. lxiv-lxvii)

The vastness of a plan which includes both a history and a criticism of society, an analysis of its evils, and a discussion of its principles, authorizes me, I think, in giving to my work the title under which it now appears—**The Human Comedy.** Is this too ambitious? Is it not exact? That, when it is complete, the public must pronounce. (p. lxvii)

> *Honoré de Balzac, ''Author's Introduction'' (1842), in his The Works of Honoré de Balzac: The Magic Skin, The Quest of the Absolute and Other Stories, Vol. I-II, edited by William P. Trent, translated by Ellen Marriage, Thomas Y. Crowell Co., Inc., 1900, pp. li-lxvii.*

### THE FOREIGN QUARTERLY REVIEW   (essay date 1843)

We are to know an author by his fruits; but those fruits we should be careful how to choose, and not take them in the spring when they are green, or in the winter when they are rotten. Judge Balzac by his **'Recherche de l'Absolu,'** his **'Père Goriot,'** his **'Eugenie Grandet,'** his **'Peau de Chagrin,'** his **'Cesar Berotteau,'** and others which have marked his place in literature: and that place will seem to you justly and deservedly of the very first rank in this class of fiction. Balzac is at once a painter of the Flemish school, and a high artist of human passion. The combination is rare indeed.

It is strongly marked in the present tale [**'Ménage de Garçon en Province'**, or **'La Rabouilleuse'**], some description of which we will therefore give. It may rank among the better specimens of Balzac's genius, and is only not among the best, because its nicety of detail in external matters is perhaps more prominent than its mastery of the secrets of the heart. The little town selected as the seat of the **'Ménage de Garçon en Province,'** is that of Issoudun in Berry; whither the poor mother of two

sons goes to implore aid of an only brother, unseen for thirty years. (p. 369)

The description of Issoudun, one of the most ancient towns of France, with its tower built by Richard Coeur de Lion, and its street, which through two thousand years has borne the name of Faubourg de Rome, and whose inhabitants assert their descent from the Romans, and have peculiar habits and peculiar features, is a masterpiece in Balzac's Flemish manner. The love of the *status quo* in this little town; the demand of its most conservative municipal council, that the high road from Paris to Toulouse should not pass through it, since it would raise the price of poultry; the ruin which threatens its wine and wool trade, since the fabrication of the first must undergo no change, and the breed that produces the other will have no amelioration; are all given in his most graphic way. Best of all is the stagnation of the inhabitants themselves: that stagnation found where there is no love of art or pursuit of science; which spreads and desolates like a marsh, to whose level all who enter must bring down their intellectual wants, if they would not feel them mere ''perilous stuff which weighs upon the heart;'' where each lives ensconced in his own walls, walking up and down within them with the useless activity of a caged animal in a Zoological Garden, till she or he dies: often of some malady wanting a name: *the effect of the air.* (p. 370)

[In **'Un Ménage de Garçon en Province;'**], Balzac keeps somewhat too much on the revolting side; in contrast to which the artist, his mother, and Madame Hochon, are sketched too lightly, though with a touch most bright and pure. The ignoble scenes are dwelt on too long, and recur too often. Some trivial matters, too, lengthen and weary to little purpose: those, for instance, which detail the mischievous tricks of the association to which Max belongs. The noble struggles of the artist had on the whole interested us more, and instructed us better, than the base success of the thief and bully, the unnatural son and dishonest brother. Philip, if not overdrawn (for we trace admirably, step by step, his way from vice to crime), is at least one of the odious exceptions which are hardly profitable to contemplate. The conception of Joseph, on the other hand, is true and beautiful. The genius unacknowledged, the devotion uncomprehended, the affection unreturned: while even the parent he supports looks on the fortunate egotist as the clever man of the family, and wonders and admires, not at the long struggles and light reward of Joseph, her youngest son, but that her eldest, Philip, should obtain the cross of honour! The miser, of a different race from him we knew in **'Eugenie Grandet,'** is graphic also; particularly at the wedding dinner, where Gritte, requiring string to truss her turkey, he draws forth a coil which has seen soil and service, and repenting his gift as she reaches the door, exclaims, ''Gritte, you will return it!'' The roué Max; the imbecile Rouget; the sordid, clever, shameless woman, bent at last after all her vicious triumphs under the iron hand of Philip, till Joseph's pity and ours would fain raise even her;—are new evidences of Balzac's power and genius: of his knowledge of the heart, and his fearless exposure of those crimes and follies by which humanity is most endangered. (p. 380)

> *''Balzac's 'Provincial Bachelor's Household','' in The Foreign Quarterly Review, Vol. XXX, No. LX, January, 1843, pp. 369-80.*

### FRASER'S MAGAZINE   (essay date 1843)

[**Peau de Chagrin**] is good, and might have been wrought into a beautiful and instructive moral. Eastern fables of the kind, though coming down to us from the infancy of letters, will never lose their charm. They require, however, from the very extravagance of their first conception, a chaster fancy and a severer simplicity of style to be treated well than any other kind of work. But the first idea of M. de Balzac's tale is, we hesitate not to say, quite as worthy of credence as any incident he has raised upon it. If there is any care shewn in the production, it is a care to avoid every sentiment and every situation that might have in it a semblance of reality or of possibility; and if we could suppose any purpose in the author, we should say it was to *glorify crime*. But of this purpose we are inclined to acquit M. de Balzac. . . . He is of the number of those writers who are essentially *of the day*. Finding the horrible and the fantastic in fiction an ultra Asiatic gorgeousness, not of imagination, but of colouring, and a philosophy (if it may be so called) like the dreams of an opium-eater, popular, he has thrown himself into the prevailing vogue with great spirit, cleverness, and effect, and seems to have determined, in the wild book before us, to leave all competitors in this species of writing far behind him. In *frenzied* eloquence, and in *frenzied* imagery, indeed, he can have no rival. . . . (p. 192)

*"French Romances,"* in Fraser's Magazine, *Vol. XXVII, No. CLVIII, February, 1843, pp. 184-94.**

### [G. H. LEWES]  (essay date 1844)

There are three points of view from which the novelist may be regarded; as a Moralist, an Artist, and an Entertaining Writer. He may be unexceptionably moral, yet unequivocally dull; he may be very entertaining, yet very immoral; and he may be a great artist without being either particularly moral or immoral, also without being (to novel readers) entertaining. . . . In endeavouring to furnish hints for the just appreciation of George Sand and Balzac, we shall treat of them under these three heads; and by means of their opposite qualities we may be able to elicit distinct characteristics of both. (p. 145)

Balzac, as a painter of society, and one who has exhibited profound knowledge of the secret springs of character, ought sparingly to use the subject of adultery; first, because, if he pretends to paint society, it is a gross error to seize only one aspect of that society (and no one will pretend to say that adultery is the rule, and chastity the exception); secondly, because his very knowledge of character should supply him with sufficient materials, without his needing recourse to disagreeable and exceptional cases. . . . This is the case with Balzac, and not with George Sand. She has used the subject very sparingly; and has always painted it as a serious misfortune, the very existence of which points at a social evil to be reformed. Balzac, on the contrary, treats it as a matter of course. From his works it would be concluded that all wives are unfaithful; and that their infidelity is looked upon as only an insult to their husbands, never as a crime against society; nay, well-bred husbands do not even consider it an insult. We believe that he has written scarcely a story in which love forms the principal element, in which adultery is not introduced; and it would be ridiculous to assert that this is a faithful representation of society. He never betrays the least consciousness that his hero or heroine are guilty. The most virtuous as the most vicious equally sin in this respect. His ideal of a woman, the Lily of the Valley, has an intrigue with a boy. (p. 147)

[There] are few of Balzac's [works] that are not very decidedly immoral in tendency. Were it not for a few isolated pictures of heroism, simplicity, and silent, unostentatious virtue which

he has painted, one would be tempted to deny that he had any moral sense. As all his heroines are unfaithful, so almost all his men are rascals. While philanthropy has been so nobly advocated in the '**Médecin de Campagne;**' integrity so touchingly exhibited in '**César Birotteau;**' and devotion so depicted in '**La Maison Claes,**' it will be impossible not to acknowledge that Balzac has a very keen, a very just moral sense. But his works in general seem flat contradictions to it. He paints the deepest rascality without a murmur of indignation. His young dandies, De Marsay, Rastignac, Ajuda Pinto, and Vandenesse, are destitute of any moral principle; nor does he express any contempt for them on that score. . . . George Sand has painted men of the day, Raymon, Horace, De Lansac, and Leoni; yet no one ever doubted for an instant that these men were objects of contempt and moral reprobation. Balzac, on the contrary, draws his polished rascals in such glowing colours, and manifests such an utter insensibility to their vices, that the result is highly immoral. This is greatly owing to his aristocratic prejudices. Vice, in losing its coarseness, loses to him its hideousness. To seduce a woman, to treat her with polished brutality, to speculate upon her influence in advancing your worldly views, to leave her when tired, and to recommence with another, are the acts of a gentleman, in his opinion.

This is not all. . . . He is fond of raising disgusting images. He is prone to describe with minuteness, feelings which ought not to be described; bestowing diseases on his personages which might very well be dispensed with. In '**La Vieille Fille,**' he has described the sexual desires as agitating an old maid; in '**Le Ménage de Garçon,**' the physical effects of abstinence and incontinence. (pp. 148-49)

Balzac, on the whole, is a very dangerous writer. There are some few of his works, such as '**Eugenie Grandet,**' '**La Recherche de l'Absolu**' (also called '**La Maison Claes**'), '**Le Curé de Tours,**' '**Le Médecin de Campagne,**' '**César Birotteau,**' and some short stories, which are perfectly unexceptionable on the point of morality. The rest are all dangerous, insidious. They want delicacy, both of taste and feeling. They imply that natural manners and natural ideas are ridiculous; and that Parisian refinement alone can make a human being estimable. By dwelling on the myriad affectations (usually characterized by him as adorable) of the *dame comme il faut*, by his very talent for penetrating into the secret springs of vanity and display, he corrupts the taste of his admiring reader. He should be strictly forbidden to young women. (p. 149)

[Let us consider Balzac as an artist], under which head we include style, exhibition of character, and poetic conception. Balzac is the worst writer we ever met with, considering his immense talent. There are few Frenchmen who write so incorrectly; none more detestably. Not to speak of his neologisms, nor of his use of active verbs in passive senses, his style is crabbed, prolix, startling, and affected. French in his hands is no longer the light, idiomatic, easy, pointed, brilliant language we know it; but unwieldy, unintelligible, and perverse. French, which compensates for its comparative poverty by its inimitable grace, becomes with him inexpressive, unwieldy, and tedious. . . . [When] men set syntax, idiom, and taste at defiance, in their research after novelty of expression, it is but natural they should sometimes succeed: as perpetual punsters sometimes stumble on a random jest. Balzac is not careless, but perverse. He does not write the slipslop of Paul de Kock or Eugène Sue. His sins are deliberate; his awkwardness is studied; his incorrectness is elaborate. Words are not used in unheard of senses from ignorance, but from *parti pris*. His sentences are not distorted because his pen hesitates and his meaning staggers; but because he conceives the best way of producing an effect is to avoid the natural sequences of language. In consequence, dialogue is the element in which he seems most at ease; it is that which he writes best: because he therein imitates the style of conversation. In descriptions he is detestable; the more he labours the worse he writes; and when he attempts poetical description, he is ludicrous beyond example. . . . His attention to the dress of his persons is tediously minute; every article is described; and should they change the dress, that also merits description. (pp. 151-52)

The cause of Balzac's deficiency in poetical feeling it would be frivolous to seek; the fact it is very necessary to signalize. Much of the pleasure one might derive from his works is diminished by the perpetual sacrifice of nature to fashion. We should be much more interested in his women if we heard more of their persons and less of their milliners; and considerable lanquor would be spared did he but pay less attention to upholstery. The minuteness and gusto with which he describes dress and furniture, are without parallel. He cannot mention a single room in the house. but he must instantly make an inventory of the furniture, as if with an eye to distraining for rent. In this respect he has 'the tediousness of a king,' and the misplaced generosity of bestowing all of it on the reader. If he places you in a street, it is by a laborious accumulation of details, never by a few rapid graphic touches. . . . There are some cases in which this minuteness of detail is productive of wonderful effect, such as **'Eugénie Grandet,' 'La Vieille Fille,' 'La Recherche de l'Absolu,'** and **'Le Curé de Tours.'** In general it is only an evidence of his prosaic mind. (p. 152)

Balzac has drawn a vast gallery of portraits, in which almost every species is represented. Dandies and countesses of every shade are pictured there. Beside them stand various specimens of the middle classes, shopkeepers, lawyers, soldiers, journalists. authors, *commis-voyageurs,* and usurers, all wonderfully executed. (p. 156)

In **'Père Goriot'** he has made a bold attempt to treat the subject already handled by Shakspeare in his 'Lear.' It is meant as a psychological study of paternal affection. The work is extremely clever but extremely disagreeable. It fails in its primary object, and fails because of the prosaic nature of the author. Poets alone can treat such subjects, for they alone can feel them properly. Balzac we have shown to be destitute of poetry; and the present work would alone suffice to prove it. (pp. 156-57)

[**'Père Goriot**'s'] resemblances to 'Lear' are the thoughtless sacrifice of property to [Goriot's] daughters, their ingratitude, and the madness which it produces. In 'Lear' the passion is colossal, overwhelming; in Goriot it is petty, and creates little sympathy. . . . [The] reason of Goriot's suffering failing to interest us, is because the man himself excites no sympathy. There is nothing loveable in Goriot, nothing noble in his paternal affection. His children are hateful; but we do not resent their treatment so much as we ought, because we feel it impossible that they could have loved him. . . . Balzac, from his want of poetic instinct, has committed the enormous blunder of representing Goriot as stupid and unsympathizing except on the one subject of his children. Goriot loves passionately, irresistibly, instinctively; his love has all the characters of instinct, none of reflection: violence, tenacity, frenzy in joy as in grief, and the forgetfulness of everything else. . . . [Balzac endeavours] to make you sympathize with the passion while detesting the person; one of the greatest mistakes ever made.

In the development of Goriot's affection we have to signalize another instance of that moral insensibility which we before mentioned as occasionally manifested by Balzac. Not content with making Goriot's passion the passion of a brute, he subsequently makes it the passion of a debauchee. He describes this father as 'crouching at the feet of his daughter that he might kiss them; gazing steadfastly into her eyes; rubbing his head against her dress; in fact, performing all the extravagances of a young and passionate *lover!*' . . . This is revolting; yet by this Balzac means to excite our sympathies. He fails, and fails ignobly. (p. 157)

As entertaining writers, their popularity speaks for them. It strikes us as a very strong tribute to what is excellent in the writings of Balzac, that it should so triumph over his defects as to make him one of the most popular writers of the day; not only in France and Germany, but in England also,—not only with the idle and frivolous, but with the grave and thoughtful. He is a writer on whom with perfect truth one might bestow very high praise, and severest condemnation; the result, however, is that his merits are great enough and rare enough to outweigh his faults. It is very true that he is horribly conceited, that his affectations are thrust upon you at every step, that he writes an abominable style, that he has no poetry, no poetical feeling, that he constantly outrages moral feeling, and that he is deficient in taste. These are faults enough to crush an ordinary author. Balzac, however, is not an ordinary author. He triumphs because he has discovered the true source of human interest to lie in human nature. He eschews complicated incidents and perilous adventures, and bestows all his powers on the human beings whom he has set in action. His plots are generally of slender materials made weighty and enduring by the quantity of character and passion with which he fills them. . . . With curious minuteness but untiring interest, we are led through all the subtle windings of motive, into all the intricate obscurities of egotism. Provincial life, in all that it has of petty and monotonous, is pictured there with the distinctness of a Daguerreotype. It is impossible, from a mere exposition of the subject, to conceive the interest of the novel. This because the interest is purely human. . . . Indeed one may say that whatever is attaching in the works of Balzac is character. The charm of a flowing narrative is nowhere to be found in his writings. . . . Not only are his stories ill-constructed, rambling and diffuse; they are rendered tedious by the overloading of details, repetitions, useless explanations, and still more useless retrospections. The interest he has taken so much pains to excite is very often suffered to subside by his interrupting the narrative to introduce superfluous descriptions. . . . Nothing in Balzac has the air of inspiration. The very narrative is not allowed to be struck off at a heat. He 'builds up' a story, and, what is more, lets you see him building. (p. 160)

We readily acknowledge that, compared with the generality of his contemporaries, Balzac takes great pains, and endeavours to give his work all the finish possible, even to its smallest details; but he diminishes this merit one half by the inconsiderate exhibition of his labour. Now, no one likes to see the scaffolding obstructing the full view of a house; the result, and not the means, should alone be represented. . . . While many make the impertinent boast that their works cost them no trouble, but are 'dashed off at a heat,' Balzac seems fearful lest the public should be ignorant of the immensity of his labour. (p. 161)

[*G. H. Lewes*], *"Balzac and George Sand," in* The Foreign Quarterly Review, *Vol. XXXIII, No. LXVI, July, 1844, pp. 145-63.**

## THE WESTMINSTER AND FOREIGN QUARTERLY REVIEW
(essay date 1847)

The *Roman feuilleton* is dying out. Meanwhile, it will not have been the fault of M. de Balzac if it does not make an end worthy of itself. In his . . . novel, **'Les Parens Pauvres, La Cousine Bette,'** some of the peculiar attributes of this class of literature are carried out to an extraordinary degree of development. It is a downright nasty book, containing an ample assortment of turpitudes, adapted to every variety of vitiated taste. (p. 176)

[Cousin] Bette (the poor relation) [is] ugly, envious, and spiteful; she is at the bottom of all the intrigues and rascalities of this odious drama. The diabolical subtlety and malice with which M. de Balzac endows this country girl, suddenly transported to Paris, is surely inconsistent with the fidelity to nature on which he piques himself in his portraits.

Of course there is no such thing as poetical justice in the *dénouement;* that fashion is out of date. Mme. Hulot dies broken-hearted, and if Mme. Marneffe is punished, it is by falling a victim to the crime of another. M. Hulot, junior, a respectable *avocat,* contrives to have her poisoned. We understand that the novel has found many admirers, and that even among women of great pretensions on the score of refined taste and sentiment. A more disgusting book there is scarcely to be found in the detestable class to which it belongs, or one that more grossly outrages human nature and artistic truth. (pp. 176-77)

> *"Recent Literature of France and Germany,"* in The Westminster and Foreign Quarterly Review, *Vol. XLVII, No. 1, April, 1847, pp. 175-86.\**

## THE NORTH AMERICAN REVIEW  (essay date 1847)

With all his faults, Balzac is essentially an artist, and not a mechanic. It is, perhaps, a result of this very quality that he has found himself growing less popular. He has been unable to sympathize with the sudden moral movement of the French mind. . . . The sudden demand for works of an elevating, humanizing, intensely moral fabric, which has sprung up in Paris since the great success of Mr. Dickens in English literature, has been partially supplied by Eugene Sue, George Sand, and others; but Balzac has not set himself to the work. (p. 86)

Now it strikes us that Balzac has been writing out of himself all his life, working up the stuff which is in him, but that he is too idiosyncratic to fall in with this sudden revolution in literature. He has been very popular in France, but he has been little translated, and is but little known in England or America. We are not surprised at this, but upon the whole, if there is to be so large an infusion of French novels into our literature, we should rather recommend Balzac than either Sue or Sand. The writers who have been naturalized in this country are worse, because they are both socially and politically disorganizing. Balzac, on the contrary, is an artist. He is neither moral nor immoral, but a calm and profound observer of human society and human passions, and a minute, patient, and powerful delineator of scenes and characters in the world before his eyes. His readers must moralize for themselves. (pp. 86-7)

Balzac's pictures of society are like daguerreotypes rather than paintings. There is the same painful and indisputable resemblance, the same accurate delineation of the most minute characteristics and infinitesimal blemishes; and there is the same sombre hue and slightly distorted expression. Moreover, a casual observer might not immediately discover their extraordi-

nary merit. Like the daguerreotypes, they must be held in a certain light, and curiously pondered, or the shifting but striking portraits will not reveal themselves to the observation.

We have said, that we consider Balzac as eminently an artist, and not an artisan. It is for this reason that we have thought his books worthy of serious examination. The first romance which we ever read from his hand seized upon us with hooks of steel. It was impossible to struggle with the fascination. We felt ourselves in the power of an enchanter whom it was useless to resist. The impression made by the first was continued by every subsequent romance which we read from his pen; and although we soon became aware of some of his tricks, and soon opened our eyes to many of his foibles, yet we felt more and more convinced, that, with all his sins, we had met with a powerful, original mind, and with a consummately artistic hand.

Balzac is an artist, and only an artist. In his tranquil, unimpassioned, remorseless diagnosis of moral phenomena, in his cool method of treating the morbid anatomy of the heart, in his curiously accurate dissection of the passions, in the patient and painful attention with which, stethoscope in hand, finger on pulse, eye everywhere, you see him watching every symptom, alive to every sound and every breath, and in the scientific accuracy with which he portrays the phenomena which have been the subject of his investigation,—in all this calm and conscientious study of nature, he often reminds us of Goethe. Balzac, however, is only an artist. He walks through the world to observe, but he observes phenomena only to furnish materials for his art. Goethe we have always considered a great naturalist. His pursuit is always truth, natural truth, which he delights to track, through all its external manifestations, up to its living principles. (pp. 88-9)

Balzac stops short of Goethe, however. He is no naturalist, except to serve the purposes of his art. His object in observing nature is to furnish himself with material in his profession. Like a painter, he will stop under a *porte cochère* in a shower, and sketch you a beggar's head with the most striking accuracy, not knowing whether it is to serve at some future time for Belisarius or Judas Iscariot. (p. 89)

[Balzac] belongs peculiarly to what has been denominated the silver-fork school. He is preeminently a fashionalbe novelist by nature and education; and it is for this reason, probably, that he has been unable to modify himself to suit the prevailing taste of the times. He must work upon the stuff which is in him. Like the silk-worm, he must feed on mulberry-leaves and spin silk. His works are, after all, nothing more nor less than fashionable novels. (p. 90)

George Sand is, no doubt, a philosopher, and her style is better than that of any modern French writer; but she always reminds us of what Yorick told the Count de B. in the *Sentimental Journey,*—"The only fault I have to find with your nation is that you are too serious." Balzac takes the world as it is. He does not look for all the virtue in one place, and for all the vice in another; and we are inclined to believe he is right. (p. 93)

We have said, that what we considered the best characteristic of Balzac is his naturalist-spirit. We have also said, that he is a writer of fashionable novels. He has studied high life in Paris with the calmness of a scientific inquirer and the eye of an artist. We know no pictures of society, in any novels, which are superior to his. There is an extraordinary richness and delicacy in his coloring. He is the Petronius Arbiter of Parisian life. We cannot help being charmed with the striking elegance of his workmanship, and in accordance with the views which we have before advanced, we confess to the extraordinary fascination which he contrives to exert over his reader. . . . We find an extraordinary power in anatomizing the passions, laying bare the fibres, tracing out the most minute filaments of feeling and sensation, exerted in every one of that striking series of tales called the *Scènes de la Vie Parisienne*. The female character he has anatomized with the most wonderful accuracy. The pathology of the female heart, in particular, he has studied like a science, and he seems to display in its treatment the combined knowledge of a family physician and a father confessor. The two great genera, the *femme incomprise* and the *femme abandonnée*, he has studied in the minutest detail, and so entirely mastered, that should both races perish, he could reconstruct them out of a single scale in red sandstone, out of a single ringlet or ribbon, with the unerring accuracy of an Agassiz. (pp. 93-4)

[The] fame of Balzac must rest upon his *Scènes de la Vie Parisienne*, and *Scènes de la Vie de Province*. The first of these series is made up generally of short stories, or rather episodes, in a sort of grand epopee of Parisian life, which seems to exist unwritten in Balzac's brain. (p. 96)

[One] of the most brilliant of these episodes in the Parisian epic is the *Histoire des Treize*. . . . "The Thirteen" compose nothing more nor less than a subterranean fraternity, in which dashing nobles and generals are banded with stamped galley-slaves and distinguished pickpockets, for mutual self-improvement and common defence. . . . Balzac has an inordinate love of the atrocious, but manages it better than any of his contemporaries. His corrupt taste seems rather to belong to his epoch than to himself. More than any of the modern Parisians, he seems to us essentially to represent a literature which is *blasée*, and which, in its morbid and depraved appetite for the original and the fresh, is constantly feeding upon the monstrous. Strictly speaking, perhaps, there is nothing absolutely, new in this general conception of "The Thirteen." Yet, such is the singular power of the delineator, who produces his efforts now by a bold, startling, Caravaggio-like effect, and now by a patient accumulation of minute details, worthy of Gerard Douw or Ostade, that we defy the most phlegmatic of readers to maintain his composure through a midnight perusal of these striking narratives. The Circean power

> to lull the sense,
> And in sweet madness rob it of itself,

belongs to this juggler in an eminent degree, and he must have potent nerves who can entirely resist the fascination.

It is in these episodes that the type of the Balzac hero is most fully developed. We cannot say much in favor of this form of the heroic, although the model is somewhat original. We are not sure whether it would pass muster with Carlyle; yet certainly these heroes are not pale and conventional, like the flunky whom he abhors, but are up to any thing in the way of energetic, unscrupulous working. (pp. 96-7)

[Balzac] wishes to represent to our imagination a hero of fabulous beauty and superhuman genius, a kind of fallen archangel, walking the world in patent-leather boots, and making love to the daughters of earth, while at the same time he is in league with all sorts of desperadoes and demons below stairs. The stage on which these brilliant Parisian scenes are represented seems a sheet of polished glass spread over the flames of hell,—rather warm work, and rather slippery footing, on

which only the very adroit can maintain their equilibrium. (p. 98)

The two masterpieces of Balzac . . . are unquestionably *Eugenie Grandet* and *La Recherche de l'Absolu;* both of which are included in the *Scènes de la Vie de Province*. The story of *Eugenie Grandet* is nothing, a mere narrative of every-day life, in which the self-abnegation of woman and the egotism of man are depicted in a series of interior, exquisitely finished scenes, which inevitable suggest, to be sure, the works of the Flemish painters, but to which we are disposed to assign a much higher rank in literature than those pictures occupy in art. Moreover, there are passages of passion, strokes of nature, scenes of light and shadow, which reveal so broad and profound a knowledge of nature and of the heart, that we consider this comparison as an undervaluation of Balzac. (p. 100)

[Balzac's] excellences and defects spring mainly from two sources, which, if we were inclined to be pedantic, we would call his micrology and his neology. To his patient, minute, but artistic observation of the world before him, with its various scenes and characters, and to his constant tendency to philosophize, refine, and subtilize upon all he sees, are attributable both the fidelity of his scene and character painting, and the occasionally laughable philosophy which he expends upon trifles. Secondly, the depraved appetite for the new, which . . . seems to characterize French literature, is eminently a characteristic of his mind,—a besetting foible, which, while it has sometimes led him to fresh and sparkling fountains, has after all engendered most that is monstrous and offensive in his writings. Both these traits, however, run together. . . . His micrologic tendency, moreover, often deprives him of much of his real power. Very often, for instance, after laying bare the breast of a character in very scientific style, instead of proceeding at once to the main purposes of the autopsy, he will wander off into the most remote ramification of the nervous system, or discourse of ruptured filaments or discolored membranes, and all sorts of pathological nonsense, till you are wearied beyond endurance, and all the effect of his science is lost. (pp. 103-04)

It is perhaps [Balzac's] defective style more than anything else which will prevent his becoming a classic, for style above all other qualities seems to embalm for posterity. As for his philosophy, his principles, moral, political, or social, we repeat, that he seems to have none whatever. He looks for the picturesque and the striking. He studies sentiments and sensations from an artistic point of view. He is a physiognomist, a physiologist, a bit of an anatomist, a bit of a Mesmerist, a bit of a geologist, a Flemish painter, an upholsterer, a micrological, misanthropical, skeptical philosopher; but he is no moralist, and certainly no reformer. We have not the least intention of recommending his works for general circulation in this country; but looking at him as an artist, and from the *standpunkt* [standpoint] of his own nation and no other, we have considered him worthy, by his genius and the magnitude of his "*oeuvre*," to be noticed thus somewhat elaborately. (p. 108)

*"The Novels of Balzac," in* The North American Review, *Vol. LXV, No. CXXXVI, July, 1847, pp. 85-108.*

**CHARLES AUGUSTIN SAINTE-BEUVE** (essay date 1850)

*[Sainte-Beuve is considered to be one of the greatest French critics of the nineteenth century. For Sainte-Beuve, a literary work was inseparable from its creator, and he defined literary criticism as*

*the ''natural history of the human spirit.'' His criticism is usually praised for its thoroughness, objectivity, subtlety, and psychological understanding, yet, in writing on Balzac, Sainte-Beuve is subjective and vindictive. Although the reason for their mutual antipathy is not known, some critics suggest that it resulted either from Balzac's biased and negative review of Sainte-Beuve's critical work* Port-Royal, *or possibly from Balzac's comment that his own novel* The Lily of the Valley *was a new and superior rendering of Sainte-Beuve's novel* Volupté. *The following essay indicates their strained relations. Sainte-Beuve's comments on Balzac are refuted by Marcel Proust (see excerpt below, 1919?). In his private notebooks, Sainte-Beuve summed up his feelings about Balzac: ''Every critic has his favorite victim, whom he pounces upon and tears to pieces with particular relish. Mine is Balzac.''*]

M. de Balzac was indeed a painter of our times, perhaps the most original, the most capable, and most penetrating of all our painters. At an early date he chose the nineteenth century as his subject, as his field of observation: he plunged into it with ardor and he never again left it. Society is like a woman: it wants its features to be recorded for posterity by a painter, a painter all its own. Balzac was just that—he followed no tradition, but created new techniques and artifices of the brush to depict an ambitious, pleasure-loving society which took pride in having no ancestors and in being unlike any other. It cherished him all the more for just these accomplishments. (pp. 241-42)

The observation and depiction of an entire society is an immense theme, and M. de Balzac from an early date never shrank from the vastness of his task. Indeed, he covered his chosen field very thoroughly, exploring ever corner of it, and even found it too confining for his gifts. Not content to observe and to divine, he very often invented and dreamed. Whatever we may think of his dreams, it was primarily by his subtle and delicate observations that he won the heart of the aristocratic society to which he always aspired. *La Femme de trente ans, La Femme abandonnée, La Grenadière* were the elite guard with which he first infiltrated the bastions of upper-class life, and they made him master of the citadel at once. (p. 243)

M. de Balzac took pride in being a physiologist, and he was one certainly, though with less rigor and exactness than he imagined; but physical nature—his own and that of others—plays a great part and makes itself felt continually in his moral descriptions. I am not blaming him for this; it is a feature that affects and characterizes all the picturesque literature of our age.

But in two respects I do not follow him. In the more delicate parts of his style, I love the *efflorescence* (I am unable to find a better word) with which he infuses life into everything and makes the very page vibrate. But I cannot accept his continual abuse of this quality, under the guise of physiology. His style, often diffuse, tends to be flushed and enervated, veined with every shade of corruption. It becomes an Asiatic style (as our teachers used to say), more flawed in spots and more effete than the body of some ancient mime. (p. 245)

Another objection I have against M. de Balzac in his capacity as a physiologist or anatomist is that in this domain he imagined at least as much as he observed. A delicate anatomist of the soul, he certainly discovered new veins; he found and brought to life, so to speak, portions of lymphatic vessels which had previously gone unnoticed. But he also invented some. There is a moment in his analysis where the plexus of truth and reality ends and that of illusion begins; nor does he distinguish one from the other. Most of his readers, particularly his female readers, confuse the two just as he has confused them. This is

not the place to insist on the distinction. But it is known that M. de Balzac admitted a weakness for the Swedenborgs, Van Helmonts, Mesmers, and Cagliostros of this world: in other words, he was subject to illusion. In short, to continue my physical, anatomic metaphor, I will say: When he grasps his subject by the jugular vein, his portrayal invests it with flesh-and-blood vitality, but when he mistakes a shadow for a substance, he proceeds no less vigorously.

M. de Balzac had scientific pretensions, but what he actually had was above all a kind of physiological *intuition*. (p. 246)

[He] seemed intoxicated by his work, and the fact is, from youth onward he never really got outside it; he lived in and for it. His world was one in every sense half-observed, half-created; the characters from every station of life which he endowed with vitality were every bit as real to him as the people he met in ordinary intercourse; the latter, in the last analysis, were to him but fainter copies of his own. He had dealings with his own characters, he lived and spoke with them, and on every occasion referred to them as to people of his and your own acquaintance. He had so powerfully and distinctly endowed them with flesh and blood that once ''on their own'' in his pages, they were inseparable from their author. He was surrounded by his own characters, and at moments of enthusiasm they formed a ring around him and drew him with them into the immense round of the **Human Comedy**—which makes us a little dizzy just to watch, but which dizzied its author first of all.

M. de Balzac's is essentially a rich, copious, opulent nature; he is full of ideas, types, and inventions, continually renewed and never exhausted. Such was the power he possessed; however, he lacked the supreme power of dominating his own creation. M. de Balzac may be said to have been devoured by his own work; his talent often carried him away like a chariot drawn by four horses. I do not expect writers to be the precise image of Goethe, always serene above the battle. But M. de Balzac demanded (and in writing) that the artist plunge headlong into his work, ''like Curtius from the edge of the precipice.'' This type of talent implies a good deal of verve and passion, but also the danger of mistaking smoke for fire.

To expound his actual literary theory, however, we need only borrow his own words. For instance, in **Les Parents pauvres,** his last novel and one of his most vigorous . . . , the author's favorite ideas and all his secrets, if he ever had secrets, are expressed by one of his characters, Wenceslas Steinbock, a Polish artist. According to him, ''A great artist today is in the position formerly enjoyed by a prince; fame and fortune are his.'' But his fame is not acquired by playing or dreaming: it is the reward of stubborn, laborious application: ''You have some ideas rattling around in your head? Is that all? Well, I have some ideas, too. . . . What does it matter, what you carry around with you, if you don't put it to some use?'' That is what M. de Balzac himself believed, and that is why he never spared himself when it came to the hard work of writing. To conceive a work, he said, ''is to smoke magic cigarettes,'' but until the work has been executed, it remains an empty dream. He also said: ''Constant work is the law of art as it is of life, for art is idealized creation. This is why great artists and poets never wait for commissions or customers; they keep on producing, today, tomorrow, always. Thus they get into the habit of working hard, of perpetually meeting and surmounting difficulties; this keeps them in constant concubinage with the Muse, in touch with her creative powers. Canova lived in his studio just as Voltaire lived in his study. Homer and Phidias must have lived the same way.'' I deliberately chose this passage because, at the same time as it discloses M. de Balzac's honorable virtues of courage and hard work, it also nakedly reveals what is so ''modern'' about him, the singular carelessness with which he derogated and did violence to the very beauty he claimed to be pursuing. No, neither Homer nor Phidias lived ''the same way . . . in concubinage with the Muse.'' *Their* Muse was always chaste and severe. (pp. 246-48)

All the artists of the age were his friends, and he portrayed almost all of them magnificently in his works. He had taste in art and a real passion for works of painting and sculpture, for period pieces of every sort. . . . This is why, when he introduced masses of objects in a novel, they never seem mere inventory lists, as they would in so many writers, but have color and life. He described them with love. Even pieces of furniture are somehow alive, even the tapestries throb. He describes too much, but in most cases the spotlight falls where it should. Even if the final result falls short of accomplishing all he seems to have hoped, the reader is left with the impression of having been moved. Balzac has the gift for color and for crowded movement. This accounts for his appeal to painters, who recognize in him one of their own kind, transplanted by mistake to literature. (pp. 249-50)

Three things must be considered in a novel: characters, plot, and style. M. de Balzac excels in setting up his characters; he makes them live and he analyzes them deeply and unforgettably. He exaggerates, he piles detail on detail, but no matter—they have plenty of substance on which to feed. He introduces us to keen, gracious, pleasure-loving, gay people; on other days to very mean persons. But once we have met them, whether they are of the former or the latter type, we are sure never to forget them. He does not content himself with portraying characters to perfection, he also invents singularly apt names for them, which engrave them forever in our memories. He attached the greatest importance to finding the right names for his creations; following Sterne, he ascribed to proper names a certain ''occult power'' in harmony or in ironic contrast with the characters designated. Marneffe, Bixiou, Birotteau, Crevel, and others are by their names invested with some sort of vague onomatopoeic quality, thanks to which the person and the name resemble each other. Next in importance after the characters comes plot. In M. de Balzac it is often much less strong, goes off the track, or is exaggerated. On this score he is less successful than in his characterizations. As for style, his is sharp, subtle, fluent, and picturesque, without relation to tradition. I have sometimes wondered what effect a book by M. de Balzac would have on a well-educated man who had been nourished on ordinary good French prose in all its frugality. . . . Such a man would take a month to get back his balance after reading a novel by Balzac. La Bruyère . . . said that every thought has its own right way of being expressed—and that one must find it. M. de Balzac seems never to have heard of this remark by La Bruyère. He employs numbers of lively, restless, capricious turns of speech, but they never sum up a matter once and for all. Rather they are experimental, groping expressions. . . . Even the mold of his mind was in continual flux; it never took permanent shape. Even when he had found the form he wanted, he kept on experimenting.

Could even the most benevolent criticism—that of a friend and comrade like his Louis Lambert—have made him accept a few relatively sober ideas, in the light of which the rushing torrent of his talent might have been controlled, contained, or regulated

a trifle? Without attempting utterly to deflect him from his self-imposed paths, I should like him to have kept in mind a few axioms I believe to be essential to every art, to every literature:

> Precision is the classic writer's varnish (Vauvenargues).
>
> The work of art must express only what elevates the soul, what gives it noble pleasure, and nothing more. The artist's feeling must concentrate on this alone—all the rest is false (Bettina to Goethe's mother).
>
> Good sense and genius are of the same family; wit is merely a collateral (Bonald).

The group of writers of whom Balzac was the most productive and certainly the most inventive [M. Mérimée, Mme. Sand, Eugène Sue, and Alexandre Dumas] created their own school and influenced their times. That school gave rise to some vigorous talents, almost gigantic in dimensions; today we may venture the opinion that its power, for better or worse, has passed its apogee. . . . Let us hope that in the future our society will be given pictures that are no less vast, but calmer, more comforting. Let us hope that those who paint them will enjoy a more peaceful life, and that their inspiration will be not so much subtler as gentler, more wholesomely natural and serene. (pp. 255-56)

> *Charles Augustin Sainte-Beuve, ''Balzac'' (originally published under a different title in* Le constitutionnel, *September 2, 1850), in his* Sainte-Beuve: Selected Essays, *edited by Francis Steegmuller, translated by Norbert Guterman (copyright © 1963 by Doubleday & Company, Inc.; reprinted by permission of the publisher), Doubleday, 1963, pp. 214-57.*

## VICTOR HUGO   (eulogy date 1850)

[*Hugo, a renowned French Romantic novelist and poet, was a friend to Balzac and a pallbearer at his funeral, where he delivered the following eulogy. Hugo was the first to label Balzac's use of realism ''revolutionary.''*]

The man who has just descended into this tomb is one of those whom the public sorrow follows to the last abode. In the times where we are all fictions have disappeared. Henceforth our eyes are fixed not on the heads that reign but on the heads that think, and the whole country is affected when one of them disappears. At this day, the people put on mourning for the man of talent, the nation for the man of genius.

Gentlemen, the name of Balzac will be mingled in the luminous trace that our epoch will leave in the future.

M. de Balzac belonged to that potent generation of writers of the nineteenth century who came after Napoleon, just as the illustrious pleiades of the seventeenth century came after Richelieu, and in the development of civilization a law caused the domination of thought to succeed the domination of the sword.

M. de Balzac was one of the first among the greatest, one of the highest among the best. This is not the place to say all of that splendid and sovereign intelligence. All his books form only one book, living, luminous, profound, in which we see moving all our cotemporaneous civilization, mingled with I know not what of strange and terrible: a marvelous book, that the poet has entitled comedy, and which he might have called history; which assumes all forms and all styles; which goes beyond Tacitus and reaches Suetonius, which crosses Beaumarchais and reaches Rabelais; a book which is observation itself, and imagination itself; which is prodigal of the true, the passionate, the common, the trivial, the material, and which at moments throws athwart realities, suddenly and broadly torn open, the gleam of the most somber and tragic ideal.

Without knowing it, whether he will or not, whether he consents or not, the author of this strange and immense work is of the mighty race of revolutionary writers. Balzac goes directly to his object. He assails modern society face to face. From all he forces something: from some illusions, from others hope, from these a cry of pain, from those a mask. He unvails vice and dissects passion. He penetrates and sounds the heart, the soul, the sentiments, the brain, the abyss that each man has within him. And by a gift of his free and vigorous nature, by a privilege of the intelligences of our times,—who, having seen revolutions nearly and with their own eyes, perceive better the end of humanity and comprehend better the course of Providence,—Balzac came forth serene and smiling from those redoubtable studies which produced melancholy in Moliere and misanthropy in Rousseau.

This is what he has accomplished among us. Such is the work he has left us, lofty and solid, a pile of granite, a monumental edifice, from whose summit his renown will henceforth shine. Great men make their own pedestals: the future charges itself with their statues. (pp. 316-17)

Alas, the powerful and indefatigable laborer, the philosopher, the thinker, the poet, the man of genius, lived among us the life of storms, of struggles, of quarrels, of combats, common in all times to all great men. Today, behold him here at peace. He leaves collisions and hostilities. The same day he enters on glory and the tomb. Henceforth he will shine above all the clouds over our heads, among the stars of our country. (p. 317)

> *Victor Hugo, "Balzac" (originally a eulogy delivered in 1850), in* The International Monthly Magazine, *Vol. I, No. 3, October 1, 1850, pp. 316-17.*

## CHARLOTTE BRONTË   (letter date 1850)

Accept my thanks for some hours of pleasant reading. Balzac was for me quite a new author; and in making his acquaintance, through the medium of **Modeste Mignon** and **Illusions Perdues,** you cannot doubt I have felt some interest. At first I thought he was going to be painfully minute, and fearfully tedious; one grew impatient of his long parade of detail, his slow revelation of unimportant circumstances, as he assembled his personages on the stage; but by-and-by I seemed to enter into the mystery of his craft, and to discover, with delight, where his force lay: is it not in the analysis of motive, and in a subtle perception of the most obscure and secret workings of the mind? Still, admire Balzac as we may, I think we do not like him; we rather feel towards him as towards an ungenial acquaintance who is for ever holding up in strong light our defects, and who rarely draws forth our better qualities.

Truly I like George Sand better.

Fantastical, fanatical, unpractical enthusiast as she often is— far from truthful as are many of her views of life—misled, as she is apt to be, by her feelings—George Sand has a better nature than M. de Balzac; her brain is larger, her heart warmer than his.

> *Charlotte Brontë, in her letter to G. H. Lewes on October 3, 1850, in* The Brontës: Life and Letters, *Vol. II by Charlotte Brontë, Emily Brontë, and Anne Brontë, edited by Clement Shorter, Hodder and Stoughton, 1908, p. 175.**

## CHARLES BAUDELAIRE   (essay date 1859)

[*Baudelaire stresses the importance of the visionary aspects of Balzac's novels, rejecting the contemporary opinion of him as a realist. Baudelaire's remarks inspired a reevaluation of Balzac's works, as is evidenced in the essays by Théophile Gautier, Arthur Symons, and Ferdinand Brunetière (see excerpts below, 1879, 1899, and 1906).*]

I have often been astonished that Balzac's chief title to fame should be to pass for an observer; it had always seemed to me that his principle merit was that of being a visionary, and an impassioned visionary. All his characters are endowed with the zest for life with which he himself was animated. All his fabrications are as intensely colored as dreams. From the highest ranks of the aristocracy to the lowest dregs of society, all the actors in his *Comédie* are more eager for life, more energetic and cunning in their struggles, more patient in misfortune, more greedy in pleasure, more angelic in devotion than they are in the comedy of the real world. In a word, everyone in Balzac has genius—even the doormen. Every living soul is a weapon loaded to the very muzzle with will. This is actually Balzac himself. And as all beings of the exterior world presented themselves to his mind's eye in strong relief and with a striking grimace, he has made their forms convulsive, he has blackened their shadows and heightened their highlights. His prodigious taste for detail, which stems from an inordinate ambition to see everything and to guess everything as well as to make others see everything and guess everything, forced him, moreover, to give greater emphasis to the main lines in order to maintain the perspective of the whole. He sometimes makes me think of those etchers who are never satisfied with the biting and who tranform the main scratches on the plate into veritable ravines. This amazing natural bent has led to marvelous results. But this bent is generally considered a weakness in Balzac. Properly speaking, it is really one of his virtues. But who can boast of being so fortunately endowed and of being able to apply a method that will allow him to clothe the most commonplace things with the splendor of imperial purple? Who can do that? Now, to tell the truth he who does not succeed in doing that, accomplishes very little. (p. 170)

> *Charles Baudelaire, "Théophile Gautier" (originally published under a different title in* L'artiste, *March 13, 1859), in his* Baudelaire As a Literary Critic, *translated by Lois Boe Hyslop and Francis E. Hyslop, Jr. (copyright © 1964 by The Pennsylvania State University), The Pennsylvania State University Press, University Park, 1964, pp. 149-78.**

## HIPPOLYTE ADOLPHE TAINE   (essay date 1865)

[*The critical writings of Taine, a nineteenth-century philosopher and historian, reflect his interest in the application of scientific analysis and classification to social and psychological issues. Many critics consider the following the best nineteenth-century study on Balzac and praise its balanced evaluation of his weaknesses and strengths. Taine describes Balzac as a naturalist who combines the abilities of a philosopher, observer, and artist to create the fictional world of* La comédie humaine.]

When we speak of a man's genius (*esprit*) we mean the general shaping of his thought. There is in every one a certain ruling habit which obliges him to look here or there, which suggests to him a figure of speech, a philosophical reflection, or a jest—so that no matter what he may be working at, he falls into one of these habits by the very necessity of his nature, his mind and his taste. Savants call this method; artists call it talent. Let us examine it in Balzac.

He began in the fashion not of artists, but of savants. Instead of painting, he dissected. He did not enter into the souls of his characters violently and at a single bound like Shakespeare or Saint-Simon; he walked round and round them patiently and slowly like an anatomist, lifting a muscle, then a bone, then a nerve, and only reaching the brain and heart after he had traversed the whole cycle of the organs and their functions. . . . There was in him an archaeologist, an architect, an upholsterer, a tailor, a costumer, an auctioneer, a physiologist, and a notary: all these make their appearance in turn, each one reading his report, the most detailed in the world and the most exact. The artist listened with pains and scrupulous care, and his imagination did not take fire until he had made out of this infinite paper scaffolding a solid structure according to his idea and desire. "I am," said he, "a doctor of the social sciences." A pupil of Geoffroy Saint-Hilaire, he announced his project of writing a natural history of man [in his preface to the **"Human Comedy"** (see excerpt above, 1842)]. Animals have been catalogued, he would furnish the inventory of manners. He has done it; the history of art has never presented an idea so foreign to art, nor a work of art so great; he has almost equaled the immensity of his subject by the immensity of his erudition.

Hence numerous defects and merits; in many passages he bores many readers. . . . The artist keeps us too long; you feel like swearing at him when he keeps you waiting in the cold for an hour among a crowd of his employés. This crew, nevertheless, is nothing if not diverting. (pp. 109-12)

But the worst of it is that the book often becomes obscure. A description is not a painting, and Balzac often thinks that he has produced a picture, when he has merely given a description. His compilations reveal nothing; they are merely catalogs; the enumeration of the stamens of a flower, never brings before our eyes the image of the flower. . . . The minute explanations of Balzac leave us in quiet and in darkness. (pp. 113-14)

A final misfortune is that the description carried at too great length falsifies the impression. When the imagination perceives an imaginary character it is as if by a flash of lightning; if you linger over a trait or a feature, through a dozen lines, nothing at all is perceived. (p. 114)

Nevertheless what power there is in . . . [Balzac]! What striking qualities and what relief [his] interminable enumeration gives to the character! How we recognize him in every action and in every detail! How real he becomes! With what precision and energy he becomes imprinted in our memory! How thoroughly he resembles nature, and how perfect the illusion! (p. 116)

If he is so strong it is because he is systematic; this is a second trait which completes the savant; in him the philosopher is combined with the observer. Along with the details he sees the laws which connect them. His houses and his physiognomies are the molds in which he fashions the souls of his characters. In these all things are inter-related; there is always some passion or situation which is at the bottom of them, and which prescribes what happens. This is why they leave so powerful an impression; each action and detail concurs to drive it home;

tho innumerable, they are brought together for a unique effect. . . . Many of his plots are so skilfully contrived that one loses his way in them. . . . (pp. 118-19)

Moreover, and what is still more notable, he always has some great idea which serves as the center round which his story revolves. He may be wrong in announcing it, but the announcement does not deceive. He not only describes, he thinks. It is not enough to observe life, he understands it. (p. 120)

But what truly stamps him philosopher and lifts him to the level of the greatest artists, is the unification of all his works into a unique whole. Each novel is connected with the others, the same characters reappear; the whole is bound together; we have a drama with a hundred scenes, each one recalling the others. (pp. 121-22)

To be exact . . . is to be great. Balzac has grasped the truth because he has grasped the whole. His great talent for system has given his pictures unity as well as power, faithfulness to life as well as interest. (p. 123)

Such are the materials of the work. When the observer and philosopher has . . . heaped up the ideas and facts, the artist arrives upon the scene. By degrees he warms up; the characters take on form and color; they begin to live. After reasoning comes feeling. Balzac involuntarily divines their gestures. Their sayings, their actions take form of themselves in his brain. . . . But after what struggles, and at the cost of what labor! Balzac has none of the passion, the sudden and happy inspiration, the rich and facile divination of the true and the beautiful. By nature he is obscure; his expression is involved; his first jet is muddy, interrupted, uncertain. . . . (pp. 125-26)

His characters do not all live; sometimes in those that are most alive a false action or phrase indicates that inspiration has flagged; the fire in his furnace was not intense enough; dross has persisted and many of his finest and most muscular figures are marred and flawed. He does not merge his own personality in his characters instantly and spontaneously; this is only reached by degrees; sometimes he pauses on the way and beneath the garb of his character you perceive Balzac himself. The **"Memoirs of Two Young Married Women,"** Farrabesche in **"The Village Curate,"** Father Fourchon in **"The Peasants,"** nearly all his great men, nearly all his women, whether honest or frail, are imperfectly molded figures that should have been recast. The Parisian man of the world, the refined observer and encyclopedist, the amateur physiologist of moral diseases, the hazy philosopher, the naturalist and the mystic, pierce through these different masks. (pp. 127-28)

Usually, however, he issues out of himself and becomes his character. His rage for work triumphs over all obstacles. The artist, held in restraint by the scholar gets the upper hand. . . . [He] is haunted by his characters, obsessed by them, sees them in visions; they live and move in him with such reality and intensity that henceforth they develop of themselves with the independence and necessity of real beings. (pp. 128-29)

It was essential to have this power of illusion to create souls. Imaginary beings are born, exist and act under the same conditions as real beings. They are born of the systematic agglomeration of an infinite number of ideas, as the others are born of the systematic agglomeration of an infinite number of causes. They act through the independent and unreflecting impulse of constituent ideas, as the other act by the personal and spontaneous force of generating causes. Thus the character actually detaches himself from the author, influences him, leads him, and the intensity of the hallucination is the unique source of truth.

I believe that this species of genius is the greatest of all. There is no other that assembles more things in less space. One act, one word of Vautrin, Bixiou, Grandet, Hulot, Mme. Marneffe, implies and recalls all their natural traits and all the circumstances of their lives. You will then perceive, as in a lightning flash, vast and most unexpected truths, the psychology of temperaments, of sex, of passion, the whole man and humanity along with man: they are foreshortened abysses. (pp. 130-31)

M. de Balzac is like a painter who empties a pot of red pigment over his canvas before he begins to paint. The reader gets a headache and decides that this style is laid on too thick, that it indicates a laborious and ungraceful writer, one who is a colorist to order and in spite of himself. . . . M. de Balzac would be a poet; he is so eager that his eagerness overreaches him; he trenches on enigma. (pp. 140-41)

With [Balzac] ideas pile up and crystalize in masses, in every corner of the crucible, according to all the chances and inequalities of inspiration, without symmetrical models and improvised pell-mell; here a glowing phrase that paints a character in foreshortening; next some general maxim, in the same paragraph a flash of sarcasm, a chaos of surging metaphor, reflections and fine sentiments. . . . For such as these a word is not a cipher but an awakener of images; they scan, examine and weigh each word; meanwhile a cloud of emotions and fugitive images floats through their brain; a thousand shades of sentiment, a thousand confused memories, a thousand jumbled glimpses, a bit of melody, a fragment of landscape, entangle each other in their brain; for them the word is the sudden tocsin that summons to the vague world of vanished dreams. What a distance lies between this kind of sense and that of the grammarians! (pp. 153-55)

It is evident that this man, whatever has been said of him, or whatever he may have done, knows the language, and knows it as well as any one; only he uses it after his own fashion. (p. 162)

In his preface of the **"Human Comedy,"** Balzac announces his design of writing the *natural history* of man; his talents were in accord with this design; hence the peculiar physiognomy of his characters; as the father, so the children. When one knows in what manner an artist invents one can foresee his inventions.

In the eyes of the naturalist man is not an independent and superior reasonable being, healthy of himself and capable of attaining by his sole efforts truth and virtue, but a simple force, similar to others in kind, and influenced by circumstances as regards his rank and conduct. He loves this force for itself; he loves it in all its phases, in all its acts; provided that he can see it living he is content. (p. 163)

The ideal is lacking in the naturalist; still more is it lacking in Balzac the naturalist. . . . [He] has none of that vivid and alert imagination by means of which Shakespeare gilds and manipulates the slender threads of human destiny; he is overburdened; we behold him painfully sunken in his scientific dunghill, absorbed in the study of all the fibers of his dissection, encumbered with tools and repulsive preparations: so that when he issues from his cavern and regains the light he exhales the odor of the laboratory in which he has been buried. He lacks true nobility; delicate things escape him; his anatomist's hands pollute modest creatures; he makes ugliness more ugly. But it is

in painting baseness that he achieves a triumph. He is at home in the presence of the ignoble, and lives in its atmosphere without repugnance; he follows with an inward satisfaction the bickerings of a household, or the intrigues of finance. With equal satisfaction he develops his exploits of brute force. He is armed with brutality and calculation; reflection has endowed him with the combinations of wisdom; his coarseness deprives him of the fear of shocking his readers. (pp. 165-66)

His men of genius have his genius. Never seek among them that measured and discreet irony which is the natural weapon of reason and good taste, that delicate finesse and propriety of style, that proud and tranquil self-possession that makes the well-bred man sure of his ideas, of his manners, of his position in life. They have a kind of curdled, violent enthusiasm which surges from them, producing a maelstrom of the trivial and the poetic, the slang of the bank mingled with lyrical imagery, a sort of unhealthy tho powerful intoxication resembling that produced by a fiery, adulterated liquor. (pp. 171-72)

[These] men have been bruised and made brazen by experience; they conceive life as ugly and sordid, and it is with mixed joy and anger that they throw mud at the beautiful fabric of enchanting dreams that appears trembling upon the threshold of youth. (p. 174)

When Balzac wishes to paint virtue, religion or love, he degenerates into the heavy bombast of false sublimity, the stiff commonplace of official phraseology, the sensuality of an imagination without shame and of a passionate temperament; his fine portraits of women are elsewhere. They are those poor, grotesque, pretentious, stingy, silly creatures, Mme. Soudry, Mlle. Rogron, Mlle. Gamard, La Grande Nanon, Mlle. Cormon, and a hundred others deformed by provincial life, by trade, by household cares, bickerings, gossip, their poetry consisting of a mechanical piety, and their ideas of art limited to polishing the furniture, urged on by, and almost feeling the claws of the devil whom their great libertine of a father, Balzac, never fails to whet to his task.

They are also his intriguing women, Mme. Camusot, for example, a kind of panders in petticoats, more cruel and cunning than the other sort, full of artifice, eager for gain, implacable, more dangerous than men, because they have less scruple, less fear and stronger passions. There are still the invalids, Mme. Graslin, Mme. d'Aiglemont, delicate creatures whom ignorance, chastity and imagination have made too sensitive, and who, fallen suddenly into the common-place of life and the brutalities of marriage, languish, become exalted, are cast down, and finally fade or perish. Wherever there is any deformity or wound in question, Balzac is there; he plies his trade of physiologist; no one has so well described ugliness and misfortune, and many praise him for it, claiming that here is the whole of man. (pp. 178-79)

He has painted with infinite detail and with a sort of poetic animation the execrable vermin that swarm and wriggle in the mud of Paris, the Cibots, the Remonecqs, the Mme. Nourissons, the Fraisiers, the poisonous denizens of the dark lower depths, that, magnified by the focussed rays of his microscope, exhibit their arsenal of deadly weapons and the diabolic sheen of their infamy. . . . [He] has so wonderfully balanced and adjusted their springs of action, he has described them so naturally and made their actions seem so logical, that while detesting them, we cannot help admiring them, and, tho the imagination would fain turn away, it can not detach itself from them.

They are, in truth, the heroes of the naturalist and rude artist whom nothing disgusts; they are the curios of his gallery. You pass quickly before his unhandsome virtuous women, his pompous priests, his dull or garrulous would-be great men; real art is not to be found here; a museum is not a *musée*. But you pause before his business men and artisans, each under his glass case exhibiting both the excess and arrest of development which classify it under its species. . . . (pp. 186-88)

Balzac's philosophy has directed Balzac's art. He considered man a force; he has taken force for his ideal. He has freed it from its fetters, he has painted it in its completeness, free, released from the bonds of reason which prevent it from injuring itself, indifferent to the laws of justice which prevent it from injuring others; he has magnified it, mastered it; exploited it and put it on exhibition as worthy of the first rank; he has crowned it as hero and sovereign in the realm of monomania and villainy. (pp. 189-90)

Balzac, like Shakespeare, has painted villains of every species, those of the world and of Bohemia, those of finance and of politics, lechers and spies.

Like Shakespeare, he has described monomania in all its varieties; that of licentiousness and avarice, of ambition and science, of art, of paternal love, of passion. Endure in one what you endure in the other. We are not dealing here with practical and moral life, but with imaginary and ideal life. (pp. 213-14)

Balzac slowly lights and stirs up his furnace; we feel pain at his efforts; we partake of his painful labors in the black and smoky workshops where he prepares, by scientific means, thousands of lanterns, which he arranges in infinite variety so that their intermingled and united rays light up the whole country. At the end all embrace; the spectator looks; he sees less suddenly, less easily, less splendidly with Balzac than with Shakespeare, but he sees the same things, on as large a plane. (p. 216)

> *Hippolyte Adolphe Taine, in his* Balzac: A Critical Study, *translated by Lorenzo O'Rourke (originally published as "Balzac," in his* Nouveaux essais de critique et d'histoire, *Hachette et Cie, 1865), Funk & Wagnalls Company, 1906 (and reprinted by Haskell House Publishers Ltd., 1973), 240 p.*

## HENRY JAMES, JR. (essay date 1875)

[*James was an early, ardent admirer of Balzac's work. In a lecture delivered in 1905, he remarked that "I speak of him, and can only speak, as a man of his own craft, an emulous fellow-worker, who has learned from him more of the lessons of the engaging mystery of fiction than from any one else, and who is conscious of so large a debt to repay that it has had positively to be discharged in installments; as if one could never have at once all the required cash in hand." The following essay is a balanced, appreciative critical analysis of Balzac.*]

[It] is impossible altogether to regret that Balzac died with work still in him. He had written enough; he had written too much. His novels, in spite of their extraordinary closeness of tissue, all betray the want of leisure in the author. (p. 814)

Balzac was to be preëminently a social novelist; his strength was to lie in representing the innumerable actual facts of the French civilization of his day—things only to be learned by patient experience. Balzac's inspiration, his stock, his *fonds*, was outside of him, in the complex French world of the nineteenth century. . . . The great general defect of his manner

. . . is the absence of fresh air, of the trace of disinterested observation; he had from his earliest years, to carry out our metaphor, an eye to the shop. In every great artist who possesses taste there is a little—a very little—of the amateur; but in Balzac there is absolutely nothing of the amateur, and nothing is less to be depended upon than Balzac's taste. . . . There is something pitiful in the contrast between [his] meagre personal budget and his lifelong visions of wealth and of the ways of amassing wealth, his jovial, sensual, colossal enjoyment of luxury, and the great monetary architecture as it were of the "Comédie Humaine." Money is the most general element of Balzac's novels; other things come and go, but money is always there. His great ambition and his great pretension as a social chronicler was to be complete, and he was more complete in this direction than in any other. . . . His women . . . talk about money quite as much as his men, and not only his ignoble and mercenary women (of whom there are so many), but his charming women, his heroines, his great ladies. . . . Each particular episode of the "Comédie Humaine" has its own hero and heroine, but the great general protagonist is the twenty-franc piece.

One thing at any rate Balzac achieved during these early years of effort and obscurity: he had laid the foundations of that intimate knowlege of Paris which was to serve as the basis—the vast mosaic pavement as it were—of the "Comédie Humaine." Paris became his world, his universe. . . . (pp. 815-16)

[Balzac's] books are singularly void of personal revelations. They tell us a vast deal about his mind, but they suggest to us very little about his life. It is hard to imagine a writer less autobiographic. This is certainly a proof of the immense sweep of his genius—of the incomparable vividness of his imagination. (p. 817)

Balzac had evidently an immense kindliness, a salubrious good nature which enabled him to feel the charm of all naïf and helpless manifestations of life. That robustness of temperament and those high animal spirits which carried him into such fantastic explorations of man's carnal nature as the "Physiologie du Mariage" and the "Contes Drôlatiques"—that lusty natural humor which was not humor in our English sense, but a relish, sentimentally more dry but intellectually more keen, of all grotesqueness, and quaintness, and uncleanness, and which, when it felt itself flagging, had still the vigor to keep itself up a while as what the French call the "humoristic"—to emulate Rabelais, to torture words, to string together names, to be pedantically jovial and archaically hilarious—all this helped Balzac to appreciate the simple and the primitive with an intensity subordinate only to his enjoyment of corruption and sophistications. I do wrong indeed to say subordinate; Balzac was here as strong and as frank as he was anywhere. I am almost inclined to say that his profoundly simple people are his best—that in proportion to the labor expended upon them they are most lifelike. . . . What he represents best is extremely simple virtue, and vice simple or complex, as you please. In superior virtue, intellectual virtue, he fails; when his superior people begin to reason they are lost—they become prigs and hypocrites, or worse. (pp. 821-22)

There are two writers in Balzac—the spontaneous one and the reflective one—the former of which is much the more delightful and the latter the more extraordinary. It was the reflective observer that aimed at colossal completeness and equipped himself with a universal philosophy. . . . Balzac's beliefs, it must be confessed, are delicate ground; from certain points of view, perhaps, the less said about them the better. His sincere, personal beliefs may be reduced to a very compact formula: he believed that it was possible to write magnificent novels, and that he was the man to do it. He believed, otherwise stated, that human life was infinitely dramatic and picturesque, and that he possessed an incomparable analytic perception of the fact. His other convictions were all derived from this, and humbly danced attendance upon it; for if being a man of genius means being all in one's productive faculty, never was there such a genius as Balzac's. . . . The chief point is that he himself was his most perfect dupe; he believed in his own magnificent rubbish, and if he made it up, as the phrase is, as he went along, his credulity kept pace with his invention. This was, briefly speaking, because he was morally and intellectually so superficial. . . . The moral, the intellectual atmosphere of his genius is extraordinarily gross and turbid; it is no wonder that the flower of truth does not bloom in it, nor any natural flower whatsoever. The difference in this respect between Balzac and the other great novelists is most striking. When we approach Thackeray and George Eliot, George Sand and Turgenieff, it is into the conscience and the mind that we enter, and we think of them primarily as great consciences and great minds. When we approach Balzac we seem to enter into a great temperament—a prodigious nature. He strikes us half the time as an extraordinary *physical* phenomenon. His robust imagination seems a sort of physical faculty, and impresses us more with its sensible mass and quantity than with its lightness or firmness. (pp. 822-24)

He had a sense of this present, terrestrial life which has never been surpassed, and which in his genius overshadowed everything else. . . . There is nothing in all imaginative literature that in the least resembles his mighty passion for *things*—for material objects, for furniture, upholstery, bricks and mortar. The world that contained these things filled his consciousness, and being, at its intensest, meant simply being thoroughly at home among them. . . . To get on in this world, to succeed, to live greatly in all one's senses, to have plenty of *things*—this was Balzac's infinite; it was here that his heart came in. It was natural, therefore, that the life of mankind should seem to him above all an eager striving along this line—a multitudinous greed for personal enjoyment. . . . If he had been asked what was, for human purposes, the faculty he valued most highly, he would have said the power of dissimulation. He regards it as a sign of all superior people, and he says somewhere that nothing forms the character so finely as having had to exercise it in one's youth, in the bosom of one's family. . . . In place of a moral judgment of conduct, accordingly, Balzac usually gives us an aesthetic judgment. (pp. 824-25)

This overmastering sense of the present world was of course a superb foundation for the work of a realistic romance, and it did so much for Balzac that one is puzzled to know where to begin the recital of what he owed to it. It gave him in the first place his background—his *mise en scène*. This part of his story had with Balzac an importance—his rendering of it a solidity—which it had never enjoyed before. . . . The place in which an event occurred was in his view of equal moment with the event itself: it was part of the action; it was not a thing to take or to leave, or to be vaguely and gracefully indicated; it imposed itself, it had a rôle to fill; it needed to be made as definite as anything else. There is accordingly a vastly greater amount of description in Balzac than in any other writer, and the description is mainly of towns, houses, and rooms. . . . I, for my part, have always found Balzac's houses and rooms extremely interesting; I often prefer his places to

his people. He was a profound connoisseur in these matters; he had a passion for bric-à-brac, and his tables and chairs are always in character. (p. 825)

The portrait of the Maison Vanquer and its inmates [in **"Père Goriot"**] is one of the most portentous settings of the scene in all the literature of fiction. In this case there is nothing superfluous; there is a profound correspondence between the background and the action. (p. 826)

[Balzac's portraiture of people is his] strongest gift, and it is so strong that it easily distances all competition. Two other writers on this line have gone very far, but they suffer by comparison with him. [Charles] Dickens often sets a figure before us with extraordinary vividness; but the outline is fantastic and arbitrary; we but half believe in it, and feel as if we were expected but half to believe in it. . . . But behind Balzac's figures we feel a certain heroic pressure which drives them home to our credence—a contagious force of illusion on the author's own part. The imagination that produced them is working at a greater heat; they seem to proceed from a sort of creative infinite, and they help each other to be believed in. It is pictorially a vaster, sturdier, more systematic style of portraiture than Turgenieff's. This is altogether the most valuable element in Balzac's novels; it is hard to see how the power of physical evocation can go further. (p. 827)

One of the most striking examples of Balzac's energy and facility of conception and execution on this line is the great gallery of portraits of the people who come to the party given by Mme. de Bargeton, in **"Les Illusions Perdues."** These people are all mere supernumeraries; they appear but on this occasion, and having been marshalled forth in their living grotesqueness, they stand there simply to deepen the local color about the central figure of Mme. de Bargeton. When it lets itself loose among the strange social types that vegetate in silent corners of provincial towns, and of which an old and complex civilization, passing from phase to phase, leaves everywhere so thick a deposit, Balzac's imagination expands and revels and rejoices in its strength. In these cases it is sometimes kindly and tender and sympathetic; but as a general thing it is merciless in its irony and contempt. . . . [Balzac, in] pictures of small middle-class ignorance, narrowness, penury, poverty, dreariness, ugliness physical and mental, is always invidious. He grudges and hates and despises. These sentiments certainly often give a masterly force to his touch; but they deepen that sense, which he can so ill afford to have deepened, of the meagreness of his philosophy. (p. 829)

Balzac's figures, as a general thing, are better than the use he makes of them; his touch, so unerring in portraiture and description, often goes wofully astray in narrative, in the conduct of a tale. Of all the great novelists, he is the weakest in talk; his conversations, if they are at all prolonged, become unnatural, impossible. . . . It is not meant by this, however, that the story in Balzac is not generally powerfully conceived and full of dramatic stuff. Afraid of nothing as he was, he attacked all the deepest things in life and laid his hand upon every human passion. He has even to be complete—described one or two passions that are usually considered unmentionable. He always deals with a strong feeling in preference to a superficial one, and his great glory is that he pretended to take cognizance of man's moral nature to its deepest, most unillumined, and, as the French say, most *scabreux* [dangerous] depths—that he maintained that for a writer who proposes seriously to illustrate the human soul there is absolutely no forbidden ground. . . . Balzac's masterpiece, to my own sense, if we must choose, is

**"Le Père Goriot."** In this tale there is most of his characteristic felicity and least of his characteristic infelicity. . . . **"Le Père Goriot"** holds so much, and in proportion to what it holds is, in comparison with its companions, so simple and compact, that it easily ranks among the few greatest novels we possess. Nowhere else is there such a picture of distracted paternal love, and of the battle between the voice of nature and the constant threat of society that you shall be left to rot by the roadside if you drop out of the ranks. In every novel of Balzac's, on the artistic line, there are the great intentions that fructify and the great intentions that fail. In **"Le Père Goriot"** the latter element, though perceptible, comes nearest to being a triumph. Balzac has painted a vast number of "careers"; they begin in one story, and are unfolded in a dozen others. He has a number of young men whom he takes on the threshold of life, entangles conspicuously in the events of their time, makes the pivots of contemporaneous history. . . . The man whose career is most distinctly traced is perhaps Eugène de Rastignac, whose first steps in life we witness in **"Le Père Goriot."** The picture is to some extent injured by Balzac's incurable fatuity and snobbishness, but the situation of the young man . . . bears a deep imaginative stamp. The *donnée* of **"Le Père Goriot"** is typical; the shabby Maison Vauquer, becoming the stage of vast dramas, is a sort of concentrated focus on human life, with sensitive nerves radiating out into the infinite. (pp. 830-31)

It is the opinion of many of Balzac's admirers, and it was the general verdict of his day, that in all this the greatest triumphs are the characters of women. Every French critic tells us that his immense success came to him through women—that they constituted his first, his last, his fondest public. . . . Balzac is supposed to have understood the feminine organism as no one had done before him—to have had the feminine heart, the feminine temperament, feminine nerves, at his fingers' ends—to have turned the feminine puppet, as it were, completely inside out. He has placed an immense number of women on the stage, and even those critics who are least satisfied with his most elaborate female portraits must at least admit that he has paid the originals the compliment to hold that they play an immense part in the world. It may be said, indeed, that women are the keystone of the **"Comédie Humaine."** If the men were taken out, there would be great gaps and fissures; if the women were taken out, the whole fabric would collapse. (p. 832)

His reader very soon perceives, to begin with, that he does not take that view of the sex that would commend him to the "female sympathizers" of the day. . . . His restrictive remarks would be considered odious; his flattering remarks would be considered infamous. He takes the old-fashioned view—he recognizes none but the old-fashioned categories. Woman is the female of man, and in all respects his subordinate; she is pretty and ugly, virtuous and vicious, stupid and cunning. . . . The *métier de femme* includes a great many branches, but they may all be summed up in the art of titillating in one way or another the senses of man. Woman has a "mission" certainly, and this is it. . . . Balzac's women—and indeed his characters in general—are best divided into the rich and the poor, the Parisians and the rustics. His most ambitious female portraits are in the former class—his most agreeable, and on the whole his most successful, in the latter. (pp. 832-33)

[The] greatest thing in Balzac cannot be exhibited by specimens. It is Balzac himself—it is the whole attempt—it is the method. This last is his unsurpassed, his incomparable merit. That huge, all-compassing, all-desiring, all-devouring love of

reality which was the source of so many of his fallacies and stains, of so much dead weight in his work, was also the foundation of his extraordinary power. The real, for his imagination, had an authority that it has never had for any other. . . . He is an enormous tissue of contradictions. He is at once one of the most corrupt of writers and one of the most naïf, the most mechanical and pedantic, and the fullest of *bonhomie* and natural impulse. He is one of the finest of artists and one of the coarsest. Viewed in one way, his novels are ponderous, shapeless, overloaded; his touch is graceless, virulent, barbarous. Viewed in another, his tales have more color, more composition, more grasp of the reader's attention than any others. . . . He believed that he was about as creative as the Deity, and that if mankind and human history were swept away, the **"Comédie Humaine"** would be a perfectly adequate substitute for them. (pp. 835-36)

> *Henry James, Jr., "Honoré de Balzac," in* The Galaxy, *Vol. XX, No. 6, December, 1875, pp. 814-36.*

### THE NORTH AMERICAN REVIEW   (essay date 1877)

[*Correspondance de H. de Balzac, 1819-1850*] throws a great deal of light on the circumstances of [Balzac's] career, admitting us into his confidence with regard to his hopes and disappointments in the most unreserved way. It is sometimes said by the cynical that every great man nowadays writes his letters to the address of posterity; but this would be by no means true of Balzac, for it is easy to see that there was no such intention lurking in his mind when he scratched off the hasty letters which make up the best part of these two volumes. The greater number were written on business matters,—about his debts, his plans, his books,—for there has seldom lived a man more engrossed in his work than he. . . . His letters are full of nothing but the most sordid anxieties; they are really painful reading; there is almost no interruption of their monotonous expression of hope and consequent disappointment. (pp. 314-15)

His letters to [Madame Hanska], like all the others, are full of the particulars of his business troubles, but they show, of course, a side of his character which did not find full expression elsewhere. It would not be easy to make out from Balzac's novels what sort of a man he was; certain qualities that he had are, to be sure, prominent in his writings,—his immense vitality, and his wonderful passion for material things; but in his letters we see, besides, more simplicity than the reader of his tales, brought into contact with every variety of wrong-doing, would expect to find. . . . [The] letters to Madame Hanska are, in a way, the most interesting of the collection. They are fuller and less concerned with business than the others, and in them he speaks more at length regarding his emotions and interests. (p. 316)

The many letters which were written about his work never treat of its literary side, but only of its relation to the business matters which were forever pursuing him. This is their most marked peculiarity. He planned his novels beforehand, and attacked them with the utmost vigor. . . . He seems never to have regarded his work except as so much merchandise to be carried to the highest market and sold on the best terms. The depressing circumstances of his life made this natural enough, for he was always poor and always longing for wealth, and a man who worked so hard at writing novels would surely seek recreation in something else than writing letters; but the fact yet remains that here was one of the greatest men of modern times—for even those who dislike him must acknowledge his greatness—who regarded literature very much as a brickmaker must regard brickmaking. It was a trade, an occupation which made him more than a manual slave. It is surprising that, driven as he was by sordid cares, he should have filled so many of his novels with the expression of what was his constant daydream, a life of solid material ease? (pp. 317-18)

*"Balzac's Correspondance," in* The North American Review, *Vol. CXXIV, No. CCLV, March-April, 1877, pp. 314-18.*

## THÉOPHILE GAUTIER  (essay date 1879)

[*The following is an intimate portrait of Balzac's life based on Gautier's long-standing friendship with Balzac. By describing Balzac as a "seer," Gautier corroborates the "visionary" concept suggested by Charles Baudelaire (see excerpt above, 1859).*]

[Balzac] was conscious of that faculty of intuition which he possessed in so high a degree, and without which, the realization of his work would have been impossible. Balzac, like Vishnu, the Indian god, had the gift of *avatar*, that is to say, of incarnating himself into different bodies, and of living in them as long as he wished; but the number of the *avatars* of Vishnu is fixed at ten, those of Balzac are countless, and still more, he had the power to incite them at will.

Although it may seem singular to say it in the full light of this nineteenth century, Balzac was a *seer*. His merits as an observer, his acuteness as a physiologist, his genius as a writer, do not suffice to explain the infinite variety of the two or three thousand types which play a rôle in the **"Human Comedy."** He did not copy them, he lived them ideally, he wore their clothes, he contracted their habits, he environed himself with their surroundings, he was, for the time being, their very selves. Hence come these well-sustained, logical personages, never belying themselves, never forgetting themselves, endowed with an interior and profound existence.

This faculty, Balzac possessed only for the present. He could transport his thought into a marquis, into a financier, into *bourgeois*; into a man of the people, into a woman of the world, into a courtezan, but the shadows of the past did not obey his call; he never would have known, like Goethe, to evoke from the depths of antiquity, the beautiful Helen, and make her dwell in the Gothic manor of Faust. With two or three exceptions, all his work is modern; he has assimilated the living, he has not resuscitated the dead. (pp. 189-90)

*Théophile Gautier, "Honoré de Balzac," in* Famous French Authors: Biographical Portraits of Distinguished French Writers *by Théophile Gautier & others (copyright by R. Worthington, 1879), Worthington, 1879, pp. 174-251.*

## [W.D. HOWELLS]  (essay date 1886)

We can be glad of it even in a writer of our time, but it would be hard to forgive a contemporary for a bit of theatricality like that which . . . Balzac offers us in *The Duchesse de Langeais*. It is worse, if anything could be worse, than *Père Goriot*—more artificial in motive, more malarial, more oblique in morals. In fact, the inversion of the principles of right and wrong, the appeal made to the reader's sympathy for the man who cannot ruin the married coquette he loves, is as bad a thing as we know in literature. But it has its value as part of the history of Balzac's evolution which was curiously fitful and retarded. It is a survival of romanticism, and its Sworn Thirteen Noblemen, who abduct the Duchess at a ball and bring her back before supper, and who are pledged to defend and abet each other in all good and ill, are the sort of mechanism not now employed outside of the dime fictions.

It must by no means be supposed, in fine, that because Balzac was a realist, he was always a realist. As a matter of fact, he was sometimes a romanticist as flamboyant as Victor Hugo himself, without Victor Hugo's generous sympathy and noble faith; and we advise the reader that a more depraving book could hardly fall into the hands of the young than *The Duchesse de Langeais*—more false to life, more false to art. . . .

It is droll to find Balzac, who suffered such bitter scorn and hate for his realism while he was alive, now become a fetich in his turn, to be shaken in the faces of those who will not blindly worship him. But it is no new thing in the history of literature: whatever is established is sacred with those who do not think. (p. 973)

*[W. D. Howells], "Editor's Study," in* Harper's New Monthly Magazine *(copyright © 1886 by Harper's New Monthly Magazine), Vol. LXXII, No. CCCCXXXII, May, 1886, pp. 972-76.\**

## OSCAR WILDE  (essay date 1886)

Many years ago, in a number of *All the Year Round*, Charles Dickens complained that Balzac was very little read in England, and although since then the public have become more familiar with the great master-pieces of French fiction, still it may be doubted whether the **"Comédie Humaine"** is at all appreciated or understood by the general run of novel-readers. It is really the greatest monument that literature has produced in our century, and M. Taine hardly exaggerates when he says that, after Shakespeare, Balzac is our most important magazine of documents on human nature. Balzac's aim, in fact, was to do for humanity what Buffon had done for the animal creation. As the naturalist studied lions and tigers, so the novelist studied men and women. Yet he was no mere reporter. Photography and proces-verbal were not the essentials of his method. Observation gave him the facts of life, but his genius converted facts into truths, and truths into truths. He was, in a word, a marvellous combination of the artistic temperament with the scientific spirit. The latter he bequeathed to his disciples; the former was entirely his own. The distinction between such a book as M. Zola's "L'Assommoir" and such a book as Balzac's **"Illusions Perdues"** is the distinction between unimaginative realism and imaginative reality. . . . [Balzac] was of course accused of being immoral. Few writers who deal directly with life escape that charge. His answer to the accusation was characteristic and conclusive. "Whoever contributes his stone to the edifice of ideas," he wrote, "whoever proclaims an abuse, whoever sets his mark upon an evil to be abolished, always passes for immoral. If you are true in your portraits, if by dint of daily and nightly toil, you succeed in writing the most difficult language in the world, the word immoral is thrown in your face." The morals of the personages of the **"Comédie Humaine"** are simply the morals of the world around us. They are part of the artist's subject-matter, they are not part of his method. If there be any need of censure it is to life not to literature that it should be given. Balzac, besides, is essentially universal. He sees life from every point of view. He has no preferences and no prejudices. He does not try to prove anything. He feels that the spectacle of life contains its own secret. . . .

And what a world it is! What a panorama of passions! What a pell-mell of men and women! It was said of Trollope that he increased the number of our acquaintances without adding to our visiting lists; but after reading the **"Comédie Humaine"** one begins to believe that the only real people are the people who have never existed. Lucien de Rubempré, le Père Goriot, Ursule Mirouët, Marguerite Claës, the Baron Hulot, Mdme. Marneffe, le Cousin Pons, De Marsay—all bring with them a kind of contagious illusion of life. They have a fierce vitality about them: their existence is fervent and fiery-coloured: we not merely feel for them, but we see them—they dominate our fancy and defy scepticism. A steady course of Balzac reduces our living friends to shadows, and our acquaintances to the shadows of shades. (pp. 29-30)

> *Oscar Wilde, "Balzac in English" (originally published as "Balzac's Novels in English," an unsigned essay in* Pall Mall Gazette, *Vol. XLIV, No. 6706, September 13, 1886), in his* The Artist As Critic: Critical Writings of Oscar Wilde, *edited by Richard Ellmann (© Richard Ellmann, 1968, 1969), W. H. Allen, 1970, pp. 29-32.*

## GEORGE MOORE (essay date 1889)

As a traveller in the unknown East, standing on the last ridge of the last hill, sees a city, and in awe contemplates the walls fabulous with terraces and gates, the domes and the towers clothed in all the light of the heavens, so does the imaginative reader view the vast sections into which the **Human Comedy** is so eloquently divided—scenes from private life, scenes from provincial life, scenes from Parisian life, scenes from political life, scenes from military life, scenes from country life, philosophical studies, analytical studies, &c. These are the streets and thoroughfares which intersect and divide this great city of thought; below each division, the titles of the volumes rise like spires and pinnacles, and unconsciously the reader passes from story to story like a sightseer from bridges to palaces through streets and gardens inexhaustible. (p. 491)

I have not yet been able to understand criticism as an exact science, and still hold that the best and most interesting critic is he who attempts no more than to tell through his author the story of his own soul. I have always felt that even the first steps in criticism as an exact science, viz., to prove that Shelley was a better poet than Tupper, are as far beyond my powers as they are beyond my desires, therefore I shall not even try to define Balzac's position in the literary firmament, as some of my learned brethren would say, and shall continue writing this paper with no higher aim than a truthful telling of my own feelings towards this great man.

Balzac re-created all things. There was in him a greater Dickens, a greater Thackeray, a greater Eliot, a greater Fielding, a greater Edgar Poe. And this is an occasion to say that notwithstanding all that has been said about Baudelaire's indebtedness to Edgar Poe, the only French writer touched at all with the true spirit of Poe's genius was Balzac, and he, because he seems to have boxed the compass of the human mind, from Rabelais to Spinoza, from Dickens to Herbert Spencer, from Swedenborg to Miss Austin.

His criticism of life seems to me as profound as Thackeray's is trivial and insignificant, and as beautifully sincere and virile as George Eliot's is canting and pedantic; and to-day it is more

living than when he wrote, for he was enormously, incomprehensibly in advance of his time and able by intuitive knowledge of the inherent qualities of things to divine all latent possibilities. . . . (pp. 491-92)

The abnormal is found in all great writers; it is not their whole flesh, but it is their heart. The abnormal must always be felt, although it may rarely form the subject of picture or poem. To make the abnormal ever visible and obtrusively present is to violate the harmony of Nature; to avoid the abnormal is to introduce a fatal accent of insincerity. But Balzac's mind being absolutely pure, and his genius wholly valid, he was led to give the abnormal exactly the same prominence in the **Human Comedy** as it has in Nature; and his treatment and comprehension of it was no wise inferior to his treatment and comprehension of the great and primal emotions. Balzac has called genius a terrible malady: he was qualified to define it; yet there is a marked element of health in all great work. Shakespeare's genius was unquestionably healthier than that of any of his contemporaries, yet he wrote the Sonnets; Balzac's genius was unquestionably saner than any of his contemporaries, if we except Hugo's, and yet Balzac wrote **La Fille aux Yeux d'Ors, La dernière Incarnation de Vautrien, Une Passion dans le Désert, Seraphita** and **Sarrasene**. (pp. 498-99)

It may be argued that *Vanity Fair* is superior to the **Père Goriot** and that the *Mill on the Floss* is a greater work than **Eugenie Grandet**, but it cannot be contended that Thackeray or Eliot, or even Dickens, came in their shorter works within range of such marvels as **Jesus Christ en Flandres, Une Vieille Fille, La Maison Nucingen** or any other handful of stories that may be gathered on the endless shore of the **Human Comedy**. The **Human Comedy** is littered with stories, and each is a supreme invention, and each reveals absolute power to attain the end desired even if it be inexcusable. (p. 501)

Many, no doubt, think that Shakespeare, Milton, Dante, and Goethe, were greater writers than Balzac. Personally I can imagine nothing greater, but that by the way. The point I should like to bring out clearly and distinctly is that if Balzac is not judged fit to dispute the highest place with Shakespeare, the only deficiencies that may be urged against him are verbal deficiencies. It is certain that of all imaginative writers he ruled over the greatest variety of subjects, peopling his vast empire with a greater number of human souls and ideas. It is certain also that the criticism of life contained in his fifty volumes is at once the most comprehensive, the most elaborate, the most philosophic attempted by any writer of imaginative literature, and these facts being granted, and I hardly see how they can be disputed, my point cannot be gainsaid—namely, that if the first wreath be given to Shakespeare it is accorded for purely verbal excellences. (p. 503)

To me there is more wisdom and more divine imagination in Balzac than in any other writer; he looked farther into the future than human eyes could see. . . . Some will deem this hysterical and exaggerated praise, but only those who do not know the master, or those who think they know him because they have read the **Père Goriot**. To arrive even at a fragmentary and superficial power you must have read at least thirty of the fifty volumes which go to make up that city of thought so well named **The Human Comedy**. As God is said to have created Adam from a handful of clay, so did Balzac create the French novel. Flaubert, Zola, Daudet, Goncourt, Bourget, Maupassant, and Henry James have only taken and developed that part of Balzac which individually they superficially represent. I am at a loss to say from what root Balzac sprang. To compare for a moment any of our novelists with him would be, as every man of letters knows, absurd! Shakespeare is the only writer that can be pitted against him, and as I understand criticism more as the story of the critic's soul than as an exact science, I say that I would willingly give up *Hamlet, Macbeth, Romeo and Juliet,* &c., for the yellow books. (pp. 503-04)

George Moore, *"Some of Balzac's Minor Pieces,"* in The Fortnightly Review, n.s. Vol. XLVI, No. CCLXXIV, October 1, 1889, pp. 491-504.

## W. D. HOWELLS  (essay date 1891)

[An astute] critic will not respect Balzac's good work the less for contemning his bad work. He will easily account for the bad work historically, and when he has recognized it, will trouble himself no further with it. In his view no living man is a type, but a character; now noble, now ignoble; now grand, now little; complex, full of vicissitude. He will not expect Balzac to be always Balzac, and will be perhaps even more attracted to the study of him when he was trying to be Balzac than when he had become so. In *César Birotteau,* for instance, he will be interested to note how Balzac stood at the beginning of the great things that have followed since in fiction. There is an interesting likeness between his work in this and Nicolas Gogol's in *Dead Souls,* which serves to illustrate the simultaneity of the literary movement in men of such widely separated civilizations and conditions. Both represent their characters with the touch of exaggeration which typifies; but in bringing his story to a close, Balzac employs a beneficence unknown to the Russian. . . . It is not enough to have rehabilitated Birotteau pecuniarily and socially; he must make him die triumphantly, spectacularly, of an opportune hemorrhage, in the midst of the festivities which celebrate his restoration to his old home. . . . It is very pretty; it is touching, and brings the lump into the reader's throat; but it is too much, and one perceives that Balzac lived too soon to profit by Balzac. The later men, especially the Russians, have known how to forbear the excesses of analysis, to withhold the weakly recurring descriptive and caressing epithets, to let the characters suffice for themselves. All this does not mean that *César Birotteau* is not a beautiful and pathetic story, full of shrewdly considered knowledge of men, and of a good art struggling to free itself from self-consciousness. But it does mean that Balzac, when he wrote it, was under the burden of the very traditions which he has helped fiction to throw off. He felt obliged to construct a mechanical plot, to surcharge his characters, to moralize openly and baldly; he permitted himself to "sympathize" with certain of his people, and to point out others for the abhorrence of his readers. This is not so bad in him as it would be in a novelist of our day. It is simply primitive and inevitable, and he is not to be judged by it. (pp. 18-20)

*W. D. Howells, in a chapter in his* Criticism and Fiction *(copyright © 1891 by Harper & Brothers), Harper & Row, 1891, pp. 18-20.*

## GEORGE SAINTSBURY  (essay date 1895)

[*Saintsbury was instrumental in introducing Balzac to the English-speaking world. He edited an early translation of* La comédie humaine *and wrote prefaces to each of its volumes. The following is excerpted from his general preface to the entire collection. According to Saintsbury, Balzac's greatness rests on his ability to combine detail, observation, and imagination. Thus Saintsbury*

*unites the critical trends that have praised Balzac either as a realist or as a visionary.*]

*'Sans génie, je suis flambé!'*

Volumes, almost libraries, have been written about Balzac; and perhaps of very few writers, putting aside the three or four greatest of all, is it so difficult to select one or a few short phrases which will in any way denote them, much more sum them up. Yet the five words quoted above, which come from an early letter to his sister when as yet he had not 'found his way,' characterise him, I think, better than at least some of the volumes I have read about him, and supply, when they are properly understood, the most valuable of all keys and companions for his comprehension.

'If I have not genius, it is all up with me!' A very matter-of-fact person may say: 'Why! there is nothing wonderful in this. Everybody knows that genius is wanted to make a name in literature, and most people think they have it.' But this would be a little short-sighted. . . . [What] Balzac felt (whether he was conscious in detail of the feeling or not) when he used these words to his sister Laure, what his critical readers must feel when they have read only a very little of his work, what they must feel still more strongly when they have read that work as a whole—is that for him there was no such door of escape and no such compromise. He had the choice by his nature, his aims, his capacities, of being a genius or nothing. He had no little gifts, and he was even destitute of some of the separate and divisible great ones. In mere writing, mere style, he was not supreme; one seldom or never derives from anything of his the merely artistic satisfaction given by perfect prose. His humour, except of the grim and gigantic kind, was not remarkable; his wit, for a Frenchman, curiously thin and small. The minor felicities of the literature generally were denied to him. *Sans génie, il était flambé.* . . . (pp. ix-x)

There are two things . . . which it is more especially desirable to keep constantly before one in reading Balzac—two things which, taken together, constitute his almost unique value, and two things (I think it may be added) which not a few critics have failed to take together in him, being under the impression that the one excludes the other, and that to admit the other is tantamount to a denial of the one. These two things are, first, an immense attention to detail, sometimes observed, sometimes invented or imagined; and secondly, a faculty of regarding these details through a mental lens or arrangement of lenses almost peculiar to himself, which at once combines, enlarges, and invests them with a peculiar magical halo or mirage. The two thousand personages of the *Comédie Humaine* are, for the most part, 'signalled,' as the French official word has it, marked and denoted by the minutest traits of character, gesture, gait, clothing, abode, what not; the transactions recorded are very often (more often indeed than not) given with a scrupulous and microscopic accuracy of reporting which no detective could outdo. Defoe is not more circumstantial in detail of fact than Balzac; Richardson is hardly more prodigal of character-stroke. Yet a very large proportion of these characters, of these circumstances, are evidently things invented or imagined, not observed. And in addition to this the artist's magic glass, his Balzacian speculum, if we may so say (for none else has ever had it) transforms even the most rigid observation into something flickering and fanciful, the outline as of shadows on the wall, not the precise contour of etching or of the camera. (pp. xliii-xliv)

The effect of this singular combination of qualities, apparently the most opposite, may be partly anticipated, but not quite. It results occasionally in a certain shortcoming as regards *vérité vraie,* absolute artistic truth to nature. Those who would range Balzac in point of such artistic veracity on a level with poetical and universal realists like Shakespeare and Dante, or prosaic and particular realists like Thackeray and Fielding, seem not only to be utterly wrong but to pay their idol the worst of all compliments, that of ignoring his own special qualifications. The province of Balzac may not be—I do not think it is—identical, much less coextensive, with that of nature. But it is his own—a partly real partly fantastic region, where the lights, the shades, the dimensions, and the physical laws are slightly different from those of this world of ours, but with which, owing to the things it has in common with that world, we are able to sympathise, which we can traverse and comprehend. Every now and then the artist uses his observing faculty more, and his magnifying and (since there is no better word) distorting lens less; every now and then he reverses the proportion. (pp. xliv-xlv)

This specially Balzacian quality is, I think, unique. It is like—it may almost be said to *be*—the poetic imagination, present in magnificent volume and degree, but in some miraculous way deprived and sterilised of the specially poetical quality. By this I do not of course mean that Balzac did not write in verse: we have a few verses of his, and they are pretty bad, but that is neither here nor there. The difference between Balzac and a great poet lies not in the fact that the one fills the whole page with printed words, and the other only a part of it—but in something else. If I could put that something else into distinct words I should therein attain the philosopher's stone, the elixir of life, the *primum mobile,* the *grand arcanum,* not merely of criticism but of all things. It might be possible to coast about it, to hint at it, by adumbrations and in consequences. But it is better and really more helpful to face the difficulty boldly, and to say that Balzac, approaching a great poet nearer perhaps than any other prose writer in any language, is distinguished from one by the absence of the very last touch, the finally constituting quiddity, which makes a great poet different from Balzac.

Now, when we make this comparison, it is of the first interest to remember—and it is one of the uses of the comparison, that it suggests the remembrance of the fact—that the great poets have usually been themselves extremely exact observers of detail. It has not made them great poets; but they would not be great poets without it. . . . But the great poets do not as a rule *accumulate* detail. Balzac does, and from his very accumulation he manages to derive that singular gigantesque vagueness—differing from the poetic vague, but ranking next to it—which I have here ventured to note as his distinguishing quality. He bewilders us a very little by it, and he gives us the impression that he has slightly bewildered himself. But the compensations of the bewilderment are large.

For in this labyrinth and whirl of things, in this heat and hurry of observation and imagination, the special intoxication of Balzac consists. Every great artist has his own means of producing this intoxication, and it differs in result like the stimulus of beauty or of wine. Those persons who are unfortunate enough to see in Balzac little or nothing but an ingenious piler-up of careful strokes—a man of science taking his human documents and classing them after an orderly fashion in portfolio and deed-box—must miss this intoxication altogether. It is much more agreeable as well as much more accurate to see in the manufacture of the *Comédie* the process of a Cyclopean workshop—the bustle, the hurry, the glare and shadow, the steam and sparks of Vulcanian forging. (pp. xlv-xlvii)

In part no doubt, and in great part, the work of Balzac is dream-stuff rather than life-stuff, and it is all the better for that. What is better than dreams? But the coherence of his visions, their bulk, their solidity, the way in which they return to us and we return to them, make them such dream-stuff as there is all too little of in this world. If it is true that evil on the whole predominates over good in the vision of this 'Voyant,' as Philarète Chasles so justly called him (and I think it does, though not to the same extent as I once thought), two very respectable, and in one case very large, though somewhat opposed divisions of mankind, the philosophic pessimist and the convinced and consistent Christian believer, will tell us that this is at least not one of the points in which it is unfaithful to life. If the author is closer and more faithful in his study of meanness and vice than in his studies of nobility and virtue, the blame is due at least as much to his models as to himself. If, as I fear must be confessed, he has seldom succeeded in combining a really passionate with a really noble conception of love, very few of his countrymen have been more fortunate in that respect. If in some of his types—his journalists, his married women, and others—he seems to have sacrificed to conventions, let us remember that those who know attribute to his conventions such a powerful if not altogether such a holy influence that two generations of the people he painted have actually lived more and more up to his painting of them.

And last of all, but also greatest, has to be considered the immensity of his imaginative achievement, the huge space that he has filled for us with vivid creation, the range of amusement, of instruction, of (after a fashion) edification which he has thrown open for us to walk in. It is possible that he himself and others more or less well-meaningly, though more or less maladroitly, following his lead, may have exaggerated the coherence and the architectural design of the *Comédie.* But it has coherence and it has design; nor shall we find anything exactly to parallel it. . . . Every [volume of the *Comédie*] bears the marks of steady and ferocious labour, as well as of the genius which had at last come where it had been so earnestly called and had never gone away again. It is possible to overpraise Balzac in parts or to mispraise him as a whole. But so long as inappropriate and superfluous comparisons are avoided and as his own excellence is recognised and appreciated, it is scarcely possible to over-estimate that excellence in itself and for itself. He stands alone; even with Dickens, who is his nearest analogue, he shows far more points of difference than of likeness. His vastness of bulk is not more remarkable than his peculiarity of quality; and when these two things coincide in literature or elsewhere, then that in which they coincide may be called, and must be called, Great, without hesitation and without reserve. (pp. xlvii-xlix)

*George Saintsbury, "Honoré de Balzac," in* The Wild Ass's Skin (La peau de chagrin) *by H. de Balzac, translated by Ellen Marriage, J. M. Dent and Co., 1895, pp. ix-xlix.*

## ÉMILE FAGUET (essay date 1898)

*[After assessing Balzac's literary importance, Faguet turns to a discussion of his influence at the turn of the century. Faguet discusses the elements of Balzac's popular appeal and the social and literary conditions that fostered his popularity.]*

Balzac was a *realist* in the good sense of the word, a pre-eminent, an incomparable realist. He had a marvellous power of creating living beings, beings who resemble us (one does not necessarily imply the other); and this, to my mind, constitutes his originality in his own day and his imperishable title to fame.

Balzac was more than a realist, he was (pardon the seeming pedantry of word, for I cannot find another so apt)—he was a *demographer.* I mean by this that he not only portrayed individuals, but that, in his novels, he almost continually conjured up before our eyes the life of a society, a whole nation, our nation; that he understood this life as a whole, and that he showed it to us as it was. He depicted it as an immense concourse of millionaire candidates and functionary candidates; on the one side the ferocious rush for money, on the other the equally ferocious, but more skilfully conducted rush for billets. . . . Balzac saw very clearly what ambition was becoming in a country turned democratic and remaining centralized. It was becoming—it has now become—incessant and universal intrigue. Balzac reflects this state of things exactly. The importance of connections, the constant preoccupation with making and keeping up friendships, with influences to be brought to bear, with "machines to be set going," as Molière has it, with recommendations to be extorted—all this is to be found on every page. (pp. 723-24)

Balzac was a *French classic.* I mean by this that, like Corneille, like Racine, like Molière, and *more than these,* he was a simplifier in the portrayal of character. With him a character is almost always *a single passion,* a colossal, dominating, tyrannical passion which invades the whole man, enslaves him body and soul, presses all his faculties into the service of its designs, and urges the being it so bestrides and spurs through all adventures, over all precipices even to madness and death. That is for Balzac very often, nearly always, a character.

Balzac was, with respect to a whole side of his work, a romanticist, or, to speak much more correctly, a *romanesque.* Realistic and real as he otherwise was, he loved to make abrupt swerves and sudden leaps into sheer fantasy and imagination. His personages are subject to sudden fortunes and unforeseen changes of destiny. Yesterday they were poor wretches on the bottom rung of the social ladder; to-day—we do not very well see why—they are at the head of society. They are, in themselves, heroes of romance quite as fantastic as the Knights of the Round Table. They perform miracles of will and energy (*Peau de Chagrin, Illusions perdues*) in comparison with which the exploits of the knights of olden time are mere child's play. They do exactly what they wish, and they wish all they dream. Nothing is beyond their desire, and they fulfil the whole of their desire with a will-power as inexhaustible as the art of a magician. There is a good deal of the *Thousand and one Nights* in Balzac. Only the *Thousand and one Nights* are the dream of an indolent people who would fain happen on diamond mines while out for a stroll; and the works of Balzac are the dream of an energetic people who would attain to fortune and glory at the expense of a short but stupendous and unheard-of effort of which they believe themselves capable. That is what I call the *romanesque* of Balzac. (pp. 724-25)

> *Émile Faguet, "The Influence of Balzac," translated by Richard Arthur, in* The Fortnightly Review, *Vol. LXIII, May 1, 1898, pp. 723-36.*

## ARTHUR SYMONS (essay date 1899)

[*Symons is generally considered the foremost critic of the French Symbolist movement. The following essay, published at the height of his involvement with the Decadent movement, employs the perceptive, subjective approach evident in his prominent critical study,* The Symbolist Movement in Literature. *Like Charles Baudelaire (see excerpt above, 1859), Symons terms Balzac a visionary rather than a realist.*]

The first man who has completely understood Balzac is Rodin, and it has taken Rodin ten years to realise his own conception. France has refused the statue in which a novelist is represented as a dreamer, to whom Paris is not so much Paris as Patmos; "the most Parisian of our novelists," Frenchmen assure you. It is a hundred years this month since Balzac was born: a hundred years is a long time in which to be misunderstood with admiration.

In choosing the name of the *Human Comedy* for a series of novels in which, as he says, there is at once "the history and the criticism of society, the analysis of its evils, and the discussion of its principles," Balzac proposed to do for the modern world what Dante, in his *Divine Comedy,* had done for the world of the Middle Ages. Condemned to write in prose, and finding his opportunity in that restriction, he created for himself a form which is perhaps the nearest equivalent for the epic or the poetic drama, and the only form in which, at all events, the epic is now possible. . . . [To-day] poetry can no longer represent more than the soul of things; it has taken refuge from the terrible improvements of civilisation in a divine seclusion, where it sings, disregarding the many voices of the street. Prose comes offering its infinite capacity for detail; and it is by the infinity of its detail that the novel, as Balzac created it, has become the modern epic. (p. 745)

Balzac worked contemporaneously with the Romantic movement, but he worked outside it, and its influence upon him is felt only in an occasional pseudo-romanticism, like the episode of the pirate in *La Femme de Trente Ans.* His vision of humanity was essentially a poetic vision, but he was a poet whose dreams were facts. Knowing that, as Mme. [de Staël] has said, "the novel should be the better world," he knew also that "the novel would be nothing if, in that august lie, it were not true in details." (p. 746)

To Balzac manners are but the vestment of life; it is life that he seeks; and life, to him, is but the vestment of thought. Thought is at the root of all his work, a whole system of thought, in which philosophy is but another form of poetry; and it is from this root of idea that the *Human Comedy* springs.

The two books into which Balzac has put his deepest thought, the two books which he himself cared for the most, are *Séraphita* and *Louis Lambert.* . . . I have never been able to feel that *Séraphita* is altogether a success. It lacks the breadth of life; it is glacial. True, he aimed at producing very much such an effect; and it is, indeed, full of a strange, glittering beauty, the beauty of its own snows. But I find in it at the same time something a little factitious, a sort of romanesque, not altogether unlike the sentimental romanesque of Novalis; it has not done the impossible, in humanising the most abstract speculation, in fusing mysticism and the novel. But for the student of Balzac it has extraordinary interest; for it is at once the base and the summit of the *Human Comedy.* . . . *Séraphita* is a prose poem in which the most abstract part of that mystical system, which Swedenborg perhaps materialised too crudely, is presented in a white light, under a single, superhuman image. In *Louis Lambert* the same fundamental conceptions are worked out in the study of a perfectly human intellect, "an intellectual gulf," as he truly calls it; a sober and concise history of ideas in their devouring action upon a too feeble physical nature. In these two books we see directly, and not through the coloured veil of human life, the mind in the abstract of a thinker whose power over humanity was the power of abstract thought. They show this novelist, who has invented the description of society, by whom the visible world has been more powerfully felt than by any other novelist, striving to penetrate the correspondences which exist between the human and the celestial existence. . . . [The] whole world is alive with meaning for [Balzac], a more intimate meaning than it has for others. . . . And so, in his concerns with the world, he will find spirit everywhere; nothing for him will be inert matter, everything will have its particle of the universal life. One of those divine spies, for whom the world has no secrets, he will be neither pessimist nor optimist; he will accept the world as a man accepts the woman whom he loves, as much for her defects as for her virtues. Loving the world for its own sake, he will find it always beautiful, equally beautiful in all its parts. Now let us look at the programme which he traced for the **Human Comedy,** let us realise it in the light of this philosophy, and we are at the beginning of a conception of what the **Human Comedy** really is.

This visionary, then, who had apprehended for himself an idea of God, set himself to interpret human life more elaborately than anyone else. He has been praised for his patient observation; people have thought they praised him in calling him a realist; it has been discussed how far his imitation of life has the literal truth of the photograph. But to Balzac the word realism was an insult. Writing his novels at the rate of eighteen hours a day, in a feverish solitude, he never had the time to observe patiently. It is humanity seen in a mirror, the humanity which comes to the great dreamers, the great poets, humanity as Shakespeare saw it. And so in him, as in all the great artists, there is something more than nature, a divine excess. (pp. 748-49)

Balzac's novels are full of strange problems and great passions. He turned aside from nothing which presented itself in nature; and his mind was always turbulent with the magnificent contrasts and caprices of fate. A devouring passion of thought burned on all the situations by which humanity expresses itself, in its flight from the horror of immobility. To say that the situations which he chose are often romantic is but to say that he followed the soul and the senses faithfully on their strangest errands. . . . To Balzac, humanity had not changed since the days when Oedipus was blind and Philoctetes cried in the cave; and equally great miseries were still possible to mortals, though they were French and of the nineteenth century.

And thus he creates, like the poets, a humanity more logical than the average life; more typical, more sub-divided among the passions, and having in its veins an energy almost more than human. He realised, as the Greeks did, that human life is made up of elemental passions and necessity; but he was the first to realise that in the modern world the pseudonym of necessity is money. Money and the passions rule the world of his **Human Comedy.**

And, at the root of the passions, determining their action, he saw "those nervous fluids, or that unknown substance which, in default of another term, we must call the will." No word returns oftener to his pen. For him the problem is invariable. Man has a given quantity of energy; each man a different quantity: how will he spend it? A novel is the determination in action of that problem. And he is equally interested in every form of energy, in every egoism, so long as it is fiercely itself. . . .

Baudelaire has observed profoundly that every character in the **Human Comedy** has something of Balzac, his genius [see excerpt above, 1859]. To himself, his own genius was entirely expressed in that word "will." It recurs constantly. . . . (p. 750)

The joy of the human organism at its highest point of activity: that is what interests [Balzac] supremely. How passionate, how moving he becomes whenever he has to speak of a real passion, a mania, whether of a lover for his mistress, of a philosopher for his idea, of a miser for his gold, of a Jew dealer for masterpieces! His style clarifies, his words become flesh and blood; he is the lyric poet. And for him every idealism is equal: the gourmandise of Pons is not less serious, not less sympathetic, not less perfectly realised, than the search of Claës after the Absolute. "The great and terrible clamour of egoism" is the voice to which he is always attentive; "those eloquent faces, proclaiming a soul abandoned to an idea as to a remorse," are the faces with whose history he concerns himself. He drags to light the hidden joys of the *amateur,* and with especial delight those that are hidden deepest, under the most deceptive coverings. He deifies them for their energy, he fashions the world of his **Human Comedy** in their service, as the real world exists, all but passive, to be the pasture of these supreme egoists.

In all that he writes of life, Balzac seeks the soul, but it is the soul as nervous fluid, the executive soul, not the contemplative soul, that, with rare exceptions, he seeks. He would surprise the motive force of life: that is his *recherche de l'Absolu;* he figures it to himself as almost a substance, and he is the alchemist on its track. (pp. 751-52)

And of this visionary, this abstract thinker, it must be said that his thought translates itself always into terms of life. Pose before him a purely mental problem, and he will resolve it by a scene in which the problem literally works itself out. It is the quality proper to the novelist, but no novelist ever employed this quality with such persistent activity, and at the same time subordinated action so constantly to the idea. With him action has always a mental basis, is never suffered to intrude for its own sake. . . .

But Balzac will make no detour, aims at an open and an unconditional triumph over nature. Thus, when he triumphs, he triumphs signally; and action, in his books, is perpetually crystallising into some phrase, like the single lines of Dante, or some brief scene, in which a whole entanglement comes sharply and suddenly to a luminous point. (p. 752)

[It] cannot be denied, Balzac's style, as style, is imperfect. It has life, and it has idea, and it has variety; there are moments when it attains a rare and perfectly individual beauty. . . . [Yet, in some passages] the failure in style is equivalent to a failure in psychology. That his style should lack symmetry, subordination, the formal virtues of form, is, in my eyes, a less serious fault. I have often considered whether, in the novel, perfect form is a good, or even a possible thing, if the novel is to be what Balzac made it, history added to poetry. A novelist with style will not look at life with an entirely naked vision. He sees through coloured glasses. Human life and human manners are too various, too moving, to be brought into the fixity of a quite formal order. There will come a moment, constantly, when style must suffer, or the closeness and clearness of narration must be sacrificed, some minute exception of action or psychology must lose its natural place, or its full emphasis. (pp. 752-53)

The novel as Balzac conceived it has created the modern novel, but no modern novelist has followed, for none has been able to follow, Balzac on his own lines. Even those who have tried to follow him most closely have, sooner or later, branched off in one direction or another, most in the direction indicated by Stendhal. (p. 753)

Balzac takes a primary passion, puts it into a human body, and sets it to work itself out in visible action. But since Stendhal, novelists have persuaded themselves that the primary passions are a little common, or noisy, or a little heavy to handle, and they have concerned themselves with passions tempered by reflection, and the sensations of elaborate brains. It was Stendhal who substituted the brain for the heart, as the battle-place of the novel; not the brain as Balzac conceived it, a motive-force of action, the mainspring of passion, the force by which a nature directs its accumulated energy; but a sterile sort of brain, set at a great distance from the heart, whose rhythm is too faint to disturb it. We have been intellectualising upon Stendhal ever since. . . . (p. 754)

Thus, coming closer, as it seems, to what is called reality, in this banishment of great emotions, and this attention upon the sensations, modern analytic novelists are really getting further and further from that life which is the one certain thing in the world. Balzac employs all his detail to call up a tangible world about his men and women, not, perhaps, understanding the full power of detail as psychology, as Flaubert is to understand it; but, after all, his detail is only the background of the picture; and there, stepping out of the canvas, as the sombre people of Velazquez step out of their canvases at the Prado, is the living figure, looking into your eyes with eyes that respond to you like a mirror. (pp. 754-55)

Balzac, like Scott, died under the weight of his debts; and it would seem, if one took him at his word, that the whole of the *Human Comedy* was written for money. In the modern world, as he himself realised more clearly than anyone, money is more often a symbol than an entity, and it can be the symbol of every desire. (p. 756)

A great lover, to whom love, as well as every other passion and the whole visible world, was an idea, a flaming spiritual perception, Balzac enjoyed the vast happiness of the idealist. Contentedly, joyously, he sacrificed every petty enjoyment to the idea of love, the idea of fame, and to that need of the organism to exercise its forces, which is the only definition of genius. I do not know, among the lives of men of letters, a life better filled, or more appropriate. (p. 757)

> Arthur Symons, "Balzac," in The Fortnightly Review (reprinted by permission of Contemporary Review Company Limited), n.s. Vol. LXV, No. CCCLXXXIX, May 1, 1899, pp. 745-57.

**WALTER LITTLEFIELD** (essay date 1902)

It is hardly worth while to write of Balzac as a dramatist for the sole purpose of showing why he made a comparative failure, in this respect, in his own day, or to account for the neglect that his *théâtre* has subsequently suffered. . . . [The] plays of Balzac represent a phase of his development which is worthy of more attention than it has hitherto received. . . .

With the exception of "**Z. Marcas**," "**La Cousine Bette**," "**Le Cousin Pons**," and a few remarkable fragments such as "**Une Rue de Paris et son Habitant**," [by 1840 Balzac] had already written all that was distinctive in his great encyclopaedia of Gallic manners. What might be called his playwriting period began early in 1840 and extended practically to the end of his life. (p. 246)

Years before the idea of the "**Comédie Humaine**" was conceived, he had begun a great classic tragedy based on the career of Cromwell. But his mind was not that of a poet, and versification palled upon him until it wrought havoc with his imagination and analytical perception. "Ideas crowd upon me," he wrote to his sister in those days of youthful enthusiasm, "but I am stopped continually by my lack of any gift for verse writing." . . . ["**Cromwell**"] was a futile, gigantic effort, but its building had taught him patience, and had stimulated his energy and thought, which were presently to find expression in another form. And so, twenty years later, being no longer a slave of the chains of prosody and the three unities, he felt confident that he could carve out a dramatic statue with his own familiar tools.

And here it may be noted that had he attempted an absolute application of his methods to dramatic art, it is certain, that while his failure in his own time might not have been less overwhelming than it was, he would have left us dramas which, in kind, were later to be written by Sardou and Zola. We have no means of knowing whether he ever thought it possible to employ consistent realism on the stage. All we know is that he took the *théâtre* of his day as he found it, without examining the possibilities of its development, or without realizing that it might be within his power and fame to produce a revolution. Aside from his fading appreciation of the French classic drama, his point of view in 1840 was entirely that of the pit. His ignorance of the psychology of the theatre was only a little less profound than his ignorance of stage-craft.

This was the condition of his mind when he submitted "**Vautrin**" to [be produced]. . . . (p. 247)

So far as Vautrin and the whole plot and movement of the play are concerned, Balzac made a compromising capitulation to the popular taste, yet here and there, in the dialogue and in the situations between the Duc de Montsorel and his heart-broken wife, doomed to expiate a fault she did not commit, the analyzer of curious destiny writes far over the heads of those whose impressionable hearts have been swayed by the purely theatric achievements and personality of Vautrin. (p. 248)

"**Les Ressources de Quinola**" is full of exciting scenes, and wrapped in the winding and unwinding of tangled threads. If Quinola may appeal to the masses through his shrewdness, homely wit, artfulness, and honest devotion to his master, in the same way, that master, Fontanarès, fighting against the dark destiny that finally overwhelmed him, is full of a higher human interest. . . . In these days of problem plays and realism it is impossible to say what would be the reception of "**Les Ressources de Quinola**" by a Parisian audience. Still it should be remembered that the underlying motif of the play is realistic and tragically human; on the surface it is an incoherent and fantastic melodrama with an ending which deals a fatal blow to the simple minds who had imagined all along that the true lovers would be reunited, that the adventuress would meet the fate of all stage adventuresses, and that the genius of the real inventor of the first steamboat would triumph over the pseudo-savants of his day and the Spanish Inquisition. (pp. 249-50)

In the third play which Balzac wrote, "**Paméla Giraud**," we see that he has entirely surrendered to the influence of the mere episodical drama of his day. Both plot and characters are entirely conventional. It is like a play of Scribe without that author's knowledge of stage-craft. . . . [Its success when first produced] would now be impossible to repeat owing to the lack of imagination displayed in the piece [and] its histrionic defects. . . . It is as much unlike Balzac in everything as can easily be imagined.

Not so **"La Marâtre,"** however, which just misses being a true forerunner of the modern French realistic *théâtre*. In it, had Balzac been as true to himself in incident and dialogue as he was in abstractly sketching a drama of great human passion, he might, and very certainly would, have produced a masterpiece of its kind. But here and there and particularly at the end he sacrificed a great dramatic incident to the purely sensational and theatric. . . . Still, in spite of the sensational, rhetorical gaud of the piece, its elemental conceptions are of a high dramatic order. . . . (p. 250)

[When Balzac submitted **"Le Faiseur"** for production, the theatre] management, believing that the success of **"La Marâtre"** rested on its romantic and sensational phases rather than upon the analysis of passions, wanted to transform the new play into a melodrama and thereby still further obliterate the individuality of the author. But Balzac remained obdurate. Whether through pride or because he had at last recognized in **"La Marâtre"** the elements of a realistic *théâtre* and hoped to come into his own in **"Le Faiseur,"** he declined to meet the wishes of the manager. . . . After his death the [play was produced as **"Mercadet"**] . . . in an altered and shortened form. Its success was instantaneous and prolonged and its hundredth performance was marked as a great gala occasion.

Paradoxical as it may seem, it owed its chief success to those very unnatural and melodramatic qualities against the interpolation of which Balzac had so strenuously combated. His material, however, had been moulded into an admirable working play of considerable popular interest. (p. 254)

[Even] to the last the stage, from which he had expected to receive so much fame and profit, proved little more than a source of worriment to him. He developed, however. There can be no doubt of that. Had he lived, he might have established a distinctive *théâtre* of his own which would have borne the same relation to life that his novels do. His tendencies pointed that way. **"Paméla Giraud"** marks the limit of his subservience to popular devices, but **"La Marâtre"** and **"Mercadet"** contain flashes of originality and genius, and lacked only a master stage manager, independent of the influences of his time, to shape them into consummate pieces of dramatic realism. Balzac missed being a great playwright by a narrower margin than his biographers seem inclined to appreciate. (p. 255)

> *Walter Littlefield, "Balzac As a Playwright," in* The Critic, *New York, Vol. XLI, No. 3, September, 1902, pp. 246-55.*

**FERDINAND BRUNETIÈRE** (essay date 1903)

Balzac's short stories, which we call in French *nouvelles*, are, generally speaking, not the best-known or the most popular part of his work; nor are they the part best fitted to give a true and complete idea of his genius. But some of them are none the less masterpieces in their kind; they have characteristics and a significance not always possessed by their author's long novels, such as **"Eugénie Grandet"** or **"Cousin Pons"**; and finally, for this very reason, they hold in the unfinished structure of **"The Human Comedy"** a place which it will be interesting to try to determine. . . .

[Though composed] to order and as a piece of hack work, **"An Episode under the Terror"** is in its artistic brevity one of Balzac's most tragic and most finished narratives. **"La Grande**

**Bretèche"** . . . as at first only an episode inserted among the more extended narratives of which it made part . . . , and brief as it is, Balzac nevertheless rewrote it three or four times. It is therefore anything but an improvisation. Yet no other of these short stories can give more vividly than **"La Grande Bretèche"**the impression of a work sprung at once in full completeness from its author's brain, and conceived from the very first in its indivisible unity. But, precisely, it is one of the characteristic traits of Balzac's genius that we hardly need to know when or for what purpose he wrote this or that one of his novels or stories. He bore them all within him at once— we might say that the germ of them was pre-existent in him before he had any conscious thought of objectivizing them. His characters were born in him, as though from all eternity, before he knew them himself; and before he himself suspected it, his **"Human Comedy"**was alive, as confusedly moving, was slowly shaping itself, in his brain. This point must be clearly seen before he can be understood or appreciated at his true value. . . . [The interest of Balzac's novels and stories] is not limited to themselves. They bring out one another's value and significance, they illustrate and give importance to each other; they have, outside themselves, a justification for existence. (p. 306)

The *nouvelle* differs from the *conte* in that it always claims to be a picture of ordinary life; and it differs from the novel in that it selects from ordinary life, and depicts by preference and almost exclusively, those examples of the strange, the rare, and the extraordinary which ordinary life does in spite of its monotony nevertheless contain. It is neither strange nor rare for a miser to make all the people about him, including his wife and children, victims of the passion to which he is himself enslaved; and that is the subject of **"Eugénie Grandet."** It is nothing extraordinary for parents of humble origin almost to be disowned by their children whom they have married too far above them, in another class of society; and that is the subject of **"Father Goriot."** But for a husband, as in **"La Grande Bretèche,"** to wall up his wife's lover in a closet, and that before her very eyes; and, through a combination of circumstances in themselves quite out of the ordinary, for neither one of them to dare or be able to make any defence against his vengeance—this is certainly somewhat rare! Then read **"The Conscript,"** or **"An Episode under the Terror"**; the plot is no ordinary one, and perhaps, with a little exaggeration, we may say it can have occurred but once. Such, then, is the field of the *nouvelle*. . . . [All that makes life's] surprises, its differences, its *startlingness*, so to speak—all this is the province of the *nouvelle*, bordering on that of the novel yet distinct from it. Out of common every-day life you cannot really make *nouvelles*, but only novels—miniature novels, when they are brief, but still novels. In no French writer of the last century, I think, is this distinction more evident or more strictly observed than it is in **"The Human Comedy"**; and unless I am much mistaken, this may serve to solve, or at least to throw light on, the vexed question of Honoré de Balzac's *naturalism* or *romanticism*.

In the literal and even the etymological sense of the word *naturalism*—that is, without taking account of the way in which Émile Zola and some other Italians have *perverted its nature*— no one can question that Balzac was a naturalist. . . . [Balzac] will always be the living incarnation of naturalism. . . . And surely, if to be a naturalist is to confine the field of one's art to the observation of contemporary life, and to try to give a complete and adequate representation thereof, not drawing back or hesitating, not abating one tittle of the truth, in the depiction of ugliness and vice; if to be a naturalist is, like a portrait-painter, to subordinate every aesthetic and moral consideration to the law of likeness—then it is impossible to be more of a naturalist than Balzac. But with all this, since his imagination is unruly, capricious, changeable, with a strong tendency to exaggeration, audacious, and corrupt; since he, as much as any of his contemporaries, feels the need of startling us; since he habitually writes under the dominion of a kind of hallucinatory fever sufficient of itself to mark what we may call the romantic state of mind—romanticism is certainly not absent from the work of this naturalist, but on the contrary would fill and inspire the whole of it, were that result not prevented by the claims, or conditions, of observation. A romantic imagination, struggling to triumph over itself, and succeeding only by confining itself to the study of the model—such may be the definition of Balzac's imagination or genius; and, in a way, to justify this definition by his work we need only to distinguish clearly his *nouvelles* from his novels.

Balzac's *nouvelles* represent the share of romanticism in his work. **"La Grande Bretèche"** is the typical romantic narrative, and we may say as much of **"The Unknown Masterpiece."** The observer shuts his eyes; he now looks only within himself; he imagines ''what might have been''; and he writes **"An Episode under the Terror."** It is for him a way of escape from the obsession of the real:

> The real is strait; the possible is vast. . . .

[Reality] does find its way into his *nouvelles* by way of exactness in detail, but their conception remains essentially or chiefly romantic; just as in his long novels . . . his observation remains naturalistic, and his imagination perverts it, by magnifying or exaggerating, yet never intentionally or systematically or to the extent of falsifying the true relations of things. Shall I dare say that by this act he belongs to the family of Shakespeare? . . . [His] *nouvelles,* his short stories, are his "Tempest," his "Twelfth Night," and his "Midsummer Night's Dream."

This comparison . . . may serve to bring out one more characteristic of Balzac's *nouvelles*—they are philosophic; in **"The Human Comedy"** it is under the title of **"Philosophic Studies'** that he brought together, whatever their origin, such stories as **"A Seashore Drama,"** **"The Unknown Masterpiece,"** and even **"The Conscript."** By so doing he no doubt meant to imply that the sensational stories on which they are based did not contain their whole significance; that he was using them merely as a means of stating a problem, of fixing the reader's attention for a moment on the vastness of the mysterious or unknown. . . . (pp. 307-09)

Thus we see what place [his *nouvelles*] hold in **"The Human Comedy."** Balzac's short stories are not, in his work, what one might be tempted to call somewhat disdainfully ''the chips of his workshop.'' Nor are they even, in relation to his long novels, what a painter's sketches, rough drafts, and studies are to his finished pictures. He did not write them by way of practice or experiment; they have their own value, intrinsic and well-defined. . . . He conceived them for their own sake; he would never have consented to give them proportions which did not befit them. The truth of the matter is that by reason of their dealing with the exceptional or extraordinary, they are, in a way, the element of *romantic drama* in Balzac's **"Comedy"**; and by reason of their philosophic or symbolic significance, they add the element of mystery to a work which but for them would be somewhat harshly illumined by the hard light of reality. (p. 309)

*Ferdinand Brunetière, ''Balzac's Short Stories,'' in* The Critic, *New York, Vol. XLIII, No. 4, October, 1903, pp. 306-09.*

**JEAN CARRÈRE** (essay date 1904?)

Genius is an occult power; but we may say of the genius of Balzac that there is something magical about it. To listen to him is to belong to him. Happy, or unhappy—as you will—the man who enters the enchanted palaces of his work. He is overcome and carried away. He becomes a captive, without resistance and without will, passing, breathless, from labyrinth to labyrinth, so subtly fitted with his bonds that, far from perceiving them, he is intoxicated by his slavery and dreads deliverance. (pp. 72-3)

[Any] man who has the courage to search . . . in his soul, after carefully reading Balzac, will discover in the depths of his being a vague uneasiness, as if he had just left some busy and noisy city, after traversing one by one its hot, sombre streets, its casinos and festive drawing-rooms flooded with light and noise, and solitary rooms where despised genius and virtue keep themselves far from the crowd. He feels that he is in a troubled atmosphere, in which mingle the mustiness of vice, the acrid odour of crime, the hot breath of violent ambition and victorious passion, and—here and there—the light perfume of hidden lilies. He is very far from the sunny and bracing atmosphere that spreads from the works of a Homer, a Vergil, a Dante, a Shakespeare, or a Rabelais. (pp. 73-4)

But perhaps it would be wrong to remain too long under the first impression that Balzac makes upon us. Perhaps he has but ventured into the dark depths of life in order to light them up with his blazing torch. After all, the poet has the absolute right to go where he pleases. There is no place into which he may not penetrate. He may, as Dante did, brave the panthers and tigers that guard the gates of hell. He may, as Shakespeare did, sit on the witch's stool. All that we ask is that, wherever he goes, he shall be himself, superior to the passions that surround him: luminous in the shade, calm in the tumult, moved but never disturbed, merciful but never an accomplice, his head always radiant and divine, even when his feet sink in all the slime of humanity.

Such the poet remains: such he must make us, whom he dominates. He must give us his own talisman in order that we may pass with him through the circles into which he takes us. Like Dante by the side of Vergil, we must walk unscathed with him through all the turmoil of the damned. (p. 74)

Is that the state of soul in which we come from the works of Balzac? We have only to ask it to find the disturbing influence of the *Human Comedy* increasing within us.

Yes, I know quite well what the answer will be: that in Balzac there is everything—evil as well as good, cupidity and self-denial, blackguards and heroes, frightful ambitions and delicate souls, the whole of life, in a word, and that it is for us to make our choice in this infinitely varied microcosm. (p. 75)

What is the dominant note of [Balzac's] work, and what does it do in our souls? That is the only question that matters. The rest is but idle chatter of the schools.

The dominant note of Balzac's work is the exaltation of social life in its most tortured, its harshest and vainest elements. Do not let us be led astray by confused theories. Let us see things in their raw truth. Who are Balzac's favourite heroes, the men upon whom he spends all the magic of his imagination, whom he follows through life with a visible tenderness? Are they lofty idealists, disdainful of honours and material pleasures, athirst for justice and beauty, ready to attempt everything for the accomplishment of something great? Are they liberators of souls, inspirers of noble actions, men of self-denial, devotion, and self-sacrifice? Oh no! Men of that type may appear in his works, but their voices are stifled by the victorious clamours of others to whom he awards all the splendours and all the triumphs, others who alone are heard by the crowd in the end. I mean that brilliant and blustering group of which Rastignac is the most illustrious example.

Rastignac! There is the supreme hero of Balzac, the man who dominates and synthesises his work as Ulysses does that of Homer, Prometheus that of Aeschylus, and Aeneas that of Vergil. Rastignac, that accomplished model of ferociously elegant adventurers! Rastignac, and the whole troop of young wolves following at his heels for the secret plunder of life, those are the beings whom Balzac cast alive into the circulation of souls; and he will bear for ever the lamentable responsibility for them.

I agree that he created others. But just examine these others and see what little weight they have in the **Human Comedy** beside the handsome adventurers. It is a distressing fate for our poet, an unalterable condemnation of his glory, that he could never draw the silhouette of a really great man without some failure which makes it ridiculous, while he caresses and makes perfect the figures of his bandits. (pp. 75-6)

There is a more powerful being than Rastignac himself, a hero whose majestic stature rises above all the others. And this titan of Balzac's epic, victorious like Agamemnon, subtle and wise like Ulysses, bold like Achilles, a creator like Aeneas, so colossal that we stand open-mouthed before his "genius" (for he *is* a genius), is the formidable Vautrin; Vautrin the thief, Vautrin the forger, Vautrin the poisoner, Vautrin the assassin, Vautrin the convict turned policeman.

Those are the real paladins of the **Human Comedy**; all the others, all the virtuous chimeras, are but wavering shadows.

Do not tell me that Balzac is not responsible for this state of things; that it is not his fault if the world belongs to unscrupulous scoundrels rather than to noble characters and generous hearts. Do not tell me that he has been merely the passive mirror of life, the faithful painter of a social order, the gifted scribe of sovereign truth.

He a mirror? He a painter? He a mere collector of documents? What folly—or what sophistry! No writer was ever more inventive, more theoretical, more of a generaliser, more completely creative than Balzac. It was from his own brain that he derived his world. and he propped it up constantly by reasoning. He could not describe a trousers button without at once developing a theory of costume in all ages. His work teems with general ideas; often they clog the narrative. He could, as he willed, make the children of his brain higher or lower. He could arrange his creation according to any hierarchy that pleased him. He had the sovereign faculty of directing, according to his own soul, the sentiments which his heroes evoke in us.

Very well, I ask if in the whole of his work there is a single page in which one detects on the part of Balzac a shudder of revolt or disgust at his bold and ferocious adventurers? Does he endeavour to put us on our guard against the brilliant world in which he places their development? Quite the contrary. How

he caresses them! How he discovers at every step they take some marvellous and indisputable theory to sustain and encourage their march to fortune! He loves them, these favourite heroes of his. He loves them, not as a great-hearted poet, full of pity, may lose every living thing, even when it has fallen into the most servile moral decay. No, he loves them as they are, and for what they are. He likes them to be handsome, to be bold, to please, to shine, to succeed.

Above all, to succeed; for that seems to be, in Balzac's eyes, the one aim of human life. . . . There is no longer any indignation at intrigue or roguery. Such things belong to another age. Now we admire the man who wins, whatever path he has taken. (pp. 77-9)

If, then, we would sum up what remains to us from all the immense work of the **Human Comedy,** the spell of which has bound us for fifty years, we find, in the last analysis, a most pernicious state of mind, most ferociously earthly and material, most removed from all nobleness, heroism, and idealism. It is a state of mind that we may resume in two words: blind admiration of good fortune, frenzied cultivation of success. (pp. 79-80)

> *Jean Carrère, "Honoré de Balzac," in his* Degeneration in the Great French Masters: Rousseau—Chateaubriand—Balzac—Stendhal—Sand—Musset—Baudelaire—Flaubert—Verlaine—Zola, *translated by Joseph McCabe (originally published in* Revue hebdomadaire, 1902-1904), T. Fisher Unwin, Limited, 1922, pp. 71-86.

### FERDINAND BRUNETIÈRE   (essay date 1906)

[*The following discussion on the morality of Balzac's work is taken from Brunetière's full-length study on Balzac. Brunetière's discussion of the morality of Balzac's work is, in fact, a defense of the author's naturalism. He outlines Balzac's role in the development of the novel, the historical significance, aesthetic value, and social bearing of his novels, his influence on other writers, and his place in literature. Brunetière contends that those who labeled Balzac immoral were challenging his basic conception of art, which Brunetière defines as the right of the novel to "represent life in its entirety"; thus, while Brunetière does acknowledge that the question of ethics is pertinent, he considers the charge of immorality often leveled against Balzac to be an aesthetic rather than ethical problem. In considering Balzac a naturalist rather than a visionary, Brunetière disputes Charles Baudelaire and Théophile Gautier (see excerpts above, 1859 and 1879). He is later refuted by Benedetto Croce (see excerpt below, 1923).*]

In giving . . . an exact and complete representation of life, it was difficult for Balzac to avoid the reproach of "immorality"; and accordingly he did not escape it. . . . To what extent does he deserve it? I must look into this somewhat closely, for I fear, to speak the truth, that there is here a question of a rather serious misapprehension, and that there is a mistake, not only as to what must be called by the name of "morality in art", a vague and ill-defined thing, but as to the very conditions of the novel. Ought a "representation of life" to be more "moral" than is life itself? (pp. 201-03)

In what, then, does this immorality consist? And are we, together with Sainte-Beuve [see excerpt above, 1850], to see it in what he called the "Asiatic character" of Balzac's style? (p. 203)

For my part, I do not consider that anywhere in his work does Balzac's style, whatever one may think of it otherwise, have

those qualities of seduction, of immodest and graceful perverseness, of subtle penetration, and expert *fluidity*, that Sainte-
Beuve ascribes to it. There is in the very nature of Balzac an
inborn *indelicacy*, or, if one might so express it, a *non-delicacy*,
which is the contrary of the flexibility and refinement which
such qualities would imply. But there is one thing that is seen
with wonderful clearness—and especially for having been seen
during the very lifetime of Balzac, or nearly so—and that is
the connection between his "manner of writing" and his "immorality", inasmuch as they both are necessary consequences
of his conception of the novel. The irregularity of his style and
the immorality of his work go hand in hand; and they do so,
perhaps, solely because of the very resemblance of his novels
to life.

I am tempted to believe this when I see that under the name
of immorality he is reproached for subjects like that of *Old
Goriot, La Rabouilleuse, Cousin Pons,* or *Cousin Bette,* which,
I admit, are not stories

for little girls
Whose bread is cut in slices small;

but which, none the less, stand in the first rank of his masterpieces, and from which no moralist would venture to propose
to cut anything away. I will admit, furthermore, that in a
general way, in *The Human Comedy,* Balzac's scoundrels and
villains, or his eccentrics, . . . conduct themselves in a way
quite different from that of his "well-bred people", and especially do they stand out more prominently, Balzac's well-
bred people too often resemble perfect blockheads: his David
Séchard, for instance—although sublime—or his two Birotteaus; and the virtue of some of his heroines, Eugénie Grandet,
for example, or Agathe Rouget, is not free from a certain
amount of simpleness. What more shall I say? That his pessimism "makes ugliness uglier"? That in his work crime or
vice is not often enough punished, nor is virtue always sufficiently rewarded? And that humanity, however little we may
think of it, is yet better than the idea of it which we get from
*The Human Comedy?* It is, indeed, a little of all this that is
meant when one speaks of the immorality of the Balzac novel;
and even if he were guilty on all these counts, which is not at
all proved, I should still defend him from this reproach of
immorality. (pp. 204-06)

[Under] the name of immorality, is it not Balzac's conception
of art which is disputed and resisted? Is it not the right which
the novel has claimed, since Balzac, to the "total representation
of life", which is refused recognition? (p. 208)

[It is] evident that in reproaching Balzac for the "immorality"
of some of his subjects, or the more subtle immorality which
consists in describing the morals of his "monsters" as he would
the most indifferent objects—with the same composure and the
same "objectivity"—it is his conception of the novel for which
he is reproached, and the right of the novel itself to be a
"representation of life" is what is disputed. . . . [It] is very
clear to me that there is a question of ethics involved; but a
problem of aesthetics is not to be solved by a question of
ethics—one shrinks from it; and the fact that truth is unpleasant,
or even unbearable to contemplate, is not sufficient ground for
condemning it when it appears in the novel. (pp. 213-14)

[If] the novel has the right to "represent life in its entirety",
it then must have the same liberty as history, which, as far as
I know, has never been reproached for telling us the whole
truth about things and men of the past. I say that this—the
right of representing life in its entirety—is the right, nothing

more, but nothing less, that Balzac claimed; and he forever
won it for the novel. Not only has the novel the right to "represent", as does history, "life in its entirety", but this right,
since Balzac, is properly its *raison d'être,* and it could not be
disputed without bringing back this literary form to the mediocrity of its classic character.

If we accept this definition of the novel, there will hardly be
more than two ways of being "immoral" left the novelist, or
even, as with the historian, only one way; and that will be to
err, voluntarily or involuntarily, in regard to the relative importance of facts in the life of humanity as a whole. . . . [This]
is precisely what Balzac was careful not to do, and what one
ought to admire in his *Comedy,* or, to express it better, in the
plan of his *Human Comedy,* is the endeavour that he made to
proportion the number and importance of his studies to the real
importance of things. If he was mistaken in the number or the
true nature of the springs by which men are moved; if he did
not give prominence enough to the passions of love; and if,
on the other hand, he gave too much to hate, avarice, and
ambition, that is another matter! But he endeavoured to make
no mistake; the question ceased to be a question of morality;
and undoubtedly it is no fault of his, but that of the society of
his day, if, in the picture of it which he left us, the representation of vice is more "copious", if I may so speak, than is
that of virtue.

Furthermore, did he go too far in this representation of vice?
And did he, in his novels—which would be another way of
being "immoral"—dwell, with a complacency that is in bad
taste, on certain details which we are all agreed should be
merely outlined? . . . Balzac's "immorality", in truth, is only
a form of his "coarseness" or "vulgarity". (pp. 215-17)

Evidently, it is easy to be neither "coarse" nor "vulgar" when
one portrays, on the stage or in the novel, only "very distinguished" persons, who, amid most sumptuous furniture or
aristocratic scenery, converse only on very gallant or elevated
subjects. But one cannot always succeed; and it has happened
that even Balzac failed in this respect just when it was especially important for him to succeed, and when, moreover, he
spared neither the subtleties of his analysis nor the efforts, or
rather contortions, of his style. . . . [It] is in a general way
that Balzac is "coarse", as he is "vulgar", almost without
being aware of it, and simply because there are things that are
beyond him, which is, in every art, the true and, I will venture
to say, the only right way of being vulgar and coarse. . . .
[One] can create neither a Gaudissart nor a Bixiou without
having some of their traits. But what a pity it would be if we
had neither Bixiou nor Gaudissart! And if these really are types
of their time, should we wish that Balzac had kept them out
of his work on the ground of their not being sufficiently distinguished persons?

Here again, if we accept the novel as a "representation" of
life, whose first merit lies in its exactness, the same question
recurs: "Did Balzac go too far? And does life, which a moment
ago did not appear to us more immoral as it is to be found in
his work than it is in reality, appear in his work 'coarser' or
more 'vulgar' than nature?" I repeat that I do not believe it.

I make allowance for his temperament, which had nothing
aristocratic about it, in spite of his doctrines, and whose inborn
vulgarity neither Madame de Berny nor the Countess Hanska
succeeded in modifying in any marked degree. But the real
explanation, which is not given by most of his critics, is that,
the object of the novel being to "represent life", the "model"

changed in the time intervening between Le Sage's *Gil Blas* and Balzac's **Cousin Bette**. Or, in still other words, the evolution in the history of the modern novel, which was Balzac's great work, is itself but the expression of an evolution in manners which was taking place at the same time; and herein, precisely, lies Balzac's incomparable originality. While around him his rivals in popularity, when they do not, as did Dumas or Eugène Sue, write simply to entertain, or, even less than that, to exploit their talent, copy from the life of their time only, so to speak, what had been copied at all times—which method allows us to-day to compare, for instance, *Manon Lescaut* with *The Lady with the Camellias (La Dame aux Camélias)*—Balzac devotes himself to the new characters, the singularities "as yet unseen", which his time offers to his observation; and this is precisely what readers brought up on the classics find it extremely hard to forgive him. That which displeases them in his manner of conceiving and representing life is the very thing that shocks them in his style, which they consider, if I may so express it, scandalously "modern". But the same considerations continue to justify him, and if his portraits are good likenesses, we therefore ought not to reproach Balzac alone, or him chiefly, on account of his "coarseness" or "vulgarity". (pp. 218-21)

The Balzac novel is "vulgar" to the extent that life itself has become vulgar in the last two centuries by submitting to new requirements; and it is "coarse" to the extent that, even if we are not singly and individually coarser than our fathers, it cannot be denied, however, that modern civilisation has, in a general way, developed coarseness.

Is this what has sometimes been meant in speaking of the "democratic" character of Balzac's work? . . . Balzac's novels are democratic because of the meeting and mingling of all social conditions which is to be found in them, including those which, before Balzac, were portrayed only to be turned into ridicule. They are democratic because of the means used to succeed, which have nothing, or almost nothing, in common with those used, for instance, in the *Memoirs (Mémoires)* of Saint-Simon. They are democratic because of the nature of the sentiments by which the characters are prompted. . . . They are democratic on account of the qualities as well as the defects of a style in whose torrent are indiscriminately mingled expressions taken from the slang of all trades, metaphors derived from the exercise of all professions, and puns and jokes picked up in all sorts of environments. They are democratic, furthermore, from the very air one breathes in them, the glittering promises of fortune and success they hold out to youth, and the manner in which the gratification of all desires is offered as a prize to the equalitarian instinct, nobody being forbidden the satisfaction of his ambition, or having it restrained by any prejudice. And, lastly, they are democratic because of their exactness in reproducing the might of that social movement whose prodigious and rapid spread, in spite of all opposition and obstacles, will no doubt be accounted in the future the essential and characteristic phenomenon of the nineteenth century. (pp. 221-24)

My conclusion, then, as regards the "morality" of Balzac's novels, is that they are, properly speaking, neither "moral" nor "immoral", but simply what they are and what they had to be, inasmuch as they are a "representation" of the life of his time. They are immoral as history and life are immoral. . . . [It is not Balzac's] "morality" that one incriminates in that case; it is the conception that he has formed of his art, and what is contested is the value or "legitimacy" of that conception. (pp. 224-25)

Balzac intended to give us a complete representation of the society of his time: we therefore have the right, we are even bound, to ask ourselves if he did so. . . . [A] defect in the ninety-seven works—novels or short stories—which constitute **The Human Comedy** is their amazing and disappointing inequality. The fault no doubt lies in Balzac's strange and furious methods of composition, and in the more than abnormal conditions of improvisation, haste, and excitement under which . . . he brought forth his work. (p. 261)

As a writer Balzac is not of the "first rank", nor is he even one of those of whom it may be said that they received from heaven, at their birth, the gift of "style"; and, in this respect, no comparison is possible between him and some of his contemporaries—George Sand, for instance, or Victor Hugo. "While thinking well he often expresses himself badly," has been said of Molière. This might also be said of Balzac; and he also too often succeeds in expressing his thought only by means of "a multitude of metaphors which come very near being nonsense". This is because, like Molière, . . . he works rapidly; but, in addition to this, he revised his work; he corrects his novels on twelve or fifteen sets of proofs, one after the other; he adds, takes out, transposes, and superposes upon the first expression of his thought what seems to him to be "better style"; his "style" comes to him as an afterthought, as does his wit, because in a novel both wit and style are expected; and, . . . just as in attempting to be witty he often fails to exhibit good taste, in like manner in attempting to display "style" he at times forgets the proper meanings of words, and often the rules of grammar and the very laws of French syntax. (pp. 268-69)

To-day the prevailing question above all others is to know what a writer's purpose may be; and when, as with Balzac, it is not the "realisation of beauty" but the "representation of life", we fully understand that, in this particular case, we cannot demand of the copy qualities which are not in the model. Therefore what we must first ask ourselves is not whether Balzac's style is "correct" or whether it is "pure", but if it is "lifelike", or, rather, if it makes what it represents "live"; the rest is an entirely subsidiary matter. Would any one say, on the strength of this, that George Sand "writes better" than Balzac? I am willing then, also, to concede it, and I began by saying it; but of all the characters whom we encounter in the novels of George Sand, do you know of one as "lifelike" as are Balzac's characters? That is the whole question! And the answer has become easy. If Balzac's style animates and vivifies, by I know not what means of his, all that he wishes to represent, he therefore accomplishes his object; and Balzac, to speak the truth, neither "writes badly" nor "writes well", but he writes "as he had to write"; and one cannot, in my opinion, without contradiction reproach him for "irregularities", for this is possibly the only condition under which his style can "live".

The only thing that can be said—from the point of view of the history of the French language—is that **The Human Comedy,** while contributing to modify deeply the previous idea of style, did not mark, and will not mark in the future, an epoch in the evolution of the language; and it is precisely in this that as a writer Balzac is not of the first rank. They who are writers of the first rank are those who, without disturbing the current of a language, or turning it from its time-honoured course, modify that current; and who teach us to draw new tones from an instrument consecrated by tradition. . . . Balzac, evidently, does not belong to that family. He may, so to speak, have treated the language in his own way, and modified the notion of style by assigning to the art of writing an object entirely different from its real one; he has had no influence, properly speaking, on the art of writing, and his style as a writer has had no imitators. It lacked the ''power'' for this, or at least a certain degree of power, and especially ''originality''. His finest pages, which are not very numerous, or, rather, which it is not easy to detach and isolate from their context or framework, are beautiful, but not for and by reason of inimitable and unique qualities of style. One does not find displayed in these pages that gift of verbal invention which is so characteristic of a natural genius for style. And, in order fully to assign to him his final place in the history of French prose, it will suffice to say, in conclusion, that all those qualities which are lacking in him—and for the absence of which I do not reproach him—are precisely the qualities of a Victor Hugo.

But if as a writer he is not of the first rank, perhaps I have a right to say, at the close of this study, that such is not at all his case as a novelist, and that no greater has been known in European literature. . . . From whatever point of view Balzac's novels are studied, and whether—as I have just done—one tries to show what they contain and what is to be found in them alone, or, conversely, and as is often done, whether one attempts to recognise in *Eugénie Grandet* or in *César Birotteau,* in *A Bachelor's Establishment* or in *Cousin Bette,* qualities which are considered to be essential to any novel, their value is always the same, and nothing can be ranked above them. Add to this that it is these books which determined, as it were, the formula from which the novel deviated, later on, only to its very great detriment. . . . (pp. 271-75)

There is no higher fame, nor, I will say, any more lasting fame, for a great author than to have thus made himself, in a way, forever inseparable from the history of a literary form! But when, in addition, like a Balzac or a Molière, he has fixed the ''models'' of that form, he may without doubt be sure that he will live in the memory of men, and that no change in fashion or taste will prevail against his work.

For this reason I believe that for a long time to come Balzac will continue to be ranked as the master of the novel. Emancipation from the influence of *The Human Comedy* will take place only along the lines indicated or foreseen by Balzac; and when, perhaps, some day—just as happened in the case of Molière's successors—this influence shall be thought too tyrannical or too burdensome, the only way to shake it off will be to return to the observation and ''representation of life''; and that will still be doing homage to Balzac. This is why I really do not see, in literature, in the nineteenth century, any influence comparable or superior to his. . . . Balzac holds supreme power in the novel, not alone in France, but even abroad! And it may be said with truth that when we tire of reading him, of rereading and admiring him, it will no doubt be because the novel itself will have begun to grow tiresome. (pp. 275-76)

> *Ferdinand Brunetière, in his* Honoré de Balzac, *translated by Robert Louis Sanderson (translation copyright, 1906 by J. B. Lippincott Company; originally published as* Honoré de Balzac, *Calmann-Lévy, 1906), Lippincott, 1906, 316 p.*

## GEORGE SAINTSBURY   (essay date 1917)

[Balzac's miscellaneous work concerns] us least. It shows Balzac as a failure of a dramatist, a critic of very varying competence, not a particularly effective *writer* merely as such, not possessed of much logical power, but having pretty wide interests and abundantly provided with what we may call the odd tools of the novelist's workshop. As a correspondent his writing has absolutely none of what may be called the ''departmental'' interest of great letter-writers—of Madame de Sévigné or Lady Mary, of Horace Walpole or Cowper; its attraction is not epistolary but wholly autobiographic. And it is only fair to say that, despite Balzac's immense and intense self-centredness, it leaves one on the whole with a much better opinion of him as a man than might be derived from his books or from the anecdotes about him. To adapt one of the best known of these, there was, in fact, nothing real to him but Honoré de Balzac, Honoré de Balzac's works and schemes, and, in rare cases (of which Madame Hanska was the chief), Honoré de Balzac's loves. These constituted his subject, his universe of thought and feeling, of action and passion. But at the same time he stands apart from all the other great egotists. He differs from those of whom Byron is the chief in that he does not introduce himself prominently in his fictitious creations. He does not, like those who may take their representative in Goethe, regard everything merely as it relates to his personality. His chief peculiarity, his unique literary character, and, it may be added at once, his greatness and his weakness, all consist in the fact that he evolves a new world out of himself. (pp. 154-55)

But, it has been said, and the saying has been attributed to no less a critic than M. Faguet, there are no ''general ideas'' in Balzac [see excerpt above, 1898]. One can only reply, ''Heavens! Why should there be?'' . . . They are not quite absolutely forbidden to him, though he will have to be very careful lest they get in his way. But they are most emphatically not his business, except as very rare and very doubtful means to a quite different end, means absolutely insufficient by themselves and exceedingly difficult to combine with the other means which—more or fewer of them—are not only sufficient but necessary. The ''slice of human life,'' not necessarily, but preferably ordinary, presenting probable and interesting characters, connected by sufficient plot, diversified and adorned by descriptive and other devices, and abundantly furnished with the conversation of men and women of this world, the whole forming such a whole as will amuse, thrill, affect, and in other ways, to use the all-important word once more, *interest* the reader,—that is what is wanted. (pp. 155-56)

It is all the more unreasonable to demand general *ideas* from Balzac himself, because he is so liberal of general *imagery*, and what is more, general *prosopopoeia*. Be the Balzacian world real, as some would have it to be, or be it removed from our mundane reality by the subtle ''other-planetary'' influence which is apparent to others, its complexity, its fullness, its variety, its busy and by no means unsystematic life and motion, cannot be denied. Why on earth cannot people be content with asking Platonism from Plato and Balzacity from Balzac? (p. 156)

Although Balzac is in a sense one of the most intensely individual of all novelists, his individuality, as in a very few others of the greatest cases, cannot be elicited from particular works. Just as *Hamlet* will give you no idea of the probable treatment of *As You Like It,* so *Eugénie Grandet* contains no key to *La Cousine Bette.* Even the groups into which he himself rather empirically, if not quite arbitrarily, separated the *Comédie,* though they lend themselves a little more to specification, do not yield very much to the classifier. The *Comédie,* once more, is a world—a world open to the reader, ''all before him.'' Chronological order may tell him a little about Balzac, but it will not tell him very much about Balzac's work that he cannot gain from the individual books, except in the very earliest stages. There is no doubt that the **Oeuvres de Jeunesse,** if not very delightful to the reader (I have myself read them not without pleasure), are very instructive; the instruction increases, while the pleasure is actually multiplied, when you come to **Les Chouans** and the **Peau de Chagrin.** But it is, after a fashion, only beyond these that the true Balzac begins, and the beginning is, to a large extent, a reaction from previous work in consequence of a discovery that the genius, without which he had acknowledged that it was all up with him, did not lie that way, and that he had no hope of finding it there. Not that there is no genius in the two books mentioned; on the contrary, it is there first to be found, and in **La Peau** is of the first order. But their ways are not the ways in which he was to find it—and himself—more specifically.

As to **Argow le Pirate** and **Jane la Pâle** (I have never ceased lamenting that he did not keep the earlier title, **Wann-Chlore**) and the rest, they have interest of various kinds. Some of it has been glanced at already—you cannot fully appreciate Balzac without them. But there is another kind of interest, perhaps not of very general appeal, but not to be neglected by the historian. They are almost the only accessible body, except Pigault-Lebrun's latest and Paul de Kock's earliest, of the popular fiction *before* 1830. . . . (pp. 157-58)

I really do not think any one ought to talk about Balzac who has not at least gained some knowledge of them, for many of their defects remained with him when he got rid of the others. These defects are numerous enough and serious enough. The books are nothing if not uncritical, generally extravagant, and sometimes (especially in **Jean Louis**) appallingly dull. Scarf-pins, made of poisoned fish-bones (**Argow le Pirate**), extinction of virgins under copper bells (**Le Centénaire**), attempts at fairy-tales (**La Dernière Fée**) jostle each other. The weaker historical kind figures largely in **L'Excommunié** (one of the least bad), **L'Israëlite, L'Héritière de Birague, Dom Gigadas.** There is a **Vicaire des Ardennes** (remarkably different from him of Wake-field), which is a kind of introduction to **Argow le Pirate,** and which, again, is not the worst. When I formerly wrote about these curious productions, after reading them, I had not read Pigault-Lebrun, and therefore did not perceive, what I now see to be an undoubted fact, that Balzac was, sometimes at least, trying to follow in Pigault's popular footsteps. But he had not that writer's varied knowledge of actual life or his power of telling a story, and though he for the most part avoided Pigault's *grossièreté,* the chaotic plots, the slovenly writing, and other defects of his model abode with him.

There are not many more surprising things . . . to be found in literary history than the sun-burst of **Les Chouans** after [the] darkness-that-can-be-felt of the early melodramas. Not that **Les Chouans** is by any means a perfect novel, or even a great one. Its narrative drags, in some cases, almost intolerably; the grasp of character, though visible, is inchoate; the plot is rather a polyptych of separate scenes than a connected action; you see at once that the author has changed his model to Sir Walter and think how much better Sir Walter would have done the thing. But there is a strange air of "coming alive" in some of the scenes, though they are too much separated, as in the case of the finale and of the execution of the rather hardly used traitor earlier. These possess a character of thrill which may be looked for in vain through all the ten volumes of the **Oeuvres de Jeunesse.** Montauran *is* a hero in more than one sense, and Mlle. de Verneuil is still more a heroine. Had Balzac worked

her out as he worked out others, who did not deserve it so well, later, she might have been one of the great characters in fiction. Even as it is, the "jour sans lendemain," which in one sense unites, and in another parts, her and her lover for ever, is one of the most really passionate things that the French novel, in its revival, had yet seen. (pp. 159-60)

The second blast of the horn with which Balzac challenged admission to the inner Sanctuaries or strongholds of the novel, **La Peau de Chagrin,** had that character of *difference* which one notices not seldom in the first worthy works of great men of letters—the absence of the mould and the rut. **Les Chouans** was a Waverley novel Gallicised and Balzacified; **La Peau de Chagrin** is a cross between the supernatural romance and the novel of psychology. It is one of the greatest of Balzac's books. The idea of the skin—a new "wishing" talisman, which shrinks with every exercise of the power it gives, and so threatens extinction at once of wishing and living—is of course not wholly novel, though refreshed in detail. But then nothing is wholly novel, and if anything could be it would probably be worthless. The endless changes of the eternal substance make the law, the curse, and the blessing of life. In the working out of his theme it may possibly be objected that Balzac has not *interested* the reader quite enough in his personages—that he seems in a way to be thinking more of the play than of the actors or the audience. His "orgie" is certainly not much of a success; few orgies in print are, except when they are burlesqued. But, on the other hand, the curiosity-shop is splendid. Yet it is not on the details of the book, important as these have been allowed to be throughout Balzac, that attention should be mainly concentrated. The point of it is the way in which the necessary atmosphere of bad dream is kept up throughout, yet with an appropriate contrast of comparatively ordinary life. A competent critic who read **Les Chouans,** knowing nothing about its author or his work, should have said, "Here is more than a promising craftsman"; reading **La Peau de Chagrin** in the same conditions he should have said, "Here is a great, though by no means a faultless, artist." One who read both ought to have had no doubt as to the coming of something and somebody extraordinary. (pp. 160-61)

George Saintsbury, "Beyle and Balzac," in his A History of the French Novel (to the Close of the 19th Century): From 1800 to 1900, Vol. II, *Macmillan and Co., Limited, 1917, pp. 133-75.**

**MARCEL PROUST**  (essay date 1919?)

[*Proust's collection of critical and autobiographical essays, from which the following has been excerpted, details Proust's objections to Charles Augustin Sainte-Beuve's systematic and biographical approach to literature. Unlike Sainte-Beuve, who saw no distinction between an artist's life and work, Proust considered a novel the expression of the author's most private and hidden life and believed that it could not be understood by examining the details of an author's public persona. Proust emphasized, too, the importance of intuition to literary criticism. In the essay excerpted below, Proust addresses Sainte-Beuve's failure to comprehend Balzac's genius (see excerpt above, 1850). Proust suggests that Sainte-Beuve criticized and misunderstood "the very greatness of Balzac's achievement," namely, the vastness and variety of* La comédie humaine.*]*

One of the writers of his day that Sainte-Beuve was wrong about, is Balzac [see excerpt above, 1850]. You look down your nose. You don't care for him, I know. And there you have some right on your side. The vulgarity of his mind was so massive that a lifetime could not leaven it. It was not only when he was no older than was Rastignac at the outset of his career that he set before him as his goal in life the gratification of the most grovelling ambitions—or at least, confused these ambitions so thoroughly with other and better ones that it is almost impossible to disentangle them. . . . (p. 157)

I say nothing of the vulgarity of his language. It was so inherent that it even contaminated his verbal resources and made him use expressions that would jar in the most careless conversation. (p. 158)

You have sometimes thought Flaubert vulgar in the light of some of his collected letters. But at least there is no vulgarity in Flaubert himself, for he understood that the writer's life is centred in his work, and that the remainder only exists "to provide an illusion to describe." Balzac puts the achievements of life and of literature on exactly the same level. "If the *Comédie Humaine* does not make a great man of me," he writes to his sister, "this achievement will" (the achievement of his marriage to Mme. Hanska).

But if you come to think of it, the verisimilitude of some of his pictures may be due to that same vulgarity. Even in those of us whom high-mindedness specifically impels to reject vulgar motives, to condemn and disinfect them, those motives may exist, fundamental though transfigured. In any case, though an ambitiously-minded man should feel an ideal love—even though his ambitious thoughts may not be transfigured by it—that love, alas! is not the whole of his life and often is no more than the few best days of his youth. It is with that part of himself alone that a writer composes his book; but there is a whole part which is left out. And so what force of truth we acknowledge when we see Vandenesse or Rastignac impulsively falling in love, knowing that Vandenesse and Rastignac are cold-hearted climbers whose whole lives have been ambition and scheming; and again when these youthful romances of theirs (yes, almost more their romances than Balzac's) are forgotten things which they only refer to with smiles, with the smiles of those who have really forgotten, and the love-affair with Mme. de Mortsauf is discussed by third parties, or even by the hero himself, just as if it were any other adventure, and without even a sense of grief that its remembrance should not have filled their whole lives. To reach such a degree of truth to life—life as the worldly and experienced know it, where it is agreed that love is fleeting, a youthful vagary, that ambition and lust have more than a hand in it, that one day all that kind of thing won't seem very important, etc.—to show that the most romantic feelings may be no more than a play of refracted light transfiguringly directed on his ambitions by the ambitious man himself and to show this, consciously or unconsciously, in the most compelling way, that is by showing objectively as the bleakest of adventurers the man who himself, subjectively, sees himself in his own eyes as a romantic wooer; this, perhaps was a privilege granted in return for, or even conditional on, the author precisely and quite naturally conceiving the noblest feelings in such a vulgar way that when he supposed he was describing the fulfilment of a life-long dream of happiness he actually told us about the social advantages of that marriage. Here there is no call to differentiate between his letters and his novels. If it has often been said that his characters were real people to him, and that he seriously debated if so and so were a better match for Mlle. de Grandlieu, or for Eugénie Grandet, one can say that his life was a novel which he set about in exactly the same spirit. There was no dividing line between real life (which as you and I think, is not real) and the life in

his novels (which for the writer is the only true life). In the letters to his sister where he talks about the possibilities of this marriage to Mme. Hanska, not only is everything built up like a novel, but those involved are placed, analysed, described, seen as factors in the development of the plot, as if in one of his books. (pp. 159-61)

Just as his sister, his brother-in-law, his mother (the mother for whom, much as he adores her, he feels none of that touching humility of those great men who always remain children where their mother is concerned and forget, as she does, that they are geniuses) interest us as characters in that novel of his life: *Un Grand Mariage,* so, in the same way, his pictures, whether those in his collection or those he saw at Wierschownia, most of which were to go to the Rue Fortunée—are "characters in fiction" too. Each of them calls forth those historical disquisitions, those picture-lover's reviews, that admiration that turns quickly into illusion, exactly as if it hung not on Balzac's walls but in the collections of Pons, or of Claës, or in the Abbé Chapeloud's modest library. . . . And he does not describe the furniture of Cousin Pons or of Claës with more affection, more realism, more illusion, than he describes his pictures in the Rue Fortunée or those at Wierschownia. (pp. 162-63)

Because of this half-baked realism, too fabulous for life, too prosaic for literature, we often get very much the same kind of pleasure from Balzac's books that we get from life. It is not mere legerdemain when Balzac, wanting a list of eminent doctors or eminent artists, hotchpotches the names of real men with those of characters in his books, saying: "He had the genius of a Claude Bernard, a Bichat, a Desplein, a Bianchon." . . . Quite often these real persons are but the more real for it. The livingness of his characters is due to Balzac's art, but the satisfaction this affords him is non-artistic. He speaks about them as though they were real people, and really celebrated. . . . (pp. 165-66)

Sainte-Beuve blames Balzac for having magnified the Abbé Troubert, who finally becomes a sort of Richelieu, etc. Balzac did the same thing with Vautrin and many others. This is not merely a way of adding splendour and stature to these characters and presenting them as the finest of their kind . . . : it is also the fault of one of Balzac's most cherished theories, the theory of the great man to whom greatness of circumstances has been denied, and because his real objective as a novelist is precisely that: to be the historian of the unhistoried, and to study certain characters of historic dimensions just as they manifest themselves while lacking the historical factor which would impel them to greatness. As long as this is how Balzac sees them, it does not disconcert us; but when Lucien de Rubempré, on the point of killing himself, writes to Vautrin, "If God wills it so, these mysterious beings are Moses, Attila, Charlemagne, Mahomet or Napoleon. But if he leaves these gigantic instruments to rust beneath the ocean of a generation they are no more than Pougatcheff, Fouché, Louvel, or the Abbé Carlos Herrera. Farewell, then, farewell to you, who on the right path could have been more than a Ximenes, more than a Richelieu, etc.," Lucien talks too much like Balzac, and leaves off being a real person, distinguishable from all others. And in spite of the amazing variety of Balzac's characters, and their amazing degree of personal identity, this, for one reason or another, sometimes happens. (pp. 166-67)

We recognize Balzac in such passages, and we smile, not unkindly; but because he can be recognised, all the details that were intended to make the characters of his novels more like people in real life, have the opposite effect. The character lived;

Balzac so plumes himself on it that he mentions, quite needlessly, the sum of her dowry, and her connections with other characters in **La Comédie Humaine,** who are thus put on the footing of living people. . . . Though the impression made by the trickster's, or the artist's, vitality is deepened, it is at the expense of the impression made by the vitality of the work of art. A work of art, for all that; and though it is a trifle eked out with all these overconvincing details, all this Musée Grévin business, they too are fuel to its fire, and something is made of them. And as all this relates to an epoch, records its outward habiliments and judges very acutely on what lies beneath, when its interest as a novel is exhausted, it begins a new life as a historical document. (pp. 167-68)

So in reading Balzac we can still feel and almost gratify those cravings which great literature ought to allay in us. With Tolstoi, the account of an evening party in high society is dominated by the mind of the author, and, as Aristotle would say, we are purged of our worldliness while we read it; with Balzac, we feel almost a worldly satisfaction at taking part in it. His very titles carry the stamp of actuality. While with many writers the title is more or less of a symbol, an emblem that must be understood in a wider and more poetical sense than a reading of the book would warrant, with Balzac it is more apt to be the other way about. (pp. 168-69)

Style is so largely a record of the transformation imposed on reality by the writer's mind that Balzac's style, properly speaking, does not exist. Here Sainte-Beuve is completely off the scent. "This style which is often titillating and melting, enervated, flushed and streaked with all manner of hues, this delightfully corrupted style, thoroughly Asiatic, as our teachers used to say, and in places more dislocated and more pliable than the limbs of a Greek pantomimist." Nothing could be less accurate. . . . [In Balzac] all the elements of a style which is still to come exist together, undigested and untransformed. It is a style that neither suggests, nor mirrors; it explains. It explains, moreover, by the aid of images which are intensely striking but do not fuse with the rest, and which convey what he wants to say as we convey something in course of conversation—if we happen to be conversational geniuses—without concerning ourselves as to whether what we say is out of keeping or an interruption. As he will say in a letter: "Good marriages are like cream; a mere nothing will turn them sour," it is by images of this sort—striking, that is, and apt, but discordant, explaining instead of suggesting, and refractory to any considerations of beauty or fitness—that he will get his effects. . . . (pp. 169-70)

Balzac makes use of all the ideas that come into his head, and does not try to resolve them into a way of writing where they would be in keeping with each other and with what he intended them to suggest. No, he states them baldly, and however eccentric or however unlikely a simile may be, besides being unfailingly apt, in it goes: "M. du Châtelet was like one of those melons that ripen from green to yellow in a single night." "It was impossible not to compare M. X. . . . to a frozen viper."

As he had no conception that literary style is a particular medium where things that are topics for conversation, subjects for study, etc., should not be incorporated in a crude state, he dogs every word with what he thinks of it, and the ideas it calls up in him. If he mentions an artist, he immediately says what he knows about him, as though in a footnote. . . . And so he puts in all manner of reflections which because of that natural vulgarity of his are often commonplace, and take on a rather comic quality from being artlessly plumped down in the middle of a sentence; the more so, as terms such as "peculiar to," employed for the specific purpose of defining or elucidating something said in parenthesis, give them an added pomposity. (pp. 172-73)

To love Balzac! Sainte-Beuve, who was so fond of defining what it meant to love someone, would have had his work cut out for him here. For with the other novelists, one loves them in submitting oneself to them; one receives the truth from a Tolstoi as from someone of greater scope and stature than oneself. With Balzac, we know all his vulgarities, and at first were often repelled by them; then we began to love him, then we smiled at all those sillinesses which are so typical of him; we love him, with a little dash of irony mixed in our affection; we know his aberrations, his shabby little tricks, and because they are so like him we love them. (pp. 178-79)

> *Marcel Proust, "Contre Sainte-Beuve: Sainte-Beuve and Balzac" (1919?), in his* Marcel Proust on Art and Literature 1896-1919, *translated by Sylvia Townsend Warner (© 1958 by Meridian Books, Inc.; reprinted by permission of Georges Borchardt, Inc., as agents for the author; in Canada by the Literary Estate of Sylvia Townsend Warner and Chatto & Windus Ltd.; originally published as* Contre Sainte-Beuve, Librairie Gallimard, 1954), Meridian Books, 1958, pp. 157-89 [published in England as his* By Way of Sainte-Beuve (Contre Sainte-Beuve), *translated by Sylvia Townsend Warner, Chatto & Windus, 1958].\**

## STEFAN ZWEIG (essay date 1920)

[*Zweig considers Balzac to be one of the three great novelists of the nineteenth century, with Charles Dickens and Fedor Dostoevski. Zweig states in his introduction to* Master Builders: A Typology of the Spirit *that the great novelist "is a universal artist, who constructs a cosmos, peopling it with types of his own making, giving it laws of gravitation that apply to it alone. . . ." In the following essay, Zweig praises the scope and versimilitude of the world of* La comédie humaine *and focuses on its inhabitants, Balzac's "monomaniacs." Because of these characters, who are motivated by passions other than erotic love, Zweig credits Balzac with developing "the concept of the novel as an encyclopaedia of the inner universe."*]

Balzac seeks to simplify the world in order to subdue it to his dominion, and to confine it within the walls of his magnificent prison-house, **La comédie humaine.** Thanks to this process of distillation, his characters become types, are always an abridged edition of a plurality from which an implacable artist has shorn everything superfluous or immaterial. Straightforward passion is the motive force, the unmixed type is the actor, an unpretentious environment is the setting, for **La comédie humaine.** He concentrates, inasmuch as he adapts the centralized administrative system to literary ends. Like Napoleon, he confines the world within the frontiers of France, and makes Paris the centre of the universe. Within this circle, again, in Paris itself, he draws many circles; one around the nobility, another around the clergy; others around manual workers, poets, artists, men of science, and so on. . . . His world is poorer than the actual world; but it is more intense. For his characters are distillates; the passions he depicts are pure elements; his tragedies are condensations.

Like Napoleon, he begins by conquering Paris. Then he sets about conquering France, province by province. Every department sends its representative, as it were, to Balzac's parliament. (pp. 10-11)

The conquest of the world effected in *La comédie humaine* is just as unique in the history of literature as Napoleon's conquests in the history of modern times; Balzac seems to grasp the whole of life in his two hands. As a boy he dreamed of conquering the world, and nothing is more potent than an early resolve which realizes itself in action. (p. 12)

His heroes resemble their progenitor, for they are all inspired with the idea of world conquest. A centripetal force drags them away from provincial life into Paris. The great town is their battlefield. The lure of the metropolis has brought this army thither; virgin souls, untested as yet, full of raw energies for which they seek an outlet. Here, needy but ambitious, they jostle one another, destroy one another, clamber up the social ladder, tumble back again into oblivion. . . .

The first lesson Balzac's young people have to learn is ruthlessness. They know that their numbers are excessive, and that they must therefore gobble one another up "like spiders in a pot," as Vautrin observes. The weapon with which their youth has armed them must be tested in the fires of experience; and it is only those who survive the ordeal who are "right." (p. 13)

All Balzac's heroes experience . . . a crisis on their march through life. Every one of them becomes a soldier in the war of all against all, pressing eagerly forward over the bodies of the slain. Each has to cross the Rubicon, each has to experience his Waterloo. Balzac shows us that the same fights take place no matter where we are, whether in palaces or in huts or in taverns; that under the garments of priests, doctors, soldiers, lawyers, the same impulses rage. (pp. 17-18)

It is precisely this murderous and suicidal warring of energies which stimulates Balzac to the exercise of his art. To depict energy, striving towards a goal, as the expression of a conscious and vital will, not in its effect but in its essence—such is the passion that possesses him. So long as this energy is intensive, he cares little or not at all whether it be good or bad, whether it be wasted energy or energy turned to good account. Intensity of purpose, will, these are everything, because they are the inherent qualities of man: success and fame are nothing, for they are subject to chance. (p. 18)

In Balzac's view, to measure the actual effects is the duty of the historian; to exhibit the causes, and to depict intensity, fall to the lot of the imaginative writer. Power becomes tragical only if it does not reach the goal. (p. 19)

Balzac does not depend upon drapery for his effects, any more than he has recourse to the exotic or to the remote annals of history for his settings. What he relies upon is the super-dimensional, the enhanced intensity of an emotion unified through singleness of purpose. He realizes that a feeling does not become important until it can remain unimpaired, in its full force; that a man is great only in so far as he concentrates on a goal, does not fritter away his energies on incidental desires, but allows his ruling passion to imbibe the juices of all the other emotions, growing strong through robbery and a fierce disregard of conflicting claims. . . . (p. 21)

It is such monomaniacs of passion whom Balzac has portrayed; persons who conceive of the world under the aspect of one single symbol, who are constant to one aim amid the great whirl.

The basic axiom of his theory of energetics is a kind of mechanics of the passions: the belief that every life expends an equal sum of energy, no matter upon what illusions it dissipates the volitional appetite; no matter whether it uses them up slowly in the course of a thousand excitements, or cherishes them thriftily for a time, in order to lavish them on one headlong ecstasy; no matter whether the fire of life burns quietly and steadily, or flames up in an explosion. . . . For a work which aims at the depiction of types, at the presentation of none but pure elements, monomaniacs are alone of importance. The feeble among mankind are of no interest to our author. He cares only for people who cling to their life illusion with every nerve and muscle of their bodies; who concentrate all their thoughts upon it, whether that illusion be love or art, avarice or self-sacrifice, courage or indolence, politics or friendship. Whatever the symbol may be, they must embrace it wholeheartedly.

These "hommes à passion," these fanatical believers in a religion of their own creation, glance neither to right nor to left. They talk in many tongues to one another, but do not understand one another's language. (pp. 21-2)

[Among] the passions there are none of greater and none of lesser importance; one does not take precedence over the others, any more than there exists a hierarchy among landscapes and dreams. None are too lowly. (p. 23)

Balzac cuts the world out into figurines, paints suitable scenery, and then pulls the strings and makes the marionettes play the parts he has assigned to them. To accomplish all this is his own ruling passion! (p. 24)

For Balzac was himself one of those monomaniacs he delighted to portray! Discouraged by an unresponsive world which did not appreciate his first efforts in the field of literature, he withdrew into himself and created a symbolic world. This world was to belong to him, to be governed by him, to cease when he himself ceased. . . . [Reality] interested him merely in so far as it provided fuel to set the wheels of his own world in motion. (p. 25)

No other artist succeeds in losing himself in his work as perfectly as Balzac, none has a more confident belief in his own dream, none allows hallucination to carry him so near to the boundary of self-deception. He sometimes found it almost impossible to curb his excitement once the machinery had been set in motion; image and reality seemed to him equally concrete; and he could not always draw a sharp line between his inner world and the world outside. . . . Perhaps the only thing which differentiates those vivid and lasting hallucinations from the hallucinations of a madman is that Balzac's imaginary figures were subject to the same causal determinisms as those that prevail in the domain of objective reality. His characters seem indeed, to have knocked at the door of his study, and to have passed from the outer world into the world of his books.

But his absorption in his work was tantamount to monomania in its persistence, its intensity, and its concentration. His industry was a veritable fever, an intoxication, a delirium. (pp. 26-7)

[The] exceptional power of intuitively knowing all things, is the essence of Balzac's genius. In respect of the familiar talents of the literary artist—the faculty to range qualities, to give order and coherency to characters, the power to bind and to loose—he was not strikingly endowed. There is a distinct temptation to say that he was not so much an artist within the meaning of the act as a genius. . . . [We] are here confronted with so stupendous a power that, like a mighty lord of the jungle, it refuses to be tamed; it is beautiful as a forest, a torrent, a thunderstorm; it has the quality of all those things whose aesthetic value lies in the intensity of their manifestations. (p. 42)

**La comédie humaine** has no inner cohesion, no definite plan. Indeed, the work is as lacking in a definite plan as life itself is—in Balzac's estimation. It does not aim at pointing a moral, nor it it intended to give a survey of the manners and customs of those days. In its own mutability, it is meant to portray the everlasting mutability of persons and things. It ebbs and flows rhythmically, like the tides. (p. 43)

With him began—and were it not for Dostoeffsky we might say "ended" as well—the concept of the novel as an encyclopaedia of the inner universe. His predecessors knew of only two ways whereby the reluctant machinery of events could be set in motion: chance, acting from without; or love, working from within, and bringing a succession of erotic incidents in its train. Balzac showed the working of another prime motive force than the erotic. For him, desire assumed two aspects: love, in the true meaning of the word, affecting a few men and all women who happen to be born under its star, who live for love, and who die with their hearts still full of passion-fraught longing; and ambition. It was only the latter kind of desire that had genuine interest for him. But we owe a debt to Balzac's genius for having demonstrated that those energies which find release in eroticism are not the only species of impulses; that the vicissitudes of other passions are no whit less enthralling; that, without in any way scattering and wasting the primitive forces, desire can assume other forms than those of love and may contain other symbols for our enlightenment. Balzac, manipulating all the urges underlying human nature, was able to give them an amazing multiplicity of expression.

But he fed his novels with reality from an additional source. As portrayer of his contemporaries and as statistician of the relative, Balzac devoted the minutest study to the moral, political, and aesthetic values of things. Above all, he paid close attention to those values which today constitute an almost universal standard and are regarded as wellnigh absolute. In a word, he investigated money values, and introduced them into his novels. (pp. 45-6)

No one can afford to ignore Balzac's work. The eighty volumes which comprise his literary achievement, represent an epoch, a universe, a whole generation. Never before had so vast an enterprise been deliberately undertaken, never has the temerity of a man's unbounded will been better requited. (p. 47)

Had Balzac been able to complete his stupendous scheme, his work would have passed into the realm of the inconceivable. It would have become a monster, scaring subsequent writers by the magnitude of its inaccessibility. As it is, it acts as a stimulus without parallel, and serves as a magnificent example for all those whose creative will is pointed towards the unattainable. (p. 48)

> *Stefan Zweig, "Balzac" (originally published under a different title in his* Drei Meister, Insel-Verlag, 1920), *in his* Master Builders: A Typology of the Spirit, *translated by Eden Paul and Cedar Paul (translation copyright © 1939, copyright renewed © 1966, by the Viking Press, Inc.; reprinted by permission of the Estate of Stefan Zweig), Viking Penguin Inc., 1939, pp. 1-48.*

## PERCY LUBBOCK   (essay date 1921)

> [*Lubbock assesses several of Balzac's narrative devices. Unlike most critics, Lubbock dislikes Balzac's use of recurring characters and maintains that they do not add a sense of continuity to the novels.*]

If one plunges straight into Balzac, at the beginning of criticism, it is hard to find the right line through the abundance of good and bad in his books; there is so much of it, and all so strong and staring. It looks at first sight as though his good and his bad alike were entirely conspicuous and unmistakable. His devouring passion for life, his grotesque romance, his truth and his falsity, these cover the whole space of the **Comédie** between them, and nobody could fail to recognize the full force of either. He is tremendous, his taste is abominable—what more is there to say of Balzac? (pp. 203-04)

Such is the aspect that Balzac presents, I could feel, when a critic tries to face him immediately; his obviousness seems to hide everything else. But if one passes him by, following the track of the novelist's art elsewhere, and then returns to him with certain definite conclusions, his aspect is remarkable in quite a new way. His badness is perhaps as obvious as before; there is nothing fresh to discover about that. His greatness, however, wears a different look; it is no longer the plain and open surface that it was. It has depths and recesses that did not appear till now, enticing to criticism, promising plentiful illustration of the ideas that have been gathered by the way. One after another, the rarer, obscurer effects of fiction are all found in Balzac, behind his blatant front. He illustrates everything, and the only difficulty is to know where to begin.

The effect of the generalized picture, for example, supporting the play of action, is one in which Balzac particularly delights. He constantly uses it, he makes it serve his purpose with a very high hand. It becomes more than a support, it becomes a kind of propulsive force applied to the action at the start. Its value is seen at its greatest in such books as **Le Curé de Village, Père Goriot, La Recherche de l'Absolu, Eugénie Grandet**—most of all, perhaps, in this last. Wherever, indeed, his subject requires to be lodged securely in its surroundings, wherever the background is a main condition of the story, Balzac is in no hurry to precipitate the action; that can always wait, while he allows himself the leisure he needs for massing the force which is presently to drive the drama on its way. Nobody gives such attention as Balzac does in many of his books, and on the whole in his best, to the setting of the scene; he clearly considers these preparatory pictures quite as important as the events which they are to enclose.

And so, in **Père Goriot**, all the potent life of the Maison Vauquer is deliberately collected and hoarded up to the point where it is enough, when it is let loose, to carry the story forward with a strong sweep. By the time the story itself is reached the Maison Vauquer is a fully created impression, prepared to the last stroke for the drama to come. Anything that may take place there will have the whole benefit of its setting, without more ado; all the rank reality of the house and its inmates is immediately bestowed on the action. . . . Balzac's care in creating the scene, therefore, is truly economical; it is not merely a manner of setting the stage for the drama, it is a provision of character and energy for the drama when it begins.

His pictures of country towns, too, Saumur, Limoges, Angoulême, have the same kind of part to play in the **Scènes de la vie de province**. When Balzac takes in hand the description of a town or a house or a workshop, he may always be suspected, at first, of abandoning himself entirely to his simple, disinterested craving for facts. There are times when it seems that his inexhaustible knowledge of facts is carrying him where it will, till his only conscious purpose is to set down on paper everything that he knows. He is possessed by the lust of description for its own sake, an insatiable desire to put every detail in its place, whether it is needed or no. . . . [When] he has finished his lengthy research among the furniture of the lives that are to be evoked, he has created a scene in which action will move as rapidly as he chooses, without losing any of its due emphasis. He has illustrated, in short, the way in which a pictorial impression, wrought to the right pitch, will speed the work of drama—will become an effective agent in the book, instead of remaining the mere decorative introduction that it may seem to be.

Thus it is that Balzac was able to pack into a short book—he never wrote a long one—such an effect of crowds and events, above all such an effect of time. Nobody knows how to compress so much experience into two or three hundred pages as Balzac did unfailingly. I cannot think that this is due in the least to the laborious interweaving of his books into a single scheme; I could believe that in general a book of Balzac's suffers, rather than gains, by the recurrence of the old names that he has used already elsewhere. It is an amusing trick, but exactly what is its object? . . . The theory is, I suppose, that the characters in the background and at the corners of the action, if they are Rastignac and Camusot and Nucingen, retain the life they have acquired elsewhere, and thereby tell the life of the story in which they reappear. We are occupied for the moment with some one else, and we discover among his acquaintance a number of people whom we already know; that fact, it is implied, will add weight and authority to the story of the man in the foreground—who is himself, very likely, a man we have met casually in another book. It ought to make, it must make, his situation peculiarly real and intelligible that we find him surrounded by familiar friends of our own; and that is the artistic reason of the amazing ingenuity with which Balzac keeps them all in play. (pp. 204-08)

[I question] whether the density of life in so many of his short pieces can really owe anything to the perpetual flitting of the men and women from book to book. Suppose that for the moment Balzac is evoking the figure and fortunes of Lucien de Rubempré, and that a woman who appears incidentally in his story turns out to be our well-remembered Delphine, Goriot's daughter. We know a great deal about the past of Delphine, as it happens; but at this present juncture, in Lucien's story, her past is entirely irrelevant. It belongs to another adventure, where it mattered exceedingly, an adventure that took place before Lucien was heard of at all. As for his story, and for the reality with which it may be endowed, this depends solely upon our understanding of *his* world, *his* experience; and if Delphine's old affairs are no part of it, our previous knowledge of her cannot help us with Lucien. It detracts, rather, from the force of his effect; it sets up a relation that has nothing to do with him, a relation between Delphine and the reader, which only obstructs our view of the world as Lucien sees it. Of the characters in the remoter planes of the action (and that is Delphine's position in his story) no more is expected than their value for the purpose of the action in the foreground. That is all that can be *used* in the book; whatever more they may bring will lie idle, will contribute nothing, and may even become an embarrassment. The numberless people in the *Comédie* who carry their lengthening train of old associations from book to book may give the *Comédie,* as a whole, the look of

unity that Balzac desired; that is another point. But in any single story, such of these people as appear by the way, incidentally, must for the time being shed their irrelevant life; if they fail to do so, they disturb the unity of the story and confuse its truth.

Balzac's unrivalled power of placing a figure in its surroundings is not to be explained, then, by his skill in working his separate pieces together into one great web; the design of the *Human Comedy,* so largely artificial, forced upon it as his purpose widened, is no enhancement of the best of his books. The fullness of experience which is rendered in these is exactly the same—is more expressive, if anything—when they are taken out of their context; it is all to be attributed to their own art. (pp. 208-10)

Balzac, it cannot be denied, had frequent cause to look about him for whatever means there might be of extenuating, and so of confirming, an incredible story. His passion for truth was often in conflict with his lust for marvels, and the manner in which they were mixed is the chief interest, I dare say, of some of his books. See him, for example, in the *Splendeurs et Misères des Courtisanes,* trying with one hand to write a novel of Parisian manners, with the other a romance of mystery, and to do full justice to both. Trompe-la-Mort, the Napoleon of crime, and Esther, the inspired courtesan, represent the romance, and Balzac sets himself to absorb the extravagant tale into a study of actual life. If he can get the tale firmly embedded in a background of truth, its falsity may be disguised, the whole book may even pass for a scene of the human comedy; it may be accepted as a piece of reality, on the same level, say, as *Eugénie Grandet* or *Les Parents Pauvres.* That is evidently his aim, and if only his romance were a little less gaudy, or his truth not quite so true, he would have no difficulty in attaining it; the action would be subdued and kept in its place by the pictorial setting. The trouble is that Balzac's idea of a satisfying crime is as wild as his hold upon facts is sober, so that an impossible strain is thrown upon his method of reconciling the two. Do what he will, his romance remains staringly false in its contrast with his reality; there is an open gap between the wonderful pictures of the town in *Illusions Perdues* and the theatrical drama of the old convict which they introduce. Yet his method was a right one, though it was perverse of Balzac to be occupied at all with such devices, when he might have rejected his falsity altogether. (pp. 211-12)

> *Percy Lubbock, in a chapter in his* The Craft of Fiction *(reprinted by permission of Jonathan Cape Ltd, on behalf of the Estate of Percy Lubbock), Cape, 1921, pp. 203-19.**

### BENEDETTO CROCE  (essay date 1923)

[*In his historical approach to Balzac's work, Croce disputes Ferdinand Brunetiére's contention that the author was "objective," "naturalistic," and a disciple of "a methodical application of natural science" (see excerpt above, 1906). Croce maintains that Balzac had an "ardent imagination" that is the source of the romanticized and exaggerated nature of* La comédie humaine.]

Everyone knows that Balzac as a young man devoured the most extravagant romantic literature both in French and English, adventures, conquests, discoveries of treasure, crimes, ghostly apparitions, hallucinations, and that he himself wrote novels of the same sort, and that he was never able to do without such marvellous tales, introducing them more or less freely and sometimes in profusion into many of the works of his maturity.

But Balzac does not do otherwise than give an extraordinary aspect to what is ordinary, middle-class and popular even in those novels and in that series of novels which Brunetière considers to be "objective" and "naturalistic" [see excerpt above, 1906]. No portrait of character or surroundings but he exaggerates it to the extent of making it altogether marvellous and fantastic, whether he is telling the story of a former officer of Napoleon like Philippe Brideau, or representing Goriot's paternal affection, or the house of father Grandet or the shop of the *chat qui pelotte*. He takes hold here and there of some bits of reality in order to make of them an object of fascination for himself and to enter by means of them into a dream of the unbridled and immense, through which he progresses, half in admiration, half in terror, as though immersed in an apocalyptic vision. To take this for "a methodical application of natural science" is really somewhat singular. . . . (pp. 273-74)

Balzac's ardent imagination not only forbade to him scientific observation, for which Brunetière praised him, but was so violent and voracious as to disturb his very work as an artist, and this point must be made clear, as it supplies guidance in the critical reading of his fiction. (p. 275)

How, then, can it be said that the ardour of Balzac's imagination, which seems to be so favourable to artistic production, yet acted injuriously upon that art? The reason is that in the delicate process of artistic creation, the imagination which embodies and dominates the impressions and the passions of reality must be kept clearly distinct from the fancy which avails itself of the intuitions of the imagination for its own enjoyment, entertainment or bitter alleviation. Balzac's case was precisely so, for with him what is described as his imaginative ardour really contained two diverse activities acting in two different ways under one name, in the one case inspiring him to artistic creation, in the other deforming the art produced or begun to be produced. One feels that Balzac was a poet in the best sense of the word, from the vigour with which he represents characters, situations and surroundings, from the perfection of the forms that burst forth from his stirred imagination. (pp. 275-76)

[Balzac] generally proceeds with energetic genius, like a true artist, but gradually in the course of the work, instead of leaving his creations free to follow the law of their true being and so create the companionship, the surroundings, the kind of action, beginning, middle and end that are implied in their fundamental notion, and consequently to moderate attemper and take on their proper tone, he compels them to follow the law of his own rapacious temperament, of Honoré de Balzac, whose taste lies in the direction of passions pushed to the extreme, of violent and intransigent conflicts, of colossal undertakings, of astonishing clevernesses and infernal complications, of astounding successes, all of which he enjoys immensely and intensifies, in order to extract from them yet more enjoyment.

It has been said and repeated (and I think Sainte-Beuve is responsible for the statement [see excerpt above, 1850]), that in Balzac the characters are excellent, the action less good and the style vicious. This further empirical utterance of criticism must be corrected by means of the exact theory, namely, that the three things are one, and that one of them cannot be exempt from the defects of the other, and the defects of all must be brought home to a common origin. This common origin is to be found in Balzac's psychological disposition already described, owing to which he capriciously applies movement to his creations, thus making the characters of his personages revolve rapidly and grow vertiginously upon themselves, be-

coming ever more and more mad about themselves, and then, having attained the summit of this process of expansion, they turn into the opposite of what they were, or reveal other qualities in an unexpected way, which are contradictory or out of harmony with their former qualities. Their actions, owing to this same vertiginous rapidity, either lose all logical consistency, and, in their efforts to develop the characters, assume the customary form of the serial novel, or else they too all of a sudden also collapse and languish, and the style, which is all one with those actions and characters, falls from simple and robust plasticity into feebleness and languishment, or assumes the tone of explanation and comment. The characters do not attain to the harmony of discordant concord, and therefore the action does not unfold itself naturally and the style is not rhythmical.

Any one of Balzac's novels selected from among the best offers ready proofs of such inequalities and disharmonies; but I shall limit myself to *Eugénie Grandet,* which is reputed to be the most perfect of all, or one of the most perfect. After the wonderful picture of the country house and of the family surroundings in which flourish the gentle affections of the youthful Eugenia, who is there that does not feel that father and mother Grandet and Eugenia herself are being turned into fixed rhetorical types? Father Grandet is no longer a miser in his humanity, but a madman. . . . (pp. 276-78)

[With a maniac for a] father and a character without character such as the bethrothed cousin, the story of Eugenia, which promised to turn out moving and poetical, loses itself in the insignificant. It seems that the author, who has spent his best strength in forcing characters and oppositions to an extreme, lacks the breadth to represent the drama which he had been preparing. So the story rushes along and what should have been represented is announced as having already happened. . . Worse still, the style becomes impoverished, and here and there assumes the appearance of a school exercise. . . . (p. 278)

[Notwithstanding] deformation, inflation and the abandonment of the end of art, which is very common in him, his art was most vigorous, and is strewn throughout with acute thoughts and observations, which vary its attractiveness. But Balzac never or only on rare occasions attained to aesthetic serenity. I admit that I remained astonished at an Italian comparison between him and Alexander Manzoni . . . , where Balzac is held to be audacious and fruitful, Manzoni timid and sterile, astonished above all that anyone could have thought of making such a comparison, but worse than astonished at seeing that not even Manzoni's divine equality of level had been sufficient to throw into a clear light the artistic vice with which was afflicted Honoré de Balzac. (pp. 279-80)

*Benedetto Croce, "Balzac," in his* European Literature in the Nineteenth Century, *translated by Douglas Ainslie (reprinted by permission of the Literary Estate of Benedetto Croce; originally published as* Poesia e non poesia: Note sulla letteratura europea del secolo decimonono, *G. Laterza & Figli, 1923), Alfred A. Knopf, 1924, pp. 267-80.*

**GEORGE MOORE**   (essay date 1924)

[In *La Comédie Humaine,* new] faces meet us at every turn; hundreds of human souls float round and round as if in a vortex, the usurer everywhere governing his own section as he governs it in life. We find all types of men and women: peasants working in fields and drinking in the inns, courtesans in the streets and in palaces, old men preyed upon by unscrupulous women, who in turn are the victims of unscrupulous young men. Balzac was a great harvester and his sheaves were souls: poets who waste their talents in love-dreams, diners-out who waste theirs in quips. As we read on, volume after volume, our wonder increases. . . . (pp. 32-3)

*Les Secrets de la Princesse de Cadignan* might be entitled: *The Seduction of Genius by Experience.* It is animated by a sublime comprehension of the fascinating perversities of cerebral passion, and the confiding simplicities of a great man, who, wearied like Faust, with learning, desires the repose and consolation of love. *Les Secrets de la Princesse de Cadignan* might also be entitled: *The Philosophy of the Drawing-room.* It is the drawing-room in essence. The Princess is a being born of the drawing-room; she has been formed and coloured by the drawing-room as an insect by the chemical qualities and the colour of the plant upon which it lives. Her ideas of love, literature, art, and science are drawing-room ideas of love, literature, art, and science. The intonations of her voice, and every inflection of accent, have been produced by the drawing-room. Her weariness of life is drawing-room weariness of life. She is a creature of the drawing-room as the horse is a creature of the stable, as the eagle is of the cliff. (p. 37)

Although somewhat lost amid numberless chefs-d'oeuvre, although rarely cited as a striking example of Balzac's genius, *Une Vieille Fille* is one of the first among the minor pieces. It seems to me to epitomise the resources of a mind profound and, at least in the conception of a subject, sensible to art. In *Une Vieille Fille* we meet a certain philosophic criticism peculiar to Balzac, and three characters conceived with imaginative incisiveness and executed with an alertness of thought only to be found in his very best work, and some two or three dramatic moments. (pp. 41-2)

One excellent reason for believing that the genius of Balzac can be approached through the minor pieces is the existence of the *Curé de Tours,* for unlike many of Balzac's short stories it is not a novel reduced to the limits of a short story—a bundle of events excellently well imagined, but hastily arranged, showing bad cutting and awkwardly sewed seams on every side. It begins at exactly the right point; the development proceeds without long waits; nowhere is there an unnecessary line; and the art it recalls is that of Turgenev. Balzac had many qualities; he was everything in turn, even delicate, and in the *Curé de Tours* the means are even slighter than the dropping of a handkerchief. (p. 51)

The story is one of pure observation—a great mind directed on what is commonly termed the minutiae of life. But are not things only great and small in proportion as we think of them? Is not the world but man's thought, and in the envelope of Balzac's mind the little folk in the city of Tours rise up at once as large, as mean, and as pathetic as life itself. . . . (p. 53)

The story is fortunate in every way. Besides the even more than usually brilliant envelope of thought in which Balzac never failed to enfold all he wrote, the *Curé de Tours* is well written. The composition is balanced within and without and so evenly that no one of the epigrams that light up the pages starts out of its setting or frets, or for one moment fatigues the eye. (pp. 53-4)

After the *Curé de Tours* perhaps the most celebrated among the minor pieces is *Massimilla Doni.* Balzac himself held this story in the highest esteem, but it is disjointed and ill-proportioned; and it may be that the musical criticism enabled him

to overlook these faults. On the subject of digression we should be indulgent, if the digression be interesting or valuable. But the eulogy of the *Moses in Egypt* shows no critical discernment, and an innocent notation of his own impressions would have been more interesting than crude technical praise of a work that has not stood the test of time; to be quite plain, only the criticism of the craftsman is valid. A cabinet-maker will always know more about the leg of a table than a tailor or candlestick-maker.

It has been said that Balzac had not time to live; it might be added that he had not time to think. Thoughts came to him intuitively, as the song comes to a bird, and it is not unlikely that one of the vulgarly seductive phrases of the *Moses* haunted his ear, and generated in his mind a scheme for a musical novel. (pp. 54-5)

[The intrigue] savours of comic opera. So beautiful a theme—a young man hesitating between the real and the ideal—should have been worked out on the simplest and most natural lines, and that the beauty of highest tribute we can pay to Balzac. *C'est du mauvais romantisme,* but the grip of Balzac is so intense that truth is transferred from reality to art. (p. 56)

*Le style c'est l'homme,* is an old saw, one that has been repeated in and out of season, and my excuse for citing it is that perhaps no better exemplification of it could be found than Balzac were all literature ransacked for vindication of its truth. . . . He wrote well, magnificently when the inspiration was by him; nobody was ever more continuously inspired, and he always had something to say, wherefore he revised to say more, never taking surreptitious pleasure in the art of writing, and his method, like every other, has advantages together with many disadvantages. . . . It has been said that Balzac had not time to live; it might be added that Balzac had not time to *write.* He lived in ideas; ideas were always about him—ideas on all subjects; and writing was merely the operation of noting them down. In Balzac there is neither question of good style nor of bad style; he simply did not *write;* he registered his ideas, and his ideas are always so interesting that you read without noticing the ruts of verbal expression he slips into. (pp. 57-8)

Balzac lived in the midst of the romantic movement, and had his genius not been high and durable it would have succumbed and been lost in the romantic current in which so much genius was lost. But the realistic and critical method of which he was inventor and creator, lived too strongly in him, and the romance that swept about him only tended to purify and ventilate the abundance of his genius; it was the romantic movement that saved him from drifting among the mud-banks and shallow shores of Naturalism. (p. 58)

*George Moore, in a chapter in his* Conversations in Ebury Street *(© J. C. Medley & R. G. Medley 1924; copyright renewed © 1952 by C. D. Medley; reprinted by permission of the Literary Estate of George Moore), William Heinemann, 1924 (and reprinted by Chatto & Windus, 1969, pp. 30-60).*

**F.C. GREEN** (essay date 1931)

It is usual to dismiss *Jane la Pâle* . . . along with [Balzac's] other early novels as the regrettable and somewhat inexplicable indiscretion of a young genius who has not yet found himself. Yet in spite of its glaring crudities, *Jane la Pâle* is well worth reading as a precocious example of the Balzacian conception of passion. Briefly, it is a study of the tenacity and the ineffable unselfishness of love in the hearts of two romantic women. . . .

What is really remarkable is that Balzac almost succeeds in convincing the reader of the probability of these dramatic events: they appear as the logical result of a dynamic passion fastening like a Fury upon a human life, twisting it into the queerest shapes. To Balzac, as to the abbé Prévost, the passion of love is a thunderbolt that can in a moment destroy the carefully erected edifice of principles and experience which we call a good education. (pp. 168-69)

Balzac did not merely magnify the passions of his characters; he revealed as no other novelist has ever done the surprising extent of the social zone which can be devastated by the influence of an unbridled passion.

Balzac viewed passion, then, essentially as an anti-social force, and here lies precisely one of his claims to originality as a novelist. Others, like Prévost in his *Manon Lescaut* and Rousseau in his *Nouvelle Héloïse,* had portrayed the classic conflict between passion and reason, but the tragic consequences affected only one or two individuals. Balzac, on the other hand, with his greater vision, reveals the repercussions of a passion the gratification of which produces unhappiness in the most unexpected quarters. His work acquires thereby an almost cosmic significance. It is doubly tragic, since it frequently reveals not only the terrible punishment that overtakes the guilty man, a punishment out of all proportion to his fault, but also the suffering which overtakes innocent people who are associated with him by economic or other ties. (pp. 172-73)

Before Balzac, the French novelist had practically confined his attention to one passion, love, and thereby he gave a false interpretation of life. Balzac, whilst appreciating the great part played by love in human existence, reduced it to its proper proportions and threw light on other motives of conduct. The dreadful avarice of a Grandet; the foolish social ambition of César Birotteau; the blind inferiority complex of Cousine Bette; the inordinate paternal love of Goriot; the perverted family instinct of De la Baudraye; the Mephistophelian love of evil for the sake of evil incarnated in Vautrin; the intellectual passion of a Claës in his mad search for the Absolute; the romantic cravings of a Louise de Chaulieu; the sinister and obscure vindictiveness of the abbé Troubert: these themes indicate to a slight extent the gulf which separates Balzac from his predecessors, and enable us to measure in some degree the fertility of his creative genius. (p. 175)

Much has been written about Balzac's realism: his novels, it is said, reflect real life. But if one means by this that Balzac is content to transcribe into novelist's language the multitude of human emotions, actions and physical facts that make up Life the definition is sadly inadequate. . . . [For Balzac, the] dynamic source of all human activity is passion. "Passion," he said, "is all humanity. Without it religion, history, the novel, art would be useless." So all his novels, besides being faithful reflections of some aspect of social life, are also illustrations of the workings of a passion. Balzac does more than reflect life: he interprets it, and this is surely the highest function of the novelist. *Les Paysans* shows admirably the cumulative and resistless force of a combination of petty passions which in the course of time break down and destroy a social system that has behind it all the authority of law and government. (pp. 176-77)

There is in many of Balzac's characters a tigerish cruelty like Troubert's [in *Curé de Tours*], a thoroughness in their destructive methods which makes them, like Troubert, dissatisfied until they have completely annihilated their enemies. For to Balzac, passion is an incurable thing, implacable as the Fate of the Ancients. If you examine the structure of his great characters you will observe they change for evil, rarely for good. The truly passionate characters seldom indulge in death-bed repentances, and this is well observed. . . . Vautrin is an exception, for on the death of his protégé, Lucien de Rubempré, he renounces his feud against society and becomes an element of order and repression, an ending which appears at first sight banal and improbable. In reality this dénouement is the only one consistent with probability. Vautrin's original obsession was to avenge himself on society, and the young poet Lucien was the instrument which he fashioned for this purpose. But Lucien became his creation, the living expression of all that Vautrin dreamed he would be and never was—his "visible soul." As he saw the young poet develop, Vautrin's idea of vengeance gradually yielded to a greater passion, the passion of the artist for his masterpiece, nay, even more gigantic than this for was he not moulding a human destiny? Lucien is imprisoned and, in despair, commits suicide. Vautrin, like Macbeth when his magical defences collapse, realises for the first time that there are limitations even to his daemonic genius for corruption. He is too old to begin again, and, moreover, he has glimpsed behind the organisation called society and inscrutable directive force compared to which his own efforts seem futile and puny. There are two courses open, resignation or suicide, and he chooses the former. Vautrin had set himself up as a god and he committed the supreme blasphemy of attempting to enslave the will of a fellow-man. The destruction of his creation, Lucien, by a greater power is a magnificent example of poetic justice.

Balzac is the first great French writer to break away from the aristocratic attitude towards society so typical of the *ancien régime.* He is also the first to emphasise the economic interdependence of the various classes, and to throw into light the tremendous part played by money in human existence. . . . In this new society, as Balzac saw it, the dominating passion was the lust for money, whether as an end in itself or as a means to the gratification of other passions. The power of money obsessed him to an extraordinary degree, and this attitude of mind was fortified by his personal experience of law and debt. (pp. 179-82)

In *Eugénie Grandet* the question of money seems to overshadow the novel as the figure of the miser overshadows Saumur, like some great tree which makes a desert of its environment. But interwoven with the story of Grandet's monstrous avarice is the lyric poem of his daughter's love for her cousin Charles. But for the miser's character this would be the banal story of a pure love unrequited, the sad but common tale of a desertion. . . . The real drama lies not in the sinister picture of Grandet's financial activities, not in the slow cancerous spread of his avarice as it permeates the social organism, but in the clash of two characters, in the sudden volcanic outburst of resistance in the daughter, a resistance inspired by love and reinforced by that tenacity of will which she has inherited from her father. . . . In the duel between avarice and love, love wins. The dénouement contains the tragedy, which is that the object on whom this great love is lavished is pitifully unworthy. And so Eugénie, after soaring for a brief and glorious moment into the empyrean, flutters broken-winged back to the drab reality of Saumur. (pp. 183-84)

By an extraordinary feat possible only to a genius, [Balzac] was able to adapt the artistic procedure of the great dramatists to the purposes of the novel. Whilst retaining the minute descriptive method of the novelist who, unlike the playwright, is practically unhampered by considerations of space and time in his character construction, he succeeded in imparting to his creations the stature, the universality and the intensity which one had hitherto associated with a Shakespeare, a Corneille or a Moliére. No novelist, French or English, prior to Balzac, achieved this. Gil Blas, Tom Jones, Des Grieux are not to be compared with the great Balzacian types like Goriot, Vautrin or Grandet. And the reason for this relative and very honourable inferiority is that they are too human. This is no paradox. Of course, Balzac excels as a novelist of manners: as a painter of the manifold and seething human activities composing social life he has few rivals. But his great figures are superhuman. No one in real life was ever a miser on the plane of a Grandet. Nor was there in real life a man so possessed by the mania of paternal love as a Goriot, or a criminal of the immensity of a Vautrin. If we would find parallels we must go to great drama, where Harpagon, Lear and Mephistopheles present the superhuman qualities reproduced by the great Frenchman. Balzac benefits by that state of mind peculiar to those witnessing great drama. For the moment, petty and local considerations of probability, drawn from our limited experience of life, are swept aside as we behold the actions of a being who is just human enough to appeal to our understanding and sufficiently superhuman to captivate our imagination. Reason assures us that no such being exists, but imagination persuades us that he might; and, after all, the immediate appeal of art in fiction as in drama is not to the reason but to the emotions. The rational verdict comes as an after-thought, but then the effect desired by the artist has already been attained. (pp. 194-95)

> F. C. Green, "Balzac," in his French Novelists:
> From the Revolution to Proust, J. M. Dent & Sons
> Ltd., 1931, pp. 163-95.

## ALBERT THIBAUDET (essay date 1936)

Balzac, the greatest creator of living creatures who ever existed, looked into the face of the mystery of creation and plumbed it in its depths. We know how prominent a place was held for him by "Faustian natures," devotees of alchemy, of discovery, of work, a Glaës or a d'Arthez. But the *natural* form of creation is what provides the material for the official registers. It is fatherhood. In the work of every writer of genius there is always one creation that has the function of a profound message and that serves as a primary cell. In Balzac everything takes place as if this function had been that of *Le Père Goriot.*

Not only because *Le Père Goriot* already includes the majority of Balzac's key characters—Vautrin, Rastignac, Bianchon, the Nucingen household—but also because le Père Goriot is primarily the title character and the mystery of fatherhood. Montaigne said that he would rather have fathered a child in trafficking with one of the Muses than with his wife. But the second of these traffickings is the carnal symbol of the first, as tradition makes the couple of the Song of Songs the symbol of the union of God and his Church. *Le Père Goriot* could have been created only by the father of Father Goriot, the "Christ of fatherhood," by the genius of paternity and the paternity of genius. "When I became a father," Goriot said, "I understood God." This is an extraordinary remark that takes us to the source of Balzac's creation. The presence of God, the acquiescence of God are as obvious, as necessary, as absolute in Balzac's work, full like a day of the Creation, as the absence, the nonexistence, of God in the work of Marcel Proust, the day-to-day record of a world that is disintegrating. Competition

with the official registers is the external, conventional description that implies, internally and in reality, collaboration with the Creator and that "*Imitation de Dieu le Père*" that is latent in *La Comédie humaine.*

Goriot is a victim of fatherhood because he is a father in the flesh, a father of individuals, a father from selfishness. The phrase, "Christ of fatherhood," means his passion, what he was made to suffer by the two daughters for whom he made himself a sacrificial victim. He loved his daughters totally, overpoweringly, he was the slave of their wills and their passions, and that is why he died desperate and destroyed. In a letter to Mme. Hanska, Balzac said that *Massimilla Doni, Louis Lambert* and *Le Chef-d'oeuvre inconnu* represented "work and execution killed by the overabundance of the creative principle." And the insistence with which he returned to this theme shows the degree to which he felt in this a peril in his own nature. Similarly, in Goriot the human and moral function of fatherhood is done to death by the abundance of this creative principle, which is a terrible gift for man if no discipline intervenes to reduce it, to contain it, and utilize it. (pp. 196-97)

If Goriot's fatherhood is seen as a symbol of the creative fatherhood of genius, Vautrin will appear as an enormous satanic parody of it. The substructures of *La Comédie humaine* are Christian substructures, those of a world in which the devil and hell exist. Among the visions that Balzac brought into the literary universe there is the social hell, the lower depths of capitals, the lower depths of human nature, the prisons. Prison has its hero [in Vautrin] as Milton's hell had him in Satan. (p. 198)

> Albert Thibaudet, "Balzac," in his French Literature
> from 1795 to Our Era, translated by Charles Lam
> Markmann (English translation copyright ©1967 by
> Harper & Row, Publishers, Inc.; reprinted by per
> mission of the publisher; originally published as his
> Histoire de la littérature française de 1789 à nos jours,
> (copyright 1938 by Librairie Stock, Paris), Stock,
> 1936), Funk & Wagnalls, 1968, pp. 195-211.

## GEORGE LUKÁCS (essay date 1949)

> [Lukács is considered one of the foremost Marxist critics of the
> twentieth century. His analysis of Balzac's The Peasants praises
> its realistic depiction of social and economic forces. In defining
> Balzac's achievement, Lukács asserts that "he manages to show
> us the whole development of French capitalism after the revolu
> tion, the decline of the nobility, and above all the tragedy of a
> peasantry once liberated and then for a second time enslaved by
> the revolution—the tragedy of the peasant smallholding."]

[In *The Peasants*], the most important [novel] of his maturity, Balzac wanted to write the tragedy of the doomed landed aristocracy of France. It was intended to be the keystone of the series in which Balzac described the destruction of French aristocratic culture by the growth of capitalism. The novel is indeed such a keystone, for it goes into the economic causes which brought about the ruin of the nobility. Earlier, Balzac had depicted the death-struggle of the aristocracy as it appeared in the hinterland of Paris or of some remote provincial towns, but in *The Peasants* he takes us to the theatre of war itself, to the economic battlefield on which the struggle between aristocratic landowner and peasant farmer is fought out to the bitter end. . . .

Yet, for all his painstaking preparation and careful planning, what Balzac really did in this novel was the exact opposite of what he had set out to do: what he depicted was not the tragedy of the aristocratic estate but of the peasant smallholding. It is precisely this discrepancy between intention and performance, between Balzac the political thinker and Balzac the author of *La Comédie Humaine* that constitutes Balzac's historical greatness. (p. 21)

It was in **The Peasants** that Balzac, after long preparation, depicted for the first time the actual impact on each other of the social classes of the countryside. Here the rural population is shown realistically in a rich variety of types, now no longer as the abstract and passive object of Utopian experiments but as the acting and suffering hero of the novel.

When Balzac, in the fulness of his creative powers, approached this problem with his own most personal method, he provided in his quality of writer a devastating criticism of the opinions which he in his quality of political thinker stubbornly held to the end of his life. For even in this novel his own point of view is the defence of the large estate. "Les Aigues," the Comte de Montcornet's aristocratic seat, is the focal point of an ancient traditional culture—which in Balzac's eyes is the only possible culture. . . .

This perspective determines the tragic, elegiac, pessimistic keynote of the whole novel. What Balzac intended to write was the tragedy of the aristocratic large estate and with it the tragedy of culture. (p. 27)

Balzac painted this tragedy of the aristocratic large estate with all the richness of his literary genius. Although he depicts the land-hungry peasants with the greatest political hostility ("a Robespierre with one head and twenty million arms"), yet, as the great realist that he is, he gives a monumental and perfectly balanced picture of the forces locked in struggle on both sides. . . .

From the outset Balzac presents the struggle raging around the aristocratic large estate not merely as a duel between landowner and peasant, but as a three-cornered fight between three parties all pitted against each other; the small-town and village usurper-capitalist takes the field against both landowner and peasant. A great variety of types are introduced to represent each warring camp and they bring into play every economic, political, ideological and other weapon in support of their cause. (p. 28)

This triangle, in which each party fights the two others, forms the basis of Balzac's composition and the inevitability of this double-fronted struggle of each of the three parties, in every phase of which one aspect of the struggle necessarily predominates in accordance with the immediate economic compulsions acting on each party, gives the composition its richness and complexity. The action swings to and fro from the nobleman's castle to the peasant tavern, the bourgeois apartment and the small-town café, and this restless shifting of the scene and characters give Balzac the opportunity of showing up the basic factors of the class struggle fought out in the French countryside. (pp. 29-30)

The destruction of the nobility—Balzac's ideological and political starting-point—was only one aspect of this total process, and however biassed Balzac may have been in favour of the nobility, he saw quite clearly the inevitability of its extinction, nor did he fail to see the internal decadence, the moral deterioration of the nobility in the course of this process. In several historical studies he uncovered the origins of this eclipse of the nobility. He rightly regarded the transformation of the feudal nobility into a court nobility, its transformation into a par-

asitic group with dwindling socially necessary functions, as the basic cause of its extinction. The French revolution and the capitalistic development it unleashed were merely the final stage of this process. The more intelligent among the nobility themselves knew well enough that their end was inevitable. (p. 40)

In Balzac's writings social forces never appear as romantic and fantastic monsters, as superhuman symbols (as e.g. later in Zola). On the contrary Balzac dissolves all social relationships into a network of personal clashes of interests, objective conflicts between individuals, webs of intrigue, etc. He never, for instance, depicts justice or the courts of law as institutions independent of society and standing above it. Only certain petty bourgeois characters in his novels imagine the law courts to be that. A law court is always presented by Balzac as consisting of individual judges whose social origins, ambitions and prospects the author describes in great detail. Every participant in the proceedings is shown enmeshed in the real conflicts of interest around which the lawsuit in question is being fought; every position taken up by any member of the judiciary depends on the position he occupies in this jungle of conflicting interests. (p. 41)

It is against such a background that Balzac shows the workings of all the great social forces. Each participant in these conflicts of interest is, inseparably from his own purely personal interests, the representative of a certain class, but it is in these purely personal interests and indivisibly from them, that the social cause, the class basis, of these interests finds expression. Thus, precisely by stripping the social institutions of their apparent objectivity and seemingly dissolving them into personal relationships, the author contrives to express what is truly objective in them, what is really their social *raison d'être:* their functions as bearers of class interests and as the instruments of enforcing them. The essence of Balzac's realism is that he always reveals social beings as the basis of social consciousness, precisely through and in the contradictions between social being and social consciousness which must necessarily manifest themselves in every class of society. This is why Balzac is right when he says in **The Peasants:**

> Tell me what you possess and I will tell you what you think.

This profound realism permeates Balzac's creative method down to the smallest detail. We can here indicate only a few main points in connection with this.

For one thing, Balzac never confines himself to a trivial photographic naturalism, although on every essential point he is always absolutely true to life. In other words he never makes his characters say, think, feel or do anything that does not necessarily arise from their social being and is not in complete conformity with both its abstract and its specific determinants. But in expressing some such intrinsically correct thought or feeling, he always refuses to keep within the limits of the average power of expression of the average representative of a certain class. In order to express some socially correct and deeply conceived content, he always seeks and finds the most clear-cut, the most trenchant expression, such as would be quite impossible within the limits set by naturalism. (pp. 41-2)

[Balzac] gives expression only to the things which really struggle to manifest themselves as social and individual necessities. This expression, transcending the limits of the trivial, but ever true in social content, is the hall-mark of the old great realists, of Diderot and Balzac, in contrast with the realism of their modern epigones whose stature dwindles more and more as time goes by. It would have been impossible to give a complete picture of French capitalist society even by means of the innumerable characters and human destinies which figure in *The Human Comedy*, had not Balzac always sought and found the essentially right expression, on the highest plane, for all their multiple interconnections.

The realism of Balzac rests on a uniformly complete rendering of the particular individual traits of each of his characters on the one hand and the traits which are typical of them as representatives of a class on the other. But Balzac goes even further than this; he also throws light on the traits which different people belonging to different groups within *bourgeois* society have in common from the capitalist viewpoint. By stressing these common traits—which he does very sparingly and only on crucial points—Balzac clearly demonstrates the intrinsic unity of the social evolutionary process, the objective social bond between apparently quite dissimilar types. (p. 43)

It is this quality of Balzacian realism, the fact that it is solidly based on a correctly interpreted social existence, that makes Balzac an unsurpassed master in depicting the great intellectual and spiritual forces which form all human ideologies. He does so by tracing them back to their social origins and making them function in the direction determined by these social origins.

Through this method of presentation ideologies lose their seeming independence of the material life-processes of society and appear as part, as an element of that process. (p. 44)

Balzac uses these forms of characterization to indicate, concretize and deepen, both on the personal and on the social plane, the diversities existing between individuals of the same social type. In Rigou, for instance, Balzac creates a most interesting addition to the great gallery of misers and usurers to which Gobseck, Grandet, Rouget and others belong; he is the type of the Epicurean miser and usurer, who is concerned with scraping and saving, hoarding and swindling, like those others, but who at the same time creates an extremely comfortable life for himself. Thus he marries an old wife for her money, the latter to enmesh the whole village in a web of usurious debt and the former to provide himself with young and beautiful mistresses without incurring any expense. Again and again he picks out the prettiest girl in the village, engages her as a servant, seduces her by promising to marry her as soon as his old wife is dead, and when he tires of her, discards her and gets himself another.

The basic rule which Balzac follows is to focus attention on the principal factors of the social process in their historical development and to show them in the specific forms in which they manifest themselves in different individuals. That is why he can demonstrate concretely, in any detached episode of the social process, the great forces that govern its course. In *The Peasants* he describes the struggle for the breaking-up of the great estate without ever going beyond the narrow limits of the estate itself and the neighbouring small town.

But when he shows the decisive social essence of the men and groups fighting for and against the parcelling of the Montcornet estate, when he draws a picture of this basic feature of provincial capitalism, then within this narrow framework, he manages to show us the whole development of French capitalism after the revolution, the decline of the nobility, and above all the tragedy of a peasantry once liberated and then for a second time enslaved by the revolution—the tragedy of the peasant smallholding. (p. 45)

Showing the revolutionary working-class was quite beyond the range of Balzac's vision. Hence he could depict the despair of the peasantry but not the only possible way out of it. Balzac could not foresee the results arising from the disappointment of the peasant smallholder, i.e. that as a consequence of this disappointment "the whole edifice of the state, built up on these same smallholdings, collapses and the chorus is taken up by the proletarian revolution without which its solo part would turn into a song of death in every peasant nation" (Marx). Balzac's genius showed itself in that he depicted this despair and disillusionment realistically as an inevitable necessity. (pp. 45-6)

> *George Lukács, "Balzac: 'The Peasants',"* in his Studies in European Realism: A Sociological Survey of the Writings of Balzac, Stendhal, Zola, Tolstoy, Gorki, and Others, *translated by Edith Bone (copyright 1950 Hillway Publishing Co.; originally published under a different title in his* Der russische Realismus in der Weltliteratur, *Aufbau-Verlag, 1949), Hillway Publishing Co., 1950, pp. 21-46.*

## MARTIN TURNELL    (essay date 1950)

An interest in crime and a highly personal form of melodrama are two of Balzac's most striking characteristics. Melodrama is usually a matter of 'character' and 'situation'; but though there is plenty of this sort of melodrama in Balzac, his personal melodrama is a property of language. . . . (p. 211)

The rhetorical tricks, the feverish tone and the lurid adjectives reveal a curious taste for violence and squalor for their own sake. The novelist does his utmost to dramatize experience, to turn people and places into a spectacle which is designed to take the reader's breath away. His characters lose their humanity and become monsters; a sordid street scene assumes an impossibly sinister air. It is difficult not to feel that there is something specious and unreal about the performance—particularly in the fanciful suggestion of the old maid's secret vices—but the melodramatic element belonged to the man and his age.

For Balzac was a novelist of the Romantic Movement or, to put it more accurately and less charitably, he was a product of the Romantic dissolution. As soon as we open one of his books, we are aware that there has been a break with the main French tradition, that the eighteenth-century virtues, which contributed largely to the success of Constant and Stendhal, have been lost and that nothing satisfactory has taken their place. French rationalism was not always the brilliant advantage that it is usually said to have been, particularly in the novels of Voltaire and Laclos, but it was vastly preferable to the cloudy theosophy on which the young Balzac was brought up. A certain measure of scepticism and a critical outlook in a novelist are salutary and necessary. They give him poise and enable him to sift and test his experience. They were singularly lacking in Balzac. Their absence meant that he had little protection against the disruptive tendencies of his age, that he was far too much the product of his environment and that far too much that was transitory and perishable went into his books. His vitality has been much admired, and it is right to say at the outset that it is his greatest single asset. We may doubt, however, whether it always sprang from the great novelist's need to create. It was diluted by less admirable elements which were characteristic of the age and it often degenerated into an urge to write, to use language for the discharge of violent, unrelated feelings. . . . (pp. 211-12)

The moral that emerges from the novels seems to be that in nineteenth-century society it is practically impossible to be honest and successful. César Birotteau is outwitted by unscrupulous business rivals while a usurer like Gobseck or a crooked banker like Nucingen carry off the prizes. . . . We cannot escape the conclusion that Balzac's choice of heroes like Flaubert's was the reflection of something that was lacking in himself.

This, however, is only one side of Balzac's criticism. Although he excelled in portraits of misers—the people who love money for its own sake—money is very often regarded as a means to an end and it becomes the symbol of the deepest aspirations of a particular society. The idea that money is power is the dynamic behind many of the novels. Money means women, luxury and happiness. . . . The transfer of wealth from the nobility to the middle and lower-middle classes explains the collapse of the old ruling class and the emergence of a new; it is at the bottom of that *déclassement* which permeates Balzac's world no less than Proust's. In this world nothing can compensate for the lack of money or for insufficient money; but if money is an obsession so is lust. Crevel, Hulot and Rubempré—young and old alike—want money because money can buy women. The less money they possess, the more violent, the more insatiable becomes the desire for rapacious and expensive women; and it is this that leads to disaster and collapse, to the loss of any and every form of moral integrity and finally, in the case of Hulot, to crime against the State. (p. 217)

[Balzac's] books record the progress of the Romantic misfit in an urban civilization. For behind all the excesses and exaggerations—intellectual and material—of the *Comédie humaine* is the Romantic pursuit of the experience which transcends all other experiences, the absolute of spiritual and material satisfaction which lures on his characters, usually with the voice of the 'sirens' of Restoration society, and brings them to destruction. The myth which turns up again and again in the novels is the myth of 'hidden treasure' which Balzac borrowed from the adventure stories. His characters are divided not merely into 'good' and 'bad', but into 'haves' and 'have-nots'. The drama centres round the efforts of the wicked 'have-nots' to obtain possession of the 'treasure' which simple, worthy men have amassed by industry and ability. The Vautrins, Philippe Bridaus, Nucingens and Gobsecks are simply different incarnations of the 'explorers', 'pirates' and 'buccaneers' of the treasure-trove stories. (p. 218)

In the famous Foreword to the *Comédie humaine* [see excerpt above, 1842], Balzac claimed to have given a realistic account of the whole of French society. One of the difficulties of the undertaking has always seemed to me to be the gap between the setting and what the novelist was pleased to call the 'drama' in which the characters are involved. I now want to suggest that there are corresponding gaps inside the characters themselves. It must, I think, remain one of the most serious criticisms of Balzac that like Gaudissart all his characters have an 'envelope' which can be left at the door and 'picked up again on leaving'. There is a gap between the *personae*, which are manipulated so surprisingly in the novels, and the humanity underneath. . . . Balzac himself worked from outside and believed that once he had 'observed' externals he had arrived at a comprehension of the interior. This explains the technique of the novels which scarcely varies from one book to another. First we have the scene or décor, then the transition—not always very well managed—from bricks and mortar to the individual. Finally, an attempt is made to establish continuity between the man and the milieu.

We do not expect, nor do we want, a novel to be a biography of an imaginary person. We are not greatly concerned whether the characters are 'lifelike' and we do not care what becomes of them when we close the book. We do, however, expect them to be coherent. For it is only when they are coherent that they can assume a place in the pattern which the novelist is trying to create. It is here, it seems to me, that Balzac fails. When we look into it, we find that his characters only hold together by tricks which conceal or are intended to conceal their fundamental incoherence. We are very conscious—sometimes oppressively conscious—of the physical appearance of people and things. We see the ageing Hulot furtively putting on his corset and tinting his whiskers. We certainly hear, even if we do not understand, Nucingen's peculiar patois or Grandet's devastating stutter as he moves round the dark, cold house at Saumur. We appreciate the condition of the characters, the soldiers, bankers, merchants, poets, and harlots. Nor can we fail to know about their supposed moral qualities. For Balzac is as explicit about their moral qualities as he is about their incomes. . . . Nearly all his characters are divided into 'angels' and 'demons', into black and white. Their moral qualities are recorded like mathematical signs. They make their entry with a plus or a minus—there is naturally no middle term—in front of them. (pp. 219-20)

[There] must be something wrong with a novelist whose characters can be summed up as completely as Balzac's are in a death-bed epigram. The source of the weakness lies partly in the theory outlined in the Foreword, that just as there are 'zoological species', so there are 'social species'. He regards his characters' 'condition' as an absolute. They are all endowed with a charge of powerful anonymous 'passion' which must find an outlet and which is entirely uncontrollable. The form and the effects of this 'passion' are determined by the characters' 'condition'. This produces the famous 'monomania'—Balzac repeatedly uses this or some similar term—which is in itself a reflection of the limitations of his psychology. Goriot is completely absorbed by his obsession with his daughters, Grandet by money, Hulot by women. They cease, as one of the characters in *La Cousine Bette* puts it, to be men and become 'a temperament'. The trouble is that the characters only 'live' in so far as they have become 'a temperament' which means that they are only partly alive. Balzac cannot show us a man's personality being gradually corroded by an obsession. the 'monomania' is an intellectual concept which is 'imagined before the character himself' and imposed on the humanity which we never really see. When the monomania is not operating the characters turn into marionnettes because there is no correspondence between their actions and the inner man. But the virtual elimination or suppression of the whole range of 'normal' of emotions does give them their mobility and a misleading appearance of unity.

This method is less of a handicap in the provincial novels where Balzac is, for valid reasons, dealing with a simplified mentality; and in the minor characters it becomes the source of a positive strength. His picture of provincial life is less searching than Flaubert's, but he grasped the essentials and there is continuity between the characters and their milieu. We not only have the impression that the characters have been formed by the society in which they are living; we see that there is a relation of cause and effect between the gossip, intrigue, jealousies and petty spite of a provincial community and the desire of a sensitive woman to make her escape, of a wealthy spinster to find a husband or of an ignorant priest to become a canon. . . . It would no doubt be going too far to use the term 'moral drama' of the *Vieille fille* and the *Curé de Tours,* but the books are a success largely because they are studies of weakness instead of vice and because the novelist does not apply the criterion of right and wrong to every action. Mlle Cormon's desperate hunt for a husband shows that she has lost her sense of proportion and Birotteau's covetousness is hardly in keeping with his calling, but they are not among the deadly sins. Their misfortunes spring from the fact that people with a particular failing happen to be living in a particular community where they prove fatal.

The minor characters are an essential part of the novels, but their role is similar to that of the *confidents* in seventeenth-century tragedy. They are there to pander to the weaknesses and vices of the principals, to set the machinery of the 'monomania' in motion. It is therefore only necessary for them to exhibit a limited range of impulses and they are drawn with a firmness and coherence which are lacking in the principals. When the principals degenerate into 'a temperament' and sacrifice family and honour in order to buy 'love', we feel that too much is being left out; but it seems perfectly natural for the courtesan to sell herself to the highest bidder in order to obtain money, luxury and position. . . . [There] is something very precarious about the principal characters. We feel that if they deviated by a fraction of an inch from the rigid plan, made a false move, uttered a single word out of character or simply became 'ruffled', the whole apparatus would collapse. (pp. 220-22)

There can be little doubt that Balzac was conscious that he was hampered by the lack of a sufficiently expressive vocabulary, and this explains his continual over-emphasis and his melodrama. . . .

Balzac's use of adjectives . . . illuminates not only the shortcomings of Balzac's own novels, but the changes which took place in the French language after the disintegration of the classical tradition. (p. 223)

[With] the classic writers the individual word rarely loses its separate identity and is seldom used merely for emphasis. Now the spoken language tends to blur these nice distinctions; and we find that, unlike the great masters of French prose, Balzac nearly always uses his streams of adjectives for emphasis and that he substitutes words for the qualities and feelings they ought to signify. The description of the furniture at the Maison Vauquer is a perfect instance:

> Pour expliquer combien ce mobilier est vieux, crevassé, pourri, tremblant, rongé, manchot, borgne, invalide, expirant. . . .

> [In order to explain the extent to which the furniture is old, cracked, rotten, trembling, worm-eaten, one-armed, one-eyed, invalid, dying. . . .]

It is clearly an example of Balzac's attempt 'to go one better'. The first five adjectives are the only ones which can properly be applied to furniture and we feel already that they are too many. The last four carry us further and further from the scene that the novelist purports to be describing and the impression becomes progressively more blurred and confused. (p. 225)

Balzac's use of adjectives cannot be dismissed as a mere flaw in his style. The weakness is central and radical. It is a sign not simply of lack of analytical power and of that insight which is indispensable to the great novelist, but of a tendency of all feelings to reduce themselves to their simplest elements until

they sometimes become practically indistinguishable from one another.

In fairness to Balzac, however, it must be emphasized that there is a credit side to the account. His work is deficient in many of the qualities which are native to all good prose, but his verbal inventiveness and even the torrents of adjectives are the sign of an immense, though often ill-directed, vitality. (p. 226)

We can read Balzac in small doses and enjoy him as a storyteller, and he produced a number of 'short range' works of art. But the tiny impact of the *Comédie humaine* on the adult reader—on the reader who properly expects a novel like any other form of art to provide him with an important experience—seems to me to be out of all proportion to its vast bulk. We cannot escape the impression that Balzac's outlook was fundamentally immature and that it was this which led him to express himself through simple or deliberately simplified figures. Henry James, we remember, spoke of 'a certain heroic pressure which drives them home to our credence'; but he made a damaging reservation when he added, 'a contagious illusion on the author's part' [see excerpt above, 1875]. For the 'heroic pressure' remains ill-defined and unattached, and it is difficult to see that any pattern, any conception of the good life, emerges from the *Comédie humaine.* Balzac's monomaniacs are in the last analysis the disinherited and degenerate offspring of Corneille. The impulse, which in more propitious times produced Rodrigue and Polyeucte, produces in a commercial society nothing better than Vautrin. Our abiding impression is, indeed, that 'there is something there', but something which because he was too much the product of his environment, Balzac failed to put across. (p. 246)

*Martin Turnell, ''Balzac,'' in his* The Novel in France: Mme de La Fayette, Laclos, Constant, Stendhal, Balzac, Flaubert, Proust *(copyright 1950 by Martin Turnell; reprinted by permission of the Literary Estate of Martin Turnell), Hamish Hamilton, 1950, pp. 209-46.*

**PETER QUENNELL**   **(essay date 1952)**

It is fortunate that the unexpectedness of Balzac's gifts should have been in direct proportion to their incompleteness. Suddenly we come face to face with *Le Lys dans la Vallée,* a story that—dangerous though it may be to compare two arts so different as writing and painting—recalls a panel picture by some French master of the early Renaissance, given the sentiment and subject-matter of a more troubled age. The effect produced is extraordinarily fresh and clear and brilliant. As in some of his most memorable long short stories, Balzac is content to expend all his genius upon the analysis of a single situation and to allow the interest of that situation to excuse itself. He had reason to feel satisfied when the story was finished. (pp. 138-39)

In scale and theme, *Le Lys dans la Vallée* is equally limited. Its story—well, that it shares with half a dozen other excellent French novels; for it is concerned with the protracted passion of a very young man for a virtuous but passionate married woman. . . . But *Le Lys dans la Vallée* has not yet ''dated''; and, though characteristically—even delightfully—the work of a period, the narrative also exists on a far less impermanent plane. Apart from his somewhat unfortunate expeditions into downright melodrama, and his generally disastrous flights into the realms of metaphysical speculation, for Balzac the truly romantic was always the concrete. He loves to situate his personages in a definite place and time, establish their genealogies and fix their incomes. He understands that human beings have two sorts of existence. They have an inner life, but simultaneously they live and express themselves through the material objects—through the houses and furniture and small personal belongings—among which their time is spent. Balzac's "realism" is essentially poetic. It has nothing about it of that dull exhaustive naturalism which appals and overwhelms us in the Goncourts or Zola. He shows us the outer world transfigured and irradiated by its human significance. Thus the little white ancient château on the hillside, with its small symmetrical façade and five windows looking south over the silvery Indre, becomes immediately the expression of its mistress's life—isolated, obscure, modest but beautifully ordered. And then, there is the first glimpse of Madame de Mortsauf's drawing-room, its panelled walls painted in two shades of grey, the white-and-gold porcelain vases on the chimney piece, the white curtains and the drab chaircovers plainly edged with green.

The appearance of M. de Mortsauf is cleverly calculated. Here is a life which, as revealed in its outward equipment, might seem to leave no loophole for discord, unhappiness or moral *malaise*. M. de Mortsauf enters; and the illusion dissolves. Years of life abroad as an *émigré* have broken his spirit. It is true that he is still energetic and industrious but spiritual vitality and physical health have alike deserted him. He is restless, embittered, remorseful, the uneasy husk of a man, a self-tormenting tyrant who preys on his family. . . . (pp. 139-40)

[The story's] charm depends in part on the flow of a simple harmonious narrative, and the flashes of acute observation by which it is enlivened: in part on the development and parallel prolongation of a number of complementary but opposing themes. Death and life rub shoulders at the château of Clochegourde; and Madame de Mortsauf, struggling against the principle of dissolution and decay that she observes in her children and her husband, expends to no purpose the resources of her strength and beauty. Then, there is the conflict engendered by the narrator's love—a passion equally pure and sensual, devoted and selfish, doomed by its own sterility yet sublime in its uselessness. . . . [Though] Balzac's personages are sometimes irritating, and though from talk they often descend to delivering speeches, they never lose their shape in the imagination. The effect may be a little absurd; but so is passion itself. Madame de Mortsauf is still a woman despite her virtues; and the fact that, at the very end of her blameless life, she should snatch greedily but ineffectually at the idea of happiness, before relapsing into the attitude of conventional piety, helps to illustrate her career of suffering in its true perspective. She, too, had been voluptuous, passionate, fallible. The measure of her moral triumph is the extent of her misery.

The celestial Venus demands an earthly counterpart. Lady Dudley, with whom Félix takes refuge from his idol's exclusive and exhausting platonism, is one of Balzac's most fascinating minor characters. . . . (pp. 141-42)

Yet, though Lady Dudley may be phantasmagoric, she has a poetic truth. And here, I think, we begin to approach the secret of Balzac's creative genius—his faculty of assimilating the real and temporal without permitting himself for a moment to become its slave. No writer has ever been more unashamed, more superbly unselfconscious. We have only to compare Balzac and Flaubert (a martyr of his own sensitiveness and literary good taste) to feel again the superiority of Balzac's gift. Balzac's taste was variable or non-existent. His psychology was

erratic (though almost invariably sound). He was occasionally vulgar; but his vulgarity was pitched in the heroic key. Put side by side with the masterpieces of the modern novelist, who tempers alarming realism with disarming sentimentality, who purveys intellectualism in a predigested form or who attempts to suffocate the critical faculty beneath a weight of words, Balzac's achievement is the more astonishing. He could write very long books which seem as brief as **Les Illusions Perdues,** or short books which seem as full and packed with meaning as **Le Lys dans la Vallée.** All bear the stamp of that poetic veracity which discards naturalism for the "super-realism" of the greatest literature. (pp. 143-44)

> *Peter Quennell, "'Le lys dans la vallée'," in his* The Singular Preference: Portraits & Essays *(reprinted by permission of Curtis Brown Ltd), William Collins Sons & Co Ltd), Collins, 1952, pp. 138-44.*

### SAMUEL ROGERS (essay date 1953)

[*In his study* Balzac and the Novel, *Rogers considers* La comédie humaine *a unified work that must be considered in its entirety. He attempts, therefore, to present a broad picture of Balzac's work to provide a framework for the reader's general knowledge of individual works. The following excerpt is taken from his discussion of narrative technique.*]

For a long time one of the stock remarks to make about Balzac was that he wrote badly; one still hears it, though not so often. Even from the first there were those who, refusing to judge his style by the standard of classical French prose, realized the force, the variety, and above all the vitality of his writing. Taine and Gautier [see excerpts above, 1865 and 1879], neither of whom can be said to have had no feeling for language, were among that number. Like everything having to do with form, style for Balzac was a means to an end. (pp. 140-41)

Neither Balzac nor Stendhal had any idea of creating a kind of abstract beauty by his manner of writing. If we are looking for harmony, evenness, or purity of style, we should not turn to **La Comédie humaine**. . . . [It] is when Balzac begins lecturing us that his writing is most apt to become stilted or turgid. On the other hand, he is at his best when he is speaking through someone else: Madame Cibot or Madame Vauquer, Père Grandet or Père Goriot. Then, of course, the style is no longer his; it is the living speech of a hundred different characters; and if he can find for them all a wonderful spate of words, he can also charge with horror, humor, or pathos the shortest and simplest phrase. We may take as an example César Birotteau's, "Je ne suis pas bien" [I am not well], when with the ideal music—the faraway memory of his one triumphant evening—still ringing in his ears, he is too near death to realize that he is dying. Often there is not the definite boundary line one would expect between Balzac's own style and that of his characters. (pp. 141-42)

As Gautier realized, Balzac does not hesitate to pick his vocabulary or his metaphors from any source; he makes use of "every kind of technical term, every kind of slang, scientific, artistic, theatrical." If most often, except when his characters speak, the expression does not strike us as "inevitable," it may suggest to us something of the indeterminacy of life itself. (pp. 142-43)

There is in Balzac's writing a tremendous freedom and sweep, a constant element of surprise. We know from his correspondence that he often felt baffled in his struggle to find words. We can see from a glance into any of his novels that he was sometimes defeated, though we can also see, from passages of clear, sharp, and eloquent writing, that he was often triumphant. (p. 143)

Baudelaire speaks of Balzac's "prodigious taste for detail" [see excerpt above, 1850], and we cannot read one of his novels or stories without noticing it for ourselves. "People who insist upon immediate interest," he remarks in **Les Paysans,** "will say my explanations are too long." In the Preface to the first edition of the *Scènes de la Vie privée,* he writes: "The author firmly believes that details alone will henceforth determine the merit of works improperly called novels"—improperly so called because the term *roman* might suggest something frivolous. What Balzac wants to do is to show us the very process of human activity. (pp. 143-44)

Such passages inform us not only that he was quite aware of what he was doing, but also that he realized its dangers. When he wanted to tell an anecdote for its own sake, he could be as bare and swift as Mérimée; I think especially of the remarkable group of very short stories in **Conversation entre onze heures et minuit.** But as a rule the effect he is seeking depends on elaboration. (p. 144)

[It] is in the novels that the use of detail is most striking. It is the living density of their texture that makes us believe in the real existence of the streets and houses, of the fields and towns, of the society from which the characters emerge, and of those characters themselves. We know the Maison Vauquer as well as any of the boarders could know it; we know the general "tone" of the boarders as a group because we have been shown each one so carefully, and knowing this we can get the full effect of Père Goriot's social decadence and can sympathize with Eugène's efforts to break away. (p. 145)

Sometimes the detail is used to emphasize the central theme of the story. In reading **La Recherche de l'absolu** for the first time, we may wonder why the house should be so minutely described. It is only after finishing the book that we see how the densely crowded picture of that house, with so much that has come down from the past, sharpens the contrast with the mad dispersal of what had taken so long to accumulate. **Les Paysans** begins with a detailed description of the château of Aigues, its gardens and its vast park. As we first read it, we cannot be aware of how that picture sets off the misery of the surrounding peasants, how the lovely dreamlike place will soon become a fortress withstanding the most ominous and persistent siege. The structure of the book demands that as we read about the peasants we keep a positive sense of the château: it is like a prolonged organ point without which the whole superstructure of thematic material would lose much of its meaning.

Balzac has then a genius for imagining detail and the art of making it coalesce into the massive blocks out of which his novels are built; but he does not always succeed in avoiding the danger of which he was himself aware. The reader must force his way at times through cluttered and obscure trails.

Most often this is the result of Balzac's entire belief in the reality of his own characters. Massimilla Doni becomes so fascinated, and Balzac with her, in analyzing Rossini's *Moses* for a visiting Frenchman that she continues, with few breaks, for some twenty pages; Gambara lovingly describes his own opera act by act; we are forced to read Lucien's complete review of the play in which Florine and Coralie appear. We should be glad to take Balzac's word for most of this. . . . [He] cannot resist the temptation to go on and on, just as the characters

themselves would do if they could buttonhole a listener. (pp. 145-47)

There is still another kind of obstruction the reader sometimes encounters: I mean Balzac's habit of commenting upon the situation he has imagined. In the midst of Lucien de Rubempré's strange vision, just before his suicide, Balzac remarks: "Today medicine is so willing to admit the phenomena of hallucinations that this mirage of our senses, this strange faculty of our minds, can no longer be questioned." Then he discusses its possible causes in a dozen more lines. The reader completely believes in the hallucination. Balzac does not drag it in as the result of any theory; it must have come to him intuitively as he identified himself in those moments with the defeated and crushed young man. But after he has created it, he looks at it in surprise, wonders how he thought of it and how it may be explained. Balzac's supplementary explanations, even when not in themselves ponderous, rarely add to our belief in the reality of what he is explaining. They are more apt to make us impatient and thereby diminish or destroy that belief. (pp. 148-49)

When we consider the structure of Balzac's novels, there are such a number of different effects, each one obtained by appropriate means, that it is impossible in a few pages to give more than a general idea of the way he subordinates his swarming detail to the overall shape of the story. . . . In spite of the number of accessories and characters, Balzac's subjects are most often basically simple; order and unity are achieved, even though the struggle to reach them may have left its trace. (p. 154)

The structure of a Balzac novel is an arrangement of lighted surfaces minutely rendered and pits of suggestive shadow. At first glance, noticing the detailed treatment of the objects in full light, we may think: here is a solid realist; he leaves nothing to the imagination. But presently, as our eye is attracted to the shadows, we realize that it is largely they that give meaning to the picture, that the lighted planes are often used as screens to suggest what may be existing in the spaces they conceal. Just as the climax of a piece of music, the very heart of the meaning, may be expressed by a pause, a silence, so the inmost center of a story may not be put into words. (p. 155)

No novelist has been more concerned with the passing of time than Balzac, and none before **La Comédie humaine** had used such varied means to suggest it. The plunging into the midst of things and then returning to the past, for the sake of concentration and chronological perspective, has been a familiar device in poetic narration since Homer. (p. 165)

It is to give us a sense of the moving present, with the wake of the past curling and seething behind it, that Balzac treats chronology with such boldness and freedom. (p. 166)

If one were to make any generalization about Balzac's time schemes (and always there would be many exceptions), it would, I think, be this: he is apt to surround the central scenes of his novels and stories, which cover a relatively short period (a few weeks, or months, or perhaps a few years), with a glimpse of the past and what is, in relation to that center, the future. This prologue and epilogue do not merely illumine the central scenes but emphasize their real existence in the *present* by showing them in relation to the past from which they emerge and the future into which they dissolve, that future which they themselves will color and explain once *they* have become the past. At the beginning of **Eugénie Grandet,** for example, after Balzac has described the house in Saumur, he tells us how Monsieur

Grandet made his fortune. Such a passage is not mere "exposition," something that must be gone through before we reach the story; it is an essential part of the story. The pages that describe Grandet's rise do not drag; they move very quickly, covering years in violent foreshortening, and are balanced by the swiftness of the narrative at the end, after Grandet has died and the main drama, between himself and Eugénie, is over. (pp. 168-69)

Some critics have thought that Balzac constructs his novels as a playwright would construct a drama to be acted upon the stage. Though I think this idea is mistaken, it is easy to see how it arose. If Balzac reveals his characters largely through their talk and actions, if the central part of each book is composed of a number of scenes each one quite fully developed, what could be more simple than to tie a few such scenes together and make a play out of the novel? Of course this has often been done, sometimes with ludicrous results. . . . Of all the plays, only *Le Faiseur* and *L'Ecole des ménages* give the impression that Balzac really enjoyed writing them.

The reason for this is clear. Balzac's characters take on their reality from the detail with which they are presented, from the space in which he has bathed them, and from the time through which they move—in other words, from the very form and texture of the novels that contain them. All these things must be sacrificed in a play. Most of the detail must be omitted; the space the writer had created becomes the actual space enclosed by painted scenery on the stage; the sense of time collapses, except for the short stretches coinciding with the action as performed. (pp. 169-70)

[Balzac's scheme for unifying his novels by the systematic use of recurring characters] might be described as doing for the whole series, on a grand scale, what Balzac had done separately in almost every part. When we think of *La Comédie humaine* as a single work, such novels as *Les Chouans* and *Une Ténébreuse Affaire* give us more fully the sense of the immediate past of which we are reminded as we read of the youth of Colonel Chabert or Père Grandet or Père Goriot. Each novel itself becomes one of the lighted shapes, so carefully presented, which pattern the surrounding shadow in most of the individual books, and that shadow becomes the space that exists between them. When the characters reappear, they do not step out of nowhere; they emerge from the privacy of their own lives which, for an interval, we have not been allowed to see. (pp. 181-82)

As soon as we have penetrated a short way into *La Comédie humaine,* we feel that each book is charged not only with its own life but with the life of the whole. In the same glance we see both Paris and the provinces, and in both we see a multitude of people all *at that very moment* living. A brief reference recalls a detailed scene, and each drama becomes more intense because we place it in the midst of other dramas. It is the flow of time with its constant repetition and change, the spread of space with its recurring patterns and its variety, and yet the continuity of both, the interrelationship of the different parts of each, that Balzac recreates for us in *La Comédie humaine;* and what is this sense of the continuity in which all life exists but the sense of History itself? (p. 184)

Although each novel has its own pattern, *La Comédie humaine* was never finished. Balzac listed the titles of books he meant to write, to be included in this or that part; but even if he had lived to write them all, he would still have been seeing new stories, imagining new people. As it exists, then, this great

work has not the clear proportions of a sonata movement. It is more like a gigantic but uncompleted fugue, developing episode after episode with no hint of an end. Perhaps, since history itself has no end, it is appropriate that it was not finished; that, with the sense it gives us of the past forever flowing into and coloring the present, there is no line fixed between itself and the future. (p. 187)

*Samuel Rogers, in his* Balzac & the Novel *(copyright, 1953, by the Regents of the University of Wisconsin; copyright, Canada, 1953; copyright renewed © 1981 by Samuel Rogers), The University of Wisconsin Press, 1953, 206 p.*

**HERBERT J. HUNT**   (essay date 1959)

[*In the preface to his* Balzac's "Comédie humaine," *Hunt, a noted Balzac scholar, states that the aim of his book "is to give a descriptive history of* La comédie humaine; *to watch Balzac's purpose unfolding from 1829 to 1848, and to put the individual works into their general chronological context and their relationship with one another. . . ." This study provides comments on all of* La Comédie humaine *including Balzac's famed 1842 preface (see excerpt above), and a critical summary that documents Balzac's enduring importance.*]

Félix Grandet [of the novel *Eugénie Grandet*], cooper, landowner and mayor of Saumur, is Balzac's first notable illustration of the psychology expounded in his philosophical novels: the relentless application of the will towards a given end, in this case the acquisition and conservation of gold. . . . [He] stands out as the most complete expression of avarice in human shape to be found in literature. Allowing for the difference of form and scope between comedy and the novel, Balzac has here attained a classicism akin to that of Molière. Félix Grandet has in common with Harpagon the fact that everything in him—physiognomy, gesture, thought, tricks of speech, grimaces, reflexes and actions—reveals and expresses the master-passion. (pp. 64-5)

The difference from Molière is that Grandet's avarice is no matter for laughter, nor is his vice suspended in a vacuum. Grandet's financial operations have their repercussions throughout Saumur, and the reactions of its inhabitants to them are recorded: he is a triumphant amasser of wealth who inspires fear, envy and respect in a community of similarly acquisitive beings. But more important is the effect of his miserliness on life in the dark cheerless house which reflects Grandet's mania in its most intimate details. The tyranny of this passion produces a sort of paralytic torpor in wife, daughter and servant. Yet the essence of the story is to show how that tyranny comes to be challenged and eventually defeated through an unexpected event: the arrival from Paris of the handsome nephew, Charles Grandet, a few hours before his father's bankruptcy and suicide. For Grandet this is an occasion to show his mettle in cheating his dead brother's creditors. For Eugénie, it means an awakening to life and individuality. The submission of Mme Grandet is absolute. Eugénie's pity and love for Charles (who turns out to be worthless, as we should expect) change her into a critic of her father and an unhesitating rebel. (pp. 65-6)

Although the figure of 'le père Grandet' dominates the work, it does not throw Eugénie into the shade. She is Balzac's first study of a middle-class girl since Augustine Guillaume [in *La Maison du chat qui pelote*], but more effective because the study is less rapid and because the development of Eugénie's character is more consistently related to a single background. She begins as one of Félix Grandet's living chattels. She is also a pawn in the game of financial chess played out between two affluent and influential families of Saumur, the Cruchots and the Grassins. As the prospective heiress of a millionaire. . . , she is a prize to be fought over. . . . But through the power of virginal love she loses the passivity and spinelessness which Balzac was inclined to associate with maidenly virtue. As the struggle becomes more intense it becomes more and more clear that she is her father's daughter. . . . In her personal habits, as a mature woman, her father's traits reappear in her.

Like many of Balzac's works, *Eugénie Grandet* began as a *nouvelle,* and only in course of composition acquired the dimensions of a novel—chiefly because the time-factor was becoming more important for one who was discarding static for dynamic psychology, and combining the latter with the depiction of manners. The work is universally popular as one of his most characteristic masterpieces. Its structure is impeccable. It affords an excellent example of the art of preparation by whose means carefully proportioned items of description and incident are coordinated until the essential action is unleashed. Also it well illustrates the art of winding up a story, for the conclusion achieves that happy blend of subjectivity and objectivity, of sympathy and sardonic detachment which shows Balzac at his best. (pp. 66-7)

*La Rabouilleuse* is the grimmest story of human wickedness that Balzac ever wrote; so much so that the attitude of moral censure which he maintains throughout the book, reinforced by the frequency of the epithet 'horrible'' which he applies to his villain's exploits, scarcely attenuates the impression of black pessimism which remains with the reader after he has closed the book. Yet this long work contains enough incidents and scenes to lighten the sombre tone of the 'rake's progress' with glimpses of normal existence, including those of the Bohemian life in which Philippe Bridau mixes as his increasing depravity reduces his mother to despair and rouses his brother to fury or contempt. (p. 342)

Has Balzac forced the tone, yielded to his craving for the melodramatic, and made his villian too competent and too promptly triumphant? We should remember that Balzac's aim was not only to emphasize the weakness of maternal authority and the impotence of human justice, unsupported by religion, to curb individual rapacity, but also to show how the real qualities of a man of action may be misapplied in a society which has no use for them. When action is needed Philippe is alert, resolute and fearless. It may also be felt that Jean-Jacques Rouget is too spineless and Flore Brazier at once too domineering and too malleable; that the scenes of the successive *ménages à trois* (the Rouget—Flore—Gilet association followed by the Rouget—Flore—Bridau combination) are too lurid and too nauseating to count as scenes from real life. Yet the addition of Flore Brazier to Balzac's tribe of harpies is an interesting one. Hitherto the novelist, seasoning reprobation with more than a pinch of admiration, had shown such creatures using their charms and wiles victoriously and to their own advantage. The fact that Flore Brazier's technique in reducing Rouget to pathetic submissiveness is the technique of all women, from the duchess to the prostitute, is urged as an excuse for what Balzac calls 'la crudité de cette peinture'; but he had never before gone so far, not even in *Un Prince de la Bohème,* in studying the victimizer in her alternative role of victim. Philippe Bridau bends Flore to his will with the utmost cynicism. . . . It is true that 'la Rabouilleuse' is nothing better than a peasant drab, who in happier circumstances might have been harmless and even blameless; she cuts a poor figure in comparison with her vivacious and resourceful Parisian sisters. (pp. 342-43)

One of Balzac's astonishing qualities is that, however restive his readers may become as intricacies of plot and improbabilities of situation develop, he can, like the Ancient Mariner, hold their attention to the end. This quality helps to make up for the many flaws in *Splendeurs et misères.* Undeniably the action of the story is extravagant. What of the characterization—that of Lucien, for example? With all his effeminate beauty, with all the wit and power of fascination Balzac would persuade us he possesses, he is a mere cat's-paw, whose role in the novel is little more than to parade his charm, arouse feminine sympathy and passion, submit unprotestingly to Vautrin's schemes, and inspire in Esther van Gobseck the passionate fidelity which leads her and him to their deaths. . . . Certainly Balzac himself finds Lucien seductive, and brings in the consensus of many of his other characters to support him. But does Lucien's presence in this work, or even in *Illusions perdues,* enable the reader to feel his charm? There is sometimes a discrepancy between what Balzac alleges certain of his characters to be and what they reveal themselves to be by their words and actions. Is Lucien as poet, wit and ladies' man anything but a postulate?

I think that only the view we obtain of him through Esther, that embodiment of the 'rehabilitation' thesis, would enable us to decide in his favour. As the plot of the novel depends on her, it was right that Balzac should take great pains at the start to show this unhappy girl in all her pathetic naïvety. The scene in which the false Abbé remonstrates with her after saving her from asphyxiation in her shabby and untidy lodgings is a memorable one. It affords a vivid insight into the feelings of a degraded creature who is only too conscious of her degradation and has vainly attempted to lift herself from the mire. (pp. 362-63)

As for Esther herself, it is impossible not to admire the skill with which Balzac shows the *fille de joie* [prostitute] peeping out under the veil of the repentant sinner. Later on she reverts momentarily to type when she exhibits the vulgar vivacity and *savoir-faire* needed for the purpose of working on Nucingen and finally states her terms with professional candour. Nucingen, though he keeps his recognizable features as a ruthless financier . . . is amusing, but hardly acceptable in his role of impassioned wooer. (p. 364)

What shall we say of Vautrin, as the adoring patron of a young man whose spinelessness any intelligent person must needs descry, and as the miraculously efficient, omniscient and omnipotent demon of criminality? Is he anything but a model for the writer of gangster stories?

There has been much speculation over the nature and extent of his homosexuality. . . . Vautrin has a mania for devoting himself to handsome young men—Franchessini, Rastignac, Raoul de Frescas (if we may take the play *Vautrin* into account). He is a woman-hater. His contempt for Esther is scarcely mitigated by his recognition in her of a serviceable tool. . . . Yet it is precisely the feminine weakness in Lucien, his dependence on others, that most attracts Vautrin: Lucien is 'une femme manquée'. This, as well as his vendetta against society, is what has called forth all his protective instincts. Not that there is anything jealous or possessive in his love for Lucien. The feeling he has for him is at once paternal and maternal: 'mon fils' is his favoured mode of address to him; but '. . . je suis *Mère,* aussi'. His paroxysm of grief on learning of his suicide resembles Goriot's ravings for his daughters on his deathbed. All this is significant enough, but it is gratuitous to suppose that it was only Balzac's discretion that prevented him from suggesting physical depravity between the two.

Vautrin is much more interesting in his role of converted rebel. In this connection there leaps to the mind a comparison between Vautrin as an enemy, then as a guardian of society, and Victor Hugo's Javert in *Les Misérables*—the inexorable bloodhound driven to suicide by the realization that there is a law of love and mercy superior to the penal code. From *Splendeurs et misères* can be culled many pages which are not less gripping and graphic than those of his great contemporary, and of which Hugo may well have taken stock. They are those in which Balzac gives picturesque descriptions of prison-life and types of criminal, suggests ideas for the revision of criminal procedure and the reform of prison conditions. Vautrin's denunciation, in conversation with Granville, of the harshness of society to a law-breaker, once condemned, is well in harmony with the ideas which inspired the creator of Jean Valjean. . . . Vautrin thus acquires additional symbolic value as a criminal whom society discourages from the amendment of his ways. (pp. 364-66)

One lays down *Splendeurs et misères* with mixed impressions. So vast a work could scarcely fail to illustrate some of the great novelist's weaknesses—errors of taste, life presented in too glaring colours, and some inconsistency in the scale of moral values. Nevertheless two considerations may be put forward in its defence. One is the fact that, in the eighteen-forties, Balzac's contemporaries were inclined to regard this kind of subject as lending itself to objective and 'realist' treatment. Eugène Sue's novel of criminal life, *Les Mystères de Paris*, had created a sensation. . . . Now it would be an insult to Balzac to equate him with Eugène Sue. Even his most lurid imaginings are redeemed, if not transfigured, by his gift for evoking personages (however improbable they may be), by his brilliance in dialogue and by a style which, though not impeccable, is that of a great writer. But while Balzac despised Sue, he also envied his success, and was not adverse from the idea of trying to eclipse him in his chosen domain. (p. 367)

The other consideration which may be urged in defence of *Splendeurs et misères* is a matter of general rather than literary history. When criticizing Balzac's policemen we should remember that they are all more or less modelled on the Vidocq type of ex-convict, emerging from a period when the clever criminal was a useful if not indispensable asset to rulers and regimes. (p. 368)

[Balzac advocates] a preventive justice to forestall crime. In fact, adhering to his oft-expressed view that political expediency rises above private morality, he regrets the disappearance of arbitrary power since the establishment of constitutional government. There can be no doubt that, in writing *Splendeurs et miséres des courtisanes,* one of his purposes was to show what anarchy under the apparently calm surface of social life can result from the inability of the executive to go beyond the formalities of the law. (p. 369)

If we allow for those 'Grand Guignol' features in *La cousine Bette* which put Balzac again in competition with Eugène Sue, we can but recognize that this is one of the outstanding novels of the **'Comédie Humaine'**. It has been hailed as the first 'roman naturaliste' of the century. By 'naturalism' is usually meant the unflinching study of human nature at its worst: a function which Taine, the brothers Goncourt and Zola imposed on the

novel after 1850. *La cousine Bette* fairly deserves the epithet. . . . (p. 379)

First there is the turmoil of hatred and rancour stirred up in the heart of a frustrated old maid, forty-two at the beginning of the action, and the potentialities for long-matured and unrelenting malevolence which such frustration may confer. . . . Not that [Bette] is virginal of soul; she is chaste simply because she is unattractive; she enjoys through the instrument of her vengeance, the pretty and vivacious Valérie, whom she loves to the point of arousing scandalous gossip among the neighbours, the power over men which she can never hope to wield directly. (p. 380)

The second great achievement of Balzac is the study of senile eroticism. The Hulot case is an extreme one: today we should call it pathological. Even at sixty-seven he has years of woman-hunting before him. At the end of his Odyssey as a libertine, minutely recorded in the novel, he has reached seventy-five, and is still incorrigible. (p. 381)

The third 'naturalist' aspect of *La cousine Bette* is the attention he concentrates on the horde of Parisian women engaged in 'the oldest profession in the world'. . . . *La cousine Bette* parades a miscellany of . . . captivating parasites—Josépha Mirah the opera-ginger, Jenny Cadine the actress, Malaga the circus-rider, the dancers Héloïse Brisetout and 'La Carabine', Olympe Bijou and Cydalise, two neophytes who are guided into Hulot's orbit, and that pathetic waif, Atala Judici. (p. 382)

The Hulot women, who are also important characters, stand of course in a very different category. Hortense is a positive and attractive girl who faces with dignity the distressing situation in which Bette's machinations put her. As for her mother, Balzac's conception of this model wife, grateful to her husband for raising her to high social rank, and forgiving 'unto seventy times seven', was dictated by the opposite of 'naturalist' considerations. No doubt his instinct as an artist urged him to unflinching revelation of human depravity, and he was unquestionably sincere in his piquant assertions that the tales he told and the situations he depicted contained in themselves their own morality. Yet his claim to be philosopher and reformer, and the sentimental disposition which he kept on surprisingly good terms with his Rabelaisian humour, would not let him rest content with Olympian objectivity. And so the moralizing intention is well to the fore in this remarkably varied novel. (pp. 383-84)

Whatever incidental criticisms one may make of *La cousine Bette,* it remains a great novel. The pathos and horror of the story in its broad lines did not prevent Balzac from displaying his gift for satiric and sardonic observation. He gives us yet another variant of the self-complacent bourgeois in the person of Crevel, and a provincial understudy of Crevel, a stupid one, in Philéas Beauvisage. He keeps himself well in hand over the matter of topographical descriptions; a notable one, though short, is that of the clusters of sordid houses neighbouring the Louvre. The novel contains some 150 characters. Great scenes abound—Balzac himself was very proud of them—and more than ever one notices the predominance of dialogue over flat narration: the action moves on through conversations and interviews. In these later years Balzac was giving more and more attention to the theatre, and one cannot deny his ability to stage, at any rate within the framework of the novel, scenes of decisive power and vividness. (pp. 386-87)

[The action of *Le cousin Pons*] is more simple and concentrated. It is as powerful in its general conception as *Le père Goriot.*

It is one of his most tragic subjects. The wealth and subtlety of observation it contains and the maturity of the moral experience it reveals bear the stamp of his highest genius. (p. 387)

*Le cousin Pons.* . . . , while it is one of the saddest of Balzac's tales, is in its essence one of the most human, and also one of the most profound. Practically all the pauses in narration are pertinent to the development of the action. Even the long digression on fortune-telling, while affording one more proof of the fusion of scientific determinism with unscientific credulity in Balzac's philosophy, leads to an excellent scene in which Mme Fontaine goes through her tricks with her gigantic toad Astoroth and her black hen Cléopâtre. The account of Pons' funeral and the preparations for it, reminiscent of similar pages in *Ferragus,* are not only entirely relevant, but poignantly pathetic. A wry humour enhances their effect. . . . A rueful pity furnishes the inspiration behind such passages, just as a kindly sympathy is behind the description of the quarter and rooms in which Topinard, his as yet unofficial wife Lolotte and their three children reside. If Balzac had set himself to the task of portraying working-class life, there is no doubt that his genius would have served him well. Seldom has he shown elsewhere greater competence in his conception of character and the depiction of background, greater fertility and variety in conjuring up new figures, greater artistry in preparing and staging his climax, or a greater appropriateness of style. (pp. 394-95)

[Balzac's] treatment of the novel is all-embracing. He lacked the perfectionism of a Flaubert—the deliberate, obstinate attention given to language, style and structure as the sole possible avenue to a consummate artistry envisaged as the end of creative endeavour. But he had his own art of composition. He has in general a way of building up his subject, of arriving at the heart of his theme, of assembling and releasing the moral and material forces operating in human lives, which imparts unequalled vigour and conviction to his tales. He has pre-eminently the talent for surprise, that surprise which results from a slow and sometimes laborious preparation of an action culminating in a precipitous surge of events, narrated as a rule though a dialogue which is superlatively dramatic. He was right in characterizing his stories as 'scenes' and the whole body of his work as a 'comédie'. With him the novel becomes an original kind of drama, but a drama enriched with all the contributory facts and factors which it is not possible to represent on the stage. And if it is a comedy rather than a tragedy, in spite of his acute awareness of the tragedy, both splendid and sordid, that haunts human effort and human ambition, it is because he is also constantly aware of all that is deflatingly comic in human experience. He is a humorist as well as a dramatist. In his laughter are the echoes of Rabelais, Molière, Sterne and Beaumarchais.

Drama presupposes psychology. Though Balzac lacks the subtlety of a Stendhal or a Proust, the habit of viewing continuously from inside which also distinguishes a Henry James or a Joyce; though he seems to go from the exterior to the interior, to present human reality as objectively observed rather than intuitively sensed; although (or because?) his conception of character is concrete and classical and his instinct for what he calls 'typisation' exceptionally strong, he has pierced through to the core of human nature and shown it as it is: potentially good, potentially bad, rarely neutral, often mediocre, capable of great extremes, but always human and therefore never entirely alienated from human sympathy. And if the note of determinism is conspicuous in the working-out of his characters, they do often

take control—he himself testified to this during the composition of *La cousine Bette*—and exhibit in themselves that element of the incalculable and the unforeseen which baffles deterministic explanation and gives them the depth and mystery inherent in the human person. (pp. 452-53)

*Herbert J. Hunt, in his* Balzac's "Comédie humaine" *(© H. J. Hunt, 1959), The Athlone Press, 1959, 506 p.*

## E. J. OLIVER (essay date 1960)

[In] 1832, the year which gave the philosophical disquisitions of *Louis Lambert* and the grave art of *Le Curé de Tours,* Balzac issued the first ten stories of the *Contes drolatiques,* in the tradition and language of Rabelais.

Yet this contrast itself was already evident in Rabelais, in whom deep scholarship and gross humour were so inextricably combined that they seemed to spring from one and the same root, a Renaissance delight in everything that is human. So the figure of Rabelais marvellously clarifies the mind of Balzac, who becomes more credible when he is considered as a belated man of the Renaissance, for all the works of which, particularly on its Italian side, he had an admiration so passionate. The range of his interests, his scientific curiosity, his combination of deeply religious feelings with eager sensuality, his long periods of uninterrupted labour broken by orgies of indulgence, his superstition, his omnivorous reading, the strange fusion in him of revolutionary impulses and traditional loyalties, the love of detail, his union of realism with high ideals, his adoration of woman and the variety of his affairs with women, the alternate humility and arrogance of his relations with the great—these are some of the traits with which the Renaissance has astonished posterity. If in Balzac they seem more incongruous than astonishing, it is because his character is more comprehensible set against the stronger passions of the sixteenth than in the respectable frame of the nineteenth century. (p. 100)

[Balzac] is very different, certainly, from the gay monks and nuns of the *Contes drolatiques,* situated in the Touraine of three hundred years before. Yet there is the same absence of religious reference. Shocking though some of their escapades are, these religious are recognizably brothers and sisters of those in medieval scandals, when funny stories about them were no more attacks on religion than schoolboy howlers are attacks on schools. But these droll stories are not chiefly concerned with them: they are chronicles of life and love in the castles of the Loire in their golden age, the joyous Renaissance. Not all these stories are funny; some, those in which there is the truest love, are extreme in tragedy. . . . (p. 106)

Certainly the same qualities are apparent in [the *Contes drolatiques* as in *La Comédie humaine*], the same power, the same love of detail, particularly in descriptions of fine stuffs and dresses, the same wit and the same ruthlessness in the pursuit of character and tragedy. There is even one quality in the *Contes drolatiques* which lightens the substance of *La Comédie humaine,* as the Renaissance itself illuminates the figure of Balzac—the combination of serenity and realism. Many, particularly English, readers of Balzac's novels have found a darkness and a drabness in them, despite the brilliance of his duchesses or the gaiety of his dandies. Their background has the darkness of Paris in his period, before the Haussmann reconstruction had broadened the streets and turned it into a city of light. Their characters are attended by debts and fatalities and death. Yet even those most aware of these sombre tones admit the vitality which transfigures them with a sort of joy that no shadows can extinguish. These novels are evidently by the author of the *Contes drolatiques,* for their realism never troubles the serenity of their atmosphere: they are the work of the Balzac who, to Lamartine, judged the world from such a height that it was no more than a bubble.

Similarly the *Contes drolatiques,* for all their gaiety, have their own grimness of realism. Often in them the gay and the grave pass as naturally into each other as day and night. The second of the stories, *Le Péché véniel,* is one of the gayest and grossest in the fun it has with the ignorance of a young bride who, married to an aged husband, is perplexed by her failure to conceive a child. Yet there is a delicacy of sentiment in her tenderness for a young page and in her affection for her husband. . . . The ending has the tenderness, at once serene and tragic, of a medieval tale. Yet the last story of the first ten, *L'Apostrophe,* is no less medieval in another sort, with its famous conclusion when the husband, about to run his sword through his wife's lover, is halted by her impassioned plea, "Do not kill the father of your children."

Such contrasts of tenderness and coarseness, the tragic and the grotesque, spires and gargoyles, were common enough in the older art and literature of Europe. . . . This spirit presides over the *Contes drolatiques,* and it is typical of Balzac's absorption in it that he should have written them in the French of the sixteenth century, the rich language of Rabelais, still encrusted with medieval elements.

The longest of the stories, *Le Succube,* which some have judged the best, is itself placed well back in the Middle Ages, in the year 1271, and it is an extraordinary reconstruction of a medieval trial. A series of documents, the testimony of witnesses, unrolls the accusation against a girl who has been brought back from the Holy Land and put into a convent under the name of Sister Clare. She is variously described as a Saracen, an Egyptian, and Zulma the Mauretanian. The charge against her is that of being a demon in the body of a woman, a succuba. (pp. 108-10)

[The] extraordinary mixture of cosmology, lust, and superstition, which all had some power in the imagination of Balzac, concludes with the words, "This teaches us not to abuse our body but to make use of it for our salvation." To most of the stories he points a moral, sometimes ironic, sometimes straight, sometimes a maxim of worldly prudence, but in these stories, as in all his work, he is essentially a historian, and both the point and the judgement are closely adapted to the reality of the action. In fact, the same realism is as evident in the grossest of these tales as in the most serious of his stories. *Le Succube,* in particular, has a relation to the most brutal of his short stories, which have given him a place in all anthologies of terror; *La Grande Bretèche,* in which a woman denies that her lover is concealed, and her husband has his hiding-place bricked up, burying him alive; *Le Réquisitionnaire,* in which a mother prepares for her son a room which is requisitioned for the secret agent sent to arrest him; or, most horrible of all, *El Verdugo,* in which the young heir of a family convicted for insurrection in war is spared on condition that he acts as executioner to the rest of the family, including his mother and sisters, who successfully plead with him to agree, that the family name may survive in him—a story with an appropriately Spanish setting.

The brutality of these horrors has something in common with the grossness of the *Contes drolatiques,* for the tragedy is as direct as the laughter. (pp. 110-11)

[A] respect for natural feelings lies at the centre of his work. It prompted the book which made his name, the *Physiologie du mariage,* which might be described as a Declaration of the Rights of Women, which are the rights of natural feelings, perhaps more important to the happiness of society than the political rights of men—or women. It was not from any romantic or chivalrous ideal that Balzac became the champion of women, but from a realist's estimate of their importance in private life, the scenes of which were both the seed and the opening of *La Comédie humaine.* As his charity began at home, so it naturally began with women.

Emotion, intimate understanding of character, vitality, charity—these were Balzac's gifts, all summed up and magnified in his master-quality—the importance with which he endowed every aspect and every incident of human life. There is nothing trivial in Balzac, nothing indifferent. . . . Perhaps this is the rarest and most useful gift in a novelist, as many writers, in the emphasis which they give to certain facets of life or character, project a dulness or an obscurity above others. By describing a society, instead of a type, a class, or an intellectual scheme, Balzac achieved a wholeness and a unity in his reflection of life which remains unique. It is this which has made him acceptable even to the most austere Marxists, tempted to reproach other nineteenth-century novelists for the narrow limits of their material. Yet for Balzac the point of this importance is personal. It is not only that he describes the struggle of a woman against temptation as more important than the greatest of historic battles; in this concentration of human sympathy he never neglects the history, the economics, the religion which deform or inspire his characters. (pp. 202-03)

*E. J. Oliver, in his* Balzac, the European *(© E. J. Oliver, 1959; reprinted with permission from Andrews and McMeel, Inc.), Sheed and Ward, Inc., 1960, 209 p.*

### MAURICE BEEBE   (essay date 1964)

[*Beebe's study combines literary history and criticism to examine Balzac's artistic temperament and creative process. Beebe traces the novel's development as a portrait of the artist. Beebe contends that the artists in Balzac's fiction, considered as a group, "enable us to understand how Balzac was able to maintain a balance between observable reality and visionary insight." His comments on the theme of the artist as creator support the view presented by Albert Thibaudet (see excerpt above, 1936.)*]

We are more conscious of aura in Balzac than in many other novelists because he took the trouble to create a fictive world which, however similar to the real world it may seem to be, is nonetheless uniquely personal. A private world at once better (more logically controlled) and worse (more evil and distorted) than the real world, it is not depicted in its entirety in the novels Balzac lived to write; but whereas many novelists give us recognizable fragments of the world they and we know only in part, Balzac's novels are fragmentary reflections of a world which we feel he knew in its entirety, a world which was somehow within him before he created it in fiction. Thus for any one work of Balzac the author has, in the other books of his series, a readymade frame of reference. Characters reappear naturally from book to book, and, in spite of the artificiality of a scheme which was imposed after many volumes of the series were already written, the novels complement one another in a remarkably consistent way. Balzac, faithful to his vision, *had* to be consistent.

Although Balzac's aura gains much from his private world, it is not entirely dependent upon it. (James, Dickens, Dostoevsky have their characteristic auras without using recurring characters or imposing a private sociology.) Aura may be discerned in the individual works of the *Comédie humaine,* though we cannot be sure that it is characteristicly Balzacian unless we are familiar with many of the other works as well. How often we are struck by the casual way in which Balzac warms up to his subject, how, in a typical novel, he begins by describing a scene in exhaustive detail, brings on to this setting an individual with an obviously dominant trait, describes him physiologically (sometimes even phrenologically), pauses to analyze his personality, and yet, in spite of this mechanical progression, manages to convey the illusion of life. In a good Balzac novel things suddenly come into focus. When the light is not working, the picture of life is blurred. (pp. 177-78)

Although it is usually assumed that Balzac began with a generalized type in mind, then illustrated it, I suspect that he did just the opposite. He began with elaborate descriptions because only by first visualizing his characters was he able to interpret and understand them. Just as he proceeded almost always from physical appearance to moral nature, he seems to have determined the type only after he had *seen* the individual. His approach was inductive, a deliberate observing of something already within his vision. Many details in his descriptions are irrelevant to the context; usually his inserted essays on such topics as the manufacture of paper or the legal procedure of bankruptcy are like the cetological chapters in [Herman Melville's] *Moby-Dick* in that they give us more information than we really need to understand the action in the story. Yet these descriptions and digressions are never entirely irrelevant, for they are the means by which Balzac keeps us aware of his posted presence in his works, his control over the materials of his fictive world. Unity in a Balzac novel depends not on the complete dramatic relevance of detail, but on our awareness of the creator in whom every detail has its source and who brings all details into relation.

Balzac's well-known method of working—the hours from midnight to eight in the morning, the monkish robe, the black coffee made from a special oriental formula, the precise ordering of his working tools, and his trancelike state—constituted a ritual whereby, isolated from the world and free from distractions, he could become completely absorbed in the visional world of his creating. (pp. 178-79)

Balzac believed that solitude led to loss of self and the gift of second sight, the ability to enter the lives and thoughts of others. But if Balzac was able to enter the selves of others, he brought to them much of himself. . . . Not any one artist stands as the surrogate for Balzac's creative self, but all together; considered as a group, they enable us to understand how Balzac was able to maintain a balance between observable reality and visionary insight. (p. 179)

*Le Chef-d'oeuvre inconnu* opens with the visit of Nicolas Poussin and Frenhofer to the studio of François Porbus. Frenhofer criticizes a recent painting by Porbus, remarking that the throat seems a "dead" thing. Porbus replies that he studied the throat with great care in the model, and Frenhofer responds indignantly, "The mission of art is not to copy nature, but to give expression to it! You are not a base copyist, but a poet! . . . We have to grasp the spirit, the soul, the features of things and beings." Frenhofer then demonstrates that he can make a painting seem alive, for he takes one of Porbus' brushes and, with "passionate ardor" but few strokes, makes the necessary

alterations in the throat. Intrigued and curious, the young Poussin learns from Porbus that Frenhofer, though little known, is the greatest of living painters and that for years he has worked on a painting of Catherine Lescault which he will permit no one to see. However, when Poussin and Porbus finally gain access to the old man's studio, they see on his canvas only a conglomeration of colors and a mass of chaotic lines. "On drawing nearer," though, "they spied in one corner of the canvas the end of a bare foot standing forth from that chaos of colors, of tones, of uncertain shades, that sort of shapeless mist; but a lovely foot, a living foot! They stood fairly petrified with admiration before the fragment, which had escaped that most incredible gradual, progressive destruction." Overhearing the two painters discuss his work, Frenhofer realizes that what is in his mind's eye is not on his canvas. That night, after burning all his paintings, the disillusioned Frenhofer dies.

The perfect foot suggests, however, that Frenhofer is not a false visionary. For a time at least he did grasp an ultimate reality, and Balzac leaves little doubt that he believes in the validity of Frenhofer's quest, in the existence of an ideal which may be captured. The perfect foot is a typical touch of Balzacian irony. . . . (p. 181)

Further evidence that Balzac believed in the reality of Frenhofer's ideal is given in his repetition of the theme in several later stories. Frenhofer the painter and Balthazar Claes the alchemist [in *La Recherche de l'absolu*] are joined by Gambara the musician [in *Gambara*], Seraphita the religious mystic [in *Séraphita*], and Louis Lambert [in *Louis Lambert*] in Balzac's gallery of visionaries. Just as Frenhofer seeks the core of reality beneath appearance so that he can represent it in painting and Balthazar Claes seeks the basic element common to all things so that he can create matter, so Gambara would discover the celestial powers that cause the sensuous effects of music. Once he attains a vision of the ideal, however, his music seems only noise to earthbound mortals and he is forced to compose for himself alone. The closer Louis Lambert comes to understanding the secret of the universe, the more insane he appears to be; and his ultimate insight, like Balthazar's cry of "Eureka!", is reserved for the moment of death. . . . In all these works, the visionaries have a passion for unity which forces them to seek the link between spirit and matter, but once they learn the secret—as several do—they are unfitted for life. Balzac thought highly of these stories, and though he wrote them during the 1830's, the first of his two decades of serious effort, he placed them at the end of the *Comédie humaine* as if to illustrate a Dantean progression from the diabolical to the divine, from self-interest (**"Scenes of Private Life"** is the first grouping) to self-transcendence in a vision of absolute unity.

Just as the artist's vision of the ideal may unfit him for life, his love of mortal pleasures and worldly glory may unfit him for art. Such is the theme of *La Peau de chagrin.* The story deals with Raphael de Vallentin, an impoverished young writer who sets himself a three-year apprenticeship in a Parisian garret, much as Balzac did, where he writes the *Treatise on the Will* that Balzac is said to have composed as a schoolboy. The treatise completed, he falls in love with Fedora, a beautiful but cold lady of fashion who, Balzac states explicitly, symbolizes Society. (pp. 182-83)

Balzac apparently chose the name Raphael for his hero to suggest his artistic nature. . . . [If] Raphael's name suggests the artist Raphael, who is said to have been a self-indulgent seeker of pleasure but who overcame self in his art, so the shagreen is a symbol large enough to include not only life and will, but also art. It is as if Balzac realized that in the creation of art as in the pursuit of pleasure one could use up life and sacrifice self to imaginative participation in the life of others. Inability to have his will drives Raphael to contemplate suicide; the shagreen gives him the power to realize whatever he wills, but that power, the story reveals, is but an alternate form of suicide. *La Peau de chagrin,* like Balzac's other literary works, was Balzac's own fatal skin. (p. 185)

The lives of Raphael and Louis coincide generally with the earlier life of Balzac. But while their lives are brought to an end within the works, Balzac's went on. On the one hand, *La Peau de chagrin;* on the other, *Louis Lambert* and *Le Chef-d'oeuvre inconnu*—here we find Balzac's concept of his alternate selves, the Balzacs who might have been. For the Balzac who maintained a perilous balance between the real and the ideal, we must turn to other artists in other works.

Balzac was himself so balanced between the two extremes that he could work concurrently on the most ethereal of his philosophical tales and the most realistic of his social studies. Although he wrote works of both types, his best stories are those in which he combined the opposing strains. Such a work is the story of Lucien de Rubempré in *Illusions perdues* and its sequels. Of the many works in the *Comédie humaine* none is more central and inclusive, yet wide-ranging—and none presents a more convincing picture of the artist *in* society— than the Lucien series. The scene shifts between Paris and the provinces; the story includes a variety of character types, and ranges in social perspective from the criminal underworld through the Paris of the journalists and the courtesans, the world of business and finance, to the upper reaches of fashionable society. Many of the characters who play important roles in other novels make fleeting appearances in the series, which therefore provides a convenient focus on the whole world of the *Comédie humaine.* (p. 186)

Balzac assures us that Lucien has the talent and sensibility of a true poet. His bright, flashing eyes, his wild, curling hair, and his slight physique suggest the stereotyped artist of fiction, but if there is "divine graciousness" transfusing his white brows, there is also a short, weak chin which to Balzac the physiognomist signified not only "matchless nobleness" but also deficient will power. . . . Lucien's tragedy is not so much that he is victimized by a money-hungry society, as Georg Lukàcs [see excerpt above, 1949] and other socially oriented interpreters of the novel suggest, as that he is himself too weak to withstand temptation. "It should be observed," Balzac says, "that there are certain natures in which a really poetic temper is united with a weakened will; and these while absorbed in feeling, that they may transmute personal experience, sensation, or impression into some permanent form, are essentially deficient in the moral sense which should accompany observation." (pp. 187-88)

[Because Lucien's genius-ideal] is an artist, it is fitting that Vautrin should say of himself, "I am a great poet, but I don't write my poems; they consist of deeds and feelings." A man of sensibility, like his disciple Svidrigailov in Dostoevsky's *Crime and Punishment,* a follower of Rousseau and what he calls the Anti-Social Contract, Vautrin even takes on the stature of a kind of god: "I take upon myself to play Providence and I will direct the will of God.". . .

If Vautrin is surrogate for Balzac in his role as spinner of plots and controller of a world, his existence in the *Comédie humaine* betrays the sense of guilt which Balzac as a pious Catholic must have felt: art is associated with crime as the archcriminal's attempt to replace God is associated with the playing at god of the world-creating artist. Balzac, like Hawthorne, realized that the artist may commit the sin of appropriating people from the world of observable reality for the sake of his controlling vision; the artist may violate the souls of others in making them adhere to his need for unity within his artistic structure. He may be guilty of the very sins with which he charges the society from which he keeps aloof. Thus Vautrin, when he is captured, is no longer artist, God, or Satan so much as he is simply "the type of a degenerate nation, of a people at once savage, logical, brutal and facile." Vautrin, warring against society, becomes that which he hates. . . . (p. 189)

The opposite foil, counter to Vautrin and society, is represented by "Le Cénacle." This group is composed of seven regular members, plus Lucien de Rubempré and Louis Lambert, contrasting types who are only temporary associates. Although their interests and professions vary, the members have certain character traits which set them apart from the rest of society. "Genius," says Balzac, "is one and the same for all and resembles nothing so much as its self.". . . All have the profound self-respect and dedication to vocation which enable them to accept poverty rather than compromise with society. Their hand-to-mouth existence in the Latin Quarter, good-hearted fellowship, and spirited arguments (for they share only a similar character, not the same philosophy) stamp them as perhaps the first Bohemians in fiction. . . . (pp. 189-90)

Only two of the regular group, Joseph Bridau, a painter, and the writer d'Arthez, are artists proper. Bridau, who is said to derive from Delacroix, plays a more important role in *La Rabouilleuse.* In this scathing indictment of a "society based on money values, on the glorification of success as an end to be obtained by fair means or foul," Joseph Bridau is the only thoroughly sympathetic character, intended obviously to balance the scales against his older brother Philippe and the other scheming, selfish people who dominate the story. . . . Often victimized by his brother and completely ineffective in his attempts to regain his rightful inheritance, Joseph Bridau "practises art for the sake of art," and though he is indifferent to worldly success, the lottery of fate, which is the pervasive symbol of the novel, ultimately throws everything into his hands.

Somewhat less emotional than Joseph Bridau, Daniel d'Arthez is equally dedicated to his profession and similarly absorbed in his work. His "life was entirely devoted to his work. He saw society by glimpses only; it was a sort of dream for him. His house was a convent. He led the life of a Benedictine, with a Benedictine's sober rule, a Benedictine's regularity of occupation." (pp. 190-91)

Thus we have met the four main types of artist in Balzac's fiction: the men of sensitivity like Raphael de Valletin and Lucien de Rubempré, the visionaries like Frenhofer and Louis Lambert, the dedicated and singleminded men of genius like d'Arthez and Bridau, and the artist as world-controller and would-be God in Vautrin. If we ask which of the four stands for Balzac, we should perhaps have to admit that no one type explains his uniqueness. Balzac, it is clear, embodied traits of all four types, and it is only by considering their relationship to one another that we can discover the sources of that "projected light" which gives us the peculiarly Balzacian aura.

"My best inspirations," Balzac wrote, "have ever come to me in moments of anguish." The Lucien type stands for the power of suffering, the suicidal impulse, which in Balzac took the form of self-imposed failures. Time after time, on the verge of success and financial independence, Balzac would leave his study and plunge into business projects, politics, and love affairs. Almost invariably he would fail and have to return, burdened with debts and frustration, to the sanctuary of his monastic cell where, in his absorption with work, he could forget his anguish. . . . Like other writers, Balzac worked best when he had to; if he had succeeded in his schemes to make a million or marry a wealthy heiress, we should not have had the **Comédie humaine.** Thus, Frenhofer is a failure as a painter—and he fails if for no other reason than that he destroys his masterpiece—because he was born rich and could afford to indulge his search for absolute perfection. The Lucien type stands also for an indispensable element in Balzac's psychological make-up, the need to suffer. Balzac's men of genius have to suffer because, as he wrote Madame Hanska, "observation is the result of suffering." Louis Lambert "suffered at every point where pain could seize upon flesh or spirit" until "like martyrs who smile at the stake, he escaped to the heaven which thought opened to him." More appropriately Balzac dramatized the link between suffering and observing in Lucien and Raphael, who are surrogates for Balzac's intense desire for glamor, social status, and the love of a beautiful woman; who, in other words, seek success not in their garrets but in that world which meant only anguish for Balzac. The Luciens do not, however, stand for something entirely negative. Adherence to what he had observed of the real world, in which he had suffered, was necessary if Balzac's writings were to achieve recognition, allow him as a man of honor to pay his debts, and keep him from the fate of a Frenhofer.

Balzac was saved too from the fate of a Lucien or a Raphael, who are entrapped by the world of observable reality. A part of Balzac knew that success and love in the real world, however desirable, are illusory and that "life is within us and not without us; that to rise above our fellows for the purpose of commanding them is only to magnify the career of a schoolmaster; and that men who are strong enough to lift themselves to the level at which they can enjoy the sight of worlds ought not to turn their gaze upon their feet." *The sight of worlds*—the one physical trait which all Balzac's true men of genius have in common is the hawk eye. . . . His worldly geniuses—the Luciens, Raoul Nathans, and Camille Maupins of his fiction—have flashing, penetrating eyes, but his more profound geniuses have eyes like those of Louis Lambert: "Sometimes clear and wonderfully penetrating, at other times of heavenly sweetness, the eyes grew dull, deadened, colorless, when he yielded himself up to contemplation." The first is the eye of the observer; the second, of the visionary. "When it pleases me to do so," Louis Lambert says, "I draw a veil before my eyes. I retire within myself and find a darkened chamber, where the events of nature reproduce themselves in purer forms than those under which they first appeared to my exterior senses."

Balzac's visionaries often have the power of second sight. . . . In **Seraphita** and **Louis Lambert** Balzac calls this gift "specialism" and defines it as "a sort of inward vision which penetrates all things.". . . (pp. 192-94)

For such a visionary, internal and external vision blend, and dreams become indistinguishable from realities. . . . The desire for unity, his impatience with the fragment, his ambition for all-embracing possession help us to understand the philosophy expressed in **Louis Lambert:** "The Universe is, then, variety in Unity. Motion is the means, Number is the result.

The end is the return of all things to Unity, which is God." If this sounds like the Poe of *Eureka*, it is because both writers are in the tradition of romantic occultism which stretches from Goethe, Novalis, and Swedenborg to Blake to the American transcendentalist to the French Symbolists to the "religion of consciousness" of Henry James. To break down the barriers between world and ego, subject and object, is the aim of all these writers.

Balzac's desire for complete unity is equivalent to the single-mindedness which we have found best represented by d'Arthez and Bridau in his gallery of artists. But whereas these artists seek to remain aloof and uncommitted, Balzac had something of Raphael and Lucien as well, and could never completely separate society from his visional world. Balzac, for all his indictment of a world dominated by selfishness, was no champion of alienation. To deny any part of the whole would be a confession of failure, a denial of the all-pervading unity of things. It is perhaps Vautrin who best represents Balzac's own nature as a creative artist. The way in which the archcriminal manipulates people, spins plots, changes from pursued to pursuer, controls the lives of others but is himself vulnerable—this suggests something of the divine-human fusion, the artist as God and man creating worlds in which the subjective and the objective blend and cause becomes indistinguishable from effect, that lies behind Balzac's depiction of his artists and is responsible for the peculiar aura of the Balzacian world.

For all the greatness of Balzac's accomplishment, however, we must remember that, like Vautrin, he ultimately failed to subject real life to the power of his will and vision. He succeeded in molding his work and giving it the design of a systematic and generalized anatomy of society; nonetheless, life kept slipping from his grasp. Characters sometimes change from work to work as if they had a free will of their own in opposition to their creator's will. But even more important, Balzac had to spend himself in order to write at all, and he exhausted himself—his fatal skin—before he exhausted his materials. *The Comédie humaine*, in spite of its largeness, remains a fragment, for Balzac did not live to write the synthesizing work that would have done for his series of novels what *Le Temps retrové* does for Proust's *A la Recherche du Temps perdu*. Only a partial reflection of his total vision remains in the novels he left. (pp. 195-96)

> *Maurice Beebe, "Honoré de Balzac: The Novelist As Creator," in his* Ivory Towers and Sacred Founts: The Artist As Hero in Fiction from Goethe to Joyce *(reprinted by permission of New York University Press; copyright © 1964 by New York University),* New York University Press, 1964, pp. 175-96.

## V. S. PRITCHETT (essay date 1964)

The small house on the cliff of Passy hanging like a cage between an upper and lower street, so that by a trick of relativity, the top floor of the Rue Berton is the ground floor of the Rue Raynouard, has often been taken as a symbol of the life of Balzac. . . . Two houses in one, a life with two front doors, dream and reality; the novelist, naïve and yet shrewd, not troubling to distinguish between one and the other. Symbol of Balzac's life, the house is a symbol of the frontier life, the trap-door life of the great artists, who have always lived between two worlds. . . . At this house in the worst year of his life, the least blessed with that calm which is—quite erroneously—supposed to be essential to the novelist, Balzac wrote **[Le Cousin Pons]** and **La Cousine Bette,** respectively the best constructed and the most fluent and subtle of his novels. (pp. 327-28)

Balzac is certainly the novelist who most completely exemplifies the "our time" novelist, but not by his judgments on his society. He simply *is* his time. He is identified with it, by all the greedy innocence of genius. The society of rich peasants brought to power by revolution and dictatorship, pushing into business and speculation, buying up houses and antiques, founding families, grabbing at money and pleasure, haunted by their tradition of parsimony and hard work, and with the peasant's black and white ideas about everything, and above all their weakness for fixed ideas, is Balzac himself. He shares their illusions. Like them he was humble when he was poor, arrogant when he was rich. As with them, his extravagance was one side of the coin; on the other was the face of the peasant miser. The cynic lived in a world of romantic optimism. We see the dramatic phase of a century's illusions, before they have been assimilated and trodden down into the familiar hypocrisies. To us Balzac's preoccupation with money appears first to be the searching, scientific and prosaic interest of the documentary artist. On the contrary, for him money was romantic; it was hope and ideal. It was despair and evil. It was not the dreary background, but the animating and theatrical spirit. (pp. 329-30)

[In *Le Cousin Pons*,] Balzac examined the dossier of human nature with the quizzical detachment of some nail-biting, cigar-stained Chief of Police who is going rapidly up in the world; who has seen so many cases; who thanks heaven that he does not make the moral law and that a worldly Church stands between himself and the Almighty. Passion, even when it is a passion for the best food, always becomes—in the experience of the Chief of Police—a transaction; Pons trades the little errands he runs on behalf of the family for the indispensable surprises of the gourmet. In the pursuit of that appetite he is prepared to ruin himself where other men, more voluptuously equipped by nature, will wreck themselves in the capture and establishment of courtesans. Sex or food, money or penury, envy or ambition—Balzac knows all the roads to ruin. If only men and women were content with their habits instead of craving the sublimity of their appetites.

But *Pons* is a type. He is a poor relation. (pp. 334-35)

Look at the delightful Pons. His character has so many departments. He is an old man, an ugly man, an outmoded but respected musician, a dandy survived from an earlier period, a collector of antiques, a poor man, a careful man, a simple man who is not quite so simple. . . . Pons is the kind of character who, inevitable, becomes fantastic in the English novel simply because no general laws pin him down. He would become a static "character." Instead Balzac takes all these aspects of Pons and mounts each one, so that Pons is constructed before our eyes. We have a double interest: the story or plot, which is excellent in suspense, drama and form—this is one of Balzac's well-constructed novels, as it is also one of the most moving—and the exact completion, brick by brick, of Pons and his circle. There are the historical Pons—he is an *incroyable* left-over from the Directoire—the artistic Pons, the financial Pons, the sociable Pons, the moral Pons, and in the end Pons dying, plundered, defiant, a man awakened from his simplicity and fighting back, the exquisitely humble artist turned proud, sovereign and dangerous in his debacle. Pons is a faceted stone, and part of the drama is the relation of each facet with the others. . . . We have the portrait of a man who in every trait suggests some aspect of the society in which he

lives. The history of his time is explicit in him. Yet he is not a period piece. A period piece is incapable of moral development and the development of a moral theme is everything in the novels of Balzac, who facilitates it by giving every character not merely a time and place, but also an obsession. (pp. 335-36)

Balzac is the novelist of our appetites, obsessions and our *idées fixes*, but his great gift is his sense of the complexity of the human situation. He had both perceptions, one supposes, from his peasant origins, for among peasants, as he was fond of saying, the *idée fixe* is easily started; and their sense of circumstance overpowers all other consideration in their lives. A character in Balzac is thus variously situated in history, in money, in family, class and in his type to begin with; but on top of this, Balzac's genius was richly inventive in the field least exploited by the mass of novelists: the field of probability. (pp. 337-38)

I do not know that I would put anything in *Le Cousin Pons* above the first part of *La Cousine Bette*, though I like Pons better as a whole. Pons is the old bachelor. Bette is the old maid. The growth of her malevolence is less subtly presented than the course of Pons's disillusion, because Balzac had the genius to show Pons living with a man even simpler than himself. One see two degrees of simplicity, one lighting the other, whereas Bette stands alone; indeed it may be complained that she is gradually swamped by the other characters. She is best in her obscurity, the despised poor relation, the sullen peasant, masculine, counting her humiliations and her economies like a miser, startling people with her bizarre reflections. . . . Bette is a wronged soul; and when her passion does break, it is, as Balzac says, sublime and terrifying. Her advance to sheer wickedness and vengeance is less convincing, or, rather, less engrossing. It is a good point that she is the eager handmaid and not the igniting cause of ruin; but one draws back, incredulously, before some of her plots and lies. Acceptable when they are naïve, they are unacceptable when they fit too efficiently the melodramatic intrigue of the second part of the book. But the genius for character and situation is here again. (p. 339)

No one has surpassed Balzac in revealing the great part played by money in middle-class life; nor has anyone excelled him in the portraits of the parvenu. Henry James alone, coming at the zenith of middle-class power, perceived the moral corruption caused by money; but money had ripened. It glowed like a peach that is just about to fall. Balzac arrived when the new money, the new finance of the post-Napoleonic world was starting on its violent course; when money was an obsession and was putting down a foundation for middle-class morals. In these two novels about the poor relation, he made his most palatable, his least acrid and most human statements about this grotesque period of middle-class history. (p. 340)

*V. S. Pritchett, "Poor Relations," in his* The Living Novel & Later Appreciations *(copyright © 1964 and 1975 by V. S. Pritchett; reprinted by permission of Literistic, Ltd.), revised edition, Random House, 1964, pp. 327-40.*

## F.W.J. HEMMINGS (essay date 1967)

[*Hemmings describes* La comédie humaine *as Balzac's attempt to depict and comprehend the changing world. In his preface, Hemmings defines the aim of his study. He proposes to examine what he considers "the two terms of the dialectic underlying* La comédie humaine . . . *individual visions, ambitions, and nostalgias acting on, colliding with, modified by the solid-seeming yet disintegrating rock of society.'' The following is taken from Hemmings's discussion of several works that focus on Balzac's view of married life.*]

The title *Scènes de la vie privée* was first used by Balzac in 1830 for a two-volume collection of short stories (half a dozen in all), the purpose of which was avowedly didactic. The previous year he had scored a considerable success with a waggish and cynical treatise, *Physiologie du mariage;* the 1830 collection dealt similarly with the subject of matrimony, but soberly and rather more chastely. If certain remarks in his Preface are to be taken at face value, these stories—in which he had ''attempted to depict with fidelity the events that follow marriage or precede it''—were designed to constitute a manual suitable for enlightened mothers to give to their marriageable daughters, the author believing that ''it is far less imprudent to put markers at the dangerous passages in life, as watermen on the Loire drive willow branches in the sandbanks, than to leave them hidden from the eyes of the inexperienced.''

In the circumstances, it is hardly surprising that such charm as these stories might once have possessed has faded, or at least taken on an irremediably period air, almost—though not quite—to the same degree as has that of Maria Edgeworth's *Moral Tales,* which they recall and which may have partly inspired them. (pp. 35-6)

There is one story, however, to which these strictures do not apply. Entitled, in 1830, *Gloire et malheur,* it was subsequently rechristened, for the first edition of *La Comédie humaine, La Maison du chatqui-pelote,* with reference to the street sign, a cat playing rackets, hanging over the old-fashioned linen draper's establishment that is the story's principal setting. The work, slight as it is, has the great merit of presenting a convincing and warmly human picture of the mercer and his family. The life of these lower middle class people is shown as unspeakably monotonous, though not felt by them as being so; the annual stock taking is a great event, a visit to an art gallery a momentous outing. But the shopkeeper's family, narrow though their horizons are, have a poetic appeal for a stranger with an eye for the picturesque. (p. 36)

*La Maison du chatqui-pelote* is both a study of incompatibility in marriage and a warning against disregarding parental advice in one's choice of a life's partner, which is a particular case of defying the authority of the family. (p. 37)

[Let us take] a brief look at a somewhat uncharacteristic work, the *Mémoires de deux jeunes mariées.* Written some twelve years later than the original *Scènes de la vie privée,* it introduces a new theme. . . : the threat to marriage and the family posed by romantic love. Balzac chose an already outmoded form, the novel-by-letters, in order to trace the parallel but opposed life stories of two convent-school friends. (pp. 44-5)

The *Mémoires de deux jeunes mariées* is a *roman à thèse* on the theme of ''sense and sensibility,'' but Renée's good sense is so unbearably smug, Louise's sensibility so wildly extravagant, that the sermon is finally robbed of all effect. A few of the maxims in Renée's letters serve, however, as useful clues to Balzac's thought on the central question he was raising. It is worth observing that Renée is a student of [the Royalist political philosopher Louis de] Bonald in between her pregnancies. As she sees it, Louise is a mere child of nature; society, in thwarting nature, perfects the individual in accordance with the divine will. So ''every married woman learns to her cost

the social law, which at many points is incompatible with the laws of nature.'' The family is a hierarchical structure, not an association or a partnership. ''There exists an equality between two lovers which I think can never manifest itself between husband and wife, under penalty of social disorders and irreparable harm.''. . . [That] passionate love can endure is a fiction invented by romantic poets. ''Nature and society are in league to destroy the existence of absolute felicity, something which is contrary to nature and society alike.'' In her last letter, which is addressed not to Louise (who is by now dead) but to her husband, Renée sums up the whole of this bleak philosophy in a single, uncompromising statement: ''Marriage cannot be founded on passion, nor even on love.'' This is not just an antiromantic sally: it has its sour logic. If passion is supremely a force rooted in egoism, a manifestation of the individual libido, it clearly has no place in the social arrangement that marriage is, an arrangement designed to enable society to progress toward its own ends and not to offer a way of self-fulfillment to its particular members.

Granted that the thesis has a certain rough common sense behind it, still it has to be acknowledged that Balzac's presentation of it in these early works is crude and conspicuously devoid of humanity and true understanding. (pp. 45-7)

*La Femme de trente ans* is one of the less worthy products of the romantic sensibility and one of the weakest novels of *La Comédie humaine.* Balzac, for once, was playing to the gallery, and though he was not normally given to self-criticism (at any rate in his letters to Mme Hanska), he spoke of this work with something like embarrassment. It is, nevertheless, not possible to dismiss it entirely as a reversion to the tasteless potboilers that he had published under pseudonyms at the beginning of his literary career; it has its interest, arising from the evident conflict between his didactic purpose and his human sympathies, which side with his heroine to a degree that all but nullifies the moral lessons he appears to have wanted to inculcate.

Sainte-Beuve, in the grudging tribute he paid Balzac on the latter's death [see excerpt above, 1850], asserted that he owed the high reputation he enjoyed in aristrocratic society to the delicacy of his portraits of ladies of refinement who had passed their first youth. (p. 50)

[It] is true that, with a few exceptions (Eugénie Grandet springs immediately to mind), Balzac's older women are more memorable than his rather insipid virgins, his Modeste Mignons, his Ursule Mirouets, with their flawless skins and their innocent stratagems.

With all this goes an immense and genuine compassion for these maturer heroines. For all the austerity of his antifeminist principles, Balzac was a feminist at heart, as his women readers instinctively recognized. He was acutely aware of the injustice of those very institutions that he was convinced he must defend and uphold. (pp. 52-3)

Balzac acquired during his lifetime an extraordinary reputation for his apparently uncanny insight into [the] hidden stresses of conjugal life that might arise from nothing more than the sudden surfacing of a suppressed antipathy for the servitudes of the marriage bed, or from some vague idealism that failed to find satisfaction in the humdrum fulfillment of matrimonial duty. *Honorine* and *Une fille d'Eve,* two short novels, are both studies of such intimate dramas that, until the imperceptible motivations at work are analyzed, appear inexplicable. The virus that can attack a superficially ''happy union'' is invisible to all eyes except the novelist's. In revealing it to us, Balzac was fulfilling a far more important function than the self-imposed one of champion of middle-class morality; he was guiding his readers through those curtained chambers of the soul where aversions and sympathies are born and grow, quite beyond the reach of a crude psychology that judges by appearances. (p. 55)

The lyric perfection of **Honorine** arises from the sense it gives us of unstated and understated tragedy; and the tragedy itself is genuine since, in the last resort, neither Octave nor Honorine can be held altogether guilty: to require either that he should have suppressed his passion, or that she should have crushed her distaste, would alike be unreasonable. In delineating this situation without issue, Balzac reaches far beyond his mundane preoccupations with the proper duties of wives and the place of love in marriage, to attain to an almost Racinian intensity of feeling in a work dealing with a sphere of moral life into which no one before had trespassed.

Compared with Honorine's angelic delicacies, the all-too-human willfulness of Mme Félix de Vandenesse makes her the true "daughter of Eve" of the book's title, though she too, like Honorine, is an idealist. There is a perceptible difference in tone between the two works: *Une fille d'Eve* is not a tragedy, but a somewhat wry comedy, for in this instance the heroine's husband is successful in rescuing her from the consequences of her idealism. *Une fille d'Eve* comprises, besides, a valuable study of the overlapping spheres of politics, journalism, and high finance; in other words, it is much more firmly rooted than **Honorine** in the normal world of **La Comédie humaine**. (pp. 59-60)

The same theme, that of the foolish woman saved from straying, was used again by Balzac in **La Fausse Maîtresse**, with the variation that it is not the husband who intervenes to save his wife from adultery, but the lover, paradoxically, who takes action to stop the woman from committing an infidelity. (p. 64)

**Honorine, Une fille d'Eve, La Fausse Maîtresse** form a group embodying an identical theme: the threat posed to a harmonious married life by the virus of romantic passion. All three heroines could be fairly described by that slighting term "children.". . . Honorine is unaccountable, Marie-Angélique is irresponsible, Clémentine is positively perverse. The heroes, on the other hand—Octave, Félix, Thaddeus—are prodigies of forgiveness and understanding.

But Balzac knew that his was not the whole truth. Over the five years (1838-43) during which he composed **Honorine, Une fille d'Eve**, and **La Fausse Maîtresse**—besides the *Mémoires de deux jeunes mariées*—he also wrote two novels, **La Muse du département** and **Béatrix**, which embody studies of women possessed of considerable strength of character, even though they manifest their independence of spirit outside the sanctified circle of married life. Dinah de La Baudraye breaks away from her husband, Félicité des Touches never takes one. Both are in every way superior to any of the men whose paths they cross. (pp. 67-8)

It cannot be denied that [*La Muse du département*] leaves a bitter taste. There is no nobility in any of the three members of the triangle—husband, wife, or lover—but it cannot be said either that any of them is particularly satanic. None gives proof of that energy, for good or evil, that is the hallmark of the typically Balzacian character; at the most, they possess pertinacity in the pursuit of their ends, but these ends are petty, limited, unexciting. **La Muse du département** is perhaps, of all Balzac's novels, that which accords best with the later aesthetic

of naturalism, especially as practiced by the minor naturalists. (pp. 68-9)

The subtitle [of **Béatrix**], **Les Amours forcés,** was a play on the phrase *travaux forcés* (penal servitude). The letters T. F. were branded on the shoulders of convicts at this time, and Balzac did indeed imagine an alternative title for his novel, *Les Galériens* (the galley slaves). His theme was the plight of two lovers who embark on an affair that causes a grave scandal in society and then find that out of pride they are forced to act out in public the drama of the romantic couple counting the world well lost for love, though in private they are heartily tired of one another and would like nothing better than to separate. (p. 72)

Even when allowance is made for the preconceptions on the subject prevalent in his day, it is hard not to find irritating Balzac's all-too-frequent pontifications on the proper destiny of woman and the way in which so often he manipulates his plots in order to prove that her subjection to her lord and master is divinely ordained. But this insistently male approach, for all its occasional injustice and insensitivity, was balanced by a rare penetration and a genuine understanding of the painful predicament of woman in the society of his age. It was when he was discussing Sainte-Beuve's first and only novel, *Volupté*, in one of his discursive letters to his future wife [Mme Hanska], that Balzac was led to enunciate his most intimately held opinion regarding the relations between the sexes. *Volupté* was founded on the situation that Balzac himself was to enlarge on, a year later, in *Le Lys dans la vallée*: a young man experiencing a passionate love for a married woman who responds, but remains physically faithful to her husband. (pp. 78-9)

[*Le Lys dans la vallée*] has always had its devotees, but for most tastes it is too long, too lush, and too high-flown. Balzac's decision to have the story related by Félix himself was a serious error of judgment, attributable perhaps to the desire to beat Sainte-Beuve on his own ground (*Volupté* is the life story of Amaury told by himself). *Le Lys dans la vallée* is the only novel in **La Comédie humaine** written in the form of the fictional autobiography; by adopting this convention, Balzac immediately sacrificed one of his principal assets, the godlike insight into the minds of his characters. Félix can only guess at Mme de Mortsauf's true feelings, which she is at pains to conceal from him; and we see her indistinctly through his hesitant, dazzled, and clouded vision. Only the husband, M. de Mortsauf, emerges as convincing and lifelike. . . . It was necessary, of course, that the heroine of **Le Lys** should be given a husband at once unattractive and a little pathetic, in order to enhance the merit of her resistance to Félix de Vandenesse's suit, and at the same time to make convincing her refusal to desert her husband. (pp. 80-1)

But strip away the unpleasantness and the affectation, and there remains at the center of *Le Lys dans la vallée* an expression of the predicament of the married woman tempted by passion which has no adequate counterpart anywhere else in **La Comédie humaine**. Mme de Mortsauf overcomes the temptation; her marriage, at least, withstands the virus of passion, and this permits her two children to grow up happily. (pp. 81-2)

Whether or not she has been a loser, it is certain that the social order has been the gainer. For all its faults, **Le Lys dans la vallée** brings us back once more, and with agonizing insistence, to the central dilemma of **La Comédie humaine**: which set of demands should prevail, those of the individual or those of the community? Where the individual is a married woman, the answer in most of the cases considered [here] is clear: the situation she is in requires that she should comply with the demands of the community at whatever cost to herself. In *Le Lys dans la vallée* this answer is not given with the assurance that we find elsewhere. The contrary ethic, the romantic, Byronic, satanic doctrine, which asserts the supreme value of self-fulfillment, is proclaimed by Félix (not, admittedly, the most disinterested of advocates): "So long as love recoils before a crime, it appears to us to accept limits, and love must be limitless." (pp. 82-3)

*F.W.J. Hemmings, in his* Balzac: An Interpretation of "La comédie humaine" *(copyright © 1967 by Random House, Inc.; reprinted by permission of the publisher), Random House, 1967, 189 p.*

## PETER W. LOCK (essay date 1967)

With the publication of *Le Père Goriot* in 1834 Balzac triumphantly asserted his powers as the creator of a complex fictional world. As early as 1829 he had resolved to group several independent works under a collective title *(Scènes de la vie privée),* and he became increasingly absorbed by the problem of integrating his rapidly expanding stock of novels and short stories into a single, unified structure. In *Le Père Goriot* the process of unification was carried decisively forward; it was in this novel that Balzac brought together a number of themes previously treated separately, and undertook for the first time the systematic exploitation of characters whom he had already set in motion in other works. Eventually all the novels published since 1829 were to be drawn together under the heading of the *Comédie humaine* whose thematic unity would be strengthened by the movement of characters from one novel to another. *Le Père Goriot* thus marks an important moment in Balzac's career, and it also provides an excellent vantage point from which to survey the larger pattern of the *Comédie humaine.* (p. 7)

On entering *Le Père Goriot* the reader is faced with a dozen or so pages of detailed description of the pension and its inhabitants. In order to reach the latter, he must thread his way through a maze of rooms and pathways, and negotiate a mass of furniture and other objects which have cluttered up the place for the past forty years. Unlike Stendhal who confessed himself bored by the task of providing 'le pittoresque', Balzac revelled in the business of establishing settings, and he pokes and rummages his way through the musty boarding-house with ebullient yet purposeful curiosity. His contemporaries had already expressed their impatience (shared by some modern readers) at this revolutionary kind of stocktaking, and Balzac acknowledges their criticism . . .—only to ignore it! And we may well consider him right to do so. . . .

On the simplest level the establishment of a particular sense of place brings the fictional world into focus and provides an air of authenticity and solidity. The reader . . . is gradually drawn into a world which, superficially at least, resembles the world he inhabits. Streets and monuments are named, distances calculated, familiar objects encountered. All the senses are involved in the exploration of a reality which is clearly perceived and forcibly made present. (p. 16)

Implicitly and explicitly, Balzac exploits his opening description as a preparation for the appearance of characters and the unfolding of the action. Once assimilated, the powerful image remains in our minds throughout the novel, and serves as a perpetual indication of a certain level of existence. In describing Rastignac's visit to Goriot's room later in the novel . . . , Balzac needs only to repeat a few of the motifs already established . . . in order to evoke the full degradation of the old man's situation. Rastignac, confronted by this misery, recoils in horror; here, and at other moments in the novel . . . , he compares his squalid surroundings with the magnificent luxury of the houses he visits. He obscurely recognizes that the boarding-house represents a trap, possibly even a tomb; should he lose his nerve and momentum, he is likely to be condemned to join those whose failure he despises.

When Balzac [refers] to the dining-room in the boarding-house . . . it is as if he were speaking of the curious collection of boarders, the majority of whom, half-submerged in their surroundings, seem to be composed of the very substance which imprisons them. In presenting Madame Vauquer, Mademoiselle Michonneau and Poiret, Balzac carries over into the portraits elements of the décor, dehumanizing his characters, depriving them of importance and value. (p. 17)

Against this sombre background Balzac presents his major characters, using terms borrowed from painting to stress relations within the general picture. (p. 18)

Balzac's general framework permits flexibility and variety. Rastignac is introduced by a few deft strokes of colour (blue, black, white); at this stage he is no more than a potentiality, a personality as yet unmarked by the passions which set their stamp on most of Balzac's figures. Minor characters seem adequately summed up in a paragraph; it is as if they had condemned themselves to such definitive treatment: the portrait is almost in the nature of an epitaph. Goriot, on the other hand, is given in a series of sketches which vividly chronicle his decline; Vautrin gets a couple of pages—and yet remains elusive. (p. 19)

Stripped of its accessory detail, the action of *Le Père Goriot* is seen as an assembly of powers which, laboriously mobilized, converge, irrupt and destroy. The characters, though they have the semblance of real persons, are best considered as forces, to be discussed in terms of movement and trajectory; the novel is an experiment in the dynamics of contagion and antagonism. Structurally, there is a marked opposition between the lengthy introductory section and the quick movement of the drama which begins to accelerate away as the predominantly panoramic method of the exposition yields to the narrower focus of scenic representation. From the beginning of Chapter II the action takes on an almost uninterrupted forward march and there is an increasing compression of the time sequence down to the last chapter where the events recorded take place on five successive days. The multiple strands which make up the fabric of the action are woven together by means of confrontations, linking actions and summarizing scenes; there is a strong sense of an order being imposed from above which results in an atmosphere of tension and strain far removed from the spontaneous naturalness of a Stendhal. An extensive use of dialogue increases the theatricality of the novel; it often seems, though, that the characters even when addressing one another are in reality engaging in self-expression rather than communication. The overall impression is of urgency—and solitude. (pp. 23-4)

In *Le Père Goriot* money is a unifying factor and a common denominator, and the general theme is constructed from scores of sharply observed details and suggestive transactions. Exact calculations permit the reconstruction of the dismal life of the boarders. . . . There are notable examples of hoarding, spending and lending: Madame Vauquer has stealthily amassed 40,000 francs (roughly equivalent to £8,000 today), Goriot indulges in suspicious prodigality, and Vautrin, the outlaws' Nucingen, occasionally floats a short-term loan to the boarders. (p. 26)

Sudden possession of income results in an immediate transformation of the individual. On receiving from his parents a replenishment of funds, Rastignac's energy and confidence redouble; it is as if life is renewed within him . . . . Later in the novel when we are given a contrasting image of disintegration as Rastignac recklessly squanders his substance . . . , there is again the indication that more than money is at stake. And this is certainly true in the case of Goriot whose life drains away as he desperately attempts to keep pace with his daughters' relentless demands. Money is not only the sign of success but the symbol of energy. (p. 27)

Passion, like money, is a force which actively works upon Balzac's humanity, galvanizing, tyrannizing, destroying. In many instances it leads to a transformation of the individual, raising even the most humble to sudden splendour. The portrait of Victorine indicates a pale, sickly creature, passive and melancholy; love alone, remarks Balzac, would cause a redemptive quickening of life. . . . Such a transformation does in fact later occur; Rastignac provokes in Victorine an 'explosion de sentiment' which causes a momentary radiance . . . ; in a subsequent scene her face is surrounded by an 'auréole de bonheur'. . . . Goriot is similarly transfigured by emotion; from a dull-witted, self-absorbed automaton, he becomes, when his soul is filled with love for his daughters, illuminated by the passion which possesses him. . . . [At] such privileged moments the characters seem to move beyond their terrestrial condition and ascend towards a state of pure spirituality. (pp. 27-8)

Ennobling or degrading, violent emotion profoundly affects rational conduct and self-control. Even the poised and eloquent Madame de Beauséant is thrown into disarray by its 'despotism' . . . and rendered speechless (like Goriot and like Madame Vauquer) by its impact. . . . (p. 29)

In demonstrating the multiple effects of passion on his characters, Balzac creates in *Le Père Goriot* an atmosphere of tension and violence. His scientific investigations led him to consider emotion not as an abstraction but as a substance or fluid of galvanizing power whose origins are uncertain and whose consequences are unpredictable. At times passion seems to have an existence independent of persons. . . . His characters, subjected to this omnipresent force, are engaged in continuous warfare and a struggle for survival. Defeat attends those who fail to achieve lucidity or self-dominion; victory goes to the calculating and the unscrupulous, the capitalists of passion who exploit the feeling of others while retaining control over their own. Spontaneity, sensitivity and idealism are outmoded, profitless values. . . .

Confronted by corruption and the destructive pressures of a mechanical existence, Balzac's characters are forced to make a choice and a decision; Vautrin, oversimplifying, indicates the alternatives: 'ou une stupide obeissance ou la révolte' [either stupid submission or revolt]. . . . Madame de Beauséant, Goriot and Vautrin himself all take a stand in an attempt to rise above circumstances and to create and preserve an independent vision of reality. The aristocrat, the bourgeois and the criminal, though they inhabit spheres which seem to have little in common, are linked by their reactions to society and by their efforts to establish a world of their own making. (p. 31)

Vautrin's attitude is the most extreme; rejecting contemporary morality, law and justice, he reduces society to the lowest possible level and expresses his view of it with devastating clarity. . . .

Balzac's major characters are basically extremists whose defiance goes well beyond a rejection of social attitudes and patterns. Madame de Beauséant, faced with the possibility of abandonment, refuses to accept that her love can be less than eternal. Having glimpsed the ideal, she attempts to perpetuate its presence; confronted with failure, she prefers solitude to compromise. Goriot is afflicted by desire to transcend the limits of space and time; obstinately refusing to accept the limitations of the human condition, he revolts against the implacable process of life itself. (p. 32)

In pursuing their quest for victory over time and human frailty, both Goriot and Vautrin assume exalted rôles. Goriot's fanatical paternal drive causes him to compare himself to God, immanent in his creation. . . . Vautrin towers above his creatures and while vicariously participating in their success remains separate from them, transcending the results of his handiwork. (p. 33)

In this respect, the controlled and lucid Vautrin would seem to come closer to Balzac's ideal creator. A manipulator of persons who possesses uncanny powers of intuition and divination, an artist in crime who read Cellini, a 'poet' whose poetry consists of actions and emotions . . . , he seems to represent an equilibrium between dictatorial aloofness and passionate involvement. And yet there are disquieting elements which have been too readily ignored by those who would make of Vautrin a reflection of Balzac himself. Even on a literal level, Vautrin lacks the omnipotence we have the right to expect from one who usurps the function of Providence. (p. 34)

From *Don Quixote* to Joyce's *Ulysses* the theme of the formative journey has been a central preoccupation of fiction. Some novelists have chosen to trace the total pattern of their hero's existence; others have dwelt on a crucial stage in his development. Balzac's system of interlocking novels enables him to combine these two approaches: in *Le Père Goriot* he concentrates on the initial steps in Rastignac's career which is then developed in other works throughout the *Comédie humaine*.

The action of *Le Père Goriot* occupies less than three months, and this might seem too brief a span in which to speak of the formation of a hero. And yet the intensity and compression of the events described and the profound impact they make on Rastignac's character and outlook compensate for the brevity of the experience. Naturally perspicacious, Rastignac quickly succeeds in assimilating the lessons received and in transforming knowledge into action; from a naïve and clumsy provincial he becomes, in the space of a few weeks, an experienced, agile and disillusioned man of the world. Though his youthful dreams are demolished by the nightmare of Paris, he is able to generate the necessary force to preserve himself, if not from contamination, at least from total defeat.

Balzac does not content himself with an unimpassioned charting of Rastignac's journey. Whereas he tends to remain exterior to the other characters, he enters the mind of his hero, dramatizing the movement of intelligence and conscience. Moreover, he does not hesitate to make comments on Rastignac's progress, to pass judgment and to generalize from the particular instance. A pattern emerges here: experience, meditation, commentary. Rastignac, subjected to a test, reflects upon his performance; the author then surveys and judges both achievement and assessment. There is a sense of progression, evaluation and unification: isolated events and themes are drawn together by the experience of the hero and the commentary of the narrator. Rastignac is brought into contact with the other major characters while the focus remains on his thoughts and actions. (pp. 35-6)

The structure of *Le Père Goriot,* like that of the *Comédie humaine,* is based on Balzac's deeply rooted tendency to express experience in antithetical terms. In *Le Père Goriot* two worlds are juxtaposed, the static unit of the boarding-house and the dynamic, disruptive confluence of Parisian society. Hostilities are uncovered between warring factions—daughters against father and against each other, criminal against society, idealistic youth against a cynical and corrupt civilization. And these basic patterns are complicated by moral and psychological conflicts within the characters themselves. Individuals who appear to represent a single attitude are in reality the theatre of opposing forces: noble passion versus perversion in Goriot, instinct versus control in Vautrin, idealism versus corruption in Rastignac, generosity versus egoism in Delphine. And Balzac's rhetoric, while apparently reducing experience to a series of unambiguous formulae, in fact increases the complexity and density of his world by establishing a network of conflicting comments and judgments which compel the reader to involve himself in the action of the novel and to form his own conclusions. (pp. 60-1)

Balzac's world, though primarily an independent repertory with its own index and cross-references, is also a vast directory which provides a record of a critical period in French history. Concentrating primarily on the fortunes of a triumphant bourgeoisie, Balzac found himself facing the problem which was to confront his successors: if the novel is to be concerned with the recording of contemporary experience, how can it attain dignity and value in a society whose dominant class, obsessed with material possessions, is moving towards mediocrity and conformity? Balzac's response, as historian and as novelist, is to inject significance into the lives of ordinary persons who become the representatives not only of basic human tendencies but also of social and historical forces. Thus in *Le Père Goriot* Vautrin is both the personification of temptation and the incarnation of anarchy. . . . Rastignac's career demonstrates the manner in which the impoverished nobility integrated itself into the new society, accepting alien values. Goriot takes us through Revolution and Empire and shows how, by skilful manipulation and a good sense of timing, a simple workman could earn a fortune and place his daughters in positions of social prominence. Balzac thus surveys and judges his society which he represents in terms of movement, assimilation and conflict; the old order has been destroyed and is being replaced by a society which lacks purpose and direction. The Goriot family, ruptured by greed and passion, and casting off the authority of the father, may be taken as a symbol of the country as a whole. (p. 62)

Balzac's energetic response to the life he observes and the forms he creates continues to strike a compelling and original note. In *Le Père Goriot* he demonstrates his ability to establish a firm and idiosyncratic hold on reality, to forge connections between individual characters and universal forces, and to discover a form appropriate to his passion for drama. The novel's strength lies not in the passive mirroring of things as they are, but in intensification and amplification; and Balzac convinces us of the value of imaginative distortion. Involving us in a

process of elaboration, demolition and reconstruction, he compels us to come to terms with his vision of life and to reflect upon the limitless possibilities of fiction. (p. 64)

> *Peter W. Lock, in his* Balzac: "Le père Goriot" *(©
> Peter W. Lock 1967), Edward Arnold (Publishers)
> Ltd, 1967, 64 p.*

**GRETCHEN R. BESSER**　(essay date 1969)

[*Besser states that "throughout his work, Balzac gropes toward
an understanding of genius, propounding various definitions, isolating different components of genius, in a continuing attempt to
unravel the mystery surrounding the creative mind." Her study
examines Balzac's concept of génie (genius) by studying both his
didactic comments on genius and their embodiment in the superior
individuals of* La comédie humaine.]

[As we delve] into Balzac's concept of genius and intellectual superiority, we become aware that the appellation of "genius," in his viewpoint and in his terminology, is reserved almost exclusively for the type of outstanding, productive individual whom we should nowadays more probably refer to as the "creative artist" or "creative personality." These men, who arise in numerous areas of art and science within the world of the *Comédie humaine,* are all designated alike as "artists," whatever their domain—whether it be poetry, chemistry, painting, music, medicine, or affairs of state. Their outstanding common denominator is their capacity for creative thought, which is frequently reinforced by their original contributions to human progress.

Balzac appears to distinguish between two categories of exceptional characters. On the one hand, he presents the true man of genius as noted above, the creative thinker in his highest manifestation, a superior being who appears to have little kinship with the rest of mankind, and to inhabit a sphere uniquely his own. On another plane of pre-eminence, Balzac depicts those exceptional persons who, either because of the power they wield, or as a result of their financial position and prestige, or on account of the intense or exclusive nature of their passion, or even by dint of their uncommon virtue, stand out from the teeming masses of humanity and, because they crop up so frequently in the pages of the *Comédie humaine,* give rise to the impression that Balzac's world is populated by a race of supermen. It is the prevalence of these larger-than-life personalities that prompted Baudelaire to make his well-known remark to the effect that all of Balzac's characters share a spark of his genius [see excerpt above, 1859].

These latter characters are seen to dominate men and events and, often enough, to rule the contemporary scene, but they are not, strictly speaking, "geniuses"—at least, not according to Balzac's scrupulous use of the term. They include such rapacious sharks of finance as Nucingen, Rastignac, du Tillet, and Gobseck, who have achieved their ascendancy over other individuals through the power which wealth provides, and who have attained their positions of prominence through a combination of financial acumen, unscrupulous tactics, and undeviating purpose. Among this group may be numbered Henri de Marsay, who is successful at every enterprise he undertakes, including attainment of the highest political eminence—in contrast, let us say, to a man of genius like Marcas, whose innate talents are actually superior, but who lacks the vigorous self-propulsion to reach the top. Closely allied is the Société des Treize, . . . of which de Marsay is a member, and which also includes Armand de Montriveau and Ferragus.

Other exceptional individuals who occupy an important place in the Balzacian world—men like Félix de Vandenesse, who is ranged among the "remarkable" men of his time, or like the trio of good friends, . . . Counts Granville, Sérisy, and Bauvan, all influential men in the magistracy and in the government—are outstanding not merely because of the lofty positions they hold in society, but also by virtue of their moral qualities. Hereupon we encounter, within the context of the exceptional individual as such (but excluding the true man of genius) certain gradations of superiority. In one instance, we find the brute superiority of extreme power, wealth, or prestige, usually achieved through unprincipled drive and ambition, and embodied in a host of "social climbers," of whom the top echelon is composed of Nucingen and his cohorts. Next in the scale, we note the afore-mentioned men of integrity, conscience, and high moral resolve, who also dominate society and their peers. More often than not, this second group comprises members of the aristocracy, who, by virtue of the entrenched social position they enjoy, are exempt from frantically clawing their way up the ladder of success, and who still cling to an antiquated tradition of "noblesse oblige."

Beyond them lies still another group, whose supremacy is not predicated upon their social status or dominance over other men, but is uniquely based on their moral courage and spiritual sanctity. These men and women rise above the rest of mankind by virtue of their "saintliness," through an excess of selflessness and sacrifice. The prime model for these paragons of virtue and benevolence is constituted by the Frères de la Consolation, headed by Madame de la Chanterie. Others of this godly *confrérie* are Dr. Benassis, repentant sinner and benefactor of an entire countryside, and his feminine counterpart, Véronique Graslin (whose mother claims that she deserves to be canonized). . . .

It is chiefly the women of the *Comédie humaine* who display virtue to a rarefied degree—devotion, selflessness, and nobility of character being the criteria of their "superiority." We can count off such models of heroic duty and self-abnegation as Henriette de Mortsauf, Adeline Hulot, and Madame Claës, not to mention the courtesans, Esther and Coralie. Dinah de la Baudraye, "la Muse de Sancerre," is derided by Balzac for her intellectual aspirations; it is not in the "cultural" pretensions of a provincial blue-stocking that she gives evidence of her superiority, but rather in her devoted sacrifice to the man she loves, in her nobility of character and the rare qualities of her soul.

The only woman of superior intellectual achievement and ability, who approaches the concept of creative genius, is Camille Maupin, and she is presented (in analogy with George Sand) as a woman whose qualities are essentially masculine. She lives outside the pale of social convention, not so much because she suffers from the anathema that is normally attached to genius—for Balzac does not allow that she is an actual genius, but only a highly-talented person—but rather because she has chosen to set her steps along a path that, for woman at least, is judged to be unnatural and contrary to society's best interests. In Balzac's view, the rôle of a woman, even of a superior one, is to conform to the dictates of society, and to fulfill her function as wife and mother. . . . Camille Maupin ultimately comes to the realization that she has been mistaken in the destiny she has carved for herself. At the end, when she is preparing to enter a convent, this woman, the most forceful, perspicacious and talented of all Balzac's heroines, the only woman who has achieved any form of creative production in her own right,

belatedly realizes the importance of bowing to society's ways. . . . (pp. 239-42)

Balzac does not allot a choice to women. Invariably, when a woman decides to strike out on her own and to defy convention, she comes to grief. A dismal fate awaits Louise de Chaulieu, who . . . embodies a form of rebellion against society's strictures, in contrast to her more conservative friend, Renée de l'Estorade. Although she champions a course of individualism and freedom, ultimately Balzac has her repudiate her nonconformist conduct. In the end, both she and Camille Maupin acknowledge that they have adopted an unwise and unhappy pattern of life. There is no redemption possible, not even in the potential excellence of the work that the female "genius" may produce. (pp. 242-43)

Glory in art and in the realm of intellectual creation is solely a male prerogative. The greatest distinction along these lines for which a woman can hope lies in inspiring and succoring a man of genius. Modeste Mignon is obsessed by the ambition to serve as companion and confidante to a poet or an artist, to devote herself to his comfort and to console him in his moments of martyrdom and solitude. . . . In this way, Modeste feels that she can partake of the genius's reflected glory. (p. 243)

Balzac's attitude concerning woman's rôle vis-à-vis genius is buttressed by his personal experience, especially in the maternal devotion and inspiration of Laure de Berny. . . . Devotion to a great man constitutes the highest destiny for a woman; although this idea is expressed mockingly by the princesse de Cadignan, it is a frequently-repeated tenet of Balzac's belief.

What of the great man himself, the creative genius? Unlike the outstanding individuals whose superiority rests upon a purely material type of power, or on a highly-developed moral character, the man of genius *per se* is occupied primarily in the domain of the intellect; his aspirations and accomplishments lie in the realm of creative activity. Superior though men like Gobseck or Nucingen or de Marsay may be, their "omnipotence" is achieved in their authority over other men, and their "omniscience," so to speak, is of prosaic affairs—the world of high finance, the ins and outs of business, the intimate and sordid details of people's lives, of those who have come to them for aid. On a different plane altogether stand the men of genius, who possess the highest form of intellectual development and spiritual concentration of which a human being is capable.

The first character to appear in Balzac's work who prefigures these later men of genius is the early hero of *Sténie*, Jacob del Ryès, on whom his creator has showered such an abundance of native gifts that these must certainly be interpreted as a naïve form of wish fulfillment on Balzac's part. Del Ryès embodies an ideal of perfection that few subsequent heroes will be able to match; he has multi-faceted accomplishments, being a writer, musician, and philosopher; in addition, he is handsome, wealthy, and successful in love. He appears to be the living personification of Balzac's two greatest desires, "être célèbre et être aimé [to be famous and to be loved]" and in the happy possession of so many attributes, in the realization of the author's fondest hopes, he serves as a model for the two greatest and most successful creative geniuses of the *Comédie humaine*, Daniel d'Arthez and Joseph Bridau. These two men, both artistic creators of the highest rank, illustrate Balzac's message about the early stages of genius and its subsequent development—the irresistible vocation, the poverty-stricken beginnings, the persistent labor, the misunderstanding and lack of appreciation, the triumphant dreams of glory which carry them over the roughest places. Then comes the ultimate, apocalyptic success—the painting hailed as a masterpiece, the book applauded as a classic, the reputation secured, the fortune acquired, even the personal life crowned with love. (pp. 243-45)

The seekers after the absolute are men of genius in equal measure, but their endeavors do not meet with the success that Balzac bestows on the others. Frenhofer, the great theorist of art, the incomparable painter whose technical ability is almost supernaturally perfect, is defeated by his search for ultimate excellence; Gambara, the inspired composer, writes his greatest music when his rational faculties are benumbed by alcohol, and in his lucid state imagines harmonies that are far ahead of his time—with the result that in either case he fails, either in his own eyes or in those of his contemporaries; Balthazar Claës, slave to his love of science, finds that his passion-ridden search for the essential unity of matter comes to an end at the very moment of his death. Louis Lambert embodies to an outstanding degree the intellectual and emotional characteristics essential to the creative genius: the mental brilliance, the prodigious memory, the almost morbid sensitivity, the intuitive faculties that are virtually equivalent to the supernatural endowment of "second sight." In addition, he enjoys supreme qualities of virtue—loyalty, modesty, patience, and innate nobility of soul. His promise is never totally fulfilled, if one accepts the conclusion that he went mad in the end. If, however, one embraces Balzac's mystique of "spécialité," it is possible to say that Lambert achieved the highest goal for which genius can aspire, spiritual absorption into the fundamental unity of the cosmos.

Linking the coterie of creative geniuses with the group of dominant, superior individuals is the protean figure of Vautrin, who in a way partakes of the dynamics of both. With his intelligence, sang-froid, and irresistible will, marshalled to serve a specific philosophy of power, he is the personification of omnipotence, governing as he does both men and events. At the same time, he is an inverted sort of artist; he is the semi-divine and yet semi-satanic creator of men. Instead of inventing creatures of fantasy, like the novelist, products of his mind and his imagination, he works directly from life; the people that he shapes and fashions to his liking are not characters in a book, but live human beings. In this respect, he shares the prerogative of the divinity, and even, in a curious way, surpasses Balzac, his author. For whereas Balzac is confined to an imaginary world, and to the creation of fictional characters, Vautrin works directly in the medium of flesh and blood; he lives in and through the real-life persons whom he is pleased to "create" and to manipulate. Therefore, in a way, he achieves a degree of power that even Balzac, fervent admirer of Napoleon and of his comparable ability to shape men's lives, cannot hope to emulate.

Just as Balzac marks a distinction between talent and genius, as two gradations in the qualities requisite for artistic excellence; just as he differentiates between two levels of genius, performing genius and creative genius; so he establishes a demarcation—not explicitly stated, but discernible in the process of investigation—between the superior individuals who populate his universe in remarkable numbers and the rare men of genius, the creative thinkers. (pp. 245-46)

> *Gretchen R. Besser, in her* Balzac's Concept of Genius: The Theme of Superiority in the "Comédie humaine" *(© 1969 by Librairie Droz), Librairie Droz, 1969, 286 p.*

## ADDITIONAL BIBLIOGRAPHY

Balakian, Anna. "Swedenborgism and the Romanticists." In her *The Symbolist Movement: A Critical Appraisal,* pp. 12-28. New York: Random House, 1967.*
    A brief examination of the romantic and surrealistic elements in Balzac's works. Balakian considers *La Recherche de l'absolu* to be "one of the most illuminating examples of Romanticism in France."

Barthes, Roland. *S/Z.* Translated by Richard Miller. New York: Hill and Wang, 1974, 271 p.
    Analyzes the text of Balzac's story "Sarrasine" and presents Barthes's inquiries into the structure of the story's narrative. This analysis provides, as Richard Howard states in his preface, "a convinced, euphoric, even a militant critique of what it is we do when we read."

Bersani, Leo. "The Taming of Tigers (Balzac and *Le lys dans la vallée*)." In his *Balzac to Beckett: Center and Circumference in French Fiction,* pp. 24-90. New York: Oxford University Press, 1970.
    A detailed study of all of the forms of passion in *Le lys dans la vallée.* Bersani attibutes the success of the novel to Felix and Henriette's ability to contain their desires.

Bertault, Philippe. *Balzac and "The Human Comedy."* Translated by Richard Monges. New York: New York University Press, 1963, 212 p.
    Combines critical insight into Balzac's ideas with an analysis of his technique.

Bowen, Ray P. *The Dramatic Construction of Balzac's Novels.* Eugene, Oreg.: University of Oregon, 1940, 128 p.
    A scholarly treatment of the classical sources and dramatic structure of Balzac's novels.

Brandes, George. "Balzac." In his *Main Currents in Nineteenth Century Literature: The Romantic School in France, Vol. V,* pp. 158-204. New York: The Macmillan Co.; London: William Heinemann, 1906.
    A comprehensive survey of Balzac's life and work that includes biographical information and stylistic and thematic evaluations of his ideas and individual works.

Brooks, Peter. "Balzac: Representation and Signification." In his *The Melodramatic Imagination: Balzac, Henry James, Melodrama, and the Mode of Excess,* pp. 110-52. New Haven, London: Yale University Press, 1976.
    Describes Balzac's melodramatic technique, vision, and ultimate goal. Brooks believes that Balzac aimed, in his art, to "achieve a victory over repression, over ordinary life and reality."

Butor, Michel. "Balzac and Reality." In his *Inventory: Essays,* edited by Richard Howard, translated by Remy Hall, pp. 100-13. New York: Simon and Schuster, 1969.
    A laudatory stylistic discussion that outlines Balzac's means of organizing and representing reality. Butor particularly praises Balzac's use of recurring characters and their ability to authenticate his fictional world.

Dargan, Edwin Preston. *Honoré de Balzac: A Force of Nature.* Chicago: The University of Chicago Press, 1932, 87 p.
    A brief, biographical-critical study presenting Balzac as "a predominant personal force in the writing of fiction, and particularly that type of fiction which is at the same time a sort of social history."

Dargan, E[dwin] Preston, Crain, W.L., and others. *Studies in Balzac's Realism.* Chicago: The University of Chicago Press, 1932, 213 p.
    A collection of studies that defines realism and evaluates the realistic technique of several Balzac novels.

De Casseres, Benjamin. "Balzac: The Clumsy Titan." In his *Forty Immortals,* pp. 163-69. New York: Seven Arts Publishing Co., 1926.
    A description of Balzac's genius.

Duclaux, Mary. "Balzac." In her *The French Procession: A Pageant of Great Writers,* pp. 176-90. London, Leipzig: T. Fisher Unwin, 1909.*

    Identifies and discusses the distinct intellectual and creative skills of Balzac and Sainte-Beuve.

Faguet, Émile. *Balzac.* Translated by Wilfrid Thorley. 1918. Reprint. New York: Haskell House Publishers, 1974, 264 p.

    An appreciative critical study of Balzac's ideas, style, characters, technique, and world view. Faguet concludes with a discussion of Balzac's reputation in late-nineteenth-century France.

Festa-McCormick, Diana. *Honoré de Balzac.* Boston: Twayne Publishers, 1979, 187 p.

    A modern critical survey of Balzac's oeuvre.

Frijling-Schreuder, E.C.M. "Honoré de Balzac—A Disturbed Boy Who Did Not Get Treatment." In *The Literary Imagination: Psychoanalysis and the Genius of the Writer,* edited by Hendrik M. Ruitenbeek, pp. 379-89. Chicago: Quadrangle Books, 1965.

    A psychoanalytic assessment of Balzac's unhappy youth tracing the effect of his upbringing on his later life and creativity.

Frye, Prosser Hall. "Balzac." In his *Literary Reviews and Criticisms,* pp. 19-28. 1908. Reprint. New York: Gordian Press, 1968.

    An essay of mixed views on Balzac's work that praises his humor, vivid portraits, and creativity, and yet censures his sensationalism, style, and lack of form.

Giraud, Raymond. "Balzac the Great Compromiser." In his *The Unheroic Hero in the Novels of Stendhal, Balzac and Flaubert,* pp. 93-131. New Brunswick, N.J.: Rutgers University Press, 1957.

    An investigation of the bourgeois world which is depicted in Balzac's novels.

Gozlan, Léon. *Balzac in Slippers.* Translated by Babette Hughes, Glenn Hughes, Madelaine Boyd, and John O'Neill. New York: Robert M. McBride & Co., 1929, 351 p.

    An early biography, first published in 1865, in which Balzac's close friend affectionately describes their experiences together.

James, Henry. "The Lesson of Balzac." In his *The Question of Our Speech: The Lesson of Balzac; Two Lectures,* pp. 55-116. Boston, New York: Houghton, Mifflin and Co., 1905.

    An astute and imaginative critical essay in which James acknowledges his debt to Balzac.

Kanes, Martin. *Balzac's Comedy of Words.* Princeton, London: Princeton University Press, 1975, 299 p.

    A thematic study that considers the role of language in *La comédie humaine.*

Levin, Harry. "Balzac and Proust." In his *Contexts of Criticism,* pp. 110-30. Cambridge: Harvard University Press, 1958.*

    A stylistic comparison of Balzac and Proust.

Levin, Harry. "Balzac." In his *Gates of Horn,* pp. 150-213. New York: Oxford University Press, 1963.

    A scholarly study of the quality of realism in Balzac's works.

Marceau, Felicien. *Balzac and His World.* Translated by Derek Coltman. New York: The Orion Press, 1966, 548 p.

    A perceptive guide to the characters and themes of *La comédie humaine* by the Belgian novelist and dramatist.

Maurois, André. "Ideal and Sensual Love—Heroines of Balzac." In his *Seven Faces of Love,* translated by Haakon M. Chevalier, pp. 149-74. New York: Didier, 1944.

    A sketch on Balzac's loves and their influence on his life and work. Maurois considers Balzac's female characters to be some of the most psychologically accurate portraits of women in literature.

Maurois, André. *Prometheus: The Life of Balzac.* Translated by Norman Denny. London: The Bodley Head, 1965, 573 p.

    A clear, concise, and accurate biography. In outlining his decision to write this biography, Maurois indicates his awareness of the limitations of the genre: "We know that the works cannot be accounted for by the life, and that the greatest events in the life of a creative artist are his works." Yet Maurois later indicates his view of the importance of the genre as he notes that "by a ceaseless process of osmosis, the acts and thoughts and encounters of Monsieur Honoré de Balzac nourished the *Comédie humaine.* We shall seek to discern some aspects of that mysterious alchemy."

Maurois, André. "Balzac." In his *The Art of Writing,* translated by Gerard Hopkins, pp. 91-115. New York: E. P. Dutton & Co., 1960.

    A study of *César Birotteau* which, according to Maurois, is "one of the finest and most terrible of all the dramas presented in the *Comédie Humaine.*" Maurois praises Balzac's elevation of a simple bourgeois tradesman to a noble tragic figure.

Oliver, E. J. *Honoré de Balzac.* Masters of World Literature Series, edited by Louis Kronenberger. New York: The Macmillan Co.; London: Collier-Macmillan, 1964, 190 p.

    A thematic study of *La comédie humaine* with detailed commentary on several novels.

Peck, Harry Thurston. "Balzac and His Work." *Cosmopolitan* XXVII, No. 3 (July 1899): 238-45.

    Summarizes and defines Balzac's importance at the turn of the century.

Poulet, Georges. "Balzac." In his *The Interior Distance,* translated by Elliott Coleman, pp. 97-152. Baltimore: The Johns Hopkins Press, 1959.

    Analyzes the Balzacian ego and its manifestations in his heroes.

Prendergast, Christopher. *Balzac: Fiction and Melodrama.* London: Edward Arnold, 1978, 205 p.

    Combines a theoretical discussion of Balzac's use of melodrama with detailed textual criticism.

Pritchett, V. S. *Balzac.* New York: Alfred A. Knopf, 1973, 272 p.

    A beautifully illustrated, informative, and well-written biography that is concerned with all aspects of Balzac's life, including his childhood and family, his relations with his publishers and with women, his dream of success, and his obsession with his work. Pritchett considers Balzac a genius.

Pugh, Anthony R. *Balzac's Recurring Characters.* Toronto, Buffalo: University of Toronto Press, 1974, 510 p.

    A comprehensive reference guide to Balzac's recurring characters, tracing their development throughout Balzac's oeuvre.

Royce, William Hobart. *A Balzac Bibliography: Writings Relative to the Life and Works of Honoré de Balzac.* Chicago: The University of Chicago Press, 1929, 464 p.

    An exhaustive listing of Balzac criticism through 1927.

Royce, William Hobart. *Balzac As He Should Be Read.* New York: Auguste Giraldi, 1946, 47 p.

    A short pamphlet by the noted bibliographer of Balzac. This compilation is designed to assist the newcomer to Balzac and lists his works in what Royce considers "their logical order of reading according to *time of action.*"

Sand, George. "Chapter Eleven." In her *My Life,* translated by Dan Hofstadter, pp. 201-18. New York: Harper & Row, Publisher, 1979.*

    A personal reminiscence by the noted French novelist, who was a contemporary and friend of Balzac.

Sandars, Mary F. *Honoré de Balzac: His Life and Writings.* New York: John Lane Co., 1914, 312 p.

    A biography of Balzac, based on his correspondence with *l'Étrangère.* Sandars finds much of his life to be shrouded in mystery.

Weber, Samuel. *Unwrapping Balzac: A Reading of "La Peau de Chagrin."* Toronto: University of Toronto Press, 1979, 180 p.

    A detailed and intricate explication of *La peau de chagrin.* Weber challenges the traditional view of Balzac as a realist.

Yeats, W. B. *"Louis Lambert."* In his *Essays: 1931 to 1936,* pp. 63-74. Dublin: The Cuala Press, 1937.

A speculation on Balzac's metaphysical background and its potential influence on *Louis Lambert*.

Zola, Émile. "Chaudes-Aigues and Balzac" and "Jules Janin and Balzac." In his *The Experimental Novel and Other Essays,* translated by Belle M. Sherman, pp. 330-41, 342-48. 1893. Reprint. New York: Haskell House, 1964.

An examination of the views of two mid-nineteenth-century critics who condemned Balzac's plots, style, and morality. In these essays, Zola belittles Chaudes-Aigues and Jules Janin and the late-nineteenth-century critics of Balzac's naturalism.

Zweig, Stefan. *Balzac*. Translated by William Rose and Dorothy Rose. New York: The Viking Press, 1946, 404 p.

A warm and sympathetic biography that demonstrates Zweig's high regard and affection for Balzac, whom he considered to be "the greatest writer of his age." This work, which Zweig expected to be his *magnum opus*, was left unfinished at the time of his death.

# Vissarion Grigoryevich Belinski

## 1811-1848

(Also transliterated as Vissarión; also Grigorevich, Grigor'-yevich, Grigor'evich, Grigorévich, Grigorevič; also Belinsky, Belínsky, Belinskij, Byelinsky, Byelínsky, Bielinski, Belinskii, Bělinskii) Russian critic, essayist, journalist, dramatist, and poet.

The most influential Russian literary critic of the nineteenth century, Belinski initiated a new trend in critical thought by combining literary appreciation with an exposition of progressive philosophical and social theory. Hailed as the "founder of revolutionary democratic criticism in Russia," he was the primary spokesman in the Russian intelligentsia's campaign against serfdom, autocracy, and orthodox religion. He believed that only works of art could perform the function of educating society, and he stressed the importance of a national literature that would reflect universal humanitarian concerns. "Culture," Belinski wrote, "is the immediate effect of our literature upon the understanding and the morals of society." In the 1840s, his insistence that literature both mirror life and promote social reform formed the theoretical basis of the Natural School in Russian literature.

Belinski was born in Sveaborg, in what is now Finland. In 1816, his family moved to Chembar, a small village in the province of Penza, where his father served as a district physician. At the age of fourteen, after private tutoring in Chembar, Belinski entered the gymnasium at Penza. In 1829, he was admitted to the University of Moscow on a government grant. Though a serious student, Belinski resented academic strictures; he found intellectual stimulation, instead, in the philosophic circle of Nicholas Stankevich and Alexander Herzen. Stankevich and Herzen introduced Belinski to the idealism of Friedrich Schelling, a German romantic philosopher who exercised a profound influence on Belinski in the early part of his career. While still a student, Belinski wrote *Dmitri Kalinin*, a drama in which he severely criticized serfdom. The university censors rejected the drama, labeling it violent and revolutionary, and Belinski was expelled before obtaining his degree. After his expulsion, Nikolai Nadezhdin, a professor at the university and editor of the progressive journal *Teleskop (The Telescope)*, invited Belinski to write for his review.

Belinski's first important essay, "Literaturnye mechtaniia" ("Literary Reveries"), is a survey of Russian literature steeped in the ideas of German romanticism. Expounding on the views of Schelling, Belinski proclaimed that reality was the manifestation of an absolute moral idea. By asserting the supremacy of spiritual values over the material, he called upon the artist, whose source of inspiration was the divine idea itself, to transcend and beautify the visible world. In the early 1830s Belinski advocated the doctrine of "art for art's sake": he acknowledged that literature could be effective as propaganda but first he demanded that it be beautiful.

In 1836, *The Telescope* was suppressed for publishing a subversive article, and Belinski briefly supported himself by tutoring. A year later, with the help of Michael Bakunin, a master dialectician and proponent of German idealism, he founded *Moskovsky Nablyudatel (The Moscow Observer)*. In

1839, the journal failed, and Belinski moved to St. Petersburg where he joined the staff of the influential review *Otechestvennye Zapiski (Notes of the Fatherland)*. Belinski's association with Bakunin resulted in a brief philosophic conversion to the ideas of Georg Wilhelm Friedrich Hegel. Bakunin's misinterpretation of Hegel's axiom, "all existing is rational," led Belinski to defend the existing social order, which he had previously denounced. In reviews of Fedor Glinka's *Sketches on the Battle of Borodino* and Vasili Zhukovsky's "The Anniversary of the Battle of Borodino," published in *Notes of the Fatherland* in 1839, Belinski declared that autocracy and serfdom were necessary phases of evolution. In "Mentsel, kritik Gete" (Menzel, Critic of Goethe), published in *Notes of the Fatherland* in 1840, Belinski set forth an argument for pure art: since, according to Hegel, the real was rational, the artist could not attempt to criticize reality. Late in 1840, Belinski began to doubt the validity of Hegel's theory and, after much deliberation, rejected Hegel in favor of a form of humanitarian socialism.

Belinski was the chief critic for *Notes of the Fatherland* until 1846 when he resigned his post and began to write for *Sovremennik (The Contemporary)*. Critics generally agree that his most memorable contributions to Russian literature were produced in the 1840s. During these years, Belinski's humanitarian socialism determined his approach to literature. He demanded that artists depict life truthfully because he believed that only a realistic portrayal of the social evils existing in Russia could be effective in awakening the national conscience. While Belinski stressed content rather than form in literature, he never failed to praise the beauty of a work of art. In a series of eleven articles on the works of Alexander Pushkin written between 1843 and 1846, Belinski commended Pushkin for his artistic perfection and acknowledged his significant contribution to the progress of Russian literature; but he also relegated his work to a bygone era because of its inadequate representation of reality.

In the last phase of his career Belinski championed Nikolai Gogol, Mikhail Lermontov, and, to some extent, Fedor Dostoevski as heralds of Russia's new naturalistic literature. It was Lermontov's despairing view of life in *A Hero of Our Time* which led Belinski to abandon the theory of "art for art's sake." Subsequently, in a review of Gogol's *Dead Souls*, Belinski praised Gogol for making the sordid and base the subject of literature and for concentrating his attention on Russia's masses. Later, when Gogol published *Selected Passages from Correspondence with Friends,* a reactionary work contradicting Gogol's earlier humanitarian beliefs, Belinski was outraged. He interpreted the work both as a personal betrayal and an apology for the existing social order. In his famous letter, "Pis'mo k Gogolyu" ("To N. V. Gogol, 3 July 1847"), he attacked Gogol for his apostacy and condemned serfdom, autocracy, and orthodoxy. Belinski wrote the letter in Salzbrunn, Germany where he was undergoing treatment for tuberculosis. Freed from the threat of censorship, he was able to express his most radical ideas. Though banned in Russia, the letter was published surreptitiously and became the credo of liberal-minded intellectuals in the last half of the nineteenth century. Despite his disappointment with *Selected Passages,* in Belinski's last article, "Vzglyad na russkuyu literaturu 1847" ("A View on Russian Literature in 1847"), he presented Gogol as Russia's greatest naturalist and the most important figure in modern Russian literature. Twentieth-century critics contend that Belinski overestimated the realism and social import of *Dead Souls* by imposing his own theories upon the novel. He is also criticized for misreading Dostoevski's *Poor Folk* as a novel in the naturalist tradition. Nevertheless, Belinski's conception of naturalism is regarded as the seed of nineteenth-century realism.

The contradictions in Belinski's philosophy has inspired a wide variety of interpretation. Many critics distinguish well-defined periods in Belinski's development; others feel such a rigid classification ignores the fact that Belinski often borrowed ideas from philosophical theories he had supposedly abandoned. In the Soviet Union, on the basis of his atheism and utopian socialist leanings, he is revered as a progressive political thinker whose opinions presaged the approach of Soviet criticism. Elsewhere, his ideologic position continues to arouse debate. A few scholars deny any political motivation on Belinski's part. Some find a unifying thread in Belinski's aesthetics in his continuing search for a definition of reality.

Although Belinski achieved no consistent critical outlook, he is uniformly praised for his sensitivity to artistic perfection and early recognition of some of Russia's finest writers. He is often credited with establishing Pushkin's preeminence in the history of Russian literature. However, his judgments on foreign authors are deemed prejudicial and overly emotional. Belinski's success is partly attributed to his ability to incite enthusiasm for his ideas with the force of his convictions; his

passionate articles earned him the name "furious Vissarion." While modern critics praise his critical insight, they consider Belinski's style verbose and repetitive. Some believe he encouraged neglect of aesthetic standards, and consider him responsible for the inattention to form which characterized Russian journalism in the latter part of the nineteenth century.

Belinski died of tuberculosis on May 26, 1848. Despite the brevity of his life, he changed the tone of Russian literary criticism by broadening it to include the discussion of moral and political questions. Though his disciples, most notably Nikolai Dobrolyubov and Nikolai Chernyshevsky, focused almost exclusively on the utilitarian aspects of his critical theory, Belinski is responsible for shifting the focus of Russian literary criticism from aesthetic considerations to social concerns.

## PRINCIPAL WORKS

"Literaturnye mechtaniia" (essay) 1834; published in journal *Molva*
  ["Literary Reveries" published in *Selected Philosophical Essays,* 1948]
"Mentsel, Kritik Gete" (essay) 1840; published in journal *Otechestvennye Zapiski*
"Pis'mo k Gogolyu" (letter) 1847
  ["To N. V. Gogol, 3 July 1847" published in *Selected Philosophical Essays,* 1948]
"Vzglyad na russkuyu literaturu 1846" (essay) 1847; published in journal *Sovremennik*
  ["A View on Russian Literature in 1846" published in *Selected Philosophical Essays,* 1948]
"Vzglyad na russkuyu literaturu 1847" (essay) 1848; published in journal *Sovremennik*
  ["A View on Russian Literature in 1847" published in *Selected Philosophical Essays,* 1948]
*Dmitri Kalinin [first publication] (drama) 1900?; published in *Polnoye sobraniye sochineii*
*Polnoye sobraniye sochineii.* 13 vols. (essays, drama, and poetry) 1900-48
*Selected Philosophical Essays* (essays) 1948
**Belinsky, Chernyshevsky, and Dobrolyubov* (essays) 1962

*This work was written in 1831.

**This work also includes essays written by Nikolai Chernyshevsky and Nikolai Dobrolyubov.

---

## N. A. DOBROLYUBOV (essay date 1859)

[*Dobrolyubov, a leading radical critic of the mid-nineteenth century, was one of Belinski's chief followers. With Nikolai Chernyshevsky, he embraced Belinski's belief that literature should express progressive social ideals. In this eulogistic essay, Dobrolyubov welcomes the first Russian publication of Belinski's collected works and hails him as the "incarnation" of Russia's social development.*]

Whatever happens to Russian literature, no matter how luxuriantly it may blossom forth, Belinsky will always be its pride, its glory, its adornment. To this day his influence is felt in everything beautiful and noble that appears in our country; to this day every one of our foremost literary men admits that for a considerable part of his development he is indebted, directly or indirectly, to Belinsky. . . .

[No] news that we receive can be so glorious as the news that the works of Belinsky are being published. . . . How many pure and happy moments his essays will recall to our minds—the moments when we were full of youthful, selfless impulses, when Belinsky's vigorous words opened for us an entirely new world of knowledge, reflection and activity! Reading him we forgot the pettiness and vulgarity of everything around us, we dreamed of different people, of different activities, sincerely hoped one day to meet such people and rapturously promised to devote ourselves to such activities. . . . (p. 171)

[On] acquainting themselves with him the readers will be convinced that much of what they admired in others belongs to him, came from him; many of the truths upon which our opinions now rest were asserted by him in a fierce struggle against the ignorance, falsehood and malice of his opponents and amidst the somnolent apathy of an indifferent public. . . . Yes, Belinsky is the incarnation of our highest ideals; and Belinsky is the incarnation of the history of our social development. . . . (p. 172)

> *N. A. Dobrolyubov, "The Works of V. Belinsky" (1859), in his* Selected Philosophical Essays, *edited by M. Yovchuk, translated by J. Fineberg (originally published as* Izbrannye filosofskie proizvedeniia, *edited by M. T. Yovchuk, Gos. izd.-vo. Polit. litri., 1948), Foreign Languages Publishing House, 1956, pp. 171-73.*

### IVAN TURGENEV  (essay date 1869)

[*Belinski's favorable review of Turgenev's poetry in the May, 1843 issue of* Notes of the Fatherland *initiated a friendship between the two which lasted until Belinski's death. Here, Turgenev speaks highly of Belinski and cites his "almost infallible" aesthetic sense, "unusually profound" judgment, and "grasp of what was of major importance at a given juncture" as those qualities which made him a brilliant literary critic.*]

Belinsky undoubtedly possessed the chief qualities of a great critic, and if in the sphere of knowledge and learning he had to fall back on the assistance of his friends and take their words on trust, he had not to seek anyone's advice in the sphere of criticism; on the contrary, others sought his advice; the initiative always remained with him. His aesthetic sense was almost infallible; his judgment was unusually profound and it never became obscure. Belinsky was not deceived by appearances or surroundings, he never submitted to any influences or ideas; he instantly recognized the beautiful and the hideous, the true and the false, and pronounced his verdict with fearless courage, pronounced it outspokenly, without any reservations, warmly and powerfully, with all the impetuosity and assurance of conviction. Anyone who witnessed the mistakes in criticisms made even by men of outstanding intellectual abilities . . . , could not help feeling respect for Belinsky's precise judgment, correct taste and *instinct*, for his ability to 'read between the lines'. . . . [At] the appearance of a new talent, a new novel, poem or short story, no one, either before Belinsky or better than he, ever gave a more correct appraisal or said a truer, or more decisive word. Lermontov, Gogol, Goncharov—was he not the first to point them out and explain their significance? And how many others! (p. 113)

Another remarkable quality of Belinsky as a critic was his grasp of what was of major importance at a given juncture, of what

demanded an immediate solution, of what was going to be 'the talk of the town'. . . . Belinsky realized perfectly well that in the conditions under which he had to work he must never go out of the range of purely literary criticism. . . . [He] saw and understood very clearly that in the development of every people a new literary epoch comes before any other, that without experiencing and going beyond it, it is impossible to move forward, that criticism in the sense of challenging lies and falsehoods must first subject to analysis literary events and—it was precisely *that* that his duty as a writer demanded of him. His political and social views were very strong and decidedly trenchant; but they remained in the sphere of instinctive sympathies and antipathies. I repeat: Belinsky knew that there could be no question of applying them, of putting them into practice; and even if it were possible, he had neither the necessary training nor the necessary temperament for it; he knew that, too, and with the practical understanding of the role he had to play, that was so characteristic of him, he restricted the sphere of his activities himself, confining it within certain set limits. . . . On the other hand, as a *literary* critic he was exactly what the English describe as *the right man in the right place*, which cannot be said of his successors. It is true, though, that their task was much more difficult and more complicated. (pp. 115-16)

It goes without saying that Belinsky's understanding of his time and his vocation did not interfere with the expression of his deepest convictions that could be apprehended in every word of his articles, particularly as his negative activity in the field of criticism was entirely in tune with the role he would most certainly have chosen in a politically developed society. He alone and a few of his friends knew what his feelings and thoughts were, but what he did and what he published was kept rigorously and strictly within the limits of literary values and was devoted to them exclusively. (p. 117)

Another remarkable quality of Belinsky as a critic was that, as the English say, he was always 'in earnest'. He never jested with the object of his researches, nor with his reader, nor with himself, and he would have repudiated the latest all too prevalent fashion of indulging in jeering as unworthy thoughtlessness or cowardice. . . . His irony was very heavy and clumsy; it turned at once into sarcasm and was all too prone to hit the nail on the head. He did not sparkle with wit either in his conversation or with his pen; he did not possess what the French call *esprit;* he did not dazzle by a skilful exhibition of dialectical powers; but he possessed that irresistible force which is the result of honest and unflinching thought, and it expressed itself in an original and, after all, an absorbing fashion. Although completely lacking what is usually described as eloquence and although quite frankly unable and unwilling 'to paint the lily' or indulge in fine phrases, Belinsky was one of the most eloquent of men, if 'eloquence' is to be understood in the sense of a force of conviction. . . . (pp. 123-24)

Belinsky, needless to say, was not an admirer of the principle of 'art for art's sake'; and it could hardly have been otherwise when the whole trend of his thoughts is taken into consideration. (p. 124)

Belinsky was much too intelligent, he had much too much common sense to deny art, to fail to understand not only its great significance, but also its very naturalness, its physiological necessity. Belinsky recognized in art one of the fundamental manifestations of the human personality, one of the laws of our nature, a law whose validity was proved by our daily experience. He did not admit of art only for art's sake in the same way as he would not admit of life only for life's sake; it was not for nothing that he was an idealist. Everything had to serve one principle, art as well as science, but in its own special way. The truly childish and, besides, not new, 'warmed-up' explanation of art as an imitation of nature he would have deemed worthy neither of a reply nor of his attention; and the argument of the superiority of a real apple over a painted one would not have made any impression on him because this famous argument loses any validity the moment we apply it to a well-fed man. Art, I repeat, was for Belinsky as much a legitimate sphere of human activity as science, as society, as the State. . . . But from art as from any other human activity he demanded truth, vital, living truth. . . . In the domain of art, however, he felt at home only in poetry and literature. (pp. 124-25)

Generally speaking, Belinsky's best articles were written at the beginning and towards the end of his literary career; in the middle of it he went through a period lasting two years in the course of which he stuffed himself with Hegelian philosophy and, failing to digest it, kept scattering its axioms, its familiar theses and technical terms . . . everywhere with feverish zeal. . . . But that flood soon subsided, leaving only good seeds behind and Belinsky's splendid, clear and sensible Russian language reappeared once more in all its courageous and artless simplicity. . . . He had no time to polish his style, to weigh and think over every expression, and that was why he willy-nilly became somewhat prolix; but he was far from becoming long-winded. . . . Belinsky's articles, for all their shortcomings, remained literary works and did not become transformed into flaccid conversation pieces, into puffed-up variations on hackneyed themes. . . . (pp. 126-27)

> *Ivan Turgenev, "Reminiscences of Belinsky" (1869), in his* Literary Reminiscences and Autobiographical Fragments, *translated by David Magarshack (reprinted by permission of Farrar, Straus and Giroux, Inc.; copyright © 1958 by Farrar, Straus & Cudahy, Inc.; originally published as* Literaturnye i zhiteishie vospominaniia, *1934), Farrar, Straus and Cudahy, 1958 (and reprinted as* Turgenev's Literary Reminiscences and Autobiographical Fragments, *translated by David Magarshack, Faber and Faber, 1959, pp. 105-39).*

## F. M. DOSTOIEVSKY   (essay date 1873)

[*In the following assessment of Belinski, Dostoevski refers to the breach in his relationship with the critic after Belinski dismissed Dostoevski's novel* The Double *as nonrealistic art because it contained elements of the fantastic. Dostoevski concedes, however, that Belinski possessed "wonderful insight" and an "unusual faculty for becoming profoundly imbued with an idea."*]

My first novel, *Poor People,* delighted [Bielinsky] (subsequently, approximately one year later, we parted for various reasons which, however, were most insignificant in every respect); yet, at the time, during the first days of our acquaintance, having attached himself to me with all his heart, he hastened, with a most naïve precipitancy, to convert me to his creed.

I do not at all exaggerate his ardent attraction to me, at least during the first months of our acquaintance. I found him a passionate socialist, and, straight off the bat, he embarked upon atheism. This, namely, his wonderful insight and his unusual faculty for becoming profoundly imbued with an idea, is to me very significant. Some two years ago, the International

prefaced one of its proclamations with this straightforward, meaningful statement: "Above all, we are an atheistic society"—that is, they started with the very essence of the matter. Such was also Bielinsky's prelude.

Treasuring above everything reason, science and realism, at the same time he comprehended more keenly than anyone that reason, science and realism alone can merely produce an ant's nest, and not social "harmony" within which man can organize his life. He knew that moral principles are the basis of all things. He believed, to the degree of delusion and without any reflex, in the new moral foundations of socialism (which, however, up to the present revealed none but abominable perversions of nature and common sense). Here was nothing but rapture. Still, as a socialist, he had to destroy Christianity in the first place. He knew that the revolution must necessarily begin with atheism. He had to dethrone that religion whence the moral foundations of the society rejected by him had sprung up. Family, property, personal moral responsibility—these he denied radically. . . . Doubtless, he understood that by denying moral responsibility of man, he thereby denied also his freedom; yet, he believed with all his being . . . that socialism not only does not destroy the freedom of man, but, on the contrary, restores it in a form of unheard-of majesty, only on a new and adamantine foundation.

At this juncture, however, there remained the radiant personality of Christ himself to contend with, which was the most difficult problem. As a socialist, he was duty bound to destroy the teaching of Christ, to call it fallacious and ignorant philanthropy, doomed by modern science and economic tenets. Even so, there remained the beatific image of God-man, its moral inaccessibility, its wonderful and miraculous beauty. But in his incessant, unquenchable transport, Bielinsky did not stop even before this insurmountable obstacle. . . . (pp. 6-7)

With this warm faith in his idea, Bielinsky was, of course, the happiest of all human beings. Oh, in vain it was said later that had Bielinsky lived longer, he would have joined the Slavophile doctrine. He would never have ended with that. Perhaps, he would have ended by emigrating, that is, if he had lived longer and if he could have managed to emigrate; if so, now, he, a tiny and enraptured little old fellow, with his original warm faith precluding any slightest doubt, would be hanging around somewhere at conventions in Germany and Switzerland, or he might have enlisted as adjutant to some German Madame Hegg, rendering petty services in connection with some feminine problem. (p. 8)

> *F. M. Dostoievsky, "Old People," in his* The Diary of a Writer, Vol. I, *edited and translated by Boris Brasol (translation copyright 1949 Charles Scribner's Sons; copyright renewed 1976 Maxwell Fassett, Executor of the Estate of Boris Brasol; reprinted with permission of Charles Scribner's Sons; originally published as* Dnevnik pisatelia, *1873), Charles Scribner's Sons, 1949 (and reprinted by George Braziller, 1954), pp. 4-9.*

## P. V. ANNENKOV   (essay date 1880)

[*Annenkov, a Russian critic of the mid-nineteenth century, was a contemporary and intimate friend of Belinski, Nikolai Gogol, Alexander Herzen, and Mikhail Bakunin. His memoirs of the decade beginning in 1839, which focus on Belinski's activities, were originally published in the liberal periodical* Vestnik Evropy, *Nos. 1-5, 1880. In his study of Belinski's ideological development, Annenkov concentrates on those factors that influenced*

*Belinski to abandon Georg Wilhelm Friedrich Hegel's basic principle of the identity of reality with truth and reason. He concludes that Belinski was ultimately concerned with "forging Russian life into a full-fledged worker for enlightenment, in endowing it with all the powers and educative principles which formed Europe's best and surest workers."*]

[Belinsky's **"Literary Reveries—An Elegy in Prose"**] attracted attention owing to the verve with which it was written and the way it characterized periods and personalities, making them quite unlike their usual and, so to speak, canonical presentation in our literature courses. The lyrical tone of the article plus a philosophical coloring borrowed from Schelling's system gave it particular originality. It was all youth, daring, fervor, as well as full of blunders which the author himself subsequently acknowledged. But everything about it did reveal the fact that new intellectual demands on Russian literature and on Russian life in general had arisen. (p. 1)

The boldness of the article consisted not so much in its investigations as in the principles and postulates to which the critic gave voice and which underlay his investigations. The article tended, rather, to place persons and things under threat of exposure, making good that threat with respect only to a very few of them. (p. 2)

[Belinsky] was in these early stages still just an echo of all the views, judgements, and criticisms existing at the core of the [Moscow circle of intellectuals] and existing without the slightest suspicion of their disparity and incompatibility. That is why Belinsky's ecstatic article, with its distinctive erraticalness, its tendency to fly off in all directions, and lack of central focus, could constitute a mixture, still unconscious, of states of mind having the least possible affinity with and resemblance to one another. A purely Slavophile idea and an idea of a purely Western variety advanced side by side. . . . (pp. 2-3)

The liberalism of the amorphous circle of friends was also represented in the article, and represented quite fully by the proposition lying at its very basis, according to which our literature was a matter of the chance emergence and conjunction of a few people, some more, some less talented, of whom society had no special need and who themselves could get along materially and morally without society. (pp. 3-4)

In short, Belinsky's famous first article, his maiden speech, perfectly expressed the intellectual condition of the young people of the time, in whom trends of every description lived at close quarters with one another as if in some primordial paradise, seeing no cause for disassociation and having no apprehensions about their mutual cordiality and intimacy. The bond uniting them was an identical love of learning, of the world, of free thought, of homeland. (p. 4)

Belinsky's work, the work of his thought inspired to seek constantly ideals of morality and the grand philosophical solution to life's problems—this work went on without abating. . . . It must be accounted a piece of extreme good fortune that the censors of the day missed seeing in the Belinsky of those early stages a moral philosopher who, under pretext of analyzing works of Russian literature, was concerned exclusively with attempts to discover sound conceptual bases on which a rationally ordered personal and social existence could be built. (p. 6)

The first attempt to treat the constituents of the Moscow intellectual circle critically and to subject the circle to an analysis that would have the result of sorting out the diverse elements composing it was laid down . . . by Belinsky in [an article

entitled] **"On the Literary Criticism and Views of the *Moscow Observer*."** As a polemic, this article belongs among the masterpieces of the author; with respect to the vividness of its colors and the high relief of its conclusions, it has not lost, we believe, a certain degree of interest even today. (p. 15)

[In] a review of F. N. Glinka's book, *Sketches of the Battle of Borodino* and a bibliographical account of Zhukovsky's "The Anniversary of Borodino" [Belinsky] believed that he was merely making logically correct deductions from Hegel's basic principles and impeccably applying them to living fact, to reality. . . .

Belinsky had the idea of using the unveiling of the Borodino monument to affirm the wisdom of the Hegelian aphorism on the identity of Reality with Truth and Reason and to analyze the fertile sum and substance of that postulate. But from the very first . . . it became apparent that excessive generalization of the rule could lead to outlandish conclusions, to stark and egregious misconceptions. (p. 18)

[In **"Menzel, Critic of Goethe"**], subduing with all the force of his contempt the low-caliber minds that minutely picked over what pleased and what displeased them in the panorama of history, Belinsky established special rights and privileges, even a special morality, for great artists, great lawmakers, for geniuses in general, who were empowered to devise special roads for themselves and to lead their contemporaries and all mankind along those roads without regard for their protests, perturbations, sympathies and antipathies. No more complete a withdrawal in favor of the privileged and elect of Fate could possibly be professed. Admittedly, the article was written with vigor and expertise and did contain a number of valid comments, now part of our common fund of knowledge, such as, for instance, his comment on the aptness and historical importance of unpremeditated feeling among the masses of the people and his comment about the intimate connection always obtaining between the strivings of great minds and the instincts of society, and the like. However, all this could not mitigate the article's fundamental, sophistical character as an attempt at complete suppression of critical attitudes toward social questions. (pp. 19-21)

[Traces of Belinsky's] ordeal of initiation [into Hegel's logic] are in evidence in his articles of 1838. His style of writing, formerly exuberant and spontaneous, became, in the *Moscow Observer* of 1838, irresolute and nebulous, as if it were withering under the strain of its preoccupation with philosophical terms, their explication . . . , their adaptation into Russian and interpretation of their meaning for the Russian reading public. At times, this weak and nondescript style of writing did attempt to take on a semblance of spontaneity, did attempt to conceal the scholastical bonds hampering its free movement and to make a show of being bold and free despite the chain with which it had consented to be bound. These were flashes corresponding to . . . momentary protests against [Hegel's] theory. . . . On the whole, however, the *Moscow Observer*, as Belinsky's organ, beginning in 1838, presented a woeful picture, over the course of several months, of that extraordinary and unique thinker in the humiliating position of an initiate suffering exhaustion and debilitation under the impact of a cruel intellectual discipline that, though it was draining his strength, he stubbornly persisted in imposing on himself and refused to regard as punishment. (pp. 29-30)

[Contrary] to the whole tenor and all the conclusions of the [Hegelian] doctrine which Belinsky had accepted and made his own, propositions smacking of heresy kept bursting forth from under his pen. Through these heretical outbursts, with their suggestion of rebellion against principles oppressive to his intellect, were expressed Belinsky's critical powers, powers temporarily held in check and kept in hiding, awaiting the end of the philosophical pogrom before coming out in the open once again in all their brilliance. (p. 35)

[It] also happened during this same period that Belinsky would bring to bear, in his struggle against oppressive conditions of metaphysical despotism, not merely outbursts and sporadic activations of his critical faculty but also whole carefully thought-out judgments and verdicts that went against the grain of the theory and all its interpreters. (p. 36)

[In **"The Russian Tale and the Tales of Gogol"**] he did not give advice to [Gogol], did not sort out what in the author was worthy of praise and what deserving censure, did not criticize some feature on the grounds of doubtful accuracy or relevance for the work and approve another as contributing to the work's pleasure and profit. Instead, basing himself on the essence of Gogol's talent and the *worthiness of his view of life*, he simply announced that, in Gogol, Russian society had a *great writer* in the offing. (p. 41)

It can well be supposed that Belinsky was using Gogol to test the fundamental principles, distinctive features and elements of Russian life, and was anxious to clarify where the artist's works stood with respect to his, Belinsky's, own philosophical views and how they could be made compatible. We must here take note that it is extremely difficult to date the change and radical shift in Belinsky's outlook with any accuracy. . . . [The] influences of his friends—Lermontov and Gogol figure not inconsiderably. . . . Under the effect of the poet of real life, such as Gogol was then, Belinsky's philosophical optimism was bound to disintegrate once he compared it with pictures of Russian reality. No logical strategies could have helped avoid disaster—he had either to concur with the artist from whom he could expect many more new works in the same spirit or to abandon him as a writer who failed to understand the life he was depicting. Moreover, Gogol's criticisms crowned a series of criticisms incited earlier by the very nature of life around him and Belinsky's own critical intelligence. Of course, Gogol was not at all responsible for giving Belinsky a truer conception of Hegel's famous formula about the identity of Reality and Reason which liberated his mind from a philosophical delusion, but Gogol did drive the point home. And it was in that way Gogol repaid the critic for all that he had received from him toward clarifying his true professional calling. (pp. 43-4)

Belinsky's superb analysis in 1840 of the novel *Hero of Our Time* remains the monument of his efforts at construing Lermontov's attitude of mind in the best sense. In it, saving Pechorin from being charged with the wild and erratic behavior, the cynical escapades of a relentlessly swaggering and self-justifying egotism, which would have made him an anti-aesthetic and so, according to Belinsky's theory, also immoral figure, Belinsky found an hypothesis able to supply a key to the rational explanation of the hero's most heinous acts. What Belinsky wrote, accordingly, was a consummately artful and eloquent, purely legalistic defense of Pechorin. The hypothesis he found consisted in the idea that Pechorin was not yet a complete man, that he was undergoing phases of his own development which he took to be the ultimate conclusion of his life, and that he himself misjudged himself, imagining that he

was a dire creature born only to be the executioner of his fellow men and the polluter of any kind of human existence. (p. 46)

[Lermontov] never said a single word without its reflecting a feature of his personality in the process of its formation. . . . He forged straight ahead and showed no intention at all of changing his haughty, scornful, and, at times, cruel attitudes toward the phenomena of life in favor of some other, more just and humane conception of them. Prolonged observation of that personality, as well as of others akin to it in the West, cast into Belinsky's soul the first seeds of that later doctrine which recognized that the time of pure lyric poetry, of sheer pleasure over the images, spiritual revelations, and inventions of creative art, had passed and that the only poetry belonging to our age was the poetry reflecting its disjointedness, its spiritual ailments, the deplorable state of its conscience and its spirit. (p. 47)

The aesthetic articles . . . which followed the Menzel article were the fruit of his Petersburg meditations. Glimmers of Belinsky's former orientation still adhered in many of their passages, but it was with these articles that the extraordinary critic reemerged into the literary arena in full possession of his thought and his engaging style. All his abilities, the whole force of his congenital literary perspicacity awoke. His articles were no mere periodical reviews—they were virtually events of the literary world of the time. All of them helped establish new points of view on things; they were read voraciously; they made a deep, indelible impression on the contemporary reading public . . . despite whatever traces of former, not wholly relinquished, beliefs might have been found in them and despite the fact that the author himself subsequently renounced certain of their propositions and verdicts on account of their immoderate gusto and excessive loftiness. Belinsky the critic-artist was genuinely a man of power and authority who was able to bring others under his sway. . . . [Each of his 1840 reviews after the Menzel article] conducted a sort of masterful dissection of the work considered—the work's whole inner structure was laid bare with a vividness and tangibleness that provided a pleasure sometimes equal to, and sometimes even exceeding, the pleasure one experienced reading the original work itself. It was a reproduction of the work, only a work now refracted, so to speak, through the soul and aesthetic sensibility of the critic and acquiring from this contact a new life, a greater freshness, and a profounder expression.

Thus, in his artistic-aesthetic criticism of 1840, Belinsky found a way out of the entanglement of his philosophical dogmatism. (p. 48)

Perhaps nowhere else did the most striking qualities of Belinsky's aesthetic criticism . . . find expression to so marked a degree as in [his] analysis of [Gogol's] *Inspector General,* wherein Belinsky contrasted the play with [Aleksandr Griboyedov's] *Woe from Wit*. In it, Khlestakov's every impulse and those of the mayor, his wife, his daughter, indeed of the comedy's cast of characters altogether, were perused with the perseverance of a theoretician-psychologist solving a knotty problem which someone has posed him. Each intimation of their personalities, often consisting in some single word or momentary feature, was seized upon with an inspiration equivalent, one might say, to the artist's own. The whole progression of the author's creative thinking was analyzed to the nth degree, and the reader of the article cannot help feeling that he is present in some laboratory of criticism where all the designs, devices, and pervasive schemes of the artist's craftsmanship are precipitated before his eyes. It was as if the secrets of another man's work did not exist for Belinsky. (p. 50)

By the end of 1840, Belinsky had ceased deriving moral good from the complete abrogation of one's own personality, of one's "I," and the transference of one's whole self into the expanse of infinite *love,* as was the case in his first (Schellingian) period of development; nor did it consist in the *understanding* of one's own self as the highest creative factor in the activity of Universal Reason and Supreme Idea, as was its Hegelian interpretation. Infinite *love* and absolute *understanding* of one's spiritual essence as principles out of which issued all the precepts of life were supplanted by a different and single agent. Now, moral good for Belinsky consisted in the aesthetic cultivation of one's own self, i.e., in acquiring a sensibility for the True, the Good, and the Beautiful, and developing an invincible, organic revulsion for ugliness of any shape or kind. . . . It was his belief that study of the basic ideas in the creative works of true artists could serve as a good device for elevating one's self to the level of Rational Man and Purified Personality. For him, all these basic ideas were, at the same time, revelations of the moral world. From analysis and assimilation of them, society would experience little by little the emergence of a moral code, an unwritten code, without marble tablets or charters, but one better able than those others to take hold in the individual consciousness and better able to bring order to a man's inner way of life and, through the individual man, to the way of life of whole generations. To this informal code of moral precepts, each new artist of genius would contribute, so to speak, some new feature, some new detail, culled directly from observation and definition of elements of man's spiritual nature. Side by side with existing and functioning, written and unwritten, necessary and unnecessary laws of communal life and good order, another law would take shape, immeasurably more luminous, rational and serious, which people aesthetically developed would follow. A man cultivated on the world view of great artists, poets, philosophers, thinkers ultimately would become capable of creativity himself in the domain of moral ideas, would discover new principles of truth and promulgate them, submitting to them in his own behavior and making others do likewise. Belinsky came upon a great many profound ideas on this ground, abandoned by him in the final stage of his career for a different one. . . . (pp. 58-9)

It is essential to bear in mind that Belinsky had completely adopted, for his own use, Hegel's division of moral principles into two realms: the *ethical (Moralitat),* to which he relegated more or less well-conceived rules of communal life, and *morals* proper *(Sittlichkeit),* which, in his conception, embraced the very laws governing man's spiritual world and engendered ethical needs and notions. Having become the sponsor of those ideas in Russian life, Belinsky began his long and noble campaign of assailing what he called moralizing or moral sophistry in literature and in the various manifestations of our society generally. When his graphic and straightforward style of writing returned to him after something of a hiatus, he pursued incessantly his vigilant campaign of running down moral sophistry, which had then assumed a position of dominance with us in the theater, in all branches of literature and life, seeing that it served people as a means whereby they could hide their spiritual nakedness and attempt to delude themselves and others on the matter of their moral vacuity. Everything smacking of seemly but, in fact, dastardly moralizing rhetoric, with its desire to supplant obvious facts with a specious interpretation of them; everything bearing the stamp of wishy-washy, vacuous sententiousness calculated to obtain by cheap means, without

trouble or effort, a reputation for honesty and decency; everything, finally, smacking of Chinese kow-towing to the good old days and fanatic loathing for the efforts of the new age— all these things were stigmatized by Belinsky with the tag "moralizing" or "moral sophistry," and were assailed by him with a courage truly extraordinary for those days. (p. 60)

Belinsky so insinuated himself, we venture to put it, into the authors he studied that he was continually discovering their covert, unuttered thought, continually correcting them when they forsook or deliberately obscured it, and continually divulging their ultimate expression, which they themselves were afraid or unwilling to make. Revelations of that sort were the strongest side of his criticism. Thus, in many foreign, predominantly economic and social writers, he surmised the direction they would or must take. . . . And as concerns people active in Russian affairs, it hardly needs to be said that he almost infallibly defined their entire future activity on the basis of the first signs they supplied of it. (p. 105)

The position he took on the Slav question had the same source as the position he chose regarding things Slavic in general. The reason for his negative attitude toward the question was once again his assumption that it screened an attempt to glorify unsophisticated national cultures and an effort, with some hope now of success, to oppose them to the consciously elaborated principles of European thought. Indeed, the attempt this time could rely on that spontaneous sympathy for oppressed ethnic groups and peoples, which was bound to exist, and did exist, among the Russian public. No one was more predisposed to sympathy of that kind than Belinsky, but at the thought that there might be a scheme here—a scheme to elevate modest folk creativity with its superstitions, delusions, and unconscious flashes of truth to a level equal to, or even higher than, the carefully thought out bases and principles of European sophistication—at that thought alone Belinsky dismissed all other considerations. . . . (p. 110)

[Belinsky's adversaries] declared him a petty and scarcely *altogether unself-seeking* centralist and bureaucrat. He indeed was a centralist, but not in the sense which his enemies maintained—not in favor of some already existent order of things, but in favor of that distant order of things which he conceived in the form of a union of all the nations of Europe on the grounds of one common civilization under the aegis of one set of laws for rational existence. . . .

In his ecstatic exposition of his hopes for the development of Europe Belinsky deluded himself about many things, as time proved, but he deluded himself valorously. . . . Belinsky was so jealously protective of the good accumulated by the old and the new European civilization that he looked with mistrust at exemplary and extraordinary works of cultures other than, and alien to, Europe and was very reserved in his comments about them. (p. 111)

Yet, however important all these questions may have been and however striking the polemic to which they gave rise, they could not for a minute overshadow in Belinsky's eyes the purely Russian question which for him had then become wholly focussed on one name, Gogol, and on Gogol's novel *Dead Souls*. This novel afforded criticism the only arena in which it could contend with an analysis of things pertaining to social life and mores; and Belinsky held fast to Gogol and his novel as to some sudden and unexpected assistance. It seemed as if he considered it the mission of his life to make the content of *Dead Souls* immune to any supposition that it harbored in it anything other than a true picture, artistically, spiritually, and ethnographically speaking, of the contemporary situation of Russian society. He exerted all the powers of his critical mind in the effort to repudiate and destroy attempts to entertain any conclusions from the famous novel other than, and tending to mitigate, the harsh, ruthlessly critical conclusions that directly issued from it. After all his digressions into the region of European literatures, into the region of Slavdom and the like, he returned from the field of those more or less successful battles to his perennial, domestic cause once again, all the more invigorated by his preceding campaigns. The domestic cause in question consisted primarily in routing from the literary arena once and for all, if possible, both the irresponsible, venal, and self-centered revilers of Gogol's epic and also its ecstatic partisans who claimed to see in it something other than that for which it actually allowed. He tirelessly pointed out, both by word of mouth and in print, what the right attitudes toward it were, urging his auditors and readers at every opportunity to think over, but to do so seriously and sincerely, the question as to why types of such repulsiveness as were brought out in the novel made their appearance in Russia, why such incredible happenings as were related in it could come about in Russia, why such statements, opinions, views as it conveyed could exist in Russia without horrifying anyone.

Belinsky believed that a conscientious answer to those questions could become, for a man who made the effort, a program of action for the rest of his life, and especially could have the effect of laying a solid foundation for his mode of thinking and for a proper judgment about himself and others.

To this same time also belongs the appearance in Russian letters of the so-called "Natural school" which ripened under the influence of Gogol—Gogol interpreted in the way Belinsky interpreted him. One could well claim that the real father of the Natural school was—Belinsky. This school had nothing else in mind than to point up those details of contemporary and cultural life which could not yet be pointed out and analyzed in any other way, whether by political or by scientific investigation. Let us note, incidentally, that the term "Natural" was given the school by the coryphaeus of the pompous, trite, and pseudo-beneficent interpretation of Russian life, Bulgarin, but out of enmity for Belinsky it was welcomed and adopted even by persons deeply averse to Bulgarin's literary and critical activity. It is still today in common use among us despite its origin and its meaninglessness. (pp. 112-13)

Belinsky inclined more and more toward avowing the great importance of what he called "belles lettres," that variegated, clever, and absorbing body of semi- and nonfiction such as existed in all European countries, constituting just as vital an element of their social development as works of imaginative literature, and often serving as a guidebook to the understanding of the latter. This introduction, on Belinsky's part, of a new factor into the domain of art and his equipping it with citizenship papers did not amount to betraying the critic's earlier positions in 1840-45, but only to something supplementing them. . . . To desire the rise of belles lettres and not to give them the significance of ultimate judge of all contemporary problems meant, for Belinsky, simply to desire an exchange of ideas, and a sorting out of essential materials in expectation of a solution of those problems by science and creative art when their time comes. The first stirrings of such belles lettres Belinsky discerned precisely in [Herzen's *Who is at Fault*], a fact which he once made public in an analysis of it where, without attaching any artistic importance to it, he placed it very

high as the work of an intelligent, observant, and cultivated man. (pp. 148-49)

What was new and peculiar was the critic's recognition that society's preceptors were now not only the geniuses or the major talents, as was the case before, but also the whole nameless mass of men of letters and men of public affairs engaged in dealing with the issues of their life and age to the best of their ability and understanding. (p. 149)

The disagreement [between the "Slavs" and the "Europeans"] amounted ultimately to the question of the cultural capabilities of the Russian people, and this question proved to be so formidable that it laid down an impassable demarcation line between the parties. (p. 157)

[By 1846 Belinsky] could no longer help but see that the doctrine on nationality, as a factor leading to a change of the prevailing conditions of national existence, had a very serious side to it; only on the basis of that doctrine was the possibility afforded of speaking of the mistakes made by Russian society in detriment to the honor and dignity of the state. (p. 159)

No later than 1847, Belinsky was . . . speaking of the absurdity of opposing nationality to the universal development of mankind, as if these two things were supposed, without fail, to exclude one another whereas in fact they constantly coincided. The universal development of mankind could not express itself otherwise than through one or another nationality, the terms were even unthinkable one without the other. He developed his idea in detail in the article, **"Survey of Literature in 1846."** . . . [Belinsky expounded] the view that just as an individual, who has not stamped the imprint of his own spirit and own substance on the ideas and notions he has come by, would never be an influential person, so also a nation which has failed to communicate some special, unique mark and expression to the moral bases of human existence would always remain an inert mass usable for the performance on it of any sort of experiment. (p. 160)

Belinsky's famous letter to Gogol which has now lost much of its original color . . . in its own time rang out through intellectual Russia like a trumpet blast. Who would believe that, when Belinsky wrote it, he was no longer the champion in search of battles that he once had been, but, on the contrary, a man half subdued who had lost his faith in the value of literary feuds, journalistic polemics, treatises on the trends of Russian thought, and reviews aimed at destroying more or less rickety literary reputations? His thinking had already turned to a sphere of ideas of another order and was concerned with the new, emerging definitions of the rights and obligations of man, with the new *truth* proclaimed by economic doctrines which was liquidating all notions of the old, displaced truth about the moral, the good, and the noble on earth, and was putting in their place formulas and theses of a purely rational character.

Belinsky had long since become interested . . . in these manifestations of the spirit of inquiry of modern times, but he never gave a thought to any application of them to the Russian world, where not so much as the alphabet for deciphering and understanding their language as yet existed. He had only come to the conclusion that the activity of developing the individual person in search of latitude and freedom for his thought must be accompanied by participation, to the furthest possible degree, in the study of the properties and elements of that stream of political and social ideas into which the civilization and culture of Europe had now been cast. It was for the sake of facilitating this work, indispensable for any, however slightly, thinking and *conscientious* person, that Belinsky had begun considering the idea that Russian literature should be the place to establish the fundamental points of view on European affairs from which the independent work of criticism and free investigation of all their content could begin in Russia.

There was only one thing that Belinsky could not abide: his composure and coolheaded deliberation abandoned him the instant he encountered a judgment which, on the pretext of the indefiniteness or questionableness of European theories, disclosed a covert intention to disparage the efforts and initiatives of the epoch, to ignore the integrity of its strivings, and to cover all its work with ridicule on the basis of precisely those obsolete traditions responsible for bringing everybody to the present state of affairs. On coming across rhetoricians or defamers of such a sort, Belinsky would lose his temper, and Gogol's book, *Correspondence with Friends*, was, as everyone knows, thoroughly permeated with a spirit of distrust and an outrageous contempt for the contemporary intellectual movement, which, moreover, he poorly understood. In addition, it served potentially as a brake on plans for peasant reforms then emerging in Russia. . . . (pp. 207-08)

[With] his new attitude of mind, the perturbations and squabbles of the Russian literary circles, in which Belinsky had quite recently taken so lively a part, retreated to the background. . . . He had so far departed from the frame of mind of the circle that he found it possible to be fair, and he finally rid himself of all his deep-rooted, virtually obligatory aversions which formerly were accounted literary and political duties. (p. 209)

Belinsky's whole outlook consisted in the conception of life and civilization as forces ordained to furnish man with the *fullness of spiritual and material existence*. He judged the relative merit and importance of epochs, of people and their works, according to the quantity of ideas and notions able to promote the realization of that fullness of rational existence which hovered before his eyes in the form of an ideal. Any reservation, omission, or concealment of any one of the elements essential for the attainment of that fullness, whether a premeditated act or the consequence of oversight, equally aroused his critical alertness. He himself constantly and conscientiously undertook the analysis and definition of genuine and spurious psychological and social agents claiming to satisfy all the needs of the mind and of development. In his evaluation of the one and the other kind, he was liable to be excessively excitable at times and to classify their colors, under the influence of enthusiasm or indignation, with a certain lack of proportion, but the documents on which his judgment was based were always authentic ones, fortified with the evidence of history and by rigorous investigations of the science concerned with the ideal and real needs of human nature. The satisfaction of these needs, without intentional exclusions prompted by the calculations and requirements of various theoretical constructs, was what he considered the task of civilization and its mission. Turning from general expression to the particular applications of this same outlook, it should be said that Belinsky demanded of each idea, image, doctrine, and literary work in general that came to his attention a fullness of content eliminating the very possibility of questions and supplements. But such totally integrated manifestations of art and thought were rare occurrences, and for the most, one had to make do with works which were far more notable for their number of omissions rather than of discoveries in the area of themes they had selected. Strictly speaking, all his literary criticism—no matter how hard it tried to hide behind diplomatic qualifications and evasions, to which Belinsky, as

the times required, had recourse no less than anybody else—was, in fact, nothing but a series of reinstatements, restorations, and justifications for various forgotten or artificially debased features of civilization, psychological and cultural necessities of individual and communal existence. This work became part of Belinsky's habitual thought and—what is particularly important—was often directed by him onto his own person, which fact readily explains his frequent changes of points of view on things that so astonished and perturbed his enemies. (pp. 220-21)

What was it that motivated this aesthetician par excellence? Of course, primarily his noble heart in search of means to render assistance to the primary, urgent needs of progress, a progress that had still not even begun for the mass of his fellow countrymen, and, after that, the whole selfsame search for the fullness of an ideal and real model for life and thought. Behind this supposed literary activity, there opened for him the whole vast field of European civilization with its elaborations and accretions gained over the course of so many centuries. He never took his eyes from it. Not a single one of the experiments—old or new—that had been applied there, not a single positive result already given by those experiments would this passionate soul have been willing to do without. The final goal of all his requirements and guidance consisted in forging Russian life into a full-fledged worker for enlightenment, in endowing it with all the powers and educative principles which formed Europe's best and surest workers. (p. 222)

> *P. V. Annenkov, in his* The Extraordinary Decade, *edited by Arthur P. Mendel, translated by Irwin R. Titunik (copyright © by The University of Michigan 1968; originally published as* Literaturnye vospominaniya, *1960), University of Michigan Press, 1968, 281 p.*

**P. KROPOTKIN**  (lecture date 1901)

To say that Byelínskiy . . . was a very gifted art-critic would . . . mean nothing. He was in reality, at a very significant moment of human evolution, a teacher and an educator of Russian society, not only in art—its value, its purport, its comprehension—but also in politics, in social questions, and in humanitarian aspirations. (p. 288)

When Byelínskiy first began to write he was entirely under the influence of the idealistic German philosophy. He was inclined to maintain that Art is something too great and too pure to have anything to do with the questions of the day. It was a reproduction of "the general idea of the life of nature." Its problems were those of the Universe—not of poor men and their petty events. It was from this idealistic point of view of Beauty and Truth that he exposed the main principles of Art, and explained the process of artistic creation. . . .

Holding such abstract views, Byelínskiy even came, during his stay at Moscow, to consider, with Hegel, that "all that which exists is reasonable," and to preach "reconciliation" with the despotism of Nicholas I. However, under the influence of Hérzen and Bakúnin, he soon shook off the fogs of German metaphysics. . . . (p. 289)

Under the impression produced upon him by the realism of Gógol, whose best works were just appearing, he came to understand that true poetry *is* real: that it must be a poetry of life and of reality. And under the influence of the political movement which was going on in France he arrived at advanced political ideas. He was a great master of style, and whatever he wrote was so full of energy, and at the same time bore so truly the stamp of his most sympathetic personality, that it always produced a deep impression upon his readers. And now all his aspirations towards what is grand and high, and all his boundless love of truth, which he formerly had given in the service of personal self-improvement and ideal Art, were given to the service of man within the poor conditions of Russian reality. He pitilessly analysed that reality, and wherever he saw in the literary works which passed under his eyes, or only felt, insincerity, haughtiness, absence of general interest, attachment to old-age despotism, or slavery in any form—including the slavery of woman—he fought these evils with all his energy and passion. He thus became a political writer in the best sense of the word at the same time that he was an art-critic; he became a teacher of the highest humanitarian principles. (pp. 289-90)

> *P. Kropotkin, "Political Literature, Satire, Art-Criticism, Contemporary Novelists" (originally part of a series of lectures delivered at The Lowell Institute, Boston, in March, 1901), in his* Russian Literature, *McClure, Phillips & Co., 1905 (and reprinted by Benjamin Blom, 1967), pp. 263-317.**

## THOMAS GARRIGUE MASARYK   (essay date 1913)

[*Masaryk rejects the theory that Belinski's ideological development can be divided into separate, mutually exclusive periods and posits that Belinski's theory of aesthetics is a mixture of the ideas of German idealism and Russian realism. He stresses that Belinski's belief in the importance of a national literature is not peculiar to the Slavophile doctrine; rather, his conception of nationalism in literature is firmly grounded in the ideas of the German romantic philosophers Friedrich Schelling and Georg Wilhelm Friedrich Hegel.*]

It was Bělinskii's way to take up new foreign ideas with great enthusiasm, but this enthusiasm was soon succeeded by a phase of sober criticism. During the stage of transition he was apt in his literary compositions to continue to expound his older views, whilst in letters and conversations the new faith was already fermenting. Letters and criticisms must therefore be weighed one against the other, for whereas in the letters things are cooked over a hot fire, in the criticisms they are served comparatively cold. Hence the interpretation of Bělinskii is difficult, and divergent opinions are possible. Moreover, about persons his views were liable to frequent and rapid changes.

Some biographers and literary historians distinguish three periods in Bělinskii's development. The first, extending to the year 1840, was that in which he was engaged in the recognition of reality, with Hegel's assistance. From 1840 to 1847 he was devoted to the struggle for western culture and social institutions. In 1847 occurred a sort of slavophil conversion, leading to a campaign on behalf of nationality.

This classification is extremely superficial. As regards the third period, it is obvious that a recognition of the importance of nationality is not peculiar to slavophilism. We need only recall that in 1847 appeared the [*Letter to Gogol*] directed against Gogol, a convert to Orthodoxy, for this will suffice to convince us that Bělinskii was no slavophil. . . . If in 1847 (it was really in 1846) Bělinskii experienced a new crisis, it was of a different kind, for at this epoch he became somewhat unsympathetic towards socialism.

Agreement with the slavophils in certain respects is characteristic rather of the first of the alleged phases. At the university

Bělinskii, having been made acquainted by Pavlov with the work of Schelling, passed under romanticist influences, but simultaneously Nadeždin drew his attention to the pitfalls of romanticism, and his youthful drama [*Dmitri Kalinin*] is permeated by this cleavage of views. Through renewed acquaintanceship with Schelling and German philosophy in Stankevič's circle he came in certain important respects to share the opinions of the slavophils, and employed some of the expressions which the slavophils had made current. (pp. 351-52)

Despite the derivation of much of his thought from German philosophy, in aesthetics Bělinskii was an empiricist. Art, he declared, existed before aesthetics, and aesthetics therefore must be guided by art, and not conversely. Bělinskii had no theory of aesthetics worked out in all its details; he was concerned almost exclusively with poesy and the written word, his realism leading him to advocate the characteristic view that the poet thinks in pictures. But he did not fail to emphasise also the work done by the poet in the field of thought. In 1842 he wrote that living contemporary science had become the foster-mother of art, for without science talent was weak and enthusiasm lacked energy. (pp. 370-71)

These views remind us of Schelling, but also of Hegel, for in aesthetics as in philosophy Bělinskii was influenced by both the German thinkers. The giving of art precedence over practice and theory is Schellingian, and when the author is in this vein we are told that the good is based upon aesthetic sentiments; but after Bělinskii has made acquaintance with Hegel his tendency is rather to range the beautiful beside religion and philosophy, and to insist that the beautiful too is moral.

We find echoes of Schelling and Hegel, in addition, in the conflict between romanticism and classicism which continues unceasingly in Bělinskii's mind, and which Russian realism hoped to bring to an end. But Bělinskii himself is as little successful here as in his attempts at a more precise demarcation between subjectivism and objectivism in general. On the one hand we are told that art, as the product of genius (genius being appraised à la Schelling) is subjective; yet at the same time he assures us that art is objective and must be nothing else. During the years when Bělinskii was idolising reality it was natural that in the sphere of aesthetics he should insist that art must represent reality alone.

The question whether art may have a purpose, exercised Bělinskii's mind greatly. At one time he would insist that art must never be tendentious, and yet shortly afterwards he would say that art pure and simple must be supplemented by tendentious belletristics, for this was extremely useful.

Bělinskii never failed to esteem the beautiful, the artistic, most highly; but as his mind matured he came more and more to look for ideas, for thought-content, in works of art. This thought-content, he insisted, must derive from society viewed as a whole.

Literature, in particular, is to Bělinskii the consciousness, or the growth into consciousness, of the people. He adopts the theory which is referable to Schelling that the poet is the orator, the instrument, of his nation. . . . Bělinskii never failed to advocate the view that the poet's gifts must be such as to enable him to sympathise directly with the ideas and the spirit of his age, for Bělinskii regarded the poet as the instrument, not of party or sect, but of the hidden ideas of society as a whole. In accordance with Hegel's teaching, he declares it to be the poet's mission to give expression, not to the individual and fortuitous, but to the universal and necessary. (pp. 371-72)

In contradistinction to the slavophils and the romanticists Bĕlinskii's conception of nationality was not mystical, and in individualistic fashion he attached more importance to individual poets, this determining his critical outlook towards folk-poetry. All he could see in Russian folk-poetry was childish lispings, sound without sense; and for the like reason he considered prepetrine literature practically valueless because it had not yet awakened to consciousness. (pp. 372-73)

Bĕlinskii's enthusiasm for Europe has led the historians of literature to regard as a lapse into slavophilism his disquisitions upon nationality, formulated in 1847. . . . This is erroneous. . . . In the opening period of his literary activities he declared himself opposed to cosmopolitanism, and continued to hold this view throughout life.

Whilst in his first critical writing [*Literary Reveries*] he said that Russia did not yet possess a literature, he subsequently came to recognise Russian literature as an independent and notable entity. (p. 373)

As historian (and before all he was historian of literature) Bĕlinskii was unable to arrive at a unified result concerning the tasks of history and in especial those of the history of literature. Hegel's influence did not make itself felt in any consistent application of the dialectic method. Nor can we discover in Bĕlinskii's work unified and distinctly formulated theories regarding the motive forces of historical development. Bĕlinskii was neither sociological expert nor philosophical historian, although he took frequent occasion to express his views concerning the evolution of Russia. . . . All his efforts were directed towards the intensification of Peter's great work, which Bĕlinskii regarded as the necessary civilising impulse coming from without. . . .

Bĕlinskii directed the rising generation into the political and social path, and contrasted the freedom of democracy with the absolutism of theocracy. . . . [He] had a remarkable understanding of the way in which men's minds could best be stirred despite the pressure of the Nicolaitan censorship. He felt democratically. Even though often enough he uttered complaints against the masses, he had ever before his eyes the reading public and the difficult and responsible mission of the Russian author. His humanitarian teaching was necessarily directed towards readers and not towards illiterates, but he was well aware that in point of character the cultured man may be no higher than the uncultured. (p. 374)

Bĕlinskii became political, social, and philosophic leader of the younger generation. His work, it is true, was that of literary critic, but for him criticism applied, not to books, but to the life which, as he said, was mirrored in literature. . . . Bĕlinskii touched upon the most important and profoundest problems of his time. Half unconsciously, with the aid of his philosophy of religion, he preached the political and social revolution under the very eyes of Nicholas' censors. (p. 375)

[In] Bĕlinskii . . . there dwelt two souls. From the aesthetic outlook he embodied the contrast between romanticism and realism, even though for Bĕlinskii himself this was a contrast between two utterly divergent outlooks on the universe. Romanticism was for him the inner mystical world of mankind, and by mysticism he practically meant the same thing as religion. The struggle with and concerning romanticism was therefore the struggle with and concerning religion. On one side was the yearning for faith, the faith that can move mountains; on the other side were reason and negation. (p. 377)

*Thomas Garrigue Masaryk, "Westernism: V. G. Bĕlinskii," in his* The Spirit of Russia: Studies in History, Literature and Philosophy, Vol. 1, *translated by Eden Paul and Cedar Paul (originally published as* Russland und Europa: Studien über die geistigen Strömungen in Russland, *1913), George Allen & Unwin, 1919 (and reprinted by Allen & Unwin, 1967, pp. 336-83).*

## LEON TROTSKY (essay date 1924)

[*Trotsky's classification of Belinski as a political revolutionary who, had he lived in the twentieth century, would have become a member of the Politburo, presages the approach of George Lukács (see excerpt below, 1949).*]

Our authors complain that there are no "Belinskys". . . . Of course Belinsky is referred to here not as a person, but as the representative of a dynasty of Russian social critics, the inspirers and directors of the old literature. . . . The historic rôle of the Belinskys was to open up a breathing hole into social life by means of literature. Literary criticism took the place of politics and was a preparation for it. But that which was merely a hint for Belinsky and for the later representatives of radical publicism, has taken on in our day the flesh and blood of October and has become Soviet reality. If Belinsky, Tchernischevsky, Dobrolubov, Pisarev, Mikhailovsky, Plekhanov, were each in his own way the inspirers of social literature, or, what is more, the literary inspirers of an incipient social life, then does not our whole social life at the present time with its politics, its press, its meetings, its institutions, appear as the sufficient interpreter of its own ways? We have placed our entire social life under a projector, the light of Marxism illumines all the stages of our struggle and every institution is critically sounded from all sides. To sigh for the Belinskys under such a condition, is to reveal—alas!—the isolation of an intelligentsia group, entirely in the style (far from monumental) of the most pious populists of the left. . . . "There are no Belinskys." But Belinsky was not a literary critic; he was a socially-minded leader of his epoch. And if Vissarion Belinsky could be transported alive into our times, he probably would be . . . a member of the Politbureau. And, furious, he would most likely start drawing a cart-shaft. Did he not complain that he whose nature was to howl like a jackal, had to emit melodious notes? (pp. 209-10)

*Leon Trotsky, "Proletarian Culture and Proletarian Art," in his* Literature and Revolution, *translated by Rose Strunsky (copyright, 1925, by International Publishers Co., Inc.; reprinted by permission of The University of Michigan Press; originally published as his* Literatura i revoliutsiia, *Gosudarstvenoy izdatelstva, 1924),* International, 1925, pp. 184-214.**

## D. S. MIRSKY (essay date 1927)

[*Mirsky's essay is one of the first objective assessments of Belinski's critical strengths and weaknesses. He expresses the opinion of many later critics when he describes Belinski as "the true father of the intelligentsia, the embodiment of what remained its spirit for more than two generations—of social idealism, of the passion for improving the world, of disrespect for all tradition, and of highly strung, disinterested enthusiasm."*]

In 1834 [Belínsky] published the famous *Literary Musings,* which may be regarded as the beginning of Russian intelligentsia journalism. In it and in his subsequent articles Belínsky displayed from the outset that eminently pugnacious and en-thusiastic temperament which earned him the nickname of the ''furious Vissarión.'' His articles were inspired with a youthful irreverence for all that was old and respected in Russian letters, and an equally youthful enthusiasm for the new ideas of ide-alism and for the creative forces of the young generation. He rapidly became the bogy of the conservative and the leader of the young. (p. 172)

[''Conservative Hegelism''] was only a transient stage in Be-línsky, and by 1841 his ideas assumed their final form, his-torically the most important. This last change was owing partly to the influence of the way Hegel's thesis was interpreted by the ''Left Hegelians''; partly to that of Herzen and his social-ism; but above all it was a natural reaction of the ''furious'' critic's temperament, which was that of a fighter and a revo-lutionary. Henceforward Belínsky became the moving spirit of the progressive Westernizers and the herald of the new liter-ature, which was to be neither classical nor romantic, but mod-ern. That literature should be true to life and, at the same time, inspired by socially significant ideas, became his principal de-mand, and Gógol and George Sand its fullest incarnations. In 1846-7 Belínsky had the gratification of seeing the birth of a school of realistic literature that precisely answered to the ideals he had heralded. (p. 173)

[Belínsky's letter to Gógol] is full of passionate and wounded indignation at the ''lost leader'' (Gógol had never really been a leader), and is perhaps the most characteristic statement of the faith that animated the progressive intelligentsia from 1840 to 1905. (p. 174)

Belínsky's historical importance can scarcely be exaggerated. Socially he marks the end of the rule of the gentry, and the advent of the *raznochinstsy* to cultural leadership. He was the first in a dynasty of journalists who exercised an unlimited influence on Russian progressive opinion. He was the true father of the intelligentsia, the embodiment of what remained its spirit for more than two generations—of social idealism, of the passion for improving the world, of disrespect for all tra-dition, and of highly strung, disinterested enthusiasm.

There is much to be said both for and against Belínsky. It remains to his lasting credit that he was the most genuine, the most thoroughgoing, the most consistent of literary revolu-tionaries. He was inspired by a love of the immediate future, which he foresaw with wonderful intuition. Perhaps never was a critic so genuinely in sympathy with the true trend of his times. And, what is more, he discerned almost unerringly what was genuine and what meretricious among his contemporaries. His judgments on writers who began their work between 1830 and 1848 may be accepted almost without qualification. This is high praise for a critic, and one that few deserve. In his judgments of the literature of the preceding age and generation, he was handicapped by party feeling, or rather by certain too definite standards of taste which, to our best understanding, were wrong. He understood only a certain kind of literary excellence (it happened to be practically the only kind practiced by men of his generation) and was blind to other kinds. He judged the writers of the eighteenth century and of the Golden Age from the point of view of his own idealistic realism. The selection he made of them imposed itself on Russian literary opinion for two thirds of a century. We have emancipated ourselves from it. But from his point of view it was admirably judicious and consistent. His judgments of foreign literature were on the whole much less happy, which is hardly astonishing considering his linguistic limitations. All said and done, he

cannot be denied the name of an exceptionally sensitive and prophetic critic.

His faults, however, are also serious. First of all comes his style, which is responsible for the dreadful diffuseness and untidiness . . . of Russian journalese (I mean high journalese) in the second half of the nineteenth century. Certainly no writer of anything like Belínsky's importance ever wrote such an execrable lingo.

Secondly, the message of Belínsky as a critic is hardly capable of kindling any enthusiasm today. Not that the civic note he introduced in the forties was avoidable or harmful. It was necessary, and it was in tune with the times. The civic attitude to literature in the later years of Nicholas I's reign was shared by all who were of any value, and was merely an expression of civic conscience. It is his *literary* doctrine that is difficult not to quarrel with. He was not entirely responsible for it, but he was, more than anyone, effective in so widely propagating it. It was Belínsky, more than anyone else, who poisoned Russian literature by the itch for expressing ideas, which has survived so woefully long. It was he also who was instrumental in spreading all the commonplaces of romantic criticism—inspiration, sincerity, genius, and talent, contempt for work and technique, and the strange aberration of identifying imag-inative literature with what he called ''thinking in images.'' Belínsky (not as the civic, but as the romantic, critic) is largely responsible for the contempt of form and workmanship which just missed killing Russian literature in the sixties and sev-enties. It is, however, only fair to say that, if the most influ-ential, Belínsky was not the only man who contributed to the infection. The weight of the sin rests on the whole generation. (pp. 174-76)

> *D. S. Mirsky, ''The Age of Gógol'' (originally pub-lished in his* A History of Russian Literature from the Earliest Times to the Death of Dostoyevsky (1881), *Alfred A. Knopf, Inc., 1927), in his* A History of Russian Literature from Its Beginnings to 1900, *ed-ited by Francis J. Whitfield (copyright © 1958 by Alfred A. Knopf, Inc.; reprinted by permission of the publisher), Vintage Books, 1958, pp. 127-76.**

## GEORGE LUKÁCS (essay date 1949)

[*Lukács is considered one of the foremost Marxist critics of the twentieth century. In his study of Belinski, Lukács contends that Belinski fully accepted the ideas of Utopian Socialism in the last phase of his career and asserts that he viewed the emergence of Gogolian realism as evidence of the ''growing intensity of the democratic-revolutionary struggle against absolutism and feu-dalism.'' In focusing on Belinski's concern for political and social reform, Lukács echoes Leon Trotsky (see excerpt above, 1924)*]

Bielinski, the founder of revolutionary democratic criticism in Russia was a contemporary and equal of the greatest European thinkers of the pre-1848 period. (p. 98)

Bielinski's development runs in many respects parallel to that of Heine. But the coincidences by no means rested on any psychological kinship—one could scarcely imagine a greater contrast than that which existed between the human and literary characters of Heine and Bielinski—but rather on a relative similarity of the historic conditions and tasks confronting them. Both great thinkers advanced as far as their social milieu per-mitted, but Bielinski is more resolute and radical than Heine.

Originally he was more strongly influenced by orthodox Hegelianism than Heine, but overcame it on the other hand more thoroughly and more profoundly. Hence, the materialist influence on him of Feuerbach was stronger and his acceptance of the ideas of Utopian Socialism, especially of its social criticism, clearer and more decided. He resembles Heine, however, in that neither of them, although they accepted much of the doctrines of philosophical materialism, ever repudiated the Hegelian dialectic, like Feuerbach himself and especially his philosophical followers and successors. Bielinski retained the great historical perspectives of the Hegelian dialectic and thereby stands in the foremost rank of the most advanced European vanguard in the great world-view crisis that convulsed Europe in the period preceding 1848. (p. 99)

Above all, we owe to Bielinski the really adequate appreciation of Pushkin and of his central, leading position in modern Russian literature; the recognition of the fact that new Russian literature began with Pushkin and found in him its first classic, unsurpassed to this day in artistic perfection. And it was again Bielinski who won for Lermontov the place in Russian literary appreciation which was his due.

But Bielinski also knew that even while Pushkin was still alive, a new period had begun in Russian literature, the period of modern realism, the period of Gogol. His appreciation of Pushkin as artist and poet was closely linked with this division of Russian literature into well-defined periods. Bielinski's conception of Russian literature closely resembles Heine's conception of the evolution of German literature. Both insist that the great central figures of the classic period, Goethe in Germany, Pushkin in Russia, stand higher in artistic merit than the representatives of the realistic period. When Heine speaks of "the end of the period of art" he sharply differs from those critics . . . who thought to advance the new, realistic democratic literature by minimizing the importance of Goethe. In this Bielinski followed Heine: he opposed with the greatest vigour Menzel's attack on Goethe. His conception of Pushkin's artistic perfection is dialectic in the best sense of the word. He regards it by no means as a mere formal impeccability, but as a harmonic unity of the artistic principles with the faithful reproduction of all the phenomena of life. It was not by chance that in his analysis of Pushkin's *Onegin* Bielinski described this work as "an encyclopaedia of Russian life"; he derived Pushkin's artistic perfection from this all-embracing universality of his reproduction of life.

In Bielinski's view, the emergence of the Gogolian period, the struggle for the triumph of Gogolian realism, coincided with the growing intensity of the democratic-revolutionary struggle against absolutism and feudalism. . . . According to Bielinski the great social and political importance of Gogol's realism lay in its merciless exposure of the social realities of its time and in its faithful mirroring of the harsh discordances of life. In Gogol's art this is not some alien tendency grafted on literature from outside. Absolutism, tyranny, feudalism made everyone's life so terrible and inhuman that the faithful reproduction of daily life was in itself the most effective propaganda. (pp. 108-09)

But it is not only in respect of Gogol's art that Bielinski was the critical and historical interpreter of the new period in Russian literature. Many of his contemporaries, critics as well as poets, complained—as did later the contemporaries of Chernyshevski and Dobrolyubov—that the critic Bielinski tore everything to pieces but created nothing "positive." It is quite true that Bielinski, with his critical analyses, destroyed the

literary career of many of his contemporaries. But in these controversies posterity has invariably endorsed Bielinski's judgment; there is not a single instance on record in which an author whom the great critic had subjected to one of his violent attacks had been later proved undeserving of such treatment. The alleged cruelty of Bielinski's criticism was just as much a thunderstorm that cleared the air in Russian literature as that of Lessing's had been in German literature. And Bielinski lived to see the first works of the new realist generation appearing before the Russian public. Here the inexorable critic is transformed into a sensitive, understanding and enthusiastic discoverer of new talent, who acclaimed the appearance of Turgenyev, Goncharov, Dostoyevski with great warmth. It was Bielinski who helped these great realist writers to occupy the places due to them in Russian literature. (p. 110)

> *George Lukács, "The International Significance of Russian Democratic Literary Criticism," in his* Studies in European Realism: A Sociological Survey of the Writings of Balzac, Stendhal, Zola, Tolstoy, Gorki, and Others, *translated by Edith Bone (copyright 1950 Hillway Publishing Co.; originally published under a different title in his* Der russische Realismus in der Weltliteratur, *Aufbrau-Verlag, 1949), Hillway Publishing Co., 1950, pp. 97-125.\**

## MARC SLONIM (essay date 1950)

In his [review of Vasili Zhukovsky's] **'The Anniversary of the Battle of Borodino,'** Belinsky declared that all existing forms of social and political life were justified and should be looked upon as inevitable links in the glorious chain of Divine Reason. Implicitly he admitted the necessity of autocracy, serfdom, and reaction against which he was morally protesting. . . . [Shortly] afterwards Belinsky himself started to re-examine his own theory. . . . [After] a painful crisis Belinsky rejected Bakunin's interpretation of Hegel. In his new articles he proclaimed that the interests of living human beings ought to constitute the point of departure for all practical philosophy. Liberty, individual or collective, is the prerequisite of any spiritual development. . . . Logical abstractions do not correspond to historic realities. Man himself creates values, which serve as touchstones in his scrutiny of reality. Beauty, justice, and truth should not remain superior to life; we must change life itself in order to make it truthful, just, and beautiful. This is the true purpose of individual and collective existence, and all of us must fight to attain the goal.

Thus, the formal disciple of Schelling and Hegel affirmed his conversion to ideas of humanitarian socialism. In the 'forties, and particularly toward the end of his life, in 1848, Belinsky's philosophy was strongly influenced by positivistic tendencies. . . . Belinsky's socialism had a strong moral tinge. . . . He dreamt of the day when all men would be brothers, when there would be no more senseless conventions and no capital punishment, when there would be neither kings nor subjects, neither rich nor poor. As far as Russia was concerned, Belinsky saw her salvation in reforms, in enlightenment, and in the progress of civilization and humanity. (pp. 137-38)

Belinsky's philosophy determined his approach to literature. He started a tradition of literary criticism based on a system of general ideas, and this school, of which he certainly remained the unchallenged leader, left a deep mark in Russian artistic and intellectual life. His influence on contemporary writers and his role in Russian letters were tremendous. (p. 139)

Belinsky was the first to broaden the scope of criticism and to forge it into a powerful factor of intellectual life. His essays in the Moscow papers and later, after he had moved in 1839, in the St. Petersburg reviews, always aroused passionate discussions and stirred public opinion. At the beginning of his career Belinsky had followed the trend of esthetic criticism; subsequently he adopted the method of historical analysis without sacrificing his philosophical approach. The purpose of a true critic, according to Belinsky, was to uncover the basic idea of each work of art, to establish its relationship with the environment in which it was conceived and, finally, to examine how the main idea had been expressed esthetically.

Belinsky had always wanted to write a history of Russian literature, and his essays, embracing its past as well as his times, are valid even today. He assigned their rightful positions in Russian culture to Lomonossov, Derzhavin, Karamzin, Zhukovsky, and others. His interpretations of the work of his contemporaries and particularly his essays on Pushkin, Lermontov, Gogol, Dostoevsky, and Goncharov were also a part of his all-embracing visions. After his anti-Hegelian revolt he emphasized the necessity of a sociological approach, insisting on the fact that each individual writer reflects the society in which he lives. In the 'forties all his writings stressed two main points: he developed his theory of art as an expression of national spirit and he declared himself a partisan of 'naturalness in literature,' thus paving the way from Romanticism to Realism. . . . He rejected shallow imitations of foreign patterns, while warning against chauvinism and pseudo-nationalism. (pp. 139-40)

In his last essay, **'A Survey of Literature in 1847,'** Belinsky reaffirmed his concept of the social significance of art. . . . The Natural school he defined as 'the sense and soul of Russian literature.' (pp. 140-41)

Belinsky made writers and readers aware of the national significance of literature and of its impact on the life of their country. His patriotism, however, was totally devoid of any aggressiveness. A liberal and a socialist, Belinsky led a campaign against national complacency, attacked the official doctrine of autocracy, Orthodoxy, and national customs, laughed at narrow-minded Slavophiles, and satirized those who considered long beards, old-fashioned clothes, and bread-cider insignia of nationality. Widely read in European and American literature (he wrote a eulogistic article on Fenimore Cooper), he declared himself a Westernizer and pleaded for permanent co-operation with Europe. He believed that Russia ought to rebuild her institutions on foundations of the European principles of human dignity, freedom, and political and social democracy. . . .

The great critic maintained and developed the radical tradition of the intelligentsia. He led the fight against despotism, serfdom, hypocrisy, narrow-mindedness, and reaction, and only his premature death saved him from prison or exile. (p. 141)

[Belinsky's writings] carried the readers away by their torrential flow of thoughts, by the emotional qualities of his style. . . . [He] underrated his unusual literary gifts. The great critic, as Turgenev has remarked in his *Memoirs*, possessed an infallible esthetic sense [see excerpt above, 1869]; he was able to grasp immediately the essence of each work of art, to judge in a flash the individual traits of each writer. His response to poetic beauty was quick and spontaneous; his evaluations, expressed with warmth and strength, were keen, challenging, and sincere. (p. 142)

> *Marc Slonim, "Dreamers and Philosophers," in his*
> The Epic of Russian Literature: From Its Origins

*through Tolstoy (copyright 1950 by Oxford University Press, Inc.; renewed 1977 by Tatiana Slonim; reprinted by permission of Oxford University Press, Inc.), Oxford University Press, New York, 1950, pp. 124-42.\**

## ISAIAH BERLIN   (essay date 1955)

[The name Vissarion Grigorievich Belinsky] became the greatest Russian myth in the nineteenth century, detestable to the supporters of autocracy, the Orthodox Church, and fervid nationalism, disturbing to elegant and fastidious lovers of western classicism, and for the same reasons the idealised ancestor of both the reformers and the revolutionaries of the second half of the century. In a very real sense he was one of the founders of the movement which culminated in 1917 in the overthrow of the social order which towards the end of his life he increasingly denounced. There is scarcely a radical Russian writer—and few liberals—who did not at some stage claim to be descended from him. . . . [He] is the father of the social criticism of literature, not only in Russia but perhaps even in Europe, the most gifted and formidable enemy of the aesthetic and religious and mystical attitudes to life. Throughout the nineteenth century his views were the great battlefield between Russian critics, that is, between two incompatible views of art and indeed of life. He was always very poor, and he wrote to keep alive, and, therefore, too much. Much of his writing was composed in fearful haste, and a great deal is uninspired hackwork. But in spite of all the hostile criticism to which he has been exposed from his earliest beginnings as a critic (and let me add that Belinsky is to this day the subject of heated controversy—no other figure dead for over a century has excited so much devotion and so much odium among Russians), his best work is in Russia regarded as classical and immortal. In the Soviet Union his place is all too secure, for (despite his lifelong war against dogma and conformism) he has there long been canonised as a founding father of the new form of life. But the moral and political issue with which he was concerned is, in the west, open still. (pp. 152-53)

[He] was, despite his detractors' charges of lack of authentic capacity, acutely sensitive to pure literary quality, to the sounds and rhythms and nuances of words, to images and poetical symbolism and the purely sensuous emotions directed towards them, yet that was not the central factor of his life. This centre was the influence of ideas; not merely in the intellectual or rational sense in which ideas are judgements or theories, but in that sense which is perhaps even more familiar, but more difficult to express, in which ideas embody emotions as well as thoughts, inarticulate as well as explicit attitudes to the inner and to the outer worlds. This is the sense in which ideas are something wider and more intrinsic to the human beings who hold them than opinions or even principles, the sense in which ideas constitute, and indeed are, the central complex of relations of a man towards himself and to the external world. . . . It is ideas and beliefs in this sense, as they are manifested in the lives and works of human beings—what is sometimes vaguely called ideology—that perpetually excited Belinsky to enthusiasm or anxiety or loathing, and kept him in a state sometimes amounting to a kind of moral frenzy. He believed what he believed very passionately, and sacrificed his entire nature to it. When he doubted he doubted no less passionately, and was prepared to pay any price for the answers to the questions which tormented him. These questions were, as might be supposed, about the proper relation of the individual to himself and to other individuals, to society, about the springs of human action and feeling, about the ends of life, but in particular about the imaginative work of the artist, and his moral purpose.

All serious questions to Belinsky were always, in the end, moral questions: about what it is that is wholly valuable and worth pursuing for its own sake. To him this meant the question of what is alone worth knowing, saying, doing, and, of course, fighting for—if need be, dying for. The ideas which he found in books or in conversation were not for him, in the first place, intrinsically interesting or delightful or even intellectually important, to be examined, analysed, reflected about in some detached and impartial fashion. Ideas were, above all, true or false. If false, then like evil spirits to be exorcised. All books embody ideas, even when least appearing to do so; and it is for these that, before anything else, the critic must probe. . . . [Belinsky's method] illustrates the beginning of a new kind of social criticism, which searches in literature neither for ideal 'types' of men or situations (as the earlier German romantics had taught), nor for an ethical instrument for the direct improvement of life; but for the attitude to life of an individual author, of his milieu, or age or class. This attitude then requires to be judged as it would be in life in the first place for its degree of genuineness, its adequacy to its subject-matter, its depth, its truthfulness, its ultimate motives. (pp. 155-57)

Books and ideas to Belinsky were crucial events, matters of life and death, salvation and damnation, and he therefore reacted to them with the most devastating violence. (p. 157)

Naturally, with a temperament of a Lucretius or a Beethoven, Belinsky as a critic was, unlike his western contemporaries, neither a classically pure connoisseur of Platonic forms like Landor, nor a sharp, pessimistic, disillusioned observer of genius like Sainte-Beuve; he was a moralist, painfully and hopefully sifting the chaff from the grain. If anything seemed to him new or valuable or important or even true, he would fly into ecstasies of enthusiasm and proclaim his discovery to the world in hurrying, ill-written, impassioned sentences, as if to wait might be fatal because the attention of the vacillating public might be distracted. (p. 158)

As a critic he remained, all his life, a disciple of the great German romantics. He sharply rejected the didactic and utilitarian doctrines of the function of art, then enjoying a vogue among the French socialists. . . . (p. 160)

Belinsky altered his opinions often and painfully; but to the end of his days he believed that art—and in particular literature—gave the truth to those who sought it; that the purer the artistic impulse—the more purely artistic the work—the clearer and profounder the truth revealed; and he remained faithful to the romantic doctrine that the best and least alloyed art was necessarily the expression not merely of the individual artist but always of a milieu, a culture, a nation, whose voice, conscious and unconscious, the artist was, a function without which he became trivial and worthless, and in the context of which alone his own personality possessed any significance. . . .

And yet, despite his historicism—common to all romantics—Belinsky does not belong to those whose main purpose and skill consist in a careful critical or historical analysis of artistic phenomena, in relating a work of art or an artist to a precise social background, analysing specific influences upon his work, examining and describing the methods which he uses, providing psychological or historical explanations of the success or failure of the particular effects which he achieves. Belinsky did indeed now and then perform such tasks; and was, in effect, the first and greatest of Russian literary historians. But he

detested detail and had no bent for scrupulous scholarship; he read unsystematically and widely; he read and read in a feverish, frantic way until he could bear it no longer, and then he wrote. This gives his writing an unceasing vitality, but it is scarcely the stuff of which balanced scholarship is made. Yet his criticism of the eighteenth century is not as blind and sweeping as his detractors have maintained. (p. 161)

[A] capacity for lasting literary verdicts is not where his genius lay. His unique quality as a literary critic, the quality which he possessed to a degree scarcely equalled by anyone in the west, is the astonishing freshness and fullness with which he reacts to any and every literary impression, whether of style or of content, and the passionate devotion and scruple with which he reproduces and paints in words the vivid original character, the colour and shape, above all the moral quality of his direct impressions. His life, his whole being, went into the attempt to seize the essence of the literary experience which he was at any given moment trying to convey. He had an exceptional capacity both for understanding and for articulating, but what distinguished him from other, at least in this respect equally gifted, critics, Sainte-Beuve for example, or Matthew Arnold, was that his vision was wholly direct—there is, as it were, nothing between him and the object. . . . [He] used to pounce upon a writer like a bird of prey, and tear him limb from limb until he had said all he had to say. His expositions were often too prolix, the style is uneven and sometimes tedious and involved; his education was haphazard, and his words have little elegance and little intrinsic magic. But when he has found himself, when he is dealing with an author worthy of him, whether he is praising or denouncing, speaking of ideas and attitudes to life, or of prosody and idiom, the vision is so intense, he has so much to say, and says it in so first-hand a fashion, the experience is so vivid and conveyed with such uncompromising and uninterrupted force, that the effect of his words is almost as powerful and unsettling today as it was upon his own contemporaries. He himself said that no one could understand a poet or a thinker who did not for a time become wholly immersed in his world, letting himself be dominated by his outlook, identified with his emotions; who did not, in short, try to live through the writer's experiences, beliefs, and convictions. In this way he did in fact 'live through' the influence of Shakespeare and Pushkin, Gogol and George Sand, Schiller and Hegel, and as he changed his spiritual domicile he altered his attitude and denounced what he had previously praised, and praised what he had previously denounced. . . . If ever there lived a man of rigorous, indeed over-rigorous, and narrow principle, dominated all his life by a remorseless, never-ceasing, fanatical passion for the truth, unable to compromise or adapt himself, even for a short time and superficially, to anything which he did not wholly and utterly believe, it was Belinsky. (pp. 162-63)

He arrived at no final or consistent outlook, and the efforts by tidy-minded biographers to divide his thought into three or more distinct 'periods', each neatly self-contained and coherent, ignore too many facts: Belinsky is always 'relapsing' towards earlier, 'abandoned', positions; his consistency was moral, not intellectual. (p. 163)

He was an uncouth provincial when he arrived in Moscow. . . . Moscow did, to some degree, soften and civilise him, but there remained to the end a core of crudeness, and a self-conscious, rough, sometimes aggressive tone in his writing. This tone enters Russian literature, never to leave it. Throughout the nineteenth century it is the distinguishing characteristic of the political radicals impatient of the urbanity of the non-political or conservative intelligentsia. (p. 176)

[Left-wing] writers of a later day inevitably tended to imitate the defects of his qualities, and in particular the brutal directness and carelessness of his diction as a measure of their own contempt for the careful and often exquisite taste of the polite *belles lettres* against which they were in such hot rebellion. But whereas the literary crudities of such radical critics of the 60s as Chernyshevsky or Pisarev were deliberate—a conscious weapon in the war for materialism and the natural sciences, and against the ideals of pure art, refinement, and the cultivation of aesthetic, non-utilitarian attitudes to personal and social questions—Belinsky's case is more painful and more interesting. He was not a crude materialist, and certainly not a utilitarian. He believed in his critical calling as an end valuable in itself. He wrote as he spoke—in shapeless, over-long, awkward, hurrying, tangled sentences—only because he possessed no better means of expression; because that was the natural medium in which he felt and thought. (p. 178)

[Spontaneity] of feeling and passionate idealism are in themselves sufficient to distinguish Belinsky from his more methodical disciples. Unlike later radicals, he was not himself a utilitarian, least of all where art was concerned. Towards the end of his life he pleaded for a wider application of science, and more direct expression in art. But he never believed that it was the duty of the artist to prophesy or to preach—to serve society directly by telling it what to do, by providing slogans, by putting its art in the service of a specific programme. . . . Belinsky, like Gorky, believed in the duty of the artist to tell the truth as he alone, being uniquely qualified to see and to utter, sees it and can say it; that this is the whole duty of a writer whether he be a thinker or an artist. Moreover he believed that since man lives in society, and is largely made by society, this truth must necessarily be largely social, and that, for this reason, all forms of insulation and escape from environment must, to that degree, be falsifications of the truth, and treason to it. For him the man and the artist and the citizen are one; and whether you write a novel, or a poem, or a work of history or philosophy, or an article in a newspaper, or compose a symphony or a picture, you are, or should be, expressing the whole of your nature, not merely a professionally trained part of it, and you are morally responsible as a man for what you do as an artist. (pp. 181-82)

He was wildly erratic, and all his enthusiasm and seriousness and integrity do not make up for lapses of insight or intellectual power. He declared that Dante was not a poet; that Fenimore Cooper was the equal of Shakespeare; that *Othello* was the product of a barbarous age; that Pushkin's poem *Ruslan and Lyudmila* was 'infantile', that his *Tales of Belkin* and *Fairy Tales* were worthless, and Tatyana in *Evgeny Onegin* 'a moral embryo'. There are equally wild remarks about Racine and Corneille and Balzac and Hugo. Some of these are due to irritation caused by the pseudo-medievalism of the Slavophils, some to an over-sharp reaction against his old master Nadezhdin and his school, which laid down that it was inartistic to deal with what is dark or ugly or monstrous, when life and nature contain so much that is beautiful and harmonious; but it is mostly due to sheer critical blindness. He did damn the magnificent poet Baratynsky out of hand, and erased a gifted minor contemporary of Pushkin—the lyrical poet Benediktov—out of men's minds for half a century, for no better reason than that he disliked mere delicacy without moral fervour. And he began to think that he was mistaken in proclaiming the

genius of Dostoevsky, who was perhaps no more than an exasperating religious neurotic with persecution mania. His criticism is very uneven. His essays in artistic theory, despite good pages, seem arid and artificial and conceived under the influence of Procrustean German systems, alien to his concrete, impulsive, and direct sense of life and art. . . .He was the more erratic because he took pride in what seemed to him freedom from petty qualities, from neatness and tidiness and scholarly accuracy, from careful judgement and knowing how far to go. He could not bear the cautious, the morally timid, the intellectually genteel, the avoiders of crises, the *bien pensant* [optimistic] seekers of compromise, and attacked them in long and clumsy periods full of fury and contempt. Perhaps he was too intolerant, and morally lop-sided, and overplayed his own feelings. He need not, perhaps, have hated Goethe quite so much for his, to him, maddening serenity, or the whole of Polish literature for being Polish and in love with itself. And these are not accidental blemishes, they are the defects inherent in everything that he is and stands for. To dislike them overmuch is ultimately to condemn his positive attitude too. The value and influence of his position reside precisely in his lack of, and conscious opposition to, artistic detachment. . . . (pp. 183-84)

Because his consuming passion was confined to literature and books, he attached immense importance to the appearance of new ideas, new literary methods, above all new concepts of the relation of literature and life. Because he was naturally responsive to everything that was living and genuine, he transformed the concept of the critic's calling in his native country. The lasting effect of his work was in altering, and altering crucially and irretrievably, the moral and social outlook of the leading younger writers and thinkers of his time. He altered the quality and the tone both of the experience and of the expression of so much Russian thought and feeling that his role as a dominant social influence overshadows his attainments as a literary critic. (p. 184)

*Isaiah Berlin, "A Remarkable Decade" (originally published as "A Marvellous Decade: (II) 1838-48, German Romanticism in Petersburg and Moscow," in* Encounter, *Vol. 5, No. 12, December, 1955), in his* Russian Thinkers, *edited by Henry Hardy and Aileen Kelly (copyright © 1948, 1951, 1953, 1955, 1956, 1960, 1961, 1972, 1978 by Isaiah Berlin; reprinted by permission of Viking Penguin Inc.),* The Viking Press, *1978 (and reprinted by Penguin Books, 1979) pp. 150-85.**

## RENÉ WELLEK (essay date 1955)

[Wellek proposes that in the last stage of Belinski's career he "embraced the mystique of time and progress" which led him to believe that literature evolved naturally, according to the "automatic fateful progress" of history. Wellek's formulation of Belinski's final position is disputed by Victor Terras (see excerpt below, 1974) but echoed by R. H. Stacy (see excerpt below, 1974).]

Belinskii, on questions of theory, must be considered as a follower of German romantic criticism, of the whole body of aesthetic thought elaborated by Herder, Goethe, Schiller, the Schlegels, Schelling, and Hegel. One cannot, however, make Belinskii an adherent of any single one of these authors. He was never a Hegelian, in a strict sense, in aesthetics, as he does not share Hegel's view of the imminent demise of art and has no sympathy for his nostalgic exaltation of the Greeks and of Greek sculpture as the highest summit of art. One cannot distinguish neat periods in Belinskii's critical thought: there was no definitely Fichtean, Schellingian, Hegelian, or Feuerbachian period in his criticism. From the beginning of his writing, starting with the **"Literary Reveries"** . . . to [**"Survey of Russian Literature for 1847"**], Belinskii uses the same categories, concepts, and procedures, the same basic theoretical idiom, whatever his shifting philosophical opinions or whatever his political convictions. Only in the last five years of his life can one discover a definite change. And even this change occurs in the same tradition and runs exactly parallel to the change which the followers of German speculative thought went through both in Germany and in other countries. Belinskii's evolution is, in this respect, roughly similar to that of Arnold Ruge, De Sanctis, Carlyle, or even Taine, who all absorbed the German conceptions and later modified them in favor of what they considered a closer approach to empirical reality, to facts, to science, to national and social needs of the time. I cannot see on what grounds Belinskii, at least in his critical thought, can be described as a "materialist" or even "realist" in the sense in which the French began to use this term as a literary slogan after 1857.

Belinskii begins his career by proclaiming literature to be the "expression of the national spirit, the symbol of the inner life of a nation, the physiognomy of a nation." This is, of course, a concept imported from Germany. The point of Belinskii's **"Literary Reveries"** is . . . a negative one: the Russians hitherto do not have a literature which truly expresses the national spirit. Belinskii severely criticizes the aristocratic "artificial" literature of the eighteenth century and also refuses to recognize Russian folk literature as truly expressive of a national spirit. He felt strongly its involvement in a serf civilization from which he wanted Russia to emerge into the light of freedom. Thus he argues against two things: the bookish derivative literature of the eighteenth century, and the popular folklore and local color nationalism of the Russian romanticists. His own ideal of literature, from the very beginning of his writings, is suggested by the terms national, genuine, natural, real. But what is meant by "naturalness" and "reality"? Surely not anything, at least in these early writings, which even remotely resembles later nineteenth-century realism. By "real" poetry, Belinskii means Shakespeare and Scott. Shakespeare, he says, "reconciled poetry with real life," and Scott, "the second Shakespeare, achieved the union with life." Truth and reality mean essential truth, inner reality, the truth of imagination. Belinskii sets no limits to the poet's themes and devices: he admires Shakespeare's *Tempest,* is in raptures over the dream in Gogol's "Nevskii Prospect," and praises Gogol's "Old World Landowners" for "not being copied from reality, but achieved by feeling in the moment of poetic discovery." Belinskii exalts the "objective" poet, Shakespeare or Goethe, who reproduces and mirrors the universe in its totality. . . . About 1840, Belinskii reached the stage of complete identification with the German theories. . . . Art, one hears, should serve society. . . . Art serves society by serving itself. Art purifies reality. Reality, often dark and ugly, is illuminated and harmonized in the poet's vision. Naturalism is expressly disparaged. "One can naturally describe a drinking party, an execution, the death of a drunkard who fell into a cesspool, but such descriptions lack a rational idea and aim." Only "rational reality" exists for the artist: he transforms ordinary reality by his ideals. Poetry, Belinskii declaims rapturously, is the quintessence of life, the poet is the organ of universal life, lives in everything, becomes everything. It is ludicrous to ask him to serve current needs. He does not imitate nature but rather competes with

her. Art is higher than nature. One could hardly wish for a more complete repertory of German romantic phrases with a definite touch of Schelling at a time when Belinskii is supposed to have been in his Hegelian period.

But in [the article] on Lermontov's *Poems* . . . , Belinskii begins to expound views which proved ultimately destructive of this position. He declares what would have been acceptable as such to any of these Germans: "The greater the poet, the more he belongs to the community in which he was born, the closer is the development, tendency, and character of his talent tied up with the historical evolution of society." But this evolution is now conceived as a progress toward reflection and subjectivity. The assumption is made (though never argued) that the progress of society and literature must be toward reflection and subjectivity, contemporaneity and immediate relevance. Belinskii recants his earlier praise of Goethe, deploring now his lack of historical and social pathos, his satisfied acceptance of reality. Subjectivity and contemporaneity are now accepted, at least as a historical necessity. Somewhat tortuously, all these arguments are put forward to justify Lermontov's poetry of despair and revolt.

Shortly afterwards, in 1842, Belinskii still tried to reconcile the objective idealism of the Germans with the historical relativism, the belief in contemporaneousness and progress, which he began to hold side by side. Art is concerned with the eternal truths of existence, while subject to the process of historical evolution. In criticism there is first an aesthetic judgment which decides whether a work of art is worthy of the attention of historical investigation. Belinskii sees no conflict between historical and aesthetic criticism: each requires the other, and cannot exist without the other. Neither does he see any conflict between aesthetic and social demands on a writer. He declares somewhat blandly, that it is easy to reconcile art with service to the community. The poet must be a citizen, a child of his society and age; he must adopt its interests, fuse his desires with those of his society. The serious conflicts between society and art of the following hundred years are not even seen as a possibility.

In 1843, however, Belinskii embraced the *mystique* of time and progress completely. He still agrees that the aim of criticism is to distinguish between the temporal and the eternal, the historical and the artistic, but he now assigns this task neither to the critic nor to aesthetics, but to the "historical movement of society itself." This view is used to buttress the main conclusion of his long series of articles on Pushkin: Pushkin belongs to a bygone and superseded stage of Russian literature and society while Lermontov satisfies a new and superior time. The assumption has become that of an automatic fateful progress, a higher and higher rising of the wave of the future. Even critical opinion can form itself only by time and from time. Responsibility for art is shifted to society. The materials ready-made for the poet's use by society have become the determinant of his work. Rather naïvely, Belinskii declaims about the happy Greeks who saw beautiful men in the streets at every step and the Italians of the Middle Ages, who had Madonna-like women as models for their paintings. Pushkin, he analogizes, "appeared in a time when it was for the first time possible to have poetry in Russia." This type of pronouncement may seem merely a comfortable hindsight, an irrefutable but meaningless assertion that things could not have been different. But it also implies not only a trust in the stream of history, but a praise of Russian life and its awakening toward freedom. (pp. 382-85)

["**Survey of Russian Literature for 1846**" and "**Survey of Russian Literature for 1847**"] formulate Belinskii's final position most memorably. He now has come to emphasize standards of naturalistic lifelikeness. He definitely rejects the fantastic as an artistic device when he criticizes Dostoyevsky's "The Double." "It can have its place only in lunatic asylums, not in literature. It is the business of doctors and not of poets." Belinskii even goes so far as to demand the "closest possible resemblance of the persons described to their models in real life." Gogol is praised for concentrating his attention on the crowd, the mass, the ordinary people. The inundation of literature by peasant types is defended; literature, he now argues, "facilitated the appearance in society of this movement (in favor of the serfs) rather than merely reflected it. Literature anticipated it rather than merely succeeded in keeping abreast of it." Belinskii seems to give up his former view of literature as a reflection of society which it can never transcend or outstrip. He seems to assign it a role of leadership, even of anticipatory divination. The strength of modern art, he finds, is "in nobly undertaking to serve the interests of society." Again and again Belinskii asserts his confidence in progress. . . . (p. 385)

Soviet criticism and the whole tradition of radical thought since Chernyshevskii find here the earliest local justification of their general point of view. But the image is a grossly simplified one. It ignores the bulk of Belinskii's earlier writings and it ignores the many reservations even in these last two articles. Belinskii did not become simply the propounder of a realistic art which is to serve a specific social and didactic purpose. In his attack on the doctrine of art for art's sake, Belinskii recognizes that "art must be first art and only afterwards can it be the expression of the spirit and drift of the society of a given age."

He rejects what seems to him both bad extremes: art for art's sake and didacticism. He argues that pure art is a dreamy abstraction which has never existed anywhere. . . . Belinskii . . . does not attack the autonomy of art as understood by Kant and Schiller, who would never have doubted its great role in world history and would never have thought of it as sensual pleasure. What Belinskii is arguing against is rather a purely ornamental hedonistic view of art. He disapproved also of didacticism. It is cold, dry, and dead. . . . Even in the very last article ["**Survey of Russian Literature for 1847**"], Belinskii emphasizes the difference between art and science or philosophy. The poet speaks in images and pictures, shows things and does not prove them. Belinskii by no means thinks of "naturalism" merely in terms of accuracy and even of insight into social realities. He sees that, in a work of art, "reality must have passed through imagination," that imagination must create "something whole, complete, unified, and self-contained." We must always keep in mind the fact that Belinskii precedes the victory of nineteenth-century realism and naturalism. What he is arguing against is pseudoclassicism, still a force in Russia, and romanticism, which Belinskii thinks of as conservative medievalism and folklore worship, or as fantastic and gruesome claptrap. Within the fold of "realism" he includes writers as diverse in their procedures and techniques as Shakespeare, Scott, Cooper, George Sand, and Dickens abroad. In Russia the "natural" school means Gogol and any writer who seems to Belinskii to have created something substantial, "real," natural. He praises the rather humble beginnings of local-color realism, in sketches of Petersburg and peasant stories, and is interested in novels which raise and debate social questions. But he does not lose his critical sense.

Thus Herzen's *Who Is to Blame?*, a book which appealed to his ideology very strongly, is still said not to be a work of art, not a real novel but rather a document. One usually hears of Belinskii's rejection of Pushkin's fairy tales and Dostoyevsky's "The Double" as instances of his prejudice against nonrealistic art, but one should remember that he also praised [Pushkin's] *The Bronze Horseman, The Stone Guest,* and even *Rusalka,* almost unreservedly, and that his objections to "The Double" are not merely those of realism. He criticized "The Double," not unreasonably after all, for Dostoyevsky's inability to master the overflow of his great powers, to define and limit the artistic development of his conception.

Belinskii, we must conclude, was a critic steeped in the views of the German theorists and firm in his hold on their central doctrine: art is concrete, sensuous knowledge; a work of art is an organic whole; the artist is the unconscious creator of a world of imagination on the analogy of nature. Art is the expression of a nation and age, is "characteristic" of that nation and age and should be so. In the last years of his life, however, Belinskii experienced a change: it was undoubtedly caused by his turn toward political radicalism; it may have had something to do with a religious crisis. It is closely parallel to the development of many of his contemporaries, especially the Young Hegelians. With them, just as with Belinskii, the "spirit" of Hegel lost its meaning as a force penetrating into the mysteries of the universe. It was replaced by the "spirit of the time," by the idea that man's mind is merely an expression of social and historical reality. . . . Belinskii proclaimed reality his God and embraced a *mystique* of time, a blind trust in progress. In his last stage, Belinskii advocated "naturalism" in the sense of a description of Russian social conditions by realistic techniques and with a social purpose which would help in organizing public opinion hostile to the regime. But he did not lose his generally firm hold on the nature of art nor his fervent devotion to the cause of Russian literature. However much we may disagree with many of his particular judgments today— his low ranking of Russian folklore, his underestimation of Russian eighteenth-century literature, his disparagement of the remarkable poets around Pushkin, his excessive praise for contemporary celebrities like George Sand, James Fenimore Cooper, and Béranger—we must admire Belinskii's great achievement in defining the status of Pushkin, Gogol, and Lermontov, and in welcoming the early promise of Dostoyevsky, Turgenev, Goncharov, and Nekrasov. In spite of the necessity, for reasons of censorship, of making criticism the vehicle for much general discussion on politics, society and morals, in spite of the prevailing conditions of magazine writing which encouraged a tendency to diffuse description, repetition, digression, incessant polemics, and rhetorical overemphasis, Belinskii must be admired as a genuine critic who kept up aesthetic standards rigorously and firmly to the last. Belinskii, almost singlehanded, established the position of literary criticism as a public force in Russia.

Belinskii had one very important historical function: he transmitted the ideas of German idealism to the tradition of Russian criticism. He was the authority for the critics of the fifties and sixties though they tried to ignore or minimize the idealistic elements in their master. Later Marxist criticism could appeal to Belinskii: in him, certainly, they found the view of literature as evolving automatically with society, the *mystique* of time, which came to them also from Marx and Engels, since all three have their common source in Hegel. The Marxists could also find an advocacy of realism in the last stage of Belinskii's writings, which, though far removed from their own conceptions, was sufficiently social in its emphasis to allow its assimilation. Belinskii thus set a mark on Russian criticism which even today has not been completely obliterated. (pp. 385-88)

> *René Wellek, "Social and Aesthetic Values in Russian Nineteenth-Century Literary Criticism (Belinskii, Chernyshevskii, Dobroliubov, Pisarev)" (a revision of a paper delivered at Arden House between March 26-28, 1954), in* Continuity and Change in Russian and Soviet Thought, *edited by Ernest J. Simmons (copyright © 1955 by the President and Fellows of Harvard College; excerpted by permission), Cambridge, Mass.: Harvard University Press, 1955, pp. 381-97.* *

### E. LAMPERT   (essay date 1957)

The words Belinsky chose were quite inadequate to describe his thought. Language itself seems to have been for him the failure to say exactly what he meant, and he tried unsuccessfully to create a new language: he wrote the worst Russian of any contemporary writer of his stature. It was obscure, confused, long-winded, untidy and crude, although glowing and pungent at the same time. (p. 49)

[Belinsky] was a man made furious by injustice and prevarication, by sham and moral pretexts, by the sufferings and unallayed pain of the human lot, rather than a philosopher or even a literary critic in the accepted sense of the word. It earned him the epithet of "furious Vissarion" . . . ; and the school of thought and of literary criticism issuing from him had all the qualities of a "furious" school. Strictly speaking, however, he founded no school and left no body of disciples to carry on some specific line of thought or investigation. Yet he was largely responsible for the dominant concern with moral problems and moral conflicts in Russian writers. (p. 51)

His own judgment was both hampered and deepened by a sense of the brutality and indifference of the world, by a sense of being in the midst of things, too close to things, pressed upon by reality. If he had succeeded in standing aside from himself, he would have achieved greater balance and clarity of vision and, certainly, better control, but he would have lost in freedom, spontaneity and closeness to humanity. In fact he wrote best and most spontaneously when the pressure was hardest to bear. One has learned to expect outbursts of blustering, sentimentality and melodrama from those in great bitterness and frustration. With Belinsky they freed his imagination and produced vividness, pathos and a certain melancholy. . . . [He] lacked that sense of humour which comes from detachment, from weighing up things and circumstances against the absolute of the imagination. . . . He had, however, a trenchant if somewhat coarse irony. . . . His great seriousness never led him into pomposity. In praise and blame he was extravagant, fiery, pugnacious, biassed and courageous. (pp. 51-2)

[His] articles . . . were largely improvised. . . . He had no time, or even inclination, to polish his style, to weigh up or think over every statement and expression and lapsed continually into verbosity. (pp. 56-7)

Belinsky strove to relate himself to the world and to relate the world to himself. It may be said that the inconsistencies and contradictions of his changing outlook were evidence of a conflict within him, and, perhaps, of a conflict which lies at the very heart of human existence: they could not and did not, therefore, render him guilty of betraying himself. This makes nonsense of any rigid chronological interpretation of his thought,

of any attempt to force his intellectual development into defined periods. . . . (pp. 60-1)

To Belinsky [Gogol's *Selected Passages from a Correspondence with Friends*] was nothing less than treason to the cause to which he believed Gogol to have dedicated his art. The violence of his reaction was partly due to the painful memories of his own defection in the past; but, whereas for Belinsky "reconciliation with reality" was a circuitous way of being brought into life and of recovering his sense of humanity, for Gogol it proved a revenge on life and a way of utter dehumanization. By the time he was writing his *Letter to Gogol*, . . . there was little left for Belinsky to idealize in the world in which he lived. There was no longer time or room to surrender to the dreams of paradygmatic Russia, or of any other paradygmatic world, not even that which opened up before him in his inspired Moscow Circle days. (pp. 96-7)

The greater the esteem in which Belinsky held Gogol, the deeper and more intense his indignation at Gogol's pious fraud was bound to be. He did not even spare him the charge of insincerity; and in view of the ghastly countenance of the very thing to which Gogol was paying homage, it cannot cause surprise that his sincerity was not accepted, although Belinsky did in fact realize how profoundly unhappy Gogol must have been when he wrote his book. (pp. 98-9)

[Belinsky's *Letter to Gogol*] was not merely a rebutter of the opinions of Gogol turned reactionary. As such it was effective but by no means remarkable. Its real importance lay in Belinsky's exposure of the utter emptiness and monstrosity of that ideal of the "good" which, in Gogol's own words, has lost its goodness, in his critique of the illusory value of those values with whose help Gogol, and with Gogol a major section of Russian society, attempted to sanctify a vulgar and ruthless world. He was warning Gogol that this "good" is a result, a symptom and a mask of a diseased body and a diseased soul, as well as a fetter for and drug against their regeneration. (p. 99)

Belinsky made no claims to be either a philosopher or a social and political thinker. His thoughts on philosophical, social and political matters, important though they were for him and important though they may be found to be for us, were haphazard, wayward and disjointed thoughts, reflecting the varying pressures to which he was constantly open from within and from without. But in one sphere alone Belinsky's preoccupations showed purpose and authority, and this was literature, to which his whole life was devoted. . . . (p. 100)

He frequently fell a victim to extremes, to precipitate conclusions, to violent likes and dislikes; he was impelled to fight his truly decisive battles in other than artistic fields, while trying simultaneously to explain the intricacies of Pushkin's and Lermontov's poetry. Sometimes, when he disagreed on fundamental issues, he was ready to reject what a writer had to say before considering what was said, for it is the writer himself whom he rejected. Yet he did so not for lack of imagination, for lack of plurality of aesthetic experiences, but because he could not assume a multiple loyalty. And even in his denials he did not fail to preserve a sense of artistic discrimination and an ability to discern talent. His errors of literary judgment were few and far between, but then even such a perfect artist as Pushkin was subject to them, not to mention Tolstoy and Dostoevsky. Belinsky's verdicts on Lermontov, Gogol, Goncharov, Turgenev, Dostoevsky and many others provide evidence of his extraordinary instinct. He was endowed, above all, with the gift of sympathy and even more with that of empathy, which enabled him to feel himself into his authors, think their thoughts, suffer their emotions, rather than attend to his own reactions—a gift all the more surprising in view of the more than usually extreme and passionate character of these reactions. He knew, as Turgenev testifies from personal experience and as Dostoevsky somewhat grudgingly admits [see excerpts above, 1869 and 1873], how to encourage, with candour and generosity, the first literary attempts of young and inexperienced authors, when they showed the slightest sign of talent; and, with equal candour, how to criticize their subsequent performance if they showed signs of deterioration, mercilessly exposing errors in taste, conception or execution, and exploding literary presumptions.

Belinsky's best essays are those dealing with Russian rather than foreign literature, and they belong especially to the beginning and the end of his career as literary critic. He started by philosophizing about literature, his thought turning, as seems to have become customary among philosophers of art, largely upon the question whether aesthetic judgments are subjective or objective, whether they express the personal preferences and prejudices of the judge or refer to some intrinsic quality possessed by the work under judgment. In accordance with his early idealistic views, his own discussion of literary works was based on the assumption that art enables us to perceive a reality which lies outside that of which we are normally aware, that it arouses emotions which are not of this world. . . . In his literary criticism Belinsky was, in fact, professing and applying the faith which the world owes not so much to romantic idealism as to a somewhat battered Platonism—the faith in an Absolute Beauty throned above the earth like an Alabaster Lady on a cloud and, from time to time, coming down to earth to generate the heat of the artist's fancy. This moved him to almost unqualified hostility towards every kind of "tendency" in art: he even repudiated Schiller, to whom he was devoted in his youth, because he suspected him of being tendentious. Poetry became for him primarily a stream of indefinite suggestions, an expression of unencumbered inspiration, a way of saying nothing in particular. . . . But even in his advocacy of "pure art" he was anything but "pure": he could only be partial in his very demand for objectivity, polluting purity and enjoying the privilege of sacrificing it to his own passionately held point of view. (pp. 101-02)

Belinsky was increasingly showing an appreciation of the purpose and the consequent limitation of mere fantasy. He began to apply his at the time favourite criterion of "sincerity" to the effusions of romanticism itself, to set aside inappropriate ideas and feelings in his aesthetic evaluations, to disapprove of what he called "romantic dishevelment". He sensed that fantasy is only justified and successful when it uses its freedom to discover a new logic in which the uses and abuses of our world are still mirrored. This enabled him to write at this early period some of the most illuminating criticism of Russian folklore . . . all of which show that he was by no means assuming literary inspiration to be an automatic passport out of the tangible, human world.

In the long run "pure literature" proved to Belinsky as impossible as "pure philosophy", and just as he was not afraid to associate the practice of philosophy with the promotion of opinion, one sees him linking literature with the function of prophecy and witness. The principle of "art for art's sake" gives place to that of art for life's sake. He is led more and more to emphasize, sometimes almost to exaggerate, a grave

and dedicated attitude to art of which the **Letter to Gogol** provides the most outspoken example. This new attitude, evident in Belinsky's writings ever since he joined the Petersburg *Annals of the Fatherland* and which became the *leitmotif* of his literary criticism from the middle of the 'forties, was for him, after many evasions, a way of becoming human again. It was also Belinsky's contribution to the rise and growth of "realism", which dominated imaginative writing in Russia throughout the latter half of the nineteenth century, from Gogol to Chekhov, and even to Gorky, constituting Russia's great legacy to European literature. Indeed, he may be regarded as its true progenitor and prophet. . . . The problem which Belinsky, and with or through him Russian nineteenth-century literature as a whole, brought to light was the problem of the freedom of the writer and his commitment in the world. (pp. 102-03)

Whether art is art can only be determined by artistic standards. The only "Absolute" that can inspire an artist is the "Absolute" of his creativity, hidden within it, rather than persisting in some independent validity outside it. And it is through being vowed to this Absolute that his work has power to move us.

But to separate the creative act of man from extraneous pressures, from religious and social infringements, and the pulpits of human opinion is not to separate it from humanity. The "perfect creator", the "pure artist" are, as Belinsky observed, fictions leading to sterile dreams, which have been the opium and the undoing of so many artists. Every creator makes something from the world in which he lives, even while rising above it or rejecting it. He must needs ask about his own attitude towards the world, towards history, towards his fellow-men, no less than towards himself. The sources of his activity are in life itself, whether that life be evil or good. Perhaps more than any other artist the imaginative writer is first of all a literary humanist. He creates human beings who suffer all that men are capable of suffering in a given situation, and his skill lets us know them as we know ourselves. He communicates the forces which move men to love and to hate, to act and to speak, to accept and to refuse.

Nowhere perhaps has this twofold character of creative activity been enacted with such intensity as in Russian literature of the nineteenth century, for Russia knew little of the world in which men could simply sit back and enjoy their freedom from anxiety and their unobtrusive and civilized pleasures of life, where literature and the arts themselves were a means of hiding the issue in question. (pp. 103-04)

Lermontov became for [Belinsky] the embodiment of his own protest against the flattening and mendacious worldliness which invades human life and pervades what he described in curiously modern terms as "commercialized literature", the embodiment of his own search for freedom, wch saves man both from effete solitude and from the compulsive mediocrity of the crowd.

In using literature for prophetic ends he was breaking down the isolation of the writer, and yet he could not refuse to look into the deep. A prophet turns his attention upwards and outwards, as well as inwards and downwards: he is in conflict with society, unacknowledged and ill-used by it, and, at the same time, he is committed to it, bearing the burden of the world outside, forecasting the world's future, bringing judgment and promise of renewal. The solitude of the prophet, alike as a witness of divine revelation and as a social reformer, an artist or a thinker, does not belong to the small and secure world of aesthetes, of select cultural *élites*, or of thinkers confined within their mental isolation. He is not hugging himself in his inner dreams, either violent or beatific. Indeed, he is not free to do anything separately or to be anything separately: his mission is to serve his fellow-men even while rebelling against them. Yet he fulfils, not the demands of his environment, but of truth, and receives his charge, not from society, but for it. It is in this sense that Belinsky spoke of literature as a means of spiritual communion between people, and that for him only those ideas could give true inspiration to the artist which promote communion between men.

What Belinsky found increasingly impossible to accept was a literature which cultivates the constriction of experience and shuts all doors to human distress. . . . He could not bear literary men with stuffed ears, no longer listening to life, but only talking about it, and spinning intricate, delicate or even beautiful cobwebs; and his own literary criticism became more and more concerned with the value of literature for living.

He felt no need, therefore, to concentrate on technical discussion and would not allow aesthetic criteria where false moral choices have been made. This is not to say that he was incapable of pure literary analysis or that he was unaware of subtleties and complications beyond mere utility. His account of Pushkin's *Stone Guest,* or the later essay on Griboedov's *Woe from Wit* (which contains more about Gogol than Griboedov), particularly the analysis of the *Story of How Ivan Ivanovich Quarrelled with Ivan Nikiforovich,* is convincing evidence of Belinsky's extraordinary exploratory and interpretative gift. But as a rule, he looked first at what was being said, and only secondarily at how it was said. The criterion was: is it on the side of humanity and truth? If it was not, Belinsky tended to discard it and to give a vigorous exposition of what he considered to be the real need, with the ensuing temptation, least of all evident in his later criticism, to succumb to vagueness, dilating and unhelpful rhetoric. Yet any attempt to substitute ''tracts for novels'', as he put it, or ''to make books instead of creating them'', to rely on the title of a book for the book's literary value, met with immediate dissent on his part. What he expected was the building up of the meaning or the idea by the literary technique, the mode of argument, the use of language, character, scene, so that in the end the ''teaching'' is the presentation, and *vice versa.* He was looking in a writer, especially in a novelist, for an ability to create depth, to make a particular situation, a fragment, even a detail extend into a wider range and deepen until the horizon is no longer within sight, until the particular acquires a universal human significance.

His articles of literary criticism provoke thought, but they do not, on the whole, irradiate our reading, or create an atmosphere in which literature can merely be pleasing. They are not an exercise in the free play of natural gaiety, in amusement and urbanity. To be that would have required a different world from the one in which he lived or, perhaps, different from any world inhabited by men—a world reduced to the manageable status of a still-life, with an abundance of beautiful things and human beings lounging amongst them. The world in which he lived provided no such opportunities, and even when it did, he could never forget ''the nightmares of history''. Life for him became more exacting than writing. And so it became for the whole of Russian nineteenth-century literature from Gogol onwards. (pp. 105-07)

*E. Lampert, ''Vissarion Belinsky (1811-1848),'' in his* Studies in Rebellion *(© by Routledge & Kegan Paul Ltd.), Routledge and Kegan Paul, 1957, pp. 46-107.*

**THELWALL PROCTOR**   (essay date 1969)

Belinskij's almost immediately recognized preeminence as a critic resulted not from the freshness and originality of his ideas but from his ability to express effectively and attractively the intellectual currents of his day. In addition to giving vigorous expression and an individual turn to ideas which he had made his own, Belinskij waged unremitting warfare against those critics who continued to defend earlier points of view. (p. 39)

Belinskij has often been acknowledged as the central figure of his time. . . . The reason for this lies rather in the representativeness than in the consistency of his ideas. This centrality of position accounts, at least in part, for Belinskij's influence during his lifetime, and it has a bearing upon the lack of a comprehensive system in his thinking. . . . In his work, all the ideas of his period, all those opinions which were to result later in wide divergences of position, found expression.

If the centrality of Belinskij's ideological position helps to explain his influence upon his contemporaries, it also helps to explain Belinskij's prestige with posterity. Precisely because of the diversity of the ideas which he expressed at one time or another, succeeding generations of writers of a wide spectrum of convictions have been able to appeal to him as an authority. (p. 43)

The difficulty of such a complex attitude toward art as Belinskij's lies in reconciling [art's] assorted functions: expressive, educative, judgmental, and theurgic. Belinskij's interest in the expressive function of art led him to champion realism; his interest in the educative and judgmental functions led him in the direction of publicistic art; his interest in its theurgic function nudged him in the direction of *tendencioznyj* [tendentious] literature. The difficulty of reconciling these functions is already implicit in Belinskij's criticism; it was to become more explicit in the work of his successors.

The multiplicity of functions which Belinskij assigned to the artist accounts for the contradictions apparent in Belinskij's aesthetic theory. (p. 47)

Belinskij energetically opposed ''pure'' art, art divorced from any except aesthetic considerations. Theoretically, Belinskij took the position that such art had never existed and could not exist. The attempt to limit art to purely aesthetic expression meant to clip its wings, to impose upon it humiliating and artificial limitations which merely crippled it. . . . Belinskij's aesthetic sense, however, did not permit him to regard aesthetic considerations as irrelevant, though they ceased to be paramount. Theoretically, according to Belinskij, a work of art could satisfy both aesthetic demands and social needs. The balance of aesthetic and social interests proved unstable, even for Belinskij. Though Belinskij frequently protested against didactic art, toward the end of his life . . . he was willing to admit privately that if a choice had to be made between aesthetic quality and social relevance, then he was willing to sacrifice aesthetic quality.

Belinskij's literary theories tended to encourage realism. Writers were urged to devote their attention to life as it was lived around them, to focus their interest on contemporary Russian life and its problems, to forge a close link between literature and life. Through such social analysis, literature fulfilled its function of assisting in the definition of the national life. But, much as Belinskij was interested in encouraging writers to describe and analyze contemporary life, he was not interested solely in objective description, in recording, classifying, defining. It was characteristic that Belinskij welcomed writers who described Russian life in such a way as to arouse dissatisfaction with it. Thus the writers of whom Belinskij approved and those who were influenced by his attitudes tended to be, implicitly or explicitly, highly critical of the Russian life to which they gave expression, and a "condemnatory" tone colored a good deal of Russian writing from Belinskij's day on. It is not surprising that Belinskij encouraged such works, for his own conviction was that the conditions of Russian life were intolerably unsatisfactory, and his theory of art emphasized the role of the artist as the implacable critic of what *is* and *ought not to be*.

Related to the condemnatory aspect of literature was Belinskij's cultivation of humanitarianism, his sympathy for human suffering, his interest in enlarging and extending the bounds of human sympathy, his emphasis on man's inhumanity to man, his demand for social justice. As humanitarian sympathy broadened, additional areas of Russian life came to be treated in literature. One aspect of Belinskij's humanitarianism was his insistence that Russian literature, which had devoted its principal attention to the upper social classes, give more attention to the lower layers of the social hierarchy. This demand, in addition to expressing Belinskij's humanitarianism, also tended in the direction of realism, as this term is usually understood.

Both Belinskij's attitude toward Russian life and his demands on Russian literature implied, it is true, a criticism of Russian life, but this criticism was not purely negative and destructive, as some of his opponents contended. If Belinskij himself criticized, protested against, condemned the actualities of Russian life, this was only a denial of what *is* in the interests of what *ought to be*. (pp. 48-9)

At the time when Belinskij was writing, the question as to whose was the greater authority, the critic's or the writer's, had not yet become pressing. Belinskij's position was that both critic and artist serve the nation. Final authority thus resides in the nation, and neither critic nor artist is exclusively invested with oracular preeminence as the voice of the nation. . . . Though Belinskij held that the critic could help the artist by pointing out his defects, he believed that criticism was based upon art, rather than *vice versa*. He argues that the most significant criticism is that which attempts to arrive at new theory based on the artist's practice. Though he later shifted his position, he at one time argued that the critic should not approach a work of art with preconceived standards but should be particularly sensitive to what is new. (pp. 49-50)

In Belinskij's view, the principal duty of the critic lay in acting as the artist's interpreter (a position which subordinates the critic to the artist). He referred to the critic as the *guverner* (mentor) of society, and in this role, the critic's function is to exert influence upon the public, not upon the artist. In this role, it is the critic's business to discern the basic idea of a work and then to show how that basic idea animates the whole. Still, one can discern the seeds of a different position in Belinskij's contention that the task of art is to represent what exists—that of the critic, to determine whether or not he has done so. So long as the critic and the artist substantially agree, . . . no difficulty arises, but in case of serious disagreement, the critic has declared his right not to accept the artist's version of reality. (p. 50)

Belinskij's work served as a point of departure for both publicistic and *tendencioznyj* literary criticism, though the latter note is to be heard only tentatively and toward the very end of Belinskij's career.

In both cases, Belinskij's literary criticism was polemical. . . . From the beginning to the end of Belinskij's career, his articles had a marked polemical tone, either simply destructive of old ideas as outworn or combatting them in the interest of new ideas, more or less specific. The polemical tone was one of Belinskij's lasting legacies to Russian literary criticism.

The heritage which Belinskij left to Russian literary criticism was . . . rich, complex, and composed of unstable, contradictory elements. To it must be attributed a shift from a predominantly literary point of view toward one oriented to a concern with society. However, in spite of his hostility to the idea of "pure" art, aesthetic considerations were of sufficient importance to Belinskij so that they have been considered as basic in his attitude toward art. . . . (p. 51)

Belinskij's legacy to Russian literary criticism was not only ideological. To it he contributed also certain of his personal characteristics and qualities: a receptivity to new intellectual currents as they made themselves felt in Western European thought, ethical fervor and an urgent sense of dedication, extremism, an appetite for polemics, and a personal style. (p. 52)

> *Thelwall Proctor, "Vissarion Grigorevič Belinskij (1811-1848)," in his* Dostoevskij and the Belinskij School of Literary Criticism *(© copyright 1969 in The Netherlands. Mouton & Co. N. V., Publishers, The Hague.; reprinted by permission of the author), Mouton Publishers, 1969, pp. 33-64.*

## C. V. PONOMAREFF   (essay date 1970)

One of the most difficult problems in Belinskij's critical essays is the wealth of terminology, which at first sight thwarts the establishment of any unity at all in his thinking. On closer inspection, however, it becomes clear that the various terminology, far from disrupting Belinskij's essential processes of thought, unifies them into one integrated whole. (p. 145)

Belinskij's ontology was idealist. In approaching empirical reality, he could not conceive of it other than through the idealist focus which was the result of his ontological premises. Whether he discussed empirical reality in terms of its aesthetic reproduction, its historical development, its human potential, or simply in terms of the conclusions reached through a critical analysis of a specific literary work, he always idealized it. By "idealized," I mean to suggest that he assigned an ideal form or value to whatever came under consideration. In other words, he tried to reduce the manifold variety of empirical reality to the essentially *typical* and the significantly *general* by means of abstraction.

Belinskij assigned the function of idealizing the world to the poet who, as a truly creative artist or genius imbued with divine instinct, was promoted to the position of a highly sensitive discerner and interpreter of the moral absolute Spirit at work in the universe. In this capacity he was the pivot in Belinskij's system of idealization.

As early as 1834, it was the inspired poet who could express the all-pervasive absolute moral Idea, thereby becoming moral himself. At the moment of inspiration, the poet was always imbued with *razum*, with moral consciousness of the absolute Essence. Whatever aspects of empirical reality he chose or was impelled to depict as a poet, they were always significant and moral, for his source of inspiration was the moral Idea itself.

As a result, his creative work could not help but influence his readers morally and significantly.

Belinskij viewed the creative process in terms of unconscious or spontaneous organic inspiration, which was the immediate power enabling the poet to penetrate to the essence of whatever he was inspired to depict. Belinskij referred to inspiration as the sudden penetration of *istina* or Truth, as the source of all creation, it was the madness or *razumnost'*—that which is morally conscious—of the gods.

Only inspired poetic creativity could unify empirical experience into an ideal experience which alone was *real*. Being a poet therefore presupposed a certain ideal approach to empirical reality. It meant that a poetic harmonious unity was imposed upon the empirically accidental diversity. Only such a reduction of empirical data could give form and unity to parts of the external world of nature. Consequently, by subjecting empirical reality to his inspired creative idea which spontaneously selected, combined, and unified the typical, the characteristic, the common features of the world around him, the poet was able to express its essence, making empirical reality beautiful and poetic. In this creative process, the poetic spirit reduced the facts of life to their general significant idea, thereby creating an artistic whole. (pp. 147-48)

The literary critic in Belinskij's system of thought had, not unlike the poet, the innate capacity to discover the real, by reducing empirical reality to an ideal reality. . . .

Belinskij's theory of poetry remained a constant in his critical work. But the pure continuum of his aesthetic thought was marked by the introduction of diverse terminology. Thus, in 1844, for instance, he introduced *ličnost'* 'personality' as a new literary critical criterion, reflecting his preoccupation at the time with personal dignity, human worth, and enlightened humaneness, a preoccupation which had already come to the fore explosively in his letters to Botkin in 1841. But though he seemed to replace *razum* or the absolute moral Idea with *ličnost'*, human personality fulfilled essentially the same function in literary criticism as *razum*. (p. 148)

It was significant, however, that, in attempting to discover whether or not a work of art had *ličnost'*, Belinskij fell back on the use of his previous aesthetic criteria which had determined the presence of *razum* in art—criteria such as, for instance, that a work of art had to be an unconsciously inspired poetic unity expressing moral or divine absolute genesis or *razum*. As a result *ličnost'*, as a critical operating tool in art and literature, was itself *predetermined* by the very poetic principles it expressed. . . . But though *razum* and *ličnost'* were by essential nature identical, the specific emphasis on personality did signify a shift of critical focus from a more abstract intuition of the moral Idea as pervasive universal presence to its more concrete embodiment in *poetic character*. . . . (pp. 148-49)

Nor were there any sharp breaks in Belinskij's views of the poet as a creative artist. Only his function in society underwent a change. From his earlier statement that a purpose was bad for poetry, he slowly came around to the view that art divorced from life is socially useless and insignificant. But he was forever at pains to affirm that even socially useful art had to be the product of poetic genius. The demands of art had to be satisfied first. Art and life must be fused in a work of art, either of them alone being insignificant either socially or aesthetically. . . .

Belinskij's view of Russian historical development was motivated by the assumption that for a country to make an original contribution to humanity, it had to have its own *organic* history, i.e., its own national historical development. . . .

*Narodnost'* [human historical development], itself an ideal concept, was in the main expressed through the medium of art (literature in particular). The function of art, thanks to the poet's unique gifts, was to express the mainsprings behind Russia's historical development, to reveal what was essentially motivating Russia's destiny. (p. 149)

The relation of the poet to society, was of course basically the same relation as held between art and *narodnost'*, except that the scale of reference was much wider, the poet's potential greater and more all-embracing, approaching a point where he could transcend his own national limitations and become universal in his art. The shorter the gap between a work of art and its potential universality (its common universal humanity), the more it was an expression of *istina*. Thus Puškin, Goethe, but above all Shakespeare had in fact created works of universal significance, expressed the truth of being.

On the national scale art expressed only a part of the universal essence of being or *istina*. But, again, art had to express life, for a work of art which was not national could not be considered to be a genuine work of art at all. In fact, the true poet could not help but be national (or *razumnyj*) in his work, even though as a creative artist he was not subjected to society, but was free to obey the poetic laws of his own creative impulses.

As to the relation between aesthetics and history, the relation of the poet to society, the creative artist, in depicting historical reality, was creatively idealizing (abstracting) the various manifestations of life into a general idea or essence *(narodnost')*. The essence expressed an ideal relation between the facts of existence and the poetic consciousness, the existential facts themselves in the process becoming much more real than the actual empirical reality which gave rise to them. Unfortunately, the poet had to create in a world of intuitive vagueness, for as Belinskij himself admitted, he could not say what made up the spiritual substance of the Russian people, though he had faith in their unique, organic, national originality. (pp. 149-50)

Without the poet's unique genius, that is to say, without what was essentially poetic intuitive perception conjuring up its own metamorphoses of reality and thereby transmitting ideal moral values through the medium of art, Belinskij's universe would have become a meaningless chaos without beauty or substance. Russia's own destiny, the cultural essence behind Russian historical development, with its original contribution to be made to humanity *(narodnost')*, would have been swallowed up by a jumble of insignificant facts lacking all teleological cause. Russian man would have remained forever doomed to an unconscious animal state, never to attain that highest possible degree of civilized moral consciousness *(razumnost')* of which at present only the poet in his work was a precursor. And "literature" would have been a glassy mirror for dead souls. (p. 154)

Since, however, the theoretical idea of the vital function of poetic genius was Belinskij's innate a priori assumption and since, moreover, he himself did possess unique power of poetic vision in order to be able to function as a critic *vis à vis* his own theoretical constructs, the very nature of his critical idealist focus was of necessity *poetic*. Only such an elect state, endowing him with the very energies of the poet, could invest him with that indomitable authority with which he could render all the natural, historical, social, moral, and artistic manifestations of empirical reality meaningful—by transforming and reducing them to their ideal forms.

Consequently, Belinskij's intuitive and transfiguring powers of poetic vision geared to the ideal stimuli of a universal moral Idea or consciousness (razum) which stood for truth (istina) and which made his or the poet's natural critical function central to the envisaging of an all-pervasive moral ideate, and the resulting ideal relations established between Belinskij's poetic consciousness and any earthly subject, made for that unifying philosophically poetic thread which runs through Belinskij's critical work from beginning to end. (pp. 154-55)

> C. V. Ponomareff, "Configurations of Poetic Vision: Belinskij As an Idealist-Critic," in Slavic and East European Journal (© 1970 by AATSEEL of the U.S., Inc.), n.s. Vol. XIV, No. 1, Spring, 1970, pp. 145-59.

## VICTOR TERRAS  (essay date 1974)

[In refutation of René Wellek (see excerpt above, 1955) Terras argues that Belinski derived his conception of reality "not from any Hegelian 'mystique of time' . . . but from a social ideal" which did not "seem to be immanent either in the empirical Russian reality of the times or in the naturalistic literature dealing with it."]

It is characteristic of Belinskij and the critical tradition which he established not to be satisfied with any kind of impressionist or formalist interpretation of literature, but to judge it on the basis of a philosophy which would create a distinct pattern of relationships between the work of art, its constituent parts, its creator, and the world at large. Belinskij knew that a critic must have talent, just as a poet must. But he believed that the critic should approach a work of art armed with native aesthetic sense, as well as good taste and erudition, and with certain general ideas. (p. 32)

To be a critic, Belinskij says [in a review of A. V. Nikitenko's "Discourse on Criticism"], means "to seek and to discover in a particular phenomenon the universal laws of reason, according to and through which a living, organic relationship exists between the particular phenomenon and its ideal.". . .

At the beginning of his Fifth essay on Puškin . . . Belinskij gives yet another outline of his theory of literary criticism. . . . Again he stresses that only a happy combination of intuitive grasp and theoretical analysis can produce good criticism. He suggests that a critic's first step should be a careful study of the poetic work in his charge, followed by an intuitive grasp of the poet's creative personality. Once he has come to understand the poet, the critic seeks to establish just how well the poet's idea has been expressed in his creation. The degree to which a poet's spirit is realized in his work is the measure of its artistic value. Finally, the critic determines the universal validity, import, and value of the poetic idea under his scrutiny. Thus, as a theorist, Belinskij is in 1844 as strong an exponent of "philosophic" and "organic" criticism (both terms are used by Belinskij) as he had been during his early, Schellingian period (1834-37). (pp. 32-3)

For Belinskij, a work of art consists of its form, the excellence of which depends on the talent of its creator and is recognized by the critic's intuition, and its content, the value of which lies in its objective historical importance and reveals itself to the philosopher-historian's understanding. (p. 33)

The question is not whether Belinskij possessed a consistent philosophy which may have served as a basis for his critical pronouncements; it is safe to say that he did not. Some would assert that the theoretical views held by Belinskij during a certain period of his life represent the "true" Belinskij, while opinions held by the critic at other times are to be either disregarded or challenged as aberrations. . . . Such selective use of Belinskij's heritage is dishonest. It is also self-defeating, for even a cursory study of Belinskij's writings will reveal that he often expresses the "wrong" view in the same breath with the "correct" view. (pp. 34-5)

The question is: Was Belinskij at all times merely the advocate and popularizer of whatever philosophic or aesthetic doctrine had most recently caught his fancy, or was the intricate development of his theoretical views an organic process with a constant basis in the critic's own intellect? (p. 35)

Belinskij's conception of the creative mind was a dynamic one. In his early, very Hegelian refutation of Wolfgang Menzel's criticism of Goethe ["Menzel, Critic of Goethe"] . . . , Belinskij points out that true humanity is always in a state of flux, that true life is constant movement, steady development, and that the advance toward Truth is strewn with errors, contradictions, and negations. And, the greater and more profound a human mind, the more prone it is to error. . . . Belinskij retained this view until the end of his life. (pp. 35-6)

The question is then whether the corpus of Belinskij's aesthetic thought, full of changes, reversals, and contradictions, indeed mirrors the organic growth of an aesthetic philosophy which should rightfully bear his name. (p. 36)

Belinskij's aesthetic theory is anchored in certain constants which he never questioned. To use a mathematical simile, Belinskij's conception of the work of art and its relationship to objective reality is like a differential equation, where the variables may assume quite different values both absolutely and relatively, yet within definite limits.

Among Belinskij's constants we find an organic and dialectic, rather than mechanistic or formalist, conception of the genesis and structure of the work of art, as well as of its relation to life at large; the notion that a work of art is the realization of an idea, a dialectic fusion of the "real" and the "ideal"; and hence, the notion that a work of art has two aspects—an ideal content which coincides with the historical life of the artist's nation and of mankind, and a concrete form which is a manifestation of the aesthetic sense and a product of the artist's genius. In the ideal aspect, Art is free, autonomous, and absolute; in the concrete form, it is determined by the laws of history. There is the belief that aesthetic intuition parallels and even anticipates the teleology of history, and, in connection with the last point, an extremely high opinion of the social role of the artist. Finally, Belinskij's love and respect for art must be considered an important factor in any evaluation of his theoretical views. . . . [He] was biased in favor of great art, in fact, of anything that deserved the name of art.

Within this framework, spectacular shifts occur in Belinskij's views. During his Hegelian period . . . Belinskij favors objective over subjective art. Thereafter, in his famous review of Gogol''s Dead Souls . . . , for example, he begins to make concessions to the subjective element, meaning an ideological tendency or social message, in art. In his last years, he much prefers the ideologically committed Herzen to the "objective artist" Gončarov. And yet, Belinskij never relinquishes the notion that art must possess both an ideal content and a real form: rhetoric, abstract philosophizing, preaching, allegory, on the one hand, and photographic naturalism, contentless entertainment, uncontrolled effusions of emotion, on the other, are nonart, as far as Belinskij is concerned, useful perhaps, and deserving of a place in life and in literature, but nonart. (pp. 36-7)

Another point to be kept in mind when dealing with Belinskij's lack of consistency is that he, even by virtue of being a Hegelian, is a dialectic thinker. He does not fear contradiction and sees in the negation of a given thesis not so much its cancellation, the reduction of a truth to a nontruth, as an advance to a new truth. Moreover, the old truth just challenged and declared invalid will some day return on a higher level of understanding, and its negation in turn negated. (pp. 38-9)

On a more mundane level, Belinskij was, at least most of the time, a practitioner of *la critique du jour,* a literary critic and a publicist at the same time. Certain inconsistencies in his writings and some outright logical and factual blunders, irrelevancies, and unsupported assertions must be seen in the light of these extrinsic circumstances. One cannot fairly hold Belinskij to the letter of his writings the way one can and should do in treating a scholar's literary criticism. (p. 39)

Belinskij's world view always remained "organic." To the end of his life, he never doubted the unity and interrelatedness of all that is: one universe, one life, one mankind, one historic process. His **"Survey of Russian Literature in 1847"** contains an example: "Certainly life is divided and subdivided into a multitude of aspects, each of which possesses a certain independence; however, these various aspects are fused with one another in a living pattern . . . , and there is no clear demarcation line separating them. No matter how hard you try to split up life, it will still remain an integral whole." . . .

As a corollary of this view, Belinskij—along with German objective idealism, and romantics everywhere—saw all art as one. He and most of his epigoni liked to refer to works of literature as "works of art," and to writers as "artists." There was a strong presumption shared by virtually everybody with this trend of thought—and Belinskij was no exception—that a critic who had proven himself as a connoisseur of one branch of art, usually poetry, was therefore entitled to an authoritative opinion in matters relating to other art forms, painting, for example, and other branches of literature such as the drama. At any rate, Belinskij was always a strong defender of the essential unity of all art forms. . . .

Belinskij's entire career represents a search for a definition of "reality". . . . That art was to represent the reality of life Belinskij never doubted for a moment. . . . (p. 77)

Belinskij always took for granted that art and literature were serious things, as serious as anything in life. He scornfully rejected any suggestion that the purpose of art might be to entertain, to amuse, to help to forget "real life." He would associate this approach to art with the frivolous and immoral eighteenth century: it was simply passé, not worthy of a refutation. Belinskij refused to concern himself with a writer like Alexandre Dumas (*père*), in spite of his wide popularity in Russia. The point is that such refusal stemmed not from Dumas's inferior craftsmanship (alleged or real) but from the absence in his works of any connection with "reality." Belinskij was willing to discuss at length works which, from a literary and artistic viewpoint, were inferior to Dumas's but were in some way concerned with "real life." The novels of Eugène Sue were examples. This particular position of Belin-

skij's has been held by most Russian literary critics ever since. It was seriously challenged only by the Formalists of the 1920s.

Belinskij's reasoning as he rejects Gogol''s *Selected Passages from a Correspondence with Friends* . . . is characteristic. In that book Gogol' had said many things that Belinskij believed to be false and insincere. Also, the book apparently was not a literary masterpiece. From these two premises, Belinskij jumps to the conclusion that "nothing that is false, affected, unnatural can ever be masked; rather, it is always mercilessly cut down . . . by its own banality." . . . In other words, Belinskij is convinced that by virtue of having departed from the truth of life, Gogol' had . . . ceased being an artist.

Belinskij's attitude toward the autonomy of art . . . is not as ambivalent as it might appear from a casual juxtaposition of his many seemingly conflicting statements on this matter. Belinskij's basic position, never abandoned, is that art, while an autonomous and *sui generis* function of the human spirit, and an end in itself, is organically linked with moral, intellectual, social and national life. Any attempt to set it apart from the other areas of human life is either illusory or sterile. By the same token, any tampering with the autonomy of art, any attempt, no matter how well-intentioned, to give art a "direction" from without is bound to fail. [In **"Survey of Russian Literature in 1847"**] Belinskij rejects as equally "bad extremes" . . . both "didactic, doctrinaire, cold, arid, dead art, the products of which are nothing but rhetorical exercises on given themes" . . . and "pure art," which he sees as a kind of "intellectual China, with sharply defined boundaries separating it from everything that is not art in the strictest sense of that word." . . . (pp. 78-9)

At the root of Belinskij's conception of the analogy between art and reality lies the assumption, usually tacit, but sometimes explicit, of a cognitive capacity inherent in artistic creation. Needless to say, this is one of the principal traits that links Belinskij with the Neoplatonic "organic" tradition. (p. 79)

It follows from Belinskij's realization of the specificity of aesthetic cognition that "poetic truth" . . . must not *formally* coincide with empirical truth as revealed by science, scholarship, and historiography. . . .

Belinskij, like Hegel, refuses to follow Kant and many of Kant's followers who derive, from a belief in the *sui generis* character of the aesthetic process, a special realm or independent domain of "art for art's sake." A truth derived by way of intuition is not, for Belinskij, of a different order than one arrived at through scientific investigation or logical deduction.

On the other hand, at least toward the end of his career Belinskij (unlike Hegel) tended to derive aesthetic merit directly from the alleged objective truthfulness and social relevance of a work of literature. (p. 82)

Belinskij, like Hegel, had been from the beginning a staunch defender of realistic art. He had always felt that art should deal with contemporary reality. But the earlier Belinskij had displayed a lively concern and indubitable talent for grasping and formulating the "ideas" which were apparently moving that reality. . . . During the last few years of his life Belinskij seems to have lost his grip on these "ideas," or perhaps his faith in their reality. For example, he had immediately sensed the drift of Lermontov's *Hero of Our Time*, recognized Pečorin as a new social type, and correctly understood his historical significance. But when faced with Dostoevskij's equally significant novels *Poor Folk* and *The Double,* Belinskij, even though he actually called *Poor Folk* "the first Russian social novel," was unable or unwilling to speculate on their broader social and historical significance, producing what was essentially a psychological interpretation.

Instead, the later Belinskij pays more and more attention to naked, empirical reality. He now perceives the history of Russian literature as a long struggle, once unconscious and now conscious, "to get closer to life, to reality and consequently, to become original, national, Russian.". . . (p. 88)

Belinskij also believed that this process had found its completion in the works of Gogol' and the Natural School, in which ordinary Russian life was dealt with directly and in Russian terms. In the critic's later writings one will find many instances in which he commends relatively mediocre authors for their devotion to simple and unadorned truth, or actually suggests that even a writer of modest talent can achieve excellent results if he is determined to make his works an honest mirror of reality. (p. 89)

We have . . . in the later Belinskij a conception of reality which derives its ideal aspect not from any Hegelian "mystique of time" (to use René Wellek's term) [see excerpt above, 1955] but from a social ideal which, at this stage in the development of Russian society, does not seem to be immanent either in the empirical Russian reality of the times or in the naturalistic literature dealing with it. In other words, the later Belinskij is intent upon turning Russian literature into the bearer of a progressive social, or even socialist, ideology, while there is still no basis for such a tendency in Russian reality. Thus, he has in effect a dialectic conception of the relationship between literature and reality. On the one hand, his insistence on "realism" in literature means that realism depends, for much of its content, on the condition of the society which it mirrors. But on the other hand, the role of literature as an active factor of social change makes society depend on literature. What is even more surprising, Belinskij often enough seems to see things exactly in these dialectic terms, and quite consciously so. (p. 90)

Belinskij . . . described a full circle, or spiral, in his conception of the relationship between "art" and "reality." He had begun by crediting art with the expression of the ideal inherent in reality, without paying much attention to the fact that art was itself largely responsible for the very existence of these ideal values. He had then gradually expanded the range of art's contacts with reality to a point where it embraced even those aspects of reality that are least congenial to art: sordid, trivial, "everyday" life. But in so doing he reached a point where he had to transcend this reality and introduce ideal values from the outside in order to breathe life into the art which represented it. Belinskij's initial metaphysical conception of art ultimately becomes an ideological one. (p. 91)

> *Victor Terras, in his* Belinskij and Russian Literary Criticism: The Heritage of Organic Aesthetics *(copyright © 1974 The Regents of the University of Wisconsin System), The University of Wisconsin Press, 1974, 305 p.\**

## R. H. STACY   (essay date 1974)

[*Stacy states that Belinski viewed literature "as the result of a historical process, progressing through a series of genres from the lyric to the drama and the novel."*]

[Vissarion Belinsky's] position as the "father" of Russian criticism is upheld in the Soviet Union largely because of his emphasis on the ideological and sociological content of works of art (as opposed to merely aesthetic or formalist analysis) but also because of his generally radical outlook (the Soviet Union now tolerates only dead radicals) and his atheism. But Belinsky was a great critic, and, though he unwittingly founded a "school" of lesser epigones . . . , his work deserves careful consideration. To dismiss him because the Soviets pay homage to him would be tantamount to dismissing Pushkin because his poetry is read—and presumably even loved—by Communists.

Fallible, however, he certainly was, especially in his judgments of foreign writers. Thus his favorite foreign novelist was George Sand, he felt that Eugène Sue had more talent than Balzac, and he once expressed the opinion that E.T.A. Hoffmann was to be ranked with Shakespeare and Goethe. And his harsh criticism of Shevchenko, the great Ukrainian poet, though due in large part to a congenital Great Russian prejudice, must be viewed as a serious blot upon his reputation as a critic. (pp. 41-2)

The influence of German idealism on Belinsky is profound, and he began his career as a critic under the aegis of Schelling's *Naturphilosophie*. Passage after passage in Belinsky, though the subject under discussion is almost always Russian literature, shows the German background: art is an organic whole; literature is the expression of the national spirit; the poet "thinks in images"; etc. But he is not completely subservient to German ideology: he dislikes, in general, Slavic folklore and speaks derogatively of oral literature, shows no nostalgic affection for *die alten Griechen* [the ancient Greeks], and even in his Hegelian period does not share the German philosopher's view of the coming demise of art. One of the remarkable aspects of Belinsky's criticism, in fact, is, despite all the German influence, its surprising homogeneity over the years so far as categories and procedures go. (pp. 44-5)

[Belinsky's style] is often ponderous and diffuse, frequently involved in elementary explanation, with numerous and abrupt digressions and repetitions and long-forgotten quarrels with long-forgotten personalities. In short, except for a *caput mortuum* [obsolete item] well worth extracting, it has all the defects of ephemeral journalism. (p. 45)

Amongst specific literary concepts which have become associated with or colored by Belinsky's activities, we may note here the term "belletristics" . . . to which he gave new currency in the Russian critical language. But in the Russian usage this term does not signify merely "belles lettres" or artistic literature; it refers rather . . . to a mixed genre, half-publicistic and half-artistic, involving not only a concern for aesthetic and cultural values but also a preoccupation with ideological, political, and moral didacticism. In addition, Belinsky was particularly instrumental in introducing into Russian criticism a good deal of abstract philosophical and metaphysical terminology coined on the basis of German models, a fact noted—and parodied—by his contemporaries. . . .

There are three distinct periods in Belinsky's career as a critic. During the first period (1834-38) his criticism, in addition to showing a marked German influence, is brash, radical, and bellicose. . . . During the short *détente* period (1838-41) Belinsky became a "right" Hegelian, adopting the famous formula, "All that is real is rational and all that is rational is real." To the astonishment and chagrin of his friends, he now accepted (as the formula demanded) the social order which he had earlier so bitterly attacked, and he concerned himself briefly with more universal and less polemical themes. But he soon saw his error (it was characteristic of Belinsky to admit error), and from 1841 until his premature death he considered art as a criticism of life (in the sense of social reality). (p. 46)

This periodization of Belinsky's criticism has a significant counterpart in his views of Schiller. Until about 1838 Belinsky was generally rapturous in his praise of Schiller. . . . During the subsequent Hegelian period of "reconciliation with reality" he frequently, in stronger and stronger terms, expressed his disillusionment with Schiller. . . . And then, after the short-lived Hegelian phase, he returns to his earlier ardor. . . . (p. 47)

Perhaps the best-known example of Belinsky's critical reaction is seen in his response to two early works by Dostoevsky, *Poor Folk* and *The Double*, both published in 1846. The first novel was enthusiastically hailed by Belinsky as a work of social protest and in the Gogolian "naturalist" tradition. . . . But it is not a "proletarian" novel, and Belinsky, in effect, misread the work, exaggerating the sympathy shown the poor and quite neglecting the essentially—although still embryonic—Dostoevskian psychological analysis. As for *The Double*, which still strikes the modern reader as inchoate and unsuccessful, this work Belinsky dismissed and castigated—not as mere *ébauche* [sketchwork], however, but as lunatic fantasy. For Belinsky, who demanded in so many words that there be the closest possible resemblance between literary characters and their "models" in real life, the fantastic and the grotesque had no place in Russian literature. And although we can see how, in emphasizing social content and didacticism and in rejecting the fantastic (which provides numerous occasions for ambiguity and irony,) Belinsky anticipates modern Soviet canons of judgment, still it is surprising that he felt the way he did in view of his particular conception of literary realism. (pp. 47-8)

Belinsky, who recognized the greatness of Gogol but who ranked him high because of the "realistic" exposure and satire of the seamy side of Russian life, seized upon the term "natural" and used it in a laudatory sense and as a synonym for "realistic." But the interesting thing is that, when it comes to defining realism, Belinsky writes: "A man drinks, eats, and dresses—this is a world of phantoms . . . but a man feels, thinks, and recognizes himself as an organ, a vessel of the spirit, a finite particle of the general and infinite—this is the world of reality." . . . But Belinsky's definition, although of course it may be quoted in support of literature as a vehicle for supposedly "universal" ideas (and in this sense it fits very well into the Hegelian Marxist-Leninist tradition), may also be read as a defense of the very technique which Dostoevsky essayed in *The Double* and which Kafka perfected in *The Metamorphosis*. (p. 48)

[What] Belinsky was getting at in his definition of, and other statements about, realism was this: that, whereas what we call naturalism represents an indiscriminate inclusion of events simply because they occur, realism represents a discriminate view of reality, i.e., reality ordered in the mind of the artist on the basis of a particular . . . philosophy. This is the soundest way of looking at realism. . . . (p. 49)

Closely related to Belinsky's views on realism is his distinction . . . between "real" and "ideal" poetry (or art in a more general sense). This again represents the adoption of German aesthetic theory, since the above distinction was Friedrich Schlegel's, while Schiller's earlier and better known distinction between "naive" and "sentimental" poetry makes essentially

the same point. On the basis, then, of the formula, "Realism deals with life, idealism with ideas," Belinsky distinguishes between works like *Don Quixote* . . . and *Eugene Onegin* as "real" poetry and Goethe's *Faust* as "ideal" poetry. He especially exalts Shakespeare and Scott. Art for Belinsky is necessarily related . . . to real life rather than being based upon abstract concepts of beauty, theory, or (as we might say today) myth; and Shakespeare's works, mirroring reality as they do, represent the acme of non-idealistic creation. But Belinsky's thought in this area as well shows two tendencies. On the one hand he increasingly emphasizes works of literature as organic wholes exhibiting the Hegelian "sensuous expression of the Idea"; he praises Gogol in "Old World Landowners" for *not* copying from reality and for creating types which, while remaining individuals, assume universal significance. "Art," Belinsky goes so far as to say, "purifies reality." On the other hand, while still holding that the function of criticism is to distinguish between the temporal and the eternal, he elaborates (in articles on Lermontov and Pushkin) what René Wellek has called a "mystique of time" [see excerpt above, 1955]: he sees literature as the result of a historical process, progressing through a series of genres from the lyric to the drama and the novel. History itself determined that Pushkin would eventually turn, as in fact he did, to the novel and that Lermontov would write drama. Though Belinsky's "official" Hegelian period was brief, these notions show the lasting influence on his thought of Hegelian meliorism and historical determinism.

Quite frequently in his articles Belinsky will merely exclaim enthusiastically over the beauty or—more often—the veracity of a passage . . . ; occasionally he will dissect and analyze, but very often this is apt, in a manner which has been called "typically Russian," to be rather a labored treatment of a literary character as if he or she were a real person with a past and a future than a stylistic or aesthetic analysis. (pp. 49-50)

Belinsky distinguishes, as have many critics, between the artist and the belletrist: the former is the rare creator who supplements reality (whose works are "more real than reality itself") and the latter is the imitator. . . . Yet the belletrist is not summarily dismissed. "Great and exemplary works of art and science," Belinsky writes, "have been and will continue to be the only elucidators of all problems of life, knowledge, and morality. But until such works appear, works which often keep us waiting long, the activity of belles lettres is essential. During the long intervals their function is to occupy, nourish, and inspire minds which would be doomed to idleness." (p. 52)

Needless to say, Belinsky stresses content. . . . Though he recognizes the stature of Lomonosov (whom he would call a belletrist of genius), Belinsky refers to his poems as having merely historical interest and nothing more. It is here, perhaps, in his outspoken emphasis on content that Belinsky's views are most clearly opposed by modern criticism in the West and by a series of critics in Russia. . . . Belinsky cites the case of Rabelais as a writer who has had lasting significance and appeal by virtue only of the content of his fiction; but we would disagree and hold that it is rather his style and language that are determining factors.

Finally, from the Russian Marxist-Leninist point of view, Belinsky was the founder of what is called "democratic literary criticism." . . . [Though] we may appreciate and sympathize with the moral zealousness and earnestness of Belinsky, though we might hope he would be, were he able to observe the execrable scene in Russia, amongst the first to condemn it, still we must remember that it was Belinsky who wrote the following words: ''People are so stupid that they must be led toward happiness by force.'' . . . (pp. 52-3)

> *R. H. Stacy, ''Belinsky,'' in his* Russian Literary Criticism: A Short History *(copyright © 1974 by Syracuse University Press), Syracuse University Press, 1974, pp. 38-54.*

---

## ADDITIONAL BIBLIOGRAPHY

Bowman, Herbert E. *Vissarion Belinski, 1811-1848: A Study in the Origins of Social Criticism in Russia*. Harvard Studies in Comparative Literature, vol. XXI. Cambridge: Harvard University Press, 1954, 220 p.

> An authoritative critical analysis of the development of Belinski's thought which aims to ''present the total Belinski'' and to ''give all that one needs to know in order to understand him.'' Bowman discusses Belinski's most important essays and letters in relation to the intellectual and cultural context of Russia during the first half of the nineteenth century.

Davies, Ruth. ''Four Rebels in Search of a Revolution.'' In her *The Great Books of Russia*, pp. 101-35. Norman, Okla.: University of Oklahoma Press, 1968.*

> A short summary of Belinski's ideology emphasizing those aspects of his thought that remained consistent throughout his career. Davies portrays Belinski as a man who crusaded against mysticism, scepticism, and superstition in a humanitarian effort to create a better future for the people of Russia.

Kostka, Edmund. ''V. G. Belinsky's War on German Idealism.'' *Rivista di Letterature Moderne e Comparate* 16 (1963): 5-19.

> A study of Belinski's changing aesthetics as reflected in his altering sentiments toward Friedrich Schiller. Kostka discusses Belinski's initial enthusiasm for Schiller's *Die Rauber*, his eventual disgust with abstract realism, and his later acceptance of Schiller's romanticism.

Mathewson, Rufus W., Jr. ''Belinsky: 'My Heroes Are the Destroyers.' '' In his *The Positive Hero in Russian Literature*, 2d ed., pp. 25-45. Stanford: Stanford University Press, 1975.

> Describes Belinski's career as a ''restless hero-quest'' and asserts that his basic attitudes toward heroes derived from his concept of realism and his advocacy of a literature of criticism and negation. Mathewson finds that Belinski most admired ''exposers and destroyers among the men of thought and imagination'' whose ''liberating destructiveness'' hastened the disintegration of the reigning order.

Matlaw, Ralph E. Introduction to *Belinsky, Chernyshevsky, and Dobrolyubov: Selected Criticism*, edited by Ralph E. Matlaw, pp. vii-xx. New York: E. P. Dutton & Co., 1962.*

> A brief biographical-critical study that focuses on the development of Belinski's theory of art.

Poggioli, Renato. ''The Tradition of Russian Realism.'' In his *The Phoenix and the Spider: A Book of Essays about Some Russian Writers and Their View of the Self*, pp. 1-15. Cambridge: Harvard University Press, 1957.*

> Contends that Belinski erred in labeling Gogol the father of Russian realism. Poggioli suggests that Belinski exaggerated the accuracy and social import of Gogol's works in an effort to substantiate his theory of naturalism.

Ponomareff, C. V. ''V. G. Belinskii's Romantic Imagination.'' *Canadian-American Slavic Studies* 7, No. 3 (Fall 1973): 314-26.

> Argues that Belinski was a morally inspired poet ''camouflaging his poetic sight with the garb of literary criticism.'' Ponomareff attempts to show that Belinski's second critical article on the works of Alexander Pushkin, written in 1843, was an extension of his poetic imagination as expressed in his plays *Dmitri Kalinin* and *Piatidesiatiletnii diadiushka, ili strannaia bolezn*.

Scherer, John L. ''Belinskij and the Hegelian Dialectic.'' *Slavic and East European Journal* 21, No. 1 (Spring 1977): 30-45.

> Defends the unity of Belinski's aesthetics by showing how an application of the Hegelian dialectic to his writings can resolve the apparent contradictions in his thought. Standard literary approaches which divide Belinski's criticism into distinct phases and reversals fail, Scherer concludes, because they ignore Belinski's kaleidoscopic vision of reality.

Smirnova, Zinaida Vasil'evna. *The Socio-Political and Philosophical Views of V. G. Belinsky*. Moscow: Foreign Languages Publishing House, 1955, 62 p.

> Advances the theory that Belinski was a progressive thinker whose sociopolitical and philosophic views in the 1840s were a combination of revolutionary democracy, utopian socialism, and materialism. Smirnova stresses the importance of Belinski's use of dialectics to substantiate his revolutionary democratic ideas; in the spheres of philosophy, sociology, aesthetics, and literary criticism he employed the dialectic to develop his arguments against serfdom, mysticism, autocracy, and orthodox religion. Smirnova contends that Belinski was a great literary critic because he strove, through criticism, to promote revolutionary theory.

Weber, Harry B. ''Belinskij and the Aesthetics of Utopian Socialism.'' *Slavic and East European Journal* 15 (Spring 1971): 293-304.

> A discussion of Belinski's utopian socialist aesthetics as reflected in four essays he wrote for the journal *Fiziologija Peterburga* in the 1840s.

Wellek, René. ''Russian Criticism: Vissarion Belinsky.'' In his *A History of Modern Criticism, 1750-1950: The Age of Transition, Vol. 3*, pp. 240-64. New Haven, London: Yale University Press, 1965.

> An expanded version of Wellek's ''Social and Aesthetic Values in Russian Nineteenth-Century Literary Criticism: Belinskii, Chernyshevskii, Dobroliubov, Pisarev'' (see excerpt above, 1955) which includes a more detailed discussion of the development of Belinski's ideology. Wellek describes the shifts in Belinski's philosophic orientation and shows how these changes were reflected in his essays.

# John Esten Cooke

## 1830-1886

American novelist, historian, biographer, essayist, short story writer, poet, and editor.

Cooke was a popular Southern author during the Civil War period. Though best remembered for his early works, which are nostalgic glorifications of colonial and pre-Revolutionary Virginia, in his later novels, Cooke wrote of the Civil War and its effect on postbellum Virginia society. All of his works are affirmations of his unfaltering loyalty and devotion to his birthplace. His goal was to fashion a history of Virginia in his fiction and non-fiction as colorful and memorable as James Fenimore Cooper's depiction of the American Indian and William Gilmore Simm's account of the American Revolution in South Carolina. Cooke wrote, "I believe that any merit of my writing has been, and will be found in the fact that I am *Virginian*, and *Cavalier*."

Descended from an established Virginia family, Cooke was born in Winchester, and spent his childhood at his mother's plantation in the Shenandoah Valley. When he was nine years old, his family moved to Charleston, where he attended the Charleston Academy. Later the family moved to Richmond, where Cooke lived until the outbreak of the Civil War. The Shenandoah Valley furnished the background for many of his border romances, while his later life in Richmond society inspired such works as *The Virginia Comedians; or, Old Days in the Old Dominion* and *Ellie; or, The Human Comedy*.

Cooke's oldest brother, the poet Philip Pendleton Cooke, had a profound influence on his decision to pursue a literary career. Prompted by his father, a prominent attorney, John began to study law at age sixteen, but his admiration for Philip's literary accomplishments and his own extensive reading quickened his desire for a literary career. In 1848, Cooke began what was to be a long association with John R. Thompson, the editor of *The Southern Literary Messenger*. Cooke contributed unsigned and pseudonymous reviews, poems, and short articles to this journal as well as to *Harper's Magazine*. By 1852, he left his father's law practice to devote himself fully to writing.

During the 1850s, Cooke produced several romantic novels which portray the colonial life of Virginia. Most critics concur that the best of these are *The Virginia Comedians* and *Henry St. John, Gentleman, of "Flower of Hundreds," in the County of Prince George, Virginia: A Tale of 1774-'75.* His acknowledged masterpiece, *The Virginia Comedians*, successfully depicts the historical era of pre-Revolutionary Virginia. This portrait of the various social classes results in a richness of characterization which is not displayed in any of his later works. Some critics, however, dismiss Cooke's portrayal of women, the lower classes, and particularly the slaves as merely superficial sketches or absurd caricatures.

During the Civil War, Cooke served in the Confederate Army on the staff of General J.E.B. Stuart. His experiences as a soldier later provided the basis for numerous romances, biographies, and essays on the war. In *Surry of Eagle's-Nest; or, The Memoirs of a Staff-Officer Serving in Virginia* and its sequel, *Mohun; or, The Last Days of Lee and His Paladins: Final Memoirs of a Staff-Officer Serving in Virginia*, Cooke blended

fact with fiction in an interpretation of Virginia's role in the Civil War. These novels secured his reputation among both Northern and Southern audiences. Although he had written biographies of Stonewall Jackson and Robert E. Lee, it was in these works that Cooke brought historical characters to life. *Surry of Eagle's-Nest* was Cooke's most financially successful novel; however, many attribute its popularity to its timeliness rather than to any intrinsic artistic value. Although critics find the story entertaining, they fault the work's sensationalism and failure to distinguish between myth and reality, weaknesses which become increasingly apparent in Cooke's later fiction. *The Heir of Gaymount* was not a popular success, but modern critics praise its depiction of the problems of Reconstruction.

Discouraged by the popular failure of *The Heir of Gaymount*, Cooke turned once again to the imaginative evocation of the past. He was, however, unable to attain his former success with antebellum subjects. In his last efforts, Cooke tended toward melodrama and exaggeration. As his inventiveness dwindled, he borrowed plots, episodes, and phrases from his earlier publications, resulting in a redundancy which critics condemned. Cooke is consistently faulted for the rapidity of his composition and a lack of revision and critics generally agree that the stock characterization, thin plots, and repetition of incidents found in his later works are the result of this carelessness.

Cooke's popularity diminished with the advent of a more realistic approach to fiction in the late nineteenth century. Though much of his work now seems outmoded, some twentieth-century critics feel that Cooke has been judged too harshly. He is still considered important as a spokesman for the South and as an author who promoted the idealized view of antebellum Virginia society. As a romantic novelist and chronicler, Cooke celebrated Virginia's land, its people, and its past. His novels, despite their artistic flaws, have always been found entertaining. Critics applaud his graceful, spirited style, his optimism, and his purity of sentiment. What Richard Henry Stoddard wrote of Cooke at his death is both a comment on his rise to popularity in the mid-nineteenth century and an explanation for the rapid decline of his reputation: "His books have the charm of elegant comedy, the pathos of pastoral tragedy, sparkles of wit, flashes of humor, and everywhere the amenities of high breeding."

(See also *Dictionary of Literary Biography*, Vol. 3: *Antebellum Writers in New York and the South.*)

PRINCIPAL WORKS

*Leather Stocking and Silk; or, Hunter John Myers and His Times: A Story of the Valley of Virginia* (novel) 1854
*The Virginia Comedians; or, Old Days in the Old Dominion* (novel) 1854
*Ellie; or, The Human Comedy* (novel) 1855
*The Last of the Foresters; or, Humors on the Border: A Story of the Old Virginia Frontier* (novel) 1856
*Henry St. John, Gentleman, of "Flower of Hundreds," in the County of Prince George, Virginia: A Tale of 1774-'75* (novel) 1859
*Surry of Eagle's-Nest; or, The Memoirs of a Staff-Officer Serving in Virginia* (novel) 1866
*\*Fairfax; or, The Master of Greenway Court: A Chronicle of the Valley of the Shenandoah* (novel) 1868
*Hilt to Hilt; or, Days and Nights in the Shenandoah in the Autumn of 1864* (novel) 1869
*Mohun; or, The Last Days of Lee and His Paladins: Final Memoirs of a Staff-Officer Serving in Virginia* (novel) 1869
*The Heir of Gaymount* (novel) 1870
*A Life of General Robert E. Lee* (biography) 1871
*Pretty Mrs. Gaston, and Other Stories* (short stories) 1871
*The Virginia Bohemians* (novel) 1880
*Virginia: A History of the People* (history) 1883
*The Maurice Mystery* (novel) 1885

*This work was originally published serially as *Greenway Court; or, The Bloody Ground* in *The Southern Literary Messenger* in 1859.

---

***THE SOUTHERN LITERARY MESSENGER*** (essay date 1855)

["*Ellie; or, the Human Comedy*,"] though a book of a high order of intellectual and dramatic merit, is not such an one as the author should be content to rest his fame upon. It bears the marks of haste in composition and seems to have been sent off to the press just as it came from the author's facile pen. . . . But with all its faults, it is clearly such an effort as none but a superior mind could ever have accomplished. That reader must be very little under the influence of genuine pathos who can follow the heroine through her bravely fought struggle with penury and temptation and not feel the moisture gather about his eyes, and that nature must be sadly hardened against good impressions which does not recognise in the pictures of humble but sincere piety that are presented in "**The Human Comedy**," a new illustration of the "beauty of holiness." A more touching conception of innocence and purity than Ellie herself, we do not remember in the course of our readings. . . .

The denouement [however] is sadly deficient in a good old poetic justice. . . . Unless Mr. Cooke means to give us a sequel in which the young lady shall be seen "married and settled," we submit that Ellie has been badly treated and the reader defrauded of a pleasurable excitement that by every rule of fictitious composition he was entitled to expect.

With regard to the treatment of the drama of "**Ellie**," we think Mr. Cooke might justly be held to a stricter fidelity to fact in respect of his scenes and incidents. We have neither picture galleries nor operas in Richmond, nor does the snow ever fall to a depth consistent with the sleigh-ride so dashingly described in the first Chapter of the third Book. But this is a trivial affair and we mention it only as something to be borne in mind in his next appearance.

In delineation of character, the same power is now and then exhibited in "**The Human Comedy**" which gave us such vivid and life-like portraitures in the "**Virginia Comedians**," while passages of real eloquence and brilliancy are scattered throughout its chapters.

*A review of "Ellie; or, the Human Comedy," in* The Southern Literary Messenger, *Vol. XXI, No. 8, August, 1855, p. 519.*

---

***PUTNAM'S MONTHLY: A MAGAZINE OF LITERATURE, SCIENCE AND ART*** (essay date 1855)

After Mr. Cooke's *Youth of Jefferson*, and several admirably graphic sketches of the Old Dominion . . . , we confess to having read his *Ellie; or, Comedy of Life*, with no little disappointment. It has no interest as a story, nor merit in its characterizations. The principal figure is a marvelously good girl, of the Little Nell species—a type of character of which we are heartily tired; while the other figures are so obviously made up, that they are quite insignificant as representatives of men and women. It was needless for the author to disclaim as he does in the preface, any designs upon actual personages: for his characters are automata and not living souls. But the greatest deficiency in this work is in dialogue or conversation. A great deal of it consists in the rapid interchange of monosyllables and short phrases, such as "Yes," "No," "What," "Who," "When," "Truly," &c., which is very tiresome; while the longer talk is generally vapid. If the Richmond society is accustomed to such an interchange of speech, it must be dreadfully vacuous. Mr. Cooke's previous writings, such as we have read, have so much genuine truth, vivacity, and force of observation in them, that we have had a difficulty in persuading ourselves that this novel could be by the same hand. He must try again, and write about ancient Virginia, not that of the present day. (pp. 319-20)

*A review of "Ellie; or, Comedy of Life," in* Putnam's Monthly: A Magazine of Literature, Science and Art, *Vol. VI, No. XXXIII, September, 1855, pp. 319-20.*

## [JOHN R. THOMPSON]  (essay date 1856)

For a novel of more than four hundred pages there are fewer changes of scene and less of incident in [the "**Last of the Foresters**"], than any other that we can call to mind. The characters are scarce a dozen in number, and carry on the plot (which from its simplicity can hardly be called so, without a misuse of terms,) in Winchester, or its immediate vicinity; and though the ante-revolutionary period selected by the author gives promise of stirring border occurrences in the course of his story, we have nothing of action more exciting than a village disturbance between the German and Irish residents, ending in a broken head or so, and a plentiful effusion of beer.

From what we have said, the reader may, perhaps, suppose that we do not think highly of the "**Last of the Foresters.**" As a dramatic work, we do not, but to quote the author's own language, "it would be unjust to apply to this volume the tests which are brought to bear upon an elaborate romance." It is rather a series of sketches of scenery and character—a succession of little comedies in village life—than a grave attempt to lay bare the motives of human conduct in another age and under other circumstances than our own. The hero is a white boy, who, having been stolen by the Indians in infancy, is thrown into intimate association with the whites before reaching manhood. . . . How this boy, Verty, was impressed by the conventional existence upon which he thus entered, how his wild, restless nature was softened and subdued by the tender eyes and loving heart of the fresh and beautiful Redbud, and how he came at last to play the part of a good, quiet citizen of colonial Virginia—all this Mr. Cooke has told with infinite skill, though the sweet shadows of the youthful lovers glide past us rather as the images of the poet in an atmosphere of unreal brightness, than as creatures of flesh and blood, in the world around us. Jinks . . . and Roundjacket . . . are more like life. . . . As for Ralph Ashley and Miss Fanny, they are two as utterly insipid young persons as can be found, making love to each other, in the whole range of fiction.

The charm of the "**Last of the Foresters,**" which makes it delightful midsummer reading, is to be detected in the humor running over the surface of the author's style, like rippling sunshine over a lake, and in the rare perception of the "beauties of nature" . . . which betrays itself in so many exquisite landscapes to vary the pictures in the artist's gallery. The pomp of Virginia woods, and the fires of our autumnal sunsets, have never been painted so gorgeously anywhere else as in Mr. Cooke's pages.

In dismissing this volume, and commending it to the reader, we may say that, while it seems to us eminently successful, it does not indicate any higher degree of talent, or farther reach of genius, than the very first novel Mr. Cooke ever wrote. He is wonderfully facile with the pen, and with his fun, his pathos, his eye for pictorial effects in the external world, and his quick apprehension of the superficial in character, we believe he could produce just such books every ninety days—books doing him great credit and affording us no small degree of entertainment, but not such as we have reason to believe him capable of writing, with greater care and more painful elaboration. Mr. Cooke writes too rapidly and revises too little. By devoting a longer time to the construction of his plots, and by studying the subtler workings of the human heart, he would be able, in our judgment, to enrich the literature of his country with works of fiction that would long survive the period that brought them forth.

*[John R. Thompson], in a review of "The Last of the Foresters; or, Humors on the Border: A Story of the Old Virginia Frontier," in* The Southern Literary Messenger, *Vol. XXIII, No. 2, August, 1856, p. 158.*

## *PUTNAM'S MONTHLY: A MAGAZINE OF LITERATURE, SCIENCE AND ART*   (essay date 1856)

The *Last of the Foresters,* by John Estin [*sic*] Cooke, . . . is equal to the best of Mr. Cooke's former writings. It is greatly superior to *Ellie,* though it has some of the same faults, particularly in the conversations, which are merely ejaculatory or unmeaning. His descriptions, both of localities and characters, are full of animation, with a strong local flavor, and with now and then a touch of true poetic feeling. The Verty and Redbud, who are the principal personages of his drama, are a success, and leave a distinct impression, as well as a pleasant memory in the mind. Nor are the other figures destitute of verisimilitude and interest. The story itself abounds in incident.

*A review of "Last of the Foresters," in* Putnam's Monthly: A Magazine of Literature, Science and Art, *Vol. VIII, November, 1856, p. 539.*

## [JOHN R. THOMPSON]  (essay date 1859)

All Mr. Cooke's excellencies and all his faults appear in ["**Henry St. John**"]. The chief merit of it is to be found in the faithful and minute reproduction of the social habitudes of a past age which is associated with the brightest renown of Virginia and in which moved the most illustrious of her sons. The pictures of life and manners which it presents, highly coloured as they are, have been drawn from materials carefully collected and conscientiously employed, and Mr. Cooke has shown the skill of the true artist in filling up the cold historic outlines and causing the canvass to glow with the freshened tints of a bygone, almost forgotten period. His selections from the poet's corner of the old Gazette are not only most happy, but they have been ingeniously introduced, while the stirring scenes of the first act of the Revolutionary drama at Williamsburg are interwoven with the story with a fine dramatic effect. When we say in addition to this that the richness and animation of Mr. Cooke's style mark almost every page of "**Henry St. John,**" the reader will feel assured that in our judgment it is a work both meritorious and entertaining.

We must qualify this sincere praise, however. . . .

The book is not altogether truthful or squared to probability in respect of its descriptions and incidents. (p. 316)

We should justly condemn a historical painting in which, however faithfully the accessories might have been executed, the artist had bestowed his whole attention upon the two principal figures, leaving the others but hastily sketched, and with no more of life in them than the lay figures of his studio. And yet this is just what Mr. Cooke seems to us to do. Not without a considerable power of delineation, he makes his hero and heroine probable beings enough, though with more than the ordinary silliness of lovers; they act from human motives, are moved by human joys and sorrows, are touched with a feeling of earthly infirmity, and do now and then cheat us into a belief in their actual existence. But he goes no further. The rest of the *dramatis personae* are not men and women at all, they are but automata, the lifeless representatives of certain follies or peculiarities. . . . Indeed there is so much flatness of characterization in Mr. Cooke's novels, that they remind us of those stereoscopic views in which two figures are vividly represented against a painted background where all the effect of perspective is lost.

The plots of Mr. Cooke's novels are singularly ill-contrived. He is not wanting in invention, and understands effect as well as any one. . . . [But in **"Henry St. John"**] the reader is kept in no state of pleasing and excited doubt, alternating between satisfaction and despair, as to the fate of the heroine, and the incidents which conduce to the catastrophe are mostly forced and unnatural. Mr. Cooke would seem to have gone on writing chapter after chapter of a particular story, without the least notion himself of how it was all to end, until the immense piles of MS. before him, warned him of the necessity of a conclusion, and then to have resorted to abductions, thunder-storms, pistols, house-burnings and all the other properties of the melodrama. We attribute this rather to want of study than to want of invention. Mr. Cooke writes too fast and publishes without proper revision.

In dismissing **"Henry St. John,"** we cannot but pay the high tribute of our admiration to the purity of sentiment which distinguishes the highly poetic and animated style of our author. It is easy to see that the atmosphere of his fancy is a healthful atmosphere. He has the heartiest sympathy with what is honest and pure and of good report. And though an occasional extravagance may be found in his descriptive passages, the style is uniformly as chaste as the sentiment. (pp. 316-17)

> *[John R. Thompson], in a review of "Henry St. John, Gentleman, of 'Flower of Hundreds' in the County of Prince George, Virginia: A Tale of 1774-75," in* The Southern Literary Messenger, *Vol. XXIX, No. 16, October, 1859, pp. 316-18.*

## RUSSELL'S MAGAZINE (essay date 1859)

[When we] read the first paragraphs of the **"Prologue"** [to **"The Virginia Comedians"**] . . . , the glow of the style, the flush and fervour of warm imaginations, an almost tropic luxuriance of imagery and description, first caught the attention, and then absorbed the mind.

Here, we said, is a truly bold, free and vigorous writer, of picturesque power, keen observation, and rarely delicate sensibilities. What an eye for the rich aspects of nature! How subtly, and yet with what gorgeous strength he paints the autumn sunsets and the autumn woods! In fact, the whole **"Prologue"** is a prose-poem, steeped in the colours of the warmest fancy, and redolent, so to speak, of the "Odours of the South!"

We were hardly less fascinated by the story which succeeded it—a narrative of vivid interest, of rapid, often dramatic action, coherent, and graphic in its characterization, and, although in technical phrase, somewhat inartistically "put together," yet, upon the whole, so life-like in its pictures of society, (the society of the "Old Dominion" a century or more ago), and exhibiting so much of reserved force, as well as present and active imagination, that we at once perceived that a writer of true genius had stepped upon the stage of authorship.

That [Mr. Cooke] was a Southerner we could not doubt, for a certain proud loyalty to Virginia, a minute acquaintance with

her history, and the magnificent scenery of her forests and mountains, and, above all, the free, almost careless exuberance and richness of his style, appeared to indicate his birth-place, and association with an impetuous, high-spirited and noble people. (pp. 285-86)

[Mr. Cooke] composes with marvellous rapidity.

In somewhat *less* than five years, a series of "Historical Romances," besides several beautiful love tales, have been contributed by him to the literature (the *best part* of the literature) of the South and the country. . . .

Mr. Cooke is most successful in his purely descriptive, or his purely passionate scenes. Although possessed of a very "pleasant humour," he is apt in his lighter portraitures, whether of men or things, to be diffuse, and occasionally to exaggerate, so that the result verges upon caricature. . . .

It is the fashion with many recent novelists altogether to eschew *a plot*. . . . (p. 286)

Mr. Cooke, we are glad to say, does *not* belong to *this* class of writers.

He perceives clearly, and he acts upon the perception, that "a plot" in the drama, or the novel, is only a succinct phrase to express *that harmoniousness of general conception*, whereby the separate details are brought into the close union, and arranged according to the natural sequence of events as they occur in our actual lives.

In other words, he repudiates, in his practice (and doubtless, upon a stern, artistic principle), the superficial theory which conveniently ignores *invention*, and would modestly substitute for it a species of narrow, spasmodic vigour, wholly destitute of the capacity to generalize and to create what may rightly be considered *a representative* character, or a typical picture of some remarkable era of time.

The truth of this observation is signally exemplified in the plan of [**"Henry St. John, Gentleman"**]. . . . In the author's own words, "his volume has two themes—two aims; the story of a man and a woman; the history, also, of a period in the annals of a Nation."

But it must not be supposed that to accomplish his ends, Mr. Cooke (as some feebler artist might have done) resorts to *separate* streams of narrative; on the contrary, the story of his "man and woman" not only runs parallel to, but is constantly mingling most naturally with, the larger stream of political events.

Thus, his novel is a consistent and unique portraiture of the society, and characteristic features of an anti-revolutionary age, as modified by the customs, opinions and passions of a peculiar locality. (pp. 286-87)

We confess to a sentiment of the liveliest gratification, when we reflect that the *two novelists* in this country (Wm. Gilmore Simms and Jno. [sic] Esten Cooke), upon whose shoulders the mantle of the American Scott (Fenimore Cooper), has fallen, belong to the South; are imbued with southern feeling, passion, patriotism; proving, by every additional work, that they are "true sons of the soil," and destined to transmit the characteristics and the fame of their native land to a far-distant posterity. (p. 288)

> *A review of "Henry St. John, Gentleman of 'Flower of Hundreds', in the County of Prince George, Vir-*

ginia: A Tale of 1774-75," in Russell's Magazine, Vol. VI, No. III, December, 1859, pp. 285-88.

### JAMES WOOD DAVIDSON   (essay date 1869)

Captain [Cooke] stands well among the novelists of our country; not so voluminous as Simms or Cooper, but ranging with them in the quality of much that he wrote years ago, before haste had impaired his style; and standing, in some respects, with Washington Irving and Hawthorne, not greatly inferior to either. (p. 105)

[*The Youth of Jefferson*] is replete with elegant portraiture, and partakes largely of the author's characteristic tone,—cheerfulness and spirit, pouring the sunshine of sentiment over the playful stream of vivacity. . . .

The girl-heroine [of *Ellie*] is intended to illustrate the author's theory of heart-goodness—the beauty of a pure young life— that is very attractive, but perhaps a trifle hyper-sentimental. (p. 106)

A Southern critic has pronounced [*Henry St. John, Gentleman*] "by great odds, the best American historical novel," and there are weighty reasons for the opinion. The strong characters are very strong, but are never indecent, grossly profane, or otherwise shocking in their language. The author has the faculty of showing you this kind of people without quoting the *ipsissima verba* of their blasphemy or smut. In this, Captain Cooke differs from Dr. Simms, of South Carolina, in whose hands Smith and Muggins follow the example of "our army in Flanders." The style in general is graceful, facile, and often elevated; and is a fair specimen of Captain Cooke's literary style. (p. 107)

[*Surry of Eagle's Nest*] is a charming book, and clears up much of the fog that had gathered around [historical] characters in the uncertain tradition of newspapers. While *Surry of Eagle's Nest* is Captain Cooke's most entertaining novel, it is not his best; but the time, the opportuneness of its appearance, gives it the advantage over all in the matter of popularity. (p. 108)

The main fault, after haste, that the critics found with [*Lee and His Lieutenants*], is one that attaches in a greater or less degree to all Captain Cooke's historical works,—an undue expansion and importance given to everything Virginian. It is as if he were too near such objects, and the eye necessarily takes in a *microscope* outline. One gathers the idea that many things of equal if not greater importance than some mentioned, have been omitted, because *covered*, so to speak, to the eye of the narrator, by some intervening Virginian object. I am wholly unwilling to intimate the slightest depreciation of the Old Dominion, . . . but the reading public may be excused for becoming restive under the implicit depreciation of everywhere else, even though so noble a state as Virginia be the gainer. (p. 109)

To say that it is thoroughly, if not intensely Virginian, is the highest praise I feel free to bestow upon [*Fairfax*]. That truthfulness to nature is its best feature. . . . [The plot] is not complicated; and the strength of the fiction lies, as it does in most of this writer's books, in the rapid action and in the spirited episode. There is everywhere a want of elaborate polish and careful art-study. The stirring times portrayed, it is true, demand less of these than would be available in spheres where mere action was less the characteristic of the life. . . . Critics have found fault with the author for introducing the great Washington, though only as a promising young man, into the field

of fiction, claiming that the character is too high and sacred for such manipulation. This objection strikes me as simply absurd; and is a symptom of such abject hero-worship, that the surprise one feels at meeting it at this day is modified by disgust. Captain Cooke's use of Washington appears to me both proper and creditable to the book, viewed as a work of art. But the work as a whole is hasty, and bears marks of having been hurried up beyond the natural and graceful speed of the writer. It is less than the earlier successes of Captain Cooke warrant us in expecting. (pp. 109-10)

*James Wood Davidson, "John Esten Cooke," in his The Living Writers of the South, Carleton, 1869, pp. 105-12.*

### HARPER'S NEW MONTHLY MAGAZINE   (essay date 1870)

Mr. John Esten Cooke has been actuated by a very commendable spirit in writing the *Heir of Gaymount* . . .—viz., a desire to teach the F.F.V.'s [First Families of Virginia] the value of hard work. He has evidently studied the agricultural books and papers to good advantage, and makes a romance out of cabbages and corn and grape-vines such as only the believers in the five-acres-enough style of literature will be able to credit. Certainly since the era of the Arabian Nights such farming was never known as that of Edmund Cartaret. However, spite of its inherent absurdity, the story is entertaining reading. . . . It is a story to be read when you want no temptation to mental excitement or mental activity of any sort; to be read to-day and forgotten to-morrow.

*A review of "Heir of Gaymount," in* Harper's New Monthly Magazine *(copyright © 1870 by* Harper's New Monthly Magazine*), Vol. XLI, No. CCXLV, October, 1870, p. 787.*

### THE LITERARY WORLD   (essay date 1872)

[*Doctor Vandyke*] is a story of Virginia life, more than a century ago. . . . [It] deals with high society, abounds in enthusiastic descriptions of Virginia lordliness and hospitality, and is rich in the elements of tragedy. Mr. Cooke delights to recall the old days of Virginia's colonial greatness, to portray—with intelligent skill and graphic effect, it must be admitted—the social pleasures of the place and time. . . .

[Dr. Vandyke] is a well-drawn character, and goes far toward lifting the story above the level of commonplace. The author credits him with the discovery of an anaesthetic—what it was does not appear—which he employed as chloroform is now used, and with like effect. This seems to be a serious anachronism, and the author's defence of it does not mend the matter.

The other characters in the story are in no wise remarkable. . . . The most curious, and perhaps the most exciting pages of the book are those in which Honoria's "eating the dumb-cake"— a process by which a girl is supposed to be enabled to see the face of her future husband—is described; but the account of Dr. Vandyke's strategy by means of which Honoria was disabused of her fearful hallucination, is admirably written. Though there is too much tragedy and mystery in this book to suit some readers, it is quite entertaining; and, so far as it goes, no doubt fairly reports some phases of Virginia life in the last century. Yet most readers will recognize a certain thinness, or want of substance in the plot, which, with the materials at the author's command, might have been easily supplied. They will remark, too, the author's failure to account for the implied sympathetic connection between the visions of Lord Ruthven and Honoria—a failure which seriously mars the artistic symmetry of the story. It is worthy of note, also, that the moral tone of the book is by no means high—that none of its personages illustrate and exemplify ennobling philosophy; not a lesson is to be learned from its pages.

> *A review of "Doctor Vandyke," in* The Literary World *(copyright 1872 by L. C. Page & Company (Inc.)), Vol. III, No. 4, September 1, 1872, p. 55.*

## THE ATLANTIC MONTHLY    (essay date 1877)

*Canolles* is an old-fashioned story of the Revolutionary period. To veteran novel-readers, accustomed to elaborate plots and subtle delineations of character, Mr. Cooke's art will not be entirely satisfying. They will smell the *dénoûment* afar off; and they will smile, perhaps, instead of tremble when, after the failure of all imaginable efforts to relieve him, the hero is led out to be shot. They know that there is to be a rescue or a reprieve . . . , and the last page will give assurances that the heroic stock is in a fair way of being perpetuated. But even to such knowing readers the story will not be without interest. . . . With all its shortcomings the story is thoroughly healthy and hearty; and it will be quite sure to interest the boys who are fond of Cooper, Kennedy, and Gilmore Simms. (p. 631)

Mr. Cooke would perhaps claim that his novel has a purpose, namely, the cultivation of a States rights spirit. But no federalist and no believer in Mr. Boutwell's theory of subordinating the State to the United States authorities need fear its influence in a political way. (p. 632)

> *A review of "Canolles: The Fortunes of a Partisan of '81," in* The Atlantic Monthly *(copyright © 1877, by The Atlantic Monthly Company, Boston, Mass.), Vol. XL, No. CCXLI, November, 1877, pp. 631-32.*

## THE INDEPENDENT    (essay date 1879)

Mr. John Esten Cooke, who can never give up writing about the old colonial days of Virginia, has produced an excellent book for boys in his *Stories of the Old Dominion*. . . . No bright boy who has once begun it will be likely to tire of it from beginning to end, for its heroes are numerous and the narratives have all the charm of stories that are told for the sake of the story alone. Virginia in the Old Dominion days was the most romantic and chivalrous of the colonies, and Mr. Cooke has not had to go begging for his material. The adventures . . . are true stories that offer sufficient variety of action and achievement to give any writer an opportunity to create a book which will prove a good one.

> *A review of "Stories of the Old Dominion," in* The Independent, *Vol. XXXI, June 5, 1879, p. 10.*

## MARGARET J. PRESTON    (essay date 1880)

[*The Virginia Bohemians*] is *post bellum,* and turns a good deal upon the troubles aroused by a band of somewhat desperate characters who distilled and traded in illicit whisky. . . . Several of the most dramatic scenes in the volume have to do with these wild mountaineers; and one of them, Daddy Welles, is about the most original and piquant personage of all the moving panorama. Mr. Cooke has astonishing skill in mingling and intermingling interminable plots; he drives his winged horses four-in-hand, and yet never seems to get the reins entangled.

In the present tale there are no less than four distinct love stories; and so well managed are they that the reader cannot say that one takes precedence of another, either in interest or execution. It is hard to determine who is the heroine, who is the hero, of the tale. This crowding of his canvas is perhaps somewhat of a fault in Mr. Cooke; the attention of the reader is distracted by the multitude of characters, and it is not possible to finish up each group with that artistic fidelity which justice to himself demands. His touches, however, are so effective that each portrait stands out with clear distinctness. Juliet Armstrong, among the feminine characters, is charmingly drawn and delightfully consistent throughout. . . . The most powerful creation of all is the Lefthander, the very vagueness of whose great looming outline renders his personality more mysterious. Mr. Lascelles, the *bête noir* of the book, is scarcely reconcilable with the fine old family, so proper in every respect, of which we find him a son.

The numberless minute details in which Mr. Cooke portrays the peculiar Old Virginia plantation manners and ways are absolutely true to nature, and this gives his book the added value of an almost photographic verity. The homes he describes are the real Old Virginia homes; the interiors he sketches are from the life, and the planters, like General Lascelles, are of that hospitable, knightly race that has now almost passed away. (pp. 207-08)

Sometimes we are disposed to think that [Mr. Cooke] is too hurried; for he is singularly careless occasionally as to his literary workmanship. Not, as it would seem, from any inability to make it otherwise; but from mere rapid writing. And sometimes, we must be allowed to say, we find him indulging in platitudes which a little careful revision would have obliterated. Still we have much pleasure to thank him for in adding to our stock of more distinctively Southern literature, and we hope for many more books from his facile pen, touched with the same rich life-coloring peculiar to *The Virginia Bohemians*. (p. 208)

> *Margaret J. Preston, in a review of "The Virginia Bohemians," in* The Literary World *(copyright 1880 by L. C. Page & Company (Inc.)), Vol. XI, No. 13, June 19, 1880, pp. 207-08.*

## THE ATLANTIC MONTHLY    (essay date 1880)

[One] may look to the easy-going stories of Mr. John Esten Cooke, and find examples of a story-telling art curiously faithful to traditions undisturbed by recent literary development. In reading, for instance, *The Virginia Bohemians,* although the scenes are *post bellum,* one faintly recalls the once popular tales of Kennedy, and is affected by forms of art very much as when, in real life, he finds himself once more in a stage-coach,—not the tally-ho of a fantastic revival, but the actual vehicle which has rumbled over country roads from necessity. Mr. Cooke takes us into a valley lying between ranges of the Blue Ridge, and, gently removing us from the roar or cities and too close reminder of the restless life of the day, spins a pleasant web about the fortunes of a few characters who are equally removed with us from actual experience. . . . Mysteries are created and solved, relationships are constructed out of apparently unpromising material, the right heroes rescue the right heroines, and no doubt is left as to the final disposition of each character. There is something agreeable in the thin veil of romance which covers the whole story. We have stepped into the story-teller's world as it used to be, and out of that realistic inclosure which modern fiction would fain have us accept as a clever substitute for the world we live in. Mr. Cooke gives us county and town names, and paints his scenery with an air of candor and affection; we only smile, and assure him that it is all the same; the Virginian Bohemia answers every purpose, whether he has described it or imagined it. The country and the characters, even including the civilly treated United States marshal, are all pleasantly unreal, and that is what we ask for in his book. There is a consistency of unreality about it. It is the real country of the novel as distinguished from the hard city to which we have become accustomed. (pp. 827-28)

> *"'Dr. Heidenhoff's Process', and Other Novels,"*
> in The Atlantic Monthly *(copyright © 1880, by The*
> *Atlantic Monthly Company, Boston, Mass.), Vol.*
> *XLVI, No. 6, December, 1880, pp. 824-38.\**

## THE CRITIC AND GOOD LITERATURE   (essay date 1884)

**'The Virginia Comedians'** is a very old-fashioned novel, and it is very, very long. . . . [The] style of writing is the 'old school.' Naturally enough, we find here no trace of the curious commingling of the opposite styles of Trollope and Tourguéneff, such as give so strange a savor to the fictions of Mr. Henry James. Here is to be seen, as plainly as possible, the influence of [Charlotte Brontë's] 'Jane Eyre' and of some of the later novels of Lord Lytton. The story is somewhat sprawling and escapes from the reader, and the disappearance of hero and heroine at the end of the first volume does not help to retain the rambling interest. Yet the picture of life in Virginia a hundred and twenty years ago is entertaining and instructive; and many of the incidents of the story itself are exciting. It is well to note that Mr. Cooke has not been kind or fair to the character of Lewis Hallam, to whom we owe the introduction of the drama into these coasts. If we may believe Dunlap, Hallam was very far from being the feeble and disreputable person Mr. Cooke presents to us.

> *A review of "The Virginia Comedians,"* in The Critic
> and Good Literature, *n.s. Vol. I, No. 7, February*
> *16, 1884, p. 76.*

## HARPER'S NEW MONTHLY MAGAZINE   (essay date 1884)

[*Bonnybell Vane*] is a delightful [tale], rich in romantic incidents and in fine delineations of the picturesque phases of society that existed in the Old Dominion on the eve of the Revolutionary War, and rich also in historic memories of the times that tried men's souls, and in speaking portraitures of the grand men who first pioneered the people of the ancient colony in their resistance to tyranny and then valiantly led them in their heroic struggle for independence. It is impossible to read Mr. Cooke's impassioned and sympathetic story without coming under the spell of the noble contagion which it so graphically depicts.

> *A review of "Bonnybell Vane," in* Harper's New
> Monthly Magazine *(copyright © 1884 by* Harper's
> New Monthly Magazine*), Vol. LXVIII, No.*
> *CCCCVIII, May, 1884, p. 975.*

## THE LITERARY WORLD   (essay date 1885)

[Mr. Cooke's *Pokahontas* is] a literary masterpiece of imitation . . . ; a telling so just to the supposed facts, and at the same time so apt in its uses of the imagination and of the feelings, that we hardly know whether to call it fiction or history. Mr. Cooke, as narrator, with great and adroit good taste, puts himself behind the person of Anas Todkill, a brave and trusty follower of Capt. John Smith at Jamestown . . . , who is made the mouthpiece of the pretty tale. Its manner is true to its subject. . . . [The] adventures of the Indian maiden with Smith and Rolfe are related in full with singular sweetness. . . .

Mr. Cooke has caught the tone and spirit of his subject in a remarkable degree, and the success of his handling of it is almost classic. The simplicity, naturalness, and tenderness of the story make it very touching. (p. 113)

> *A review of "My Lady Pokahontas,"* in The Literary
> World *(copyright 1885 by L. C. Page & Company*
> *(Inc.)), Vol. XVI, No. 7, April 4, 1885, pp. 112-13.*

## MARGARET J. PRESTON   (essay date 1886)

It was with a quickened pulsation of heart, and with a sense of personal loss, that Virginians learned, a fortnight since, of the unlooked-for death of John Esten Cooke. . . . He has done more within the last two decades to illustrate and honor the Colonial, the Revolutionary and the Four-years' War, and the unique domestic and social life and history of his Motherland, than any man who has lived within its borders. . . .

John Esten Cooke was still in the prime of his powers; his last two or three works were among his best; his **'Virginia'** is the best compendium of the history of his State that I have ever seen. It has none of the dryness of mere annals: there is a glow about it from beginning to end, which makes it attractive even to quite young readers, and it has a dramatic quality which is very charming. **'My Lady Pokahontas'** is the tenderest and most poetical rendering of the true story of the young Indian Princess which has ever been set forth. . . . His **'Surrey of Eagle's Nest'** will always remain as a kind of classic with the people of his native State; for it deals so largely with the personal experience of Mr. Cooke as he came into the close relation of staff-officer to Gen. J.E.B. Stuart, and as he was thrown into personal contact with Gen. Stonewall Jackson, and the knightly Ashby, that it contains much of the material out of which history is made. Mr. Cooke did not set himself to write a novel in its pages; but to give, as an eye-witness, the scenes of his story. . . .

I do not claim for him that his literary style was as correct and polished as it might have been, or that his novels were built up on the most artistic principles. But I do say for him that he was chivalrous in his devotion to the land of his birth, and at the same time singularly devoid of bitter feeling toward those who differed from him sectionally and politically; that he was remarkably successful in the vivid and actual portrayal of Virginia life and manners, both under the old *régime* and the new; and that he was so specially saturated with the spirit of the Colonial days, to whose study and delineation he gave untiring attention, that his reproductions of the old life are absolutely faithful to time and circumstance. Thackeray himself, not being 'to the manner born,' is far less accurate; in his 'Virginians' he gives us pictures of the Colonial life and of the boyhood of Washington, which are very wide of the reality. Cooke's **'Fairfax'** is a far truer portraiture of the same period. It is in the minute rendering of the peculiar life of the South, in his absolute truthfulness of detail from the side-lights which Mr. Cooke throws upon his pictures, that the value of his works consists. He always wrote of what was as familiar to him as his daily breathing. In the full sense of the word, his books are racy, and have the very fragrance of the soil. . . . Although Mr. Cooke's works have been more widely read at home than elsewhere, Virginians of the most cultivated class have perhaps been more disposed to be critical in regard to the faults of his literary style than other readers; from the very fact that Love, instead of being blind, is Argus-eyed, and in its pride and jealousy makes too much of peccadilloes.

> *Margaret J. Preston, "A Virginian of the Virginians," in* The Critic, *New York, n.s. Vol. VI, No. 146, October 16, 1886, p. 181.*

## CHARLES F. RICHARDSON  (essay date 1889)

The best novel written in the Southern States before the civil war is "**The Virginia Comedians**" of John Esten Cooke. Its author, like Simms, was an inveterate book-maker, and belonged distinctly to the romantic-sentimental school, not the realistic. He aimed to produce novels and novelettes of incident or passion, rather than sketches of local scenes and characters. The past of Virginia was more vivid, in his mind, than her present. But his stories are not sensational, in the sanguinary sense. . . . [Cooke's] masterpiece ["**The Virginia Comedians**"] is a series of historic pictures, warmed by bygone sunshine and given true spirit by the sympathetic promptings of the maker's heart. If "background" is needed in our fiction, it assuredly is here. . . . If we seek color and action in a varied society, Thackeray himself asked no better, though he understood the scene and time less perfectly. Cooke, a fierce fighter in the war, was as sensible and kindly as Lee at its close, nor in his books did he display Simms' silly contempt for his Northern betters, nor Cooper's or Poe's angry hatred of New England. . . . [This] "Virginian of the Virginians" . . . left his state no unworthy literary legacy. . . . ["**The Virginia Comedians**" does not] cease to interest those who turn, from time to time, to the study of a phase of life not less attractive because its antique grandeur now seems as faded and thin as the garreted satins in which it once was resplendent. (pp. 401-03)

> *Charles F. Richardson, "The Lesser Novelists," in his* American Literature, 1607-1885: American Poetry and Fiction, Vol. II *(copyright by Charles F. Richardson 1888), G. P. Putnam's Sons, 1889, pp. 390-412.**

## CARL HOLLIDAY  (essay date 1906)

Perhaps the most widely known and most popular novelist the South has ever had was John Esten Cooke. . . . In his early work imitative to some degree, in his later productions hasty unto negligence, he nevertheless possesses qualities that lift him high above the common run of fiction writers and make him at his best, the companion of Irving and Cooper. In not a few ways he resembles these two men; for he unites in his writings the gentler traits of the one with the more strenuous character of the other. A love of lingering description and the charm of wild activity are in him well mingled. (p. 275)

Some of his stories are not read today; some are not even heard of; but, when all this is said, there remain for posterity such permanent works as *Virginia Comedians, Stories of the Old Dominion, Surrey of Eagle's Nest, Henry St. John, Gentleman,* and *Hilt to Hilt.* These, by their vividness, their forceful char-

acters, and the very power of their movement, will not soon pass away. (p. 276)

[Cooke depicts] the quaint phases of the old life, of the Virginia life when it was in its bloom, when Washington, Jefferson, Patrick Henry, the Randolphs, the Lees, and a host of others whose names are household words, lived and wrought for the nation. True to nature, as he saw it, he is picturesque at all times.

Whether he is always true to life is an open question; for the stricture is too frequently true of him, as of those he unconsciously imitated, that "wizards, gloomy barons, French dancing masters, fair young maidens, lamiae, Christian big-Injuns, savage halfbreeds, secret panels, mysterious packages, thunder, duelling, and desperation are thrown into the cauldron, stirred with a pen, and spiced with genuine love for the grand old Blue Ridge and romantic Massanutten." That he does love wild scenes cannot be denied; the healthy blood of a new race was in him. Yet the spirit that rushes and swirls in many of his narratives is higher than that of mere violence. Thus, in *The Virginia Bohemians,* the description of a fight with the moonshiners has a dramatic quality that mere bombast and sensationalism can never impart. (pp. 277-78)

However weak in some respects Cooke may be, he is an admirable character-builder. In his earlier work he was in full sympathy with Cooper and Simms in that he had great admiration for the "natural" man. . . . But he does not fail to see the beauty of which the cultured soul is capable, and therein, especially in his portrayal of the gentle yet courageous spirit of woman, he far surpasses Cooper. Few indeed are the female characters in American fiction more lovable and more touchingly pictured than Beatrice Hallam, the actress, in *Virginia Comedians.* For another instance of this mingling of strength and elegance, that strongest of all his characters, Henry St. John, is worthy of praise. Using large canvases for his portrayals of society, the characters that he creates are ever distinct, vivid, intensely living.

His faults, it has been hinted, are plain. He too often lapses into sentimentality; he sometimes mistakes bravado for bravery; he is tainted with sensationalism; he is often too romantic; he does not at all times face squarely the sterner phases of life; he is frequently in haste; he forgets, in his interest in the tale, the demands of art. And, in spite of it all, his work is good— it is excellent. The words of praise bestowed upon *Virginia Comedians* might be applied most justly to others of his many volumes: "The whole book is redolent of youth and poetic susceptibility to the beauties of nature, the charms of women, and the quick movement of life." He is ever cheerful; hope never leaves him. Even in *Surrey of Eagle's Nest,* written in 1866, when the South was one vast field of wretchedness and despair, there is the same strong call for courage and a belief in a future victory. Such a writer could not have come at a more needed time.

Why, then, has his fame diminished? The question is answered in his own words: "Mr. Howells and the other realists have crowded me out of the popular regard as a novelist, and have brought the kind of fiction I write into general disfavor. I do not complain of that, for they are right. They see, as I do, that fiction should faithfully reflect life, and they obey the law, while I was born too soon and am now too old to learn my trade anew. But in literature, as in everything else, advance should be the law, and he who stands still has no right to complain if he is left behind." Such indeed is the cause of his neglect. He was essentially a romanticist, not a realist. He did not write to prove theories; he was simply a teller of stories. Unlike the later fiction, his tales do not blindly follow where a merciless destiny leads them; for he at all times considers it best that his characters should "live happy ever afterwards." (pp. 279-80)

> *Carl Holliday, "John Esten Cooke" (originally published in a slightly different form as "John Esten Cooke As a Novelist," in* The Sewanee Review, *Vol. XIII, No. 2, April, 1905), in his* A History of Southern Literature, *The Neale Publishing Company, 1906 (and reprinted by Kennikat Press, Inc., 1969), pp. 275-81.*

### CARL VAN DOREN   (essay date 1921)

It is true that one successor of Cooper upheld for a time the dignity of the old-fashioned romance. John Esten Cooke . . . cherished a passion as intense as Simms's for his native state and deliberately set out to celebrate its past and its beauty. *Leather Stocking and Silk* and [*The Last of the Foresters*] . . . , both narratives of life in the Valley, recall Cooper by more than their titles; but in *The Youth of Jefferson* . . . and its sequel, *Henry St. John, Gentleman* . . . , Cooke seems as completely Virginian as Beverley Tucker before him, though less stately in his tread. All three of these novels have their scenes laid in Williamsburg, the old capital of the Dominion; they reproduce a society strangely made up of luxury, daintiness, elegance, penury, ugliness, brutality. At times the dialogue of Cooke's impetuous cavaliers and merry girls nearly catches the flavor of the Forest of Arden, but there is generally something stilted in their speech or behavior that spoils the gay illusion. Nevertheless, *The Virginia Comedians* . . . may justly be called the best Virginia novel of the old régime, unless possibly [John Pendleton Kennedy's] *Swallow Barn* should be excepted, for reality as well as for color and spirit. No other book, of fact or fiction, so well sets forth the vision which in the days immediately before the Civil War Virginians cherished of their greater days on the eve of the Revolution. . . . [In *Surry of Eagle's Nest*] and the related tales *Hilt to Hilt* [and *Mohun*] . . . , as well as in numerous later novels, he continued to practise the old manner which grew steadily more archaic as the rough and ready dime novel, on the one hand, and the realistic novel, on the other, gained ground. Toward the end of his life he participated, without changing his habits, in the revival of the historical romance which began in the eighties, but he still seemed a belated dreamer, the last of the old school rather than the first of the new. (pp. 111-13)

> *Carl Van Doren, "Blood and Tears," in his* The American Novel *(reprinted with permission of Macmillan Publishing Company; © 1921 by Macmillan Publishing Co., Inc.; copyright renewed 1949 by Carl Van Doren), Macmillan, 1921, pp. 109-24.\**

### JOHN O. BEATY   (essay date 1922)

[John Esten Cooke, Virginian *is the only book-length critical study of Cooke. An objective assessment of Cooke's flaws and weaknesses, Beaty's statements are generally echoed by later critics. Beaty remarks that "Cooke's fluency was the cause of his chief faults" and notes that his historical fiction, particularly his Civil War novels, suffered becuase "in treating actual persons he does not always distinguish between what might have happened and what is generally known not to have happened." Beaty praises* The Virginia Comedians *as a work which "should be neglected*

by no serious student of American fiction," and commends Cooke for his depiction of the "various classes of individuals who formed the Virginia of 1765." He concludes that Cooke, despite his distaste for revision and his tendency toward sensationalism, "achieved more than a modicum of distinction."*]

Irving was the literary grand old man of Cooke's youth, and *Leather Stocking and Silk* owes him more than a little. . . . The style of the book is Irvingesque, particularly in passages which contrast the old with the new in the life of the Virginia border. . . . The Cooper influence was more obvious but less subtle. The "Leatherstocking Tales" suggested the title, and as a border tale the novel belongs to the school in which Cooper holds primacy.

This initial volume exemplifies Professor Brander Matthews's statement that an author, in his first book, tries to tell everything he knows. (p. 34)

*Leather Stocking and Silk* is, in spite of its scant four hundred pages, divided into three parts and ninety-five chapters. As might be expected from such a structure and the heterogeneity of sources, the plot . . . is somewhat weak. . . . *Leather Stocking and Silk* possessed some real merits which pointed to better subsequent work. The easy, graceful, flowing style is little inferior to the author's best achievement. The book has a certain value as social history. Some of the conversations sparkle; they are essentially transcripts from life, as may be seen from actual conversations recorded in the diaries. . . . [An] atmosphere of kindliness . . . pervades the entire composition, and reflects the temperament of the genial author, who says "to the reader:" "If the book be found entertaining and (above all else) the spirit of it pure, the writer will be more than satisfied." The first of these wishes was perhaps not realized. *Leather Stocking and Silk* split in halves the great decade which began with [William Thackeray's] *Vanity Fair* and ended with [George Eliot's] *Adam Bede;* but Cooke, unlike his fellow-countryman Hawthorne, did not share largely in the great novel-writing power then abroad in the English-speaking world. Fitting it is, however, that the second wish should have been expressed in the preface of his first book. It was fulfilled to the letter. In a score of novels and hundreds of shorter compositions he did not make use of an impure word or situation. (pp. 35-7)

[*Fairfax*, a novel nearly completed in 1853 but not published until 1859,] is markedly more entertaining than *Leather Stocking and Silk* and is a not wholly unworthy forerunner of *The Virginia Comedians*. . . . [However, a] great weakness of Cooke's historical fiction is in *Fairfax* seen for the first time. In treating actual persons he does not always distinguish between what might have happened and what is generally known not to have happened. He discredits the essential historical truth of his narrative by giving a son to the bachelor Fairfax. (pp. 37-8)

[*The Virginia Comedians*] should be neglected by no serious student of American fiction. It is of value to the social historian, is interesting to the student of the early American theater, and should prove fascinating to those who take delight in things pre-Revolutionary. At the opening of the thirty-second chapter of the second book Cooke states that he "aims at presenting in a brief and rapid manner, some view, however slight, of the various classes of individuals who formed that Virginia of 1765." This inclusion of "various classes" marked a decided advance in Virginia fiction, the writers of which had seen in Colonial Virginia chiefly cavaliers and servants. The low-class characters are not, however, successfully drawn. They either are meagerly sketched, lack the appearance of reality, or are portrayed merely in a subordinate relation to some superior person. Cooke was never skilful in his delineation of the negro. . . .

With these reservations Cooke achieved his aims notably. The middle-class Waters family is well portrayed. The upper part of society is brilliantly depicted. (p. 41)

Apart from the main plot *The Virginia Comedians* offers some interesting digressions in the way of comic scenes and sketches from colonial life. Tag as parson and schoolmaster is well conceived. Notable also are the accounts of the governor's ball, the Williamsburg fair, and the development of liberal sentiment in politics.

If a prospective reader decides from the first few pages whether or not he will go on with a book, John Esten Cooke is under a disadvantage. *The Virginia Comedians* is supposed to be arranged from or based on a manuscript work written by a Mr. C. Effingham, who refers to Champ as his "respected ancestor," but is otherwise not identified. Cooke as editor begins with a few pages supposedly by the "author of the ms.," and then explains that he will simplify, "give more artistic point to certain passages," and omit some "unnecessary and superfluous portions." This complex beginning . . . is likely to perplex the casual reader and is unfortunately characteristic of many of the author's books. But Cooke here plays up to the part admirably. Few writers who shift from one supposed character to another are more skilful in escaping a stylistic identity. (pp. 44-5)

Cooke preserves a superb detachment; he rarely if at all intrudes his personality. . . . Cooke had studied his field and, without apology or praise, presented his characters as he conceived them to have existed. In this respect his work is on a plane with *Tom Jones* [by Henry Fielding] and *Vanity Fair*. . . . (p. 46)

[*The Virginia Comedians*] was Cooke's only work to appear on the professional stage. His novels have far too many characters, too much sweep and pageantry, for successful condensation in a three-hour talking piece. If the cinema had existed in his time he might have won fame and fortune as a scenario writer. His crises are normally brought about by accidents, runaways, or rescues from drowning, rather than by the subtleties of conversation or the development of a mental attitude. In their shift back and forth from public events to the fortunes of a set of lovers, Cooke's best books before and after the war are of the same mold as the motion picture, *The Birth of a Nation*. (pp. 46-7)

*The Youth of Jefferson* affords pleasant reading for those who like a quaintly imagined reconstruction of the past and are not averse to having historical personages doctored to suit a novelist's purposes. . . . [Cooke's] accounts are not definitely authentic, although an atmosphere of essential truth pervades the work. . . . Cooke's humor is never of the broad, racy kind which is often regarded as typical of the United States; it is delicate, playful, fanciful, at most provocative of a smile. (pp. 49-50)

[*The Last of the Foresters*] is a rather unsatisfactory performance. Although it is far better than *Leather Stocking and Silk* in plot construction, and gives some passably good pictures of Valley life, it is rendered disagreeable by a very maudlin love affair. . . . The style of the book is characteristic of the author's more subjective vein and is commendable; but its gracefulness and limpidity are not able to counteract the effect of an unending redundancy. (p. 51)

Nothing complimentary can be said of the central romance, but the Ashley-Fanny, Jinks-Sallianna, Roundjacket-Lavinia approaches and understandings are by no means disagreeable. They save the novel from being a welter of insipid sentimentalism. . . . Cooke always shared the medieval-born admiration of the frail woman. Could the girl who caught cold at a mere foot-wetting really have been so attractive? Why should not Mrs. O'Calligan, "young and handsome, strong and healthy," have been given at least a chance of being a subsidiary heroine? As the third book written in a very busy year, *The Last of the Foresters* was probably an indiscretion of a tired author who was never at all capable of self-criticism. . . . (p. 52)

*The Last of the Foresters* retained suggestions of *The Virginia Comedians*. [*Ellie*] was, on the contrary, completely of the mid-nineteenth century type which depicts the patiently endured sorrow of penniless Christian childhood. [It] is hardly notable in any respect except for the rapidity of its composition, but it is in one key, and avoids the repetitions and the love-drivel of *The Last of the Foresters*. . . . In his attack on certain social ills as well as in his depiction of Ellie, Cooke was influenced in a general way by Dickens. The novel may, in a last analysis, be best described, however, as a very lengthy tract—and an excellent one. (pp. 55-6)

[Perversion] of historical fact is one of the chief faults of [*Henry St. John*] which is in most respects a worthy sequel to *The Virginia Comedians*. The portrayal of Dunmore and his entourage is brilliantly done; there is true splendor in the depiction of the last stand of the arrogant alien Governor of Virginia. Cooke on the whole builds rather largely on facts, always of course handling them freely, but sometimes in too much detail. . . . (p. 59)

In this late Colonial trilogy—the two parts of *The Virginia Comedians*, and *Henry St. John*—Cooke achieved the finest product of his career. He attained his difficult goal. He accomplished the imaginative reconstruction of the life of a past period with sufficient charm and power almost to warrant his being called a great social historian. (p. 60)

Throughout his career Cooke wrote poetry, and his poems attracted some attention. He was frequently referred to as a poet rather than a novelist. . . . [This] would seem to indicate that Cooke had considerable poetic ability, but such was hardly the case. The mid-century was not over-critical; a wholesome theme was nearly all that was demanded. Cooke's rapidity of composition was responsible for his chief shortcomings. His poems not only frequently lack the fine finish of perfection, but are sometimes faulty in rime and meter. Such of them as escape technical carelessness are mildly acceptable, but few exhibit marked vigor or originality. (p. 66)

[*Surry of Eagle's-Nest*] is at once a reflection of its author's faults and an earnest of what he might have achieved. If Cooke had forgotten his overworked Irvingesque habit of "editing" a supposed manuscript, had left out the Mordaunt-Fenwick plot, had even left out the big events of history, and—as he first intended—had given in his fluent, agreeable style an account of his experiences, his book might have been of perennial interest. In its actual form *Surry* has too much history to be excellent fiction; and it mingles the real Farley, Pelham, and others with fictitious persons of the same and higher rank to such a degree that as history it is sometimes confusing and in small details actually misinforming. The attempted blending of two distinct elements, a wildly improbable Gothic tale and a record of a career in the Civil War, results in a species of romance for which no large numbers of later general readers—boys perhaps excepted—are likely to have a pronounced taste.

The composition of *Surry* occupied about six weeks, and the results of the haste are plainly seen. Portions of [his *Life of Stonewall Jackson*] are incorporated bodily. There are stylistic faults. Rapidity of composition may be blamed for such banalities as a "long farewell to the only woman he had ever loved." . . . *Surry* was above all else a timely book. It was not penned with the care expected in a great modern historical novel. It must, however, have afforded pleasant reading to many a veteran; for it showed the war not as a failure, but as a superb adventure, the very participation in which was a mark of honor. Even to-day it is an agreeable volume for Southerners and others who are interested in the Civil War, like a stirring tale, and do not read too critically. (pp. 93-5)

Uneven as it is in quality, *Wearing of the Gray* is nevertheless both interesting and of solid value. . . . A pleasing touch is given by the author's frequently addressing the unknown persons who crossed his path in the war. . . . Unfortunately some of the papers are fiction and not history. "**Longbow's Horse**," for instance, concludes with a reference to Colonel Surry and May Beverley, characters in *Surry of Eagle's-Nest*. The inclusion of already published articles causes several anecdotes to be repeated. . . . The separate origin of the articles results also in a style of unusual redundancy. . . . A small but unnecessary flaw is the use of "natale solum," "gaudium certaminis," "immedicabile vulnus," and "perdu," where English words are available. (pp. 99-100)

[*Mohun*] requires no detailed comment for its merits and defects are those of *Surry*. . . . The greatest value of the work lies in its depiction of the dogged determination of the lessening band of "Lee's Miserables" as they faced defeat, and in the admirable representation of the civilian classes in Richmond. . . . The style of the book is facile and not uniform in texture. It sometimes has a tinge of the yellow-back; but in places, as in the invocation to the field of Gettysburg, exhibits an ornate splendor. To one who reads Cooke's works in their chronological order, a large portion of the military matter is now familiar, and the lack of variety in expression begins to pall. Again and again are found such phrases as "hilt to hilt" and "hammer and rapier," to cite only those figures which give names to books. (pp. 105-07)

The *Life of General Robert E. Lee* is, in its portraits, illustrations, and maps, and its type and binding, a fitting companion to the [*Life of Stonewall Jackson*]. In method and style the two biographies are . . . nearly identical. . . . [In the *Life of General Robert E. Lee*] almost no attention whatever is paid to the years before 1861 or after 1865. For battles and other national events one can have recourse to a history; a biography should reveal at least a few personal idiosyncrasies. . . . In Cooke's *Life* the great general is, at the close of five hundred pages, still but a distant figure passing on horseback. The military leader may have been revealed; the man is largely unknown. In such matters as he does admit, Cooke distributes emphasis rather poorly. . . . It must be borne in mind, however, that Cooke produced this book rapidly to meet a sudden popular demand, and made use of only such facts as he knew or could discover easily. (pp. 107-08)

It seems almost a loss to the world that the young captain of artillery, an already famous novelist, should have written his

biographies without regard to style or sufficient data, and above all should have vitiated notes of the utmost value by blending with them an outworn strain of fiction. What an opportunity he lost! (p. 108)

In the eight years from 1870 until the death of his wife Cooke produced a half-score of books which, in their setting and time, varied from the seventeenth century England of *Her Majesty the Queen* to the contemporary America of *Pretty Mrs. Gaston*. The novels of this decade are more nearly forgotten than those of any other period of Cooke's activity, but while they are not notable they do not deserve aggressive condemnation. They are in many cases good of their kind, and doubtless gave satisfaction to such of their readers as did not peruse them with too critical an eye.

Among these novels there is one, not the best of the lot, considered as literature, which stands out as of the highest interest. *The Heir of Gaymount* contains an almost complete record of Cooke's response to his environment in the years immediately following the war. (p. 121)

[Its] commonplace plot fails to reveal the true character of *The Heir of Gaymount*, and does not explain its importance to a person interested in Cooke or in contemporary attempts at solving the problems of Reconstruction. In the first place Carteret [the heir of Gaymount] is plainly Cooke. . . .

More important even than this reflection of the author is the book's preaching of the doctrine of work as a remedy for the South's troubles. (p. 124)

[The] value of [*The Heir of Gaymount*] as a document is conspicuously lessened by [Cooke's] failure to consider the negro. Between diatribe and ignoring there is little to choose. (pp. 127-28)

[*Out of the Foam*] is really an excellent story of its type. It has elements of adventure, mystery, and terror. It presents living embodiments of physical and moral ugliness in combat with brave and estimable persons in whose triumph one becomes something more than quietly interested. To secure a reader's approval a novel must be a masterly study appealing to the intellect and reflecting true criticism of life, or, failing this, must be either delightful or sensational. *Out of the Foam* is neither masterly nor delightful, but it is highly sensational, and can withal be put down unfinished less easily than some of its author's better books. (p. 130)

As a tour-de-force attempting to reproduce an atmosphere of the past, *Her Majesty the Queen* is of the manner of [Thackeray's] *Henry Esmond*, and, like *Esmond*, contains references to contemporary notables in politics and literature. . . . The work aimed to afford a panorama of its period, but unfortunately lacks the little details indicative of a firsthand knowledge of the ground. The style is fluent and the incidents are well handled, but there are no high places—the narrative remains on a dead level. (p. 131)

[In *Dr. Vandyke* there are] few traces of Cooke's antebellum manner. The story is wildly melodramatic. . . . Cooke fabricates a plot which is typical of his later manner, and owes many incidents to his previous work. . . . [In spite of] superficial local details, the story is not at all a reflection of Virginia life. It is not to be compared with *The Virginia Comedians*, the historical period of which it shares. (pp. 132-33)

*Pretty Mrs. Gaston* is a pleasant conventional story. . . . The book deserves neither praise nor blame. It served its temporary purpose, and is now forgotten. It is mildly diverting, but is of no interest as a record of life and manners, for it is Virginian only by the author's statement. The persons are as conventional as the plot, and the events might have been localized at any spot where English-speaking people congregate. (pp. 133-34)

*Justin Harley* begins with a description of certain members of several old Virginia families, but these worthies are soon involved in the meshes of tawdry melodrama. The book not only exemplifies the impossibility of Cooke's going back at this period of his life to the style of *The Virginia Comedians,* but shows vividly how his inventiveness was flagging. . . . The novel has, however, a few portraits worthy of appearing in the *Virginia Comedians* gallery. (pp. 135-36)

Like a number of Cooke's stories, *Canolles* begins with the conventional yet effective opening, the man on horseback at sunset, and in other respects seems equally hackneyed—especially to one who has read all its predecessors. In its love and war adventures it has elements decidedly suggestive of *Surry;* in its free handling of early American history it harks back to *The Virginia Comedians.* Its appearance in print marked the culmination of another stage of Cooke's literary career, for he was never again to produce a novel in the field or in the manner of either of these two important works. (pp. 137-38)

The twenty-one stories [in *Stories of the Old Dominion*] cover the more dramatic episodes of Virginia history in the Colonial and Revolutionary periods, and are entertainingly told. When not true to facts, they are true to tradition, and show Cooke to have achieved his desire of doing a serious and valuable piece of work. . . . Cooke's style was always clear and direct, but here he made a special effort to be "simple." The unnecessary pains resulted in no greater cramping of his style than an occasional superfluous explanation of an easy term, such as: "It was proclaimed on coins, that is, pieces of money." A few defects of this nature do not, however, obscure the merit of a book some of whose chapters are charming as well as vigorous. Perhaps it was no hard task to give the flavor of romance to the story of Captain John Smith; but other figures are as effectively handled. (p. 147)

For true local color, *The Virginia Bohemians* holds primacy among Cooke's novels. . . . The two churches [of Piedmont], the town pump, the blacksmith shop with the crowd of small boys, the village store with a porch full of idlers awaiting the stage—all these are excellently presented, especially in the chapter entitled "Piedmont wakes up." This part of the novel is of "photographic accuracy to Virginia life," as Margaret Junkin Preston described it. Of nearly equal merit is Cooke's description of the circus and its effect on Piedmont. Here, however, he exhibits a habit which is one of the main characteristics of another Southern writer, Mrs. Augusta Evans Wilson: he parades his learning in numerous literary and historical allusions and in the use of foreign and unanglicized words. In a single short paragraph, for example, there are a half-dozen allusions, and "aura," "populus," "ennui," and "élite," appear. Of the plot, nothing need be said save that it inclines to Cooke's more complicated type and fails to share the freshness of the setting. (pp. 148-49)

[*Virginia; A History of the People*] is strictly a history of Colonial Virginia and the state's part in founding the nation. For the first two centuries of Virginia history, Cooke's volume is an excellent manual, accurate enough for the ordinary reader and intensely interesting. The author preserves a fine balance between the sweeping events of war at one extreme and the depiction of the quiet life of the people at the other, and, without a vigilant regard for the whole truth, succeeds, like Macaulay, in giving to history the glamor of fiction. (p. 150)

Cooke's fluency was the cause of his chief faults. He wrote far too rapidly for his training and talents. . . . [He] had not received a university education, and the want of it is seen in much that he wrote. He disliked revision, and consequently shows an occasional irregular sentence. He produced contiguous passages and contiguous chapters of vastly unequal merit. He was weak in invention; many incidents in his later works are copied from some earlier production. He failed to adapt his characters to his setting. His world-traveled, melodramatic heroes and villains are out of place in a Virginia background. Most of his female characters are of one pattern and are particularly weak. They are described as delicate, sprightly "little beauties," but to the reader they appear immature and colorless. Throughout his career Cooke made the mistake of writing on subjects with which he was not wholly familiar. . . . In his later years his worst work paid best. This seeming anomaly encouraged a natural taste for sentimentality and sensationalism and shut him off from achieving his finer possibilities. . . . Cooke, nevertheless, achieved more than a modicum of distinction. His style is uniformly clear and agreeable. He usually had an eye for the picturesque. His movement is rapid and his dialogue is normally true to life. In everything he wrote, there is an element of sprightliness, dash, and manliness. Cooke was a gentleman-romancer who wrote while the spell of composition was upon him and devoted himself to his family and friends instead of revising his manuscript. (pp. 158-59)

> *John O. Beaty, in his* John Esten Cooke, Virginian *(copyright 1922 by Columbia University Press; copyright renewed © 1949 by John O. Beaty; reprinted by permission of the publisher), Columbia University Press, 1922 (and reprinted by Kennikat Press, 1965), 173 p.*

**ARTHUR HOBSON QUINN** (essay date 1936)

The plot [of *Leather Stocking and Silk*] is weak and the conversations are interminable, but the book is important historically because it represents the comfortable middle class of foreign extraction of which little is said in Southern romance. The mountaineers are brought in also, picturesque in their dances and merrymaking. . . . (pp. 126-27)

That Cooke's second published novel, *The Virginia Comedians* . . . , is his best, was due to the fact that it was inspired by his love for the past of Virginia and his interest in the theatre. . . . Cooke knew that what is needed in romance is not facts but color, contrast and life, and these he gave in full measure. . . . That the struggle in the mind of Beatrice Hallam against the charm of [Champ] Effingham [the hero-villain] would have puzzled an actress of the eighteenth century may be quite true, but Cooke is hardly to be criticized, for he gave us a situation that rarely fails to appeal. As usual, he put too much into his novel, the book falls apart in the middle, and the approach of the Revolution is hardly worked into the lengthy plot. . . . [*The Last of the Foresters*] is simply a conventional love story. . . . The efforts at humor are best treated with silence. *Henry St. John* . . . is a sequel to *The Virginia Comedians,* and is concerned with the opening of the Revolution in Virginia. . . . Cooke has drawn well the part which social organization played before and during the Revolution. (pp. 127-28)

The best part of the novel [*Fairfax*] deals with the love of a half-breed, ''Yellow Serpent,'' for Bertha Argal, who is really insane. The way in which his passion appeals to her although she does not love him, and the clever use she makes of it to rescue her companions are quite effectively pictured. (p. 128)

[In *Surry of Eagle's Nest*] Cooke painted a remarkable picture of the war in Virginia up to the Battle of Chancellorsville in 1863. His talent for endowing historical characters with personal life brings Stonewall Jackson, ''Jeb'' Stuart, Turner Ashby, Pelham, and other Confederate leaders vividly into a struggle in which they live bravely and many die gloriously. . . . The calm critic, especially if his ancestry was on the other side of the struggle, cannot help smiling at the inevitable flight of the Union cavalry in every skirmish, and Cooke's figures concerning the relative numbers of the forces engaged would make any impartial historian gasp. But even in the extraordinary interview between McClellan and Surry, in which the former calmly discusses his plans with a captured prisoner, the attitude of McClellan toward the South is quite fairly represented, and a more accurate estimate of McClellan's abilities is given than would have appeared in a Northern novel in 1866. It is this sense of reality in the general atmosphere and in vivid scenes such as the death of Jackson which made *Surry* one of the best pictures of the Civil War in American fiction. It was superior to *Hilt to Hilt* . . . , in which Cooke continued the memoirs of Colonel Surry. . . . [In this novel he] claims that he is telling only facts, but certainly the climax, in which Captain St. Leger Landon, bound and about to be executed, leaps upon his enemy and seizes his throat in his teeth, has rarely been exceeded in the annals of melodrama. There are no great historic figures here to lift the story into permanent interest.

In *Mohun; or The Last Days of Lee and his Paladins*, . . . Cooke continued to tell his story through the eyes of Surry. . . . There is a complicated family quarrel and the Union and Confederate secret services are confusing rather than dramatic elements. But nowhere in fiction are we given as realistic a picture of the closing days of the war in Richmond. (pp. 128-29)

[*The Heir of Gaymount*], while not significant in its character drawing, . . . has a certain interest because of its reflection of Cooke's own experiences after the Civil War. The hero, Edmund Carteret, faced with ruin, rejects the old easy going methods of agriculture which had impoverished the South, and represents the spirit which through variation of crops pointed to the future. Unfortunately Cooke was ahead of his time here, and his methods of telling the story were still the old ones. . . . The uneven quality of Cooke's work can be seen in a comparison of *Out of the Foam* . . . , one of the most absurd of his stories, laid in England during a war with France, [with *Her Majesty the Queen*] . . . , a romance of the days of Charles I, which is quite readable. To be sure, it is a Cavalier of Virginia of 1860 whom he is describing, and not a Cavalier of England in the 1640's. But there are some strong scenes. . . . [*Doctor VanDyke*] a mystery tale of no especial value. *Canolles; or, The Fortunes of a Partisan of '81* . . . , while not equal to Cooke's best stories, is unique in the romances dealing with the Revolution. . . . In 1880 Cooke tried to imitate *The Virginia Comedians* with [*The Virginia Bohemians*]. . . . But he was not able to throw the romantic glamour about Mignon and her supposed father, the ''Left Hander,'' with which he had invested the Hallam Company. There are some good touches, however, especially the description of the writer who is forgotten. (pp. 129-30)

*My Lady Pokahontas* is neither history nor fiction and is artificial and dull. Cooke must have had little sense of humor, for

when he takes Pokahontas to England he draws an amazing scene at the Globe Theatre in which Shakespeare and Smith converse and in which the playwright acknowledges that he has drawn Miranda from Pokahontas! Cooke's last long novel, *The Maurice Mystery* . . . , is a long drawn out attempt on the part of a son, Haworth Dacis, to relieve his father's memory of the stain of murder. Cooke had no great ability in the creation of mysteries, although he was fond of them. He belonged to a school of writing which believed that suspense could be secured by postponing the explanation and by putting up straw men to be knocked down. He does not, however, deserve the comparative neglect which has befallen him, for he was a born story-teller; that he came belated into a period in which his methods no longer prevailed was his misfortune. (p. 131)

*Arthur Hobson Quinn, ''The Development of Idealistic Romance,'' in his* American Fiction: An Historical and Critical Survey *(© 1936, renewed 1963, excerpted by permission of Prentice Hall, Inc., Englewood Cliffs, NJ 07632), D. Appleton-Century Company, Inc., 1936, pp. 102-31.**

**CARVEL COLLINS** (essay date 1944)

John Esten Cooke is well known for his biographies of General Lee and Stonewall Jackson and for his many novels and stories, but he has an additional distinction: he was one of the pioneer authors of fiction about the Southern mountains, and he participated in the transition from the early fiction to the local-color stories of the last decades of the nineteenth century—stories which, although often keeping the romantic plots of the earlier period, were important in the development of American literature because they gave emphasis to a new realistic treatment of their characters' surroundings.

It is too frequently said that Mary Murfree, under her penname of ''Charles Egbert Craddock,'' discovered the Southern highlander for fiction. . . . But several authors explored the region before Miss Murfree, and one of the most prolific as well as one of the earliest was John Esten Cooke. (p. 82)

In 1851 *The Messenger* . . . printed the first of his mountain pieces and started him on three decades of writing about the highlands of the South. These sketches of praise for the scenery of western Virginia—**''Recollections of Sully,'' ''Shadows of the Pine Forest,''** and **''Shadows of the Mountain Pine''**—were by no means realistic. . . . Nor at this early stage in his development as a writer about the mountains did Cooke describe the ordinary mountaineers who appeared in later fiction, for the people of these sketches had a ''breakfast room.''

But almost at once—in 1852—*The Messenger* printed Cooke's first mountain story, **''Peony.''** This account of how a free school improved the life of a community of mountaineers is historically important in the development of mountain fiction; for it was a remarkably early presentation of the mountains as a region with its own characteristics, and the story, crude as it was, is noteworthy for so early letting almost all the main characters be people of the region, the schoolmaster being the only lowlander.

The next year, however, Cooke reverted for a time to the older attitude toward the mountaineer. In *Leatherstocking and Silk*, . . . the mountain hunter John Myers, like the hunter in Tucker's *Valley of the Shenandoah* of almost thirty years earlier, was not the mountaineer we meet in later fiction: Cooke did not change him from the frontiersman of the earlier stories.

Nor in *The Last of the Foresters* . . . did Cooke depart from the tradition.

But in 1859 he began a succession of novels and stories all of which touched on the same motif—the mountains as a place to which men could retreat from the world—and in this series Cooke made steady progress in the direction of the realism which was an essential part of the later fiction. In the first of this chain of stories, *Greenway Court,* which appeared in *The Messenger* in 1859, Cooke used the mountains as the fittingly romantic setting in which to place the Wizard of Massinutton, a fantastic scientific recluse. In *Surrey of Eagle's Nest* . . . , Mordaunt, who had wandered in exotic parts of the world, came with his silent Arabian servant to find in the Southern mountains a seclusion which he left—in Cooke's novel *Mohun*—only because he felt he should fight for the Confederacy. But Cooke began to put the mountains to less romantic use: in **"A House in the Blue Ridge"** (1874) which used the region as a retreat for a slightly less glamorous recluse than Mordaunt . . . ; in **"Owlet"** (1877) in which a hermit died leaving his daughter to grow up with an old mountaineer in a miserable hut. And four years later Cooke's reduction of the romance in this succession of stories reached its end in **"The Sumac Gatherers"** (1881) in which a prosaic lawyer retreated to the hills in bankruptcy.

Despite the increasing realism of these accounts of highland recluses, in them Cooke did not quite achieve local-color treatment of the mountains. But in 1879 he published **"Moonshiners,"** which, of all his stories, comes nearest to completing the transition to the newer form. This story has many elements found in the fiction of the mountain local-color movement. . . . Cooke's story points out the isolation of the mountaineers, their clannishness, their suspicion of strangers, and their bravery and independence—the chief characteristics with which the "localists" endowed them. And this story shows Cooke to be to some extent still the pioneer, for it is an early treatment of illicit distilling in the hills—a theme which, along with feuds and the War, was to be one of the stock elements of the hundreds of works of mountain local-color. (pp. 82-4)

Miss Murfree was only two years old in 1852 when John Esten Cooke, by publishing **"Peony"** in *The Messenger,* became one of the pioneers in discovering that the mountains were a unique setting for fiction. . . . [In **"Moonshiners"**] he almost completed the transition to local-color and certainly came nearer to producing a mountain story of the later type than did any other author who had been trained before the sixties. (p. 84)

> Carvel Collins, *"John Esten Cooke and Local-Color,"* in The Southern Literary Messenger, *Vol. VI, No. 1, January-February, 1944, pp. 82-4.*

**ALEXANDER COWIE** (essay date 1948)

[*Cowie's* The Rise of the American Novel, *from which the following excerpt is taken, is an important study of the development of the American novel. Cowie discusses Cooke's hasty, careless method of composition, his dependence on Cooper, and his "forte . . . in powdered romance of an older era." Labeling* The Virginia Comedians *"a pretty flimsy story," and pointing out the superiority of the novels of John Pendleton Kennedy and William Gilmore Simms, he refutes Charles F. Richardson's claim that the work is the " best novel written in the Southern States before the civil war " (see excerpt above, 1889). Cowie does not agree with the majority of critics regarding* The Virginia Comedians; *he describes the characters as "little more than types" and criticizes Cooke's use of cliches and his reliance on fantastic melo-*

*drama. He does note, however, that the novel "contained enough of the elements of good story-writing to become the prototype of many later Virginia novels." Cowie regards* Fairfax *as "second only to the* The Virginia Comedians *and* Surry of Eagle's-Nest *as the "first and best of the War novels."*]

[*The Virginia Comedians*] has been called the "best novel written in the Southern States before the civil war" [see excerpt above by Richardson, 1889]. Such an encomium it can scarcely lay claim to in the face of the brilliant and substantial productions of Kennedy and Simms, but it contained enough of the elements of good story-writing to become the prototype of many later Virginian novels that, however inaccurate in their report of actual conditions, have satisfied an enormous public appetite for light romantic tales of the Old Dominion. (p. 464)

Though Cooke's imitation of Cooper is obvious even in the titles of his books and in the names of his characters, he utilized one avenue to popularity which for Cooper always remained secondary, namely, the love story. *The Virginia Comedians* is first of all a story of the love fortunes of Champ Effingham. . . . The novel is one of incident and "drama," for as the author avowed, he was not equal to giving it that "nice finish which is the cameo-work of literature." Accordingly characters are little more than types and their actions are reported in well-worn expressions that were clichés even in Cooke's time. Over and over again contempt is expressed by the "curling lip," mental agony by the "writhing lip," and honest love by a "chaste salute" on the mistress' brow. These are harmless iterations, but there is less excuse for the ranting melodrama in which Champ is constantly involved. His actions are incredible even in romance. Twice he actually tears at his breast until his fingers are "stained with blood." His persecution of Beatrice exceeds not only the bounds of realism but even the looser bounds of romantic plausibility. He is wholly unconvincing, and in fact he has much in common with those insolent, blasé scions of wealth in the domestic novel of that day who conduct themselves in the most incredibly malicious, dissipated, and even criminal fashion, only at the end to be united to sweet, trusting girls.

*The Virginia Comedians* is then a pretty flimsy story that captivated readers in its day by its clever arrangement of picturesque properties in a traditionally romantic area. Its historical aspect gave it badly needed ballast, but, one must believe, did not greatly add to its vogue. The unrest of a period when there was growing resentment against British oppression is used as a theme in the somewhat tedious conversations between Charles Waters and the "man in the red cloak," who is supposed to figure Patrick Henry. At the end of the book an exciting scene reveals Colonial hostility to the Stamp Act. Notwithstanding these, however, and frequent allusions to the *Virginia Gazette,* the Old Theatre of Williamsburg, and the Raleigh Tavern, as well as a number of incidents intended to illustrate manners, the historical background is a trifle thin. Cooke aimed to be picturesque rather than thorough. Naturally he made no such rounded study of eighteenth-century Virginia as Kennedy did of a later period; nor does his command of language in any way invite comparison with Kennedy's. Cooke did not even have the knack of giving his speech that archaic quality which so adds to the charm of Churchill's *Richard Carvel,* and the characters speak in an idiom not far different from the conventional idiom of Cooke's own day. . . . Yet his gifts, such as they were, were well enough fused to make *The Virginia Comedians* almost a household title in the period just before the Civil War. It is still good reading, but it has been somewhat overrated while other Southern novels have had to struggle for their due. (pp. 464-66)

The quality of [Cooke's] writing never fluctuated markedly: he wrote no great books and no books without at least a modicum of merit. On the whole those novels which he wrote before the Civil War are of greater value than his later productions. . . .

More than most of Cooke's books, [*The Last of the Foresters: or, Humans on the Border*] seems to have suffered from rapidity of composition. A more substantial book was *Fairfax: or, The Master of Greenway Court.* . . . Despite its use of old conventions, *Fairfax* is a very readable story—probably second only to *The Virginia Comedians* among Cooke's novels. (p. 467)

The first and best of the War novels was *Surry of Eagle's Nest.* . . . Military matters are merged with romance . . . and Surry is at last provided with the usual colorless heroine employed by Cooke. The novel made money for the author, but artistically Cooke failed to fuse "a wildly improbable Gothic tale and a record of a career in the Civil War" [see excerpt above by Beaty, 1922]. Between *Surry of Eagle's-Nest* and its sequel (*Mohun*) appeared an undistinguished war novel, *Hilt to Hilt.* . . . Rebuked by a Boston critic for rhetorical extravagances, Cooke resolved in *Hilt to Hilt* never to "be florid or exaggerated any more," but stylistically he failed to evince any real reform. . . . All these stories had a certain topical value, and all displayed flashes of a talent that (one believes) might have shown to better advantage had the author been willing to spend more than a month or two on a novel. Even so, Cooke was not quite at his best in handling materials so close to his own experience as those of the Civil War. No one of these stories compares favorably as an account of military maneuvers with, for example, Hervey Allen's *Action at Aquila.* . . . Crane's brilliantly written *The Red Badge of Courage* was, of course, a type of novel quite beyond the range of Cooke's powers. (pp. 468-69)

It was clear now that Cooke's forte lay in powdered romance of an older era. Yet *The Heir of Gaymount* . . . , his first book after *Mohun,* attempted to fictionalize the author's own experiences after the War. Problems of finance and agriculture come up for consideration, but *The Heir of Gaymount* did not turn out to be an important "Reconstruction" novel. . . . Several other novels followed, but they revealed Cooke's inability to establish himself in an important new category or to reopen a profitable old one. (p. 469)

[Cooke] resembled Simms in his theory of the historical romance. He too realized that after the historian has raked the past for factual data regarding wars and dynasties, many apparently unimportant materials could be gleaned with which the novelists might recreate the form and color of history. . . . In this aim Cooke succeeded admirably when he treated old Virginia in his earliest stories. More than Simms he stressed color and atmosphere. He also took more liberties with historical fact than Simms—probably to his own disadvantage. But, as far as his Confederate stories are concerned, the Civil War was too close to him to respond to the same treatment that had succeeded in *The Virginia Comedians* and *Fairfax.* And when later he returned to olden times, he had somehow lost the formula which would enable him to recreate the old atmosphere. Moreover literary movements in the 1870's and 1880's called for new abilities to which he could not adapt himself. . . . The same detachment which permitted him to recognize his own limitations is shown in his ready vein of humor both in his novels and in articles. He was adept at parody and raillery. (pp. 470-71)

[Cooke's] "ultimate literary ancestor" was Scott, but neither Scott nor Cooke's nearest relative among Virginians, Caruthers, was apparently a close model for him. Cooper, however, was an early ideal, and he was never completely out of Cooke's mind. Yet Cooke lacked Cooper's robustness, and he showed more interest in the amenities of life than did Cooper. Simms, whom Cooke resembled in his voluminous and speedy production, was a writer of much more original force. With gentle and picturesque Irving, Cooke was a trifle more in line, but he was prone to sustained melodrama of a type that Irving would soon have escaped from with a jest. Cooke drew from all these writers. He also had a weather eye open for the sentimental novels of the 1850's—those of Mary Jane Holmes, Elizabeth Wetherell, and Mrs. Southworth—whose code of propriety he strictly observed, and whose reeking sentiment he occasionally equalled. Along with his gracefulness went a certain almost feminine softness which manifested itself in a love of small domestic detail. He also, it is very likely, learned part of his craft from the example of Thackeray, whose *Esmond* had appeared in 1852. The historical romance of Thackeray at its poorest has an infusion of tea-partyish sentiment that appears also in Cooke's writing. And it was probably this same softness, this delicacy, which, when crossed with a slightly forced gusto and robustness, gave the guise of novelty to his chef-d'oeuvre, *The Virginia Comedians.*

The novelty of Cooke brought him many readers, and it inaugurated a new tradition of Virginia novels grounded in picturesqueness and sentiment. . . . Now, when the novels of Miss Glasgow and others have revealed Virginia in more realistic outline, Cooke's type of romance seems artificial as well as outmoded. He was a facile writer of no great force or originality who reached quick success by stumbling upon a rich vein. But when that was exhausted he had neither the capacity for discipline nor the imagination to operate successfully elsewhere. . . . To compare him with Scott or Cooper or Simms is to draw attention to his essentially light gift. It is better to say that he was a writer of moderate talents who fed a harmless appetite for gingerbread romance without a grievous sacrifice of the ideals of good writing. (pp. 471-72)

*Alexander Cowie, "Experiment and Tradition," in his* The Rise of the American Novel *(copyright, 1948, 1951 by American Book Company), American Book Company, 1948 (and reprinted by American Book Company, 1951), pp. 447-504.**

## JAY B. HUBBELL (essay date 1954)

[*Hubbell's* The South in American Literature: 1607-1900 *is considered a standard work on that subject. Hubbell states that although "Cooke was the first important novelist to treat the Civil War in fiction," he was "still too facile and too uncritical of his work to become a great novelist." Like Alexander Cowie (see excerpt above, 1948), Hubbell remarks that Cooke's method of blending fact with fiction did not lend itself well to his first-hand accounts of the Civil War.*]

[In *The Virginia Comedians,* Cooke,] though less the aristocrat than his brother, could not help casting a glamour over some of the planter families, but his yeomen are well drawn. Negroes and poor whites he was never able to treat with much success. Like Thackeray's *The Virginians,* Cooke's romance breaks in two in the middle and becomes two separate stories, which with *Henry St. John, Gentleman* . . . may be regarded as a trilogy. Cooke thought of himself as writing in the spirit of a social historian, imaginatively reconstructing a great period in American history. As a social historian of Virginia, he is markedly inferior to Ellen Glasgow. (p. 514)

[Cooke] would probably not have developed into a really important writer even had the war not interrupted his work. (p. 515)

Of the seven books which he wrote dealing with the war not one is the book he should have written—a plain, straightforward account of what he had experienced, for no other writer on either side had seen so much of what was really memorable. His lives of Jackson and Lee are hurriedly written accounts of battles rather than substantial biographics. (p. 518)

Cooke was the first important novelist to treat the Civil War in fiction. . . . [However, he] was still too facile and too uncritical of his work to become a great novelist. . . . The war was too close for him to see it through the romantic haze in which it was wrapped for Thomas Nelson Page. In Cooke's imagination the Revolution was still the romantic period in Virginia's history. In his Civil War novels he felt it necessary to adopt ''the Reade-Collinsish style of mystery and sensation'' and to import into rural Virginia outlandish villains who figure in plots made up chiefly of the outworn machinery of mystery and intrigue. Perhaps because of the inferior periodicals which alone would accept his work, he found in his later years it was generally his poorer novels that paid him best. In *Surry* and *Mohun* history and fiction refuse to blend, and in consequence each novel breaks into long sections in which historical and fictitious events are treated separately. No writer of Cooke's ability, however, could treat such fresh and interesting materials as the battles and leaders of Lee's army without accomplishing something better than I have suggested. His pictures of Ashby, Pelham, Stuart, and Jackson are memorable. In the flood of Civil War literature it is not easy to find anything better than Cooke's best historical passages. His account of the war—and this explains in part his success—is remarkable for the almost complete absence of bitterness toward the North. In some respects his romances set the pattern for later Civil War fiction, notably in picturing a Virginia family divided by the war. (pp. 518-19)

[In *The Heir of Gaymount*], a book which cost him much labor, he tried to do something similar to what Ellen Glasgow was to do much more successfully in *Barren Ground*: to show how by scientific methods a planter could make money out of an estate reduced to forty acres. . . . Cooke, however, could not even here keep out mystery and sensation: it is a buried treasure, discovered by solving a cryptogram in Poe-like fashion, that gives the planter his financial independence. (p. 519)

Cooke was too ready to concede the field to the realists and to admit that romance represents an inferior mode of writing. He should have . . . reminded himself that the taste for romance, temporarily in abeyance, was certain to return. In fact, under the leadership of Stevenson, it had already begun to revive before Cooke's death. By using the romantic materials of Colonial Virginia in *Justin Harley* [and *Canolles*], . . . the old-fashioned romancer had anticipated Mary Johnston in *Prisoners of Hope* (1898) and *To Have and To Hold* (1900). He never, however, quite succeeded in equaling *The Virginia Comedians,* published when he was only twenty-four. He had failed to develop into the writer he had promised to become. In later years his inventiveness flagged, and he repeated incidents and resorted still oftener to the tricks of tawdry melo-

drama. In *The Virginia Bohemians* . . . , however, he employed with partial success the newer methods of the local colorists, and in *My Lady Pokahontas* . . . he treated with charm a theme which Thomas Dunn English had urged upon him years before. (p. 520)

[*Virginia: A History of the People*] is not to be described as scholarly, for here, as in his romances, Colonial Virginia is seen through a golden mist; but it is written with all the charm and skill of Cooke at his best, and when he is at his best there are few American historians who write with half his charm. The century following the Revolution, however, is only sketched; except for the Civil War years, the later history of Virginia did not lend itself to Cooke's romantic method of treatment. (p. 521)

> *Jay B. Hubbell, ''John Esten Cooke,'' in his* The South in American Literature: 1607-1900 *(copyright © 1954 by Duke University Press, Durham, North Carolina), Duke University Press, 1954, pp. 511-21.*

### MATTHEW C. O'BRIEN (essay date 1976)

Despite the quality of *Wearing of the Gray* . . . [and *Mohun*, the body of work Cooke composed after the Civil War] is flawed by sentimentality, a hastiness of construction, and by an overall failure to revise and rewrite, a lifelong artistic bane of Cooke. The near-impenetrable haze of nostalgia he cast over the ''Lost Cause,'' moreover, does not redound to his literary credit.

Long before the firing on Sumter, however, the Virginian's prolific pen had been at work on an earlier segment of the Old Dominion's history. In his antebellum writings, . . . he journeyed back into the Colonial past to deal with such questions as his home state's Cavalier heritage, the growth of a native aristocracy, and the rise of the democratic spirit in the years preceding the American Revolution. (pp. 259-60)

Cooke's imaginative journeying into this other era was catalyzed by a glance at a surviving relic—a sword, an old waistcoat, a copy of the *Virginia Gazette,* a mouldering doublet. So powerful is the aura of the artifact, so compelling are the associations it arouses, that for Cooke a type of reverie takes place in which the past does indeed come to replace the present, the ''new'' Virginia becomes the ''old'' again.

What alternative does the past offer, even if it is reached through mere reverie? Cooke focuses again and again on the vigor, the pomp, the chivalry of that ''knightly age'' when Cavaliers held sway in Virginia. . . . Metaphorically, he identifies the difference between past and present in terms of the types of dance which found favor in each: the minuet, to which Cavaliers and ladies gracefully bowed and curtsied, represented courtesy, respect, and chivalric devotion; the polka, the current rage, was, in Cooke's estimation, coarse, graceless, and crude.

To be sure, a good deal of embellishment marks Cooke's composite portrait of the eighteenth-century Virginia gentry. Too often, it seems, his James River and Northern Neck plantations are unrealistically fashionable; their inhabitants, in silken garments, ruffles, and powdered wigs, preside over many a cotillion and banquet. . . . Cooke at times tended to see culture and refinement everywhere. Elegance, wealth, and hospitality undoubtedly existed in good measure then and there, but Cooke occasionally mythologizes in a way which runs counter to historical evidence.

To accuse Cooke of being an unwitting glorifier of this old regime, however, as some critics have done, is not altogether accurate. In fact, Cooke himself was a descendant of the Virginia aristocracy, and may have gazed back somewhat nostalgically to the epoch of his forefathers, but a democratic impulse caused him to disdain the evils and inequities of the class system. Indeed, his recognition that there were definite levels in Colonial society set him apart from many a Southern romancer. At times he implied that any man, regardless of class, could become a "cavalier" if he possessed the requisite virtues of honesty, courage, and charity.

Moreover, he refused to make over his legitimate Cavaliers into plaster-of-Paris saints to be blindly idolized. He insisted on filling in what he termed "the dark shade in the picture," and examining the faults of his aristocrats within a larger historical perspective. . . . To disdain the common man, to scorn his attempts to improve his lot, are mortal sins in Cooke's moral system. Thus the infamous Lord Dunmore, who is a prominent character in *Henry St. John, Gentleman* . . . , becomes a Cavalier-turned-madman, a villain who attempts to crush the forces of independence by stirring up the tribes on the Western frontier to aid him in his dictatorial campaign. (pp. 260-61)

What Cooke demanded of his Cavaliers was the proper combination of an aristocratic heritage and a democratic outlook, high spirit tempered by compassion for the downtrodden. Not surprisingly, he found such attributes in George Washington, who appears as a central figure in . . . *Fairfax*. It was the last, and most certainly the best, of Cooke's antebellum Shenandoah Valley novels.

There is, as in Cooke's best work, an historical basis for the action, which here occurs in 1748 in and around Winchester. . . . The actual events which lend verisimilitude to the novel are the struggle between Winchester and Stephensburg to be named county seat and the preparations of the settlers in the face of an impending Indian attack.

These, however, remain secondary to a characteristically involved series of romantic relationships between historical and fictional characters. (pp. 261-62)

Just as typical of a Cooke novel as these romantic entanglements is his preoccupation with the components of "Cavalier" conduct and the essence of nobility. What he regarded as the most fortunate combination of personal attributes and heredity is seen here in the characters Falconbridge and the young Washington, both "stout-hearted and stout-armed cavaliers." . . . (p. 262)

Another "true gentleman" in the novel, though he possesses not a shred of noteworthy ancestry, is the "borderer" Wagner. Like Hunter Myers of *Leather Stocking and Silk* . . . and Verty in *The Last of the Foresters* . . . , he enjoys neither inherited title nor cultural refinement, yet in his embodiment of natural goodness he rivals even Washington himself. . . . Though coarse and inarticulate, he displays a most appealing type of backwood chivalry as he becomes the mainstay of the settlers in their defense against the savages. . . . Acting together, Cooke seems to say, the aristocratic but down-to-earth Washington and the frontiersman Wagner represent the best in Virginia society. (p. 263)

[Cooke's literary] path, strewn with millions of words, a host of frail heroines and scheming villains, a goodly dose of fortunate coincidence, led forth up to the Civil War and after to locate Cooke finally in a secure, if minor, position in the realm of Southern letters. In a figurative sense, though, the path twisted back into the dim days of the past, into a Golden age of Cavaliers in which nobility—not greed—reigned supreme. But he was neither a blind nor uncompromising glorifier of the old regime. . . . For him, nobility transcended class, title, and background. (p. 265)

*Matthew C. O'Brien, "John Esten Cooke, George Washington and the Virginia Cavaliers," in* The Virginia Magazine of History and Biography, *Vol. 84, No. 3, July, 1976, pp. 259-65.**

---

## ADDITIONAL BIBLIOGRAPHY

Cohen, Hennig. "Autobiography of John Esten Cooke." *American Literature* XXX, No. 2 (May 1958): 234-37.
    Contains an autobiographical sketch in which Cooke asserts that he and his works are best described as "cavalier."

Hubbell, Jay B. "Notes and Documents: The War Diary of John Esten Cooke." *Journal of Southern History* 7, No. 4 (November 1941): 526-40.
    A discussion of Cooke's military career which includes excerpts from his Civil War diary.

Starnes, Lucy Gaylord. "Scribe of the Old Dominion." *Virginia Cavalcade* XIII, No. 2 (Autumn 1963): 32-7.
    A biographical sketch which depicts Cooke as the quintessential Virginian.

# Nikolai Alexandrovich Dobrolyubov

## 1836-1861

(Also transliterated as Nicholas, Nikolay, Nikolaj, Nikoláy; also Aleksandrovič, Aleksandrovich, Alexándrovich; also Dobroliubov, Dobroljubov, Dobroljúbov, Dobrolúboff, Dobrolúbov) Russian critic, essayist, poet, and editor.

One of the most influential Russian literary critics of the nineteenth century, Dobrolyubov is noted for his contribution to the philosophy of Russian revolutionary socialism. Along with Vissarion Belinski and Nikolai Chernyshevsky, he helped to redirect Russian critical thought in the 1850s by integrating revolutionary political theory into his literary criticism. Using a radical, anti-aestheticist approach, he emphasized the utilitarian aspects of literature and stressed the critic's responsibility for calling attention to the inequalities of the class system in Russian society and the need for social revolution.

Born in Nizny Novgorod (now Gorky), Dobrolyubov was deeply affected by his family's poverty and strict religious dogmatism. His father, an orthodox priest, instilled in him a love of learning and discipline. Complying with his family's wishes, he studied first in a theological seminary, and subsequently graduated from the St. Petersburg Pedagogical Institute in 1857. The interest in education, science, anthropology, and journalism that he acquired there remained strong throughout his life. Dobrolyubov's desire to make others aware of the mistreatment of serfs by the landed gentry in Russia inspired his interest in journalism. As a student, he began contributing articles to *Sovremenik (The Contemporary)*, an influential journal of the radical left founded by Alexander Pushkin and dedicated to the popularization of contemporary European socialist thought. By 1857, Dobrolyubov had become, under his mentor Chernyshevsky, one of *The Contemporary*'s chief literary critics. He also served as editor of its critical and bibliographic sections, and contributed to *The Whistle*, a satirical supplement to *The Contemporary*, and to the journal *The Spark*. The political tenor of Dobrolyubov's literary reviews so infuriated the novelist Ivan Turgenev that he, among others, refused to contribute to *The Contemporary*.

Influenced by Jeremy Bentham, John Stuart Mill, François Fourier, Alexander Herzen, Belinski, and Chernyshevsky, Dobrolyubov promoted a materialist-utopian view of art, and believed that literature should serve a social purpose. "The value of a writer or a book is determined by the degree to which they express the aspirations of an age or of a people," he wrote. Dobrolyubov asserted that a literary work should first reflect all aspects of reality and, second, should embody an interpretation and a judgment of reality. The task of the critic, in turn, would be to expose the deeper meaning inherent in the work, and to encourage a sense of social responsibility. A good critic, Dobrolyubov contended, could inspire revolution by focusing the readers' attention on the apathy of the gentry toward the enslavement of the serfs.

Dobrolyubov's most famous essays reflect his moral fervor. In "Unizhonnye i oskorblyonne," a review of Fedor Dostoevski's novel *The Insulted and the Injured*, and "Tiomnoye Tzarstvo" ("The Kingdom of Darkness"), a review of Alexandr Ostrovski's play *The Storm*, Dobrolyubov praises the authors for their

accurate portrayal of characters trapped by their social positions. In "Kogda zhe prediot nastroyashchi den?" ("When Will the Day Come?"), a review of Turgenev's novel *On the Eve*, Dobrolyubov ridicules most of the novel's characters for being "toothless squirrels," and asks when Russia will produce strong men and women capable of revolution.

In his most notorious essay, "Chto takoye Oblomvschina?" ("What is Oblomovism?"), a review of Ivan Goncharov's novel *Oblomov*, Dobrolyubov interpreted Oblomov as the typical representative of the idle Russian gentry, and attacked the self-absorption of the Russian liberals. He maintained that they had become so decadent through their indifference and ineffectuality that revolution was inevitable. Contemporary critics who shared Dobrolyubov's leftist sentiments lauded his campaign for social reform under the guise of literary criticism. However, most critics severely reprimanded him for his polemicism, his insensitivity to literary aesthetics, and especially for his political interpretations of theme, symbol, and characterization. For instance, Dobrolyubov's reading of Katerina's suicide in Ostrovski's *The Storm* has been widely criticized: while most view her suicide as desperate and pathetic, Dobrolyubov presented it as a noble act of revolutionary defiance through which Katerina escapes her social niche. Yet, despite the misgivings of many of his contemporaries, his critical and philosophical works served to educate the Russian revolutionaries of the latter half of the nineteenth century, and today  Soviet critics cite Dobrolyubov, along with Belinski and Chernyshevsky, as a precursor of the theories of Soviet realism.

PRINCIPAL WORKS

*"Chto takoye Oblomvschina?"    (essay)   1859
  **["What Is Oblomovism?" 1956]
*"Tiomnoye Tzarstvo"   (essay)   1859
  **["The Kingdom of Darkness," 1956]
*"Kogda zhe prediot nastroyashchi den?"   (essay)   1860
  **["When Will the Day Come?" 1956]
*"Unizhonnye i oskorblyonne"   (essay)   1861
*Sobranie sochineniia*. 4 vols.   (essays and poetry)   1885
*Dnevniki* (diaries)   1932
*Izbrannye filosofskie sochineniia*. 2 vols.   (essays)   1948
*Stikhotvorenia*   (poetry)   1948
*Selected Philosophical Essays*   (essays)   1956

*These essays were originally published in the journal *Sovremenik*.

**These essays were translated and published in *Selected Philosophical Essays* in 1956.

---

**P. KROPOTKIN   (lecture date 1901)**

Dobrolúboff [did not have] a very definite criterion of literary criticism, or . . . a very distinct programme as to what was to be done. But he was one of the purest and the most solid representatives of that type of new men—the realist-idealist, whom Turguéneff saw coming by the end of the fifties. Therefore, in whatever he wrote one felt the thoroughly moral and thoroughly reliable, slightly ascetic "rigourist" who judged all facts of life from the standard of—"What good will they bring to the toiling masses?" or, "How will they favour the creation of men whose eyes are directed that way?" His attitude towards professional aesthetics was most contemptuous, but he felt deeply himself and enjoyed the great works of art. He did not condemn Púshkin for his levity, or Gógol for his absence of ideals. He did not advise anyone to write novels or poems with a set purpose: he knew the results would be poor. He admitted that the great geniuses were right in creating unconsciously, because he understood that the real artist creates only when he has been struck by this or that aspect of reality. He asked only from a work of art, whether it truly and correctly reproduced life, or not? If not, he passed it by; but if it did truly represent life, then he wrote essays *about this life;* and his articles were essays on moral, political or economical matters—the work of art yielding only the facts for such a discussion. This explains the influence Dobrolúboff exercised upon his contemporaries. Such essays written by such a personality were precisely what was wanted in the turmoil of those years for preparing better men for the coming struggles. They were a school of political and moral education. (pp. 291-92)

> *P. Kropotkin, "Political Literature, Satire, Art-Criticism, Contemporary Novelists" (originally part of a series of lectures delivered at the Lowell Institute, Boston, in March, 1901), in his* Russian Literature *(copyright, 1905, by McClure, Phillips & Co.), McClure, Phillips & Co., 1905 (and reprinted by Benjamin Blom, 1967), pp. 263-318.*

**A. BRÜCKNER   (essay date 1905)**

[*The Contemporary*] gained colour after 1855, and with it the new periodicals that appeared—the *Russian Speech, Russian Messenger,* &c. This colour was given them less by their *belles lettres* than by their critical portion, which, indeed, was the outcome of the former but aimed at objects which had nothing to do with it—this is the strength and weakness of Russian criticism. Its strength in that the ostensibly "literary" or even "aesthetic" criticism became a moral and socio-political power: it delighted in making use of those literary productions which were suited to the spreading of its ideas and deliberately neglected others often far more important in a literary sense; it relegated aesthetics to ladies' society, and turned its critical report into a sort of pulpit for moral and social preaching. This most "warlike" criticism, one-sided and purposeful, achieved a colossal effect among the young men, to whom the essays of a Chernyshévsky, Dobrolúbov, and a Písarev became revelations, the language of eloquent and fiery agitators, not critics. Therein also lay its weakness, prejudice, and perverseness. One must never let oneself be deceived by its judgments: it extolled or decried the author and his work . . . not because of the value or no value of his performance, but for his opinions, his ideas—nay, for the journal in which he published his work. Thus this criticism is often, in spite of all its giftedness, its zeal and fire, only a mockery of all criticism. The work only serves as a peg on which to hang their own views. (p. 322)

To [Chernyshévsky,] the passionate, headlong controversialist who despised no means of confounding his opponent or taking him by surprise, the cool, sober, solid Dobrolúbov was inferior in originality of conception, in solidity of historical attainment . . . , and in breadth of view, but was far his superior in clearness, logicalness, vividness of description, and aesthetic feeling (he himself had a poetic gift), and in wit and humour as well. Even his literary interests were primarily journalistic: pedagogical and philosophical literature—nay, even the political phenomena of foreign countries . . . attracted him in reality more than poems, novels, and comedies, but his analyses of Goncharóv's "Oblómov," Turgénev's "On the Eve," and Ostróvsky's comedies are among the most brilliant of his writings; only they are not literary or aesthetic analyses in our sense. (p. 326)

The women in "Oblómov," for instance, do not concern him at all, as he does not wish to be a judge of women's hearts. In return he seeks out the Oblómov type all through literature, and shows that [Griboyédov's Chátsky, Pushkin's Onêgin, Lermontov's Pechórin, and Turgenev's Rúdin] are but Oblómovs in disguise. He gave it all out so clearly and convincingly that he made the young generation enthusiastic, for it recognised in this realism, this condemning of all idealism, the only security for successful development. (pp. 326-27)

> *A. Brückner, "Modern Times (1855-1905)," in his* A Literary History of Russia, *edited by Ellis H. Minns, translated by H. Havelock (originally published as* Geschichte der russischen Litteratur, *1905), T. Fisher Unwin, 1908, pp. 312-37.*

**THOMAS GARRIGUE MASARYK   (essay date 1913)**

[*The term "raznočinec," which Masaryk mentions below, was used to describe a new and growing cultural force in Russia in the 1850s, the plebian or classless intelligentsia. Men like Dobrolyubov, Nikolai Chernyshevsky, and Vissarion Belinski, who felt excluded from the established circles of aristocratic intellectuals, prided themselves on their humble social backgrounds and on the knowledge they had acquired through experience rather than through study. Masaryk maintains that Dobrolyubov's identification with the "raznočintsy," more than any other influence, was responsible for the formulation of his social philosophy.]*

Dobroljubov's activities were not of long duration, but they gave a rich yield. He was animated with an enthusiastic and inspiring love for intellectual liberty, and he fought to introduce the light into the Old Russian "realm of darkness" (his analysis of Ostrovskii's dramas depicting the mercantile classes). Writing of Gončarov's *Oblomov,* he described Oblomov as the issue of this darkness and as characteristic of the Russians in general; but the errors, he said, were those of one already struggling towards the light. . . . The effect of Dobroljubov's essays was all the greater because he had a closer and more realistic knowledge of Russian conditions than was possessed by his friend and teacher [Černyševskii] and because, too, he had in the highest degree the gift of satire.

Dobroljubov turned away from the "phantasmagorias of the orientalist imagination"; he turned to Bělinskii (of the last phase) and to Herzen; in this way, like Černyševskii and his radical contemporaries in general, he came to Feuerbach and the Hegelian left. He now adopted the political views of Černyševskii, and in the latter's review secured a free platform for the expression of his ideas. (p. 20)

As materialist and utilitarian, Dobroljubov could not fail to ask himself the question whether there was any justification for art in general and for literary criticism in particular, to ask himself whether literary criticism was "work" in the sense in which work was demanded by Černyševskii. In Dobroljubov's critical writings we often feel that this question is troubling him, and his answer does not always set doubts at rest. Whereas at first his judgment of Puškin coincided with that of Černyševskii, who, despite his admiration for Puškin considered the latter's work lacking in realist content, Dobroljubov's later opinions concerning the utility of poets, and of Puškin in especial, have a harsher ring. But a closer examination of Dobroljubov's studies leads us to recognize that all he insisted upon was a clear distinction between art and pseudo-art. Only the genuine artist, the truly great artist, has a justified existence, for he alone in his creative work is so permeated with the truth of life that simply by his faithful reproduction of facts and relationships he furnishes for us a solution of the problems we are endeavouring to solve. According to Dobroljubov, persons of mediocre talent must be content with subordinate parts, must serve in the interests of propaganda. It is true that the question arises who is to decide concerning the quality of the talent; who is to decide when an artist is to be classed as mediocre and excluded from the circle of Dobroljubov's recognised great ones, from the company of Dante, Shakespeare, Byron, and Goethe. Of those named, Dobroljubov esteems Shakespeare most highly, considering that his work marks a new phase in human development.

This realistic valuation of art does not differ greatly from the views of the romanticists, who could not stress the greatness of the artist's influence more strongly than did these realists, the reputed enemies of art. In matters of detail, too, we can discover points of contact between the two schools. Dobroljubov, for instance, considers that the natural, that nature, is psychologically manifested in instinct, instinct being to him the all-powerful energy of nature. Similarly, he gives a psychological explanation of the suicide of Katerina in Ostrovskii's *The Storm.* I do not myself think that instinct as a blindly working force takes us very far in the way of explanation, and

this apart from the consideration that the theory is out of harmony with the high valuation of reason and culture which Dobroljubov shares with Černyševskii. Manifestly here Feuerbach's philosophy, and the endeavour to attain to a purely empirical and materialistic psychology, are at work.

According to Dobroljubov (and Černyševskii), the critic's task as propagandist mainly consists in a kind of reperception of artistic truth, and this led Dobroljubov to prize above all those works of art wherein the artist has revealed himself. It is continually urged against Dobroljubov that he was unjust to Puškin, but on the other side we must point out that he took delight in Gončarov. He admires Gončarov, not merely on account of the latter's creation of the Oblomov type, but he praises this writer's repose and objectivity and his superiority to the passions and influences of the moment. The desire to be swept along by the current "is Oblomovist, and arises from the wish always to have a leader even in matters of sentiment." As propagandist, Dobrolujbov exhorts us to judge poets by their theories of life. (pp. 20-2)

Following Černyševskii, Dobroljubov shows how the individual's merits and defects derive from the social environment. In his hands, aesthetic criticism becomes an analysis of the family, of classes (mercantile and aristocratic), and of social institutions in general. He condemns Russian patriarchalism, which enslaves the family and above all enslaves woman; and he endeavours in Katerina's suicide to discover a manifestation of the folk-soul unbemused by official morality. To selfish merchants and nobles he holds up the mužik, the folk, as models. In the political field he condemns as Oblomovism, not aristocracy alone, but liberalism as well, with its unpractical culture. (pp. 22-3)

In Dobroljubov's characterisation, the liberals appear as "superfluous persons," who begin with Puškin's Onegin and are subsequently represented by Turgenev's types and by Gončarov's Oblomov—dragging out a miserable existence whether in literature or in real life. These cultured and hypercultured individuals are affected with the malady of Oblomovism, they suffer from the paralysis and morbidity of civilisation. Dobroljubov here succumbs to a paroxysm of Rousseauism, and accuses Puškin of remaining too much aloof from the folk. The peasant, says Dobroljubov, is physically and mentally vigorous and healthy, in contrast with the "superfluous" weaklings. Černyševskii by no means shared this favourable opinion of the mužik, and would have rejected it as romanticist. Nor do we find the theory consistently carried out by Dobroljubov; but we have to remember that the mercantile "kingdom of darkness" was peopled for him by "living corpses" (Katerina's husband being among the number), and that he looked upon these Russians of the mercantile classes as persons remote from civilisation.

In this criticism and analysis of literary and socio-political types, Dobroljubov is one-sided and lacking in precision. Moreover, we can detect a certain vacillation, for despite his campaign against the Oblomovs and superfluous persons, he is almost mastered by an enthusiasm for [the Russian philosopher] Stankevič. If, he tells us, most of the members of human society were to resemble Stankevič, no struggles, no sufferings, and no privations, would be necessary—"those privations which unduly utilitarian persons are so fond of expecting from others." We here see the utilitarian discovering that the utilitarians are in the opposite camp.

Dobroljubov's pen, Dobroljubov's realistic criticism, became a political weapon. In his literary critiques the written word was actually transmuted into deeds—opponents declared, into deeds of violence. Doubtless much was said during the heat of battle which would better have been left unsaid, but we must not forget what weapons of word and deed the nihilists' opponents used! Dobroljubov was a fighter; this was his mission and this was the service we owe to him. In his study of Stankevič, he finely tells us upon what he is waging war, and it is, "the constrained and artificial virtue of inner falsehood towards oneself." Dobroljubov fought this fight honourably. We may perhaps note here and there in his polemic the seminarist's touch, that of the preacher or the professor. From his days as a theological student there had clung to him a tinge of the hermit spirit; yet his judgment and condemnation of the world, of society, was not religious but political. Though we learn from his diary that as a student he aspired in ethical matters to be guided by the stoics Cato and Zeno, he shows us often enough that he failed to adhere to his principles. Do we note in him, in fine, a touch of the Oblomov?

Dobroljubov never attempted a philosophical elaboration of his principles. He accepted Černyševskii's materialism without making any strict examination of its foundations. . . . Dobroljubov was nourished almost exclusively on Russian literature; European philosophers were practically unknown to him. Moreover, his interest lay rather in the direction of practical ethics than in those of abstract philosophy, as we may learn from his essay directed against the pedagogic principles of Pirogov.

Nor did Dobroljubov acquire his political and socialistic principles in the philosophic field. It is evident from the essays against Cavour and in favour of Owen that he was here wholly dependent upon Černyševskii. Besides, his socialism was the fruit of personal experience. Dobroljubov was the embodiment of the poor raznočinec, was the man who in his own frame had had experience of the blessings of poverty. (pp. 23-5)

Dobroljubov did not contribute any strongly original ideas to the general stock, but he was an energetic literary propagandist, such as the time needed. (p. 25)

> *Thomas Garrigue Masaryk, "Realism and Nihilism, Černyševskii and Dobroljubov, Pisarev: Dobroljubov Continues Černyševskii's Literary Criticism," in his* The Spirit of Russia: Studies in History, Literature and Philosophy, Vol. 2, *translated by W. R. Lee & Z. Lee (© George Allen & Unwin Ltd; originally published as* Russland und Europa: Studien über die giestigen Strömungen in Russland, *1913), second edition, Allen & Unwin, 1955, pp. 19-25.*

### D. S. MIRSKY   (essay date 1927)

Although all [Dobrolyúbov's] criticism is about works of imaginative literature, it would be grossly unjust to call it literary criticism. Dobrolyúbov had, it is true, a certain sense of literary values, and the choice of works he consented to use as texts for his sermons was, on the whole, happy, but he never so much as attempted to discuss their literary aspects. All his most famous articles—*What Is Oblomovism?* (Goncharóv's *Oblómov*), *A Kingdom of Darkness* (Ostróvsky's early plays), *A Ray of Light in the Kingdom of Darkness* (Ostróvsky's *Thunderstorm*), *When Will There Be Really Day?* (Turgénev's *On the Eve*)—are criticisms of Russian life as reflected in those works. His task was to create a democratic intelligentsia that would be inspired by faith in progress and a desire to serve the people and that might take the place of the romantic and aesthetic,

lazy and ineffective, educated gentry—of which he regarded Oblómov as the true incarnation. All Old Russia—the gentry, the merchants, the traditions of Church and State—he hated with equal violence, and to tear the intelligentsia and the people away from everything connected with old times was his one aim. (p. 226)

> *D. S. Mirsky, "The Age of Realism: Journalists, Poets, and Playwrights" (originally published in his* A History of Russian Literature from the Earliest Times to the Death of Dostoyevsky (1881), *Alfred A. Knopf, Inc., 1927), in his* A History of Russian Literature from Its Beginnings to 1900, *edited by Francis J. Whitfield (copyright © 1958 by Alfred A. Knopf, Inc.; reprinted by permission of the publisher), Vintage Books, 1958, pp. 215-55.\**

### M. YOVCHUK   (essay date 1948)

[*Yovchuk provides a detailed treatment of Dobrolyubov's philosophical and social theories. He particularly stresses Dobrolyubov's role in the development of Russian democratic literature, and his belief that art can transform society.*]

The life and work of Nikolai Alexandrovich Dobrolyubov constitute one of the most vivid and remarkable pages in the history of Russian culture and Russian philosophy. (p. v)

Dobrolyubov—eminent and versatile thinker, author of remarkable works on philosophy and sociology, aesthetics and literary criticism, ethics and pedagogics—was and remains the pride of the Russian people and of all the peoples of the U.S.S.R. (p. vi)

His first literary essays in the field of philosophy—the philosophical "assignments" on which he worked while at the ecclesiastical seminary, in particular, his **"Reflections on the Resurrection of Bodies,"** evidently written in 1852—indicate that already in his early youth he was inclined towards materialism, shared the views of Bacon and Herzen on the role of experience in man's cognition of the outside world, and preferred materialism in philosophy and materialistic natural science to the religious world outlook. (pp. vi-vii)

Already in his first literary production, written while he was at the Central Pedagogical Institute (**"The Russian Historical Novel," "A Few Biographical and Bibliographical Notes on Pushkin," "Some Comments on Didacticism in Stories and Novels,"** etc.), Dobrolyubov showed that he possessed uncommon talent as a publicist, a critical mind in which democratic convictions were taking shape. (p. viii)

Many of Dobrolyubov's critical essays on literature [written for *Sovremennik* following his graduation from the Institute]—in particular **"What Is Oblomovshchina?" "Realm of Darkness," "A Ray of Light in the Realm of Darkness," "When Will the Day Come?" "From Moscow to Leipzig," "Features for the Characterization of the Russian Common People," "The Organic Development of Man in Connection with His Mental and Spiritual Activities," "Russian Civilization as Concocted by Mr. Zherebtsov"**—were valuable contributions to the treasury of Russian and world culture. (pp. viii-ix)

It can be confidently asserted that not a single Russian or West-European thinker of the period before Marx produced, at so early an age, such first-class works as those that came from the pen of Dobrolyubov. Not one of them succeeded in so short a period in working out such a profound, integrated and many-sided world outlook as Dobrolyubov did during the four years of his literary activity. (p. x)

Dobrolyubov's theoretical work, all his activities as a publicist and literary critic, were prompted by the desire to prove the necessity of a democratic revolution in Russia and of rebuilding society on new, and as he thought, on socialist lines. The philosophical basis of his revolutionary-democratic views was provided by the materialist theory and the dialectical principle of universal development, which he propagated in the censored press from the beginning of his literary activities.

In order that the ideas of philosophical materialism and dialectics could capture the minds of progressive people in Russia and lead them to the struggle for the transformation of society, it was necessary to liberate the public mind from the influence of idealistic philosophical systems and the metaphysical method of thinking. (p. xi)

He urged the necessity of freeing literature and life from the influence of the religious "allegories" which appeared at the time "when mankind, not yet conscious of its inner strength, was entirely under the influence of the external world and, influenced by an inexperienced imagination, saw some mysterious power in all things."

In all his works of literary criticism he attacked mysticism in literature and philosophy and ridiculed the fruitless dreaming of the mystics and their isolation from real life. (p. xii)

Like Herzen, Belinsky and Chernyshevsky, Dobrolyubov regarded dialectics as the logical foundation of the revolutionary world outlook, as the "algebra of revolution."

Dobrolyubov's dialectical method revealed itself not in the shape of abstract logical formulae and categories, but in his analysis of the social phenomena of his time, and also in his philosophical and aesthetical analysis of literary works.

In examining the character of popular art, he associates that art with reality, the environment in which it arose and developed. He strongly opposed the metaphysical method of thinking in literature and art which is satisfied with a simple description of casual facts and phenomena divorced from the whole of surrounding circumstances. "To tear a fact out of living reality," he wrote, "and to put it on a shelf side by side with dusty folios, or to classify a few fragmentary, casual facts on the basis of schoolbook logical divisions, means destroying that vitality which lies in this very fact when put in connection with surrounding reality."

Thus, he regarded popular legends as a reflection, expressed in the thoughts and sentiments of the people, of the circumstances under which the people live.

In his essay **"What Is Oblomovshchina?"** Dobrolyubov revealed the inseverable connection that existed between the slave-serf system that prevailed in Russia, the life of the gentry, and the intellectual and moral stagnation among the landlord class. Examining "Oblomovshchina" in connection and in interaction with the environment in which it arose, he started out from the premise that truth is always concrete, and that everything depends upon conditions, time and place.

Dobrolyubov vividly depicted the interdependence of social phenomena, and of how people's actions are conditioned by their environment in his essays **"Realm of Darkness"** and **"A Ray of Light in the Realm of Darkness,"** in which he critically analyzed the works of Ostrovsky. (p. xxiii)

Dobrolyubov's essay **"The Degree to Which Popular Tradition Has Participated in the Development of Russian Literature,"** is a model of the dialectical approach to the development of poetry. When mankind, he says, was entirely under the influence of the external world and was not yet conscious of its strength, its poetry, or rather the monstrous images of mythology, reflected man's oppression by the frightful forces of nature. Subsequently, as man began to become conscious of his importance and to utilize the forces of nature in his own interests, poetry began to assume anthropomorphic forms. When war brought gains and trophies for some and slavery and oppression for others, poetry began to laud the victors and extol the obedience of slaves and vassals. What at one time was the product of its age, subsequently contradicts the truth of life and becomes monstrous and meaningless. "What has outlived its time," concluded Dobrolyubov, "no longer has any meaning. . . . The Greek gods may have been beautiful in ancient Greece, but they are revolting in the French tragedies and in our odes of the last century. The appeals of the knights of the Middle Ages may have roused hundreds of thousands of men to go and fight the heathens, to liberate the Holy Places, but the same appeals, repeated in Europe in the 19th century, would rouse nothing but laughter."

Dobrolyubov not only upheld the dialectical method as a theoretical principle; with the aid of dialectics he smote the enemies of revolutionary democracy who urged that Russia must preserve the "immutable foundations" of her life, which have existed from the days of antiquity, and reject all innovations. (pp. xxv-xxvi)

Dobrolyubov called upon Russian society to rise up and fight conservatism and routine; he contrasted movement and life to the "stagnation of the marsh." . . . (p. xxvi)

In laying new paths in literature and art, Dobrolyubov tried with the aid of the dialectical method to prove the necessity of active art, and he advocated the creation of works of art that would not only truthfully portray actual reality, but also inspire progressive people to change this reality. (p. xxvii)

Like Robert Owen, Saint-Simon, and the other ideologists of utopian socialism whose theories Dobrolyubov critically assimilated, he took as his premise that a man is neither good nor bad at birth, but only potentially one or the other. A man is born with the ability to receive impressions from the outside world. Owing to this, a man who lives in a definite environment yields to its influences and effects. To enable men to abandon bad actions and habits, it is necessary to change the social environment in which they live and develop, to change the character of social relationships.

These premises make Dobrolyubov akin to the ideologists of utopian socialism, but his utopian socialism differed fundamentally from West-European utopian socialism. He stood for the class struggle and, like Herzen and Chernyshevsky, inseparably combined the ideas of socialism with the ideas of revolutionary democracy. He believed that it was impossible to establish socialism unless power passed into the hands of the masses of the people. (p. xxxiii)

Unlike the idealist enlighteners, Dobrolyubov understood that no ideology by itself can change the structure of society. The fact that progressive people in society have become aware of the needs that have matured in society can lead to the satisfaction of these needs only as the result of the practical activities of men; but this will take place only if the activities of the men who have become aware of society's needs go beyond the limits of the purely ideological sphere.

Dobrolyubov sharply criticized the idealists who are of the opinion that "literature directs history, that it [changes states, rouses or tames people], even alters national customs and character, especially poetry—oh, poetry, in their opinion, introduces new elements into life, creates everything out of nothing." Actually, literature is not the legislator but the mouthpiece of social interests. (p. xxxvii)

In the endeavour to awaken the democratic consciousness of the masses of the people and to rouse them for a struggle against tsarism and serfdom, Dobrolyubov turned his gaze and hopes to literature and literary criticism. Following V. G. Belinsky and N. G. Chernyshevsky, he strove to blaze new paths in the development of Russian literature and art; he tirelessly and passionately fought for the creation of a truly popular literature. As he conceived it, this literature was to reflect surrounding reality truthfully and comprehensively, sign the death warrant of the old, feudal order and ideas, and inspire all the virile and progressive forces of the Russian people to wage a struggle for the freedom and happiness of the toiling masses, for the progress of popular culture. To Dobrolyubov and Chernyshevsky fell the great honour in the 1850's of fighting for a Russian literature that would deal with the people and pursue definite ideological aims, in opposition to the efforts of the liberal writers, to isolate literature from the revolutionary struggle and become dispassionate "servants of the muses." (p. xli)

In Dobrolyubov's literary essays the aesthetical principles of Russian revolutionary democracy found vivid expression.

To him, *realism* was the first and chief principle of aesthetics. He fought tirelessly for the realistic trend in literature and art, and demanded that works of art should truthfully reflect all sides and all the contradictions of actual reality. Life does not proceed according to literary theories; on the contrary, literature changes in accordance with the trend of life, he argued. (pp. xli-xlii)

In his essay **"A. S. Pushkin"** he revealed the road to realism for Russian literature. Formerly, he said, Russian poets wrote odes to court festivals and similar events with which the people were not concerned; later they turned to humanistic ideas, but understanding them in an extremely abstract manner, they dropped into sentimentality; ignoring real distress, they lamented over imaginary sorrow, paying homage to prevailing vice, they denounced non-existent vice and extolled ideal virtue. Becoming convinced that the real world was not so good, Russian poetry found consolation in some ephemeral, nebulous world, in the sphere of shades, apparitions and other phantoms. Dropping into mysticism, our poetry of that time strove towards the transcendental and the unknown, and regarded the sinful world as being unworthy of its attention. Pushkin had succeeded in freeing Russian literature from the rule of these trends, and in his works the real Russian world was revealed for the first time. . . . "Pushkin was able to comprehend the true needs and the true character of the life of the people."

Pushkin, discovering the real but as yet unexplored world, was unable to see all its imperfections, and did not make a strict analysis of reality; but his poetry paved the way for a new, realistic trend in literature. (pp. xlii-xliii)

Dobrolyubov's most important principle in aesthetics was the pursuit of an ideal. *The pursuit of a lofty ideal in art* is a

guarantee that art will develop and, at the same time, a condition for its social utility.

Dobrolyubov worked out his revolutionary-democratic theory of art in the course of his struggle against the bourgeois-aristocratic idealistic theory of "art for art's sake." . . . (p. xliii)

He expressed the hope that literature would become imbued with the lofty ideal of liberating toiling humanity and thus become one of the motive forces of social development. . . .

At the very beginning of his activities as a literary critic, Dobrolyubov called upon authors and critics to utter a new, democratic word in science and art, "to spread in society a bright outlook, truly noble convictions." The pursuit of an ideal is the indispensable and determining factor in the contents of every work of literature and art, he argued; and he strongly urged the necessity for a close alliance between art, science and philosophy. This idea he brought out in exceptionally strong relief in his essay **"Realm of Darkness."** (p. xliv)

A vitally important principle of Dobrolyubov's aesthetics was his effort *to make literature and art play an active role in the transformation of society*. In his opinion, the object of works of art should be not only to depict in artistic images the most important aspects of reality, but also to reveal their interconnection in the present, determine their trend of development in the future, and inspire men to wage a conscious struggle for the realization of that future.

Dobrolyubov entertained the hope that a *people's party* in literature would be formed in Russia, i.e., that a democratic literature would spring up that would inspire the people and rouse them for a struggle for the transformation of society. (p. xlv)

Dobrolyubov's aesthetics were based on the consistent pursuit of the principle of *the popular in art*. In his opinion, art is one of the forms of the spiritual life of the people. Genuine works of art express the life, the world outlook of the people.

Truly popular works of art are not only those which depict the lives of the lower estates and classes of society. All works of art which depict the lives of the different classes of society are truly popular, provided, however, they are imbued with humanistic ideas, with sympathy and respect for the people.

Dobrolyubov did not reach a correct understanding of partisanship in literature, but he clearly saw that in the society of his day, "even poetry has been constantly affected by the spirit of parties and classes."

The principles of revolutionary-democratic aesthetics which Dobrolyubov advocated, his struggle for realism in art, for art that pursued definite ideals, that was popular and played an active role in transforming society, were of enormous importance in the development of Russian democratic literature. (pp. xlv-xlvi)

Nikolai Alexandrovich Dobrolyubov is dear to the hearts of the Soviet people, and of progressive people everywhere, as a great revolutionary democrat, an outstanding figure in Russian democratic culture and a brilliant forerunner of Marxism in Russia. (p. xlvi)

*M. Yovchuk, "The Philosophical and Socio-Political Views of N. A. Dobrolyubov," in* Selected Philosophical Essays *by N. A. Dobrolyubov, edited by M. Yovchuk, translated by J. Fineberg (originally published as* Izbrannye filosofskie proizvedeniia, *edited by M. T. Yovchuk, Gos. izd.-vo. Polit. litri., 1948),*

*Foreign Languages Publishing House, 1956, pp. v-xlvi.*

## GEORGE LUKÁCS  (essay date 1949)

[*Lukács is considered one of the foremost Marxist critics of the twentieth century. In his study of the Russian revolutionary democratic critics, Lukács defends Vissarion Belinski, Nikolai Chernyshevsky, and Dobrolyubov from the charge that they cared little for literature as art. Lukács asserts that "these allegations are based on nothing more than that these great critics were sharply opposed to many prejudices still current in modern literary criticism." Praising them for their "passionate advocacy of genuine democratic principles," Lukács grants them an important place among those who helped "literature and literary criticism to rise to the great problems of the epoch."*]

The classical leaders and representatives of [the] new upsurge of democratic thought [in mid-nineteenth-century Russian literary criticism] were the two great heirs to Bielinski's lifework: Chernyshevski and Dobrolyubov. . . .

Throughout the fifties [the] political division [between the Russian liberals and democrats] was reflected in every ideological sphere, from philosophy to literature. Chernyshevski and Dobrolyubov were the ideological leaders of the radical democrats in their struggle against the flabby and submissive philosophy of the liberals. (p. 100)

[The] new upsurge of revolutionary democracy in Russia thus took place in politically and socially more advanced conditions than those in which Bielinski fought his ideological battle a decade earlier. This higher level of the political struggle is apparent in all the writings of Chernyshevski and Dobrolyubov. The most striking new feature of their literary activities was that they now directed their criticism not only against the traditional enemies of freedom but also against their own unreliable allies, the liberal *bourgeoisie* and its ideological representatives. In Bielinski's eyes the chief enemy was still the despotism of autocracy and feudal reaction. Chernyshevski and Dobrolyubov attacked these forces no less resolutely than their master, but in their time another problem had already arisen: the differentiation in the camp of the opponents of absolutism and feudalism, the incipient split between liberalism and democracy.

This new situation naturally affected the philosophical foundations of the new critical school. Chernyshevski and Dobrolyubov no longer, like Bielinski, based themselves on Hegel's philosophy, but on the materialism of Ludwig Feuerbach. Their social criticism was to a large extent determined by the analysis of *bourgeois* society given by the classics of Utopian Socialism. . . . Chernyshevski and Dobrolyubov took up a more realistic, and less ideological attitude to history and historical thought. They were also witnesses of the decadence of Hegelian philosophy, its degradation into a philosophy of liberal compromises. (pp. 100-01)

This position of Chernyshevski and Dobrolyubov is unique in the history of nineteenth-century thought. (p. 101)

If one is to understand the significance and historical place of Chernyshevski's and Dobrolyubov's militant materialism, one must take [the] general historical situation of philosophy into consideration. Chernyshevski and Dobrolyubov are to this day the last great thinkers of revolutionary-democratic enlightenment in Europe. Their work is to this day the last great, inwardly unbroken offensive thrust of the democratic philosophy of enlightenment. Both were enthusiastic adherents of Feuerbach's materialism, but in their social philosophy, their social criticism and their conception of history they far outrun their teacher [Bielinski] who was himself much more interested in natural science and the materialist solution of purely philosophical problems and who in the ideological sphere had subjected only religion to a concrete analysis. (p. 102)

Thus Chernyshevski and Dobrolyubov have done much more than merely to apply the philosophy of Feuerbach to new spheres. They, too, were naturally unable to carry their last principles, their methodology, forward into a dialectical-materialist philosophy. And because they went beyond Feuerbach in their practical philosophy without completely transcending his philosophical principles, their methodology had of necessity to contain many contradictions. But even these contradictions were of a fruitful nature because they pointed towards the future. Chernyshevski's and Dobrolyubov's revolutionary genius manifests itself precisely in the fact that whenever they examined social facts and historical correlations and drew revolutionary conclusions from them, they never allowed themselves to be hampered by their own conscious philosophy, by the limits of mechanistic materialism. (pp. 102-03)

Chernyshevski and Dobrolyubov were genuine, fearless and uncompromising revolutionaries, in the sense in which Marat or St. Just were revolutionaries in the days of the French revolution. . . . And they were true democrats for they put the total liberation of the suffering people above all other considerations and for the sake of this liberation they did not flinch from any unforeseen course the form of social evolution might take. . . . It is this faith in the people, this devotion to the oppressed and exploited masses that constitutes the revolutionary-democratic greatness of Chernyshevski and Dobrolyubov. Here they parted company with even the best of their Liberal contemporaries and here lies the basis of the ideological conflict between them and the Liberals.

The depth of this democratic-revolutionary feeling in Chernyshevski and Dobrolyubov is the foundation on which the greatness of their literary criticism rests. These criticisms always served the end of the liberation of the plebs, always pointed towards the revolutionary way of emancipating the peasantry. Latter-day academic literary historians went so far as to say that Chernyshevski's and Dobrolyubov's literary criticism was merely a means of eluding the vigilance of Tsarist censorship and smuggling revolutionary ideas into the masses in this disguise.

Such a conception is of course quite incorrect, mainly because it contains a narrow and one-sided conception of what revolution is and of the tasks revolutionary ideologies have to fulfil. Chernyshevski and Dobrolyubov, like all truly great democratic revolutionaries before them, always conceived a social cataclysm, a revolution in the universalist sense, as a radical change in all human relations and in all human manifestations of life, from the most massive economic foundations to the highest forms of ideology. Seen from this angle, literature can of course no more be an end in itself than philosophy or even politics. Throughout their life Chernyshevski and Dobrolyubov sought for ways of revolutionary change and in all manifestations of human activity they looked for the tendencies which would advance or hinder the great changeover. What they longed for was ever the universal freedom of men to develop their faculties in every direction. In this respect they remained true disciples of Feuerbach and of the great thinkers of the Enlightenment. (pp. 103-05)

The difference between them and the old thinkers of the Enlightenment lies in the fact that Chernyshevski and Dobrolyubov could historically and philosophically gain insight into and digest the period following upon the great French revolution. Hence they were not confronted with a problemless "empire of reason" like the thinkers of the Enlightenment in the eighteenth-century. They saw that the great French revolution had not swept away the contradictions of *bourgeois* society but had raised them to a higher level and reproduced them in enhanced form. Thus they could look at the obstacles to the liberation of the popular masses with fewer illusions and much more concretely than their great precursors, but for this reason their final outlook is also more full of contradictions than that of the earlier thinkers of the Enlightenment. But these contradictions are the fruitful contradictions of life itself, the fearless recognition and philosophical assimilation of which makes Chernyshevski's and Dobrolyubov's writings so exciting and interesting. (p. 105)

Chernyshevski's and Dobrolyubov's conception of society strives to go beyond [the] limits of mechanistic materialism. That is why we find in the concrete analysis of certain phenomena by them a striking and lively dialectic, although the epistemological principles of their philosophy derive from Feuerbach's mechanistic materialism. This contradiction which can often be observed in the history of philosophy, is very conspicuous in them, but is by no means the first instance of such a contradiction. (pp. 105-06)

[The] observation and recognition of the contradictory movement of society, its evolution by contradiction, determines the nature of Chernyshevski's and Dobrolyubov's critical writings. This is of course much too general a statement. It indicates merely why and how Chernyshevski and Dobrolyubov concerned themselves with social problems, but not why literary criticism occupied a central position in their literary activities. (p. 106)

Bielinski, Chernyshevski and Dobrolyubov were all engaged in a bitter struggle against the "aestheticist" critics of their time, against those who consciously or unconsciously advocated "art for art's sake," who attempted to separate the conception of artistic perfection from the realistic reproduction of social phenomena, and who regarded art and literature as phenomena independent of social strife and untouched by it. In contrast to such ideas, Bielinski, Chernyshevski and Dobrolyubov laid the greatest emphasis on the connection between literature and society. For them life itself was the criterion for artistic beauty; art grew out of life and creatively reproduced it; the fidelity and depth of this reproduction was the true measure of artistic perfection.

Closely related to this conception is their basic idea that life itself, deeply conceived and faithfully reproduced in literature, is the most effective means of throwing light on the problems of social life and an excellent weapon in the ideological preparation of the democratic revolution they expected and desired. Inasmuch as the great Russian critics concerned themselves with the origins, the nature, the value and the effect of literature, inasmuch as they strived to deepen, widen and accelerate by their positive and negative criticism the practical, revolutionary influence of literature, their work can rightly be described as publicistic criticism. (p. 107)

Diderot and Lessing, Bielinski, Chernyshevski and Dobrolyubov concerned themselves with genuine great artistic values. . . . [It] was these critics who established the scientific

foundations of Russian literary history, demarcated its periods and gave valid appreciations of its great figures. (p. 108)

[It] is Chernyshevski and Dobrolyubov who are the theorists, critics and historians of the Gogolian period of literature, the period of the great Russian realists of the nineteenth century. . . . [They] have given us a profound and comprehensive analysis of the greatest representatives of Russian realism, who were their contemporaries. It is to their work as critics that the correct appreciation of the personalities of Turgenyev, Goncharov, Saltykov-Shchedrin, Ostrovski, Dostoyevski and of the works they produced in the 'fifties of the nineteenth century is chiefly due. They welcomed with the same understanding and enthusiasm the first appearance of the younger generation of realists, as Bielinski in his time welcomed the writers who in Chernyshevski's and Dobrolyubov's day were in their maturity. (p. 110)

Bielinski, Chernyshevski and Dobrolyubov always insisted that literature must never be detached from the evolutionary process of life itself; that every work of art must be regarded as a product of the social struggle and playing a more or less important part in it. The methodological consequence of this premise is that every work of art is considered as a reflection of social life. The essence of Bielinski's, Chernyshevski's and Dobrolyubov's critical method is therefore to juxtapose life and literature, the original and the reflection. This conception of art as a mirror of reality is a common trait of all aesthetic theory based on a materialist philosophy. (p. 111)

Bielinski, Chernyshevski and Dobrolyubov brought to light the deepest, most hidden problems of Russian social evolution and made them the subject of their analyses. In comparing the "originals" thus found with their artistic counterparts, they obviously could not be satisfied with a mere naturalist reproduction of the surface of life; on the contrary they flayed any such attempt with the most biting irony. They demanded of the writers that in faithfully depicting the everyday destinies of men they should demonstrate the great problems agitating Russian society, and those decisive, fateful social forces which determine its evolution.

This way of posing the problem naturally determined the method of Bielinski's, Chernyshevski's and Dobrolyubov's negative criticisms. Such comparisons of "original" and reflection as we have just described, are in themselves a devastating criticism of all literature devoid of content. (pp. 111-12)

The great Russian critics sharply reject all psychological quibbles, that false and misleading expedient of the literary theory of decadent periods in which explanations for works of art are sought in the mental peculiarities or biographical circumstances of their authors. (p. 112)

[The] Russian revolutionary-democratic critics emphatically refused to dive into the poets' soul and to regard works of art from that viewpoint, as the product of a mysterious creative subjectivity. For them the starting-point is the finished work of art and its relation to the reality which it mirrors, is for them the proper subject of criticism. Dobrolyubov says: "What the author intended to express is much less important for us than what he really did express, possibly unintentionally, simply as a result of the correct reproduction of facts as he saw them." In another passage we read: "A work of art may be the expression of a certain idea, not because the author had this idea in mind while he was producing it, but because he was impressed by certain features of reality from which this idea automatically arises."

It is precisely this objectivism that many critics and historians of literature in the period of the decline of the arts regard as an anti-aestheticist trend. This entirely false opinion is a result of the pseudo-aesthetic prejudices of a period of decline. For it is precisely by means of this method that Bielinski, Chernyshevski and Dobrolyubov were able to throw light on what the writer had really created, and why in happy moments of creative inspiration he had been able to raise what he had seen and formed high above the barriers of his own subjective opinions or prejudices. The true nature of artistic creation was thus explained here for the first time, in contrast to the psychologising mystifications of the subjectivist school of aesthetics. (pp. 113-14)

The appeal to reality, the materialist theory of mirroring the objective world through the medium of human consciousness, through art, science and philosophy . . . does not by any means lead the great Russian critics towards an intellectualisation of art and even less towards its mechanical politization—but on the contrary towards establishing the independence of art, not of course in the sense of the subjectivistic-idealistically inflated spurious isolation found in the theories of the post-1848 period of decline, but in such a manner that in demonstrating the interdependence of art and life and in showing the real function of art in the process of social evolution, they facilitate the philosophical understanding of the true independence of art.

Thus did the great Russian critics, in contrast to the modern, narrow, subjectivist, distortingly aestheticist overestimation of art, establish the true and epoch-making part played by art in the history of mankind. (p. 115)

Chernyshevski and Dobrolyubov . . . reject all probing into the so-called 'depths of the poet's soul.' In its place they put the basic question: how does the evolution of the community itself create typical problems and typical characters, how are certain types which mutually supplement each other and develop each other to a higher plane, spontaneously produced by the process of social evolution itself. In his analysis of Goncharov's novel *Oblomov*, Dobrolyubov gives a classical example of this new critical method. He shows the growing discontent and opposition of the Russian nobility and gentry in its evolution from Pushkin's *Onegin* to Goncharov's *Oblomov*. He shows how the unity of the social process necessarily and spontaneously produces cognate problems for all men actively participating in it and demonstrates how several great writers (in accordance with their own social position, time, and personality) depicted different stages in the development of this type and the typical conflicts in which it was involved, until at last the type found its historical and aesthetical completion in Goncharov's *Oblomov*. (p. 116)

The discovery and revelation of the social and historical significance of such typical characters and typical destinies are the main task Bielinski, Chernyshevski and Dobrolyubov set themselves in their work as critics. (p. 117)

[Dobrolyubov] violently attacked the so-called "laws of dramaturgy" in an analysis of one of Ostrovski's plays. But if we read the whole article, what do we find? What Dobrolyubov attacked so sharply was the niggling, formalistic, academic dramaturgy, which attempted to slaughter Ostrovski's new, revolutionary, realistic plays on the grounds that they broke these laws. When Dobrolyubov analysed Ostrovski in detail, he deduced concretely and critically, without any abstract theoretical discussion—the new principles of dramaturgy by means of which Ostrovski succeeded in putting on the stage with great power and profound effect important trends of his time.

Essentially Dobrolyubov's method is thus to re-establish and defend the laws of aesthetics—laws periodically changing their forms of manifestation—against the danger of academic-abstract modification. (pp. 117-18)

[The] methodology of Russian revolutionary-democratic criticism . . . is of the greatest importance even today. It would be a grievous error to consider Bielinski, Chernyshevski and Dobrolyubov merely historically, as prominent representatives of a past epoch, who have now ceased to be a live and effective force. The exact opposite is the case. If in the present profound crisis in the evolution of mankind we are to advance towards a genuine literary culture, if we want literature and literary criticism to rise to the level of the great problems of the epoch, then we can and must, today more than ever before, learn a great deal from Bielinski, Chernyshevski and Dobrolyubov. (p. 123)

The history of criticism in the past centuries shows that its great periods, its immortal figures were linked—and not by accident— with the passionate advocacy of genuine democratic principles. Thus did Diderot and Lessing act in the eighteenth century achieving an influence extending far beyond the confines of their own country; Bielinski, Chernyshevski and Dobrolyubov occupied a similar position in the history of aesthetical thinking in the nineteenth century, although they have not as yet made any impression outside Russia. But the social scene and the demand for its reproduction in literature are such that a universal recognition of their international significance can only be a question of time and that not long. (p. 125)

*George Lukács, "The International Significance of Russian Democratic Literary Criticism," in his* Studies in European Realism: A Sociological Survey of the Writings of Balzac, Stendhal, Zola, Tolstoy, Gorki, and Others, *translated by Edith Bone (copyright 1950 Hillway Publishing Co.; originally published under a different title in his* Der russische Realismus in der Weltliteratur, *Aufbrau-Verlag, 1949), Hillway Publishing Co., 1950, pp. 97-125.* *

### HENRY GIFFORD  (essay date 1950)

[Dobrolyubov] was vowed to destroy the old order, which never held any illusions for him. . . . [He] had his eyes wholly on the future—a future which he was never fated to come in sight of, being only twenty-four when he died.

The most famous of a few striking articles which he wrote for *The Contemporary* was . . . **'What is Oblomovism?'** The literal answer, of course, is that Oblomovism was a word coined by Oblomov's energetic friend Stolz to characterise the indolence and apathy of Oblomov. But in this article Dobrolyubov seizes upon Oblomovism as the keyword to describe Russian life, or, more precisely, the life of the landowning class which had produced all the heroes of Russian literature so far. Oblomov, lying on his divan, and dreaming his idle dreams, may not appear very significant in himself. But all the same he deserved to have a novel, in four considerable parts, written about him, because he is the residue of Onegin and all the others. Dobrolyubov puts the character of Oblomov to a searching examination. What are the leading traits of Oblomov?

First, there is his proverbial indolence. Oblomov has been brought up to rely on Zakhar, and on three hundred other Zakhars, to do everything for him. . . . So, in time, he looked to others to do the work, while he, a gentleman, sat back with folded hands. Not that he didn't dream of action. There were moments when he longed for some great crisis, so that he could step forward and save humanity. Fortunately, the great crisis was far off: it dissolved when he ceased thinking of it. The activity of ordinary life repelled Oblomov. He had infinite dreams, and infinite excuses.

And then, there was his passion for liberty—if you could call anything so negative by the name of passion. Oblomov prided himself on not having to work, or make decisions. (pp. 148-50)

As Dobrolyubov points out, many of these traits can be found in Onegin, and the other heroes. (pp. 150-51)

What has been said of Onegin could be said generally of Pechorin, Beltov and Rudin. Dobrolyubov carries the attack farther, and shows that Oblomov is the 'superfluous man' in his true colours. All these unhappy gentlemen, with their splendid hopes and petty performance, are no different from Oblomov. It was a point of view that Herzen could not see, and he felt that the 'superfluous men' had been necessary in their hour. But Dobrolyubov's charge, all the same, has a certain melancholy truth. What had been half veiled in Onegin was now clear enough in his descendant, Oblomov. The type had developed, and run to seed. And all those young men who, in a later day, lived and talked like Onegin or Pechorin, were really playing Oblomov. His were the attitudes, the ideas, the gospel of the 'superfluous men', carried to their logical end. The shadow of Oblomov lay over Russian society. (p. 151)

Towards the end of his essay, Dobrolyubov puts the question which Gogol had once asked: 'Where is the man who can say in the very language of the Russian soul this all-powerful word "Forward"?' As yet, he concludes, there is no sign of this man. But Russia awaits him, even though, for the moment, Oblomov's is the prevailing spirit, and Oblomovka is the true image of Russia. (p. 153)

All the same, Stolz was intended, as Dobrolyubov said, to be the antidote to Oblomov. For the first time, a figure has come on the scene who is fully disciplined. Every movement in Stolz is directed to some end; he has a firm and lively step; his attitude towards life is simple; he believes in work and concentration. . . .

As a pattern of something not yet realised, Dobrolyubov could accept Stolz. But he was emphatic that so far no such men existed; they had nothing firm under their feet. (p. 156)

> Henry Gifford, "The Road to the Vyborg Side" and *"In Search of the New Man,"* in his *The Hero of His Time: A Theme in Russian Literature, Edward Arnold & Co., 1950, pp. 133-53, 154-76.**

### RENÉ WELLEK (essay date 1955)

[*Wellek here disputes the contention of earlier critics that Dobrolyubov was influenced by Ludwig Feuerbach. In addition, he maintains that Dobrolyubov is not really interested in literature for its own sake, but that "in practice he succumbed to simple didacticism and even to crude allegorizing to serve his polemical purposes." He views Dobrolyubov primarily as a revolutionary, and feels that for Dobrolyubov, as for Nikolai Chernyshevsky and Dmitri Pisarev, "literature was only a weapon in the battle."*]

The continuity between Belinskii and the [Russian] critics of the [eighteen-fifties] and sixties—Chernyshevskii, Dobroliubov, and Pisarev—is obvious. Still, they differ sharply from their master, however sincerely they may have thought that they were only developing the ideas and conceptions of his last stage. The intellectual atmosphere had changed greatly: Belinskii had grown in the shadow of German idealism and had never abandoned its basic doctrines on art and history. Chernyshevskii, Dobroliubov, and Pisarev had no understanding of the German romantic views. Their philosophy precluded this: it is frequently called Feuerbachian and considered identical with that of the latest stage of Belinskii. But I cannot see any evidence that these writers adopted the specific doctrines of Feuerbach, a highly sentimental fervid theologian, imbued with Hegel's way of thinking. They must rather be described as materialistic monists, most deeply influenced by popularizers of the scientific outlook, such as Vogt, Moleschott, and Büchner, and by the English Utilitarians. (p. 388)

Dobroliubov was as little interested in art as his master [Chernyshevskii], though he wrote much more exclusively on belles-lettres. But he applied more consistently, more systematically and consciously the point of view indicated by Chernyshevskii. Dobroliubov never tires of repeating the view expounded by Chernyshevskii, that literature is only a mirror of life, which reflects, but cannot change, reality. (p. 391)

But at times, Dobroliubov modifies his thesis about art as the mere passive mirror of society. Literature helps to clarify existing tendencies in society. It may be useful in "quickening and giving greater fulness to the conscious work of society." It is an "auxiliary force, the importance of which lies in propaganda, and the merit of which is determined by what it propagates and how it propagates it." Dobroliubov even recognizes that artists became the historical leaders of mankind who symbolize, like Shakespeare, an entire phase of human development. Thus Dobroliubov runs the gamut from complete pessimism to messianic hopes: from the view that literature is a passive mirror of society to the view that it incites to direct action. He is caught in a net of conflicting views: his theoretical conviction that literature is mere words which cannot affect reality, his doctrinaire determinism, and the practical impossibility of the resignation implied, the need to demand from literature a discussion of what he considered new and progressive ideas in the hope that they might, in the end, prevail.

Surveying the history of Russian literature, Dobroliubov displays the same hesitation: on the one hand the development of literature is said to reflect the changes of society passively and inertly; on the other, it seems to him shameful that literature has not expressed what he considers the real needs of the nation. Dobroliubov wants an all-national literature, above classes, parties, and cliques, but recognizes that Russian literature has hitherto appealed only to a small reading public. He wavers in his hopes for the future between a romantic conception of nationality as something uniquely Russian, and a literature written for the peasant masses, representing them and comprehensible to them. But Dobroliubov merely raises the question of popular art: in his criticism he is rather occupied with one problem, the truth to life of the novels and plays he discusses. Dobroliubov made a real contribution to the theory of the social study of literature. He apparently for the first time thought clearly of "social types" as revealing an author's world view, independently of or even contrary to his conscious intentions. The attitude of a writer must be sought for in the living images he creates. "In these images the poet may, imperceptibly even to himself, grasp and express an inner meaning long before his mind can define it. It is precisely the function of criticism to explain the meaning hidden in these images." The conscious intention of an author remains a secondary question. This method of studying social types or heroes, with its dismissal of what today is called "The Intentional Fallacy," seems a valuable technique: it distinguishes between an overt and a latent meaning of a work of art somewhat as, in different philosophical contexts Engels, Freud, Pareto, or Mannheim distinguish them. Social types such as the gentleman or the intellectual had begun to attract consideration in French literary criticism. . . . The German romantic critics had discussed the great mythic types of humanity: Hamlet, Faust, Don Quixote. The Schlegels had dismissed conscious intention as a criterion of value. But these motifs had not yet coalesced as they did in Dobroliubov.

Unfortunately, Dobroliubov was unable to keep steadily to his central insight. In practice he succumbed to simple didacticism and even to crude allegorizing to serve his polemical purposes. Oblomov, in [**"What is Oblomovshchina?"**], is declared a "key to the riddle of many manifestations of Russian life." "Oblomovka is our motherland: a large portion of Oblomov is within every one of us." Dobroliubov sees the continuity between Oblomov and the type of "superfluous man" depicted in Onegin and Pechorin, yet he wanted to dismiss these two fictional heroes as belonging to a dead past. "They have lost their significance, they have ceased to mislead us with their enigmatic mystery." But instead of trying to analyze Oblomov, Dobroliubov dismisses him as a "disgusting nonentity," holding him up as a kind of warning example, a bogyman, an allegory of Russian indolence and backwardness. He has lost sight of the book and the figure.

Similarly, Dobroliubov analyzes the plays of Ostrovskii, using them to document tyranny, oppression, ignorance, superstition, and downtrodden resignation. Only the heroine of Ostrovskii's *Storm*, Katerina, seems to him the "representative of a great national idea," a "reflection of a new movement of national life." He glorifies her suicide in the Volga as "the height to which our national life is rising in its development." He sees it as "a challenge to the power of tyranny." But if my own reading of the play is anywhere near the text, Katerina must rather be considered a pitiful figure, dominated by dark instinct. . . . [To] make Katerina, an adultress and a suicide, a superstitious ignorant woman pursued and crushed by a sense of doom, into a symbol of revolt, seems the very height of what could be called "loss of contact" with the text. Anything must serve the cause and if it does not, it must be made over to fit it. Similarly, Turgenev's *On the Eve* is merely used as a pretext to call for a Russian Insarov. An ominous "the day will come" concludes the piece. Only in Dobroliubov's last essay on Dostoyevsky's *Insulted and Injured* can one discern some progress of sensibility. He suddenly recognizes the role of imagination. An artist is not a "photographic plate." "He supplements the isolated moment with his artistic feeling. He creates a whole, finds a vital link, fuses and transforms the diverse aspects of living reality." The poet's work is "something that must be so, and cannot be otherwise." Though Dobroliubov is puzzled by Dostoyevsky's novel and denies even that it is art, the power of Dostoyevsky's imagination had its effect. But unfortunately, Dobroliubov died in the year of this article . . . , aged not yet twenty-six. (pp. 391-93)

[We] should recognize that [Chernyshevskii, Dobroliubov, and Pisarev] were not primarily interested in literature at all. They were revolutionaries, and literature was only a weapon in the battle. They did not see that man is confronted with questions which surpass those of his own age: that the insight art provides into the full meaning of existence does not necessarily grow out of his immediate social preoccupations. As critics they constantly lose sight of the text, confuse life and fiction, treat figures in novels as if they were men or women in the street, or allegorize a fictional character, make it evaporate to represent some generalization such as the decadent aristocrat, the desire for freedom, the new man. They constantly succumb to two not unrelated fallacies: naturalism and intellectualism. They have lost hold on the concrete universal, the fusion of the particular and general in every work of art, which Belinskii had understood. Content and form are divorced with them: the unity of the work of art is broken up, imagination is reduced to a mere combinatory power. Art, in short, is denied as a value in itself. It is distributed between the despised sensual pleasure of form and a purely intellectual or hortatory content. Art is, at bottom, superfluous. (p. 396)

But this tendency, destructive of the very nature of art and literary criticism, should not make us ignore the real contribution of the three critics to a social study of literature. Their analysis of social types was something important, also methodologically. Besides, one must recognize that Russia at that time was actually producing a social novel, that poetry then was derivative, and the drama rather a reflex of the novel. Our critics helped to define and describe the nature of the social novel, the obligation of the writer toward social truth, his insight, conscious or unconscious, into the structure and typical characters of his society. It seems a pity that they did so in narrow local terms, shackled by their gross utilitarianism. The noise of the battle deafened them. (pp. 396-97)

*René Wellek, "Social and Aesthetic Values in Russian Nineteenth-Century Literary Criticism (Belinskii, Chernyshevskii, Dobroliubov, Pisarev)" (a revision of a paper delivered at Arden House, March 26-28, 1954), in* Continuity and Change in Russian and Soviet Thought, *edited by Ernest J. Simmons (copyright © 1955 by the President and Fellows of Harvard College; excerpted by permission), Cambridge, Mass.: Harvard University Press, 1955, pp. 381-97.*

**VLADIMIR SEDURO** (essay date 1957)

[In **"Downtrodden People,"** Dobrolyubov] displayed extraordinary sensitivity toward the characters in Dostoyevski who have exaggerated pride and discerned in them hidden sparks of that flame of protest which blazes in the souls of "downtrodden people." Those utter derelicts, as they seemed, who, when put to test, proved capable of fighting "for their rights" were especially understandable to him. (p. 14)

Dobrolyubov saw in Dostoyevski the faculty for detecting living people with living souls in his dulled, numb heroes. . . . Even in Dostoyevski's earliest fiction Dobrolyubov found the one feature which runs through all Dostoyevski's work to the end, namely, compassion for man. The realization by man of his legitimate right to be himself and to find genuine, complete, and independent expression of his personality was the driving force in the behavior of Dostoyevski's heroes. The impossibility of preserving their individuality leads them to bitterness, withdrawal from the world, or even to madness, but more often "simply to quiet torpor, to the suppression of human nature in themselves, to the frank recognition that they are something much lower than a man." (p. 15)

Neither before nor after Dobrolyubov did Russian critical thought of the nineteenth century rise to such a height of keen penetration into the secret of Dostoyevski's writings. The character of Golyadkin and his heroic madness, which was the self-sacrifice of a zealot in behalf of the lofty estate of man, a protest against the unjust conditions of life, an explosion of the insulted human dignity lying hidden in his secret inner world, found their interpreter in Dobrolyubov. (pp. 15-16)

Dobrolyubov was interested not so much by the formal aspect of Dostoyevski's fiction—the still not fully developed art of the novel—as by the author's extraordinary insight into the previously unknown world of the insulted and injured man of the time. In his keen and subtle analysis of the complex psychology of Dostoyevski's characters, with their tangled lives and their gloomy feeling about life, the critic expressed concern for the lot of the downtrodden people and anxiety over the failure of efforts to curb the forces striving to extinguish the sparks of human dignity. (p. 17)

The critic regarded Dostoyevski as an impartial artist, detached from controversies and theories of the day, who observed and depicted reality "without thinking at all whom this will benefit, for what idea it will prove useful." On the other hand, the transmutation of facts of life into art gives them such force as a generalization that "afterwards there can be no doubts whatever in respect to the entire range of similar phenomena." Proceeding from this premise, Dobrolyubov, here as much publicist as literary critic, grouped the personalities and types of characters found in Dostoyevski and arrived at answers to the questions raised throughout his writing.

In his examination of the character of Ikhmenev in *The Insulted and Injured* and of the ineffectuality of the latter's protest against the injustice inflicted upon him by the prince, who was protected by "connections and the police regime," the critic prompted the reader to seek a way out of the circumstances that had been created for Dostoyevski's heroes:

> Does it thus follow that the position of these unhappy, downtrodden, insulted, and injured people is completely hopeless? Can they do nothing but keep silent and endure, and, reduced to the condition of a dirty rag, tuck away their unvoiced feelings in its most obscure folds?

Dobrolyubov's radical trend of thought had brought him to unequivocal answers, but censorship forced him to hedge at this point, to say that he would not enlarge upon the subject and that it would be naïve to expect him to answer these questions, which were fraught with the accursed and still vexed problems of the times. He deliberately limited his task to the classification of the downtrodden, insulted, and injured characters, pointing out that there were many of them in the middle strata of society, that they had a hard life in both the moral and physical sense, that underneath their apparent outward resignation they never ceased feeling bitter over their circumstances, that their irritation and protest were easily aroused, and that they longed for a way out.

The critic's conclusion is full of sincere indignation, sympathy, and desire to help shape a consistent philosophy of life out of the feelings which Dostoyevski's characters had about their world. In the muffled beat of life among them Dobrolyubov, filled with dreams of a better Russia, heard precisely what he yearned to hear. Restraining himself from forecasts too far beyond the bounds of literary criticism, he nevertheless found reassurance in the actual trends of his time—the emergence into the social and cultural arena of extraordinary forces from the people, chiefly the middle classes, as represented by Dobrolyubov himself, those of similar persuasion among the

men of the sixties, and even Dostoyevski; and the heartening signs that new masses were awakening and coming to a realization of their cultural, social, and political role. . . . With a wary eye on the censor, he called cryptically upon his readers to give themselves to the revolutionary current. . . . (pp. 18-20)

As a *raznochinets*, Dobrolyubov clearly alluded to those like himself who were less crushed by their circumstances, and appealed to them to look more closely at this third force coming to life among Dostoyevski's characters. Here to a certain extent the political thinker in Dobrolyubov involuntarily gained the upper hand over the critic, as in the case of all those writing for the journals of the 1860s. Dobrolyubov was the leading exponent of such social and publicist critical literature of the period. His great interest in public affairs, coupled with a deeply analytical mind, contributed much to his understanding of the complexities and contradictions of Dostoyevski. Dobrolyubov was the first to open up the new world of Dostoyevski for later Russian scholarship and, indeed, it may be that no other Dostoyevski critic has ever surpassed him in insight. (pp. 20-1)

> *Vladimir Seduro, "The Early 'Radical' Critics," in his* Dostoyevski in Russian Literary Criticism: 1846-1956 *(copyright © 1957 Columbia University Press; reprinted by permission of the publisher), Columbia University Press, 1957, pp. 3-38.\**

**RUFUS W. MATHEWSON, JR.**   (essay date 1958)

*[Matthewson discusses Dobrolyubov's search for a new kind of Russian hero capable of revolutionary action. He states that "the quest for the hero gives a focus to all Dobrolyubov's moral, social, political, and literary concerns, and to his brief, hectic career as well."]*

[N. A. Dobrolyubov] is the eternal, perhaps one should say the professional, youth of the Russian revolutionary movement. His brief career . . . summarizes all the virtues and vices of the youthful radical. For his partisans, then and now, he expressed the energy, the optimism, the critical brilliance, and the refreshing anger against injustice that characterize the best of the radical ethos. To his enemies, his brilliance was arrogant precocity, his optimism callow, and his anger and energy were expressed in a blind urge to destroy. In all the senses that radicalism is youthful, Dobrolyubov comes down to us a classic example. In this role he was a compelling figure in his own time. (p. 46)

Dobrolyubov's indebtedness to Belinsky is direct, heavy, and explicit. He felt a strong spiritual kinship with his predecessor, that "pride, glory and adornment" of Russian literature, and his intellectual dependence on Belinsky is evident in everything Dobrolyubov has to say about the nature of art and society. Frequently he gave sharp, dogmatic utterance to ideas which had been half-understood or unexplored premises for Belinsky. Dobrolyubov presents restatements of Belinsky's three key premises, optimism, typicality, and service, indicating that they are central in his own thought. (p. 47)

If Dobrolyubov sharpened some of Belinsky's ideas, he also reduced the range of his interests and eliminated the contradictions, always in favor of the prescriptive element, always to the detriment of literature's independence. There is no doubt that the narrow, systematized version of Belinsky used by Soviet critics had its beginnings here. That literature performs a kind of secondary service in the intellectual activities of the day is stated far more uncompromisingly by Dobrolyubov than by Belinsky. . . .

The writer is given no leeway to distort or falsify; nor, though he works under the guidance of an idea, is he permitted to inject this idea as learned from a philosopher into his work. It must be verifiable against an objective norm, usually described simply as "real life." Literature, then, is accountable to experience, but the principal reason for this restriction is that its propagandist function is impaired by falsification. . . . (p. 48)

Though the writer may end by agreeing with the philosopher, he must proceed to his conclusion by a different route. In comprehending social discontent, for example, the philosopher will analyze facts and then proceed to formulate general principles which will aid in the removal of the unrest. But "the author-poet . . . noticing the same discontent, paints such a vivid picture of it that it attracts universal attention, and of itself suggests to people what it is they need."

Both aspects of the truth have the same final purpose: the abolition of the unacceptable present and its replacement by a better future. . . . The writer becomes a kind of prophet, and even when his expectations turned out to be premature, they still were to be considered "true" at the moment they were expressed. (pp. 48-9)

Dobrolyubov was stimulated by widespread restlessness and by the rising note of agitation which preceded the Emancipation Act of 1861. He found evidence in life and in literature to justify his optimism and to validate his philosophy of social action. In addition to the belligerence among the leftist intellectuals, there were strong "murmurings" from the people. And nothing seemed to offer a stronger guarantee that one era was about to give way to another than the discovery that a revolution was taking place in the personalities of Russia's men of conscience:

> No matter where you look, everywhere you will find an awakening of personality (a claim for its legitimate rights), a protest against violence and tyranny (in most cases still timid, indefinite, ready to hide, but for all that) already making its existence felt.

This new kind of person was a symptom of impending change as well as the agent who was to carry it out. Also, by all the tenets of Dobrolyubov's creed, he was an obvious candidate for the role of the literary hero. The quest for the hero gives a focus to all Dobrolyubov's moral, social, political, and literary concerns, and to his brief, hectic career as well.

Dobrolyubov's controversial manifesto, **"What Is Oblomovism?"** was intended to proclaim the ceremonial burial of the superfluous man. Looking back over thirty years of the new Russian realism, Dobrolyubov claimed to have made a striking discovery about Russian literary heroes. Using Goncharov's *Oblomov* as his point of departure, he generalized angrily about the unvarying pattern of weakness, egotism, and inactivity these heroes describe. . . . These imagined figures are treated as *descriptions* of types in the real world and their common crime is their failure to act morally and effectively in the fictional semblance of the real world. Dobrolyubov is perfectly clear about this: Oblomovism is a moral and social disease widespread in Russian life itself. Literature has done its job well in exposing and diagnosing the illness. But life has moved on and literature must bestir itself to catch up. (pp. 49-50)

"We need men of action and not of abstract . . . argument," Dobrolyubov wrote in his review of Turgenev's *On the Eve*, which bears the characteristically impatient title, **"When Will the Day Come?"** Correct principles have become common property, and now await the kind of men who will put them into practice.

The successor to the superfluous man had a name and a set of characteristics before he had been reliably reported to exist: he was called "the new man." As first conceived, he was in one sense a development beyond his predecessors, and in another sense—notably in his thirst for action—a direct antithesis to them. (p. 51)

But Dobrolyubov's tireless scrutiny of literature indicated that the image of the positive hero was disappointingly elusive. He suspected at times that the new type existed only in his own expectations. At other times, he indicated that he was very close to finding him, or that the hero had been discovered in some incomplete form, or that a careless author simply had not known a hero when he saw him. Then again, Dobrolyubov seemed ready to conclude that the circumstances of Russian life were still exercising their harsh sovereignty over the growth of the new moral personality, and, though the public expected him and the movement of history guaranteed that he would come, he had not yet reached maturity. But Dobrolyubov persisted in the certainty that the new moral type must ultimately come to exist.

According to Dobrolyubov's optimal expectations, the new man, freed of the curse of inertia when he became aware of his condition, would know his own strength, who his enemies were, and how to attack them. Factual knowledge of his environment, which had become widespread by this time, was not the only resource available to the man who thirsted to act. He was blessed with a generous endowment of "natural" goodness and strength, and a vivid emotional awareness of his "natural" rights. These resources, if they managed to survive the gauntlet of the Russian environment, including the adverse effects of a false educational system, would supply him with the energy and courage to put his principles into practice, and to make use of his knowledge.

These natural attributes of character which are the birthright of all men are described variously by Dobrolyubov at various points in his work, but they have one common denominator: they are the virtues that overcome inertia and lead to fearless, direct action. (pp. 51-2)

Presumably, suicide registers in an ultimate way an individual's determination and capacity to act. It did not seem absurd, apparently, to the angry young revolutionary to consider suicide or martyrdom as "healthy" acts of rebellion. Although he never said it in so many words, he seems at times to be making the even more absurd proposal that suicide is a kind of program for social action. Dostoevsky may well have found his cue here when he created Kirillov, the brilliantly absurd philosopher of self-destruction in *The Possessed,* who hoped to liberate men from their fear of death and of God by his own exemplary suicide. Dobrolyubov had no such grandiose intentions but the gesture of angry defiance is the same in each case, and it seems plausible to read Kirillov as a grotesque extension of Dobrolyubov's light-minded views on self-destruction. As a plain tactical matter it would seem that Dobrolyubov's heroes are a little too ready to die to do the cause much good.

Suicide, in Dobrolyubov's uncomplicated understanding of it, signifies a simple kind of virtuous strength, which is found in abundance among the common people. Dobrolyubov is not suggesting that the new hero will be from the lower orders. He is saying, rather, that the new man in his search for moral strength should learn from the people in whose name he finds the ultimate justifications for his acts. It is the grievances of the common people that dignify his efforts, it is their terrible anger that he must arouse, and their strength that he must direct. They may provide, too, in the example of their lives, the answer to the fatal breakdown of character which paralyzed the potential leaders of preceding generations.

With this blueprint in hand, Dobrolyubov set out in search of the hero of his time among current literary portraits. A number of examples are rejected out of hand. Any suggestion of the superfluous man's faint heart is unacceptable because history has rendered it obsolete. Also invalid are all efforts by writers to inject their own abstract notions of Russian valour into an imagined protagonist. The character must have genuine moral stature, must be capable of action, and must be presented in compelling and verifiable detail.

Anany, the peasant hero of Pisemsky's *A Bitter Fate,* is dismissed as absurd. . . . Goncharov's Stolz (in *Oblomov*), one of the most deliberate efforts to create a wholly positive, emblematically good man, is dismissed on two counts: the limited, mundane quality of his morality, and the abstractness of his literary portrait. (pp. 53-5)

[Stolz] moves "in a mist," without effective motivation, without an inner life that explains his self-confident behavior.

Turgenev's *On the Eve* was carefully scrutinized for traces of the new Russian heroism. Insarov, the central male figure, is disqualified on technical grounds—he is a Bulgarian, not a Russian! In addition, he suffers from the blurred delineation that mars the image of Stolz. (p. 55)

Eliminated from the Russian hero competition on a technicality, Insarov is nevertheless useful to Dobrolyubov as a yardstick against which to measure the Russians in the same novel. They are more brilliant and more complex than Insarov, and men of equally lofty moral aims. Yet they do not act. They still measure their private interests against the interests of society—a meaningless dichotomy for Insarov—and keep their highly developed sense of principle intact by never risking it in action. (p. 56)

Dobrolyubov's conclusions are gloomy. There is no arena in Russia for Insarov's kind of heroism. In addition, the hostile environment has begun to disfigure the moral character of potential heroes from the earliest days of their education. Only a clear-cut, unambiguous cause could provide the scope for action which would release the latent energies of the men of good will. Dobrolyubov veers close to despair. . . . The individual's struggle to reach the threshold of heroic public service is itself a work of heroism, but he has so often suffered serious moral injury in this preliminary battle that the absence of a goal when he finally arrives causes him to succumb to his wounds or waste his remaining energies in trivial activities, "playing the Don Quixote." (pp. 56-7)

Not all the Russian characters in *On the Eve* are "toothless squirrels." There is one person who has moved beyond the stage of indoctrinated paralysis that afflicts the Russian men in the novel. This individual, together with two others, the creations of Goncharov and Ostrovsky, the dramatist, form, in composite, the most complete profile of the new man Dobrolyubov was able to find. Curiously, it is a woman's face that

emerges. Dobrolyubov arranges three literary heroines, typical of the impulsive, straightforward feminine figures in Russian literature since Pushkin's Tatyana, in an ascending order of virtue and effectiveness. Beginning with Olga in *Oblomov*, proceeding to Elena in Turgenev's *On the Eve*, and ending with Katerina in Ostrovsky's *Storm*, he thought he had discovered the basic trend toward stronger, more resilient characters. Though not yet fully developed, they were the first authentic images of the new type. (p. 57)

[In] her hopeless effort to win Oblomov's love and reclaim him from sloth, [Olga] displays genuine moral strength; she is determined, ready to defy convention, and the picture of a vital "natural" woman in love. . . . She has, in addition, recognized one face of the ubiquitous internal enemy in the pitiable and, "repulsive" figure of Oblomov and has fought strenuously against it. Finally, Dobrolyubov praises her because her defeat has not seriously discouraged her. (pp. 57-8)

[In *On the Eve*, Elena's] sensitivity to the suffering of others and a habit of questioning dominant values have prepared her for purposeful activity. . . . Her one major act, . . . her marriage to the Bulgarian activist, Insarov, is carried out with exemplary courage and directness, and in open defiance of social convention. . . . [The] example of her virtuous behavior in these personal matters indicates the trend toward more and more effective people, specifically, toward a Russian Insarov. . . .

Dobrolyubov sees [Katerina's suicide in *Storm*] as an act of defiance, not of despair, the only unblocked path to her liberation. Her refusal to submit to a way of life which smothers all her "natural" strivings is interpreted as the moral equivalent of an act of political rebellion. (p. 58)

The central virtue she possesses is one which is lacking in the noblest and most brilliant of her superfluous predecessors. With a mind uncluttered by abstractions, she is motivated solely by the "instinctive consciousness of her inalienable right to life, happiness, and love." Her awareness of her rights is so urgent that she meets and passes the supreme test of her courage, the willingness *to risk* death. Convinced that her death symbolizes an ultimate challenge to the existing order, Dobrolyubov insists that it is a "joyous" and "inspiring thing," serving notice to tyranny that "it is impossible to live any longer with its violent and deadening principles."

The problem of the hero's need to break through the encircling environment comes into focus in recapitulation. Knowledge, both factual and theoretical, is a first requirement for the new man. But this need has long been met. First principles have been enunciated; facts to buttress them have been gathered and analyzed; and the hard-won legacy of Belinsky's generation is by now common property. Enough people have survived the Russian environment intact, and have reached an understanding of the need for radical change. Now the formula for social consciousness has been brought to the verge of completion as Dobrolyubov conceived it: from fact to idea to intention to longing and finally to action. The last was the most difficult step of all, the insuperable barrier for all the superfluous men. Since Dobrolyubov was sure that knowledge of the laws of history must lead to action, it is clear that an essential ingredient is still missing. It is, we are told, the inner moral strength of individuals which will finally set the mechanism of change in motion. (p. 59)

Action is generated in the individual's awareness of the discrepancy between the "natural strivings" of his heart and the repeated, senseless violations of human dignity in Russian life. The "natural" man, the vital, wholehearted person who has preserved his total human birthright, confronted with intolerable conditions, will simply refuse to submit to them.

The hero's moral personality contains the program and the means for action, as well as the guarantee of its success. The hero, in a sense, *is* the revolution. Discussion of doctrine and of action groups—parties, cells, circles, unions—was proscribed in the press. But the impatient Dobrolyubov suggests that as soon as the new hero has appeared in sufficient numbers, the process of change will be launched without the need for further preparations. This man, in whom such extravagant hopes were invested, would not be alone—any number could join his ranks; the virtues and the ideas that would motivate him were available to all, even the illiterate; and he would have willing followers among all oppressed sections of the population. (p. 60)

It is well to remember that Dobrolyubov frankly disqualifies himself from the traditional offices of literary criticism. "The main task of the literary critic," he wrote, "is to explain the phenomenon of reality which called a given artistic production into being." This explains the fact that he ignored the problem of incorporating the new affirmative hero in conventional literary forms. He assumed, apparently, that the new hero would succeed the tragic-pathetic figures of the superfluous era without difficulty on the formal level. The new literature would be better simply because it reflected a more advanced social morality. The writer, expected to produce a condensed record of Russian life, had only to worry about the accuracy of his eye and the soundness of his judgment in discerning the true, the typical, and the significant. Dobrolyubov never dwelt at length on problems of conflict or suspense, or of dramatic resolution, whether tragic, comic, affirmative, or inspirational. The degree of his indifference is made clear in his misreading of Ostrovsky's *Storm*. He simply overlooks the fact that Katerina kills herself in a mood of despair, not of defiance. By this ingenious misinterpretation in which he is encouraged by his peculiar view of suicide, he reads his own topical concerns into the play and converts it from a conventional tragic drama into an inspirational document with a kind of happy ending. Dobrolyubov simply felt that an heroic death moved people to admiration. In one of his first prescriptions for the new man he pointed out that he must be unafraid of death, but that if he does die (whether or not by his own hand) the example of his defiant courage, as recorded in some sort of literary communiqué, will surely summon others to fill the gap he has left. (p. 62)

> *Rufus W. Mathewson, Jr., "Dobrolyubov: Beyond the Superfluous Man," in his* The Positive Hero in Russian Literature *(with the permission of the publishers, Stanford University Press; © 1958, 1975 by the Board of Trustees of the Leland Stanford Junior University), Columbia University Press, 1958 (and reprinted by Stanford University Press, second edition, 1975, pp. 46-62).*

## R. H. STACY (essay date 1974)

Having replaced Chernyshevsky as literary critic on the staff of *The Contemporary*, [Dobrolyúbov] repeated *ad nauseam* and with exceeding little grace the tenets of his predecessor. Still, despite the overriding pressure of his rigidly utilitarian convictions, he was exceptionally gifted and he shows a considerably keener critical judgment than Chernyshevsky. He comes close to elaborating a critical theory of types, and his name is inseparably linked with two themes in Russian literature and criticism, "Oblomovism" (*Oblomovshchina*) and the "Superfluous Man" (*lishnij chelovek*). In one essay (on Dostoevsky's *The Insulted and the Injured*) there is even outlined a "holistic" view of the poet's function and an intimation of the catalytic role of the imagination in an almost Coleridgean sense: "The poet creates a whole; he finds the vital link, fuses and transforms the diverse aspects of living reality." (p. 60)

In **"What Is Oblomovism?"** he uses the notorious indolence and acedia of the hero of Goncharov's novel [*Oblomov*] . . . mainly as a text for an extended social criticism of Russian life, a procedure which he candidly admits will disturb "true" critics. But some of the formal qualities of the novel are touched upon (and disparaged): e.g., the relentless repertory of detail (the description of the ink and paper used in writing a letter) and the attention paid (in a manner Gogol brought to hilarious perfection) to "peripheral" characters. And he notes the "role" played by Oblomov's famous dressing gown. . . . As a brash young critic of very radical persuasions (we must remember that he died at the age of twenty-five), Dobrolyubov too frequently uses a somewhat heavy-handed sarcasm. . . . (pp. 60-1)

Dobrolyubov's name is also associated with the dramatist Ostrovsky and he has two articles on his work, **"The Kingdom of Darkness"** and **"A Ray of Light in the Kingdom of Darkness."** In the former, Dobrolyubov expatiates on the type of the domestic merchant-tyrant, the *samodur*, and, as if he were a historian rummaging through source documents, he tries to get at the underlying social factors. Dobrolyubov loses sight of the play as a piece of dramatic art requiring exceptional technical skill on the part of the artist, and he regards it essentially as a corpus of sociological data. The economic dependence of certain characters on others is more important than stagecraft. The other essay, on Ostrovsky's *The Storm*, centers around Katerina (the unfortunate heroine of the play) whom Dobrolyubov sees as a symbol of "a great national idea"—in effect, the symbol of revolution; an interpretation, as René Wellek puts it, "that seems the very height of what could be called 'loss of contact' with the text [see excerpt above, 1955]."

One of Dobrolyubov's most apparent weaknesses as a critic— even in the context of Russian Civic criticism—is seen in his tendency to discuss literary characters as if "they" were real persons, actually existing in a social milieu, with a past history and a contingent future, a procedure which is futile and inane. Of course he is not unique in this respect (for example, the word *Hamlet* in a matrix of other words has received similar treatment in the West); but he represents, as does Chernyshevsky, an extreme development. (p. 61)

On the credit side, Dobrolyubov's principal contribution is his notion of social types based upon the assumption that the types of characters which a particular author creates in his fiction (or the types created by various authors in a given literature or literary period) reveal, more accurately than any stated or implied intentions, the actual outlook and philosophy of the writer. "What an author intended to say," writes Dobrolyubov "is much less important for us than what he really did say, possibly without realizing it, simply as a result of the correct representation of the facts as he saw them." But this concept has been expressed by other critics and theoreticians, from William Blake (on Milton) to Rozanov and Shestov (on Dostoevsky), while Kant has some similar remarks on this point in his *Critique of Pure Reason*. (p. 62)

> *R. H. Stacy, "The Civic Critics," in his* Russian Literary Criticism: A Short History *(copyright © 1974*

*by Syracuse University Press), Syracuse University Press, 1974, pp. 55-65.**

## ADDITIONAL BIBLIOGRAPHY

Matlaw, Ralph E. Introduction to *Belinsky, Chernyshevsky, and Dobrolyubov: Selected Criticism,* edited by Ralph E. Matlaw, pp. vii-xx. Bloomington, London: Indiana University Press, 1962.*
> Provides a general introduction to the criticism of Vissarion Belinski, Nikolai Chernyshevsky, and Dobrolyubov. Matlaw condemns Dobrolyubov for his tendency to treat characters in literature as if they were real individuals, and for his polemical interpretation of literature.

Proctor, Thelwall. "Nikolaj Aleksandrovič Dobroljubov (1836-1861)." In his *Dostoevskij and the Belinskij School of Literary Criticism,* pp. 90-116. The Hague, Paris: Mouton, 1969.*
> A comparative study of the literary criticism of Dobrolyubov and Fedor Dostoevski. Proctor finds that, despite Dostoevski's misgivings about Dobrolyubov's critical approach, the two writers shared the belief that the ultimate goal of literature ought to be a humanitarian one.

Slonim, Mark. "The Critics and the Nihilists." In his *The Epic of Russian Literature: From Its Origins through Tolstoy,* pp. 203-18. New York: Oxford University Press, 1950.*
> Briefly examines Dobrolyubov's writings in the context of the "revolutionary democracy" of the 1860s. Slonim asserts that Nikolai Chernychevsky and Dobrolyubov "determined the tendency and the tone of literary criticism for generations to come."

Weinstein, Fred. "The Origins of 'Nihilist' Criticism." *Canadian Slavic Studies* III, No. 2 (Summer 1969): 165-77.
> An analysis of Dobrolyubov's personality in relation to his theory of Oblomovism. Weinstein argues that although Dobrolyubov understood the necessity for emotional control in social revolution, he himself was unable to maintain emotional stability and therefore tended to lapse into Oblomov-like inertia.

# (Sarah) Margaret Fuller

## 1810-1850

(Later Marchesa d'Ossoli) American critic, essayist, translator, travel writer, and poet.

A distinguished critic and early feminist, Fuller played an important role in the developing cultural life of the United States during the first half of the nineteenth century. As a founding editor of the Transcendentalist journal, *The Dial*, and later as a contributor to Horace Greeley's *New York Tribune*, she was influential in introducing European art and literature to the United States. She wrote social, art, and music criticism, but she is most acclaimed as a literary critic; many rank her with Edgar Allan Poe as the finest of the era. In addition, her *Woman in the Nineteenth Century* is recognized as the first full-length American feminist treatise. Yet in her own day, Fuller was known chiefly for her forceful personality and for the series of instructive conversations that she led in Boston between 1839 and 1844. After her death, critics tended to dwell on the colorful circumstances of Fuller's life, and on her association with the better-known New England Transcendentalists, notably Ralph Waldo Emerson. Fuller was rarely granted careful critical attention until the 1960s, when a renewed interest in Transcendentalism and feminist history prompted a reappraisal of her literary achievement. While modern commentators generally agree that her writing style is prolix, they recognize Fuller as a pioneering critic, feminist, and thinker.

Fuller was the eldest child of a Harvard-educated lawyer who was prominent in Massachusetts politics, and who eventually served in the United States Congress. Disappointed that his first child was not a boy, Timothy Fuller was determined to educate his daughter as if she were a son, and he schooled her from an early age in a rigorous curriculum. Before she reached her teens, Fuller had mastered Latin and was thoroughly familiar with the works of William Shakespeare, Miguel de Cervantes Saavedra, and Molière. Noting later that this regimen caused her chronic ill health, Fuller remarked regretfully that she had had "no natural childhood."

As a young woman, Fuller joined the intellectual circles of Boston and Cambridge, and befriended members of the Harvard class of 1829. The Boston Brahmins admired her erudite conversation, and were arrested by her imposing, demanding, sometimes sarcastic, and often droll personality. In 1833, the family moved to rural Groton, where Fuller was responsible for running the household and tutoring the younger children in the family. She also pursued her own study of German literature and philosophy, particularly the works of Johann Wolfgang von Goethe. She became seriously ill in 1835, and soon after she recovered, her father suddenly died, leaving her to help support the family.

Fuller's three-week stay the following summer with the Emersons in Concord marked the beginning of a mutually-influential, often-chronicled relationship. Fuller hoped to create with Ralph Waldo Emerson an ideal friendship, one which would combine spiritual and intellectual intimacy. Fuller, however, resented Emerson's remoteness and accused him of being "on stilts," while he was uncomfortable with her as-

sertiveness and what he termed her "rather mountainous ME." Nevertheless, the two shared thoughts, philosophies, and critiques, and when Fuller died, Emerson confided in his journal that "in her I have lost my audience."

In 1836, Amos Bronson Alcott hired Fuller to teach French and Latin at his progressive Temple School, but the position was too taxing, and she transferred the following autumn to the Greene Street School in Providence, Rhode Island. There she completed her first published book, *Conversations with Goethe in the Last Years of His Life*, a translation of *Gespräche mit Goethe in den lezten Jahren Seines Lebens*. Tremendously influenced by Goethe's writings and philosophies, Fuller shared his devotion to self-culture and his striving to become "extraordinary, generous-seeking." Fuller never finished a proposed biography of Goethe, but her critical essays on his work are considered to be among the most sensitive ever written.

In 1839, Fuller and her family were reunited in Jamaica Plain near Boston, and that autumn she began to recruit participants for her series of conversations for women. Lydia Maria Child, Caroline Sturgis, Maria White, and Sophia Peabody, among others, attended the conversations, which focused on such topics as mythology, art, and equal rights for women. In addition to showcasing Fuller's natural dramatic flair, the series provided the Fuller family income. During the same period, from

1840 to 1842, Fuller was both the editor of *The Dial* and its major contributor. In addition, she took part in planning the Transcendentalist Brook Farm community; however, she was disenchanted with farm life after her experience in Groton, and chose not to live at Brook Farm, although she visited frequently. The outspoken, sensual character, Zenobia, of Nathaniel Hawthorne's *The Blithedale Romance,* is considered by many to be a portrait of Fuller.

After relinquishing her *Dial* editorship to Emerson, Fuller joined James Freeman Clarke and his sister on a trip to the Midwest and Great Lakes regions, which she recounted in *Summer on the Lakes, in 1843.* Generally well-received, the book brought Fuller to the attention of Greeley, who asked her to join the *Tribune* as its literary critic. Some note that comforming to a journalistic style and newspaper deadlines helped Fuller to condense her rambling prose style. At the same time, living in Manhattan sharpened her awareness of the need for social reform, a concern that she expressed in her later political writings. Greeley published *Woman in the Nineteenth Century,* an expanded version of an essay originally printed in *The Dial.* Controversial in its philosophy, and in its discussion of prostitution and women criminals, the book sold well in spite of mixed reviews.

In 1846, Fuller made a long-anticipated trip to Europe. Greeley assigned her to send the *Tribune* dispatches, which were collected later in *At Home and Abroad; or, Things and Thoughts in America and Europe,* and she thus became America's first paid female foreign correspondent. In England, Fuller was received by William Wordsworth, Thomas De Quincey, and Thomas Carlyle, among other celebrities. The emphatic Fuller did not fail to impress the British. According to a famous anecdote, she once announced, "I accept the universe," to which Carlyle reportedly retorted, "By gad, she'd better!"

Fuller eventually settled in Italy, where she became involved with Giovanni Angelo Ossoli, an impoverished, unintellectual marquis eleven years her junior, who was active in the liberal cause to win Italy's independence. Their son was born in September, 1848, and they secretly married the following summer. Fuller and her husband continued to serve the liberal cause, and during the French siege of Rome she took charge of a military hospital. After the fall of the republic to France in 1850, the family set sail for the United States. After a difficult journey, their ship sank within sight of Fire Island, New York. Their child's body was recovered, but Fuller and her husband were never found. Fuller's nearly-completed manuscript of a history of Italy, which many believe would have been her greatest work, was also lost in the wreck.

For many years after she died, her secret marriage and tragic death dominated studies of Fuller. *Memoirs of Margaret Fuller Ossoli,* compiled with additional commentary by her friends Emerson, Clark, and William Henry Channing, was an attempt to erase Fuller's reputation as an overbearing egotist, and to diminish the scandal surrounding her last years. The work, however, created a portrait of a pious, timorous creature unrecognizable as Fuller, while underplaying her scholarly and literary achievements. The courtly, condescending tone established by this work dominated Fuller criticism for many years, and it is only in the past few decades that scholars have begun to assess her contribution to America's feminist and intellectual history. Her admirers agree with Henry Wadsworth Longfellow, who remarked that "it is easy enough now to say and see what she then saw and said, but it demanded

insight to see and courage to say what was entirely missed by that generation."

(See also *Something about the Author,* Vol. 25, and *Dictionary of Literary Biography,* Vol. 7, *The American Renaissance in New England.*)

PRINCIPAL WORKS

*Conversations with Goethe in the Last Years of His Life*
[translator] (conversations) 1839
*Günderode* [translator] (letters) 1842
*Summer on the Lakes, in 1843* (travel essay) 1844
*Woman in the Nineteenth Century* (essay) 1845
*Papers on Literature and Art* (criticism) 1846
*Memoirs of Margaret Fuller Ossoli* (memoirs) 1852
*Woman in the Nineteenth Century and Kindred Papers
Relating to the Sphere, Conditions, and Duties of
Woman* (essays) 1855
*At Home and Abroad; or, Things and Thoughts in America
and Europe* (essays, travel essays, and letters) 1856
*Life Without and Life Within* (essays, criticism, and poetry)
1860
*Torquato Tasso* [translator] (drama) 1860; published in
*Art, Literature, and the Drama*
*Margaret and Her Friends; or, Ten Conversations with
Margaret Fuller upon the Mythology of the Greeks and
Its Expressions in Art* (conversations) 1895
*The Writings of Margaret Fuller* (essays, travel essays,
criticism, letters, and memoirs) 1941
*The Letters of Margaret Fuller.* 2 vols. (letters) 1983

---

**[CALEB STETSON]** (essay date 1844)

[*An acquaintance of Fuller, Stetson grants* Summer on the Lakes, in 1843 *a mixed review. He praises Fuller's "subjective tendency," a trait that Edgar Allan Poe also admires (see excerpt below, 1846), but faults her pedantic and unnatural style, a point that recurs throughout Fuller criticism.*]

We took up [*Summer on the Lakes in 1843*] with eager expectation. Knowing the extraordinary endowments of its author, we looked for an uncommon book, and we were not disappointed. It is indeed an uncommon book, not at all like an ordinary journal of travel. . . .

It is a work of varied interest, rich in fine observation, profound reflection and striking anecdote. It breathes throughout a spirit of perfect benignity and love—generous, humane, and free from prejudices of every kind. In regard to all things and persons that come under her notice—especially the character of the native Indians, of whom she has collected many fine stories before unknown to us,—it would be difficult to find a writer so liberal, just and discriminating. . . .

Miss Fuller's book is in a high degree subjective. It is not so much a description of the beautiful lake scenery in the midst of which she passed the summer months, looking upon all things with the eye of a poet and artist, as a record of her own impressions and of the recollections they called up. Accordingly, amidst scenes so novel and striking she writes not from without, but from within. It is not that she overlooks the nature which smiles or frowns around her. She often gives us descriptions of such beauty as to show that she has an eye and a heart for everything lovely or grand in the external creation. But evidently she is much more occupied with what is passing in her own soul, than with the objective realities which present themselves to the senses. . . .

We notice this subjective tendency of the writer as a peculiar excellence. It gives to her work its most remarkable characteristic. We can never anticipate what she will say, from knowing her point of view and the objects which surround her. She throws her own being into the outward world and gives it a new character. (p. 274)

This reflective tendency often draws into her journal things quite unlooked for and most remote from her field of observation—things connected by no apparent link of association with the objects which seem to fill her eye and mind. These underground associations, unintelligible to those who are not in the secret of her thoughts, sometimes give an air of pedantry to her remarks. We are persuaded that she has a mind too noble to wish to display her rich stores of knowledge for the sake of display, and therefore we find it difficult to account for the introduction of so many allusions to classic antiquity, to Europe and its arts, manners and literature. It appears often strained, unnatural, out of place. Tales also unexpectedly appear—such, for instance, as the German story of the "Seeress of Prevorst"—which have no connexion with the scenes she visited, except the accidental fact that they occurred in the course of her reading or were called up from the depths of her memory by some mysterious association. Such portions of her work might have been written as well at Boston, Rome, or Constantinople, as on the shores of our Western waters.

There is often a certain stiffness, an unnaturalness, in the style of the work. We are unable to suppose that it proceeds from defective taste in a person of so fine a culture. It results perhaps from over-carefulness and severity in a mind unwilling to trust to natural and simple impressions, and allow them to utter themselves in their own way. She does not let her thought or emotion write itself out. We cannot help feeling that the intellect is too predominant—that she is too conscious of style—that she writes under the constraint of an artistic view, in conformity with some ideal that is not congenial with her nature and does not allow it free action. She seems to be afraid of the simple utterance of a first impression or thought, as if it had not weight or firmness enough to go out of her hands without elaborate refining and re-coinage. Accordingly we find something cold, stately, almost *statuesque*, in her language. It has not the warmth of life which her heart would give it, if she would yield herself trustingly to its impulses with less of intellectual criticism. It reminds us sometimes of Coleridge, sometimes of Walter Savage Landor; yet we see no marks of imitation. It seems to us rather, that in aiming to be classical she loses sight of nature, or too sternly represses its genuine instincts in obedience to some law which she has prescribed to herself. The beautiful flower must not bloom out spontaneously with its own shape and hue; it must be fashioned into some preordained form and its colors be retouched, before it is fit for exhibition. We make these remarks with diffidence, for we mistrust our taste and judgment when we find ourselves presuming to criticise a writer whose mind is so full of manifold forms of beauty and grace. (pp. 275-76)

> [*Caleb Stetson*], *in a review of "Summer on the Lakes, in 1843," in* The Christian Examiner and Religious Miscellany, *n.s. Vol. II, No. II, September, 1844, pp. 274-76.*

## [ORESTES A. BROWNSON]   (essay date 1844)

> [*Brownson was the editor of* Brownson's Quarterly Review, *and a longtime detractor of Fuller. Here he refers derisively to her interest in Transcendentalism and German literature, and recommends "the firm, old-fashioned Catholic faith in the Gospel" as a means of freeing her literary powers. While he does concede that* Summer on the Lakes, in 1843 *is "marked by flashes of a rare genius," he "detests [Fuller's] doctrines," and therefore does not commend her writings.*]

[Miss Fuller's] writings we do not like. We dislike them exceedingly. They are sent out in a slipshod style, and have a certain toss of the head about them which offends us. Miss Fuller seems to us to be wholly deficient in a pure, correct taste, and especially in that tidiness we always look for in woman. Then, we detest her doctrines. We know nothing more abominable. She is a heathen priestess, though of what god or goddess we will not pretend to say. She is German, heart and soul, save so far as Germany may retain traditionally somewhat of Christianity. We believe no person has appeared among us whose conversation and writings have done more to corrupt the minds and hearts of our Boston community. For religion she substitutes Art; for the Divinity who has made us, and whom we should worship, she would give us merely the Beautiful; and for the stern morality of the Gospel, such principles as we may collect from the *Wahlverwandtschaften* [by Johann von Goethe, and his] *Correspondence with a Child.* She is, in fact, the high-priestess of American Transcendentalism, and, happily, ministers now at an almost deserted fane.

We admit that she has read much and variously; but her notions are crude, and the materials she has collected lie fermenting in her intellectual stomach, and generate all manner of strange and diseased fancies. She is ill at ease. She has no quiet, no repose. She has no faith, no hope. She now reminds us of the old heathen Euripides, now of the modern skeptic, Byron, and finally, of the cold indifferentism of Goethe dashed on the warm woman's heart of Bettina Brentano. We see in her a melancholy instance of the fate which awaits a gifted woman in an age of infidelity. All she needs, to be the ornament of her sex, and a crown of blessing to her country, to be at peace with herself and the world, is the firm, old-fashioned Catholic faith in the Gospel. Her soul would then burst its fetters, all her powers would find free scope, and her heart the rest after which it yearns.

[Her *Summer on the Lakes, in 1843*] is characteristic. It is marked by flashes of a rare genius, by uncommon and versatile powers, by sentiments at times almost devout; but after all it is a sad book, and one which we dare not commend. Alas! it is melancholy to contemplate the noble victims sacrificed to the Moloch, Doubt; still more sad, when the sacrifice is made by priests aping the forms of Faith, and the vestments of Piety! (pp. 546-47)

> [*Orestes A. Brownson*], *in his review of "Summer on the Lakes, in 1843," in* Brownson's Quarterly Review, *Vol. I, No. IV, October, 1844, pp. 546-47.*

## L.M.C. [LYDIA MARIA CHILD]   (essay date 1845)

> [*Child was an American author, editor, feminist, and abolitionist, and an avid participant in Fuller's conversations for women. In the following review, she praises Fuller's intellect, and asserts that the "rough" style of* Woman in the Nineteenth Century "*does not arise from affectation . . . ; it is the defect of a mind that has too many thoughts for its words.*"]

[*Woman in the Nineteenth Century*] will be likely to excite a good deal of remark, for and against. It is from the pen of Margaret Fuller, a woman of more powerful intellect, comprehensive thought, and thorough education, than any other American authoress, with whose productions I am acquainted. Her style is vigorous and significant, abounding with eloquent passages, and affluent in illustration; but it is sometimes rough in construction, and its meaning is not always sufficiently clear. This does not arise from affectation, or pedantic elaboration; it is the defect of a mind that has too many thoughts for its words; an excess by no means common, either in men or women. She is a contralto voice in literature: deep, rich, and strong, rather than mellifluous and clear.

The book in question is written in a free energetic spirit. It contains a few passages that will offend the fastidiousness of some readers; for they allude to subjects which men do not wish to have discussed, and which women dare not approach. But the clean-minded will not sneer; for they will see that the motive is pure, and the object is to ennoble human nature.

> *L.M.C. [Lydia Maria Child], in a review of "Woman in the Nineteenth Century," in* The Broadway Journal, *Vol. 1, No. 7, February 15, 1845, p. 97.*

## [CHARLES F. BRIGGS]   (essay date 1845)

[*In one of the most overtly sexist appraisals of Fuller, Briggs questions her ability to represent women in* Woman in the Nineteenth Century. *"Woman is nothing but as a wife," he writes. "How, then, can she truly represent the female character who has never filled it?" Briggs criticizes the lewd subject matter, poor construction, and inflated style of the book. In his 1846 sketch of Fuller, Edgar Allan Poe disavows Briggs's essay, terming it "silly, condemnatory criticism" (see excerpt below).*]

That Miss Fuller is justly chargeable with wasting the time of her readers, her most devout admirer cannot deny. [*Woman in the Nineteenth Century*] consists of two hundred pages, but all that it contains of her own suggesting, might be fairly compressed into a third of the space. The title is a misnomer to begin with. . . . We keep looking for woman of the nineteenth century, but we only find a roster of female names from Panthea to Amelia Norman. The propriety of the title is the more doubtful from the following passage in her preface.

> By man, I mean both man and woman. I lay no especial stress on the welfare of either. I believe the welfare of the one cannot be effected without that of the other. My highest wish is that this truth should be distinctly and rationally apprehended; and the conditions of life and freedom recognised as the same for the daughters and the sons of time.

The style is somewhat stilted, but the thought is just and philosophical, and proves Miss Fuller to be a thinking, right-judging person. Why could she not, then, since she thinks so correctly, call her book, Man, or Society in the Nineteenth century, and so plead in a straight forward manner in behalf of man, without any specialities about woman's rights or woman's wrongs, as though she had either rights or wrongs, which are not also the rights and wrongs of men. We certainly did not expect from a woman of Miss Fuller's natural and acquired powers, the wretched cant which we hear so often from men, who, having no claim upon man, seek for the sympathies of women, and from women, who, having as little claim upon the sympathies of men, try for it by speaking in the name of their sex, about woman's mission, woman's influence, and woman's rights; and we have not been disappointed; she seems to entertain a wholesome horror of the whole tribe of shallow canters. But then, if we do not misapprehend her, which we are not sure of, she has errors of her own which are more dangerous, because not so shallow as the others. She forgets, or rather seems to forget, that God created man male and female, notwithstanding the declaration in her preface, which we suspect, contains, like the postscript of a woman's letter, the fact which she intended to put into the body of her work. She is dissatisfied that women are not men, and takes offence at the term "women and children"; words which to us sound sweeter for being spoken together. She is offended that women should esteem it a compliment to be called masculine, while men consider it a reproach to be called feminine. "Early I perceived," she says, "that men, in no extremity of distress, ever wished themselves women." Of course not. It is the law that woman shall reverence her husband, and that he shall be her head. We may love those whom we protect, but we can never wish ourselves in their place, although we naturally wish to be like those from whom we receive protection. . . . Miss Fuller says:

> I have urged on woman, independence of man, not that I do not think the sexes mutually needed by one another, but because in woman, this fact has led to an excessive devotion, which has cooled love, degraded marriage, and prevented either sex from being what it should be to itself or the other. . . . That her hand may be given with dignity, she must be able to stand alone.

This, we conceive to be the radical error of Miss Fuller's reasoning, and directly opposed to the law of nature, of experience and revelation. She says,

> A profound thinker has said, that no married woman can represent the female world, for she belongs to her husband. The idea of woman must be represented by a virgin.

He was a very shallow thinker, or a joker. It would be as reasonable to say that none but a deaf man could give a true idea of music. Woman is nothing but as a wife. How, then, can she truly represent the female character who has never filled it? No woman can be a true woman, who has not been a wife and a mother. These are not accidental characters like those of mistress and servant, which may be thoroughly understood without being acted; but they are the natural destiny of woman, and if she is kept from them, her nature is distorted and unnatural: and she sees things through a false medium. Her report, therefore, of a character which she never filled, must be received with distrust.

It is not easy to discover from Miss Fuller's essay what her precise ideas of the true relation of man and woman are; although on some points she is sufficiently distinct. Mrs. Jamieson, with true womanly feeling, said that she would prefer being Mary of Scotland to Elizabeth of England; but Miss Fuller would prefer being the termagant Queen and swearing by "God's teeth." Colonel Emily Plater and Madame George Sand sound pleasantly in her ears. "If you ask me what offices women may fill," says Miss Fuller, "I reply any; let them be sea captains if you will." Very good, let them. We have a queen of England, and England claims to be mistress of the seas; let us have a woman Admiral. But we take sides with Spinoza, and answer that woman cannot command. She lacks the chief qualities of a commander. She cannot invent. She is an apt imitator, but she cannot originate; and therefore we have no fears that we shall ever see woman in our halls of legislature, or in command of our ships or armies. (pp. 130-31)

• • • • •

The great defect of [*Woman in the Nineteenth Century*] is a want of distinctness. We can easily discover that her chief concern is to help remove the evils which afflict society; but we cannot discover any hints of the means by which they may be removed. She is sufficiently learned, sufficiently vigorous, and sufficiently earnest, but not sufficiently plain and direct. We have too much of the Scandinavian mythology and the Greek tragedy, and too little of what the book professes to deal with—woman in the nineteenth century. The most direct writing is on a topic that no virtuous woman can treat justly, because she must of necessity be imperfectly informed; it is exceedingly painful to read a portion of her work, which we feel must have been painfully produced; and though we cannot but respect her for her courage in printing it, we regret that she should have felt herself bound to do so, since no good can possibly result from it. There are a thousand existing evils in society which a woman may freely censure, and a thousand topics of pervading interest which she may freely discuss, with profit to her sex, without verging towards those that the innocent had better not know the existence of. We wish that Miss Fuller had loosened the fibula of her arrows, and let them fly at the practices which are, indeed, the direct causes of the lewdness which she deplores, instead of treating of the lewdness itself, which she can only know by hearsay, and of course but imperfectly comprehend. (p. 145)

There are many admirable little episodes in the book, which ever and anon appear, like springs of sweet water bubbling out of a sterile soil, and charm us by their sparkles and music. There are too few of passages like the following:

> Only in a clean body can the soul do its message fitly. The praises of cold water seem to me an excellent sign of the age. They denote a tendency to the true in life. . . .
>
> (pp. 145-46)

These passages are of greater import than Miss Fuller seems to be aware of, or she would dwell longer upon them, and draw more profitable reflections from them than she has done. The well-being of the body is the great end of all moral teaching, and if this truth were most distinctly comprehended, the moral preacher would not so often preach to so little purpose. . . .

There are some things in Miss Fuller's book, which startle us by their strange sound, and set us a-thinking what they can possibly mean; for instance: "if there were more Marys there would be more virgin mothers;" and some others, equally enigmatical. . . .

Miss Fuller writes vigorously, but womanly; she has gathered together the materials for a very profitable book; but they are so loosely arranged, and so pervaded with threads of error, that as a whole we doubt whether the work will be productive of much either of good or of evil. It will, however, have one good effect. It will cause her to be more generally known than she has been; for although the reading public have been familiar with her name since the first appearance of the "Dial," they have had but an imperfect conception of the exact quality of her mind. (p. 146)

[*Charles F. Briggs*], *in reviews of "Woman in the Nineteenth Century," in* The Broadway Journal, *Vol. I, Nos. 9 and 10, March 1 and 8, 1845, pp. 130-31; 145-46.*

**EDGAR A. POE**   (essay date 1846)

[*Poe, the influential novelist, poet, and short story writer, is generally considered to be the finest mid-nineteenth-century American literary critic. His review of Fuller is noteworthy for his assertion that her style "is everything a style need be," and for his generally objective and generous assessment of Fuller's critical and literary ability. He stresses that the "silly, condemnatory" article on Fuller that had appeared anonymously the previous year had not been written by him, but by Charles Briggs (see excerpt above, 1845)*].

At present, [Miss Fuller] is assistant editor of "The New York Tribune," or rather a salaried contributor to that journal, for which she has furnished a great variety of matter, chiefly critical notices of new books. . . . [Her review of Professor Longfellow's works] did her infinite credit; it was frank, candid, independent—in even ludicrous contrast to the usual mere glorifications of the day, giving honor *only* where honor was due, yet evincing the most thorough capacity to appreciate and the most sincere intention to place in the fairest light the real and idiosyncratic merits of the poet.

In my opinion it is one of the very few reviews of Longfellow's poems, ever published in America, of which the critics have not had abundant reason to be ashamed. . . .

"Woman in the Nineteenth Century" is a book which few women in the country could have written, and no woman in the country would have published, with the exception of Miss Fuller. In the way of independence, of unmitigated radicalism, it is one of the "Curiosities of American Literature," and Doctor Griswold should include it in his book. I need scarcely say that the essay is nervous, forcible, thoughtful, suggestive, brilliant, and to a certain extent scholar-like—for all that Miss Fuller produces is entitled to these epithets—but I must say that the conclusions reached are only in part my own. Not that they are too bold, by any means—too novel, too startling, or too dangerous in their consequences, but that in their attainment too many premises have been distorted and too many analogical inferences left altogether out of sight. I mean to say that the intention of the Deity as regards sexual differences—an intention which can be distinctly comprehended only by throwing the exterior (more sensitive) portions of the mental retina *casually* over the wide field of universal *analogy*—I mean to say that this *intention* has not been sufficiently considered. Miss Fuller has erred, too, through her own excessive objectiveness. She judges *woman* by the heart and intellect of Miss Fuller, but there are not more than one or two dozen Miss Fullers on the whole face of the earth. Holding these opinions in regard to "Woman in the Nineteenth Century," I still feel myself called upon to disavow the silly, condemnatory criticism of the work which appeared in one of the earlier numbers of "The Broadway Journal." That article was *not* written by myself, and *was* written by my associate Mr. Briggs [see excerpt above, 1845].

The most favorable estimate of Miss Fuller's genius (for high genius she unquestionably possesses) is to be obtained, perhaps, from her contributions to "The Dial," and from her "Summer on the Lakes." Many of the *descriptions* in this volume are unrivaled for *graphicality*, (why is there not such a word?) for the force with which they convey the true by the novel or unexpected, by the introduction of touches which other artists would be sure to omit as irrelevant to the subject. This faculty, too, springs from her subjectiveness, which leads her to paint a scene less by its features than by its effects. (p. 72)

[In her account of Niagara Falls, for example,] the feelings described are, perhaps, experienced by every (imaginative) person who visits the fall; but most persons, through predominant subjectiveness, would scarcely be conscious of the feelings, or, at best, would never think of employing them in an attempt to convey to others an impression of the scene. . . .

[Miss Fuller's prose style] is always forcible—but I am not sure that it is always anything else, unless I say picturesque. It rather indicates than evinces scholarship. Perhaps only the scholastic, or, more properly, those accustomed to look narrowly at the structure of phrases, would be willing to acquit her of ignorance of grammar—would be willing to attribute her slovenliness to disregard of the shell in anxiety for the kernel; or to waywardness, or to affectation, or to blind reverence for Carlyle—would be able to detect, in her strange and continual inaccuracies, a capacity for the accurate.

> "I cannot sympathize with such an apprehension: the spectacle is *capable* to swallow *up* all such objects."

> "It is fearful, too, to know, as you look, that whatever has been swallowed by the cataract, is *like* to rise suddenly to light."

> "I took our *mutual* friends to see her."

> "It was always obvious that they had nothing in common *between them*." . . .

These are merely a few, a very few instances, taken at random from among a multitude of *wilful* murders committed by Miss Fuller on the American of President Polk. She uses, too, the word "ignore," a vulgarity adopted only of late days (and to no good purpose, since there is no necessity for it) from the barbarisms of the law, and makes no scruple of giving the Yankee interpretation to the verbs "witness" and "realize," to say nothing of "use," as in the sentence, "I used to read a short time at night." (p. 73)

In spite of these things, however, and of her frequent unjustifiable Carlyleisms, (such as that of writing sentences which are no sentences, since, to be parsed, reference must be had to sentences preceding,) the style of Miss Fuller is one of the very best with which I am acquainted. In general effect, I know no style which surpasses it. It is singularly piquant, vivid, terse, bold, luminous—leaving details out of sight, it is everything that a style need be.

I believe that Miss Fuller has written much poetry, although she has published little. That little is tainted with the affectation of the *transcendentalists*, (I use this term, of course, in the sense which the public of late days seem resolved to give it,) but is brimful of the poetic *sentiment*. Here, for example, is something in Coleridge's manner, of which the author of "Genevieve" might have had no reason to be ashamed:—

> A maiden sat beneath a tree;
> Tear-bedewed her pale cheeks be,
> And she sigheth heavily.

> From forth the wood into the *light*
> A hunter strides with carol *light*,
> And a glance so bold and bright.

He careless stopped and eyed the maid:
> 'Why weepest thou?' he gently said;
> 'I love thee well, be not afraid.'

> He takes her hand and leads her on—
> She should have waited there alone,
> For he was not her chosen one.

> He *leans* her head upon his breast—
> She knew 'twas not her home of rest,
> But, ah, she had been sore distrest.

> The sacred stars looked sadly down;
> The parting moon appeared to frown,
> To see thus dimmed the diamond crown.

> Then from the thicket starts a deer—
> The huntsman, seizing *on* his spear
> Cries, 'Maiden, wait thou for me here.'

(pp. 73-4)

To show the evident carelessness with which this poem was constructed, I have italicized an identical rhyme (of about the same force in versification as an identical proposition in logic) and two grammatical improprieties. *To lean* is a neuter verb, and "seizing *on*" is not properly to be called a pleonasm, merely because it is—nothing at all. . . .

[Miss Fuller's] personal character and her printed book are merely one and the same thing. We get access to her soul *as* directly from the one as from the other—no *more* readily from this than from that—easily from either. Her acts are bookish, and her books are less thoughts than acts. Her literary and her conversational manner are identical. Here is a passage from her **"Summer on the Lakes:"**—

> The rapids enchanted me far beyond what I expected; they are so swift that they cease to *seem* so—you can think only of their *beauty*. The fountain beyond the Moss islands I discovered for myself, and thought it for some time an *accidental* beauty which it would not do to *leave*, lest I might never see it again. After I found it *permanent*, I returned many times to watch the play of its crest. In the little waterfall beyond, Nature seems, as she often does, to have made a *study* for some larger design.

(p. 74)

Now all this is precisely as Miss Fuller would *speak* it. She is perpetually saying just such things in just such words. To get the *conversational* woman in the mind's eye, all that is needed is to imagine her reciting the paragraph just quoted. . . . [Imagine a person] looking you at one moment earnestly in the face, at the next seeming to look only within her own spirit or at the wall; moving nervously every now and then in her chair; speaking in a high key, but musically, deliberately, (not hurriedly or loudly,) with a delicious distinctness of enunciation—speaking, I say, the paragraph in question, and emphasizing the words which I have italicized, not by impulsion of the breath, (as is usual,) but by drawing them out as long as possible, nearly closing her eyes the while—imagine all this, and we have both the woman and the authoress before us. (pp. 74-5)

*Edgar A. Poe, "Sarah Margaret Fuller," in* Godey's Lady's Book, *Vol. XXXIII, No. 5, August, 1846, pp. 72-5.*

*GRAHAM'S MAGAZINE*   (essay date 1846)

Miss Fuller is a lady of large acquirements, fine powers, and earnest, honest purpose. No one can read her [*Papers on Literature and Art*] without doing justice to her talents and intentions. But with all her merits she has one fault which essentially mars the pleasure of reading her writings, especially her critiques. We allude to a certain dogmatism of tone in enunciating her judgments, a dogmatism often supported by nothing more than "the lady's reason," as it is ungallantly called. This is most evident in her essay on American literature. Her decisions in this essay are pronounced in a style half petulant, half oracular, often inexpressibly amusing rather than particularly edifying. She announces trite truths as though they were new thoughts, and debatable paradoxes as though they were admitted facts. The criticism, too, is the criticism of a *clique*— a kind which is calculated to do more injury to our "infant" literature than the universal puff or universal libel system. A few authors are selected, who happen to be greater favorites in "our set" than with the public, and they are studiously cried up as the true prophets of the land, and their unpopularity ascribed to their original merit. All the rest are imitators or echoers, and however stamped with public approbation are placed on a low round of the ladder of precedence. These decisions are supported with a host of canting expressions, hateful to gods and men; and are calculated to rouse in the public an antagonist feeling, which, in the end, will depress the unjustly exalted below their real merit. . . . We sincerely wish that a few of Miss Fuller's favorites were as popular as some of those she dislikes. But we do not wish to see them march into popularity over the bodies of their equals or superiors.

In this essay R. W. Emerson is called "the sage of Concord." Now it happens that Mr. Emerson not only possesses one of the subtlest of human intellects, but a sense of the ridiculous exquisitely acute. What must be his sensation on reading his new title? . . . Mr. Lowell's volumes, we believe, have passed through more than one edition, and he enjoys no small portion of public favor, but how awful must be his depression when he learns from Miss Fuller, that "to the grief of some of his friends, and the disgust of more, he is absolutely wanting in the true spirit and tone of poesy;" that his verse is "stereotyped;" (by the type and stereotype foundry?) that his "thought sounds no depth." We do not see why a man should grieve or disgust his *friends,* because he wants the true tone or spirit of poesy, as friendship has been known to exist toward persons lacking even the power of versification. The attack on Lowell is sufficiently authoritative, insulting, and unsustained by fact or principle; but the criticism on Longfellow is even spiteful. It is the ugliest looking thing in Miss Fuller's volume. It is as inconclusive as it is petulant. The real fault in Longfellow is, that his poetry has passed through many editions, that his genius has been fully acknowledged by his countrymen; that his poems are in the memories of thousands who never read or heard of young William Ellery Channing. We agree with Miss Fuller that the latter has many fine and deep touches of genius; but is it Longfellow's fault that he is not read?

The essay on American literature, therefore, we, in imitation of Miss Fuller's own oracular method, pronounce a piece of adulterated humbug: adulterated, because, with a great deal which will never be believed beyond her own literary circle, it contains a little which has never been doubted by anybody, and is in fact the merest commonplace of the newspapers. All who are praised therein we warn not to be unduly elated; all who are condemned need not commit suicide or profane language. All Mutual Admiration and Mutual Assurance Societies are strictly forbidden to retort upon Miss Fuller and her "worthies" the wrongs they have received in her essay; remembering, in the words of a pious poet, that their "little hands were never made to tear each other's eyes." . . .

But the value of the present book does not rest on the **"Essay on American Literature."** It contains some dozen other papers, which we cheerfully admit to be valuable contributions to the literature of the day, and to be well worthy of being printed in their present elegant form. . . . They well entitle Miss Fuller to a high rank among contemporary authors, as a good writer, an independent thinker, and diligent student. We trust her present publication will be sufficiently successful to induce her to collect another series of her miscellaneous writings, and thus redeem the promise she makes in her preface. In case, however, her future volumes are devoted, like the present, almost exclusively to foreign writers, and present their claims to attention with as much warmth, we hope that she will dispense with another essay on contemporaries, berating them for not being more American in feeling. Her own mind has been so completely bathed in foreign literatures, that she appears much better as an appreciating critic of them, than as a depreciating satirist of the literary efforts of American authors.

*A review of "Papers on Literature and Art," in* Graham's Magazine, *Vol. XXIX, No. 5, November, 1846, p. 262.*

*THE ATHENAEUM*   (essay date 1846)

Popular analytics as applied to literature and art occupy a considerable space in the library of the day. They express those trains of speculative meditation which, falling short of what the severity of science demands, yet lifted considerably above the level of ordinary thinking, engage at present so many of those student minds that are begotten of German literature. To the higher class of such minds that of the author of [*Papers on Literature and Art*] unquestionably belongs. It is true, the vices of the school in which she has matriculated appear profusely throughout her pages; yet it is but justice to admit that the intrinsic merits which they disclose—and these are of no common order—predominate, on the whole. When the balance is struck, a large surplus of gratification remains to the reader.

Not that perhaps the author tells us any new truth, or sounds the limited depths over which she holds her course as fully as she might. It is the spirit in which her mission is accomplished—the free yet reverential and elevated tone which, with slight interruption, reigns throughout,—the original mood, if not the original thought—that constitute her merits. Nor are these light claims. Raphael has been called Divine for pourtraying such qualities. The writer who paints them shall have his apotheosis too—varying in dignity according to his place in the Pantheon of Genius. There is a "touch of divinity" about Margaret Fuller.

Having, however, thus far rendered our acknowledgments to the author of these papers, we must turn even thus early to the less grateful task of remonstrating with her on those waywardnesses and perversities which the *Dii minores* [lesser gods] of literature will sometimes practise upon us mortals, and for which she also must be held largely responsible. . . . Were they peculiar to this author only, we should probably dismiss them with a passing remark; but being, as they are, the sins also of that corporation of writers who seek to Teutonize and stultify the English tongue, we feel it to be a duty to denounce them as far as in us lies. This forced amalgamation of foreign modes of thought and expression,—or rather the parody of those modes—with our own, is in fact the sum and abstract of those offences. . . .

[Under enthusiasts of German literature, an] extreme contempt of the lucid arose. Common intelligibility was held as backsliding, and perspicuity as filthy rags. A rhapsodical outpouring of sublime nonsense became the order of the day; and the beggarly elements of sense and purpose were so thoroughly repudiated by these fifth-monarchy men of letters, that their ravings might have been read backwards or forwards, occidentally or orientally, by Anglo-Saxon or by Arab. . . .

This plague must be stayed. Not, however, by prescribing what would promote its opposite—the shallow-clear [transcendentalism]. That despotic purism which seeks to restrain the infinite progress of thought within fixed *formulae* of expression is, if possible, a still grosser violation of the prerogative of mind than the licentiousness to which we have been alluding. . . .

In fine, the real antidote for all this is what the mystics themselves are ever prescribing, but never acting on,—namely, sincerity and truthfulness, heart-capacity as well as head;—in a word, the will and the ability to be in earnest. (p. 1287)

Now, it is for the occasional indulgence in these vices,—the sins of a wavering faith, one not yet thoroughly sincere or earnestly in earnest, much as she may deem it to be so,—that we must hold the author of these **'Papers'** responsible. She is naturally too genuine and healthy-minded to make them the rule; but is just enough tainted by the pestilential contagion described above, to make them the exceptions. For example, the following rhapsody which appears in the first Dialogue of the first volume between the Poet and the Critic:—

*Critic*. Dost thou so adore Nature, and yet deny me? Is not Art the child of Nature, Civilization of Man? As Religion into Philosophy, Poetry into Criticism, Life into Science, Love into Law, so did thy lyric in natural order transmute itself into my review.

*Poet*. Review! Science! the very etymology speaks. What is gained by looking again at what has already been seen? What by giving a technical classification to what is already assimilated with the mental life?

*Critic*. What is gained by living at all?

*Poet*. Beauty loving itself,—Happiness!

*Critic*. Does not this involve consciousness?

*Poet*. Yes! consciousness of Truth manifested in the individual form.

*Critic*. Since consciousness is tolerated, how will you limit it?

*Poet*. By the instincts of my nature, which rejects yours as arrogant and superfluous.

*Critic*. And the dictate of my nature compels me to the processes which you despise, as essential to my peace. My brother, (for I will not be rejected) I claim my place in the order of nature. The Word descended and became flesh for two purposes, to organize itself, and to take

cognizance of its organization. When the first Poet worked alone, he paused between the cantos to proclaim, 'It is very good.' Dividing himself among men, he made some to create, and others to proclaim the merits of what is created.

*Poet*. Well! if you were content with saying, 'it is very good,' but you are always crying, 'it is very bad.'

And "very bad," this most assuredly is. Not, however, worse than what follows to the end of the dialogue,—to no one single line of which can we say "very good," or even indifferently good. . . . [It] would seem as if the author regarded such passages as these as her best credentials. Their being placed in the van of her array—a preliminary paper—leads to that inference. We think, however, that long before "ten years"—the period which, when alluding to the "crudities" of earlier pieces which she had "outgrown," she assigns to herself for hereafter outgrowing those that may blemish what she writes at this day—she will have put away the childish things contained in the above extract, and along with them several others of the same class which appear in these volumes. To a mind so inherently honest and earnest as hers we would not pay the ill compliment of allotting more than a tithe of that time, for that consummation. She will also, we think, perceive within that interval that the ambitious and affected style—the euphuism of the mystics—has led her into other faults as well as those of obscurity, and caused her to lay down wrong doctrine and misinterpret true. When we would walk on stilts, we are prone to stumble and fall. We cannot pass the sinews and muscles of our motivity through our wooden legs. Consequently, they stump and straddle and totter and trip. . . . Indiscriminate praise is as gross injustice as indiscriminate censure. . . . Things may be both good and bad and throughout a variety of modifications of each; and here critical equity is distributive, and does not make its awards worthless by decreeing either a promiscuous ovation or a promiscuous penalty. Of this the author herself is at times unconsciously sensible,—unwarily illustrating it by her own practice when she occupies the critic's tribunal. It must, however, be admitted that she is generally on her guard in this respect; and, by the profuse application of the "very good" principle alone, commits much injustice, straining "the quality of Mercy" in defiance of the Bard, until she makes *it* the substance and Equity the accident. Indeed, in the Dialogue under consideration, being a special pleader from the first and not a judge, she makes an *ex parte* statement for her client the Poet throughout; and a wish to indulge in the affectedly familiar vein—a favourite with fanatics, whether puritan divines or Germanized mystics—combining with that bias this "very bad" kind of thing which we have extracted, is the result. Had it not been for these influences, the maxim which the author would have laid down would, we conceive, have been simply expressed after this manner,—viz., that genuine criticism, when pronouncing on meritorious works, has in the generality of cases the tendency to note the excellencies and to overpass the defects. But this unaffected way of stating the case would have expunged the mystic metaphors of the Incarnation and the Creation—consummations that, perhaps, some might think devoutly to be wished—would have caused the supposed essential of obscurity to evanesce, and eliminated the "very bad" portion:—and hence, it was not adopted.

The false doctrine enunciated in the paragraph which we have just been examining is again repeated a few lines further on.

Here the "dogmatic replaces the familiar" as the vehicle of expression. The Poet issues his ukase after this fashion,—"If one object does not satisfy you, pass on to another, and say nothing,"—unless the critic can cry "very good," we suppose. We do not, however, find the author following her own advice. With her, it is "Mind what I say, but not what I do:" for when . . . she reviews Mr. Allston's pictures—which, on the whole, she very much admires,—and finds amongst them several that do not satisfy her, she does not pass on and say nothing, but very properly stops at each and says something, very much to the purpose, and pretty tolerably severe too. She is, in fact, again off her guard here; and acts instinctively on the true principle, instead of her own false canon. As to the Critic in this Dialogue—who sure enough is a very poor creature, not a giant made by the author to be slain, but a puppet set up to be demolished—he is bullied by the Poet from beginning to end. To the "pass on, say nothing" command, he merely falters out, in euphuistic accents, the following commonplaces of his craft:—"It is not so that it would be well with me, &c.; I must examine, compare, sift, and winnow, &c., until I find the gold," &c. It is not "well with him,"—as the sequel proves. In a word, the Poet smothers him. (pp. 1287-88)

We could have wished to have had a less meagre account of American literature than is given in these volumes. But we shall look forward to the author's fulfilment of the pledge which she has given in her Preface—namely, that "a year or two hence she hopes to have more to say upon this topic, or the interests it represents, and to speak with more ripeness both as to the matter and the form." The sooner the better. We shall have great pleasure in renewing, at an early period, our acquaintance with Margaret Fuller:—and, though hers is a mind that must ever be in progress, the next one or two years, we venture to predict, will be a *per saltum* stage of that progress—and will greatly accelerate the "ripening" process not only as regards American literature but several other subjects also. In fact, "one or two *hours* of critical self-examination would suffice to determine her upon felling at once these foreign and fantastically carved shrubberies "both of matter and form,"—which at present shut out in great measure the rays of her genius; and would thus enable it to shine fully on the fruits which it would ripen. (p. 1289)

> *A review of "Papers on Literature and Art," in* The Athenaeum, *No. 999, December 19, 1846, pp. 1287-89.*

## [JAMES RUSSELL LOWELL]   (poem date 1848)

[*Lowell was a celebrated American poet and essayist. His* Fable for Critics *is a book-length poem featuring thinly-disguised critical portraits of his literary contemporaries, and is noted by twentieth-century critics for the extent to which personal bias influenced some of his judgments. Referring to Fuller as "Miranda," the name of a character that appears in her* Woman in the Nineteenth Century, *Lowell portrays her as pompous, arrogant and egotistical. Commentators note that Lowell is reacting here to an earlier review in which Fuller described him as "absolutely wanting in the true spirit and tone of poesy." In a review of the* Fable, *Edgar Allan Poe remarked that Lowell had "obviously aimed his "Fable" at Miss Fuller's head."*]

Miranda came up, and said, "Phoebus! you know
That the Infinite Soul has its infinite woe,
As I ought to know, having lived cheek by jowl,
Since the day I was born, with the Infinite Soul;
I myself introduced, I myself, I alone,

To my Land's better life authors solely my own,
Who the sad heart of earth on their shoulders have taken,
Whose works sound a depth by Life's quiet unshaken,
Such as Shakespeare, for instance, the Bible, and Bacon,
Not to mention my own works; Time's nadir is fleet,
And, as for myself, I'm quite out of conceit"—

"Quite out of conceit! I'm enchanted to hear it,"
Cried Apollo aside. "Who'd have thought she was near it?
To be sure, one is apt to exhaust those commodities
One uses too fast, yet in this case as odd it is
As if Neptune should say to his turbots and whitings,
'I'm as much out of salt as Miranda's own writings'
(Which, as she in her own happy manner has said,
Sound a depth, for 'tis one of the functions of lead).
She often has asked me if I could not find
A place somewhere near me that suited her mind;
I know but a single one vacant, which she,
With her rare talent that way, would fit to a T.
And it would not imply any pause or cessation
In the work she esteems her peculiar vocation,—
She may enter on duty to-day, if she chooses,
And remain Tiring-woman for life to the Muses."

Miranda meanwhile has succeeded in driving
Up into a corner, in spite of their striving,
A small flock of terrified victims, and there,
With an I-turn-the-crank-of-the-Universe air
And a tone which, at least to *my* fancy, appears
Not so much to be entering as boxing your ears,
Is unfolding a tale (of herself, I surmise,
For 'tis dotted as thick as a peacock's with I's).
*Apropos* of Miranda, I'll rest on my oars
And drift through a trifling digression on bores,
For, though not wearing ear-rings *in more majorum,*
Our ears are kept bored just as if we still wore 'em.

(pp. 72-4)

> [*James Russell Lowell*], *in his* A Fable for Critics: Or, Better, a Glance at a Few of Our Literary Progenies from the Tub of Diogenes *(copyright, 1848, by George P. Putnam), Putnam's, 1848 (authorship acknowledged and reprinted by Houghton, Mifflin and Company, 1891, 101 p.).*\*

## ELIZABETH BARRETT BROWNING   (letter date 1852)

[Madame Ossoli] was a most interesting woman to me, though I did not sympathise with a large portion of her opinions. Her written works are just *naught*. She said herself they were sketches, thrown out in haste and for the means of subsistence, and that the sole production of hers which was likely to represent her at all would be the history of the Italian Revolution. In fact, her reputation, such as it was in America, seemed to stand mainly on her conversation and oral lectures. If I wished anyone to do her justice, I should say, as I have indeed said, 'Never read what she has written.' The letters, however, are individual, and full, I should fancy, of that magnetic personal influence which was so strong in her. I felt drawn in towards her, during our short intercourse; I loved her, and the circumstances of her death shook me to the very roots of my heart. The comfort is, that she lost little in this world—the change could not be loss to her. She had suffered, and was likely to suffer still more. (p. 59)

> *Elizabeth Barrett Browning, in a letter to Mrs. Jameson on February 26, 1852, in her* The Letters of

Elizabeth Barrett Browning, Vol. II, *edited by Frederic G. Kenyon, Smith, Elder, & Co., 1897, pp. 57-60.*

### THE NEW QUARTERLY REVIEW    (essay date 1852)

Margaret Fuller was one of those he-women who, thank Heaven! for the most part figure and flourish, and have their fame on the other side of the Atlantic. She was an intellectual Bloomer of the very largest calibre. She was an encyclopaedia in cerulean stockings. She understood Socrates better than Plato did, Faust better than Göethe did, Kant's Philosophy better than Kant did—an acquirement by the way not, perhaps, so very, very, difficult—astronomy much better than Adams or Leverrier, ethics better than Aristotle, rhetoric, logic, poetry, better than any professor in any Yankee college. But, alack! the difference between an encyclopaedia bound in calfskin, and an encyclopaedia moving in blue stockings! Every fact, word, thought, idea, theory, notion, line, verse, that crowded in the cranium of Margaret Fuller was a weapon. They shot from her in season and out of season, like pellets from a steam gun. She bristled all over with transcendentalism, assailed you with metaphysics, suffocated you with mythology, peppered you with ethics, and struck you down with heavy history. . . .

Mrs. Ossoli is dead, and a committee of Yankee memoir writers have combined to work her apotheosis [in *Memoirs of Margaret Fuller Ossoli*]. Here she sits upon a cloud, blown by these panting, puffing fame-givers. The bombastic eulogy, well-flavoured as it is by American slang, would be amusing from its exaggeration; but, alas it disgusts by its vulgarity.

Of course this mighty mass of mind never did anything worth recording. She translated some German and Italian, and helped to edit an American transcendental periodical, but nothing more did Margaret Fuller do. The strong-minded lady, however, forced all she knew upon everybody, and obtained an awful respect in society. We question after all whether Margaret Fuller, whom even one of her biographers admits knew very little indeed of one of the authors she vapours most about—Shakespeare, had more solid useful learning than many a well-informed English lady, who is quite content to remain a woman and not to be a prodigy. (p. 168)

We need hardly say that we do not recommend this book to English family reading. It is false in style and sentiment, and, although free from glaring improprieties, and, perhaps, not amusing enough to be very likely to be read, still we think it is not a nice book for English ladies, and not an entertaining book for English gentlemen. (p. 170)

*A review of "Memoirs of Margaret Fuller Ossoli," in* The New Quarterly Review, *Vol. I, No. II, 1852, pp. 168-70.*

### R. W. EMERSON    (essay date 1852)

[*Emerson, the leading American Transcendentalist philosopher, was a close friend of Fuller and an editor of her* Memoirs, *from which the following is drawn. His comments on Fuller are courtly and guarded. He stresses her love of art and nature, her talent for friendship, and, like many of her contemporaries, particularly praises her conversation. "[Margaret's] powers and accomplishments," he states, "found their best and only adequate channel" in this medium.*]

Margaret's love of art, like that of most cultivated persons in this country, was not at all technical, but truly a sympathy with the artist, in the protest which his work pronounced on the deformity of our daily manners; her co-perception with him of the eloquence of form; her aspiration with him to a fairer life. As soon as her conversation ran into the mysteries of manipulation and artistic effect, it was less trustworthy. I remember that in the first times when I chanced to see pictures with her, I listened reverently to her opinions, and endeavored to see what she saw. But, on several occasions, finding myself unable to reach it, I came to suspect my guide, and to believe, at last, that her taste in works of art, though honest, was not on universal, but on idiosyncratic, grounds. (pp. 267-68)

She was very susceptible to pleasurable stimulus, took delight in details of form, color, and sound. Her fancy and imagination were easily stimulated to genial activity, and she erroneously thanked the artist for the pleasing emotions and thoughts that rose in her mind. So that, though capable of it, she did not always bring that highest tribunal to a work of art, namely, the calm presence of greatness, which only greatness in the object can satisfy. Yet the opinion was often well worth hearing on its own account, though it might be wide of the mark as criticism. Sometimes, too, she certainly brought to beautiful objects a fresh and appreciating love; and her written notes, especially on sculpture, I found always original and interesting. (p. 268)

[That] susceptibility to details in art and nature which precluded the exercise of Margaret's sound catholic judgment, must be extended to more than her connoisseurship. She *had* a sound judgment, on which, in conversation, she could fall back, and anticipate and speak the best sense of the largest company. But, left to herself, and in her correspondence, she was much the victim of Lord Bacon's *idols of the cave,* or self-deceived by her own phantasms. I have looked over volumes of her letters to me and others. They are full of probity, talent, wit, friendship, charity, and high aspiration. They are tainted with a mysticism, which to me appears so much an affair of constitution, that it claims no more respect than the charity or patriotism of a man who has dined well, and feels better for it. . . . In our noble Margaret, her personal feeling colors all her judgment of persons, of books, of pictures, and even of the laws of the world. This is easily felt in ordinary women, and a large deduction is civilly made on the spot by whosoever replies to their remark. But when the speaker has such brilliant talent and literature as Margaret, she gives so many fine names to these merely sensuous and subjective phantasms, that the hearer is long imposed upon, and thinks so precise and glittering nomenclature cannot be of mere *muscae volitantes,* phoenixes of the fancy, but must be of some real ornithology, hitherto unknown to him. This mere feeling exaggerates a host of trifles into a dazzling mythology. But when one goes to sift it, and find if there be a real meaning, it eludes search. Whole sheets of warm, florid writing are here, in which the eye is caught by "sapphire," "heliotrope," "dragon," "aloes," "Magna Dea," "limboes," "stars," and "purgatory," but can connect all this, or any part of it, with no universal experience.

In short, Margaret often loses herself in sentimentalism. That dangerous vertigo nature in her case adopted, and was to make respectable. As it sometimes happens that a grandiose style, like that of the Alexandrian Platonists, or like Macpherson's Ossian, is more stimulating to the imagination of nations, than the true Plato, or than the simple poet, so here was a head so creative of new colors, of wonderful gleams,—so iridescent, that it piqued curiosity, and stimulated thought, and communicated mental activity to all who approached her; though her perceptions were not to be compared to her fancy, and she made numerous mistakes. Her integrity was perfect, and she was led and followed by love, and was really bent on truth, but too indulgent to the meteors of her fancy. (pp. 279-80)

[Margaret's] powers and accomplishments found their best and only adequate channel in her conversation;—a conversation which those who have heard it, unanimously, as far as I know, pronounced to be, in elegance, in range, in flexibility, and adroit transition, in depth, in cordiality, and in moral aim, altogether admirable; surprising and cheerful as a poem, and communicating its own civility and elevation like a charm to all hearers. She was here, among our anxious citizens, and frivolous fashionists, as if sent to refine and polish her countrymen, and announce a better day. She poured a stream of amber over the endless store of private anecdotes, of bosom histories, which her wonderful persuasion drew forth, and transfigured them into fine fables. Whilst she embellished the moment, her conversation had the merit of being solid and true. She put her whole character into it, and had the power to inspire. The companion was made a thinker, and went away quite other than he came. The circle of friends who sat with her were not allowed to remain spectators or players, but she converted them into heroes, if she could. The muse woke the muses, and the day grew bright and eventful. Of course, there must be, in a person of such sincerity, much variety of aspect, according to the character of her company. Only, in Margaret's case, there is almost an agreement in the testimony to an invariable power over the minds of all. I conversed lately with a gentleman who has vivid remembrances of his interviews with her in Boston, many years ago, who described her in these terms:—''No one ever came so near. Her mood applied itself to the mood of her companion, point to point, in the most limber, sinuous, vital way, and drew out the most extraordinary narratives; yet she had a light sort of laugh, when all was said, as if she thought she could live over that revelation. And this sufficient sympathy she had for all persons indifferently,—for lovers, for artists, and beautiful maids, and ambitious young statesmen, and for old aunts, and coach-travellers. Ah! she applied herself to the mood of her companion, as the sponge applies itself to water.'' The description tallies well enough with my observation. I remember she found, one day, at my house, her old friend Mr. ——, sitting with me. She looked at him attentively, and hardly seemed to know him. In the afternoon, he invited her to go with him to Cambridge. The next day she said to me, ''You fancy that you know ——. It is too absurd; you have never seen him. When I found him here, sitting like a statue, I was alarmed, and thought him ill. You sit with courteous, *un*confiding smile, and suppose him to be a mere man of talent. He is so with you. But the moment I was alone with him, he was another creature; his manner, so glassy and elaborate before, was full of soul, and the tones of his voice entirely different.'' And I have no doubt that she saw expressions, heard tones, and received thoughts from her companions, which no one else ever saw or heard from the same parties, and that her praise of her friends, which seemed exaggerated, was her exact impression. We were all obliged to recall Margaret's testimony, when we found we were sad blockheads to other people. (pp. 311-13)

*R. W. Emerson, ''Visits to Concord'' (1852), in* Memoirs of Margaret Fuller Ossoli, Vol. I *by Margaret Fuller Ossoli, edited by Arthur B. Fuller & others, revised edition, The Tribune Association, 1869, pp. 199-316.*

**HORACE GREELEY**   (essay date 1852)

My first acquaintance with Margaret Fuller was made through the pages of 'The Dial.' The lofty range and rare ability of that work, and its un-American richness of culture and ripeness of thought, naturally filled the 'fit audience, though few,' with a high estimate of those who were known as its conductors and principal writers. Yet I do not now remember that any article, which strongly impressed me, was recognized as from the pen of its female editor, prior to the appearance of **'The Great Lawsuit,'** afterwards matured into the volume more distinctively, yet not quite accurately, entitled **'Woman in the Nineteenth Century.'** I think this can hardly have failed to make a deep impression on the mind of every thoughtful reader, as the production of an original, vigorous, and earnest mind. **'Summer on the Lakes,'** which appeared some time after that essay, though before its expansion into a book, struck me as less ambitious in its aim, but more graceful and delicate in its execution; and as one of the clearest and most graphic delineations, ever given, of the Great Lakes, of the Prairies, and of the receding barbarism, and the rapidly advancing, but rude, repulsive semi-civilization, which were contending with most unequal forces for the possession of those rich lands. I still consider **'Summer on the Lakes'** unequalled, especially in its pictures of the Prairies and of the sunnier aspects of Pioneer life. (pp. 152-53)

[Margaret's] earlier contributions to the Tribune were not her best, and I did not at first prize her aid so highly as I afterwards learned to do. She wrote always freshly, vigorously, but not always clearly; for her full and intimate acquaintance with continental literature, especially German, seemed to have marred her felicity and readiness of expression in her mother tongue. While I never met another woman who conversed more freely or lucidly, the attempt to commit her thoughts to paper seemed to induce a singular embarrassment and hesitation. She could write only when in the vein; and this needed often to be waited for through several days, while the occasion sometimes required an immediate utterance. (p. 154)

I think most of her contributions to the Tribune, while she remained with us, were characterized by a directness, terseness, and practicality, which are wanting in some of her earlier productions. Good judges have confirmed my own opinion, that, while her essays in the Dial are more elaborate and ambitious, her reviews in the Tribune are far better adapted to win the favor and sway the judgment of the great majority of readers. But, one characteristic of her writings I feel bound to commend,—their absolute truthfulness. She never asked how this would sound, nor whether that would do, nor what would be the effect of saying anything; but simply, 'Is it the truth? Is it such as the public should know?' And if her judgment answered, 'Yes,' she uttered it; no matter what turmoil it might excite, nor what odium it might draw down on her own head. Perfect conscientiousness was an unfailing characteristic of her literary efforts. (pp. 157-58)

*Horace Greeley, in an extract from ''New York'' (1852), in* Memoirs of Margaret Fuller Ossoli, Vol. II *by Margaret Fuller Ossoli, edited by Arthur B. Fuller & others, revised edition, The Tribune Association, 1869, pp. 152-63.*

**RUFUS WILMOT GRISWOLD**   (essay date 1852)

*Woman in the Nineteenth Century* is one of the most brilliant of the many books on the intellectual and social position of woman that has been published. It is difficult, however, to understand what is its real import, further than to the extent that the author was ill satisfied that there should be difference in the rank and opportunity of the sexes. That there should be some difference in their sphere she seemed not unwilling to allow. Like the rest of that diverting company of women who have contemplated a nullification of certain of the statutes of nature, she would but have choice of places and vocations.

*Summer on the Lakes* evinces considerable descriptive power, and contains some good verses. Her remarks in this work upon the Indians, and that part of our ethnological literature which relates to them, are very superficial and incautious. . . . [When her book was composed, Miss Fuller] had been about one week west of Buffalo, and had seen perhaps a dozen vagabond Indians across the streets of Detroit and Chicago.

The *Papers on Literature and Art* contain a short essay on Critics, in which she gives a brief exposition of her views of criticism. It is followed by some dozen papers, several of which are admirable in their way. They are all forcible, and brilliant in a degree; but frequently pointed with pique or prejudice.

She was fond of epigram, and showed everywhere a willingness to advance any opinion for the sake of making a point. Thus, in a review of Mr. Poe's writings, she makes the observation that "no form of literary activity has so terribly degenerated among us as the tale," because it gave opportunity to remark "that everybody who wants a new hat or bonnet takes this way to earn one from the magazines or annuals." But no fact is more generally understood by those who have paid any attention to the advancement and condition of letters here, than that the exact reverse of this is true. She rarely attempted particular or analytical criticism, but commended or censured all books with about an equal degree of earnestness, being generally most severe upon those of home production, excepting a few by personal friends.

She had remarkable quickness, but not much subtlety of apprehension; general, but not solid acquirements; and an astonishing facility in the use of her intellectual furniture, which secured her the reputation of being one of the best talkers of the age. Her written style is generally excellent,—various, forcible, and picturesque,—though sometimes pedantic and careless,—very much like that of her conversation, and probably a result of but the same degree of labour. (pp. 537-38)

> *Rufus Wilmot Griswold, "S. Margaret Fuller," in his* The Prose Writers of America: With a Survey of the Intellectual History, Condition, and Prospects of the Country, *revised edition, A. Hart, 1852 (and reprinted by Garrett Press, Inc., Publishers, 1969), pp. 537-38.*

## [GEORGE ELIOT]   (essay date 1855)

[*Eliot was an English novelist and essayist whom Fuller had met during her visit to England. In the following review, Eliot compares* Woman in the Nineteenth Century *with Mary Wollstonecraft's feminist work,* Rights of Woman. *While Eliot faults Fuller's occasional obtuseness of style, she praises her for painting women "as they are." A year after this essay appeared, Eliot reviewed Fuller's* At Home and Abroad; or, Things and Thoughts in America and Europe *for the same periodical (see excerpt below, 1856).*]

*Woman in the Nineteenth Century* . . . has been unduly thrust into the background by less comprehensive and candid productions on the same subject. Notwithstanding certain defects of taste and a sort of vague spiritualism and grandiloquence which belong to all but the very best American writers, the book is a valuable one: it has the enthusiasm of a noble and sympathetic nature, with the moderation and breadth and large allowance of a vigorous and cultivated understanding. There is no exaggeration of woman's moral excellence or intellectual capabilities; no injudicious insistance on her fitness for this or that function hitherto engrossed by men; but a calm plea for the removal of unjust laws and artificial restrictions, so that the possibilities of her nature may have room for full development. . . . (p. 988)

It is interesting to compare this essay of Margaret Fuller's . . . with a work on the position of woman, written between sixty and seventy years ago—we mean Mary Wollstonecraft's *Rights of Woman.* . . . There are several points of resemblance, as well as of striking difference, between the two books. A strong understanding is present in both; but Margaret Fuller's mind was like some regions of her own American continent, where you are constantly stepping from the sunny "clearings" into the mysterious twilight of the tangled forest—she often passes in one breath from forcible reasoning to dreamy vagueness; moreover, her unusually varied culture gives her great command of illustration. Mary Wollstonecraft, on the other hand, is nothing if not rational; she has no erudition, and her grave pages are lit up by no ray of fancy. In both writers we discern, under the brave bearing of a strong and truthful nature, the beating of a loving woman's heart, which teaches them not to undervalue the smallest offices of domestic care or kindliness. But Margaret Fuller, with all her passionate sensibility, is more of the literary woman, who would not have been satisfied without intellectual production; Mary Wollstonecraft, we imagine, wrote not at all for writing's sake, but from the pressure of other motives. So far as the difference of date allows, there is a striking coincidence in their trains of thought; indeed, every important idea in the *Rights of Woman,* except the combination of home education with a common dayschool for boys and girls, reappears in Margaret Fuller's essay. (pp. 988-89)

[Some] of the best things [Margaret Fuller] says are on the folly of absolute definitions of woman's nature and absolute demarcations of woman's mission. "Nature," she says, "seems to delight in varying the arrangements, as if to show that she will be fettered by no rule; and we must admit the same varieties that she admits." Again: "If nature is never bound down, nor the voice of inspiration stifled, that is enough. We are pleased that women should write and speak, if they feel need of it, from having something to tell; but silence for ages would be no misfortune, if such silence be from divine command, and not from man's tradition." . . .

Unfortunately, many over-zealous champions of women assert their actual equality with men—nay, even their moral superiority to men—as a ground for their release from oppressive laws and restrictions. They lose strength immensely by this false position. . . .

Both Margaret Fuller and Mary Wollstonecraft have too much sagacity to fall into this sentimental exaggeration. Their ardent hopes of what women may become do not prevent them from seeing and painting women as they are. (p. 989)

> [*George Eliot], "Margaret Fuller and Mary Wollstonecraft," in* The Leader, *Vol. 6, October 13, 1855, pp. 988-89.* \*

## [GEORGE ELIOT]   (essay date 1856)

Every reader of Margaret Fuller's Life must have felt the superiority of the letters she wrote from Italy over her earlier journals and correspondence. A straining after some unattained effect had given way to calm vigour, and magniloquence to noble simplicity. It was clear that the blossoming time of her nature had come. Her affections had been drawn into their proper channel; her intellect had found its proper soil in the deep rich loam of European civilization, and her wide sympathies had found a grand definite object in the struggles of the Italian people. . . .

[In *At Home and Abroad; or, Things and Thoughts in America and Europe*], it is again the letters written from Italy which chiefly arrest us. They have indeed a double value, a value not only biographical, but historical. A description, however fragmentary and imperfect, of the events in Rome from 1847 to 1849, written on the spot by a foreign resident who could both feel and think forcibly, must have an interest quite apart from any special interest in the writer. It will bring those events nearer to the imagination of the ordinary reader, and help him to make a picture of what has hitherto perhaps been a rough diagram in his mind; and to the historian in search of materials it is likely to contribute some valuable touches. . . . [These letters] have no great merit considered as literature, and we could probably have afforded to neglect them, if Margaret Fuller's manuscript *History of the Italian Revolution* had been rescued from the waves; but being, as they are, the only result left to us of her experience and observation in Rome, they are precious. . . .

[Fuller] observed what went forward in the Roman streets with the feeling of an artist, as well as of one who ''loved the people well,'' and her descriptions have often a fine mixture of the pathetic and the picturesque.

> [*George Eliot*], *''Margaret Fuller's Letters from Italy,'' in* The Leader, *Vol. VII, No. 321, May 17, 1856, p. 475.*

## VERNON LOUIS PARRINGTON (essay date 1927)

[*Parrington, whose sympathetic, laudatory account of Fuller's life and career appeared in his survey of American literature, was one of the first twentieth-century critics to reassess Fuller's achievement.*]

The fame of Margaret Fuller has waned greatly since her vivid personality was blotted out in the prime of her intellectual development. Misunderstood in her own time, caricatured by unfriendly critics, and with significant facts of her life suppressed by her friends out of a chivalrous sense of loyalty, the real woman has been lost in a Margaret Fuller myth and later generations have come to underestimate her powers and undervalue her work. Yet no other woman of her generation in America is so well worth recalling. She was the completest embodiment of the inchoate rebellions and grandiose aspirations of the age of transcendental ferment; for to the many grievances charged against the times by other New England liberals, she added the special grievance of the stupid inhibitions laid upon women. Transcendental radical and critic, like Emerson and Thoreau and Parker, she was feminist also; and to the difficult business of freeing her mind from the Cambridge orthodoxies, she added the greater difficulty of freeing her sex.

The written record that Margaret Fuller left is quite inadequate to explain her contemporary reputation. In no sense an artist, scarcely a competent craftsman, she wrote nothing that bears the mark of high distinction either in thought or style. Impatient of organization and inadequately disciplined, she threw off her work impulsively, not pausing to shape it to enduring form. Yet she was vastly talked about, and common report makes her out to have been an extraordinary woman who creatively influenced those with whom she came in contact. Like Alcott, her power lay in brilliant talk. Her quick mind seems to have been an electric current that stimulated other minds to activity. . . . (p. 418)

Margaret Fuller was the first since Mary Wollstonecraft, fifty years before, to undertake a reasoned defense of the claims of woman to emancipation from man-made custom. [*Woman in the Nineteenth Century*] was a somewhat shocking book to fling at respectable Boston bluestockings—male as well as female—for not only did she discuss equality of economic opportunity and equality of political rights for women, but she went further and spoke frankly about sex equality, marriage, prostitution, physical passions—pretty much everything that was taboo in Boston society. It was a bold thing to do, needing more courage even than to engage in a Fourieristic onslaught upon the conventions of private property. Only a first-class rebel would have had the temerity to offer such morsels to wagging tongues. (p. 424)

[Fuller] plunged vigorously into the work of criticism, never perhaps very successfully, certainly never with high distinction. Her judgments were penetrating and individual, she awakened some Cambridge animosities by her comment on certain Cambridge poets, but she was not a notable critic. A fine craftsmanship she never attained. A light touch she could never command. (pp. 424-25)

Margaret Fuller's tragic life, despite its lack of solid accomplishment, was an epitome of the great revolt of the New England mind against Puritan asceticism and Yankee materialism. She was the emotional expression of a rebellious generation that had done with the past and was questioning the future. Not a scholar like Theodore Parker, not a thinker like Thoreau, not an artist like Emerson, she was a ferment of troubled aspiration, an enthusiasm for a more generous culture than New England had known—the logical outcome of the romantic revolution which, beginning with Channing's discovery of humanitarian France, and leading thence to idealistic Germany, was to break the indurated shell of life in New England, and release its conscience and its mind. She was the spiritual child of Jean Jacques [Rousseau] even more than of Goethe. (p. 425)

The rebel pays a heavy price for his rebellions, as Margaret learned to her cost. She suffered much in her daily life, but it was her art that suffered most. She was evidently a far richer nature than her printed works reveal. Intense in her extravagant demands upon life, a radical humanitarian in all her sympathies and instincts, generous in response to whatever was fine and high, living unduly an inner life as became a daughter of Puritanism—Margaret Fuller was too vivid a personality, too complete an embodiment of the rich ferment of the forties, to be carelessly forgotten. The deeper failure of her career—its vague aspirations and inadequate accomplishment—was a failure that may be justly charged against the narrow world that bred her. Perhaps no sharper criticism could be leveled at New England than that it could do no better with such material, lent it by the gods. (p. 426)

> *Vernon Louis Parrington, ''Margaret Fuller: Rebel (1927),'' in his* Main Currents in American Thought, an Interpretation of American Literature from the Beginnings to 1920: The Romantic Revolution in America, 1800-1860, *Vol. 2 (copyright 1927 by Har-*

court Brace Jovanovich, Inc.; renewed 1955 by Vernon L. Parrington, Jr., Louise P. Tucker, Elizabeth P. Thomas; reprinted by permission of the publisher), Harcourt Brace Jovanovich, 1930 (and reprinted by Harcourt Brace Jovanovich, 1958), pp. 418-26.

### ROLAND CROZIER BURTON (essay date 1944)

[*In his survey of Fuller's writings on drama, painting, sculpture, dance, and music, Burton finds Fuller to be a better critic of literature than of the fine arts. He states that, while Fuller "perceived many of the issues of aesthetics," she did not pursue these ideas far enough "to suggest thorough assimilation of sources." Burton proposes that Fuller's inferiority as a critic of the fine arts may be partially due to her strong literary background, which caused her to judge all the arts by literary standards.*

*Despite misgivings about Fuller's fine-arts criticism, Burton acknowledges her acumen as a literary critic, and recognizes her contribution to American culture. He assessed her achievement in the preface to his unpublished doctoral dissertation: "First, . . . she was an eloquent pleader for the cause of continental literature. Second, . . . she made accurate, intuitive estimates of the worth of her American contemporaries. Third, she accomplished something toward the separation of moral judgment and aesthetic judgment, and thereby helped to prepare the way for sounder aesthetic criticism. Fourth, by insisting . . . upon the close relationship between art and society, she contributed toward winning, from a materialistic social order, some respect for art."*]

Although Margaret Fuller remains of interest chiefly because of her literary criticism, as a transcendental exponent of the unified aesthetic sensibility, she frequently touched upon the drama, painting, sculpture, the ballet, and music. . . . [Fuller's criticism of the fine arts], sometimes purely incidental but frequently quite extended, . . . entitle her to the status of a pioneer American critic of the arts. In this less familiar province she often speaks with less warranted authority than in literature, but her comments are no less significant in revealing her traits of mind. (p. 18)

[In her critical arguments, Fuller] made use of Reynolds' distinction between the sublime and the beautiful; of Rousseau's theory of emotional states evoked by natural beauty; of Lessing's pronouncement upon the expression of pain and transitory emotion; of Schiller's discrimination between the naïve and sentimental and between classic harmony and romantic discord; of A. W. Schlegel's delimitation of the boundaries between finite and infinite aspiration; of Novalis' identification of poetry with absolute reality; and, most important of all, of Goethe's injunction, which she freely applied in all the arts, "To appreciate any man, learn first what object he proposed to himself; next, what degree of earnestness he showed with regard to attaining that object." Each of these points of reference served its turn in the attempts by which "we do not seek to degrade but to classify an object by stating what it is not," without, at the same time, being "constrained by the hard cemented masonry of method."

Fundamental to her conception of unity in the arts is the idea, borrowed from the more romantic theorists, relating to the organic succession of forms. In this context Margaret Fuller found the botanical analogy particularly appropriate: "There is, perhaps, a correspondence between the successions of literary vegetation with those of the earth's surface, where, if you burn or cut down an ancient wood, the next offering of the soil will not be in the same kind, but raspberries and purple flowers will succeed the oak, poplars the pine." Comparison

of her various papers shows that she consistently adhered to this belief that each particular age would bring forth its own characteristic form of artistic expression. According to the principle, she found the drama most alien to the introspective tendencies of the day. . . . It belonged, rather, to the age of Elizabeth, when an appreciation of individual greatness had pervaded society. Contemporary architecture and sculpture, which received little of her attention, evinced to her no more than imitative power, as did painting, in which her low estimate did not, however, prevent a more sustained interest. In poetry she found hopeful portents, especially in that verse which foreshadowed the future greatness of the common man; and she praised the ballet extravagantly, partly because she saw in it "body made pliant to the inspirations of spirit," and partly because of her abhorrence of the prudery which had objected even to exhibitions of statuary. . . . (pp. 18-19)

More illuminating in revealing ideas and attitudes are Margaret Fuller's attempts to order and synthesize her impressions of painting, an art toward which she exhibited one of her most consistent inclinations. Landscape painting, wherein character and incident are subordinated, appeared to give her the most difficulty. Evidently placing it in an inferior category, she was content with representation rather than expression or interpretation. By this criterion she judged Allston's scenes: "Here the painter is merged in his theme, and these pictures affect us as parts of nature, so absorbed are we in contemplating them, so difficult is it to remember them as pictures." (p. 19)

As a means of classifying paintings, Margaret Fuller used the terms "sublime" and "beautiful"—terms obviously derived from Sir Joshua Reynolds' *Discourses*. Judging by the tone of her comments on ideal portraits, she placed such works—and, inferentially, landscapes—in the inferior category of the Beautiful. . . .

In the "grand historical style," which she associated with the Sublime, she considered Allston's best attempts "imposing rather than majestic." Here, only Raphael and Michelangelo, as workers in the pictorial and plastic arts, completely met her expectations. Raphael was the apostle of the Finite, "whose life is all reproduced; nothing was abstract or conscious." Michelangelo was the prophet of the Infinite. (p. 20)

There is traceable, among the disparate and variously oriented statements on the pictorial and plastic arts, a slight tendency toward growth that is unique in her aesthetic criticism. Early in her career, during the flush of her Goethean enthusiasm, she expanded her favorite critical standard into a logical absurdity. Comparing Martin's "Destruction of Nineveh" with one of Raphael's Madonnas, she asserted that if "the one is intended to excite the imagination, and the other to gratify the taste; that which fulfills its object most completely must be the best, whether it give me pleasure or no."

A more rewarding use of her sources is recorded in 1840, when, obviously under the influence of Lessing, she considered the expression of pain and emotion. She found Allston's "Massacre of the Innocents" unpleasant. . . . Five years later, however, she had grown to believe that this same depiction of human agonies might contribute to a deeper experience. Writing on "The Nubian Slave," . . . she said: "It is only necessary that pain and dread should be subordinated to some meaning of a permanent dignity, and we think it is so in this instance." That the fluctuations of opinion should at length attain this higher level of comprehension betokens a maturation of viewpoint not discernible in relation to the other arts.

Such lack of fulfilment is most notable in her criticism of music. Her theory of organic succession in the arts proclaimed music as the most authentic and original voice of her own age, the culmination of finite aspiration, and the glorious expression of modern yearning toward the infinite. In her gallery of individual heroes—Goethe, Wordsworth, Shelley, Emerson, and the like—she admired a musician, Beethoven, the most consistently and least critically.

In moments of highest enthusiasm she felt that music could supplant, not only the other arts, but other fields of human knowledge as well: "What other arts indicate and Philosophy infers, this all-enfolding language declares." Her exaltation of music, as reflected in her writing, does not appear to be implemented by soundness of knowledge or acuteness of perception. (pp. 20-1)

Her praise of "the *Sehnsucht* [yearning] of music", her confusion of musical, with conceptual, ideas; and her almost complete indifference to harmonic and formal structure—all corroborate an impression which is further strengthened by her frequent preoccupation with the incidental matters of financial support, the decorum of audiences, and the personal mannerisms of concert artists: music was for her, in spite of pretensions to the contrary, little more than a sensuous pleasure and a stimulant toward free imaginative association with all elevating experiences. (p. 21)

In extenuation of Margaret Fuller's relative inadequacy as a critic of the arts, one might cite the paucity of opportunities for enjoyment of the arts other than literature. A listing of the cultural resources of Boston and New York during the 1830's and 1840's, while quantitatively impressive, would not be remarkable for quality. Margaret Fuller did her best with what was available; indeed, her willingness to generalize was out of proportion to her actual experience with works of art. All that she had to say bore some of the naïveté and freshness of novel experience. . . . Her remarks on painting and sculpture were based chiefly upon her study of the Athenaeum casts and the Flaxman and Retzsch engravings. Her musical experience was bounded by the music lessons of her childhood, the oratorios that she heard in Boston, and the occasional concerts and operas that she attended in New York. Her reading "about" the arts was much richer than her experience "with" the arts.

The riches of her literary background as compared with her restricted acquaintance with kindred arts suggests a fundamental weakness of her criticism in these other fields. All of them were judged in terms of literature. However powerful the emotional stimulus awakened by a particular work, she remained somewhat perplexed until she could discover a literary theme. Were not all forms of art simply languages by which "the presence of the highest genius makes all mediums alike transparent"? She drew from this principle a corollary that the "language" must of necessity be a literary language. "What does the picture mean to say?" she queried, upon inspecting Allston's "Witch of Endor"; and, upon finding the artist's reading of the text at variance with her own, she disparaged the painting as conveying "no distinct impression." With facile assurance she translated the meaning from one art to another. Concerning Beethoven's "Fifth Symphony," she said: "What the Sibyls and Prophets of Michel Angelo demand, is in this majestic work made present to us." Again, in encompassing the Creation theme, she found that her own imagination, fired by the scriptural text, was more nearly adequate to the conception than was either a literary, a musical, or a sculptural

transcription: "Haydn fell short of Milton, who falls short of what we know how to expect." (pp. 22-3)

The pervasive literary standard, blurring the distinctions among the arts and uniting them under a false premise, operated to prevent the formulation of a genuinely "comprehensive" aesthetic theory.

Margaret Fuller's critical essays are the adventures of an active and intelligent but essentially unspeculative mind in a strange field. The conflicts and cross-purposes that in her literary criticism are seemingly transcended—resulting in singularly just estimates of individual writers—are brought to the surface in her criticism of the other arts; and the basic weakness becomes apparent. Though her appraisals of such men as Longfellow, Lowell, Poe, and Emerson were at variance with the majority opinion of her own day and notably prophetic of significant twentieth-century estimates, her opinions in these other fields lapsed into the genteel orthodoxies of her own time and ours.

In its entirety Margaret Fuller's criticism of the arts bears the impress of a mind that seeks to assert the unity of the aesthetic sensibility and to base the criticism of art on broadly comprehensive principles. She perceived many of the basic issues in aesthetics. Inquiries concerning representation versus expression, the Sublime and the Beautiful, content versus form, the distinction between aesthetic and conceptual ideas, the sociological implications of art, moral versus aesthetic judgment— all are adumbrated in her published writings; yet none of these questions can be pursued far enough to suggest thorough assimilation of sources, if, indeed, the pursuit does not at length reveal a contradictory attitude. By brushing aside all sustained and systematic investigation of any one of her hypotheses, and by relying entirely upon what she thought to be her individual intuitions, she involved herself in contradictions, ambiguities, and false assumptions, ending in the very type of conventionality that she professedly disliked. (p. 23)

> *Roland Crozier Burton, "Margaret Fuller's Criticism of the Fine Arts" (copyright © 1944 by the National Council of Teachers of English; reprinted by permission of the publisher and the author), in* College English, *Vol. 6, No. 1, October, 1944, pp. 18-23.*

## RENÉ WELLEK (essay date 1965)

[*Wellek considers Fuller's critical work to be a "solid achievement," particularly her judgments of her American peers. He proposes that Fuller comes closer to "the generous, frank, and somewhat overfervid spirit of young Germany and liberal France" than to the rarefied spirit of her two idols, Johann Wolfgang von Goethe and Ralph Waldo Emerson.*]

[From a historical perspective, Fuller's critical work for the *Dial* and her reviewing for the New York *Daily Tribune*] are a solid achievement. Transcendental phraseology tinges it only superficially, and even her turgid and often high-pitched and sentimental rhetoric should not divert attention from her basic good sense and her clear critical discernment. The **"Letter to Beethoven"** written seventeen years after the composer's death, in which she speaks of the "swell of her soul as deep as thine," is happily not characteristic of her work. Actually Miss Fuller reflected more concretely on the nature and office of criticism than any of her American contemporaries, and she faced literary works more intimately and more frequently than anyone else in the New England group. (p. 179)

Margaret Fuller spoke out bravely and reviewed her American contemporaries severely. She recognized the problem of nationality and individuality, the novelty of the American synthesis of Europe, but sadly reflected that she would not be "present at the gathering-in of this harvest." . . . Hawthorne she recognized as "the best writer of the day." Though she had been a victim of Poe's critical asperity, she had a sense of his talent: the "intellect of strong fiber," the "well-chosen aim," the virtuosity of the poems. The New England poets fared in her hands almost as badly as in Poe's: Longfellow is imitative and artificial, "a dandy Pindar"; Lowell is "absolutely wanting in the true spirit and tone of poesy."

Her views of the English poets are less sure. She is taken in by Bailey's *Festus* and by Henry Taylor's tragedy *Philip van Artevelde,* and she understandably ranks Elizabeth Barrett "above any female writer the world has yet known." On the other hand, she was also one of the first admirers of Robert Browning in America. (pp. 179-80)

Sentimentality permeates her survey of the French novel. . . . George Sand—the "glow of her heart"—and Eugène Sue come in for praise; but she has some admiration for Vigny's tales and for Balzac, though she calls the latter a "heartless surgeon" and "a Mephistopheles." (p. 180)

Goethe was the one writer who occupied her most. . . . She makes much of [his] aristocratic sympathies and Olympian heartlessness but penetrates always to the works themselves. . . . Her Goethe is the classical Goethe, the sage whom she criticizes for lacking insight into the Emersonian "sacred secret," but admires for his worldly wisdom and toleration, his knowledge of human nature and art. "As a critic on art and literature, not to be surpassed in independence, fairness, powers of sympathy, and largeness of view," Goethe helped emancipate her from strait-laced morals and sentimental piety. She did not succeed completely. In spirit she comes closest not to Goethe, with his universality, not to Emerson, with his rarefied vision, but rather to Bettina [von Arnim] and George Sand—in short, to the generous, frank, and somewhat overfervid spirit of Young Germany and liberal France. (pp. 180-81)

> *René Wellek, "American Criticism," in his* A History of Modern Criticism, 1750-1950: The Age of Transition, Vol. 3 *(copyright © 1965 by Yale University), Yale University Press, 1965, pp. 150-81.*\*

**ANN DOUGLAS**   (essay date 1977)

[*Douglas discusses Fuller's journalistic writings, proposing that through newspaper writing, Fuller was able to improve her style and to discover the material that she wrote about best: history rather than literature.*]

Both Margaret Fuller's detractors and her admirers in her own day and since knew that she could talk incomparably better than she could write. . . . (p. 329)

There are many possible reasons for Fuller's over-reliance on the spoken medium during much of her adult life in America, not least of which was the fact that she was a woman. In a society that offered little encouragement for intellectual women, Fuller needed the stimulus of a present audience to dare to display her full powers. She had been denied the self-confidence needed for long-term productivity, for working without the reassurance of immediate attention and approval. . . . "When I meet people," she explained, "it is easy to adapt myself to them, but when I write, it is into another world." She could only believe such an audience existed when she saw it in front of her. (pp. 329-30)

As a journalist in New York, she altered her concept of her audience; they were less the people she wanted to have see and hear her, than the people she wished to talk to about something. And, significantly and appropriately, she began, though with little awareness of it, to change her style.

Fuller was no happier with herself as a writer in New York than she had ever been. Yet her most perceptive friends noted a difference—a welcome simplification, force, and point in her prose. . . . [In] her transcendental period she was using her writing too entirely as a vehicle for herself for it to be successful. This is not to imply that she was obsessed with the personal in a helplessly subjective fashion, although Emerson and other male friends at times hinted such was the case. It was rather that her aspirations were in some not altogether illegitimate way Messianic; and she had nothing for a Messianic vehicle but herself, even while she was rightly convinced of her own inadequacy. Journalism both satisfied and deflected Fuller's need for personal communication. Its relative informality was congenial to her; she believed it to be in style and tone very close to "conversation." The compulsion to meet a daily deadline freed her from the fears entailed for her in consciously attempting a large-scale achievement. Her instinct for self-defeat was incorporated into the conditions of success: she could not really look at what she was doing; she wrote it, and it was printed. And she had a subject outside herself. As a newspaperwoman, Fuller's attention could be less on the struggle between Margaret-in-person and Margaret-on-paper, and more simply and powerfully on what she wanted to say. Finding a form of indirection, she found direction.

*Woman in the Nineteenth Century* is journalism in the best sense, as the more consciously reporting yet more romanticized *Summer on the Lakes* is not. . . . [In *Woman in the Nineteenth Century*] Fuller was discovering not just her style, but her material. Significantly, Fuller's subject was current events—history, not literature. The literary criticism she did for Greeley represents some of her best work, but she had done excellent literary criticism for the *Dial*. Her new sense of excitement is felt most vividly in the [*Herald Tribune*] pieces on slavery, prisons, labor. As she extended and deepened her perception of national life, she became increasingly aware that current American pre-eminence was based on abuse of various classes of people, most notably blacks, immigrants (who formed the bulk of the working classes), Indians, and above all, women. She spoke for these groups with force and indignation; her subject was oppression.

Fuller's deepest concern, moreover, lay with the subtle forms of status oppression that she as a woman had always known rather than with brutal and overt economic exploitation. She is at her most compelling and astute in *Summer on the Lakes* when she analyzes the cause of the white man's low estimate of the Indian. "The aversion of the injurer for him he has degraded," Fuller calls it. She was acutely alive to the tragic irony that the whites, in order to justify their own inevitable rapacity and destructiveness, were determined to destroy the Indian's sole remaining possession, his self-respect. *Woman in the Nineteenth Century* revealed that she saw male-female relations as another version of the same dynamic. She was most sensitized, and most indignant, before that part of the rationale of oppression which tells its victim, whether Indian or woman: you merited no better. Her characteristic crusade was against the myths so integral to status oppression: that all Indians are by nature lazy and drunken, that all women are incapable of intellectual effort and naturally seek domestic life. Herself tentatively disavowing an image which she had long confused with her identity, as a journalist Fuller naturally took on a kind of muckraking role: her desire and her claim was to have seen for herself, to be able authoritatively to separate hard "facts" from self-serving "talk."

Fuller's new capacity for self-analysis was manifest in her increasing dislike of the popular forms of "eloquence." As she became more aware of the discrepancy between myth and reality in her society, she grew equally convinced that most Americans did not want to be enlightened; they welcomed a culture of sheer verbosity. The proliferating July Fourth orations of florid self-congratulation infuriated her. On the national birthday in 1845, she issued a counterblast: America has shown "that righteousness is not her chief desire, and her name is no longer a watchword for the highest hopes to the rest of the world," she announced. She was still Timothy Fuller's daughter; her standard was always that set by the American Revolution. In 1845, she lamented: " 'More money! more land' are all the watchwords they [modern Americans] know. They have received the inheritance earned by the fathers of the revolution, without their wisdom and virtue to use it. But this cannot last." Fuller was calling for historical rebirth, "not merely . . . revolution but . . . radical reform," such as she increasingly realized her country could neither provide nor tolerate. Her battle against her culture's substitution of rhetoric for action could not be fought at home. (pp. 340-42)

Fuller responded passionately to Italy from the moment she arrived. . . . [Her] Italy was not the Italy of her predecessors or her contemporaries. Indeed, the culmination of her life work was in her protest against their view of Italy, in her monumental effort in her *Tribune* dispatches and her now-lost history of the Roman republic to translate Italy for Americans from the realm of "literature" back into the realm of "history." (p. 344)

[In her newspaper dispatches from Italy] Fuller wielded the oratorical tradition in which she had been trained with new skill and authority. She had never been more rhetorically impressive than when she passionately redeemed the legacy of the founding fathers by translating it in terms of the socialism which had become her creed:

> There is no peace. . . . It would appear that the political is being merged in the social struggle: it is well. Whatever blood is to be shed, whatever altars cast down, those tremendous problems must be solved, whatever be the cost! . . . to you, people of America, it may perhaps be given to look on and learn in time for a preventive wisdom. . . . You may, despite the apes of the past who strive to tutor you, learn the needs of a true democracy. You may in time learn to reverence . . . the true aristocracy of the nation, the only real nobles—the LABORING CLASSES.

At her finest moments in her late dispatches, Fuller went beyond rhetoric to achieve an "eloquence" more genuine than any which had marked her transcendental period. Here is her memorable description of Rome after the French occupation:

> I . . . entered the French ground, all mapped and hollowed like a honeycomb. A pair of skeleton legs protruded from a bank of one bari-

cade; lower, a dog had scratched away [the] light covering of earth from the body of a man, and discovered it lying face upward all dressed; the dog stood gazing on it with an air of stupid amazement.

The change is a simple but crucial one. Fuller is no longer wordy. More confident of her identity, she no longer needs to flood her subject with herself. She has learned the style of understatement in which facts are allowed to speak for themselves.

In the last years of her life, Fuller no longer thought of her work as critical or even journalistic, but as "historical." She never fully defined these terms, but it is possible to guess at her meaning. She was always moved by the great achievements of art, and the architecture and painting of Italy gave her intense pleasure. Yet she was proud to measure the distance between herself and her culture when she could write a friend at home that she, a woman, found "art . . . not important to me now." To judge this remark rightly, one must put it in its cultural context. At the time Fuller was working on her (now lost) account of the Roman Revolution in 1849 and 1850, other American feminine writers had already published travelogues like Lydia Huntley Sigourney's *Pleasant Memories of Pleasant Lands* (1842), thin pastiches of quotation-laden eulogies and reminiscences of encounters with literary lions. . . . Little wonder that Fuller exulted that she would return to America from revolution-torn Europe, not perhaps more "cultured," but "possessed of a great history." In her mind, "art" was somehow bad, "history" somehow good; that she felt little need to amplify such a painfully simplified view is a measure of her society, her own antagonism to its values, and the energy she devoted to the expression and maintenance of her anger. She clearly believed that "art" was increasingly functioning in American culture as a diversion from the pressing problem of the socio-economic order, and that "history" suggested active participation in the revolutionary changes necessary to transform and better that order. For distinctions more complex and more profound than these, she had no time. (pp. 345-47)

*Ann Douglas, "Margaret Fuller and the Disavowal of Fiction," in her* The Feminization of American Culture *(copyright © 1977 by Ann Douglas; reprinted by permission of Alfred A. Knopf, Inc.), Knopf, 1977 (and reprinted by Avon Books, 1978, pp. 313-48).*

## MARGARET VANDERHAAR ALLEN (essay date 1979)

[Fuller's] gift for poetic communication seldom found an effective voice in her poems. Many other Transcendentalists, like Fuller, aspired to poetry but succeeded in prose. Her lyric poems are often moralistic or pious, filled with undigested sadness and dejection. Unable to break out of eighteenth-century diction and conventions, she disparaged her verses as "all rhetorical and impassioned." . . . Fuller knew that much of her poetry was occasional poetry and said that "for us lesser people [she meant less than geniuses like Goethe or Byron], who write verses merely as vents for the overflowings of a personal experience," it is inexcusable to take the public for a confidant by means of autobiographical poetry not sufficiently universalized and objectified to be of lasting merit. . . . As always, Fuller's self-criticism was too harsh. The passion and tension in **"The Captured Wild Horse,"** the delicate harmony of **"To Miss R.B.,"** the good-humored self-mockery in **"Imperfect Thoughts,"** and the frank paganism and rationalism of

**"Thoughts on Sunday Morning,"** to mention only a few, make them well worth reading.

Fuller's infatuation with the German Romantics probably contributed to her inability to find a wholly satisfying form for her utterance. Many German Romantics spoke as she did of dissatisfaction with "mere" words, a wish to go beyond existing forms and wield "an enchanter's mirror." . . . Fuller, in describing the kind of poetry she wanted to write, was describing something like the poetry that the French Symbolists developed later in the century. . . . [She] anticipated the Symbolists. Once again her ideas were far ahead of her time. But she could not write the poetry she envisioned. "In earlier years I aspired to wield the sceptre or the lyre; for I loved with wise design and irresistible command to mould many to one purpose, and it seemed all that man could desire to breathe in music and speak in words, the harmonies of the universe. But the golden lyre was not given to my hand, and I am but the prophecy of a poet." (pp. 70-1)

For Fuller ever to have produced a body of finished work of high artistic standards, she would have had to discipline herself in ways for which she was neither inclined nor prepared. When Poe admonished her for slovenly grammar and carelessness with detail, he did so justly. Fuller lacked a formal education, particularly in writing, where mastery comes easily to no one. . . .

Fuller's carelessness with detail often makes her writing seem impromptu, or amateurish. She knew how far short she fell of her own standards. "How can I ever write with this impatience of detail? I shall never be an artist; I have no patient love of execution; I am delighted with my sketch, but if I try to finish it, I am chilled. Never was there a great sculptor who did not love to chip the marble." (p. 72)

Fuller's unwillingness or inability to execute a longer work made the essay or some other short form inevitable. Though the essay allows a more personal, less systematized writing, she found it unsatisfying. "What a vulgarity there seems in this writing for the multitude," she once exclaimed. "We know not yet, have not made ourselves known to a single soul, and shall we address those still more unknown? Shall we multiply our connections and thus make them still more superficial?" (p. 73)

Although she remained unsatisfied with the form of the journalistic essay, and although she continued to regard inspiration as necessary to produce works of enduring merit, she did produce "something excellent" in her *Tribune* work. The best essays have maturity, breadth of viewpoint, command of subject, and incisiveness of language. Fuller criticized Emerson for being aloof, remote, otherworldly. And although her own writing expressed a deepened understanding of the world and a compassionate involvement in it, she still evaluated it by the elitist criteria of her refined New England literary acquaintances; she lamented the failure of her work to meet standards that she had outgrown. Fuller's severe self-criticism and her disparagement of her work thus encouraged posterity to think of her writings as an inferior footnote to the annals of her life.

Fuller's obvious limitations as a writer should not blind us to her strengths. She had not mastered long written forms, but she commanded the vivid, succinct sentence; she ranks with the best writers of her age as an epigrammatist. Her style was vigorous, forceful, and persuasive, as Poe said. And she exercised her descriptive powers and sense of drama not only in her public writings but in her letters and private journals as

well. Her letters and journals have been published only in fragments, often so heavily interpolated (as in the *Memoirs*) that their essential qualities are blurred by editorial judgments. These private writings half-reveal, half-create both her inner life and her sense of the life around her, in all its hidden struggles, its drama and flashes of meaning and moments of exaltation and structurelessness and boredom—the process itself, inescapably personal, not the abstraction from the process.

In the best of Fuller's prose, thought comes alive. Her mind worked in harmony with her emotions and nerves and senses, as well as her abstract reasoning faculties. Rarely does she fail to illuminate her chosen subject. Often she uses the exhortatory mode, a characteristic of most Transcendentalists' style, which probably grew out of their consciousness of being intellectual and cultural missionaries, and out of their pervasive clericalism, which found its proper element in the sermon. But even when exhorting, Fuller's writing is a product of a keenly conscious intelligence, "one of those on whom nothing is lost," in Henry James's famous phrase. (pp. 73-4)

Fuller's use of the metaphor best reveals her essentially poetic imagination. She had that image-making faculty, the eye for resemblances that Aristotle called the hallmark of the true poet, the one indispensable gift that cannot be imparted by anyone else. Fuller invariably used metaphor to tell her meaning. In her poorer work the metaphors are murky, high-flown, or strained in effect, but in her best writing they are controlled, pointed, and clarifying.

For example, when revolution was brewing in Europe and the United States was convulsed with tensions rising out of slavery and the Mexican War, she wrote:

> Altogether, it looks as if a great time was coming, and that time one of democracy. Our country will play a ruling part. Her eagle will lead the van; but whether to soar upward to the sun or to stoop for helpless prey, who now dares promise? At present she has scarce achieved a Roman nobleness, a Roman liberty; and whether her eagle is less like the vulture, and more like the Phoenix, than was the fierce Roman bird, we dare not say. May the new year give hopes of the latter, even if the bird need first to be purified by fire.

The bird image changes from eagle to vulture to phoenix: because each of these birds is strong, dominating, and impressive, inspiring awe or respect, the image points up America's importance and leadership position among nations. In metamorphosis, the image evokes national pride (the noble, aspiring eagle), anger and disgust (the predatory vulture), and hope for the future after purification by fire, which prophesied the Civil War. (pp. 74-5)

Like other Transcendentalist writers, Fuller took most of her analogies from nature. . . . It is a mistake to look to her writing for the Thoreauvian or Wordsworthian style; she neither deifies nature nor embraces it as an escape from social intercourse. But no one who reads [*Summer on the Lakes*], her journals, or her poems can miss her awareness and love of nature. She often seemed self-conscious when trying to focus *primarily* on nature, and the self-consciousness damages the effect. She wrote best of the natural world seeing it interwoven with human thought, human activity, and human feeling—not as a mere backdrop, but as an essential nourishing and esthetic element of life. Thus, though Emerson made supercilious judgments about Fuller as a nature writer, he did not see how essentially nature entered her writing, as a constant source of metaphor on which she drew to illuminate even the most abstract subjects. . . . (pp. 75-6)

Fuller was the prophecy of a poet, not a fully realized one, but she did not fail as a writer. Because of its vitality and power to excite, much of her work ranks with the best discursive prose of her age. An important purpose of writing is to communicate interior life, and with the publication of her journals and letters, we will at last be able to balance public statement with private expression and understand what Fuller was trying to tell us. That her writings have lapsed into obscurity is a misfortune they do not deserve. In Margaret Fuller's writings I have found endless illumination, disquiet, and delight, for they show me the world through her eyes, mind, and emotions. (p. 77)

> *Margaret Vanderhaar Allen, in her* The Achievement of Margaret Fuller (*copyright © 1979 by The Pennsylvania State University*), *The Pennsylvania State University Press, University Park, 1979, 212 p.*

## MARIE MITCHELL OLESEN URBANSKI (essay date 1980)

[*In the following excerpt from her full-length study of* Woman in the Nineteenth Century, *Urbanski asserts that Fuller's feminist treatise is not as formless as some critics maintain; rather, it "partakes of the major characteristics of transcendental art." Urbanski discusses Fuller's syllogistic reasoning, her subjectivity, and her reliance on oratorical rather than written tradition in writing* Woman in the Nineteenth Century.]

The first impression a reader may get from a hasty perusal of Margaret Fuller's *Woman in the Nineteenth Century* is one of effusiveness and formlessness. Containing a display of erudition that is impressive, it is prolix, as was the work of many transcendentalists and other writers of the past century. . . . In the midst of its verbosity, it is still possible to see more of a pattern in *Woman* than has been maintained [by critics]. Its basic structure is that of the sermon, which is appropriate, because *Woman*'s message is hortatory. Its complexity and apparent lack of form are due to its dual nature. Within the sermon framework, *Woman* partakes of the major characteristics of transcendental literary art. (p. 128)

According to precepts generally accepted by the transcendentalists, a work of literature grows out of experience and hence is organic. As Coleridge, a romantic, wrote: "The organic form is innate; it shapes, as it develops itself from within." And Keats, using a nature metaphor, explained that good poetry grew as naturally as the leaves on a tree. Emerson later used this concept, saying a poem is "a thought so passionate and alive that like the spirit of a plant or an animal it has an architecture of its own." The basic assumption of transcendental art is of the "superiority of the spirit to the letter." Art as inspiration meant that the word became one with the thing. Ultimately, the "transcendental theory of art is a theory of knowledge and religion as well." Hence transcendental expression must coalesce the seer and spectacle into one, an organic whole. Margaret Fuller, the observer, united the spectacle—her experience—with that of all other women into the final fusion of *Woman in the Nineteenth Century*. (pp. 134-35)

As early as 1826 Sampson Reed published his "Observations on the Growth of Mind," setting forth transcendental literary thought. He wrote: "Syllogistic reasoning is passing away," leaving nothing behind but a demonstration "of its own worth-

lessness." Both Julia Ward Howe and Arthur W. Brown pointed out that there was no systematic parallelism in *Woman;* however, Fuller did not intend that there should be. By not following a rigidly organized pattern of syllogistic reasoning, she was merely demonstrating that she had accepted the transcendentalist aesthetic theory that, as a member of the club, she had helped to shape. The movement of her treatise is not parallel but soaring and circular. Its dominant mode of composition is an unfolding from the subconscious in a form of spiraling thought patterns. One of her recurrent themes is an optimistic refrain that appears in a mood of confidence, disappears in a burst of admonition, and later reappears in a form of wavelike undulation characteristic of transcendental writing. Moreover, the polarities of optimistic expectation (symbolized by the epigraph, "The Earth waits for her Queen") and impatient anger (symbolized by, "Frailty, thy name is Woman") have an ebb and flow rhythm to them. She may begin in a lull with a mundane matter such as the problem of a poor widow whose husband has died leaving no will and accelerate in intensity to the sublime "ravishing harmony of the spheres," or start at the crest of the wave as it flows back to the sea. From practical application of her sermon, the thought patterns of *Woman* soar back to the world of the spirit. Instead of syllogistic reasoning, order comes from the authority that the certitude of intuition brings.

A characteristic of transcendental literature, which *Woman* reflects, is subjectivity—the individual as the center of the world. At times this method suggests a free association of ideas. One authority requires that another be included; one mythological figure suggests another. Ultimately the thought patterns lead from the conscious, to the subconscious mind, to the transcendental wellspring of truth, the divine intuition. Fuller used her own experience as representative of the experience of all women—that indeed the lot of woman is sad, that all women need and, in fact, should aspire to the same self-culture and fulfillment that she herself had desired. She began *Woman* by using the conventional "we" but she changed to "I" after only fifteen pages. Later she alternated between "we" and "I." She gave an account of her youthful education by her father under the guise of the persona, Miranda, as an example of an independent girl who was respected for being self-reliant. Fuller told this story by means of an imaginary conversation in which the "I" takes the role of the foil to Miranda's explanation of her youthful training in self-reliance, so unusual for a girl of that day. . . . In her subjectivity there are times when she almost linked herself with the queen that the earth awaits. If not the queen directly, she associated herself in her description of Miranda with the woman of genius, possessor of the magnetic electrical element (intuition), who has a contribution to make to the world—"a strong electric nature, which repelled those who did not belong to her, and attracted those who did." . . . By looking into her own soul, she saw reflected there the problems and the frustrated aspirations of other women: "but what concerns me now is, that my life be a beautiful, powerful, in a word, a complete life in its kind. Had I but one more moment to live I must wish the same." . . . Starting from her own angle of vision, she unfolded her hopes to the world, and she concluded her treatise as a prophet:

> I stand in the sunny noon of life. Objects no longer glitter in the dews of morning, neither are yet softened by the shadows of evening. Every spot is seen, every chasm revealed. Climbing the dusty hill, some fair effigies that once stood for symbols of human destiny have

been broken; those I still have with me show defects in this broad light. Yet enough is left, even by experience, to point distinctly to the glories of that destiny; faint, but not to be mistaken streaks of the future day. . . .

Thus her subjectivity became universal as she linked her own experience to that of the experience of all women and prophesied that in the future life would be better for them.

The tone of *Woman* reinforces the idea that Fuller was writing a didactic work. At times the tone admonishes the audience to act; at other times it is declamatory, but dominantly it is conversational. Although its voice patterns are conversational, the archness of Fuller's diction and tone is transcendental. Today, the mannerism of Fuller's speaking style may sound affected. Nevertheless, many people who knew Fuller said that her chief talent was as a speaker, so it is not surprising that instead of syllogisms, many phrases contain the emotive power of a conversation, of which she would have been the star. Her writing technique included both questions and answers in a debate form, but it also revealed the hallmark of the accomplished conversationalist: a flair for the dramatic. At best her conversational technique suggests breathless ejaculations rather than sentences. In a kind of accelerating excitement, she used the hortatory style: "Let us be wise, and not impede the soul. Let her work as she will. Let us have one creative energy, one incessant revelation. Let it take what form it will, and let us not bind it by the past to man or woman, black or white. Jove sprang from Rhea, Pallas from Jove. So let it be." . . . Then her tone changes to one of intimacy. Her writing sounds as if she were talking to a small group and studying the reaction of her audience. (pp. 135-37)

In effect, [Fuller often] seemed to be anticipating objections. Her most famous suggestion combines a speaking conversational style with her flair for dramatization: "But if you ask me what offices they may fill, I reply—any. I do not care what case you put; let them be sea-captains, if you will." . . . Her frequent use of dashes suggests the pause used by accomplished speakers. (p. 138)

Whether that of a preacher, orator, or confidante, the tone of *Woman* expresses the spoken word. Hence many of Fuller's images relate to sound. . . . She used music as a means of expressing the divine: "Then their sweet singing shall not be from passionate impulse, but the lyrical overflow of a divine rapture, and a new music shall be evolved from this many-chorded world." . . . Or she saw woman as a bird with clipped wings that desires to fly and sing: "no need to clip the wings of any bird that wants to soar and sing." . . . That she frequently preferred sound imagery to that of sight is again indicated by her final poem:

> For the Power to whom we bow
> Has given its pledge that, if not now,
> They of pure and steadfast mind,
> By faith exalted, truth refined,
> *Shall* hear all music loud and clear,
> Whose first notes they ventured here. . . .

Another type of rhetorical device that Fuller often used is imagery derived from organicism, which implies movement, growth, expansion, or fruition. Her argument rested on the "law of growth." She used phrases such as *ampler fruition, fruitful summer,* or *plants of great vigor will always struggle into blossom*. She liked movement related to the life force symbolized by the heart: "I must beat my own pulse true in

the heart of the world; for *that* is virtue, excellence, health." . . . And the cycles of nature—the flowing of streams, the waxing moon, and noon-morning-dawn imagery—are favorites.

Yet despite her frequent choice of auditory and organic imagery, her work's salient characteristic is its great use of references to literature, history, religion, and mythology. These references are used primarily as an exemplar for her readers to emulate, as recognized authority to support her topic, or as allusions to Holy Writ.

Since the structure of *Woman* is sermon-like, Fuller used biblical allusions as the major support for her near-rhapsodic religious vision of the great potentialities of men and women. She derived her thematic exhortation—"Be ye perfect"—from Matthew 5:48, from which she deleted "therefore." On occasion she quoted directly from the Bible: "This is the Law and the Prophets. Knock and it shall be opened; seek and ye shall find." . . . From traditional Christian theology she derived a reference to the deadly sin of sloth. Phrases that connote Calvinism, such as "doomed in future stages of his own being to deadly penance," can be found in *Woman*. Elements of the providential doctrine appear: "Yet, by men in this country, as by the Jews, when Moses was leading them to the promised land, everything has been done that inherited depravity could do, to hinder the promise of Heaven from its fulfillment." . . . (pp. 138-40)

Fuller employed biblical and religious allusions in the usual way to clarify meaning and as the wellsprings of her treatise. In addition, she cited contemporary writers—feminists, socialists, and transcendentalists—to buttress her argument that women could play a broader role in society. Her use of allusions to outstanding women from all recorded time, however, was complex. Their use is not an affectation but an intrinsic part of her way of thinking and the rhetorical method she adopted in order to make her point. Her allusions not only clarify her meaning but also serve as models of conduct to inspire or instruct women. Examples used as affirmations are taken from poetry, such as Britomart; from history, such as Aspasia; from mythology, such as Isis and Iduna or Sita in the *Ramayana;* from folklore, such as Cinderella; or from more contemporary life, such as the Polish Countess Emily Plater. Instead of cataloging lists of words, as Emerson suggested and Whitman did, her technique was to catalog women. She barely escaped creating an encyclopedic effect because she appears not to have wanted to leave anyone out. She admitted she "may have been guilty of much repetition." . . . It could be argued that Fuller should have been more selective, but on the other hand, through sheer weight of numbers, the women cited from the ages become a catalog that is an evocation, a challenge to men to remove "arbitrary barriers" through proof that women can succeed. (pp. 140-41)

[Fuller's] plethora of examples represents a remarkable amount of scholarship, and [she] delved into countless sources in her search for answers. Although written in nineteenth-century language with some words as outmoded as *purity* and *delicacy* and a conversational style that might be considered affected, her work is surprisingly modern in its concepts. Her brilliant treatise presents and prefigures such modern ideas as the need for role models. Fuller searched beyond Judeo-Christian patriarchy for the feminine principle and the earth mother. She posited an androgenic quality in all people, a need to do away with sexual stereotyping. In essence, Fuller's creation becomes the archetype of woman, of "The Woman in the Nineteenth

Century," and of any woman who has aspired, who has wondered and been thwarted but who has still refused to compromise. Fuller's archetypal woman knows that in any compromise, she compromises not only herself but everyone else as well; and that men who become exploiters suffer and lose their humanity themselves.

As with all scholarly and complex literature, reading **Woman** calls for active participation from readers. Also, since **Woman** is a highly suggestive work, readers must be receptive to its message. Both Edgar Allan Poe [see excerpt above, 1846] and Henry David Thoreau said that Fuller's writing and speaking voice were one. A careful scrutiny of **Woman** reveals the dynamism and insights that Fuller's conversation praised, and readers who are willing to become engaged in the profundity of her thought processes will be amply rewarded.

Essentially **Woman** is an affirmation, a witness to the possibilities within women and men who discover within themselves their spirituality and permit it to grow. It is a call for excellence. The first obstruction, the self, is on trial. Beginning with the individual, who must take responsibility for her or his own life, **Woman** envisions a world that would correspondingly reflect this changed self. Ultimately, **Woman** transcends the issue of woman's rights. Paradoxically, after preaching self-reliance for women, it becomes a philosophic message on the interdependence of all people.

*Woman in the Nineteenth Century*'s philosophic framework is predicated on universals; principles of right and wrong do indeed exist. Margaret Fuller was not ashamed to preach because she believed an individual could reshape her or his life—in fact, could approach perfection. (pp. 143-44)

As the major inspiration of the feminist movement of the nineteenth century, Fuller engendered ideas that were catalytic to those who followed her. Many of her concepts are surprisingly modern. Due to the influence of Jung, much of the later twentieth-century literary criticism has been concerned with the use of myth. Fuller's **Woman,** which explored Scandinavian, classical, and biblical myths as a method of explaining the complexity of the human personality, is a precursor of mythic study. Psychologically intuitive, she understood the androgenous nature of sexuality and the conflict between women's need to love and their need for artistic expression, which often thwarted creative women. Her interest in Fourier is significant because of his psychological form of socialism, which considered an individual's emotional needs as important as his physical needs. **Woman** is of contemporary value as a starting point for feminist consciousness raising. Each woman is prompted to look within herself, at her past, and at her future goals. Ultimately it involves male consciousness raising, too, as a man is given to understand that he becomes psychically crippled when he enslaves others. (pp. 169-70)

Margaret Fuller realized that ultimately she represented the meaning of the transcendental age:

> The destiny of each human being is no doubt great and peculiar, however obscure its rudiments to our present sight, but there are also in every age a few in whose lot the meaning of that age is concentrated. I feel that I am one of those persons in my age and sex. I feel chosen among women. I have deep mystic feelings in myself and intimations from elsewhere.

She incarnates the transcendental age. Her life and her work express American aspirations at their loftiest. Her **Woman** em-

bodies the early American hope for a new Eden, the innocent ideal that, based on right principles, a just society is possible. (p. 170)

**Woman** is more than just a successful piece of protest propaganda that served its purpose as a means of arousing public opinion in its day. It has much to offer present and future generations of readers. Of all of the feminist writing, it is the most complex and the most spiritual. *Woman in the Nineteenth Century* most clearly delineates that it is in the interest of men as well as women that woman be able to fulfill herself. . . . (pp. 170-71)

> *Marie Mitchell Olesen Urbanski, in her* Margaret Fuller's "Woman in the Nineteenth Century": A Literary Study of Form and Content, of Sources and Influence *(copyright © 1980 by Marie Mitchell Olesen Urbanski; reprinted by permission of Greenwood Press, a Division of Congressional Information Service, Inc., Westport, CT), Greenwood Press, 1980, 189 p.*

## ADDITIONAL BIBLIOGRAPHY

Alcott, A. Bronson. "Margaret Fuller." In his *Concord Days,* pp. 77-9. Boston: Roberts Brothers, 1888.
> Brief appreciation of Fuller as a thinker and an advocate of women.

Anthony, Katharine. *Margaret Fuller: A Psychological Biography.* New York: Harcourt, Brace and Co., 1921, 220 p.
> A Freudian interpretation of Fuller's life that is too specialized and speculative to be a completely reliable factual source.

Barbour, Frances M. "Margaret Fuller and the British Reviewers." *New England Quarterly* (December 1936): 618-25.
> Briefly assesses coverage of Fuller in the British press from 1846 to 1852. Barbour notes that only one reviewer acknowledged Fuller's critical acumen and that the majority of commentators stressed Fuller's personality rather than her writing.

Bell, Margaret. *Margaret Fuller.* New York: Charles Boni, 1930, 320 p.
> A fictionalized biography, notable chiefly for Eleanor Roosevelt's brief introduction which warmly praises Fuller and her work.

Blanchard, Paula. *Margaret Fuller: From Transcendentalism to Revolution.* New York: Delacorte Press, 1978, 370 p.
> Thorough general biography written from a feminist viewpoint. Blanchard's expressed purpose is to expose modern readers to Fuller, to correct the distortions about Fuller's public image, and to view Fuller's life "through the eyes of another woman, living in the 1970s, with an awareness of the questions raised about women in the past decade."

Braun, Frederick August. *Margaret Fuller and Goethe.* New York: Henry Holt and Co., 1910, 271 p.*
> A study of Goethe's influence on Fuller's personal and intellectual development. Braun also discusses Fuller's interpretation of Goethe's works and her role in introducing German literature and culture to the United States.

Brooks, Van Wyck. "Alcott, Margaret Fuller, Brook Farm." In his *The Flowering of New England: 1815-1865,* rev. ed., pp. 228-51. New York: E. P. Dutton & Co., 1940.*
> Brief, laudatory account of Fuller's life and career, focusing on the romantic aspects of her nature.

Brown, Arthur W. *Margaret Fuller.* Twayne's United States Authors Series, edited by Sylvia E. Bowman. New York: Twayne Publishers, Inc., 1964, 159 p.
> A biographical study which attempts to present a balanced portrait of Fuller as a critic, journalist, reformer, and notorious person-

ality. Brown's was among the first studies to credit Fuller for her pioneering work as a journalist.

Chevigny, Bell Gale. *The Woman and the Myth: Margaret Fuller's Life and Writings.* Old Westbury, N.Y.: The Feminist Press, 1976, 500 p.

An anthology containing Fuller's own writings, her contemporaries' writings on her, and Chevigny's informative commentary. The collection is designed to trace "the struggle to conceive and act out of free womanhood, by showing how . . . Fuller construed her problem and by examining, one at a time, the various identities she assumed in an effort to resolve the struggle."

Clarke, James Freeman. *The Letters of James Freeman Clarke to Margaret Fuller.* Edited by John Wesley Thomas. Hamburg: Cram, de Gruyter & Co., 1957, 147 p.*

Letters from Fuller's lifelong friend and the editor of the journal, *The Western Messenger.* The collection provides valuable biographical information and criticism of Fuller's writing, particularly of her contributions to the *Messenger.*

Deiss, Joseph Jay. *The Roman Years of Margaret Fuller.* New York: Thomas Y. Crowell Co., 1969, 338 p.

Detailed account of Fuller's years in Italy, especially noteworthy since these had been covered less thoroughly in the earlier biographies. In depicting the personal and political events of her Roman years, Deiss quotes frequently from Fuller's travel letters to the *Tribune.*

Frothingham, Octavius Brooks. "The Critic: Margaret Fuller." In his *Transcendentalism in New England: A History,* pp. 284-301. New York: G. P. Putnam's Sons, 1886.

Concise biographical and critical portrait containing many passages from the writings of Fuller and her contemporaries.

Greeley, Horace. "Margaret Fuller." In his *Recollections of a Busy Life,* pp. 169-91. New York: J. B. Ford and Co., 1868.

Biographical sketch and reminiscence by Fuller's editor at the *Tribune.*

Hawthorne, Julian. *Nathaniel Hawthorne and His Wife, Vol. I.* Boston: Ticknor and Co., 1884, 505 p.*

Biography of Nathaniel and Sophia Hawthorne by their son, including several references to Fuller, notably Nathaniel Hawthorne's well-known letter deriding "clownish" Giovanni Ossoli and terming Fuller a "great humbug." The letter, which had been expurgated from earlier editions of Hawthorne's journals, prompted articles in defence of Fuller in several publications.

Higginson, Thomas Wentworth. *Margaret Fuller Ossoli.* Rev. ed. Boston: Houghton, Mifflin and Co., 1892, 323 p.

A general account of Fuller's life that helped to correct the distortions of her *Memoirs.* This book was first published in 1884.

Howe, Julia Ward. *Margaret Fuller, Marchesa Ossoli.* Boston: Little, Brown, and Co., 1905, 298 p.

A sympathetic portrait of Fuller's character and personality, first published in 1883.

MacPhail, Andrew. "Margaret Fuller." In his *Essays in Puritanism,* pp. 116-67. London: T. Fisher Unwin, 1905.

A sardonic assessment of Fuller's life and career. Although he does credit her with "courage, good sense, and insight" in her literary criticism, MacPhail chides Fuller and her associates for perpetrating a romantic myth about Fuller's life.

Myerson, Joel, ed. *Margaret Fuller: An Annotated Secondary Bibliography.* New York: Burt Franklin & Co., 1977, 272 p.

An authoritative listing of books, essays, articles, and incidental pieces published about Fuller, from her time through 1975.

Myerson, Joel, ed. *Margaret Fuller: A Descriptive Bibliography.* Pittsburgh: University of Pittsburgh Press, 1978, 163 p.

Complete bibliography of Fuller's own writings, including her contributions to newspapers and periodicals.

Myerson, Joel, ed. *Critical Essays on Margaret Fuller.* Critical Essays on American Literature, edited by James Nagel. Boston: G. K. Hall & Co., 1980, 289 p.

An anthology of reviews and studies of Fuller written by her earliest commentators as well as modern scholars, including Edgar Allan Poe, James Russell Lowell, Granville Hicks and Martin Duberman. The comments are often biographical and personal and reflect the tone of the majority of Fuller criticism. Myerson's introduction offers a good overview of the history of criticism of Fuller.

Rosenthal, Bernard. "*The Dial,* Transcendentalism and Margaret Fuller." *English Language Notes* VIII (September 1970): 28-36.

A discussion of the content and policies of *The Dial* during Fuller's tenure as editor. Rosenthal asserts that *The Dial* does not reflect New England Transcendentalist thought in general. He notes that "it instead largely reflects one extraordinary woman's intellectual interests."

Showalter, Elaine. "Women Writers and the Double Standard." In *Woman in Sexist Society,* edited by Vivian Gornick and Barbara K. Moran, pp. 323-43. New York, London: Basic Books, 1971.*

An analysis of critical responses to women writers in the nineteenth century. Although it does not specifically deal with American literature, the study provides an understanding of the social, intellectual, and moral prejudices that these female authors faced.

Smith, Bernard. "The Criticism of Romance." In his *Forces in American Criticism: A Study in the History of American Literary Thought,* pp. 66-113. New York: Harcourt Brace Jovanovich, 1939.*

An early, appreciative appraisal of Fuller as a critic. Smith praises her "sound judgment and good taste," and describes her best criticism as "more nearly in the direction of modern thought than the 'sane,' uninspired, unadventurous essays of the respectable pendants and journalists of her day."

Wade, Mason. *Margaret Fuller: Whetstone of Genius.* New York: The Viking Press, 1940, 304 p.

Well-written, general biography, although lacking complete footnotes to sources. Recent commentators have noted Wade's bias against Fuller's "masculine" nature; nonetheless, this remains one of the clearest and most comprehensive of modern Fuller biographies.

Wellek, René. "The Minor Transcendentalists and German Philosophy." *New England Quarterly* XV, No. 4 (December 1942): 652-80.*

A study of the relationship between German philosophy and the minor New England Transcendentalists, including a brief discussion of Fuller. This article concludes that her interest in German thought was aesthetic, rather than philosophical.

Wellisz, Leopold. *The Friendship of Margaret Fuller D'Ossoli and Adam Mickiewicz.* New York: Polish Book Importing Co., 1947, 40 p.*

An account of Fuller's relationship with the Polish poet and professor, Adam Mickiewicz, based on ten letters from their correspondence.

# Elizabeth Cleghorn Gaskell

## 1810-1865

(Born Elizabeth Cleghorn Stevenson; also wrote under the pseudonym of Cotton Mather Mills, Esquire) English novelist, biographer, novella, sketch, and short story writer, poet, and essayist.

One of the most popular writers of the Victorian era, Gaskell is principally remembered today for her achievements in the minor English classics *Cranford* and *Wives and Daughters: An Every-day Story*. Gaskell's early fame was established by *Mary Barton: A Tale of Manchester Life,* in which she spurred the conscience of industrial England by truthfully depicting the suffering and disillusionment of Manchester working people during the 1830s and 1840s. While *Mary Barton* retains interest as a social novel, critics consider *Cranford* and *Wives and Daughters* to be her finest artistic achievements. In these novels, Gaskell united her considerable powers of observation with genial humor and gentle pathos to create portraits of early nineteenth-century provincial life that are considered to be among the best in English letters.

Gaskell's fiction was deeply influenced by her upbringing and by her marriage. When Gaskell was an infant, her mother died, and she was raised by her maternal aunt in Knutsford, a small Cheshire village that served as the prototype for the rural societies that she depicted in *Cranford, Wives and Daughters,* and numerous short stories and novellas. In 1832, she married William Gaskell, a Unitarian clergyman, with whom she collaborated on the poem "Sketches among the Poor" in 1837. Gaskell's involvement in her husband's ministry in industrial Manchester inspired her first novel, *Mary Barton*. This sympathetic and accurate depiction of the plight of Manchester's destitute factory population won Gaskell a large, admiring audience. Charles Dickens, John Ruskin, Thomas Carlyle and other renowned contemporaries cultivated her friendship. Two years after *Mary Barton* appeared, Gaskell contributed the short story *Lizzie Leigh: A Domestic Tale* to the first number of Dickens's journal, *Household Words*. Throughout the next two decades, many of Gaskell's novels, novellas, essays, and short stories appeared in *Household Words* as well as Dickens's other journal, *All the Year Round*.

Two controversies troubled Gaskell's literary career. In 1853 she offended many of her readers with *Ruth*, an exploration of seduction and illegitimacy. Although critics praised the soundness of the novel's moral lessons, several members of Gaskell's church congregation burned the book, and it was banned in many libraries. Following the 1857 release of *The Life of Charlotte Brontë*, she was charged with misrepresentation. When her sensational account of Branwell Brontë's involvement with a married woman could not be substantiated, she issued a public apology; her publishers removed the biography from circulation, and its most offensive passages were revised. As Brontë's friend of three years, Gaskell had relied on Charlotte's own accounts for much of the material in the book. She was mortified by the allegations of dishonesty, and did not attempt another full-length work until 1863. Although Gaskell's subsequent works were all well received, *Wives and Daughters* was most highly praised. This serialized novel was near completion when Gaskell died in 1865.

Compassion for human frailty and suffering and faith in mutual understanding as a vehicle of reconciliation are the trademarks of Gaskell's "social novels." Along with a realism free of sentimentality, these characteristics give particular power to *Mary Barton* and *North and South*, in which Gaskell explored the issues dividing the manufacturing and working classes of Manchester in the 1830s and 1840s. *Ruth* applies the principles of Christian love to moral and social dilemmas, compelling readers, as an early reviewer noted, "to recognize, to love and reverence God's grace in the sinner." While some feel that it is marred by prolixity and a sometimes cloying pathos—shortcomings noted in all of Gaskell's social novels—many critics compare *Mary Barton* favorably with Benjamin Disraeli's *Sybil* and Charles Kingsley's *Alton Locke*, its closest counterparts in Victorian social literature.

In her later fiction, Gaskell subdued the pathos of the social novels. Uniting her refined sensibility with light, ironic humor, she produced a genial narrative tone which complemented her portraits of small provincial communities. "Mr. Harrison's Confessions" and *My Lady Ludlow* are the best-known shorter works of this kind, while *Cranford* and *Wives and Daughters* are the most important and popular novels. In these works, the gradual accretion of commonplace details of everyday life replaces the customary formal properties of plot and structure. Characters are therefore especially prominent in the provincial stories, and critics have singled out Cynthia Kirkpatrick of *Wives and Daughters* and *Cranford*'s Miss Matty as Gaskell's finest creations. Graphic, sensuous descriptions of the English countryside grace her pictures of rural life. For the evocative beauty of the physical settings described in *Sylvia's Lovers*, *Cousin Phillis*, and *The Life of Charlotte Brontë*, Gaskell is often compared with Thomas Hardy.

Gaskell's critics have been consistent in their enthusiasm for individual works such as *Cranford*, *Wives and Daughters*, and *Cousin Phillis*, but they continue to debate the extent and nature of her overall achievement. Early critics cited charm, femininity, and truthfulness as her chief assets, qualities that are more personal than artistic. This attitude prevailed into the early 1930s, when T. S. Eliot stated that Gaskell had made "a literary virtue" out of "simple goodness." Succeeding commentators portrayed her as an occasionally brilliant minor artist whose creative potential was limited by submission to Victorian mores. Influenced by several major studies of Gaskell's life and works published in the 1960s, critics are currently engaged in a reassessment of her achievement, relying on close analysis of the thematic and structural dimensions of her art.

While scholars continue to debate the precise nature of Gaskell's talent, they also reaffirm the singular attractiveness of her best works. Regarded as brilliant by her admirers and merely delightful by her detractors, Gaskell will no doubt continue to command critical attention as a respected minor figure in English letters.

(See also *Dictionary of Literary Biography*, Vol. 21, *Victorian Novelists Before 1885*.)

PRINCIPAL WORKS

"Sketches among the Poor" [with William Gaskell] (poetry) 1837; published in journal *Blackwood's Magazine*
*Mary Barton: A Tale of Manchester Life* (novel) 1848
*Lizzie Leigh: A Domestic Tale* (short story) 1850
*The Moorland Cottage* (novella) 1850
"Mr. Harrison's Confessions" (short story) 1851; published in journal *The Ladies' Companion*
*Cranford (novel) 1853
*Ruth* (novel) 1853
*Lizzie Leigh and Other Tales* (short stories) 1855
*North and South* (novel) 1855
*The Life of Charlotte Brontë* (biography) 1857
*My Lady Ludlow* (novella) 1858
*Right at Last and Other Tales* (short stories) 1860
*Sylvia's Lovers* (novel) 1863
*Cousin Phillis* (novella) 1864
*Wives and Daughters: An Every-day Story* (unfinished novel) 1866
*The Novels and Tales of Mrs. Gaskell*. 11 vols. (novels, novellas, short stories, poetry, essays, sketches, and biography) 1906-19
*The Letters of Mrs. Gaskell* (letters) 1967

*This work was originally published as a series of sketches in the journal *Household Words* in 1851-53.

---

[ELIZABETH CLEGHORN GASKELL]  (essay date 1848)

[*The following is taken from the preface to* Mary Barton, *in which Gaskell discusses her purposes in writing the novel. Disclaiming knowledge of economic principles, she characterizes her work as an attempt to express the suffering and disillusionment of Manchester's workers.*]

Three years ago I became anxious . . . to employ myself in writing a work of fiction. . . . I had already made a little progress in a tale, the period of which was more than a century ago, and the place on the borders of Yorkshire, when I bethought me how deep might be the romance in the lives of some of those who elbowed me daily in the busy streets of the town in which I resided. I had always felt a deep sympathy with the care-worn men, who looked as if doomed to struggle through their lives in strange alternations between work and want; tossed to and fro by circumstances, apparently in even a greater degree than other men. A little manifestation of this sympathy, and a little attention to the expression of feelings on the part of some of the work-people with whom I was acquainted, had laid open to me the hearts of one or two of the more thoughtful among them; I saw that they were sore and irritable against the rich, the even tenor of whose seemingly happy lives appeared to increase the anguish caused by the lottery-like nature of their own. Whether the bitter complaints made by them of the neglect which they experienced from the prosperous—especially from the masters whose fortunes they had helped to build up—were well-founded or no, it is not for me to judge. It is enough to say, that this belief of the injustice and unkindness which they endure from their fellow-creatures taints what might be resignation to God's will, and turns it to revenge in many of the poor uneducated factory-workers of Manchester.

The more I reflected on this unhappy state of things between those so bound to each other by common interests, as the employers and the employed must ever be, the more anxious I became to give some utterance to the agony which, from time to time, convulses this dumb people; the agony of suffering without the sympathy of the happy, or of erroneously believing that such is the case. If it be an error that the woes, which come with ever returning tide-like flood to overwhelm the workmen in our manufacturing towns, pass unregarded by all but the sufferers, it is at any rate an error so bitter in its consequences to all parties, that whatever public effort can do in the way of merciful deeds, or helpless love in the way of "widow's mites" could do, should be done, and that speedily, to disabuse the work-people of so miserable a misapprehension. At present they seem to me to be left in a state, wherein lamentations and tears are thrown aside as useless, but in which the lips are compressed for curses, and the hands clenched and ready to smite.

I know nothing of Political Economy, or the theories of trade. I have tried to write truthfully; and if my accounts agree or clash with any system, the agreement or disagreement is unintentional. (pp. lxxiii-lxxiv)

> [*Elizabeth Cleghorn Gaskell*], in a preface to her Mary Barton and Other Tales, *Chapman and Hall, 1848 (authorship acknowledged and reprinted in her* The Works of Mrs. Gaskell: "Mary Barton" and Other Tales, Vol. I, *edited by A. W. Ward, Smith, Elder & Co., 1906, pp. lxxiii-lxxiv*).

**MARIA EDGEWORTH**  (letter date 1848)

[*A popular novelist, Edgeworth was one of the many English writers of the period who commented on* Mary Barton. *Subsequent critics such as Samuel Bamford and Edna Lyall (see excerpts below, 1849 and 1897) shared Edgeworth's admiration for Gaskell's depiction of the human costs exacted by industrialization, while others reiterated her criticism that Gaskell overused death as a source of pathos in her fiction (see excerpts below by Marjory A. Bald, 1923, and Anne Kimball Tuell, 1932).]*

[There] is no bodily or mental evil to which flesh is heir which [the author of **Mary Barton**] cannot describe most feelingly—The evils consequent upon over manufacturing or over population or both conjoined and acting as cause and effect—the misery and the hateful passions engendered by the love of gain and the accumulation of riches, and the selfishness and want of thought and want of feeling in master manufacturers are most admirably described and the consequences produced on the inferior class of employed or unemployed workmen are most ably shewn in action—There is great discretion in the drawing [of] the characters of the Carson family—in not exaggerating—Jem is a delightful noble creature and not over colored. John Barton too is admirably kept up from 1st to last—and Mary herself is charming—from not being too perfect— . . . Here are no such faultless nor any such vicious monsters as the world ne'er saw—But all such as have been seen and are recognised by all who have thought and by all who can feel—all who can look inwardly at their own minds or outwardly at the world we live in—

The story is ingenious and interesting—The heroine is in a new and good difficulty between her guilty father and her innocent noble lover—It is a situation fit for the highest Greek Tragedy yet not unsuited to the humblest life of a poor tender girl—heroism, as well as, love in a cottage—(pp. 108-09)

I am sorry that [Mary] and her lover emigrate—I think the poetic justice and moral of the story would have been better and as naturally made out by Jem's *good character* standing against the prejudice suspicion or envy of his fellow workmen as I really believe it would have done—and it would more shew the effect of good conduct in workmen and inspire hope for the future better without its being improbable that the noble conduct of Jem should have made such impression on the rich man and the master manufacturers that they took the case of the workmen for his sake into consideration. . . .

The fault of this book is that it leaves such a melancholy I almost feel hopeless impression. (p. 109)

All that can be done is to prevent the labourers from being made slaves and to deter the masters from becoming tyrants—Such a powerful writer as the author of **Mary Barton** could tend to this beneficial purpose by his pathetic representations and appeals to the feelings of pity and remorse—But I doubt whether this has been effected by the present tale—*Emigration* is the only resource pointed out at the end of this work, and this is only an escape from the evils not a remedy nor any tendency to reparation or improvement. (pp. 109-10)

I *feel* that there are too many deaths in the book—Death is an evil common to all and not a peculiar moral punishment and the mere contemplation of the difference between the death bed *hour* of the bad and the good is not according to my view a sufficient motive for the survivors—to make it advisable for a good moral writer to have recourse to this source of pathos.

[Not] only there are too many deaths but too many living creatures in this book—The reader's sympathy is too much divided—cannot flit as fast as called upon from one to another without being weakened. The more forcible the calls and the

objects of pity the more the feelings are harassed and in danger of being exhausted. (p. 110)

*Maria Edgeworth, in a letter to Miss [Mary] Holland on December 27, 1848, in* Bulletin of The John Rylands Library *(© The John Rylands Library, 1935), Vol. 19, 1935, pp. 108-10.*

### SAMUEL BAMFORD   (letter date 1849)

[*A Manchester weaver by trade, Bamford gained local celebrity as an advocate of working-class causes. In his letter to Gaskell, Bamford praises* Mary Barton *as a faithful, compelling record of the life and sentiments of Manchester's working-class population.*]

[In **Mary Barton** you] have drawn a fearfully true picture: a mournfully beautiful one also have you placed on the tables of the drawing rooms of the great, and good it must there effect; good for themselves, and good also I hope for the poor of every occupation.

You are a genius, of no ordinary rank. . . . It seems to me that you have begun a great work and I do hope you will not be discouraged from going on with it. You have opened and adventured into a noble apartment of a fine old dwelling house and on one of the English oaken pannels [*sic*] you have worked a picture from which the eyes cannot be averted nor the hearts [*sic*] best feelings withdrawn. A sorrowfully beautiful production it is, few being able to contemplate it with tearless eyes.—I could not, I know. (pp. 106-07)

Some errors may certainly be detected in the details of your work, but the wonder is that they are so few in number and so trifling in effect. The dialect I think might, have been given better, and some few incidents set forth with greater effect, but in describing the dwellings of the poor, their manners, their kindliness to each other, their feelings towards their superiors in wealth and station, their faults, their literary tastes, and their scientific pursuits . . . you have been very faithful; of John Bartons, I have known hundreds, his very self in all things except his fatal crime, whilst of his daughter Mary, who has ever seen a group of our Lancashire factory girls or dress makers either, and could not have counted Mary? Nor is Jem Wilson, and I [am] proud to say it, a solitary character in the young fellows of our working population, noble as he is. . . .

Dear Madam, Give us some more of your true and touching pictures. . . . (p. 107)

*Samuel Bamford, in a letter to Mrs. Gaskell on March 9, 1849, in* Bulletin of The John Rylands Library *(© The John Rylands Library, 1935), Vol. 19, 1935, pp. 106-07.*

### [WILLIAM RATHBONE GREG]   (essay date 1849)

[*Mary Barton* portrays manufacturers as indifferent to the concerns and conditions of their employees, a characterization which antagonized the manufacturers. In the following review, Greg expresses many of their objections. He maintains that Gaskell's depiction of the relationship between laborers (operatives) and employers is false; according to him, the workers are not as embittered, nor the manufacturers as insensitive as Gaskell has depicted them. Greg states that *Mary Barton* only exacerbated dangerous popular prejudices against the manufacturing class.]

'**Mary Barton**' is a work of higher pretensions than an ordinary novel. It aims not only at the delineation of the joys and sorrows, the loves and hatreds of our common humanity, but it professes also to give a picture of the feelings, habits, opinions, character and social condition of a particular class of the people,— a class, too, which has of late years attracted a great share of public attention, and has probably been the subject of more misconception and misrepresentation than has fallen to the lot of any other. (p. 402)

The literary merit of the work is in some respects of a very high order. Its interest is intense: often painfully so; indeed it is here, we think, that the charm of the book and the triumph of the author will chiefly be found. Its pictures and reflections are, however, also full of those touches of nature which 'make the whole world kin:' and its dialogues are managed with a degree of ease and naturalness rarely attained even by the most experienced writers of fiction. We believe that they approach very nearly, both in tone and style, to the conversations actually carried on in the dingy cottages of Lancashire. The authoress— for 'Mary Barton' is understood to be, and indeed very palpably is, the production of a lady—must not be confounded with those writers who engage with a particular subject, because it presents a vein which they imagine may be successfully worked— get up the needful information, and then prepare a story as a solicitor might prepare a case. She has evidently lived much among the people she describes, made herself intimate at their firesides, and feels a sincere, though sometimes too exclusive and undiscriminating, sympathy with them. In short, her work has been clearly a 'labour of love,' and has been written with a most earnest and benevolent purpose. We can conscientiously pronounce it to be a production of great excellence, and of still greater promise.

But it must also be regarded in a more serious point of view. It comes before us professing to be a faithful picture of a little known, though most energetic and important class of the community; and it has the noble ambition of doing real good by creating sympathy, by diffusing information, and removing prejudices. To its pretensions in these respects, we regret that we cannot extend an unqualified approbation. With all the truthfulness displayed in the delineation of individual scenes, the general impression left by the book, on those who read it as mere passive recipients, will be imperfect, partial, and erroneous. Notwithstanding the good sense and good feeling with which it abounds, it is calculated, we fear, in many places, to mislead the minds and confirm and exasperate the prejudices, of the general public on the one hand, and of the factory operatives on the other. . . . [Considering] the extraordinary delusions of many throughout the south of England respecting the great employers of labour in the north and west; as well as the ignorance and misconception of their true interests and position, which are still too common among the artisans of many of our large towns,—the effect of the work, if taken without some corrective might, in these quarters, be mischievous in the extreme. And this must be our apology for pointing out, in some detail, both the false philosophy and the inaccurate descriptions which detract so seriously from the value of these most interesting volumes.

But first we must indulge ourselves in the more pleasing task of noticing the beauty and fidelity with which the authoress seizes on and depicts those bright redeeming features which still characterise our operative population. . . . First among these must be reckoned what Monckton Milnes so justly calls 'the sacred Patience of the poor.' (pp. 403-04)

[Their] predominant characteristic has always been a submissive hopefulness, often an almost stoical endurance, and as

soon as times mended, there has been generally even too speedy a forgetfulness of past troubles.

This admirable feature in the artisan character, the authoress of 'Mary Barton' has discovered and delineated in the cases of George Wilson and Old Alice; though, from the circumstance of the discontented man, John Barton, being the more prominent person, the erroneous impression would be conveyed to the reader, that patience is the exception, and ill-humour and vindictiveness the rule,—especially among the stronger and more thoughtful natures. (p. 405)

Another feature in the character of the operative poor, perhaps even lovelier and brighter than their wonderful patience under suffering, is their mutual helpfulness and unbounded kindliness towards each other. To this virtue our authoress has done full justice. . . . (p. 406)

But we are putting off the unpleasant part of our duty. There are representations made—at least impressions left—by the book before us which we have signalised as inaccurate and full of harm. Some of these we must proceed to notice: and first among them, the exaggeration of describing an animosity against masters and employers as the common quality and characteristic of the operative population. The narrative imports that the angry and vindictive feelings by which the soul of John Barton is absorbed, are constant and pervading. (p. 411)

It is unquestionably and unfortunately true that sentiments of animosity of this description do exist in a considerable degree, and in a degree which varies with the times. All that we contend for is, that they are exceptional, not general—local, limited, and transient,—and certainly not entertained by the working population at large. As a picture of an individual,—that is, of the feelings of this or that person,—John Barton is unhappily true to the life; as the type of a class, though a small one, he may be allowed to pass muster: but to bring him forward as a fair representative of the artisans and factory operatives of Manchester and similar towns generally, is a libel alike upon them and upon the objects of their alleged hatred. (pp. 411-12)

There is, too, it seems to us, a double error, both an artistic error and an error of fact, in representing a man of Barton's intelligence and habits of reflection and discussion, to be so ignorant of the first principles of commercial and economic science. . . . Probably this arises from the writer's acknowledged unacquaintance with social and political economy herself, and from her ignorance how far the rudiments of these sciences have been mastered by the more thoughtful and the better educated artisans of our large towns. But indeed the lights and shades are thrown too strongly on everything relating to John Barton. . . . [He] is painted as utterly unconscious, even to the last, of his own improvidence and of its sinister influence on his condition. Instead of drawing from his privations those lessons of warning and remorse which, to an intellect like his, must have been as patent as the day, they are merely made to heap up fresh fuel for that funeral pile to which his senseless and vindictive passion is at last to set fire. (p. 413)

How came it never to occur to the authoress, or to her hero, that had Mr. Carson (who is represented as having raised himself from the operative class) thought as little of saving as John Barton, who so envied and so wronged him, their condition and their sufferings, when the period of distress arrived, would have been precisely equal? It was, in truth, because the one had been prudent and foreseeing, and the other confident and careless—because the one had busied himself about his work, while the other had busied himself about unions and politics, that their positions, when the evil day came, which came alike to both, were so strangely contrasted. (p. 415)

The whole book, too, is pervaded by one fatally false idea, which seems to have taken possession of the writer's mind, and can scarcely fail to be impressed with equal vividness on the merely passive reader, [namely] that the poor are to look to the rich, and not to themselves, for relief and rescue from their degraded condition and their social miseries. An impression more utterly erroneous, more culpably shallow, more lamentably mischievous, it is difficult to conceive. (p. 419)

The plain truth cannot be too boldly spoken, nor too frequently repeated: the working classes, and they only, can raise their own condition: to themselves alone must they look for their elevation in the social scale; their own intellect and their own virtues must work out their salvation; their fate and their future are in their own hands,—and in theirs alone. (p. 420)

There are several minor points in which the authoress of **'Mary Barton'** has laid herself open to serious criticism, which want of space compels us to pass by. Two, however, we must notice. The first is the countenance she gives to the trite and shallow error, that labour is a curse,—that the poor are to be pitied for the obligation to daily toil which their state imposes, and that the poor *only* are ordained to toil. These popular misconceptions . . . carry with them the seeds of much mischief. The very expression so commonly employed—'*condemned* to labour'—conveys a radically false view of human nature. It implants in the mind of the poor man the idea that the condition of his existence is a hardship; and in the mind of the rich the still more fatal fallacy, that idleness is a dignity and a privilege. Two worse errors could scarcely take possession of the popular mind. . . . (p. 423)

The second of the two faults in **'Mary Barton,'** to which we have referred, is this. There is an impression left by it upon the mind—an impression, too, which is the legitimate and inevitable result of the statements and the descriptions it contains—which yet is so unfounded and so unjust as almost to expose the writer to the charge of culpable misrepresentation. It would be impossible for any one to read **'Mary Barton,'** and take from it his opinion of the relations between rich and poor in the manufacturing towns, without coming to the conclusion . . . that there exists an entire want of kindly feeling between them,—that the sufferings of the operatives are entirely disregarded by their employers, and that no effort is made to relieve them, even in times of the severest pressure. Now every one acquainted with the districts in question will bear us out, when we affirm that no representation can be further from the truth. The writer sinks, as if ignorant of them—and we hope she is—a whole class of facts, of which, however, it is scarcely possible that she should have been totally uninformed. For it is notorious, that in no town are there better organised or more efficient charities than in Manchester. . . . [In] so resolutely ignoring all the kindness felt for the people, and all the willing and anxious assistance rendered to them by their employers, the authoress of **'Mary Barton'** has borne false witness against a whole class,—has most inconsiderately fostered the ill-opinion of them known to exist in certain quarters—and has, unintentionally no doubt, but most unfortunately, flattered both the prejudices of the aristocracy and the passions of the populace.

The basis of the book—the master idea which pervades it—is the old dispute between capital and labour—as to the *distri-*

*bution* of that wealth which is the joint production of the two. The operative is represented as utterly bewildered by seeing his employer, to all appearance, steadily and rapidly advancing in the world, in spite of the vicissitudes of trade; while he himself, in consequence of those vicissitudes, is left to struggle, and often to struggle in vain, for daily bread. He is said to be disgusted and enraged at that *unequal division* of the profits of their combined exertions, in which alone he can find the explanation of this irritating difference in their lot. Now, it is unqestionably true that this feeling does exist in the minds of many operatives; though the intensity and the prevalence of it are both exaggerated. It is manifest, too, that the writer before us shares in the feeling. . . . (pp. 425-27)

When [economic] matters are duly weighed . . . , we do not believe that any man, whether operative or not, could conscientiously come to the conclusion, that the master manufacturers—abusing their advantages in the labour-market—have generally engrossed a larger proportion of profit than of right belongs to them. (p. 429)

[In] concluding, we must again express our sense of the high literary merit of the work, and our conviction also, that both its value and its chance of lasting popularity would have been far greater, had the writer endeavoured to represent the real position of the operative classes, rather than the inaccurate and distorted view of that position as taken by the sour and envious among them; had she, while depicting the distress and privation which they are so often called upon to endure, drawn attention also to those intellectual and moral deficiencies by which this distress is so often caused or aggravated; had she dealt out one measure of kindliness and severity to the rich and poor; and had she spoken of the bitter and malignant feelings she had dramatised, less as sparing and excusing them than as perceiving and deploring their injustice. (p. 434)

> [William Rathbone Greg], in a review of "Mary Barton: A Tale of Manchester Life," in The Edinburgh Review, Vol. LXXXIX, No. CLXXX, April, 1849, pp. 402-35.

**[WILLIAM ELLIS AND MARY TURNER ELLIS]** (essay date 1849)

['Mary Barton'] is a most striking book. . . . It is an appropriate and valuable contribution to the literature of the age. It embodies the dominant feeling of our times—a feeling that the ignorance, destitution and vice which pervade and corrupt society, must be got rid of. The ability to point out how they are to be got rid of, is not the characteristic of this age. That will be the characteristic of the age which is coming. . . .

[Compare this] **'Mary Barton'** of 1849, with [an] imaginary 'Mary Barton' of 1899. The tale in pathos, good feeling, powerful narration and graphic description, will not surpass the present—it cannot. But the writer will be able to breathe guiding knowledge, as well as kindly emotions, into her story. Not only will impulses and aspirations be warmed and ennobled, but understandings will rise satisfied and improved from its perusal. (p. 48)

That John Barton should have had the discontent, engendered by want, increased to hatred towards the class of rich employers, is not strange nor forced [considering his history]. The patience and long-suffering of the industrious poor, left in the ignorance which we see, are more strange than the conclusions to which John Barton arrives, and which lead him an unwilling agent, step by step, to the crime, the incidents connected with which form the striking interest of the story. (p. 51)

A very admirable picture of the state of feeling among the unemployed workmen who formed themselves into bands of trades' unionists and chartists, is given. (p. 53)

[With] power and truth is [Mr. Henry Carson's] thoughtless immorality drawn—a portrait of that large number whose morals are only of, and for a class—merely conventional. (p. 56)

[Mary's] speedy regret after her hasty refusal of Jem Wilson's hand; her conviction of the sincerity of his affection, and the consciousness that it was not unreturned by herself; are all most admirably told. . . .

Her errors, that had their source more in the temptations to which the gift of her natural beauty exposed her, than in any serious levity of conduct, are drawn with delicate discrimination. . . . (p. 57)

From the hour of her departure to seek the only man who can prove that Jem Wilson was not in Manchester when the murder [of the young Mr. Carson] was committed, and during the subsequent trial, the interest becomes intense—so life-like, so unexaggerated, that fiction disappears. . . . (p. 58)

[We] must not pass altogether in silence the admirably pourtrayed and sustained characters of [Jane Wilson, Alice, Job Legh and his granddaughter, the boy Charley, and Ben Sturgis and his wife]. . . . The unhappy Esther . . . also claims a parting word. Her misery calls largely upon our commiseration. (p. 59)

To sum up: we can hardly trust ourselves to speak of the merits of this work as they deserve to be spoken of. By many of the descriptions we have been perfectly enchanted, as we have been melted by the calls upon our sympathy and pity. But when we have laid down the absorbing tale . . . and returned to the every-day duties and wants of life, looking around us upon the similar scenes which might be painted in every neighborhood, we seem to pine for the writer of 1899. We are even emboldened to ask why the author of **'Mary Barton'** should not be— we are even inclined to think that she will be—that writer. Her diffidence and modesty will alone prevent it.

She says in her preface, ''I know nothing of political economy, or the theories of trade. I have tried to write truthfully; and if my accounts agree or clash with any system, the agreement or disagreement is unintentional'' [see excerpt above, 1848].

She is evidently labouring under the mistaken notion that there is something very difficult, dark, and mysterious in political economy. Let her emancipate herself from that error. . . . [Political economy] particularly recommends itself to all who crave either for self-improvement or for the improvement of others, by the breadth and simplicity of its elementary principles. (pp. 59-60)

Political economy, we may also tell this generous and sympathizing writer, has some principles applicable to the edification and enlightenment of the rich. By the assistance of his ill-understood science, she may even ease herself of some of her own desponding feelings, and teach the rich how to benefit, as well as the poor how to be benefited. (p. 61)

> *[William Ellis and Mary Turner Ellis], in a review of ''Mary Barton: A Tale of Manchester Life,'' in* Westminster and Foreign Quarterly Review, *Vol. LI, No. 1, April, 1849, pp. 48-63.*

## ELIZABETH BARRETT BROWNING    (letter date 1850)

[In Mrs. Gaskell's **'Mary Barton,'** there] is power and truth— she can shake and she can pierce—but I wish half the book away, it is so tedious every now and then; and besides I want more beauty, more air from the universal world—these classbooks must always be defective as works of art. . . . [The] style of the book is slovenly, and given to a kind of phraseology which would be vulgar even as colloquial English. Oh, it is a powerful book in many ways. You are not to set me down as hypercritical. Probably the author will write herself clear of many of her faults: she has strength enough. (p. 472)

> *Elizabeth Barrett Browning, in her letter to Mary Russell Mitford on December 13, 1850, in* The Letters of Elizabeth Barrett Browning, Vol. I, *edited by Frederic G. Kenyon, Smith, Elder, & Co., 1897, pp. 470-75.**

## GEORGE ELIOT    (letter date 1853)

**'Ruth,'** with all its merits, will not be an enduring or classical fiction—will it? Mrs Gaskell seems to me to be constantly misled by a love of sharp contrasts—of ''dramatic'' effects. She is not contented with the subdued colouring—the half tints of real life. Hence she agitates one for the moment, but she does not secure one's lasting sympathy; her scenes and characters do not become typical. But how pretty and graphic are the touches of description. . . . [And there is] the rich humour of Sally, and the sly satire in the description of Mr Bradshaw. Mrs Gaskell has certainly a charming mind, and one cannot help loving her as one reads her books. (p. 86)

> *George Eliot, in a letter to Mrs. Peter Alfred Taylor on February 1, 1853, in her* George Eliot's Life As Related in Her Letters, Vol. I, *edited by J. W. Cross, William Blackwood and Sons, 1885 (and reprinted in* The George Eliot Letters: 1852-1858, Vol. II *by George Eliot, edited by Gordon S. Haight, Yale University Press, 1954, pp. 85-6).*

## [GEORGE HENRY LEWES]    (essay date 1853)

[*In his review of* Ruth, *the noted journalist and critic Lewes represents the novel as an unusually candid and morally satisfying treatment of the subject of seduction. His assertion that the moral teaching in the novel is unostentatious is at variance with Marjory A. Bald's claim that, in* Ruth, *''Mrs. Gaskell seems to be overwhelmed by her own earnestness'' (see excerpt below, 1923).*]

[**''Ruth''**] is a story of seduction—a subject of the most delicate nature that can well be taken up; being one which has rarely if ever been looked fairly in the face; and one on which, of all others, it is the rarest to hear a rational word spoken. . . . [Mrs. Gaskell approaches the subject] like a woman, and a truly delicate-minded woman; with a delicacy that is strong in truth, not influenced by conventions. In **''Ruth''** there is no confusing of right with wrong; no tampering with perilous sympathies, no attempt to make a new line of action such as the world's morality would refuse to warrant, but a clear insight into the nature of temptation, and wise words of exhortation to those who have fallen—showing them, that no matter what clouds of shame may have gathered around them, they may still redeem themselves if they will only rise and do honestly the work that still lies before them to be done, and that, in every position, however dark or degraded, there is always a certain right course which, if followed, will lead them once more into light. (p. 476)

[Ruth is seduced] under such "extenuating circumstances," that the question of "guilt" is reduced to a point of casuistry. . . . We think, for the object Mrs. Gaskell had in view, the guilt should not have had so many extenuating circumstances, because as it is, Ruth, although she has much to regret, cannot in her conscience have much to repent. But this by the way: Ruth is seduced, and therefore has practically incurred all the penalties of social reprobation. (p. 477)

Poor Ruth is abandoned . . . ; she has no resource but suicide. Succour comes, however, in the shape of the Bensons—a dissenting clergyman and his sister—who, pitying her forlorn condition, and believing in her real goodness, agree to adopt her into their own family till she be able to earn a living for herself.

In the midst of their unostentatious self-denying charity a touch of human weakness shows itself: partly from the desire to spare Ruth's feelings and save her from the terrible tongues of a provincial town, and partly to save themselves and make their task smoother and easier, they agree to pass her off as a distant relative—a widow. Admirable is the stroke of nature by which Ruth cannot be made to feel "sorry" that she is to have a baby! This revelation . . . is to the young girl nothing but a source of joy. It is new life, new strength, new hope! Admirable also is Miss Benson's confession to her brother, that she cannot help enjoying the novelty of "filling up the outline they had agreed upon, and inventing a few details of Ruth's widowhood."

Yielding to the temptation of this piece of specious worldly wisdom is the one flaw in an otherwise perfect act of Christian charity, and its consequences are ably worked out. There is no strain to save the moral, all follows naturally upon one false step taken at the onset. . . . (pp. 479-80)

[Ruth's love for her child] is made the main influence which strengthens her to rise up under her load of shame, and begin her life afresh. . . .

The author has treated this phase of the history of a fallen woman with immense truth and delicacy. She has separated the consequences of an action from the action itself. The natural and pure relationship between a mother and her child ought not to be considered as poisoned and vitiated, because the antecedents of that relationship are to be regretted; it is an opportunity afforded to her of rehabilitating her life, by nobly and courageously accepting the responsibility she has incurred, and qualifying herself to discharge the trust committed to her. If women who have placed themselves in Ruth's position only could find the moral courage to accept the duties entailed upon them by their own conduct, it would much lessen the misery and social evil that now follows in the train of illicit connexions.

Under the influence of her new duties, and the instructions of Mr. Benson, [Ruth] . . . becomes, in all respects, an educated gentlewoman. Nature had already made her a "born lady." We confess that, for the sake of the teaching, we should have preferred having Ruth more homely, and less richly endowed in good qualities and good looks. We should have preferred a more simple trust in the principle involved, and less attempt to interest and propitiate the reader by all manner of graceful accessories. (p. 480)

The working up of the concluding scenes is beautiful, and yet they are so simple and unexaggerated, that they haunt the reader like a reality. The author has gone into no vituperation of Ruth's

seducer, but he is so drawn as to suggest all that could be said; the interview between him and Mr. Benson, by the side of Ruth's dead body, satisfies the requirements of poetical justice. He is none the less miserable and contemptible that he does not know himself to be so.

The moral, or morals of **"Ruth"** . . . are legible enough. The first is, that if women are to have their lives rehabilitated, it must be through the means of women, who, noble and pure in their own lives, can speak with authority, and tell them that in this world no action is final; and that, to set the seal of despair and reprobation upon any individual during any one point of his career, is to blot out the inner life by which we live. The second moral is suggested in the untruth by which the Bensons endeavoured to shield their protegée. . . . *They faced the truth, and yet were afraid lest others should face it!* Had they confronted conventionalism, they would have awed and conquered it. . . . The Bensons have but suffered for their want of reliance on truth, and the moral of the whole is plainly this,—however dark and difficult our course may seem, the straight path of truth is the only one to lead us through it into the light.

**"Ruth,"** then, besides being a beautiful novel, satisfies the highest moral sense by the pictures it suggests. It is a sermon, and of the wisest, but its teaching is unostentatious. We need only allude in passing, to the wonderful beauty of some of the descriptions; to the clear truthful portraiture of the characters, especially Sally, Bradshaw, his meek Wife, and the sensible Farquhar, and to the somewhat common-place incidents by which the novel is carried on. . . . [But] we must protest against one portion of the work, which strikes us as being conventional and unnatural: we allude to the intensity of grief with which Ruth's child is afflicted on hearing that his mother has not been married. (pp. 483-84)

No child would at once realize . . . such shame, even were it a fact, that illegitimacy in actual life *did* bring with it disgrace, so that the illegitimate child must "go forth branded into the world, with his hand against every man's, and every man's hand against him;" the least reflection will tell Mrs. Gaskell that in our day no such brand affects the illegitimate child. And as to Leonard's anticipating this social degradation, to render *that* intelligible to the reader there should have been scenes of insult and opprobrium from his companions and world at large, to make him bitterly aware that the misfortune of his birth was regarded as a brand. (p. 485)

> *[George Henry Lewes], in a review of "Ruth: A Novel," in* The Westminster Review, *Vol. LIX, No. 116, April, 1853, pp. 474-91.**

### [J. M. LUDLOW]  (essay date 1853)

> *[In Ludlow's opinion, Gaskell had written a "good, righteous, true book" in* Ruth. *While he regards the length of the work as a serious artistic defect, Ludlow praises* Ruth *as a natural and realistic account of seduction and its consequences. David Cecil later cited the novel as evidence of Gaskell's inability to convey passion in her characters (see excerpt below, 1934).]*

The most marking characteristic of [**"Ruth"**] . . . is its perfect simplicity, truthfulness, its following out, step by step, of nature in all its parts, together with its exquisite purity of feeling in dealing with a subject which so many would shrink from. For instance, the latter part of the first volume shews us Ruth living with her seducer at a Welsh inn—a grand opportunity for commonplace moralists to picture to us terrible struggles of conscience in one or both of them—the debasement of the one, the corrupting influence of the other. The wife and mother who wrote "**Ruth**" does no such thing. Ruth is still the simple girl, country-bred, delighted with the new sight of mountain-scenery, with all her sympathies not deadened, but heightened, by the new power which has been developed in her, the entire devotion of a most humble, most trustful love. Mr. Bellingham is no Don Juan, but a young gentleman with a new toy, which he very much admires for its beauty, but sometimes grows tired of. . . . And yet, when the bitterness of trial is come, and with it the inculcation of a higher morality, not by the reproof, but by the example, the love, the self-devotion of a Dissenting minister and his sister, . . . Ruth is able to look back upon this period of outward sunshine and inward ignorance as one of guilt and sinfulness, and bears her life-long penance of self-abasement always . . . as the just wages of her fault. . . . Another exquisitely natural development of circumstances alike and of character is shewn in the well-meaning untruth of the Dissenting minister and his sister as to Ruth's history. . . . The perfectly simple, necessary, logical evolving of consequence after consequence is here obvious to anyone. You see that the temptation to the first falsehood is almost irresistible; you feel instinctively that, sooner or later, it must be found out. You know that the more blameless is Ruth's conduct, the more she will justify the world's good opinion in her assumed character as a widow, and the more dreadful will be the shock of the discovery of her sin, the more bitter the world's anger at having been so deceived in her.

The dramatic power of the authoress of "**Mary Barton**" was not to be doubted. But what marks "**Ruth**" is her extreme sobriety in the wielding of it, the common incidents out of which she evolves it, the distinctive abstinence from exaggeration in her most highly-wrought and pathetic passages. (pp. 151-53)

The perfect naturalness of development in the story of Ruth results necessarily in a perfect clearness of purpose, from whatever side the work is looked at; a purpose not ticketed in the shape of a moral, but inwoven with the whole texture of the book. . . . That purpose, so far as respects the Bensons . . . is the inculcation of the plain old English maxim, "tell the truth and shame the devil." Let us have no charitable Jesuitry, it tells us, no doing of evil that good may come; no paltering with the world's prejudices. If you want it to admire a self-devoted woman, don't flatter it by telling it she is a respectable widow, whereas she is nothing but a poor betrayed girl; compel it to love and reverence God's grace in the sinner; it is only thus that you will daunt its Pharisaical pride.

Again, in the unfolding of Ruth's character another truth shines out, clear and bright as day . . .—the truth which the Church of England has boldly embodied in her service of the churching of women, every word of which is as applicable to a harlot who has become a mother as to the Queen of England on her throne—the truth that "children and the fruit of the womb are an heritage and gift which cometh of the Lord." . . . [Ruth] is made a noble Christian woman by the very consequences of her sin. . . . The new sense of responsiblity which [her child's] birth brings forth, the feeling of the wrong she has done to him, of the joy which he is to her, . . . of the good to which she must train him, these are the means of her sanctification. (pp. 154-55)

But the tracing out of the influence of Ruth's motherhood upon herself is but a part, we take it, of the larger and more general purpose of the book—of that lesson which it inculcates, along with every penitentiary, ill or well regulated, in the world, for those who choose to read the lesson—that, as the sin of unchastity in the woman is, above all, a breaking up or a loosening of the family bond—a treason against the family order of God's world—so the restoration of the sinner consists mainly in the renewal of that bond, in the realization of that order, both by and through and around herself. . . . [The authoress of "**Ruth**"] goes at once to the root of the matter, and places poor erring Ruth in a family, between a brother and sister, and their old servant, with her wronged innocent child before her for a monument of past sin and life-long duty. And thus the erring girl, as we said, grows up into a noble Christian woman. . . . (pp. 155-57)

The characters in "**Ruth**" are all real characters, even when, like Mr. Benson, Mr. Farquhar [and Jemima Brandshaw] . . . , they grow slowly upon our view, half-riddles at the first. But long before the book is over we know them all well, and could tell each again out of a thousand. . . . And the scenery and the society in which they move are equally real. (pp. 158-59)

We shall not stop to notice one or two provincialisms of style. . . . We might caution [the authoress] . . . against the too frequent use of eulogistic epithets, such as "pretty, beautiful," &c., which grow to be almost catchwords. A graver artistical defect, as it seems to us, lies in the length of the work, and in the eking out of it by the love-story of Jemima and Mr. Farquhar. This, indeed, is in itself almost perfect, and wrought out with the truth and finish of a Miss Austen. But the character of Ruth herself and her fortunes are of too overwhelming an interest to allow us to dwell with complete satisfaction on this side-plot. . . . It is quite possible that it may have been introduced as a relief to others, nay, that it may have been worked out by the writer as a relief to herself, from the intense painfulness of the main plot. But this would only show that that painfulness has been—not overstrained . . .—but over-lenghtened. (pp. 159-60)

There are, indeed, many who will object to the painfulness of "**Ruth**" as a positive defect. (p. 160)

The novelist's true answer seems to be:—I have to paint God's world as I find it, and above all, to shew others those portions of it on which I think they ought to look. . . . It might have been far pleasanter for me, as for you, . . . to have left [Ruth] . . . the wife of a loving husband, a happy and prosperous mother. But look around you, and ask yourself how often the complete spiritual restoration of a fallen woman, as I have depicted it, is ever accompanied by complete worldly restoration? Or ask yourself rather, how seldom either will occur alone; and then see if in shewing you the painfuller picture, I have not shewn you also the truer one.

And we venture to think that the authoress would be right in so pleading. (pp. 161-62)

We certainly do not feel qualified to teach ethics to the authoress of "**Ruth.**" But there is one point of her story on which we have felt some moral doubt. . . . Is she quite sure that Ruth has the right, when Mr. Donne offers to marry her, and give their son all the advantages of his position, to reject his offer? (p. 162)

We do not deny that Ruth's rejection of Mr. Donne is natural, and we acknowledge it just. We doubt whether it be Christian, whether, in God's eye, she be not his wife, and forbidden to turn from him when he turns to her; whether, in fact, her refusal of him be not simply the sign that she has not self-sacrifice enough in her to devote her life to the man who has wronged her, though she may have self-sacrifice enough to die for him. (p. 163)

If we compare ["**Ruth**"] with the author's other works, and especially with "**Mary Barton,**" we shall find it presents itself under some new aspects. . . . "**Mary Barton,**" although deeply true to human nature in its essential constitution, and not in its evanescent phenomena, was yet an *occasional* novel, if we may so call it. Its main interest lay in those terrible class-rivalries, and class-hatreds, and class-miseries, which are the direct outgrowth of the manufacturing system, while as yet unsoftened, unpurified, unharmonized, by Christian duty and Christian love. . . . But in "**Ruth,**" the occasional element occupies the very smallest possible space. . . . Although we hear of Ruth, while at the Bensons, earning a little money by plain needlework, the writer takes no trouble to conduct us to the warehouse, to shew us the needlewomen waiting for orders, and the foreman bullying or fining them. She knows well that such scenes would but distract us *here* from her main purpose. . . We shall be all the better disposed another time, if she choose it, to acknowledge the truth of some work having for its object the delineation of some of those special social evils of which she knows so much, by this evidence of her entire freedom from all cant of philanthropy. (pp. 163-64)

"**Ruth**" is far more finished, more even, more artistic and less melodramatic . . . than "**Mary Barton.**" There is also developing more and more in the writer, as the "**Moorland Cottage**" gave evidence already, a very striking power of describing the aspects of nature, such as is equalled by very few of the writers of the day. We might take for instances . . . the scene, from the story of Ruth's excursion to Wales with her lover, in which, standing by a sheltered mountain-pool, he decks her hair with water-lilies . . . ; and again, the description of Ruth's watching by night at the Welsh inn during her lover's illness, when shut out of his room by his mother.

But there is another quality developed in "**Ruth,**" of which we saw only the faint glimmerings in "**Mary Barton,**"—humour. . . . Now there *was* a quiet subdued humour in "**Mary Barton,**" especially in the scenes between old Job and Will Wilson the young sailor. But in "**Ruth**" there is one character genuinely humorous, the old maid-servant Sally; besides a good deal of the same quality about the strong-minded Miss Benson. (pp. 164-65)

A more delicate bit of humour is to be found in the wise conversation between Mrs. Bradshaw's two youngest girls as to the signs and tokens of love in their sister Jemima. . . . It is indeed observable, that the humour of "**Ruth**" . . . disappears before the end of the book. . . . The last we see of Sally in "**Ruth**" is . . . a piece of homely pathos, quite as true and characteristic as her earlier humour. (p. 166)

On the whole, we take it, our authoress has written a good, righteous, true book; such a book as shews that she has taken her calling as an author in Christian earnest, and means to go on in it from strength to strength; such a book as befits her own sweet spirit, and will make her, if possible, somewhat more loveable to all who love her already. (p. 167)

*[J. M. Ludlow], in a review of "Ruth: A Novel," in The North British Review, Vol. XIX, No. XXXVII, May, 1853, pp. 151-74.*

### THE ATHENAEUM   (essay date 1855)

[The Athenaeum *here recommends* The Life of Charlotte Brontë *as "one of the best biographies of a woman by a woman which*

*we can recall to mind." The journal retracted its recommendation when Gaskell's statements linking Branwell Brontë's "wrecked life" with his involvement with a married woman could not be substantiated (see excerpt below, 1857). The controversy surrounding the biography marked the nadir of Gaskell's literary career.]*

[This year] will produce few better tales than '**North and South.**' . . . The Author of '**Mary Barton**' possesses some of an artist's best qualities. She *will* be attended to, having never as yet written without engaging the reader's interest, whether he agrees with or dissents from her philosophies. Her dialogue is natural,—her eye for character is keen. She enjoys humour, obviously,—she calls out pathos skilfully. Few things have been met in modern fiction more touching than the fading away of the poor girl to whom Margaret Hale attaches herself on removing from the South to a manufacturing town in Lancashire. . . . The Author of '**Mary Barton**' seems bent on doing for Lancashire and the Lancashire dialect what Miss Edgeworth did for Ireland and Scott for the land across the border. There has been no use of English *patois* in English fiction comparable to hers. She has strong Lancashire sympathies, too:—if they be class-sympathies such as propel her to a somewhat disproportionate exposure of the trials and sufferings of the poor, her excess is a generous one, and not accompanied by that offensive caricaturing of her more "conventional" heroes and heroines, which must always bring the sincerity of the caricaturist displaying it under question.

In another point the Author of '**North and South**' is open to remonstrance. She deals with difficulties of morals needlessly, and too fearlessly, because . . . the riddle propounded cannot be solved in fiction; and because by all one-sided handling of such matters . . . there is always a danger of unmooring the eager and the inexperienced from their anchorage. . . . It should be added, however, that the tenor and tissue of our author's writings are such as to satisfy us that no wilfulness has been in her mind, but an earnest, if a mistaken, desire to do good.

*A review of "North and South," in The Athenaeum, No. 1432, April 7, 1855, p. 403.*

### THE ATHENAEUM   (essay date 1857)

By all, [the '**Life of Charlotte Brontë**'] will be read with interest. As a work of Art, we do not recollect a life of a woman by a woman so well executed. (p. 427)

[Not] till now has the world learnt that the efforts by which [her] indomitable will at last reached its aim were made while Miss Brontë was ministering to her father . . . , and during years while her heart was torn with anxiety on behalf of her brother,—a man who became a drunkard, to drown the remorse consequent on a wrecked life. . . . Mrs. Gaskell has told the whole dismal story, without hesitation or suppression, too emphatically for any one dealing with it to forbear from comment. (p. 428)

[Mrs. Gaskell's] has been a labour of love (a little, also, of defence),—and [she], we repeat, has produced one of the best biographies of a woman by a woman which we can recall to mind. (p. 429)

*A review of "The Life of Charlotte Brontë," in The Athenaeum, No. 1536, April 4, 1857, pp. 427-29.*

## G. H. LEWES    (letter date 1857)

[*In his letter to Gaskell, Lewes praises* The Life of Charlotte Brontë *for its moral lessons and its vivid delineation of Brontë's inner life and her physical surroundings at Haworth parsonage.*]

[Your **'Life of Charlotte Brontë'**] will, I think, create a deep and permanent impression; for it not only presents a vivid picture of a life noble and sad, full of encouragement and healthy teaching, a lesson in duty and self-reliance; it also, thanks to its artistic power, makes us familiar inmates of an interior so strange, so original in its individual elements and so picturesque in its externals—it paints for us at once the psychological drama and the scenic accessories with so much vividness—that fiction has nothing more wild, touching, and heart strengthening to place above it.

The early part is a triumph for you; the rest a monument for your friend. (p. 137)

> *G. H. Lewes, in a letter to Mrs. Gaskell on April 15, 1857, in* Bulletin of The John Rylands Library *(© The John Rylands Library, 1935), Vol. 19, 1935, pp. 136-37.*

## SHIRLEY [PSEUDONYM OF JOHN SKELTON]    (essay date 1857)

Mrs. Gaskell has done her work well [in ***The Life of Charlotte Brontë***]. Her narrative is simple, direct, intelligible, unaffected. Her descriptions of the Yorkshire uplands and of the people who live there are vivid and picturesque. She dwells on her friend's character with womanly tact, thorough understanding, and delicate sisterly tenderness. Once or twice there is a burst of uncontrollable indignation against those who blunderingly misunderstood or wilfully maligned. The extracts from the letters are excellently selected. And they are remarkable letters. . . . Many parts of the book cannot be read without deep, even painful, emotion. . . . Still, we feel as we read, that though trying and distressing in many ways, it is a life always womanly. And we are thankful that such a life . . . should have been written by the writer of ***Ruth***. No one else could have paid so tender and discerning a tribute to the memory of Charlotte Brontë. (p. 577)

> *Shirley [pseudonym of John Skelton], "Charlotte Brontë," in* Fraser's Magazine, *Vol. LV, No. CCCXXIX, May, 1857, pp. 569-82.**

## CHARLES KINGSLEY    (letter date 1857)

[*Kingsley's* Alton Locke *and* Yeast, *pioneer works in the English social novel, are frequently compared with Gaskell's later efforts in* Mary Barton *and* North and South. *In his letter to Gaskell, Kingsley hails* The Life of Charlotte Brontë *as a welcome vindication of Brontë's character. Prior to the publication of the biography, little was known about Brontë's personal life, and readers had associated the passions and events depicted in her novels with Brontë's own experiences.*]

Let me renew our long interrupted acquaintance by complimenting you on poor Miss Brontë's **'Life.'** You have had a delicate and great work to do, and you have done it admirably. Be sure that the book will do good. It will shame literary people into some stronger belief that a simple, virtuous, practical home life is consistent with high imaginative genius; and it will shame, too, the prudery of a not over cleanly, though carefully white-washed age, into believing that purity is now (as in all ages till now) quite compatible with the knowledge of evil. I

confess that the book has made me ashamed of myself. 'Jane Eyre' I hardly looked into, very seldom reading a work of fiction—yours, indeed, and Thackeray's are the only ones I care to open. 'Shirley' disgusted me at the opening: and I gave up the writer and her books with the notion that she was a person who liked coarseness. How I misjudged her! (pp. 269-70)

Well have you done your work, and given us the picture of a valiant woman made perfect by sufferings. I shall now read carefully and lovingly every word she has written. . . . (p. 270)

> *Charles Kingsley, in a letter to Mrs. Gaskell on May 14, 1857, in his* Charles Kingsley: His Letters and Memories of His Life, *edited by F. E. Kingsley (copyright by Scribner, Armstrong & Co, 1877), revised edition, Charles Scribner's Sons, 1877, pp. 269-70.*

## THE ATHENAEUM    (essay date 1857)

We are sorry to be called upon to return to Mrs. Gaskell's **'Life of Charlotte Brontë,'**—but we must do so, since the book has gone forth with our recommendation. Praise, it is needless to point out, implied trust in the biographer as an accurate collector of facts. This, we regret to state, Mrs. Gaskell proves not to have been. . . . [The] *Athenaeum* advertises a legal apology, made on behalf of Mrs. Gaskell, withdrawing the statements put forth in her book respecting the cause of Mr. Branwell Brontë's wreck and ruin. These Mrs. Gaskell's lawyer is now fain to confess his client advanced on insufficient testimony. The telling of an episodical and gratuitous tale so dismal as concerns the dead, so damaging to the living, could only be excused by the story of sin being severely, strictly true; and every one will long have cause to regret that due caution was not used to test representations not, it seems, to be justified. It is in the interest of letters that biographers should be deterred from rushing into print with mere impressions in place of proofs, however eager and sincere those impressions be. They *may be* slanders, and as such they may sting cruelly.— Meanwhile, the **'Life of Charlotte Brontë,'** we apprehend, must undergo modification ere it can be further circulated.

> *A review of "The Life of Charlotte Brontë," in* The Athenaeum, *No. 1545, June 6, 1857, p. 727.*

## [DAVID MASSON]    (essay date 1865)

The world of English letters has just lost one of its foremost authors. Another of the writers I have known has passed away in the person of Mrs. Gaskell; and I think this magazine would scarcely be worthy of itself unless it contained some short notice of the authoress of **"Mary Barton."** . . . (p. 153)

Neither necessity, nor the unsatisfied solitude of a single life, nor, as I fancy, an irresistible impulse, threw her into the paths of literature. She wrote, as the birds sing, because she liked to write; and ceased writing when the fancy left her. And the result of this was, that all her works have, in their own way, a degree of perfection and completeness rare in these days, when successful authoresses pour out volume after volume without pause or waiting. . . . One of the chief charms of her writings is the enjoyment she shows throughout in all the pleasures of home and family; but still, in all her works, there is a certain subdued weariness, as though this world would be a very dreary one if we were not all to rest ere long.

I take it that the fact of her literary life having begun so late explains, to a great extent, both her strength and her weakness as a novelist. There is no sign of haste and immaturity about any of her novels. Her style was never slovenly; her word-painting was perfect of its kind; and her characters had none of the exaggeration so universal almost amidst women writers. Everybody who ever read "**Cranford**," knows the inhabitants of that little sleepy town as well as if he had been in the habit of paying visits there for years. We are on speaking terms with all the personages of "**Wives and Daughters**;" we can see the Gibsons, and Hamleys, and Brownings, as well as if we had called upon them yesterday. But, somehow, we never get further than an intimate acquaintance. . . . [An] authoress, the passion time of whose life had gone by before she began to write fiction, must always lack something of that dear-bought experience which, for good or evil, is to be acquired only in the spring-tide of our existence. (p. 154)

Of all her works, [the "**Life of Charlotte Brontë**"], viewed as a literary production, is, to my mind, the ablest. As a biography, it is almost unequalled. "Currer Bell" may or may not have been all that her biographer fancied: but, as long as her books are read, she will survive in the memory of men as Mrs. Gaskell painted her—not as she seemed to those who knew her less intimately and perhaps less well. . . . Passion, as I have said, lay out of her domain; and both "**Ruth**" and "**Sylvia's Lovers**" rested on a delineation of passions with which the writer was either unable or, as I rather believe, unwilling to grapple firmly. The literature of passion can only be treated worthily by persons who, whether for good or bad, are indifferent to the thought how their work may be judged by the standard rules of the society in which they move; and this was not the case with one of the most sensitive and delicate-minded women who ever wrote in England. (p. 155)

It is not a slight matter that an author can look back at the last glimpse of life, and feel that he has left behind him no written word which can make those who read it otherwise than better; and this acknowledgment is justly due to Mrs. Gaskell. Other novelists have written books as clever, and many have written books as innocent; but there are few, indeed, who have written works which grown-up men read with delight, and children might read without injury. It is impossible to determine now the exact position which Mrs. Gaskell will hold ultimately amongst English writers of our day. It will be a high one, if not amongst the highest. . . . [If] I had to say which of those novels we talk most of now will be read when we all are dead and buried, I should give the preference to "**Cranford**" and "**North and South**," above novels which I deem to excel them in innate power. These pleasant homeland stories—these vivid delineations of the lives of common men and common women, will survive, as long as people care to know what our England was at the days in which our lot is thrown. Within the last few years we have lost greater English writers than Mrs. Gaskell; we have greater still left; but we have none so purely and altogether English in the worthiest sense of that noble word. (p. 156)

> [David Masson], "Mrs. Gaskell," in Macmillan's Magazine, Vol. 13, No. 74, December, 1865, pp. 153-56.

## [FREDERICK GREENWOOD] (essay date 1866)

> [Greenwood served as editor of The Cornhill Magazine, Gaskell's publisher for Wives and Daughters. His commentary was appended to the last installment of the unfinished novel.]

[The] regrets of those who knew [Mrs. Gaskell] are less for the loss of the novelist than of the woman. . . . But yet, for her own sake as a novelist alone, her untimely death is a matter for deep regret. It is clear in [her] novel of **Wives and Daughters**, in the exquisite little story that preceded it, **Cousin Phillis**, and in **Sylvia's Lovers**, that Mrs. Gaskell had within these five years started upon a new career with all the freshness of youth, and with a mind which seemed to have put off its clay and to have been born again. . . . [Few] minds ever showed less of base earth than Mrs. Gaskell's. It was so at all times; but lately even the original slight tincture seemed to disappear. While you read any one of the last three books we have named, you feel yourself caught out of an abominable wicked world, crawling with selfishness and reeking with base passions, into one where there is much weakness, many mistakes, sufferings long and bitter, but where it is possible for people to live calm and wholesome lives; and, what is more, you feel that this is at least as real a world as the other. The kindly spirit which thinks no ill looks out of her pages irradiate; and while we read them, we breathe the purer intelligence which prefers to deal with emotions and passions which have a living root in minds within the pale of salvation, and not with those which rot without it. This spirit is more especially declared in **Cousin Phillis** and **Wives and Daughters**. (p. 13)

We are saying nothing now of the merely intellectual qualities displayed in these later works. Twenty years to come, that may be thought the more important question; . . . but it is true, all the same, that as mere works of art and observation, these later novels of Mrs. Gaskell's are among the finest of our time. There is a scene in **Cousin Phillis**—where Holman, making hay with his men, ends the day with a psalm—which is not excelled as a picture in all modern fiction; and the same may be said of that chapter of [**Wives and Daughters**] in which Roger smokes a pipe with the Squire after the quarrel with Osborne. There is little in either of these scenes, or in a score of others which succeed each other like gems in a cabinet, which the ordinary novel-maker could "seize." There is no "material" for *him* in half-a-dozen farming men singing hymns in a field, or a discontented old gentleman smoking tobacco with his son. . . . [But] it is just in such things as these that true genius appears brightest and most unapproachable. It is the same with the personages in Mrs. Gaskell's works. Cynthia is one of the most difficult characters which have ever been attempted in our time. Perfect art always obscures the difficulties it overcomes; and it is not till we try to follow the processes by which such a character as the Tito of [George Eliot's] *Romola* is created, for instance, that we begin to understand what a marvellous piece of work it is. To be sure, Cynthia was not so difficult, nor is it nearly so great a creation as that splendid achievement of art and thought—of the rarest art, of the profoundest thought. But she also belongs to the kind of characters which are conceived only in minds large, clear, harmonious and just, and which can be portrayed fully and without flaw only by hands obedient to the finest motions of the mind. Viewed in this light, Cynthia is a more important piece of work even than Molly. . . . And what we have said of Cynthia may be said with equal truth of Osborne Hamley. The true delineation of a character like that is as fine a test of art as the painting of a foot or a hand, which also seems so easy, and in which perfection is most rare. In this case the work is perfect. Mrs. Gaskell has drawn a dozen characters more striking than Osborne since she wrote **Mary Barton**, but not one which shows more exquisite finish. (pp. 13-14)

Mrs. Gaskell was gifted with some of the choicest faculties bestowed upon mankind; . . . these grew into greater strength and ripened into greater beauty in the decline of her days; and . . . she has gifted us with some of the truest, purest works of fiction in the language. (p. 15)

> [*Frederick Greenwood*], *in a review of "Wives and Daughters: An Every-Day Story," in* The Cornhill Magazine *(© John Murray 1866), Vol. XIII, No. 73, January, 1866, pp. 11-15.*

## HENRY JAMES   (essay date 1866)

[*In his review of* Wives and Daughters, *James provides what is perhaps the most insightful reading of the novel. Expressing particular admiration for the subtlety of Gaskell's narrative technique, he places* Wives and Daughters *among those few works "which will outlast the duration of their novelty and continue for years to come to be read and relished for a higher order of merits."*]

We cannot help thinking that in **"Wives and Daughters"** the late Mrs. Gaskell has added to the number of those works of fiction—of which we cannot perhaps count more than a score as having been produced in our time—which will outlast the duration of their novelty and continue for years to come to be read and relished for a higher order of merits. Besides being the best of the author's own tales—putting aside **"Cranford"**, that is, which as a work of quite other pretensions ought not to be weighed against it, and which seems to us manifestly destined in its modest way to become a classic—it is also one of the very best novels of its kind. So delicately, so elaborately, so artistically, so truthfully, and heartily is the story wrought out, that the hours given to its perusal seem like hours actually spent, in the flesh as well as the spirit, among the scenes and people described, in the atmosphere of their motives, feelings, traditions, associations. The gentle skill with which the reader is slowly involved in the tissue of the story; the delicacy of the handwork which has perfected every mesh of the net in which he finds himself ultimately entangled; the lightness of touch which, while he stands all unsuspicious of literary artifice, has stopped every issue into the real world; the admirable, inaudible, invisible exercise of creative power, in short, with which a new and arbitrary world is reared over his heedless head—a world insidiously inclusive of him (such is the *assoupissement* of his critical sense), complete in every particular, from the divine blue of the summer sky to the June-bugs in the roses, from Cynthia Kirkpatrick and her infinite revelations of human nature to old Mrs. Goodenough and her provincial bad grammar—these marvellous results, we say, are such as to compel the reader's very warmest admiration, and to make him feel, in his gratitude for this seeming accession of social and moral knowledge, as if he made but a poor return to the author in testifying, no matter how strongly, to the fact of her genius.

For Mrs. Gaskell's genius was so very composite as a quality, it was so obviously the offspring of her affections, her feelings, her associations, and (considering that, after all, it *was* genius) was so little of an intellectual matter, that it seems almost like slighting these charming facts to talk of them under a collective name, especially when that name is a term so coarsely and disrespectfully synthetic as the word genius has grown to be. But genius is of many kinds, and we are almost tempted to say that that of Mrs. Gaskell strikes us as being little else than a peculiar play of her personal character. In saying this we wish to be understood as valuing not her intellect the less, but

her character the more. Were we touching upon her literary character at large, we should say that in her literary career as a whole she displayed, considering her success, a minimum of head. Her career was marked by several little literary indiscretions, which show how much writing was a matter of pure feeling with her. Her **"Life of Miss Brontë"**, for instance, although a very readable and delightful book, is one which a woman of strong head could not possibly have written; for, full as it is of fine qualities, of affection, of generosity, of sympathy, of imagination, it lacks the prime requisites of a good biography. It is written with a signal want of judgment and of critical power; and it has always seemed to us that it tells the reader considerably more about Mrs. Gaskell than about Miss Brontë. In [**"Wives and Daughters"**] this same want of judgment, as we may still call it in the absence of a better name, presuming that the term applies to it only as it stands contrasted with richer gifts, is shown; not in the general management of the story, nor yet in the details, most of which are as good as perfect, but in the way in which, as the tale progresses, the author loses herself in its current very much as we have seen that she causes the reader to do.

The book is very long and of an interest so quiet that not a few of its readers will be sure to vote it dull. In the early portion especially the details are so numerous and so minute that even a very well-disposed reader will be tempted to lay down the book and ask himself of what possible concern to him are the clean frocks and the French lessons of little Molly Gibson. But if he will have patience awhile he will see. As an end these modest domestic facts are indeed valueless; but as a means to what the author would probably have called a "realization" of her central idea, *i.e.*, Molly Gibson, a product, to a certain extent, of clean frocks and French lessons, they hold an eminently respectable place. As he gets on in the story he is thankful for them. They have educated him to a proper degree of interest in the heroine. He feels that he knows her the better and loves her the more for a certain acquaintance with the *minutiae* of her homely *bourgeois* life. Molly Gibson, however, in spite of the almost fraternal relation which is thus established between herself and the reader—or perhaps, indeed, because of it. . . . commands a slighter degree of interest than the companion figure of Cynthia Kirkpatrick. Of this figure, . . . the editor of the magazine in which the story originally appeared speaks in terms of very high praise; and yet, as it seems to us, of praise thoroughly well deserved [see excerpt above by Greenwood, 1866]. To describe Cynthia as she stands in Mrs. Gaskell's pages is impossible. The reader who cares to know her must trace her attentively out. She is a girl of whom, in life, any one of her friends, so challenged, would hesitate to attempt to give a general account, and yet whose specific sayings and doings and looks such a friend would probably delight to talk about. This latter has been Mrs. Gaskell's course; and if, in a certain sense, it shows her weakness, it also shows her wisdom. She had probably known a Cynthia Kirkpatrick, a *résumé* of whose character she had given up as hopeless; and she has here accordingly taken a generous revenge in an analysis as admirably conducted as any we remember to have read. She contents herself with a simple record of the innumerable small facts of the young girl's daily life, and leaves the reader to draw his conclusions. He draws them as he proceeds, and yet leaves them always subject to revision; and he derives from the author's own marked abdication of the authoritative generalizing tone which, when the other characters are concerned, she has used as a right, a very delightful sense of the mystery of Cynthia's nature and of those large proportions which mystery always suggests. The fact is that genius is always difficult to formulate, and that Cynthia had a genius for fascination. Her whole character subserved this end. Next after her we think her mother the best drawn character in the book. Less difficult indeed to draw than the daughter, the very nicest art was yet required to keep her from merging, in the reader's sight, into an amusing caricature—a sort of commixture of a very mild solution of Becky Sharp [from William Makepeace Thackeray's *Vanity Fair*] with an equally feeble decoction of Mrs. Nickleby [from Charles Dickens's *Nicholas Nickleby*]. Touch by touch, under the reader's eye, she builds herself up into her selfish and silly and consummately natural completeness.

Mrs. Gaskell's men are less successful than her women, and her hero in this book, making all allowance for the type of man intended, is hardly interesting enough in juxtaposition with his vivid sweethearts. Still his defects as a masculine being are negative and not positive, which is something to be thankful for, now that lady-novelists are growing completely to eschew the use of simple and honest youths. Osborne Hamley, a much more ambitious figure than Roger, and ambitious as the figure of Cynthia is ambitious, is to our judgment less successful than either of these, and we think the praise given him in the editorial note above-mentioned is excessive. He has a place in the story, and he is delicately and even forcibly conceived, but he is practically little more than a suggestion. Mrs. Gaskell had exhausted her poetry upon Cynthia, and she could spare to Osborne's very dramatic and even romantic predicaments little more than the close prosaic handling which she had found sufficient for the more vulgar creations. Where this handling accords thoroughly with the spirit of the figures, as in the case of Doctor Gibson and Squire Hamley, the result is admirable. It is good praise of these strongly marked, masculine, middle-aged men to say that they are as forcibly drawn as if a wise masculine hand had drawn them. Perhaps the best scene in the book (as the editor remarks) is the one in which the squire smokes a pipe with one of his sons after his high words with the other. We have intimated that this scene is prosaic; but let not the reader take fright at the word. If an author can be powerful, delicate, humorous, pathetic, dramatic, within the strict limits of homely prose, we see no need of his "dropping into poetry," as Mr. Dickens says. It is Mrs. Gaskell's highest praise to have been all of this, and yet to have written "an everyday story" . . . in an everyday style. (pp. 153-59)

> *Henry James, "Mrs. Gaskell" (originally published as an unsigned review of "Wives and Daughters," in* The Nation, *Vol. II, No. 34, February 22, 1866), in his* Notes and Reviews, *edited by Pierre de Chaignon la Rose, Dunster House, 1921 (and reprinted by Books for Libraries Press, Inc., 1968; distributed by Arno Press, Inc.), pp. 153-59.*

***BRITISH QUARTERLY REVIEW*** (essay date 1867)

It is hardly possible to read a page of [Mrs. Gaskell's] writing without getting some good from it. The style is clear and forcible, the tone pure, the matter wholesome. Under her guidance we are always taken into cleanly company, and need never feel ashamed to say where we have been. . . . She is never afraid of degrading her subject by homely details, and on whatever she touches she leaves the artist-mark of reality. Other novel-writers of her generation have more poetry, more scholarship, more grace, eloquence, and passion, but in the art of telling a story she has no superior—perhaps no equal. (pp. 399-400)

[In] more than one of her stories Mrs. Gaskell takes up the parable of Dives and Lazarus with the avowed object of telling one half of the world how the other half lives, that knowledge may breed sympathy, and sympathy bring about redress for those sufferings which arise from ignorance, misconception, or wilful wrong. She by no means thinks it her mission simply to amuse. (p. 400)

Mrs. Gaskell's vocation was that of a peacemaker. She compels us to feel not how different men are, but how much they are alike when the accidents of wealth and poverty are put by. She utters her voice often through tears, but always to a most wise and Christian purpose, and throughout '**Mary Barton**' her cry is for Patience with the Poor. . . . The literary merits of the story are great, but the moral of it, the deep, direct, earnest intention that underlies the story . . . , is its most forcible part. (p. 401)

[With the introduction of Harry Carson's murder] the dramatic interest of the story quite runs away with its morality. Jem Wilson, falsely accused of the murder and brought to trial, gets a safe deliverance in one of the finest scenes of the book, but the real criminal goes unpunished of human justice, the wickedness of his act is dissimulated, and the law is mocked. . . . [We] would rather . . . that the murderer of Harry Carson had expiated his crime upon the gallows, a warning and example to others, tempted and tried as he was tempted and tried, at whatever cost of feeling to writer and readers. . . .

'**North and South**' is a second illustration of the quarrel between Manchester masters and operatives as it was in the times that are past. But here the quarrel is incidental to another story, designed to set forth the different fibre of Hampshire and Lancashire men—to the distinct advantage of the latter. It is easy to see where Mrs. Gaskell's heart is, and where also was her truer and fuller knowledge at this period of her career. (p. 405)

['**North and South**' includes] some of those sweet descriptive bits of country which betray that if Mrs. Gaskell's lot was cast in murky Manchester, her imagination made its brightest holidays in the woods and fields. (p. 406)

John Thornton plays hero admirably to Margaret Hale's heroine, and they begin in the most promising way with a little aversion. How this aversion becomes interest, admiration, and something more, is the substance of the story; and a perfectly charming story it would be, but for what strikes us as a wanton degradation of Margaret by putting her into circumstances where she is driven to think a lie better policy than the truth—necessary, indeed, to save her brother's life—a tricky expedient for raising interest which blemishes more than one of Mrs. Gaskell's works. . . .

The subordinate characters in '**North and South**,' chiefly factory-folk, are touched in with force and distinctness, and this remark applies no less to '**Mary Barton**,' than to all the later productions of our author. (p. 407)

Mrs. Gaskell has written many things of greater power and more vivid interest than [the stories grouped together in '**Cranford**'], but nothing that will better bear to be read over and over again. They are rich in her peculiar humour, her sense of fun, and warm throughout with her genuine womanly kindness. Akin to these are numerous short tales . . . , amongst which we may instance as most striking, '**Lizzie Leigh**,' '**The Grey Woman**,' and '**Mr. Harrison's Confessions**.' . . . (p. 411)

We shall now pass forward to '**Ruth**,' in order of publication Mrs. Gaskell's second great work, written in . . . her second manner, and, of all her novels, perhaps least our favourite. . . . ['**Ruth**'] attracts the dangerous admiration of a self-indulgent young gentleman of three and twenty. . . . [He] entices her easily over the threshold of temptation, soon to abandon her in that wilderness of sorrow and suffering, where society has decreed that women who have once left the straight paths of virtue shall wander all their days outcast, branded, apart. Whether this decree of society is Christian, wise, fair, is the hard problem Mrs. Gaskell sets us to consider and to solve in the sad story of '**Ruth**.' (pp. 411-12)

We may say here, once for all, that in its rigour of social law against wantonness we believe [society] is right. There are men and women always ready, always willing to mitigate the law and receive to mercy those who, like Ruth, have sinned in ignorance, passion, and youth. But they distinguish. Few hearts would not be pitiful to such a case as hers. . . . [As] individuals it will be good to bear in mind that we can never do amiss in restraining harsh and bitter speech to the tempted, lest we urge mere weakness to wickedness, or in holding out a hand to help the fallen to a chance of redemption. . . .

Ruth's life from the time she stands forth to the little world of Eccleston as the betrayed mother of a bastard child is exquisitely sorrowful, exquisitely touching. . . . We are touched with so much pity as the last, that we are almost moved to erase our previous strictures. But let them stand. (p. 415)

[Mrs. Gaskell's '**Life of Charlotte Brontë**' is] one of the fullest yet simplest and most touching records in our language. . . . (p. 417)

Mrs. Gaskell's fine appreciation of scenery, especially of the wild, bleak hill-country of Yorkshire and Lancashire, enables her to set before us in vivid relief the moorland parsonage of Haworth, where Charlotte Brontë was born and died. . . . The biography was almost universally accepted as tender, just, and true, and if it has appeared to some that the happy-tempered, genial, motherly writer did not get at the core of the recluse, all whose joys were spiritual, all her miseries physical and external, it may arise from the fact that their personal intimacy was not close, more than from the lack of sympathy. A biography, written so immediately on the death of its subject, risks many perils, and of these it cannot be said that Mrs. Gaskell steered quite clear even of the most obvious. Reading the book now, we are impressed with the intense pain and mortification it must have inflicted on living persons, and with the absence of the judicial spirit which would have discerned that there must be something to be said on the other side of those matters of fact of which we are shown but one. . . . [Coming] to the story with a calm mind, after the lapse of ten years, we are not always so far influenced by Mrs. Gaskell's power of narrative that we cannot perceive primary causes other than those she sets forth to account for the family tragedy she has to record. . . . It is to be observed that in the selection made from Miss Brontë's letters, we have no word of causes, but only of consequences; that she lays no blame anywhere, and offers no plea in extenuation of the misconduct which made her home worse than a prison-house. Whether it was fair to reveal a half-truth with insinuations, where it was impossible to reveal the whole truth, is a matter for private rather than for critical opinion. In a literary point of view, we think the interest and reality of the life might have been retained with much less of painful reflection upon persons beyond the four walls of Haworth parsonage. But with all its over-statements or under-statements, the work undoubtedly remains what it was pronounced to be at the time of its publication, 'one of the best

biographies of a woman by a woman,' that we possess [see excerpt above from *The Athenaeum,* April 1857].

We come now to Mrs. Gaskell's novels in her last manner, '**Sylvia's Lovers,**' and '**Wives and Daughters,**' with the exquisite short story of '**Cousin Phillis**' between. . . . ['**Sylvia's Lovers**'] demonstrates Mrs. Gaskell's] art of thoroughly clothing her conceptions in flesh and blood, of putting into their mouths articulate speech, individually appropriate, so that we are impressed by them, and moved as by the doings and sufferings of men and women whom we have actually known. As we read, they are not fictitious characters to us, but persons whose sentiments, motives, conduct, we feel inclined to analyze and discuss as if they had a literal bearing upon our own. (pp. 417-19)

[The story of '**Sylvia's Lovers**' is] as true as it is pathetic, and as beautiful as true.

'**Cousin Phillis**' is less remarkable for story than for consummate grace and delicacy of execution. Here we escape the shock of soul-destroying sorrows; we breathe sweet country air amongst good people who live above the temptations of an evil world; people to whom God has given neither riches nor poverty, but a full measure of content; who live laborious days, rising with a prayer, lying down with a blessing. The characters are few but instinct with vigour and action. (p. 423)

With '**Wives and Daughters**' we bring our reviewal of Mrs. Gaskell's works to a close. . . . In this story of every-day life her literary art attained its highest excellence. The moral atmosphere is sweet, bracing, invigorating; the human feeling good and kind throughout. We do not hesitate to pronounce it the finest of Mrs. Gaskell's productions; that in which her true womanly nature is most adequately reflected, and that which will keep her name longest in remembrance. This generation has produced many writers whose books may live long after them as pictures of manners in the reign of good Queen Victoria; but we call to mind none save Mr. Thackeray, Mr. Dickens, George Eliot, and Mr. Anthony Trollope, in their best moments, to whom the future will be so much indebted for its knowledge of how we lived and moved in the middle of the nineteenth century, as to Mrs. Gaskell. (p. 424)

There are characters in ['**Wives and Daughters**'] as difficult to portray as ever novelist attempted, and Mrs. Gaskell's success in portraying them is as great as ever novelist achieved. We have no wish either to add or to diminish—they are perfect in their strength and in their weakness—people whom we know and think of as if they were our personal acquaintances. . . . [All] the women are natural. . . . And if the women are excellent, the men are no less admirable. We do not know that it has ever been charged on Mrs. Gaskell that she drew her characters from life, but they are all so distinctly individualised that a real model might have sat for each portrait. (pp. 425-26)

[The] merit of ['**Wives and Daughters**'] is that it carries out its name—it is a story of such simple loves and doings and sacrifices as we see around us; it progresses by days and weeks and months and years as our lives progress; it is not rounded into any completeness of plot, though each event grows out of its predecessors as inevitably as real events grow, and brings about its natural results, in the fulness of time, such as we anticipate will be brought about. . . . [The] genius which created Mary Barton and Ruth, Margaret Hale and Mr. Thornton, Cousin Phillis and Sylvia Robson, had lost none of its fire, none of its force when its work was suddenly arrested by death. (p. 426)

[We] keenly regret that the world will have no more amusement, no more wise instruction from the same masterly pen. Mrs. Gaskell leaves a place vacant in the literary world, as Thackeray left a place vacant the year before her—as all men and women of genius and power like theirs, do leave vacant places which never seem to find quite adequate successors. (p. 429)

*"The Works of Mrs. Gaskell,"* in British Quarterly Review, *Vol. XLV, No. XC, April 1, 1867, pp. 399-429.*

### EDNA LYALL [PSEUDONYM OF ADA ELLEN BAYLY]  (essay date 1897)

Of all the novelists of Queen Victoria's reign there is not one to whom the present writer turns with such a sense of love and gratitude as to Mrs. Gaskell. This feeling is undoubtedly shared by thousands of men and women, for about all the novels there is that wonderful sense of sympathy, that broad human interest which appeals to readers of every description. (p. 119)

The enormous difficulties which attended the writing of a biography of the author of "Jane Eyre" would, we venture to think, have baffled any other writer of that time. . . . [But] it would . . . be hard to find a biography of more fascinating interest [than the **"Life of Charlotte Brontë"**], or one which more successfully grappled with the great difficulty of the undertaking. (p. 120)

[The novels] are not only consummate works of art, full of literary charm, perfect in style and rich with the most delightful humour and pathos—they are books from which that morbid lingering over the loathsome details of vice, those sensuous descriptions of sin too rife in the novels of the present day, are altogether excluded.

Not that the stories are namby-pamby, or unreal in any sense; they are wholly free from the horrid prudery, the Pharisaical temper, which makes a merit of walking through life in blinkers and refuses to know of anything that can shock the respectable. Mrs. Gaskell was too genuine an artist to fall either into this error or into the error of bad taste and want of reserve. She drew life with utter reverence; she held the highest of all ideals, and she dared to be true.

How tender and womanly and noble, for instance, is her treatment of the difficult subject which forms the *motif* of **"Ruth"**! How sorrowfully true to life is the story of the dressmaker's apprentice with no place in which to spend her Sunday afternoons! . . . It is so natural that the girl's fancy should be caught by Henry Bellingham . . . ; so inevitable that she should lose her heart to him. . . . But her fall was not inevitable, and one of the finest bits in the whole novel is the description of Ruth's hesitation in the inn parlour when, finding herself most cruelly and unjustly cast off by her employer, she has just accepted her lover's suggestion that she shall go with him to London, little guessing what the promise involved, yet intuitively feeling that her consent had been unwise. (pp. 124-26)

The selfishness of the man who took advantage of her weakness and ignorance is finely drawn because it is not at all exaggerated. Henry Bellingham is no monster of wickedness, but a man with many fine qualities spoilt by an over-indulgent and unprincipled mother, and yielding too easily to her worldly-wise arguments. (pp. 127-28)

The sadness of the book is relieved by the delightful humour of Sally, the servant. The account of the wooing of Jeremiah Dixon is a masterpiece; and Sally's hesitation when, having found her proof against the attractions of "a four-roomed house, furniture conformable, and eighty pounds a year," her lover mentions the pig that will be ready for killing by Christmas, is a delicious bit of comedy. (pp. 130-31)

[**"Mary Barton"**] was the first of the novels, . . . and this powerful and fascinating story at once set Mrs. Gaskell in the first rank of English novelists. . . . Like [Charles Kingsley's] "Alton Locke," it has done much to break down class barriers and make the rich try to understand the poor. . . . The secret of the extraordinary power which the book exercises on its readers is, probably, that the writer takes one into the very heart of the life she is describing. (p. 133)

[We] venture to think that **"Mary Barton,"** which for nearly half a century has been influencing people all over the world, owes its vitality very largely to the fact that Mrs. Gaskell knew the working people of Manchester, not as a professional doler out of tracts or charitable relief, not in any detestable, patronising way, but knew them as *friends*.

This surely is the reason why the characters in the novel are so intensely real. . . . How entirely the reader learns to live with [Mary] in her brave struggle to prove her lover's innocence! One of the most powerful parts of the book is the description of her plucky pursuit of the good ship *John Cropper,* on board of which was the only man who could save her lover's life by proving an alibi.

But it is not only the leading characters that are so genuine and so true to life. Old Ben Sturgis, . . . [his wife, Job Legh, John Barton, old Mr. Carson]—all these are living men and women, not puppets; while in the character and the tragic story of poor Esther we see the fruits of the writer's deep knowledge of the life of those she helped when released from gaol.

But Mrs. Gaskell looked on both sides of the question. In **"North and South"** . . . she deals with the labour question from the master's standpoint, and in Mr. Thornton draws a most striking picture of a manufacturer who is just and well-meaning. . . . The main interest of this book lies, however, in the character of the heroine, Margaret. . . . By far the most dramatic scene is that in which, to enable Frederick to escape, Margaret tells a deliberate falsehood to the detective who is in search of him. The torture of mind she suffers afterwards for having uttered this intentional lie, and the difficult question whether under any circumstances a lie is warrantable, are dealt with in the writer's most powerful way. (pp. 134-36)

[The] greatest of all Mrs. Gaskell's works [is] . . . the inimitable **"Cranford."** For humour and for pathos we have nothing like this in all the Victorian literature. It is a book of which one can never tire: yet it can scarcely be said to have a plot at all, being just the most delicate miniature painting of a small old-fashioned country town and its inhabitants. (pp. 136-37)

There is an air of leisure and peacefulness in every page of the book, for there was no hurrying life among those dignified old people. (p. 137)

In the whole book there is not a character that we cannot vividly realise. . . . One and all they become our life-long friends, while the book stands alone as a perfect picture of English country town society fifty years ago.

Mrs. Gaskell's shorter stories are scarcely equal to the novels, yet some of them are very beautiful. "Cousin Phillis," for example, gives one more of the real atmosphere of country life than any other writer except Wordsworth. (pp. 139-40)

Among the short tragic stories, the most striking is one called "The Crooked Branch," in which the scene at the assizes has almost unrivalled power; while among the lighter short stories, "My French Master," with its delicate portraiture of the old refugee, and "Mr. Harrison's Confessions" . . . are perhaps the most enjoyable. (pp. 140-41)

"Wives and Daughters" will always remain as a true and vivid and powerful study of life and character; while Molly Gibson, with her loyal heart and sweet sunshiny nature, will, we venture to think, better represent the majority of English girls than the happily abnormal [heroines] . . . of present-day fashion.

In Mr. Gibson's second wife the author has given us a most subtle study of a thoroughly selfish and false-hearted woman. . . . Wonderfully clever, too, is the study of poor little Cynthia, her daughter, whose relations to Molly are most charmingly drawn. (p. 141)

Few writers, we think, have exercised a more thoroughly wholesome influence over their readers than Mrs. Gaskell. Her books, with their wide human sympathies, their tender comprehension of human frailty, their bright flashes of humour and their infinite pathos, seem to plead with us to love one another. Through them all we seem to hear the author's voice imploring us to "seize the day" and to "make friends.". . . (pp. 144-45)

> *Edna Lyall [pseudonym of Ada Ellen Bayly], "Mrs. Gaskell," in* Women Novelists of Queen Victoria's Reign: A Book of Appreciations *by Mrs. Oliphant, Mrs. Lynn Linton, Mrs. Alexander, & others, Hurst & Blackett, Limited, 1897, pp. 117-45.*

## PAUL ELMER MORE   (essay date 1908)

[*More, who admires many qualities in Gaskell's works, suggests that, even in her social novels, Gaskell was a writer conscious of her art. This view was also advanced by Kathleen Tillotson (see excerpt below, 1954), but it was challenged by David Cecil and H. P. Collins (see excerpts below, 1934 and 1953). Unlike Cecil, Collins, and David Masson (see excerpt above, 1865), More praises Gaskell's ability to portray passion in her characters.*]

[In Mary Barton, Mr. Carson] becomes in his own way a reformer. His new desire was "that a perfect understanding, and complete confidence and love, might exist between masters and men; . . . and to have them bound to their employers by ties of respect and affection, not by mere money bargains alone; in short, to acknowledge the Spirit of Christ as the regulating law between both parties."—How strangely old-fashioned the phrases sound; how far we have removed our theories from that simple trust! (pp. 76-7)

The moral of North and South is the same as that of Mary Barton. . . . But it must not be supposed that the didactic purpose is unpleasantly prominent in either tale. Mrs. Gaskell wrote, not because she had a lesson to inculcate, but because her heart was moved by the blind suffering about her and her mind absorbed by the problem of . . . contending characters.

Nor is the colour of the stories one of unrelieved darkness. Especially there is a play of light in [North and South], in the pretty opening idyl at Helstone. . . . And when the heroine is transplanted from this southern home to the grime and stress of a great northern factory town, there is the contrast of two civilisations, meeting and contending for her soul—the old ideal of leisurely manners and the modern of stripped efficiency. And Margaret Hale herself is one of the heroines of fiction we cherish as we cherish the memory of women known in our youth. . . . Mr. Thornton himself, the self-made master who resents any interference with the control of his money, and his men, is an ably-drawn character. The bending of his stern spirit to human charity toward his workmen, by his love for Margaret, is told with consummate skill, and yet in the end the reciprocal yielding of Margaret has a touch of something not entirely agreeable; beauty such as hers needs to be enveloped by strength, but by more of fineness too.

In one respect Margaret, like the other heroines of Mrs. Gaskell's books, is sketched with a touch less feminine than masculine. They are all creatures of passion, yet we feel that their choice in love is not so much personal and voluntary as the result of that life-force which beats through the world, and of which they are the passive instruments. They are like vessels charged with a subtle and dangerous fluid; and this, I take it, is rather man's way of contemplating women. And when, as it does in Sylvia's Lovers, this unregarding force takes for its vehicle a girl made up of little vanities, what can the consequence be but a life broken by the clashing of its own strength and weakness—perhaps in the end a pathetic self-abnegation? One feels this union of traits at the first glimpse of Sylvia as she comes down from the hill-home to the sea-town—in her childlike delight at the thought of buying a new cloak, in the nimble vitality of her body. (pp. 77-80)

And with this portrayal of passion there goes an entire chastity of language—the *púdor* of true art which would represent the beauty and the devastating attraction of this force without evoking the corresponding physical emotion in the reader or beholder. . . . Read the pages where Philip watches his Sylvia at the spinning wheel, or where Kinraid observes her knitting, and again at her household work, moving "out of light into shade, out of shadow into the broad firelight"—the nature of her attraction is made sufficiently clear, but there is never a disturbing suggestion. (pp. 80-1)

[If] we analyse the charm of Cranford, it will be found to depend largely, I think, on a feeling of unreality, or, more precisely, of proximity to the greater realities of Manchester. This contrast was a part of Mrs. Gaskell's own life; she made use of it deliberately in North and South, and it gives their peculiar tone to the idyllic tales, as may be seen clearly enough by comparing her country with Jane Austen's. What impresses one in Miss Austen's books is a feeling of stability; Governments may fall in London, but any change in the manners and occupations of this provincial folk is inconceivable. In Cranford just the contrary is true. Here the grace is of something that has survived into an alien age, and is about to vanish away; there is a tremulous fragility in its beauty.

Cranford is flawless in a way, but not more so than Cousin Phillis, while its colours are altogether paler. Indeed, one scarcely knows how to praise the gem-like beauty of the later pastoral [Cousin Phillis] without using language that might seem to place it too high as a literary work. "A Protestant clergyman is perhaps the finest subject for a modern idyl that can be found," wrote Goethe of [Oliver Goldsmith's] The Vicar of

*Wakefield,* and the words are even more applicable to Mrs. Gaskell's minister Holman. (pp. 81-2)

[The meeting of Holman, Phillis, and her father in the fields] is a rare scene, whose dignity verges on the humorous, and which only a writer conscious of her art would have dared venture upon. (p. 84)

In the end one is tempted to ask why this pastoral tale has failed to establish itself among our classics. One compares it, perhaps, with *The Vicar of Wakefield.* . . . Why is it that [*Cousin Phillis*] with all its overtones of beauty and sentiment, does not rank with its plainer rival? We are more deeply stirred by the events of **Cousin Phillis** than by that of *The Vicar,* yet we feel that a hundred years from now Goldsmith's work will be read with the same kind of interest as to-day, when Mrs. Gaskell's shall be all but forgotten. May it not be just the emotional qualities of **Cousin Phillis** which prompt one to give it so brief a period of life? Somehow the sentimental appeal has a dull trick of losing its effect in an astonishingly short time, . . . whereas Goldsmith's just mixture of satire and sentiment, his freedom from superfluous baggage, his eighteenth-century cleanness of style, have the preservative quality of Attic salt. (pp. 84-5)

> *Paul Elmer More, "Mrs. Gaskell," in his* Shelburne Essays, fifth series *(copyright, 1908, copyright renewed © 1935, by Paul Elmer More; reprinted by permission of the Literary Estate of Paul Elmer More),* G. P. Putnam's Sons, 1908, pp. 66-85.

## MARJORY A. BALD (essay date 1923)

[*In her examination of pathos in Gaskell's fiction, Bald acknowledges the "over-powering" effect of Gaskell's early, unrestrained compassion, but she discerns in the later works evidence of a deliberate and "matured and beautiful" emotional reticence.*]

It is interesting to consider which faculty came first to Mrs Gaskell—compassion or humour. It will probably be acknowledged that her compassion was at first more evident, though it needed to grow side by side with humour before it could attain to its perfection of delicacy and insight.

*Mary Barton* shows us Mrs Gaskell's pathos as yet undisciplined by humour. It is genuine, no doubt, but how dreadfully overpowering! . . . Death comes back and back to the story. It is like an overhanging scourge.—[Yet] Mrs Gaskell's treatment of bereavement is often singularly beautiful. . . . We notice how gently Mrs. Gaskell handles the superstition of those watching over the dying twins, and trying not to "wish" them; she looks on with a mind free from disdain or impertinent curiosity.—The passing of Davenport is infinitely more heart-rending. We see more of the physical aspect of death, and for a moment we are reminded of Tolstoi's resolute mind to shirk nothing of the grim truth. But Mrs Gaskell never remains shrinking over the physical horror; she follows it up with some spiritual beauty or tenderness. . . . (p. 122)

It was not only death that stirred Mrs Gaskell to sympathy. She had an instinctive reverence for all ties of human affection. (p. 123)

The sympathy which George Eliot achieved by discipline seems to have come to her by nature.

It is impossible, in a short paragraph, to do anything like justice to the wonderful concentrated passion which beats through *The Heart of John Middleton.* There is something peculiarly search-ing in its stern candour, and the compressed energy which strains through its plain, curt phrases. Yet John remembered little things, almost irrelevant, in the midst of so much fierceness; all through we feel this contrast between gentleness and violence—particularly in the trifling domestic details which give a strange reality to the record of turbulent passion. . . . There may be a slight overbalancing of the emotion in the account of little Grace and her message. . . . If it is a flaw, it is the only one. (p. 124)

The pathos of **Cranford** finds its centre in the person of Miss Matty. It is not usual to find so much patience for colourless, inefficient people, wanting in "push." Jane Austen never showed such daring. Her central figures were all of them young, and most of them sprightly. Charlotte Bronte thought she was running great risks when she chose a plain heroine; but Jane Eyre was young, and as well she was clever. Miss Matty was old and diffident. . . . Mrs Gaskell always showed a very tender reserve in speaking of her tragedy. As Miss Matty herself kept silence, her creator seems to have felt that any outspoken comments would be jarring. (p. 125)

[*Ruth*] attempted larger matters with far less success. . . . In *Ruth* she was struggling to find her way. It was an ambitious attempt, which gave her exercise; though imperfect itself, it was her only way of winning through to something better. It is hard to say exactly what is wrong with this book. We always feel that the emotion is laboured, and often that it is forced. Mrs Gaskell seems to have been overwhelmed by her own earnestness. She felt it necessary to explain so much that would have been better left for granted. There is too much soliloquy, and too little silence. We should never have been told every word of Ruth's confession to Leonard. We sometimes wonder whether a real mother would have used such words—and so many of them—to a real child; but in any case it seems a breach of privacy for anybody else to hear them. This passage typifies the emotional defects of the novel as a whole. (p. 127)

[*North and South*] marks a distinct advance. We no longer feel that we are being artificially prompted to emotion. As in *Ruth,* Mrs Gaskell was tackling a big subject, but with a surer control. In *Mary Barton* she treated the sorrows of the poor with a noble sympathy. Here the impression is deepened by the greater justice with which she adds the sorrows of those who are not actually destitute. We feel Boucher's wretched misery all the more acutely for knowing that his class does not possess the monopoly of suffering. Moreover in *Mary Barton,* Mrs Gaskell showed pity for the "deserving" poor; its characters were people whom we could heartily respect. In the later book her pity was broader and more tolerant. Though she could not respect Boucher, she recognised the fact that even weak and foolish men are worthy of pity. . . . (p. 128)

[The] theme of voluntary renunciation, which would have appealed strongly to George Eliot's type of sympathy, was rare in Mrs Gaskell. Yet [in *Half a Lifetime Ago*] she wrote in the unaccustomed strain, heart-taught, and with a stateliness quite equal to George Eliot's. (p. 129)

[In *My Lady Ludlow* we see] that intermediate state between pathos and humour in which Mrs Gaskell approached so closely to Charles Lamb. . . . [She] most closely resembled Lamb, not in her actual humour, which was not nearly so obstreperous; not in her deliberate pathos, for this, though present in Lamb, was extremely rare; but in the recognition of things which are at once laughable and pitiful, without being contradictory. (p. 130)

The central emotion [in *Sylvia's Lovers*] is concerned with Daniel's arrest and trial. . . . Most moving and searching of all is that wonderful twenty-seventh chapter where we live through the long, last day of suspense. . . . Little domestic details fill our hearts with the reality of that never-ending morning. . . . It shows us Mrs Gaskell's own growth in reticence and delicacy, that she told us so little. . . . We know that Sylvia and her mother went to York, and we are vaguely informed what happened there; but we are not taken along with them. In her earlier novels Mrs Gaskell might have led us every step of the agonising journey. Here she was stronger and wiser. She showed us Bell and Sylvia growing towards their ordeal; and she let us see them when they returned, changed for life. She felt— and so do we—that it would hardly be decent to pry further into their tragedy. (pp. 131-32)

The pathos of **Cousin Phillis** shows the same matured and beautiful reticence. Phillis could not speak of her secret happiness; still less of her secret grief. (p. 132)

Finally we come to **Wives and Daughters.** We can never neglect this book if we are looking for examples of Mrs Gaskell's finest achievement. Here again mere words of pity were very much reduced. (p. 133)

There are few death-bed details. (p. 134)

[When his son Osborne died, the] Squire could not speak. Molly silently gave him a spoonful of soup, and his speech was released in a jerk. But he made no set "book" speech, only six startling words; "He will never eat again—never."

It is not seemly to make comments on such utterances. It is enough to say that they were made, and then leave them in their sacred poignancy. (pp. 134-35)

Summing up the general development of her pathos, we need say only this: It began in freedom of speech; it matured into deliberate reticence which suggested whole worlds of emotion outside the province of human utterance. A few ideas are brought captive across the frontiers of speech simply to represent that multitude of passions and emotions lying beyond in the wild, dark, voiceless spaces of the human spirit. (p. 135)

> Marjory A. Bald, "Mrs. E. C. Gaskell," in her
> Women-Writers of the Nineteenth Century, *Cambridge at the University Press, 1923, pp. 100-61.*

**ANNE KIMBALL TUELL**    (essay date 1932)

[*Like Marjory A. Bald (see excerpt above, 1923), Tuell focuses on Gaskell's artistic development. According to Tuell, Gaskell progressed from an early indulgence in bathos to an increased reliance on her instinctive ability to detect the "little springs of laughter's source" in human conduct, thus investing her later work with a "fuller humanity" and opening to her a "broader, firmer art, . . . an art comfortable, leisurely, sane with a genial and cleanly tolerance."*]

Seldom is a writer more beloved [than Mrs. Gaskell] for one book or perhaps for two. But if we will trouble ourselves to rummage among her plentiful writings, we come with odd regret, as at a pleasure almost missed, upon a multitude of stories dear to her contemporaries, known to us only in name or perhaps not at all. We find them pale from long sojourn in the dark places of neglect—but still alive with a curious modernity of power set in a quaintness of style and taste. Here is a world unquestionably of the past. . . . But it is a world in

itself which seems to touch, by a strange contradiction, the borders of the eighteenth and the twentieth centuries.

At our first stroll beyond the close-hedged paths of Cranford, the voices of the past sound far clearer than the complex medley of to-day. We are in an authentic world of human folk but not a part of it, present at actual doings and yet invisible, as some of us feel with our glasses on. But we need the glasses; it is hard even then to realize that Mrs. Gaskell belongs to the heyday of the modern novel. And our sense of anachronism comes naturally from her limitation. . . . Mrs. Gaskell is apt to show a singular pliancy, bending with intuitive suavity to the predilections of her readers, to those secret indulgences of which they are perhaps unconscious, modestly regardless, at least in early years, that her own instinct would be a better guide. Dickens might carry the public by storm, Thackeray sting it to a healthy resentment; but in so far as it was well-disposed, Mrs. Gaskell, delicately sensitive to circumstance and environing influence, would conform to it with a gracious and yielding complaisance. Hence appears in her work that contradiction of retrocession and progress, of vagueness and distinction of aim, which baffles an attempt at strict analysis, except in so far as it is found always feminine, refined by a high-bred and effective womanhood. (pp. 61-2)

[With] her earnestness for "the human with its droppings of warm tears," Mrs. Gaskell is the truest daughter of her time. . . . We watch helplessly at the deaths of happy children, noisy an hour ago; at the despair of the fierce grown tame by suffering. . . . (p. 70)

Her unsparing tenderness, always poignant and appealing, never contemptible, does sometimes exceed the modesty of nature. It may be that the world has not grown hard-hearted—has learned only a reticence necessary to art. The fervent spinning of a long agony intrudes on the privacy of pain. We seem like spectators pausing from curiosity at an accident. We feel a little vulgar; if we can do nothing about it, we ought to pass on. Certainly Mrs. Gaskell is not here at her best. She knew well how to develop the logic of experience, to make a moral result sufficient punishment for a cause of weakness; yet was too often willing to drag a chain of fortuitous calamity, "plague, pestilence, and famine, battle, murder, and sudden death." (pp. 70-1)

But Mrs. Gaskell doubtless knew what she was about. . . . Pathos is the low-built foundation of her art; without it the world would never have come to love her for a gentle lady with a merry heart. Seeking acquaintance with diversity of grief, but listening and alert for better news of herself, she followed with energy a lively series of experiments, sometimes failing, sometimes succeeding, but working, although by no means steadily, towards a more complete freedom of faculty. An unusual amplitude of scope is evident from the first. In her early popular novels, **Mary Barton** and **North and South,** she can claim a sympathetic and unprejudiced intelligence for the struggles between the labourer and the employer. Sometimes she skirts the edge of a darker field, though lacking as a rule command of the stern silences. So in **A Dark Night's Work** the secret of hidden crime waits its revelation with punishment terribly out of proportion to the original guilt. In **The Doom of the Griffiths** there passes through the gloomy quarrel of father and son a faint foreshadow of Stevenson. And at least in Sylvia's father, Daniel Robson, surly, dogged Yorkshireman, rude creature of his bleak home, stubborn unto death, she reaches near the inner circle of that miserable tragedy of stupidity, more strongly treated by the greater George Eliot.

Once by an amusing accident, in *The Grey Woman*, she produces a tale not of pity but of terror, well worth reading as a contribution to the list of tremors which English fiction has offered for cure of the man who knew not how to shiver. (pp. 71-2)

But a blood-boltered narrative at best could be for Mrs. Gaskell only an adventure. She was prompt to learn that her feet were straying if they passed along ungentle ways. . . . Accepting her mission to be the voice of pity's entreaty, she found pity's answer in the reaction of loving mirth, which is pity's release and escape. (p. 73)

The grace to detect the little springs of laughter's source was the sure result of her fundamental excellence, through which she is, in a measure, always great and always modern,—her instinct for the significant detail. Even in the most searching of her pathetic appeals the sincerest "tears of things" are tears of the little things. Not at her scenes of excessive pain do we shrink, which, ruthless in their extremity of grief, yet fail of tragedy's reserve. It is harder to notice Jem's pockets, bulging with oranges for the stricken children, or Alice Wilson's loving fingers as she handles the box packed for her by her mother so many years ago. (pp. 73-4)

Her cheer is but the eternal relish for the discovery of common traits of nature drawn again with the fine clearness of porcelain. A life may be infinitely pitiful and infinitely absurd, so fragile, so unreasonable, so genuine. To recognize the human truth of an oddity in character or situation is to have a good jest for ever. Hence the wholly winsome laughter which saves and corrects the sentimentality of the early *Cranford*—at a familiar foible, a meek stubbornness, a serene prejudice, a shrinking delicacy, faint as an aged scent. . . . And again, in that more farcical Cranford, the Duncombe of *Mr. Harrison's Confessions*, the laugh rings clear, like a sweet field wind. But it rings always low with the self-effacement of high breeding, for Mrs. Gaskell never shows more mirth than she is mistress of. (pp. 74-5)

Instinct, again, rather than deliberate effort, guided Mrs. Gaskell's fine choice of pictorial setting. Tireless ever in her zest for detail, exquisitely responsive to sense impression, she could create a convincing rightness of surrounding, imagined with the force of a lesser Hardy. . . . [She escapes] from triviality in the rare firmness of her pastoral, the almost elemental simplicity of her country scenes. . . . With all her inclination for the elegant refinements she has usually the wit to prefer the homely. . . . (pp. 75-6)

Peculiarly precious to Mrs. Gaskell seems the suggestion of an interior. At times she shows an almost Dutch appreciation for the effect of light and colour beyond a foreground of shade, a vista through cool rooms and opening casements of a bright old-fashioned garden. . . . (p. 76)

[The] human detail, the separate flavour and importance of each private experience, became with Mrs. Gaskell's growth of supreme importance to her. She would be hurt to know herself classed to-day somewhat as an antiquarian novelist, a lover of the old and the odd for the sake of age and oddity. Age was venerable to a mind like hers, if only as a shade of past life, sanctified by a gathering cluster of intimate associations; but age was readily absorbing to her artist self just because the habit of time sharpens and simplifies a personality to a clarity of distinctness. For the same cause she delighted in an eccentricity, not as an accident but as an accentuation of humanity. (p. 77)

So to Mrs. Gaskell there was opening a broader, firmer art, where "warm tears" should at last have no occasion to drop, an art comfortable, leisurely, sane with a genial and cleanly tolerance. Such is the fuller humanity of the unfinished *Wives and Daughters*, well stocked with a normal and pleasant society of worthy folks, not too clearly marshalled after their kind but uncommonly interesting to know. (p. 78)

Anne Kimball Tuell, "Mrs. Gaskell," in her *A Victorian at Bay* (copyright, 1932 by Anne Kimball Tuell), *Marshall Jones Company, Inc., 1932, pp. 61-80.*

## DAVID CECIL  (essay date 1934)

[*In his detailed assessment of her work, Cecil characterizes Gaskell as a gifted but minor artist whose "femininity" limited her intellectual and creative powers. H. P. Collins later attributed Gaskell's limitations to her religious background and environment (see excerpt below, 1953).*]

The outstanding fact about Mrs. Gaskell is her femininity. (p. 207)

In an age whose ideal of women emphasized the feminine qualities at the expense of all others, she was all a woman was expected to be. . . . As Trollope was the typical Victorian man, so Mrs. Gaskell was the typical Victorian woman.

This gives her books a place of their own in English literature. It is not a place outside their period. The fact that she was so Victorian makes her books Victorian. As much as Trollope— and as much as Dickens and Thackeray for that matter—she admired innocence and industry and a warm heart, disliked harshness and flippancy and loose living. As much as they, she preferred those who were good and let who would be clever. Her talent, too, is a Victorian talent, fertile, intuitive, uncritical. Her rambling, unequal, enthralling novels, full of providential chances and comic character-parts and true love rewarded in the last chapter, are typical Victorian novels. Only with a single difference. Her novels are Victorian novels, for the first time transposed into the feminine key. (pp. 208-09)

Now it is not to be denied that this did in some measure detract from her stature as a novelist. For one thing, it meant that her work was wholly lacking in the virile qualities. Her genius is so purely feminine that it excludes from her achievement not only specifically masculine themes, but all the more masculine qualities of thought and feeling. She was very clever; but with a feminine cleverness, instinctive, rule-of-thumb; showing itself in illuminations of the particular, not in general intellectual structure. The conscious reason plays little part in her creative processes. She could not build a story round a central idea, like Meredith, or argue from her particular observation to discover a general conception of the laws governing human conduct, like Thackeray. Nor could she describe intellectual characters. (p. 209)

Her emotional capacity is no less feminine than her intellectual. She is not a powerful writer. She could no more express the crude, the harsh or the violent than she could speak in a bass voice. And if the plot involves her in a situation which calls for the expression of these qualities, if Mary Barton is to bear witness at her lover's trial for murder, or Margaret Hale to confront a mob of starving cotton workers, athirst for their master's blood, Mrs. Gaskell's imagination ceases abruptly to function. The characters suddenly lose life and individuality and assume the stilted postures of puppets in a marionette show. Even such repressed intensities as might reasonably be supposed to come within her view, even such violent emotions as ladies in vicarages did feel, are beyond Mrs. Gaskell's imaginative range. She knew the Brontës well, but she does not put anyone like them into her books. . . . Bitterness and disillusion are as remote from Mrs. Gaskell's comprehension as violence. Every discord is resolvable to her; the most hardened sinner has his soft side. Though she often ends a story sadly, she never ends it grimly. (p. 210)

Mrs. Gaskell's femininity imposed a more serious limit on her achievement. It made her a minor artist. Of course, there is no inevitable reason why a normal woman should be a minor artist, even a normal Victorian woman. It is true Mrs. Gaskell lived a narrow life, but Jane Austen, living a life just as narrow, was able to make works of major art out of it. . . . Her achievement may cover a more confined area of experience than that of Dickens, but within this area it was of equal power and quality. Mrs. Gaskell's art, even at its highest, is not. She could express what she thought and felt better than the average Englishwoman of her day, but she did not think or feel more than they did. Her vision was not in a supreme degree intense. And the fact that she lived in a confined life tended to diminish such intensity as it had. She cannot, as Jane Austen did, make one little room an everywhere; pierce through the surface facts of a village tea-party to reveal the universal laws of human conduct that they illustrate. If she writes about a village tea-party, it is just a village tea-party; indeed, she emphasizes its surface peculiarities, its placidity, its remoteness. It is not so much that her talent is narrow as that it is slight. She has humor and pathos and poetry, but all in a relatively temperate degree. Beside that of the great masters her drawing seems a little tentative, her tints a little faint. (p. 211)

Limitations, however, are not defects. And within her limitations Mrs. Gaskell was just as successful a novelist as the greater Victorians. She has the merits of her school: its creative vitality, the unflagging, infectious zest that rivets the reader's attention in a single sentence and carries him captive through a hundred thousand words of narrative. She has the Victorian variety of tone; grave and comic, the lyrical and the pathetic, chase each other across her pages, checkering their clear surface with an incessant delightful play of shadow and sunshine. Finally, she has the most precious of the Victorian qualities. She has the artist's imagination.

For to say that she is a minor artist compared with Dickens or Thackeray is not to say that she is less an artist. . . . As much as Dickens, she opens the door into a new and living world.

And it is a world with its own especial attractions. Mrs. Gaskell has the merits as well as the defects of her limitations. Her particular kind of femininity endowed her imagination with certain virtues that those of her contemporaries are without. Taste, for instance; the Victorian lady was brought up before all things to be careful not to offend against the canons of good taste. And so apt and dutiful a pupil as Mrs. Gaskell profited to the full by this instruction. She was sometimes weak and often uninspired; she did not know how to be awkward, obtrusive or over-florid. In consequence, she can write on the most delicate subjects without jarring on the reader's susceptibility. She can be sweet without silliness, and arch without vulgarity. Over regret for old love, the beauty of helpless innocence, the tenderness of mothers, all the treacherous emotional swamps in which a thousand writers have sunk, overwhelmed in glutinous gush, she passes unscathed. . . . And though like Trollope she is sometimes dull, unlike him she is never commonplace. Her unfailing literary good breeding in-

vests her flattest pages with a sort of gentle distinction. (pp. 212-13)

[She also] has the feminine command of [visual] detail. (p. 213)

And her psychological observation is as sharp as her visual. (p. 214)

[This] power of observation enabled her to make the most uneventful scenes interesting. What could be less promising as a subject than that visit to Miss Barker, which occupies a whole chapter in the brief novel of *Cranford*—a tea-party of dull old women, all of whom know each other well, and at which everything goes off just as was expected. Yet it is one of the most entertaining scenes in English fiction. For over every inch of its drab surface quivers and gleams the play of Mrs. Gaskell's microscopic, incessant, ironical observation.

This feminine eye for detail is closely associated with a feminine subtlety. It is an innocent, even an unconscious subtlety. Mrs. Gaskell was far too unintellectual to analyze her impressions. She just sat down and described what she saw. But this, within the limited area of her vision, was a great deal. For endowed as she was with acute perceptions, and compelled to exercise them in a society which forbade people to show their true selves except through a thick veil of manners, she acquired a power to divine a situation, to assess a character by the slightest and most fleeting indication. (pp. 215-16)

Mrs. Gaskell is the only Victorian novelist who exhibits this sort of penetration. (p. 216)

But though Mrs. Gaskell was subtle, she was not sophisticated. Here we come to her fourth asset—her freshness of outlook. Cloistered like a young girl in her convent of peaceful domesticity, she never lost the young girl's eager-eyed response to the world. . . . Her mental palate, fed always, as it were, on the fruit and frothing milk of her nursery days, kept a nursery simplicity and gusto. And in consequence her whole picture of life is touched with a peculiar dewy freshness, shimmers with a vivifying, softening spring light. It does not matter that she had nothing very new to say. As a matter of fact her most elaborate descriptions are concerned with hackneyed subjects, summer gardens, picturesque village streets. And her sentiment is as unoriginal as her objects of admiration: regret for childish happiness, pity for lonely old age. Nor does she exhibit these hoary perennials of literature from a new angle. . . . But the unsophisticated, whole-hearted way in which she responds to her inspiration enables her successfully to dare the danger of the obvious. . . . No matter how trite what she wishes to say, she says it as if for the first time; and we, caught by the youthful infection of her spirit, listen to it as if for the first time too.

This freshness is Mrs. Gaskell's most significant quality, for it gives its distinguishing twist to all her other qualities. . . . Other writers have been subtle and fastidious—other writers have been fresh. But no others have been both, exactly in the way she is. (pp. 216-18)

Nor is this charm a minor weapon in Mrs. Gaskell's armory. She cannot take our attention by storm—she has not the force— she must win it by peaceful means. And win it she does. (p. 218)

Mrs. Gaskell's sex and circumstances limited her range of subjects as they limited her range of mood. . . . [The] life of the poor among themselves, the teeming, squalid, vivid life of the democracy that surges through the pages of Dickens, she does not understand at all. Equally, though she can give us an entertaining vignette of the Countess of Cumnor condescending at a country garden-party, she draws no such full-length portrait of the great world of rank and fashion as we find in [Trollope's] *Phineas Finn.* Still less had she Thackeray's knowledge of the outcasts and parasites of society; disreputable Becky Sharps, raffish Captain Deuceaces. The range of her effective creative vision is confined to the home life of the professional classes and the country gentry.

Even here it has its limitations. For it excludes half humanity. Mrs. Gaskell cannot draw a full-length portrait of a man. This is, of course, true up to a point of most women novelists. But of none, not even of Charlotte Brontë, is it so glaringly true as of Mrs. Gaskell. . . . She was incapable of appraising them with the keen eye of Jane Austen; and when she has to draw them her hand falters. Her great characters are all women, and women whose lives have little connection with men. . . . Moreover, they are exhibited, not in their relations with men— her heroines' love affairs are treated with perfunctory conventionality—but mainly in their relations with other women. . . . "Cranford," says Mrs. Gaskell, "is in possession of the amazons." And this statement is true of the whole world of her creative achievement. Mrs. Gaskell's best books are concerned with home life in its feminine aspect.

All the same, within its limits Mrs. Gaskell's picture of life is convincingly solid, vivid and true. . . . [Like] Trollope's, Mrs. Gaskell's world is real largely in virtue of the reality of its social structure. Of course, her vision of it is nothing like so complete as that of Trollope, for she saw it from a less central standpoint. But, within her smaller range, it is as convincing as his—and more delicate. Her eye for detail, her feminine subtlety, combined to give her an exquisitely fine perception of social distinctions. (pp. 218-21)

Knowledge of social differences implies knowledge of snobs, and in her small way Mrs. Gaskell describes snobs as well as Thackeray himself. She had a rosier outlook on human nature, but it does not make her account less penetrating. It makes it more truthful. . . . She brings out the often-forgotten fact that a snob may be a human being—and quite a creditable representative of his species.

Mrs. Gaskell's world does not, however, exist primarily in virtue of the reality of its social structure; like all other imaginary worlds, it lives by its characters. . . . When she leaves her own ground for that of George Eliot and tries to describe an "unusual" girl of serious interests and independent character, like Margaret Hale, the result is only a monument of maidenly priggishness. Her convincing heroines—Phillis Holman, Molly Gibson—are typical Victorian heroines . . . : gentle, unintellectual, domesticated. But they are more living to us [than the heroines of Dickens, Thackeray, and Trollope]. For the fact that Mrs. Gaskell was a woman prevented her from shrouding their figures in a dehumanizing mist of masculine sentiment, as Dickens and Thackeray did, while it enabled her to realize them more intimately than Trollope. . . An author like Trollope, who is oblivious of . . . trifles, is thus only able to make his heroine fully alive in her moments of crisis. Mrs. Gaskell, hawk-like to read every slightest indication, makes her live all the time. (pp. 222-24)

Finally, Mrs. Gaskell's peculiar combination of simplicity and subtlety enables her to communicate her heroines' charm better than Trollope. It is not an easy charm to "put across.". . . [The attraction of Molly and Phillis] lies wholly in their girlish freshness, the natural sweetness and delicacy of their dispo-

sitions. . . . [But they] bloom in Mrs. Gaskell's pages as freshly, delicately sweet as violet buds with the dew on them. And their charm is beautifully differentiated. (pp. 224-25)

But Mrs. Gaskell's girls are not all simple. Her masterpiece in this kind, Cynthia Kirkpatrick, is of a more elusive type. . . . Her apparent contradictions are the expression of a single principle of action. She is a natural hedonist—a character whose every act is directed by the instinctive love of pleasure. Since hers is an amiable disposition with a naturally refined moral taste, this means that her acts are often good ones. But she could not go on acting well, if it involved her in anything unpleasant; nor could she stop herself acting badly, if she was enjoying it. (pp. 225-26)

It is a wonderful portrait, and it is unique in Mrs. Gaskell's work. It is unique in Victorian fiction, too. The sirens of Thackeray and Trollope and Charlotte Brontë . . . are just heartless, frivolous baggages. To find a parallel to Cynthia we must leave the English novel and go to the Irina, the Madame Odintsov of Turgenev. Of course, Cynthia is a slight affair compared with these. . . . We do not see her in her maturity; her sensual side, which by all the laws of psychology must have been a strong one, is rigidly suppressed. Nor does Mrs. Gaskell draw her with Turgenev's intellectual understanding. Her subtlety is as unconscious here as everywhere else; she did not analyze Cynthia, she just tells us what she said and did. But Cynthia is essentially of the same complex and fascinating family as Turgenev's heroines; and Mrs. Gaskell tells us what she said and did so subtly and fully that her character is equally clear. (pp. 226-27)

Mrs. Gaskell's other great characters are of a type less completely her own. They are semi-comic character parts in the regular English tradition. But Mrs. Gaskell's character parts have their own individuality. In them we see the tradition modified by her peculiar powers and limitations. (pp. 228-29)

Mrs. Gaskell, then, is primarily a domestic novelist. Confined to the drawing-room, it is the people and things in the drawing-room that she sees most completely. But she sees other things as well. . . . Indeed, she is the first novelist before the time of Hardy who tried to make a whole novel out of [the inspiration of the English rural scene]. . . . (pp. 235-36)

She saw the [country] laborers and the laborers' wives and village maidens with the acuteness she saw everything, but she saw them only as they appeared to the minister's wife—in their best clothes and on their best behavior. Of the primitive savagery, the animal passions, that underlay their superficial placidness, she knew nothing. In consequence her rural scene is a little too good to be true. Her cottages are too picturesque, her farmers too jolly and rubicund, her village maidens altogether too blooming and innocent. Her picture of rural life is less real, not only than Hardy's, but than her own picture of middle-class domestic life.

All the same, it is not a false one; no artificial Arcadia of beribboned china shepherdesses and periwigged sheep. She may not have seen all the facts, but those she saw were true facts. She idealizes only by omission. (p. 237)

[Though] she may be blind to the harsher moods of nature, she can convey its gentle ones perfectly. . . . And she appreciates the gentler facets of country life as acutely as those of its setting. No English writer indicates better its placidity, the slow simple regularity of those primitive activities which are its occupation—sowing, reaping, milking, cider-making. Only

Hardy has an equally discriminating appreciation of its antique customs and ceremonies and naïve merrymakings, its local and traditional superstitions. (p. 238)

Mrs. Gaskell's technical powers are as typical of her school and personality as the rest of her achievement. Her form, indeed, is less obviously faulty than that of her contemporaries. . . . [Her] every episode has its part to play in the development of the plot; her most memorable characters are the chief actors in the stories in which they appear. All the same, she is not a faultless craftsman; her books are often too long. She never seems to have realized that a slight inspiration like hers should be embodied in a slight structure, that you cannot paint a life-size portrait in water-colors. . . . We find ourselves unable to respond for hundreds of pages together to a stimulus at once so mild and so monotonous.

Besides, the structure of her stories is, as in Dickens, a framework imagined separately from the characters; not, as in the masterpieces of form . . . , their inevitable product. And her plots are not always good in themselves. They have the usual Victorian faults: they are often improbable and stagey, relying on coincidence and unexpected strokes of fortune. . . . (p. 240)

Mrs. Gaskell's style is better than her form; indeed, it is one of her chief glories. It is not, of course, a great style; it lacks the spare athletic vigor of the best plain stylists, and the magnificence of the best elaborate ones. Moreover, her want of intellectual grasp makes it at times both loose and wordy. But in its way it is as important an agent in her achievement as Thackeray's own. It is the same sort as his; that English, at once pure and colloquial, easy and fastidious, introduced into English by the eighteenth-century essayists. It has all their elegance and consistency, yet it has its own flavor. Mrs. Gaskell's feminine sensibility shows itself as much in her choice of words as in her treatment of her material. Her every page has its happy descriptive image, its graceful turn of phrase, and her characteristic flexibility, too. . . . (p. 241)

Style, poetry, humor, pathos, sensibility to nature, knowledge of character; the recital of Mrs. Gaskell's virtues brings us to the same question as did those of the other Victorians. Why has she not got more reputation: with twenty times the talent of most novelists, why is she not read twenty times as much? Alas, the answer is the same. Like Dickens' and Charlotte Brontë's, Mrs. Gaskell's work is as faulty as it is inspired, and for the same reason. Like them she commits the novelist's most fatal fault, she writes outside her range. For she too was the instinctive, uncritical child of an instinctive, uncritical age, ignorant alike of the laws governing her art and of her particular capacities and limitations. When her imagination was fired, she had no idea that she ought to find a form appropriate to it. She just fitted it as best she could into the form commonly used by the novelists of her day.

And this was a form that involved a great deal of material outside her imaginative range. Men's characters, for instance; the sort of plot Mrs. Gaskell chose for herself almost always entailed full-length portraits of men. And the result was disastrous. Her elderly men, indeed, are not so bad. . . . They are character-parts, and as such give scope to her humor; while their only serious emotions are their relatively sexless family affections. . . . But they are lively vignettes, rather than full-length portraits. . . . As for her young men, they are terrible; either wooden stock types of manly character . . . [or] imperfectly disguised Victorian women, prudish, timid and demure, incapable of regarding any question except in its personal as-

pect, addicted to cozy fireside confidences, inclined to admonish their sweethearts with the tender severity of a mother.

Again, the plot of the typical Victorian novel contained dramatic incidents, so Mrs. Gaskell's plots often contained dramatic incidents. But such incidents involved those violent and masculine emotions she could least express. Her dramatic episodes—the murder in *Mary Barton,* the riot in *North and South,* the press-gang scenes of *Sylvia's Lovers*—are utterly unlike such episodes in real life. They are melodrama; and bad melodrama at that. (pp. 242-44)

It was not just the convention of her time that led Mrs. Gaskell into melodrama. And here we come to the second cause of her failure to keep to her proper range. Her natural disinclination to do so was increased by her moral views. . . . A large part of her work is inspired, not by the wish to embody an artistic conception, but to teach her readers what she considered an important moral lesson. This need not, of course, have been fatal to her. A moral lesson can be a work of art; Tolstoy's often were. But the subject of Tolstoy's lesson and the subject of his inspiration happened to coincide. Mrs. Gaskell's never did.

The moral lessons she thought important dealt with subjects outside her imaginative range. Sociological subjects for one thing. . . . [Mrs. Gaskell] was horrified by the bad conditions in which the poor lived, and by the un-Christian spirit that possessed both employers and employed. She therefore wrote both *Mary Barton* and *North and South* in order to expose these evils and suggest a remedy. It would have been impossible for her if she had tried, to have found a subject less suited to her talents. It was neither domestic nor pastoral. It gave scope neither to the humorous, the pathetic nor the charming. Further, it entailed an understanding of economics and history wholly outside the range of her Victorian feminine intellect. And the only emotions it could involve were masculine and violent ones. Mrs. Gaskell makes a creditable effort to overcome her natural deficiencies . . . , but all in vain. Her employers and spinners are wooden mouthpieces, not flesh-and-blood individuals; her arguments are anthologies of platitude; her riot and strike scenes are her usual feeble melodrama.

She does no better when in *Ruth* she turns the light of her reforming eye on the sexual morality of her time; calls down the wrath of mankind on the injustices consequent on a dual standard for men and women. Any story illustrating such a theme requires in its teller a capacity to express passion, an understanding of man's attitude to this, his most masculine activity, and an acquaintance with the animal side of character. Mrs. Gaskell cannot convey passion, did not understand men at all; while the society in which she had grown up had made it a primary purpose to see that a respectable woman like her should know as little of the animal side of life as possible. (pp. 244-46)

[Moral fervor] was nearly fatal to poor Mrs. Gaskell. For it meant that to an extent unparalleled among Victorian novelists, she wasted her time writing about subjects that did not inspire her. . . . A great part of her work is artistically worthless, unlit by that flame of creative imagination which alone could make it living literature today. *North and South* is not living literature, though it is the most elaborately finished and largely conceived of her books. *Ruth* is not, though it is the most serious in intention. For both books are primarily sociological pamphlets. *Mary Barton* is irradiated by gleams of her humor and poetry, but these are only a small and inessential part of its scene. . . . Three novels alone of her huge output, *Sylvia's Lovers, Cranford, Wives and Daughters,* and one short *nouvelle, Cousin Phillis,* make up her significant achievement; only they are conceived predominantly within her range. (pp. 248-49)

[In] spite of minor blemishes, these four stories are of the imperishable stuff of our literature. Character and incident alike stir and shimmer with the energy of the true creative imagination. It may not be the greatest kind of imagination. *Sylvia's Lovers* and *Cousin Phillis* in particular, expressing as they do Mrs. Gaskell's slighter pastoral inspiration, are not great, in any sense of the word. But they have their peculiar charm; gleaming, delicate-hued little bits of luster pottery unlike anything else in the varied museum of English letters. *Wives and Daughters* and *Cranford* are not exactly great either. But they express a stronger side of Mrs. Gaskell's talent. And they have their place among the classic English domestic novels. Of the two, *Wives and Daughters* reaches the greater heights. The characters of Cynthia and Mrs. Gibson are Mrs. Gaskell's masterpieces. There is nothing so remarkable in *Cranford,* but in it she has found for once a form proper to her inspiration, short, episodic, exclusively concerned with women; and it is the most consistent of her works. Her humor, her pathos, her exquisite charm, appear in it almost unalloyed; hardly a word of it but is still as fresh as the day it was printed.

But so are the other stories for that matter, all three of them—as fresh as this morning's roses. (p. 250)

> David Cecil, "Mrs. Gaskell," in his Early Victorian Novelists: Essays in Revaluation *(copyright 1935 by The Bobbs-Merrill Company, Inc.; copyright renewed © 1962 by David Cecil; used by permission of the publisher, The Bobbs-Merrill Company, Inc.; in Canada by Constable & Company Limited), Constable, 1934 (and reprinted by Bobbs-Merrill, 1935, pp. 207-50).*

## H. P. COLLINS  (essay date 1953)

[*In his response to A. B. Hopkins's* Elizabeth Gaskell: Her Life and Works, *(see Additional Bibliography), Collins challenges Hopkins's promotion of Gaskell as a major novelist. Rejecting Hopkins's claim that Gaskell's work is remarkable for its variety, dramatic power, and modernity, Collins portrays Gaskell as a "rather wasted woman of genius" whose environment and religious background impeded the intellectual detachment essential to producing great art. Collins shared many of the views set forth by David Cecil (see excerpt above, 1934).*]

[Elizabeth Gaskell] was intensely feminine without the usual feminine resources, and a Romantic without the Romantic's enthusiasm. Although she was not intellectually capable of seeing life steadily or whole, and equally incapable of intellectual detachment, her vision was unusually direct. Experience made an unbroken, unalleviated impact on her mind, her feelings, her nerves. She had no faculty of distortion, of that distortion which transmutes the artist's feeling. Perceived things, perceived values, did not change from one shape to another in her mind. (p. 61)

Hers was the naked sensibility, and in her writing so far as it is valid we are always conscious of the simple impact of life upon her. She had no real defences, no real artifice, and in literary creation, which 'disrealizes and realizes, realizes and disrealizes' she is ultimately ingenuous. Any complexity she has—and art does not go far without complexity—is in herself, it is not fashioned in the creative process. . . . Cynthia Kirkpatrick, Elizabeth Gaskell's masterpiece, is . . . photographic. Detailed observation has had little or no part in the making of her, she is conditioned by pure sensibility. (pp. 61-2)

Elizabeth was far from a pure artist; but she was without arrière-pensée [hidden motives] *as an artist.* So long as she stuck to reality, it was a reality never manipulated. Her sensibility was pure, as it was naked and defenceless. (p. 62)

She had abounding humour in perception and a delicate irony. . . . But she was not adept at turning the humour or irony on her own moral presuppositions. As long as she remained upon the social surface she was neither dull nor turgid—*Cranford,* for example, is singularly free of sentimentality. But neither the humour nor the irony became quite a harmonious expression of the complete personality. She was a Victorian, not a contemporary of Jane Austen's, and the abysses of Romantic suffering had opened before her feet. *Emma* is genuinely self-contained, *Cranford* is arbitrarily self-contained. The classicist correspondence between life and the individual had become untenable. (p. 64)

The receding tide of Romanticism did not leave Elizabeth Gaskell safe and sound on the shores of Victorian certitude and compromise. She was left there, but not safely. The brilliant, rather flashy and insensitive novelists of early Victorianism, Disraeli, Bulwer Lytton, the young Dickens himself, emphasize by contrast Elizabeth Gaskell's subfusc quality; but at this distance of time the contrast should help us to understand her inhibitions. She had not their assurance, for 'on instinct' she could not accept any suppositions comparable with theirs, or indeed any suppositions at all, beyond mere moral conventions. Just the transparency which makes her admirable spiritually makes her unsatisfactory artistically.

For unsatisfying, in the wider sense, she remains—how much less enjoyment she gives than, for instance, Trollope. . . . She lacked the intellectual control that could have made her last novel a tenderer and greater *Middlemarch.* The conventional moral strain in her could not tolerate the play of free intelligence. . . . [She] could not achieve the 'poetry' of the self-intoxicated Protestant Brontës because her sensibility was nourished only on negative [unitarian] beliefs. Her spirit was disciplined, not released; but the disciplined spirit can only find peace on a plane lower than that of imaginative creation. (p. 65)

She did not *think* hard enough; and collaterally she took experience too hard. She was not a true satirist—she did not half-create, in the way of real satire, the social tensions she exploited. She suffered them, vicariously, and conscience, not exhilaration, took charge. But the end of literature, as Longinus said long ago, is not persuasion but rapture. All Elizabeth's fine sincerity and all her faults are clear in her first book, *Mary Barton.* . . . [It] has no merits which were not realized more artistically in *Ruth* and *North and South.* . . . (pp. 65-6)

[*North and South*] is an admirable study of the conflict between Hampshire grace and industrial individualism, and it has in Margaret Hale a quite brilliant heroine; but there is still the failure to come to a point intellectually, the pulled punch of the unassured moralist. . . . It is not so much that there is evasion of realities in religion and realities in sex, as that the author is not *deliberately conscious.* The impulse to completeness is lacking: the writer all-too-conscientiously bludgeons herself with violent and disagreeable incident, not too well reproduced, but she does not focus passion intellectually.

It is not surprising that Elizabeth's strongest, truest and least inhibited feeling should have been for *place* and the atmosphere of place. The chief character in several of her novels is Manchester; Knutsford . . . is far more widely celebrated than any of her men and women, and everywhere the influence of her country scenes broods as a gracious presence over her work. With places she is never uncomfortable, never lapses into the moral or morbid. The element that really gives *The Life of Charlotte Brontë* its abiding readability—and after all it has never been superseded—is her feeling for windswept Haworth and the Yorkshire moors, not her rather limited sympathy with, and knowledge of, the disorderly Brontë genius. Through the whole of her real work, from the lovely opening of *The Moorland Cottage* to the rural interludes of *Wives and Daughters,* she never falters in her appreciation of the English scene and—what is perhaps a little surprising—she never subjectifies it. One famous novel, *Sylvia's Lovers,* seems to me to combine a complete triumph in animating inanimate nature, whether land or sea, with an equally complete failure in dialogue and human character. (pp. 66-7)

It does not seem to me that Elizabeth Gaskell was very remarkable for variety of any kind: she exhibits the one consistent merit of being Elizabeth Gaskell. Her unvaried, unveiled sensibility is the strength and limitation of everything she wrote. To try one's hand at too many genres is not the same thing as to do many things well. She did very few things well, but her quality was unmistakable. The supremely good things, surely, are her sensitiveness, sympathy with human nature, humour, playfulness, and insight into not-too-complex character, above all acute feeling for the beauty of the English scene at its best. But her vision of life was confined within her own *instinctive* feminine sympathies; she never created an objective, dramatized world in which men and women live without revealing the lineaments of their creator. . . . *Cousin Phillis* is a delightful book, with singularly few faults proceeding from any flaw in the artistic purity, but all the time we cannot help feeling that this is happening in the world of Elizabeth Gaskell, it is conditioned by the consciousness of an early Victorian woman of rather restricted moral and intellectual scope. (pp. 68-9)

[Though] Elizabeth is always tender and (in her artistic passages) true, she is not really strong, if that implies secure and detached mastery, and surely not 'dramatic' which would involve an altogether more restrained and deliberate technique of presentation. We cannot suspend our belief that we are being told a story. . . . Drama requires not only a sense of character, but a sense of development and situation. Elizabeth Gaskell's figures rarely develop through experience; and she is not good at crises. (p. 69)

She remains, like her men and women, fast bound within the confines of her temperament. *Wives and Daughters,* which is, after all, a masterpiece, exhibits a growth in care and a psychological deepening—she had been gradually abandoning her moral pot-boiler novel—and there is a sustained delicacy and subtlety in the handling of Cynthia Kirkpatrick rarely rivalled in English fiction between the time of Richardson and the dawn of the modern psychological novel. And the insight is set off with a lightness, a sparkle without hardness or malice, which even Jane Austen does not quite attain. Within the range of what her author herself once rather naively called 'mild literature' Cynthia is complete and perfect. Her mother, the second Mrs. Gibson, is a recognized success in the comical-nasty, and as the presentation of her steers perfectly between the boisterous and the low-toned, achieving a consistent vivacity of light satire, she must be ranked very high in the order of non-dramatic comedy. Elizabeth Gaskell's humour does not have

its being in the world of Rabelais or Molière, it does not reach out to include sex and religion and vice; but the comedy of *Wives and Daughters* is far from artificial: it amuses through sensitivity and not by a designed suspension of sensitivity. It is not only spontaneous, it is naturally related to a serious theme, though it is as comedy that the book survives in the reader's memory. . . . Though the novel has little vital action or progress, it revolves very smoothly—far more convincingly than any of its forerunners. The Gaskell stories are not driven forward by the compulsive power of any inner idea, but in *Wives and Daughters* there is an almost unflagging buoyancy and sparkle which atones for the want of deliberate form.

Future generations will enjoy *Cranford* just as we do—and rightly—and it seems probable that they will preserve *The Life of Charlotte Brontë* for its haunting Yorkshire atmosphere and *Cousin Phillis* as a singularly pure and tender idyll, redolent of our lost rural civilization in its last years. . . . [But] it is on *Wives and Daughters* that her claim to rank as something more than a minor classic must rest. It merits a place among the masterpieces of our great age of fiction, even if . . . it is the least pretentious place of all. The mood of the twentieth century is far from favourable to Elizabeth Gaskell, her *tone* in fiction is unsophisticated and démodé; the style is neither intellectually modulated nor terse and colloquial and it is unlikely that a culture already impatient of convention will ever be well attuned to it. . . . But she was fairly certain to fall a victim to conventionality, which she had neither the passion nor the intellectual guile to withstand. A freer way of expression would not have made her a liberated artist. She wanted passion, positive faith, the resources of the cultivated ego. . . . But, however much she may disappoint us as an artist, however much we may feel the hiatus between the innate capacity and the achievement, we can gratefully acknowledge a writer free of all essential falsity. . . . [And] we can recognize in this attractive, lovable, rather wasted woman of genius one who reflected with absolute honesty (though the mirror was sometimes blurred) the life around her. Her great contemporaries, with their wider vision, who have given us so much more delight, also mislead us more vitally. In her social judgment, Elizabeth Gaskell never lost proportion. (pp. 70-2)

> *H. P. Collins, "The Naked Sensibility: Elizabeth Gaskell," in* Essays in Criticism, *Vol. III, No. 1, January, 1953, pp. 60-72.*

### KATHLEEN TILLOTSON (essay date 1954)

[*Citing its appeal to universal themes and its integrity as a work of art, Tillotson argues that* Mary Barton *transcends the limitations of the documentary social novel or "novel with a purpose."*]

[*Mary Barton*] is the outstanding example—outstanding in merit as in contemporary fame—of a kind of novel which first clearly disengaged itself in the [1840s]: the novel directly concerned with a social problem, and especially with the 'condition-of-England question'; and because it transcends that kind; alike in motive and effect, it is far more than a 'tract for the times'. The same social conditions, and something of the same anxiety about them, inspired *Sybil* and *Yeast* and *Alton Locke;* but Mrs. Gaskell differs from Disraeli and Kingsley in having no axe to grind. A wider impartiality, a tenderer humanity, and it may be a greater artistic integrity, raise this novel beyond the conditions and problems that give rise to it. (p. 202)

It is partly because it is a novel which starts from 'individuals' that *Mary Barton* stands out from the run of 'novels with a purpose'. It is not less truthful than others of its kind, nor less passionate; but it is also, as befits a woman's novel, more purely compassionate; 'the poetry is in the pity'. But there is no patronage or condescension towards suffering. The denizens of the 'other nation' are neither harrowing victims nor heroic martyrs; they are shown in their natural human dignity. . . . (pp. 202-03)

The grimmest episode in **Mary Barton,** John Barton's visit to the Davenport family, dying of fever in their cellar dwelling, could easily have been merely documentary and detachable; instead it is made an essential stage in Barton's experience, part of the warp of the novel. As often with Mrs. Gaskell's descriptions, it makes its effect by slow persistent accumulation; the reader is enmeshed in its detail before he is aware, and engaged as a complete human being, not a politician or philanthropist. [With Disraeli's *Sybil,* the] reader's response to Devilsdust and to the tommy-shop is simple and immediate: these conditions are wrong and should be altered by legislation. . . . The sufferings of the characters in **Mary Barton** evoke this response and something more. The Davenports could have a better drained and ventilated dwelling and law or charity should see that they do not starve because the mill is closed: but with John Barton we are left aware of

> how small, of all that human hearts endure,
> That part which laws or kings can cause or cure.

Not small indeed, but not all; beneath this is the hard core of irremediable suffering 'permanent, obscure, and dark', in John Barton's sense of the mysterious injustice of man's time-bound existence. To counter-act this there must also be a reconciling power; the sense that 'we have all of us one human heart'. . . . Manchester life is the life of men and women stirred by the primary human affections, and made in the divine image. On this simple intuition the novel is built.

It has therefore a more complex unity than that of social purpose, a unity rather of theme and tone. But first of all, it has the unity of a single character . . . [John Barton]. He is central both to the mere narrative, and to the theme of class antagonism; both reaching their climax in the eighteenth and exactly half-way chapter, 'Murder'. But he is also bigger than the events, even than the clashing social forces which they represent; rebelling against more than society; marked with the same tragic irrationality as [Thomas Hardy's] Michael Henchard, Mayor of Casterbridge. . . . [John Barton's story] is the timeless history of how a man full of human kindness is hardened into (and by) hatred and violence. This defines the rising curve of the story. . . . But, as he says on his deathbed after he has confessed the murder, 'All along it came natural to love folk, though now I am what I am . . . I did not think he'd been such an old man—Oh! that he had but forgiven me.'. . . [Mr. Carson] does forgive, and John Barton dies in the arms of the man whose son he has murdered. And this points to the book's true theme: not this or that feature of industrial society is being criticized, but its whole principle, excluding any human contact between masters and men; and the hope of betterment lies not in this or that reform, but in the persistence, against all odds, of humanheartedness. (pp. 209-12)

[Mary] subsides at times into the novel-heroine of the period— though the greater freedom of her class gives her more scope for action. Her emergence as active and heroic heroine after the murder . . . makes her dominate the narrative for the latter half of the novel; but her relation to its theme seems too weakly

developed. The rivalry of her two lovers, the master and the man, and her vacillation between them, her relation to her father, the threatening parallel between her and Esther, all have thematic possibilities that are only roughly suggested. . . . [In] her alone of the characters one sees the prentice hand. (pp. 213-14)

[Job Legh] is more than a minor character; he is the point of rest in the narrative, and in the theme, the embodiment of 'the gentle humanities of earth' and of the practical possibilities of the Christian ethic. . . . [It is he] who appeals for Mr. Carson's forgiveness, he who presses home the social and spiritual lesson after John Barton's death. . . . (p. 219)

A novelist of narrower purpose might have didactically emphasized the difference between Job Legh and John Barton. But Mrs. Gaskell holds the balance fairly between John Barton's bitter protest and Job Legh's acceptance of his lot; resignation to the power of the masters and to the divine will are not confused. (p. 220)

John Barton and Job Legh may perhaps stand not only for different yet related aspects of 'Manchester life', different responses to life's hardships, but for the defiant courage and persistent loving-kindness that are seen now colliding, now cooperating, in all Mrs. Gaskell's novels. Courage to give utterance to unfamiliar points of view—that of the workman driven to violence; of the stern self-made factory-owner; of the seduced girl and the parson who protects her; but always with the purpose, unconscious perhaps, of promoting sympathy, not sharpening antagonisms; between regions, classes, sexes, generations; on the quiet assumption that to know is to understand, to forgive, and even to respect.

Not even George Eliot shows such reverence for average human nature as Mrs. Gaskell; and this is evident from her earliest work. . . . [She] accepts, and not ruefully, the ordinariness of people and the dailiness of life. Already in her first novel the minor characters . . . are solid and distinct; each character, however small, has its scale of moral values, and its social medium; all are closely associated with the domestic detail of their surroundings. . . . This unheightened truthfulness establishes confidence, so that we are ready to accept her 'big scenes'—the chase down the Mersey, the murder trial; like the bank failure in **Cranford,** they seem simply emergencies which must occasionally arise in ordinary life and which test character. And more: this almost pedestrian truthfulness is already accompanied by something spacious: her common flowers of human nature are rooted in earth, but over them arches 'the divine blue of the summer sky' [see excerpt above by Henry James, 1866].

It would be better then to remove from **Mary Barton** the old tag of 'novel with a purpose', implying social, extra-artistic purpose. It was indeed, more perhaps than any other of the time, a novel with a social *effect;* but Mrs. Gaskell wrote, then as always, not with her eye on the effect, but as one possessed with and drenched in her subject. . . . (pp. 221-22)

> *Kathleen Tillotson, " 'Mary Barton' " (a revision of a lecture originally delivered at the University of London in 1949), in her* Novels of the Eighteen-Forties *(reprinted by permission of Oxford University Press), Oxford University Press, Oxford, 1954, pp. 202-23.*

### EDGAR WRIGHT (essay date 1965)

[*In his* Mrs. Gaskell: The Basis for Reassessment, *Wright seeks to demonstrate that Gaskell's work exhibits the thematic unity and technical development associated with novelists of stature. His comments on the "world of Cranford," excerpted below, reflect his contention that, in all of her major novels, Gaskell "develops her central interest in observing and analyzing the various aspects of individual emotion and behaviour, as controlled by social custom and belief, that combine to form a unified or disorganized society."*]

[The standard objection to *Cranford*] is that it is not a novel, and is hardly to be ranked as fiction; that it is a set of reminiscences thinly disguised as fiction, something like Conrad's *The Mirror of the Sea* but carried slightly further in its method. . . . That it is fiction should be obvious as we follow the story line of each episode, and the gradual linking of episodes into a larger structural unity, while increasing our acquaintance with the relatively few characters round whom and through whom *Cranford* grows. Anecdotes and incidents . . . are taken from life or local legend, but Mrs. Gaskell has no hesitation in altering facts and reshaping events to suit her purpose. (pp. 102-03)

[The] first episode is slight, simple and unoriginal, a mixture of pathos, mild melodrama and happy ending. Yet the unobtrusive and undemanding nature of the story is its virtue; it is admirably suited to permit the narrative of daily incident and custom which carries it along and provides the real interest. . . .

[It] is around Miss Matty that the episodes develop until they have finally limned her history and character in a narrative that accumulates unity as it proceeds. And all the time the delicate nuances of behaviour in the circumscribed society and its small country town are being described in incidents that, whether trivial or major within the narrative, keep proportion to the social scene. (p. 104)

*Cranford* makes its initial impression by its tone and by the sheer felicity of incident and dialogue. The narrative attitude is one of humour, a humour based on sympathy and affection laced with common sense and a nice eye (or ear) for observation. It admits that life can be serious, but the narrative viewpoint is just sufficiently detached to keep events in proportion, and to refuse to act as though a recognition of what is serious necessarily involves solemnity or joylessness. The observation is shrewd; it notes what is amusing without poking fun. Above all it is the sort of humour that is possible only in an environment in which the general run of events is pleasant, and the inhabitants are free from the continual presence of hardship and the daily evidence of man's inhumanity to man. Given such surroundings, it is possible to concentrate on the minor details of life—one's own and one's neighbour's. (p. 105)

[Two] principles—propriety and humanity—. . .directly control Cranford conduct. The book is a portrayal of a community where these principles govern action; there may be argument on the interpretation of propriety (never about humanity) but it is unthinkable that any other basis of conduct can exist. It is because of this that *Cranford* is in its essence, not simply in its background and detail, different from the Manchester stories, in which propriety and humanity are present but can also be conspicuously absent. Drumble, the great manufacturing town only twenty miles from Cranford, is mentioned just often enough to keep us aware that other attitudes exist. It is at Drumble that the Town and Country Bank in which Miss Matty's small savings are invested stops payment, an impersonal attitude to obligations, which Miss Matty quietly refutes by changing Farmer Dobson's now worthless note into sovereigns.

It may be considered that *Cranford*, in its assumption of the unquestioned acceptance of such principles is an idealization, but we are kept aware of other attitudes. (pp. 105-06)

The implication all the time is that clear notions of duty and behavior can achieve all that is necessary—if everybody acts by them. *Cranford* ultimately arrives at the same conclusion as *Mary Barton,* but it starts from the opposite direction.

Because of its assumptions there is no need to preach, we are given the illustration without the sermon. The third and vital principle, Religion, on which all else is based, is not discussed because it is accepted and acted on. It appears therefore only where it is natural to find it, at the death-bed of Miss Brown for example, taking its place without strain or emphasis in the dialogue of people whose Christianity is so native to them that they would be surprised, and rather shocked, at any suggestion of a need to proclaim it, let alone defend it. (p. 107)

The impression we are encouraged to get of Cranford is of an old-fashioned place a generation ago, though clear indications—such as the reading of the current number of *The Pickwick Papers* and the passage of time after that—show that the calendar time is roughly contemporary. But the narrative threads move back to the late eighteenth century, and Cranford is shown as a continuity, a surviving as well as a present reality personified particularly in Miss Matty. Yet in a hundred little touches . . . change is suggested. Cranford is not static, it has to accept interference from the outside world. Its whole tenor indicates for example a gradual shifting of the social balance, 'dubious' members such as Betty Barker, Mrs. Fitz-Adam and the 'vulgar' Mr. Hoggins are admitted, as their worth is accepted. The point is that the values of the traditional outlook are maintained. (pp. 107-08)

It is over simple to accept *Cranford* as a nostalgic idealization, though to some extent it has this quality. Yet only to some extent; in spite of its lightness of treatment it is informed by a serious concern for known and trusted standards, and this has supplied part of its strength to survive. Nor is life itself idealized. Its characters suffer, life is unfair to them. (p. 108)

It is no more possible than it is with Manchester to define in rigid and precise terms exactly what Cranford 'stands for' [in Mrs. Gaskell's fiction], but we can see the principles and feelings which govern it. It is associated with pleasant and tranquil surroundings, a sense of security and stability, a way of life guided by order, custom and a clear vision of right and wrong in great and small things, free equally from the poverty and the desire for 'progress' that occupied the nervous energy and time of the new industrial society. It is a world in which there is leisure for humanity and social obligations, and sufficient means to support them. Moreover it is not a remote ideal. Cranford as a town and a society may ignore a few awkward facts, but it represents a type that existed alongside the new materialism. It was possible to make a choice.

Two further qualities which as it were tinge the Cranford world may be referred to in rounding off this account of its essence. One [is] . . . the stability of its class structure. In *Cranford* the characters all know their place, and all accept without hesitation the general scheme of things. In practice we are hardly aware from the book of any section of Cranford except the genteel one—for the servants are part of the gentility, mirror-images reflecting views and beliefs, more conscious of the niceties of position than their mistresses. . . . (p. 112)

The other quality is the presence of the countryside, which is part of the physical charm of Cranford. While it is true that

Cranford is a country town, the country is very much a background and barely mentioned. When it occurs, as in the journey out to Thomas Holbrook's farm, it is domesticated and humanized. 'The fragrant smell of the neighbouring hayfields came in every now and then,' no more. (p. 113)

During the period up to the publication of *North and South* Mrs. Gaskell had turned frequently to the Cranford world as a relief from the industrial [Manchester] society in which she lived and which she was writing about. Much of this turning away may be regarded as a form of escape achieved by the expression, through fiction, of her preference. Occasionally she varies the physical milieu, making it more specifically country, although still a Cranford type of country. The story of **'My French Master'** for example is set vaguely on the edge of a forest. . . . Sometimes, as in **'Morton Hall'**—set on the outskirts of Drumble—she gives extra rein to her interest in local tradition and legend, moving the story back to give a perspective of event and continuity. Characteristically these stories are not essentially happy ones; Mrs. Gaskell . . . did not attempt to escape from the harsh aspects of life itself, and the Cranford tales vary from the near farce of **'Mr. Harrison's Confessions'** to the sombre shading of **'Morton Hall'**. But they all have in common a background of happiness and humour, an actual or potential pleasure seen in the physical setting and its society. (pp. 114-15)

After *North and South* (more strictly, after the *Life*), Mrs. Gaskell turned away with almost decisive completeness from the Manchester world. She gives up with it the attempt to deal with the 'big' problems and broad issues, and paradoxically universalizes her work by restricting it to the individual problems of life in a small community. For by doing this she is able to ignore external pressures which, as the reader realizes only too well, cannot be interpreted in terms of individual behaviour other than by a process of simplification which may with some truth be labelled as a romantic idealization. . . . Once the decision had been taken she was free to regard her work solely from the point of view of the novelist; it is as a novelist and not as a moralist that she succeeds or fails in her later work; even the apparent exception of the feeble didacticism which closes *Sylvia's Lovers* is largely a novelist's failure. *My Lady Ludlow, Sylvia's Lovers, Cousin Phillis* and *Wives and Daughters* are expressions of Cranford values, stages in her progress to the final and full expression of the Cranford world in its complexity and strength, while showing it as a durable form of society capable of standing the pressure of other attitudes. There is also little doubt that living in Manchester had depressed and influenced her; her later years of greater independence, travel and the contacts which fame brought, allowed fuller vent to her natural outlook. (p. 118)

*Cranford* and the early stories which share its context all tend to look back, depicting a society set in its ways; it is a world of the middle-aged. . . . In her later work the centre of interest gradually switches to the young and to the adaptable. The Cranford ethos is not lost, nor is the setting with all that it stands for, but the small section of society whose attitudes and behaviour occupy the whole of the early book has retreated into the background of *Wives and Daughters*, represented by the Miss Brownings. Old-fashioned, slightly comic in their rigidity of outlook, bewildered by strange patterns of behaviour and thought, they are still respected for their principles and loved for their goodness. They are the hereditary custodians of manners and ethics who need to be propitiated by all sections of society, even by the modern and aristocratic Lady Harriet,

and who have handed on the principles to be adopted and adapted by the next generation. The novelist now catches not merely a whole society but one in the process of change, evolving without discontinuity from its less complex predecessor.

Mrs. Gaskell insists on humanity as well as propriety, and as the context of her work broadens, her insight into human nature and feeling deepens. . . . Her humour found its natural outlet through her examination of 'propriety' and her sensibility in the 'humanity', while her art as a novelist as well as her views as an individual found their full expression in the fusion of the two aspects. (pp. 118-19)

> *Edgar Wright, "The World of 'Cranford'" (originally published in a slightly modified form as "Mrs. Gaskell and the World of 'Cranford'," in* The Review of English Literature, *Vol. VI, No. 1, January, 1965), in his* Mrs. Gaskell: The Basis for Reassessment *(© Oxford University Press 1965; reprinted by permission of Oxford University Press), Oxford University Press, London, 1965, pp. 102-119.*

### ARTHUR POLLARD (essay date 1966)

Mrs Gaskell wrote both short and long short stories. Hence it is difficult to criticize her achievement as though it represented a body of work in a single manner. I propose therefore to say something about those pieces whose length is more conformable to our notions of the short story and then to consider the longer ones later. . . . Time and again [in her really short stories] Mrs Gaskell is much too leisurely in her introduction. This shows itself, for instance, in tales which depend on the fulfilment of prediction. The beginning represents a move backward in time—over nine generations in **'The Doom of the Griffiths'** and two centuries in **'Morton Hall'** . . . , for example; and too much space is given to describing the original prediction. A similar failure in a tale of longer scope is to be found in **'A Dark Night's Work'** . . . , where far too much attention is given to the history of Ellinor Wilkins' father's career. What matters for the tale is his downfall and the murder he commits. . . . (pp. 175-76)

Besides the shortcomings which arise from the working out of what is predicted, there are those which stem from what is predictable. Sometimes inadequacy of this kind does not matter much, because the strength of the tale lies in aspects other than those of plot. Events, however, sometimes turn out almost too good to be true. Thus in **'Six Weeks at Heppenheim'** we are not surprised that Thekla eventually marries her employer, nor in **'Lizzie Leigh'** that Lizzie is found, nor again in **'The Crooked Branch'** . . . that the worthless son returns to rob his parents' home; but whereas in the first two cases absence of narrative surprise does not matter much, in the last it is more serious, since **'The Crooked Branch'** has fewer resources to rely upon once its plot has come under criticism. **'Right at Last'** . . . is inadequate in another way. Admittedly the really short story is limited in opportunity to establish character, but in this tale Mrs Gaskell, after the manner of many a modern detective-story writer, ultimately convicts the least likely character, about whom we have not only not had the smallest hint of suspicion but we have also been told of his extreme reliability. Lest it should be thought that Mrs Gaskell cannot do right in this regard, let it be said that what is really required is what I would call appropriate surprise, that is, an outcome not foreseen but yet in character with what has gone before. This she achieves in **'Half a Life-time Ago'** in which Susan Dixon finds her love of long years ago dying, and then comforts and protects his widow and her family. (pp. 176-77)

The short tale was, generally speaking, too short for Mrs Gaskell; she needed room in which to spread herself. There was, however, another source of trouble. Too many of her short stories were written to order. . . . (p. 177)

['**A Dark Night's Work**'] is inadequate, as Mrs Gaskell herself thought it to be, and it will serve well for considering the insufficiencies of plot as they are exemplified in her longer works. Others of the *nouvelles* are deficient in plot-structure. . . . '**A Dark Night's Work**' has its qualities, but they are not those of plot. Its pace is in general too slow and uneven. Too much is made of too little. Above all, it conveys no sense of internal necessity, no sense that it has to be what it is. Its virtue consists in just those qualities which represent Mrs Gaskell's strength elsewhere, in evocation of atmosphere, understanding of characteristic behaviour and demonstration of her kindly philosophy of life. The same basic fault, flabbiness in plot-structure, is found again in both '**The Grey Woman**' and '**The Poor Clare**'. The former has the materials for an exciting story. . . . Mrs Gaskell instils some sense of excitement into the latter half of the tale . . . , but the introduction is altogether too leisurely and the method of narration, allegedly, by letter is both long-winded and retrospective and as a result lacks some of the vividness it might otherwise possess. '**The Poor Clare**' is again one of those tales that take so long to start that the reader is puzzled about its direction. (pp. 178-79)

By contrast with the tales referred to in the previous paragraph, three may be singled out for their achievement—'**Lizzie Leigh**', '**Half a Life-time Ago**' and '**Lois the Witch**'. The scope and method of each is different. The first is the shortest. It begins in an atmosphere of suffering and mystery, a dying father forgiving his absent daughter. . . . The story is of a mother's love which is ultimately rewarded, but the daughter is not so simply wicked as she at first appears. The mother's anxious search is paralleled by Lizzie's no less anxious watch over the daughter that as a prostitute she could not keep but had left to be found and cared for by Susan Palmer. The coincidence of the latter's engagement to Will Leigh is acceptable within the story, and even if the baby's death may seem a moral imposition on the tale, it does not detract from the structural unity and neatness of organization. The use of an obviously moral ending is displayed in many of Mrs Gaskell's tales; acceptance of its presence is almost a necessary condition in reading her work. Critically speaking, we need to question not its presence, but its appropriateness, the way in which the moral arises from the ending and the way in which that ending proceeds suitably from what has gone before. The criterion, that is, is related to the degree of imposition. (pp. 179-80)

For unity of tone and structure, ['**Half a Life-time Ago**'] is wellnigh perfect. Everything fits—the place, the character, the events. Like '**Lizzie Leigh**', it catches our attention at once with a reference to what life has done and to the unspoken pity that those who have known Susan Dixon long enough have for her. . . . [But] whereas '**Lizzie Leigh**' goes forward into the future, this tale explains the past that has made this woman what she is. . . . The success of this tale depends crucially upon its central character, but others also fit perfectly, for Mrs Gaskell knew the place and the people. (pp. 181-82)

Setting, plot and character coalesce with even greater aptness in the quite different tale of '**Lois the Witch**'. . . . [This story] possesses an intensity unusual in Mrs Gaskell's short stories.

There is little relaxation of narrative pressure, and even what there is is usually there to provide a prelude by which to impress us the more strongly by what follows. Realization of environment, disposition of incident, control of pace, opposition of characters, all go to make this one of the most convincing of her short stories.

Much of the power of this piece and of '**Half a Life-time Ago**' derives from characterization. Indeed, Mrs Gaskell never seems to have much trouble with plot when she is able to imagine her characters fully and precisely. . . . Most of Mrs Gaskell's eccentrics are women. She imagined the characters of women far better than those of men, and the eccentric is a type which makes great demands upon strength. . . . Openshaw [of '**A Manchester Marriage**'] is as near eccentricity as any of Mrs Gaskell's male characters. . . . He is neatly balanced by his quite ordinary wife; and his love for her child develops an appropriate sympathy for him in the reader. . . . It is the mark of a good story that it should seem to possess the ability to reveal more than it does, and when it does reveal, that its revelation is as exact as we would expect it to be. This is what happens in '**A Manchester Marriage**', and it happens largely because Openshaw contains within him resources that never seem extended to their limits.

In '**Six Weeks at Heppenheim**' with its restrained delineation of Thekla . . . , we encounter another precisely imagined character and condition. It is a quiet tale, of the kind in which Mrs Gaskell excelled, not without its pathos nor its comedy. . . . The sense of participation in suffering helps us better to understand the sufferer, and the nearness of the narrator to Thekla in '**Six Weeks at Heppenheim**' helps to make her sympathetic. Her goodness to him, his understanding of her position, the expression of the reader's own hopes and fears by the narrator himself all contribute to this effect. The principal success of the characterization of Thekla derives then not so much from what she is, for she is quite a simple character, but rather from the way in which she is regarded.

Thekla, however, also belongs very much to the circumstances and environment of the tale. The interaction of individual and surroundings is evident in all of Mrs Gaskell's best work. Sometimes atmosphere and environment, ways of life and attitudes to life, give a sense of solidity to character as in the Lake District tale of Susan Dixon. At other times the effect is almost directly opposite, an alienation of character from environment, producing a sense of instability and crisis as in '**Lois the Witch**'. The worlds of both these tales are hard and trying in their different ways. Those of other stories are quieter, more serene, in the popular mind perhaps more typical of Mrs Gaskell. This is the case, for instance, with *My Lady Ludlow*, *Cousin Phillis* and '**Mr Harrison's Confessions**', which together with *The Moorland Cottage* we may consider now as representing their author's broad achievement in the realm of the *nouvelle*. (pp. 182-87)

[*The Moorland Cottage*] is really a simple story of a family in which the worthless boy, Edward Browne, is favoured by his mother at his sister Maggie's expense. Mrs Gaskell skilfully exploits the contrast in character and treatment between brother and sister. . . . The development of the plot shows how Mrs Gaskell can rely quite adequately upon the most economical resources. The end is therefore all the more unsuitable. It is out of accord both from the point of view of plot-structure and tone. It is both melodramatic and improbable. . . . Maggie herself succeeds as a character because of the manifest sincerity with which she has been imagined, but like Molly Gibson [of

*Wives and Daughters*], for whom she looks much like a trial sketch, she does seem occasionally almost too good-tempered, too self-sacrificing, too long-suffering, too forgiving. . . . Mrs Browne is the greatest success of the work, and she too was to be a predecessor for a fuller portrait, probably the greatest of all Mrs Gaskell's creations, that of Mrs Gibson in *Wives and Daughters.* Another way in which the air of convincing verisimilitude is maintained in this tale is by its use of dialogue; Mrs Browne's criticism is particularly well done with its suggestions of her petulance, partiality and small-mindedness. The more Mrs Gaskell seems at home with her characters, the more she is prepared to rely on dialogue to convey her effects. (pp. 187-88)

['**Mr. Harrison's Confessions**'] is almost as episodic as *Cranford* and its world is much the same. It is allegedly the story of Surgeon Harrison's wooing of his wife, but all Duncombe comes into it with its rounds of visiting, picnics, dinners and illnesses. All the fuss and the goodwill of small-town society is conveyed, and there is plenty of variety in the incidents. . . . In this story the autobiographical standpoint adds to the comedy and to the pleasantness of the work. Harrison is able to laugh at himself. At the same time, by the variety of situations in which she places him and the sense of his learning from the experience with which she endows him, Mrs Gaskell is able to produce a fully rounded character.

In evoking the atmosphere of place in '**Mr Harrison's Confessions**' she relies considerably upon the group of women characters she creates—the imperious Miss Tomkinson, the simpering and affected Miss Caroline, the spiteful Miss Horsman. *My Lady Ludlow* also depends much upon its chief women characters, Lady Ludlow herself principally, of course, but also Miss Galindo, one of the best of Mrs Gaskell's minor characters. . . . [One] might well argue that the events hardly matter in themselves, and that their sequence is only minimally necessary. Character is what matters, and what people say and do, and think of what other people say and do. . . . In *My Lady Ludlow* Mrs Gaskell creates a whole village-society from the lady of the manor down to the poacher Gregson. She shows how each regards the other, delineating the relationships of parson and lady of the manor, agent and mistress, lady of the manor and other independent ladies in the village, parson and labourer and so on. Altogether, a sense of depth is given to the circumstances of the story. It does not therefore matter that so little seems to happen. She is re-creating the very being of the society she describes. (pp. 188-91)

The world of *Cousin Phillis* is, on the whole, a happy one; critics often describe it as idyllic. It is marred by the heroine's illness, but even then we have to admire the goodness, tenderness and concern of all around her. Mrs Gaskell's achievement here has the appearance of that perfect spontaneity which marks the consummate artist. Setting is lovingly and attractively drawn, characters are exact even down to the farm-labourers who make but two or three appearances, plot is scanty yet sufficient, tone is perfectly modulated throughout, the author's own attitude is generous and kindly without any hint of deliberate moralizing. The whole work has about it the perfection of a delicate piece of china, but it has also abundant human warmth. It crowns its author's achievement in the realm of the short story and the short novel. This achievement came at the end of a long and sometimes uneven progress. It shows that here too, as in her novels, Mrs Gaskell appeared to have become endowed with new energy and new vision in her last years.

The overall achievement is so mixed, the degree of her own interest so varied, that it is difficult briefly to estimate Mrs Gaskell's work as a writer of short stories and *nouvelles*. What can be said is that, generally speaking, her powers of plot-construction were not strong enough to make her a predominantly successful author in these kinds. Where a simple plot will suffice, she does quite well. Often, however, she finds herself trying to do too much with too little. Her strength lies rather in her ability to create character, to evoke mood, to establish a sense of place. In her best tales her success derives from the fact that her characters belong to the atmosphere and environment in which she has set them. Usually they are found in surroundings which she knew well herself, but occasionally, as with '**Lois the Witch**', an alien world is powerfully imagined. What remains lastingly memorable is the succession of characters Mrs Gaskell created—Susan Dixon, Lois, Maggie Brown, Thekla, Holman, Phillis and a host of other—characters as sympathetic as she herself was. They represent aspects of their creator's own moral vision of life. (pp. 192-93)

> *Arthur Pollard, in his* Mrs Gaskell: Novelist and Biographer *(copyright © 1965 Arthur Pollard; excerpted by permission of the President and Fellows of Harvard College), Cambridge, Mass: Harvard University Press, 1966, 268 p.*

### ENID L. DUTHIE (essay date 1980)

> [*Duthie maintains that, although Gaskell was essentially a "natural" writer who was not primarily concerned with considerations of form, she did learn to refine and exploit the formal aspects of her art.*]

Elizabeth Gaskell was not primarily concerned with considerations of form. The themes that dominated her work were those that suggested themselves to her naturally, out of her own experience of life, and naturalness was her chief criterion in presenting them to her readers. She expressed herself on paper as fluently as she did in conversation. But it is not as easy to achieve naturalness on paper as in the spoken word. It was only through writing that she learned how to develop the kind of art that was her own, and to progress, in the seventeen years of her literary career, from the powerful but uneven *Mary Barton* to the finished mastery of *Wives and Daughters*. (p. 177)

For her, imagination was not so much a 'strong, restless faculty' as a lively and consoling one. She possessed, like Charlotte Brontë, amazing powers of observation—which, in her case, had been exercised over a wide field—a wonderfully retentive memory and a keen intelligence. Her attitude to her art was typical of the balance of her nature; she enjoyed it, allowed it to develop naturally, and gradually learned how to increase its effectiveness through greater complexity and a greater measure of control, which never endangered its inherent spontaneity.

The story-telling gift was hers from the first, and she did not minimise its importance. . . . [Her] novels have unity and conscious design. The original rough sketch of her first novel *Mary Barton* still exists to bear witness to the preliminary planning involved. Like any creative artist, she inevitably modified the original plan, but the essential outline of the plot is there.

But for her the writing of fiction involved very much more than this. To use her own metaphor, the outline of the plot was only the 'anatomical drawing' of the artist; he must give it muscle and flesh. . . . [The most salient quality of her art was] the power to realise not only the great crucial scenes but a multiplicity of smaller ones which are also 'events' in their own right, happenings and conversations which, as in real life, are all in their own way a series of minor crises, unobtrusively but surely helping to shape the onward course of the action. (pp. 178-79)

Where it was necessary to introduce the natural setting, or to give information about the social or industrial background, Elizabeth Gaskell encountered no difficulty, since she never dealt with themes in which she was not keenly interested and with which she was not thoroughly familiar. . . . Where the moral implications of a situation were involved, her concern that they should be correctly understood sometimes betrayed her into a didacticism which brought her into the foreground as a conscious moralist. Charming as she was, in this character she did not please all her Victorian readers and can alienate modern ones. (p. 180)

Although all her writings throw light on her artistic development, it is in the full-length novels that it can be seen most clearly. There is a wide difference between the artistic achievement of *Mary Barton,* considerable as it is, and the art of *Wives and Daughters*. . . . (p. 181)

The growth in artistry is very evident in the increase in power and originality shown in the composition, which progresses through some initial uncertainties to the structural mastery of *North and South* and the finished symphonies of the final novels. *Mary Barton* has, instead of a wholly integrated action, what is really a combination of two different plots. In the first part, though dramatic scenes do occur, the author builds up to the crisis of the murder largely through a sequence of those seemingly everyday yet significant scenes in the handling of which lay her truest originality. After the commission of the murder, at a point little more than halfway through the action, the interest shifts to Mary's dramatic search for the missing witness, who must be found within a few days, if her lover's life is to be saved. Once this is achieved, there is a natural diminution of tension, and the eventual return and death of the long absent John Barton have the character of an epilogue rather than the natural conclusion of the action. *Ruth* has a simpler plot and . . . the interest is concentrated throughout on the heroine. Scenes of dramatic confrontation occur, but within a domestic context. But there is a certain monotony in the linear plot, and readers have questioned the inevitability of the tragic conclusion. Far more assured is the handling of a much more complex subject in *North and South,* where the two main protagonists at the same time represent two widely differing cultures. The Milton environment brings them together, involving Margaret Hale in the industrial unrest which is Thornton's natural element. The complex plot never becomes confused because its basic pattern is established by the gradual growth in understanding between Margaret and Thornton. Dramatic crises do occur but the chief interest lies in the progress towards final reconciliation. . . . *Sylvia's Lovers* has a simpler plot . . . , but its simplicity is endowed with an epic quality by the rugged grandeur of the setting, the intensity of the passions involved and the prestige of a historical epoch, that of the Napoleonic Wars. . . . The composition of *Wives and Daughters* represents a higher level of achievement than in any of the other novels. For over seven hundred pages the author succeeds without apparent effort in holding the reader's interest with her 'everyday story' of the doctor's daughter, where dramatic scenes are few and life moves at a leisurely pace. Her narrative has none the less the 'unity, life and colour' she judged essential and moves so naturally towards its conclusion that, when it breaks

off unfinished, no one is left in any doubt as to how it would have ended.

The progressive subordination of the dramatic element in the novels does not mean that Elizabeth Gaskell had not a sense of drama. All born storytellers have. The account of the search for the missing witness in *Mary Barton* is compelling in its force. She possessed to the full the power to awaken suspense, and to prolong it till it becomes almost unendurable. . . . Yet she was right to develop her own technique as a novelist and to judge that there, though not necessarily in her shorter tales, high drama should be, as she had most often found it to be in real life, a matter of relatively rare occurrence. But in relying increasingly, for the interest of her narrative, on a multiplicity of minor events rather than on the number of major ones, she was opting for a technique that made considerable demands on her skill. It was necessary that the minor events should all be felt to have a bearing on the development of the action, and that they should be introduced in such a way as to make their significance clear. To achieve this, she relied to a considerable extent on her great skill in using a pattern of contrast. (pp. 181-83)

Elizabeth Gaskell introduces both significance and variety into the narration of the many small crises which only slowly and cumulatively build up to major ones. She also enlivens her narration by frequent variations in tone. Only in *Mary Barton* did the tragic nature of her subject almost preclude the exercise of her gift of humour, though occasionally it asserted itself irrepressibly even there. Normally her balanced attitude to life enabled her to see the comic element latent in many of the occurrences that make up everyday existence. (p. 183)

Another resource of which she makes good use in her leisurely plots is the importance of the time factor. A sequence of small events gives her the opportunity to convey that sense of being imprisoned in a quagmire of difficulties which most people experience at some time in their lives. . . . The comparative rarity of major happenings can produce an illusory sense that time is standing still. (p. 184)

Through the leisurely action of her novels, Elizabeth Gaskell lets her characters reveal themselves as they would do in the course of everyday life. One of the triumphs of her characterisation is the way in which she uses the small and apparently trivial to throw light on feeling and motive. . . . Even the minor characters, who are only 'minor' in relation to the particular circumstances involved, reveal themselves by small but significant acts. (p. 185)

Dialogue is another unfailing means of characterisation in the Gaskell fiction. . . . From *Mary Barton* onwards Elizabeth Gaskell uses reported conversation to reveal the minds and hearts of her people. . . . Dialogue can also become at times the voice of the community; the neighbours who gather round Barton before his departure for London voice the grievances of their submerged world. In this first work there are occasional faults of tone; Mary sometimes fails to convince when speaking of her love, and Esther's speech can descend to melodrama. But there are few such lapses in the subsequent works. (pp. 185-86)

When she lets her people express themselves in speech and action, Elizabeth Gaskell's characterisation cannot be faulted. When it becomes necessary to describe their unspoken thoughts and feelings she is, in her first novels, less at ease. The role of omniscient narrator came less naturally to her than that of the interested spectator, concerned to report speech and action. . . . There is a great advance in the ability to portray the inner life of the characters from *North and South* onwards. In her later novels Elizabeth Gaskell enters into the consciousness of her central characters not with the intellectual equipment of the philosopher but with the intuitive insight of the painter of genius. (pp. 186-87)

It was in the relationship of art and ethics that Elizabeth Gaskell encountered her most serious problems. The religious theme is the most basic in her work, the common factor that underlies all the others. In her first novels her anxiety to make her own outlook clear led her at times perilously near to contradicting, by explicit moralising statements, the impression given by the work in general. In *Mary Barton* her early account of Barton's resentment when he sees employers continuing to live in comfort while economic depression brings the workers to destitution is immediately followed by a qualifying statement: 'I know that this is not really the case; and I know what is the truth in such matters; but what I wish to impress is what the workman feels and thinks.' This remark is obviously motivated by the desire to be fair to both sides, and above all by the fear of appearing in any way to incite class warfare, which is in opposition to the Christian ideal of reconciliation. But it is ineffective in the context and is contradicted by the whole tenor of the novel; there is no sign that the Carsons and their fellow mill-owners are deprived of any material comfort, and every evidence of the extreme privation of the workers. (pp. 187-88)

*Cranford* is the most distinguished representative in her work of a different genre, the collection of related episodes, held together by a first-person narrator and a common social setting, which she had first essayed in **'Mr. Harrison's Confessions'** and to which she returned . . . in *My Lady Ludlow*. The first-person narration, the form most often used by Charlotte Brontë, was one she used less frequently, never in her full-length novels and never for subjective reasons. But the presence of a personal narrator offered certain advantages to an author who was anxious to appear thoroughly familiar with the setting and society described and yet to avoid any undue assumption of omniscience. The narrator in each of these works is someone who comes originally from outside and is at first aware of the novelty of different surroundings, but who very soon absorbs the atmosphere of the place to the point of becoming almost as much a part of local society as anybody else. Such a formula conforms to Elizabeth Gaskell's wish that the author should not intrude himself into his description and yet affords opportunity for social comment more directly humorous, or compassionate, or both, than is possible in the third-person narrative. . . . *Cranford* began as a self-contained sketch, **'Our Society at Cranford'**, but the succeeding episodes effortlessly maintain the same atmosphere and the same ethos. In the little community itself the central character is undoubtedly Miss Matty, not the narrator, Mary Smith. Yet unobtrusively it is Mary Smith who directs our attention, answers our questions, shows us what calls for laughter or compassion. Though a very self-effacing narrator, she is something more than the 'prim little Mary' that Mr. Peter considers her. She is nearer to the 'well-to-do and happy young woman' she once calls herself. She is nearer still to Elizabeth Gaskell as she surveys the human comedy in her letters, wise, witty and compassionate. *Cranford* is not a subjective work, but perhaps in that hidden affinity lies the true secret of its charm. (pp. 190-91)

The nouvelle, or short novel, [also has] an important place in [Elizabeth Gaskell's] total achievement. The shorter form pre-sented hazards for an author with her need to evoke clearly the physical and social environment but offered, if handled successfully, corresponding advantages by encouraging concision in one so naturally fluent as to be sometimes diffuse. **'The Moorland Cottage'**, her first treatment of the genre, avoids the danger of too leisurely a start and anticipates *Wives and Daughters* in its subject matter, but it is marred by an obviously hurried and melodramatic conclusion. The poignant tale **'Lois the Witch'** is, however, a powerful example of the short novel. It belongs to the period between the *Life of Charlotte Brontë* and *Sylvia's Lovers,* when the tone of Elizabeth Gaskell's work tended in any case to be sombre, but it is unique in its tragic force, to which the greater concision of its form certainly contributes. The note of doom is clearly struck near the outset. . . . Every detail of the physical and mental environment points to the inevitability of disaster from the moment when [Lois] arrives at the home of her New England relatives. The brief epilogue, combining realistic acceptance with the sense of incurable grief, is the fitting conclusion to a tale of almost unbearable poignancy. **'A Dark Night's Work'**, written a few years later, has neither the same force nor the same artistic cohesion, though its subject matter is not lacking in interest. The action takes too long to get under way, the dramatic crises are unevenly distributed in the course of the usually uneventful narrative and there is a lack of inevitability about the artificially cheerful conclusion. None of these criticisms apply to *Cousin Phillis*, whose art shares the maturity of the final masterpiece, *Wives and Daughters,* and yet has qualities of its own, due to the difference in form. Where *Wives and Daughters* involves us slowly, without our knowing it, in the tissue of the story, *Cousin Phillis* allows us the pleasure of consciously appreciating the perfect symmetry of a tale whose unfolding stages are clearly marked by basic harmonies. . . . The use of a first-person narrator enhances the unity of this quiet idyll but here the young narrator, unobtrusive though he is, develops through his sympathy with Phillis, and becomes increasingly skilled in interpreting the emotions she strives to conceal. This exquisite pastoral, which has Virgilian overtones and something of the afterglow of an Italian summer, is perhaps the most finished example of Elizabeth Gaskell's art.

She was also attracted to the short story. Her first published essay in the genre, **'Libbie Marsh's Three Eras'**, appeared prior to *Mary Barton* and throughout her writing career she frequently returned to it. It was, however, what might be termed paradoxically the long short story which attracted her most, for even here she needed a certain amount of space for the development of her themes. . . . Elizabeth Gaskell normally prefers, even in [her] shorter tales, to study not simply a crisis but the conditions which led up to it and its perhaps long delayed repercussions. (pp. 192-93)

Elizabeth Gaskell is most successful [with the short story form] when she adopts as the pattern of her story the natural stages of a human life. In **'Lizzie Leigh'**, **'The Well of Pen-Morfa'**, **'The Heart of John Middleton'** and **'Half a Lifetime Ago'** the story develops naturally through the hopes and illusions of youth and the conflicts of adult life to the final acceptance which characterises maturity. **'Half a Lifetime Ago'**, an unforgettable study of the quiet heroism of a Cumbrian 'Stateswoman', is probably Elizabeth Gaskell's finest achievement in this genre. (p. 194)

The love of drama was natural to Elizabeth Gaskell. . . . But her dramatic sense really finds its best expression in the novels, where scenes of violent confrontation are powerfully handled and secrets in the past lives of the characters unexpectedly revealed, but never without such crises having been in fact skilfully prepared. In some of the 'long' short stories, like **'Crowley Castle'**, the emphasis falls all too heavily on the sensational. . . . Elizabeth Gaskell is happier when she combines drama with the occult. **'The Old Nurse's Story'** is a remarkable artistic achievement. The gradual awakening of the narrator to the presence of the occult in the shape of ghostly music, 'which did one no harm', is followed by her experience of the presence of the phantom child, who possesses the power to lure her own charge to her death on the fells. The suspense is comparable in degree to that evoked by Henry James in 'The Turn of the Screw'. . . . (pp. 194-95)

The short story properly so called was less suited to Elizabeth Gaskell as a writer than the more extended version. . . . [The] best of her really short stories are in fact the interpolated anecdotes and reminiscences in her longer works, where they occur naturally in the course of reported conversation. . . .

The desire to narrate was the mainspring of Elizabeth Gaskell's art, but her keen interest in social phenomena in general, both in the present and in the past, inspired a number of articles . . . which constitute another example of the versatility of her genius. (p. 195)

[Yet her] non-fictional writings, though always thematically interesting, show that Elizabeth Gaskell is primarily a narrator rather than an essayist. Where her material calls for a plan involving abstract considerations, she is not entirely at home. . . . In her fiction, on the contrary, she proves herself both sociologist and historian, able to reproduce the very structure of life in contemporary Manchester or Knutsford, or in eighteenth-century Whitby. . . . Her views on society and history find their natural place in her fiction, from which they emerge with admirable clarity.

Elizabeth Gaskell's use of language is governed by the same belief in naturalness which is her basic guide in the composition of her work. She distrusted the 'unusual fineness of language' which some people assume in society, and which effectively puts an end to any natural conversation. She was equally an enemy of the pedantic. . . . [Her] criterion of naturalness meant that it must always be appropriate to the situation. And since she dealt with a variety of situations, she was as versatile in her style as she was in her methods of composition.

The use of regional setting and atmosphere necessarily involved variations in spoken language. Regional dialect is a sustained feature of her style. . . . From **Mary Barton** onwards it recurs, attaining its highest development in **Sylvia's Lovers**, but appearing also in many of the shorter works. . . . The language spoken by Elizabeth Gaskell's characters shows indeed all the subtle variations that exist between the speech of different social groups. (pp. 197-98)

When, instead of reporting the conversation of her characters, Elizabeth Gaskell writes in the capacity of narrator, her style is guided by the same ideal of naturalness. At its best and most characteristic, it shows no straining after effect, no self-consciousness. The interest is concentrated on 'the thing let seen'. Her fluency had its dangers, however, and, when not writing at her best, she could sometimes become diffuse. . . . Experience, and her own love of order, gradually showed her how to exercise a firmer control when describing situations that held possibilities of sentimentality and melodrama. (p. 198)

The lack of artistic restraint, in the earlier works, is most evident where the author's intense moral seriousness, and her

genuine compassion, cause her to intervene personally to point a lesson with unnecessary emphasis. (p. 199)

The greater control which Elizabeth Gaskell gradually acquired as a narrator was something she never needed to learn where description was concerned. . . . The sheer felicity of her language, whether she paints the interior of a dingy court or a summer day in the Welsh mountains, never fails. It is seen in her work from the beginning. (pp. 199-200)

The same descriptive power continues to manifest itself in all the many landscapes and interiors of her novels and tales, and never more charmingly than in the last work, **Wives and Daughters**. It was so much a part of her genius that she exercised it whenever she could, in her occasional articles as well as in her fiction. (p. 200)

Naturalness is the essence of Elizabeth Gaskell's art. In the form of her work, as in its matter, she had the same aim, to reproduce life as she saw it. She believed that it was a unity, but a unity in diversity. She did not attempt to impose any artificial pattern; she allowed her themes, and they were always the same basic themes, to express themselves in the ways that seemed most appropriate, confident in the underlying harmony that was audible to her even in moments of crisis. Other writers have been more devoted to art for itself, or more concerned to use it in the service of a philosophy. For her it was part of life, as life was part of a more divine whole. She could paint all that met her eyes 'with the careless, triumphant hand of a master', but her greatness stems even more surely from her unfailing belief in what she described as 'the infinite and beautiful capacities of human nature'. (p. 201)

*Enid L. Duthie, in her* The Themes of Elizabeth Gaskell *(© Enid L. Duthie 1980), Rowman and Littlefield, 1980, 217 p.*

---

## ADDITIONAL BIBLIOGRAPHY

Berke, Jacqueline, and Berke, Laura. ''Mothers and Daughters in *Wives and Daughters:* A Study of Elizabeth Gaskell's Last Novel.'' In *The Lost Tradition: Mothers and Daughters in Literature*, edited by Cathy N. Davidson and E. M. Broner, pp. 95-109. New York: Frederick Ungar Publishing Co., 1980.

An enlightening study of mother-daughter relationships in *Wives and Daughters*. According to the Berkes, the novel is informed by a profound concern with the nurturing of children and its effect on individuals and society.

Easson, Angus. *Elizabeth Gaskell*. London: Routledge & Kegan Paul, 1979, 278 p.

A general critical survey of Gaskell's major novels, short stories, *The Life of Charlotte Brontë*, her miscellaneous writings, and letters.

Ffrench, Yvonne. *Mrs. Gaskell*. London: Home & Van Thal; Denver: A. Swallow, 1949, 112 p.

A succinct survey of the Gaskell canon. Ffrench's work is a distinctive mix of conventional interpretation, blunt censure, and shrewd analysis.

Ganz, Margaret. *Elizabeth Gaskell: The Artist in Conflict*. New York: Twayne Publishers, 1969, 313 p.

Detailed critical analysis of Gaskell's fictional and biographical work. The qualities of the writer's humor are examined closely in this study, for Ganz maintains that humor was Gaskell's vehicle for sublimating and transcending the conflict between instinct and convention that vitiated her creativity.

Gérin, Winifred. *Elizabeth Gaskell: A Biography*. Oxford: The Clarendon Press, 1976, 318 p.

An insightful, thorough biography that relies heavily upon the 1967 edition of *The Letters of Mrs. Gaskell* to provide the first complete account of Gaskell's personal life. Gérin maintains that Gaskell's correspondence demonstrates the close relationship between her life and writings; he states that "now we can have a view of Mrs. Gaskell temperamentally as well as intellectually capable of the wit and charm of *Cranford*, of the wide and deep perception of *Wives and Daughters* . . . and yet also harassed like other women . . . —a very complete human being in short."

Gosse, Edmund. "The Early Victorian Age (1840-1870)." In his *A Short History of Modern English Literature*, pp. 334-59. New York, London: D. Appleton and Co., 1924.*

States that Gaskell produced "one or two short books which are technically faultless," and suggests that the diverseness of her works and a lack of "personal magnetism" caused her ample literary gifts to be undervalued. A. B. Hopkins cites Gosse's criticism in her defense of Gaskell's achievement (see annotation below).

Hopkins, A. B. *Elizabeth Gaskell: Her Life and Work*. London: John Lehman, 1952, 383 p.

Places Gaskell among "the upper levels, close to the major novelists whose books can still be read with pleasure and profit." Hopkins's study influenced the modern reassessment of Gaskell's literary contribution.

Lansbury, Coral. *Elizabeth Gaskell: The Novel of Social Crisis*. New York: Barnes and Noble Books, 1975, 219 p.

A detailed analysis of the major novels and *The Life of Charlotte Brontë* that encourages the appreciation of Gaskell as a "master of psychological realism" and a "social historian of unusual prowess."

Lucas, John. "Mrs. Gaskell and Brotherhood." In *Tradition and Tolerance in Nineteenth-Century Fiction: Critical Essays on Some English and American Novels*, edited by David Howard, John Lucas, and John Goode, pp. 141-205. London: Routledge and Kegan Paul, 1966.*

A highly-regarded essay on Gaskell's treatment of social problems in *Mary Barton* and *North and South*. Lucas maintains that, guided by a peerless imaginative honesty in her exploration of social conflict, Gaskell confronted implications in these works discordant with her liberal, middle-class convictions and ultimately "retreated from the abyss" to which she had been drawn.

Mews, Hazel. "Women Awaiting Marriage (2): The Brontë Sisters, Elizabeth Gaskell, George Eliot." In her *Frail Vessels: Woman's Role in Women's Novels from Fanny Burney to George Eliot*, pp. 69-125. London: The Athlone Press, 1969.*

Examines Gaskell's treatment of the changing role of women in Victorian society. Mews's study offers original commentary on Gaskell's heroines and on the social dimensions of her art.

Minto, W. "Mrs. Gaskell's Novels." *Fortnightly Review* 16 (1 September 1878): 353-69.

Discusses the moral purposes that inform Gaskell's writing. In his essay, Minto directly challenges W. R. Greg's strictures concerning the inflammatory purport of *Mary Barton* [see excerpt above, 1849].

Rubenius, Aina. *The Woman Question in Mrs. Gaskell's Life and Works*. Essays and Studies on English Language and Literature, edited by S. B. Liljegren, vol. V. Upsala, Sweden: A.-B. Lundequistska Bokhandeln, 1950, 396 p.

Identifies issues of particular importance to women in Gaskell's fiction and examines these issues against the background and conditions of her society. Rubenius claims that Gaskell "was well aware of many of the special problems of early Victorian women" brought about by the Industrial Revolution and "publicized by pioneers of women's rights." In documenting these special problems, Rubenius demonstrates their role in Gaskell's life as well as their reflection in her work.

Sanders, Gerald DeWitt. *Elizabeth Gaskell*. 1929. Reprint. St. Clair Shores, Mich.: Scholarly Press, 1971, 267 p.

A biographical and critical study of Gaskell's literary career. The critic's recognition of Gaskell's status as a professional writer is a distinguishing feature of this early study.

Selig, Robert L. *Elizabeth Gaskell: A Reference Guide*. Reference Guides in Literature, edited by Peter A. Brier. Boston: G. K. Hall & Co., 1977, 431 p.

A comprehensive annotated bibliography of critical commentary on Gaskell's life and works published from 1848 to 1974.

Sharps, John Geoffrey. *Mrs. Gaskell's Observation and Invention: A Study of Her Non-Biographic Works*. Fontwel!, England: Linden Press, 1970, 693 p.

An exhaustive study of Gaskell's writings. Sharps analyzes the elements of creation and observation in her works, and praises her ability as a perceptive commentator of society. He maintains, however, that while she "sought to observe what she had invented, and what she had invented owed much to her prior observations," Gaskell's works lack a capacity to "see into the life of things."

Shorter, Clement K. "Mrs. Gaskell and Charlotte Brontë." *The Bookman* III, No. 4 (June 1896): 313-24.*

Provides a factual and critical account of Gaskell's approach to her subject in *The Life of Charlotte Brontë*. Shorter is the source of the frequently-quoted statement that the *Life* "still commands a place side by side with Boswell's *Johnson* and Lockhart's *Scott*."

Waller, Ross D., ed. "Letters Addressed to Mrs. Gaskell by Celebrated Contemporaries." *Bulletin of the John Rylands Library* 19 (1935): 102-69.

Presents, in a "somewhat arbitrary arrangement," a selection of Gaskell's correspondence from contemporary notables. The letters of John Ruskin, Matthew Arnold, George Eliot, Thomas Carlyle, Elizabeth Barrett Browning, Dante Gabriel Rossetti, Maria Edgeworth, George Henry Lewes, and Charles Dickens are of special interest to the student of Victorian literature.

Whitfield, A. Stanton. *Mrs. Gaskell: Her Life and Work*. London: George Routledge & Sons, 1929, 258 p.

An early biographical and critical survey. In its appreciation of Gaskell's artlessness and its emphasis on the pleasing matter and manner of her works, Whitfield's "Surview" (Chapter XI) typifies the predilections of Gaskell's critics from 1865, the year of her death, into the 1920s. This work also provides a comprehensive bibliography of the editions of Gaskell's works.

# Nikolai (Vasilyevich) Gogol

## 1809-1852

(Born Gogol-Yanovsky; also transliterated as Nikolay; also Vasilevich, Vasil'yevich, Vasilievich, Vasilyevitch; also Gogol', Gógol; also wrote under the pseudonyms of V. Alov and Rudy Panko) Russian novelist, dramatist, short story writer, essayist, critic, and poet.

Gogol was an initiator of the Russian Naturalist movement. He began to write when a new literary focus was developing in Russia, one that described the lives of the lower classes of society. Gogol explored contemporary social problems, often in a satiric fashion. His imaginative, extravagant language contrasted with the simple, pure, poetic diction of such writers as Alexander Pushkin, and his work presaged a new literary age in Russia. His best-known works, the novel *Mërtvye dushi* (*Dead Souls*) and the drama *Révizor* (*The Inspector General*), are universally praised as masterpieces of Russian Naturalism.

Born into a family of Ukrainian landowners, Gogol was sent to boarding school, where he developed an interest in literature and drama. He performed in amateur productions and, upon graduation, hoped to find employment as an actor. However, his audition at the Bolshoi theater in St. Petersburg was unsuccessful, and his attempts to sell his writing also failed. He eventually used his own money to publish his long epic poem *Hans Kuechelgärten*, but when the poem received only negative reviews, Gogol collected all the remaining copies and burned them.

Soon after, he obtained a civil service position in St. Petersburg and began writing *Vechera ná khutore bliz Dikanki* (*Evenings on a Farm near Dikanka*), a volume of folk tales set in his native Ukraine. These stories, a lively mixture of realism and fantasy, depict the world of the Cossack peasant. The stories met with immediate acclaim and brought Gogol to the attention of both Pushkin and the critic Vissarion Belinsky. Belinsky had earlier championed Pushkin, and now recognized similar promise in Gogol. Gogol found in Pushkin his strongest literary inspiration, and the period of their association from 1831 to 1836 was Gogol's most productive period. The older poet sensed Gogol's satirical powers and provided him with the ideas for both *Dead Souls* and *The Inspector General*. In 1836, *The Inspector General* was produced in St. Petersburg. Though the play was an indictment of Russian bureaucracy, it passed the rigid censorship of the time because Czar Nicholas I had read and admired the drama. He ordered all his ministers to attend the premiere and announced, as the final curtain fell: "Everyone has got his due, and I most of all." However, despite the czar's official sanction, the play was violently attacked by a number of influential people who denied that it contained a single honest character.

Stung by the criticism of *The Inspector General*, Gogol moved to Italy in 1836, and, except for two brief visits home, remained abroad for twelve years. Most of this time was spent writing *Dead Souls*. Originally planned as a light, picaresque novel, Gogol decided instead to create an epic in several volumes that would depict all elements of Russian life. The liberal Russian critics called *Dead Souls* a true reflection of life, and gave Gogol the title of "supreme realist." Realism, according to

Belinsky, required a simple plot, a faithful representation of everyday life, and a humorous exposure of the negative aspects of Russian society. Belinsky saw in *Dead Souls* the embodiment of these ideals, and considered it a plea for Russian writers to fight for civilization, culture, and humankind. Gogol's subsequent collection *Sochinenya* included his well-known short story "Shinel" ("The Overcoat").

Upon completing *Dead Souls*, Gogol began a sequel in which he intended to depict the moral conversion of his protagonist Chichikov. He finished the second part after ten years, but its creation had driven him to a state of nervous collapse and, in 1845, he burned the manuscript. Two years later he composed *Vybrannye mesta iz perepiski s druzyami* (*Selected Passages from Correspondence with My Friends*), a reactionary work which reflects his growing religious and moral fanaticism. These selections condone serfdom and the Czar's policies, and also discuss his reasons for burning the second part of *Dead Souls*. His friends condemned the book, but the harshest denunciation came from Belinsky, who, in a scathing letter to Gogol, accused him of being a "preacher of ignorance."

Following the critical failure of *Selected Passages*, Gogol recommenced the second section of *Dead Souls*. He had fallen, however, under the influence of Matthew Konstantinovsky, a maniacal priest who insisted that Gogol again burn his manuscript and enter a monastery. Gogol agonized over the decision, but finally complied, convinced that this act would save him from damnation. He began a fast to cleanse his soul, and died shortly thereafter. Following his death, a small portion of the second part *Dead Souls* was discovered and published, but critics generally agree that the sequel does not reveal the mastery of the first section. Though Gogol's critical appeal waned in his final years, his funeral brought out thousands of mourners. Commenting on the throngs, a passerby asked "Who is this man who has so many relatives at his funeral?" A mourner responded, "This is Nikolai Gogol, and all of Russia is his relative."

Gogol's influence on Russian literature has continued in the twentieth century and is most evident in the poetry of the Russian Symbolists. Such poets as Andrey Bely and Aleksandr Blok cite Gogol's rich prose and "visionary" language as embodiments of supreme fantasy. Yet many critics maintain that Gogol's mixture of realism and satire has proved most influential and remains his greatest achievement. Dostoevski acknowledged Russian literature's vast debt to Gogol by stating simply, "We all came from Gogol's 'Overcoat'."

## PRINCIPAL WORKS

*Hans Kuechelgärten* [as V. Alov]  (poetry)  1829
*Vechera ná khutore bliz Dikanki* [as Rudy Panko]  (short stories)  1831
    [*Evenings in Little Russia,* 1903; also published as *Evenings on a Farm near Dikanka,* 1906]
*\*Arabeski*  (essays and short stories)  1835
    [*Arabesques,* 1981]
*Mirgorod*  (short stories)  1835
    [*Mirgorod,* 1842]
*Révizor*  (drama)  1836
    [*The Inspector General,* 1892; also published as *The Government Inspector* in *The Government Inspector and Other Plays,* 1927]
*Mërtvye dushi*  (novel)  1842
    [*Tchitchikoff's Journeys; or, Dead Souls,* 1886; also published as *Dead Souls,* 1915]
*Sochinenya.* 2 vols.  (short stories, dramas, and novel)  1842
    [*The Works of Nikolay Gogol.* 6 vols., 1922-28]
*Zhenit'ba; Sovershenno neveroyatnoye sobitye*  (drama)  1842
    [*The Marriage: An Utterly Incredible Occurence* published in *The Modern Theatre,* Vol. IV, 1955-60]
*Igroki*  (drama)  1843
    [*The Gamblers* published in *The Modern Theatre,* Vol. III, 1955-60]
*Vybrannye mesta iz perepiski s druzyami*  (essays and letters)  1847
    [*Selected Passages from Correspondence with My Friends,* 1969]
*Letters of Nikolai Gogol*  (letters)  1967

\*This work includes the short story "Taras Bulba"; also published as "Taras Bulba" [revised edition], 1842.

ALEXANDER PUSHKIN   (letter date 1831)

I have just read *Evenings by the Dikanka* [*Vechera ná khutore bliz Dikanki*]. It astonished me. Here is real gaiety, which is sincere, unforced, without affectation, without pomposity. And in places what poetry! What sensibility! All that is so unusual for our contemporary literature that I have not yet come to my senses. I have been told that when the publisher came into the printing works where the *Evenings* were in the press, the compositors began to suppress their giggles and snorts, covering their mouths with their hands. The foreman explained their hilarity, confessing that the compositors were dying of laughter in setting up his book. Molière and Fielding would doubtless have been glad to have amused their compositors. I congratulate the public on a truly gay book, and sincerely wish the Author success in the future. For God's sake take his side if the reviewers, in their customary manner, attack the *indecency* of his expressions . . . It is high time that we laughed les précieuses ridicules [the ridiculous affectations] of our literature to scorn, those people who are for ever talking of their 'fair readers', which they have never had, of the highest social circles, to which they are not invited. . . .

> *Alexander Pushkin, in an extract from a letter to the editor of the* Russky Invalid Literary Supplement, *No. 79, 1831, in his* Pushkin on Literature, *edited and translated by Tatiana Wolff (translation © 1971 by Tatiana Wolff; reprinted by permission of Methuen & Co. Ltd), Methuen, 1971, p. 299.*

ALEXANDER PUSHKIN   (essay date 1836)

Our readers will of course remember the impression made on them by the appearance of [*Evenings on a Farm near Dikanka*]: everyone was delighted by this vivid portrayal of a singing and dancing tribe, by the fresh pictures of the Malorossian scene, by the gaiety which was at once naïve and cunning. How astonished we were to find a Russian book which made us laugh, having not laughed since Fonvizin's time! We were so grateful to the young author that we willingly forgave him the unevenness and incorrectness of his style and the incoherence and improbability of some of the stories, leaving these defects as a perquisite for the critics. The author has justified such indulgence. From that time he has continually developed and improved. He published *Arabesques,* in which is found his 'Nevsky Prospect', his richest work. This was followed by *Mirgorod,* in which everybody greedily lapped up both the 'Old-world Landowners' —that humorous, touching idyll, which makes one laugh through tears of sorrow and tenderness, and 'Taras Bulba', the opening of which is worthy of Walter Scott. Mr. Gogol is still advancing. We desire and hope to have the occasion of speaking of him in our review.

> *Alexander Pushkin, in his review of "Evenings on a Farm near Dikanka" (originally published under a different title in* Sovremennik, *April 11, 1836), in his* Pushkin on Literature, *edited and translated by Tatiana Wolff (translation © 1971 by Tatiana Wolff; reprinted by permission of Methuen & Co. Ltd), Methuen, 1971, p. 381.*

VISSARION BELINSKI   (essay date 1842)

*[Belinsky saw Gogol as a uniquely Russian author, and believed that he heralded a new era in Russian literature. Belinsky here maintains that there is little humor in* Dead Souls *and, praising*

*the realistic dimension of the novel, states that "everything here is serious, quiet, true, and profound."*]

No doubt Gogol will soon be praised by those very people who scorned us for praising him and who now, given the lie by the unprecedented success of *Dead Souls,* are like drowning men clutching at straws. . . .

Now everybody has become wise, even people who were born stupid, and they will all be able to make the egg stand on the table. After the appearance of *Dead Souls* there will be many literary Columbuses who will find it easy to discover a great new talent in Russian literature, a great new Russian writer: Gogol.

Gogol was the first to look boldly and directly upon Russian reality; and if to this is added his profound humor, his unlimited irony, it becomes clear why for a long time he was not understood and why it was easier to love him than to understand him. . . . [We] shall limit ourselves to a general expression of our opinion of the worth of *Dead Souls*—that great creation.

Our literature, in consequence of its artificial beginning and unnatural development, has been condemned to become a spectacle of fragmentary and most contradictory phenomena. We have already said more than once that we do not believe there exists a Russian literature in the sense of a written expression of a historically evolving national consciousness. But we see here a wonderful beginning of a great future, a series of disconnected flashes, which are as brilliant as lightning and as broad and sweeping as the Russian soul, but still only *flashes.* All the rest which constitutes our day-to-day literary activity has little or no relation to these flashes except perhaps the relation of shade to light and dark to shine. Gogol began his career while Pushkin was still alive, and when the latter died he fell silent, it seemed for good. After *The Inspector* he published nothing until the middle of the present year. During this interval of his silence, which so saddened the friends of Russian literature and so gladdened the literary hacks, there dawned and then died out on the horizon of Russian poetry the bright star of the talent of Lermontov. After *A Hero of Our Time* there appeared in the journals . . . a few more or less noteworthy stories, but . . . nothing which constitutes a permanent literary achievement. . . . And suddenly, in the midst of this triumph of mediocrity . . . there appears a purely Russian, a national creation, drawn from the secret places of the life of the people . . . a creation incomparably artistic in conception and execution, in the personalities of its characters and in the details of Russian life—and at the same time profound in its meaning. . . . In *Dead Souls* the author has taken such a huge step that everything which he has written up to now seems weak and pale in comparison. We consider the author's greatest success and greatest step forward to be that everywhere in *Dead Souls* one feels and, as it were, touches his subjectivity. Here we do not mean that subjectivity which by its narrowness or limitation disfigures the objective reality of what the author portrays; but that profound, vast, and human subjectivity which reveals in the artist a man with an ardent heart, a sympathetic soul, and an independent spiritual personality—that subjectivity which does not allow him to remain in apathetic indifference aloof from the world which he depicts, but forces him to experience in his *living soul* the manifestations of the external world, and thereby to breathe a *living soul* into them. . . . This pathos of subjectivity in the poet appears not only in . . . highly lyrical digressions; it appears continually, even in the midst of recounting the most prosaic subjects. . . .

An equally important step forward in Gogol's talent is seen by us in the fact that in *Dead Souls* he has completely abandoned the Ukrainian element and has become a national Russian poet to the full extent of that word. At every word of his poem the reader can say:

*Here is the Russian spirit, this smells Russian!*

This Russian spirit is felt in the humor, in the irony, in the author's expressions, in the broad sweep of emotion, in the lyricism of the digressions, in the pathos of the whole poem, and in the personalities of the characters, from Chichikov to Selifan . . . , in the policeman who, by the light of the lantern, half asleep, kills a bug between his fingernails and then goes back to sleep. We know that the prudery of many readers will be offended at seeing in print what is so close to them in their personal lives and will call obscene such tricks as the bug crushed on a fingernail; but that means they do not understand the poem, which is based on the pathos of reality as it exists. . . .

*Dead Souls* will be read by everybody but will no doubt not please everybody. Among the many reasons why, is the fact that *Dead Souls* does not fit the popular conception of a novel as a story in which the main characters fall in love, separate, and then get married and live rich and happy. . . . Moreover . . . *Dead Souls* demands study. In this regard it should again be repeated that humor is understandable only to a person of some depth and maturity. The popular mind doesn't understand or like it. . . . The majority of our people understand "humor" and "the comic" as buffoonery, as caricature, and we are convinced that many will seriously . . . say and write that Gogol was joking when he called his novel a poem. . . .

. . . It was not in fun that Gogol called his novel a "poem," [nor] did he mean by that a comic poem. Not the author but his book has told us so. We find nothing farcical or funny in it; by no word of the author's have we noted any intention to amuse the reader: everything here is serious, quiet, true, and profound. . . . There can be no greater error or grosser misunderstanding than to look upon *Dead Souls* as a satire. [Despite Gogol's powerful lyrical passage on the troika of Russia, some] will see in *Dead Souls* a spiteful satire, resulting from coldness and indifference to what is native, to what is national. . . . As for us, we on the contrary would accuse the author of too much emotion uncontrolled by calm and reasonable reflection . . . rather than of a lack of love and warmth for the native and the national. We speak of several places—fortunately few and unfortunately glaring—in which the author makes hasty judgments of the nationality of foreign races and without much reserve gives himself over to dreams about the superiority of the Slavic race over others. We think that it is better to leave to each his own and, while realizing one's own worth, to be capable of respecting the worth of others also. (pp. 158-61)

*Vissarion Belinski, in an extract from a review of "Dead Souls" (1842), in* Vissarion Belinski, 1811-1848: A Study in the Origins of Social Criticism in Russia *by Herbert E. Bowman (copyright © 1954 by the President and Fellows of Harvard College; copyright renewed © 1982 by Herbert E. Bowman; excerpted by permission), Cambridge, Mass.: Harvard University Press, 1954, pp. 157-63.*

**NIKOLAI GOGOL**   (letter date 1843)

[If] I had not been in a hurry to publish the manuscript [of *Dead Souls*] and had kept it for a year, I would then have seen myself that it should not appear in the world in such a slovenly condition. Indeed, the very epigrams and the ridicules aimed at me were necessary to me, even though at first they cut me to the quick. Oh, how we need these continual nips and this abusive tone, and these sarcastic jibes which pierce us through! So much pettiness is hidden in the depths of our soul, so much paltry self-love, so much touchy, nasty vanity, that at every moment we ought to be pricked, struck, beaten by all possible arms, and we must every moment thank the hand striking us.

I would have wished, however, for a little more criticism, not on the part of men of letters, but on the part of people of busy lives, on the part of practical people; as ill luck would have it, except for the men of letters nobody answered.

Meanwhile, *Dead Souls* made a great deal of noise, aroused much grumbling, cut many to the quick by its jibes, by its truth and justice, and by its caricature; it discussed an order of things which we all daily have before our eyes; it is full of blunders, anachronisms, and obvious ignorance of many subjects; indeed, cutting and offensive things were designedly placed in it: perhaps some one will rate me properly and in swearing and wrath tell me the truth of what I have attained.

If one soul had raised his voice! Anyone could have. And sensibly! . . . On the occasion of *Dead Souls,* another incomparably more interesting book than *Dead Souls* could have been written by a mass of readers, and it could have taught not only me but the readers themselves, because—nothing may conceal this sin—we all know Russia very badly.

And if but one soul had begun to speak out in public! It was exactly as though everything had died out, as though Russia in fact was inhabited not by living but by *Dead Souls.* And they reproach me for knowing Russia badly! As though, by the strength of the Holy Spirit, I ought unfailingly to know everything that is done in all its corners—to learn it without having been taught! But by what means could I learn, I, a writer, already condemned by the vocation of a writer to a sedentary, secluded life, I, who am sick besides, and therefore compelled to live far from Russia, by what means could I learn? I could not learn from men of letters and journalists who are themselves secluded desk people. For a writer there is only one teacher—his readers. But the readers refused to teach me. I know that I will have a terrible account to render to God for not having performed my work as I should have, but I also know that others will render an account for me. And I do not speak in vain. God sees that I do not speak in vain! (pp. 96-8)

*Nikolai Gogol, in a letter to an unidentified recipient in 1843, in his* Selected Passages from Correspondence with Friends, *translated by Jesse Zeldin (translation copyright © 1969 Vanderbilt University Press; originally published as* Vybrannyîa Mîesta iz perepiski s druz'îami, Canxmnemepoypis, 1847), *Vanderbilt University Press, 1969, pp. 96-8.*

## NIKOLAI GOGOL   (letter date 1846)

[*Gogol's failing mental health is evident in this letter defending his decision to destroy the second part of* Dead Souls.]

The second part of *Dead Souls* was burned because it was necessary. "Lest the seed die, it will not live again," says the Apostle. It is first necessary to die in order to be resurrected. It was not easy to burn the work of five years, produced with such painful effort, where each line was the result of a shock,

where was much of what had constituted my best thoughts and had occupied my soul. But all has been burned, and, further, at that very time when, seeing my own death before me, I desired so much to leave after me something which would be a better reminiscence of myself. I thank God for having given me the strength to do it. Immediately that the flame had carried away the last pages of my book, its content suddenly was resurrected in a purified and lucid form, like the Phoenix from the pyre, and I suddenly saw in what disorder was what I had considered ordered and harmonious. The appearance of the second volume in the form in which it was would sooner have done harm than good. It is necessary to consider not the enjoyment of some lovers of art and men of letters, but all the readers for whom *Dead Souls* was written. To describe some fine characters who are supposed to demonstrate the nobility of our race would lead to nothing. It would only arouse empty pride and vanity. . . . [There] are times when it is not possible to turn society, or even one generation, towards the beautiful, so long as it is not shown the depths of its present abasement; there are times when one may not even speak of the sublime and the beautiful, if the way and roads to it for everyone are not shown clear as day. This last circumstance was badly and weakly developed in the second volume of *Dead Souls,* where it should have been the chief thing, and therefore it was burned. Do not judge me and do not draw conclusions: you would be in error, like those of my friends who, having made their ideal writer out of me, acccording to their idea of a writer, began to demand that I answer to their created ideal. God created me and did not hide my purpose from me. I was not at all born to produce an epoch in the sphere of literature. My business is simpler and lower: my business is above all what every man must think about, not just myself. My business is *the soul and the durable things in life.* That is why the form of my actions must be firm, and what I write must be firm. There is no need for me to hurry; let others hurry! I burn when it is necessary to burn, and, probably, I act as I must, because I never start anything without prayers. . . . It is He Who by pride, ailments, and obstacles has quickened the development of my powers and my thoughts, without which I would never have conceived my work, it is He Who has formed the greater half of it in my brain, it is He Who will give me the strength to accomplish the rest—and put it down on paper. I am decrepit in body but not in soul. In my soul, on the contrary, everything is getting stronger and becoming firmer; my body also will get stronger. I believe that, if the right time comes, in several weeks I will accomplish that on which I have spent five sick years. (pp. 108-10)

*Nikolai Gogol, in a letter to an unidentified recipient in 1846, in his* Selected Passages from Correspondence with Friends, *translated by Jesse Zeldin (translation copyright © 1969 Vanderbilt University Press; originally published as* Vybrannyîa Mîesta iz perepiski s druz'îami, Canxmnemepoypis, 1847), *Vanderbilt University Press, 1969, pp. 108-10.*

## NIKOLAI GOGOL   (letter date 1847)

[*When* Selected Passages *appeared, Vissarion Belinsky published a virulent review of the work in the journal* Sovremenik (The Contemporary). *In the review, which is not available in English, he expressed his contempt for Gogol's strange new beliefs. In the following letter, written in response to Belinsky's article, Gogol defends his beliefs, stating that Belinsky viewed* Selected Passages *"with the eyes of an angry man and therefore took almost everything the wrong way."*]

I read your article about me in the second number of *The Contemporary* with sorrow. I was not sorrowful because of the abasement in which you wanted to display me before all, but because the voice of a man who is angered at me can be heard in it. And I did not want to anger even a man who does not love me, all the less you whom I always thought of as a man who loved me. I didn't in the least have in mind distressing you in any passage of my book. I still cannot understand how it happened that to the last man everyone in Russia has become angry at me. . . . You looked at [*Selected Passages from Correspondence with Friends*] with the eyes of an angry man and therefore took almost everything the wrong way. Ignore all those passages which are still a riddle for many, if not for all, and turn your attention to the passages which are comprehensible to every sensible and reasonable man, and you will see that in much you are mistaken.

It was not for nothing that I implored everyone to read my book several times, foreseeing all these misunderstandings in advance. Believe it—it is not easy to judge a book in which the personal spiritual history of a man is involved, a man who is not like others and, in addition, a secretive man who has long lived within himself and suffered from the inability to express himself. . . . [How] can one draw the conclusion that the critics who have spoken of my merits were inaccurate from my saying that there is much that is accurate in the critics who have spoken of my shortcomings? There can be such logic only in the head of an angered man who continues to look only for that which can anger him, who does not calmly survey the subject from all sides. Well, what if for a long time I was keeping in mind and considering how to start talking about those critics who spoke about my merits and who, apropos of my works, spread many fine thoughts about art. And if I wanted to define impartially the merit of each and those delicate shadings of aesthetic sensibility with which each of them was more or less gifted in his own way? And if I was just waiting for the time when I would be able to talk about that or, more accurately, when it would be *proper* to talk about that—so that it would not be said afterwards that I was guided by some selfish goal and not by a feeling of impartiality and accuracy? Write the harshest critiques, apply all the words that you know to abase a man, to promote the ridicule of me in the eyes of your readers without sparing the most sensitive strings of, perhaps, a very tender heart—my soul will endure all this, although not without pain and the throes of sorrow. But it is painful for me, very painful (I say this to you truthfully), even when an evil person harbors personal malice against me—not just a good man, and I always considered you a good man. There is an honest statement of my feelings. (pp. 176-78)

> *Nikolai Gogol, in his letter to V. G. Belinsky on June 20(?), 1847, in his* Letters of Nikolai Gogol, *edited by Carl R. Proffer, translated by Carl R. Proffer with Vera Krivoshein (translation copyright © by The University of Michigan 1967; originally published in* Polnoe sobranie socinenij, Vols. X-XIV, 1937-52), *University of Michigan Press, 1967, pp. 176-78.*

## V. G. BELINSKY (letter date 1847)

[*The following excerpt is taken from one of the best-known letters in Russian literature. Belinsky here details the depth of betrayal he felt toward Gogol upon the publication of* Selected Passages. *Gogol had provided a model of what Belinsky valued in literature: "salvation not in mysticism, asceticism, or pietism," but in the successes of civilization, enlightenment, and humanity." To Belinsky,* Selected Passages *displayed a narrow-minded attitude that he felt contradicted Gogol's earlier work. Belinsky had praised the realism of Gogol's earlier work, and condemned the elements of fantasy, romance, and spiritualism evidenced in* Selected Passages. *Later, this letter was circulated, and its appeal for realism in literature earned it the title of the Manifesto of Russian Realism. Belinsky's denouncement proved to be a great influence on subsequent evaluation of* Selected Passages.]

You are only partly right in regarding my article as that of an *angered* man: that epithet is too mild and inadequate to express the state to which I was reduced on reading your book. . . . One could endure an outraged sense of self-esteem, and I should have had sense enough to let the matter pass in silence were that the whole gist of the matter; but one cannot endure an outraged sense of truth and human dignity; one cannot keep silent when lies and immorality are preached as truth and virtue under the guise of religion and the protection of the knout.

Yes, I loved you with all the passion with which a man, bound by ties of blood to his native country, can love its hope, its honor, its glory, one of its great leaders on the path toward consciousness, development, and progress. And you had sound reason for losing your equanimity at least momentarily when you forfeited that love. I say that not because I believe my love to be an adequate reward for a great talent, but because I do not represent a single person in this respect but a multitude of men, most of whom neither you nor I have set eyes on, and who, in their turn, have never set eyes on you. I find myself at a loss to give you an adequate idea of the indignation your book has aroused in all noble hearts, and of the wild shouts of joy that were set up on its appearance by all your enemies— both the nonliterary—the Chichikovs, the Nozdrevs, and the mayors—and by the literary, whose names are well known to you. You see yourself that even those people who are of one mind with your book have disowned it. Even if it had been written as a result of deep and sincere conviction, it could not have created any impression on the public other than the one it did. And it is nobody's fault but your own if everyone (except the few who must be seen and known in order not to derive pleasure from their approval) received it as an ingenious but all too unceremonious artifice for achieving a sheerly earthly aim by celestial means.

Nor is that in any way surprising; what is surprising is that you find it surprising. I believe that is so because your profound knowledge of Russia is only that of an artist, but not of a thinker, whose role you have so ineffectually tried to play in your fantastic book. Not that you are not a thinker, but that you have been accustomed for so many years to look at Russia from your *beautiful far-away;* and who does not know that there is nothing easier than seeing things from a distance the way we want to see them; for in that *beautiful far-away* you live a life that is entirely alien to it; you live in and within yourself or within a circle of the same mentality as your own that is powerless to resist your influence on it.

Therefore you failed to realize that Russia sees her salvation not in mysticism or asceticism or pietism, but in the successes of civilization, enlightenment, and humanity. What she needs is not sermons (she has heard enough of them!) or prayers (she has repeated them too often!), but the awakening in the people of a sense of their human dignity lost for so many centuries amid dirt and refuse; she needs rights and laws conforming not to the preaching of the church but to common sense and justice, and their strictest possible observance. . . . The most vital national problems in Russia today are the abolition of serfdom and corporal punishment and the strictest possible observance of at least those laws that already exist. This is even realized by the government itself (which is well aware of how the landowners treat their peasants and how many of the former are annually done away with by the latter), as is proved by its timid and abortive half-measures for the relief of the white Negroes and the comical substitution of the single-lash knout by a cat-o'-three tails.

Such are the problems that prey on the mind of Russia in her apathetic slumber! And at such a time a great writer, whose astonishingly artistic and deeply truthful works have so powerfully contributed toward Russia's awareness of herself, enabling her as they did to take a look at herself as though in a mirror—publishes a book in which he teaches the barbarian landowner to make still greater profits out of the peasants and to abuse them still more in the name of Christ and Church. . . . And would you expect me not to become indignant? . . . Why, if you had made an attempt on my life I could not have hated you more than I do for these disgraceful lines. . . . And after this, you expect people to believe the sincerity of your book's intent! No! Had you really been inspired by the truth of Christ and not by the teaching of the devil you would certainly have written something entirely different in your new book. You would have told the landowner that since his peasants are his brethren in Christ, and since a brother cannot be a slave to his brother, he should either give them their freedom or, at least, allow them to enjoy the fruits of their own labor to their greatest possible benefit, realizing, as he does, in the depths of his own conscience, the false relationship in which he stands toward them.

And the expression *"Oh, you unwashed snout, you!"* From what Nozdrev and Sobakevich did you overhear it, in order to present it to the world as a great discovery for the edification and benefit of the peasants, whose only reason for not washing is that they have let themselves be persuaded by their masters that they are not human beings? And your conception of the national Russian system of trial and punishment, whose ideal you have found in the foolish saying that both the guilty and innocent should be flogged alike? That, indeed, is often the case with us, though more often than not it is the man who is in the right who takes the punishment, unless he can ransom himself, and for such occasions another proverb says: *Guiltlessly guilty!* And such a book is supposed to have been the result of an arduous inner process, a lofty spiritual enlightenment! Impossible! Either you are ill—and you must hasten to take a cure, or . . . I am afraid to put my thought into words! . . .

Proponent of the knout, apostle of ignorance, champion of obscurantism and Stygian darkness, panegyrist of Tartar morals—what are you about! Look beneath your feet—you are standing on the brink of an abyss! . . . That you base such teaching on the Orthodox Church I can understand: it has always served as the prop of the knout and the servant of despotism; but why have you mixed Christ up in it? What have you found in common between Him and any church, least of all the Orthodox Church? He was the first to bring to people the teaching of freedom, equality, and brotherhood and to set the seal of truth to that teaching by martyrdom. And this teaching was men's *salvation* only until it became organized in the Church and took the principle of Orthodoxy for its foundation. The Church, on the other hand, was a hierarchy, consequently a champion of inequality, a flatterer of authority, an enemy and persecutor of brotherhood among men—and so it has remained to this day. . . . Hence, can it be that you, the author

of *Inspector General* and *Dead Souls,* have in all sincerity, from the bottom of your heart, sung a hymn to the nefarious Russian clergy whom you rank immeasurably higher than the Catholic clergy? Let us assume that you do not know that the latter had once been something, while the former had never been anything but a servant and slave of the secular powers; but do you really mean to say you do not know that our clergy is held in universal contempt by Russian society and the Russian people? About whom do the Russian people tell dirty stories? Of the priest, the priest's wife, the priest's daughter, and the priest's farm hand. Does not the priest in Russia represent the embodiment of gluttony, avarice, servility, and shamelessness for all Russians? Do you mean to say that you do not know all this? Strange! According to you the Russian people is the most religious in the world. That is a lie! The basis of religiousness is pietism, reverence, fear of God. Whereas the Russian man utters the name of the Lord while scratching himself somewhere. He says of the icon: *If it isn't good for praying it's good for covering the pots.*

Take a closer look [at the Russian people] and you will see that it is by nature a profoundly atheistic people. It still retains a good deal of superstition, but not a trace of religiousness. Superstition passes with the advances of civilization, but religiousness often keeps company with them too; we have a living example of this in France, where even today there are many sincere Catholics among enlightened and educated men, and where many people who have rejected Christianity still cling stubbornly to some sort of god. The Russian people is different; mystic exaltation is not in its nature; it has too much common sense, a too lucid and positive mind, and therein, perhaps, lies the vastness of its historic destinies in the future. (pp. 83-7)

I shall not expatiate on your panegyric to the affectionate relations existing between the Russian people and its lords and masters. I shall say point-blank that panegyric has met sympathy nowhere and has lowered you even in the eyes of people who in other respects are very close to you in their views. As far as I am concerned, I leave it to your conscience to admire the divine beauty of the autocracy (it is both safe and profitable), but continue to admire it judiciously from your *beautiful far-away:* at close quarters it is not so attractive, and not so safe. (p. 87)

Another thing I remember you saying in your book, claiming it to be a great and incontrovertible truth, is that literacy is not merely useless but positively harmful to the common people. What can I say to this? May your Byzantine God forgive you that Byzantine thought, unless, in committing it to paper, you knew not what you were saying. . . . But perhaps you will say: "Assuming that I have erred and that all my ideas are false, but why should I be denied the right to err and why should people doubt the sincerity of my errors?" Because, I would say in reply, such a tendency has long ceased to be a novelty in Russia. Not so very long ago it was drained to the lees by Burachok and his fraternity. Of course, your book shows a good deal more intellect and talent (though neither of these elements is very richly represented) than their works; but then they have developed your common doctrine with greater energy and greater consistence; they have boldly reached its ultimate conclusions, have rendered all to the Byzantine God and left nothing for Satan; whereas you, wanting to light a taper to each of them, have fallen into contradiction, upholding, for example, Pushkin, literature, and the theater, all of which, in your opinion, if you were only conscientious enough to be consistent, can in no way serve the salvation of the soul but can do a lot toward its damnation. . . .

You have placed yourself too high in the regard of the Russian public for it to be able to believe you sincere in such convictions. What seems natural in fools cannot seem so in a man of genius. Some people have been inclined to regard your book as the result of mental derangement verging on sheer madness. But they soon rejected such a supposition, for clearly that book was not written in a single day or week or month, but very likely in one, two, or three years; it shows coherence; through its careless exposition one glimpses premeditation, and the hymn to the powers that be nicely arranges the earthly affairs of the devout author. That is why a rumor has been current in St. Petersburg to the effect that you have written this book with the aim of securing a position as tutor to the son of the heir apparent. Before that, your letter . . . became known in St. Petersburg, wherein you say that you are grieved to find that your works about Russia are misinterpreted; then you evince dissatisfaction with your previous works and declare that you will be pleased with your own works only when the Tsar is pleased with them. Now judge for yourself. Is it to be wondered at that your book has lowered you in the eyes of the public both as a writer and still more as a man? . . .

As far as I can see, you do not properly understand the Russian public. Its character is determined by the condition of Russian society in which fresh forces are seething and struggling for expression; but weighed down by heavy oppression, and finding no outlet, they induce merely dejection, weariness, and apathy. Only literature, despite the Tartar censorship, shows signs of life and progressive movement. That is why the title of writer is held in such esteem among us; that is why literary success is easy among us even for a writer of little talent. The title of poet and writer has long since eclipsed the tinsel of epaulettes and gaudy uniforms. And that especially explains why every so-called liberal tendency, however poor in talent, is rewarded by universal notice, and why the popularity of great talents that sincerely or insincerely give themselves to the service of orthodoxy, autocracy, and nationality declines so quickly. . . . And you are greatly mistaken if you believe in all earnest that your book has come to grief not because of its bad trend, but because of the harsh truths alleged to have been expressed by you about all and sundry. Assuming you could think that of the writing fraternity, but then how do you account for the public? Did you tell it less bitter home truths less harshly and with less truth and talent in *Inspector General* and *Dead Souls*? Indeed, the old school was worked up to a furious pitch of anger against you, but *Inspector General* and *Dead Souls* were not affected by it, whereas your latest book has been an utter and disgraceful failure. (pp. 88-9)

I would tell you, not without a certain feeling of self-satisfaction, that I believe I know the Russian public a little. Your book alarmed me by the possibility of its exercising a bad influence on the government and the censorship, but not on the public. . . .

Your conversion may conceivably have been sincere, but your idea of bringing it to the notice of the public was a most unhappy one. The days of naïve piety have long since passed, even in our society. It already understands that it makes no difference where one prays and that the only people who seek Christ and Jerusalem are those who have never carried Him in their breasts or who have lost Him. He who is capable of suffering at the sight of other people's sufferings and who is pained at the sight of other people's oppression bears Christ within his bosom and has no need to make a pilgrimage to Jerusalem. The humility you preach is, first of all, not novel, and, second, it savors on the one hand of prodigious pride, and on the other of the most shameful degradation of one's human dignity. (p. 90)

And what language, what phrases! "Every man hath now become trash and a rag"—do you really believe that in saying *hath* instead of *has* you are expressing yourself biblically? How eminently true it is that when a man gives himself wholly up to lies, intelligence and talent desert him. If this book did not bear your name, who would have thought that this turgid and squalid bombast was the work of the author of *Inspector General* and *Dead Souls*? (pp. 90-1)

Were I to give free rein to my feelings this letter would probably grow into a voluminous notebook. I never thought of writing you on this subject, though I longed to do so and though you gave all and sundry printed permission to write you without ceremony with an eye to the truth alone. . . . I cannot express myself by halves, I cannot prevaricate; it is not in my nature. Let you or time itself prove to me that I am mistaken in my conclusions. I shall be the first to rejoice in it, but I shall not repent what I have told you. This is not a question of your or my personality; it concerns a matter that is of greater importance than myself or even you; it is a matter that concerns the truth, Russian society, Russia. And this is my last concluding word: If you have had the misfortune of disowning with proud humility your truly great works, you should now disown with sincere humility your last book, and atone for the dire sin of its publication by new creations that would be reminiscent of your old ones. (pp. 91-2)

> *V. G. Belinsky, in a letter to N. V. Gogol on July 15, 1847, in* Belinsky, Chernyshevsky, and Dobrolyubov: Selected Criticism, *edited by Ralph E. Matlaw (copyright, ©, 1962, by E. P. Dutton & Co., Inc.; reprinted by permission of the publisher, E. P. Dutton, Inc.), Dutton, 1962, pp. 83-92.*

## NIKOLAI GOGOL   (letter date 1847)

*[The following letter, which was never mailed, is Gogol's response to Belinsky's vitriolic letter in which he had condemned* Selected Passages *as "turgid and squalid bombast" (see excerpt above, 1847). Gogol here defends his ideals and intentions, and concludes with a half-hearted gesture toward reconciliation with Belinsky.]*

How shall I begin my answer to your letter? I will begin it with your very own words: "Come to your senses, you are standing on the edge of an abyss!" How far you have wandered from the true road, what an inside-out view of things you have! In what a crude, ignorant sense you have taken my book! How you have interpreted it! Oh, may the holy powers bring peace into your suffering, tormented soul. (p. 179)

What a strange delusion you are in! Your lucid intellect has been befogged. Such a wrong view you have taken of the meaning of my works. My answer is in them. When I wrote them I held in reverence everything which man should hold in reverence. In my work there is no dislike and mockery of authority, not of the basic laws of our country, but of perversion, of deviations, of incorrect interpretations, of bad application of them, of the scabs which have accumulated, of a life inappropriate to it. I have never mocked that which forms the basis of the Russian character and its great powers. There was mockery only of triviality unnatural to its character. . . . Even though I have observed Russian man more than you, although a certain gift of clairvoyance could help me, I did not blind myself; my eyes were clear. I saw that I was still not mature enough to contend with the most powerful characters, with events which were above those which had appeared in my works formerly. Everything could seem exaggerated and forced. This happened in my book which you attacked so violently. You glanced at it with inflamed eyes, and you saw everything in it the wrong way. You did not see it for what it was. I am not going to defend my book. How can I answer any of your charges when they all miss the point. (pp. 179-80)

How can I defend myself against your attacks when the attacks are irrelevant? My words to the emperor reminding him of the sacredness of his calling and his high duties seemed lies to you. You call them flattery. No, each of us should remember that his calling is sacred—all the more the emperor. Let him remember what a stern answer will be demanded from him. But if the calling of each of us is sacred, then all the more the calling of the one who has received the difficult and terrible lot of caring for millions. Why remind one of the sacredness of a calling? Yes, we must even remind each other about the sacredness of our duties and calling. If one doesn't do this, man will sink into the muck of material concerns. You say, incidentally, that I sang a song of praise to our government. Nowhere did I sing. I said only that the government consists of us ourselves. We attain higher ranks and constitute the government. If then the government is a huge band of thieves, or do you think that none of the Russians know that? (pp. 180-81)

Why did it seem to you that I also sang a song of praise to our vile, as you put it, clergy? Was it my saying that the preacher of the Eastern Church must preach by means of his life and deeds? And why are you possessed by such a spirit of hate? I have known very many bad priests, and I can tell you a multitude of amusing anecdotes about them—perhaps more than you can. But on the other hand I have also met those whose great deeds and holy lives amazed me; and I saw that they are a creation of our Eastern Church and not of the Western one. Therefore, I did not in the least render up a song of praise to the clergy who have disgraced our church, but to the clergy who have evaluated our church.

How strange this all is! How strange my position is—that I have to defend myself against attacks which are all directed neither against me nor against my book! You say that you read my book seemingly a hundred times, while your own words prove that you haven't read it once. (p. 181)

What am I to answer you to the biting remark that the Russian peasant is supposedly not inclined to religion, and that when he talks about God, he scratches himself below his back with the other hand, a remark which you utter with such self-confidence—as if you had spent your entire life in the society of the Russian peasant. What is there to say to this when the thousands of churches and monasteries which cover the Russian land speak so eloquently. They are built not with the gifts of the rich, but with the donations of the poor, those very people who you say talk about God with disrespect, and who share their last kopek with the poor and God, who bear bitter privation about which each of us knows, in order to have the opportunity of giving earnest alms to God. No, Vissarion Grigorevich, it is impossible for one who has lived his whole life in Petersburg to judge about the Russian people, one who has busied himself with the light magazine articles and novels of those French novelists who are so prejudiced that they don't want to see that

truth comes out of the Gospels and who do not notice what an ugly and trashy way they use to depict life. Now, allow me to say that I have more right than you to start talking about the Russian people. All my works, at least according to unanimous conviction, show a knowledge of the Russian character; they reveal a man who has been observant with the people and, therefore, already has a gift of understanding their life—about which much has been said—which you yourself confirmed in your critical articles [see excerpt above, 1842]. (p. 183)

You say that Russia has prayed long and in vain. No, Russia has not prayed in vain. When it prayed, it was saved. It prayed in 1612 and was saved from the Poles; it prayed in 1812 and was saved from the French.—Or do you call it prayer when one out of a hundred prays, and all the rest go on a spree like mad from morning till night at all kinds of shows and spectacles, mortgaging the last of their property to enjoy all the comforts with which this dunderheaded European civilization has endowed us? (pp. 184-85)

Leave this world of those who have become insolent, which is half-dead, for which neither you nor I were born. Allow me to remind you of your former works and writings. Allow me also to remind you of your former path. The man of literature exists for something else. He ought to serve art, which introduces a higher reconciliatory truth into the soul of the world—not hostility; love for man—not bitterness and hate. Again take up the calling from which you have wandered with the thoughtlessness of a youth. Begin your study from the beginning again. Take up those poets and sages who educate your soul. (p. 185)

You took my words about literacy in a narrow, literal sense. These words were spoken to a landowner whose serfs are tillers of the soil. Why it was even amusing to me when you understood my words to mean I was attacking literacy. Just as if that were the question now when this question was already decided by our fathers long ago. Our fathers and grandfathers, even the illiterate ones, decided that literacy was necessary. That is not the point. The idea which runs through my entire book is this: how can we enlighten the literate first (rather than the illiterate), how first of all to enlighten those who have close contact with the common people (rather than the common people themselves), all these minor civil servants and officials who are all literate and who are nevertheless guilty of many abuses. Believe this—it is more necessary to publish for these gentlemen the books which you think are useful for the common people. (pp. 185-86)

God knows, perhaps there is some truth in your words. I will tell you only that I have received about fifty different letters about my book; not one of them resembles another, there are not two people whose opinions about one and the same subject are in agreement; what one refutes another asserts is correct. And besides that, there are equally noble and intelligent people on every side. So far I have seen only one thing as an indisputable truth—the fact that I do not know Russia at all, that much has changed since I was there, and that now I have to learn almost everything that is there anew. And from all this I have drawn the conclusion for myself that I should not publish anything—not only not *living images,* but not even two lines of any writing whatever—until such time as I go to Russia and see a great deal with my own eyes and feel it with my own hands. I see that those who have reproached me with ignorance of many things and not taking into consideration many aspects have revealed to me their own ignorance of much, their own failure to consider many aspects. . . . The coming age is the age of reasonable awareness; it weighs everything without passion, taking all sides into consideration—without which it is impossible to discover the reasonable middle road of things. It orders us to scan things with the many-sided glance of an old man, not to show the zealous nimbleness of a knight of past times; we are children in the presence of this age. Believe me, both you and I are guilty before it in equal degrees. Both you and I have gone over into excess. At least I admit this, but do you admit it? Exactly as I lost sight of *contemporary* affairs and a multitude of things which should have been considered, exactly in the same manner you too lost sight; as I *concentrated* within myself too much, you *scattered your energies* too widely outside yourself. As I need to learn much that you know and I do not know, so you too need to learn at least part of what I know and which you wrongfully disdain. (pp. 186-87)

With all my heart I wish you spiritual tranquility, the first blessing without which it is impossible to work and act reasonably in any field of endeavor. (p. 187)

> *Nikolai Gogol, in his letter to V. G. Belinsky, July-August, 1847, in his* Letters of Nikolai Gogol, *edited by Carl R. Proffer, translated by Carl R. Proffer with Vera Krivoshein (translation copyright © by The University of Michigan 1967; originally published in* Polnoe sobranie socinenij, *Vols. X-XIV, 1937-52), University of Michigan Press, 1967, pp. 179-87.*

## V. G. BELINSKY   (essay date 1848)

[*In his final essay on Gogol, Belinsky transcends his scorn for* Selected Passages (*see excerpt above, 1847*) *and offers a positive assessment of Gogol's place in Russian literature. He acknowledges Gogol's "originality and independence," which, he states, "[distinguish] him from all Russian writers." He ultimately calls Gogol uniquely Russian, free from theory or influence.*]

It was with the appearance of *Mirgorod* and *Arabesques* . . . and of the *Inspector General* . . . that Gogol's full fame began, as did his strong influence on Russian literature. Of all the opinions about this writer expressed by admirers of his talent, the most remarkable and closest to the truth seem to belong to [Vasili Plaksin,] a man who is not at all one of his admirers and who, in a moment of some sudden inspiration . . . uttered the following in praise of Gogol:

> All Gogol's works reveal him to possess self-confidence, a striving to do things his own way, a sort of deliberate and mocking disdain of previous knowledge, experience and standards; *he reads only the book of nature, studies only the world of realities;* hence his ideals are natural and simple to the point of nakedness; to use the expression of Ivan Nikiforovich, one of his characters, they appear before the reader in a state of nature. The beauty of his creations is always new, fresh and striking; *his errors are almost repellent (?); seeming to have forgotten history, he, like the ancients, begins a new world of the arts,* invoking it from the limbo of nihility into an *undisguised (?), chaotic (?!)* state; that is why his art does not know, does not understand, what modesty is; he is a great artist who knows no history and has seen no models of art.

In this lyrically confused eulogy, the author has, despite himself, expressed the most characteristic feature of Gogol's tal-

ent—originality and independence, which distinguishes him from all Russian writers. (p. 410)

Gogol had no models to follow, no predecessors either in Russian or in foreign literatures. All theories, all literary traditions were against him, because he was against them. To understand him one had to get them all out of one's head, to forget their existence—and that for many would have meant being born again—dying and arising from the dead. To make our idea clearer, let us see in what relation Gogol stands to the other Russian poets. Of course, even in those of Pushkin's works that represent pictures foreign to the Russian world there are, without doubt, Russian elements, but who will point them out? How prove that such poems as *Mozart and Salieri, The Stone Guest, The Covetous Knight* and *Galub* could have been written only by a Russian poet and that no poet of another nation could have written them? The same can be said of Lermontov. All Gogol's works deal exclusively with the world of Russian life and he has no rivals in the art of portraying it in all its truth. He tones down and embellishes nothing for the sake of ideals or any preconceived ideas, or some habitual bias, as for example Pushkin did in his *Eugene Onegin* where he idealized the life of the landowners. Of course, the predominant feature of his works is negation; to be valid and poetical, every kind of negation must be made in the name of an ideal—and this ideal, with Gogol, as with all other Russian poets, was not his own, that is to say, not native, since our social life had not yet taken form or established itself sufficiently to be able to supply literature with this idea. But one must agree that, as far as Gogol's works are concerned, it is entirely out of the question to ask: how prove that they could have been written only by a Russian poet, that they could not have been written by a poet of another nation? (pp. 411-12)

Gogol is one of the few who completely avoided the influence of any theory whatsoever. Though able to understand art and admire it in the works of other poets, Gogol nevertheless went his own way, following the profound and true artistic instinct with which nature had so richly endowed him, and refusing to be lured by other men's successes into the net of imitation. This, of course, did not give him originality, but it enabled him to preserve and give full expression to the originality which was an attribute and quality of his personality, and, consequently, like talent, a gift of nature. Because of this he seemed to many to have entered Russian literature from without, whereas he was really an essential fact in this literature, a prerequisite of the entire trend of its development. (pp. 413-14)

> *V. G. Belinsky, "A View on Russian Literature in 1847" (originally published under a different title in* Sovremennik, *1848), in his* Selected Philosophical Works, *Foreign Languages Publishing House, 1948, pp. 395-490.**

## IVAN TURGENEV   (essay date 1852)

Gogol is dead! What Russian heart will not be deeply moved by these words? He is dead. Our loss is so cruel, so sudden that we still cannot believe it. At a time when all of us could still hope that he would at last break his long silence, that he would gladden, exceed our impatient expectations, this fatal news came! Yes, he is dead, the man whom we now have the right, a bitter right conferred on us by his death, to call great; the man who by his name marked an epoch in the history of our literature; the man we are proud of as one of our glories! He is dead, struck down in the prime of life, at the height of his powers, without finishing the work he has begun, like one of the noblest of his predecessors. His loss renews our grief for those unforgettable bereavements, as a new wound awakens the pain of old ones. This is not the time nor the place to speak of his merits—that is the business of future criticism; let us hope that it will understand its task and appraise him with that impartial judgment, filled with respect and love, with which people like him are appraised before posterity. . . . The thought that his remains lie in Moscow fills us with a kind of sorrowful satisfaction. Yes, let them lie there, in the heart of the Russia he knew so well and loved so well, loved so ardently that only thoughtless and short-sighted people do not feel the presence of that loving flame in every word uttered by him! But what is so hard to bear is the thought that the last and most mature fruits of his genius are irretrievably lost to us—and we hear with horror the cruel rumours of their destruction. . . .

We need hardly speak of those few people to whom our words will appear exaggerated or altogether misplaced. . . . Death has a purifying and reconciling force; slander and envy, hostility and misunderstanding—they all fall silent before the most ordinary grave; they will not break the silence before Gogol's grave. Whatever the place history finally allots to him, we are certain that no one will refuse to repeat after us: May he rest in peace, may the memory of his life be everlasting! Eternal glory to his name! (pp. 146-47)

> Ivan Turgenev, "A Letter from Petersburg" (1852), *in his* Literary Reminiscences and Autobiographical Fragments, *translated by David Magarshack (reprinted by permission of Farrar, Straus & Giroux, Inc.; copyright © 1958 by Farrar, Strauss & Cudahy, Inc.; originally published as* Literaturnye i zhiteishie vospominaniia, *1934), Farrar, Straus and Cudahy, 1958 (and reprinted as* Turgenev's Literary Reminiscences and Autobiographical Fragments, *translated by David Magarshack, Faber and Faber, 1959, pp. 146-47).*

### [C. E. TURNER]   (essay date 1868)

Admirers of the modern sensational novel, in whose eyes tragedy is inseparably connected with 'ermine-tippets, adultery, and murder' must look upon the tales of Gogol as insipidly commonplace, and exhibiting a sad poverty of imagination. Nothing can exceed their simplicity of plot. In most of them there is an entire absence of intrigue. What is the subject of his **'Old-Fashioned Farmers'**? Two country boors, living in a dull round of thoughtless content, spend their sixty or seventy years in drinking and eating, eating and drinking; and when they have eaten and drunk their fill, die off. Utterly incapable of the slightest intellectual effort, ignorant of all the higher impulses of nobler aspirations that dignify our nature, unconscious of any pleasure beyond the satisfaction of those instincts which man shares in common with the beast of the field,—what interest can there be in the record of life like theirs? All the emptiness, poverty, and bare nakedness of their existence is exposed; not a single detail in their petty, monotonous career, each to-morrow, the deadening counterpart of yesterday is forgotten or passed over; and yet, such is the power of art, when exercised on even the most trivial of themes, that what in unskilled hands would have sunk into a revolting burlesque, becomes with Gógol the source of truest poetry and kindliest humour.

Combined with, and a natural consequence of this simplicity of plot, we observe in Gógol a rare fidelity of human nature in the delineation of his characters. They are not heroic, gifted with superhuman virtues of superhuman vices. It requires no great genius to sketch incarnations of wild devilry or embodiments of perfection. They are not extraordinary people, still less fancy portraits, but living realities; to many of whom we feel that we could give their true name. It is this which arouses our interest in the humblest and the meanest among them; we perceive that they are no painted puppets put into certain postures at the whim and caprice of the showman, but through every change of circumstance they are allowed to develope themselves naturally, and without the author's controlling intervention. . . . [We] seem to have known them one and all in real life. Let their story be told however briefly, we feel able to supply some trait in their history which the author has failed to give, relate some additional anecdote about them which the writer has forgotten or passed over.

The next feature in the writings of Gógol of which we would speak is one which, on a first perusal, we are apt to imagine constitutes their sole, or at least chief, recommendation. We refer to their humour. And when we speak of Gógol's humour, we wish the word to be understood in its widest and most comprehensive sense. For though in its source it is one springing from a deep conviction of the vanity of all that is human, it is most varied in its manifestations. At times he will surrender himself to some wild fancy so extravagantly absurd, that no writer less daring than himself would ever have used it to move our laughter, and hold us spell-bound as he describes Vakóola's ride on the devil's back to St. Petersburg [in **'Christmas Eve'**]. . . . There is in such passages as this an abandonment to the humour of the moment which it is impossible to resist. . . . In general, however, Gógol's humour is quieter and more subdued in its tone. It is this forced absence of passion which gives such strength to Gógol's satire, and makes his irony so biting. By a single word or trifling phrase, which would seem to have fallen accidentally from his pen, he will plant the blow, aimed at the social folly or administrative abuse he is attacking, with a vigour and a certainty that renders it fatal. Thus, in the description of a general's daughter, which he puts into the mouth of a poor *tchinóvnik* [government clerk], who is infatuated with her beauty, after having made him expatiate on the charms of her person, with what exquisite banter does he sum up the cringing subserviency natural to his position in the one expressive sentence, 'Her very handkerchief breathes the essence of a general's rank!' (pp. 332-34)

In his humour, in his irony, in his language, in his thoughts, in his lyrical outburst of passionate eloquence, and in his pathos, Gógol is thoroughly Russian. And thoroughly Russian, too, are all his personages; and it were difficult to cite one trait in the national character that has not been seized upon by Gógol. His nationality, to use his own words, does not consist 'in describing the saraphan,' but is 'inspired by the very spirit of the people.' And yet, as a true artist, he did not neglect external peculiarities. Nothing can be more remarkable than the pains which he took to render his portraits true to the minutest detail. . . . So true and so outspoken is he, that he was not seldom met with the charge of being unpatriotic: as if, forsooth, patriotism consisted in a blind admiration of whatever is, and an equally blind belief that it therefore must be right. It is a charge which honest writers in every land and in every age have had to bear. 'But,' to quote Gógol's manly reply to such reproaches, 'the accusation is not founded on any sentiment so pure or so noble as patriotism. It proceeds from those who do not care to remedy an evil, but are only anxious that none should speak of the ill they do. A cowardly fear is its sole foundation, however grandly it may mask itself under the holy name of patriotism. This mask it is the mission of every honest writer to tear away, to trample beneath his feet. Writers have but one sacred duty, and that is to tell the truth, the whole truth, and nothing but the truth.' (pp. 334-35)

There are a freshness, a simplicity, and a gaiety in Gógol's descriptions of Little Russian life, which bring home to us a conviction of their unexaggerated truthfulness, even though we have never visited the country, and are ignorant of its habits, faith, and language. They are filled with those happy touches which of themselves reveal the whole character of the people with a certainty and a precision not to be attained in pages of ordinary traveller's gossip. (pp. 335-36)

'Tárass Búlba' and 'The Old-Fashioned Farmers' are two companion pictures: the one representing the complete abnegation of all activity in life; the other, the heroic energy which knows of no tranquility or rest. There is something brutal in both these lives: in the placid contentment, which nothing can ruffle or disturb so long as the animal instincts are satisfied; and in the unrestrained abandonment to the fiercest passions, which acknowledge no higher law, admit of no restraint. And where shall we find the portrait of a savage hero drawn with grander boldness in its colossal outlines, or with subtler delicacy in its minutest filling up, than in the first of these stories? (pp. 336-37)

Of Gógol's numerous tales relating to *tchinóvnik* life, 'The Cloak' strikes us as affording the best example of that knowledge of, and power to describe, the petty joys and unromantic miseries of homely, commonplace people, which form the most striking characteristics of his genius. It is impossible to read the history of 'Akákia Akakievitch,' and not be touched by the deep pathos that underlies its very insignificance, and in the one bright dream, that for a moment gladdened his dim, narrow existence, recognise the glorious probabilities with which every soul, however thwarted, however deadened, is originally endowed. (p. 340)

> [C. E. Turner], "Gógol's Works," in The British Quarterly Review, Vol. XLVII, No. XCIV, April 1, 1868, pp. 327-45.

### *THE LITERARY WORLD*   (essay date 1887)

Gogol's story of *Dead Souls* . . . may safely be classed as the author's masterpiece and as one of the enduring productions of modern literature. . . .

Notwithstanding its lugubrious title, the book is by no means a ghastly one. Tchitchikoff is a polished, insinuating scoundrel, whose undeviating effrontery and honest villainy are delightfully depicted; the "dead souls" are dead serfs, whose names he buys or begs from landed proprietors with the intention of mortgaging them to the government. The motive of the plot is at once evident. The author adopts the ingenious scheme as an excuse for a constant change of scene in harmony with his purpose, which is to pass from point to point, describing people, manners, customs, and conditions, leaving no phase of rural existence unrecorded. The book is really a narrative of travel and observation, so real are the personages, so actual the shifting scenes through which the author conducts us. And what enthusiasm, what vivacity, what unfailing humor, what clever wit, and what unsparing satire does he not display in the course of his enticing chronicle! The petty nobility, the village functionaries, the peasants—all classes are represented by ten or a hundred different types; each one of them is alive,

thinks, feels, acts, plays his or her part with undeviating truthfulness. Open the book at any point and you are at once impressed with Gogol's wonderful fertility of imagination, his profound knowledge of human nature, and his overwhelming resources as a social satirist. These qualities naturally led him into excesses. That he often resorts to caricature is evident; but this very exaggeration is self-confessed, and serves an artistic purpose. Like Cruikshank, Gogol deals in bold outlines and sharp dashes of color; yet we perceive clearly the essential veracity of all that he creates. . . .

Underneath the humor and wit and satire is the elemental pathos of a sorrowing comprehension of Russian limitations and Russian needs. Gogol saw constantly in the background as he wrote, an ideal, perfected Russia, the Russia that might be, that must be; and contrasting the real with the ideal, he mingled his laughter with tears. The humor that we find in Gogol belongs to the same order as that of Cervantes; it is based on an innate sympathy which never loses its tenderness, even when humanity shows itself in the most degraded and humiliating forms. . . .

[The *Continuation and Conclusion of Dead Souls*] has no reasonable excuse for being. It is not interesting as a literary curiosity, and as for "those people who like to have their stories complete," let them seek for mental pabulum elsewhere. Certainly the person who reads *Dead Souls,* with or without continuations and conclusions, "to see how the story ends," is doomed to a toilsome task terminating in condign disappointment.

> "Gogol's 'Dead Souls'," in The Literary World (copyright 1887 by L. C. Page & Company (Inc.)), Vol. XVIII, No. 7, April 2, 1887, p. 101.

### ARTHUR TILLEY   (essay date 1894)

At first sight the majority of [the tales collected in "Evenings at a Farm near Dikanka"] seem to be purely romantic in type, the supernatural element playing a large part in them. In "A Terrible Revenge," a Cossack story, it runs utterly riot. But in the others we find behind the naïve hocus-pocus of devils and witches a carefully drawn background of Little-Russian life; indeed the supernatural element itself is only an additional trait of national character. Very noticeable are the magnificent descriptions of scenery, true lyrical outbursts, which testify to the writer's passionate love for his native land. The most celebrated are that of the Dnieper in "A Terrible Revenge," that of the Ukraine night in "The May Night," and that of a hot summer's day at the beginning of "The Fair at Sorochintsi." One of the stories, "Ivan Feodorovitch Sponka and his Aunt," stands by itself. The supernatural element is entirely absent; it is a purely realistic picture of Russian country life, and though there is as little attempt at a plot as there is in its companions, the characters are drawn with great care and incision. Sponka is one of those negative, nondescript, unheroical heroes in whom Gogol delights, but the aunt is a notable woman, of marked energy and originality. (p. 490)

"Proprietors of the Olden Time" [from the collection entitled "Mirgorod"] is a masterpiece of its kind. It is a simple sketch of an old couple—a sort of Philemon and Baucis—who live in a country house far from the world, with no ideas beyond eating and drinking and loving one another, and showing hospitality to chance guests.

"The Story of how Ivan Nikiforovitch and Ivan Ivanovitch Quarrelled" is almost as admirable a picture of town life as the other is of country life. It has more movement than its companions, and there is some attempt at a story. Ivan Ivanovitch and Ivan Nikiforovitch were dear friends, till one day Ivan Ivanovitch called Ivan Ivanovitch a gander, and they went to law, but there were many delays, and the case was never decided. This is all the story; but it is admirably told. The tone is more comic than in the country idyll, the irony is more pronounced, and, though it is perfectly good-natured, it has a spice of malice which reminds one of La Fontaine. The comic effect is often heightened by the grave, matter-of-fact air with which the most absurd things are said.

Most effective, too, is the adoption of an intimate button-holing tone which, by means of skilful little touches, helps to create the illusion that the narrator is telling something that he actually saw. Finally, it should be noticed that as well as the story last mentioned, it concludes in a somewhat melancholy key, and that the more laughable story is at bottom the sadder of the two; for the years roll on and the two old friends are never reconciled. . . .

["Taras Bulba"] is Gogol's first attempt at something more ambitious than a short tale. The outcome of his grandfather's stories and of his own studies in Little-Russian history and folk-lore, it is a striking picture of the life of the Zaporozhian Cossacks in the sixteenth century. Readers of it have complained of its too-palpable imitations of Homer; but of Homer Gogol knew little or nothing, and the apparent Homeric reminiscences are due partly to the folk-songs which form the basis of much of his narrative, and partly to the naïve freshness of his genius, with its natural capacity for vivid and soul-stirring narrative. Truly has the book been called the Little-Russian epic. Though in many respects it differs widely in manner from the works of our own great epic novelist, it recalls him in the vigor and color of the descriptions and the rapid movement of the narrative. Taras Bulba himself is cast in a heroic mould. His manners are barbarous, even to ferocity, but by his love for his country, his devotion to his comrades, and his heroic death, he compels our sympathy and admiration. A romantic love-story serves like a thread of gold to relieve the deep hues of the main texture. (p. 491)

[The volume "Arabesques" contains] amongst other miscellaneous pieces, four stories of no great merit. "Nevski Prospect" opens with a masterly description of the street from which it takes its name. "The Portrait" is a fantastic tale, in the manner of Hoffmann, which promises well at the outset, but dies away to nothing. It is chiefly noticeable for the absence of the fun and kindly irony which had hitherto distinguished Gogol's humor. "The Memoirs of a Madman" has plenty of fun on the surface, but it is a gloomy tragedy at bottom, for it is the self diagnosis, in the shape of a diary, of the growing madness of a humble government clerk. There is something, no doubt, of personal recollection in the story, and, alas! something of prophecy. . . . [Two subsequent] short stories, "A Nose" and "The Calash," [are] both sharp satires in the guise of high comedy, the one of St. Petersburg, the other of provincial life. It is this vein of humor, this blending of laughter and irony, which appears fully developed in his well-known play, "The Inspector." . . . The simplicity of the plot has provoked a smile from more than one countryman of Scribe and Sardou, but the plot is a mere peg on which to hang a scathing satire on the corruption of Russian official life. A rollicking farce on the surface, at the bottom it is bitter, serious truth. (pp. 491-92)

Regard for humble or commonplace people, regard for apparently insignificant details—these are two of the leading features which the Russian realistic school has inherited from Gogol. The first feature is especially conspicuous in his story of "The Cloak." (p. 494)

"We all started from Gogol's story of 'The Cloak,'" said [Dostoïevsky]. . . . It is very true. That note of sublime pity is to be found alike in Turgéniev, and Dostoïevsky, and Tolstoy. . . .

The second feature, the careful observance of details, which at first sight appear trivial and insignificant, has been somewhat misunderstood both by imitators and critics. The thumb of the tailor in "The Cloak," which had "a deformed nail, thick and strong as a turtle's shell," has raised a contemptuous smile. But it should be noticed first that what Gogol asks his friend to send him are notes, not of every kind of detail, but of "incidents bearing upon human nature," and secondly, that he only uses for the purpose of his art those incidents and details that are really characteristic. . . . Another characteristic, not only of Gogol's, but more or less of the whole Russian school, is consciously affected by some would-be realists, as if it were an essential quality of realism. I mean the absence of a plot, or at best the barest pretence of a story as a framework upon which to construct studies of human character and society. . . . [However,] it is not the absence of plot which makes a story realistic, but the realism of a story, or rather the realistic handling of human character, which makes the absence of plot endurable. Further, . . . Gogol's execution is always lively, pregnant, and artistic. (p. 495)

Another conspicuous feature which Gogol has in common with his successors is his passionate love for his country. It is this very love which makes him so keenly alive to her faults. Like the Athenians and the French, the Russian writers combine with intense patriotism great frankness in their observations on national shortcomings. In Gogol this love of his country often . . . takes the form of magnificent descriptions of natural scenery. . . .

Gogol was essentially a humorist; that is to say, he viewed the topsy-turvydom of life rather with sympathetic laughter than with savage indignation or scientific neutrality. But the quality of his humor underwent a considerable change during the ten years which separated "Dead Souls" from the "Evenings at the Farm near Dikanka." He began as an observer of the human comedy; he ended as a lasher of national vices. His earliest mood resembles the gentle malice of Jane Austen, his latest has the bitterness, though not the savageness, of Swift. Truly he said that after "The Inspector" he was no longer the same man. His self-imposed task of stemming the tide of national corruption proved, as well it might have done, too much for his strength. He had not that inexhaustible reserve of good humor, which enabled Molière, when he found the world crying out on him, to turn the laughter against himself and produce his masterpiece. He became himself not a misanthrope, for his pity for human nature saved him from that, but a melancholy recluse. And it is noteworthy that the more serious and bitter his criticisms of life became the more he laughted outwardly. "The Inspector" is on the surface a roaring farce; in "Dead Souls," if the laughter is not so loud, it is, so to speak, more out of place. Even Molière grows serious in the presence of a Tartuffe or a Don Juan, but Gogol in "Dead Souls" laughs at fools and villains alike. . . . (p. 496)

It is, in fact, often a forced laughter. "Amidst laughter which is visible to the world I drop invisible tears," says Gogol, in words which are inscribed on his statue at Nyezhin; but in "Dead Souls" the tears are sometimes visible behind the laughter.

And if the laughter is somewhat forced the realism is also forced; it has become conscious and militant. Gogol contrasts in one place the happy lot of the idealist with the hard, ungrateful task of the realist, whose business it is to make a picture out of the sordid and contemptible elements of life. His realism does not consist in seeing only shadows. "Dead Souls" may be a true picture in the sense that it represents actual facts, but it cannot be a complete one. Even in Russia, under the Czar Nicholas, there must have been some public honesty, some domestic unselfishness. Thus, from the point of view of truth, and still more from that of art, the picture wants lights. Gogol, in short, has ceased to "see life steadily and see it whole." But, in spite of some elements of weakness, he is a great genius. The amount of his work, practically finished by the time he was one-and-thirty, is naturally not great; but take the best of it—take "Taras Bulba," "The Inspector," "Dead Souls," and the best of the short stories, and you get a marked impression of strength and variety. There is truth, humor, imagination; he unites, in a rare degree, power with delicacy of observation; his touch is as light as it is firm. (pp. 496-97)

Arthur Tilley, "Gogol, the Father of Russian Realism" (reprinted by permission of the Literary Estate of Arthur Tilley), in The National Review, London, Vol. XXIII, No. 137, July, 1894, pp. 650-51.

## DMITRY MEREZHKOVSKY (essay date 1906)

[A prominent member of the Russian Symbolist movement, Merezhkovsky valued Gogol as a mystic and spiritual writer. In the following, he maintains that Gogol's work ultimately displays "the great struggle of Man with the Devil."]

In Gogol's religious outlook, the Devil is a mystical essence and a real being, in which eternal evil, a denial of God, has been concentrated. Gogol the artist investigates the nature of the mystical essence in the light of laughter; Gogol the man contends with this real being using laughter as a weapon: Gogol's laughter is man's struggle with the Devil.

God is the infinite, the beginning and end of all being. The Devil is the denial of God and consequently the denial of the infinite as well, the denial of all beginnings and ends. The Devil is something that is begun and is left unfinished, but purports to be without beginning or end. The Devil is the noumenal median of being, the denial of all heights and depths—eternal planarity, eternal banality. The sole subject of Gogol's art is the Devil in just this sense, that is, the Devil as the manifestation of "man's immortal banality," as seen beneath the specifics of place and time—historical, national, governmental, social; the manifestation of absolute, eternal, universal evil—banality sub specie aeternitatis. (pp. 57-8)

Everyone can perceive evil in great violations of the moral law, in rare and unusual misdeeds, in the staggering climaxes of tragedies. Gogol was the first to detect invisible evil, most terrible and enduring, not in tragedy, but in the absence of everything tragic; not in power, but in impotence; not in insane extremes, but in all-too-sensible moderation; not in acuity and profundity, but in inanity and planarity, in the banality of all human feelings and thoughts; not in the greatest things, but in the smallest. Gogol did for the moral dimension what Leibnitz had done for the mathematical: he discovered, we might say,

the differential calculus, the infinitely great significance of infinitely small magnitudes of good and evil. (p. 58)

Gogol's two principal heroes—Khlestakov, in The Inspector General, and Chichikov, in Dead Souls—are two contemporary Russian selves, two hypostases of eternal and universal evil, of man's immortal banality. . . .

The inspired dreamer Khlestakov and the worldly entrepreneur Chichikov: concealed behind these two diametrical opposites is a third self which unites them: the self of the Devil "without a mask," "in a tail-coat," "in his own true form," the self of our eternal alter ego, who shows us our reflection in himself, as in a mirror, and says: "What are you laughing at? You're laughing at yourselves!" (pp. 59-60)

Khlestakov is not only a real human being, but a "phantom" as well: "he is a phantasmagoric figure," Gogol says, "who, mendacious deception incarnate, was carried off in the troika Heaven knows where." The hero of "The Overcoat," Akaky Akakievich, becomes a phantom, just like Khlestakov, only not in life but after death—a corpse who frightens passers-by at the Kalinkin Bridge and pulls off their overcoats. And Poprishchin, the hero of "Diary of a Madman," becomes a fantastic, phantom figure, "Ferdinand VIII, King of Spain." All three start from the same point: they are minor civil servants in St. Petersburg, depersonalized cells in the vast body of the state, infinitely tiny parts of an infinitely great whole. And from this starting-point—the almost total ingestion of a living human personality by a dead impersonal whole—they thrust out into emptiness, into space, describing three parabolas, each different but all equally monstrous: the first a lie, the second madness, the third a superstitious legend. In all three cases, the personality avenges itself for being negated as a reality; rejecting reality, it takes its vengeance in spectral, phantasmal self-assertion. Man tries to be something other than what he is, because he does not wish to be, he cannot be, he should not be—nothing. (pp. 61-2)

Intellectually and morally, Khlestakov is by no means a complete nonentity. "Khlestakov," as Gogol defines him, "is an adroit person, completely comme il faut, intelligent, perhaps even virtuous"—not too intelligent or too virtuous, to be sure, but not too stupid or wicked, either. He has a most ordinary sort of mind, a most ordinary sort of worldly conscience—common and lightweight. He embodies everything that has now become voguish and will later prove vulgar. He is fashionably dressed and he also speaks, thinks, and feels according to fashion. "He belongs to a circle of people who apparently are in no way different from other young people," as Gogol remarks. He is like everyone else; his mind, his soul, his words, his face: all are like everyone else's. (p. 63)

But the main forces that impel and control him reside not in his social, mental or moral self, but rather in his impersonal, unconscious, elemental being—in his instincts. Pre-eminent among them is the blind animal instinct of self-preservation—an unbelievably ravenous hunger. "I've never been so hungry in all my life. . . . Ugh, I even feel sick. . . ." This is not the simple hunger of a peasant who is satisfied with his daily bread, but the hunger of a lord and master. In asserting his right to satisfy this hunger, Khlestakov is very much aware of his social position: "you explain to him [the inn-keeper] in all seriousness that I need to eat. . . . He thinks that just because a peasant like himself can go a whole day without eating, other people can do the same. That's ridiculous!" "I want to eat, I need to eat"—by now this is something absolute and infinite in Khlestakov's essential nature. In any event, it is his natural beginning and end, his primary and ultimate truth.

Nature, having endowed him with this need, has also armed him with a special power for satisfying it—the power of the lie, of pretense, of knowing how to appear to be something other than he is. And this power, once again, resides not in his intellect, not in his will, but in the innermost recesses of his unconscious instinct. (pp. 63-4)

Khlestakov's lying has something in common with the artist's power of invention. He intoxicates himself with his fancies to the point of utter self-oblivion. Least of all has he any practical goals or advantages in mind. His is a disinterested lie; it is lying for lying's sake, art for art's sake. At this moment he asks nothing of his listeners—only that they should believe him. He lies innocently, guilelessly, and is the first to believe himself, the first to deceive himself: this is the secret of the spell he casts. He lies and he feels: this is good, this is true. For him, as for any artist, *what does not exist* is more beautiful and therefore more true than truth itself. (p. 64)

Another characteristic of his—equally primordial and elemental—is connected with lying. ''I have,'' he acknowledges, ''an extraordinary lightness of thought.'' Not only his thoughts but his feelings too, his actions, his words, even his ''slender and delicate physique''—his entire being—manifest an ''extraordinary lightness.'' He seems to have been entirely ''spun from air.'' He barely touches the ground: at any moment he may flutter up and fly away. (p. 65)

Epicurean free-thinking, regenerated pagan wisdom, the principle of ''enjoy life while you are alive''—Khlestakov condenses all this into an aphorism that conveys a new and affirmative wisdom: ''After all, that's what life is for—to pluck the flowers of pleasure.'' How simple, how easy for everyone to grasp! Will not this emancipation from all bonds of morality later become the Nietzschean and Karamazovian ''There is no good or evil, all is permitted''? In both cases, the origin is the same: the wings of the eagle and the wings of the gnat struggle against the same universal laws of gravity. (pp. 66-7)

This, then, is what his mind encompasses. Everything with three dimensions he reduces to one or two—to utter planarity and banality. All this has become so voguish because it is so vulgar. He abbreviates every idea to the ultimate, lightens it to the ultimate, discards the beginning and the end, leaving only an infinitely tiny point in the middle. What once had been the summit of a mountain ridge now becomes a speck of dust swept along the highway by the wind. There is no feeling so noble, no idea so profound that it cannot be reduced to dust by the abrading and weathering action of Khlestakov's genius for making everything small and light. (p. 67)

Gogol intends us to believe that [the actual official from St. Petersburg] who appears like a *deus ex machina*, like an angel in the medieval mystery plays, is a bona-fide inspector general, the incarnation of fate, the conscience of mankind, the justice of Heaven. However, we do not see him; for us he remains an even more illusive and ghostly figure than Khlestakov. But if we had caught a glimpse of him, then who knows? Perhaps the two ''officials from St. Petersburg,'' great and small, might have borne a strange resemblance to one another after all. . . .

''From St. Petersburg by imperial command'': this is what deafens everybody, like a thunderclap—not only the characters in the play, not only the audience, but apparently even Gogol himself. A command from St. Petersburg? From where else

indeed but St. Petersburg, that most ghostly, foggy, fantastic of all cities on the globe, would all this issue and spread over Russia: the stupefying fog, ''life's dreadful murk,'' the ''Egyptian darkness,'' the Devil's mirage, in which nothing can be seen except ''what look like pigs' snouts instead of faces, and nothing else?'' Are not both inspectors general, the first and the second—the simple registry clerk and the real generalissimo—equally legitimate offspring of the same Table Ranks, products of the same ''St. Petersburg period'' of Russian history?

Furthermore, is not this whole monstrosity of a provincial town a part of the great, all-Russian polity and its citizenry, is it not a miniature image of St. Petersburg itself, reversed but absolutely accurate, as in a drop of water? St. Petersburg brought this town into being out of nothingness. By what right, from what superior height can St. Petersburg then pass judgment on it and mete out punishment to it? What had actually happened in the St. Petersburg of Gogol's time that could have burst not in a Khlestakovian but actually in a divine thunderclap over this tiny Sodom of a town? (pp. 73-4)

*The Inspector General* was not completed; it was not fully apprehended by Gogol himself, and it was not understood by the audience. The denouement is merely brought off according to the conventions of the stage; it is not a real, not a religious denouement by any means. One comedy is brought to an end; another one, higher and far more amusing and terrible, begins, or ought to begin. We will never see this particular comedy on the stage; but it is being played off stage, in life, in actuality, to this very day. In fact, Gogol was aware of this to some extent. ''*The Inspector General* has no ending,'' he said. We might add: *The Inspector General* is endless. Its laughter is not grounded in time and history; rather, it is the endless and enduring laughter of the Russian *conscience* at the Russian polity of its day.

''In the last analysis,'' as Gogol himself says, through the lips of one of the characters in the piece entitled ''The Denouement of *The Inspector General*,'' ''in the last analysis something . . . I can't really explain it to you—something monstrous and gloomy remains, a certain feeling of terror created by the disorder in our lives. The gendarme's appearance in the door, the way everyone is petrified by the words announcing the arrival of the real inspector general, who is to wipe them all off the face of the earth and annihilate them utterly—this is all somehow inexpressibly terrible.''

But really, why is it so terrible? Does not this mute scene also contain some deep prototypical meaning, like everything else in *The Inspector General*? (pp. 74-5)

Khlestakov is carried off in the troika into an indeterminate expanse, into emptiness, into the void from which he, void and emptiness incarnate, has emerged—into nothing. And while everything real and existent, past and present, freezes into immobility and stands petrified in mindless horror at the inevitable final appearance of the mystical Derzhimorda, only the phantasmal Khlestakov, endued as he is with ''an extraordinary lightness of thought,'' sweeps off, forever moving, into the immeasurable expanses of the future. (p. 75)

What is the meaning—to use Gogol's own words—of this ''horror-inspiring motion'' on the one hand, and this horror-inspiring lack of motion, on the other? Can it really be that the petrified Russian polity, fettered not in chains of iron but in ''Egyptian darkness,'' is all of Russia, past and present? That Khlestakov, flying off to the Devil's domain somewhere, is the Russia to be? Massive heaviness and diaphanous lightness—the actual banality of what is now and the phantasmal banality of what will be—these are two equally lamentable ends that are being pursued by Russia, two equally dreadful roads that lead to the Devil, to emptiness, to nihilism, to nothingness.

In this sense, Gogol's comparison of Russia to a speeding troika, at the end of *Dead Souls,* has a horribly mocking ring to it that Gogol himself did not anticipate. . . . The demented Poprishchin, the quick-witted Khlestakov, and the commonsensical Chichikov are the ones carried off by this symbolic Russian troika in its terrible flight into boundless space or boundless emptiness. "A horizon without end. . . . Russia! Russia! I behold thee. . . . What does this boundless space portend? Is it not here, in thee, that a boundless idea will come to birth, since thou thyself are without bounds? Is it not here that a titan will come to life, where there is space for him to develop his powers and stride about?" Alas, the answer to this pitiless question was given by Gogol's prophetic laughter! Only two "heroes of our time" appeared before his eyes, two titans born of the boundless expanses of Russia, like gigantic visions, like "hideous decaying specters with melancholy faces"— Khlestakov and Chichikov.

The principle of motion or progress predominates in Khlestakov; in Chichikov, the principle of equilibrium or stability. Khlestakov's strength lies in the lyrical outburst, in intoxication; Chichikov's strength lies in judicious composure, in sobriety. Khlestakov possesses an "extraordinary lightness," Chichikov an extraordinary weightiness and solidity of mind. Khlestakov is a contemplative; Chichikov is an activist. For Khlestakov everything desirable is real; for Chichikov everything real is desirable. Khlestakov is an idealist; Chichikov is a realist. Khlestakov is a liberal, Chichikov is a conservative. Khlestakov is the poetry, Chichikov the prose of real life in contemporary Russia.

But all these obvious contrasts notwithstanding, their essential natures are identical. They are the two poles of a single force; they are twin brothers, offspring of the Russian *middle* class and the Russian nineteenth century, the most average and bourgeois of all centuries. The essential nature of each is the eternal median, "neither this nor that," utter banality. Khlestakov affirms what does not exist, Chichikov affirms what does exist— and both are equally banal. Khlestakov conceives projects, Chichikov carries them out. The illusive Khlestakov proves to be responsible for very real events in Russia, just as the real Chichikov is responsible for the very illusive Russian legend of "dead souls." These, I repeat, are two contemporary Russian men, two hypostases of eternal and universal evil—of the Devil. (pp. 75-7)

For Chichikov, there is nothing vulgar and ostentatious about the power of money; it is an inner power, a power of the spirit, of thought, of will, of a kind of disinterestedness, heroism, and self-sacrifice. In Part 2 of *Dead Souls,* the Prince—who, like the second inspector general, has arrived "from St. Petersburg by imperial command"—berates Chichikov in the presence of two hefty gendarmes: "You will be taken to jail this very instant and there you will await the disposition of your fate, along with the lowest of scoundrels and thieves." Chichikov protests: "I am a human being, Your Excellency!" And then to Murazov: "I had to earn my daily bread with my blood. I earned every kopeck by patience stained with blood, so to speak, through toil and labor—not by fleecing anyone or embezzling public funds, as some people do. . . . Where is

the justice of Heaven? Where is the reward for my patience, for my exemplary persistence? . . . I had to overcome so much, I had to endure so much! Every single kopeck was earned, you might say, with all the strength of my soul!" For him, there is something absolute, even, it almost seems, infinite, almost religious, in the idea of money. (pp. 78-9)

So-called *comfort,* that is, the fairest flower of today's industrial-capital, bourgeois system, comfort, which is served by all the forces of nature that science has subdued—sound, light, steam, electricity, every invention, every art—this for Chichikov is the ultimate crown of the earthly paradise. . . . Not rapture, or luxury, or intoxication, or the pinnacle of happiness, but merely an average well-being, a modicum of plenty for spirit and body, "peaceful prosperity." . . . (p. 80)

Instead of felicity, well-being; instead of nobility, propriety— that is to say, an external and relative virtue, because for Chichikov, as a true positivist, there is nothing absolute in either good or evil. Inasmuch as man's only definite goal and his greatest good on earth consists of "peaceful prosperity," and the only way of reaching it is through acquisition, then all morality is subordinate to this goal and this good, for "once the goal is chosen, you have to push on, stopping at nothing." "Onward, onward! Excelsior!" This, the battle cry of modern progress, is the cry both of Khlestakov and of Chichikov. (p. 81)

For all his deep conservatism, Chichikov is also a Westerner in part. Like Khlestakov, he feels that in the backwoods of provincial Russia he is a representative of European enlightenment and progress. This attests to Chichikov's close ties with the "Petersburg period" of Russian history, with the reforms of Peter the Great. Chichikov is attracted to the West; he seems to sense that his power and his future "kingdom" are located there. "That's what it would be good to get into," he says as he dreams of entering the customs service; "the border is nearby, and so are enlightened people. And what a stock of fine Holland-linen shirts I could get hold of!" (pp. 82-3)

Russian culture—and this has been the case ever since Peter the Great—plucks only Khlestakovian "flowers of pleasure" from universal culture, and skims off only the choice cream or foam: the finer fruits of Western European enlightenment enter Russia along with other "fancy goods," on just the same basis as Holland-linen shirts. . . . Chichikov selects what he wishes from world culture, and anything else that is too profound or too exalted he reduces to two dimensions, with the same ease as Khlestakov, he lightens, abridges, and flattens it to the ultimate possible degree. (p. 83)

[Gogol wrote:]

> When I began to read him the first chapters of *Dead Souls,* Pushkin, who had always laughed while I read (he liked to laugh very much), gradually became more and more somber, and finally grew positively gloomy. And when I finished reading, he said, in an anguished voice: "Lord, how sad our Russia is!" At this point I understood just how horrifying was the aspect in which darkness could be presented to people. . . .

*Dead Souls* leaves us with the same impression as *The Inspector General:* that it is "something monstrous and gloomy," that "all this is somehow inexpressibly terrible." Even in Pushkin's luminous and childlike heart this feeling of fear, though at first drowned out by laughter, gradually kindled in an ominous glow. It was not sadness and not tears, but actually fear through laughter. (p. 89)

[In] *Dead Souls,* just as in *The Inspector General,* an "Egyptian darkness" descends, "pitch-black night amidst broad daylight," a "stupefying fog," the Devil's mirage in which nothing can be seen except pigs' snouts instead of human faces. And most horrible of all is that these "hideous decaying specters with melancholy faces" that glare at us, these "children of non-enlightenment, these Russian freaks," are, in Gogol's words, "taken from our very own soil," from actual Russian life. For all their illusiveness, they are "of the same body as we ourselves": they are we, as we are reflected in some demonic yet undistorted looking-glass.

In one of Gogol's early stories, "**A Terrible Vengeance,**" "the dead men gnaw at the dead man," they are "pale, very pale, one taller than another, one bonier than another." Among them is "another, taller than the rest, more terrible than the rest," a dead man who has "grown immense in the earth." Likewise, in *Dead Souls,* Chichikov, an "immense dead man," grows and rises up amidst the other dead men, and his physical human form, refracted through the fog of the Devil's mirage, becomes an immense specter. (p. 90)

The two greatest "monsters," who were closer to Gogol and more terrible than any others in his eyes, and whom he therefore pursued with all the anger he could muster, were Khlestakov and Chichikov. . . .

In Gogol there was perhaps even more of Chichikov than of Khlestakov. He could have said both to Chichikov and to Khlestakov what [Dostoevsky's character] Ivan Karamazov says to his Devil: "You are the incarnation of me, myself, though of only one side of me . . . the incarnation of my thoughts and feelings, but only the vilest and most stupid of them. . . . You are myself, me, only with a different face." But Gogol did not say this, he did not perceive, or simply did not wish or dare to perceive, his own Devil in Chichikov, perhaps in fact because Chichikov had detached himself from Gogol and gained real independence to a much lesser degree than had Khlestakov. Here the truth and power of laughter suddenly betrayed Gogol: he took pity on himself in the image of Chichikov. (p. 99)

Just as Ivan Karamazov wrestled with the Devil in his nightmare, so Gogol wrestled with the Devil in his work, which was also a nightmare of sorts. "These nightmares have oppressed my own soul. Only something already present in my soul could have emerged from it." And the important thing in his soul was "a concern that people should have a good, hearty laugh at the Devil." Did he succeed? Ultimately, who was laughing at whom in Gogol's work—man at the Devil, or the Devil at man?

In any event, the challenge was accepted, and Gogol sensed that he could not decline to fight the duel, that it was too late to back out. But this terrible struggle, which had begun in art and in a contemplativeness divorced from life, had to be decided in life itself, in real activity. Before vanquishing eternal evil in the world outside, as an artist, Gogol had to vanquish it within himself, as a human being. This he understood, and he did in fact shift the scene of battle from his work into his life: in this battle he saw not only his vocation as an artist, but also the business of life, the business of the soul.

Nevertheless, Gogol's own contemplativeness already contained the beginning of activity, his very words the beginning of the "business." Here he stands in contrast to Pushkin:

> Not for life's stir and agitation
> Have we been born, nor to make gain
> Or war, but rather for sweet sounds,
> For inspiration, and for prayer.

Gogol did acknowledge the eternal truth of this Pushkinian precept—the truth of contemplativeness—but at the same time he also saw the other truth, antithetical but equally eternal— the truth of action. And here Gogol embodied the inevitable transition of Russian literature and the Russian mind from art to religion, from great contemplativeness to great activism, from word to deed—a transition that is being completed among us only now, in our own times. (pp. 100-01)

Pushkin summons us away from battle; Gogol summons us into battle. This of course is the battle against eternal evil for eternal good, man's ultimate battle with the Devil. The martial spirit in Gogol is just as ingenerate and genuine as is the spirit of peace in Pushkin; there is no self-betrayal or self-renunciation on Gogol's part here: he is as true to his own nature as is Pushkin to his. (p. 101)

[In] this war with himself—as everywhere else—Gogol remained faithful to his own nature, to his true inner nature; yet he could not help but make the transition from "imagination" to "actuality," from word to deed: "my business is the *soul* and the *solid business of life.*" Art he abandoned for test and trial; the Pushkinian attitude of prayer and sacrificial offerings left off; the Gogolian attitude of struggle and self-sacrifice began. The poet disappeared; the prophet emerged.

And at the same time, this marked the beginning of Gogol's tragedy—*incipit tragoedia* [here begins the tragedy]; the beginning of this struggle with everlasting evil, with banality, no longer in creative contemplativeness, but in religious activity; the great struggle of man with the Devil. (p. 102)

> *Dmitry Merezhkovsky, "Gogol and the Devil" (1906; previously published as "Gogol i chert,"" in* Polnoe sobranie sochinenii, *Vol. X, 1911), in* Gogol from the Twentieth Century: Eleven Essays, *edited and translated by Robert A. Maguire (copyright © 1974 by Princeton University Press; excerpts reprinted by permission of Princeton University Press), Princeton University Press, 1974, pp. 57-102.*

**ANDREI BELY** [PSEUDONYM OF **BORIS NIKOLAEVICH BUGAEV**] (essay date 1910)

[*Bely, a prominent Russian Symbolist, explains Gogol's literary appeal from a dramatically Symbolist viewpoint. He cites Gogol's ability to create a world simultaneously real and unreal, and praises his innovative language. Bely's full-length study on Gogol, which is not available in English, provides one of the first considerations of Gogol in schools of literature other than Realism.*]

A song so innate, close to our hearts, entrancing our souls, and yet always distant and indistinct—that is Gogol's song.

And a horrible, heart-gripping laughter which sounds like laughter from a graveyard, and nevertheless it troubles us, as if we too were dead men—a dead man's laughter, Gogol's laughter!

"A song struck up in the distance, the distant tolling of a bell, which fades away . . . the endless horizon . . . Rus, Rus!" (*Dead Souls*) and a line earlier—on the "*boundless plain*" "a *soldier on horseback, carrying a green box with grapeshot and the insignia of a certain artillery battery"* **(Dead Souls)**. Two visions, two ideas; but also two creative desires; here is one of them: *"To clothe it* [i.e., the song. Trans.] *in the moonlit wondrous night and its silvery shimmer, and in the warm luxurious breath of the South. To pour over it a glittering stream of the sun's bright rays, and let it be filled with unbearable brilliance."* (Meditation . . . concerning an unwritten play.) And the other desire consisted in *"dashing off"* a multi-volume history of the Ukraine, without any qualifications for this task. (p. 131)

What kind of images are these? What impossibilities have created them? Everything is mixed together in them: colors, smells, sounds. Where can you find bolder comparisons, where is artistic truth more improbable? Poor Symbolists: to this day they are being rebuked by the critics for their "blue sounds"; but find me images in Verlaine, Rimbaud, Baudelaire which would be as improbable in their boldness as Gogol's. No, you cannot find them, and meanwhile people read Gogol and they don't see, they still haven't seen that we have no word in our dictionary with which to label Gogol; we have no means to measure all the possibilities which he exhausted. We still don't know what Gogol is, and although we do not see the real Gogol, his work, even when reduced by our limited perception, is closer to us than that of all the Russian writers of the nineteenth century.

What a style!

He has eyes invading the soul with singing, or else coming out like pincers, hair spreading like a pale-gray mist, water becoming dust; or else water becomes a glass nightgown, trimmed with wolf-hair, with moonlight. On every page, almost in every sentence he crosses the borders of what is some kind of new world, growing out of the soul in *"oceans of fragrance"* (**"A May Night"**), in *"floods of joy and light"* (**"Viy"**), in a *"gale of gaiety"* (**"Viy"**). From these gales, floods and oceans, when trees whisper their "drunken utterances" (**"The Lost Letter"**), when the human being flies in ecstasy like a bird . . ." *And it seemed . . . would fly right out of the world'* (**"A Terrible Vengeance"**), Gogol's songs were born. Then he wanted to *"clothe"* his son *"in the moonlit wondrous night . . . to pour over it a glittering stream of the sun's bright rays and let it be filled with unbearable brilliance"* (from Gogol's **"Notes"**). And Gogol was beginning his world edifice: in the depths of his soul a new universe was being born, such as we have not known. In floods of bliss, in gales of emotion, there erupted the lava of creativity which hardened into "high-peaked" mountains, blossoming with forests and meadows, sparkling with ponds. And these mountains are not mountains: "Isn't it the mischievous sea which has overrun its shores and tossed its waves like a whirlwind, and petrified, they have remained motionless in the air" (**"A Terrible Vengeance"**). *"These forests are not forests—they are hair growing on a wood demon's shaggy head"* (**"A Terrible Vengeance"**); *"These meadows are not meadows . . . but a green belt—girding the sky'* (**"The Terrible Vengeance"**); and that pond is not a pond: *"like a feeble old man it held the distant, dark sky in its cold embrace, covering the fiery stars with icy kisses"* (**"A May Night"**). That is the kind of earth Gogol sees, where forests are a wood demon's beard, where meadows are a belt criss-crossing the sky, where mountains are petrified waves, and a pond is a feeble old man embracing the sky. And the sky? . . . In **"A Terrible Vengeance"** Gogol has the sky filling the sorcerer's room when he calls up Katerina's soul; the sky itself comes

out of the sorcerer like a magic current. . . . That's the kind of sky we find in Gogol: a sorcerer's sky; and in that kind of sky originates his earth—a sorcerer's earth: that is why a forest turns out to be on a wood demon's head, and even a chimney *"turns into a rector;"* and for Gogol the children of this earth are the same—the earth's horrible children. They are sorcerers, a Viy, or a pannochka [young lady; refers to the witch in **"Viy"**]; their bodies are transparent, hewn from clouds. . . . That earth is not our earth; it is a cloud bank pierced by moonlight. Begin to daydream . . . and your dream will at your will change the cloud outline into a mermaid, or a devil, or a new city—and here you can even find a resemblance to St. Petersburg.

Gogol's song is a song of unbearable brilliance; and the light of this song has created for him a new, better earth where a dream is not a dream but a new life. His song is *moonlight*, which *"like a transparent veil, fell lightly"* (**"Viy"**) on the earth on which Gogol walked. *"With precious muslin damask white as snow"* (**"A Terrible Vengeance"**) Gogol has shrouded from us, and from himself, the real earth; and the folds of this muslin gave birth to the transfigured bodies, apparently *hewn* from *clouds* of flying *maidens*. In the first period of Gogol's writing reality often appears under a romantic veil of moonlight, for his reality is like the lady whose appearance could be borne only when veiled. But suddenly Gogol tears the veil from his lady—and see what Gogol turns reality into: "The cowherd let out such a laugh that it was as if two bulls were bellowing at each other simultaneously" (**"Viy"**). "Ivan Ivanovich's head resembled a radish with the tail down; Ivan Nikiforovich's head resembled a radish with the tail up . . ." "Ivan Ivanovich had . . . tobacco-colored eyes, and a mouth . . . somewhat like the letter V; Ivan Nikiforovich had . . . a nose shaped like a ripe plum" ". . . and now the whole lower part of our assessor's face is a ram's head, so to speak . . . and really for a most trifling reason: when his dear departed mother was in labor a ram came up to the window, and the devil put it into his head to let out a bleat" (**"The Litigation"**).

That's reality for you! After bodies hewn from clouds glitter, he has a ram's ugly face crawling out and bellowing at us like two bulls, then radishes crawl out with tails up and tails down, with tobacco-colored eyes; and they begin not to walk but to scuttle, or to mince and sidle; and what is most horrible of all is that Gogol makes them express themselves in a delicate manner. These *"radishes"* wink with their tobacco-colored little eyes, sprinkle their speech with the words "if it please you," and Gogol does not simply tell us about them but reports on them with a strange desperate sort of joviality; the lower part of the assessor's face is not a ram's head, but *"so to speak"* a ram's head—*"so to speak"* for the most trifling reason: because at the moment of the assessor's birth a ram walked up to the window—a horrible "so to speak."

At this point Gogol is called a realist—but, by all that's holy, where is there any reality here? Here we face not humanity but prehumanity. . . . (pp. 131-33)

[All] these mincing, shuffling busybodies, these Pererepenkos, Golopupenkos, Dovgochkhuns, and Shponkas are not people, but radishes. There are no such people, but as the crowning horror, Gogol makes this *menagerie* or *turnip patch* (I don't know what to call it) dance the mazurka, take snuff from each other and even worse—experience mystical ecstasies, as one of his radishes—Shponka—experiences ecstasy, while looking at an evening sunbeam. Even worse: he has amphibians and reptiles buying human souls. But under just what skies does the life of these creatures take place? *"If . . . it hadn't turned as dark in the field as under a sheepskin coat,"* Gogol remarks in one place. *"It's as dark and desolate* (at night) *as in a wine cellar"* (**"The Lost Letter"**). Gogol knew how to open up the sky, because his heroes were getting ready to take a run and fly out of the world; but Gogol also knew another sky, like a sheepskin coat and like the lid of a wine cellar. And behold, no sooner does he remove the muslin of his fancies from the world than you are no longer in the clouds, but here on earth, and this *"here"* of the earth turns into *something* under a sheepskin coat, and you into a bedbug or a flea, or (worse yet)—into a radish, stored in the cellar.

And already another of Gogol's fairy tales begins, the opposite of the first. Gogol did not know people. He knew giants and dwarfs. Neither did Gogol know the earth—he knew a mist "hewn" from moonlight, or a black cellar. And when he combined the cellar with the boiling moon foam of clouds, or when he combined a radish with creatures flying in the air—he arrived at some sort of strange semblance of the earth and its people. This earth is not our earth: the earth suddenly begins to run out from under our feet; or it turns out to be a coffin, in which we, corpses, are suffocating. And these people are not our people: a Cossack is dancing—you look closely: a fang protrudes from his mouth; an old woman is gulping down dumplings—you look: she's flown up the chimney; an official is walking along Nevsky Prospect—he looks: his own nose is walking toward him. . . . Gogol had lost contact with what we call reality. Someone had jerked the earth out from under his feet. There remained in him the memory of the earth: The earth of humanity had decomposed into ether and manure; and the creatures inhabiting the earth had been transformed into disembodied souls, seeking new bodies for themselves. Their bodies are not our bodies. They are a cloud mist, pierced by moonlight, or they have become *radishes* in human shape, growing in the manure. And all the best human emotions (such as love, pity, joy) have for him gone off into the ether. It is characteristic that we do not know what woman Gogol loved, or whether he loved at all. When he describes a woman, she is either a vision or a cold statue with breasts *"lusterless, like unglazed porcelain,"* or a lewd woman, mincing in the night toward a seminary student. Is it possible that woman as such does not exist but only an old hag or a mermaid with *porcelain breasts* hewn from clouds?

When he teaches about human emotions, he moralizes and even worse: he warns the department heads to remember that he is, as it were, an official of the Department of Heaven, and in Nicholas' Russia he foresees, as it were, *"a new city descending from heaven to earth."*

Does Gogol rejoice? No, Gogol's face grows dark with the years, and Gogol dies from fear.

Such are his inexpressible, tender emotions: in his love fantasies there is no longer love— / it is some kind of world ecstasy, but a disembodied ecstasy; on the other hand, ordinary human emotions are for him the emotions of collarbuttons and radishes winking at each other. And everyday life is a madhouse. (pp. 133-35)

I don't know what Gogol is: a realist, a symbolist, a romanticist or a classicist. Yes, he saw all the dust motes on Ivan Ivanovich's coat so distinctly, that he turned Ivan Ivanovich himself into a dusty cloak. The only thing he didn't see in Ivan Ivanovich was his human face. Yes, he saw real aspirations, human emotions; so clearly did he perceive the deep inex-

pressible roots of these emotions, that the emotions became emotions no longer of human beings but of some sort of still bodiless creatures. (p. 135)

They say Gogol is a realist—he is. They say he is a symbolist—he is. His forests are not forests; his mountains are not mountains. He has mermaids with bodies of clouds. Like a romanticist, he was attracted to devils and witches and, like Hoffmann and Poe, he introduced the fantastic into reality. If you wish, Gogol is a romanticist; but hasn't Gogol's epic also been compared to Homer?

Gogol is a genius, whom you cannot possibly approach through scholarly definitions. I have a predilection for symbolism. Consequently it is easier for me to seek the features of Gogol's symbolism. The romanticist will see in him a romanticist; the realist—a realist.

But let's take a look not at literary schools, but at Gogol's soul; the sufferings, torments, and raptures of this soul reach such heights on the human (or rather superhuman) path, that it is blasphemous to measure these heights with our yardstick. And indeed, does one use a yardstick to measure the heights above the clouds and the morass of bottomless marshes? Gogol is the morass and the height, the mud and the snow; but Gogol is no longer the earth. Gogol had a score to settle with the earth. The earth had perpetrated her *terrible vengeance* upon him. Our normal emotions are not Gogol's emotions: love is not love; gaiety is anything but gaiety. Laughter—what kind of laughter do we find here: simply a roar at Ivan Ivanovich's cloak, and at that, a roar as if *"two bulls standing opposite each other were bellowing simultaneously."* Gogol's laughter changes into a tragic roar, and some kind of darkness falls heavily upon us out of that roar:*"And it will roar against him on that day like the roaring of the furious sea; and he will look at the earth—and, beyond darkness and distress, and the light is darkened in the clouds,"* says Isaiah (5:30). Gogol had come up to some strange boundary of life, beyond which he heard a roar; and this roar Gogol turned into laughter. But Gogol's laughter is a sorcerer's laughter; Gogol takes a look at the earth, bursts out laughing—*"and behold, darkness and distress,"* although the sun is shining, *"rows of fruit trees, sunk in the crimson of the cherries and in the sapphire sea of plums, covered by a lead coating."* That's how Gogol arranges the earth's surface with fairy-tale magnificence in his realistic stories. . . . (pp. 135-36)

Yes, in his images, in his relationship to the earth, Gogol transcended the limits of art. He wandered in the garden of his soul, and blundered into a place where a garden is no longer a garden and the soul is not a soul. Deepening the artistic aspect of his nature, Gogol went beyond the limits of his personality, and instead of utilizing this broadening of his personality for artistic goals, Gogol threw himself into the abyss of his alter ego—he set out on paths which one must not enter without a definite, occultly worked out way, without an experienced guide. Instead of combining his empirical self with the world-self, Gogol broke the bond between the two selves—and a black abyss appeared between them. One self would be horrified by the contemplation of collarbuttons and radishes, the other self would fly in the immensity of the world—out there beyond the heavenly vault. (p. 137)

His rapture is a wild rapture; and the sweetness of his inspirations is a wild sweetness; his lips do not smile, but *"leer in a laugh of bliss."* The Cossack dances—and suddenly *"a fang protrudes from his mouth"* (**"A Terrible Vengeance"**). *"The* *rubies of her lips are boiled onto his very heart''* (not love—some kind of vampirism!). In all the ecstasy which transfigured both Gogol and the world (''the grass seemed to be the bottom of some kind of clear . . . sea (**''Viy''**)—in all this ecstasy there is *''an excruciating, unpleasant and at the same time sweet sensation''* (**''Viy''**), or a *''piercing, agonizing sweet delight''*—in a word, a *''hellishly sweet''* (**''Viy''**), but not a divinely sweet sensation. And therefore the transfigured brilliance of Nature begins to frighten. . . . And when the earth is transfigured, so that distances changed just outside Kiev *''appeared the blue waters of the Liman, beyond the Liman . . . the Black Sea . . . the Galician land could be seen''*), why ''does one's hair stand on end'' and why does the *''hellishly sweet''* sensation culminate in the horse turning his head, and—a miracle!—laughing? Gogol's ecstasy culminates not in the mystery of love but in a wild dance; everything is transfigured not in love but in a dance of madness; truly—Gogol is in a bewitched spot. . . . Gogol had a vision; he saw the Countenance, but he had not transfigured himself so as to be able to look upon the Countenance with impunity, to hear the call of the beloved Soul, whose voice in the words of Revelation *''is like the sound of many waters.''* This sound became for Gogol a *''roaring,''* the brilliance of transfiguration became *''wolf-hair''* and the soul a *''witch.''* Hecate and the bewitched animals did not touch those who were being initiated into the mystery rites, when they left the Eleusinian temple. But they gnawed Gogol, as the dead men gnawed the sorcerer. And the countenance seen by Gogol did not save him. This *countenance* became for him the *''horseman in the Carpathians.''* And from him Gogol fled. ''In the cloud before him shone someone's *wondrous face.''* (pp. 138-39)

Gogol loves Russia, his native country. He loves her as a lover loves his beloved. *''Rus! What do you want from me? What inscrutable bond is concealed between us?''* (**Dead Souls**). Gogol loves a Russia which no one else knows. Gogol loves Russia with an ancient love. His relation to her is like the sorcerer's relation to his daughter Katerina; Gogol uses sorcery on her: *''Why do you look like that; . . . My eyes are alight with unnatural power''* . . . What a tone, what jealous tyranny—Gogol is putting a sorcerer's spell on Russia. Throughout his life, she is a mysterious image for him, and, nonetheless, his mistress. . . . Inscrutably, unnaturally Gogol, perhaps more than any other Russian writer, is bound to Russia, and he is bound by no means to the Russia of the past, but to today's Russia, and even more to tomorrow's.

Isn't everything that is happening to us, to our land, to our nation, a dream; just recently our native land was illumined by a strange brilliance, so that from Moscow there became visible the Liman and the Black Sea and a mysterious horseman. And now, even on a sunny day, when there are no clouds, someone's terrible shadow flashes: a shadow of horrible provocation coming from the depths of the soul, from the depths of the earth. Everything has become strange and unintelligible; and our country is gripped by a deadly longing; both here and there a wild dance of strange gaiety, of strange oblivion goes on. And like the Carpathian Mountains, the storm clouds of disaster hover over us: on those mountains is an unknown avenger. And a strange wall arises from the depths of our soul: Rus! What do you want of us? What calls and sobs and grips our hearts? . . . We do not know. . . .

We are facing the veil of the future, like neophytes facing the temple: Soon the veil of the temple will be rent in twain—what will gaze out at us: Hecate and ghosts? Or the soul of our nation, the Soul of the populace wrapped in a shroud?

Gogol was the first to approach this mystery rite, and a dead man stood up before him. Gogol died.

But now we stand before the same vision—the vision of Death. And that is why Gogol's vision is closer to us than anything that has been said about our country. We must remember that the veil of Death will fall away only when we purify our souls for the great mystery rite. (pp. 140-41)

When discussing Gogol it is impossible not to say at least a few words about his style. One could write many learned volumes on the style and use of words in Gogol's works. And just as Gogol's realism consists of two fairy tales about the prehuman and the superhuman earth, so is also the natural fluency of his style composed of two kinds of unnaturalness. It consists of the most intricate jeweler's work with words, and at that of such kind that it remains completely incomprehensible how Gogol could, while piling marvel upon marvel of technical artistry so that the fabric of his speech is a series of technical tricks—how Gogol could, precisely by means of these tricks, express the ecstasy of a living soul. Such is one side of Gogol's stylistics, interrupted at times by a crude (even ungrammatical) turn of speech or by an extremely crude, absurd, or even vulgar device. Such meaningless epithets as *''wondrous,''* *''splendid,''* or *''enchanting''* decorate Gogol's style, and in themselves express nothing; but in combination with the most refined similes and metaphors they impart a particular charm to Gogol's style. Who doesn't remember the striking story about Captain Kopeykin; but take the trouble to observe the technical trick of the approach: the completely banal account of the misadventures of the unfortunate captain is interrupted literally after every other word by the insertion of the expressions *''do you see,''* *''so to say,''* and so on.

Precisely through this crude device Gogol achieves dazzling expressiveness. Gogol's style is simultaneously pre-cultural and, in addition, it surpasses in its refinement not only Wilde, Rimbaud, Sologub and the other ''decadents,'' but often even Nietzsche. (p. 141)

[His] stylistics reflects the subtlest and most refined soul of the nineteenth century. Gogol's superhuman torments were reflected in superhuman images; and these images evoked in Gogol's writing a superhuman formal achievement.

Perhaps Nietzsche and Gogol are the greatest stylists in all of European art, if by style is understood not only the use of words, but also the formal reflection of the soul's life rhythm. (p. 143)

> *Andrei Bely [pseudonym of Boris Nikolaevich Bugaev], ''Gogol,'' translated by Elizabeth Trahan (originally published under a different title in his* Lug zelenyi, *1910), in* Russian Literature Triquarterly *(translation © 1972 by Ardis Publishers), No. 4, Fall, 1972, pp. 131-44.*

## IVAN YERMAKOV (essay date 1923)

[*A psychoanalyst, Yermakov was strongly influenced by Sigmund Freud. Using Freud's concept of the creative process as the basis of his analysis, Yermakov draws a general picture of Gogol's psyche. He maintains that Gogol, like Freud, understood the significance of dreams and thus revealed his characters primarily through their own dreams.*]

Gogol's fantastic tale **''The Nose''** occupies a special position among those works of his which are linked, if not exactly by the same theme, then by the tormenting questions he put to himself and endeavored to resolve. Included in this group are a number of his best stories, such as "Viy," "The Tale of How Ivan Ivanovich Quarrelled with Ivan Nikiforovich," "The Nose," "The Overcoat," and "Diary of a Madman." To be sure, it is to some extent arbitrary and artificial to lift just a few stories out of the corpus of Gogol's works, all of which are organically interconnected; for . . . the theme of "The Nose" had long been in the making, in stories where the nose itself had not yet been assigned the role of protagonist. This fact makes it clear that Gogol did not borrow his theme from elsewhere, as literary historians suppose; he was not simply echoing certain literary fashions of the beginning of the nineteenth century; rather, he responded to them, interpreted them, and gave them a particular form, out of an inner need and compulsion to do so. (p. 158)

In his letters and his works of fiction, Gogol betrays an irrepressible need to observe, describe, and castigate the shortcomings of others and of himself as well. In neither case is he free, for he is obeying the command of his unconscious. Gogol torments himself in order to have the right to torment others.

All of a writer's works are nothing more than a confession and self-revelation. Gogol—and he speaks of this specifically in "An Author's Confession"—saw his works as a kind of mirror in which he scrutinized and studied himself. This, it seems to me, explains his narrative method, his use of colloquial language and skaz, [a form of narration in which the speaker's style is as significant as the story], and his habit of putting himself into everything he wrote. The clash of two opposing tendencies in the confession—one revealing, the other concealing—produced a compromise solution to the task that Gogol set himself, and forced him to resort to jests, puns, and unfinished utterances. The attempt to say what cannot be directly expressed in civilized society leads to ambiguity and to witticism. Gogol regarded his works as a confession, an exhibition, for all to see, of something important and significant. (pp. 159-60)

In the complex and interesting course of Gogol's search for his unique, Gogolian self, there is a natural demarcation of two phases, although they are very intimately interconnected. The first is one of open self-ridicule; the second finds him directing his gaze more deeply into the hidden recesses of his own experiences and seeking out "nastiness" there. "The Nose" is one of Gogol's confessions that belongs to this second phase, along with "Viy," "The Overcoat," "Nevsky Prospect," and others.

Two sides of Gogol's personality are revealed in the first phase of the development of his work as a satirist: his attempt to depict both comic and terrible things. Here his tendency to try to discredit other people does not go beneath the surface, and his humor is sometimes not of a very high order. He does hit on some very apt names and situations for his characters; but we also constantly find many awkward and rough-cast attempts, such as Dovgochkhun, Pupopuz, Krutoryshchenko, and others.

The second phase is marked by greater care in the selection of such names; the dark and terrible side of life, which was localized in the countryside in the **Dikanka** stories, is now transformed into universal evil, of which every man is the vehicle.

In the first stage, the writer participates in the stories himself, he consistently does the narrating, as if he were retelling old tales and adapting himself to the people he is talking about, putting himself, as it were, on their level. But in the second

stage the situation changes. To be sure, Gogol hews to the same narrative method as before. But fundamentally new is his focus on himself, his desire to reveal and identify in himself the same traits he sees in others. In other words, there comes a time in the development of Gogol's work when, preoccupied with self-purification and self-analysis, he gradually shifts to the confessional form until finally, and with complete consistency, he entitles one of his last works "An Author's Confession." As this inner development proceeds, Gogol begins to take a different view of his early works, which had made him famous overnight. He does not find in them what is now most important to him: the *spiritual* element, which attracts him and fills his life above anything else. (pp. 160-61)

[Two] opposing and endlessly conflicting tendencies underlay Gogol's art: self-depreciation and self-exaltation. The conflict was explicitly reflected not only in what Gogol wrote, but also in the way he wrote, in the style and the imagery he used. . . .

In his early works Gogol liked to introduce and even elaborate on heroic themes, together with themes drawn from ordinary life. For example, **Taras Bulba,** "Al-Mamun," "Rome," and others contain epic descriptions and characterizations that might well have been taken from Homer. These two styles—the one intense and epic, the other commonplace—intertwine throughout all his writings, for instance in "Diary of a Madman," in **Dead Souls,** and, as we shall see, in "The Nose" as well, even though they are concealed there.

There is something very significant about the ease with which noble and ignoble themes interweave and unfold in tandem. (Gogol's follower, Dostoevsky, brought this tendency to full flower.) Very often such themes develop in unexpected ways; but they grip us, they seem to dull our critical faculties, and we do not notice how outwardly unmotivated and unexpected they are. Among such instances we should include the so-called lyrical digression at the beginning of "The Overcoat" and those in **Dead Souls**—the passage in chapter eleven, for example, where the courier gallops by, shouting imprecations and shattering the reverie into which the writer has fallen. (p. 162)

In his art [Gogol] constantly moves between two abysses, falling now into one, now into the other. This is what some critics see as his tendency toward the extreme, the ultimate. These two natures are the masculine and the feminine, the active and the passive, the holy and the sinful, the pregenital and the genital. Laughter and tears, pleasure and pain are expressed simultaneously in Gogol's works; and the coexistence of these two opposing tendencies is intimately linked with his sexual experiences and is marked both by auto-erotism and by fear or bitter repentance for such self-gratification. Active behavior is repressed and directed against the self. (pp. 162-63)

In moving toward the extreme, or the ultimate, Gogol, like many fantasts, consistently starts from reality, from some story he has been told, from anecdotes or incidents current in society. He fixes an inquisitive eye on the world around him as he studies man—his words, his gestures, his expressions, and, above all, his nose, to which he attaches a special and very vital significance. One could compile a whole little anthology from the passages in Gogol's works that mention the nose, so tirelessly does he describe the taking of snuff, nose-blowing, and so on. (p. 163)

We must . . . study "The Nose" from the viewpoint of that most unusual work of Gogol's, "An Author's Confession." A confession is a serious act. . . . [Gogol] is faced with the equally important task of neither revealing nor concealing anything completely. These two opposing drives give rise to conflicting needs. They very often cross and produce so-called compromise solutions, which end up as puns and double entendres. . . . (p. 191)

Feeling absolutely unrestricted, and burning with a desire to repent, Gogol sought an opportunity to bare everything that lay in the depths of his soul, and to make a confession as a great sinner. The most blasphemous scenes, the most unforgivable similes, the most cynical images and possibilities pass before his mind's eye; it is his tremendous capacity for self-analysis which allows him to accept them and to regard their exposure as a heroic deed. To discern these conflicting drives within himself, to bring them out for himself and even for all to see, to invite laughter and ridicule and to know that he is "laughing at himself"—this is what makes it possible for Gogol to confess and reveal himself to the ultimate. It is at this ultimate—this realm of our basic, archaic self, this primitive fabric on which the patterns of our life are later embroidered, this dark, unknown, nether-world of the mind into which man is usually so ready to cast everything he finds cumbersome in his conscious life—it is here that the most contradictory drives come into collision and prove to be identical. Here the same word, the same symbol takes on two completely different meanings at the same time. Here religious fervor is blasphemy, things of the greatest value are valueless, good deeds are evil and sinful. Only after he has reached this ultimate, only after he has brought forth the essence of this basic self can a writer free himself from everything accidental and temporary, touch and understand the innermost secrets of the soul, and then forge a truthful and genuine image of man, and thereby a work of art.

But perhaps there is something dubious about this approach. Perhaps "The Nose" is simply a joke, a trifle, with none of the serious purposes that we have indicated here. (pp. 191-92)

[The] problem posed in "The Nose" is a sexual one. It throws light on the question of the autonomy of man's sexual activity as symbolized by the separate existence of the nose. (The same thing can be seen in the quarrel between the two Ivans.) Sexual activity asserts its rights, which run counter to the urgings of the ego and the norms of society. The thing that cannot be displayed or talked about without shame and embarrassment—"the nose"—itself evokes a feeling of shame and embarrassment if it is not in its proper place, between the two cheeks. The result is an insoluble problem: it is uncomfortable to have a nose but just as uncomfortable not to have one: the two situations are equally discrediting and disgraceful. (p. 192)

In trying as best we can to decipher "The Nose," we must say that two things underlie the story: the fear of castration, which goes along with the repressed wish to possess an enormous sex-organ; and the desire for unlimited erotic pleasures. These desires lead to aggressive acts directed against social life and cultural values, and must be repressed. However, a frivolous individual like Kovalyov is not guided by anything except his own egotistic interests. His activities run counter to the demands of civilized life. They create a feeling of guilt in him which he does not wish to recognize, but which reveals itself to him in the form of an extremely oppressive dream (the dream of castration). But it has been only a dream; on awakening, Kovalyov tries to ignore his painful experiences, and he resumes his interrupted activities. We find him making fun of a military man whose nose is the size of a waistcoat button; he is even buying the ribbon of some order, but it is not known

why, since he has not been so honored. In other words, life has once again fallen into its old rut. The mysterious disappearance of the "nose" remains as mysterious as ever to Kovalyov. (p. 194)

Something that could have brought about catharsis, awareness, purification, further growth and development, a turning point in life (an "annunciation"), has been lost beyond recall. The laughter in the story is suffused with tears, the bitter tears of the author: no, man will not become aware of all his vileness, he will not understand what he is really like. Even in the case of a "learned" collegiate assessor such as Kovalyov, the unconscious attempt to reveal his essential inner self in the form of images and actions has passed without leaving a trace.

In keeping with the structural requirements of the humorous story, Gogol is obliged to bring off a happy ending. But somehow, we feel like saying, as he himself does at the end of **"The Two Ivans"**: "It's a dreary world, my dear sirs!"

All these surprisingly perceptive discoveries are the result of the same process we observe at work in psychoanalysis: one must be honest and courageous when faced with oneself. Gogol possessed a sufficiency of honesty and therefore succeeded in bringing out a great many things in his own mind and the minds of others, things which need much more extensive elucidation and analysis.

For the present, however, we can draw two conclusions from our analysis of **"The Nose."** First of all, what strikes the reader as being mere chance, "nonsense," a dream yet not quite a dream; what makes Ivan Yakovlevich and Kovalyov constantly test themselves to see whether they are asleep or losing their minds—all this has its own logic and has been skilfully prepared by the author. From here it is only a step to the assertion that sleeping and dreaming are not such nonsense after all. The statement that the nose was found by a near-sighted police officer with a mother-in-law who could not see anything either is fraught with significance. Does it not say that the real meaning of the loss of the nose can be discovered and revealed only when a person is near-sighted, when he can see nothing but his own nose, or, in other words, nothing but a dream?

[Second], Gogol's characters frequently carry on meaningless conversations that would hardly be conceivable for normal people. Evidently they do not understand what they are saying or why. But it is just such utterances which best characterize individuals; in psychoanalysis they are called free associations, and they reveal that area of the mind that contains drives which man cannot understand but which nonetheless determine his actions. (pp. 195-96)

["The Nose"] makes it clear that Gogol grasped the significance of the dream as a phenomenon that threatens us and compels us to give serious thought to ourselves. He discerned the possibility of crisis in Kovalyov's petty and intimidated soul—in his useless running around and in his cynical attitude toward women. He created a tragedy, a tragicomedy, and thereby posed the question: what is more important, the sexual or Kovalyov? Is the sexual subordinate to Kovalyov, or Kovalyov to the sexual? The nose comes off by itself and declares its independence of Kovalyov; so far as it is concerned, Kovalyov is nothing more than a carriage for it to ride in. Kovalyov laughs at himself for being foolish enough to take a dream for reality. He does not notice that it is precisely his predicament in the dream which perhaps does more than anything else to expose the emptiness of his life and the humiliation of being utterly dependent on his own nose. Whenever it seems as if the meaning of these events is about to be revealed, everything is shrouded in fog. Kovalyov is not allowed to see; he does not want to see the person who is to blame for everything: himself.

Gogol says that although such cases are rare, they do happen: this is a subtly ironic commentary on people who do not understand the significance of dreams, and who consider outer reality truer than inner. But Gogol understands. He takes the fashionable ''nosological'' theme which intrigued so many writers before him, and does something more with it than simply reshuffle its familiar components. And he is able to make us understand what every person is tormented by, and what must be resolved and grasped so that man can free himself from the power of the dark forces of primitive instinct. He seems to be refusing to give a solution; he leaves the reader baffled; but any attentive eye can see that Gogol knows something about why such dreams occur; and he prods us into ''action,'' into making an effort to see our own dreams in Kovalyov's dream and hearken to the voices that challenge us to evaluate the life and activity of such an individual. (pp. 197-98)

*Ivan Yermakov, ''The Nose'' (originally published as ''Nos,'' in his* Ocherki po analizu tvorchestva N. V. Gogolya, *1923), in* Gogol from the Twentieth Century: Eleven Essays, *edited and translated by Robert A. Maguire (copyright © 1974 by Princeton University Press; excerpts reprinted by permission of Princeton University Press), Princeton University Press, 1974, pp. 156-98.*

## JOHN MIDDLETON MURRY (essay date 1924)

Over and over again, in reading **''The Overcoat,''** we come upon sentences and paragraphs in which we feel, as it were, a new life stirring, the birth of a new sensitiveness to human experience. The range of man's responsiveness is being definitely extended.

This sense of new possibilities that he gives us is Gogol's great fascination. Old limitations are breaking down; the face-to-face vision of eighteenth-century ''common sense'' is giving way not so much to a new method as to the potentiality of many new methods. Gogol now looks more intently at what is before him, now he glances altogether sideways. His scrutiny is sometimes more microscopic, sometimes more fantastic than that of his predecessors in his own country and abroad. He looks harder, and he looks from a different direction. But indeed he glances rather than looks. He opens the new window just long enough for the vision to excite us; then he turns abruptly aside and opens another. We have not time to see the whole world as we do through the eyes of the greatest, but we have many glimpses. They are unsettling, for Gogol's eyes are restless. We feel that he is being driven on by a greater power: he has no time to pause. On this side and that he leads us to a brink and turns abruptly away. He sets our imaginations racing and pulls them up short at the crucial leap. What he does to us must in some sort have happened to himself, so that we might describe him also as the man of a racing imagination. And the moment we have written those words we remember the strange description of the racing *troika* with which **''Dead Souls''** rushes to its illimitable end.

Gogol's work is essentially incomplete; because of that it is the more exciting, so exciting in its peculiar way that we can not only see the Russian literature we know springing out of

its beginnings, but we have glimpses also of a literature which not even the Russians have achieved. There is what we can only call a ''mad'' streak in Gogol; and madness, applied to the human imagination, is an unsatisfactory term, the more unsatisfactory since we are using it to define a queer imaginative tempo in Gogol by which the first things at moments are brought perilously near to the last. It might be argued that Dostoievsky himself followed this particular road of Gogol's opening to the bitter end. But there is, or there seems to be, a real difference between them. The ''mad'' element in Gogol's vision is not an inevitable extension of the intellectual and the speculative as it is in Dostoievsky. Gogol's is not a mind considering the problem of evil and pain with an implacable imaginative logic. The tremendous discipline of Dostoievsky is not his at all. Gogol's fantasmagoric vision is more immediate and more primitive. When things and creatures begin to loom before his mind, they are not embodied principles; they are more elemental. They are grotesque and gigantic and comic; they are terrifying, also.

The more we feel that Dostoievsky's sentence [''We all came out of **''The Overcoat''**] is true, the more definitely we feel that the seeds contained in certain pages of **''Dead Souls,''** and in such an extraordinary story as **''The Nose,''** did not come to fruition. These possibilities were never fulfilled. Perhaps they never could have been; perhaps, in fact, they are not there. But so much undoubtedly was there that it is wiser to allow the benefit of the doubt. **''The Nose,''** for instance, persists in appearing as something rather more than crude comic fantasia. . . . [When] Major Kovalyov goes to the newspaper office to advertise for his missing nose, and is taken aback at being told that such an advertisement can not possibly be accepted, the story remains within the limits of an excellent fantastic invention. But when the Major, with his face muffled, stops ''as tho rooted to the spot before the door of a house,'' the ''mad'' streak is suddenly visible.

> Something inexplicable took place before his eyes: a carriage was stopping at the entrance; the carriage door flew open; a gentleman in uniform, bending down, sprang out and ran up the steps. What was the horror and at the same time the amazement of Kovalyov when he recognized that this was his own nose!

The effect which this makes in its place and context, upon one mind at least, is queer indeed. It is, perhaps, only an Aristophanic invention, but it is so curiously sinister. The last thing we feel inclined to do is to laugh. It should, it *ought* to, be uproariously funny; but it is not funny in the least. It is impressive, indeed, but in quite another way. And this, after all, is only a single instance, and in some respects rather a crude one, of a kind of vision which is continually manifesting itself in Gogol, and is invariably disconcerting when it does.

Again, consider the tailor's toe-nail in **''The Overcoat.''** It sticks in the mind first because there is another famous toe-nail in Russian literature. It belonged to Dmitri Karamazov, who gazed at it with a disgusted fascination when he was arrested at Mokroe. One wonders whether Dostoievsky had a subconscious memory of Gogol. But they are very different toe-nails. That of Gogol's tailor was almost a thing-in-itself. It had no relation to Akaky Akakievitch's consciousness, as Dmitri's had to his.

> The feet, as is usual with tailors when they sit at work, were bare; and the first object that

caught Akaky Akakievitch's eye was the big toe, with which he was already familiar, with a misshapen nail as thick and as strong as the shell of a tortoise.

That is all; but it is surprizing and more than a little frightening to discover how monstrous that toe-nail is, and how monstrously it abides in the memory. It dwarfs the tailor and his room.

But this is not the Gogol from whom Russian literature descended. This is the Gogol of the most disturbing parts of "Dead Souls," and not of "The Overcoat," even tho the toe-nail comes in that story, simply because Gogol found it impossible to be only one thing at a time. After all, he was Gogol, and not, save for the purposes of literary history (which are always laudable but never essential), the original germ of Russian literature. "The Overcoat" itself, which is in this historical context a "realistic" story, telling of the disaster of a creature "whose cause no one had championed, who was dear to no one, of interest to no one, who never even attracted the attention of the student of natural history," is in right of its own reality something different. That is quite clear from the fact that there is plenty of room in it for the quest of the dead Akaky Akakievitch, who, with scant courtesy and a total forgetfulness of what was due to a general, roughly pulled off the overcoat of the civil councillor who had refused to help him in his search for the overcoat he had lost. That unseemly ghost is not at all discordant in Gogol's own story; but he had no place in the literature which derived from it. Ivan Karamazov's Devil, Kolya's Black Monk are quite another kettle of fish. Gogol's ghost was just a ghost; Dostoievsky's and Chekhov's were projections of a consciousness.

Russian literature took what it wanted from Gogol, and it did not want the whole of him. It is hard to say quite how central to Gogol was the part it took. Probably the pound of flesh was pretty near the heart; but it was on one side of it, and there were the other sides. Nevertheless, in the description of Akaky Akakievitch at his work as copying-clerk, we can hear not only faint intimations of the note which was to be sounded, but the very voice itself. (pp. 110, 176)

Perhaps not the whole of Russian literature can be derived from ["The Overcoat"] but the whole of Dostoievsky can. And probably that is what Dostoievsky really meant. (p. 176)

> *John Middleton Murry, "A Youthful Story that Started a Literature" (reprinted by permission of The Society of Authors as the literary representative of the Estate of John Middleton Murry), in* The Literary Digest International Book Review, *Vol. II, No. 2, January, 1924, pp. 110, 176.*

### D. S. MIRSKY (essay date 1927)

The significance of Gógol is twofold—he is not only a great imaginative writer; he is a supremely interesting individuality, a psychological phenomenon of exceptional curiosity. This psychological side still remains, and will probably always remain, very largely a mystery. I am not here concerned with it, except in so far as it is directly connected with the nature of his creative work. But as a writer Gógol is not twofold in the sense Tolstóy or Dostoyévsky is. There is no common *literary* measure between his imaginative work and his miscellaneous and moralistic writings. The latter are remarkable only as they throw light on the psychological, human personality of Gógol. The early essays contained in *Arabesques* are

rhetoric pure and simple, of a kind that is but the manure for the really magnificent rhetoric of such early stories as *The Terrible Vengeance* or *Tarás Búlba.* The *Correspondence with Friends* is painful, almost humiliating, reading, in spite of the occasional flashes of imagination that break through its heavy and poisonous mist. The critical pages, with their sometimes genuinely and sublimely imaginative appreciation and impressionistic portraits of Russian poets (especially of his favorites Yazýkov and Derzhávin), may be alone singled out for praise. Of the writings of his last years, the commentary on the liturgy is derivative and irresponsible. While *The Author's Confession* is notable as a human document of considerable importance, it has no claim to comparison with the *Confession* of Tolstóy. Still, even in these writings the unique, unrepeatable personality of Gógol is always present in the labored, consciously original style, with its constant suggestion of the presence of unconquered chaos and disorder.

His imaginative work is a very different business. It is one of the most marvelous, unexpected—in the strictest sense, original—worlds ever created by an artist of words. If mere creative force is to be the standard of valuation, Gógol is the greatest of Russian writers. In this respect he need hardly fear comparison with Shakspere, and can boldly stand by the side of Rabelais. Neither Púshkin nor Tolstóy possessed anything like that volcano of imaginative creativeness. The enormous potency of his imagination stands as a strange contrast (or complement) to his physical sterility. . . . Woman was to him a terrible, fascinating, but unapproachable obsession, and he is known never to have loved. This makes the women of his imagination either strange, inhuman visions of form and color that are redeemed from melodramatic banality only by the elemental force of the rhetoric they are enshrined in, or entirely unsexed, even dehumanized, caricatures.

The main and most persistent characteristic of Gógol's style is its verbal expressiveness. He wrote with a view not so much to the acoustic effect on the ears of the listener as to the sensuous effect on the vocal apparatus of the reciter. This makes his prose intense and saturated. It is composed of two elements, romantically contrasted and romantically extreme—high-pitched, poetic rhetoric, and grotesque farce. Gógol never wrote simply—he is always either elaborately rhythmical or quite as elaborately mimetic. It is not only in his dialogue that the intonations of spoken speech are reproduced. His prose is never empty. It is all alive with the vibration of actual speech. This makes it hopelessly untranslatable—more untranslatable than any other Russian prose.

The other main characteristic of Gógol's genius is the extraordinary intensity and vividness of his *sight*. He saw the outer world romantically transformed; and even when he saw the same details as we do, they acquired such proportions in his vision as to become entirely different in meaning and measure. Gógol's pictures of nature are either romantically fantastic transformations (like the famous description of the Dnepr in *The Terrible Vengeance*) or strange mounds of detail heaped on detail, resulting in an unconnected chaos of things. Where he is absolutely supreme and definitive is in his vision of the human figure. His people are caricatures, drawn with the method of the caricaturist—which is to exaggerate salient features and to reduce them to geometrical pattern. But these caricatures have a convincingness, a truthfulness, an inevitability—attained as a rule by slight but definitive strokes of unexpected reality—that seems to beggar the visible world itself.

I have alluded to the great and exceptional originality of Gógol. This does not mean that numerous influences cannot be discerned in his work. The principal of these are: the tradition of the Ukrainian folk and puppet theater, with which the plays of Gógol's father were closely linked; the heroic poetry of the Ukrainian *dumy*, or Cossack ballads; the *Iliad* in the Russian version of Gnédich; the numerous and mixed traditions of comic writing from Molière to the vaudevillists of the twenties; the novel of manners from Lesage to Naréžhny; Sterne, chiefly through the medium of German romanticism; the German romanticists themselves, especially Tieck and E.T.A. Hoffmann; the "furious school" of French romanticism, with, at its head, Hugo and Jules Janin, and their common master, Maturin—a long and yet incomplete list. (pp. 154-56)

The first part of [*Evenings on a Farm near Dikánka*] (containing *Soróchinsky Fair, St. John's Eve, The May Night, or The Drowned Girl*, and *The Lost Charter*) together with two of the four stories of the second part (*Christmas Night* and *The Charmed Spot*) are the early Gógol. They are much simpler, less sophisticated and tense, then anything he wrote later. Their fun, which was what attracted the reader above all, is simple and unadulterated. Their romance is somewhat youthfully operatic but free from sophistication. Their devilry is gay and lighthearted. The picture they give of Ukraine is of course quite fantastic, but it was so attractive, at once so prettily romantic and so hugely funny, that not even the Ukrainians themselves (except till much later) remarked all the absurdities, all the supreme disregard for (and ignorance of) reality displayed by Gógol. . . . The stories themselves depend for the humor on the stock characters of the Ukrainian puppet theater; for the spook and romance on the various fictions of chiefly German romanticists. Gógol is present in the blend of the two elements, in the verbal intensity of the style, in the vivid convincingness of the largely fantastical dialogue of the comic figures, in the unique, physical infectiousness of the laughter.

Of the remaining two stories in the second part of *Evenings, The Terrible Vengeance* is a creation of the purest romantic imagination. Strongly redolent of foreign romanticism and full of reminiscences of the Cossack songs, *The Terrible Vengeance* is, in a certain sense, a masterpiece. It is Gógol's greatest effort at purely ornate prose. The beautiful rhythmical movement is sustained without breach or flaw from beginning to end. The story is gruesome and creepy, and at a first reading almost intolerably impressive. It is one of his very few stories where humor is entirely absent. (pp. 156-57)

Gógol's stories of everyday life of contemporary Russia are introspective—not in the sense that he analyzed and described his psychic experience as Tolstóy, Dostoyévsky, or Proust did, but because his characters are exteriorized and objectivated symbols of his experience. His inferiority complex and his deep roots in the animal, or rather vegetable, life of a rural squiredom gave these symbols the form of caricatures of grotesque vulgarity. The aspect under which he sees reality is expressed by the untranslatable Russian word *póshlost*, which is perhaps best rendered as "self-satisfied inferiority," moral and spiritual. But other subjective aspects may be discovered in his realistic stories—in particular what we might call a "sterility complex," which makes its appearance in the very first of these stories, in *Iván Fëdorovich Shpónka and His Aunt*. . . . (p. 158)

Gógol took scant interest in reality as such but relied for the creation of his characters entirely on his unaided imagination. But he was a realist in the sense that he introduced (as details and as material) innumerable elements and aspects of reality that had hitherto not possessed the freedom of literature. He

was (like Tolstóy, Górky, and Andréyev, after him) a great lifter of taboos, a great destroyer of prohibitions. He made vulgarity reign where only the sublime and the beautiful had reigned. This was *historically* the most important aspect of his work. . . .

In his attitude towards "vegetable life" Gógol oscillated between sympathetic complacency and scornful irony. The sentimental and sympathetic attitude is most fully expressed in the **Old-World Landowners** (in *Mírgorod*), where the vegetable humors of the old pair, their sloth, their gluttony, their selfishness, are idealized and sentimentalized. The purely ironic attitude is expressed with equal purity in the other realistic story of *Mírgorod—The Story of How Iván Ivánovich Quarreled with Iván Nikíforovich*. It is one of the greatest of Gógol's masterpieces. His comic gift (always verging on impossible caricature and impossible farce) appears in its absolute purity. But like almost all his later stories it results ultimately in a vision of depressingly hopeless gloom. (p. 159)

Gógol's greatness as a dramatist rests chiefly on the *Revizór*, doubtless the greatest play in the Russian language. It is not only supreme in character drawing and dialogue—it is one of the few Russian plays that is a play constructed with unerring art from beginning to end. The great originality of its plan consisted in the absence of all love interest and of sympathetic characters. The latter feature was deeply resented by Gógol's enemies, and as a satire the play gained immensely from it. *Revizór* was intended as a *moral* satire against bad officials, not a social satire against the *system* of corruption and irresponsible despotism. But quite apart from the author's intention, it was received as a social satire, and in the great oppositional movement against the despotism of Nicholas I and the system of bureaucratic irresponsibility, its influence was greater than that of any other single literary work. In their great symbolic and comprehensive popularity the characters of *Revizór* stand by the side of those of *Dead Souls*. They are less obviously geometrical, and, the characterization depending entirely on the dialogue, more supple and human. . . . As for the central character, Khlestakóv, the supposed inspector general himself, he is as subjective and introspective as Chíchikov. If in Chíchikov Gógol exteriorized all the vegetable elements of his self, in Khlestakóv he symbolized the irresponsibility, the light-mindedness, the absence of measure, that was such a salient trait of his own personality. But, like Chíchikov, Khlestakóv is entirely "transposed," entirely alive—the most alive of all the characters of Russian fiction—meaningless movement and meaningless fermentation incarnate, on a foundation of placidly ambitious inferiority. As for the dialogue of *Revizór,* it is above admiration. There is not a wrong word or intonation from beginning to end, and the comic tensity is of a quality that even in Gógol was not always at his beck and call. (pp. 160-61)

[*Marriage*] is very different from *Revizór*. It is not satirical, and it is loosely built, with dialogue greatly dominating over action. It is pure fun, though undoubtedly on a Freudian foundation (the same sterility complex as in **Shpónka**). The characters and the dialogue are marvelous. For here, unfettered by any message, Gógol gave free reign to his grotesque, mimetic imagination and surpassed himself in the exuberance of his comic creation. The remaining play, **The Gamblers,** is inferior to the two great comedies. It is an unpleasant play, inhabited by scoundrels that are not funny, and, though the construction is neat, it is dry and lacks the richness of the true Gógol.

On the stage, as in fiction, Gógol's action, historically, was in the direction of realism. Here as elsewhere he was an opener of doors, an introducer of hitherto forbidden material. (pp. 161-62)

*D. S. Mirsky, "The Age of Gógol" (originally published in his* A History of Russian Literature from the Earliest Times to the Death of Dostoyevsky (1881), *Alfred A. Knopf, Inc., 1927), in his* A History of Russian Literature from Its Beginnings to 1900, *edited by Francis J. Whitfield (copyright © 1958 by Alfred A. Knopf, Inc.; reprinted by permission of the publisher), Vintage Books, 1958, pp. 127-76.* *

## VASILY GIPPIUS  (essay date 1936)

[*Gippius's book* Gogol *is considered by many critics to be the finest work on the author in any language. Gippius's abstract style is characteristic of much Russian criticism in the 1930s, 1940s, and early 1950s, though he is not affiliated with any specific literary movement. In this essay Gippius emphasizes the literary craftsmanship of* The Inspector General *and considers Gogol's political opinions from an aesthetic viewpoint.*]

A rough general formulation of the concept of life that is reflected in Gogol's writings of the 1830's would be: "confusion." What gives Gogol's stories their impact as exposés is precisely their portrayal of reality as a tangled web of misunderstandings, in which nothing is located where it should be. Self-satisfied vulgarians and "kind-hearted beasts," who contribute, all unsuspectingly, to this general confusion, are the butts of Gogol's laughter. Those who are endowed with somewhat greater awareness lose their minds, like Poprishchin ("**Diary of a Madman**"), or perish, like Piskaryov ("**Nevsky Prospect**"); it is the philistines like Pirogov (also "**Nevsky Prospect**") who flourish. This persistent return to the theme of confusion (which is carried to a grotesque extreme in "**The Nose**") constitutes Gogol's strength and his weakness. It is a strength because his realistic method enabled him to reflect the actual contradictions in the society of his time. It is a weakness because even though he reached the point where he could observe "confusion" and understand its tragi-comic nature, he could not explain why it existed. (pp. 229-30)

*The Inspector General* offers a new variation on this same theme of confusion. The basic situation, as set forth in the first act, shows people who are occupying positions for which they are not suited—self-satisfied philistines on whom the destinies and the very lives of people depend ("injustices that are perpetrated in places and situations where justice, above all, is required of men"). Then a new, and this time intentional, "confusion" appears and grows apace: the "whippersnapper" Khlestakov finds himself in the position of a person of consequence, and the mayor daydreams his way up to a general's rank in St. Petersburg. All these misunderstandings—real and apparent—are dealt a blow at the very end of the play, and Gogol, with great artistic tact, does not reveal its full implications.

Gogol intended not only that "Khlestakovism" should be a generalized and typical phenomenon, but that it should also serve as a commentary on the "confusion" of life. Khlestakov's philosophy is that of vulgar epicureanism; it is translated, with the utmost accuracy, into the language of basic physiology when he says: "I like to eat. After all, that's what life is for—to pluck the flowers of pleasure." . . . Meanwhile, the "power of general fear" creates a person of consequence out of this nonentity (see Gogol's "Advance Notice" to the actors). This is possible because of his particular traits of character ("he is rather dim-witted, and, as the saying goes, there's no Tsar in his head"). He is ready to enter into any situation and adjust

to any: for him the boundaries between the real and the imaginary are easily obliterated. He is therefore capable of skimming over the waves of life's confusion, while unwittingly playing the leading role in it.

Khlestakov's inner vacuity and passivity are precisely the qualities which ensure that an appropriately negative evaluation of confusion will be made. If he were a deliberate cheat . . . , or if he were in general an actively negative character, then the point of the exposé would be blunted. Instead of confusion arising from society itself and being therefore *typical*, there would be just an artificial muddle created by the malevolence of a particular individual: it would be an *exceptional* phenomenon, not a typical one. (pp. 230-31)

As a social being and as an individual, Khlestakov is typical, not exceptional. He is a minor St. Petersburg civil servant from a landowning family of modest means. But as the other characters in the play see him, he belongs to high society. Indirectly, this case of mistaken identity makes possible a criticism (although muffled) of that society as it is refracted through its unwitting representative. (p. 232)

As regards the central group of characters—the "six provincial civil servants"—there is nothing in Gogol's basic conception that would emphasize their belonging specifically to the *gentry*. They are completely detached from the economic and social relations that are characteristic of owners of land and serfs. Conversely, Bobchinsky and Dobchinsky have no official position but are fully integrated into the general *civil-servant* type (cf., e.g., Dobchinsky's remark: "When an important person speaks, you feel afraid"). The theme of duty to the state, implicit in the play, is never treated specifically as a problem of duty on the part of the *gentry*. Likewise, there is nothing about Khlopov that identifies him specifically as not of gentle birth; nothing distinguishes him from the collective that is headed by the mayor. (pp. 232-33)

The impression of solidarity (or, as it were, of "chorality") created by the collective consisting of the officials (and other members of the gentry who are part of the system) is reinforced by the *mise-en-scène* of each act (except the second), by the polyphonic structure of the dialogue, and to an even greater extent by the fact that a more or less independent function is assigned to those characters who are the least individualized: the postmaster, who is described as "simple-hearted," and Bobchinsky and Dobchinsky, who are the "two town chatterboxes." . . . Conversely, those who are more individualized and are created by a more or less complex combination of traditional traits have no independent function in the play. Such are the judge, Lyapkin-Tyapkin, a hunting enthusiast and sententious free-thinker; and Zemlyanika, a cheat, flatterer, and gossip. Neither one exerts any direct influence on the development of the plot: Zemlyanika's attempts to muddy the waters and set Khlestakov against the other officials come to naught. (pp. 233-34)

In the cast of characters, another social group is set in opposition to the group of officials: the oppressed citizenry, the merchants and townspeople. Gogol shows his originality here as well, in the ability to use individual characters in such a way as to create the impression of a collective united by shared attitudes and functioning as a unit in the play. At first, this collective offers only passive resistance to the collective of bigwigs headed by the mayor ("The merchants and the ordinary folk are saying terrible things about me"). Then this collective tries to take on the mayor directly. Nothing comes of it, of course, and this only heightens the general confusion. In itself, the creation of a collective agent in this play was an important achievement on Gogol's part; but he makes it considerably more complex. As the plot develops, we see that the ordinary folk, though a collective, are not an integral whole. To Gogol's mind as well, the merchants and the townspeople are two different categories. The merchants occupy an intermediate position: they are oppressed by the powers that be (the gentry) and are prepared to make open (and collective) protest; but as soon as conditions change, they strike a bargain with the civil-servant/gentry group, that is, with the head of this group, the mayor. The townspeople are shown as being utterly defenseless. The author's attitude toward each of these groups is hereby clearly indicated. For the townspeople his sympathy is unqualified. For the merchants, it is qualified; it stops at the point where (to his mind) these two groups begin to be differentiated within the one big ''chorus'' of oppressed and protesting citizens. The merchant-group is singled out of the ''chorus'' at large, and becomes itself an object of exposé and satire from two directions: (1) as allies of the mayor's group and as collaborators in his shady dealings, they are censured along with the gentry and the officials . . . ; (2) the strong censure of the merchants is made even more pointed by the fact that the author himself maintains the class attitude of a member of the gentry and regards the merchants as a group that is alien and inferior, both socially and culturally. (pp. 234-35)

We see that the grouping of characters according to social identities does not aim at preaching any specific messages about society or describing manners and mores as such. It is subordinate to the one theme that organizes the entire play: that of official abuses, and the related (though contrasting) potential theme of *true* service to the state. (pp. 236-37)

Gogol's method of plot-making depended on the fundamental elimination of positive character types. Three things disappeared in *The Inspector General:* (1) the stereotypes of plot and theme that were routine in the comedy immediately preceding Gogol (for example, the ''rivalry'' of good and bad characters, or the ''unsuccessful undertaking''); (2) the unsophisticated social didacticism; and (3) the division of the dramatis personae into exemplars of virtue and vice. (pp. 249-50)

[In] abandoning the ''springs'' that had long moved both the satirical and the light comedy, Gogol had to find new principles which would enable him to bring about [a] unity of the satirical and the comic not only in the general tenor of the play and in the delineation of individual characters, but also in the development of the plot itself, in the very dynamics of the comedy. And Gogol found fruitful principles in the vaudeville and the vaudeville comedy: the dynamics of misunderstanding, and exposés based on a false point of view.

In itself, the device of ''point of view'' easily acquires a comic function: it refracts the entire play through a double angle of vision, and forces us to combine things that cannot be combined, thereby creating a comic effect. Because of this, contradictory elements can coexist on the stage: contradictory as to situation (an inspector general and a man who is passing through town just by chance), as to social level (a bigwig and a simple registry clerk), and as to psychology (a ''fine fellow'' who is at the same time a ''good-for-nothing''). They coexist because the viewpoint held by some of the characters, on the one hand, and the viewpoint held by the audience, on the other, are antithetical. This puts the entire plot on two planes, at the very least. These two planes, however, form a unity within a duality, inasmuch as the audience holds the key to the interplay

of these points of view, and establishes the necessary correlations between the ''real'' and the apparent.

Thus, the basic plot, which the audience perceives as the true one, is paralleled by another plot, an internal one, which is false by virtue of the false viewpoint held by the characters who open the play—the officials. This false plot has its own internal system of roles: (1) the principal agents, that is, the mayor and his group; (2) their enemies, the ordinary townsfolk; (3) the inspector general, whose potential actions in any given situation are not immediately apparent, but who, as a potential defender of the ordinary townsfolk, is presumably one of the ''enemies.'' This false plot develops out of the rivalry between the ''virtuous'' group of zealous officials and the ''negative'' group of ordinary townsfolk, in other words, out of a situation that was typical of the pre-Gogolian sentimental comedy. But, while making his negative heroes play out a sentimental comedy, Gogol at the same time makes the reader perceive everything that goes on as a light comedy. Gogol himself hinted at this double purpose in his **''Advance Notice''** to the actors: ''The audience, being at a remove, sees the vanity of their efforts. But they themselves are by no means joking, and they do not have the slightest idea that anyone is laughing at them.''

The audience identifies the false plot and evaluates it accordingly. The conflict between the two groups that are antagonistic as to class is maintained in the true plot as well, but the positive and negative viewpoints are interchanged, just as Gogol intends. Of primary concern now is the exposé of Khlestakov, that zero entity who in the false plot functions sometimes as a potential enemy and sometimes as a reliable ally.

The problem of the comedy's satirical function is also resolved in this way. It is only in the most primitive types of comedy (which are, however, very common in the vaudeville) that the misunderstanding is either fully motivated by specific attributes of the psychologies of individual characters (absent-mindedness, gullibility, or outright stupidity), or is not psychologically motivated at all (it is just a convergence of chance happenings). Naturally, the way the misunderstanding develops makes it impossible to attribute what happens to malevolent individuals and to draw the appropriate moralistic conclusions. But this very fact opens the way for sociopsychological motivations, especially in cases where the falseness of the viewpoint depends (as it does in *The Inspector General*) on a difference in social levels, which in turn depends not on the personal qualities of errant individuals, but rather on ''confusion'' of a social nature. Vyazemsky proposed that misunderstandings could be explained by the proverb: ''Fear has big eyes''; but from the viewpoint of the author's basic conception, this can be done only if we have in mind not the cowardice of the mayor and the other officials as individuals, but rather cowardice as seen in the context of social satire.

At the same time, the rivalry, which is parodied in the false plot, shows its truly satirical side to the audience. Even when seen from the mayor's false point of view, this rivalry does not become nothing but a contest between ''malevolent'' and ''benevolent'' individuals; rather, it is interpreted as a social conflict. This makes it all the more necessary to create a corresponding impression in the true plot, i.e., from the point of view held by the audience. The motif of the rivalry is preserved when it is interpreted as it should be by the audience, although it is not this that determines the development of the plot. On the other hand, because it is interpreted by the audience, and because it has a satirical function, it does to some extent lose its comic function as such. However, in the fabric of the play as a whole, this loss is imperceptible, since the true and false points of view do not exist separately, but form a unity. Thus, the device of the *unity of contradictory points of view* is fundamental and decisive for Gogol's whole system of comedy. For it brings about *the unity of the satirical and the comic* in a concrete way. (pp. 251-53)

The first act of **The Inspector General** creates the original false point of view; the second builds situations on it; the third and the beginning of the fourth provide a certain respite in the forward movement of the plot, and are concerned, on the one hand, with putting the final touches on the characterizations and, on the other, with consolidating the false point of view even further. And here Gogol departs from the practice of the writers of vaudevilles, who had no need to make consolidations of this sort, for the rapid tempo and the small dimensions of the vaudeville required rapid denouements as well. The middle one-and-a-half acts are structured as a comedy of character, with its sudden disruptions and restorations of point of view. This is possible because the main character, Khlestakov, is more passive than active, and has no point of view of his own. (p. 254)

The dialogues in Act IV serve not only to delineate character but also to prepare for the climax. The false plot is now concerned not only with the characterization of Khlestakov (Act III had been devoted to that), but also with the apparent success of the other characters, which brings the false inspection-motif to an end. At the same time, the false plot becomes considerably more complex than before. In the first three acts, it developed entirely from the point of view of the mayor and his group; but here it depends on the intersection of two very different false points of view: (1) that of the officials; (2) that of the merchants and townspeople. (In this particular case, the merchants and townspeople are united by a commonly held false point of view.) Taken by itself, each of these false points of view has both a satirical and a comic function—satirical because each motif rests on a contradiction that is seen by the author for what it really is; comic because each motif is paralyzed by the false point of view. The intersection of contradictory points of view strengthens the unity of the comic and satirical function even more.

The role of Khlestakov as the false inspector general really ends here; the love "vaudeville" at the end of Act IV merely adds some details. The introduction of this vaudeville into the fabric of the play deserves attention if only because Gogol, in his theories of the drama, regarded the love-intrigue as being incompatible with the aims of high social comedy, and insisted that it must be abandoned. But it is quite obvious that the love episode in Act IV has absolutely nothing in common with the traditional love-intrigue; on the contrary, it eliminates the intrigue by parodying it. (p. 255)

From the point of view of the mayor's group, the comedy is brought to an end in keeping with the stock formula of the triumph of the virtuous—i.e., of his excellency the inspector general and "such a fine person" as Maria Antonovna, the daughter of the selfless and zealous governor of the town. At the same time, everything happens "in a most respectable and refined way"; and whenever the patent discrepancy between the sentimental motifs of the false plot and the vaudeville motifs of the true plot becomes obvious, it is promptly eliminated by Anna Andreyevna's remarks, just as easily as is the discrepancy between Khlestakov's engagement and his departure. (p. 256)

From the true point of view (the audience's), Khlestakov's engagement and departure represent not a denouement but a culmination. If from the mayor's point of view the movement of the comedy has depended on the way the rivalry develops (with a group of enemies in all four acts, and with the inspector general in the first two), then from the point of view of the audience it develops out of the way the misunderstanding and unmasking are brought off, with the motifs of the rivalry being interpreted satirically at the same time.

The satirical function of the misunderstanding is now basically at an end. The misunderstanding has helped point up the things that were to be satirized: in the speeches ("interpolated novellas," in their own way) made by the characters from the lower level of society, in the emotionally agitated orders and reminiscences of the mayor, and in the information that is communicated in the remarks made by the mayor's colleagues. (pp. 257-58)

Gogol's particular version of [the] final unmasking may appear to be rather ineffectual. But it is entirely in keeping with the purposes of a social comedy as Gogol conceived of them. A graphic "shaming of the guilty party" might have been necessary in plots [like those of Molière's] *Tartuffe* or [Grigory Kvitka-Osnovyanenko's] *Visitor from the Capital* . . . , which depended on points of view that were not clearly established and on sudden reversals in the roles of accuser and defender. But in **The Inspector General** there is no need for this sort of thing. The audience has long since established its point of view (negative and satirical) toward the mayor and his group and toward Khlestakov—although far less satirical energy has been expended on the latter, precisely because he is an individual *character*, and, moreover, a character who is assigned only a weak social function. But in order to realize the satirical idea to the fullest, it is important that the provincial powers that be (the primary object of the satire) should be brought together, both at the very beginning and at the very end of the play. Gogol does even more, by putting an even larger collective into the final scenes—the "milieu" which has existed only by implication throughout the play but which has in fact determined the way the mayor and his group have behaved. Once again, this illustrates—and in a most convincing way—that the town is a collective unity, and that the behavior of the officials is determined not by the evil intentions of individuals, but by a community of "manners and habits of common-sense philosophy." (Similar tendencies can be seen in other works that Gogol wrote at about the same time—the play *Marriage,* and the stories **"The Two Ivans," "The Nose,"** and **"The Carriage"**; later, in *Dead Souls,* the contradiction between individual and social attributes is brilliantly eliminated.) There is a very significant detail here: the merchants are included in this collective, although class antagonism toward them on the part of the others is inevitably emphasized.

Finally, the ending of **The Inspector General** gives us a glimpse of the third point of view that is operative in the comedy: that of the author. As it turns out, then, the comedy exists not just on one plane—as it does from the point of view of the characters (which is why the denouement does not coincide with the engagement of Khlestakov and the mayor's daughter); not just on two planes, as it does for a certain time within the point of view of the audience (which is why the denouement does not coincide with the postmaster's reading of Khlestakov's letter to Tryapichkin), but on three planes. (pp. 258-59)

*Vasily Gippius, "The Inspector General: Structure and Problems" (originally published as "Problematika i kompozitsiya 'Revizora'," in N. V. Gogol: Materialy i issledovaniya, edited by Vasily Gippius,*

1936), in Gogol from the Twentieth Century: Eleven Essays, *edited and translated by Robert A. Maguire (copyright © 1974 by Princeton University Press; excerpts reprinted by permission of Princeton University Press), Princeton University Press, 1974, pp. 216-65.*

**DMITRY CHIZHEVSKY**  (essay date 1938)

[*Chizhevsky emphasizes the craftsmanship and technical significance of "The Overcoat." He also details the study of "skaz", a form of narration used in this story and commonly employed in Russian literature of the period, in which the speaker's style is as significant as the story.*]

In ["The Overcoat"], the same virtually meaningless word is repeated with extraordinary frequency: *"even."* Within the thirty-two to forty pages that "The Overcoat" takes up in the usual editions of Gogol, this little word crops up no fewer than seventy-three times. Moreover, in some places, it is especially frequent: we run across it three, four, and even five times on a single page. Is this just accidental? (pp. 296-97)

First of all, repetition of exactly the same word is characteristic—in Gogol and in other writers—of conversational speech or *skaz,* as the literary historians now call it. In "The Overcoat"—and we must mark this well—the story is, to all appearances, told not by Gogol himself but by a narrator whom Gogol very deliberately keeps at a certain distance or remove from himself. Here Gogol follows the narrative technique of *Evenings on a Farm Near Dikanka* and *Mirgorod.* He uses various devices to emphasize that the story is being told by some narrator (who is not himself further characterized). For example, he uses parenthetical expressions such as: "nothing is known of that"; "I don't remember from what town"; "Akaky Akakievich was born—if my memory doesn't betray me—sometime on the night of March 22"; "it's hard to say on precisely what day." . . .

Gogol employs digressions for the same purpose. For example, at the very beginning of the story—"In the department of . . ."—the narrator breaks off: "But it's better not to specify in just which department"—and twenty lines of digression follow, after which the story begins all over again: "And so, in a certain department there worked a certain clerk. . . ." (p. 299)

But the narrator is made to resemble Akaky Akakievich in a certain way. This is done by the repetition of certain unnecessary words. For example, in place of words which modify substantives in an expressive and meaningful way, we find qualifiers which have no meaning whatsoever; "a certain" ("a certain police inspector," "a certain director," etc.); "some . . . or other" ("some attitude or other," "some town or other," etc.); "something or other"; "somehow or other"; etc. Gogol himself draws attention to his hero's way of speaking: "It must be noted that Akaky Akakievich expressed himself for the most part in prepositions, adverbs, and last but not least, in particles of a kind that have absolutely no meaning. And if the matter was very complicated, he even had the habit of not finishing a sentence at all." . . . (pp. 299-300)

The impoverishment of the narrator's diction is therefore no accident. Obviously Gogol was unable to bring it all the way down to the level of the speech of Akaky Akakievich. . . . [The] result would have been no story at all. However, Gogol does to some degree make his narrator's diction resemble that of his heroes. This is the purpose of the peculiar impoverishment of the language of "The Overcoat." Such impoverish-

ment would seem to contravene the fundamental, intrinsic law of every work of art, which necessarily strives to achieve the greatest possible richness, fullness, and plenitude. But in this case, the possibilities for a richness and fullness of diction are obviously limited by the inarticulateness that is so characteristic of the narrator and the heroes. (p. 300)

The later development of the naturalistic style in Russian literature provides examples of such language which go far beyond the modest first steps that Gogol made. Examples from Dostoevsky are the speech patterns of Makar Devushkin, in *Poor Folk,* and of the anonymous narrator of *The Double.* On certain pages a reader who has not grasped the author's intention sometimes feels some irritation: why make narrators out of stammerers like these? (pp. 300-01)

The comic element in Gogol consists of a distinctive play of oppositions, or antitheses, between something meaningful and something meaningless. These antitheses alternate, so that one particular thing—a phrase, a word, an idea—which has seemed to make sense suddenly proves to be nonsense; or, vice versa, what has seemed like nonsense proves to make good sense. Among such instances of word-play is the way in which "even" is used. "Even" introduces an intensification, a heightening: it marks a tension, an anticipation; and if no heightening follows, if the thing that is anticipated does not come off, we feel thwarted and surprised, and Gogol has achieved a comic effect. Instead of intensification, Gogol sometimes introduces a "zero meaning" after "even" (meaningless phrases are very common in Gogol); and sometimes we are surprised by a slackening instead of an intensification. Thus there is an alternation of the serious and the humorous; and if a rise in the level of diction is given special emphasis by highly emotional and rhetorical intonation, then even ordinary diction looks like nonsense: having soared too high into the realm of intense emotion, the diction suddenly breaks off and everything ends in nothing, in trivialities—exactly the opposite of what the reader was anticipating. (pp. 302-03)

In "The Overcoat," the word "even" very often . . . introduces phrases and ideas which lack the anticipated logical connection or perhaps in fact any connection at all with what precedes. Thus, "even" robs what is meaningful of its meaning. And what seems meaningful is not always so: such is Gogol's artistic plan here. Some examples: "The clerk's surname was Bashmachkin. From the name alone it is already clear that it was derived from the word for shoe [*bashmak*]; but when, at what time, and in what manner it derived from 'shoe'—of this nothing is known. His father, his grandfather, and *even* his brother-in-law, and absolutely all the Bashmachkins wore boots, merely having them resoled about three times a year." After the first break in logic—the transition to the brother-in-law, who, after all, is not a blood relative of Akaky Akakievich—there follows still another break—the transition to the soles [*podmyotki*], a word that bears absolutely no resemblance to the name Bashmachkin.

Similar breaks in the logical train of thought, all introduced by "even," go along with the narrator's distinctive ideas about the relation of the weather and fate to the higher levels of the Russian "table of ranks." The St. Petersburg cold makes "the forehead ache and tears come to the eyes . . . *even* in those who occupy higher positions"; or: "Various misfortunes are strewn on the path of life not only of titular, but *even* privy, actual, court and all other councilors, *even* those who give no counsel to anyone, nor themselves take it from anyone." . . . (pp. 303-04)

[Through this device, Gogol] reveals the insignificance of the realm or segment of life that he is depicting. What comes after "even" proves to be trivial and insignificant. This means that in this particular realm of life, insignificance, emptiness, "nothingness" are represented as being significant and essential. (pp. 305-06)

A story gains in psychological intensity when the author moves close to his hero. It is precisely in the interest of getting closer that Gogol introduces a narrator, who takes everything seriously. The same effect is achieved in "Diary of a Madman" through the diary form, which affords the reader a glimpse into Poprishchin's soul. Dostoevsky brings it off in *Poor Folk,* by having his hero write letters. In his Ukrainian stories Gogol gets close to his heroes with amazing ease, and even merges with them through his narrators (Foma Grigorievich, in "St. John's Eve") and through his use of two levels of language: literary Russian saturated with Ukrainianisms. (pp. 308-09)

The task of establishing a close identity with the hero and his inner world is far more difficult in "The Overcoat." . . . [It] is much harder to depict emptiness, insignificance, and nothingness than great and elevated things. It would have been utterly impossible to have Akaky Akakievich himself tell about his own adventures and experiences. It is really not so easy to create a type of narrator who is close to Akaky Akakievich.

Nonetheless Gogol does try to transport us into the inner world of his hero wherever he can, and to show us how Akaky Akakievich looks at life. To a large extent, Gogol shows us the angle from which Akaky Akakievich views the world by means of those everlasting "evens." "Even" indicates how many things and people there are in the world that the poor clerk looks up at from below. After all, "even," logically, points to things or objects which are higher, elevated, significant, unattainable. And as it happens, there is a great deal that lies in this higher realm as far as Akaky Akakievich and the narrator of his story are concerned: overcoats with beaver collars and velvet lapels; state councilors, court councilors and other councilors who are not subject to the operations of those laws of nature and fate that a poor clerk is. This is also the world of the other characters in the story: a new overcoat is an unusual event not only for Akaky Akakievich but for his tailor as well.

The small world or microcosm of a poor clerk is a big world for him precisely because it is filled with objects that he looks up at from below. It is just this sort of existence that Gogol wished us to understand; hence the innumerable "evens" that mark out the configuration of the hero's inner world, his spiritual posture. The small world—the big world: it is on this antithesis that the movement of the entire story depends. "The Overcoat" is built on the oscillating rhythm of contrasting experiences. Gogol transports us into Akaky Akakievich's little world; we cannot remain there, because we do not find it easy to reincarnate ourselves as Akaky Akakievich. Over and over again our own awareness that his world is a microcosm shatters any illusion that we are in a big world and are experiencing a profound tragedy which decides the matter of the hero's life and death. (pp. 309-10)

"The Overcoat" represents one stage in the development of a theme which is so characteristic of Russian literature—that of the poor clerk. Next to "The Overcoat," the best-known stories in this genre are those of Dostoevsky . . . : *Poor Folk, The Double,* "A Faint Heart," and "Mr. Prokharchin."

Of all the versions of this story (which have been numbered at around two hundred by literary historians), Gogol's is the most successful and effective. . . . However, if social protest really were at the center of the story, would Gogol not have achieved a much greater effect by drawing a portrait of an individual of depth and complexity working in a low-level job? Let us not forget that in his youth Gogol himself had to snatch time for his literary labors from sterile and inane office work. Of course, a reading of Gogol's story as a moral, ethical protest ("I am your brother") is more in line with his own moralizing tendencies; but is Akaky Akakievich a literary type who can successfully illustrate the idea of "I am your brother" to the reader? One does not, after all, have to be particularly snobbish to refuse to see a brother in Akaky Akakievich, whose life is a pitiable and ridiculous tragedy. Should not Gogol have understood that the plot of the story and the mind of Akaky Akakievich being what they are, many, very many readers have to acknowledge Akaky Akakievich not as a brother but, at most, as some very distant relative? (pp. 310-11)

The idea that every human being is our brother was axiomatic in Gogol's Christian view of life and he deemed it necessary to remind us of that at the beginning of the story. But actually, if we read even this passage carefully, without any preconceived ideas, the person who comes out as a human being, as a counterweight to the inhumanity of Akaky Akakievich's fellow clerks, is not Akaky Akakievich himself, but that same young man for whom "everything seemed to change." The theme of "The Overcoat" is much more closely associated with a problem that is central to Gogol's view of life: that of "one's own place." (p. 311)

[Gogol speaks of Akaky Akakievich's overcoat] in a language of passion and love, in an erotic language; and there is no doubt that he does so intentionally:

> He had even grown quite accustomed to going hungry in the evenings; but he did partake of spiritual nourishment, for his thoughts were constantly on the eternal idea of the future overcoat. From that time on, his very existence seemed to become somehow fuller, as if he had gotten married, as if some other person were present with him, as if he were no longer alone but were accompanied by some agreeable helpmeet who had consented to walk the road of life with him. This helpmeet was none other than the new overcoat, with its warm padding and its sturdy lining, something that would never wear out. . . . Nevertheless, just before the end of his life he was visited by a radiant guest in the guise of an overcoat, which for a brief moment enlivened his drab existence.

The reader is apt to interpret such lines more as a mockery of the poor clerk than as an expression of real sympathy or as evidence of a feeling of brotherhood for him. But it is only in this "erotic" context that certain small details in Gogol's story become intelligible. For example, the thief does not merely strip Akaky Akakievich of his coat but, for some reason or other, says: "But this coat belongs to me!" Is not this nocturnal robber a variant of the powerful-rival type in love stories? Love for the overcoat is the only thing that is capable of arousing any erotic feelings in Akaky Akakievich. He runs after a charming lady, and studies an erotic picture in a shop window. And is not the appearance of a ghost searching for an overcoat a kind of parody of the romantic "dead lover" who rises from the grave in quest of his bride? (pp. 312-13)

The theme of "The Overcoat" is the kindling of the human soul, its rebirth under the influence of love (albeit of a very special kind). It becomes evident that this can happen through contact with any object—not only with one that is grand, exalted, or important (a heroic deed, one's native land, a living human being such as a friend, a beloved woman, etc.), but also with one that is common and ordinary too. . . . And it is not only love for what is grand and important that can destroy a man or pull him down into a bottomless pit; so too can love for an insignificant object, once it has become the object of passion, of love. (p. 315)

[In] "The Overcoat" the hero's fervor is of a lower order than anywhere else in Gogol. Yet Akaky Akakievich does have a fervor; he displays the object of this fervor—the overcoat—to his fellow workers and rejoices that he can show himself in it "even in the evening." The intensity of his enthusiasm for the object of his fervor somehow places him in the ranks of Gogol's other heroes, both serious and humorous. He has something in common with Gogol's fops, accumulators, and unhappy lovers. (pp. 316-17)

Gogol not only wished to present Akaky Akakievich as our "brother"; the main purpose of "The Overcoat" was to point to the danger that lurks even in trivia, even in the daily round: the danger, the destructiveness of passion, of passionate enthusiasms quite apart from the object they attach to, even if that object is only an overcoat. For Gogol, the word "even" serves as the means for emphasizing this basic idea. "Even" carries our thoughts to the heights, like an arrow, like an irrepressible thrust of passion, only to let them fall, all the more impotent, and plunge into the common ruck. Akaky Akakievich's impotent aspiration is directed at an unworthy object and is toppled from an illusory height ("even") by the Devil, who is the one responsible for providing such a prosaic yet fantastic goal for this aspiration.

And Akaky Akakievich's aspiration, his earthly love, does conquer death itself; this means, for Gogol, the utter loss of self, a loss that extends even to the life beyond the grave. By returning from the other world to the cold streets of St. Petersburg, Akaky Akakievich shows that he has not found peace beyond the grave, that he is still bound, heart and soul, to his earthly love. The illusory victory of earthly love over death is therefore really the victory of the "eternal murderer," the evil spirit, over man's soul. Gogol's story of the poor clerk is not humorous, but terrible. (pp. 320-21)

> *Dmitry Chizhevsky, "About Gogol's 'Overcoat'"*
> *(originally published as "O 'Shineli' Gogolya," in*
> Sovremennye Zapiski, *Vol. LXVII, 1938), in* Gogol
> from the Twentieth Century: Eleven Essays, *edited*
> *and translated by Robert A. Maguire (copyright ©*
> *1974 by Princeton University Press; excerpts re-*
> *printed by permission of Princeton University Press),*
> *Princeton University Press, 1974, pp. 295-322.*

## VLADIMIR NABOKOV  (essay date 1944)

[*Although Nabokov's study of Gogol is primarily biographical, critical sections are scattered throughout. Nabokov considers Gogol to be a strongly visual writer who excels primarily as a stylist. He concludes that Gogol's work "is a phenomenon of language and not one of ideas."*]

Gogol was a strange creature, but genius is always strange; it is only your healthy second-rater who seems to the grateful reader to be a wise old friend, nicely developing the reader's own notions of life. Great literature skirts the irrational. *Hamlet* is the wild dream of a neurotic scholar. Gogol's *The Overcoat* is a grotesque and grim nightmare making black holes in the dim pattern of life. The superficial reader of that story will merely see in it the heavy frolics of an extravagant buffoon; the solemn reader will take for granted that Gogol's prime intention was to denounce the horrors of Russian bureaucracy. But neither the person who wants a good laugh, nor the person who craves for books "that make one think" will understand what *The Overcoat* is really about. Give me the creative reader; this is a tale for him.

Steady Pushkin, matter-of-fact Tolstoy, restrained Chekhov have all had their moments of irrational insight which simultaneously blurred the sentence and disclosed a secret meaning worth the sudden focal shift. But with Gogol this shifting is the very basis of his art, so that whenever he tried to write in the round hand of literary tradition and to treat rational ideas in a logical way, he lost all trace of talent. When, as in his immortal *The Overcoat*, he really let himself go and pottered happily on the brink of his private abyss, he became the greatest artist that Russia has yet produced.

The sudden slanting of the rational plane of life may be accomplished of course in many ways, and every great writer has his own method. With Gogol it was a combination of two movements: a jerk and a glide. Imagine a trapdoor that opens under your feet with absurd suddenness, and a lyrical gust that sweeps you up and then lets you fall with a bump into the next traphole. The absurd was Gogol's favorite muse—but when I say "the absurd," I do not mean the quaint or the comic. The absurd has as many shades and degrees as the tragic has, and moreover, in Gogol's case, it borders upon the latter. It would be wrong to assert that Gogol placed his characters in absurd situations. You cannot place a man in an absurd situation if the whole world he lives in is absurd; you cannot do this if you mean by "absurd" something provoking a chuckle or a shrug. But if you mean the pathetic, the human condition, if you mean all such things that in less weird worlds are linked up with the loftiest aspirations, the deepest sufferings, the strongest passions—then of course the necessary breach is there, and a pathetic human, lost in the midst of Gogol's nightmarish, irresponsible world would be "absurd," by a kind of secondary contrast.

On the lid of the tailor's snuff-box there was "the portrait of a General; I do not know what general because the tailor's thumb had made a hole in the general's face and a square of paper had been gummed over the hole." Thus with the absurdity of Akaky Akakyevich Bashmachkin. We did not expect that, amid the whirling masks, one mask would turn out to be a real face, or at least the place where that face ought to be. The essence of mankind is irrationally derived from the chaos of fakes which form Gogol's world. Akaky Akakyevich, the hero of *The Overcoat*, is absurd *because* he is pathetic, *because* he is human and *because* he has been engendered by those very forces which seem to be in such contrast to him.

He is not merely human and pathetic. He is something more, just as the background is not mere burlesque. Somewhere behind the obvious contrast there is a subtle genetic link. His being discloses the same quiver and shimmer as does the dream world to which he belongs. The allusions to something else behind the crudely painted screens, are so artistically combined with the superficial texture of the narration that civic-minded Russians have missed them completely. But a creative reading of Gogol's story reveals that here and there in the most innocent descriptive passage, this or that word, sometimes a mere adverb or a preposition, for instance the word "even" or "almost," is inserted in such a way as to make the harmless sentence explode in a wild display of nightmare fireworks; or else the passage that had started in a rambling colloquial manner all of a sudden leaves the tracks and swerves into the irrational where it really belongs; or again, quite as suddenly, a door bursts open and a mighty wave of foaming poetry rushes in only to dissolve in bathos, or to turn into its own parody, or to be checked by the sentence breaking and reverting to a conjuror's patter, that patter which is such a feature of Gogol's style. It gives one the sensation of something ludicrous and at the same time stellar, lurking constantly around the corner—and one likes to recall that the difference between the comic side of things, and their cosmic side, depends upon one sibilant.

So what is that queer world, glimpses of which we keep catching through the gaps of the harmless looking sentences? It is in a way the *real* one but it looks wildly absurd to us, accustomed as we are to the stage setting that screens it. It is from these glimpses that the main character of *The Overcoat,* the meek little clerk, is formed, so that he embodies the spirit of that secret but real world which breaks through Gogol's style. He is, that meek little clerk, a ghost, a visitor from some tragic depths who by chance happened to assume the disguise of a petty official. Russian progressive critics sensed in him the image of the underdog and the whole story impressed them as a social protest. But it is something much more than that. The gaps and black holes in the texture of Gogol's style imply flaws in the texture of life itself. Something is very wrong and all men are mild lunatics engaged in pursuits that seem to them very important while an absurdly logical force keeps them at their futile jobs—this is the real "message" of the story. In this world of utter futility, of futile humility and futile domination, the highest degree that passion, desire, creative urge can attain is a new cloak which both tailors and customers adore on their knees. I am not speaking of the moral point or the moral lesson. There can be no moral lesson in such a world because there are no pupils and no teachers: this world *is* and it excludes everything that might destroy it, so that any improvement, any struggle, any moral purpose or endeavor, are as utterly impossible as changing the course of a star. It is Gogol's world and as such wholly different from Tolstoy's world, or Pushkin's, or Chekhov's or my own. But after reading Gogol one's eyes may become gogolized and one is apt to see bits of his world in the most unexpected places. I have visited many countries, and something like Akaky Akakyevich's overcoat has been the passionate dream of this or that chance acquaintance who never had heard about Gogol.

The plot of *The Overcoat* is very simple. A poor little clerk makes a great decision and orders a new overcoat. The coat while in the making becomes the dream of his life. On the very first night that he wears it he is robbed of it on a dark street. He dies of grief and his ghost haunts the city. This is all in the way of plot, but of course the real plot (as always with Gogol) lies in the style, in the inner structure of this transcendental anecdote. In order to appreciate it at its true worth one must perform a kind of mental somersault so as to get rid of conventional values in literature and follow the author along the dream road of his superhuman imagination. Gogol's world is somewhat related to such conceptions of modern physics as the "Concertina Universe" or the "Explosion Universe"; it is far removed from the comfortably revolving clockwork worlds of the last century. (pp. 140-45)

*Vladimir Nabokov, in his* Nikolai Gogol *(copyright 1944 by New Directions; renewed 1971 by Vladimir Nabokov; reprinted by permission of The Literary Estate of Vladimir Nabokov), New Directions, 1944 (and reprinted by New Directions, 1961), 172 p.*

## PHILIP RAHV (essay date 1949)

Like Flaubert, Gogol is an inverted Romantic trying to resolve the tension between actuality and romance, between the deflation and inflation of life's vital illusions, by the most rigorous application of rhetorical and stylistic force, by exploiting the necromantic properties of language so as to establish some kind of psychic control and a measure of moral poise, however precarious. In wholly different ways both of these literary artists used language as a shield against chaos and as a therapeutic resource; and both were compelled to create prodigious images of negation even as they inwardly yearned to utter the saving, the positive, the loving word. Thus Flaubert, who began as a Romantic, was inclined from the outset to idealize love; yet what he actually wrote is novels about the destructive effects of love and its power to entangle us in fatal illusions. The theme of love was of course closed to Gogol by his prohibitive fear of sexuality, but in his own chosen themes he too was compulsively driven to expose precisely that which he would have liked to portray in glowing colours. Starting from the invulnerably naive premise that it was his task to idealize the feudal-bureaucratic order of imperial Russia and to paint an idyllic picture of the rural squires, what he in fact produced is a picture so grotesquely satiric that it could easily be made to serve as an instrument of social disruption. Flaubert found his ideal enemy in the bourgeois, whom he tirelessly berated, while Gogol, inasmuch as in his time the Russian bourgeois existed as no more than an embryo in the body politic, seized on the government official and on the parasitic landlord as types whom he could paralyze with his satiric virus and then fix forever in the monstrous tableau his imagination constructed. (pp. 240-41)

It is not difficult to recognize in Gogol some of the features of Dostoevsky's underground man, in particular the split between sickly, spiteful vanity on the one hand and aspirations toward truth and goodness on the other. Some Russian scholars have surmised that Dostoevsky had Gogol in mind in his portrayal of Foma Fomich, the buffoon-like protagonist of his long story "The Friend of the Family." Whether this surmise is correct or not, there is indeed something in Foma Fomich's insufferably didactic tone, in his outrageous preaching of virtue and uplift that reminds us irresistibly of Gogol's vainglorious and clownish bombast in that incredible book, *Selected Passages from the Correspondence with Friends,* probably the most implausible work ever produced by a writer of genius.

The truth is that Gogol was quite aware of his own "underground" traits, and he spoke more than once of "the terrible mixture of contradictions" of which his nature was composed. This master of language, the first truly important artist of Russian prose, strove with might and main to overcome what he regarded as the morbid negativism of his relationship to life, a striving pitiful in its futility; for as he himself admitted in **"The Author's Confession,"** his real predilection was "for bringing out the trivialities of life, describing the vulgarity of mediocrity . . . and all those small things which generally remain unobserved." What is missing, however, in this self-analysis of Gogol's is any hint of the astonishing comic sense that enabled him to invest mediocrity and smallness of soul with a superreal quality that ultimately acts to liberate us and restore us to our humanity. The one thing that Gogol failed to believe in is that laughter cures. (pp. 241-42)

Gogol was in no sense a cultivated man of letters. He appeared on the literary scene like an utterly unexpected and rude guest after whose departure life at home could never again be the same. It does not matter that the rude guest's performance was not quite understood for what it was, that a critic like Belinsky [see excerpts above, 1842, 1847, and 1848], for instance, could cite this performance as an overriding example of the writer's assumption of responsibility to society, of his civic consciousness and fidelity to the factually real. What was then chiefly overlooked in Gogol was the fantastic gratuity of his humour and his transcendence of the limited social motive through the unearthly and well-nigh metaphysical pathos of a supreme creation like **"The Overcoat."** For in truth Baschmatskin, the little copying clerk who is the hero of that story, attains a stature far greater than that of any mere victim of an unjust social system. He is a timeless apparition of humanity *in extremis*, of man homeless not only in his society but in the universe. There is one story in American literature, Melville's "Bartleby the Scrivener," which has a spiritual affinity with **"The Overcoat."** But it is no more than affinity. Melville's story, for all its profound overtones, lacks the inner coherence, the resonance, and marvellous stylization of Gogol's masterpiece. (p. 242)

> *Philip Rahv, "Gogol As a Modern Instance," in his* Image and Idea: Fourteen Essays on Literary Themes *(copyright 1949 by Philip Rahv; copyright renewed © 1976 by Betty T. Rahv; reprinted by permission of the Literary Estate of Philip Rahv), New Directions, 1949 (and reprinted in* Russian Literature and Modern English Fiction: A Collection of Critical Essays, *edited by Donald Davie, The University of Chicago Press, 1965, pp. 239-44).*

## EDMUND WILSON  (essay date 1952)

Gogol's style is a variety of that viscous prose which—for reasons rather difficult to understand—was so popular in the early nineteenth century. . . . A paragraph seems a mere clot of words, which might almost as well be read backward as forward and in which the contrived rhythms have the air of being ends in themselves, since they are always forcing the reader to stop and pay attention to them instead of carrying him along. This style must have been due to some very strong pressures, for it is shared by a relatively careless writer who worked on a big scale, like Balzac; and even by a popular writer, like Scott, who did want to tell a story. The settings of the stage in Balzac, the antiquarian preliminaries of Scott, are often mare's-nests of this littered non-functional style, which combines the facetious with the pompous, clumsily handled actualities with jaunty mythological allusions. Now, Gogol is the master of the mare's-nest. Though he may seem to be merely stirring round and round his thick and nutritious pages, as if they were the strawberry boiled preserve, or the *kasha* to be eaten with currants or honey, or the dough full of hazelnuts and poppyseeds for one of the fancier forms of the rich polymorphous Ukrainian bread that his country people are always eating, this invariably results in a finished dish, which contributes to a well-arranged dinner. The Russian genius for movement, which is one of the great features of Russian literature—I make no apology in this connection for continually changing the metaphor—never allows Gogol's prose to get

really stuck; there is always a drama on foot that you know will not let you down, and in the meantime the rhapsodies, the inventories, the interpolated anecdotes, and the huge, Homeric similes that are whole short stories in themselves are managed with a great sense of rhetoric, so that they do not hold anything up, and they always become in some curious way organic parts of the story. With so much that might be stifling or stagnant, like the life that Gogol depicts, there is always something else that creates suspense—an element of the passionate, the *détraqué*, that may startle us at any moment. In these pages, which in style resemble the tangled forests and the overgrown gardens that are a recurrent motif in Gogol's work, from his earliest goblin tales to Plushkin's estate in **"Dead Souls,"** astounding transformations take place: a devil will suddenly appear at the turn of a paragraph, a treasure will be revealed—though the treasures are mirages arranged by the devils—but, as is not always the case with the Gothic novels or the Hoffmannesque tales from which Gogol derived, these visions have a force of emotion, an intense identity and life of their own, that make even Poe seem cerebral and such fancies of Hawthorne's as the Minister's Black Veil and the Black Sabbath of Young Goodman Brown mere phantoms of woven words. (pp. 41-2)

[In **"Dead Souls,"** we] are submerged in the messy and stuffy and smelly and run-to-seed life of landowners who are drunken and quarrelsome, moping and ineffective, brutal and self-assertive or crazily acquisitive or stupidly grasping. After an opening almost Pickwickian, with a man putting up at an inn, this strange book, which never ceases to be humorous, leads us into a domain of horror: another and ranker jungle that is also a stagnant morass. Gogol wallows, like his characters, in the paragraphs of a cluttered, apparently phlegmatic style that has now been brought to perfection; yet this style has a persistent undercurrent of sadness, of disgust, of chagrin; it condemns and it undermines. There is still the same queer suspense that is sometimes disrupted by violence but is never completely relieved. (p. 47)

Gogol's life was full of absurdities. . . . Ten days before his death—at the insistence, perhaps, of his priest—he burned up the Second Part of **Dead Souls,** on which he had spent years of work, then declared that this had been a mistake, that the Devil had induced him to do it.

The typical situation in Gogol is the sudden falling-out of the bottom of some impressive construction that we have watched being elaborately built. You have, thus, the dissolution of the old-world landowners; the loss of Taras Bulba's sons; the explosion between the two Ivans; the theft of the overcoat in the famous later story; the cataclysmic discoveries, too late, in the plays, of the large-scale imposture of **"The Inspector General"** and of the confidence game in **"The Gamblers,"** the abject jumping out the window of the fiancé of **"Marriage"** at the moment when, with infinite difficulty, his betrothal has been achieved; the breakdown of Chichikov's fraudulent traffic just in his hour of triumph when he is fêted as the toast of the town. So Gogol and his great book, at the moment when Turgenev says that all attention in Russia was centered on him and it, unexpectedly collapsed together.

Gogol presents an unusual case of a frustrating impasse of the spirit, a hopeless neurotic deadlock, combined with a gusto for life, an enormous artistic vitality. . . . [There is] . . . no doubt that Gogol's defeat was bound up with his lifelong failure to arrive at any satisfactory sexual life. Fear of marriage is made the comic theme of the story of **"Shponka and His Aunt,"** deliberately left unfinished, and of the rather inferior comedy "**Marriage**," and Gogol's difficulties in this connection appear in another kind of theme, which he never succeeds in developing: that of the ideal woman, seen briefly and adored from afar—the maidenly *pensionnaire* who makes such an impression on Chichikov; the Italian beauty who gleams in the crowd for the hero of the projected novel on Rome. The magnificent opening of this novel has far more of positive inspiration than anything that has survived from the Second Part of "**Dead Souls**." Gogol's longing for a feudal world becomes somewhat more sympathetic when it is dramatized in the person of an Italian prince returning from impoverished exile to discover for the first time his native Rome, but at the moment when it at last becomes necessary, after the long, the monumental buildup, to bring the prince into direct relations with the dazzling Annunziata, the story abruptly breaks off. In "**Viy**," of the Mirgorod series, the traveler and the beauty—both Gogol and his heroes are always traveling—do engage, but with a fatal result, and that this fatal result was inevitable to Gogol's vision of life is shown by the turn that he seems to have given to the folk tale from which he derived the story. This is a version of the vampire legend in which a young man must stand watch for three nights by the body of a dead woman, who at midnight comes to life and attacks him. Gogol says that he has followed the folk tale exactly, but in the versions of this story included in the collection of Afanasiev, the Russian Grimm, the young man is always able to defend himself with the Psalter and the sign of the Cross, and finally defeats the witch; and, from these and from the habits of folk tales in general, we may assume that it is Gogol himself—the solid Ukrainian background, more or less realistically presented, is certainly very much Gogol's—who is responsible for making his student succumb at the third vigil and fall dead with fright when the vampire calls in the reinforcements of Hell (just as, in "**Taras Bulba**," the young Andréy is destroyed through the irresistible spell that has been cast on him by the Polish princess). It should be noted that the girl is revenging herself. She had fastened herself first on the student in the shape of an old hag, and he had only got rid of her by beating her to death, at which point she had been forced to reveal herself as the typical Gogolian beauty, intimidating and unattainable. In a final ironic scene, the boy's former companions on the walking trip that has had for him this tragic end—back in college now and warming over their cups—are discussing his fate at their ease. Not having had to share his ordeal, they decide that if he had not been yellow, the witch could have done him no harm: "You've only got to cross yourself and spit on her tail, and nothing can happen to you!" But this rite had never worked for Gogol. It was always the Devil who appeared to him, never the Savior he hoped for, and when the feminine apparition toward whom he aspired comes at all close to any of his heroes, she proves to be a devil, too.

It was only to Dostoevsky, in the next generation, that the Christian revelation came. It is one of the striking features of the continuity of Russian literature that Dostoevsky should not only show strongly the literary influence of Gogol but that he should even give somewhat the impression of being haunted by Gogol's devils and even of saving Gogol's soul. (pp. 48-51)

*Edmund Wilson, "Gogol: The Demon in the Over-grown Garden" (reprinted by permission of Farrar, Straus and Giroux, Inc.; copyright © 1952 by Edmund Wilson; copyright renewed © 1980 by Helen Miranda Wilson; originally published in* The Nation, *Vol. 175, No. 23, December 6, 1952), in his* A Window on Russia: For the Use of Foreign Readers, *Farrar, Straus and Giroux, 1972, pp. 38-51.*

## VSEVOLOD SETCHKAREV   (essay date 1953)

[*Setchkarev's study provides an in-depth analysis of all Gogol's major works and concentrates primarily on his artistic merits rather than his personal life. Setchkarev, however, does take into account Gogol's spiritual crisis, which he considers a decisive influence on Gogol's later works. According to Setchkarev, before his crisis Gogol developed an artistic philosophy based on the idea that art should fulfill the concerns of religion.*]

Gogol deals with a problem [in "**The Portrait**," from the collection *Arabesques*] that was to torment him all his life: evil is capable of infecting even artistic inspiration. Through this means it does the greatest harm, for they are indeed the best who engage in the arts or take pleasure in them. How great, therefore, is the responsibility of the artist, how he must control his actions! Nature, which has passed through an artistic consciousness and thus resulted in the work of art, is raised to a higher sphere of universal validity; but there is a limit beyond which art leaves its proper domain. The highest mastery of art gives the artist the means to go beyond this limit, to advance beyond art to the ultimate, to the first causes of Nature, into that reality which is the basis of all reality that is perceptible to the senses. The artist who reaches this stratosphere of art "steals something that cannot be produced by human action; he tears from life something living which animates the original." And this original reality, which is perceived by the artistic imagination, when strained to the utmost and propelled by a blow from without, it flies off its axis, is truly terrible. It is revealed to him "who thirsts for this reality, when in his desire to comprehend beautiful Man, he opens him up with his scalpel and catches sight of the repulsive Man within."

Thus, basically the same theme as in the Dikanka tales is present here: beneath the surface of the beautiful world the chaos of evil bubbles, and according to God's decree the world is to end after it has been tempted by Satan. The older the world, the stronger the power of the devil. "Wonder, my son, at the terrible power of Satan," says the old monk, "he will permeate everything: our works, our thoughts, yes, even the inspiration of the artist. Countless will be the victims of this hellish spirit who lives on earth invisible and shapeless." And is there any escape? "No" is the unspoken answer, for according to God's laws, so it is to be; the reprieve gained by the pious artist in years of renunciation is only a rare exception, attained through the intercession of the Mother of God. But the world is drifting helplessly toward its destruction—no sanctity is capable of saving it. But Gogol is less concerned here with the religious problem, for which reason he carelessly leaves the question open. It is the problem of the essence of art that excites him, and nowhere do we perceive so clearly his struggle to find a definition of that irrational effect produced on men by a great work of art as in this tale. The description of the good picture that causes the radical change in Chertkov is an example of these efforts. The "inexpressibly expressible" is the formula he comes upon. He is aware of the difficulty of the creative process; he knows how much work is involved in producing the apparently simple in art, for "everything unforced and light for the poet and painter is attained only forcibly and is the fruit of great exertions." Only one who dedicates himself to pure art will be able to achieve something great. The artist must serve art alone; if he lives only for his work, it can happen that in a mystical experience, knowledge of the coherence of the world within the divine order is revealed to him—but only if he does not strive for this knowledge, but rather serves art alone and dedicates himself to his work.

It is not hard to see that Gogol is here following the romantic conception of art. (pp. 125-27)

Gogol built up his material with great stylistic skill. ["**The Portrait**"] consists of two parts, which are not apparently connected with each other, but stand next to one another like two unrelated tales, yet in both of them, the mysterious picture is the center point; the first only becomes comprehensible after a reading of the second as an episode explaining the fatal effect of the picture. The author's tone is serious, and only at times are there flashes of satiric light (e.g., the policeman, the distinguished lady and her daughter) or traces of Gogol's humorous stylistic devices (e.g., "slight disagreements" used to designate absolute contradictions in the chatter of the lady . . .). In the second part, which is narrated by the "buyer," any attempt to have the language sound like that which is really spoken is given up, so that the scattered apostrophes produce a jarring effect. Several uncertainties in expression, false pathos ("He threw himself on his knees and was completely transformed into prayer"), and superfluous sentimentalities, especially in the religious scenes, prove that Gogol was not entirely successful here with the serious, solemn style which he later worked so hard to perfect. (pp. 127-28)

[In "**Nevsky Prospect**,"] Gogol simultaneously combines two different literary genres: the gruesome naturalistic *feuilleton* of late French romanticism with its strongly sentimental tendency and an anecdote recounted in the style of a farce. (pp. 128-29)

A description of the main street in St. Petersburg, Nevsky Prospect, constitutes both the beginning and the end of the whole work. Both adventures begin on this street. In the introduction the changing appearance of this avenue according to the time of day is described in an apparently admiring, positive tone—but in reality, a fair of human vanity and stupidity is passing by. As soon as the sun sets, the action of both stories immediately begins; at the end of both stories we again find ourselves in the twilight on Nevsky Prospect, just as the street lamps are being lit. And now the author shows his cards:

> Everything is deceit, everything is a dream, nothing is what it seems! . . . It lies at all times, this Nevsky Prospect, but most of all when night presses against it like a condensed mass and outlines the white and straw-colored walls of the houses, when the whole city turns into thunder and glitter, myriads of carriages swarm the bridges, the outriders shout and hop up and down on their horses, and when the demon himself lights the lamps only to show everything differently from the way it really is.

We have again come to Gogol's theme: the devil is lying in wait for Man, and there is no escape from him. The painter who thinks he sees the ideal of womanhood when he takes the beautiful exterior for the mirror of the soul is in reality meeting a whore. His dream, which he seeks to prolong by means of opium and which is turning into real life for him, cannot save him in the long run. Our life involves a contradiction between the ideal and reality, but the imagination does not have the power to deliver Man—a conception which essentially distinguishes Gogol from his literary model at this time, E.T.A. Hoffmann. The stupid, unimaginative, crude, run-of-the-mill

Lieutenant Pirogov lives more happily than anyone, as he forgets his righteous anger with some pastry and a mazurka, and on the next day is ready to go out on a new adventure of the same sort. The two dull-witted beauties who are the heroines of the two stories are also happy. (Gogol inserts a charming observation on the beauty of married people at this point.) But what terrible happiness it is! It is the happiness of the enslaved beast, for the devil already has power over such a man. Incapable of any higher impulse, his soul is paralyzed, and he will fittingly join the crowd on the streets which conceal its gaping inner emptiness beneath a brilliant appearance and vain splendor. It is again noteworthy that at this time Gogol does not speak a word about God or religiosity. His conception of the world is one-sidedly pessimistic: Evil rules. In art and in love a glimpse of salvation is granted Man; it is shining somewhere as something lofty and noble in which Man feels the need to believe. But Satan holds his deceiving prism in front of everything so that Man cannot see the truth. And what is truth? . . . Man stands in the world uncertain and alone—will he find in himself something to hold on to? Thus the Nevsky Prospect becomes a symbol of the world. . . . (pp. 129-30)

[In "**The Diary of a Madman**," Gogol again] interweaves naturalism and the fantastic in an aesthetically convincing manner. The development of the mental disturbance into delusions of grandeur as a consequence of an inferiority complex resulting from an unhappy love affair is described with realistic detail and considerable empathy. However, the hero writes his memoirs himself, and, in addition, in the madhouse—a complete impossibility. The letters of the dogs are represented as really existing and their contents are so *normal* (in contrast with the memoirs themselves), that in spite of the precision and detail of the description, one constantly feels oneself in a fantastic and unreal atmosphere. The fact that the comedy of events and ideas has a bitter aftertaste is quite understandable in view of the subject chosen. . . . (p. 133)

It would be wrong to try to see in this tale a social bias on Gogol's part. He is concerned with something higher; as the King of Spain is assuring the object of his affections of his favor, he suddenly breaks off to cry out: "Oh, she's a perfidious creature—Woman! I just now realized what Woman is. Up till now, no one had yet recognized with whom she is in love: I am the first to discover it: Woman is in love with the devil. Yes, no joking. The physicists write a lot of nonsense that she is this and that—she loves no one but the devil." Woman is the devil's tool—with Gogol, this old theme of Russian ascetic literature takes on a profound significance. Passion for earthly things is the snare of the devil, who thus changes the world into a dead-end of absurdity; and whoever succumbs to him can assert with doctrinaire gravity that the moon is usually manufactured in Hamburg and that noses inhabit it, that every cock bears a Spain under its tailfeathers and that China and Spain are one and the same country.

In Poprishchin's eyes the gruesome, extremely matter-of-fact treatment of the mentally ill in the madhouse acquires another aspect; he interprets it in his own way and ascribes a new meaning to reality. Is this not what we do in this devil-directed world? Where is the fixed point by which truth and illusion can be distinguished? Even when complete nonsense is related, the style of a factual report is brilliantly maintained. Only when the hero thinks of his beloved is it interspersed with stereotyped interjections which are intended to strengthen the artistic unity of the work as a whole. (p. 134)

Nowhere does Gogol so clearly reveal the vanity of the world as in this story. All sense of reality is abolished; and absolute nothingness rises up in its stead. All of Man's ambitious striving, which, according to Poprishchin, is caused by a worm as tiny as a pinhead in a pimple under the tongue, is senseless and causes him to consider things important which are only illusions produced by the devil. But at this time Gogol saw only the negative side; at this time he was not consciously aware of the positive side, which allows the kingdom of God's grace to appear behind the dissolved world. (p. 135)

[In "Taras Bulba" there] is no plot in the strict sense of the word. It is a description of cossack life and some cossack campaigns in which Gogol does not tie himself down chronologically (first he speaks of the fifteenth century, then of the sixteenth; at the same time, however, many details suggest that the action takes place in the first half of the seventeenth century) and also does not present any concrete events but merely generalizes and typifies the period of the Ukrainian War of Liberation against Poland (sixteenth to seventeenth centuries), its events and personalities. The whole work suffers from this use of types. Even the heroes, the cossack colonel Taras Bulba and his sons Ostap and Andriy, are abstractions which come alive only in a few episodes. On the one hand, Gogol would like to render a faithful picture "of that rough, cruel time . . .;" on the other hand, however, he wants to patriotically glorify (as is customary in the epic), and the results are idealized beasts whose deeds one reads of with a feeling of embarrassment because they lack inner truth. . . . The battle descriptions are veritable orgies of horror: an *Iliad* faithfully transposed into modern times, but without its human breath. The idea of creating a Ukrainian epic caused Gogol to turn to Homer, but he makes use only of Homer's technique of describing battles—naming of the individual names of otherwise unknown heroes along with a short biography and an account of their character and physical appearance before the description of their death, precise statement of the horrible kinds of wounds, and very detailed comparisons expressed in tensely rhythmic speech. (pp. 141-42)

Taras Bulba's character has no unity. He does not reach even the level of the stereotype of the brave warrior with the golden heart and the rough exterior for which Gogol strove; this is made impossible by his deviousness and the inhumanities which can supposedly be excused by casual references to "that cruel time," but which are not at all appropriate for the picture of a hero who is intended to be altogether admirable. His son Ostap is also a cold abstraction of heroic blamelessness. The love story involves the youngest son, Andriy, with the beautiful Polish girl, of whom Gogol can say only that "her breast, neck, and shoulders were enclosed within those sublime limits which are appointed to fully developed beauty."

Their love dialogues, moreover, strike one as only embarrassing declamations. Andriy's betrayal is not motivated from within; and even less motivated is his passivity when about to be murdered by his father. Undoubtedly one can again see in this story Gogol's old theme of the destructive power of diabolical beauty which causes one to forget all other values. (p. 142)

Serious pathos is not Gogol's forte. He immediately becomes rhetorical and hollow. It is interesting to observe how his normal style breaks through in many places (e.g., in the comparison of the captured Andriy with the misbehaving schoolboy, which is absolutely unsuitable under the circumstances, or in the enumeration of the many Pysarenkos among the cossacks). At once the tone tightens and becomes natural. Gogol also succeeds in nature descriptions which, however unreal, possess an astonishing glow. (pp. 142-43)

While in "Taras Bulba" Gogol does not succeed in organically uniting the heterogenous stylistic elements, in the third tale of the [*Mirgorod*] cycle, "Viy," he is much more successful. (pp. 143-44)

Basically, Gogol continues here the style employed in [*Evenings on a Farm near Dikanka*], but the realistic element is strengthened and the fantastic intensified to the point of uncanniness until it approaches the limits of possibility. (p. 144)

The feverish atmosphere that was so successfully maintained in "The Portrait" is conveyed here with even greater tension. Gogol achieves his effect by eliminating intermediary stages from the descriptions of motion, showing only completed states (hence the effective use of perfective verbs) and suggesting, as it were, the intervening sinking into unconsciousness. (p. 145)

[In "The Story of How Ivan Ivanovich and Ivan Nikoforovich Quarrelled" it] becomes more and more clear how unimportant the construction of a plot is for Gogol. A little anecdote is all that he needs to produce a work of art that touches all the depths of the human soul through the manner in which it is told. . . . Gogol brings into play all his humorous technical devices and thus glosses over the disturbing gravity of the plot. The catastrophe occurs in the moment of greatest peace; in the midst of harmless comedy a radical change takes place which acts like a clap of thunder and which brings a sharp change in tone along with it. The vantage point from which the author was describing the action shifts with great suddenness. The tale begun in a cheerfully ironic conversational tone ends up in hopeless pessimism. "It's tedious in this world, my friends!" This now famous concluding sentence sounds like a last judgment, like the final product of a philosophical conception of the world, precisely because it stands at the end of such a lively, such a tremendously amusing story. And this liveliness, this amusing quality—they are but a senseless confusion of human desires and strivings that appear so important and so colorful when one participates in them oneself, but seen from the outside they turn into an irrelevant grayness.

The unity of the narrative tone is brilliantly maintained. The subtitle reads: "One of the unpublished true events related by the beekeeper Red-haired [Rudy] Panko." This enables the author to ramble on with apparent freedom, to act as if he presupposes extensive knowledge of the background on the part of the reader so that only an allusion, a name suffices to make him aware of what is going on. Since in reality this is not the case, this procedure increases suspense as well as comedy.

The first chapter is devoted to the description of the two heroes of the tale. Every paragraph begins with the declaration that they are fine men, but the proofs which follow are very strange. . . . (pp. 148-49)

[This is true also of the comparison of the two Ivans, in which their] human qualities will allegedly become especially clear. At first all goes well: one is like this, the other like that; one does this, the other that; but hardly has Gogol lulled the suspicions of the reader by means of the stylistic consistency of the comparison, when we suddenly read: "Ivan Ivanovich is of a somewhat timid nature. Ivan Nikiforovich, on the other hand, has wide breeches with such wide pleats that if they were inflated, one could comfortably store the whole farm with granaries and building in them."

The irrelevance of these people and their characteristics becomes strikingly clear by means of this stylistic illogicality.

And yet after the pages of comparison, the two heroes—the lean, pretentious Ivan Ivanovich and the fat, crude Ivan Nikiforovich—stand before us as if alive. "However, in spite of a few dissimilarities, both Ivan Ivanovich as well as Ivan Nikiforovich are excellent men." Thus Gogol concludes the chapter in which, in a laudatory style, he has proven the exact opposite. In its composition, it reflects the absurdity of the world it describes.

The quarrel between the two described in the second chapter is simply the logical consequence of the conglomeration of human qualities governed by irrationality. (p. 150)

The increasing improbability reaches its climax in the theft of Ivan Nikiforovich's petition by Ivan Ivanovich's pig. This is a parody on the retardation at all costs customary in literature and a demonstration of the freedom of the author, who is able to narrate a complete impossibility in such a way that it appears completely conceivable. The episode sounds even a bit sinister: the brown pig was offered by Ivan Ivanovich in exchange for the rifle and was indignantly refused by Ivan Nikiforovich for completely nonsensical reasons . . .—and this same pig now steals the petition. "When they informed Ivan Nikiforovich of this, he said nothing and merely asked whether it was by any chance the brown one?" From this passage we become aware of the fact that the surface of the world is again cracking up and that strange things are trying to come out. But this time Gogol bypasses the subject. Ivan Nikiforovich's new, second petition so far surpasses the parody in the first two that, in the chaos of quasi-official formulations, all sense is lost. (It is amusing to compare the ways in which some translators have tried to insert their own meanings into these *intentionally meaningless sentences*.) (pp. 151-52)

[*The Marriage*] signifies a decisive break with the usual traditions of [the comedy]. Apart from a few unimportant attempts at original treatment, the comedy plot as such had become firmly established in world literature: in spite of certain complications, two lovers find their way into the harbor of marriage. . . . Love is parodied in *The Marriage*. It is surrounded with such a swarm of banalities and clichés that it produces a simply ridiculous effect. In none of the persons involved is love the driving force of his actions; it is either greed for money or convention and convenience, or perhaps sensual attraction (Podkolesin, Zhevakin), in which there is no concern for the person of the girl. (pp. 174-75)

There are above all two problems dealt with in the . . . Christian social structure and Christian art. They are closely related, for in the divinely ruled social structure demanded by Gogol, art can play only a very definite role—it submits to the hierarchy of a divine state as a servant of God, who inspires it; the artist is a priest who creates his works of art for the glory of God and preaches God's law in them. The testament, which opens the book, states: "I am a writer, and the duty of the writer is not only to provide a pleasant occupation for mind and taste; he will be held responsible if no benefit to the soul is disseminated by his works and if he leaves nothing for the edification of men."

The poet is called by God; he feels his calling within him, and it does not permit him to follow other, perhaps more lucrative professions. But this selection by God also involves obligations: "The poet must be just as blameless in the field of the word as everyone else in his own field." . . . (pp. 233-34)

Gogol wrote his *Correspondence* in a definite style, which he surely and consistently maintained and which is entirely appropriate for the positive, idyllic utopia that results. It is the combination of the unctuous calmness of the sermon with the simple tone of an idyll, of plain colloquial speech between man and man with cleverly calculated, elevated climaxes. It is not the language of one searching, nor the speech of a fanatic who wants to force his opinion on others—fanaticism and humility generally are not easily united, and Gogol consistently calls the fanatic a cancerous sore on society—but the wise tone, one that is beyond all doubt, of a person firmly convinced, who does not need to take great pains to make clear what is evident. Antitheses, exclamations, and imaginary dialogues are far more rare than repetitions, intentional assonances, polysyndeta, and archaisms; a rich vocabulary, slightly archaic in sentence structure, is handled with great skill. (pp. 242-43)

One can only make vague conjectures concerning the contents of the missing part [of the second part of *Dead Souls*]. Gogol was never a master at constructing a plot, so that the whole work probably possessed a mosaiclike character. (p. 255)

In comparison with the first part, the tone of the narrator is much more serious. This gravity appears to have increased more and more towards the end. Only on a few occasions does the comedy peek through, surprisingly enough. The scandal in connection with the will, for example, expands and spreads over the whole province: "In another part of the province the Old Believers were stirring. Someone circulated among them the rumor that the Antichrist had been born, who would not even leave the dead any peace as he went around buying up some sort of dead souls. They did penance and they sinned, and under the pretext of catching the Antichrist, they did in some non-Antichrists." This is genuine Gogol, but one clearly feels that he is forcibly restraining himself. The writer is a preacher: jokes are out of place in matters of great concern. Gogol succeeded in doing violence to his talent, but only with great difficulty; what could the burnt completed version have been like?

Looking back on Gogol's work we recognize in him a poet who succeeded in finding the only form suitable for *his* statement about the world. It is filled with a profound pessimism in regard to human nature, which, due to the influence of evil powers, is incapable of recalling its real essence, which inclines toward the good. Man is the battleground of good and evil principles, and evil is victorious in most men by means of petty trifles. Instead of recognizing himself in all and instead of bringing about an earthly paradise through love towards his actual, flesh-and-blood neighbor, everyone considers himself the center of the world, indulges in his petty passions, and does not think of the great whole. In the face of this attitude, there is place only for a knowing irony that sees the pettiness of that which deems itself great, portrays it, and smiles at it resignedly. The smaller the motives and results of human actions, the clearer the true nature of this world, which could indeed be so good. Gogol portrays these trifles with such a deep inner truth that one feels touched by the immediacy of it; he knows how to make his reader feel the essence of the real, even in what is most unreal. A wealth of inner human life moves on an extremely narrow foundation of external events, which nevertheless fascinate in spite of their triviality. "The task of the writer of novels," says Schopenhauer, "is not to relate great events, but to make little ones interesting." Gogol performed this task in perfect fashion. (pp. 255-56)

*Vsevolod Setchkarev, in his* Gogol: His Life and Works, *translated by Robert Kramer (reprinted by permission of New York University Press; translation*

## FRANK O'CONNOR  (essay date 1956)

[Gogol was] an intensely subjective writer. Though he gradually gained control over his own fantasy in the same way as Balzac did, it always remained there, intact and unmodified by observation and analysis. Like Goldsmith, he always writes of himself.

> Having taken some bad feature or other of my own, I persecuted it under a different name and in a different character, endeavouring to make it appear before my eyes as my deadly enemy— an enemy who had inflicted a terrible injury on me; I persecuted it with malice, with irony, with anything I could get hold of. Had anyone seen those monsters which came from my pen at the beginning, he would have shivered with fear.

It is this which makes him such a wonderful chronicler of Tsarist Russia. Fantasy is the folk art of every autocracy. Where decisions are arbitrary and the secret manipulations of a single official can bring about the downfall of any individual, people live in fear of the unknown. In such an atmosphere anything is possible. Gogol's clerk Khlestyakov can paralyze the administration of a whole area with fear. So, in *Dead Souls,* when the problem arises as to who Chichikov is, it is suggested that he may be a shadowy captain who lost an arm and leg in the Napoleonic wars, and when someone points out that Chichikov has two of both, the postmaster explains that "mechanical devices had been much perfected in England." He may even be Napoleon. Three years before, a prophet had appeared, "wearing bast shoes and an unlined sheepskin coat, and smelling terribly of stale fish; and he had announced that Napoleon was Antichrist and was kept on a stone chain behind six walls and seven seas, but that afterwards he would break his chains and master the whole world. The prophet was very properly jailed for this prediction, but nevertheless he had done his job and set the merchants in a flutter."

Under such a rule, authority itself takes on the quality of fantasy. (pp. 103-05)

But what are we really dealing with in these brilliant scenes? Is it autocracy or a psychological state? For all this time Gogol himself is driven on by a sense of undistributed guilt which sends him flying from place to place in the attempt to escape it. . . . [Between] Gogol's Tsar and Gogol's God there is very little difference; if anything, the heavenly Tsar is a little more capricious than the earthly one. He was able to master the personal fantasy by turning it into literature, but even the literary exercise is never with him more than a temporary expedient, nor is it ever free of the pangs of conscience in which it originated.

Our problem, then, is to decide whether Chichikov is no more than the amusing rogue of picaresque comedy (in which case the idea of his redemption is pretentious and absurd and Gogol was really insane when he attempted it) or whether he is something different, something out of the nineteenth century, a modern Everyman in whom we are expected to see an aspect of ourselves. The former view turns Chichikov into a flat char-

acter and makes the significance of the book depend upon the wonderful caricatures of men and women whom he meets on his travels; a series of disjointed episodes, disconnected not only from their sequel, but also from one another.

The second view is, I am quite sure, the correct one. It is the meaning behind the repeated statements that Chichikov was neither too young nor too old; too handsome nor too ugly; too stout nor too thin; too distinguished nor too humble. He is, in fact, the average sensual man, and before the first part of the novel was complete, Gogol no longer attempted to conceal this meaning from himself or his readers. "And if any one of you is full of Christian humility in the solitude of his heart rather than for all the world to hear, in moments of communion with himself he will ponder this weighty question in the depths of his soul: 'Is there not a trace of Chichikov in me too?'"

Chichikov is not really a rogue. He is merely Everyman playing his eternal part. His vision is consistently a snug middle-class one of wife and children, and he is particularly devoted to the children, whom—like Gogol himself—he has failed to beget. His life is really a distressful one, for though he is a clever man and even a conscientious one in a world of thieves and liars, his own little theft, his own little falsehood is forever being exposed. When we meet him, he has already lost two tidy little fortunes—one acquired in the Treasury, another in the Customs. He will also lose the fortune he acquires through his brilliant deal in dead souls. It is a foregone conclusion because essentially he is a decent man, a man whose heart can rise to the inspiration of a good landowner or a saintly merchant. Yet he cannot save himself from falling into petty acts of knavery which the real knaves exploit against him. Nothing, in fact, can settle Chichikov's problem but salvation. Hence, in principle and in spite of the critics, Gogol is right.

It is only by realizing this that we can realize the difference between Gogol's caricatures and those of Dickens and Balzac. In all of them the caricatures are produced by the addition to the realistic imagination of Jane Austen and Stendhal of the romantic imagination of Mrs. Radcliffe and Monk Lewis. All of them tend to let their characters turn into monsters. But whereas the monsters of Dickens and Balzac represent little more than passions run wild, Gogol's represent, as well as a fantasist could see it, life itself, his own life, above all, Russian life. For no more than Turgenev can Gogol resist identifying himself with his native land.

It is this which gives his caricatures such extraordinary richness compared with the puppets of Dickens and the monsters of Balzac. Gogol has an amazing power of generalizing from slight aspects of his own character in order to form the impression of a type, almost of a community. (pp. 105-07)

Pursued by guilt like Goldsmith, Gogol was haunted by some vision of childhood and home which, in the final analysis, was a vision of his mother and an Eden to which he could never return. "And as the hare whom hounds and horn pursue pants to the place from which at first he flew," when he felt the necessity for representing the redemption of Chichikov, it was to this vision of childhood innocence he returned, only to flounder in ill-digested chauvinism and religiosity. He had turned his magnificent intelligence on the passions in himself; he had not turned it on his own ideals; and when he tries to represent these, they turn out to be a life without French, without pianos, dancing or fashionable clothes—"a simple and sober life," as one of the characters describes it. Gogol's intelligence is purely negative; when he turns it on the enemies of his ideal, like the mad Colonel Koshkaryov, who has learned organization and method abroad, the fun is as good as ever; it is only when he has to depict the alternative to Koshkaryov that Gogol collapses into his chaos of negations; no lawns, no factories, no busts of Shakespeare, no porticoes, no back scratchers, no tea, no views, no . . . no . . . no . . .

Perhaps, after all, the man who sobbed after the destruction of his masterpiece was not haunted so much by the fear of hell as by the fear of his own negations. (pp. 109-10)

> *Frank O'Connor, ''Gogol's Shoe'' (a revision of a lecture delivered at Harvard Summer School in 1953 and 1954) in his* The Mirror in the Roadway: A Study of the Modern Novel *(reprinted by permission of Joan Daves, as literary agents for the author; copyright © 1956 by Frank O'Connor), Alfred A. Knopf, 1956, pp. 97-110.*

## RENATO POGGIOLI  (essay date 1963)

[Gogol himself admitted to having written **''Old-Fashioned Landowners''**] in a pastoral key: more particularly, as a kind of modern version, in Russian, or rather, in Little-Russian terms, of the ancient tale of Philemon and Baucis. (p. 54)

The opening passage starts by depicting the ''far-away villages'' of those landowners in the charming picturesqueness of their ruins, as well as in the seductive attractiveness of their way of life, now about to fall into oblivion and neglect. And it is in the sentence referring to the subtle and yet overwhelming power of suggestion which those places and their inhabitants still exercise on the visitor or the traveler that Gogol' makes the acknowledgment mentioned above: ''Without realizing it, you pass with all your feelings into *this humble, bucolic life.* . . .'' As if that hint were not enough, the writer hastens to point out the resemblance existing between the two old people of his story and the protagonists of one of the most lovely pastoral myths which antiquity bequeathed to us through Ovid and his *Metamorphoses:* ''Were I a painter, and should I wish to represent Philemon and Baucis on canvas, I would not choose other models than these.'' (p. 55)

The task of this essay is to re-examine whether the frame of reference of **''Old-Fashioned Landowners''** is pastoral in a genuine or in a specious sense, and to determine whether the parallelism between these two sets of characters, suggested by the writer and asserted by the critic, is based on a relationship of either concordance or discordance.

The first, or perhaps the last question to ask in such an inquiry is whether the author's glowing praises of the bucolic condition flow from an earnest feeling, or derive instead from a sentimental affectation, either self-conscious or not. If we do so, we must however heed an important warning: the criterion of sincerity, which has at its best only a doubtful esthetic value, is rather a poor yardstick to measure the quality of an inspiration choosing as its vehicles the bucolic, the eclogue, or the idyll. Even when it flows most spontaneously and naturally, pastoral inspiration tends to adopt conventional forms: and it would be wrong to deduce from this alone that the pastoral attitude is a sentimental pretense, a literary pose, or a poetic sham. The bucolic imperative fulfills itself not on the plane of experience, but of contemplation alone: and the artificiality of its masks or disguises is but a consequence of the pastoral dream's inability to materialize itself. Thus, if the nature of pastoral attitude lies in the very conventionality of its ideal assumptions, it would not be too paradoxical to affirm that the test of Gogol's

sincerity should be seen in his observance of the conventions of the genre, rather than in his neglect of them.

Some of the most important of such conventions concern the perspective through which the bucolic poet looks at the pastoral world. . . . It is obviously easier to sing of shepherds than to behave like one: to contemplate the bucolic way of life from without, rather than from within. This is the preferred alternative in all modern versions of the pastoral, although it is not uncommon even in the older ones; and it is also the solution chosen by the author of this tale, or, more precisely, by its narrator, who speaks as someone who once, or more than once, journeyed to an Arcadia of his own. As often happens in pastoral literature, Gogol' however merges the fiction of the pilgrimage with the idea of a recurring retreat: ''Sometimes I love to descend for a while to a sphere of life unusually solitary, where no wish ever crosses over the hedges surrounding the little yard.''

Thus, through the double frame of the journey and the retreat, Gogol' succeeds in changing the land of his heart's desire into a place which is *in,* but not *of,* this world, and which exists as a sort of dream, and perhaps as a nightmare. He locates that place in a region out of the reach of our experience through its remoteness not merely in space, but also in time. Even in this, Gogol's invention runs true to type, since the ''pastoral oasis'' is often conceived as a charming and lonely province, divided from the centers of activity and life by historical barriers, as well as by geographical ones. Gogol's awareness of this is made evident by the key words in his story, which are the epithet *starosvetskij,* meaning literally ''of an old world,'' rather than merely ''old-fashioned;'' and the noun *ugol,* signifying ''nook'' or ''corner,'' and endowed with some of the connotations of the English ''backwater.'' While the adjective refers to the inhabitants, the noun alludes to the habitat: and both imply that the way of life they suggest is both inaccessible and irrevocable. (pp. 55-6)

Gogol' opens the narrative section of his story by giving us a double portrait of Afanasij Ivanovič and Pul'xerija Ivanovna Tovstogub: and such a portrait, both physical and moral, begins with their very names. Names are very important in Gogol's fiction, as well as in pastoral literature, where, however, they are conventional rather than characterizing devices. Pastoral names, while trying to convey at first an impression of rusticity and commonness, end by producing the opposite effect of rarity and preciosity, of an elegant strangeness. The names of the two old-fashioned landowners are, however, so vulgar and coarse as to suggest not merely the plain and the ordinary, but rather the bizarre and the grotesque. This implies that Gogol's intent, whether conscious or not, was not to replace the artificial with the natural, the poetic with the prosaic, or even the serious with the ridiculous: by giving his characters names that are more absurd than funny, the author seems to project his invention beyond the boundaries of realism. That such is the case is made evident by the mannerism of the representation, and especially of the portrayal of the old couple. Even when choosing to depict the blessings, rather than the ravages of time, no realistic writer would depict old age with traits like the following one: ''The soft wrinkles on their faces were so gracefully placed that a painter would have done well to paint them.''

This detail may suffice to prove that the spirit of the tale ''demanded,'' to use for our own purpose a famous formula by Ezra Pound, not a group of marble, but ''a mould of plaster.'' We must therefore not be surprised by both the rigidity and the softness of the figures: they are lifelike and lifeless, hardly disguising their ghostly unreality under the artificial geniality of their doll-like faces. . . . To be true, the author may have emphasized the puppet-like joviality of Afanasij Ivanovič's face in order to develop again the traditional contrast between the care-worn countenances of those who live in the turmoil of the world and those who spend their lifetime in obscurity and quiet. Yet the distortion of the representation destroys any feeling of sympathy and tenderness: and notwithstanding the author's statements to the contrary, we suspect from the very beginning that his couple of characters is unlovely, as well as unlovable.

This, however, fails to deny by itself the bucolic quality of Gogol's invention, which, in its turn, seems to be enhanced by the description of the material side of the protagonists' way of life. The bucolic dispensation is grounded, so to say, on an economic utopia, which reduces all pastoral well-being to the spontaneous fertility of the soil. (pp. 56-7)

In the terms of economic science, one could say that here the process of production is taken for granted, and that the author directs our attention to the process of consumption alone. Thus, paradoxically, Gogol' produces a quasi-pastoral effect through the very opposite of the pastoral situation, which is certainly based on the spontaneous generation of the staples of life, but where self-sufficiency operates on the level of mere subsistence, so that the threat of scarcity is made void only through the rule of self-restraint. In contrast with this, here we witness instead the triumph of largeness and affluence: and the author's awareness of this fact is made evident in the passage where he defines the manners and customs of his old couple as a characteristic example of that type of life which was once led "by old, native, simple, and yet, *well-to-do* families" (italics ours). Yet, despite all this, Gogol' does not break totally the pastoral scheme, because he uses the theme of abundance and prosperity to emphasize the moral, rather than the material, well-being of the protagonists. What Gogol' gives us here is his own version of the agrarian dream: a dream according to which a moderate prosperity is not only a generous gift of nature, but also a reward for the simplicity of the soul, and for its innocence. Such a simplicity and innocence are exemplified here, as in all agrarian utopias, by a way of life free from the taint of the acquisitive spirit, as well as from the curse of money.

Pastoral or quasi-pastoral economy is patriarchal in the literal sense, since it coincides with home economics, and its rightful manager is the *paterfamilias*. Here the situation is, however, subtly and comically reversed, since the master of the house (or more exactly, the writer of the story) lays all the burden of the household on the shoulders of Pul'xerija Ivanovna. The pastoral, whether it deals with material, or with emotional and spiritual happiness, is a typically masculine dreamworld: and this divergence from the normal pattern is important enough to suggest a deviation not only from the letter, but from the very spirit, of the bucolic ideal. (p. 58)

Pul'xerija Ivanovna's husbandry shows, first of all, an excess of foresight, which is hardly a pastoral virtue, since shepherds are wont to follow the bad example of the grasshopper of the fable, spending all summer in song and dance, rather than the edifying behavior of the ant, who labors and toils to collect food and fuel for a rainy day, as insurance against poverty, famine, or a cruel winter. (pp. 58-9)

The concrete symbol of Pul'xerija Ivanovna's safe-keeping is the immense and overflowing storehouse, the main object of her cares, and the only building on the property giving the impression of beehive activity: "the administration of Pul'xerija Ivanovna consisted in an uninterrupted opening and shutting of the storeroom, in salting, drying, and baking an immense quantity of vegetables and fruits." The storeroom is the fat belly of the house, and, like all fat bellies, has its own parasites: "the magazine would not have been big enough if the servants had not consumed a good deal of produce." The very presence of such a horn of plenty suggests that the farmland growing all the produce that fills, interminably and inexhaustibly, its entrails, is a Land of Cockaigne, which in its turn is but a monstrous caricature of Arcadia's blissful fertility. (p. 59)

[One] could say that this little world is ruled by the principle of conspicuous consumption, although the formula cannot be understood in this case as meaning ostentatious waste. Yet Gogol' must speak with tongue in cheek when he claims that the old couple "needed so little," which really means that they needed nothing, except all sorts of food. Thus, the greatest understatement of this story may be seen in the narrator's assertion that "according to the old custom of old-fashioned landowners, they were very fond of eating": an ironic understatement which is perhaps due to the equivocal intent to emphasize and to attenuate at the same time the realization that what is taking place here is an exception to the pastoral rule, according to which human needs must neither sink below the minimum nor rise above the modicum level.

Thus, in an existence like this, generally dominated by an absolute passivity, there takes place every day a series of epic deeds and gargantuesque feats, seemingly out of keeping with the non-golden mediocrity, or outright meanness, which is its regular norm. The arenas of such undertakings are the kitchen and the table: two fields of activity to which the narrator devotes the main section of his tale. (pp. 59-60)

Yet it would be wrong to think that the eating feats of the old pair are evoked by Gogol' as a kind of perpetual *kermesse*. What we witness is not an orgy, but only a routine. We are shown self-indulgence without self-gratification; we watch the triumph of greediness, not of gluttony or gourmandise. The only thing that counts is the quantity of the intake, not the quality of the food; and this is why we have failed to mention any of these numberless dishes, since they are apparently unable to arrange themselves into the pattern of a menu. . . . Gogol's tale is a denial of the pastoral dispensation, where the innocent pleasures of eating are enhanced by frugality, by what one might call the hedonism of simplicity.

The way of life represented in **"Old-Fashioned Landowners"** differs from the pastoral scheme in other matters than the eating habits of its two characters. Thus, for instance, one of the main paradoxes of this story is to be seen in its being a pastoral unfolding within the four walls of a house, rather than beyond them. The indoor quality of Gogol's invention reminds us of genre painting, especially of those Flemish interior scenes, revealing through a window the closeted happiness of a couple of old burghers. And at least here, the author of this tale never seems to feel the appeal of Northern nature, which is so strong in Flemish painting, as shown by its willingness, as in Brueghel, to go outdoors and to give us the pastoral of winter in the poetry of ice and snow. (p. 61)

[The boredom and sloth that rule the Tovstogubs' house] seem to disappear when the masters practice hospitality, which is the highest of all pastoral virtues. There is no bucolic narrative failing to play up this theme: so, for instance, the story of Philemon and Baucis is built on the very fact that they are the only ones among their neighbors to welcome two unknown travelers, who could easily be mistaken for highway robbers, while they are instead Jupiter and Mercury *incognito*. To be sure, the visitors dropping in at the Tovstogubs' are not disguised gods, but ordinary people, like the narrator himself: or perhaps like the perpetual traveler of *Dead Souls,* the pleasant rascal Čičikov. (p. 62)

The two most important divisions of the pastoral are the pastoral of innocence and the pastoral of love. There are other divisions, such as the pastoral of solitude and the pastoral of the self, but they are only variants of the two main branches. Of these two, the pastoral of innocence claims a sort of primacy or priority, since bucolic love is but a quest for innocence in happiness itself. At any rate, the two categories seem to merge together when the subject of bucolic inspiration is a happy *ménage.* Strangely enough, the eclogue looks with sympathy at conjugal love only when the marriage, as well as the pair, is an old one. From this standpoint, the fable of Philemon and Baucis is so exemplary as to become an archetype.

According to such an archetype, the pair must be not only old, but also childless. The couple of Gogol' follows the traditional pattern also in this respect: "they never had any children, and all their affection was concentrated on each other." It is significant that the author speaks of affection, rather than of love; and we wonder whether the fire of passion ever burned in those two hearts, now filled only with ashes. Yet, in the absence of a child, even a pet can do. It is quite natural that a pet should later appear in a story like this, although, against what one might expect, that pet is not going to be a dog. The dog, after all, is the pastoral animal par excellence, a useful servant of his master, and a loyal guardian of his herd. But in this case, as we have already said, we have to do with an indoor pastoral, so that the dog is quite naturally replaced by a sleepy and lazy cat. (p. 63)

"**Old-Fashioned Landowners**" and the Ovidian mythological fable occupy the two opposite ends of the same poetic, and moral, scale. They differ in other matters than contingencies and circumstances. Thus, for instance, the existence of Philemon and Baucis cannot be understood in terms of the alternative between passion and habit, or rather, of the reduction of all vital values to the second element of that alternative. In their souls, passion has eased itself into a serene calm, not into a living death. Their hearts, not deadened by habit, are still able to feel, and their eyes still look at the world as if it were fresh and new. They enjoy both the "days" and the "works," and thus change idleness into leisure, which is the opposite of sloth. In all they do, they follow the golden rule of moderation, and humbly accept the law of nature, the law of alteration and alternation, with its visible symbols, the ever-changing seasons of the year. Thus they age nobly and gracefully, since their bodies grow old but their souls remain young.

It is obvious that such luminous wisdom is not only unattainable, but even inconceivable, in Gogol's gloomy world. Yet the greatest of all signs of contradiction between the fable of Philemon and Baucis and the story of Afanasij and Pul'xerija Tovstogub is to be seen not so much in the manner of their lives, as in the manner of their deaths. The pastoral hero accepts death as a sad, but not somber event, with the consoling awareness that his fellow shepherds will bring offerings of flowers to his grave, where the inscription *Et in Arcadia ego* [I too have been in Arcadia], carved in stone, will remind the passerby that there lies a shepherd who once played his oaten flute, and tended his flock. Yet the destiny of the old pair sung

by Ovid will be even better than this. . . . [The transformation of Philemon and Baucis into plants] is a pagan piety at best: a piety which in Gogol's tale is not replaced by any Christian creed or belief. The most significant trait of "**Old-Fashioned Landowners**" is its absence of religious feeling: its lack of faith, as well as of charity and hope. Faith is replaced by superstition, which is blind to the sacred, and sees the ominous, rather than the numinous, in the mystery of the world.

It is not in the visit of the gods, nor in the wonders produced by that visit, with the final metamorphosis of the two characters into trees, that we must see the real miracle of the fable of Philemon and Baucis: that miracle is but the simultaneity of their death. Goethe recognized in this the meaningful climax of the whole tale: and this is why he refused to change its ending in the highly arbitrary version of the Ovidian fable which he gave in his *Faust.* . . . Gogol' instead broke the pattern of the double death: and this is the most eloquent proof that he aimed not at a transfiguration, but at a defiguration of the mythological characters he pretended to translate into modern, and Russian, terms. (pp. 67-8)

> *Renato Poggioli, "Gogol's 'Old Fashioned Landowners': An Inverted Eclogue," in* Indiana Slavic Studies, *Vol. III (© copyright 1963 by Indiana University), edited by Walter N. Vickery and William B. Edgerton (© copyright 1963 by Indiana University), Indiana University Publications, 1963, pp. 54-72.*

### ERNEST J. SIMMONS (essay date 1965)

What has survived of the second part of *Dead Souls* is not so much of a "fragment" as its usual cursory critical handling would indicate. (p. 83)

If the transformation of the cunning rogue Chichikov into a positively good man, like Dostoevsky's Prince Myshkin in *The Idiot,* would seem to be a more suitable task for a Salvation Army worker than a literary artist, the process is not exactly foreign to the experience of life or, for that matter, the endeavors of novelists. The fact is that Gogol does not attempt to describe this process until the very end of the second part of *Dead Souls,* and there Chichikov is represented as merely experiencing a change of heart because of the misfortunes he has suffered. The real transformation was to take place in the third part, of which nothing has come down to us, and hence the bulk of the fragmentary second part is devoted to a continuation of Chichikov's efforts to lengthen his list of purchases of dead souls.

If in these efforts one expects more of the gusto and grotesquerie of the first part, then there is bound to be some disappointment. But it must be realized that such an emphasis was quite out of place in terms of Gogol's overall plan of the novel. In the second part the quality of the realism changes. There is less stress on the fantastic, more on actuality. A different set of characters and different experiences in the context of an equally real but different slice of Russian life were necessary to bring about the slow dawning of a Christian moral conscience in Chichikov. And an element of didactic moralizing was inevitable, but it is no more offensive in this scheme of things than it was later in some of the greatest novels of Turgenev, Dostoevsky, and Tolstoy.

Throughout most of the fragment there is no falling off in the further characterization of Chichikov. He pursues his travels, now in southern Russia, with Petrushka and Selifan, still bent on buying up dead serfs and an estate. His initial encounter is with Tentetnikov, the first thoroughly honest landowner to appear in the novel and a brilliantly realistic portrayal. The image may have been suggested by Pushkin's Onegin and certainly looks forward, in some of its traits, to Goncharov's Oblomov. (pp. 83-4)

[When Chichikov calls on General Betrishchyov,] Betrishchyov falls in with Chichikov's suggestion that he visit the estates of the general's relatives in the surrounding countryside, apparently with the intention of procuring more dead souls. This device provides occasions for encounters with a group of landed gentry that parallels the amazing group in the first part of the novel. The contrast is striking for now Gogol has a different purpose to serve. The moral unpleasantness of the first group is replaced by moral goodness in the second, although each is a type and has his oddities and failings which reflected those Gogol professed to see in the whole class. It would be hard to find the likes of the first group anywhere in Russian literature, but reasonable facsimiles of the second appear frequently in later fiction. They are realistically individualized, occasionally flecked with comic caricatured traits, but they never possess the grotesque features of the first group. (p. 85)

The one exception to this group is Kostanzhonglo, obviously Gogol's answer to what he regards as the national weaknesses of the whole class of landed gentry. It is at this point that Gogol first introduces a didactic moralizing element in *Dead Souls*. Kostanzhonglo is a model, self-made estate owner who has achieved remarkable success and much wealth through hard work and business acumen. He willingly offers the enraptured Chichikov an exposition of his methods and philosophy of life. In the course of stressing the doctrine of hard work, honesty in all dealings, and the charm of country existence, he attacks the stupidity, laziness, and lack of thrift of Russian landowners and the waste, corruption, and snobbishness of those who desert their estates for the city. In condemning the growing tendency of landowners to substitute for Russian initiative the latest European ideas and agricultural techniques, he echoes the Slavophils, and [in] his insistence that the farmer's simple existence is the only natural life and that on the land man is morally purer, nobler, and higher, he anticipates the thinking of Tolstoy. (p. 86)

The last section of the fragment opens with Chichikov preparing to set out on his travels again before the law catches up with him. While he is admiring himself in the mirror in a new suit of silky material in his favorite lingonberry red, the police arrive. . . . Chichikov's poise vanishes and he is reduced to an abject, cringing seeker for mercy. He ends his pathetic plea: "My whole life was like a whirlwind or a ship tossed among the waves at the mercy of the winds. I am a human being, Your Highness!" But this uniquely honest official promptly sends him to prison. (p. 88)

Is this the purpose [Gogol] had in mind when he first hit upon the vast design of *Dead Souls*—to present Chichikov as a kind of Russian Everyman, transgressing the moral and civil laws of the land, to take him through stages of crime and punishment, and in the end to lead him to redemption as an object lesson to his countrymen to go and sin no more? Was Gogol, dealing with a lesser but more typical Russian criminal than Raskolnikov in *Crime and Punishment,* anticipating Dostoevsky's doctrine of salvation by suffering? . . . Chichikov, who had traversed the long road of his inferno and purgatory, was [at the end of the fragment of the second part] prepared to seek

his salvation by good deeds—the paradise of the unwritten third part of *Dead Souls*.

It seemed desirable to dwell at some length on this substantial fragment, so often scanted by critics, not only to demonstrate the impressive scope of the total conception of *Dead Souls* and the profoundly unified and realistic treatment of its remarkable hero, but also to suggest that if this second part had only come down to us in complete and finished form, its artistic impact would probably have been as great as that of the famous first part. (pp. 89-90)

*Ernest J. Simmons, "Gogol—'Live or Dead Souls'," in his* Introduction to Russian Realism *(copyright © 1965 by Indiana University Press), Indiana University Press, 1965, pp. 44-90.*

## HUGH McLEAN   (lecture date 1968)

With some writers, . . . art is primarily a mode of perception, a vehicle for intellectual judgment and analysis of the real world. With such writers, though emotion is generally present in their attitude toward these perceptions and therefore incorporated in their artistic representation of them, the necessary artistic distancing is achieved through the operations of the critical intellect. With other writers, however—among whom I would include Gogol—art is primarily an effort to communicate what is meaningful in the world within. . . . With writers of this latter sort, the externalization of the inner world is not the conscious, rational, intellectual introspection of a Tolstoy; it is rather a direct outflow in the form of symbols from the inner world of feeling. In artists of this second type, the intellect functions not so much to understand, to conceptualize and judge, as simply to find adequate means of expression, of verbal representation. It orders the symbols, grouping them into coherent aesthetic structures. This is what is meant by artistic talent; and in *this* kind of intellectual functioning—and only this—Gogol was a great genius.

For this intellectual operation, the aesthetic organization and shaping of materials, psychological distancing is still required. The artist must be able to experience those moments of detachment, of noninvolvement, so that his judging intellect can deal with the formal and expressive problems that arise in the process of creation. Even if it is not rationally conceptualized and understood, this highly charged material from his own emotional interior must be viewed with some objectivity so that it can be adequately expressed. How did Gogol manage it? (pp. 88-9)

Gogol found two basic methods, two fundamental techniques for artistic distancing. In my opinion one of these produced much more satisfactory aesthetic results than the other, but there are those who would disagree. The two also roughly correspond to two developmental phases in Gogol's career.

The first I will call *literal* distancing: social or temporal separation of the author from his characters. . . . Gogol uses this technique in all but one of the stories in *Evenings on a Farm near Dikanka,* in "Taras Bulba" and "Vii" from *Mirgorod,* and in "The Portrait." In the stories from *Evenings,* for instance, Gogol first hides himself behind a stylized narrator, the old beekeeper Rudyi Panko, a figure both lower in class status than the author and also inseparable from that Ukrainian locale from which the author, a semi-Russified gentleman, has removed himself. (p. 90)

From the purely psychological point of view, this "literal" technique of distancing was eminently successful. Feeling safely separated and unidentified, the author could not allow these comic-opera peasants and folklore phantoms to become symbols of the private phantoms in his own unconscious and thus to represent, to stand for and express, some of the painful emotional conflicts lurking there. . . .

In "**Taras Bulba**" and "**Vii**," Gogol continued to apply the same method of "literal distancing." The latter is a supernatural horror story, of the same order as "**The Terrible Vengeance**"; the former is a historical romance about roughriding Cossack cowboys whose precise historical period is not clear, but who in any case belong to a fairly distant past. In both instances, the "literal distance" from the author, in time, class, and "reality," is very marked.

Once again, therefore, since these characters are so remote, so different from the author himself, they can be used as symbols to express feelings he might otherwise have difficulty in articulating. "**Taras Bulba**," for instance . . . , among other things illustrates Gogol's unconscious conviction of an inevitable connection between love and death, and in particular, the inevitable punishment of sexual love by death. Andriy is executed by his father, ostensibly and consciously for his treason against his fatherland, but unconsciously and symbolically for his fulfilled love for the Polish *pannochka*.

Toward the end of the second part of *Evenings,* however, Gogol developed a second technique of distancing, which in my opinion produced much more impressive artistic results. (p. 91)

This new method appears for the first time in "**Ivan Fedorovich Shponka and His Auntie**." By comparison with the other stories in *Evenings,* several unique features of "**Shponka**" are immediately apparent. . . . This Shponka is a figure with whom Gogol could (and obviously did) identify himself closely—he belonged to the same time, the same locale, the same class, the same sex, the same psychological age. Yet this same Shponka was to be used to represent some feelings that must have been acutely painful and humiliating for Gogol: his fear of women and especially his mortal terror of sexual contact with them.

Clearly a new method of distancing would be needed to enable such feelings to emerge and be expressed in art. The technique Gogol hit upon was an unusual use of his "telescope." The trick was a simple one: turn the telescope around. When we look through the wrong end, instead of magnifying the field of vision, the telescope shrinks it. Objects at the other end appear very small, insignificant, and trivial. Human beings are reduced to pygmy size and look ludicrous and absurd. And the feelings of such pygmy men seem as unimportant as those of the flies and mosquitoes we so cheerfully murder.

This reverse telescope is, of course, a metaphor. The actual literary operation that produces this shrinking effect is a complicated one, which I cannot describe in detail here. It includes a variety of devices, including irony and especially downward associations; these latter are sometimes metaphoric and sometimes metonymic, but in general Gogol's characters have much more active and meaningful relations with animals and things than with people, let alone with ideas. It is a pervasive process of *trivialization*. Surrounded with animals, vegetables, and objects, the lives and minds of Gogol's characters are filled with nothing but the most petty and insignificant concerns.

In the case of Ivan Shponka, we can observe these techniques in operation from the start. Gogol—or rather Stepan Ivanovich

Kurochka (whose last name links him with a chicken, just as Gogol's own associated him with a kind of duck)—informs us at the beginning of the story that his hero is a grown man, a former officer who four years before had retired from the Army and had come to take up residence on his estate in the Ukraine. But immediately after this single sentence about Ivan Fedorovich's present status and demesne, the narrator abruptly reverts to Shponka's childhood, when he was called not Ivan Fedorovich, but simply Vaniusha ("Johnny"). The character is thus literally shrunk before our eyes.

Gogol then proceeds to employ irony against this unfortunate lad, ostensibly lavishing praise on him for his good behavior as a schoolboy, but in fact graphically demonstrating his flabbiness, lack of spirit, timidity, and stupidity—all qualities later amply brought out in his adult behavior. (pp. 91-3)

By such means this Shponka, who otherwise might have clung too close to the author, is held far off, transformed into a pygmy man to be regarded with condescension and ridicule. Thus safely distanced, Shponka can represent the all too genuine terrors of Gogol himself. Shponka is taken in hand by his big, masculine auntie who, he fears, might thrash him as she does her peasants. Much worse than a thrashing, Auntie undertakes to force Ivan Fedorovich to marry, to live in a state of sexual intimacy with a woman. This prospect fills him with utter panic, so beautifully expressed in his famous dream. . . . (pp. 93-4)

The effect [of Shponka's dream] is indeed comic, and meant to be. But such terrors are not in themselves comic, and if Gogol actually had feelings like these, they were doubtless not comic to him. He required the reversed telescopic lens of his art to transform into comedy some very painful and humiliating feelings. But no wonder the story of Shponka had to end there, before the marriage was more than a dream; otherwise it might have been hard to keep the tragic undercurrent from breaking through. (p. 94)

In *Mirgorod* the reverse telescope is employed to the fullest extent in "**A Tale of How Ivan Ivanovich Quarrelled with Ivan Nikiforovich**," that uproarious, perfectly written story, a masterpiece of the comic grotesque. Here the process of trivialization is carried to its limits. [These] basic devices are employed: ironic effusions of admiration (Ivan Ivanovich's glorious *bekesha,* a kind of coat), association with vegetables (the two Ivans' heads look like radishes, one with the tail up, the other with the tail down), association with animals (Ivan Nikiforovich's petition is stolen from the courtroom by a pig), excessive concern with food (Ivan Ivanovich keeps a file of melon seeds wrapped in paper and labeled, "This melon was eaten on such and such a date"), and of course the idiotically trivial object of the quarrel itself, a rusty and useless rifle, itself trivialized by being absurdly hung on a line to dry.

Yet here . . . this absurdly trivial quarrel of these absurdly trivial men is really a way of saying a very sad thing: that people are hopelessly isolated from one another and that love and friendship are impossible. (p. 96)

Actually, the operation of Gogol's telescope is not so simple and straightforward as mere reversal of direction. (Few things about Gogol are simple and straightforward.) The telescopic metaphor needs adjusting. Trivialization is pretty much a constant in Gogol's mature art, but he sometimes achieves this effect not by using his telescope in reverse, but by turning it straight on. Or rather, he whirls it, alternating our image with bewildering rapidity between the shrunken, wrong-end view and a greatly magnified, straight-on one.

When the telescope in its normal position is directed at a character, you might think it would magnify him to heroic size, transform him into a figure of Titanic majesty. No doubt it could have this effect, but not in Gogol's hands. It all depends on the angle of vision and the distance of the observer from the object. If the observer is too close to a human subject, for instance, the lens will not take in the character's whole body (let alone his mind and spirit), but will single out some particular feature of his anatomy and magnify *that* out of all proportion to the rest of him. The result, as graphic artists have understood for a long time, is caricature, another mode of the grotesque.

Like many caricature artists, Gogol most frequently selects the nose for grotesque enlargement. Seen from too close a distance, magnified out of proportion to the rest of the body, this indispensable organ appears absurd, fantastic, hideous. . . . In **"Nevsky Prospekt,"** the "rather thick nose" of "the well known Schiller" is about to be amputated by the latter's friend, Hoffmann, since that nose improvidently consumes three poods of tobacco a month. And of course the most famous of Gogol's noses is magnified to the point where it can detach itself from its owner's face, wear the uniform of a State Councilor, and lead, for a time at least, a very independent life. (pp. 96-7)

In Gogol's other works the distancing techniques are basically the same and need not be analyzed here in detail. In *The Inspector General* the reverse telescope is very much in operation, since the caricature close-up—the straight-on telescope—is more or less precluded by the real distance of the spectators from the stage. But through trivialization the emotional distance can be still further increased, as Gogol parades before us this extraordinary assemblage of petty, ludicrous, and venal officials, who are somehow *gemütlich* [cordial] and appealing in their very venality. Yet here too, as in the conclusion of **"The Two Ivans,"** Gogol contrives to jerk away for a moment the telescopic lens, to shock the audience with a recognition of their fundamental spiritual identity with the pygmy characters from whom they had previously been so comfortingly distanced. (pp. 97-8)

[Perhaps] we can also find, both in *The Inspector General* and in *Dead Souls,* a greater cognitive interest in outside (nonself) materials, a real effort to epitomize in microcosm the moral state of Russian society. To some extent we could therefore say that the whirling telescope is now used for "objective" satirical purposes, rather than for enabling the author to exteriorize inner phantoms. But actually the two are combined, and . . . the either/or epistemological controversy about the "reality" of Gogol's vision cannot be resolved unilaterally in favor of either side. Both are partly right.

In *Dead Souls* one further distancing device appears, which is best described not as a telescope in either position, but as a kind of rocket ship. This is the lyric or rhetorical flight, which carries us soaring upward into the sky of fantasy. From there Gogol shows us another "Russia," not the real Rossiia he lived in nor the grotesque Russia inhabited by his pygmy characters, but a beautiful, lyrically charged country bearing the archaic, affect-laden name of *Rus*. Propelled by his exalted rhetoric, in the lyrical digressions of *Dead Souls,* Gogol increases to infinity his emotional distance from the world of Mr. Chichikov and his pygmy associates.

From this celestial vantage point Gogol seems to be saying, "This grubby world of pygmies is not all that exists beneath the firmament; there is another world of nobility, splendor, and perhaps even love." It was this other world Gogol hoped to present in the second and third parts of *Dead Souls.* But to do this successfully would have required techniques Gogol had not developed and perhaps a temperament he did not possess. For such a vision the whirling telescope would be of no use. Characters would have to be perceived as Tolstoy perceived them, straight on, in their full human shape, without being rendered either trivial or grotesque. But Gogol's lenses were not ground to reveal the world in this way, and the struggle to see brightness through his dark glass is the tragedy of Gogol's last years. (pp. 98-9)

*Hugh McLean, "Gogol and the Whirling Telescope" (originally a lecture delivered at the University of Washington in February, 1968), in* Russia: Essays in History and Literature, *edited by Lyman H. Legters (copyright 1972 by E. J. Brill), Brill, 1972, pp. 79-99.*

## LEONARD J. KENT  (essay date 1969)

There is abundant evidence that Gogol', because of his marked neuroses, projected his own needs into his works more consistently and clearly than most other authors, but what the works tell us about Gogol' is secondary. To push too hard to convert literature into a total projection of self must lead ultimately to the type of literary criticism which seeks to make Dostoevskij guilty of all the crimes he depicts in his works. (p. 54)

In some measure, Gogol's projection of self must have been unconscious. He was, thus, able to write most bitter and sincere attacks on the "incredible" contemporary interpretation of *The Inspector General,* insisting that the arrival of the real Inspector General symbolized the call to the Last Judgment and was not the final irony of an anti-bureaucratic comedy. But, on the other hand, there is also textual evidence that Gogol' was, on occasion at least, aware of the personal psychological implications of some of his works. (p. 54)

The early Gogol' is lighthearted, romantic, and unsophisticated fun, but even in his first story, the gay and fanciful *The Fair at Soročinsy,* Gogol' is not very far removed from shadow and gloom. The bright and vibrant and irreverent world of the fair—a world in which there are "a drunken Jew kneeing a woman on the rump . . . women hucksters quarreling with abusive words and gestures of contempt . . . a Great Russian with one hand stroking his goat's beard . . ."—is changed at the conclusion, the final lines making all that preceded deeply ironic, a common technique in Gogol':

> Is it not thus that joy, lovely and fleeting guest, flies from us? In vain the last solitary note tries to express gaiety. In its own echo it hears melancholy and emptiness and listens to it, bewildered. Is it not thus that those who have been playful friends in free and stormy youth, one by one stray, lost, about the world and leave their old comrade lonely and forlorn at last? Sad is the lot of one left behind! Heavy and sorrowful is his heart, and nothing can help him!

It could be argued that folklore itself often stands on the verge of melancholy, and that the tone of these lines is consistent within the context of folk legend, but the frequency of the depressing conclusion, even in the more realistic stories which are otherwise overtly humorous (e.g. *The Tale of How Ivan*

*Ivanovič Quarreled with Ivan Nikiforovič*), suggests another source, Gogol'. It is he who is "bewildered", "lost", "left behind". There is almost always a shadow spread over the gaiety. . . . For Gogol', childhood was no less an exalted stage than it was for Wordsworth or Rimbaud, but not because "trailing clouds of glory do we come / From God who is our home", nor because of childhood's "visionary gleam". For Gogol', childhood is a period of divorcement from the everyday, an escape from reality because it is not involved with it. It is a world of warm mothers and tales of long ago, especially comforting specifically because they are apocryphal. Shelley's "thorns of life" are, for Gogol', concomitant with maturity. Automatons jerk to music, move their heavy feet even as they drink to forget what they are, where they are, where they are soon to go. Their vision cannot penetrate happiness because it cannot comprehend it. Escape becomes a basic need. Reality is mitigated by encompassing it in the aura of a dream; the worlds of reality and fantasy so intermingle in many of Gogol''s stories that one wonders sometimes whether something happened or was merely imagined. Sleep is often sought, often left only with great reluctance. When Gogol' is most eloquent it is tranquility he is eulogizing. . . .

Reality, within the framework of the early stories, is romanticized, but the response to the threats of reality is rooted in the subconscious wish to escape. Tsibulja, in *The Fair*, seeking relief from "the frightening pig's snout . . . rolling its eyes as though asking', "What are you doing here, folks?'" creeps "shuddering under his wife's skirts". His position is exceptional. (pp. 56-7)

In *St. John's Eve* there is again the Gogol'ian mingling. The warm thoughts, typically, are reserved for the long ago, when, as a child, "on a long winter evening when frost crackled outside and sealed up the narrow window of our hut", Foma Grigor'evič was aware of his mother's "rocking the cradle with her foot, and singing a story which I can hear now". Even the tellers of tales were different then: Foma wishes his grandfather to eat "rolls made of fine wheat and poppy cakes . . . in the other world", but now there are only gabblers "who drive you to pick up your cap". . . .

Beneath the humor—and wonderfully rich it is!—highlighted by incipient evidence of the grotesque which in later works becomes pronounced, there is again the shadow cast by life. Foma Grigor'evič cannot completely take us in because he sustains himself with the past. His vision, moved ahead to his time, takes on, by implication, some of the pallor of the grave. His characters dance the *gopak* [a Ukrainian folk dance], but I am not certain that it is not their disengagement in time that prevents it from being converted into a *danse macabre* [dance of death].

In *A May Night, or the Drowned Maiden*, there is again a mingling of the real (which, on occasion, is not quite real—"brooding evening dreamily embraced the dark blue sky, making everything seem vague and distant") and the fantastic. There is a dream which is yet not a dream, the first of several ghoulish women in Gogol', and, related, the typical Gogol' heroine, fleshless, chiseled from alabaster or marble. (p. 58)

It is not necessary to know about Gogol''s life to appreciate the implications diffused through the text. Many later stories often reveal more sophisticated manifestations of the subconscious, manifestations primarily of literary rather than analytical value, and these are, of course, my major concern, but, with consistency, the works contain implications of disillu-

sioned romanticism, reflect an author who never matured emotionally, one who would sit with the gods because of the corrupting effects of flesh on earth, because neither emotionally nor spiritually is satisfaction to be gained from reality. (p. 59)

[*A Terrible Vengeance, Vij,* and *Taras Bul'ba*] are singularly Gogol'ian; that is, to know Gogol' is to be aware that these stories could only be his, despite their alleged debt to folk legends or German sources. The symbols are no different, the vision is now through "fine gray dust" instead of "delicate silvery mist", rivers are still slumbering, sleep is still exalted. *A Terrible Vengeance,* however, probably owing much to Tieck, is the most sophisticated of this genre. It is replete with dreams, nightmares, and a central situation that can most easily be described if we call it Oedipal. (pp. 63-4)

[The] eroticism of the story is manifest. Gogol''s frequent use of ellipses serves not as a traditional suspense-creating device, but stops the action at the very point of revelation and suspends the possibility of final conclusion.

Even without very close analysis of the possibilities latent in the story, it seems clear that sex and sexual guilt here supply at least some of the motivation; that religion (salvation, holy hermits, the Antichrist, etc.) is the façade. The potential for an interpretation other than one based on a religious allegory is inherent in the story and in its profusion of provocative symbols and symbolic situations—in its dreams, theme, plot, even in the stated characteristics of those who function within it. It is difficult to separate what Katerina dreams from what she feels or knows, or what Danilo sees from what he thinks he sees or fears to be true. The worlds of nightmare and eroticism and desire and guilt and fear and reality are so enmeshed that it is impossible to make easy distinctions between them. And we need not. Viewed in its full potential, it is much more than a simple religious allegory (which, I suspect, would have been Gogol''s interpretation). It is, rather, a dark and seething and marvelously rich fictional world, one which gains in literary merit even as it becomes more and more clear that it is not at all clear. (pp. 66-7)

Despite the possible influence of Tieck's *Karl von Berneck* and *Pietro von Albano,* it is Gogol'ian. The symbolic density and hyperbolic tone are strongly focused, the lines between dream and reality almost effaced. The conclusion is consistent: sexuality-heathenism has led to absolute chaos and destruction. For Gogol' there is no heaven on earth. Earth, at its best, merely suspends and sustains us. The pure voice from above directs us to heaven; the erotic voice which is within Everyman must be exorcised precisely because it demands to be heard.

Perhaps the erotic is implicit in the Gothic. (p. 67)

[*Vij*] has been enriched and complicated by Gogol''s unique projection of subconscious fantasies and fears. It is precisely that which we cannot exactly explain which enables the story to take that enormous step that separates the particular from the general, a superficial motif from a universal theme, the fantastic and "unreal" from the meaningful. What destroyed Xoma is a question with as many answers as the range of imagination can supply. The most obvious answer, a ghoul, will not do because we could not then explain the effectiveness of the story beyond the traditional context of "horror stories". It has about it the mystery and haunting quality of Poe's *Ligeia.* A neurotic personality has verbalized his dreams; latent in the story, they come to life when exposed to the subconscious of the reader. (pp. 69-70)

*Nevskij Prospekt* epitomizes Gogol''s total view clearly, is deeply ironic, makes use of a second hero, whose role as foil invites his interpretation as a double, the first in Russian literature. The story is realistic, introduced by those marvelous pages in which Nevskij Prospekt breathes and throbs, and comes alive; and it thereby gains in immediacy. The problem of the ultraromantic hero, Piskarev, is comprehensible even upon a perfunctory reading. He dreams and incubates dreams, and we come to know him better when we expose his subconscious to inspection. . . .

In Gogol''s world it is the romantic who fares poorly. Gogol''s world is Piskarev's, a should-be world of chivalry and celibacy: "just to touch . . . and nothing more! No other desires—they would be insolence".

The girl Piskarev thinks he is following is a divinity; the girl he is following is merely a prostitute. His pursuit is "not aflame with earthly passion": he is "pure and chaste as a virginal youth burning with the vague spiritual craving for love", imbued with "the sacred duty of chivalrous austerity". His world comes apart at the seams at "the sight of such a beauty touched by the putrid breath of vice". "Alas! by some terrible machination of the fiendish spirit, eager to destroy the harmony of life, she had been flung with satanic laughter into this terrible swamp." The "harmony of life" does not exist in reality; there are too many discordant notes, too many jagged edges that cannot fit into a predetermined pattern. This is what Piskarev is to learn. Prostitutes may indeed look like angels. (p. 74)

[Piskarev] is a "little man". His dreams outline his idea of an earthly paradise, and they are so removed from the realm of possibility that he is more pathetic than ludicrous. His fantasy world existed before the appearance of the girl. She causes it to focus into a hot, white dot, and the pain becomes acute. Piskarev, recognizable as a recurrent type in modern fiction, is an idealist who lives only on the fringe of society, a pariah who cannot enter, one who troubles those of us who live within it because he insists upon living apart. The world of reality cannot begin to compensate for the delights of the world of fantasy. (pp. 75-6)

Piskarev's dreams are conventionally romantic, but they are deeply revelatory. They enable us to move him into the capricious and spiteful world of humanity, even if he does not care to enter. (p. 76)

The story is, then, part tragedy, part comedy. Devoid of the fantastic, there is a brilliantly contrasted clash of different worlds, that of the sensitive artist and that of Pirogov the philistine. Dostoevskij understood the shallowness of Pirogov, the necessity for Piskarevs. Perhaps they are doubles, parts of each in each. Piskarev, the dreams seem to suggest, could become Pirogov; Pirogov must already be partly Piskarev. There is a common denominator—flight. Both run from reality, both dream to escape: Piskarev of what he cannot be, Pirogov of what will make him forget what the world is. His cynicism is as escapist oriented as Piskarev's romanticism. He is perhaps Piskarev turned inside out.

*Nevskij Prospekt* is a story of doubles, of paradoxes. Primarily, it concerns the threads separating and joining fantasy and reality, a world containing Pirogov-Piskarev, angel-whore, escape-punishment, misery-bliss. The dreams are critical. They make it possible to believe there is a final double, Piskarev-Piskarev.

*Nevskij Prospekt* is a story of psychologically ill men. It is Gogol''s most profound exposure of his own weaknesses. Pis-karev is a tragic figure; he will never belong to established society, but his idealism cannot descend to reality; reality, if ever the worlds truly meet, must ascend to his standards.

In *Diary of a Madman,* Gogol' is perhaps more directly involved with contemporary social reality than in any of the earlier tales. . . . It is full of references to contemporary society and Western politics, and is, therefore, partly satiric. This is important, for Popriščin's madness is in great measure directly related to the abuses of the society in which he functions.

Popriščin is a destitute clerk like Akakij Akakievič, but he cannot adjust to the same world, and because he cannot he is more sympathetically treated, the grotesque is almost suspended. A "little man", he would be important; unable to be important, he creates a fantasy world which shields him from abuse. (pp. 76-7)

The diary is pure fantasy, wildly funny. It is a detailed record of the subconscious because the world of madness is a dream, or rather, a nightmare. Madmen have *carte blanche,* and it would be absurd not to become at least a king; after all, madmen hardly ever wish to become clerks. Popriščin becomes his own double; his double tells us what he needs to become, reflects on the inadequacies and the stressfulness of the world from which he has fled. (p. 78)

Popriščin is very much like Dostoevskij's Goljadkin. He too does not belong, is without a niche. He is less than Kafka's insect; a thing without even a place. And there is a darker question beneath the surface: is there a place at all? Perhaps he does not even exist. Perhaps there is no world of reality.

There is about this story of an aura of Hoffmann's hopelessness. Popriščin is a puppet, a feeble, wistful nonentity who hardly feels the strings that activate him. He left reality without leaving a trace behind because, after all, he had nothing to leave. (p. 79)

It is in *The Portrait,* one of Gogol''s less successful stories, that his use of the subconscious, especially the dream, is most artistically successful and profound. Part of this may be due to the Hoffmannesque quality about it (it is strongly reminiscent of *Die Elixiere des Teufels*), part of this to Gogol's increasing skill in objectifying and handling the subconscious, part of this to the nature of the story and of its hero; and part of this because the major appearance of the subconscious comes relatively early in the story, and though it is affected by what follows, Gogol' is able to handle it with considerable artistic control. (p. 81)

In many ways, the use of the subconscious in *The Portrait* seems closer to the tone and quality of Dostoevskij's use of it than anything else in Gogol'. The depiction of duality in the preceding stories is, of course, one of Dostoevskij's major themes, but its delineation in Gogol' is much more artistically limited, much less profound than it is in Dostoevskij. The implications inherent in the use of the double may be essentially the same in both, but Gogol''s expression of the theme is not only less consistent, but more limited and less effective.

In *The Portrait,* however, the relative complexity of the hero (perhaps the most complex of his heroes), the quality of the interweaving of dream and reality, the symbolism of the dream, the depiction of physical symptoms anticipating the dream, its reflection forward, backward, and inward, its creation of a supernatural aura, its use as a symbolic warning and as a tension-escalating device, all seem to more closely anticipate Dostoevskij.

Gogol''s attitude toward Čartkov is somewhat ambivalent, much to the benefit of the story. Being a destitute artist, he is at first positively depicted, but his comprehension of art is imperfect because his inspiration is imperfect. He has talent, ''but no patience''. Gogol's attitude seems to be verbalized by the warning of the professor: ''Take care. The outside world begins to attract you. . . . forget about fineries . . . your own time will not fail to come''. (pp. 81-2)

The hyperbolic quality of the eyes in the portrait may be essentially Čartkov's subjectified view of them. Their major function is to haunt him to his doom, and ''the strange kind of life'' in them may represent the conscience of the artist, one part of him accusing and warning the other. The eyes, revealingly enough, haunt him not when he is painting but rather when thinking of money. Again within the context of reality, their lifelike quality is comprehensible because the narrator assures us that ''the eyes, truthfully, were particularly striking and alive''. Also, the setting itself (e.g., the moonlight playing on the eyes) serves to further such a conclusion.

The dream, and it flows over from reality, is immediately anticipated by a feeling of restlessness, thoughts of poverty ''and the miserable fate of the artist''. In a sense, then, the dream is a dramatization of his desire for wealth, a symbolization of wish fulfillment. The horror of the dream bespeaks Čartkov's own ambivalence; it is subconscious self-punishment. Most important of all, the dream enables us to see into Čartkov, and, for the first time, it becomes clear that if he is a dual man, it is yet the immoral part of him that has the upper hand now and will affect the course of what follows. (p. 82)

Dostoevskij's dreamers usually awake shrieking, and it is clear that in Gogol' and Dostoevskij the shriek performs a special literary function—it is the highest point of the tension that has been building, and it is followed by a period of calm. In *The Portrait* this calm is short-lived because the dream is yet incomplete, but it comes immediately after the dream finally ends, when not only is the usually high-strung Čartkov ''depressed and sullen as a wet rooster'', but even the room is suddenly limp. (p. 83)

The first part of *The Portrait,* much superior to the more traditionally realistic part which follows, indicates an advance in Gogol''s use of the subconscious, reveals how well it can function when thoroughly integrated into the fabric of the story being told. Here there is evidence that Gogol' was employing its manifestations in a most careful and deliberate way. But in nothing that followed was it ever to be so fully exploited again by him. (p. 84)

In Gogol', the conscious use of the subconscious is less developed, less profound, less complex than it becomes in Dostoevskij, though, in many ways, it anticipates Dostoevskij in several most important respects. Part of this is due to Gogol''s level of self-involvement; he too much subjectified his material, was himself too narrowly focused to sustain a theme in depth (even *Dead Souls* is primarily a compilation of vignettes). The intensity so marked in Dostoevskij is not lacking here, but the core of a deep and abiding and universally significant vision of life from which to build a sustained work is. Dostoevskij was extroverted enough, disciplined enough, to convert his experiences and insights into broad and complex works predicated upon a meaningful vision of life. Gogol''s canvas is too small, the sweep of the brush too restricted, the vision too distorted, the self too involved, for such achievement. But these limitations are relative.

Gogol''s works tell us more about their author than do the works of almost any other author I can think of. This accounts in part for their hyperbolic quality. There is a great consistency in his works; patterns emerge, as do attitudes and the separate ingredients of the delightful but disturbing Gogol' brew.

Gogol''s use of the double and the dream is nearly always artistically successful; their appearance is relevant to the literary quality of the stories in which they appear. Almost consistently serving beyond traditional romantic function, the dream and other manifestations of the subconscious not only enrich the potential of the works, but so dominate them that they become necessary for any meaningful interpretation. They reflect backwards, making the preceding ironic; they project ahead, coloring and shading what follows, and, crucially, they reflect inward. (p. 86)

The paradoxical, so frequent in his work, stemmed from the paradoxes in Gogol': a selfless Christ who was selfish; a loveless man who needed love; an impotent man potent in fantasy; a self-satisfied man disgusted with self; a man who cried when he laughed, laughed even while he cried.

The appearance of the subconscious serves Gogol' very well indeed. It helps us to understand a crucial attitude: ''It is a dreary world, gentlemen.'' (p. 87)

> *Leonard J. Kent, ''Nikolaj Vasil'evič Gogol','' in his* The Subconscious in Gogol' and Dostoevskij, and Its Antecedents *(© copyright 1969 Mouton & Co. N.V., Publishers, The Hague; reprinted by permission of the author), Mouton Publishers, The Hague, 1969, pp. 53-87.*

### DONALD FANGER   (essay date 1979)

[*Fanger demonstrates that characteristics from several literary movements can be distinguished in Gogol's works.*]

''Soul'' (*duša*) is one of the most frequently recurring words in Gogol's writing throughout his career. [In *Dead Souls*] its Gogolian meanings reach a new plenitude—and not only because in his time it also designated an enserfed peasant (landowners were commonly said to possess so many souls). The Gogolian usage, still uncharted, covers a spectrum that runs from regarding the soul as the seat of authentic individual being, through equating it with the unconscious, to seeing it as the organ of communication with supraindividual sources of truth and beauty, not necessarily religious. Thus in the first essay of *Arabesques* painting is rated above sculpture since the latter cannot convey ''those subtle, mysteriously earthly traits, regarding which you sense heaven filling your soul, and you feel the inexpressible.'' . . . (p. 168)

Gogol's novel is organized and dominated by the road. It begins with an arrival and ends with a departure; its concluding lines are a panegyric to the road. . . . Literally the instrument of Chichikov's quest on the level of story, it leads him to planned and unplanned encounters, and so stands for experience, perspective, movement, change, life. ''How much there is,'' Gogol writes in the last chapter, ''of the strange, and the alluring, and the transporting, and the wonderful in the word: road! And how wondrous it is itself, this road.'' . . . For all that, the road here serves neither as pretext nor as occasion for adventures. It affords *views*—of landscapes, characters, and routines, presented through ''those trivia which seem trivia only when they are put into a book.'' . . . The mirror moving down this road is, in the first place, Chichikov himself, the featureless hero ("neither handsome nor of displeasing exterior, neither too plump nor too thin," not exactly old "but not any too young." . . . (pp. 169-70)

The opacity conferred at the end by giving Chichikov biographical dimensionality is meant to explain his enterprise and so prepare the next stage of his road, on which the events of this novel have been only a way station. But it has a deeper function in making clear, retrospectively, that what was presented as Chichikov's mirroring of the characters has in fact been mutual. Manilov now appears as a hyperbolic parody of Chichikov's main quality, decorum; Korobochka represents a naive variant of his suspicious canniness in bargaining; Nozdryov shows more than comparable resourcefulness in prevarication, though his is instinctive and motiveless; Sobakevich manifests the calculating side of Chichikov, with its implicit misanthropy laid bare; and Plyushkin represents the passionate side of his acquisitiveness, showing how, unchecked, it can destroy the family life to which Chichikov so eagerly looks forward. (p. 170)

The portrait gallery of the book is thus a gallery of mirrors as well—to which, in the process of presentation, the narrator adds his own generalizing reflections. Only the author, whose voice emerges distinctly from that of the narrator at times, remains above this process, in the role of self-justifying commentator and ultimately of creator. . . .

Presentation is the work of the narrator; it embraces the projections and perceptions of the characters and offers them, embellished and in a new perspective, to be registered by the reader. The author, by contrast, appears as such, hinting at a larger enterprise of his own, as enigmatic as Chichikov's, and likening his own task to a journey. The passages where his voice dominates might collectively bear the title given Gogol's posthumous "Author's Confession," constituting as they do crucial passages in the tale of his authorship. They are all keyed to the question: why? (p. 171)

The authorial interpolations in *Dead Souls*—as opposed to narrative comment—are confessions and admonishments, pleas for sympathy and defiant complaints about probable misunderstanding. Testimony to a new conception of the writer's function, they parallel the programmatic revisions of "The Portrait" and "After the Play." But they remain outside the world of the novel, like the scattered fragments of an introduction the author feared his readers might otherwise pass by.

The world of that novel is the weedlike culture on the Russian heartland, conceived abstractly from a distance and bodied forth in disconcerting closeups, with absences commanding the same meticulous attention as presences and thereby assuming a like status; this verbal world takes its weird consistency from such ontological mixing and implies its own relation to other worlds simply by existing as it does. . . . Out of the flat miscellaneousness [of his prose], crystallizing into colorful incongruities, Gogol shows how each of the five landowners Chichikov visits—solipists all—has arranged a particular landscape reflecting his own dominant qualities. Thus the rough and solid order of Sobakevich's estate is matched by the master himself, whose very face is described as one of those on which nature took few pains, but simply hacked away from the shoulder with an ax, "and set him into the world unplaned, saying: 'It lives!'" . . . This technique is so artfully handled and so subtly sustained as to preclude brief citation; avoiding the allegorical consistency it threatens, Gogol manages to suggest the variety of nature through the range of his observation and the modulation of his emphases. (pp. 173-74)

The world of *Dead Souls* is a world of detail natural and fictive, familiar and strange—and all subtly out of joint. Even at its sharpest, this detail contributes to the general impression of indeterminacy: What time of year can it be when the peasant men sit in sheepskin coats, their women are up to their knees in a pond, Korobochka comments on a snowstorm, and the fruit trees are covered with a net to keep off the crows? . . . The people themselves become features of the landscape—Plyushkin a "rip," Sobakevich a bear, the unidentified woman in Sobakevich's house "one of those persons who exist in the world not as objects, but as foreign specks or spots on objects" (pp. 175-76)

How these details relate to each other and cohere to fulfill a serious intention is as difficult to formulate as it is easy to feel in the reading. Paraphrase misses the sustaining magic of the language—Gogol's triumph here—and so deadens. Analysis freezes the essential movement of the text, which is not lineal, thus risking arbitrariness, not to mention endlessness. Summary supposes, fatally, that plot provides a meaningful pattern. There is no single locus or level of significance adequate to account for this text in which speech events rival human events (even *generate* them), and characters who stumble momentarily into the narrative through hearsay or are invited in to make up a simile, share a quality of enigmatic, stubborn "thereness" with those whose presence is demanded by Chichikov's scheme or the narrator's *sententiae*. (p. 176)

The universe of *Dead Souls* expands and contracts in the reader's consciousness—from metaphysical intuition to densely enigmatic vocables. That is why if we pause at any point in our reading, the whole appears as an ontological puzzle. The smallest and so most apparently tractable elements—the words themselves—may call language as such into question, to such an extent can they appear freed not only from clear referential meaning but from single specifiable relevance. In this connection, the title itself is central: Biely declared that he could write dozens of pages on the tricks of narration that arise from the ambiguity of both words.

Souls in this novel are absent, displaced, or atrophied. Sobakevich pinpoints the ambiguities when he assures Chichikov that "some other crook would deceive you, sell you rubbish, and not souls"; his dead souls are select merchandise, each one "either a skilled workman or some healthy peasant." . . . For truths issue eccentrically in this book; there is no privileged source among the characters. Sobakevich's point is borne out by Chichikov's heartfelt (*"ot duši"*; literally, from the soul) reaction to the only death in the book: "There's the public prosecutor for you! He lived and lived, then up and died! And now they'll be printing in the papers that, to the grief of his subordinates and all humanity there passed away a respected citizen, a rare father, an exemplary spouse, and all sorts of things . . . But if one were actually to look into the matter carefully . . . all there really was to you was your bushy eyebrows". . . . (pp. 178-79)

[The] fundamental paradox of the novel is [this] . . . : Living people and dead ones may be clearly distinguished in the action, but the cumulative sense of the text denies this distinction, as it denies the autonomy of comedy. (p. 180)

*Dead Souls* exploits the narrative voices and devices worked out in the most Gogolian of his earlier comic writings; the text abounds with parallels, at times almost citations, from "Shponka," "Old-World Landowners," the story of the two Ivans, "The Nose," "The Carriage," all five of the Petersburg

Tales, *The Inspector General.* It is his last, most inclusive, and most intentional performance in that special mode of his own devising—half monologue, half story—by which he creates a world whose status with relation to ordinary experience remains, like the implied personality of the narrator, teasingly elusive. The world of *Dead Souls* differs only in this: because it is more ample, it shows a greater consistency, the very discontinuities suggesting a pattern, the several levels echoing each other to signal a controlling perspective over the whole design. Technique itself does not simply carry but becomes a part of theme; the humblest details take on a thematic charge.

That theme at its broadest is the amorphousness, characterlessness, purposelessness, senselessness, alternately ludicrous and ominous, of life—specifically Russian life in the first place—as material for a novelist. (p. 182)

Gogol found a key to the most puzzling of his inherent tendencies when he took contemporary Russia as his theme. Even on the strategic authorial level, that is, *Dead Souls* remains a comedy of attribution. It is a symbolic statement of what it means to live (as Gogol claimed he had written previously) without controlling consciousness, without asking "why?" and "to what end?" Here was a license for derision, or rather a serious warrant for the most ingeniously unserious presentation. No oddity, no irrelevance, no absurdity but could—given the unflagging genius of the language—contribute to the painful because concrete sense of an absence. (pp. 183-84)

Bringing time into the novel—through Plyushkin and through the biographical sketch in the last chapter that puts Chichikov, too, on the level of becoming—brought cause for mortal apprehension in the artistic sense as well as the moral. Gogol's fateful error lay in accepting and repeating Pushkin's remark that his gift was for "divining a man" on the basis of a few observed traits. It was never that. Accuracy (as the few examples show) was never in question; the gift alluded to was for *creating* a plausible and amusing portrait, one more gratuitous item in the collection of what he came here to label as dead souls. His genius lay always in eccentric but lifelike attribution—a kind that tempts one to add "expressionist" to the other anachronistic labels (symbolist, surrealist, absurdist) that fit his work better than any current in his own time. So long as Chichikov remained an enigmatic vehicle for this process of creation and exhibition, he served his author's genius perfectly by sharing Gogol's freedom of arbitrary movement at the expense of the static population of his book. Indeed, Chichikov's very quest for nonexistent merchandise that would, all the same, have an impact in his world parallels Gogol's quest to render an absence that would, by the force of the rendering, change the historical consciousness of his Russia. (pp. 189-90)

Gogol's twentieth-century appeal [is that] we are most comfortable with texts that are paradoxes and puzzles. At the same time, it explains the novel's earlier appeal and influence. As an entity at once polished and open-ended, *Dead Souls* brought together in literary form a flux of attitudes and tendencies, sights and sounds—the raw material of an unborn national self-consciousness. (p. 190)

The palpable miscellany of the book has coalesced into an abstraction, which can be questioned only rhetorically. The famous final paragraph consists almost entirely of such questions, most of them, strictly speaking, senseless: a phantom interrogation of a phantom symbol. What more fitting close to a novel that demonstrates with unprecedented brilliance the

power of form without content and action without resolution—a work that finally does invite comparison with Cervantes' in the subtlety of its comedy and the depth of its symbolism, mimicking the emptiness of life no less resourcefully than the *Quixote* had mimicked life's fullness? (p. 191)

To fit Gogol's work, the common terms of literary criticism require qualification so extensive as to amount to reconstruction; with many of the older ones, the effort is by now clearly excessive. "Realism," for example, is more prescriptive than descriptive in Gogol's case, despite the fact that his protagonists could hardly be more ordinary, their ambitions more mundane, their physical surroundings less conventionally poetic or more intimately a part of their being; for hyperbole swamps any realistic tendencies when simple narrative arbitrariness does not unhinge them. (pp. 229-30)

Among more generic terms, "satire" and "humor" have their obvious areas of relevance and no less obvious insufficiency. The aggression of satire is certainly prominent in much of the post-Dikanka work; and the Petersburg Tales, like *Dead Souls,* worry with unflagging derision the vices of vanity, complacency, obsession with rank, and propensity to gossip. But the aggression in question goes beyond these traditional targets. Gogol's text ridicules the great majority of the characters who appear in it—not for particular failings but for a radical cretinism ("insignificance") whose source is in the text's source and not in society or nature. The usual instrumentality is thus inverted: characters and phenomena that do not clearly merit artistic scourging nonetheless serve as pretexts for a presentation whose artistic merit is self-justifying and unquestionable. So, though identifiable satire cannot be considered the main thing in Gogol, the satirist's stance and the satirist's quasi-magical belief in the power of words, applied to vaguer ends, may be.

A like qualification applies to the humor of most of the post-Dikanka works. Gogol may be playful and inventive in the manner of a humorous writer, but the sympathy of a Sterne or a Dickens vanishes after **"Old-World Landowners,"** and his startling incongruities, like his passages of amusingly gratuitous play, serve an end about which one can say with certitude only that it involves a feeling of superiority in the reader as in the author. (pp. 230-31)

As for irony, it is ironic that that element in Gogol should still be awaiting its investigator, for it pervades his writing from first to last and marks it on so many levels that one might see him, in Ortega's phrase, as "doomed to irony." Ranging in kind from simple declarative ("Ivan Ivanovich is a wonderful man!") through dramatic (*The Inspector General,* **"Nevsky Prospect"**) to romantic (**"The Nose,"** *Dead Souls*). Gogolian irony serves three broad functions. It (1) proclaims the author's creative freedom, by putting off the question of his identity in the texts . . . , and in so doing it (2) turns the question to the creation itself ("Why do writers write such things?"), thus (3) producing an art through which to pose the question of the possibility of art ("creation out of nothing"). In Gogol's universe of concentric ironies, even a clearly decodable instance will promptly be translated to a larger context in which it can take on—or seem to take on—a new and perplexing ironic charge. (pp. 232-33)

The extent to which Gogol fashioned a new kind of fictional discourse is still underrated: particular words and turns of phrase, as has long been recognized, function synecdochically, small details standing for large wholes. Recognition of this is usually confined to the referential level—the waists and mustaches that parade down Nevsky Prospect, or the sidewhiskers, three-cornered hat, and sword that make up Ivan Yakovlevich's perception of the policeman at the end of the first chapter of "**The Nose.**" In fact, synecdoche plays a no less important role on other levels—the literary-conventional, the psycholinguistic, the sociolinguistic. (p. 234)

We do not, of course, turn to Gogol's writing for information on Russia (as Belinsky thought we would), and neither do his Russian readers; what has survived the possibility of topical interpretation is what tempted nineteenth-century readers into such interpretation in the first place: a sense that this writing held some deeply enigmatic authenticity. . . . (pp. 234-35)

Understanding Gogol . . . must begin with understanding the function of his language. He "broke the language barrier," as Sinyavsky puts it—not by simply *using* the language that Russians speak (or spoke), but by turning to account "his inability to speak in the ordinary way," thereby illustrating the fact that "prose, like any art, presupposes a transition to an unfamiliar language and through this exotic quality assumes a parity with poetry." So mimesis in his works is functionally illusory; the texts may evoke real objects, but the reality to which they testify is ultimately a verbal counter-reality. The Gogolian universe thus has its anti-matter . . . : it also has its suggestive concentricities, like solar systems and atoms, in the macro- and micro-structures of event, which may be mimetic happening or speech event, the agencies being respectively human emotion and phonemic interplay. (p. 235)

Since conventional form itself is a sign of conscious intentionality, the Gogolian universe begins to be constituted only after the Dikanka stories. The writing in them does, to be sure, already show Gogolian traits, but its rationale or sanction comes ready-made from familiar genres: from romantic folk tales, theater, and legend. That is why generalizations about his "essential" writings tend to exclude these pieces or to misrepresent them; and that is why later works that depend on plot seem relatively weak (***Taras Bulba***, "**The Portrait,**" *The Gamblers*, "**Rome**"), their brilliant passages notwithstanding. "**A Terrible Vengeance,**" in the way the intensity of its symbolic pattern renders the closing explanation inadequate, shows his work beginning to break free. And "**Shponka**" in its provocative "incompleteness" already exists entirely within the Gogolian universe, which consists of fluid discourse. *Mirgorod* thus is a step forward into artistic maturity precisely because it shows consistent signs of accommodating a psychological regression. What makes these stories Gogol's most intimately expressive is the constant exploitation of the child's point of view, the child's needs and emotions (framed, to be sure, by a shrewdly adult awareness in much the manner of Dickens). (pp. 237-38)

The Gogolian universe . . . models the "soul" of its creator in the radical sense of giving it its only possible perceptible form. For soul, as used here, refers ultimately to that silence out of which the writing originated, the very impulse to creation freed as far as possible from biographical contingency. So for all important purposes (and to a degree unmatched by any writer of his time) the text is Gogol and Gogol is the text, simultaneously compelling recognition and resisting definition. (p. 239)

What we . . . recognize is the unique thematic resonance his phrases take on from their participation in the characteristic workings of the larger Gogolian text. By theme here I mean something more fundamental than those recurrent objects of concern—rank, stupidity, greed, moral vacuousness . . .—all of which may be found in "reality" and in his writings alike. Behind them, organizing the rival reality that is Gogol's poetic universe and expressing only *its* laws, are certain pervasive entities which cannot be reduced to propositional statements. In fact, they manifest themselves textually as dynamic tendencies, modalities of concern, patterns of relationship. Because they comprise key elements of Gogol's artistic code and because they are not to be confused with themes as usually construed, I propose to use the terms "thema" and "themata."

The point can be illustrated by considering what I take to be a central cluster of such themata. Because they are not in their nature susceptible of direct expression, putting labels to them is bound to be quixotic, and those offered here should be taken as arbitrary, awkward, and provisional. Each of the themata in question forms a whole constellation of smaller themes (in the more usual sense); their boundaries are vague and they overlap. To the extent that they do constitute a cluster, moreover, it follows that the latter can be read in any sequence with only slightly altered effect. None of its members is clearly privileged. Each in its shifting relation to the others contributes to an implication. For present purposes they will be considered under the headings of Metamorphosis, Evasion, Identity, and Recognition. (pp. 239-40)

Sudden change dominates the Gogolian fictions from first to last. In the early stories evil spirits try on forms like actors in a wardrobe room: dogs and evil stepmothers turn into cats, and the devil goes around in human shape. (p. 240)

All such happenings carry a ready-made and quite sufficient explanation in the supernatural, specifically in traditional notions of Satan as man's adversary. Alternative explanations involving a kind of psychological allegory, though supererogatory, may appear, but never as more than hints or overtones (the incest motif in several of the Dikanka stories, and particularly in "**A Terrible Vengeance**"). As the Gogolian universe takes form, however, a transposition occurs: what was previously overtone—anxiety, obsession, the logic of dreams and fantasies—becomes dominant, and the still-prevalent metamorphoses now involve supernatural intervention only as an ambiguous, probably figurative coloration. . . . "**Viy**" is at the center of this shift, the demonic there being so overwhelmingly a psychological phenomenon as to render the falsely explanatory appeal to folklore an artistic mistake. (pp. 240-41)

[In writings subsequent to the composition of "**The Nose**"] ontological tampering that had previously required the sanction of a devil or a dreamer now needs none. Henceforth the threat of metamorphosis in one sense or another pervades the Gogolian universe (the extended similes of *Dead Souls* show its tug), built into its very fabric by a narrator who is himself protean.

To say this of Gogol's universe is to emphasize its fluid perspectivism. Figurative metamorphosis is everywhere latent alongside the "literal" (the nature of the case requires quotation marks): what a thing is depends on when and how one looks at it, and the text controls both. (p. 241)

Metamorphosis is the ramifying expression of the creation constantly going on in Gogol's universe. Its ultimate source is the creative impulse that brought that universe into being: "freshness," a conferring, fundamentally lyrical energy. For Gogol's best art itself operates a metamorphosis on its objects, taking the inconsequential and, without either ennobling or disguising it, making it a matter of discursive consequence. A universe so constituted, however, reveals a special kind of entropy. The engendering, lyrical-comic energy weakens over time (even the time of individual works). . . . (pp. 241-42)

If metamorphosis is the central process in the Gogolian universe, then the road is its central image, operating similarly on every level and evolving as the work evolves. . . . The urge to move on is always connected in one way or another with the problematics of identity, more specifically with frustrating identification from without. A basic feature of the author's life, it finds expression—sometimes direct, sometimes metaphorical—as the defining trait of the Gogolian narrative persona. ''I was fleeing from myself,'' he explained when he first bolted abroad in 1829. But this flight from self was at the same time a flight *toward* self: his identity in the present, he never tired of repeating, was nothing, his identity in the future—a textual identity to be judged by the indices of artistic creation—everything. What mediated between the two was the road. It kept fixity, accountability, knowability itself at bay. (''I travel to be traveling.'') Up to its final metamorphosis, therefore, Gogol's is not the familiar allegorical road of life, but an instrument of evasion in all the crucial Gogolian senses. (pp. 242-43)

In the major writings it is evasion that supplies the poetic energy and the implicit positive element. It does so by encoding in work after work a powerful and primitive impulse to escape that hitherto unnamed state which Gogol images as burial alive, death-in-life, mere existence where habit stifles ''soul.'' . . . Thus meaning or significance—a fundamental thematic concern in the Gogolian text—is for all its portentousness identifiable only negatively via the principle of *ne to*, a potential presence, the *ex post facto* reward and justification of an activity that is process and movement and must be pursued in a state of freedom from conventional categorization. There is the largest ground of vicarious experience in these texts: what the reader relives most importantly is, by a characteristic displacement, the experience of the author—not Nikolai Vasilievich Gogol but that self-created, textual Gogol who must be understood to be as pervasively present in his universe as God is in ours. From this it follows that Gogol's art needs to be seen not as a way of saying something (even in the sophisticated sense in which Pushkin and Tolstoy ''say'' something in their works) but as a way of *doing* something: proving its own possibility, and so legitimizing that maximalist sense of further possibilities, that faith which produced the proof.

All this concerns the shaping impulse of the Gogolian universe; but the road also has discrete organizational functions in the several works, as we have seen. At first, it breaches the boundary of a closed world which symbolizes home and childhood, and where the terms for understanding are familiar and traditional. (So even when the marvelous erupts within it, the note of bewilderment—that hallmark of the post-Ukrainian works—is absent.) Seen largely from the perspective of this world, the road communicates with what is alien and menacing: ''Everything there is not right, even the people are not the same'' (''*Tam vse ne tak, i ljudi ne te*''; ''**A Terrible Vengeance**''). An adolescent ambivalence toward this symbolic world provides the lyrical frame of ***Mirgorod,*** which opens with a nostalgic view of the road back and ends with a negative one. The Petersburg Tales, by contrast, body forth a world of adult experience, ruled by abstraction and irrelevance and as intolerably present as the earlier one was irretrievably absent, a new prison where society replaces community, temptation re-

places adventure, and illusion (except in ''**The Portrait**'') replaces magic. All are victims here, the more sympathetic being those childlike souls (Piskaryov, Akaky Akakievich) who have no worldly ambition, the rest, presented with a harsher irony, enjoying various degrees of soul-deadening success. There is no way out save through dream or fantasy. (pp. 244-45)

The closed worlds of the Ukraine and Petersburg, for all their obvious differences, have in common a stressed non-Russianness. When Gogol confronts the theme of Russia—as he does in **The Inspector General,** ''**The Carriage,**'' **Dead Souls,** and **Selected Passages**—the road becomes central and takes on a new range of meanings. Russia proper is amorphous and unencompassable; it *contains* the road and requires it. So Khlestakov and Chichikov, the heroes of the only works by which Gogol hoped to be remembered, are cast as travelers, surrogates for the author who was to proclaim in his last book, ''It Is Necessary To Travel Throughout Russia.'' With this a fateful realignment takes place between the writer and his thematics. The escape to Petersburg had led to the discovery of vocation; the escape from Petersburg signified the embrace of that vocation, and with it a commitment. If **Dead Souls** seems colder in its brilliance than any of the previous writings, it is because there alone the values of childhood and free fantasy have virtually no place. An informing nostalgia for the past has yielded to an anxious concern for the future. (p. 246)

The problematic nature of identity is, as Karlinsky puts it, ''*the* theme'' in Gogol. It operates consistently in his work on a whole series of levels, from the incidental (the civil servant who is at the same time a civil servant and an oboe in ''**Nevsky Prospect**'') to the global. That very consistency is an identifying feature of Gogol's created universe—which is to say, of his own created identity—and a key to the radical peculiarity of both.

At its most explicit the theme is represented by all those works which center on mistaken identity—first of all by the Gogolian army of impostors and impersonators who swarm out of the puppet-theater tradition and folklore through the Dikanka stories and appear, somewhat further evolved, in ''**Viy**'' and ''**The Portrait.**'' In all such cases changes of identity are clearly motivated, the merely ostensible ones psychologically and the literal ones supernaturally. (pp. 247-48)

Gogol's characters have an unquestionable individuality, and yet, by the inclusive standards of ''normal'' fiction, they are neither fully complete nor fully human—not plenipotentiary and not persons. Something is missing. They seem to lack a center of gravity . . .—or else to lack all flexibility of response, appearing as blinkered monomaniacs. The individuality in either case is unaccountably stunted and, though vivid, defies empathetic understanding. Gogol lays repeated stress on the last point while remaining ostensibly unconscious of the first. Not a voice in his textual world (not even the narrator's) represents a stable norm; the very Gogolian consistency of that world arises from the careful reader's bafflement in the face of an oddly limited, though verbally lively scene populated and presented by the oddly lobotomized.

What is in question here is the peculiar nature of identity—which is to say, of character—as represented in Gogol's writing. It may be approached first of all in terms of *function*. Because the Gogolian character is not the agent of a plot whose unfolding and resolution might represent value in itself, his actions have no constitutive value; they are secondary. (p. 249)

The image of marionettes—a recurrent one in Gogol criticism—suggests that the puzzling incompleteness of Gogolian characters may come from their existing on the borderline of two semiotic systems, appearing now as creatures of the one, now of the other, much as puppets depend for their effect on seeming to be both human and nonhuman. Their speech—and the psychological impulses that provide its themes and energy—is individual, suggestive, and quasi-realistic in its colloquialism. But the larger individuality that would normally be signaled is absent; they are fashioned psychically in just the way (the way of caricature) that Sobakevich is said to have been fashioned physically: a few broad strokes and, without further ado, they are set in motion with the exclamation: "It lives!" For this the author is responsible, as Gogol repeatedly and artfully underlines. Yet the author has taken unusual pains to baffle any quest for a clear intentionality in his text.

His works thus do and do not exist to exhibit character, just as they do and do not make use of character to convey a message. They are all in this sense trials of the word, exercises in poetic mastery whose success is to be gauged simply by the way they make readers exclaim, "It lives!" The Gogolian character takes on his peculiarity from his participation in the Gogolian enterprise. Like the works that contain him, he is an episode in an arrested evolution. The problem of his identity is inseparable from the problem of narrative and authorial identity (the first consistently masked, the second consistently evaded); that is why the texts insist on it. The reader's problem is to find a point of view adequate to comprehend the sustained exhibition of creatures more than half mired in solipsism. And that problem too—of the perceiver and the perceived—is encoded within the text.

Motifs of vision play a central role in Gogol's creations from first to last, most strikingly in the early works where the supernatural and the uncanny dominate. Not only do annihilating glances seal the doom of Khoma Brut in **"Viy"** and of Chartkov in **"The Portrait."** Lightning darts regularly from the eyes of young beauties, signaling the ineffable, intolerable, and indescribable. In **"Woman,"** the first publication to be signed with Gogol's name, it is said of Alkinoya that "the lightning of her eyes wrenched loose one's whole soul." . . . (pp. 251-52)

The threat of the identifying look . . . is ubiquitous in Gogol's poetic universe. Narration itself is responsive to that threat; hence those ingenious shifts by which the narrative voice, for all its ironic use of the pronoun "I," nonetheless eludes identification. At the origin of the Gogolian creation and pervading it is an impulse to simultaneous exhibition and concealment which may best be understood in light of Sartre's disquisition on *le regard d'autrui* [the look of Other]. In Sartre's terms the sense of self in solitude is a sense of free possibility which is condensed and narrowed into self-consciousness when it is made an object by "the look of the Other": The Other, as perceiving glance, "transcends my transcendence." "In order for me to be what I am, it suffices merely that the Other look at me. My transcendence becomes for whoever makes himself a witness of it a purely established transcendence, a given-transcendence; that is, it acquires a nature by the sole fact that the *Other* confers on it an outside. To apprehend myself as seen is, in fact, to apprehend myself as seen *in the world* and from the standpoint of the world. Thus I, who in so far as I am my possibles, am what I am not and not what I am—behold now I *am* somebody." The perceiving Other thus represents "the hidden death of my possibilities." (pp. 255-56)

Gogol's pride and sustaining faith attached precisely to his possibilities, [and] constantly he expressed fear of premature identification and judgment, insisting that his existence as a writer was a riddle whose solution lay in a constantly receding future. The early pseudonyms, like the habitual disowning of all his work to date, give clear evidence of what was at once a psychological complex in his life and, more importantly, a shaping principle of the creation that dwarfed it. Rejecting recognition of anything other than his possibilities, Gogol was, as it were, warding off the Medusa glance that might freeze him en route to their realization. His best art does the same thing, proclaiming a self-sufficiency that seems by turns absolute and provisional. (p. 256)

*Donald Fanger, in his* The Creation of Nikolai Gogol *(copyright © 1979 by the President and Fellows of Harvard College; excerpted by permission), Cambridge, Mass.: Belknap Press, 1979, 300 p.*

---

## ADDITIONAL BIBLIOGRAPHY

Brasol, Boris. *The Mighty Three: Poushkin, Gogol, Dostoievsky; A Critical Trilogy.* New York: William Farquhar Payson, 1934, 295 p.*
	An examination of Gogol and two of his literary ancestors.

Debreczeny, Paul. "Nikolay Gogol and His Contemporary Critics." *American Philosophical Society* 56, No. 3 (1966): 5-68.
	A detailed summary of the criticism written on Gogol's work up to 1848. Most of the criticism referred to is in Russian.

Driessen, F. C. *Gogol as a Short-Story Writer: A Study of His Technique of Composition.* Translated by Ian F. Finlay. The Hague: Mouton & Co., 1965, 243 p.
	A critical guide to all the stories, including detailed plot summaries and listings of major themes.

Du Puy, Ernest, "Gogol." In his *The Great Masters of Russian Literature in the Nineteenth Century,* translated by Nathan Haskell Dole, pp. 5-115. New York: Thomas Y. Crowell & Co., 1886.
	An appraisal of Gogol and his work. Du Puy identifies dreaminess and banter as the two favored pleasures of Russians and the two elements of Gogol's talent. Because of this, Du Puy believes that Gogol is Russia's most patriotic and beloved author.

Eichenbaum, Boris. "How Gogol's 'Overcoat' Is Made." In *Gogol from the Twentieth Century: Eleven Essays,* edited and translated by Robert A. Maguire, pp. 267-92. Princeton: Princeton University Press, 1974.
	A structural analysis of "The Overcoat."

Erlich, Victor. *Gogol.* New Haven and London: Yale University Press, 1969, 230 p.
	A valuable general study of Gogol's life and works, designed to provide a complete survey for the English-speaking reader of Gogol.

Kayser, Wolfgang. "The Grotesque in the Nineteenth Century." In his *The Grotesque in Art and Literature,* translated by Ulrich Weisstein, pp. 100-29. New York, Toronto: McGraw-Hill Book Co., 1957.*
	Discusses the grotesque elements in "The Overcoat" and "Diary of a Madman."

Lavrin, Janko. *Gogol.* London, New York: George Routledge & Sons, 1925, 263 p.
	A biographical and critical appreciation of Gogol's life and works. Lavrin states that his objective is "to introduce to English readers a great and complex foreign author in as simple terms as possible."

Lavrin, Janko. *Nikolai Gogol (1809-1852): A Centenary Survey.* London: Sylvan Press, 1951, 174 p.
	An appreciation of Gogol on the hundredth anniversary of his death.

Magarshack, David. *Gogol: A Life*. London: Faber and Faber, 1957, 329 p.
  A biographical study which emphasizes Gogol's artistic development. Magarshack includes a number of reminiscences by Gogol's contemporaries.

Muchnic, Helen. *The Unhappy Consciousness: Gogol, Poe, Baudelaire*. Northampton, Mass.: Smith College, 1967, 22 p.*
  A consideration of the unhappy consciousness as a unifying factor in the works of Gogol, Edgar Allan Poe, and Charles Baudelaire. According to Muchnic, the unhappy consciousness is "the alienated soul which is the consciousness of self as a divided nature."

Noyes, G. R. "Gogol: A Precursor of Modern Realist Russia." *The Nation* CI, No. 2629 (18 November 1915): 592-94.
  A brief survey of Gogol's contribution toward literary realism in Russia. Noyes briefly likens Gogol to Mark Twain and O. Henry, and identifies Gogol's creation of "clear, distinct characters" as the basis of his genius.

Proffer, Carl R. *The Simile and Gogol's "Dead Souls"*. The Hague, Paris: Mouton, 1967, 206 p.
  A detailed study of *Dead Souls* and its literary and stylistic devices.

Rowe, William Woodin. *Through Gogol's Looking Glass: Reverse Vision, False Focus, and Precarious Logic*. New York: New York University Press, 1976, 201 p.
  An examination of Gogol's creative process. Rowe emphasizes the world of vision and perception in Gogol's writings.

Slonim, Marc. "Gogol." In his *The Epic of Russian Literature: From Its Origins through Tolstoy*, pp. 159-81. New York: Oxford University Press, 1950.
  A study of Gogol's development as a man and as a writer.

Slonim, Marc. "Gogol and the Natural School." In his *An Outline of Russian Literature*, pp. 57-70. New York, London: Oxford University Press, 1958.
  Places Gogol historically within the Naturalist tradition.

Slonimsky, Alexander. "The Technique of the Comic in Gogol." In *Gogol from the Twentieth Century: Eleven Essays*, edited and translated by Robert A. Maguire, pp. 323-73. Princeton: Princeton University Press, 1974.
  An essay which analyzes the comic devices in Gogol's work.

Stilman, Leon. "The 'All-Seeing Eye' in Gogol." In *Gogol from the Twentieth Century: Eleven Essays*, edited and translated by Robert A. Maguire, pp. 376-89. Princeton: Princeton University Press, 1974.
  An analysis of visual themes in Gogol's writing.

Tsanoff, Radoslav Andrea. "The Russian Soil and Nikolai Gogol." *The Rice Institute Pamphlet* IV, No. 2 (April 1917): 121-43.
  Identifies Gogol as the first great analyst of the Russian soul, and Russia's finest humorist. The critic asserts that Gogol is responsible for the integration of realism into Russian literature.

Worrall, Nick. *Nikolai Gogol and Ivan Turgenev*. New York: Grove Press, 207 p.*
  A comparison of the dramas of Gogol and Turgenev, with particular emphasis on *The Inspector General*. Worrall includes an extensive critical bibliography.

# Jupiter Hammon

## 1711?-1800?

American poet and essayist.

Although Phillis Wheatley was long regarded as America's first black author, twentieth-century scholarship has now determined that Hammon was the first black American whose work appeared in print. His first poem, *An Evening Thought: Salvation by Christ, with Penetential Cries*, appeared in 1761 and antedates Wheatley's verse by at least nine years. Hammon's essays and poems were issued on broadsides, large sheets of paper printed on only one side. His best known work, *An Address to the Negroes in the State of New-York*, promises a just spiritual reward for obedient slaves, depicting a heaven where white masters and black slaves will be judged as equals.

Hammon's birthdate is now considered to be October 11, 1711, though many sources place his birth nearly ten years later. He was born a slave on the estate of Henry Lloyd on Long Island, and served that family for three generations. As a household slave, Hammon was given many privileges not available to other slaves. He attended primary school with Lloyd's children and learned to read and write. In 1733, Hammon purchased a Bible from Mr. Lloyd and began the religious studies which greatly influenced both his poetry and prose. The inspirational hymns of Charles Wesley, John Newton, and William Cowper also profoundly affected Hammon's verse. *An Evening Thought*, which strongly resembles eighteenth-century devotional hymns, reflects Hammon's evangelical preoccupation with salvation, righteousness, and eternal life.

After the death of Henry Lloyd in 1763, Hammon became the property of Lloyd's son Joseph, who fled with his family to Connecticut when the British took control of Long Island. In Hartford, Hammon produced four works, the most noteworthy being *An Address to Miss Phillis Wheatly* [*sic*]. Printed in 1778, this poem suggests that Wheatley's enslavement in Ethiopia, arrival in America, and conversion to Christianity were the product of divine will. The other works printed during Hammon's years in Connecticut include two essays which are commonly referred to as sermons: *An Essay on the Ten Virgins*, of which no known copy exists, and *A Winter Piece: Being a Serious Exhortation, with a Call to the Unconverted, and a Short Contemplation on the Death of Jesus Christ*, which illustrates Hammon's views on death. A third essay, *An Evening's Improvement: Shewing the Necessity of Beholding the Lamb of God*, was also printed in Hartford. It includes a dialogue in verse, entitled *The Kind Master and Dutiful Servant*, which recommends that all slaves show dutiful servitude.

Following the death of Joseph, Hammon returned to Long Island as the property of Joseph's nephew, John Lloyd, Jr. Hammon produced only one work after his return to the Lloyd estate, although it is possible that other pages of manuscript were never discovered. *An Address to the Negroes in the State of New-York* became Hammon's most popular piece. Two editions were issued during his life, and a third was published by members of the Pennsylvania Society for Promoting the Abolition of Slavery, after Hammon's death.

Although he was the first black American author, Hammon is not widely known. Many critics find his syntax weak and his use of language and theme repetitive. Still others feel that his verse is forced and imperfect in meter and rhyme. The primary reason for Hammon's obscurity, however, is most likely what Vernon Loggins calls his "conciliatory attitude towards slavery." Hammon was not an avid abolitionist, although he did urge manumission, or the emancipation of black children and adolescents, in his *An Address to the Negroes in the State of New-York*. Hammon himself, however, preferred to remain in servitude. Citing his advancing age, he stated that he "should hardly know how to take care of [himself] . . .". This view most likely discouraged the acceptance which would have saved Hammon's works from virtual obscurity.

While he is still little known today, Hammon remains important as the first black American author to appear in print. His primitive verses are considered the forerunners of Negro spirituals and abolitionist dialogues. After more than a century of neglect, twentieth-century critics now are beginning to assess Hammon's contribution to early black American literature.

## PRINCIPAL WORKS

*An Evening Thought: Salvation by Christ, with Penetential Cries* (poetry) 1761
*An Address to Miss Phillis Wheaty* [*sic*] (poetry) 1778
*An Essay on the Ten Virgins* (essay) 1779
\**A Winter Piece: Being a Serious Exhortation, with a Call to the Unconverted, and a Short Contemplation on the Death of Jesus Christ* (essay and poetry) 1782
*An Evening's Improvement: Shewing the Necessity of Beholding the Lamb of God. The Kind Master and Dutiful Servant* (essay and poetry) 1783?
*An Address to the Negroes in the State of New-York* (essay) 1787
*America's First Negro Poet: The Complete Works of Jupiter Hammon of Long Island* (essays and poetry) 1970

\*This work includes *A Poem for Children, with Thoughts on Death*.

---

## OSCAR WEGELIN (essay date 1915)

[*Wegelin is responsible for bringing to light Hammon's "An Evening Thought," thus proving that Hammon predated Phillis Wheatley as the first black American author. Wegelin states that Hammon's work is "commonplace," but stresses that had Hammon received a formal education, he might have "ranked as (Miss Wheatley's) equal if not her superior."*]

As a poet Hammon will certainly not rank among the "Immortals." His verse is stilted, and while some of his rhymings are fairly even, we can easily comprehend that they were written by one not well versed in the art of poesy. They have a sameness which is wearying to the reader and there is too much reiteration, in some cases the same or nearly the same words being employed again and again.

His verse is saturated with a religious feeling not always well expressed, as he did not possess the ability to use the right word at the proper time. Hammon was undoubtedly deeply religious, but his religion was somewhat tinged with narrowness and superstition, a not uncommon fault of the time in which he lived and wrote.

Although grammatically almost perfect, it seems certain that an abler and more experienced hand than his own was responsible for this.

Compared with the verses of Phillis Wheatley, his lines are commonplace and few would care to read them more than once. When we consider, however, that this poor slave had probably no other learning than what he had been enabled to secure for himself during his hours of relaxation from labor, it is surprising that the results are not more meagre. Although his rhymings can hardly be dignified by the name of poetry, they are certainly not inferior to many of the rhymings of his day and generation.

As before noted, his lines breathe a deep religious feeling and were written with the hope that those who would read them would be led from the ways of sin to righteousness. (pp. 19-21)

He was fond of using certain words, and "Salvation" was one of his favorites, it being made use of twenty-three times in his earliest known publication. . . .

Hammon was also fond of using marginal references from Scripture and in some of his writings they are found at every second line. (p. 21)

When we consider that he was probably without any education whatsoever, we marvel that he accomplished as much as he did. Had he had the advantages of learning possessed by Miss Wheatley, it seems possible that as a poet he would have ranked as her equal, if not her superior. His prose writings were also above the mediocre, but from the testimony of one of his printers he was evidently deficient as a speller.

He stands, however, unique in the annals of American Poetry and his works must not be too harshly judged. The disadvantages under which he composed them were probably far greater than we can imagine.

It seems, however, too bad that his verse is entirely of a religious nature. Much would have been added to its interest had he written about some of the events that were transpiring all around him during the War for Independence and the years that followed that struggle.

He seems to have been content to sing the praises of the Master whom he longed to serve and whose reward he some day expected to receive, and with that end in view he labored to instill the blessings of religion into his less fortunate brethren.

For this his memory should be honored and let the broken lines which fell from his pen be cherished, if for no other reason than that they were written by the first American Negro who attempted to give expression to his thoughts in verse. (pp. 21-2)

*Oscar Wegelin, in his* Jupiter Hammon, American Negro Poet: Selections from His Writings and a Bibliography *(reprinted by permission of the Literary Estate of Oscar Wegelin),* C. F. Heartman, 1915

*(and reprinted by Books for Libraries Press, 1969, distributed by Arno Press, Inc.), 51 p.*

**VERNON LOGGINS**   (essay date 1931)

It is an interesting coincidence that most of Hammon's poetry was published at Hartford at a time when that Connecticut town was the literary capital of America. But if the neoclassical "Hartford Wits" [a literary circle which included John Trumbull and Timothy Dwight] read his poems, they no doubt looked upon them as chaotic effusions of crude thoughts poured out in a verse not inappropriate to the cheapest balladry. To the twentieth-century mind, which places a high value on the artlessness of folk poetry, Jupiter Hammon's work takes on a new meaning. There is a strength of wild and native religious feeling in what he wrote, a strength which he achieved without conscious effort. From hearing evangelical sermons and from reading the Bible according to his own untrained fancy, he picked up strange notions regarding salvation, penitential cries, redeeming love, tribunal day, the Holy Word, bounteous mercies. His mystic Negro mind played with these notions; and, endowed with the instinct for music which is so strong in his race, he sang out his impressions in such meters as he had become familiar with in the hymns of Charles Wesley and Augustus Montague Toplady, and in such rimes as for the moment pleased his ear. Indeed, his method of composition must have been that of the unknown makers of the spirituals.

Like the spirituals, the poems of Jupiter Hammon were composed to be heard. There is evident in his verse that peculiar sense for sound which is the most distinguishing characteristic of Negro folk poetry. A word that appeals to his ear he uses over and over again, in order, it seems, to cast a spell with it. In *An Evening Thought* the word *salvation* occurs in every three or four lines. Any impressionable sinners who might have heard Jupiter Hammon chant the poem when in the ecstasy of religious emotion no doubt went away to be haunted by the sound of the word *salvation* if not by the idea. . . . [The] metrical arrangement is that of the ballad stanza with alternating rimes, a verse form which is often found in the early Methodist hymns. . . . Hammon followed this pattern in all of his poems, though not without marked irregularities. There are numerous cases of wrenched accents demanding an outrageous pronunciation. . . . [The] most interesting irregularities are the strange rime combinations—such as, *word* and *God, Lord* and *God, call* and *soul, sound* and *down.* Since we know little about how English was spoken by the Negroes on Long Island in the eighteenth century, we cannot determine how far astray Jupiter Hammon's ear was in hearing exact rimes in such combinations. We can say with definiteness that the riming words which he selected are always sonorous.

While the imagery in Hammon's poems is in general restrained, often taken bodily from the New Testament, there are unexpected turns in the thought which suggest the wild extravagance of the spiritual. The unusual association of ideas in the following stanza from *An Address to Miss Phillis Wheatly* is probably the result of a necessity for rimes:

> God's tender mercy brought thee here;
>    Tost o'er the raging main;
> In Christian faith thou hast a share,
>    Worth all the gold of Spain.

(pp. 11-13)

It must not be supposed that Jupiter Hammon was only primitive and naïve, merely a folk poet incapable of consistent and orderly reflection. *An Address to Miss Phillis Wheatly,* his second poem, written eighteen years after his first spontaneous and chaotic effort, *An Evening Thought,* shows a balanced structure of ideas. . . . Both this poem and "A Poem for Children with Thoughts on Death" are provided with scriptural glosses, and in each the thought association with the Biblical citations is fairly logical and exact. While the two earlier prose pamphlets, *A Winter Piece* and *An Evening's Improvement,* intended as sermons, are rhapsodic and incoherent, the *Address to the Negroes in the State of New-York* displays a regular and firm organization. (pp. 14-15)

[However, Hammon's] attempts at thoughtful composition, such as *An Address to the Negroes in the State of New-York,* fall low in the class of the subliterary. It is his poetry, with all of its artlessness and crudeness, which makes his name important. As the product of the uncultivated Negro imagination and temperament, his verse, slight as the body of it is, forms a unique contribution to American poetry in the eighteenth century. The reader of today is likely to find a more sincere feeling in it than in most religious verse written in America during Hammon's age. It is a quaint prelude to the rich and varied songs which were to burst spontaneously from the Negro folk a little later, songs which make up the great gift from Africa to the art of America. (pp. 15-16)

> *Vernon Loggins, "The Beginnings of Negro Authorship, 1760-1790," in his* The Negro Author: His Development in America to 1900 *(copyright 1931, 1959; Columbia University Press; reprinted by permission of the publisher), Columbia University Press, 1931 (and reprinted by Kennikat Press, Inc., 1964), pp. 1-47.\**

## J. SAUNDERS REDDING   (essay date 1939)

[Hammon's] verse is rhymed prose, doggerel, in which the homely thoughts of a very religious and superstitious man are expressed in limping phrases. Now and then his lines have a lyric swing that seems to mark them as having been chanted spontaneously in the sermons he preached. Undoubtedly some lines from "An Evening Thought" have this lyric significance. The alternately rhyming lines lend themselves very easily and nicely to religious chanting. (pp. 4-5)

Of the work of this kind, the piece addressed to Phillis Wheatley is the best. (p. 5)

On the whole, Hammon's untutored art offered but narrow scope for the fullest expression. His most substantial contribution to Negro literature prior to the Civil War is in prose, and whatever of literary merit he possessed must be looked for in his single prose piece, "An Address to the Negroes in the State of New York." This work reveals more of Hammon's workaday character than all his poetry together. The thoughts expressed in "An Address to Negroes" are not typical of the thoughts of slaves, especially those who were unfortunate enough to have had some education. (p. 6)

Hammon's life was motivated by the compulsion of obedience to his earthly and his heavenly master. Perhaps the inevitability of his position tended to wilt his moral fiber. Perhaps the beneficence of his masters lightened the burden of his bondage. Though he was the first Negro slave to publish an adverse opinion on the institution of slavery, his opinion was robbed of its force by the words "though for my own part I do not wish to be free." Perhaps it was the very weakness of the statement that recommended it for publication. (p. 7)

As to literary values, there is not much to choose between Hammon's poetry and prose. Though he was not without the romantic gift of spontaneity, he lacked any knowledge of metrics and sought only to make rhymes. In prose the artlessness of his construction, the rambling sentences, the repetitions reveal, sometimes at the expense of thought, his not unattractive personality. When he is most lucid there is force in the quaintness of his thought evocative of the highly personal flavor of early American letters. (p. 8)

> *J. Saunders Redding, "The Forerunners: Jupiter Hammon, Phillis Wheatley, George Moses Horton," in his* To Make a Poet Black *(copyright, 1939, by The University of North Carolina Press), University of North Carolina Press, 1939, pp. 3-18.\**

## JEAN WAGNER   (essay date 1963)

If the quality of [Jupiter Hammon's] verse were the only criterion we might consign him to oblivion forthwith, for his poems, inspired by the Methodist hymns of the period and taking over their phraseology, are crudely composed. Yet Hammon deserves mention above all for his first poem, "An Evening Thought: Salvation by Christ with Penitential Cries" . . . , which is very close in tone to folk poetry. It represents a halfway stage between the guileless art of the unknown composers of spirituals and the already much wordier manner of the black popular preacher. . . . [Hammon] can readily be imagined using this poem to appeal to his fellows, until the sonorous repetition of the word "salvation" at regular intervals finally stirs the rhythm that has so often channeled the religious emotions of Negroes. . . . A shifting of tonic accents and even bold syncopations characterize a poem destined to be heard rather than seen and read. Employing a subtle, complex rhythm, the preacher's voice brings the verse to life, and so he can with impunity set aside the traditional rules of prosody. Hammon probably relied on the extraordinary precision of his auditory sensibility, while remaining unaware of the process. Yet his experiment should be borne in mind, for the black poets of the twentieth century will take it up again.

One can find much less to praise in Jupiter Hammon's religious fervor, which overlaid a strange torpor in his racial sensitivity. For here we are confronted with a neophyte who has been carefully indoctrinated by his entourage and whom kindly treatment has rendered docile. He ultimately ceases even to long for the future restoration of his freedom. More curious still are his endeavors to lull to sleep the same desire in his fellow slaves by turning their thoughts away from terrestrial realities and directing them toward the joys of eternity. In "The Kind Master and Dutiful Servant," basically a dialogue on salvation and God's mercy, the great gap that separates master and slave is conscientiously insisted upon, on the lines of the "aristocratic contempt for the sodden mass of the people," a feature of the Calvinistic outlook that Hammon adopted with a somewhat naïve enthusiasm. . . . (pp. 17-18)

This passiveness and resignation obscure the genuineness of Hammon's religiosity, so that today we view his Christian faith as something alien to him. His morality also remains undeveloped, and seemingly restricted to Saint Paul's admonition: "Slaves, obey your masters!" He lets fall not a word that might be taken to criticize slavery, in which he sees only the manifestation of divine foresight and mercy. Thus the deportation of Africans to America becomes a kind of providential pilgrimage toward knowledge of the one true God. (pp. 18-19)

*Jean Wagner, in his introduction to his* Black Poets of the United States: From Paul Laurence Dunbar to Langston Hughes, *translated by Kenneth Douglas (copyright 1973 by The Board of Trustees of the University of Illinois; reprinted by permission of the author; originally published as* Les poètes nègres des États-Unis, *Librairie Istra, 1963), University of Illinois Press, 1973, pp. 3-36.*\*

### KENNY J. WILLIAMS (essay date 1970)

Although most of his poetry was published at Hartford at a time when the Hartford Wits were attempting to aid in the creation of a national literature, there is a great deal of difference between any of their works and the existing poems by Hammon. His poetry was not hampered by the rules of neoclassicism as was the work of the Hartford Wits, neither was his poetry pallid imitations of current English modes. Rather, his poetry is closer in spirit and technique to the poetry of the earlier century of New England, the poetry produced by the New England Puritans of the seventeenth century. . . . There is in Hammon's poetry a religious feeling which resulted in an intensity which he apparently achieved without conscious effort. From hearing evangelical sermons and from reading the Bible according to his own interpretations, he adapted his ideas regarding salvation, penitence, redeeming grace, God's mercy, death, and judgment day to his poems. He recorded his ideas and impressions in a poetic meter which is designed to be heard. A word which appealed to him is repeated until the very word itself seems to cast a spell. In **"An Evening Thought . . ."** the word *salvation* appears so often that the sound of the word becomes far more important than the message of the poem. (pp. 10-11)

[In **"An Evening Thought . . . ,"**] Hammon used a variation of the ballad stanza, a verse form which is often found in Methodist and in Baptist hymnals and which is the basic pattern of [Michael Wigglesworth's] *The Day of Doom*. This pattern consists of quatrains whose first and third lines are iambic tetrameter and whose second and fourth lines are iambic trimeter; the four-line stanza has a usual rhyme scheme of abcd. Although Hammon followed this pattern in most of his poems, there are instances of irregularities which can be seen in **"An Evening Thought. . . ."** In addition to his adaptation of the ballad rhyme pattern to abab, there are examples of distorted accents as well as of syncopation which occur most frequently in the iambic trimeter lines. To the twentieth century reader, Hammon's poetry seems similar to so much of eighteenth-century poetry for his work tends to employ unusual rhyming patterns and combinations. . . . When odd uses of poetic diction occur, they often result because his choice of language is an immediate outgrowth of an apparent need for rhyming patterns. (pp. 13-14)

It is apparent that most of Hammon's religious poetry is characterized by a certain naivete, and his art of versification seems little more than spontaneously rhymed doggerel; but this is the same charge which is frequently hurled at Michael Wigglesworth who also used poetry as a means of instruction and as a means of simply stating basic religious concepts. The difference between these two poets, however, rests in the difference between the complexity of the religious dogma of Puritanism which is explained by Wigglesworth and the simplicity of the more primitive forms of Protestantism. In the eighteenth century complexity of dogma and creed was not a characteristic of the Methodist and Baptist movements. . . . These more

primitive groups stressed "religion by faith" as opposed to the Puritan emphasis on "religion by reason." Wigglesworth—for example—in attempting to simplify Puritanism made its doctrines appear harsh and terrible when he placed them into ballad form; while Hammon, on the other hand, in attempting to capture the tone of primitive Christianity, seems extremely childlike in his wonder and in his awe. (pp. 14-15)

Hammon has been condemned because of his acceptance of the institution of slavery; yet, it must be remembered that he was in no position to understand it in its fullest impact. With his limited experiences in Long Island and in Hartford and with his own lot being much better than that of the average workingman of the period, it is no wonder that he tended to place all of his attention on matters of religion. While his poems are far superior to his prose works, his poetry is, after all, eighteenth-century religious poetry and does not differ too greatly from other such works of the period. His infrequent references to slavery and to his race are the only distinguishing marks of his work. The chaos of the rhythmic structure and the distortions of rhyme which appear, the sudden bursts of religious fervor, the sometimes strained poetic diction coupled with apparent sincerity are characteristics of religious poetry in America during the seventeenth and eighteenth centuries. (pp. 16-17)

*Kenny J. Williams, "A New Home in a New Land," in his* They Also Spoke: An Essay on Negro Literature in America, 1787-1930 *(copyright © 1970 by Kenny J. Williams; reprinted by permission of the author), Townsend Press, 1970, pp. 3-49.*\*

### R. RODERICK PALMER (essay date 1974)

Throughout his life, Hammon was able to reach remarkable stages of self-awareness and self-assertiveness. . . . [First] as a preacher and later as a published poet, Hammon emerged as one of the foremost and influential shapers of non-militant modes of thinking and of religious preoccupations of his people. (pp. 22-3)

In his role as a preacher, Hammon was an anathema to certain militants of his race because of his personal satisfaction in the role that he played as a pacifier and because of the proclamations of subservience that he promulgated. His exhortations, poetic in nature, decreed that the black race should endure its bondage humbly and patiently until it earned its freedom by honesty and good conduct. Hammon never advocated violence or any other militant acts to gain freedom or liberty. (p. 24)

Literary analysis of two famous Hammon sermons based on the Scriptures, **"A Winter's Piece"** and **"An Evening's Improvement,"** reveals typical patterning of simple, pedantic 18th century style. The writing is characterized by omniscient predictions and prophetic declarations, encouched in long, verbose sentences with faulty syntax. Use of archaisms, extra letters in words, a plethora of dashes and capital letters, and numerous sentence fragments further describe Hammon's rhetorical style. The prose is, at best, mediocre. The critic will readily admit, however, that the writing is simple and was no doubt easily understood by Hammon's followers. (p. 25)

Due to his fondness for preaching, the major portion, if not all, of Hammon's poetry is religious in tone and is usually dismissed by critics as being of little aesthetic value. His poetry, however, is filled with didacticisms and aphorisms. . . . [In **"An Evening Thought"**, the] reader becomes immediately aware of the contrived and forced rhymes and the poor quality of the verse patterns, which are archetypes of the early Methodist hymns. In fair appraisal, however, the critic simultaneously sees in the poet's crudely penned lines folksy themes that depict the mores of a people who envisioned a life lived righteously "on this side of Jordan" would reap rich rewards on the other side. (pp. 25-6)

Eighteen years after Hammon's first verses appeared in print, a poem entitled "A Poetical Address to Phillis Wheatley, Ethiopian Poetess," reached the reading public. . . .

In this and in all of his other poems, there are marked irregularities. The omission at times of one syllable and at other times two seems to mar the poetic line. Yet these profuse examples of syncopation, so characteristic of Negro dance rhythms, are fascinating. The stanzaic form is quatrain and the dominant metrical pattern is iambic tetrameter. Such prosody provides facile reading and almost puerile comprehension. (p. 26)

Hammon's style [in "The Kind Master and the Dutiful Servant"] is conversational in tone. Like others, this poem and especially "A Poem for Children with Thoughts of Death" are meant to touch the heart strings with repetitions, predictable rhymes, and uncomplicated structures. All of the subject matter is basically religious with intent to move the heart and spirit, not the mind nor the muscle. It is surprising that in all of his writings the reader is unable to find one statement abhoring slavery and the deprivations of the black people of his era. (p. 27)

Today, readers of Hammon's poetry and prose, in their benignancy, will surely admit that the poet possessed a workable knowledge of 18th century writing styles despite the simplistic quality of his productivity. Readers will concur, too, that his emotional involvement with religion, to the point where it approaches intoxication, as one critic puts it, was so intense that the words and the expressions are forced into verse mold almost as a procrustean endeavor.

Personally, I feel, however, that as a product of the uncultivated Negro imagination and temperament, Hammon's writing, sparse as it is and undistinguished, forms an uncommon contribution to American belles-lettres of the 18th century because of its simplicity and its honesty. (p. 28)

*R. Roderick Palmer, "Jupiter Hammon's Poetic Exhortations," in* CLA Journal *(copyright, 1974 by the College Language Association; used by permission of The College Language Association), Vol. XVIII, No. 1, September, 1974, pp. 22-8.*

## WRITING ABOUT BLACK LITERATURE    (essay date 1976)

*[The following was written by an unidentified student of Chester J. Fontenot, Jr., who revised the piece for publication in* Writing about Black Literature. *The critic's opinion represents a sharp contrast to the opinion of Bernard W. Bell (see excerpt below, 1977), who maintains that "An Evening Thought" reveals Hammon's personal resignation to slavery. According to the author of this essay, Hammon "uses ambiguous language and symbols to create a poem which subtly protests against . . . (slavery)."]*

In "An Evening Thought" Jupiter Hammon uses ambiguous language and symbols to create a poem which subtly protests against the inhuman conditions which slavery created. Hammon's language is characterized by the repetitive use of words such as "thy," "only," and "true," to suggest an emphasis on salvation from God and opposed to the corrupted version of salvation the slavemaster offered, and by the use of ambig-

uous words such as "salvation," "king," "spirit," "preparation," and "nation." These characteristics lead one to think that Hammon's poem has a dual quality: (1) on the surface the poem seems to be addressed to those who either are sinners, or who are simply misled by false versions of salvation; (2) on another level, the poem seems to be addressed to the slaves in an attempt to move them from a passive stance with regards to the master to an active, rebellion's position. (p. 116)

Hammon begins "An Evening Thought" by introducing the reader to the concept of salvation. He says, "Salvation comes by Christ alone! The only Son of God." The concept of salvation here is ambiguous—with the knowledge that Hammon was a slave, one might conclude that he is talking about salvation in two senses: (1) as a transcendence from the secular world; and (2) as an escape from slavery. If we place emphasis on certain words in the first two lines of the poem (alone and only), we can see that the second sense of salvation may be the one that Hammon is talking about here. . . . Hammon continues his usage of ambiguous language in lines 4-8; they read as follows:

> Dear Jesus we would fly to thee,
> And leave off every sin,
> Thy tender mercy well agree,
> Salvation from our King

I think that by using the word "we," Hammon is talking about slaves. The metaphor he uses to suggest union with Christ—"we would fly to thee"—implies freedom from bondage of some sort. Hammon's use of "sin" is also ambiguous. Sin can mean two things here: (1) the original sin which all men are *born* with; and (2) the sin of being *born* black. I think Hammon is using sin in the latter sense. His use of "King" to suggest both God and the slavemaster here is important. "King" suggests the slavemaster because Hammon says, "Salvation from our King." This is an ambiguous line: It can mean that God will give man salvation, or that the slaves need to be saved from the slavemaster. (pp. 116-17)

Hammon shifts his stance from that of mediator between God and slaves (or mankind) to that of a slave. He says:

> We cry as sinners to the Lord
> Salvation to obtain
> It is firmly fixt his holy word,
> Ye shall not cry in vain

The significance of this shift is that Hammon moves the poem from a critique of social conditions to an appeal to the slaves for insurrectionary action. Again, Hammon emphasizes "We cry as sinners to the Lord," as opposed to an appeal for freedom to the slavemaster. . . .

Hammon's appeal though does not seem to be in the form of a passive prayer, but of an invocation of the "nations" for action. He asks God to "turn our dark benighted souls; / Give us a true motion." One might ask here if the souls are "dark" and "benighted" because of their sins, or because of the color of their skins? If we assume the latter choice, it seems that Hammon is calling for inspiration—divine or otherwise—for all himself and other slaves to plot their paths to freedom. Hammon's language suggests freedom. He says, "O let our prayers ascend on high." The notion of upward movement combined with his previous use of the metaphor suggesting flight ("Dear Jesus we would fly to thee"), suggest transformation of social conditions and not transcendance to another ethereal world. (p. 118)

Hammon seems to write as if [a] revolution is occurring while he is writing his poem. He says . . . , "Lord unto whom now shall we go, / Or see a safe Abode." These two lines imply that the slaves are searching for alternatives to slavery (perhaps that they are considering escape by means of the underground railroad). "Unto whom now shall we go," and "safe abode," seem to suggest that the slaves are searching for a plan for escape, perhaps even for places and people to aide them in their escape. In any case, these two lines are illusions to escape from slavery by some means.

Hammon also tries to reverse the stereotypical image of the black person as damned, as not fit to sit in the presence of the Lord. He does this by referring to the slaves as "Blessed of the Lord," and by insisting that their "souls are fit for Heaven." He asks that the slaves accept the true Word of God, and that they move toward an acknowledgment of their plight. (p. 119)

Hammon's use of ambiguous language and symbols gives this poem a dual quality. I think that the poem is addressed to slaves. Hammon uses dual language and symbols to mask his intentions from the slaveholders. The poem is, only superficially, addressed to believers in Christianity who are in need of salvation. (pp. 119-20)

> "'An Evening Thought' As a Protest Poem," in *Writing about Black Literature, edited by Chester J. Fontenot, Jr. (copyright 1976 Chester J. Fontenot, Jr.; reprinted by permission of the editor), Nebraska Curriculum Development Center, 1976, pp. 116-20.*

## BERNARD W. BELL (essay date 1977)

In the case of Jupiter Hammon, we see the influence of the Bible and slavery in shaping an otherworldly view of liberty and equality that distorted his social vision. (p. 176)

Lacking the originality, ironic tension, graphic imagery, and call and response pattern of black American spirituals, [*An Evening Thought*] reveals Hammon's personal resignation to slavery and the inspiration of the Psalms and Methodist hymnals. . . .

The repetition of "Salvation" in twenty-three of the poem's eighty-eight lines does not significantly elevate the prosaic quality of the verse. (p. 177)

Hammon's unimaginative use of the meter, rhyme, diction, and stanzaic pattern of the Methodist hymnal combined with the negative image of Africa and conciliatory tone of [his] early poems reveal the poet's limitations and the costly sociopsychological price he paid for the mere semblance of cultural assimilation. . . .

The lessons of the Bible and slavery had taught him that for body and soul, black and white, individual and nation, freedom was God's alone to grant. (p. 178)

Hammon's reference to himself and his people as "Africans by nation" [in *A Winter Piece*] reflects his awareness of the duality of his identity, a duality he unfortunately sought to transcend rather than synthesize through religiosity. Appended to the sermon is the seventeen quatrain *Poem for Children with Thoughts of Death* as further testimony to the poet's piety.

The sermon and poem believed to have been written soon after *A Winter Piece* contain references to "the Present War." In *An Evening's Improvement. Shewing the Necessity of beholding the Lamb of God . . .* Hammon is true to his apolitical, religious philosophy of life. . . . [In] the second half of **"A Dialogue**

**Intitled the Kind Master and the Dutiful Servant,"** the two-page poem concluding the sermon, the poet stands above [a] battle praying for peace. . . . Banal, bloodless, unoriginal, and nonracial, these lines on Christian virtue tell us as much about the theology whites imposed on colonial blacks as they do about Hammon's warped sense of identity and poetry.

The most decisive evidence of the poet-preacher's exploitation by those who found his religious convictions a model for African-American character and behavior is found in Hammon's final discourse, *An Address to the Negroes of the State of New York.* . . . With an uncommon if not unnatural faith in God and white people, whose sinful habits, he believed, did not in God's eyes and his own condone the slaves, Hammon preaches against the sins of disobedience, stealing, lying, swearing, and idleness. Consciousness of the irony of his people's oppression by those who had waged a costly and bloody war to end their own oppression is expressed but quickly suppressed by personal resignation to slavery and otherworldliness. . . . Jupiter Hammon's importance as a poet is essentially historical and sociological, for his blind faith in the benevolence of whites and the kingdom of heaven is a vivid illustration of the ambiguous political role of too many early African-American integrationist writers and preachers whose double-consciousness was both a blessing and a curse in the struggle of blacks for independence. (pp. 179-80)

> *Bernard W. Bell, "African-American Writers," in* American Literature, 1764-1789: The Revolutionary Years, *edited by Everett Emerson (copyright © 1977 The Regents of the University of Wisconsin System), The University of Wisconsin Press, 1977, pp. 171-94.**

---

## ADDITIONAL BIBLIOGRAPHY

Baker, Houston A., Jr. "Terms for Order: Acculturation, Meaning, and the Early Record of the Journey." In his *The Journey Back: Issues in Black Literature and Criticism,* pp. 1-26. Chicago: The University of Chicago Press, 1980.*
  Addresses the role of religion in Hammon's poetry. Baker maintains that it is used as a means of conforming to and surviving in eighteenth-century white society.

Brawley, Benjamin. "The Pioneers." In his *The Negro Genius: A New Appraisal of the Achievement of the American Negro in Literature and the Fine Arts,* pp. 16-31. New York: Dodd, Mead & Co., 1937.*
  Includes a brief account of Hammon's life and works.

Brown, Sterling. "Early American Negro Poetry." In his *Negro Poetry and Drama and the Negro in American Fiction,* pp. 4-14. New York: Atheneum, 1969.*
  Considers the significance of Hammon's verse in the development of black American literature.

Kaplan, Sidney. "The Emergence of Gifts and Powers: Jupiter Hammon." In his *The Black Presence in the Era of the American Revolution: 1770-1800,* pp. 171-80. Greenwich, Conn.: The New York Graphic Society, 1973.
  An overview of Hammon's life and works. Kaplan uses extracts from Hammon's poetry and prose to illustrate the poet's views on slavery and the American Revolution.

Ransom, Stanley Austin. Introduction to *America's First Negro Poet: The Complete Works of Jupiter Hammon of Long Island,* by Jupiter Hammon, edited by Stanley Austin Ransom, pp. 11-19. Port Washington, N.Y.: Kennikat Press, 1970.
  A brief biographical introduction to Hammon and his works. Ransom describes Hammon's poetry as "sincere and enthusiastic,"

and asserts that his later prose ''unquestionably served the cause of freedom'' because it set forth the spiritual equality of master and slave.

Reese, Carolyn. ''From Jupiter Hammon to LeRoi Jones: Our Schools' 'Sins of Omission'.'' *Changing Education*, I, No. 3 (Fall 1966): pp. 30-3, 45.*

Discusses the neglect of black American authors in school curriculums. Reese describes several major groups of black writers and explains their significance to American literature as a whole.

# Jules Laforgue

## 1860-1887

French poet, short story and sketch writer, essayist, and dramatist.

Laforgue was an early experimenter in *vers libre* (free verse). A member of the French Symbolist school, he advocated abandoning popular literary conventions, and maintained that art should be the expression of the subconscious mind. Laforgue's earliest writings, particularly *Le sanglot de la terre*, resemble the poetry of Charles Baudelaire and Walt Whitman. The impressionistic language, fluid metric construction, and vivid imagery of his later works influenced such twentieth-century authors as T. S. Eliot, Ezra Pound, and Hart Crane. His "Pierrot" figure, the white-faced mime, symbolizes humor, fate, and humanity; this character personifies the themes of uncertainty and anguish found throughout Laforgue's poetry and prose. Laforgue is widely recognized for his *Moralités légendaires (Six Moral Tales from Jules Laforgue)*, a collection of short stories which parody famous literary works such as William Shakespeare's *Hamlet*. He is best known, however, for his final poems, published posthumously as *Les derniers vers de Jules Laforgue*, which firmly established his reputation as an initiator of free verse. The experimental rhythmic patterns, psychological realism, and evocative language of *Les derniers vers* provided the Symbolists with a dynamic model for their later, more refined free verse.

Laforgue was born at Montevideo, Uruguay. His father was a poor teacher from Gascony, who in 1866 sent his family to Tarbes, France, where Jules and his brother Émile attended school. Laforgue's memories of the tedious ocean voyage to Tarbes remained vivid throughout his life. It was at this time, Laforgue said later, that he first experienced the restlessness and boredom which plagued him throughout his brief life, and which greatly influenced his work.

Although exceptionally intelligent, Laforgue was a mediocre student at the Lycée Tarbes. "Stéphane Vassiliew," an unpublished short story, is a melodramatic account of Laforgue's experiences at the lycée, and his first attempt at prose. In 1876, he enrolled at the Lycée Fontanes in Paris where, although he liked the school, his work did not improve. Laforgue twice failed his baccalaureate exams, and never received a diploma.

In 1880, while studying art and working as a part-time journalist in Paris, Laforgue met Gustave Kahn, a leader of the Symbolist movement. Kahn, also a poet and editor of the periodical *Le vogue et le symboliste*, became Laforgue's mentor. Laforgue's associations with Kahn, Charles Henry, and the noted literary critic Paul Bourget were the most crucial of his career. With Bourget's help, Laforgue obtained his first job as apprentice poet-critic to Charles Ephrussi. Ephrussi, an impressionist-art collector and editor of the journal *Gazette des beaux-arts*, taught Laforgue much about art and literature and encouraged him to write. Although he generally disliked Laforgue's early, unpublished work, Bourget became Laforgue's personal literary critic during this period, and worked with Laforgue to help him improve his style. Laforgue's early work was also deeply influenced by Arthur Schopenhauer's

pessimistic philosophy and Edward von Hartmann's concept of the unconscious mind. These various influences are evident in *Le sanglot de la terre*, Laforgue's first significant poetic work.

In 1881, Laforgue accepted the position of French-reader and secretary to Empress Augusta of Prussia. For five years he traveled with the Empress and led a luxurious, leisurely life. The position was boring and rigidly-structured, however, and Laforgue did not feel a part of Parisian literary circles. *Les complaintes*, his first poetry to employ the image of the Pierrot, was published during his stay at the Berlin court. Also published during his Berlin service were *L'imitation de notre-dame la lune* and *Le concile féerique*, a verse drama which remained unperformed until four years after Laforgue's death.

Laforgue left the Berlin court in 1886 when he married Leah Lee, an English tutor. The couple moved to Paris, where a particularly harsh winter severely affected Laforgue's health. He wrote for Kahn's periodical *Le vogue*, and tried to find a publisher for *Six Moral Tales*, but was unsuccessful. Supported by loans from Bourget and Ephrussi, money from anonymous donors, and payment by friends for articles which were never published, Laforgue tried in vain to find a way to move to a warmer climate. He continued to write until the opiates given him for his illness left him too weak to eat or work. He died, at the age of twenty-seven, virtually unknown. His *Six Moral Tales,* published within weeks of his death, were immediately acclaimed.

Although Laforgue is not considered the primary initiator of free verse, he figures prominently in its development. Through his manipulation of language, rhythm, and structure, he achieved an unprecedented stylistic freedom. He also combined words from science, medicine, philosophy, and music to achieve the verbal freedom he desired. In *Les derniers vers* his stark, evocative imagery is created through a juxtaposition of common objects and sentimental, romantic ideals. Critics especially praise Laforgue's ability to convey shifting emotions through the use of precise visual imagery.

*Les derniers vers,* the most widely-discussed of Laforgue's works, is a twelve-part poem in which the intricate structure marks a technical achievement uncommon to other early Symbolist literature. According to many critics, the collection reflects an emotional maturity lacking in his earlier works; the lengthy poem displays sensitive insight into the uncertainty and anguish of the speaker's struggle to overcome his alienation from society. While essentially a critical success, *Les derniers vers* has been criticized for its lack of intellectual depth. It is often stated that although *Les derniers vers* is technically superb, the subject matter remains insufficiently developed.

Laforgue's *Six Moral Tales* is also praised for its technical finesse. Widely read after their publication and still popular today, these parodies evince a psychological realism and morality not found in Laforgue's other works. Considered by some to be overly-ornate and insufficiently dramatic, "Hamlet" is still the most popular of the stories and is often discussed by modern critics.

Laforgue's dramas are noteworthy for their influence on later Symbolist poets. *Pierrot fumiste* is a successful blend of mime and dialogue. Although it has never been performed, this satirical drama is noted for its spectacular imagery. His one-act verse drama titled *Le concile féerique* is generally criticized for its lack of characterization and plot. Performed unsuccessfully in 1891, the drama received little critical attention. While neither drama shows emotional or intellectual maturity, their dramatic construction and rhythmic patterns have influenced the works of later writers, most notably Eliot and Pound.

Whether Laforgue died before fully developing his potential is a point which critics continue to debate. Some feel that Laforgue could have eventually become the leader of the Symbolist movement, while others feel that *Les derniers vers* is the fullest possible expression of an important, though limited, genius. It is generally agreed, however, that Laforgue should be remembered for his role in the Symbolist movement and for his bold experiments in free verse.

## PRINCIPAL WORKS

*Les complaintes* (poetry) 1885
*Le concile féerique* [first publication] (verse drama) 1886
*L'imitation de notre-dame la lune* (poetry) 1886
    ["Locutions des Pierrots I, II, III" (partial translation),
    1922; published in journal *Double Dealer*]
*Moralités légendaires* (short stories) 1887
    [*Six Moral Tales from Jules Laforgue,* 1928]
*Les derniers vers de Jules Laforgue* (poetry) 1890
*\*Oeuvres complètes.* 3 vols. (poetry, verse drama, short
    stories, essays, and letters) 1902-03

*Oeuvres complètes.* 6 vols. (poetry, verse drama, short
    stories, journals, essays, letters, and sketches) 1922-
    30
*Lettres à un ami: 1880-1886* (letters) 1941
*Selected Writings of Jules Laforgue* (poetry, short stories,
    essays, letters, and sketches) 1956
*Poems of Jules Laforgue* (poetry) 1958

*This work includes *Le sanglot de la terre, Pierrot fumiste,* and *Mélanges posthumes.*

---

### REMY DE GOURMONT    (essay date 1896-98)

[Laforgue's] was a mind gifted with all the gifts and rich with important acquisitions. With his natural genius made up of sensibility, irony, imagination and clairvoyance, he had wished to nourish it with positive knowledge, all the philosophies, all the literatures, all the images of nature and art; and even the latest views of science seemed to have been familiar to him. He had an ornate flamboyant genius, ready to construct architectural works infinitely diverse and fair, to rear new ogives and unfamiliar domes. . . . (p. 206)

Many of his verses are as though reddened by a glacial affectation of naiveté; they speak of the too dearly cherished child, of the young girl hearkened to—but a sign of a true need of affection and of a pure gentleness of heart,—adolescent of genius who would still have wished to place on the knees of his mother, his "equatorial brow, greenhouse of anomalies." But many have the beauty of purified topazes, the melancholy of opals, the freshness of moonstones, and some . . . have a sad, consoling grace, with eternal avowals: forever on the same subject, Laforgue retells it in such fashion that it seems dreamed and confessed for the first time. And I think that what we must demand of the translator of dreams is, not to wish to fix forever the fugacity of a thought or air, but to sing the song of the present hour with such frank force that it seems the only one we could hear, the only one we could understand. (pp. 206-07)

[Laforgue's *Moralités Legendaires* represents] a literature entirely new and disconcertingly unexpected, giving the curious sensation (specially rare) that we have never read anything like it; the grape with all its velvet hues in the morning light, but with curious reflections and an air as if the seeds within had become frozen by a breath of ironic wind come from some place farther than the pole. (p. 208)

[Laforgue] was of those who ever look forward to finding themselves in their next work, the noble unsatisfied who have too much to say ever to believe that they have said other things than prolegomenae and prefaces. If his interrupted work is but a preface, it belongs to those which counterbalance a finished work. (p. 209)

*Remy de Gourmont, "Laforgue," in his* The Book of Masks, *translated by Jack Lewis (originally published as* Le livre des masques, *1896-98), J. W. Luce and Company, 1921 (and reprinted by Books for Libraries Press, 1967; distributed by Arno Press, Inc.), pp. 205-09.*

## ARTHUR SYMONS (essay date 1908)

*[Symons's* The Symbolist Movement in Literature *was the first book-length study of the Symbolist movement. In one of the earliest considerations of Laforgue's style, Symons points out that Laforgue's work owes "more than anyone has realized to the half-unconscious prose and verse of Rimbaud." Symons claims, however, that although the origins of Laforgue's prose in the* Six Moral Tales *can be found in "the experimental prose of Rimbaud, it carries that manner to perfection." At the root of Laforgue's art Symons finds a "great pity. . .which extends, with the artistic sympathy, through mere clearness of vision, across the world."]*

The prose and verse of Laforgue, scrupulously correct, but with a new manner of correctness, owe more than any one has realised to the half-unconscious prose and verse of Rimbaud. Verse and prose are alike a kind of travesty, making subtle use of colloquialism, slang, neologism, technical terms, for their allusive, their factitious, their reflected meanings, with which one can play, very seriously. The verse is alert, troubled, swaying, deliberately uncertain, hating rhetoric so piously that it prefers, and finds its piquancy in, the ridiculously obvious. It is really *vers libre,* but at the same time correct verse, before *vers libre* had been invented. And it carries, as far as that theory has ever been carried, the theory which demands an instantaneous notation (Whistler, let us say) of the figure or landscape which one has been accustomed to define with such rigorous exactitude. Verse, always elegant, is broken up into a kind of mockery of prose. . . . The old cadences, the old eloquence, the ingenuous seriousness of poetry, are all banished, on a theory as self-denying as that which permitted Degas to dispense with recognisable beauty in his figures. Here, if ever, is modern verse, verse which dispenses with so many of the privileges of poetry, for an ideal quite of its own. It is, after all, a very self-conscious ideal, becoming artificial through its extreme naturalness; for in poetry it is not "natural" to say things quite so much in the manner of the moment, with however ironical an intention.

The prose of the *Moralités Légendaires* is perhaps even more of a discovery. Finding its origin . . . in the experimental prose of Rimbaud, it carries that manner to a singular perfection. Disarticulated, abstract, mathematically lyrical, it gives expression, in its icy ecstasy, to a very subtle criticism of the universe, with a surprising irony of cosmical vision. We learn from books of mediaeval magic that the embraces of the devil are of a coldness so intense that it may be called, by an allowable figure of speech, fiery. Everything may be as strongly its opposite as itself, and that is why this balanced, chill, colloquial style of Laforgue has, in the paradox of its intensity, the essential heat of the most obviously emotional prose. The prose is more patient than the verse, with its more compassionate laughter at universal experience. (pp. 102-05)

In these always "lunar" parodies, *Salomé, Lohengrin, Fils de Parsifal, Persée et Andromède,* each a kind of metaphysical myth, [Laforgue] realises that *la créature va hardiment à être cérébrale, anti-naturelle* [the author is going to be boldly cerebral and anti-natural], and he has invented these fantastic puppets with an almost Japanese art of spiritual dislocation. They are, in part, a way of taking one's revenge upon science, by an ironical borrowing of its very terms, which dance in his prose and verse, derisively, at the end of a string.

In his acceptance of the fragility of things as actually a principle of art, Laforgue is a sort of transformed Watteau, showing his disdain for the world which fascinates him in quite a different way. He has constructed his own world, lunar and actual;

speaking slang and astronomy, with a constant disengaging of the visionary aspect, under which frivolity becomes an escape from the arrogance of a still more temporary mode of being, the world as it appears to the sober majority. He is terribly conscious of daily life, cannot omit, mentally, a single hour of the day; and his flight to the moon is in sheer desperation. He sees what he calls *l'Inconscient* [the unconscious] in every gesture, but he cannot see it without these gestures. And he sees, not only as an imposition, but as a conquest, the possibilities for art which come from the sickly modern being, with his clothes, his nerves: the mere fact that he flowers from the soil of his epoch.

It is an art of the nerves, this art of Laforgue, and it is what all art would tend towards if we followed our nerves on all their journeys. There is in it all the restlessness of modern life, the haste to escape from whatever weighs too heavily on the liberty of the moment, that capricious liberty which demands only room enough to hurry itself weary. It is distressingly conscious of the unhappiness of mortality, but it plays, somewhat uneasily, at a disdainful indifference. And it is out of these elements of caprice, fear, contempt, linked together by an embracing laughter, that it makes its existence. (pp. 106-08)

There is a great pity at the root of this art of Laforgue: self-pity, which extends, with the artistic sympathy, through mere clearness of vision, across the world. . . . In Laforgue, sentiment is squeezed out of the world before one begins to play at ball with it. (pp. 108-09)

He composes love-poems hat in hand, and smiles with an exasperating tolerance before all the transformations of the eternal feminine. He is very conscious of death, but his *blague* of death is, above all things, gentlemanly. He will not permit himself, at any moment, the luxury of dropping the mask: not at any moment. (pp. 109-10)

And yet one realises, if one but reads him attentively enough, how much suffering and despair, and resignation to what is, after all, the inevitable, are hidden away under this disguise, and also why this disguise is possible. Laforgue died at twenty-seven: he had been a dying man all his life, and his work has the fatal evasiveness of those who shrink from remembering the one thing which they are unable to forget. Coming as he does after Rimbaud, turning the divination of the other into theories, into achieved results, he is the eternally grown up, mature to the point of self-negation, as the other is the eternal *enfant terrible.* He thinks intensely about life, seeing what is automatic, pathetically ludicrous in it, almost as one might who has no part in the comedy. He has the double advantage, for his art, of being condemned to death, and of being, in the admirable phrase of Villiers, "one of those who come into the world with a ray of moonlight in their brains." (p. 111)

*Arthur Symons, "Jules Laforgue," in his* The Symbolist Movement in Literature *(reprinted by permission of William Heinemann, Limited), revised edition, Dutton, 1908, pp. 101-11.*

## EZRA POUND (essay date 1917)

*[Most critics agree that Pound was influenced by the works of Laforgue. In this essay, Pound calls Laforgue "an incomparable artist" who was "a master" of "good verbalism, distinct from lyricism or imagism."]*

[Laforgue] is perhaps the most sophisticated of all the French poets, so it is not to be supposed that any wide public has welcomed or will welcome him in England or America. The seven hundred people in both those countries, who have read him with exquisite pleasure, will arise to combat this estimate, but no matter. (p. 281)

Laforgue was a purge and a critic. He laughed out the errors of Flaubert, i.e., the clogging and cumbrous historical detail. He left *Coeur Simple, L'Education, Madame Bovary, Bouvard.* His, Laforgue's, **Salome** makes game of the rest. The short story has become vapid because sixty thousand story writers have all set themselves to imitating De Maupassant, perhaps a thousand from the original.

I think Laforgue implies definitely that certain things in prose were at an end. I think also that he marks the next phase after Gautier in French poetry. It seems to me that without a familiarity with Laforgue one can not appreciate—i.e., determine the value of—certain positives and certain negatives in French poetry since 1890.

He is an incomparable artist. He is, nine-tenths of him, critic— dealing for the most part with literary poses and *clichés,* taking them as his subject matter; and—and this is the important thing when we think of him as a poet—he makes them a vehicle for the expression of his own very personal emotions, of his own unperturbed sincerity. (p. 282)

I do not think one can too carefully discriminate between Laforgue's tone and that of his contemporary French satirists. He is the finest wrought; he is most 'verbalist'. Bad verbalism is rhetoric, or the use of *cliché* unconsciously, or a mere playing with phrases. But there is good verbalism, distinct from lyricism or imagism, and in this Laforgue is a master. He writes not the popular language of any country but an international tongue common to the excessively cultivated. . . . (p. 283)

> *Ezra Pound, "Irony, Laforgue, and Some Satire" (copyright 1918 by Ezra Pound; reprinted by permission of New Directions Publishing Corporation; originally published in* Poetry, *Vol. XI, No. 2, November, 1917), in his* Literary Essays of Ezra Pound, *edited by T. S. Eliot, New Directions, 1954, pp. 280-84.*

## PETER QUENNELL    (essay date 1929)

[*Quennell's* Baudelaire and the Symbolists, *first published in 1929 in a slightly different form, was the first English study of the Symbolist movement to appear after Arthur Symons's* The Symbolist Movement in Literature *(see excerpt above, 1908). In this work, Quennell explores the lives and works of eight Symbolist writers, including Laforgue. He states that Laforgue is "inimitable," but that his success essentially depends upon his "extremely limited swarm of words, busy round an equally limited stock of ideas." Martin Turnell later refuted this view, claiming that Laforgue deliberately employs an elaborate and consistent network of recurring imagery and symbolism (see excerpt below, 1948-49).*]

Jules Laforgue remains, in the truest sense, inimitable. He derived largely—often borrowing and adapting the imagery of his own early productions; for a considerable distance was travelled during the eight or nine years of his poetical life; and the progress of his journey was uninterrupted. He never allowed a procession, so to speak, of unwritten poems, to break the sequence of his written work. The sequence is clear, very clear. An extremely limited swarm of words, busy round an equally

limited stock of ideas—that must be the complaint of his detractors, a half-truth which does not lack significance. Words, images and entire friezes of imagery recur, not once or twice. Thus to limit himself was, I believe, a voluntary condition of his success. (p. 97)

Laforgue the poet and Laforgue the prose-writer are impossible to separate. His ear for the rhythms of prose had been sharpened by writing verse; and there was an endless amusement in the unexpected conjunction of melodious syllables. . . . (p. 105)

With each new effort, the poet tended to epitomize what had gone before. *Le Concile féerique* condensed earlier material. *Derniers Vers,* a sequence of twelve poems, conveniently read as one poem in twelve parts, closed the procession. The manner has been revolutionized; but, again and again, one recovers a familiar cadence, wearing an altered and improved form. *Derniers Vers* are an attempt at classicism—classicism understood not only as the resounding sententiousness of seventeenth and eighteenth century verse, but as the completeness of expression attained by a masterly innovator of any school, who appears to be moving away from tradition, whose curve of development, insensibly pressing round again into contact, exchanges a long electric flash with the past. (pp. 107-08)

Quiet application, a long process of self-discipline had made it possible for him to stand apart and appreciate the harrowing spectacle of ambitious and defeated youth, in the capacity both of actor and of reflective, impersonal spectator. He mingled the bitterness of defeat and the pleasure that comes from another sort of victory; he was detached. . . . And thus it is that, besides mirroring the futile discomfitures of adolescence, Laforgue's imagination, like one of those small circular glasses which epitomize and enrich the scattered features of some sprawling and chaotic room, supplies also a dignified context, a sober and consistent ground. Trifle as he please, Laforgue is seldom trivial. He is the supreme sentimentalist, but he is never lachrymose. An immense underlying seriousness harmonizes the ebullitions of his effervescent, abounding wit. Even his sensual reveries seem to have been laid up like pressed blossoms, dried and preserved between the chapters of an innate puritanism. (pp. 110-11)

> *Peter Quennell, "Jules Laforgue (1860-1887)," in his* Baudelaire and the Symbolists *(copyright Peter Quennell; reprinted by permission of Curtis Brown Limited), revised edition, Weidenfeld and Nicolson, 1954, pp. 97-111.*

## JAMES HUNEKER    (essay date 1929)

In [Jules Laforgue's] literary remains, slender enough as to quantity, there is little to suggest a fuller development if he had lived. Like his protagonist Arthur Rimbaud . . . , Jules Laforgue accomplished his destiny during the period when most poets are moulding their wings preparatory to flight. . . . Like Watteau, Laforgue was "condemned" from the beginning to "a green thought in a green shade." The spirit in him, the "shadow," devoured his soul, pulverized his will, made of him a Hamlet without a propelling cause, a doubter in a world of cheap certitudes and insolent fatuities. . . . Laforgue was a great despiser.

But he made merry over the ivory, apes, and peacocks of existence. He seems less French than he is in his self-mockery, yet he is a true son of his time and of his country. This young Hamlet . . . was a very buffoon; I am the new buffoon of dusty eternities, might have been his declaration; a buffoon making subtle somersaults in the metaphysical blue. He was a metaphysician complicated by a poet. . . . He possesses the sixth sense of infinity. A cosmical jester, his badinage is well-nigh dolorous. His verse and prose form a series of personal variations. The lyric in him is through some temperamental twist reversed. Fantastic dreams overflow his reality, and he always dreams with wide-open eyes. (pp. 424-25)

The phrase of Laforgue has a timbre capable of infinite prolongations in the memory. It is not alone what he says, nor the manner, but his power of arousing overtones from his keyboard. His aesthetic mysticism is allied with a semi-brutal frankness. . . . His Kingdom of Green was consumed and became gray by the regard of his coldly measuring eye. For him modern man is an animal who bores himself. Laforgue is an essayist who is also a causeur. His abundance is never exuberance. Without sentiment or romance, nevertheless, he does not suggest ossification of the spirit. To dart a lance at mythomania is his delight, while preserving the impassibility of a Parnassian. (pp. 427-28)

Perhaps his verse is doomed; it was born with the hectic flush of early dissolution, but it is safe to predict that as long as lovers of rare literature exist the volume of prose [entitled *Moralités légendaires*] will survive. It has for the gourmet of style an unending charm, the charm en sourdine [muted charm] of its creator, to whom a falling leaf or an empire in dissolution was of equal value. (p. 431)

*Moralités légendaires* contains six sections. I don't know which to admire the most, the **"Hamlet"** or the **"Lohengrin,"** the **"Salomé"** or the **"Persée et Andromède."** **"Le Miracle des Roses"** is of an exceeding charm, though dealing with the obvious, while **"Pan et la Syrinx"** has a quality which I can recall nowhere else in literature; perhaps in the cadences charged with the magic and irony of Chopin, or in the half-dreams of Watteau, color and golden sadness intermingled, may evoke the spiritual parodies of Laforgue, but in literature there is no analogue, though Pan is of classic flavor despite his very modern Weltanschauung. Syrinx is a woodland creature nebulous and exquisite. . . . The landscapes of these tales are fantastically beautiful, and scattered through the narrative are fragments of verse, vagrant and witty, that light up the stories with a glowworm phosphorescence. (pp. 432-33)

The subtitle of **"Hamlet,"** which heads the volume, is—**"Or, the Results of Filial Devotion"**—and the story, as [the American critic] Mr. Hale asserts, is Laforgue's masterpiece. Here is a Hamlet for you, a prince whose antics are enough to disturb the dust of Shakespeare and make the angels on high weep with hysterical laughter. Not remotely hinting at burlesque, the character is delicately etched. By the subtle withdrawal of certain traits, this Hamlet behaves as a man would who has been trepanned and his moral nature removed by an analytical surgeon. He is irony personified and is the most delightful company for one weary of the Great Good Game around and about us, the game of deceit, treachery, politics, love, social intercourse, religion, and commerce. Laforgue's Hamlet sees through the hole in the mundane millstone and his every phrase is like the flash of a scimitar.

It is the irony of his position, the irony of his knowledge that he is Shakespeare's creation and must live up to his artistic paternity; the irony that he is au fond a cabotin, a footlight strutter, a mouther of phrases metaphysical and a despiser of Ophelia . . . that are all so appealing. (pp. 434-35)

It is his rigorous transvaluation of all moral values and conventionalities that proclaims this Hamlet a man of the future. No half-way treaties with the obvious in life, no crooking the pregnant hinges of his opinions to the powers that be. An anarch, pure and complex, he despises all methods. What soliloquies, replete with the biting, cynical wisdom of a disillusioned soul! (p. 435)

The artistic beauty of the prose, its haunting assonance, its supple rhythms, make this **"Hamlet"** impossible save in French. Nor can the fine edge of its wit, its multiple though masked ironies, its astounding transposition of Shakespearean humor and philosophy be aught else than loosely paraphrased. Laforgue's Hamlet is of to-morrow, for every epoch orchestrates anew its own vision of Hamlet. The eighteenth century had one; the nineteenth had another; and our generation a fresher. But we know of none so vital as this fantastic thinker of Laforgue's. He must have had his ear close to the Time Spirit, so aptly has he caught the vibrations of his whirring loom, so closely to these vibrations has he attuned the key-note of his twentieth-century Hamlet. (p. 438)

> *James Huneker, "The Buffoon of the New Eternities: Jules Laforgue," in his* Essays by James Huneker *(copyright © 1929, 1957 Charles Scribner's Sons; reprinted with permission of Charles Scribner's Sons), Charles Scribner's Sons, 1929, pp. 424-38.*

**EDMUND WILSON** (essay date 1931)

[Jules Laforgue] independently developed a tone and technique—poignant-ironic, grandiose-slangy, scurrilous-naïve—which had much in common with Corbière's. . . . [And], for all his nonchalance in handling rudely the conventions of French poetry, [he was] much more a professional man of letters than Corbière. Laforgue even errs through preciosity in his fashion; what with Corbière seems a personal and inevitable, if eccentric, manner of speech, in Laforgue sounds self-conscious and deliberate, almost sometimes a literary exercise. He was tubercular . . . and dead at twenty-seven—and his gentleness and sadness are still those of a sick well-cared-for child; his asperities, his surprising images, his coquetries, his cynicism, and his impudence, are still those of a clever schoolboy. (pp. 96-7)

Yet Laforgue is a very fine poet and one of the most remarkable of the Symbolists. He and Corbière had introduced a new variety of vocabulary and a new flexibility of feeling. (p. 97)

[The] longer and more elaborate poems—**"Derniers Vers"** in the collected edition—which Laforgue was constructing at the time of his death out of more fragmentary and less mature work are certainly his most important performances: through his masterly flexibility of vocabulary and metric, he has here achieved one of the definitive expressions of the pathetic-ironic, worldly-aesthetic moods of the *fin de siècle* temperament. (p. 99)

> *Edmund Wilson, "T. S. Eliot," in his* Axel's Castle: A Study in the Imaginative Literature of 1870-1930 *(copyright 1931 by Charles Scribner's Sons; renewal copyright © 1959 by Edmund Wilson; reprinted with the permission of Charles Scribner's Sons), Charles Scribner's Sons, 1931, pp. 93-131.**

**H. R. HAYS** (essay date 1934)

Laforgue's early work is a great cry of disillusionment made all the more bitter by the fact that the period of perpetual disillusionment (the shedding of adolescence) coincided with a fairly general feeling that man had been cosmically "sold out." (p. 243)

But Laforgue grew older and found, as every one finds, that some defense is necessary against the external world, be it ever so loathsome. His defense was irony, elegance and technique. He discovered that the perfection of one's tools helps one to forget philosophy; and that a similar technique in the mind, checking, neutralizing and juggling with emotion (which is irony) diverts one's attention from the more unpleasant effects of emotion itself. He cultivated his vocabulary, the use of colloquialisms, and the invention of a diverting kind of fantasy. But during his short life he did not succeed in completely objectifying himself. The tricks and the trapeze performance are sometimes a little too aggressively clever; and one finds him sticking out his tongue with tears in his eyes. His love poems record a continual melancholy, because the shimmer of the dream cannot be preserved, and because Woman in a repetition of the same disappointment. . . .

In short, Laforgue's "chronic orphanism" lasted throughout his short life. He remained a tender Romantic at heart, his charm is grace, *gaminerie* and wistfulness. (p. 244)

> *H. R. Hays, "Laforgue and Wallace Stevens," in* The Romantic Review *(copyright © by the Trustees of Columbia University of the City of New York), Vol. XXV, No. 3 (July-September, 1934), pp. 242-48.**

### FRANCIS C. GOLFFING   (essay date 1946)

Jules Laforgue's poetic achievement depends closely on the intellectual framework that sustained it. Critics of this precocious poet usually fail to do justice to his aesthetic theory, his championship of impressionism, and his general philosophic background. Although his main distinction is doubtless that of a technical innovator, any investigation of his work should transcend the field of technique and examine the motives that prompted him to break away from the tradition of French verse. (p. 55)

The poetic qualities which Laforgue cherished most highly he was unable to find in his contemporaries; he then set out to realize them in his own verse. The man who wrote: "I eat my heart with various spiced sauces," and who, in a critical passage, asserted that the only valid aesthetic principle is our desire to escape from ennui was not likely to end up by writing academic lyrics. What he wanted was a nervous, impressionistic art; not the "straight and tedious line," but the line which was "broken a thousand times, sparkling with unforeseen twists, ready to deceive the eye, to whip and to irritate it . . . a thousand broken lines, assuming different hues, their angles vibrating in the undulations of the atmosphere." (p. 65)

To Laforgue, poetry has its natural center in the nerves. They are the only organs able to transmit the most subtle changes of our consciousness; hence all other faculties in man should be subordinated to them. The more sensitive a poet's nerves, the more likely he is to succeed artistically. . . . His constant preoccupation with this isolated aspect brings him close to the brink of monomania. Thus he speaks once of his "religious neurosis," and he even conceives of the cosmos in psychiatric terms. (pp. 65-6)

In consequence, Laforgue's poetry abjures any intellectual principle of order. . . . Chance observations, abstract notions, ironic comment—all these may be thrown together without rational coherence; an irrational coherence is supposedly guaranteed by the unity of theme, which automatically harmonizes the discordant elements. Thus, in his famous *Complainte des Pianos,* Laforgue uses popular refrains, loosely strung together, which are set off by the half melancholy half ironic comment of the protagonist. Each stanza is metrically different from the previous, and this metrical diversity serves to reflect the rapid changes of mood and the essential instability of sensory experience. A slender theme—the conflict between sensual temptation and ironic detachment—is here embroidered in an extremely delicate fashion. The movement of the whole poem is swift; the poet does not insist on any of his points, for he knows that by insisting he would become either sentimental or coldly facetious. In this instance, Laforgue was able to put his theory successfully into practice; the precarious balance is maintained throughout the poem, and something like a subterranean unity is achieved by virtue of the felicity of ordonnance. Human life can be prismatically refracted without becoming a wholly amorphous kaleidoscopic pattern; *Complainte des Pianos* attests to this. But in nine out of ten cases the balance is liable to be upset; one single word, if ill chosen, may render the whole poem either ludicrous or absurd, for there are no other qualities which could compensate the reader for such a lapse. The majority of Laforgue's more ambitious poems are vitiated by his royal disregard of argument, while his shorter pieces—notably the sonnets and octosyllabic quatrains—show to advantage his lightness of touch, his capricious wit and his perfect command of idiom. (pp. 66-7)

Some of his cadences are unforgettable; at his best he achieves a kind of erudite cosmic irony which defies any attempt at imitation; and there is a certain frail childlike charm about the whole man, perceptible mainly in the atmosphere of his verse, which somewhat tempers his intellectual presumption and the monotony of his themes. It is hard to tell whether Laforgue would ever have developed into a major poet. Personally, I have my doubts: for even though his natural endowment was great, his philosophy led him of necessity along a road that was, to say the least, unpromising; and he probably would have followed that road to its logical end. We who have read Pound's *Cantos* know that Laforgue's road leads to the triumph of reverie and to poetic disintegration. (p. 67)

> *Francis C. Golffing, "Jules Laforgue," in* Quarterly Review of Literature *(© Quarterly Review of Literature, 1946), Vol. III, No. 1, Summer, 1946, pp. 55-67.*

### MARTIN TURNELL   (essay date 1948-49)

*[Turnell here refutes Peter Quennell's earlier claim that Laforgue's use of imagery and ideas was limited (see excerpt above, 1929). Instead, Turnell argues, Laforgue employed an "elaborate system of reference and association, a sort of poetic shorthand" which created free verse "as we know it." Turnell describes* Les derniers vers *as one of "the most important poems produced by the nineteenth century," and laments the fact that Laforgue never achieved an emotional maturity commensurate with his technical virtuosity.]*

Laforgue was not the first nineteenth-century poet to write free verse. The honor almost certainly belongs to Rimbaud. . . . All the free verse written in the last century can no doubt be traced to a common impulse; but it was Laforgue who first exploited its possibilities, who introduced a distinctive personal rhythm and made it the vehicle of a fresh vision. For this reason he must be regarded as virtually the inventor of free verse as we know it. (p. 82)

The implication that his range of feeling is limited is true, but this does not mean that his use of stock imagery is a shortcoming [see excerpt above by Quennell, 1929]. One of his achievements was to have worked out an elaborate system of reference and association, a sort of poetic shorthand. The recurring image, which has been brilliantly developed in [T. S. Eliot's] *The Waste Land,* was an important part of the system.

In Laforgue's essay on Impressionism, the image of the prism decomposing light into its elements is constantly introduced. . . . [In his poetry he] takes a mood or a feeling and examines it from every possible angle, but he always returns to his starting point. Laforgue does not seem to me to describe or analyse emotion in the accepted sense; he translates feelings into precise visual images which recur again and again. They are symbols in the strict sense or, as he called them, *phrases mélodiques* [melodic phrases], which enable him to keep the different themes of his poetry simultaneously present in the mind. In his best work, the *Derniers vers,* they are used with kaleidoscopic effect, continually forming new patterns of feeling. The 'meaning' of his poetry, indeed, often lies in the relation between the symbols, in the transition from one emotion to its opposite. (p. 83)

Laforgue seldom used the device of omitting his main verbs and piling up substantives more effectively than in the [*Derniers vers*]. . . . It is a device which is common to the modern poet and the novelist of the inner monologue and it enabled Laforgue to come closer to our mental processes than any of his predecessors, to give us the *immediate* sensation of the atmosphere of a great city. (p. 84)

The *Derniers vers* are really a single poem of 816 lines which registers the changes of mood of a sensitive person living in modern urban conditions. Its great virtues are the fidelity and insight with which these changes are recorded, its great weakness the absence of the intellectual framework which gives *The Waste Land* its unity and finality. The only principle of unity is the personality of the timid, love-sick young man who bears a striking resemblance to the young man of Eliot's early work. . . . [Autumn]—it is one of Laforgue's characteristic poetical conceits—stands for the dominant mood which colours [*Derniers vers*]: the despair of the love-sick young man who is old before his time. There is an immensely effective transition from the calm, gracious, Watteauesque atmosphere of the 'harvest' to the grim lycée with the schoolchildren coughing in the freezing dormitories. The *phtisie pulmonaire* [pulmonary consumption] gives the verse its tragic note; it is not a simple cough; the children are already victims of the disease which is the scourge of the *grands centres* [great centers]. The theme is [further developed when the] . . . poet gives a picture of the squalid horror of the great city with its slums, its washing hanging out to dry, the raincoats, the chemist's shop, the 'ocean' of roofs which makes the poet think longingly of the real ocean with its real shores instead of the 'shores' of balconies. (pp. 85-6)

Laforgue's picture of city life reminds us at once of an impressionist painting and of a film in which the mobile camera pans over the ocean of roofs, climbs the balconies rising in tiers one above the other, noses in and out of backyards and windows, showing us what lies beyond the *rideaux écartés* [open curtains]; and somewhere in the back of our mind we are always conscious of the tinkling of the out-of-tune piano. In the last lines there is a reference back to the children coughing in the dormitories and the *phtisie pulmonaire*. Real suffering—Laforgue was evidently thinking of his own childhood and perhaps of the disease which killed him—is ironically reduced to the dry *statistiques sanitaires* [sanitary statistics]. The mystery of faith has been replaced by the mysterious statistics of the ravages of tuberculosis in urban civilisation; and the shortening lines leave us with the sensation of life gradually ebbing away. (p. 86)

From a technical point of view, the *Derniers vers* were one of the most important poems produced by the nineteenth century and the debt of later writers to them has been immense. This should not mislead us, however, into overestimating Laforgue's achievement as a poet. . . . He was not a poet of the same calibre as Baudelaire or Rimbaud and his technical mastery is of a different order from theirs. He was essentially a virtuoso and the *Derniers vers* sometimes make me feel like a spectator at an exhibition match applauding the brilliant transitions as one might applaud a 'lightning return'; and when it's over the appropriate comment seems to be not 'a great poem,' but 'a splendid performance.'

We must remember that Laforgue died when he was twenty-seven and that his attitude remains incomplete. His protective irony, the tendency of many of his lines to peter out and his very seductive spiritual defeatism (which had a very bad influence on his successors) are all signs of immaturity. What he would have accomplished if he had lived can only be a matter of idle speculation. . . .

It seems to me that the disparity between Laforgue's technical development and the absence of any corresponding emotional development tells heavily against him and against the view that he might have become a major poet. (p. 90)

> *Martin Turnell, "Jules Laforgue: Observations on the Theory and Practice of Free Verse," in* The Cornhill Magazine *(© John Murray 1949; reprinted by permission of John Murray (Publishers) Ltd.), Vol. 163, No. 973, Winter, 1948-49, pp. 74-90.*

### R. R. BOLGAR (essay date 1950)

[Laforgue's stories and poems] contain more novelties than the mind can accept without a definite purposive effort. His rhythm, for example, never follows a conventional or even a consistent pattern. Sometimes it is so complicated as to elude any but the most careful and sensitive ear. Then sometimes it degenerates into a crude jingle. He coins words. He attempts to popularize astonishing ideas. He is a moralist with a new system of ethics, while his sensibility, even where it is only half revealed, shocks by its strangeness. In short, everything is calculated to repel, and nothing in his work will attract, ordinary hurrying readers. Yet he is the poet whose influence can be most clearly discerned in Gide's earlier books and in T. S. Eliot's *Prufrock*. He is a poet whom his fellow writers have always admired deeply and about whom it is agreed by general consent that once you have come to know his work well, you can never again quite forget it or refuse it value. (p. 193)

In a way he was typical of an important section of his contemporaries. The great educational reforms of which the 'thirties had been so proud had come by the' seventies to impose an almost intolerable burden upon middle-class youth. . . . [These] adolescents [were compelled] to spend long years at schools and universities, where their work had no direct connection with the doings of the world around them. . . . [They] were encouraged to develop the habit of reflecting about all they did, long before they learnt how to find a blessed relief from thought in action. The self-distrust, the frustrations, the bitter loneliness, which oppressed them in consequence, were the occupational diseases of higher education in the French nineteenth-century manner. Laforgue knew all these. His life of study and isolation had lasted far longer even than was usual. He had explored all its dismal crannies. He could formulate the attitudes it engendered and express their attendant emotions with a vivid lyrical force. Thus, he was admirably fitted to speak for the nineteenth-century mind in training.

Had these been the limits of his sensibility, his work might have been more easily understood and more popular than it is. But that experience of enforced solitude, which made it possible for him to share the feelings of contemporary adolescents, also provided his genius with material for bolder and more disturbing flights. Since he had been compelled to watch society from the outside, he judged it as an outsider. A social observer who has led a normal life cannot be impartial except in spurts, however hard he tries. But Laforgue's impartiality was complete. Hence that strange characteristic of his, which the average reader finds so hard to accept, and which consists in a dispassionate readiness to question the worth of our most common, our most cherished forms of thought and feeling. When he slips, as he so often does, from the heights of a lyrical outburst down to earth in a banal cliché, his intention is generally to test a conventional emotion on the touchstone of mockery. When he demonstrates, as he so often does in the *Moralités Légendaires,* how subtly the conventions of art shape our reactions to what we hear and see, he is questioning by implication the final validity of our categories. It is evident that he regarded all human behaviour with unvarying detachment and could do this because he was not committed by habit or advantage to uphold any specific code. He was the permanent spectator who proverbially sees the most of the game. (pp. 198-99)

At the basis of all existence there is to be found, in his opinion, a Life Force whose role it is to promote change in an effort to satisfy needs which are however beyond our comprehension. This Force works through all living things, including ourselves; and with us, its promptings are to be recognized in those vigorous internal urges which we so often feel. Since these urges are habitually directed at satisfactions found in the objective external world, they have had, from the most primitive past onwards, the effect of compelling man to develop his intelligence and to construct with its aid a picture of the universe as a guide to action. Unfortunately, the practical intelligence of mankind has remained, even after the passage of countless millennia, a relatively crude instrument, permanently limited by those rough and ready categories it had built up to solve the simple problems which had been its first concern at the dawn of history. It gives us a false picture, both of our own desires and of conditions in the external world. Therefore we must supplement its activity and redress its errors. We must look beyond it to Art. For it is the function of the artist to reveal through his sensitive comprehension of the Unconscious the purposes of the Life Force. . . . [Laforgue] concluded that the only realistic course for a contemporary artistic movement was to insist, first upon destroying the intellectual tyranny of the so-called normal picture of the world, then upon modifying the common uses of language so as to make it better able to

represent the operations of the Unconscious for the benefit of the conscious mind.

His own writing exemplifies the practical application of these theories. By dissolving normality into its constituents and using these logically disconnected but still recognizable impressions to suggest psychological states, he demonstrated how a poet could satisfy by a single technique the two aims he thought desirable. That was his principal contribution to the Symbolist cause.

But when we turn from the content of Laforgue's poetry to the consideration of its form, we find that this readiness of his to abandon the common categories of thought must not be taken as proof of a similar facility of spirit in other spheres. He was one of the pioneers of free verse, and the rules he accepted for it were as rigid and exacting as the canons of the alexandrine. (pp. 200-01)

In the poems he wrote after July 1886 Laforgue faithfully observed the rules for free verse which we must now regard as imitated from Rimbaud and first formulated in all probability by Gustave Kahn: that each line was to be a unit of sense, and of such a length that it could be easily taken in without shifting the eye and easily spoken in a breath. Within the ambit of these experiments, he was something of a doctrinaire and something of a precisian. But he did not have similar feelings about the rules of syntax. . . . Language, like the common experience it represented, was regarded by him merely as a convenient instrument whose internal logic could be safely neglected. He writes as if every verb could take a direct infinitive, as if every adjective could turn into a noun. He mixes up his prepositions and sprinkles his text with overgrown adverbs. But if his syntax is sometimes unfortunate, his innovations in vocabulary are extraordinarily felicitous. (p. 202)

The great majority of these linguistic novelties occur in that curious collection of stories, the *Moralités Légendaires,* which the Symbolists regarded as the best of Laforgue's works. They strike us nowadays as over-decorated and insufficiently dramatic. But even the careless reader, if he perseveres long enough, will come away from the book with an impression, confused but lasting, which paints in his mind's eye a world of curious pageantry, brilliant with variations of light, and which revives in his memory, but freed from all the sediment of frustration, the original excitements of adolescent love. . . . Would [Laforgue] have achieved more, if he had attempted less? The answer may be yes. But then his triumph would have been more conventional, and that would perhaps have been a pity. For there are many writers of genius, but there is only one Laforgue. In any case, it was a remarkable feat to have combined an elaborate description which outmatched [J. K. Huysmans's] *A Rebours* with the lyric emotion of really good love-stories and sometimes with the thrills of murder, to have been able to move from extravagant fantasy to stingingly realistic dialogue, from the solemn exactitudes of psycho-analysis to the joys of parodying the great. For most of the stories are parodies. There is a *Hamlet* and a *Lohengrin,* while *Salomé* and *Pan et la Syrinx* echo [Stéphane Mallarmé's] *Hérodiade* and *L'Après-Midi d'un Faune.*

The Symbolist cause was one which in its hour appealed to men of very diverse temperaments and aims. Laforgue belonged to the future, to the generation of Klingsor, Toulet and Apollinaire, just as definitely as Mallarmé belonged to the Parnasse and the past. He took the first step in that campaign to remould the categories of the human consciousness which was to absorb the energies of the most original writers in twentieth-century France and whose import we are still far from understanding. Its failure, if it has failed, has been due largely to the lack of a leader. Laforgue would have possessd the requisite stature if death had given his versatile genius a chance. Had he lived, he could have dominated French poetry, as Ronsard and Hugo had dominated it, during the critical period when a new form was evolving to its yet uncharted maturity. (pp. 202-03)

R. R. Bolgar, "The Present State of Laforgue Studies," in French Studies, Vol. IV, No. 3, July, 1950, pp. 193-207.

## WILLIAM JAY SMITH   (essay date 1956)

[Smith's Selected Works of Jules Laforgue was the first book-length English translation of Laforgue's poetry and prose. In the introduction to his translation, Smith states that he hoped to achieve "the raciness and cheek of the original work" without sacrificing the "balance" of the work. He considers Les derniers vers an important influence on later French and English poetry, and characterizes Laforgue's verse as a "syncopation of feeling."]

Jules Laforgue's earliest poetic work, Le Sanglot de la terre, composed between 1878 and 1881, was in some ways the most ambitious that he undertook during his lifetime: like many a beginning writer, he projected a volume that was beyond his powers. (p. 5)

The superior poet who turns to free verse usually begins by working in form, and Laforgue shows in Le Sanglot de la terre that he was capable of composing poems in conventional modes. There are passages of extraordinary beauty, too. What is lacking, perhaps, is the very quality for which Laforgue was to become famous, that is, humor. The truth of this is borne out by the fact that the poet kept a number of these poems intact for his Complaintes, adding, after each stanza, as a kind of counterpoint, a few light-hearted verses in his later manner. Laforgue here sounds the organ note—"Marche funèbre" is the most noteworthy example—but he is seldom able to sustain it. There is something a trifle schoolboyish in the poet's angry address to the infinite heavens. . . . (p. 7)

Les Complaintes, the first volume published by Jules Laforgue during his brief life, expressed immediately and firmly a poetic personality with which succeeding generations would have to deal. The poems in the Complaintes are so very different from those of Le Sanglot de la terre that one would think at first that they were the work of another poet. But the change is not so extraordinary as it seems; it is merely a shift in tone. The poet treats the same major themes but in a minor key, the macrocosm is reduced to microcosm: the instrument is smaller, but capable nevertheless of vibrant echoes. The pale, serious young organist in the loft is replaced by the nimble, playful, sentimental organ-grinder on the street corner. The cosmic is dealt with in terms of the ordinary and everyday. . . . Lofty poetic diction gives way to popular speech; no subject is either too grand or too trivial to be treated. The romantic dirges of the early unpublished volume are replaced by complaintes, popular laments patterned after ballads of the sort people had sung for centuries. The words of the two titles are significant—sanglot [sob] and complainte [lament]—for they suggest the fact that Laforgue thought of the earth as a living and suffering thing. . . . (p. 18)

No one has been more successful than Laforgue in bringing the machinery, the shabby and sordid décor of modern life, into poetry, right down to the "marbre banal du lavabo" [banal bathroom marble]. One feels that he was compelled to make poetry out of everything, omitting, as Arthur Symons pointed out, no hour of the day or night [see excerpt above, 1908]. He does not always succeed, of course, but the attempt is impressive. Everything animate and inanimate has its rhythm and its song, clocks and foetuses, pine trees and bells, wind and stars, space and time. He attempts throughout to record a world that is living, moving, breathing, ticking, grinding. . . . It is the sounds of vie courante, "running life," like running water, that he catches in the rhythms of popular songs, nursery tunes, old refrains. (p. 19)

One of the most amusing and typical of the poems is the "Complaint of the Poor Knight Errant." . . . The Knight Errant is reduced to base reality: he is the man between the sandwich boards wandering up and down the sidewalk, and the "palaces of the soul" are the rooms at The Knight Errant, the hotel he advertises. Laforgue's genius is verbal, everything exists on the surface, but always for the sake of what lies below it. Here we have the inner man, the introvert, buttressed against the external world, but held and contained within it: the man who is literally a sandwich. (pp. 20-1)

Behind all the rhythms of these poems there is one fundamental, immediate rhythm which Laforgue strives to set down: it is the human heartbeat. This is made clear in what was probably the first complainte that he composed, the "Chanson du petit hypertrophique." . . . The poet is too close to his subject for this to be a successful poem, but it strikes the keynote of the work. The reader hears in the lines . . . exactly what the boy hears, the thumping heart and the voice of the mother calling from beyond the grave. Death is always somewhere between the lines of the poems, and accounts for their effect of urgency, their hurried manner, their staccato beat. (pp. 21-2)

[Laforgue] introduced words from every branch of human activity, mixing them together as if they naturally belonged side by side and came as readily to the tongue as the simplest child's phrase. Terms from philosophy, biology, medicine, phrases from aesthetics, sentimental song titles, words from billboards and advertisements all mingle in such a fashion that one has the impression at times that the poems are collages made up from the pages of a daily newspaper. Not content with giving existing words new meanings, the poet invents new ones whenever it serves his purpose. He combines two words of very different sense which bear some orthographical resemblance; he makes nouns of adjectives and adjectives of nouns; he turns nouns into verbs. . . . Much of the punning and verbal invention is, of coures, quite untranslatable into English. . . . Nor does it always go so well in French; far from it. . . . Laforgue himself was later to realize that he had overdone these extravagances, and yet, in his campaign against the cliché and the hackneyed phrase, he was trying for, and at times achieved, a kind of verbal freedom that had not existed in France since Rabelais. (pp. 22-3)

[L'Imitation de Notre-Dame la Lune selon Jules Laforgue] is more homogeneous and controlled [than Les Complaintes]; the tone, but for certain far-fetched conceits, is not so shrill. The poet displays extraordinary technical virtuosity, especially in his unprecedented combinations of long and short lines. But the technical skill does not exist for itself alone. The poems are frequently so slight that they seem cast in some peculiar poetic shorthand; but if we follow them carefully and pursue their recurrent themes, we find that they are integrated with a remarkable subtlety. The repeated images like pieces of isinglass stuck together hold and project an inner fire. They remind one of Laforgue's interest in Impressionist painting: the poems may be likened to the paintings of Seurat, for the images have the sparkling, mathematical precision of dots of color applied to canvas.

Of all the lunar journeys recorded in literary history surely none is stranger than that of this "honnête poète français" [honest French poet]. None has made the moon more immediate and appealing; none has better conveyed its infinite remoteness and inaccessibility. . . . The constant references to whiteness, sterility, and decay, however playful, do not spring from mere perversity, but reflect rather a concern with death as great as that of the English Metaphysical poets. The bone-white face of Pierrot, as expressionless as it is timeless, is the image of the full moon. It is also a death's-head animated by feeling.

In the theatre, Pierrot, stemming from the Italian *commedia dell'arte,* had undergone many transformations through the years. . . . [To this symbol] Laforgue gave new depth and dimension, and his creation is distinctly his own.

The Pierrot protagonists of these poems are Lenten creatures who "have nothing to do with God." Their fasting, in Christian terms, has no significance; they are priests of the unconscious. They observe the Lenten acts of piety; indeed, they are pious to a fault, total abstainers, protectors of virtue. The clowns are carnival figures who have not abandoned their masks. They have bade farewell to the flesh, and yet are obsessed by it. Like the dandies of Baudelaire in a kind of fourth dimension, they are of this world, but not of this world. They have an affinity not with the broad light of day which reveals the full outlines of the real, but rather with the unreality of moonlight, the light radiated by that high priestess, their "lady, the moon," whose maxims they bear upon their hearts. They worship the moon, and, on this earth, the moonlike mask of the Gioconda, the artist's depiction of the perfect and enigmatic lady. They are attracted by women but repelled by them at the same time. The clowns would like to confess their love, but they are aware that such a confession would be both improper and improbable: if they act, they have gone too far; and they will not, under any circumstances, be held responsible for their actions. The Prufrock of Eliot is "almost, at times, the Fool"; the clowns of Laforgue are fools pure and simple. (pp. 38-40)

Pierrot is for Laforgue a vehicle for the inner dialogue of a man of feeling. The moon which is addressed is quite explicitly the soul, the feminine side of the male personality in both its light and dark aspects, that which Jung has called the *anima.* And perhaps this explains the fascination *L'Imitation de Notre-Dame la Lune* has held for so many readers. By fixing attention on the mask of death, the poet explores all the more intensely the living mechanism; and, with psychological sureness, goes to the substratum of the psyche, and to the heart of human tension and conflict. (p. 41)

Laforgue was not a dramatist; his gift was essentially lyrical. As a poet, however, he strove for some sort of dramatic form. He was by no means unaware or uninterested in people and in the creation of character, but what he sought principally was an objectification of emotion, a distillation of the feeling inherent in human relationships. It is this that makes *Le Concile féerique,* while in some respects merely transitional, an interesting example of his mature work. . . .

*Le Concile féerique* is, in effect, an ironic study of relationship: the relationship of man to woman and woman to man, of man and woman to the world, and of the world to the universe, a study of microcosm and macrocosm. . . .

The stage Laforgue sets is classical, but one can well imagine a dance orchestra playing in the wings; in many ways, this work is more a ballet than a drama. The characters have something of the studied chic of cabaret dancers, and the dramatic action—such as it is—consists of a series of movements, forward and back, forward and back, of man and woman. The Chorus might be said to represent the human psyche, incorporating both male and female aspects. The Echo, like the voice of feeling, serves as a link between the inner and outer worlds; and the device of irony maintains the whole in balance. (p. 80)

In his poetic development Jules Laforgue alternated between retraction and expansion: no sooner had he attempted to introduce new and freer rhythms into his poems than he would return, if only briefly, to more conventional stanzas. Toward the very end of his life, however, we see him breaking down all barriers, taking liberties he had only hinted at previously, working to attain, in the prose of the *Moralités légendaires* and in the verse of the *Derniers Vers,* that effect of spontaneity, that "unwritten" quality which later writers were to associate with his name. Laforgue built things up in order to break them down. In the *Complaintes* he took many of his earlier "philosophical" poems and lightened them by the insertion of light ballad refrains; in the *Derniers Vers* he lifts lines and stanzas from his projected volume, *Des Fleurs de bonne volonté,* giving them the unusual fluid power that characterized all his final work. . . . His last poems (*Derniers Vers*) have been aptly called Laforgue's "poetic testament"; the poet put into them every thought, feeling, and image contained in his other volumes. They are in reality a single long poem, poignant and persuasive from beginning to end, totally revolutionary in form. (p. 84)

From the outset the work impresses the reader as a musical composition in which phrases recur, taken up and dropped, developed and then abandoned just at the moment when they seem to provide the key to the entire composition. . . . Indeed, throughout the *Derniers Vers,* there is a suggestion of musical accompaniment: the speaker improvises, putting down his feelings, not being wholly certain what the complete melody is to be. The sound of hunting horns is heard and lost, then heard again; church bells toll and are hushed, but reverberate through succeeding stanzas. . . . Musically, all this provides a kind of syncopation; and if the poetry of T. S. Eliot is a "music of ideas," that of Laforgue may be said to be a syncopation of feeling. . . .

The *Derniers Vers* is a complete operatic orchestration, employing all the instruments, piano, violins, horns, and, above all, the human voice, or rather, voices—the "forest voices of Wagner." It is an impressionistic orchestration, visual as well as musical. Blocks of images—"friezes of imagery" Peter Quennell calls them [see excerpt above, 1929]—sweep along to the music. But the figures on the frieze—the little girls in white on their way to mass, for example—all move endlessly in the same direction: their destination is innocence and infinity. There is reason for the repetition; the effect is cumulative. (p. 85)

Laforgue piles up objects, old newspapers, soiled linen, fashion plates, everyday banal things alongside sentimental and romantic ones; and it is as if a Victorian glass bell had shattered and tumbled its ornate flowers, shells, and mementoes on the floor: the Romantic pile is split apart, revealing the sorry frame-work beneath, the pathetic assembly of the soul. . . .

The *vers libre* of the **Derniers Vers** constitutes one of the most important starting points for all modern poetry, both French and English. (p. 86)

From the opening words, ''Blocus sentimental'' to the closing, ''nous mourrons,'' the **Derniers Vers** is a dream of youthful love in which the beloved continually escapes the grasp of the lover. Objects, beings, feelings merge with one another until one can no longer distinguish dream from reality. . . . Leaves fall and mingle with the hoardings in the gutter; legends end with the ending of the year—all go back to the earth to be turned over by the gravedigger's spade. Laforgue here achieves in poetry something which he had always sought: ''psychology in dream form.'' (p. 87)

Behind everything Laforgue wrote was an awareness of death: in the **Derniers Vers,** written at the end of his life, death had become a veritable obsession. . . . It is this obsession that makes for the poignancy of his **''Solo de Lune,''** where the poet riding at night on top of a coach, becomes pure spirit disembodied in space, flying like Ariel through the moonlit night. (pp. 87-8)

It is Laforgue's brooding over death which makes him seem so close to the English Metaphysical poets. There are important differences, however. In Donne one finds a similar kind of verbal play, but the integrating force in each poem is always intellect; whereas in Laforgue, while intellect is certainly present, the unifying force of stanza and of poem is feeling. It is true, also, that many sections of Laforgue's work are marred by an immaturity of emotion; but where he is in full control, as in his **Derniers Vers,** we have something quite unique. Thinking of its influence with respect to form, Martin Turnell has called Laforgue's last work the most important single volume published in Europe since the seventeenth century [see excerpt above, 1948-49]. Whether or not one agrees with such a sweeping statement, there can be no question of its significant relation to the development of modern poetry. (pp. 88-9)

*William Jay Smith, in* Selected Writings of Jules La-forgue *by Jules Laforgue, edited and translated by William Jay Smith (reprinted by permission of the author; copyright © 1956 by William Jay Smith), Grove Press, 1956, 287 p.*

## MICHAEL COLLIE  (essay date 1963)

[*In his* Laforgue, *which is one of the major critical studies of Laforgue's works in English, Collie calls Laforgue's contribution to the development of free verse* ''considerable'' *and* Les derniers vers ''*the only sustained expression of Laforgue's mind and imagination.*'' *He concludes that Laforgue's experimental poetry, which* ''*represents the self-conscious mind at odds with the world,*'' *simultaneously reflects discipline and innovation in rhythm and language.*]

The figure of Pierrot [in *L'Imitation de Notre-Dame la Lune*] is a guise for Laforgue, not a disguise. He has always had in mind the Gilles of Watteau, the uncommitted, passive, perceptive harlequin: everybody is taking part in the masquerade that is life, and it is his destiny to play the clown. He is not Lord Hamlet, nor an attendant Lord; he is the Fool. . . . This clown, who anticipates the unromantic, actual, suffering clowns of Picasso, is apart from the world, in a safe way. As a literary symbol, he is made to regard life with a detached, critical, but

unconcerned air, without priggishness since he is only a clown, and without the romantic gesture of the desperate nihilist. . . . The fatalism of Laforgue's Pierrot is more aggressive than that of, for example, Turgenev or Chekhov: it is more like that of Strindberg, since he proposes, though with affected indifference, not the acceptance of life as it comes, nor a resignation to the play of fate, as in Hardy, but a firm negative. Whatever is contrary to life is his. This, too, constitutes the rationale of the other dominant symbol of the poems, the moon. Though beautiful perhaps, it is not a romantic image. It is dead, cold, unchanging, remote, not implicated in generation, unmoved by gesture. (pp. 64-5)

There are essentially two kinds of poem in *L'Imitation de Notre Dame la Lune.* Firstly, there are two series of Pierrot poems (**''Pierrots I-V,** and the **''Locutions de Pierrot''**) in which the harlequin lightly addresses himself to that other world, the earth, and ironically disengages himself from the woman who wishes for a human, ordinary love. The themes remain the same, so that the poems are like the inconsequential line-drawings of a painter, complete in themselves, but contributing to nothing substantial. Some give [Laforgue] the opportunity of displaying a neat virtuosity, as in the description of Pierrot in the very first of the poems. In others, the concerns of previous poems are expressed without the old vehemence and energy, but rather with a contraction and economy of phrase which is almost impersonal. One of the best of these is the fifth poem of the Pierrot sequence. . . . [Here the] world is a scandalous place without a meaning, an isolated event, like one of a thousand throws of the dice in the game played by Love and Possibility. Despite the laconic tone of this poem, and despite Laforgue's interest in writing a controlled, dispassionate poem for the sake of doing so, (perhaps with the example of Verlaine in mind), it can be seen that the cynicism is still shadowed by a lingering moral: it is ''Ce bas monde de scandale'' [this sordid world of scandal]. Laforgue is the man for whom the world is out of joint. He does not believe in the possibility of putting it right, yet he never comes near to achieving the amoral indifference of, for example, Oscar Wilde.

Secondly, there are poems in which the theme of the volume . . . is a mere pretext for a flow of words, images and impressions. By association of idea, and by the reversal of normal expectation, Laforgue paints a word picture of an ''unreal'' subject, such as the topography of the moon, the effect of the poem being almost entirely in the words. . . . In the poem called **''Climat, faune et flore de la lune,''** the poet, who describes himself as ''vermine des nébuleuses d'occasion,'' [vermin of nebulae created at hazard] says that from his Babylon he enjoys imagining what the moon is like. It is decadent in the most immediate sense, uninformed by thought, purpose, or imaginative insight. . . . Fortunately Laforgue does not do this very frequently. Indeed only one other poem [**''Les linges, le cygne''**] can rival **''Climat, faune et flore de la lune,''** for this kind of decadence. (pp. 65-8)

The volume has a final awkwardness. Just as he had taken away from the integrity of the **''Complaintes''** by insisting both on his ''halleluia Preface'' and on the penultimate poem, **''Complainte des complaintes,''** so now he spoils his own performance by revealing his actual self, this time so nakedly that the reader is almost bound to be embarrassed or offended. . . . In the last poem in *L'Imitation de Notre Dame la Lune* which is called **''Avis je vous prie,''** Laforgue destroys the integrity of his volume as surely as the schoolgirl actress who calls to her mother in the front row that she has not really been strangled. He fears life, he says, as he fears marriage, for which he is anyway not old enough. (p. 68)

Laforgue's short stories, *Moralités légendaires*, are very similar in quality to these poems in *L'Imitation de Notre Dame la Lune*. Both the verbal texture and the imaginative attitude behind it are the same. Whatever their value, they constitute Laforgue's most important prose writing. (p. 69)

The *Moralités légendaires* are anti-romantic myths. Thus Hamlet is more interested in the play that he has written than in what he calls his "domestic situation." (p. 70)

Though not alone in doing so, Laforgue anticipates the use to which myths have been put in the twentieth century. The old story or legend is not chosen for its intrinsic interest, but because it permits an ironical, mock-heroic play on the well-known theme and gives the author the opportunity of reversing the point or moral, in this case by proposing down-to-earth though fantastic alternatives for the ancient chivalric motives of the main characters. This is one of the ways by which a writer can ease himself out of the stock attitudes of one generation, or of a particular society, and, under cover of the fable and with the protection of the irony with which he handles it, explore alternative attitudes which occur at first as the attitudes of his characters, rather than as the moral basis of his own work. . . . The stories told in the *Moralités légendaires* are loose fitting masks, exactly like the figure of Pierrot, so that they are much closer to being extended, dramatised prose poems than short stories. As expressions of [Laforgue's] personality, they propose a view of life which is essentially passive, where everything is accepted as it is, where there is nothing better than what nature has to offer, and where the only preference would be for the gesture of refusing to take part, of opting out, of refusing to be animalistic, of refusing to dream.

Even in the last story, **"Les deux pigeons,"** which is different in tone from the other since the two characters are led to realise and to acknowledge, though too late, that there has been something genuine in their relationship, there is a scoring of extreme pessimism and an exceptionally cynical and bitter twist to the conclusion. (pp. 71-2)

To a lesser extent *Moralités légendaires* anticipate the twentieth-century literary interest in myth as archetype. This is not the reason for Laforgue's adoption of a legend, but having adopted it, he so writes his new story, that the pattern or inter-relationship of character and situation tends to be Freudian, often by implication, occasionally (as in the character of Andromède with her love of the sea-Monster), by heavy emphasis. Laforgue's interest in psychology developed from his early reading of Hartmann and it is quite evident that he knows what he is doing. The epigraph to **"Salomé,"** for example, is: "Birth is a departure: death a re-entering." From this point of view, both the themes and the details of the stories, have a double significance. Thus in **"Pan et la Syrinx,"** after the momentary encounter before Syrinx is transformed, Pan consoles himself with a reed pipe, which is art; and, in **"Lohengrin, fils de Parsifal,"** the hero escapes from his marriage bed, and from the incompatibility of the relationship, by clutching at his pillow which turns into a swan and carries him away. . . . [Yet the] *avant-garde* Freudianism of the *Moralités légendaires* does not make them good short stories; nor does Laforgue's overall view of human character, whether Freudian or not. . . . Laforgue has a notion of the subject, but lacks the understanding that later goes with it. His determination to remove his characters from the world of normal expectation has the negative

virtue of saving them from lending-library silliness. In doing so, however, in a *cul-de-sac* away from the moral and spiritual actualities of everyday life, he creates for them a world as unreal as the one they have left, and weakens literature, if one takes it so seriously, by making people into gaudy, papiermaché archetypes and life an activity which, for a reason only known to decadents, atheists, existentialists, and saints, one cannot choose to live, but only to reject. Laforgue was certainly committed to the foolishness of this position, which is an illogical attempt to credit the individual with a degree of importance, and at the same time deny it absolutely. The stories, however, do not depend on these themes of repression and sexual frustration. It is Laforgue's ironic, humorous, anti-romantic handling that gives them their point, though the irony often has, as in the poems, a touch of bathos, and though the humour is more often sardonic than gay.

In any case, Laforgue's style gives the tales a quality which quite removes them from the world of serious meaning. Since the situations and scenes which he describes constitute only the fantasy world of myth, Laforgue is able to do with language what he does with the stories themselves. Normal usage is not important to him, except as something to be played upon. Extraordinary usage is the intention, and the greater part of the *Moralités légendaires* has the same verbal and imaginative texture as . . . *L'Imitation de Notre Dame la Lune*. Utter decadence is achieved, at the breaking point of meaning, as it were, when a word or phrase is taken to the extreme of extravagance, so that words are used as in the configurations of a masquerade, the spontaneity of language being altogether destroyed. (pp. 73-5)

[In the *Derniers Vers*] one can see that Laforgue's difficulty with symbol is at last resolving itself. The idea of symbol, as objective correlative, becomes important when the subject of the poem is the relationship between the poet on the one hand and the "external world" on the other, and the danger is that it will be either obscure, because relating to the poet's existence only, or for the same reason, limited in effect. An image in a poem which does not have this personal focus derives its force, not merely from the originality or inventiveness of the man who conceived it, but from the relationship, however remote, to some fixed point of reference, whether it is the explicit subject of the poem, the author's evident intention, or the reader's vague assumption of the stable world within which the image occurs. Laforgue is not a Symbolist in the strict sense of the word because the world which he imagines and recreates in his poems does not exist in symbol only, the imagination being paramount. On the other hand, the difficulty in all the early poems is that when Laforgue expresses a feeling as a definite image . . . too much is cut away for them to be fully intelligible or for the full force to be felt. He therefore has to discover a way of charting in definite terms his wholly personal attitudes: he has to find a way of letting the image be the feeling, without concealing it. This he only really achieves in the *Derniers Vers*, where the poems are long enough for there to be an interrelation of images, and consequently a greater imaginative clarity. (pp. 78-9)

These poems, *Derniers Vers*, are the only sustained expression of Laforgue's mind and imagination. They have a stamp of authority which is altogether lacking in his earlier, experimental writing: in them he discovers his own idiom to the extent that it becomes purely speculative to imagine him then moving on to something else. (pp. 86-7)

The twelve parts of the *Derniers Vers* are tone poems on the several themes of *fin-de-siècle* scepticism. They express the feelings associated with uncertainty, disbelief and anguish, not now in a dogmatic way, but evocatively, as though the intention were no longer to propose ideas, but rather to permit the world of Laforgue's imagination its proper existence, without the more juvenile emphasis and intention to shock of the earlier poems. At the same time, they are not listless, but nervously energetic, like the last paintings of Van Gogh. Their unity, for it is not a mere formality that they comprise one volume, is a homogeneousness of style. . . . But it derives also from the two principal themes, as they are brought together: on the one hand, the various elements of Laforgue's personality, now brought to focus, and therefore under a degree of control; on the other, the painting of autumn, its moods, associations, implications. (p. 89)

One can think of the *Derniers Vers* as a whole by considering the way in which the author's own thoughts and preoccupations are gradually introduced into the complex of visual impression and mood. Whereas, before, the poet's thought had often been the dominant feature of a poem, like a demonstrator collecting round himself the paraphernalia appropriate to his experiment, now a whole way of seeing becomes the poem, of which the poet's own thoughts are at first only a part. . . . Laforgue in these poems. . . is that very modern figure who lets the weaknesses of his own personality be the lens through which a faithful credible view is achieved. In moral art the limitations of personality weaken the impact of the work; in art which is taking care not to be moral, but has a different ambition, in this case impressionistic, a character who is sensitive even in an anaemic way is taken to be a greater guarantee of authenticity than his more heroic predecessors. (pp. 90-1)

Whatever reservations it might be necessary to have about Laforgue himself, there is no doubt that many of these poems are highly accomplished works. The first poem, for example. **"L'Hiver qui vient,"** is one of the most complex and powerful. A series of exclamations, free from the restriction of grammar, like the brusque, non-realistic strokes of the Impressionist painter, sketch in the atmosphere, but with a play upon words that perhaps takes the imagination by surprise. It is not the Continental system and a naval blockade in the real emergency of the Napoleonic War, but in the poet's emergency a blockade of sentiment, in which the poet's mind is trapped by the impressions of autumn, by packets from the Levant. At the same time, there is the habit of irony, and a literary self-consciousness: not the rich mists of the Keatsian autumn, but the mist of the factory chimneys in a drizzling rain. (pp. 94-5)

[It] is evident that the theoretical images of Laforgue's earlier poems have been replaced by definite and usually visual ones. This is an improvement in itself. It means also, however, that his virtuosity with words and his inventiveness have a much more substantial imaginative base. (p. 95)

The *Derniers Vers* are not worth discussing except as whole poems. A truncated tone-poem is in any case a manifest absurdity, since it is the interrelationship of the parts, and the consequent harmony, that is important. Here the interrelationship has been achieved in a particularly fine way, it being clear, over and above everything else, that free-verse as Laforgue wrote it, held firmly by assonance and rhyme, was as disciplined and controlled as any other form he might have adopted, yet unobtrusive as he had always wished. He made a style. (p. 100)

If one considers the *Derniers Vers* as a whole, it can be seen that they demonstrate only too well one of the principal dilemmas of the modern poet. From this time on, it is as though the poet has the option of writing a poem which satisfies his feeling for art or of remaining close to life as he knows it even if that entails writing a more limited kind of poem. . . . Specifically, [Laforgue] showed that it was possible to write a free-verse poem, of great musicality, where the imaginative discipline was at the very heart of the poem, and not a matter of externals; he found a way of using symbol as the direct expression of the poet's insight; and, by dint of sheer virtuosity, he moved poetry into the realm of art, in the twentieth-century sense, and away from the romantic context of moral communication.

Laforgue's contribution to the craft of poetry is therefore considerable, whereas the Pre-Raphaelites, in rather a similar position, because of their preoccupation with the past had missed the opportunity of making significant technical progress. He created a new poetic idiom simply by writing it. As a person, he represents the disengaged, *fin-de-siècle*, self-conscious mind, at odds with the world yet obliged to place trust in his own untrusting sensibility. (pp. 112-14)

> *Michael Collie, in his* Laforgue *(© 1963 Text and Bibliography Michael Collie; reprinted by permission of the author), Oliver and Boyd, 1963, 120 p.*

**MICHAEL COLLIE and J. M. L'HEUREUX** (essay date 1965)

Laforgue's first free-verse poem, **"L'Hiver qui Vient,"** is one of the most self-contained and technically accomplished of the **D.V. [Derniers Vers].** Although Laforgue wrote to Kahn . . . that he had "forgotten" to rhyme, count syllables, or create stanzas, the poem itself does not lack artistic control and unity. Liberated from the external disciplines of more formal poetry, **"L'Hiver qui Vient"** is nevertheless firmly held by the strength and unity of its theme, and by the way in which the various strands of its imagery are worked into a single rich pattern. The poem is an attempt to seize and render the elusive essence of autumn, both in its physical manifestations and in the complex of feelings, memories, and association with which, for the poet, it has become charged. The poem thus sets up a delicate balance between the concrete examples of the working of autumn (rain, wind, deserted highways, falling leaves, etc.) and the symbolic representation of what the season means to the poet (the hunting horns, the dying sun, the city district with its loneliness and misery). But in the interplay and merging of symbol and description, in the constant pointing of the irony, the distinction is blurred, so that Laforgue successfully achieves what the last line of the poem indicates is his aim: a representation of autumn which takes fully into account the sensibility of the viewer. (pp. 73-4)

[**"Le Mystère des trois cors"**] elaborates a theme introduced in **"L'Hiver qui Vient."** Once again, life, represented by the sun, is hunted to death; but the focus now shifts to the witnesses of that death, the hunting horns. Although the symbol of the hunting horns is a complex one, some of its implications may be ascertained from Laforgue's earlier references to them. In a letter to Kahn, for instance, Laforgue uses the horn to indicate the fundamental ennui of his life. . . . The hunting horn thus symbolizes on one level the hopelessness and despair of a meaningless life. (p. 77)

Like Baudelaire and Mallarmé, Laforgue [also] associates the hunting horn with the theme of death. It is in this sense that, in poem VI, the breaking-up or death of the existing social order is attended by the sound of horns. . . . In **"Le Mystère des trois cors"** it is the death of the horns themselves that constitutes the "mystery" of the title.

Lastly, the hunting horn is often the objective correlative of a sexual theme. In Laforgue's earlier poems its call is heard immediately before sexual union, as in later poems it is heard immediately before death. (pp. 77-8)

[The third poem, **"Dimanches,"**] strikes a more direct, personal note. To begin with, the poet now speaks in the first person; and one of the principal themes introduced—that of the highly introspective, sensitive individual whose very self-awareness makes him unsure of his own personality and unable to establish contact with others—is of central concern to Laforgue himself. In the *D.V.* it recurs again and again, thus forming one of the leitmotives which give the twelve poems their unity. Another personal theme introduced in this poem is also to gain increasing prominence in succeeding poems: that of the two lovers who thought of marrying only to separate. (pp. 79-80)

Also given its first statement in this poem is the important symbol of "Sunday," one which Laforgue used consistently as the exterior equivalent for his "spleen," his alienation from the world around him. For it is on Sunday, when he is himself idle, and when he sees other people occupied together in the weekly rituals of churchgoing and family reunions, that the poet most feels his own isolation and boredom. The irony of the situation lies in his awareness of the fact that, although he has nothing but contempt for the emptiness of lives filled with such mechanical routines, he cannot help feeling still the loneliness of his own position. (p. 80)

[The] second **"Dimanches"** reasserts in its vigorous opening section the original leitmotif of autumn. The image of young ladies on their way to church again conveys the melancholy of Sundays and the poet's isolation; but the focus shifts gradually to a slightly different aspect of the symbol, as the young girls come to represent womankind as a whole. Laforgue thus probes the nature both of women and of relationship between the sexes, a psychological exploration which, continued in the next poem, becomes its main and all-encompassing subject. (p. 85)

The beginning of **"Pétition"** is a variation on the closing lines of [the second **"Dimanches"**], whose bitter tone it sustains. Anatomizing the "espèce" [species] with which he is so disgusted, the poet finds little cause for optimism: love is as sterile as a fountainless square and yet full of meaningless fury like a fairground; beneath a genteel façade women are merely the instruments of sex. From this cynical outburst, the poem moves to a serious appeal—the "petition" of the title—for a more genuine and equal contact between the sexes, but the earnestness of the plea is neutralized by the irony of the fanciful last section. (p. 88)

The main theme of **"Simple Agonie"** is . . . close to *Hamlet*. . . . It is a meditation on life, on the problem "to be or not to be." The **"Agonie"** of the title holds several levels of association. It can mean the anguish . . . of the man caught in the fatalistic situation outlined in the [preceding] poems. As in those poems, that man can find no certainty or value, either in himself, since he is critical of his very ability to think or judge accurately . . . , or in society—from which he is in any case estranged . . .—and which he feels to be irremediably

corrupt. . . . But **"Agonie"** also denotes a more literal death-agony, for the protagonist in the last section is in fact dead. He—unlike Hamlet—could find no reason to continue living, since he no longer believed in or feared the "something after death, the undiscovered country." This reason, indeed all reasons, are no longer valid. . . . Lastly, the title also retains its suggestion of Christ's agony in the garden, but the coupling of "simple" and "agonie" makes this religious implication very ironical. (pp. 92-3)

[**"Sur une Défunte"**] begins to knit together some of the previously unrelated themes informing the *D.V.* as a whole. Although it is mainly concerned with the idea of the fiancée's other loves, this is no longer seen as a single, isolated event (as in **"Légende"**) but as an inevitable corollary to the lack of certainty in life. Thus it unites two main themes: the theme that man has no control over his own destiny . . . and the theme that there is no such thing as absolute value or absolute love. . . . The poet's fatalistic dilemma, his loneliness, his failure to marry are also seen as part of the larger pattern which has formed the backdrop to the *D.V.*: a pattern of isolation, despair, renunciation, autumn, death. (p. 105)

*Michael Collie and J. M. L'Heureux, "Critical Notes," in* Derniers Vers *by Jules Laforgue, edited by Michael Collie and J. M. L'Heureux (© University of Toronto Press, 1965; reprinted by permission of Michael Collie), University of Toronto Press, 1965, pp. 73-108.*

**WILLIAM JAY SMITH** (essay date 1969)

[In *Moralités légendaires*], as in his final poems, Laforgue is at the height of his inventive powers. What delight there is in these exquisitely wrought tales; what flash and sparkle of youthful genius. There is surely no prose of the late nineteenth century that is so ornate without being heavy: it is light to the occasional point of frivolity but somehow always firm; it is delicate but rarely weak. Here Laforgue works within the fulness of his orbit, and only on the sure base of sensibility could rise such intaglio of intellect. . . . [In] these tales he moves, giving dimension with a quick brush-stroke to everyday events and objects, making what is ordinary and everyday seem fantastical and strange, and what is strange and fantastical ordinary and everyday. (p. 60)

At first glance, Laforgue's purpose in the *Moralités légendaires* appears to be a stylistic one: he wishes to dispense with bombast and grandiloquence, to restore to art a sense of proportion and common sense, to wring the neck of rhetoric in his own way. But as in all his work, this stylistic purpose reflects a deeper psychological one. . . . The stories are, in a sense, a parallel development to the *Complaintes*. In the poems he attempted to cast traditional poetic and philosophical themes in common everyday popular songs; in the stories, he brings myth and lofty legend down to earth, he cuts his heroes down to size. Of course, the simplest and most direct, if not always the most effective, means of accomplishing this is through parody; indeed, the *Moralités* have been called nothing but "parodies artificielles." It is true that, at their worst, they do degenerate into a kind of schoolboy burlesque, as in **"Salomé."** The wit disintegrates in places, and we have a sense of the smart aleck, something gets between the author and his material, and the result is a series of monkeyshines. Even at his worst, however, Laforgue is never gross nor uncouth; the comedy almost always remains that of the drawing room rather than of the smoking car. But parody is not Laforgue's real purpose. The *Moralités* seem to point up no moral. . . . Laforgue would have us forget the point, for the point is always made by indirection. The moral is as much in how the thing is said as it is in what is said. And what he says in the entire book is that all the past—history, myth, and legend—exists everywhere and for all of us: we are in it, and it is in us.

The past is a living thing, and our heroes are where we find them. (pp 61-2)

Laforgue always had his personal and private reasons for depicting his heroes as he did: indeed, he put a great deal that is recognizably himself into his **"Hamlet"**; and though his heroes are at times rather hopelessly immature, they are, for all their posturing, ordinary people. In the destruction of the hero there is still something heroic that survives. With this treatment of myth, Laforgue, poetically and intuitively, hit upon a wholly modern approach; the heroes of the past must be recreated by each human consciousness in its own way; they are perpetually waiting to be reborn. (pp. 62-3)

So completely did Laforgue live through his eyes that one can almost say that he saw these tales as tone poems and assigned to each of them a certain color: black to **"Hamlet,"** red to **"Le Miracle des roses,"** white to **"Lohengrin,"** yellow to **"Salomé,"** green and gold to **"Pan et la syrinx,"** gray to **"Persée et Andromède,"** and violet to **"Les deux Pigeons,"** which Laforgue decided to eliminate from the book. Each story is bathed in its own color; and the reader has the sense as he proceeds of experiencing an entire scale of color values. The **"Lohengrin"** of Laforgue with its ice-cold lunar landscape bears many resemblances to "The Eve of St. Agnes" of Keats, and like Keats, Laforgue is aware of the emotional overtones which color can provide. The descriptive passages in the *Moralités légendaires* do not exist apart from the story; the detail, exquisite in itself, serves to move the plot forward. The landscape, in some remarkable way, actually helps to define the characters; as in a finely wrought tapestry, all is interwoven with extreme care. Salomé, in her spidery yellow muslin with its black polka dots, has a real affinity with the heavens; she is actually a manifestation of the Moon Goddess, an earthly projection of the Milky Way.

Two themes are paramount in all the tales: one is the proximity of death . . . , the other, the permanence of art. . . . Perhaps it is Laforgue's youth and his awareness of an early death, as well as of his own genius, that gives the tales, like the best of his poems, their special poignancy. (pp. 63-4)

Art *was* life to Laforgue, and he left no better testimonial to the fact than his moral tales. Art for art's sake, yes, which meant art for life's sake as well. And how paradoxical it is that there can be so much freshness of spirit in a work so artificial in nature. (p. 65)

*William Jay Smith, "The Moral of the 'Moralités',"* *in* Jules Laforgue: Essays on a Poet's Life and Work, *edited by Warren Ramsey (copyright © 1969 by Southern Illinois University Press; reprinted by permission of Southern Illinois University Press), Southern Illinois University Press, 1969, pp. 60-5.*

**HASKELL M. BLOCK** (essay date 1969)

Jules Laforgue can hardly be considered among the important French playwrights of the later nineteenth century, yet had he lived longer, he might have distinguished himself in the the-

atre. . . . In his brief but intense span of creative activity, Laforgue completed only two short dramatic compositions. These could hardly be described as representative modern plays; nevertheless, they are of high interest, both intrinsically and as part of Laforgue's poetic testament, and they have scarcely received more than passing attention, even from the poet's admirers. (p. 76)

Appropriately, the image of the clown is at the center of the first of Laforgue's plays that has been preserved, *Pierrot fumiste*. . . . It seems to have been composed—or at any rate, finished off, hastily. Squarely in the tradition of *commedia dell' arte*, the playlet probably has its immediate origins in the irreverent and farcical *saynette* [drawing room comedy] of Huysmans and Hennique, *Pierrot sceptique*, published in 1881. . . .

The same flippant and light-hearted satire [found in *Pierrot sceptique*] characterizes *Pierrot fumiste*. (p. 79)

*Pierrot fumiste* begins with mock-serious badinage and ends with a scenario. The transition from dialogue to mime is altogether in keeping with the farcical tone of the piece, but the mixture of bawdy and sentimental dialogue is so spirited and comical that one cannot help wishing the poet had not abandoned it so lightly.

*Pierrot fumiste* has not been taken seriously by many of Laforgue's admirers. . . . [We may find, however,] the same ironic and poignant comic mask in the hero of *Pierrot fumiste* as in the *Complaintes* of Lord Pierrot that constitute some of Laforgue's best poetry. . . . *Pierrot fumiste* is a striking expression of Laforgue's originality and his love of mask, mime, and farcical extravaganza, remote from any overt or tendentious preoccupation. His hero points not only to *Les Complaintes,* but to the spirited and meditative clowns of Musset, Banville, Paul Margueritte, or Apollinaire. *Pierrot fumiste* is an early attempt at theatrical exploitation of the poet's characteristic gestures and devices. A slight play but one by no means mediocre for a beginner, it reveals a talent for spectacle and farce that might have led to a significant achievement in the theatre had time sufficed. (pp. 80-1)

By far the better known of Laforgue's two published plays, *Le Concile féerique* is in fact a composite work, formed by the grouping in dialogue form of five of the poems collected for *Des Fleurs de bonne volonté,* a volume prepared by the poet in 1886 for publication but soon abandoned. (pp. 82-3)

*Le Concile féerique* is far closer to dramatic poetry than to poetic drama. There is no plot and little characterization; simply the nocturnal musings of a man and a woman before and after their sensual embrace. The lovers are surrounded by a Chorus and an Echo, whose dialogue both masks and comments on the physical act of love. (p. 83)

Laforgue's verse proverb ultimately fuses all of the voices into a single attitude. All the characters share the same ironic sophistication, along with a keen awareness of the littleness and emptiness of even the most passionate of acts. (p. 84)

Delightfully engaging in its wit and verve, *Le Concile féerique* is much too slight to carry any profound philosophical weight. Essentially a lyrical meditation, its lines could be reassigned without undue incongruity. The action is untheatrical and virtually static, and one may wonder if the poet envisaged the work as more than a literary exercise. Unquestionably, there is a significant advance in Laforgue's transposition of isolated poems from *Des Fleurs de bonne volonté* into his playlet, but the integration is artificial. The characters are mere types, and their essential relationships are not with each other but with the cosmos. What unity the work possesses lies not in traditional dramatic elements but in a wonderful coalescence of mood and language, in which the witty and ironic commentary of the supernatural observers corresponds perfectly to the behavior of the lovers and to the lovers' insight into their own condition.

It is patently unfair to read or envision Laforgue's play from the same standpoint as a modern drama of contemporary life. The capricious make-believe, ribald farcicality, and ironic sophistication that we find permeating Laforgue's poetry and earlier play are central to his dramatic art. Despite external differences, *Le Concile féerique* is not as far removed in style and tone from *Pierrot fumiste* as one may at first glance imagine. . . . Voices take the place of gestures in a setting so bare and simple that the physical stage and its attendant properties hardly seem relevant.

Was *Le Concile féerique* actually written for the stage? The absence of almost any change in the transposition from the lyric to the dramatic mode may offer convincing proof of the intrinsically dramatic character of Laforgue's poetry with its complex interplay of several voices; but poetic drama cannot be equated with dramatic poetry. (pp. 84-6)

Laforgue's best known single work, **Hamlet,** reflects [his] intimate awareness of the theatre's ways and means. A scenario as well as a *nouvelle,* it brings together soliloquy, gesture, and dramatic dialogue in depicting the vivid interplay of the real and make-believe. Hamlet is himself both actor and playwright, seeing life and art as performance and masquerade. Laforgue's **Hamlet** cries out for dramatic presentation; a skillful craftsman could turn it into an effective play. . . . In structure as well as style, **Hamlet** testifies brilliantly to the steady growth of dramatic power in Laforgue's art.

It would be over-generous to consider Jules Laforgue a great playwright *manqué,* but his love and understanding of histrionic performance helped significantly to shape and direct his poetic talent. His theatrical compositions were inspired not so much by grandiose ambition as by the desire to write something striking and new. The quest for novelty and originality made Laforgue a precursor of much that is modern in twentieth century poetry. It also might have led him to imaginative and arresting discoveries in the modern drama. (pp. 91-2)

> Haskell M. Block, "Laforgue and the Theatre," in Jules Laforgue: Essays on a Poet's Life and Work, *edited by Warren Ramsey (copyright © 1969 by Southern Illinois University Press; reprinted by permission of Southern Illinois University Press), Southern Illinois University Press, 1969, pp. 76-92.*

**RUSSELL S. KING**  (essay date 1976)

However much Laforgue's verbalism may be explained in terms of a particular sensibility, it nonetheless represented a desire to create a "new poetic language", as editors and critics have been quick to point out. . . .

Laforgue's attempt to create a new poetic expression and his obsession with linguistic experimentation are, at a most obvious level, related to his quest for originality. . . . Not surprisingly his claim to verbal originality depends on his occasional use of Joycian portmanteau words (sexciproque, violupté, élé-

phantaisiste) and his conspicuous deviations in syntax. [However] his originality [also] resides . . . in his use of cosmic imagery in his first collection of poems, *Le Sanglot de la Terre* . . . , in his special sensibility which mingled pathos and burlesque in a manner which appealed so much to T. S. Eliot, and his use of popular ballad forms in *Les Complaintes* . . . , and in his early use of *vers libres.* (p. 2)

Like Laforgue's contemporary critics, any modern reader of *Moralités légendaires* or *Derniers vers* is immediately aware that Laforgue was attempting something new. On the one hand there is in his poetry a tendency to simplicity and a conversational style apparent even in his earliest writing. On the other hand however this tendency is counterbalanced by another towards concision and obscurity. (p. 3)

The stylistic variations in Laforgue's writing in part reflect a rapid evolution which is apparent in any thematic, formal or stylistic comparison between the early *Sanglot de la Terre* and *Derniers Vers.* . . . By the time of the composition . . . of the *Moralités légendaires* [however] his idiosyncratic style (or styles) was largely and distinctively formed. . . . Already the key qualities are apparent: on the one hand those qualities which tend towards easy comprehension like clarity, simplicity, naïvety and obvious human relevance; and those which tend to difficulty: complexity of construction and unusual, novel images.

Laforgue was conscious of the difficulty of reconciling the "what one says" of naturalist writing with the "how one says it" of decadent and symbolist aesthetics. . . . The "coarseness" and "saletés de la vie" [filthiness of life] which one more readily associates with the transitive discourse and aesthetics of naturalist prose writing are to be expressed [in Laforgue's work] in the self-conscious refined style of decadent-symbolism. . . . The fusion of naturalism in subject matter, the frequent use of colloquial language and popular art forms, with decadent aesthetics provides one key to Laforgue's poetic universe.

This refinement of expression must not be associated with notions of eloquent communication, for eloquence would undermine the impression of dreamlike naïvety which Laforgue sought to convey. . . . Laforgue condemned his early *Le Sanglot de la Terre* for its excessive eloquence. . . . Eloquence [he said] belongs rather to the committed, passionate poet for whom poetry is primarily a vehicle of communication. . . . This rejection of eloquent expression in favour of neglect of form and an appearance of childlike naïvety brings Laforgue close to Verlaine. . . . Laforgue's identification with Verlaine is to be explained in a large measure by the two poets' partial adoption of impressionist aesthetics: the artistic reflection of impressions of relatively insignificant life and scenes resulting from direct confrontation with, and apprehension of, ephemeral reality, unformed by the intellect and expressed with a sense of directness and immediacy rather than in elaborate diction and traditional forms. In a sense their impressionism explains their appearance of naturalism in content and symbolism in expression. (pp. 3-5)

The adoption of free verse is not an isolated phenomenon, but must be understood with reference to Laforgue's aesthetic as a whole. Without doubt the two principal stylo-linguistic features of his writing comprise his frequent rejection of standard norms of syntax and his lexical inventions. All his poetry after *Le Sanglot de la Terre* reflects an increasingly daring rejection of conventionally accepted syntax. . . . [His] devaluation of subject matter and the simple construction or juxtaposition of ''bouts de rêverie sans suite'' [incoherent fragments of dreaming] could never adequately be adapted to the language of logical realism. (p. 6)

The absence of explanation and coordination, the transformation of normally dependent grammatical structures into independent units juxtaposed with others, the abandonment in *Derniers Vers* of traditional verse forms, a fusion of naturalist triviality with decadent refinement, all tend to create an impression of anarchy of expression and obscurity of content. However this appearance of anarchy and obscurity needed to be orientated towards some counterbalancing artistic coherence. There is an obvious thematic unity in the earlier collections: cosmology in *Le Sanglot de la Terre* and the moon in *L'Imitation de Notre-Dame La Lune*. In a letter to Léo Trézenik in which he compared himself with Tristan Corbière he insisted: ''Je vis d'une philosophie absolue et non de tics'' [I saw by means of an absolute philosophy and not one of tics]. Yet the structuring of his poetry with its thematic and grammatical discontinuity gives precisely the impression of ''tics'', however much there may be an underlying ''philosophie absolue''. This is the ''philosophy of the unconscious'' which evocatively and suggestively translates itself into a language of discontinuity and apparent disassociation. Only the intellectual analyst, as opposed to the symbolist, dadaist or surrealist poet, can retranslate the apparent anarchy into patterns of logic, which of course would destroy the poetry as poetry.

The Laforguian ''sentence'' often seems to be in a state of decomposition, a state particularly associated with social and cultural attitudes of ''decadent'' writing in the 1880's. . . . [And] the decomposition of unity between poems—as in Baudelaire's *Le Spleen de Paris* and all Laforgue's collections—is related to the decomposition of the sentence, and, in its turn, to lexical decomposition, which provides an important link between Laforgue's syntactic experimentation and his lexical peculiarities. However it would perhaps be more accurate to say that, in respect of poetry as a reflection of mental processes, Laforgue's language is intended to suggest a state of pre-composition. . . . Laforgue revised his poems by ''deconstructing'' and ''degrammaticalizing'' the conventional, comprehensible sentences into concise, deviant, juxtaposed structures. (pp. 7-8)

Within the late Laforguian poem patterning is not provided in any formal way through verse or stanza forms but through refrains and the repetition of certain lines or words at regular or irregular intervals. Similarly there is abundant parallelism and tripling of syntactic structures, particularly in vocative forms and lists of nouns. This multiplication, which often appears gratuitous, of lexical and grammatical elements within the poem parallels the patterning of thematic elements—the kaleidoscope of life—with images of the dying universe, autumn, wind, rain, boring Sundays, absence of love etc. (pp. 8-9)

Laforgue vacillated abruptly and unexpectedly, between an intellectual's desire to use language as a medium of clear and even eloquent communication and an anti-intellectual artist's rejection of ''transitive discourse''. Though his basic subject matter . . . may have coincided in a large measure with that of naturalist writing (Maupassant rather than Zola), his perception of reality and the verbal means of communicating this perception reflect rather a fusion of impressionist and decadent principles and techniques. All Laforgue's writing in fact is based on polarized tensions: between colloquial language and refined ornamentation; between banality and vulgarity, and decadent artifice; between coherence and anarchy; and between an appeal to a special coterie of initiated readers and a desire to create living heroes accessible to the general public. In this manner the poet's ''stylo-aesthetic'' novelty with its clever juggling—logopoeia—of themes and words requires a very considerable mental agility on the part of the reader. Neologisms and unusual technical terms along with syntactic innovations reflect not only a particular sensibility but also a new form of poetic expression which is a composite of realism, naturalism, impressionism, Tainian and anti-Tainian methodologies, and which anticipates aesthetic principles associated with, for example, the language and style of the Dadaists, T. S. Eliot and James Joyce. (p. 10)

> *Russell S. King, ''Jules Laforgue's Symbolist Language: Stylistic Anarchy and Aesthetic Coherence,''* in Nottingham French Studies, *Vol. 15, No. 2, November, 1976, pp. 1-11.*

---

## ADDITIONAL BIBLIOGRAPHY

Arkell, David. *Looking for Laforgue: An Informal Biography*. New York: Persea Books, 1979, 248 p.

   A casual, anecdotal approach to Laforgue's life and literary accomplishments. Arkell relies heavily upon correspondence and unpublished journal entries.

Cowley, Malcolm. ''Laforgue in America: A Testimony.'' In his *And I Worked at the Writer's Trade: Chapters of Literary History, 1918-1978*, pp. 69-81. New York: The Viking Press, 1978.

   Explores Laforgue's influence on early twentieth-century American writers. Cowley concentrates on the importance of Laforgue's style to the works of Hart Crane, T. S. Eliot, and Ezra Pound.

Newman, Frances. Introduction to *Six Moral Tales from Jules Laforgue*, edited and translated by Frances Newman, pp. 9-26. New York: Horace Liveright, 1928.

   A general discussion of the *Six Moral Tales* which includes a brief overview of Laforgue's life. Newman concludes that the *Six Moral Tales* ''are the perfection of fictions because they are growing in reality and because they are carefully and beautifully trained against the lattice of their writer's fragile and tender spirit.''

Peyre, Henri. ''Jules Laforgue: 1860-1887.'' In *The Poem Itself*, edited by Stanley Burnshaw, pp. 60-3. New York: Holt, Rinehart and Winston, 1960.

   Discerning, though brief, comments on four of Laforgue's major poems. Peyre provides the original French text, his English translation, and a short textual analysis of each poem.

Ramsey, Warren. *Jules Laforgue and the Ironic Inheritance*. New York: Oxford University Press, 1953, 302 p.

   The first English critical biography of Laforgue. Ramsey traces Laforgue's literary development from his schooldays in Tarbes to his death in Paris. He also explores the influence of philosophy and contemporary literary trends on Laforgue's writing and discusses the critical response of Laforgue's contemporaries to his work.

Ramsey, Warren, ed. *Jules Laforgue: Essays on a Poet's Life and Work*. Carbondale, Ill., Edwardsville, Ill.: Southern Illinois University Press; London, Amsterdam: Feffer & Simons, 1969, 194 p.

   A collection of essays by such critics as Warren Ramsey, Henri Peyre, Peter Brooks, and William Jay Smith. This volume includes essays which compare Laforgue's work with that of Charles Baudelaire, Stephane Mallarmé, Ezra Pound, and Samuel Beckett, as well as essays which discuss Laforgue's style, symbolism, and dramatic presentation.

Starkie, Enid. *From Gautier to Eliot: The Influence of France on English Literature: 1851-1939*. London: Hutchinson & Co., 1960, 236 p.*

 Discusses Laforgue's general influence on the development of modern literature, and the effect that his works had on the writings of Ezra Pound and T. S. Eliot.

Unger, Leonard. "Laforgue, Conrad, and T. S. Eliot." In his *The Man in the Name: Essays on the Experience of Poetry*, pp. 190-242. Minneapolis: The University of Minnesota Press, 1956.*

 Investigates the relationships between the works of T. S. Eliot, Joseph Conrad, and Laforgue. Unger illustrates the similarities between the authors and with examples from their works.

# Mikhail Yuryevich Lermontov

## 1814-1841

(Also transliterated as Yurevich, Yurievich, Yur'evich; also Lermontoff) Russian poet, novelist, dramatist, and short story writer.

Lermontov wrote during an important transitional period in Russian literature when writers began to focus on the novel rather than verse. He achieved distinction as the author of richly Romantic poetry as well as Russia's first psychological novel, *Geroi nashego vremeni (A Hero of Our Time)*. Lermontov's verse is generally considered second only to that of Alexander Pushkin, and many believe that Lermontov's prose works are among the best in Russian literature. In *A Hero of Our Time,* Lermontov continued the tradition of character study initiated in Russian literature with Pushkin's portrayal of the "superfluous man" in *Eugene Onegin.* Critics credit Lermontov with expanding upon Pushkin's "novel in verse" in his portrait of Grigory Pechorin, the novel's complex and subtle anti-hero. *A Hero of Our Time,* which is regarded as a forerunner of the novels of Leo Tolstoy and Fedor Dostoevski, ushered in what many consider the greatest age of Russian literature.

Born in Moscow, Lermontov was the son of a poor army officer of Scottish descent and a young woman from a wealthy family. His mother died when he was three years old and his maternal grandmother, who had disapproved of her daughter's marriage, adopted him. Subsequently, Lermontov's grandmother tried to alienate the boy from his father. The divisive family situation affected him deeply, and his first poems reflect his feelings of isolation and melancholy.

Lermontov's early work reflects his admiration of Lord Byron, who provided Lermontov with the prototype for his brooding, rebellious poetic persona. As a student at Moscow University, he was distant from his classmates, who included the future critic Vissarion Belinski, as well as Ivan Goncharov who was to become a leading novelist. He continued to read Byron, and emulated his work in a series of confessional poems. Set in the Caucasus, these poems focus on the themes of freedom and the conflict of good and evil. Though Lermontov's early poetry closely resembles Byron's youthful work, Lermontov's is considered more violent and extreme. He also wrote several melodramatic plays imitating Friedrich Schiller's early *Sturm und Drang (Storm and Stress)* works. The best known of these, *Ispantsy,* is fashioned after Schiller's *Don Carlos,* and is, according to most critics, verbose and overly emotional.

In 1832, Lermontov moved to St. Petersburg, where he attended the Guards Cadet Academy. While some sources maintain that he was expelled from the University for accusing his professors of incompetence, others believe he left the Academy because of an unhappy love affair. While at the Academy, he wrote little, with the exception of his "Hussar Poems," which are mildly obscene accounts of his amorous conquests. It was considered unfashionable for a cadet to express a personal interest in literature or art and Lermontov instead cultivated the image of a carefree Don Juan. He did, however, write a narrative poem, "Khadzi Abrek," which one of his professors submitted to a journal without Lermontov's permission. Ler-

montov was furious when the poem appeared, but when he received only positive comments, he agreed to publish some of his work.

In 1837, after Pushkin was killed in a duel, Lermontov wrote "Na smert' Pushkina" ("The Death of Pushkin"), an angry poem which implicates the government in the poet's death. Lermontov's friends wrote out the poem by hand, and circulated thousands of copies. Overnight, Lermontov became famous. However, government officials, angered by Lermontov's accusations, arrested him and exiled him to the Caucasus. While in exile, he composed two of his finest poems, "Demon" ("The Demon") and "Mtsyri" ("The Circassian Boy"). Both of these poems evince in musical, flowing verse Lermontov's love of the Caucasian countryside and are ranked among his finest poetry.

Lermontov returned from exile to discover that "The Death of Pushkin" had made him a celebrity. But he considered his fame a burden and avoided literary society. In 1840, his most famous work, *A Hero of Our Time* was published. The work further enhanced his reputation, but its success only encouraged his feelings of boredom and his disappointment with life. He engaged in a duel on a meaningless pretext, and was exiled once again.

*A Hero of Our Time* is composed of five narrative sketches: "Bela," "Maxim Maximich," "Taman," "Princess Mary," and "The Fatalist,' which are unified by the figure of Pechorin. The last three segments are known collectively as "Pechorin's Journal." As the title implies, *A Hero of Our Time* depicts the life and character of a man who, according to Lermontov, is typical of his age. Like the other Byronic heroes of Lermontov's work, Pechorin is a strong, independent figure, always battling the world. Life is, for him, a disappointment. At the time of its publication, most critics believed that the book was autobiographical, and that Lermontov was flaunting his own personality. In the preface to the novel's second edition, Lermontov responded to these accusations, stating that he intended Pechorin as a mirror of society's weaknesses, rather than as a self-portrait. Pechorin's failings, he suggested, are not so much a fault of the hero, but "of his own time." In contrast to his earlier Romantic work, the style of *A Hero of Our Time* is realistic and controlled, and though some critics initially questioned the novel's moral stance, most generally considered it then, as now, a masterpiece.

When Lermontov returned from his second exile, he continued to antagonize those around him; in particular, he enjoyed teasing Nikolay Martynov, an elderly major who critics believe provided the model for Grushnitsky in *A Hero of Our Time*. Ultimately, Martynov tired of Lermontov's taunts, and challenged him to a duel. When the guns were drawn, Lermontov shot into the air; Martynov fired and killed him instantly. Upon hearing of Lermontov's death, Czar Nicholas I said only, "A dog's death for a dog." While some have intimated that Lermontov's death was part of a government scheme, most now see the duel as the fulfillment of Pechorin's death wish: "Why go on living? One just goes on living out of curiosity, waiting for something new. It's absurd and annoying."

In the twentieth century, critics have generally considered Lermontov's poetry the outstanding example of Russian Romanticism. Poets such as Aleksandr Blok and Boris Pasternak emulated his innovative use of language and meter. However, it is the literary and historical importance of *A Hero of Our Time* for which Lermontov is primarily remembered. Since its publication, critics have consistently ranked it among the foremost achievements of Russian literature.

## PRINCIPAL WORKS

*Khadzi Abrek* (poetry) 1835; published in journal
    *Biblioteka dlya chteniva*
*Na smert' Pushkina* (poetry) 1837
    ["The Death of Pushkin" published in journal *Free Russia*, 1899]
*Geroi nashego vremeni* (novel) 1840
    [*The Hero of Our Days*, 1847; also published as *Sketches of Russian Life in the Caucasus*, 1853; and as *A Hero of Our Own Time*, 1854; and as *A Hero of Our Time*, 1886]
*Stikhotvoreninya* (poetry) 1840
*Socheninya.* 2 vols. (poetry, essays, and drama) 1847
*Demon* (poetry) 1856
    [*The Demon*, 1875]
*Demon. Angelj. Rusalka. Pisnia pro Kalashnikova. Mstyri. Borodino. Duma.* (poetry) 1874
*The Circassian Boy;* also published as *The Novice*, 1875 (poetry) 1875
*Ionsekia drama M. O. Lermontova* [first publication] (drama) 1880

*Maskarad* [first publication] (drama) 1891
    [*Masquerade* published in journal *Russian TriQuarterly*, 1973]
*The Angel* (poetry) 1895; published in journal *Anglo-Russian Literary Society Proceedings*
*The Song of the Merchant Kaláshnikov* (poetry) 1911; also published as *A Song of Tzar Ivan Vasiljevich, His Young Life-Guardsman, and the Valiant Merchant Kaláshnikov* in journal *Poet Lore*, 1913
*Poems of Michael Lermontov* (poetry) 1917
*Two Brothers* (drama) 1933
*The Demon, and Other Poems* (poetry) 1965
*A Lermontov Reader* (poetry and essays) 1965
*Selected Poetry* (poetry) 1965
*Sobranie sochinenii v chetyrëkh tomakh.* 4 vols. (poetry, essays, and drama) 1979-81

*This work includes the dramas *Ispantsy, Menschen und Leidenschaften, Strannji chelovekj,* and *Dva brata.*

---

## VISSARION BELINSKI (essay date 1840)

[*The influential critic Belinski initially disliked, then admired Lermontov's work. In the following essay, which assured Lermontov's critical reputation, he praises both Lermontov's poetry and* A Hero of Our Time. *Unlike his contemporaries, Belinski did not view the novel as an autobiography, but as a purely artistic and historical achievement.*]

[We] recognize in [Lermontov] a Russian poet, *national* in the highest and noblest sense of that word: a poet in whom there has found expression a historical stage of Russian society. And all his poetry of this sort is profound and significant. In it there is expressed a nature rich in the gifts of the spirit, a noble human personality. (p. 132)

[In **"Meditation" ("Duma")** the] poet speaks of the new generation, of how he looks upon it with sadness, saying that its future is "either empty or dark." . . . These verses are written in blood. They come from the depths of an outraged spirit. This is the wail, the groan of a man for whom the absence of inner life is an evil a thousand times more fearful than physical death! . . . And who among the men of the new generation will not find in it the clue to his own despair and spirit apathy and inner emptiness, and will not answer back with his own wail and groan? . . . If by "satire" we are to mean not the innocuous grin of some gay wit, but the thunder of indignation, the storm of a spirit outraged at the shame of his society, then Lermontov's **"Meditation"** is a satire, and satire is a legitimate form of poetry.

Since the time of Pushkin's appearance in our literature . . . there has come into use the new word "disillusionment." . . . This was the age of the awakening of our society to life; literature for the first time began to be an expression of society. (pp. 132-33)

Recall *A Hero of Our Time,* recall Pechorin—that strange person who, on the one hand, is tired of life, despises it and himself, believes neither in it nor in himself . . . and who, on the other hand, is in pursuit of life, who greedily seeks its sensations . . . recall his love for Bela, for Vera, for Princess Mary—and then you will understand those lines:

> And love! . . . but who is there to love? . . . and why
> love for a time?
> Yet all love is for only a day. . . .

**"How weary! how mournful!"** ["**I skuchno! i grustno! . . .**"], out of all the pieces written by Lermontov, attracted the special hostitity of the older generation. Strange people! They still think that poetry should invent instead of being the priestess of truth, that it should console with a baby's rattle instead of thundering forth the truth!

[Yet] from the spirit of that same poet who sang songs of affliction, freezing the human heart, from that same spirit there could come forth also—[a] prayerful, soothing melody of hope, of reconciliation, and of the benediction of life in the midst of life. . . . (pp. 133-34)

We shall not call Lermontov a Byron or a Goethe or a Pushkin; but we do not consider it excessive praise to say that *such poems as* **"The Water Nymph"** ["**Rusalka**"], **"Three Palm-trees"** ["**Tri Palmy**"], and **"The Gifts of the Terek"** ["**Dary Tereka**"] could be found only in such poets as Byron, Goethe, and Pushkin. . . . (p. 134)

Casting a general glance over the poetry of Lermontov, we see in it all the forces, all the elements of which life and poetry are composed. In this deep nature, in this powerful spirit, everything seems to live, everything is accessible and understandable, everything finds a response. He is the omnipotent master of the kingdom of life; he reproduces it in the manner of the true artist. He has the soul of a Russian poet: in him are alive both the past and the present of Russian life; and he has a profound knowledge of the world of the spirit. . . . There is everything, everything in the poetry of Lermontov: both heaven and earth, both paradise and hell. . . . For the present we shall call him neither a Byron nor a Goethe nor a Pushkin, for we are convinced that he will become neither the first nor the second nor the third, but—*Lermontov*. . . . Already the time is not far off when his name in literature will become a famous Russian name. . . . (p. 135)

> *Vissarion Belinski, in an extract from "The Rationalism of Reality" (originally published in its entirety under a different title in* National Notes, *Summer, 1840), in* Vissarion Belinski, 1811-1848: A Study in the Origins of Social Criticism in Russia *by Herbert E. Bowman (copyright © 1954 by the President and Fellows of Harvard College; copyright renewed © 1982 by Herbert E. Bowman; excerpted by permission), Cambridge, Mass.: Harvard University Press, 1954 (and reprinted by Russell & Russell, 1969, pp. 132-35).*

**M. YU. LERMONTOV** (essay date 1841)

[*In his preface to the second edition of* A Hero of Our Time, *Lermontov defends Pechorin, and denies that this character is patterned after himself. He further maintains that rather than being merely a portrait of one person, his novel is "a portrait of the vices of our whole generation in their ultimate development."*]

The Preface is the first and also the last thing in a book. It either explains the book's purpose or else defends it against the attacks of critics. But the reader doesn't usually care in the least about a book's moral purpose or about journalists' attacks on it, so he doesn't bother to read the Preface. It is a pity,

especially in our country, where the reading public is still so naïve and immature that it cannot understand a fable unless the moral is given at the end, fails to see jokes, has no sense of irony, and is simply badly educated. It still doesn't realize that open abuse is impossible in respectable society or in respectable books, and that modern culture has found a far keener weapon than abuse. Though practically invisible, it is none the less deadly, under the cloak of flattery strikes surely and irresistibly. (p. 19)

The present book recently had the misfortune to be taken literally by some readers and even by some journals. Some were terribly offended that anyone as immoral as the Hero of our Time should be held up as an example, while others very subtly remarked that the author had portrayed himself and his acquaintances. Again that feeble old joke! Russia seems to be made in such a way that everything can change, except absurdities like this, and even the most fantastic fairy-tale can hardly escape being criticized for attempted libel.

The *Hero of our Time* is certainly a portrait, but not of a single person. It is a portrait of the vices of our whole generation in their ultimate development. You will say that no man can be so bad, and I will ask you why, after accepting all the villains of tragedy and romance, you refuse to believe in Pechorin. You have admired far more terrible and monstrous characters than he is, so why are you so merciless towards him, even as a fictitious character? Perhaps he comes too close to the bone?

You may say that morality will not benefit from this book. I'm sorry, but people have been fed on sweets too long and it has ruined their digestion. Bitter medicines and harsh truths are needed now, though please don't imagine that the present author was ever vain enough to dream of correcting human vices. Heaven preserve him from being so naïve! It simply amused him to draw a picture of contemporary man as he understands him and as he has, to his own and your misfortune, too often found him. Let it suffice that the malady has been diagnosed—heaven alone knows how to cure it! (pp. 19-20)

> *M. Yu. Lermontov, in a preface to his* A Hero of Our Time, *translated by Paul Foote (translation copyright ©Paul Foote, 1966; reprinted by permission of Penguin Books Ltd; originally published as* Geroi nashego vremeni, *second edition, Sankmasmerbyra, 1841), Penguin Books, 1966, pp. 19-20.*

**NIKOLAI GOGOL** (essay date 1847)

Since the death of Pushkin [Russian] poetry has ceased to progress. Nevertheless, this does not mean that its spirit has died out; on the contrary, it is building up afar, like a storm; the dry and stuffy atmosphere itself announces its approach. Already somewhat talented people have appeared. But they are all under the powerful influence of the harmonious sounds of Pushkin; none is yet capable of tearing himself away from the enchanted circle traced by him and showing his own strength. Nobody has yet perceived that another time has succeeded to his, that the moods of a new life have been formed and questions posed that were never posed before; and that is why not one of them is a precious stone. It is not fitting even to name them, except for Lermontov, who went further than the others and who is already no longer among us. One perceives in him the marks of a first-rate talent: a great career might have awaited him, had there not been an unfortunate star which he chose to take for his own. Having got into a society which might justly be called temporary and transitory, like a poor plant torn from its natal soil, condemned joylessly to drift across the steppes, feeling that it could not grow in any other soil and that its fate was to wither and be lost—from his earliest age he began to express that heart-rending indifference to everything that we have perceived in no other of our poets. Joyless meetings, careless partings, strange, senseless liaisons, concluded for no reason and broken for no reason, became the subjects of his verses and furnished [Vasily] Zhukovsky occasion most correctly to define this poetry by the neologism *unenchantment.* Thanks to the talent of Lermontov, this was in fashion for a while. . . . As in former times Schiller with a light hand diffused an *enchantment* which became fashionable throughout the world, as then, under the heavy hand of Byron, there was a run of *disenchantment,* born perhaps of excessive enchantment, which also became fashionable for a time, so in turn there came *unenchantment,* the natural child of Byronic disenchantment. Its existence, it goes without saying, was of shorter duration than the others, because in unenchantment there was no attraction for anyone. Having evoked the power of some seductive demon, the poet attempted more than once to depict its image as though wishing to exorcise it by his verse. This image was not drawn definitively; it was not even invested with that seductive power over man that he wished to give it. Apparently it was the degenerate product not of his own strength but of the fatigue and indolence of a man who had struggled with it. In one of his unfinished poems, called **"Story for a Child,"** this image is more definite and sensible. Perhaps if he had finished this tale, which is his best poem, he would have rid himself of this spirit, which is his own, and of his dismal state (a mark of this shines forth in the poems **"Angel," "Prayer,"** and some others), if he had preserved a little more respect and love for his talent. But no one has ever played with his talent so lightly, nor shown such vainglorious disdain for it as Lermontov. In him we note no love for the children of his imagination. Not one line stands out in him, is carefully wrought, balanced, and concentrated upon itself; indeed, his verse has no solid personality; sometimes it vaguely recalls the verse of Zhukovsky, sometimes that of Pushkin; everywhere there is excess and verbosity. His prose works are more valuable. No one among us has written so correct, so beautiful, and so fragrant a prose. There is more of the depth and reality of life—a future great painter of Russian existence was being prepared. But strange is the fate of our poets. Only let one of them who has lost his principal vocation and purpose throw himself into another or sink into the slough of worldly considerations, where it does not suit him to be and where there is no place for the poet, and a sudden violent death tears him out of our midst. Three first-rank poets, Pushkin, Griboyedov, Lermontov, one after the other, in the sight of everyone, were stolen away by violent death in the course of a single decade, when their maturity was just blossoming, in the full development of their powers—and it surprised no one; our frivolous breed did not even shudder! (pp. 239-41)

> Nikolai Gogol, "On the Essence of Russian Poetry and on Its Originality," in his Selected Passages from Correspondence with Friends, *translated by Jesse Zeldin (translation © 1969 by Vanderbilt University Press; originally published as Vybrannyia miesta iz perepiski s druz'iami, Canxmnemepóypis, 1847), Vanderbilt University Press, 1969, pp. 199-249.\**

## V. G. BYELINSKY   (essay date 1848?)

What an abundance of power, what a variety of ideas and images, emotions and pictures! What a strong fusion of energy and grace, depth and ease, elevation and simplicity!

Not a superfluous word; everything in its place; everything as required, because everything had been felt before it was said, everything had been seen before it was put on the canvas. [Lermontov's] song is free, without strain. It flows forth, here as a roaring waterfall, there as a lucid stream.

The quickness and variety of emotions are controlled by the unity of thought; agitation and struggle of opposing elements readily flow into one harmony, as the musical instruments in an orchestra join in one harmonious entity under the conductor's baton. And all sparkles with original colors, all is imbued with genuine creative thought and forms a new world similar to none. (p. 29)

•  •  •  •  •

Invincible spiritual power; subdued complaints; the fragrant incense of prayer; flaming, stormy inspiration; silent sadness; gentle pensiveness; cries of proud suffering, moans of despair; mysterious tenderness of feeling; indomitable outbursts of daring desires; chaste purity; infirmities of modern society; pictures from the life of the universe; intoxicating lures of existence; pangs of conscience; sweet remorse; sobs of passion; quiet tears flowing in the fullness of a heart that has been tamed in the storms of life; joy of love; trembling of separation; gladness of meeting; emotions of a mother; contempt for the prose of life; mad thirst for ecstasies; completeness of spirit that rejoices over the luxuries of existence; burning faith; pains of soul's emptiness; outcry of a life that shuns itself; poison of negation; chill of doubt; struggle between fullness of experience and destructive reflection; angel fallen from heaven; proud demon and innocent child; impetuous bacchante and pure maiden,—all, all is contained in Lermontov's [lyrical poems]: heaven and earth, paradise and hell. . . . (pp. 29-30)

> V. G. Byelinsky, in an extract from "M. J. Lermontov" (1848?), in A Guide to Russian Literature (1820-1917), *edited by Moissaye J. Olgin (copyright, 1920, by Harcourt Brace Jovanovich, Inc.), Harcourt Brace Jovanovich, 1920, pp. 29-30.*

## THE NATIONAL REVIEW   (essay date 1860)

Lermontoff must be placed among those who are *par excellence* called subjective poets; for his works reflect preëminently his own soul, its joys and sorrows, its hope and its despair. His heroes are parts of himself; in fact, his poems are his biography. This is, however, by no means to be understood as an intimation that he was deficient in all those qualities which distinguish the objective poet; on the contrary, several of his poems, particularly **The Song of the Czar Iwan Wassiljewitsh, his young Lifeguardsman, and the bold Merchant Kalashnikoff,** furnish ample proofs that he was fully capable of moulding figures quite independent of his own individuality. But he was one of those natures in whom all the chords that link them with their time vibrate so strongly that their creative power can rarely free itself from the influence of personal feelings, judgments, and reflections. These natures usually appear during the decay of old forms of society, in times of transition, of general skepticism, and of corrupt morals. In them the purer spirit of mankind seems to take refuge, and to make of them its mouthpiece. They criticize and doom the follies and vices of society by the disclosure of their own wounds, errors, and struggles on the one side; and, on the other, they heal, reconcile, and redeem this corrupt world by the insight they give into that beauty and ideal perfection of human nature of which genius always holds the secret. They generally blend in one the epic and the lyric element, action and reflection, narrative and satire. [Auguste] Barbier, and above all Lord Byron, are representatives of this class of poets; and both of these, as well as his countryman Pushkin, exercised a great influence over Lermontoff. From Pushkin he got the secret of Russian verse; with Byron he shared his scorn for society; from Barbier he learned the art of bitter satire and the iron strength of expression. But these influences by no means injured his originality; rather, on the contrary, did they give it more strength and finish.

Striking in him is the realistic element, which . . . seems to form a chief feature in the literary character of [Russia] generally. With their lively impressionable natures, with their great power of observation, and the facility with which they assimilate the impressions of others, the Russians seem qualified to develop preeminently that literary realism which tends to become the basis of all modern art. Lermontoff, wherever he directed his thoughts, stands on the firm ground of reality; and to this we owe the great precision, freshness, and truthfulness of the pictures in his epic poems, as well as the conscientious exactness in the lyric ones, which are always a true mirror of the dispositions of his mind. (pp. 171-72)

His predilection for the Circassian races is undeniable, and his most beautiful works prove this; for instance, the epic poem, which, in our opinion, is superior to all his other works, as well in the treatment of the subject itself as in the exquisite beauty of the pictures and the artistic finish of the whole. The poem is entitled *Mtsiri*, which means a novice living in a monastery, his vows yet unpronounced. (p. 172)

Here, more than in any of the other epic works, we behold the poet's own individuality revealing at last the secret of his soul's life, which had been ever concealed from the eyes of men. The story . . . is obviously the story of genius, which, while longing to realize an existence full of truth and ideal beauty, is yet doomed to live in a corrupt and enslaved society, and at last, with broken wings, is destined to feel that the struggle of a single individual against the great social necessity is vain. But when this last hour of consciousness has come, Lermontoff seems to say that his spirit likewise will curse none, and go to rest reconciled; for he has at last realized that, just such as it was, his life was *his* individual life; and as a remarkable woman has said, "if we could understand all, we should pardon all."

Beautiful also, and even preferred by many to this one, is another of Lermontoff's epic poems, *Ismaïl Bey,* in which unfortunately many gaps are left, in consequence of the rude excisions of the censor. Lermontoff speaks of these with disgust in some of his verses; and it certainly was one of the reasons why he himself published but such a small number of his poems, the greater part having only been printed after his death. The subject of *Ismaïl Bey* is, again, borrowed from life in the Caucasus, and also bears witness to his admiration of the poetry and beauty of a nature and of races which have preserved their wild originality and grace, unspoiled by the touch of that civilization which became for him synonymous with corruption. The character of Ismaïl Bey himself has perhaps a little too much of the poet's own individuality, of his skeptical and speculative turn of mind, for a hero of the uncivilized world; but the description of Sarah, the Leshgian girl, is not surpassed in any of Lord Byron's most picturesque feminine sketches. . . .

[*The Demon*] possesses great beauty and is thoroughly original. . . . Whilst Goethe's Mephistophiles especially represents the spirit of boundless dissatisfaction with finite enjoyments,—

the negative spirit which is so often allied to great intellectual powers, and which seems to stir them on to continual progress; whilst Byron's Lucifer, in *Cain,* shows us the stern metaphysical skepticism which plunges into the depths of existence, and asks for the ultimate reason—Lermontoff's demon shows us rather the despairing side of evil, which has not quite lost the sense of agony at its perpetual exile from all that is good. Neither Mephistophiles nor Lucifer ever descend from the heights of their cold and satirical contempt for the existing order of things to a repentant word, nor indulge one longing for the unconscious and undoubting quietude of a soul whose belief has never been shaken; but Lermontoff's demon, on the contrary, represents expressly the anguish of evil. Through all his contempt, through all his revolt, breaks forth a deep longing for that which he has lost. (p. 174)

There are some weak points in this poem, and it is altogether less perfect in composition than [*Mtsiri*]; but, on the whole, it makes a powerful impression, and there is such a profusion of glowing imagery and artistic beauty in it, that it well deserves to rank among the first of its kind. (p. 176)

> *"Russian Literature: Michael Lermontoff" (originally published in* The National Review, London, *Vol. XI, No. XXII, 1860), in* The Eclectic Magazine, *Vol. LII, No. II, June, 1861, pp. 167-76.*

### INNOKENTY ANNENSKY   (essay date 1909)

[*Annensky is considered one of the foremost Russian critics of the early twentieth century. Like Lermontov, he wrote of life's weariness and futility and his criticism reflects his cynical attitude and sense of detachment from the world.*]

Lermontov's Dream did not repeat itself. It has remained as it was, unarticulated. Perhaps it has even been lost without a trace; at any rate, Tolstoy, the sole person who could have understood it, early chose to follow his own path, an entirely different one.

Like all true poets, Lermontov loved life in a way peculiar to him. The words "love life" do not signify here, of course, loving a bell's pealing or champagne in life. I am speaking only of that particular aesthetic emotion, that dreamlike concurrence with life, symbolized by the metaphors called forth and given life by every poet.

Lermontov loved life without ecstasy and without anguish, seriously and wisely. He did not try to elicit life's secrets, and he did not exasperate her with questions. Lermontov did not bow down before life, and, precisely because he refused to stand in judgment of life, he did not take upon himself the self-abnegations so beloved by the Russian soul.

Lermontov loved life as it came to him; he himself did not come to life. Lermontov was a fatalist before the incoherence of life, and he replied with the same haughtiness both to her temptations and to her challenges. Perhaps no less than Baudelaire, Lermontov loved stillness and contemplation, but life made him a wanderer, and, moreover, a wanderer with hired post-horses. Perhaps his feeling of freedom and his proud intellect taught him that where one cannot be strong one may at least be different.

There is no Russian poet whom you can "put away" more simply, but at the same time there is scarcely another whose rhetoric fends off *poshlost'* [vulgarity] with metallic verse as Lermontov's does, revealing bluer depths and not faltering before the repulsiveness of life as Gogol did. No other poet has had that same aerial touch to life. He is a poet for whom the dignity and independence of man are not only ethical concerns, but also an aesthetic need, a symbol of his spiritual existence which is inseparable from it. Lermontov knew how to stand on the periphery of life enamored and enchanted and yet not blending with it, not imagining himself life's master for a minute, even once. (pp. 57-8)

How strange it is after [Tolstoy, Chekhov, Baudelaire, and Gogol] to read Lermontov again, and particularly Lermontov's prose. What exactly is it that his little tale **"Taman"** offers us? Curiously, Chekhov loved **"Taman"** and dreamed, without success, of writing a story just like it. Lermontov, feeling as deeply as he did the charm of blue waves in the moonlight and the black webbing of a ship's rigging on a bright strip of the horizon, had real strength and the wisdom to allow these things to live, to shine, and play freely without overshadowing them with his own personality or compromising their beauty with freighted words or authorial compassion, leaving them all the wise charm of their disinterestedness, their singular and independent life in which I really have absolutely no place. Or, in the concluding scene, the way Lermontov deposits the blind little boy on the shore, simply to leave him there quietly and inconsolably weeping and not ever to venture a word about his own kinship with this solitary, this pointlessly sensitive, mystically superfluous creation of the capricious God of Genesis. (p. 60)

It is consoling to think that not very long ago people knew how to love life without rushing into it idiotically. What is pleasing in Lermontov are the *thing-thoughts:* the face of a blind person, the spider web of a ship's rigging, a white female figure quietly sitting by the shore, the legitimacy of disinterestedness in those things about which we only talk.

These thing-thoughts are sometimes significant, but they are *always,* without fail, luminous and aerial. This is where their charm lies. Against our will Lermontov's thing-thoughts make a striking impression after we read of banal and, in our time, inevitable fears and desires, heavily corporal, importunate, sticky, and mainly, most often only, pretentious.

Lermontov understood that if he wanted to preserve his creative *I,* then it was not necessary to enter life's cabala using all his sensitivity. For him there existed only one aesthetic connection with life—the purely intellectual.

Was Lermontov a disdainful person? He required a filter for that troubled water of the soul which we often turn on like a full fountain. If Lermontov occasionally seems cold and egotistic, this has, I think, a profound and rational justification. For the fact is that his constant self-contemplation was not a Stendhalian pose, it was his self-defense, his conscious counterpoise to the tender, Pechorin-like sensitivity of the poet.

**"Taman"** closes humorously: "Besides, what business of mine are human joys and misfortunes, me, a traveling officer and, besides, one going by hired post-horses?"

Contemplate these words. There is in them none of the Gogolian *longing,* for Lermontov knows neither his *shameful,* nor his *terrible,* nor his *boring.* He never arranges little compromises with life, as Gogol does, treating one of his clerks sympathetically, or as Dostoevsky does, embracing one of his demented creatures. Lermontov had nothing to do either with the oppressed or with aphorisms.

All of these now-so-classical Gogolian moods found scant place in his keen and ironic mind. Lermontov does not pity others, because he does not know how to pity himself. (pp. 61-2)

Death sometimes seems to me a magical midday dream, which sees far, in a calm and clear fashion. But death can and must be beautiful in another way, too, because it is the soul-child of my will and it can be, if I wish it, also a golden luminary in the harmony of the world's order. It must have an indifference about it, the indifference of Lermontov. (p. 62)

> *Innokenty Annensky, "Innokenty Annensky on Mikhail Lermontov," translated by Andrew Field (originally published in an expanded form under a different title in* Vtoraya kniga otrazhenii *by Innokenty Annensky, 1909), in* The Complection of Russian Literature: A Cento, *edited by Andrew Field (copyright © 1971 by Andrew Field; reprinted with the permission of Atheneum Publishers, New York), Atheneum, 1971, pp. 57-62.*

## VLADIMIR NABOKOV (essay date 1941)

[*Nabokov's 1958 translation of* A Hero of Our Time *is considered outstanding. He views* A Hero of Our Time *as a fine example of narrative development but ultimately finds it overrated.*]

Women prefer [Lermontov] to Pushkin because of the pathos and loveliness of his personality, singing so urgently through his verse. Radical critics, people who expect poets to express the needs of the nation, have welcomed in Lermontov the first bard of the revolution. Although he did not allude to politics in his works, what they admired in him was his violent pity for the underdog, and one pessimistic critic has suggested that had Lermontov lived he might have used his talent in the 'sixties and 'seventies to write novels with an obvious social message. Here and there, in the sobbing rhythm of some of his lines, I cannot help feeling that the tearful rhymsters of later generations . . . owe something to Lermontov's pathos in singing the death of a soldier or that of his own soul. (p. 32)

Among human beings, poets are the best exponents of the art of deception. Such poets as Coleridge, Baudelaire, and Lermontov have been particularly good at creating a fluid and iridescent medium wherein reality discloses the dreams of which it consists. A geological transverse section of the most prosaic of towns may show the fabulous reptile and the fossil fern fantastically woven into its foundation. Travellers have told us that in the mysterious wastes of Central Asia mirages are sometimes so bright that real trees are mirrored in the sham shimmer of optical lakes. Something of the effect of these manifold reflections is characteristic of Lermontov's poetry, and especially of that most fatamorganic poem of his which might bear the title: A Dream in a Dream of a Dream in a Dream. In this respect the poem is, as far as I know, perfectly unique. But curiously enough, none of Lermontov's contemporaries, least of all the poet himself, ever noticed the remarkable telescopic process of images that it contains. Here is this fourfold dream:

> I dreamt that with a bullet in my side
> In a hot gorge of Daghestan I lay.
> Deep was the wound and steaming, and the tide
> Of my life-blood ebbed drop by drop away.
>
> Alone I lay amid a silent maze
> Of desert sand and bare cliffs rising steep,
> Their tawny summits burning in the blaze
> That burned me too; but lifeless was my sleep.

And in a dream I saw the candle-flame
Of a gay supper in the land I knew;
Young women crowned with flowers. . . . And my name
On their light lips hither and thither flew.

But one of them sat pensively apart,
Not joining in the light-lipped gossiping,
And there alone, God knows what made her heart,
Her young heart dream of such a hidden thing. . . .

For in her dream she saw a gorge, somewhere
In Daghestan, and knew the man who lay
There on the sand, the dead man, unaware
Of steaming wound and blood ebbing away.

Let us call the initial dreamer $A^1$, which will thus apply to the poetical personality of Lermontov, the live summary of the mirages involved. For simplicity's sake we shall ignore the argument that it was not he who really dreamt, but the poet he imagined dreaming. He dreams of his lifeless body lying among the yellow cliffs, and this second personality we shall call $A^2$. This $A^2$ dreams of a young woman in a distant land, and here is the central and deepest point of the whole image complex, which point we shall term $A^3$. In so far as the imagined existence of the young woman is implied, her dream of $A^2$ should be called $A^4$: however, this $A^4$ is a reversion to $A^2$, though not quite identical with it, and thus the circle is completed. The dreamer drifts back to the surface, and the full stop at the end of the poem comes with the exactitude of an alarm clock.

To be a good visionary you must be a good observer. The better you see the earth the finer your perception of heaven will be; and, inversely, the crystal-gazer who is not an artist will turn out to be merely an old bore. Lermontov's long poem **"The Demon"** devoted to the lurid love-affair between a demon and a Georgian girl is built on a commonplace of mysticism. But it is saved by the bright pigments of definite landscapes painted here and there by a magic brush. There is nothing of an Oriental poet's passion for gems and generalizations here; Lermontov is essentially a European traveller, admiring distant lands, as all Russian poets have been, although they might never have left their hearths. The very love for the native countryside is with Lermontov (and others) European, in the sense that it is both irrational and founded on concrete sensual experience. "An unofficial English rose," or "the spires and farms" seen from a hilltop in Shropshire, or the little river at home which a Russian pilgrim, many centuries ago, recalled when he saw the Jordan, or merely those "green fields" a famous fat man babbled about as he died, offer a thrill of indescribable love for one's country that history books and statues in public gardens fail to provoke. But what is quite peculiar to "native land" descriptions in Russian poems is the atmosphere of nostalgia which sharpens the senses but distorts objective relationships. The Russian poet talks of the view from his window as if he were an exile dreaming of his land more vividly than he ever saw it, although at the moment he may be actually surveying the acres he owns. (pp. 34-5)

There has been a good deal of nonsense written recently by Russian critics about *The Hero of Our Time*'s being the chef d'oeuvre of the Russian novel, and thus ranking higher than, for instance, Tolstoy's *War and Peace*. It is the same kind of attitude, really a commonplace turned inside out, as when people maintain that Verlaine's whole poetical output is inferior to his religious poems. . . . (pp. 35-6)

First of all, *The Hero of Our Time* is not really a novel at all, but a group of five short stories. The first, **"Bela,"** relates the narrator's meeting the Caucasian veteran, Captain Maxim Maximych, on the road from Tiflis to Vladikavkaz; Maximych tells the story of Pechorin, who was a subaltern for a time in a fort on the mountain frontier and had a love-affair with a native girl. The movement of Lermontov's plots follows the line of least resistance, and eavesdropping is a trick extensively used by him. But in "Bela" we don't mind the device so much because the eavesdropper's story is so good. . . .

Not only new colors but the art of rendering human gestures appears with Lermontov for the first time. Maximych, after a silence, suddenly stamps on the floor: "Never shall I forgive myself one thing—why the hell did I tell Pechorin what I overheard?" And generally speaking, the character of Maxim Maximych, a simple old warrior with sound principles and broad views, is extraordinarily well suggested. (p. 36)

In the next story, **"Maxim Maximych,"** the author meets the good veteran once again and, as fate would have it (coincidence is the sister of eavesdropping), Pechorin happens to arrive at the same roadside inn. . . . Pechorin is on the way to Persia, is anxious to hurry on, and poor old Maxim Maximych is very much hurt by the casual bored greeting which his former companion gives him after all these years. With tears of anger and disappointment in his eyes, he tosses over to the author a bundle of Pechorin's manuscripts which have been in his keep, and the next three stories come from these papers, which the author, as it were, publishes after learning of Pechorin's death on his way back from Persia. (p. 37)

The next story (the first one from Pechorin's diary), **"Taman,"** is a kind of mystery story, with Pechorin playing the part of the amateur detective. One day he happens to disturb some smugglers in a lonely spot on the East shore of the Black Sea: on sunny mornings one could discern from the beach "the distant Crimean shore which stretches in a violet line with a cliff at the end." I note this sentence because this was probably the very first time that a Russian writer saw that color. The story is chiefly important for its concise, beautifully graduated, descriptive passages (a Chekhov feature), such as those referring to the hut where the hero lived, the golden sheen on the sunburnt neck of the girl who was involved in the smuggling business, and the fierce struggle in the boat. But it is not the masterpiece of Russian fiction suggested by some critics. The initial idea that the officer Pechorin, seeing people secretly carrying bundles to a boat in the night, did not leap at once to the obvious conclusion is, to say the least, unsound. But **"Taman"** has nevertheless that style, that grace, that vigor which can be achieved only by a great writer.

The story **"The Fatalist"** is merely an intensified anecdote akin to the tales of Pushkin. The longest one, **"Princess Mary,"** is probably the most important of the five. At a Caucasian watering-place, where the local ladies "are used to finding an ardent heart under a numbered army button and a cultured mind under a white cap," Pechorin and Grushnitsky are attracted by a young girl who is there with her mother. Grushnitsky is a parody of the Byronic young man—pompous, vain, full of himself, falsely *blasé,* proud of a slight wound, and flaunting a soldier's rough greatcoat. (pp. 37-8)

The story is really a medley of more or less brilliant aphorisms interspersed with illustrations in narrative form. . . . It is spoiled, as are the other stories, by the usual method employed by Lermontov in order to speed up the climax—persistent and quite unjustified eavesdropping on the part of the storyteller. (p. 38)

In Russian schools, at least in my day, a favorite theme for compositions was "Onegin and Pechorin." The parallel is obvious, but quite superficial. Pushkin's Onegin stretches himself throughout the book and yawns. Lermontov's Pechorin does nothing of the sort—he laughs and bites. With his immense store of tenderness, kindness, and heroism behind his cynical and arrogant appearance, he is a deeper personality than the cold lean fop so delightfully depicted by Pushkin.

> *Vladimir Nabokov, "The Lermontov Mirage," in* The Russian Review *(copyright 1941 by The Russian Review, Inc.), Vol. 1, No. 1, November, 1941, pp. 31-9.*

## MARC SLONIM  (essay date 1950)

Lermontov was undoubtedly the most powerful representative of Russian Romanticism. However, he did not err in stressing the fundamental difference between Byron and himself. Many of Lermontov's mental attitudes were certainly affectations, springing from his desire to 'play a role'—this was the extent of his Byronism. But while the English poet brought his artificiality and insincerity even to his poems, Lermontov was utterly sincere in his work. He never regarded poetry as a stage: he enjoyed performing romantic parts in real life—and his torments were real enough—but he was never stilted in his lyrics. His poems were an exact transcript of his thoughts and emotions. At the age of fifteen, in **'The Angel,'** he revealed one of his main themes: the discord between reality and imagination, the gap between the world he was destined to inhabit and the vision of perfection that haunted his dreams. An angel is singing while carrying a soul about to be born. The sounds remain in the young soul, and all the dull songs of earth can never replace the echo of that angel's heavenly melody. The image of the demon is the second leitmotiv of Lermontov's poetry. **'An Exile from Paradise'** symbolizes the negation of accepted values, the rebellion against 'the prison of Being.' Many critics have felt that of the two guardians of Lermontov's poetry, the Demon was stronger than the Angel. (pp. 117-18)

[It] is obvious that Lermontov's rebellion is not as infernal and sinister as some critics would like to think. Even his Demon, **The Great Exile** is a 'melancholy spirit.' Lermontov uses many Romantic images: bandits, corsairs, primitive men of passion and lust crowd his poems, but melancholy accompanies their outbursts. Lermontov is always aware of the 'tears of things' *(lacrimae rerum)* and they pain his mortal heart. His melancholy takes on the character of a national trait: he emphasizes it in the Russian landscape, in the Russian folk songs, in the Russian temperament. He himself is a 'melancholy rebel.'. . . (p. 118)

It would be presumptuous to try to explain Lermontov through any one of the themes of his poetry. His duality involved various unresolved contradictions in his nature and his work. The charm of his poetry lies in the alternation of light and shadow, in the changing colors of his moods. Lermontov, never having attained harmony within himself, stresses in his poetry discord and struggle as primary forces of the universe. He said that 'only in man can the sacred and the sinful unite' and saw in that union the cause of all human woes. It should be added that he was attracted equally by heavenly melodies and by demoniac war songs. (pp. 118-19)

Even in his early writings, Lermontov was one of the first Russian writers to deal with the problem of evil. He was well acquainted (more by intuition than through personal experi-

ence) with the 'darkness' of life and the 'nocturnal side' of human nature. There is a link connecting Lermontov with the tormented heroes of Dostoevsky. The pathological, warped, and pathetic world of suffering, of inner conflicts, and of 'accursed problems' of God, truth, immortality, morality, and cruelty, which startled the Western readers of *Crime and Punishment* and *The Brothers Karamazov* some forty years later, was already present in the works of Lermontov. Lermontov, however, was a poet, and consequently infinitely harder to translate than Dostoevsky. (p. 119)

It can be said that, beyond all his individualistic ideas, there was in Lermontov a constant quest for moral justification. His refusal to accept man, society, and the universal order was determined by his search for a higher finality, and this gives to his poetry a dynamic quality and a brilliance that enliven almost every line. This search for moral truth is even more manifest in . . . *A Hero of Our Times.* In it Lermontov relates the adventures of a young officer, Pechorin, an egotistic and wilful individual who, by his early twenties, has experienced—or so he believes—all that life has to offer. He is disillusioned and disgusted with everything. Nothing can delight his thoughts or fix his emotions. He believes in neither God nor Devil, and what others call 'ideals' or 'aims of life' are, to his cynical mind, nothing but childish illusions. Pechorin does not hesitate to sacrifice the love of women or the affection of men for the sake of amusement or a mere whim. He plunges into dangerous adventures, elopes with a Caucasian girl who is later killed by her betrothed, stakes his life on a trifle, ruins the women who adore him, and still does not succeed in overcoming his boredom and awareness of the futility of all human endeavor. At the same time he is capable of genuine feeling; he is courageous and endowed with a strong will. His main trouble is that he is continually wasting his exceptional energy and his rich potentialities. His life has no purpose, no central theme. (pp. 119-20)

Lermontov does not defend his hero. He regards him with an amazing objectivity and does not attempt to hide his vanity, his worthlessness, or the other negative traits of his character. The title of the novel, however, contains, if not a justification, at least an explanation of Pechorin. Pechorin, like [Griboyedov's] Chatsky, and Oneghin, is socially worthless; he is one of the many 'superfluous men' described by great Russian writers of the nineteenth century (especially by Turgenev and Chekhov). Many critics interpreted not only Pechorin, but his creator as well, in terms of social categories. (p. 120)

It can be hardly contested that the social and political environment was largely responsible for Lermontov's pessimism and his feeling of futility, and that his Pechorin was the product of his times. However, the poet and his hero were more than that. One cannot reproach Pechorin with the verbal sentimentality of a Chatsky or the indolent superficiality of an Oneghin. He has a strong character and he loves action. Unlike Oneghin, the dandy who depends on other people's opinions, Pechorin defies all social conventions; he is 'anarchically free,' beyond good and evil. As Dostoevsky's Raskolnikov or Ivan Karamazov later on, he discards the accepted moral values and looks for his own truth. He is actually a new hero and Lermontov, in creating Pechorin, initiated a new literary type. Dostoevsky believed that Russian literature was mainly concerned with the 'humble man,' yet he himself painted magnificent portraits of 'proud men' who all bear a resemblance to their archetype, Pechorin.

At the same time Pechorin is by no means a 'demoniac' hero. Lermontov refuses to employ the exaggerations and pompous artificialities of the Romantic school. His characterization of Pechorin is realistic and sober. Moreover, despite the autobiographical flavor of the novel, the writer does not identify himself with his creation. This objectivity in portraying his hero is extremely significant in a writer such as Lermontov.

Even more astounding is Lermontov's treatment of minor characters. Pechorin's rival in the **"Princess Mary'** chapter is Grushnitsky, a young officer, who is a caustic caricature of the affectations and pretensions of a would-be Byronic hero. In depicting Grushnitsky the author was aiming at, and actually scored a hit against, pseudo-Romanticism, the sham Byronism of Russian society and literature. Sketches of other minor characters of the book are also vigorous, deft, and realistic.

A thoroughly subjective writer, Lermontov possessed at the same time the rare gift for perfectly realistic characterization and epic narrative. (pp. 120-21)

Although Lermontov's poetry followed the path broken by Pushkin and his disciples, and although his verse is not striking for any prosodic innovations, it has great stylistic originality and presents very unusual classical features.

Pushkin achieves perfection in simplicity, and his lyrics are smooth and polished. Lermontov's verse is nervous and somewhat rugged; he intensifies his dramatic, dynamic quality by constantly carrying over the meaning from line to line (enjambement)—which breaks the sentence and gives the impression of an intermittent rhythm *(saccadé)*—by the abundance of masculine rhymes, by the frequent change of intonations, by the recurrence of coruscating, often hyperbolic images, and by contrasts, in semantics as well as in the tonality of sentences. Pushkin's poetry is light, harmonious, transparent. His best poems have the shimmering beauty of precious stones. Lermontov is sometimes almost obscure; his lines hide as much as they reveal; they have the disturbing instability of submarine depths. Lermontov wrote that 'there are words whose sense is obscure or trivial—yet one cannot listen to them without tremor.' This holds true of many of his poems. They have the magic of music and spontaneous movement. The Russian symbolists at the turn of the century pointed out the irrational elements in Lermontov's poems and the strange admixture of the demoniac, idealism, despondency, and moral anxiety which assured them a unique place even in such a variegated literature as the Russian. (pp. 121-22)

This nobleman who suffered from the political oppression of his times, this idealist who was shocked by the triviality and futility of earthly existence, this poet who absorbed and transformed European Romantic influences, remained fundamentally Russian and reflected in his works many national traits. His wistfulness and his revolt, his quest for freedom and his refusal to accept reality, corresponded to identical features of the cultured Russian society of his period. These features remained intact through many generations, and even today in the Soviet Union, where pessimistic ideas are banned and many of the feelings expressed by Lermontov are officially frowned upon, the poet is loved, widely read, and acclaimed one of the greatest and most original representatives of the true 'Russian spirit' in native literature. (pp. 122-23)

> *Marc Slonim, ''Lermontov,'' in his* The Epic of Russian Literature: From Its Origins through Tolstoy *(copyright 1950 by Oxford University Press, Inc.; renewed 1977 by Tatiana Slonim; reprinted by permission of Oxford University Press, Inc.), Oxford University Press, New York, 1950, pp. 108-23.*

## RENATO POGGIOLI (essay date 1960)

Lermontov is perhaps the most subjective of all Russian poets, the one must concerned with his own ego, with his own selfhood. In a private letter the poet once wrote: *moi, c'est la personne que je fréquente avec plus de plaisir.* [I am the person I most enjoy being with.] The statement could be extended to his poetry, but not without qualifications; Lermontov's narcissism is more pathetic than hedonistic, and the poet himself viewed it not as a blessing, but as a blight. He knew that an excessive concern with the personal and the subjective may lead not to self-cultivation, but to self-destruction, changing the artist into a parasite of the man. . . . Precisely because of this he was perhaps one of the first Russians to see in the poet's calling a predestination for suffering (''the poet's crown is a crown of thorns'') and even for damnation himself. In this he went even beyond Byron and anticipated Baudelaire, who, by the way, mentioned Lermontov in his *Journal intime* as one of the few poets he would place in a select Pantheon of his own.

Lermontov, like Baudelaire, would have rejected Pascal's claim that man is *ni ange ni bête* [neither angel nor beast]. Both his view of the world and his way of life seem to rest on the idea that the angelic and the demonic principles are constantly at war against each other in man's heart and in God's universe. It is perhaps for this reason that his most popular compositions seem to be the early lyric **''The Angel''** and the long verse tale *The Demon.* . . . While **''The Angel''** is a perfect little jewel, *The Demon* is a vast failure despite the splendor of its lyrical passages. Yet the one and the other have great significance as psychological documents, since they reflect the poet's conception of man as an exiled being, who finds his native habitat in other spheres than that of human existence, in a no-man's-land which may be either an Eden or a Hell. In another Byronic tale, *The Novice,* written against the same exotic, Caucasian background, Lermontov conveyed the sense of man's alienation from the life of his earth. . . . (pp. 30-1)

[Both *The Demon* and *The Novice* are rhapsodies] of exalted monologues, which the poet utters through the transparent masks worn by their operatic and undramatic protagonists. Thus in a sense even in *The Demon* and *The Novice* Lermontov employs one of the favorite instruments of his lyrical inspiration, which he adopts most frequently in the poems of love. That instrument is the confession device, which in the lyricism of passion the poet uses simply and directly, as a truthful image of himself and his life, as a mirror of his guilt and shame, as well as a spring of hope and a well of repentance. This is another way of saying that Lermontov's mature lyrical poetry, unlike his early Schilleresque plays and late Byronic verse tales, succeeds in reconciling in human terms that conflict of the angelic and the demonic elements which was both the trauma of his art and the complex of his psyche. Lermontov achieved an even loftier resolution of that dualism in a few brief poetic utterances shaped like prayers, fusing in a new harmony the discordant tongues of sublimity and humility. Yet prayer, like confession, still remains a personal statement, even when not a subjective one; and Lermontov reached a higher degree of poetic objectivity in his discursive ''meditations'' (the title is perhaps patterned after Lamartine), which often have the noble gnomic quality of classical verse.

Lermontov felt, however, that his song should be ''wild,'' and like most of the Romantics yielded to the passionate appeal of both indignation and enthusiasm. It was indignation that dictated his poem on Pushkin's death [*Na smert' Pushkina*], as well as the many poems treating the theme of the reciprocal hostility between the artist and society, between the poet and the world. In such poems he chose the sharp and bitter language of invective and sarcasm, and spoke and acted like a real-life imitation of Chatskij, the unhappy, idealistic hero of Griboedov's *Woe from Wit*. (pp. 31-2)

Despite its almost perfect mimesis of the legendary and heroic tone of the old popular epos, which it reproduces in the accentual rhythm of its metrical pattern, the [*Song of Tsar Ivan Vasil'evich, of his Guard Kiribeevich, and of the Brave Merchant Kalashnikov*] is a Romantic ballad, and it may well be the foremost *réussite* of European poetry in that genre. Yet the *Song* is also one of the best proofs that the late Lermontov was moving toward a more objective vision of art and life. Near the end of his all-too-short career, the poet felt the attraction both of the epic narrative in verse and of the realistic narrative in prose. . . . The most significant testimonial to the maturation of Lermontov's genius is . . . his short novel, *A Hero of Our Time*. . . . [It] is through the portrayal of his hero that Lermontov, like Pushkin before him, transcends, both artistically and morally, his earlier Byronism. The sad lesson which both authors teach through those two heroes is the same as the one that Lermontov conveyed as a maxim in one of his poems: that "we hate and love by chance," rather than by our heart's desire. Lermontov's last lyrics reveal the same poetic wisdom, an equal mastery of beauty and of truth. In "**The Angel**" the childish poet had said that for a soul coming from on high to live and suffer among men no human tune could ever replace the divine melodies; yet, just before his all-too-early death, Lermontov proved himself able to turn into "heavenly sounds" even "the wearisome songs of the earth." (pp. 32-3)

> *Renato Poggioli, "The Masters of the Past," in his* The Poets of Russia: 1890-1930 *(copyright © 1960 by the President and Fellows of Harvard College; excerpted by permission), Cambridge, Mass.: Harvard University Press, 1960, pp. 1-45.*\*

**JOHN MERSEREAU, JR.**   (essay date 1962)

[*Mersereau is a foremost Lermontov scholar. His study provides an excellent overview of all Lermontov's works.*]

**Vadim** has hereditary ties with the Gothic tale, the *Lara* variety of Byronic poems, and the early dramas of Hugo, but essentially it requires classification as a historical novel. Indeed it is rich with the clichés of this genre: two men compete for the affections of the heroine, the girl is separated from her lover by the evil machinations of the villain, there is a flight and pursuit, a faithful servant renders timely assistance, and blood is shed copiously. . . . Unlike most historical novels, however, no persons from real life appear, for Lermontov was interested in the events of the period primarily because they provided a congenial setting for the activities of his demonic hero, the avenger Vadim. . . . (pp. 37-8)

The novel differs from the usual specimens of the historical romance in that there is a lack of consistency in the depiction of the central character, who at first is presumably the hero but who ultimately becomes the villain. (p. 38)

Quasimodo, from Victor Hugo's *Notre-Dame de Paris*, may have suggested to Lermontov the "beauty and the beast" contrast represented by Vadim and his comely sister, Olga, but Vadim's insatiable lust for revenge is clearly a Byronic trait rather than one taken from the half-witted Quasimodo. A much

more important work of Hugo in so far as the delineation of Lermontov's hero is concerned is *Bug-Jargal*, one of the French writer's first works, which is, moreover, linked to *Vadim* by the theme of rebellion. (p. 40)

[There] is another progenitor who occupies an important place on Vadim's genealogical tree, namely Elshie, the Wise Wight of Mucklestane-Moor, the hero of Scott's *The Black Dwarf*. Elshie, like Vadim, first appears as a mysterious hunchback suspected of demonic powers, both exercise unusual control over others, and the lives of both are blighted by unrequited love. . . .

Vadim is a grotesque collage of scraps and pieces scissored from the darkest and bloodiest pages of romantic literature combined with autobiographical fragments of various dimensions and coloration. (p. 41)

[The] examples of realistic prose which appear from time to time in **Vadim** . . . are the most original and valuable aspect of the novel, for they are the basis of Lermontov's mature style. His development of a means of realistic expression was essentially a process of rooting out the language of frenetic romanticism to provide room for the growth of that impersonal and restrained style, seeds of which are scattered throughout this first novel.

There is another hopeful indication in **Vadim** that its author might someday break down the walls of that romanticism which, in combination with his own egocentricity, had kept his art confined within certain narrow limits. This is the element of humor, which though weakly developed and naturally not touching Vadim himself, does represent something new as far as Lermontov's works are concerned. The humor here takes the form of irony, which is directed primarily at Yury Palitsyn, Vadim's successful rival for Olga. Had Lermontov not identified with Vadim, Yury would probably have turned out just another of those handsome, dashing young officers who invariably overcome the forces of evil and marry the princess. But, although he does win the girl, the author could not let him be inherently superior to his hero, and so he divested him of his romantic halo through the use of irony. (pp. 44-5)

[**Masquerade**] is a mishmash involving gamblers, mistaken identity, the Othello theme, and, at the same time, it attempts to satirize Petersburg society in the same way that Griboedov's *Woe From Wit* satirized the Muscovites. (pp. 49-50)

The plot is implausible, the characters very flat, and the dialogue rambling and uneven. It is out of the question even to suggest comparing it with *Woe From Wit*, or Gogol's *Inspector General*.

Irrespective of its artistic worth, **Masquerade,** like the contemporaneous **The Boyar Orsha,** does show that its author was freeing himself from the fetters of his traditional themes and expanding the function of his art. In his Moscow period he had sought to manifest a purely personal *Weltschmerz* for which a completely subjective approach to the world was quite adequate. After he leaves Moscow, however, there becomes evident in his works the gradual expansion of his field of view, the development of an ability to see life as a phenomenon apart from its effect upon himself alone. There awakens in him an awareness that the negative aspects of society have broad implications, and he becomes indignant not only because of the bruises suffered by his own ego but because the ideal of life is itself besmirched by an insensate and corrupt society. And so, as in **Masquerade,** he turns to satire, seeking to correct society by reflecting its shortcomings in the mirror of his art. (pp. 50-1)

[Lermontov] has been called the poet of negation, doubt, despair, solitude, protest, and tendency, and, conversely, the poet of resignation, religiosity, and humility. The last three definitions could be substantiated by references to individual poems, but to posit them as true to the essence of his art is to ignore its dominant tenor and content.

The lyrical poems written after his first exile [in 1837]—there are less than seventy of them—are concerned with a number of themes, but the most recurrent are those of freedom, solitude, and the turpitude of society. These themes appear not only in poems where they are the organizing idea but are alluded to constantly throughout his verse. So many of these poems of the poet's last years reveal a maturity of outlook and a sense of duty not evident in his earlier works. The self-centered youth who once wrote mostly of unrequited love and dark passions now begins to raise his voice not only on his own behalf but in support of truth, freedom, honesty, dignity, and common sense. In the best tradition of Russian authors, he becomes part of the national conscience. Dismayed at the level to which his fellow man has sunk, he cries shame upon him. Contempt and scorn for society pervade such works as **"Death of the Poet,"** [**"Meditation," "Three Palms," "The First of January,"** and **"Goodbye, Unwashed Russia."**]. . . . As a poet he considers himself a prophet, and he knows that not only are prophets without honor but, in his country, often the object of severe reprisals. Nonetheless, he speaks out against the vices of his era in completely unequivocal and condemnatory terms, and he will not be silenced in spite of the obvious consequences. In fact, the accusatory tone becomes increasingly evident and the critical attitude ever more pronounced. (pp. 63-4)

Most of these works have a particular rhetorical quality which admirably suits the subject matter. Avoiding the pitfalls of pomposity or bathos, the poet expresses himself with lucidity and conviction. These poems read like prose, but prose charged with emotions of anger or sorrow. They lack intimacy, and by their very style they beg to be declaimed from the forum steps. Yet not all of Lermontov's last works are accusatory or even pessimistic. The consolation that the poet could not find in human associations was provided by nature, and at times it was even able to inspire a mood of reconciliation with life. In **"When the Yellowing Fields Billow"** . . . , scenes of the seasons lead to a vision of God, and it is the night sky of **"Alone I go Along the Road"** . . . which causes pain and troubles to be forgotten in hopes of the peaceful freedom of a sleep-like death. Again it is the nature of his homeland, its rivers, steppes, and forests that bring him to express his "strange love" for Russia in **"Motherland."** . . . (p. 65)

*Mtsyri* (Georgian for *novice*) is one of Russian literature's finest examples of romantic eloquence. Lofty and impassioned, it is the history of a soul tortured by the physical and spiritual captivity of civilization. . . . In the depiction of the romantic ideal of the fusion of nature and the human ego, the work is a real *tour de force*. (pp. 67-8)

The poem is a wonderfully unified piece, and it defies the destructive analysis of the anti-romantic critic. It must either be accepted or rejected, but it can't be picked to pieces. When the novice exultingly declares that he became friends with the storm and seized lightning with his hands, one doesn't feel that this is too extravagant, because the whole work is extravagant, in its basic concept and in the elevated flight of its verse. One

colorful scene replaces another, and the reader is borne along the waves of poetry, delighted by the view and fearful of obstacles, but the pace and emotional tension are maintained until the end. (p. 68)

Like *Mtsyri*, [*The Demon*] is the quintessence of romanticism. It is picturesque, visionary, and sensual. It is as extravagant as an ostentatious ruby, but it has a ruby's brilliance and color. If not the poet's best work, it has been one of his most popular and well-known. (p. 69)

*Mtsyri* and *The Demon*, representative of Lermontov's most successful ventures in the romantic mood, are proof enough that during his last years the fires of romanticism were far from burning out. But, at the same time, he was more than casually disposed towards realism. The lyric poems **"Borodino"** and **"Valerik,"** to mention just two, show that on occasion the poet could achieve a high degree of objectivity and convey a graphic impression of reality. Even such a poem as **"Meditation"** is more logically classified as a work of realism than of romanticism, although it was inspired by romantic indignation at the divergence between reality and the ideal. And the same is true of a number of other poems written during the final period, which, like **"Meditation,"** have the character of editorials in rhymed prose. Obviously the product of romantic disillusionment, their subject matter and its treatment link them closely with realism.

The development of Lermontov's art in its final stage is distinguished, therefore, not so much by movement towards realism, which would suggest the abandonment of romanticism, but by a broadening of the scope of his art to embrace realism. At the same time, the romantic element in his work was undergoing its own evolution. The arm-waving and teeth-gnashing aspects were being deemphasized in favor of qualities more appealing to the mature intellect. (pp. 70-1)

The arrangement of [the various parts of *A Hero of Our Time*] might at first seem capriciously complex, but a sound logic underlies it. The parts are ordered not with regard to chronology but so that the reader, proceeding from one story to the next, is presented with an increasingly intimate view of the hero. In *Bela* Pechorin is what might be termed a "hearsay" figure. That is, one learns about him only as much as the traveling author hears from the captain. In *Maxim Maximych* Pechorin is described from a closer vantage point—that of an eyewitness. The point of view then shifts from the exterior to the interior, as we learn of the hero from his own *Journal*. Here again there is a development. *Taman* is "autobiographical," but the emphasis is as much on the adventure as on its "author." *Princess Mary* concentrates more heavily upon Pechorin's motives and states of mind, and his narrative acquires the additional element of a personal confession. *The Fatalist* provides the final comment on the hero, revealing the fundamental cause for his aimless and destructive existence. Note, too, that the first story, *Bela*, and the last, *The Fatalist*, are set in overlapping chronological frames. This enabled Lermontov, despite the temporal space covered by his novel, to tie the final tale to the introductory one by reintroducing, if only momentarily, the figure of Maxim Maximych.

The thematic links between the various parts of *A Hero of Our Times*, the unity provided by the figure of Pechorin, who is the focus of attention in each of the tales, the logical development of the work considered as a whole—all this should dispel any doubts as to whether this is a novel. That there is no unifying intrigue is of little importance, because psychological novels have no particular need for an all-embracing plot. They start at a point where it pleases their authors to begin observing their heroes and end at a point where they are pleased to drop them. Incidentally, Lermontov justified the termination of his portrayal of Pechorin by the simple expedient of having his hero die, thus logically avoiding any extension of his history. (pp. 79-80)

Lermontov was aware that if the tale of Pechorin and Bela were to be told from the point of view of the simple, unsophisticated Maxim Maximych, then he would need an educated auditor who might record and publish the story, something the junior captain would never have done. Accordingly, he created this traveler, endowed him with the fortitude to cross the Caucasus, gave him a personality calculated to inspire confidence in the old veteran officer, made him a sufficiently sympathetic listener to elicit the captain's narrative—as well as retentive enough to remember it in detail—and finally caused his trip to be delayed so that he might record the story of his traveling companion. . . . (p. 82)

It is, however, in the descriptions of nature, legitimized by the fact that *Bela* is exteriorly a travel account, that the narrator's image more closely resembles that of Lermontov. In fact, in these magnificent passages devoted to the evocation of the Caucasian landscape, it is the voice of Lermontov-the-prose-poet which we hear, not that of his rather ordinary author-traveler.

In composing these descriptive passages, Lermontov made use of exactly the same elements as he did in his lyrical poems dealing with nature or in the emotional-impressionistic landscapes found in *Vadim.* With certain variations and omissions requisite for the avoidance of monotony, all of these word pictures include celestial bodies—the sun, moon, or stars—or a general term, such as "sky," "horizon," "the heavens," "the vault." There are always present clouds, mist, or smoke above a cliff, peak, ravine, crag, gorge, or mountain. Various colors or color verbs are widely used, and if there is no sound its absence is particularly mentioned. Movement, the animation of natural elements, mood-bearing adjectives are invariably ingredients. In *Bela* these landscapes are usually introduced by a subjective evaluation, such as "A wonderful place is this valley," or "And just so, I'll probably never again see such a panorama anywhere."

To intensify the emotional effect of his descriptions, Lermontov makes use of repetitions, [such] as "high, high," or "quietly, so quietly," as well as introducing adjectives which develop an emotional context in addition to a descriptive one. Verbs commonly used to describe human actions are metaphorically employed. The following example of these breath-taking panoramas is typical:

> A wonderful place is this valley! On all sides are inaccessible mountains, reddish cliffs hung with green ivy and crowned with clusters of plane-trees, yellow precipices lined by torrents, and there, high, high above is a golden fringe of snow, and below the Aragva river, having embraced another nameless stream which breaks noisily out of a mist-filled gorge, stretches in a silver thread and glistens like the scales on a snake.

Though emotionally colored and impregnated with the author's enthusiasm for Caucasian nature, these landscapes are surprisingly realistic. Stripped of their subjective components,

they are like word pictures, complete with foreground, background, horizon, and detail. Their components are much the same in each case, but the final results are not manneristic. (pp. 83-5)

The features of Maxim Maximych's personality are, for the most part, revealed indirectly in the course of his narrative about Pechorin and Bela, rather than by the traveling author. (pp. 87-8)

In delineating this character, Lermontov made full use of language as a key to personality and background. The vigorous, unadorned, idiomatic language of Maxim Maximych not only reveals the man but serves to enrich the story itself. Both his own narrative and his conversations with the traveling author are full of forceful, mordant phrases, which are typical for a soldier who has spent his whole adult life in a completely masculine environment. (p. 90)

Maxim Maximych emerges as a living personality, extremely well-motivated, subtly characterized, completely Russian, possessing peculiarities and mannerisms which one might expect of a person whose life had been spent in arduous circumstances on the Russian frontier. (pp. 90-1)

In reviving the romantic Caucasian tale by putting it in the mouth of a realistic narrator such as Maxim Maximych, Lermontov faced a stylistic problem which he did not completely surmount. If one's narrator is a simple, unsophisticated officer, his tale must be told in prosaic and naïve terms. For the most part the old captain renders his story in such a manner. There are, however, notable exceptions, in particular when he reproduces the speech of those who figure in his narrative, such as Azamat or Pechorin. Azamat's plaintive address to Kazbich, which reveals his mania to possess Kazbich's prized steed, is repeated verbatim by Maxim Maximych. Whether or not a Chechen youth would actually have spoken as Azamat does is open to question. The real point is that it is quite unlikely that the old veteran would have been able to remember and reproduce such a speech, filled as it was with florid phraseology. (p. 92)

*Maxim Maximych* is not a complete short story, for its whole meaning and importance depend upon its contiguity to *Bela,* since without the knowledge of the relationship between the captain and Pechorin revealed in that story there would be virtually no significance to their encounter in Vladikavkaz. Nor is it simply a sequel to *Bela,* for from the point of view of form *Bela* ends much more logically without such a pendant as *Maxim Maximych.* The real purpose of this epilogue to *Bela* is to present a more detailed portrait of Pechorin than that which had been given by Maxim Maximych in the previous story. (p. 97)

*Maxim Maximych* is an excellent example of a skilled raconteur's ability to exploit the potential interest of even a commonplace occurrence. Lermontov excites a desire to learn more about Pechorin . . . by arranging the story so that it has a great deal of natural suspense. The appearance of the "foreign" looking carriage followed by the lackey who is obviously "the spoiled servant of a lazy master, something on the order of a Russian Figaro," not only stimulates the curiosity of the traveling author and Maxim Maximych but also that of the reader. (pp. 100-01)

*Maxim Maximych* is an essential component of the novel. It explains and justifies the presence of the following three stories from *Pechorin's Journal* and, even more important, it enables

Lermontov to present a first-hand description of his hero. In this section the reader gets his closest objective view of Pechorin, and the impression of objectivity is in no small way increased by the careful concentration on realistic, everyday details throughout the whole episode. Of all the stories forming *A Hero of Our Times,* this one presents the least indications of its author's allegiance to romanticism. (p. 102)

In [*Taman*] virtually everything is pervaded by a romantic essence, and this is especially true of the characters, whose appearances, attributes, and actions all collaborate to deepen the romantic impression. The first of the smugglers to be encountered by Pechorin is the blind boy, about whom he immediately senses something uncanny. And indeed the boy's behavior is suspicious, for he speaks to Pechorin only in Ukrainian but to the girl in Russian, he is more sure-footed on the precipitous path to the beach than those who can see, he has an extraordinary sense of hearing. His white eyes and enigmatic smile, his unnatural abilities effectively capture the reader's attention and arouse feelings of pity, wariness, and wonder. (p. 106)

The romantic atmosphere which dominates in [*Taman*] is intensified by demonic overtones, whose presence is, of course, not surprising in view of Lermontov's enduring fascination with the Devil, demons, diabolic types and demoniacal activity. . . . The adventure at Taman is even initiated by a situational cliché favored by romantics whose plots involved Satan. In the first scene Pechorin grows increasingly irate at his fruitless search for quarters and finally demands: "Take me somewhere, you cutthroat. Even to the Devil, only somewhere!" (pp. 109-10)

Considered apart from the rest of *A Hero of Our Times, Taman* is a tale which is typical of romanticism at full blossom. Yet, in the context of the whole novel, the story assists in the further delineation of the hero's realistic portrait. It does this both directly, by Pechorin's own statements about himself, and indirectly, by revealing his reactions to persons and situations. In several places he refers to his convictions and prejudices, in others he alludes to his past and even generalizes about his fate. Describing his first encounter with the blind boy, he states: "I admit that I have strong prejudices against all people who are blind, one-eyed, deaf, dumb, legless, armless, hunchbacked, and so forth. I have noticed that there is always some strange connection between a person's appearance and his soul: it's as if with the loss of a limb the soul lost one of its senses." (pp. 110-11)

It should not be forgotten that to a large extent it is Pechorin's own nature which is responsible for the development of the action in *Taman,* for had he not been by nature curious, predisposed to interpret what he saw in a romantic light, and, as well, amenable to romance itself, there would have been no story. Indeed, it is his inquisitiveness, a certain naïve audacity, and his amorous tendencies which conspire with the situation existing at Taman—the smuggling operation—to bring about his nearly fatal adventure. Certainly, too, it is the realization of his own failure to assess correctly the position in which he found himself, thereby permitting a girl almost to drown him and a blind boy to purloin his possessions, that causes him to declare testily at the conclusion of his story: "What became of the old woman and the poor blind boy—I don't know. And then what to me are human joys and miseries, me, an itinerant officer who has, moreover, an official travel pass!"

Thus, however much the smugglers may be steeped in romanticism, Pechorin is not. In fact, the romantic lustre that he

acquired in *Bela* is considerably dulled in *Taman,* where he appears more the victim of his own gullibility than, as he would have it, a victim of fate. . . . (pp. 111-12)

Like *Bela* and *Taman, Princess Mary* can be read out of the novel's context and appreciated simply as a better than usual society tale. There is no question that it is a highly exciting and intriguing adventure story. At the same time, of all the stories in *A Hero of Our Times,* it is the one which reveals the most about the nature of the hero. The image of Pechorin that appears here is much more personal than even in *Taman,* which is also autobiographical, because in *Princess Mary* it is not the intrigue itself which is important but the actions, attitudes, and imperatives of the hero. To give depth to the portrait of his hero, to probe below the surface of action and reaction, Lermontov utilized in this story a device of characterization which may, for the sake of convenience, be called the personal confession. The term will seem less vague if we define exactly to what it is applied, namely, those stylistically distinctive passages in which Pechorin directly exposes the motives behind his actions, the facts from his past which have colored his behavior, and the whys and wherefores of his states of mind. Few of these confessions, it is important to note, reveal a penitent attitude. They are, rather, Pechorin's rationalizations or *professions de foi.* (pp. 118-19)

The popularity with Lermontov of the confessional manner is evidenced not only in *Pechorin's Journal* but throughout the whole novel. In the first story there is a long rationalization delivered by Pechorin to Maxim Maximych in which he strives to explain the withering of his love for Bela. This is the first indication that there is in the hero, remote and aloof as he is, a need to examine and justify his behavior, to unburden his soul, if not to an auditor then at least to himself, as he does in his journal. In *Princess Mary* those passages which echo the confessional tone are of two types: short personal revelations which are made *en passant* and longer passages in which Pechorin deliberately, and even mercilessly, focuses his attention on his own nature and personality. The longer confessions or avowals are formed of certain standard ingredients which give them a definite uniformity of content and tone. The development usually begins with some idea or emotion suggested by a current event. The order of the elements varies, but usually includes generalizations based on his observations of life, rhetorical questions, the disclosure of motives, statements regarding past influences and reactions, and musings on his own emotional states.

The imminence of the duel provided Lermontov with the possibility of exploiting the formula of confession to its utmost degree. Pechorin's final entry on the night preceding the meeting acquires the quality of a death-bed confession, for this is the testament of a man who in a few hours may no longer be living. And what is significant here, and at the same time so tragic, is that Pechorin admits, or rather states, that his life has been essentially pointless and empty. . . . (pp. 119-20)

As in the preceding tales, in *Princess Mary* the Caucasus forms a picturesque and congenial background for the plot, and nature is utilized to assist in intensifying the moods of the narrative. But a new function has been added, for here nature is also used to aid in the hero's characterization. Even from the passage which opens the story, it is evident that Pechorin has a deep love for the natural beauties of the Caucasus, and his affinity with nature is further developed as the story progresses. But it is in the scenes immediately surrounding Grushnitsky's death that the special role of nature is to be seen most clearly. (p. 122)

Contrary to some opinions, [these scenes do] not show weakness or lack of manly qualities in Pechorin. It is, in fact, all to his credit that he can ''cry like a child,'' for in Lermontov's hierarchy of values, children enjoyed a place of exceptional prestige. Childhood was the time of innocence, of purity, before the evil passions of adulthood blinded the vision of angels and muted the music of the spheres. Pechorin's breakdown is really a return to the natural state of childhood. His vaunted common sense disappears, his firmness and presence of mind vanish, and the man whose intellect heretofore has at every moment disciplined his feelings becomes once again an emotional child. And only when he has achieved this state of purity, as evidenced by his tears, does nature once more console him, for it is the night dew and mountain wind which then refresh his feverish brain and put his thoughts in order. There can be no question about Lermontov's opinion as to the moral right of Pechorin to kill Grushnitsky. The face of nature is beautiful and friendly until he commits this deed, and nature then rejects him. Only when he has purified himself through his tears does she once again embrace him and offer consolation.

Grushnitsky, Mary, Vera, and Werner have more involved roles than the secondary characters of the previous stories, for here they not only fulfill the needs of the plot but also serve as objective mirrors reflecting the image of the hero. At the same time, each of them acquires his own aura of reality and stands out from the pages of the journal as a ''round'' figure or, at the very least, in bas-relief.

Grushnitsky is the most complex of the supporting cast, a poseur whose every action is unnatural and whose every word is premeditated for its effect. (pp. 123-24)

Grushnitsky's soldier's greatcoat, mentioned at least eight times, is the emblem of its wearer's affectation and artificiality. As a cadet he has no reason to wear this garment, yet he finds it an essential prop for his pose of one who has been demoted to the ranks for duelling. Yet, at the same time the coat conceals the true and valuable qualities underneath: ''However, in those moments when he throws off the tragic mantle, Grushnitsky is quite pleasant and amusing,'' says Pechorin, using the word ''mantle'' both metaphorically and literally. (p. 125)

In the early part of the story, Pechorin merely records Grushnitsky's posturing and lets the young cadet's actions and appearance speak for themselves. Thus Grushnitsky, at least exteriorly, presents his own stylized portrait. As the story progresses the emphasis changes, and the naïve, romantic, and slightly ridiculous youth becomes a dishonorable conspirator in the cowardly plot to humiliate Pechorin. The transformation, although perhaps unexpected, is completely logical, for Grushnitsky is essentially a person of weak character who is unable to withstand the temptation to appear in some way superior to his successful rival. His is the fate of one ultimately brought to destruction by his own besetting sins: egocentrism, pride, envy, anger, and weakness of will. (pp. 125-26)

It is with the figure of Princess Mary . . . that Lermontov shows himself completely competent in presenting both a realistic exterior and inner portrait of a feminine character.

Mary is no stock heroine, no china doll with a saccharine personality, no damsel in distress, but rather a superior type of girl on the brink of womanhood who thinks and acts like a human being. She is not stylized—except in Grushnitsky's excited imagination, where she appears as an angel—and since we see her principally through Pechorin's eyes, she is presented without any halo of authorial sympathy or approbation. This

technical feature itself lends greater realism to her depiction. (pp. 126-27)

Mary is not merely a thrall to the whims of the hero. She has an independent existence within the frames of the story, displays a wide variety of moods, has a mind of her own, and is far from acting conventionally. When Pechorin affronts her, she does not weep a silent tear or even smoulder in secret but bursts into flame, revealing her vexation both visibly and verbally. (p. 127)

*Princess Mary* is in no way an imitative work. All of its elements, of whatever source, exist to serve the author's intention of clarifying the image of Pechorin, and this they do. There are no superfluous scenes, there is no development of plot which is not revelatory. In this story the hero steps from the shadows and stands before the reader in complete illumination, surrounded by the protesting figures of Werner, Vera, Mary, and nature itself. And in the background, but clearly visible, is Grushnitsky's grave, a mute monument to the hero's tragic activity. (p. 131)

If *The Fatalist* were consciously conceived to serve as the conclusion of the novel, we are obliged to discover within this tale some elements which would particularly justify the author's having given it this most important position. The usual assumption has been that since the story coincides chronologically with *Bela,* in putting *The Fatalist* at the end of his novel Lermontov simply intended to give the work an additional element of form by thus closing the temporal circle. This in itself, however, would not justify *The Fatalist's* cardinal position. That Lermontov so located it because he thought it technically or artistically the best selection must also be dismissed, for it is in no way superior to the preceding parts. The plot is certainly not more absorbing than those of *Bela, Taman,* or *Princess Mary,* and as for Vulich, the new character introduced here, he is only sketchily developed, particularly when compared to other secondary figures of the novel, such as Grushnitsky or Maxim Maximych. Nor does *The Fatalist* reveal anything essentially new with respect to Pechorin's personality. It only reiterates those qualities of audaciousness and contentiousness which the reader has already come to associate with him.

The title itself, *The Fatalist,* suggests the area in which we must search to find the significance of this story in connection with the novel as a whole. Indeed, it is the treatment of the theme of fate and Pechorin's relationship to this theme which explain Lermontov's having planned this story to conclude his novel. The theme of fate is found directly expressed in all of the parts forming the novel except *Maxim Maximych.* In *Pechorin's Journal,* especially, it acquires increasing importance with each succeeding page, culminating in the final tale. (pp. 135-36)

*The Fatalist* obviously deserves its position as the conclusion of *A Hero of Our Times,* for it provides what is logically the final ''key'' to the enigma of Pechorin. Whereas the preceding stories are primarily concerned with revealing the nature of his life and personality, this tale endeavors to answer the question of why he acted as he did. Having established that the alternative to a belief in fatalism is the acceptance of free will and the responsibility that it entails, Lermontov demonstrates that his hero rejects fatalism in favor of free will, as this is more gratifying to his ego, but he refuses the concomitant burden of responsibility. With the revelation of this moral deficiency, it becomes finally clear why his life is essentially aimless and often destructive. The hero's innate intelligence and dynamism combine to give him unusual personal power, but this power is neither restrained nor directed by any conviction of responsibility. His only imperatives are those dictated to him by his passions. (pp. 141-42)

Seen in its proper perspective, [*The Fatalist*] not only assumes its rightful place as a keystone in the thematic structure of *A Hero of Our Times,* thus resolving any doubts as to its role in the novel, but it also lends additional meaning to the work as a whole. Is not the problem of freedom and responsibility one of mankind's eternal and universal problems? It is true that Lermontov did not concentrate exclusively upon this matter in his novel. Rather, with a delicate poetic touch he developed the theme of freedom and responsibility through his entire work, bringing it to a culmination in his final story. (p. 142)

> *John Mersereau, Jr., in his* Mikhail Lermontov *(copyright © 1962 by Southern Illinois University Press; reprinted by permission of Southern Illinois University Press), Southern Illinois University Press, 1962, 176 p.*

### C. M. BOWRA　(essay date 1965)

Pushkin's style, with its simplicity and its strength, its effortless variety and tremendous charge of emotion, taught Lermontov how to write. He too makes every word do its work and every line say all that it can. But if Pushkin is simple, Lermontov is simpler still. He conforms, as very few poets do, to Wordsworth's prescription for the language of poetry, and does it with so unassuming an air that we hardly notice his style as such, so perfectly wedded is it to his mood and his purpose. Every word comes so inevitably and so naturally into the sentence that we mark not the choice of words but their final effect. But of course this is a triumph of style. Hardly any poets have written with quite this ease and self-effacing simplicity, and yet succeeded in being powerful and expressive. Lermontov lacks Puskin's caressing sweetness and gift for suggesting a whole complex mood, but he almost makes up for it by a sheer force which strikes us directly as a powerful response to experience. When early in the present century advanced Russian poets, eager to exploit neglected qualities of their language, claimed that Pushkin was too sweet and too Italian, they did not say the same of Lermontov, whom they regarded as a more masculine, more forcible writer. (p. xiv)

Like Pushkin, [Lermontov] longed for some unattainable freedom in which he could be uncompromisingly himself without checks or obligations, but he was born too late to think that this was even conceivable. Whatever he might desire in the depth of his being, he was convinced that he would never find it and that he was trapped in a way of life from which there was no release. This conviction, which was fully justified, was strengthened by something which had troubled him since childhood, a vague sense of homesickness for some lost happiness, a 'hunger for eternity', a longing for a supernatural exaltation. In *The Angel* . . . he gives expression to this feeling and sets forth the fancy that the soul at birth hears an angel's song and is ever afterwards haunted by it.

This sense of frustration fostered a deep discontent in Lermontov and led him even in youth to two almost inconsistent positions, a fierce scepticism and a no less fierce desire for action. The first is common enough in imaginative youth, but Lermontov held it with an uncommon force. In *The Cup of Life* he expresses with memorable pathos a sensitive school-

boy's sense of unreality in everything around him, and tells how, as we drink from the cup of life, the brim is wet with our tears until death comes and shows that it is all an illusion. . . . To escape from his melancholy uncertainties Lermontov sought excitement and adventure both in life and in imagination. The main lines on which he was to move were set in boyhood, and to them he remained constant.

Externally Lermontov was a man of the world, a frequenter of high society, feared and disliked for his cruel jokes, the author of ribald verses, the reckless, inconstant lover, the poet who claimed to have no interest in his poetry and refused to talk about it. (pp. xv-xvi)

Though Lermontov had . . . the Byronic temperament, though he read and admired Byron and learned something from him, his poetry is quite independent. He never admits to it the kind of wit which he practised so recklessly in his life and which Byron used so gloriously in *Don Juan*. When he wrote poetry, Lermontov shed his social self and became a different man. Moreoever, Byron took very little trouble with his poetry, poured it out in careless abundance, and left it at that, but Lermontov was an extremely conscientious and critical artist, who worked hard on every word and was content only with his very best. The result is that we think of him more as a poet than as a personality, or at least as a personality only because he is a poet.

Lermontov's poetry reflects his conflict with himself. He was cynical because he felt that the world had defeated him. In boyhood he had longed for some ideal, unattainable condition, and, when he failed to find it, he compromised with the world and treated it, as he thought it deserved, by going further than most men in the reckless, hard-hearted spirit which prevailed in society. But behind this we can see that his cynicism was largely due to his bitter conviction that his most cherished hopes would never be fulfilled. (p. xvii)

What his temperament and circumstances cost Lermontov, and what they did for his poetry, may be seen from his treatment of love. Like Pushkin, he fell in love often and wrote about it from many angles, but, unlike Pushkin, he says very little of its happiest or most tender moments. Sometimes indeed he seems to write in the moment of falling in love, but it is rather a moment of magic when he hears a beautiful voice which seems to promise everything. . . . We cannot doubt the genuine affection of such a poem as *We Parted*, but it is an affection salvaged from the past. From love Lermontov extracts a peculiar pathos, but it is the pathos of defeat and regret.

This sense of failure sometimes takes forms which are none the less true for their strangeness and touch of violence. Even when all is well, Lermontov is troubled by fear and suspects evil ahead, as in *Wherefore,* where his sympathy and understanding for his beloved prompt a thought of what sufferings await her. No one can claim that this was written by a cynical amorist, but it was equally not written by a man who knows the sublime confidence of being in love. Even at such moments Lermontov's insecurity spoils the happy moment (*Not For You My Love*). He seems to have been possessed by an ideal of a lost love which prevented him from ever falling fully in love again. . . . No less striking is the poem *A Dead Man's Love,* in which Lermontov dramatises himself as a corpse who still thinks of his beloved and appeals to her from the grave, saying that, just as he still remembers and loves her, so should she remember and love him. (pp. xviii-xix)

If Lermontov's tormenting uncertainties made him take a low view of life about him, they also made him take a low view of himself. So far from thinking that he was the innocent victim of a wicked world, he had few illusions about himself. He dramatised himself as a lost soul, derided by society because of some fault which he had committed. The image or myth which he found for this conviction was a demon, which personified his position. In different short poems and in the various drafts of his long poem, *The Demon,* Lermontov shows how this myth changed under his hands and passed from youthful fancies to a true record of something deep in his nature. In *My Demon,* written in 1892, the Demon is a kind of Byronic hero, whose element is storm and whose character, compounded of melancholy, bad temper, and unbelief, makes him scorn love, reject prayers, and look with indifference on blood. Two years later some of the more violent traits have disappeared, and the Demon is the poet's other self, almost his familiar spirit, who taunts him with images of perfection and presentiments of bliss to be withdrawn as soon as they are presented. Lermontov at this period hovered between two ideas, the one that he was a demon, elect of evil and proud in temper, an exile from both heaven and earth, and the other that this demon was his other self, who tormented and corrupted him but was in the last resort not his essential nature.

In the last draft of the poem, *The Demon* . . . , Lermontov tells a story which is almost autobiographical in that the Demon is his own soul with its contradictions and paradoxes. . . . The Demon is Lermontov's image of his dissatisfaction and disgust with himself, of his conviction that some final weakness of flesh or character prevents him from making the sacrifice which would deliver him from his worst impulses. His Demon is a new conception of evil. He is no Satan or Mephistopheles, as Milton or Goethe created them. He is closer to the ordinary human heart with its selfish passions, its uncontrolled appetites, its cowardly refusals, its cold absorption in itself.

In his melancholy and his misgivings Lermontov had one thing to which he could hold—his art. In the last four years of his life he strengthened and enriched it in every poem. He found the Caucasus more inspiring than St. Petersburg with its uneasy pressure of social relations. Like Pushkin, he felt free among the mountains and their primitive inhabitants, savoured with relish the local stories, and enjoyed a solitary communion with the incomparable landscape. He experimented with new metrical effects, as in *The Novice,* in which he abandons the Russian fondness for feminine endings and uses masculine endings throughout, thus giving to his verse a hardness of outline not to be found in Pushkin. His imagery, always bold for his time, becomes bolder, as when he compares the Caucasus to a giant leaning on his shield or the river Terek to a lion shaking its mane. (pp. xix-xxi)

Though he continued to write about his own problems and conflicts, [Lermontov] moved surely and confidently towards a more objective art. His early poetry is almost entirely about himself, even when it takes the form of drama or narrative, but in his later work he begins to create worlds which live in their own right and need no reference to his feelings or circumstances. In this progress he was helped by his growing command of his art and his increased trust in himself. A good example of it can be seen in his treatment of nature. In his early poetry nature plays very little part, and, when it does, it is as a background or a parallel to his feelings. But in the Caucasus he found a new approach to it and welcomed a companionship which made him forget his troubles in an unalloyed delight. Nature gave him the contrast which he needed to himself, and this explains his unusual treatment of it. He was not concerned with the 'pathetic fallacy' which attributes human feelings to natural things; he did not, like Wordsworth, find among mountains and lakes a philosophy of life; he had nothing in common with his contemporary, Tyutchev, who saw nature rent between light and darkness, between order and chaos; he lacked Hölderlin's vision of a radiant world still hallowed by Hellenic gods. For him the claim of nature was precisely that it is not human, that it has nothing in common with man. (pp. xxi-xxii)

If he shared the taste of his age for stupendous scenery, his vision of it was not half dream like Shelley's or an accumulation of fine details like Keats'. His vivid eye saw the whole scene in perspective and marked equally the main design and the significant features. If he allowed a generous measure of such description, he also made it perform an important part in his stories. One of his sublimest passages is in *The Demon,* when the Demon flies down to earth and sees the Caucasus below him, from the snow-clad peak of Kasbek, glittering like a diamond, to the rivers hurtling down rocky gorges. Here Lermontov turns a contrast which he knows in himself to stress the point of his story. The vast detachment of nature emphasises the passions in the Demon and prepares the way to his career among men. So, too, in *The Novice,* Lermontov marks the difference between the cloistered life, which his hero has hitherto led, and his sudden liberty by a contrast between the dark woods from which he emerges and the blazing scene which greets him in the heat of day. Lermontov makes nature provide an uninterested, splendidly independent antithesis to the strange ways of men and demons. It lives in its own right and gives a new dimension to the actions of which it is the stage.

Just as Lermontov transposed his own delight in nature to objective descriptions of it, so he transposed his taste for action into exciting stories. . . . [In *Borodinó*] he tells the story of the great battle through a soldier who took part in it, and displays a professional pride in a great achievement as well as an experienced knowledge of war. The poem is at once realistic and imaginative, detailed and exciting. It gives the authentic thrill of battle without any false glorification of it. It begins quietly with the preliminaries to the encounter, the occupation of a position suitable for defence, and the long wait before the French attack, when the soldiers sit and mend their coats or spit and clean their bayonets. Then comes the fight. This is objective narrative in the strictest sense. The old soldier speaks not in Lermontov's voice but his own, and there is nothing of Lermontov's characteristic sentiment in what he says. All that matters is a vivid experience as it might appeal to one who took part in it. The dramatisation is complete and masterly.

This art Lermontov exploited both in long and short poems. In the manner of Russian epic tales he wrote the *Lay of Kaláshnikov the Merchant* [*The Song of the Merchant Kaláshnikov*] in which the old devices of narrative and the traditional metre are given a new brilliance, and an exciting and tragic tale is told without any reference to the poet's own feelings. Many shorter poems show the same art. In the *Cossack Cradlesong,* which dwells with a charming grace on the mother who rocks her child in his cradle and looks forward to the time when he will be a great warrior, her characterisation, even in so short a space, is complete and satisfying. In *The Rendezvous* the speaker is a Caucasian whose beloved has betrayed him, and the theme is the moment at night when he is about to take his revenge. In *Tamára* a witch, living in a castle which is a lifeless ruin by day and a haunt of music by night when it lures travellers to their doom, may have something in common with themes of German romanticism but owes more to Caucasian legends and has their authentic air of a world haunted by mysterious, malignant spirits. In his last years Lermontov perfected his gift for poetical narrative, showing how much can be done with a few words, some significant details, and an unfailing sense of climax. Of the poets of the Romantic period he is almost alone in the remarkable objectivity of his story-telling. Whereas Byron makes his heroes reflections of himself, or Shelley presents metaphysical abstractions in human guise, or Schiller imposes his own speculative ideas on the narrative, Lermontov tells a story for its own sake and makes the most of its possibilities by exploiting its human appeal. (pp. xxii-xxiv)

[Lermontov] was tired of struggling with others and with himself, and inevitably his thoughts turned to some ideal state in which he would be freed from his troubles and yet still in some sense be himself. So in a poem written in the last year of his life he gives a characteristically vivid and concrete form to his desire. As he walks on the road at night, he contrasts the serenity of the skies with his own tormented state, his longing for peace and rest. He longs to sleep and to forget (**Lone I Walk at Night**). The fancy, which Lermontov so boldly presents, reflects a mood which is not unfamiliar to young genius when it is rent by inner conflicts or finds its load of responsibility too heavy. . . . Such is the dream which young poets invent for themselves when they find the strain of life too great. It shows how they wish to secure the impossible, to maintain their imaginative vision without its cost or its cares. (pp. xxiv-xxv)

Lermontov has a full share of the discontent which we associate with the Romantic age. If in his ordinary life it made him sarcastic and cynical, it touched his poetry in a far more serious and more human way. Behind his self-dramatisation, behind his escapes into nature or his tales of stirring action, lay his central belief in certain things of great importance, in the affections, in truth, in courage, in liberty. He saw that what mattered so much to him mattered very little to his contemporaries, and he sought to solve the conflict by despising them, as they despised him. In the end he knew that he had failed, that his glorious message meant nothing to others. In this spirit he wrote **The Prophet**, in which at the close of his life he speaks clearly about himself. In choosing the theme and the title he had no doubt Pushkin's poem of the same title in his mind. But whereas Pushkin speaks of the ineffable splendours of the poetic calling, of the visions and knowledge which it confers, of the divine force behind it and of the infinite possibilities before, Lermontov speaks of its tragic cost, of the contempt and derision which it earns from other men. His prophet lives in the wilderness and is fed by the birds, but the contrast is absolute between his communion with God and his communion with men. Lermontov's **Prophet**, like Pushkin's, reflects a lofty conception of the poet's calling, a conception to which men of the Romantic age had been led not merely by their trust in inspiration but by their belief that poetry stands for all that is best in man and is a means to redeem the world. Lermontov did not question this belief, but a hard school taught him that it would be met by misunderstanding and obloquy and that any man who held it must pay for it with his blood. (pp. xxv-xxvi)

> *C. M. Bowra, ''Lermontov,'' in his* Inspiration and Poetry *(reprinted by permission of Macmillan, London and Basingstoke), Macmillan, 1955 (and reprinted in a slightly different form as an introduction to* The Demon and Other Poems *by Mikhail Lermontov, translated by Eugene M. Kayden, The Antioch Press, 1965, pp. xi-xxvi).*

## RICHARD FREEBORN (essay date 1973)

The theme of [*A Hero of Our Time*] is vengeance. Just as Lermontov experiments with narrative techniques in a manner which suggests a vengeful rejection of the narrative conventions of his time, so his hero, Pechorin, experiments with his own life by avenging himself on society, on women, on rivals, on the caprice of chance or Providence. Despite the professions of disillusionment and the propensity for reflective self-analysis no hero in the Russian nineteenth-century novel is more keenly alerted to life than Pechorin. (p. 39)

There are two chronological layers in this novel: the 'present time' of the fiction, during which the ostensible author, who is making travel notes, journeys northwards from Tiflis to Vladikavkaz and *en route* meets the *shtabs*-captain Maksim Maksimych (who tells him the story of Pechorin and Bela), spends a night and morning crossing from the Koyshaur Valley to Kobi and the rest of the day in reaching his destination. He spends three days in Vladikavkaz, on the second of which Maksim Maksimych turns up early in the morning and Pechorin's arrival occurs towards evening, but he does not see Pechorin until the morning of the third day. The 'present time' of the fiction ends with Pechorin's departure and the author's receipt of the papers comprising Pechorin's *Journal* from the bitterly disappointed Maksim Maksimych. (pp. 40-1)

Only in **Maksim Maksimych** do the two 'times' of the novel meet, in the sense that all three narrators are gathered in one spot at the same time and therefore that Pechorin exists in the present time of the fiction. The author's description of him is nevertheless a last portrait. He dies, the author tells us in his preface to Pechorin's *Journal,* on the return journey from Persia: this is what gives the author the right to publish the papers comprising the *Journal.* Everything else, then, that we know about Pechorin derives from a 'past' time, or a time prior to the 'present time' of the fiction. (p. 41)

The precise chronology of events in the 'past time' of the fiction is at best vague. The only reasonable certainty is that the events described in the stories which comprise Pechorin's *Journal* occur in chronological order, but how these events relate to the events described by Maksim Maksimych in **Bela** is not entirely clear. A distribution of the stories according to the chronology of events would place **Taman'** first and **Princess Mary** second. Whether or not **Fatalist** precedes the events in **Bela** is a matter for conjecture. It is equally conjectural whether Lermontov intended to suggest by such a chronological ordering of the events that the Pechorin of **Princess Mary** was younger than the Pechorin of **Bela**. . . . [Lermontov] was less conscious of time, less of a historicist, than Pushkin. In his orientation, his prose style, his imagery, there is nothing of the watch-tick effect, the suggestion of a beautifully timed mechanism, which runs from word to word in Tolstoy's work and is the very pulse of his fiction. For Lermontov time was to be experimented with, and if the experimentation violated normal chronological probability this mattered less than the dramatic effect which such an experiment obtained for him in the portrayal of his hero. There is no doubt that this was his real intention, behind which lay an obviously autobiographical or subjective impulse. If the temporal element in the composition of this novel contributes little to its authenticity, then the narrator's role is essential. As readers we are asked to assume that all three narrators are honest, that their separateness as narrators fuses in the single aim of—as the opening preface puts it—creating 'a portrait composed of the vices of our entire generation, in their full development'. . . . We must assume, then, that the itinerant author with his travelling box half-full of travel notes on Georgia honestly records Maksim Maksimych's story about Bela, that Maksim Maksimych honestly remembers what he has to tell, that both of them are as honest as they can be in their observation of Pechorin and that Pechorin in his *Journal* is the soul of candour. Yet having made such an assumption, which is the automatic prerogative of readership, we are concerned to know *why* the narrators should be honest, for the authenticity of the novel must depend to a great extent on the authenticity of the narrators, on the reasons for their curiosity and the motives for their behavior. (pp. 41-2)

The content of Maksim Maksimych's story broaches the theme of vengeance which is developed by stages throughout the novel and is so essential to Pechorin's portrait. *Bela* is about plunder and vengeance and life devoid of moral principle. Just as imperial Russia was plundering the Caucasus, enforcing her authority by colonisation and military suppression, so the world to which Maksim Maksimych's story introduces us is one in which Kazbich avenges himself on Azamat for stealing his fine horse by killing Azamat's father and on Pechorin for stealing Bela, whom he also loves, by mortally wounding her. For all the melodramatic character of these events, none of the participants is portrayed as a melodramatic character. That they are all unprincipled, devoid of loyalty, guided by varying degrees of selfishness, even in the case of the wretched Bela herself, gives little cause for surprise: they are by implication different from the norm of honesty and moral good sense for which Maksim Maksimych stands. But the assumption of his narrative is that he has the literary or creative ability to give them all the lineaments of authentic characters. He knows them and in his lack of sophistication can identify with them. His limitations as narrator only become apparent when he tries to understand sophisticated—and, by extension, spurious—emotions with which he cannot readily identify. It is here that his true role as narrator becomes clear: he has, quite simply, the gift of truthful observation. (p. 51)

[The] greater part, what we learn from Maksim Maksimych about Pechorin is, naturally enough, very general in character. He is a uniform, a voice, a figure in his narrative, but faceless. We know more about Bela's appearance—'And exactly so, she was beautiful: tall, slender, her black eyes, like those of a mountain gazelle, literally peered into your soul'—than we do about Pechorin. The narrator's increasingly emotional involvement with her accounts for the touching picture of her artlessness, and her loneliness, and her despair, and finally her last tormented agony. The role which Pechorin plays in this picture is largely incidental, for naturally the narrator concentrates on the central figure in his narrative. Also, the narrator does not have any emotional affinity with Pechorin's predicament. We gain, then, from him little more than an externalised, general picture of Pechorin as one suffering from the fashion of disillusionment and boredom.

The same generalised character attaches to the portrait of Pechorin which the itinerant author gives us in the second section of the novel, *Maksim Maksimych*. The portrait is lengthy and seemingly full of particulars, but on closer examination it transpires that it is not so much the portrait of one man as a series of associations. (p. 53)

*Taman'* is arguably related more closely to *Bela* than to *Princess Mary* in what it has to tell us about Pechorin; or it may be regarded as a bridge between the external and internal, objective and subjective portrayals of the two parts of the novel. The 'finished' form of this *conte* was originally explained by

the 'author' as due to Pechorin having prepared parts of his *Journal* for the press—an explanation omitted from the final version because it could hardly have accorded with the need to emphasise Pechorin's 'sincerity'. (p. 56)

[*Taman'*] is pervaded by a sense of dreamlike inconsequence in which tenebrous figures dart from one edge to another of the mind's eye and exist for the narrator in a condition of seen but only vaguely comprehended reality, as though a gauze, a darkling glass, stood between him and them. (pp. 57-8)

The rest of the story is supplied by [Pechorin's] curiosity, narrated with that dramatic reserve which so eschews sentiment or any elaboration that it seems almost to parody its own intent. As in *Bela*, the verve and speed of narration are what redeem the story, and as in *Bela* this is also a story of vengeance: the *undina*'s attempted vengeance upon him for allowing his curiosity to involve him in the mysterious activities of the 'honest smugglers'. And the moral? The moral is precisely stated in the penultimate paragraph: 'And why on earth should fate have cast me into the peaceful midst of *honest smugglers*? Like a stone thrown into a smooth pool I disturbed their calm, and like a stone I almost went to the bottom myself!'

The moral is that he represents himself as being an agent of fate. To the 'honest smugglers' he is fate, as was Eugene Onegin to his peasants; and throughout his *Journal* Pechorin presumes to enact the same role of fate's representative, until the third and final tale sees him assuming his ultimate role of the fatalist who is committed to speculating about the possibility of predestination. But the point is that, in the longest section of his *Journal, Princess Mary*, he presumes to be an avenging fate; here he is no more than the stone of fate which disturbs the smooth surface of the smugglers' lives and almost sinks to the bottom; here his fateful influence is counter-balanced by the vengeful reaction of the smugglers to his curiosity. For the balance is all-important: Pechorin's intrusion into the midst of the 'honest smugglers' is adequately repaid by the *undina*'s attempt to drown him and the blind boy's theft of his possessions.

Yet Pechorin, it must not be forgotten, appears to have the same kind of relationship to the events that Maksim Maksimych has in *Bela*. He does not really understand what is happening. The story comes to us through an I-narrator who gives the impression of dreaming what he tells, whose apprehension of reality, whose prejudices and essentially private or subjective terms of reference cast a film of mystery over the narration. (pp. 60-1)

*Princess Mary* in its remarkable blend of society tale and confession is the greatest of Lermontov's many achievements in *A Hero of Our Time*. The significance of Pechorin—and therefore of the novel as a vehicle for his portrayal—is to be judged primarily on the basis of this section. Probably it differs chiefly from other sections in the clarity of focus and immediacy of presence with which the characters emerge from its pages. Elsewhere there is a certain blurring of the immediately present scene, due for instance to the itinerant author's fondness for the grandeur of distant perspectives, Maksim Maksimych's perhaps unclear memory, the itinerant author's apparent indifference to Pechorin when he meets him and Pechorin's vagueness about the events of the *Taman'* episode. Inevitably such blurring produces a miniaturisation of the events and personalities. Received at so many presumed removes of narrative and time, the portrait of Pechorin in *Bela* appears miniature, and particularly miniature are the problems of his disillusionment and despair—his emotional state, in fact—as recounted to us through the diminishing incomprehension of Maksim Maksimych's attitude. . . . By comparison with *Princess Mary* especially, the world of *Eugene Onegin* gives the impression of having been miniaturised to the proportions of a doll's house. But the world of *Princess Mary* seems full-scale, its sophistication fully grown. The faint air of nursery standards which lends charm and innocence to *Eugene Onegin* is gone entirely from *Princess Mary*; here the sophistication is vicious and witty, and words have the power to draw blood.

The reason for this is obviously that it is all Pechorin's own work. What is and what happens in *Princess Mary* must all be directly attributable to Pechorin. He offers what the itinerant 'author' calls 'the observations of a mature mind about itself' written in a spirit of merciless self-criticism. (pp. 61-2)

How truthful is Pechorin's picture of himself? It is probable, despite the seeming abundance of information on the subject, that we never really know what he looks like or what expression his face habitually wears. The itinerant author's portrait generalises but does not specify and the image Pechorin offers is oddly contradictory. To the impressionable Princess Mary, quoted by the even more impressionable Grushnitsky, Pechorin has 'an unpleasant heavy look' in the expression of his eyes, whereas Pechorin himself writes a day later, after his first encounter with Vera, 'in looks I am still a boy: my face may be pale, but it's still fresh.' Perhaps a pale, fresh-faced boy with an unpleasant heavy look is exactly what Pechorin was: a degree of reticence about his appearance would be only seemly in that case. But of course Pechorin is profoundly concerned with appearances and dissimulation. (pp. 62-3)

*Princess Mary* is composed of two relationships—Pechorin-Princess Mary, Pechorin-Grushnitsky—which are in their respective ways variations on the themes of love and death. If Pechorin is the seducer, or pretender to that role, in his relationship with Princess Mary, then in relation to Grushnitsky he is the executioner. To Princess Mary he represents tears and heartbreak, to Grushnitsky bloodletting and death. In both cases he tries to mitigate his vengeful role by the private justification that he is the 'indispensable character in the fifth act' who always, despite himself, 'played the miserable role of executioner or traiter'. . . . He tends to represent himself as neutral, one destined to enact a role which is not strictly of his own devising. To this extent he is as much the plaything of fate as are those who become the playthings of his own vengeance. But the source of this vengeance has its beginnings in the contradictory tensions which exist between his public image, that which offers supposed him to be, and his private self, that which remembrance of his past made uniquely his own experience. (pp. 65-6)

The 'artificial means' (*iskusstvo*) by which Pechorin has become so 'adept at the science of life' may not have brought him happiness, but they have been successful in the negative sense of making others unhappy. Vera is the object lesson in this instance. Her farewell letter admits in so many words what he had claimed for himself after their first encounter in the grotto: that he was incapable of becoming the slave of the women he loved, that he always acquired unconquerable power over their wills and hearts. He had precisely such authority over her, knowing how to make her love him and yet afflicting her with the unhappiness of which he tries so hard to rid himself. (p. 67)

Pechorin's death of the heart, however stylised and specious it may seem, is central to his dilemma. His diary is ostensibly

that of a dead man consumed by the agony of his emotional death in life. This is the private despair at the centre of his experience 'hidden beneath amiability and a good-natured smile'; but it provokes analysis of self, and from such self-analysis emerges a kind of experimental philosophy.

Grushnitsky—not Dr Werner, nor Princess Mary, nor Vera—is the catalyst for Pechorin's philosophy. He is Pechorin's *alter ego* in several senses—in the sense of the 'romantic fanaticism' which brought him to the Caucasus, where he affects a disillusionment which resembles a parody of Pechorin's crippling despair; in the sense of resembling and rivalling Pechorin in his desire to produce an effect; in the sense of being a solipsistic portrait of a novelettish hero by the novel's hero; in the sense of being the cause of the 'intrigue', without which Pechorin would not have been able to kill him; in the sense of bodying forth the ordinariness, the ingenuousness, the weakness which Pechorin sought at all costs to eradicate in himself. (pp. 67-8)

Pechorin's philosophy is obviously self-justificatory. The candour of his egoism is what endears; its viciousness is what impresses. His primary object is the attainment of happiness through the subjection of others to his will. Conversely, had the will of others been kinder towards him, he would have been kinder in turn. But he is little concerned with this side of the coin. He summarises the ideological principle which governs his attitude to life in the following way: 'ideas are organic creations, someone has said: their birth gives them form, and this form is action; he in whose head more ideas are born will act more than others.'

From this there arises, firstly, the idea that 'evil gives birth to evil . . . the idea of evil cannot enter a man's head without his wanting to apply it to reality', and, secondly, the idea that 'passions are nothing but ideas in their first stage of development'; they are like the river which begins in roaring waterfalls but later grows placid and reflective, as does man in his evolution from adolescence to maturity. (p. 68)

At the end of *Princess Mary* Pechorin asks himself why he had not chosen to follow the path which fate had opened to him, 'where quiet joys and spiritual peace awaited me'. In other words, why had he not married Princess Mary and abandoned his vengeful experiment with life and with those who fell victim to his will? No, he could not have reconciled himself to that, he says. For Pechorin there is no reconciliation with others, with society, with the destiny of the sailor cast ashore 'who pines and languishes no matter how alluring the shady groves and how bright the peaceful sun'. When he is cast ashore, in the sense of being posted away to Maksim Maksimych's fort beyond the Terek and the Cossak village which is the setting of *Fatalist*, he has no alternative but to employ the weapons which he uses in his conflict with others upon himself. He turns to experiment with himself and his own destiny. This is a natural outcome of his concern with the central significance of the will. He has to determine whether there is any pre-ordination of events; and this may only be proved by submitting his own will to the test.

Such an experiment is the central theme of the final story, *Fatalist*. It is a story roughly divided into two episodes which are separated by a lengthy passage of reflection on ancient astrology and man's present-day lack of purpose. In the first part of the story Pechorin makes a bet against predestination. He loses his bet when Vulich's pistol fails to fire, but he is intuitively sure that Vulich is destined to die. Though he rejects predestination, his intuition is fully borne out in the second part of the story by the sudden news that Vulich has been killed by a drunken Cossack. He then resolves to follow Vulich's example and experiment with his own destiny by pitting himself against the likelihood of sudden death: he breaks into the hut where the Cossack has taken refuge and succeeds in overpowering him. Hiw own death had not been decreed by the stars for that moment, it would seem, and he concludes by preferring to doubt. . . . (pp. 70-1)

There are no rules, then, no systems of belief, no moral codes in Pechorin's view of life. All is anarchic, just as for him the free exercise of will absolves him of responsibility. . . . Even if repentance is as impossible for him as it is for the murderous Cossack, since he cannot acknowledge the moral sanction which would make repentance possible, his free exercise of will is based on the premise that passions are the source of ideas which only acquire form through action. For all his speculations on the nature of life, the true centre of his life is action, the implementation and testing of his ideas; and clearly the most private, or personal, point to which all such experimentation can be taken is that at which he—or any man, for Pechorin's is at this point a universal dilemma—confronts death, of which he may be the agent or the victim, but to which he is inevitably fated.

Lermontov's novel is designed by its structure and method of portrayal to achieve exactly this penetration of the hero's inner experience. From the generalised portraiture offered by Maksim Maksimych and the itinerant author the revelatory process obviously involves an ever-deepening analysis of the real motives of Pechorin's actions, the essentially private cause of the vengeful and callous conduct which he exhibits in public. Private and public aspects coalesce in the universality of the ultimate confrontation, and the portrait can be seen, for all its reference to place and period, as universally timeless, of one age and every age, of our time as of any other. We are required only to understand the portrait, not to censure it ('we almost always forgive what we understand', the preface to the *Journal* reminds us). The relationship which the novel as a whole aims to achieve with the reader is of such a personal character that it must surely induce in the reader a self-analytical response in which, if he can relate to himself with any credibility, he must scrutinise his own heroic presumptions. *A Hero of Our Time,* after all, debunks heroism and invites the reader to reappraise his own received view of what the heroic may be. (pp. 71-2)

> *Richard Freeborn, "'A Hero of Our Time','' in his* The Rise of the Russian Novel: Studies in the Russian Novel from "Eugene Onegin" to "War and Peace" *(© Cambridge University Press 1973), Cambridge at the University Press, 1973, pp. 38-73.*

## VICTOR RIPP   (essay date 1977)

[The] disjunctive formal structure of *A Hero of Our Time* only makes most visible an issue that pervades the book at every level: the need to make fragmentary experience coherently meaningful, in both a social and personal sense. (pp. 969-70)

[In the Russian literature of the 1830's there were] various attempts made at reducing chaos to an observable subject within the book, so that the fragmentary and multipicitous nature of experience was not only depicted but explained.

In choosing his title (and in the **"Author's Introduction"**), Lermontov obliquely refers to one such attempt [see excerpt

above, 1841]. The novel to follow, Lermontov insists, will depict events and characters not only in their particularity but as reflections of the whole epoch. Not [Daniel Defoe's] Moll Flanders or [Samuel Richardson's] Pamela or any other single individual is our concern but a Hero who will embody the most general meanings. Pechorin is an emblematic figure, "a composite of all the vices of our generation in the fullness of their development." (p. 970)

It is all too obvious that Pechorin's calculatedly off-hand seduction of the naive Princess Mary is something other than a link in a scheme for the mechanical displacement of evil. His statement, and indeed all his comparable graspings after generality, thus possesses a dramatic rather than an explanatory power: it is not really meaningful but it does signal Pechorin's yearning for such a meaning as will fit the randomness of his life to a pattern. (p. 972)

[The main purpose of the author in the book] does indeed seem to be to arrange the parts into a whole, to fit the discrete episodes of Pechorin's existence into an exemplary Life. Since *A Hero of Our Time* calls out for some ordering intelligence, we are more than willing to credit the capabilities of the travelling author who collects, organizes and publishes Pechorin's recollections: he seems *ex officio* to possess an encompassing wisdom. But Lermontov (perhaps from carelessness, but to brilliant effect) has also made this travelling author remarkably resemble Pechorin. It is impossible to distinguish the styles of the chapters they respectively narrate, the two men even seem to have physical and temperamental similarities so that when they confront each other in **"Maksim Maksimich"** the effect is of mirror images uncannily converging. And the result, finally, is that all the self-confident assertions of the travelling author appear to be only cunning transformations of Pechorin's befuddlement and despair. (pp. 972-73)

[In] *A Hero of Our Time* the authorial personality is so thoroughly collapsed into the fiction as to appear swallowed by it. Even Lermontov himself, the historical Lermontov who appears in the **"Author's Introduction"** to rebut critics of the first edition of the novel, becomes subject to this process. Or rather, Lermontov seems willingly to submit to this devalorization of authorial privilege; for he has consciously made Pechorin a notorious wit, a cynical seducer, an accomplished duelist and an exile to Caucasus, all of which (as contemporaries, not knowing of the intentional fallacy, were exquisitely aware) he was himself. With all these similarities, why should there be a difference in their ability to rise above events in order to explain them?

But most surprisingly, Lermontov's ironic animadversions to the various methods by which authors expressed the architectonic impulse does not cause *A Hero of Our Time* to lapse into the obvious alternative. The fragmentary nature of experience, including the potential disorganization of every work of art, is a topic the book examines, not a force it yields to. *A Hero of Our Time* . . . exists in a most narrowly defined area, avoiding both the facile assertion of harmony and the accession to disharmony. (p. 973)

*A Hero of Our Time* belongs to an altogether different genre [than the historical novel]—Lermontov's title is, among other things, an endorsement of purely contemporary concerns. But in thus advertising a modern focus, the title must necessarily refer obliquely to the antiquarian one it replaces; and if Pechorin's problem is the bafflingly diverse impulses of contemporary man, its presentation often involves a revision of the conceptual apparatus which moved the historical novel. Specifically, the concern with some meaning overarching men's petty activities is still acute. Nor is it very important that this meaning is no longer looked for in the suprapersonal historical dimension, since this is more a matter of changing interests (questions of history having passed from fashion) than changing logical assumptions. The crucial alteration is more subtle, an altered emotional context—for what was once a naive faith in the existence of a rational order has given way to a desperate nostalgia for it.

This is most obvious in the treatment of nature. The opening section, **"Bela,"** continually alludes to the privileged status of the Caucasus as a silent, peaceful and beautiful realm, and at one point Lermontov asserts explicitly that to ascend Mt. Gud means to escape the world of man's petty activities. Vistas of the Caucasus, expressive of an eternal changelessness, seem to stand in for the stability once associated with the rationality of history. But from the first, the insistence on nature's iconic powers is sufficiently strident to arouse suspicion. And indeed when we are admonished to restrain our interest in the narrative of Pechorin's adventures in favor of listening to nature descriptions—since this "is not a novella" but "travel notes"—one informing idea becomes clear: nature and the affairs of men occupy radically different spheres, irretrievably distanced from one another.

By the beginning of **"Maksim Maksimich,"** the author's attitude has shifted to irritated ineffectuality, an expressed feeling that the fullness of nature's meaning entirely escapes his attempts to describe it. It follows that although Pechorin may often muse on the divine plan he sees signalled in the stars, the philosophical questions this raises are never resolved, not even perfunctorily. Fate may indeed determine men's every action, but Pechorin's animating idea throughout the novel is consciously to ignore, since he cannot controvert, this possibility. Pechorin obstinately refuses to make his life dependent on any external contingency; he knows that symbols of order, nature among them, only tantalize men with meanings which can never be assimilated to the concrete problems of life.

In general, *A Hero of Our Time* proceeds not merely without a symbol of the transcendent order but with a perceptible vacuum where that symbol should be. And though this atmosphere can, and often does, drive Pechorin to profound despair, his best effort is rather to tease meaning from this world which seems designed to deny him one. For Lermontov has thoroughly understood the reason the historical novel sought to present a comprehensive vision, even though he works to deflate its facile pretensions in that direction: Alone, man collapses into solipsism, and the fragmentary quality of lived experience becomes not only an undeniable aspect of life but the only one. Pechorin must therefore create his meanings, construct that extra-personal pattern that is not given by the world.

Hence the curious aimlessness of the book, a sense of uncertainty not about how to win necessary battles but about how to define a battleground in order to fight at all. **"Taman,"** for example, relates Pechorin's visit to a provincial town and his involvement, almost ending in his death, with a band of native smugglers, the blind boy, his beautiful sister and old mother, and the demonic Yanko. This cast of stock characters accurately reflects the quality of the story, which is full of excessive passion and exotic occupations. There must be some point to this episode; but we are given no hint what it is or how to respond, and Pechorin himself is content to narrate the events with no comment. Pechorin—and we with him—seem caught in a situation that is all event and no meaning, a complex intrigue with no point except continuous excitement. (pp. 978-80)

Pechorin apparently is in a privileged position relative to the other characters, capable of moving from their highly charged romantic setting to a level defined by emphatically different concerns. He is not merely a participant in the intrigue, not merely the baffled adversary of that band of smugglers. To be sure, it remains unclear precisely what Pechorin is, and precisely how much his vision encompasses. Nevertheless Pechorin has in his possession an instrument enabling him to transcend the blank sequentiality of mere experience. Self-consciousness, even if it is consciousness of oneself as hopelessly baffled, can transform sensation into knowledge.

Self-consciousness may also lead to intellectual paralysis. But this is a necessary risk, given Pechorin's options. The alternative, whether it takes the form of dangerous adventure or erotic pursuit, is a life tailing off into a desperate randomness. Thus Pechorin's feelings for both Bela and Princess Mary always threaten to degenerate into merely fitful gestures, performed with progressively diminishing energy as the stimulus loses its novelty. Pechorin has consciously—self-consciously—to struggle to turn these encounters into affairs of enduring interest. His manipulation of others during this effort is of course morally reprehensible; but his behavior also involves a manipulation of himself, a projection of his errant impulses into a role which might transform common experience into a complex drama demanding sustained attention. (p. 980)

By consciously assuming the role of a Don Juan, of a dandy, of a cynical duelist, as well as spontaneously yielding to the emotion from which these types derive, Pechorin manages to construct a sense of himself that escapes pure subjectivity; for once assumed, these roles proceed in some measure according to a conventional logic. They belong to the world as much as to Pechorin. By the same token, it is worth noting how often Pechorin's relations with others simultaneously encompass several interests and topics. The aim here also is not to find a natural situation permitting the direct expression of feeling but rather to establish a psychological environment which will disperse and check mere appetite. (p. 981)

If the short-livedness of instinctual behavior were the only issue in the novel, Pechorin's strategies might be considered reasonably successful. But this is only one aspect of the difficulty. To Lermontov the main problem of experience lies elsewhere, and it is so presented in this novel as to make Pechorin's specific efforts always incomplete. The reason that life constantly skirts chaos is only partly because feelings die quickly; it is also because it is difficult to know exactly where to direct feelings, for fully to accept the priority of individual reactions is to accept a world where everyone seems only an aspect of the self. Lermontov suggests as much when he refuses significantly to distance Pechorin from his creator. But the same apparently debilitating idea informs many relationships in *A Hero of Our Time*. Of Doctor Werner Pechorin says, "Between us there can be no exchange of feelings and thought: we know everything about each other we wish to know and we do not wish to know anything more.". . . So they sit in mute inactivity, admiring their externalized selves.

It is thus telling that throughout the book, every character who contests Pechorin, thereby assuming a degree of otherness, also always evokes in him a spontaneous admiration, sometimes even a tender regard. Kazbich's impulsive and athletic derring-do in **"Bela,"** Yanko's demonic inscrutability in **"Taman,"** Vulich's coolness in the face of death in **"The Fatalist"** all occasion Pechorin's respect—as well they might, since these are all traits he admires in himself. Though *A Hero of Our Time* is a book given over to expressions of hate and will to dominate, there is no real conflict in it, nor can there be when every potential opposing force turns out on inspection to be an aspect of the hero—who is himself an aspect of the author.

Even Grushnitskij, whom Pechorin kills in a duel, is made to appear as a sort of surrogate. Indeed, though this relationship seems to culminate in the absolute antagonism which death must suggest, it is here that Lermontov most fully reveals the nature of the bonds between Pechorin and the other characters. From their first encounter, when Pechorin echoes an epigram of Grushnitskij's, a potential for identification is signalled; but just as Pechorin alters the epigram in a way that deflates the original utterance, so does he generally stand in oblique relation to Grushnitskij. (pp. 981-82)

The duel scene where Grushnitskij passes abruptly from conniver to naive victim—while Pechorin easily describes the innermost thoughts accompanying this transition(!)—neatly symbolizes this difference in understanding. And Pechorin's killing of Grushnitskij must be seen less as the instance of gratuitous cruelty that it first appears to be than the simple privilege of knowledge. In this context an off-hand remark of Pechorin's takes on special significance. He says, "Grushnitskij does not know people and their vulnerable spots since all his life he has been occupied with his own self. His object is to become the hero of a novel." Grushnitskij is thus not only a falling off from Pechorin but a falling off in a specific direction, towards a too exclusive subjectivity. And significantly this limitation is now equated with literariness. Conversely it is Pechorin's ability to make such a comparison that marks his own encompassing vision. But of course the reference to literature does something more. It must remind us that Pechorin is himself only a literary hero, himself encompassed. He stands in the same relative position to the author as Grushnitskij does to him.

Lermontov has thus replaced the historical novel's enthusiastic assumption of a transcendent rational order with a process of gradual transcendence toward such an ideal. Only there is a final twist to Lermontov's procedure. Since much of *A Hero of Our Time* is devoted to denying any authorial pretensions to an overarching, synthesizing role, the agent who should stand at the end of this process, the author himself, can never really deliver the knowledge that has been promised. Finally there is no point of view in the book that reliably unites all the particulars of experience by organizing them in accordance with an unswerving meaning. But for Lermontov's purpose it is enough—it is precisely to the point—to show that while the resulting instability is undeniable and pervasive, total chaos is not. In brief, the informing attitude of *A Hero of Our Time* is ironic, a realization that all certainty is only apparent—except only the certainty of this realization itself. (pp. 982-83)

[*A Hero of Our Time*] does not ignore but rather emphatically acknowledges the desire to fit the fragmented aspects of life, the moments of experience, to a general pattern. If this project is ultimately and necessarily impossible, the feeling which sustains it is nonetheless fully credited, depicted as a real and reasonable aspect of man. But *A Hero of Our Time* goes beyond a naive acknowledgement of chaos to offer some relief from this existential deadlock. Though no one in the novel, from

Grushnitskij to the author, manages to pierce the opacity of the subjective experience and attain a consequent view of an overriding pattern, this dismal limitation of the self is attenuated by being made subject to a systematic scrutiny. Real transcendence of personal experience is impossible, Lermontov tells us, but by contemplating the universal urge in this direction, we can rise above the chaos that would otherwise envelope us. Irony in *A Hero of Our Time* means sincerely to live one's life as if it had that ultimate reasonableness it clearly lacks. It is a self-conscious acceptance of the limitations of knowledge which thereby extends one's knowledge, at least fractionally. (p. 985)

*Victor Ripp, " 'A Hero of our Time' and the Historicism of the 1830's: The Problem of the Whole and the Parts," in MLN (© copyright 1977 by The Johns Hopkins University Press), Vol. 92, No. 5, December, 1977, pp. 969-86.\**

---

## ADDITIONAL BIBLIOGRAPHY

Davie, Donald. "Tolstoy, Lermontov, and Others." In *Russian Literature and Modern English Fiction: A Collection of Critical Essays,* edited by Donald Davie, pp. 164-99. Chicago, London: University of Chicago Press, 1975.\*
    Discusses Lermontov's concept of "transparent prose" and his desire to depict and criticize an entire society. Davie also explores Lermontov's influence on Tolstoy.

Eagle, Herbert. "Lermontov's 'Play' with Romantic Genre Expectations in *A Hero of Our Time.*" *Russian Literature TriQuarterly,* No. 10 (Fall 1974): 299-315.
    States that the individual chapters of *A Hero of Our Time* retain elements of Romantic short stories, but that the overall structure of the work alters its Romantic function. Eagle maintains that this "deformation" signals an advance in the development of the realistic novel.

Eikhenbaum, B. M. *Lermontov: A Study in Literary Historical Evaluation.* Translated by Ray Parrott and Harry Weber. Ann Arbor: Ardis, 1981, 190 p.
    A "literary-historical" evaluation written in 1924. Eikhenbaum analyzes Lermontov's creative work as the expression of the artist's "historical individuality" rather than his "natural (psychophysical) individuality." Eikhenbaum's work is said to have been influenced by Vladimir Fisher, a prominent Lermontov scholar whose work is not available in English.

Hopkins, William H. "Lermontov's Hussar Poems." *Russian Literature TriQuarterly,* No. 14 (Winter 1976): 36-47.
    A discussion of Lermontov's "Hussar," or "Junker" poems, a group of ribald poems Lermontov wrote in school. Though these poems are generally considered coarse and unprintable, Hopkins believes that their study is important to any student seriously interested in Lermontov's stylistic transition from Romanticism to Realism.

Katz, Michael R. "Lermontov's Literary Ballads." In his *The Literary Ballad in Early Nineteenth-Century Russian Literature,* pp. 166-82. Oxford: Oxford University Press, 1976.\*
    Examines Lermontov's ballads written between 1837 and 1841, and demonstrates the influence of Vasily Zhukovsky and Pushkin. According to Katz, Lermontov draws from their language, prosody, and narrative techniques.

Kaun, Alexander. "Lermontov: Poet of Nostalgia." In *Slavic Studies,* edited by Alexander Kaun and Ernest J. Simmons, pp. 34-74. Ithaca: Cornell University Press, 1943.
    Maintains that Lermontov's most peculiar characteristic was a nostalgic heartache, "a yearning that was never to be quenched."

Kelly, Laurence. *Lermontov: Tragedy in the Caucasus.* New York: George Braziller, 1978, 259 p.

An informative historical biography which includes an appendix of Lermontov's poetry in English translation.

Kropotkin, Prince. "Pushkin: Lermontoff." In his *Ideals and Realities in Russian Literature,* pp. 39-66. New York: Knopf, 1915.*

A comparison of Pushkin and Lermontov. Kropotkin considers Lermontov to be a humanist, and discusses the proud patriotic spirit which imbues his literature.

Lavrin, Janko. *Lermontov.* London: Bowes & Bowes, 1959, 111 p.

A detailed biographical study with brief critical comments on Lermontov's works. Lavrin contends that Lermontov wanted to die, and sees his fatal duel as the fulfillment of a death wish.

Milner-Gulland, Robin. "Heroes of Their Time? Form and Idea in Büchner's *Danton's Death* and Lermontov's *Hero of Our Time.*" In *The Idea of Freedom: Essays in Honour of Isaiah Berlin,* edited by Alan Ryan, pp. 115-37. Oxford: Oxford University Press, 1979.*

Compares the masterpieces of Georg Büchner and Lermontov. The critic calls *A Hero of Our Time* "eternally modern" and considers it the first European psychological novel.

Mirsky, D. S. "The Age of Gogol." In his *A History of Russian Literature* edited by Francis J. Whitfield, pp. 122-68. New York: Alfred A. Knopf, 1949.*

Studies Lermontov in relation to the Russian Romantic movement.

Reeve, F. D. "*A Hero of Our Time.*" In his *The Russian Novel.* pp. 45-63. New York: McGraw-Hill Book Co., 1966.

Views *A Hero of Our Time* as an autobiographical study.

Turner, C.J.G. *Pechorin: An Essay on Lermontov's "A Hero of Our Time."* Birmingham, Eng.: University of Birmingham, 1978, 93 p.

A detailed study of Pechorin. Turner compares *A Hero of Our Time* to Pushkin's *Eugene Onegin,* and maintains that Pechorin develops from, rather than parallels, Pushkin's hero.

# Susanna Haswell Rowson

## 1762-1824

Anglo-American novelist, dramatist, poet, essayist, and editor.

Rowson was one of the first women to write professionally in the United States. Her novel, *Charlotte: A Tale of Truth*, achieved unprecedented popularity, exceeding 160 editions in its first three years of publication. The breadth and duration of this novel's circulation permanently influenced the reading habits of the American public. With her blend of sensationalism and didacticism, Rowson helped popularize the novel in colonial America, where novel-reading had long been considered immoral.

Rowson was born in Portsmouth, England. Her mother died during her birth, and her father, an English naval officer, was sent to Nantasket Beach, Massachusetts, shortly thereafter. In 1767, Rowson joined him, but the family was forced to return to England in 1778 because of the political tensions resulting from the Revolutionary War. Although her residence there was brief, Rowson was deeply impressed by the land and people of America. In England, Rowson worked as a governess and published four novels, as well as a number of essays and poetry. Her novels were modeled on the fashionable sentimental works of Samuel Richardson and Frances Burney; unlike Richardson's and Burney's novels, however, Rowson's early work met with little critical success. When she returned to America in 1793, she was married and a professional actress. In addition to continuing her career on stage, she composed a number of topical, patriotic theatrical pieces, including *Slaves in Algiers; or, A Struggle for Freedom*, which is noted today for its feminist overtones. Rowson eventually ended her acting career in order to open a girls' boarding school in Boston. Though she was an educator the rest of her life, she continued to write novels, as well as educational texts, poetry, and songs. In addition, she contributed regularly to journals, and became the first American female magazine editor, of the *Boston Weekly Magazine*.

Concern for the education of women pervades Rowson's work. In *Mentoria; or, The Young Lady's Friend*, she stated that her purpose in writing was to show women that "happiness can never be met with in the temple of dissipation and folly." The early novels, including *Victoria, The Inquisitor; or, Invisible Rambler, Charlotte*, and *Trials of the Human Heart*, each portray a good woman who is seduced, then realizes her error and repents her weakness. While Rowson often conformed to the conventions of the sentimental novel, she wrote in a realistic style, and insisted that her fiction was based in truth. Her later heroines are more independent and resilient. *Sarah; or, The Exemplary Wife* and *Charlotte's Daughter; or, The Three Orphans*, depict resourceful women who reconcile their problems while maintaining their personal integrity. In *Slaves in Algiers* and *Reuben and Rachel; or, Tales of Old Times*, Rowson explores the struggle against political tyranny and the fight for women's rights.

Rowson's novels were generally dismissed by her contemporaries as highly stylized, mawkish imitations of Richardson. Although *Charlotte* was a great popular success, critics belit-

tled the novel's literary and artistic merit. Later critics have praised Rowson's realistic rendering of character and situation and her skillful handling of plot. The most recent criticism generally concerns Rowson's treatment of women. While some critics believe that her use of sentimental-novel conventions reinforces a stereotype of the weak, dependent woman, others feel that Rowson's works reveal a strongly feminist sensibility. The latter group maintains that her genteel, sentimentalized novels were more than mere entertainment; rather, these critics believe that these works express her contempt for those who freely victimize women, and her belief in education and full equality for women.

Today Rowson is recognized as a pioneer in prose fiction in American literature. The popularity of her works precipitated an important change of attitude which prompted the public's acceptance of the novel. In addition, because she championed women's education, both in her novels and in her personal life, she has been noted as a leading proponent of feminism in colonial America.

## PRINCIPAL WORKS

*Victoria* (epistolary novel) 1786
*The Inquisitor; or, Invisible Rambler* (novel) 1788

*A Trip to Parnassus; or, The Judgment of Apollo on
    Dramatic Authors and Performers*  (poetry) 1788
*Mary; or, The Test of Honour*  (novel) 1789
*Charlotte: A Tale of Truth*  (novel) 1791; also published
    as *Charlotte Temple: A Tale of Truth*, 1797
*Mentoria; or, The Young Lady's Friend*  (epistolary novel)
    1791
*Rebecca; or, The Fille de Chambre*  (novel) 1792
*Slaves in Algiers; or, A Struggle for Freedom*  (drama)
    1794
*Trials of the Human Heart*  (novel) 1795
*Reuben and Rachel; or, Tales of Old Times*  (novel) 1798
*Miscellaneous Poems*  (poetry) 1804
*Sarah; or, The Exemplary Wife*  (epistolary novel)  1813
*Charlotte's Daughter; or, The Three Orphans*  (novel)
    1828; also published as *Lucy Temple*, 1842

---

### THE MONTHLY REVIEW, LONDON  (essay date 1787)

[*Victoria*] is interspersed with various little histories, verses,
&c. It is, so far to be commended, that it exhibits the ill effects
of filial disobedience and thoughtless libertinism, in striking
colours: the language is neither good nor bad; it is too much
in the common style of modern novels to deserve great commendation, though, when ranked in that numerous class of
productions, the lowest place must not be assigned to this first
born of a young writer's brain.

> A review of "Victoria," in The Monthly Review,
> London, Vol. LXXVI, January, 1787, p. 83.

### THE MONTHLY REVIEW, LONDON  (essay date 1788)

Mr. Inquisitor [in **The Inquisitor; or, Invisible Rambler**] is presented by his guardian genius with a ring; which ring, when
placed on his finger, is to render him invisible. Thus, like the
Asmodeus of Le Sage, the writer has an opportunity of viewing
the secret transactions of mankind, and of commenting on them
accordingly—that is to say, as good or evil manners may be
found to prevail.

There is nothing of novelty in the idea, nor any thing particularly striking in the execution of the work. It may, however,
be perused with profit by our youthful friends, as in some of
the stories here presented to us, the duplicity and dishonesty
so frequently to be found in the world, are exhibited with a
tolerable degree of skill. The Authoress is evidently in possession of a feeling heart. But *style*, and the various graces of
composition, are yet to come.

> A. B. . . . . t., in a review of "The Inquisitor; or,
> Invisible Rambler," in The Monthly Review, Lon-
> don, Vol. LXXIX, August, 1788, p. 171.

### THE CRITICAL REVIEW  (essay date 1791)

[*Charlotte, a Tale of Truth*] may be a Tale of Truth, for it is
not unnatural, and it is a tale of real distress. . . . The situations
are artless and affecting; the descriptions natural and pathetic.
We should feel for Charlotte, if such a person ever existed,
who for one error scarcely perhaps deserved so severe a pun-

ishment. If it is a fiction, poetic justice is not, we think, properly distributed. (pp. 468-69)

> A review of "Charlotte, a Tale of Truth," in The
> Critical Review, Vol. IV, No. 1, April, 1791, pp.
> 468-69.

### WILLIAM COBBETT  (essay date 1795)

[*In the following letter to the editors of the* American Monthly
Review, *the English critic William Cobbett sarcastically attacks
Rowson for her "sudden conversion to republicanism," accusing
her of hypocrisy and anti-British sentiment. She responded in the
Preface to her* Trials of the Human Heart *by describing him as
"a kind of loathsome reptile." The exchange was highly publicized.*]

[Mrs. Rowson] somewhere mentions "the unbounded marks
of approbation," with which her works have been received in
[America]. Whether this observation from the authoress was
dictated by an extreme modesty, or by the overflowings of a
grateful heart, is a matter of indifference; the fact, I believe,
will not be disputed, and there I cannot withhold my congrat-
ulations on the subject, either from the lady or my countrymen.
It is hard to tell which is entitled to most praise on this occasion,
she for the possession and exertion of such transcendent abilities, or they for having so judiciously bestowed on them "their
unbounded marks of approbation." (p. 83)

[*Slaves in Algiers*] may be looked upon as a criterion of her
style and manner. (p. 85)

The authoress insists upon the superiority of her sex [in this
play], and in so doing, she takes care to express herself in such
a correct, nervous, and elegant style, as puts her own superiority, at least, out of all manner of doubt. Nor does she
confine her ideas to a superiority in the *belles lettres* only, as
will appear by the following lines from her epilogue:

> Women were born for universal sway,
> Men to adore, *be silent* and *obey*.

Sentiments like these could not be otherwise than well received
in a country, where the authority of the wife is so unequivocally
acknowledged, that the *reformers* of the *reformed church*, have
been obliged (for fear of losing all their custom) to raze the
odious word *obey* from their marriage service. (pp. 85-6)

[I will] quote a sentence or two, in which our authoress speaks
highly in praise of our alacrity in paying down the ransom for
our unfortunate countrymen in Algiers.

> But there are souls to whom the afflicted never
> cry in vain, who, to dry the widow's tear, or
> free the captive, would share their last posses-
> sion.—*Blest spirits of philanthropy*, who in-
> habit my native land, never will I doubt your
> friendship, for sure I am, you never will neglect
> the wretched.

This, you must know, gentle reader, is a figure of speech, that
rhetoricians call a *strong hyperbole*, and that plain folks call
a d——d lie, we will, therefore leave it, and come to her
versification.

This is an art, in which the lady may be called passing excellent,
as I flatter myself the following verses will prove. They are
extracted from her Epilogue; where, after having rattled on for

some time, with that air folâtre, so natural to her profession, she stops short with,

> But pray forgive this flippancy—indeed,
> Of all your clemency I stand in need.
> *To own the truth*, the scenes this night display'd,
> Are only *fictions*—drawn by *fancy's* aid.
> *'Tis what I wish*—But we have cause to fear,
> No ray of comfort the sad *bosom's* cheer,
> Of many *a christian*, shut from *light* and *day*,
> In *bondage*, languish *their lives* away.

This is a little parterre of beauties.

It was kind of the authoress to tell her gentle audience, that her play was a *fiction*, otherwise they might have gone home in the full belief, that the American prisoners in Algiers had actually conquered the whole country, and taken the Dey prisoner. I confess there was a reason to fear that an audience, who had bestowed "unbounded marks of approbation" on such a piece, might fall into this error.

It was not enough to tell them that the subject of her play was a *fiction*, but she must tell them too, that it was a *fiction* drawn by *fancy's* aid. This was necessary again; for they might have thought it was a *fiction*, drawn by the aid of *truth*.

"'*Tis what I wish*."—What do you wish for, my dear lady? Do you wish *that your scenes may be fictions drawn by fancy's aid*? Your words have no other meaning than this; and if you may have another you have not told us what it is.

Being shut from *light* is the same thing as being shut from *day*, and being shut from day is being *in bondage*; either of these, then, would have been enough, if addressed to an audience of a common capacity.

*Many a Christian's* having a plurality of *bosoms* and *lives*, is an idea, that most assuredly bears in it all the true marks of originality.—The lady tells us somewhere, that she has never read the ancients: so much the better for us. . . . (pp. 86-8)

[The authoress's romances] are, in no respect, inferior to her poetic and "dramatic efforts."

Among the many treasures that the easterly winds have wafted us over, since our political emancipation, I cannot hesitate to declare this lady the most valuable. The inestimable works that she has showered (not to say *poured*, you know) upon us, mend not only our hearts, but if properly administered, our constitutions also: at least I can speak for myself. They are my *Materia Medica* [drugs], in a literal sense. A liquorish page from the *Fille de Chambre* serves me by way of a philtre, the *Inquisitor* is my opium, and I have ever found the *Slaves in Algiers* a most excellent emetic. As to *Mentoria* and *Charlotte*, it is hardly necessary to say what use they are put to in the chamber of the valetudinarian.

Before we were so happy as to have *a Rowson* amongst us, we were, or seemed to be, ignorant of our real consequence as a nation. We were modest enough to be content with thinking ourselves the only enlightened, virtuous, and happy people upon earth, without having any pretension to universal dominion; but she, like a second Juno, fires our souls with ambition, shows us our high destiny, bids us "soar aloft, and wave our *acknowledged* standard *o'er the world*."

After this, it is not astonishing that she should be called the poetess laureat of the Sovereign People of the United States; it is more astonishing that there should be no salary attached

to the title; for I am confident her dramatic works merit it much more than all the birth-day and new-year odes, ever addressed to her quondam king.

Notwithstanding all this, there are (and I am sorry to say it), some people, who doubt of her sincerity, and who pretend that her sudden conversion to republicanism, ought to make us look upon all her praises as ironical. But these uncandid people do not, or rather will not, recollect, what the miraculous air of America is capable of. (pp. 88-9)

> *William Cobbett, "A Kick for a Bite" (originally published in* The Monthly Review, *London, Vol. XVI, February, 1795), in his* Porcupine's Works: Containing Various Writings and Selections, Exhibiting a Faithful Picture of the United States of America, *Vol. II, Cobbett and Morgan, 1801, pp. 69-93.*

### THE CRITICAL REVIEW    (essay date 1800)

[*Reuben and Rachel; or, Tales of the Old Times*] is a strange medley of romance, history, and novel, in which the scenery is changed with the pantomimical rapidity of Voltaire's *Candide*. New characters and new narratives are frequently introduced; and we were in some measure surprised that a novelist of Mrs. Rowson's experience should have aukwardly thrown together, in two volumes, a number of stories sufficient (in the hands of a dexterous manufacturer) to have occupied nearly ten times the space on the shelves of a circulating library. (pp. 116-17)

> *A review of "Reuben and Rachel; or, Tales of the Old Times," in* The Critical Review, *Vol. XXVIII, January, 1800, pp. 116-17.*

### JOHN GREENLEAF WHITTIER    (essay date 1828)

We have been pleased with a perusal of [*Charlotte's Daughter; or, the Three Orphans*]. The characters which its author has introduced to our view are not so strongly contrasted as in some of her earlier productions; yet they [are] sufficiently marked to excite our interest.—Lucy Blakeney is, we think, the most interesting of the group—the progress of her gentle affections—her brief enjoyment of that happiness, which in the language of our author "is never felt but once"—and her noble resignation to the fearful necessity of quenching in her bosom a passion which could no longer be indulged with innocence, are all described with a pathos and sensibility which is peculiar to Mrs. Rowson. (p. 15)

Mrs. Rowson, has, we believe, been censured for her uniform simplicity of style and scrupulous adherence to the realities of life. She has indeed little to do with the imagination. Her pictures, simple and unadorned as they really are, doubtless appear tame and spiritless to those who are satisfied with nothing which approaches the bounds of probability. But there is a truth—a moral beauty in her writings, which harmonizes with our purest feelings—a language which appeals to the heart, not in the studied pomp of affectation, but in the simple eloquence of Nature.

Mrs. Rowson, however, was by no means a faultless writer.—In the volume before us, we could point to many imperfections both in style and incident. It should, however, be borne in mind that it was written while its author was engaged in the daily task of superintending the education of nearly one hundred pupils and that she was at the same time the conductor of that popular paper, the *Boston Weekly Magazine*.

To the admirers of *Charlotte Temple,* we recommend this volume. It deserves a place with its predecessor. (pp. 17-18)

> *John Greenleaf Whittier, "Susannah Rowson, 'Charlotte's Daughter,'" (originally published in* Essex Gazette, *May 17, 1828), in his* Whittier on Writers and Writing: The Uncollected Critical Writings of John Greenleaf Whittier, *edited by Edwin Harrison Cady and Harry Hayden Clark (copyright, 1950 Syracuse University Press), Syracuse University Press, 1950, pp. 15-18.*

## ELIAS NASON (essay date 1870)

*Charlotte Temple* is not . . . a creation of fancy, but a faithful transcription of real life, in 1774, and hence it is a living book, and criticise it as we may, the people after all will read it, weep over it and enjoy it. It appeals to the tenderest sentiments of the human heart, and sweeps across the chords of feeling as the evening breeze across the strings of the Aeolian harp. It exhibits passages of beautiful description, as the one commencing; ''It was a fine evening in the beginning of autumn''; of tender pathos, as the visit of Mr. Temple to Fleet prison, the sorrows of a mother, and the death of Charlotte; of moral sublimity, as the agonizing struggles of a wounded conscience. The character of an intriguing, heartless teacher is well portrayed in that of Madam De la Rue, and that of a fiendish libertine in that of Belcour. As to Montraville, his course and character may perhaps be too favorably described; his punishment too light. . . . (pp. 47-8)

The plot of the story is as simple and as natural as Boileau himself could desire; the denouement comes in just at the right time and place; and the reader's interest is enchained, as by magic, to the very last syllable of the book. A question has been raised as to the moral tendency of this work. I will attempt to answer it only by observing that it is a simple record of events as they transpired, as truthful as Macaulay's sketch of Charles the First, or of Lamartine's Columbus; and that whatever objection one might urge against it on the ground of immorality, might, with equal force, be brought against some of our very best works of history and biography. But let the decision be what it may, it seems quite certain that Mrs. Rowson wrote the story with the purest motive. She had seen something of the scandalous lives of the British land and naval officers of that period, and she determined to warn her fair countrywomen of their seductive arts. The bishop of London would have taken another course; but his voice would have failed to reach, as her cunning fingers did, the secret springs of the heart of the people. (pp. 48-9)

A great warm loving heart guided the fingers which portrayed the picture [of Charlotte Temple], and that is power; and ply the rules of rhetoric as we may, the people feel the power and they acknowledge it. The common mind of the common people is after all the true arbiter of the merit of the works of genius. (p. 51)

The plot of *Rebecca* is not as well contrived as that of *Charlotte Temple;* the unity not so well sustained; nor are the characters, if we except that of Rebecca, so ably drawn; yet it will ever be interesting as a faithful picture of English and American life in the days of the revolution, as a record of the trials and privations which the author herself experienced in early years, upon our guarded coast, and of the troubles no less serious which she met with while a governess. . . . (p. 56)

The *dramatis personae* [in *Trials of the Human Heart*] are by far too numerous; the plot is carelessly constructed, and the general drift of thought and sentiment, is similar to that of the leading female novelists of that period among whom Mrs. Rowson [mentioned] . . . Mrs. Frances Burney, Mrs. Bennet, and Misses Sophia and Harriet Lee, as her especial favorites. The moral bearing of the work, however, is healthful. . . . (p. 77)

[*Reuben and Rachel; or, Tales of Old Times*] was written with the design of awakening a deeper interest in the study of history which the author had pursued with great delight, and of showing that not only evil itself, but the very appearance of evil is to be avoided.

While this story presents many passages of vivid description; and several scenes of touching pathos, we nevertheless can claim but little merit for it as a work of art. The writer made her plot subservient to her desire of teaching history, and hence it ranges over a period of quite two centuries. The hero and heroine, Reuben and Rachel Dudley . . . are not introduced to the attention of the reader until the chapter closing the first volume. . . . [However,] Mrs. Rowson has breathed so much of her own generous emotion into this work, that in spite of its want of unity and the improbable incidents with which its pages abound, the interest of the reader is enchained as by the spell of an enchanter, to the last. (pp. 92-3)

The plan of [*Sarah, the Exemplary Wife*] is simple; the leading characters are few, distinct and consistent with themselves in word and action; the style is easy, flowing, natural, and sometimes truly tender and pathetic. (p. 119)

In common with the poets of her day, Mrs. Rowson frequently personifies [in her poetry] the faculties of the mind, and makes them play their scenic parts before us. Her versification is generally smooth, her images striking; but she often wrote too rapidly, sometimes too sentimentally, to write well. With much, however, that is affected, and much that bears the marks of haste, we occasionally meet with pieces rich and vigorous in thought, as they are graceful and appropriate in language. (p. 124)

The echoes of [Mrs. Rowson's] gentle voice are murmuring sweetly still. The gems she touched with beauty sparkle still. The spirit she evoked is breathing and the strings she struck are quivering still; the life she lived is eloquently speaking still, and as the tide of our national glory rolls along, will be most eloquently discoursing still; and may we not believe that when the Master shall make up his jewels at the final audit, this accomplished writer, this faithful wife, this loving teacher, this blessed almoner of God's sweet mercies to the poor, this humble, earnest and adoring Christian, will, surrounded by the radiant gems of her own polishing, and beaming in etherial light, live still! (p. 201)

> *Elias Nason, in his* A Memoir of Mrs. Susanna Rowson, with Elegant and Illustrative Extracts from Her Writings in Prose and Poetry, *Joel Munsell, 1870, 212 p.*

## CHARLES F. RICHARDSON (essay date 1889)

America, prior to 1750, had no drama, no joy of art, and no creative impulse outside of politics. (p. 284)

One poor little means of expression, nevertheless, was at length vouchsafed in fiction. However limited, timid, bigoted, inartistic, or ignorant a people may be, it is sure to have ''feelings.''

The growing sentimentalism which was to affect even the higher poetry and fiction of Germany and England made its trifling mark upon nascent American literature. In the last decade of the eighteenth century appeared **"Charlotte Temple, a Tale of Truth,"** by Mrs. Rowson—actress, playwright, poet, schoolteacher, text-book compiler, and voluminous sentimental novelist. Its pages were long bedewed with many tears of many readers; and, alone among our few eighteenth century tales, it survives to-day, if a cheap pamphlet issue, addressed to a somewhat illiterate public of readers, can be called survival. Its longdrawn melancholy is unrelieved by a touch of art; it is not even amusing in its absurdity. (pp. 284-85)

> Charles F. Richardson, "The Belated Beginning of Fiction," in his American Literature, 1607-1885: American Poetry and Fiction, Vol. II (copyright by Charles F. Richardson 1888), G. P. Putnam's Sons, 1889, pp. 282-96.*

## LILLIE DEMING LOSHE   (essay date 1907)

The earliest of Mrs. Rowson's works accessible in an American edition is **The Inquisitor or the Invisible Rambler,** professedly in the manner of Sterne. Mrs. Rowson, however, possessed little sentiment and no humor. The Inquisitor, her would-be sentimentalist, whose beneficent undertakings are furthered by a magic ring, suggests the able and efficient agent of a charity organization society. Indeed so admirable is his economy of effort, that if he rescues a betrayed and forsaken maiden, she is sure to be the long lost daughter of the penniless old soldier whom he had saved from insult the week before. . . . [**Charlotte Temple, a Tale of Truth**] established Mrs. Rowson's reputation, and still maintains it, although among a somewhat different class of readers. . . . Nothing that can heighten the sensational effect is spared,—two of the very blackest villains obtainable are employed to bring about the catastrophe. The question at once suggests itself—why should this story have survived, to linger out a dishonored old age in yellow paper covers, when all its equally harrowing contemporaries have long been forgotten? The answer lies in Mrs. Rowson's undeniable command of the sensational, and in the comparative simplicity and directness of the story itself. There are many such tales, treated merely as episodes in Mrs. Rowson's other novels, which, if worked out separately with the same brevity and workmanlike construction, might have won the same reputation. (pp. 11-12)

The more practical bent of Mrs. Rowson appears [in **Lucy Temple or the Three Orphans**] Lucy's decision to found a school instead of dying of a broken heart. The general tone of the novel is educational, in contrast to the pure sensationalism of **Charlotte.**

[**The Trials of the Human Heart**] is best described in the definition of a novel given by the translator of **Alexis,** "a concatenation of events which taken separately will be worthy of belief." In its four volumes horrors worthy of the tragedy of blood are seen domesticated in London. Mrs. Rowson's sensationalism differs from that of most of her contemporaries—from that of Mrs. Bennett for example—in its complete lack of romance. Her theme here, as in **Rebecca** and in **Sarah,** is the bitter struggle of a poor and friendless woman to maintain herself in a world in which her beauty and accomplishments are only added dangers. Meriel, the heroine, after years of vicissitudes, individually conceived with some crude force, but collectively incredible because of their number, emerges from

the ordeal, apparently with not a curl displaced, to marry her first love.

In the choice of her horrors, and in the presentation of them, Mrs. Rowson is essentially a realist, whose trick of giving vividness by touches of homely detail was probably learned from Richardson, who got it from Defoe. . . . This crude realism of situation, without any corresponding truth of character, has given Mrs. Rowson a high place among successful exploiters of domestic melodrama, and it separates her didactic sensationalism from the more politely imaginative world of her "female" contemporaries. (pp. 12-13)

> Lillie Deming Loshe, "The Didactic and the Sentimental," in her The Early American Novel (copyright, 1907 by The Columbia University Press; copyright renewed © 1935 by Lillie Deming Loshe; reprinted by permission of the publisher), Columbia University Press, 1907, pp. 1-28.*

## ARTHUR HOBSON QUINN   (essay date 1936)

[**Charlotte; a Tale of Truth**] has had a tremendous vogue in this country. . . . [This] great vogue must be attributed to that quality which delights in reading of the misery of others which by contrast makes us satisfied with our own lot.

Perhaps the most interesting aspect of Mrs. Rowson's fiction consists in its reflection of the current standards of morality. She wrote her stories primarily for morality's sake and published her collection of short tales, **Mentoria; or, the Young Lady's Friend** . . . , because she believed that her young charges should not read the novels then being written. Yet she inserts a novelette, **Marian and Lydia,** which contains a situation in which Sir George Lovemore is only prevented from incest with his own daughter by the author's violent intervention! **Rebecca; or, the Fille de Chambre** . . . is of more interest to us on account of the picture of her own life during the Revolution. . . . There is quite a touch of verity in the scenes at sea and in America, and Rebecca excites more respect than Charlotte, for she acts at times with courage and decision. The satiric picture of the heartless conduct of her mistress, Lady Ossiter, after her mother's death, is not bad by any means. (pp. 15-16)

The most extraordinary novel by Mrs. Rowson, and the one most significant in this study on account of its use of American material, was **Reuben and Rachel; or, Tales of Old Times**. . . . Fortified by a cursory glance over the history of the world, she produced a romance which proceeds with unruffled steps from Christopher Columbus through ten generations of his descendants until the heroine reaches Philadelphia about 1700. To her inventive powers the creation of letters from Columbus to his wife is nothing; nor does she bother about mere fact, time or place, for after she has led him through an imaginary conquest of Peru, she calmly tells us that he sailed back to the islands of the Caribbean Sea, thus anticipating the Panama Canal by some years. After grafting a Peruvian princess and an English gentleman upon the stock of Columbus, she plunges her third heroine, Columbia, into the religious wars of Queen Mary's reign and makes her, among other things, the mother of Sir Ferdinando Gorges. This adventurer, who played a considerable role in early New England history, appeared later several times in American literature, but Mrs. Rowson alone furnishes him with so distinguished an ancestry. (pp. 16-17)

A mere outline . . . cannot do justice to this mixture of the historical romance, the story of adventure, and the novel of sentiment and intrigue. Despite all its absurdities, she showed in this novel the calm courage of the real romancer, and while her knowledge of Indian life must have been at second hand, her rapid sketches of Quaker Philadelphia have some verity. This novel, also, reveals most distinctly that dramatic sense which was expressed even more clearly in her one extant play, *Slaves in Algiers.* (p. 18)

Mrs. Rowson's last novel was a sequel to *Charlotte,* called *Charlotte's Daughter; or, The Three Orphans. . . . Charlotte's Daughter* has not the interest of her other novels written in America, though it is not quite so hopelessly sentimental as its more famous predecessor.

Notwithstanding their obvious faults, Mrs. Rowson's novels are of real significance in the history of English and American fiction. She had a knack of compelling interest and a power of description, evident for example in scenes like the passage of the Irish Sea in *Sarah.* More important, she was, if not the creator, a vivid portrayer of the virtuous woman adventuress. While the influence of Richardson is of course apparent, her creations are not, like Pamela and Clarissa, passive recipients of persecution. She passed on to several of her heroines her own courage and resourcefulness, which are cheering in days when "females" were supposed to faint in any crisis. Before Elizabeth Bennet had routed Lady de Bourgh in [Jane Austen's] *Pride and Prejudice,* and long before [Charlotte Brontë's] Jane Eyre lived, Rebecca and Meriel had broken through the conventionality of an age which demanded that a gentlewoman should do nothing for her self. While Fanny Burney undoubtedly is one of her models, Evelina would not have met such trials with the same daring or capacity. Mrs. Rowson had to live through a great many trials before she wrote about them. One of the earliest of feminists, as her amusing epilogue to *Slaves in Algiers* proves her, Mrs. Rowson's accomplishment in the creation of her heroines is all the more remarkable because she knew so well the constitution of the English social life she depicts. It was based upon the supremacy of the male, and she accepts it. That is why, with a sure instinct, she lays the scenes of her novels largely in England, even after she had become naturalized in America. The most severe criticism of her work lies in its implicit acceptance of a cold-blooded, eighteenth-century morality, British in essence, which permitted a man of wealth to purchase any virtue he desired and accepted as inevitable the hard lot of any woman without friends or money, whom a single mistake might destroy. It would be comforting for an American to dismiss her work as foreign in tone and as unrepresentative of American character and manners. But its great popularity must unfortunately give us pause. (pp. 18-19)

*Arthur Hobson Quinn, "The Foundations of American Fiction," in his* American Fiction: An Historical and Critical Survey *(© 1936, renewed 1963, excerpted by permission of Prentice-Hall, Inc., Englewood Cliffs, NJ 07632), D. Appleton-Century Company, Inc., 1936, pp. 3-24.\**

## CONSTANCE ROURKE   (essay date 1941)

[*Rourke was the first critic to recognize Rowson's feminism. Underneath the "surface gentility" of Rowson's novels, Rourke detects an "underlying bias" which she interprets as strongly feminist. Rourke's view was disputed by later critics, such as Kathleen Conway McGrath, who claims that Rowson "consistently reinforces her society's ideas about the value of its institutions and structures" (see excerpt below, 1973).*]

Mrs. Rowson was never languid. Something big and bosomy might be discovered in her most sentimental fiction; her energy was unbounded. (p. 76)

Yet a surface gentility belonged to her career as a writer in London: she had entered upon it entirely for pecuniary reasons, but she managed to convey the idea that for her writing was only a pleasurable accomplishment. She was one of those women who are said to have a gifted pen, which somehow removes them from the coarse realm of effort. "What," said a Grub Street journalist upon meeting the dainty heroine of her *Mentoria,* undoubtedly herself, "can that young creature be an author?" But she brightly satirized this hack writer with his scissors and paste. She worked hard at her trade, and wrote one sentimental novel after another in an easy style that must have cost her some effort, none of them without some touch of originality, all of them with a distinct bias. Already Mrs. Rowson was a reformer: her novels rarely contained an irresistible story, but they always had a purpose. They also had an underlying bias. They were feminist. Mrs. Rowson looked upon the male sex with a skeptical eye. In her *Victoria,* the heroine loses her mind as a result of male scheming; indeed her delicate, distraught heroines almost invariably suffered deeply through masculine faults, failures or downright deviltry. In *Charlotte Temple,* seduction was the single primary theme upon which she harped. Written in liquid prose, pervaded by verses and songs into which the unhappy heroine slipped as easily as she slipped to her downfall, the novel was based upon facts which Mrs. Rowson took no pains to disguise. Indeed she flaunted them. Mr. Rowson's dereliction does not seem to have been directly exposed though it probably gave her momentum. . . . Poor Charlotte seems to have been a real person: her ashes are supposed to rest in Trinity Churchyard in New York. Perhaps a knowledge of these circumstances gave the novel its first great vogue in England and the United States, but only its driving energy of style could have kept it alive—and alive it is to this day. Long and plotless as her other novels are, they had motion and purpose, but none of them, not even the sequel *Charlotte's Daughter,* which trenched upon the fearful theme of incest, had the success of *Charlotte.* (pp. 78-80)

Nothing less than the popular operatic form would do for her first play, *Slaves of Algiers.* . . . But into [her] coy lines she worked a statement of her theme, that women "should have supreme dominion," and she meant it. The whole play revolved about women; they dominated the plot, the action, the outcome. Moreover, the play had an assertive rollicking note. . . . (pp. 80-1)

[Mrs. Rowson also] wrote a poem on **"The Rights of Women"**—

> While patriots on wide philosophic plan
> Declaim upon the wondrous rights of man.

If the verses were rough the equalitarian idea was expounded with firmness. (p. 85)

She was not truly a poet, but she carved a niche for herself among those American verse-makers who were long to be called poets, and she was better than many of them. She was not truly a dramatist, an actress, a novelist, nor in the full sense an educator, but in each of these roles she had managed to give momentum to broad tendencies. Mrs. Rowson died in 1824. On the walls of Boston houses in which she was surely welcome were portraits of women of a somewhat older generation to whom she must have felt akin. . . . Elegant in their stiff silks, fine mulls, pearls, elaborate headdresses, they might seem concerned only with such matters, yet clearly enough they were women of principles and ideas. Shrewd, tolerant, hardy, they belonged to a provincial society but exceeded it: in a genuine sense, with their own particular bias, they were women of the great world. They would have understood Mrs. Rowson. They would have admired the strict fashion in which she had tethered a buoyant temperament to a prolonged series of tasks. They were advocates of discipline. But they also would have relished the ebullience running so engagingly through her character, for they had *esprit*, they had belonged to the Revolution. (p. 87)

> *Constance Rourke, ''The Rise of Theatricals'' (1941), in her* The Roots of American Culture and Other Essays, *edited by Van Wyck Brooks (copyright 1942 by Harcourt Brace Jovanovich, Inc., renewed 1970 by Alice D. Fore; reprinted by permission of the publisher), Harcourt Brace Jovanovich, 1942, pp. 60-160.**

## ALEXANDER COWIE   (essay date 1948)

The story [of *Charlotte Temple*] is told rapidly and with signs of genuine power that cannot be laughed away in merriment over the inevitably ornate style in which the author wrote. (p. 12)

The harsh attitude toward fallen women which is generally associated with Puritan morality is not fully illustrated in *Charlotte Temple*. The author's reproaches of Charlotte are at least equalled by her indignation at Montraville and Belcour, especially the latter. Observing Charlotte in her wretched betrayed condition, Mrs. Beauchampe asserts that Charlotte is worth saving, for ''her heart may not be depraved,'' and even when the end is near Mrs. Beauchampe expresses a hope that Charlotte ''might recover, and, spite of her former errors, become a useful and respectable member of society.'' A far cry, this, from the common conviction that one step from rectitude should blast a girl's soul for eternity. . . . Obviously Mrs. Rowson was kinder to erring womanhood than most of her contemporaries and immediate successors among American novelists. . . . Yet Mrs. Rowson is strong in her indictment of the one really corrupt character in her story, the French governess. . . . It is easy, especially for the person without historical perspective, to laugh at the old-fashioned rhetoric of the author. It *is* amusing. When Mrs. Rowson meant that Mrs. Beauchampe wept for Charlotte, she referred to ''the pellucid drop of humanity stealing down her cheek.'' Yet to base a critical judgment of a whole book on trifles like this is illogical; over-embellished language was as much a part of the period as hoopskirts. The real question about *Charlotte,* as about any novel, is whether it has basic sincerity and power. Unquestionably it has; the wretchedness and loneliness of Charlotte and the quiet suffering of her parents are rendered with a simple vividness which can be felt even today. . . . That *Charlotte* was in constant demand throughout the nineteenth century and has had a moderate sale even at the present time is a sign of real merit in the novel.

Mrs. Rowson wrote a number of other novels which show a fair degree of skill and some originality but which for the most part deserve the oblivion which has overtaken them. *Trials of the Human Heart* . . . is a story which moves rapidly over land and sea on narrative errands which could hardly have edified conservative readers of the day. . . . [In *Reuben and Rachel: or Tales of Old Times*] Mrs. Rowson uses American history and American scenes as ingredients in a romance so fantastic and so involved that even her comparatively sober

study of the American Indian cannot redeem it. . . . In all these novels, as in a number of shorter tales, Mrs. Rowson repeatedly proved herself as an able delineator of dramatic episode with incidental realistic effects, but her plots showed that instability which was one of the principal weaknesses of the early novel. The stories are overloaded with poorly allocated episodes, and the scene shifts from place to place too rapidly to permit of orientation. Mrs. Rowson had a natural affinity with the adventure story. Her heroines are adventuresses of a superior sort, often displaying the author's own initiative and enterprise instead of the flabby passivity of many contemporary heroines. The underlying moral intention of the author is almost always felt, but Mrs. Rowson's fairly frequent use of the methods and atmosphere of what has come to be known as ''chamber-maid fiction'' raises the suspicion that she was occasionally thinking more of her own bread and butter than of a suitable intellectual diet for the young. The meek and lowly heroine of *Charlotte* was the only one of Rowson's characters who really stirred the sympathies of the public. (pp. 13-15)

> *Alexander Cowie, ''At the Beginning,'' in his* The Rise of the American Novel *(copyright, 1948, 1951, by American Book Company), American Book Company, 1948 (and reprinted by American Book Company, 1951), pp. 1-37.**

## LESLIE A. FIEDLER   (essay date 1966)

[*One of the most prominent and outspoken critics of Rowson's* Charlotte Temple, *Fiedler considers the novel ''an unwitting travesty'' of Samuel Richardson's Clarissa Harlowe. He maintains that ''the sacred power is still there, but the subtlety and passion, the style and distinction have gone.'' Richardson's ''mythic literature'' has been, according to Fiedler, transformed by Rowson into ''subliterate myth.''*]

Mrs. Rowson's *Charlotte Temple* is a book scarcely *written* at all, only in the most perfunctory manner told; yet it is the first book by an American to move American readers, and certain historians of the American novel, not themselves critics or readers of criticism, have praised it absurdly for its ''basic sincerity and power,'' or its ''simple vividness'' [see excerpt above by Cowie, 1948]. To be sure, the popularity of *Charlotte* poses a real problem. Why a book which barely climbs above the lower limits of literacy, and which handles, without psychological acuteness or dramatic power, a handful of stereotyped characters in a situation already hopelessly banal by 1790, should have had more than two hundred editions and have survived among certain readers for a hundred and fifty years is a question that cannot be ignored. It is tempting to say that popular taste given the choice between a better and a worse book will inevitably choose the worse; but this is an antisentimental simplification no more helpful than its sentimental opposite number. Only certain bad books succeed, apparently not by the simple virtue of their badness, but because of the theme they have chosen to handle badly.

Mrs. Rowson's book apparently comprises something that is not literature, though it is published in the guise of literature. It is apparent at least that the appeal of *Charlotte* is based not upon form or characterization or insight or beauty of language, not even upon the simplest skills of composition, but upon the bare bones of plot, on what its readers would call quite simply ''the story.'' That story, which it is almost impossible to retell without improving, represents in its essential form the myth or archetype of seduction as adapted to the needs of the American female audience. To Mrs. Rowson we must be grateful for having separated the archetype from its literary or pseudo-literary envelope, for having, as the scientists say, "isolated" it.

To be sure, there are some literary pretensions in Mrs. Rowson's approach—a certain self-consciousness which makes her pause occasionally to address the critic over the shoulder of the servant girl who is her ideal reader. . . . But her intended literary devices are most often as naively transparent as the pseudo-quotation from Shakespeare on her title page: "She was her parents' only joy / They had but one—one darling child." This poor, limping verse she attributes hopefully to *Romeo and Juliet;* but though she was an actress and became a teacher, she has misremembered or simply faked.

Occasionally, she strives for a kind of Biedermeier decoration, visualizing a scene in terms of the most sentimental genre painting of her day. . . . But aside from the old man with his pipe and the humbly grateful hens, nothing is visualized in the book. It is morality not art at which Mrs. Rowson consciously aims; and she desires, as she tells us disarmingly if ungrammatically, nothing more than to convince her readers "that I have not wrote a line that conveys a wrong idea to the head." She is, indeed, almost openly anti-literary in a defensive way, hinting that "trifling performances" like her own are to be preferred to "the most elegant, finished piece of literature whose tendency might deprave the heart or mislead the understanding." Her book at least is firmly committed to the notion "that vice, however prosperous in the beginning, in the end leads only to misery and shame."

There is no duplicity in *Charlotte Temple,* or at least, only the unwitting duplicity of the best-seller which confuses the wish with the fact, and presents the dreams of its readers as an account of real actions in the real world. It is a book no one could have faked, even its tender lingering over the details of vice which it presumably hates arising from an essential artlessness. As even its title declares, Mrs. Rowson's novel . . . is completely a woman's book—a tale in which female suffering is portrayed from a female point of view in order to stir female sympathy; while vice and virtue are judged by female standards. Mrs. Rowson . . . , who had been forced by her husband's failure to make herself a career and forge by her own hard work a shield of respectability, stood unequivocally on the woman's side in that war of the sexes whose existence she would not for a moment have denied. Her title declares her allegiance, her conviction that she is one of the girls. The single first name (returning to the tradition of [Samuel Richardson's] *Pamela*) suffices to describe what the book is about; and there is no ambitious subtitle to lead us up metaphysical blind alleys—only the conventional boast "A Tale of Truth." The facts related do, indeed, seem to be derived from the real-life experiences of a certain Charlotte Stanley, but Richardson had invented that person's life before she managed to live it. (pp. 93-5)

It is the Richardsonian story as it has descended through the female line in its most banal form. In Mrs. Rowson's version, however, it succeeded in projecting once and for all the American woman's image of herself as the long-suffering martyr of love—the inevitable victim of male brutality and lust. Not for nothing is Charlotte called "Temple"; she represents a cult object, a center of worship—and on her (supposed) tomb, the floral tribute of generations of girls expressed their adoration of the Great Goddess whom they could venerate only if they believed her a "real" woman like themselves.

It is the nature of American scriptures to be vulgarizations of the holy texts from which they take their cues; and just as *The Book of Mormon* caricatures the Bible unawares, so *Charlotte Temple* is an unwitting travesty of *Clarissa Harlowe.* The sacred power is still there, but the subtlety and passion, the style and distinction have gone. What was mythic literature has become subliterate myth.

Mrs. Rowson, who had little sense, of course, of the scriptural character of her best-selling book, tried to continue it in a sequel, as if it were an ordinary novel. *Lucy Temple,* however, lacked the archetypal appeal of the earlier volume; though . . . it establishes the prototype of the repentant seducer, reduced to trembling dependence and near idiocy. (p. 97)

> *Leslie A. Fiedler, "The Bourgeois Sentimental Novel and the Female Audience," in his* Love and Death in the American Novel *(copyright © 1960, 1966 by Leslie A. Fiedler; reprinted with permission of Stein and Day Publishers), revised edition, Stein and Day, 1966, pp. 74-104.\**

## HENRI PETTER  (essay date 1971)

Mrs. Rowson's tales and sketches, apart from being an individual author's work, are also an index to the fiction then popular in America. Her work can be looked upon as a deliberate collection of the ingredients that went into the making of an average novel designed to be fashionably successful and derived from earlier successes. The patterns of Mrs. Rowson's stories owe much to popular models, just as the manner used in *The Inquisitor* is borrowed from Sterne and the character named Mentoria from Fénelon's widely read *Télémaque.* From *Charlotte* to its sequel, *Charlotte's Daughter,* Mrs. Rowson adopted with more or less discretion and skill the conventional plot elements of contemporary fiction, both English and American. That fiction was largely imitative, harking back to the examples of Richardson, Fielding, Goldsmith, and Sterne. But it was not just in her novels that Mrs. Rowson made use of the situations and characters that the writers of the time so glibly manipulated. *The Inquisitor* and *Mentoria,* which cannot be termed novels, are marked more distinctly by such interchangeable elements than by the manner or plan adopted. Plainly the conventional elements of plot and characterization exercised an irresistible attraction upon a host of minor writers, including Mrs. Rowson, who lacked the imagination and inventiveness needed to inform other material. There is a simple reason why *Charlotte* was so much more successful and still reads better than the rest of Mrs. Rowson's work: in writing that book she was using material which could to some extent be called her own, and she withstood the temptation of elaborating it with borrowed additions. This is a commendable restraint considering how easily available were a large number of predictable events or clichés of behavior. (pp. 22-3)

Mrs. Rowson's novels are stories first and lessons last. The novels rely less on the writer's moral commitment than on her sense of narrative control; but *Mentoria* and *The Inquisitor* depend on the didactic continuity underlying and linking up the various episodes that constitute their story content. Though there is this difference in degree, Mrs. Rowson's didactic bent is genuinely at work in all her books. From *Victoria* to *Charlotte's Daughter* she seemed to increase her enjoyment of storytelling by the satisfaction of carrying a lesson to her readers. (p. 25)

To call forth the reader's sensitive reaction, Mrs. Rowson used in *The Inquisitor* three chief narrative means: the motifs of (1) actual or attempted seduction and adultery, (2) social prejudice and oppression, and (3) cupidity. Whether introduced separately or in conjunction, these three motifs form the main pegs upon which the novelists of Mrs. Rowson's day hung their plots. The three motifs of *The Inquisitor* and the central topic of *Mentoria* could conveniently be combined: obedient or disobedient children often had an important role to play in stories of seduction, social prejudice, and cupidity. Mrs. Rowson's novels give several instances in which girls disregard their parents' wishes and become the victims of seducers, and young men and girls brave their parents' wrath by defying the barriers between the noble and the humble, the rich and the poor. (p. 26)

[Mrs. Rowson] usually submitted to the dictates of fashion and followed the line of least resistance, choosing to put her novels together out of the parts provided ready-made for the novelist. . . . [Her heroines belong] to a tradition of novel-writing whose heroines were just feeble echoes of Richardson's Pamela or Fielding's Amelia, far too retiring and resigned to assume the individual character of [Austen's] Elizabeth Bennet or even Miss Burney's Evelina. They were in fact not characters but stereotypes, whose few facets could be seen only in stock situations.

The novel as exercised by Mrs. Rowson might be called the novel of victimization. It is a novel that relies for its success on the contrast between the readers' cozy comfort and the heroine's sorrows and insecurity. . . . Whether the reader truly sympathizes with the heroine's plight or not depends not only on the writer's skill but also to a considerable extent upon the reader's familiarity with situations similar to hers—perhaps through his own experience, but more probably because of their current use in fiction. One source of the reader's gratification may well be his resentment at the heroine's humiliations, for such indignation gives him the assurance that he knows right from wrong and stands uncompromisingly on the side of what is right. In this sense the happy endings, though they grant a relief long yearned for, frequently are an anticlimax: confirming the reader's self-righteous verdict, they also put an end to a situation in which he was called upon to take sides.

Within the group of the novels of victimization, a distinction can be made between the novel of personal struggles and suffering on the one hand and the novel of impersonal vicissitudes on the other. *Charlotte* belongs to the first class; so does its sequel, *Charlotte's Daughter*, though it does not lend itself to classification so easily. The other class includes *The Fille de Chambre, Trials of the Human Heart, Reuben and Rachel,* and *Sarah*. (pp. 28-30)

Mrs. Rowson's two epistolary novels *Trials of the Human Heart* and *Sarah* handle the form too clumsily to gain anything from it. The former book is a diary rather than an exchange of letters; significantly, some of the few letters not written by Meriel can be laid before the reader only by being included in one of Meriel's. Occasionally the author tried to make the epistolary form serve the creation of suspense by ending a letter at a critical point. . . . The various correspondents of *Trials* hardly ever refer to the same incident from their different points of view, so as to heighten its importance or bring out its diverse meanings. In *Sarah* the different letter-writers are given still less of a chance to offer their own interpretation of some oc-

currence. Their letters do not convey additional information and become tediously repetitive.

Whatever Mrs. Rowson was trying to do when she wrote **Reuben and Rachel,** the result is not brilliant. Nevertheless the book must be briefly considered here, for it is not *only* a novel of victimization. It deserves notice because of its attempt at including historical and American material. (pp. 34-5)

The New World plays an important part in this book. . . . The Indian background used by Mrs. Rowson is in itself almost an innovation in American fiction. . . . [Yet her] Indian chapters are insufficiently coordinated with the more usual parts of her novel; they read like an element deliberately introduced to give the story a dash of the uncommon and are not so much part of the narrative as a picturesque feature, rather like the Columbus material in the opening chapters. **Reuben and Rachel** is clearly not a historical novel but a poorly organized book, setting fashionable plots against a sketchy background of historical fact. Yet it may have contributed to awaken a sense of the American past and its various ante-national roots: Italian, Spanish, English; Catholic, Protestant, Quaker; native, colonial, immigrant. (pp. 35-6)

Since **Charlotte's Daughter** is designated as a sequel to **Charlotte,** it is difficult to ignore either of the novels when speaking of the other. In the moral sense, indeed, they complement each other, but as stories they adopt different plans. **Charlotte** has something tragic about it, whereas **Charlotte's Daughter** begins as a kind of fable, only to have the balance between its three main figures upset by an extraneous element. **Charlotte's Daughter** cannot stand by itself either as a narrative or as a didactic entity, **Charlotte** definitely can—the popularity which it enjoyed is sufficient proof of it.

Unlike Mrs. Rowson's other novels, **Charlotte** is, or just fails to be, a unified entity. This coherence expresses itself in the simplicity of its plot, which is especially striking to the reader who turns to **Charlotte** after reading Mrs. Rowson's other novels. In writing it Mrs. Rowson found herself treating a tale that was moving enough and had just the right attributes to be successfully turned into a novel of victimization and sentiment. She felt no need, however, to introduce into the book and the heroine's life a spectacular variety of events and characters. . . . [There] is a fair degree of plausibility and consistency both in the way in which the characters act and in the linking up of their actions. Granted that the note of sentiment and pathos is forced, especially in the over-proportioned story of the Temples and in the account of the heroine's final hours, yet thanks to Charlotte and Montraville the novel has more to recommend it than the average fiction of the time. . . . [Charlotte] retains to the end enough humanity not to tire the reader following the account of her trials. Judged by the standards of the age, Mrs. Rowson was rather reticent in her use of sentimental appeals during much of that account.

Part of our patience with the seduced heroine is due to Mrs. Rowson's treatment of Montraville. Her refusal to paint him as an out-and-out villain does much to encourage in the reader a sane approach to Charlotte. In the case of the ordinary seducer in fiction, the act of seduction is frequently the mere confirmation of his villainous nature; or it starts him for good on a career of crime because he becomes the victim of his own action, unable to free himself of its influence on his character and behavior. But Montraville is shown as a young man temporarily stifling his scruples, the better to obey an impulse dictated by his senses and vanity, yet without losing his conscience and his sensibility. He therefore shares many of the sorrows which he causes Charlotte and suffers his own as well in the dilemma of his relations with Julia. This girl is herself a useful figure in the conflict and an index to Montraville's standards. The young officer does not give up Charlotte for an unworthy rival, mean of character and desirable only for her fortune; on the contrary, Julia is a competitor whom Charlotte might have had to acknowledge under any circumstances.

If Mrs. Rowson avoided the cruder temptations of the stereotype in the central couple of *Charlotte,* she was not so fortunate with her two villains. Both Mademoiselle La Rue and Montraville's false friend Belcour perform as all seducers and calculating, immoral females should in the climate of the novel of seduction, yet neither achieves any degree of lifelike credibility. As do other female characters of Mrs. Rowson, Mademoiselle La Rue incurs the author's particular blame for assisting in the corruption of young girls.

The characters of *Charlotte's Daughter,* the heroine included, are fragmentary and sketchy. Franklin in particular suffers from not being a more conspicuous personage than the two orphans with whom Lucy is contrasted. As to Lucy and her companions, they remain remote because of what they were designed to be: three different types of girls facing the same situation at the beginning of their adult life. Lady Mary's fate is that of the heroine of *Female Quixotism,* transposed from the satirical to the tragic, to show the possible serious consequences of immoderate novel-reading. (pp. 36-8)

The best that can be said of Mrs. Rowson's style is that it is generally free of the self-conscious over-writing which many contemporary novelists indulged in. In occasional scenes of dramatic revelations and confrontations, though, she did use pathetic and melodramatic tricks of emphasis, and in some rare instances she introduced touches of the Gothic. Otherwise, she wrote rather straightforwardly. At the same time, her reticence in embellishing her pages appears to be not so much a quality as a defect, inasmuch as it prevented her writing from achieving anything like a recognizable individuality. (pp. 38-9)

Except in the cases of *Charlotte* and *Reuben and Rachel,* Mrs. Rowson remained strictly within the limits of [conventional late eighteenth-century] novel writing. In *Charlotte* she managed to infuse into a stock situation an ingredient of personal and moral vitality, giving her tale a degree of human warmth which saved it from the obvious literariness of the rest of her work. In *Reuben and Rachel* she drew attention to historical and Indian material, though her experiment did not result in an improved form of the novel. (p. 40)

> *Henri Petter, "A Novelist's Practices: Mrs. Rowson," in his* The Early American Novel *(copyright © 1971 by the Ohio State University Press; all rights reserved), Ohio State University Press, 1971, pp. 22-45.*

**KATHLEEN CONWAY McGRATH**   (essay date 1973)

Mrs. Rowson's purpose in writing [*Charlotte Temple*] was both moral and social; she begins her Preface with the statement that her book is designed "For the perusal of the young and thoughtless of the fair sex," and she continues throughout the work to address pieces of advice to that audience. (p. 22)

Admittedly, the story line, or sequence of recurrent acts in the novel is both action packed and tragedy laden—and that fact must have accounted for a good deal of the popularity of the

work, which underwent two hundred editions. The story is based upon an event which really is archetypal: an attraction between two people which is not sanctioned by society and which must therefore run its course outside of the structures of society. (p. 23)

But there is another element to be considered in this accounting: the way in which Rowson consistently reinforces her society's ideas about the value of its institutions and structures. Given the exact same story line, one can imagine numberless different points of view, countless ways of reckoning the *why* of Charlotte's tragedy. It is not hard to imagine a story along similar lines which would berate a society so narrow as to conceive of only one social form for human relationships, so unforgiving as to permit a progress of desperation like that which Charlotte endures. But Mrs. Rowson's imagination is severely limited by the prevailing social norms; she attacks neither the social rigidity of her times nor the prudery which maintained that rigidity; she turns her wrath upon the forces which seduce youngsters away from compliance with the existing social structures. I suggest that it is *because* Rowson reinforces the prevailing social norms that *Charlotte Temple* enjoyed such widespread popularity. I have no doubt that the late eighteenth and nineteenth century readers of *Charlotte Temple* enjoyed the tragic story of Charlotte; they also, I am suggesting, enjoyed being told repeatedly that the social structure in which they were caught up was firmly and rightfully rooted in human nature. Mrs. Rowson gives her readers vast amounts of moral instruction and reinforces the social status quo with her remarks in three general areas: first, the sanctity of the family; second, the sanctity of the virtue of Content; and third, the villainy of certain types of characters who detract from the sanctity of the first two. All three of these areas overlap as is to be expected, since they all derive from one consistent vision of social security with one concomitant set of fears about the dangers to that security.

Rowson presents the life of the family in idyllic tones. (pp. 23-4)

Inherent in this idyllic vision of family life are Rowson's fears of 1) irresponsible marriage and 2) marriage contracted under impulsive inclination rather than under "the precepts of religion and virtue." (pp. 24-5)

The second area in which Rowson reinforces the social *status quo* comprises her remarks on the preeminence of the virtue of Content. She is particularly concerned that women should be content with their lot in life. . . . She idolizes Lucy Temple, Charlotte's mother, because she has found Content in her marriage. Between what must have been the harsh social reality of her times and the suffering individual Rowson interposes her philosophy of Content, of not expecting too much from life. (p. 25)

The final area in which I see Mrs. Rowson moving to support the social status quo is in her definition of who the villains are in her society.

Needless to say, the villains in Rowson's scheme of things are those who would seduce "the young and thoughtless of the fair sex" away from the holy ground of the family, away from being Content with the domestic life. . . . In her narrative the monsters of seduction, LaRue and Belcour, come to utter ruin in the last few pages of the work. (pp. 25-6)

There is, of course, no definitive answer to the question of why *Charlotte Temple* achieved the immense popularity which it did achieve. But the fact that it is no longer "popular"—that is to say, that it enjoyed a historically limited popularity—suggests that its appeal rested more upon its reinforcement of a particular vision of society than upon the universality of the appeal of its recurrent events. There is something very comforting in being reassured that the structures which surround and penetrate one's life are valid structures, structures deeply rooted in human nature. (p. 26)

[Popular] literature tends to support society's ideas about itself, and therefore is subject to the same inability to see the full complexity of the truth about its social reality as society is subject to that inability. I would suggest that only literature which sees more about society than society sees about itself can endure the test of time. *Charlotte Temple* does no more than reinforce prevailing social ideas, and because it does no more than that it has passed with the passing of the age it reflects. (p. 27)

> Kathleen Conway McGrath, "Popular Literature As Social Reinforcement: The Case of 'Charlotte Temple'," in Images of Women in Fiction: Feminist Perspectives, edited by Susan Koppelman Cornillon (copyright © 1972 by the Bowling Green University Popular Press), revised edition, Bowling Green University Popular Press, 1973, pp. 21-7.

**DOROTHY WEIL** (essay date 1976)

[*In this major critical study, Weil, like Rourke (see excerpt above, 1941), treats Rowson as a feminist and maintains that she "attacked the myths and stereotypes that surrounded women and taught her reader that she could be the equal of the male in most of the important spheres of life."*]

The complete education of the young female was the consistent aim of Mrs. Rowson's literary life. From the beginning of her career, the author selected critical principles that underlined and supported her rhetorical purpose. Three topics recur in Mrs. Rowson's discussion of literary standards and goals: concern for the young female audience, the importance of instructing this audience, and the necessity to provide a realistic or natural picture of life. (p. 11)

The protagonists of all but one of the fictions are young women, the action consists of problems faced by women, and the point of view rarely departs from that of the protagonist or a female friend. . . .

The desire to teach is the organizing principle of Mrs. Rowson's work. She states this idea in her prefaces and follows it in practice. Each of Mrs. Rowson's fictional works aims at and is organized by a moral lesson (or two) with the author's brand of Christianity as the controlling doctrine. . . .

Much has been written about Mrs. Rowson's claim that *Charlotte Temple* is a "Tale of Truth." (p. 14)

Mrs. Rowson's insistence upon the factual in *Charlotte,* when placed in context, can be seen as inchoate realism, part of her avowed method, and the product of aesthetic choice. For Mrs. Rowson did not confine her claim to authenticity to *Charlotte.* She asserted that all her works were reflections of reality. She never labeled a fictional work "romance." . . . Mrs. Rowson called all her extended fictional stories "novels," indicating that she meant them to be held to the higher standard of verisimilitude and probability. Her projected design for her texts was that they too should describe the real world and combat the errors of fancy, imagination, and false doctrine. Her whole didactic scheme rests upon the idea that everything she writes is based on actuality.

The young woman must be taught certain religious and moral principles, but this task must never be accomplished by holding up visionary or chimerical pictures of the world. Mrs. Rowson's rôle as the young woman's guide requires that she give her audience an honest look at what they might experience in reality. (p. 15)

Under the banner of Christianity and with a battalion of literary forms at her command, Mrs. Rowson met the major issues concerning women, and claimed freedom for her sex. . . . Mrs. Rowson attacked the myths and stereotypes that surrounded women and taught her reader that she could be the equal of the male in most of the important spheres of life, and that she should see herself as a person capable of great achievement. Mrs. Rowson's attempt to work through the problems that such a belief entails, and her recommendations for social change, are her major themes. (p. 35)

She emphatically rejected the advice to be "mild, social and sentimental," and although she described the contemporary woman's rôle as inevitably one of influence upon the male, she insisted that women are capable of high intellectual development and success in "any profession whatever."

One aspect of woman's basic nature upon which Mrs. Rowson never wavered was her sex's equality with the male. She states her view clearly in **"Sketches of Female Biography,"** a series of vignettes of famous women in history who excelled in various ways. (pp. 36-7)

The matter of sex and temperament is somewhat more complex for Mrs. Rowson. She has been included among writers who perpetuated the myth of the delicate, sensitive, passive woman, and the lustful, brutal, active male; she does tend at times to present this view. She often uses phrases like "the delicacy natural to our sex." On the other hand, Mrs. Rowson devotes a good deal of energy to refuting feminine stereotypes. As noted, she resolves such problems by resorting to a religious standard. A Christian, she argues, should combine the softer female virtues and the harder masculine ones. She cannot quite bring herself to drop the male-female dichotomy, so she retains it and still asserts a non-sex-linked personality for women. (p. 37)

Mrs. Rowson's heroines tend to combine the "graces and gentleness" of their own sex and the "knowledge and fortitude of the other" rather than to possess a rare, specifically feminine, religious and moral sensibility. Weak, passive vessels like Charlotte and Victoria may be in good standing "in futurity," but cause themselves and others great distress in the present. The heroines Mrs. Rowson presents as models to copy possess an active moral sense, and they face up to the tribulations involved in their choices as well as any man. Rebecca, who must support herself financially, faces poverty and ignominy when she refuses on two occasions to assist her employers in immoral intrigues. In several instances the power of Christian women to influence others is given special focus. (pp. 38-9)

[In *Slaves in Algiers*], which is ostensibly organized around a patriotic theme—the enslavement of Americans by the Barbary Pirates—the courage and fortitude of women takes precedence. . . .

Fetnah explicitly rejects the concept that women are inferior to men. She has learned to appreciate liberty in spite of being the daughter of Ben Hassan, a Jew and keeper of slaves. . . . Fetnah also rejects the notion that the character of a woman should express itself differently from that of a man. (p. 39)

Fetnah is Mrs. Rowson's version of a Shakespearean comic heroine, the girl who shows her spirited, active side. In helping the plot along, Fetnah must dress in men's clothing, thus underlining her relationship to Rosalind, Viola, et al.

In the epilogue to the play, Mrs. Rowson not only assumes equality with men, but incites her female audience to claim precedence. . . .

In character and virtue, Mrs. Rowson asserted, women could rival men, and their morality should be judged by similar standards. As to intellect, men may appear superior to women, but Mrs. Rowson viewed this situation as a function of society, not nature. (p. 40)

For the most part, Mrs. Rowson works from the theory that human temperament, guided properly, can be the same in both sexes. The virtuous male, like the virtuous female, would aspire to a similar goal, a combination of the "knowledge and fortitude" of his own sex and the "gentleness" of the other. As a Christian he would make the best of the two sides of his nature. (p. 45)

With all [her] virtues and talents, the female might be expected to claim almost any social rôle, but Mrs. Rowson does not suggest such a sweeping program. The prevailing social ideal envisioned woman as a good influence upon the male, with marriage as the principal means of influence. Susanna Rowson defers to this trend, even while she recognizes that marriage will not be the lot of every woman and will provide none with an eternally comfortable haven. She does not preclude the participation of women in any other kind of activity.

Mrs. Rowson sees the rôles of men and women as complementary. . . . In all the pedagogical works, Mrs. Rowson stresses the importance of women as an influence upon men and children. . . . Her rationale for the education of women is often based on the uplifting effect educated women will have on their families. . . . Still, she stresses the value of the works of individual women, and offers some alternatives to marriage.

In the fiction, the destiny of most of the protagonists is marriage. Only a few escape husbands for useful single lives. Of course, Mrs. Rowson's novels, aside from *Victoria* and *Charlotte,* are comic in the sense that there are alternatives for the protagonists, and the final reversal of fortune moves from bad to good; and marriage is the traditional resolution of the comic plot. (p. 48)

For the woman, marriage is one more possible briar in that "thorny path of life" Mrs. Rowson offers to her audience. It may be fulfilling: one feminine type frequently encountered in the works is the generous, philanthropic, happily married woman. (p. 50)

At worst, marriage is legalized prostitution. This idea is stated in *Charlotte,* where marriage forced upon women as their only alternative is quietly attacked. . . . Mrs. Rowson continues this argument against society's insistence upon marriage in *Charlotte, Trials of the Human Heart,* and *Sarah.* (pp. 50-1)

The rights of women begin, Mrs. Rowson believed, with changes in the attitudes of society. She calls for abandonment of the stereotypes that confine the woman's world educationally and professionally, in the way men view women, and in the treatment of women by the social mores. . . .

The rights of women also include treatment from men as the equals they are and the abandonment of the image of women as children or "sex objects." (p. 60)

Women, claims Mrs. Rowson, have the right to be judged on a par with men. The sexual double standard is implicitly criticized throughout her works. (p. 61)

Susanna Rowson's religion is the controlling system from which the author's main concerns take their shape and support. As we have seen, Mrs. Rowson uses a Christian standard as the basis for her concept of temperament. Religious themes and character types recur in her work, and her treatment of these elements supports her feminist views. Mrs. Rowson's theology is a timely reaction to male-inspired church traditions demeaning to women.

Mrs. Rowson believes in the unity of Christian doctrine, and stresses the power of Christ to redeem fallen mankind. In accepting the doctrine of original sin, she takes a harder view of human nature than literary scholars have ascribed to the typical female novelist of her period. She accepts the basic sacraments and forms of the Anglican Church, but stresses the spirit over the letter of the law. Nevertheless, she does not advocate religion based purely on emotion, as many nineteenth-century sentimentalists did, but insists on the need for intellectual as well as emotional understanding of the Scriptures. (p. 65)

In her earlier efforts Mrs. Rowson uses satire to dramatize the difference between the ideals of Christianity and life as it is. She presents a world marred by the activities and attitudes of a fallen race. There is a smattering of practicing Christians who keep the world from becoming a desert, and to these the author often bows and apologizes for her harsh statements; still, human society as a whole is corrupt—the world is a Vanity Fair where the majority engage in heartless barter and the worship of false idols, especially money and rank. (p. 66)

Mrs. Rowson attempts to establish a basis upon which women might share religious life free from the many anti-female traditions of the church, which ranged from the use of Scripture to insist upon feminine inferiority to related rules giving women inferior seating and prohibiting them from preaching. But rather than confront and combat these traditions directly as Elizabeth Cady Stanton did at a riper time, Mrs. Rowson stresses the aspects of her religion likely to encourage respect for the female. . . .

While she derides formalism, Mrs. Rowson does not go to the other extreme of putting all her emphasis upon feeling in her treatment of religion. (p. 76)

Whether or not her foresight extended so far, Mrs. Rowson combines the concepts "reason and religion." . . . [Maintaining] our faith requires sense, the use of the intellect, and the faculty of reason. (pp. 76-7)

Mrs. Rowson is not anti-intellectual, but she opposes a particular point of view: skepticism. It is not an adventitious combination of traits that makes so many of the male "seducers" in the fiction freethinkers. These men cause the "ruin" of the female only if she is corrupted by their philosophy. Mrs. Rowson does not set up an opposition between the head and the heart in these encounters, but the opposition of two points of view, both of which claim reason for their side. The male seducer tries to induce his target to use her reason to justify her passions, while Mrs. Rowson tries to convince the reader to use her reason to resist such arguments and maintain her faith (purity). (p. 78)

[Mrs. Rowson's] emphasis on the Christian virtues, which anyone could practice, with or without privileges in church life, underline the equality among all people, and give support to her teaching—so necessary to the complete education of her audience—on the proper arrangement of society. (p. 80)

During the 1790s and early 1800s, Mrs. Rowson wrote several theater pieces on American subjects, as well as numerous poems and songs eulogizing George Washington and John Adams and celebrating American values, virtues, and victories. . . . The values she praises in her patriotic American efforts, democracy and freedom, are extensions of those she always advocated. A Christian society, argues Mrs. Rowson, will be a democratic society, and a democratic society recognizes the female as a participating, rational individual. She establishes this equation through her literary treatment of various nations and groups, and makes her point especially trenchant by emphatically condemning dictatorship and slavery. (p. 81)

Its few problems notwithstanding, America is, in Mrs. Rowson's view, the stronghold of freedom, and the ultimate symbol of female emancipation. All of her surveys of world history end with the celebration of the new country, in the vein of *Reuben and Rachel*. (p. 91)

While *Slaves in Algiers* may exhibit the overstatement appropriate to farce, Fetnah's vision of happiness summarizes Mrs. Rowson's view of the relation between religion, society, and sex. Fetnah, alone in a garden, says "I do wish, some dear, sweet, Christian man would fall in love with me, break open the garden gates, and carry me off." . . . Her dream is not asexual; her Christian man will "break open the garden gates," but he will not enslave her with new limitations. When Frederic, a Christian and an American (an unbeatable combination), approaches her, Fetnah asks him to take her "where there are no bolts and bars; no mutes and guards; no bowstrings and scymetars—Oh! it must be a dear delightful country, where women do just what they please." . . . (p. 97)

Certainly Mrs. Rowson uses many of the standard ingredients of the neo-Richardsonians. Seduction is a major theme and plot device. Seducers are rung in whenever the action begins to wane or a sense of time passing must be suggested. The number of would-be seducers encountered by the average Rowson protagonist would stagger the imagination of the creator of the sentimental prototype, maybe even that of his followers. However, the character of some of these villains is given believable complexity. . . . Further, Mrs. Rowson's standard seducer is as threatening as a germ at a public drinking fountain, and as easily avoided. . . . [Mrs. Rowson] does not believe in the absolute vice of the seducer and the absolute virtue of the seduced. (p. 113)

Because of the book's popularity and its reputation for evoking tears, critics most often use *Charlotte* to prove Mrs. Rowson a purveyor of sensibility rather than sense. But Mrs. Rowson foresaw the reader's proneness to enjoy the good cry *Charlotte* provides, and ignore its moral purpose. To correct this tendency, she plays the rôle of a third-person author-narrator, who takes a satirical attitude toward her own introduction of tears and suffering. . . .

According to Mrs. Rowson, sensibility in its proper form was never distinct from or divorced from the use of reason. The ability to feel compassion for others was one of the highest goods in the author's scheme of values; she rejects the stoic and the "icy sons of philosophy," whoever would overburden reason by subordinating feeling among the human faculties.

Thus in *Charlotte* the reader is cajoled to use her sensibilities to feel sympathy for Charlotte even though the protagonist's situation might be far removed from her own; but excess, morbid, uncontrolled emotions are dangerous and undesirable. (p. 115)

Feeling must be tempered by reason, sensibility with sense. Mrs. Rowson's constant concern with this balance shows that she pays more than conventional "lip-service" to the latter qualities, in spite of her use of some of the stock ingredients associated with the cult of sensibility. (p. 117)

Mrs. Rowson portrays two kinds of heroines in her fiction, the young lady of intense sensibility who is life's victim, and the robust girl with spirit who fights and endures. The first type is represented only by Victoria and Charlotte, who are sad examples of girls led astray not merely by men but by their own false views of life. They let feeling—in both cases, romantic love—run away with them. They have no practical sense, exert no active force on their situations, and are duped and ultimately driven to despair and death. They adopt the poses of the typical heroine of sensibility, moping about in Ophelia-like garments, singing songs of love and woe, and remaining aloof from reality. All the other protagonists—Mary, Rebecca, Meriel, Rachel, Sarah, and Lucy—are girls in whom sense predominates over sensibility. They may begin life susceptible, sensitive, and naive, but they learn from experience and refuse to fade at "the first rude blast." Their predominant qualities are pluck and resilience. Like Fetnah, they are "spirited ladies." (p. 119)

Solid virtues, based upon clear perception of the world as it is, are superior to the refined poses of sentiment and sensibility. In fact, the structure of Mrs. Rowson's novels indicates that she would make her lessons even stronger. The Christian virtues she teaches will not be practiced or tested in artificial situations. She *insists* that her heroines enter the real world; thus she repeats in each novel a basic confrontation: the protagonist, a woman, is ejected from a comforting but rarefied place, either spiritual or real, and is coerced into facing the realities of everyday life. (p. 120)

The allegorical quality of Mrs. Rowson's work has been touched upon in [an] earlier [comment] about society as a Vanity Fair. Mrs. Rowson establishes this dimension of the fictional and imaginary world through symbolism, satire, personification, the emblem, and allegorical names and characters. (p. 123)

The moral qualities of Mrs. Rowson's world are made concrete and pictorial by the use of personified vices, virtues, and psychological qualities. "Prudence," "Pride," and "Humanity" argue with the Inquisitor over whether he should help an old man he encounters as he travels in his coach . . . ; "indolence" gives birth to "luxury" in the early colonies (*Reuben and Rachel* . . .). The ubiquitous presence of such figures gives Mrs. Rowson's fictional world, as well as the landscape of her poetry and nonfiction, an old-fashioned static quality.

A love of the emblem by the author as well as her characters contributes to this static world. In *Reuben and Rachel,* for instance, describing the new American home of the young people, Mrs. Rowson cannot forbear slipping in the idea that the persimmon tree is emblematic of the "pleasures of the world" by being beautiful but bitter. . . . Mrs. Rowson uses the emblem somewhat more skillfully to summarize the quality of various situations, including at times the state of mind of the characters. (pp. 123-24)

The allegorical character of Mrs. Rowson's world and its relation to Vanity Fair is underscored by the author's persistent use of allegorical names and characters. One part of the heroines' names often signifies some abstract quality, while the other is taken from the everyday world. . . . A gallery of semi-allegorical *dramatis personae* possessing some degree of individuality, who are nevertheless associated by their names with their leading vice, virtue, or situation, surround the protagonists. (p. 125)

To complement her use of allegory, Mrs. Rowson develops certain techniques associated with more modern forms of realism. . . . [She] rejected the ideals of romanticism, and accepted a commonsense view of the reality of everyday life. The world may be a Vanity Fair and only a temporary resting place for [a] Christian, but it is not just a state of mind. This world as well as the next must be faced, and the young woman must develop a practical view of the problems, worldly as well as spiritual, that must be met.

In the interests of such teachings, as well as to fulfill her goals, Mrs. Rowson adopts the methods of treatment associated with literary realism. She sets her narratives in a solid, individualized time and place, and stresses the everyday quality of this world. She presents many of her settings, situations, and characters with the detail, pungency, and vividness typical of the realist. She chooses problems and choices for her characters that she thinks represent those they might actually face, and tries to present them without sentimentalizing or stressing the macabre or heroic.

Mrs. Rowson's characters never inhabit "an imaginary land." . . . The protagonists learn their lessons in ordinary places like the shires of England, in London, Soho, Bath, Brighton, New England, and Philadelphia. Their activities take place in the present. Mrs. Rowson avoids the mists of past and future—even in **Reuben and Rachel,** her one departure from the eighteenth and early nineteenth centuries, she does not romanticize the past but tries to show its connection and similarity to the everyday present. (pp. 126-27)

The creation of memorable characters was not Mrs. Rowson's forte as a writer of fiction; however, she attempts to give many of her *dramatis personae* a degree of verisimilitude. Although their activities may be ultimately traceable to the seven deadly sins or the Christian virtues, they are by and large of a human scale, neither impossibly brave and noble nor implacably evil. Their immediate motives are influenced by the world in which they live; they are as often driven by the need for financial security and respectability as by the "power of sympathy," undying love, or diabolical hatred. (p. 131)

In addition to keeping her characters within a believable scale, Mrs. Rowson is occasionally able to realize her characters through the use of psychological detail. In **Victoria**, the heroine is seen moving slowly toward melancholia as Mrs. Rowson describes her behavior and her dreams and poems. The vividness with which Charlotte's postpartum psychosis is presented enlivens Charlotte as a character. In spite of the Shakespearean overtones of the passages in which this experience is described. Mrs. Rowson must be given credit for using lifelike detail not found in the typical "mad scene" and for making the reader experience the disturbance of the heroine. . . . (p. 135)

Mrs. Rowson subjects her heroines to everyday problems as well as to romantic trials like seduction and shipwreck. Poverty is the central problem the uneducated, dependent, unprotected female must face, and nearly every Rowson heroine is subject to its rigors. Mrs. Rowson is not alone in using this ploy as part of her protagonists' experiences, but she manages to convince the reader that she knew something about the actual woes of bankruptcy. She does not romanticize nor sentimentalize poverty as many writers did. . . .

Mrs. Rowson's subject is realistic. The author realized as well as Virginia Woolf that the problems of the female in the man's world are not all spiritual, and, like Mrs. Woolf, advocated keeping an eye on one's purse as well as one's apron strings. In her presentation of the financial ups and downs of her heroines, Mrs. Rowson stresses the sordidness and horror of poverty as well as the meanness and mediocrity.

From her first novel, Mrs. Rowson was preoccupied with the real problems of making one's way in the world. (p. 142)

Mrs. Rowson's most successful creation was her persona, the "author" of the works who is never offstage for long but always hovering nearby with chalk and pointer, reward and punishment. She can clarify the moral direction of a story and cajole and direct her reader to the right point of view. She becomes a friend and model for the reader. Mrs. Rowson is her own best heroine, whose situation and responses well illustrate her feminist views.

This persona is ubiquitous. None of Mrs. Rowson's works is without some reference to the personality of the writer. The dimensions of this personality are established largely through the prefaces and are developed through the narrators and speaking voice of the various works; they are extensions of Mrs. Rowson's real personality insofar as the latter is known. The author often points out the autobiographical nature of details and episodes in the fiction and refers to her activities outside her books, but these references are very selective. Mrs. Rowson always presents herself as the penwoman and teacher, the English woman transplanted to America. The "author" attains a unity and singleness of purpose hardly possessed by the actual author. She seems more real and is more memorable than many of the dramatic characters. (p. 147)

To some degree Mrs. Rowson's literary self matures as Susanna Rowson grows older, and reflects the author's actual career, but the basic qualities of the preface and narrative speaker are consistent. . . . In an early work such as **The Test of Honour**, Mrs. Rowson presents herself as the youthful "female scribe" and shows the defiance of youth by daring her reader to question her motives in writing. . . . Over the years, the author becomes more friendly and intimate with her audience. . . .

Although the epistolary and dramatic forms Mrs. Rowson employed in half her fiction do not conveniently lend themselves to development of an authorial personality, Mrs. Rowson manages to remain visible. She is never outside her works, "paring her nails." . . .

In only one work, Mrs. Rowson adopts a mask or persona that is a distortion of the actual author, and this departure from her usual method is explained as a matter of decorum. A masculine narrator-protagonist is used in **The Inquisitor** because "a man may be with propriety brought forward in many scenes, where it would be the height of improbability to introduce a woman." . . . But only the sex of the narrator is assumed; the voice of the Inquisitor is in no way different from Mrs. Rowson's standard narrative voice. (p. 148)

**Charlotte** represents Mrs. Rowson's best use of the commenting, third-person narrator; in this novel many of the qualities of the Rowson speaking voice are blended, and the moralizing is more artfully related to the events of the story than that in *Mentoria* or William Hill Brown's *The Power of Sympathy*. The elaborate prefatory defense of the novel as both true and uplifting, and the buildup of the author as a scrupulous, dedicated guide, focus attention upon the narrator-author. *Mentoria*'s preface achieves similar goals, and although the book is basically epistolary in method, the text is frequently interrupted for direct author comment. (p. 149)

Mrs. Rowson does not provide a preface for her poetry, but the signature implies the character of the speaker when not otherwise indicated; the speaker is often specifically feminine as in **"Rights of Woman,"** always firm of opinion, and eminently capable of moral judgment—the same mentor appearing in the other works. If the poet and lyricist is not offering advice to "A Young Lady, Who Requested the Author to Write Something On Her" . . . , she is extending it to her new young country—advising it on the creation of American art (**"Commemorative of the Genius of Shakespeare"**), on war (**"Truxton's Victory"**), and on politics (**"Eulogy, George Washington"**).

Besides her ubiquity, the Rowson persona exhibits other characteristics of tone and stance that remain constant and that add the final touches to the author as the young woman's friend and model. . . . The author-mentor is feminine, highly moral, compassionate, a woman rich in both intellectual and life experience. She is by turns sweet, satirical, preachy, indignant, and accepting. Her attitude toward her readers and toward herself encourages her pupils to enter into new activities and to adopt a rounded and complete self-image.

Mrs. Rowson seems to like her audience. She has fun at the expense of her readers. She depicts them as human and fallible, not as stiff priggish little misses or monsters who need reform. She is on their side, although never on their level. . . . In the fiction, Mrs. Rowson gives the audience the elements of suspense and drama that she supposes they thirst for—with good-humored acknowledgment of their desire for entertainment. Her aims include amusement as well as instruction, for her pedagogical theory endorses the idea that students learn best when they enjoy their lessons. Her texts often include interesting anecdotes and detail. She is always concerned about keeping her readers interested. (pp. 154-55)

Mrs. Rowson writes as a woman involved in the hurly-burly of life, not tucked away in a genteel parlor. As we have seen, she claims the rôle of teacher from the first, and increasingly presents herself as someone who has experienced great trials, and survived both physically and morally. Her comments as narrator often contain notes of cynicism that show her worldly wisdom. (p. 158)

Most important of all Mrs. Rowson's characteristics is her refusal to adopt a tone of diffidence about her work at a time when so many female authors feared to be identified. Pseudonyms or such author designations as "by a lady" or "Anonymous" were very popular. . . .

Because "presumptuous" female authors were not tolerated, many contemporary women prefaced their novels with tales of decrepit parents to support or their own illness and poverty, in order to win sympathy from the critics. Mrs. Rowson never indulged in such stratagems; in fact, in *The Inquisitor*, she satirizes the practice of seeking pity. (p. 160)

Mrs. Rowson tries to bring the female out of what Simone de Beauvoir calls her "cave of immanence," that is, her condition

of dependence and passivity, which Mrs. Rowson neatly symbolizes by the grotto in which Fetnah [in *Slaves of Algiers*] refuses to remain. Through the creation of a persona, as well as through her strenuous concentration upon the problems of women, she tries to create models for her audience that will encourage them to active, full lives. (p. 161)

*Dorothy Weil, in her* In Defense of Women: Susanna Rowson (1792-1824) *(copyright © 1976 by The Pennsylvania State University), The Pennsylvania State University Press, University Park, 1976, 204 p.*

### EMILY STIPES WATTS   (essay date 1977)

[Rowson's] poems are standard neoclassical imitations—except for one important quality in several of them. As is evident from most of her poems, Rowson could jingle along in verse with the best jinglers in her day, but in several poems she struck out alone in a new prosodic direction, which she called "Irregular Verse." Warned by this term, the reader is soon aware that there are two experimental irregularities. The first is the use of a variety of stanzaic structures in no regular sequence and often in no traditional form throughout a single poem. A similar method had been used in America for some time for odes, but generally the stanzas were more regular and the topic was public. . . . Rowson attempts to use such variety of stanzaic structure in narrative and lyrical verse. It should be noted that, at about the same time Rowson was trying to experiment with her "Irregular Verse" (which seems to have derived from odes), the English Romantic poets were working out the problems which would lead to their odes.

The second irregularity is that Rowson is not regularly "jingling." She has created very uneven metrical lines, carefully balanced by more regular lines. The irregular stanzaic forms tend to emphasize further the metrical irregularities. Her prosodic explorations point to the verse of later experimenters in the nineteenth century. (p. 59)

Rowson's experiments did not continue; they never got beyond the experimental stage. Perhaps she was discouraged by her early efforts (they obviously were not successful). Nevertheless, she is the first of a number of American women to experiment with original prosodic methods, both in metrical variations and stanzaic forms. In the later nineteenth century, only Emily Dickinson was as bold as Rowson. . . . (pp. 60-1)

*Emily Stipes Watts, "1735-1804: Another Kind of Independence," in her* The Poetry of American Women from 1632 to 1945 *(copyright © 1977 by University of Texas Press), University of Texas Press, 1977, 29-62.**

### KENNETH DAUBER   (essay date 1980)

[The] claim for [Susanna Rowson's] work's Americanness is problematic. But we can see that its problems are a consequence not of its history or of its author's birthplace, but of its uncertain relation to reading and writing, its failure to define itself as within a rhetorical field, though it moves in that direction. Indeed, to uncover the problematical rhetoricity of *Charlotte Temple* is to uncover the problematic of America itself as it struggles to define its own Americanness in the years just following its political independence.

Now the genre of *Charlotte Temple* is hardly remarkable. The book is one more tale of seduction, degradation, and death of the sort popular in England and America, based ultimately on

Samuel Richardson's *Clarissa*. Similarly, for the national material: part of the action takes place . . . in the United States, but Rowson is so little interested in local color or manners that England and America are indistinguishable except in name. There is, however, a peculiar failure of authoritativeness, more than simple amateurishness, that might be seen as pre-American in that it seems to result from the absence of that established tradition of writing which English novelists of however little accomplishment always assumed. "It would be useless to repeat the conversation that here ensued; suffice it to say, that Montraville used every argument that had formerly been successful, Charlotte's resolution began to waver, and he drew her almost imperceptibly toward the chaise." This is a sort of talking of the novel rather than a writing of it. The drama, the dialogue are not rendered, but referred to. The novel has not yet achieved the authority of novel-hood. It cannot produce realities itself, but must assume a reality outside, instead. Accordingly, to establish it more securely, Rowson must invent it from the ground up, must create for it a basis in rhetoric, in consent, by appealing to the reader openly, unabashedly. . . . In effect, the reader is to write the story, though admittedly this is hardly more than a pretense. (pp. 106-07)

Though we would not have expected it, though it makes no sense if we regard the genres of **Charlotte Temple** as a conventional "novel of sentiment," there appears in the book a kind of reserve, a refusal to participate in the events represented, that is striking and otherwise hard to explain. Despite its pathetic trappings, the expected handkerchief waving, the too ready tears, the book's language is remarkably *not* overwrought. Its style, for this sort of thing, is almost, we should say, chaste. It is as if Charlotte, whom the sentimental, by softening, would enable us to take in, is so frighteningly appealing that she must forcibly be walled out. Charlotte is not, finally, us, the books tells us. Indeed Charlotte was a real person. **Charlotte Temple,** as the subtitle proclaims, is "A Tale of Truth," and truth, almost defined as rhetorical, is finally defined as historical. What Rowson says of Mrs. Beauchamp, Charlotte's friend in her troubles, is ultimately true of Rowson and her audience as well: she "returned home with a heart oppressed with many painful sensations, but yet rendered easy by the reflection that she had performed her duty towards a distressed fellow creature." . . . It is duty that saves us from the anguish of sympathy, the certainty of traditional moral and religious obligations that prevents us from having to define ourselves *by* ourselves. **Charlotte Temple** is not yet an American novel because it refuses to take on the obligations of the rhetorical revolution it comes so close to initiating. It goes so far along the rhetorical path as to ask the reader for his assent to its truth. But it refuses to admit that assent would produce truth. (pp. 108-09)

*Kenneth Dauber, "American Culture As Genre," in* Criticism *(reprinted by permission of the Wayne State*

*University Press; copyright 1980, Wayne State University Press), Vol. XXII, No. 2 (Spring, 1980), pp. 101-15.\**

---

## ADDITIONAL BIBLIOGRAPHY

Benson, Mary Sumner. "Women in Early American Literature." In her *Women in Eighteenth-Century America: A Study of Opinion and Social Usage,* pp. 188-222. New York: Columbia University Press, 1935.\*

Examines *Charlotte Temple* in relation to the social position of eighteenth-century American women. Sumner finds that Rowson conformed to sentimental novel conventions which generally emphasized women's weakness, vulnerability, and need for protection.

Halsey, Francis W. Introduction to *Charlotte Temple: A Tale of Truth,* by Susanna Haswell Rowson, pp. xix-cix. New York: Funk & Wagnalls Co., 1905.

Contains an overview of Rowson's life, and a complete bibliography of known editions of *Charlotte Temple* up to 1905. Halsey provides, in addition, the historical facts relating to the real-life Charlotte Temple, her tombstone, Montraville, and Montrésor.

Kirk, Clara M., and Kirk, Rudolf. Introduction to *Charlotte Temple: A Tale of Truth,* by Susanna Rowson, edited by Clara M. and Rudolf Kirk, pp. 11-32. New York: Twayne Publishers, 1964.

Provides a survey of criticism on *Charlotte Temple* as well as a brief history of the novel's numerous editions. The Kirks assert that *Charlotte Temple*'s similarity to other didactic and religious household texts aided its popularity.

Martin, Wendy. "Profile: Susanna Rowson, Early American Novelist." *Women's Studies* 2 (1974): 1-8.

Traces the popularity of Rowson's novels through the nineteenth century. Martin concludes that Rowson's didacticism, along with the rise of the middle class with more leisure time for women, contributed to the success of her novels.

Papashvily, Helen Waite. "The Rise of the Fallen." In her *All the Happy Endings: A Study of the Domestic Novel in America, the Women Who Wrote It, the Women Who Read It, in the Nineteenth Century,* pp. 25-34. New York: Harper & Brothers Publishers, 1956.\*

Places Rowson's novels in the tradition of the late eighteenth and early nineteenth-century American domestic novel. Papashvily notes, however, that Rowson can be viewed as a transitional figure because she moved her heroines toward greater responsibility and a sense of independence in her later novels.

Vail, R.W.G. "Susanna Haswell Rowson, the Author of 'Charlotte Temple': A Bibliographical Study." *Proceedings of the American Antiquarian Society* 42, No. 1 (20 April 1932): 47-160.

The authoritative bibliography of Rowson's works. Vail supplies bibliographies of biographical works on Rowson, her complete works, and her music. He also includes a record of Rowson's theatrical career, with a list of her dramatic roles.

# Charles Augustin Sainte-Beuve

## 1804-1869

(Also wrote under the pseudonym of Joseph Delorme) French critic, essayist, poet, and novelist.

Sainte-Beuve is considered to be one of the foremost French literary critics of the nineteenth century. Beginning his career as a champion of Romanticism, he eventually formulated a biographical and psychological method of criticism. Believing that one cannot separate a writer from his or her work, Sainte-Beuve focused on an author's life and character as well as his work. Of his vast body of writings on literature, the best known are his "Lundis" (Mondays)—weekly newspaper articles which appeared every Monday morning over a period of several decades. These essays display his desire for truth, rejection of prejudice and fanaticism, and above all, his love of literature.

Born in Boulogne, Sainte-Beuve was raised by his mother, who encouraged his early interest in literature. In school, he composed Romantic poetry, but chose to pursue a career in medicine. However, when a former professor asked him to write reviews for his literary journal, Sainte-Beuve abandoned his medical studies. Among Sainte-Beuve's early articles was an adulatory review of Victor Hugo's *Odes et ballades*. After Hugo sent Sainte-Beuve a gracious letter of thanks, the two became good friends, and Sainte-Beuve joined the *cénacle*, a literary circle which included Hugo, Alfred de Vigny and Alexandre Dumas, *père*. Under their influence, Sainte-Beuve published several volumes of Romantic poetry and *Tableau historique et critique de la poésie française et du théâtre français au seizième siècle*, a collection of literary reviews. These essays praise Hugo and his fellow Romantics, and compare them with the sixteenth-century Pléiade poets. Though critics now contend that Sainte-Beuve praised the Romantics too generously, they credit him with regenerating interest in the Pléiade. During this period, Sainte-Beuve began contributing to *Revue des deux mondes*, where he produced critical studies of authors and their works. These literary portraits, which demonstrate Sainte-Beuve's talent as an insightful biographer, were later collected and published as *Portraits contemporains*.

While the literary partnership of Sainte-Beuve and Hugo flourished, their friendship suffered when Sainte-Beuve fell in love with Hugo's wife, Adèle. Both men struggled to continue their alliance, but the breach was irrevocable. Finally, Sainte-Beuve renounced his Romantic allegiance and left the *cénacle*. Later, in his novel, *Volupté*, and his volume of poetry, *Livre d'amour*, he recreated his affair with Adèle. Although critics praise these works as convincing depictions of doomed love, they generally agree that Sainte-Beuve's critical writings are far superior to his creative efforts. Nevertheless, recent commentators praise his poetry, and cite its influence on Charles Baudelaire and Paul Verlaine.

Following his break with Hugo, Sainte-Beuve became active in a number of religious and philosophical movements, including Saint-Simonism and Catholicism. He gave a series of lectures at the University of Lausanne, which were later published as *Port-Royal*. This work charts the development of the Jansenist movement at the time of Louis XIV and is regarded as an achievement of historical insight and an embodiment of

Sainte-Beuve's critical strengths: conscientiousness, impartiality, and psychological understanding. A subsequent lecture series, *Chateaubriand et son groupe littéraire sous l'empire*, is considered equally perceptive, though not as objective. Rejecting his previous literary affiliation, Sainte-Beuve pronounces Romanticism as shallow, a reaction which is believed to stem from his unhappy break with the *cénacle*. While he usually treated his subjects with respect, he dealt harshly with François Chateaubriand and Honoré de Balzac. Balzac, in particular, had angered Sainte-Beuve by announcing that his novel, *The Lily of the Valley*, was an improved version of Sainte-Beuve's *Volupté*. About his retaliatory essay, Sainte Beuve confessed, "Every critic has his favorite victim, whom he pounces upon and tears to pieces with particular relish. Mine is Balzac."

In 1849, Sainte-Beuve returned to Paris to review books for several journals. These essays are similar to his earlier *Portraits contemporains*, but extend beyond a simply biographical format to develop, in Sainte-Beuve's words, "a natural history of the author and his work." Known as *Les causeries du lundi*, or *Monday Chats*, they reflect Sainte-Beuve's belief that one cannot comprehend literature until one understands the writer's environment and influences. In simple, accessible language, the "Lundis" display Sainte-Beuve's broad knowledge of literature and literary history. Their influence on Sainte-

Beuve's contemporaries is due in part to the growth and increasing popularity of the daily newspaper, and the essays were collected and published several times during Sainte-Beuve's lifetime. Today Sainte-Beuve's "Lundis" are still considered among the most valuable literary guides in modern letters.

Though Sainte-Beuve's critical method was generally uncontested during his lifetime, several twentieth-century critics, most notably Marcel Proust, have questioned its validity. Arguing that a literary work should be analyzed for its artistic merits from an objective point of view, they maintain that he relied excessively on biographical information and distrusted his own analytic powers. Yet few critics deny his enduring importance. In the twentieth century, Sainte-Beuve still fits his own definition of a classic: "An author who has enriched the human mind, who has actually added to its treasures and carried it a step forward, who speaks to all in a style of his own which happens also to be that of common speech."

## PRINCIPAL WORKS

*Tableau historique et critique de la poésie française et du théâtre français au seizième siècle* (criticism) 1828
*Vie, poésies et pensées de Joseph Delorme* [as Joseph Delorme] (poetry) 1829
*Les consolations* [as Joseph Delorme] (poetry) 1830
*Volupté* [as Joseph Delorme] (novel) 1834
*Critiques et portraits littéraires.* 5 vols. (essays) 1836-39
*Pensées d'aôut* [as Joseph Delorme] (poetry) 1837
*Poésies complètes* (poetry) 1840
*Port-Royal.* 5 vols. (lectures) 1840-59
*Livre d'amour* (poetry) 1843
*Portraits contemporains* (essays) 1846
*Les causeries du lundi.* 15 vols. (essays) 1851-62
  [*Monday Chats* (partial translation), 1877; also published as *Causeries du lundi* (partial translation), 1885]
*Portraits de femmes* (essays) 1852
  [*Portraits of Celebrated Women,* 1868]
*Étude sur Virgile* (lectures) 1857
*Chateaubriand et son groupe littéraire sous l'empire* (lectures) 1861
*Nouveaux lundis.* 13 vols. (essays) 1863-70
*Premiers lundis.* 3 vols. (essays) 1874-75
*English Portraits* (essays) 1875
*Les cahiers de Sainte-Beuve* (notebooks) 1876
*Selected Essays from Sainte-Beuve* (essays) 1895
*The Essays of Sainte-Beuve* (essays) 1901
*Portraits of the Seventeenth Century, Historic and Literary* (essays) 1904
*Portraits of the Eighteenth Century, Historic and Literary* (essays) 1905
*Essays by Sainte-Beuve* (essays) 1910
*Selections from Sainte-Beuve* (essays) 1918
*Mes poisons* (essays) 1926
*La correspondance générale de Sainte-Beuve* (letters) 1935-70
*Sainte-Beuve: Selected Essays* (essays) 1963
*Portraits of Men* (essays) 1972

---

## HENRI BEYLE [LATER STENDHAL] (letter date 1830)

[*Beyle, better known by his pseudonym, Stendhal, sent the following letter to Sainte-Beuve after reading the* Les consolations.

*Sainte-Beuve later published the letter in the appendix to the 1862 edition of his* Poésies complètes.]

If there was a God, I should be very content, for he would reward me with Paradise for my being the gentleman I am.

Thus I should not change my conduct at all, and I should be rewarded for doing exactly what I do.

One thing however would lessen the pleasure I get from dreaming with the warm tears which good deeds provoke: this idea of being *paid* with a reward, a paradise.

There, Sir, is what I would tell you in verse, if I could write it as well as you. I am shocked that you and your kind, who *believe in God,* imagine that to be *in despair* for three years at losing your mistress, one should have to believe in God. . . .

I believe you to be destined, Sir, for the greatest literary triumphs; but I find a little affectation in your verse still. I would prefer it a little more like La Fontaine's. You talk too much of glory. . . . Who the devil knows if glory will come! . . . Why talk of such things? Passion has it modesty, why reveal these intimate details? Why all those names? It looks like a prospectus, a *puff.*

There, Sir, is my opinion, all my opinion. I think you will be spoken of in 1890. But you will do better than the ***Consolations:*** something *stronger* and *purer.*

> *Henri Beyle* [*later Stendhal*], *in his letter to Charles Sainte-Beuve on March 26, 1830, translated by A. G. Lehmann (originally published in* Poésies, seconde partie *by Charles Sainte-Beuve, 1861-63), in* Sainte-Beuve: A Portrait of the Critic, 1804-1842 *by A. G. Lehmann (© Oxford University Press 1962; reprinted by permission of Oxford University Press), Oxford at the Clarendon Press, Oxford, 1962, p. 96.*

## SIR NATHANIEL (essay date 1853)

Readers now approaching M. Sainte-Beuve for the first time, would hardly surmise that he was, in times past, a devout adherent to the Romantic school. Once he espoused its cause, expounded its beauties, and defended its teachers. But with years that bring the philosophic mind, and that also, be it added, chill the fires and tame the hey-day blood of youth, he has been changed into a veteran of another creed, bound by other canons of taste, and sound in quite other articles of faith. Without venturing to discuss the limitless controversy suggested by such change, involving as it does so manifold an appeal to criticism in its principles, and to the illustrations of French literature at large, we shall content ourselves, at this present, with a cordial expression of interest in M. Sainte-Beuve as one of the most accomplished, graceful, refined, and withal instructive of French critics. And hereby we invite attention to his *Causeries du Lundi* . . . . (p. 490)

The France of our own day teems with [literary portrait painters]. . . . Of these, many may surpass M. Sainte-Beuve in boldness, vivid effect, and intensity of colouring. Beside the studies of not a few contemporaries, his own have a pale, sober, almost chilly tint; and admirers of the exaggerated and the pretentious will complain of a comparative absence, in his designs, of glare and glitter, and of those dashing appliances by which adventurous sketchers pander to a popular greed for something *ultra.* His style, on the contrary, is quiet, mellow, strict, and carefully toned down. Common taste will probably vote it common-place. It eschews meretricious arts; it is true to a self-imposed law of self-restraint. *Causeur* though he be by profession, M. Sainte-Beuve's *causeries* have a method, a system, a principle of limitation: the chat may not transgress certain rules, or lose itself in chaotic miscellanies and wandering mazes and passages that lead to nothing; it must not reveal a mere voluble chatterbox; it must not evaporate in the thin air of purposeless gossip, or become a disorganised mass of "bald disjointed chat." The critic reverences and magnifies his office. He is a veteran in his labour, and it is a labour of love. . . . His criticisms are excellent in moderation, clear-sightedness, and good sense. Not very profound or subtle, perhaps; yet searching and thoughtful, and with a singular and thrice-blessed freedom from the cant vices of the craft. . . . M. Sainte-Beuve brings to his work a lofty sense of its moral as well as of its intellectual requirements; he has scanned its responsibilities, and evidently seeks to employ the conscience of a careful, as well as the pen of a ready, writer. He strives to do justice to his author, his reader, and himself. . . . It is allowed that few rival him in an intimate acquaintance with the history and literature of his country during the seventeenth and eighteenth centuries—in the shifting phases of its many-coloured life—whether the *couleur de rose* of tranquil days, or the blood-stained *tricolor* of revolutionary frenzy, or any other shade and hue of social experience, before or since.

In style he is clear, classical, simple. Great and constantly repeated is his aversion to turgid, grandiose diction; great and warmly-expressed his admiration of the simplicity and purity of the school of Pascal and Bourdaloue. He has a keen eye, and a severe one, for neologisms and solecisms; he loves to expose them in their monstrosity. . . . (pp. 490-92)

In politics and ethics, those delicate points for English readers of French authors, he is cautiously conservative—not using that phrase technically, or as a party word, but as significant of his opposition to assailants of what is established and time honoured in morals and social science. The immoral in fiction, the lawless in fact, he cannot away with. Romancers who weave [a] network of false sentiment, and political theorists who never tire of playing "Much Ado about Nothing," at the state's expense and society's risk—find in him an adversary "of credit and renown." . . . He is severe on what he calls the mysticised sensualism of the *René* school of novelists, as well as the unmasked sensualism of the Sues and Paul de Kocks. In short, he enjoys and deserves the repute of a "healthy" writer.

One of the chief attractions of his *Causeries* is the series of portraits of eminent French women, to whom he assigns a foremost place. The popularity of the subject in France itself is inexhaustible; and great credit is due to M. Sainte-Beuve for the tact and discrimination with which he has approached it—without affected prudery on one side, or, on the other, anything like prurient license. He is at once the sagacious man of the world, and, as aforesaid, the "healthy" writer. (pp. 492-93)

Madame de Sévigné is neatly portrayed:—that rich and vigorous nature, healthful and ever fresh; impassioned in one direction only, in her tender enthusiasm towards her daughter; distinguished by a pervading grace all her own, a grace not indeed serene and sweet, but lively, exuberant, full of sense and even smartness, and with no one pale hue in its harmony of colours. (p. 493)

Of contemporary genius, M. Sainte-Beuve has evidently a special grudge against Lamartine and Chateaubriand. The former

he pounces upon, not indeed with the vulturous swoop, or rather perhaps the worrying tenacity, of Cuvilier Fleury (of the *Débats*), but with a resolute desire to turn him and his sentiment inside out, and show, by shaking it to the winds, what inflated falsity there is in the poet-politician's personal composition and literary compositions. This is not the time, or place, to enter at length into the justice of the strictures on the author of *Raphael;* we can only refer to the fact, that he is severely handled—his egotism roundly ridiculed—and his questionable morality more than questioned. Chateaubriand, again, is sadly "cut up," notwithstanding the liberal eulogies which besprinkle the detracting page; he is twitted with a whimsical imagination, an enormous and puerile vanity, an undue tendency to voluptuous themes, and especially—in spite of his great name as a pillar of orthodoxy—a deep-seated and desolating scepticism. He is represented as incessantly victimised by a twofold fatuity—that of the man of fashion who would be always young, and that of the *littérateur* who cannot but be ostentatious. Passion, as a poet, is freely conceded him; but what kind of passion? that which involves the idea of death and destruction, a satanic fury, mingled all the while with a subdued emotion of the pleasurable, altogether composing a strange hybrid epicureanism, peculiar to Chateaubriand, and very unwholesome for society. The unfortunate [*Memoires d'outre-tombe*] are sarcastically and searchingly interpreted, in a way infinitely displeasing to those enraptured admirers of the noble viscount, to whom their voice *d'outre tombe* came with so sepulchral a spell of fascination, and who found in their changeful records a recurring series of delights; and indeed the [*Memoires*] have the merit of diversity in matter, if not in manner. . . . (pp. 497-98)

*Sir Nathaniel, in his review of "Causeries du lundi," in* The New Monthly Magazine, *Vol. XCVII, No. CCCLXXXVIII, April, 1853, pp. 490-98.*

### CHARLES AUGUSTIN SAINTE-BEUVE (essay date 1862)

[*In the following essay, which was collected in* Nouveaux lundis, *Sainte-Beuve justifies the biographical basis of his critical method. He states his belief that "tel arbre tel fruit—the fruit is like the tree. Thus the study of literature leads me naturally to the study of human nature."*]

I have often heard the reproach made to modern criticism, especially my own, that it has no theory to speak of, that it is entirely historical, entirely individual. Those who are most favorably disposed to me have been kind enough to say that I am a fairly good judge, but a judge without a code. However, I do have a method; and although I did not give it an a priori theoretical formulation, it took shape as I practiced my criticism, and I have found it confirmed by a long series of applications.

Beginning with my very first critical essays, I instinctively came upon this method. At a very early date it was already as though natural to me; and for years I have always followed it, varying it according to the subject treated. It never occurred to me to make a secret of it or to claim it as my discovery. (p. 281)

Literature, literary production, as I see it, is not distinct or separable from the rest of mankind's character and activity. I may enjoy a work, but it is hard for me to judge it independently of my knowledge of the man who produced it, and I am inclined to say, *tel arbre, tel fruit*—the fruit is like the tree. Thus the study of literature leads me naturally to the study of human nature.

In the case of the older writers, our information is inadequate. In most instances, we cannot reconstruct the man from his writings; especially is this the case with the truly ancient authors, those of whom we possess only mutilated statues. We are thus reduced to commenting on the work, to admiring it; we can only imagine the author, the poet, behind it. (pp. 281-82)

The situation is entirely different in the case of the moderns, and the critic who adapts his method to his means has other duties here. To know another man, and to know him well, particularly if he is a prominent or famous man, is a great thing, not to be scorned.

Our study of human nature is still at the data-gathering stage; at best, we have descriptions of individuals and of a few types. However, a day will come—I believe I have discerned its coming in the course of my observations—when a science of human nature will be constituted, and the great orders and species of minds will be sorted out. Then, on the basis of a mind's principal characteristics, it will be possible to deduce several others. No doubt it will never be possible to achieve in the case of man what can be achieved in the case of animals and plants: human nature is more complex. It possesses what is called "freedom," and this always presupposes a great mobility of possible combinations. However that may be, I imagine that eventually the science of the moralist will be constituted on a broader foundation. . . . What we achieve is mere monographs, detailed observations; yet I sense the presence of connections and relationships; and a more comprehensive, more luminous understanding, with a sharp eye for detail, will one day be able to discover the great natural divisions in which the various families of minds belong.

However, even once the science of minds has been organized along the lines here adumbrated, it will always be so delicate and so intricate a matter that only those with a natural vocation and talent for observation will be able to make much of it. It will remain an *art* requiring a skillful artist, just as medicine requires medical tact in the man who practices it, as philosophy should require philosophical tact in those who call themselves philosophers, as poetry is accessible only to poets.

Thus I conceive of someone possessing such talent, being able to make out groups or families of writers (for we are dealing with literature), being able, indeed, to make them out almost at first sight and capable of grasping their spirit and their life. To such a one this would be his true vocation; he would be a good naturalist in the vast domain of the human spirit.

Suppose we set out to study a superior man, or merely a man distinguished by his productions, a writer whose works we have read, and who is worth the trouble of being examined thoroughly. How should we go about it so as not to omit anything important or essential, and to progress farther than the old theoreticians, not being taken in by conventional phrases and fine sentiments? How can we arrive at the truth, as we do in the study of nature?

It is very useful to begin at the beginning and, whenever possible, to place the superior or distinguished writer in his own country, among his own people. If we knew his lineage thoroughly, physiologically speaking, including his remoter ancestors, we should gain much light on the essential hidden quality of his mind, but these deeper roots most often remain obscure

and elusive. Whenever they do not escape us completely, we gain a great deal by observing them.

We surely recognize the superior man, at least in part, in his parents, especially in his mother, the more immediate and more certain parent; also in his sisters, in his brothers, even in his children. In all these we encounter essential traits which, in the great individual himself, are often masked by being too condensed or too closely welded; his own substance may appear more visibly, in a less complex state, in others of his blood: nature herself has performed the analysis. (pp. 282-84)

Take sisters, for instance. Chateaubriand had two sisters. According to him, one of them possessed imagination, but it was superimposed upon an underlying stupidity, and must have come close to pure extravagance. His other sister, on the contrary, was divine (Lucile, the Amélie of *René*). She possessed an exquisite sensibility and an affectionate, melancholy sort of imagination, without the sometimes compensating, and sometimes exaggerated features that characterized Chateaubriand's own imagination. She died insane, by her own hand. The elements which, at least in his talent, were combined and linked and kept in a certain balance, were separated and disproportionately divided between his sisters. (p. 284)

Once we have learned as much as possible about the origins of an eminent writer, his parents and nearest relatives, an essential point to be determined, after examining his education and studies, is his first *milieu,* the group of friends and contemporaries among whom he was living when his talent first manifested itself, took shape, and matured. Whatever his subsequent achievements, he will always show the influence of this early group.

Since I often use the term "group," it may be useful to define the sense in which I do so. By "group" I do not mean the fortuitous, artificial assemblage of men of parts, but the natural and as it were spontaneous association of young minds and young talents—not necessarily similar, but of the same "flight" and the same spring, come to flower under the same sun, who feel themselves to be born, with variations of taste and vocation, for a common task. Thus the little company of Boileau, Racine, La Fontaine, and Molière about 1664, at the beginning of the *grand siècle:* here you have the group par excellence—all geniuses! (pp. 285-86)

Very great individuals dispense with groups: they serve as centers themselves, people gather around them. But it is the group, the association or alliance, with its active exchange of ideas and spirit of perpetual emulation in the presence of one's equals, that provides a man of talent with his outward setting, all his development, and all his value. There are talents who belong to several groups, who never stop traveling through successive milieus, perfecting themselves, being transformed, or being deformed. In such cases of shifting affiliations, of slow or sudden conversions, it is important to note the hidden and constant spring, the persistent motive force. (pp. 286-87)

Criticism based on a first reading, on first impressions, will always be important, as well as the opinions of the fashionable and academic criticism. Such passion for thoroughness, as all this implies, is no cause for alarm: there are times and places for it, as well as times and places where it would be inappropriate. (p. 287)

However, analysis involves a kind of emotion, too; indeed, one might say that it has an eloquence of its own and even a poetic quality. Those who know a writer of talent and appreciate him only when he has been fully developed, or in his last works, who did not see him in his youth, at the moment when he first took wing, will never form a complete and natural idea of him, the only living kind. . . . [For] the critic who studies a talent, there is no greater pleasure than to surprise it in its first fire, its first flights, to catch it in early morning, in all the freshness of youth. For the art lover and man of taste, the first state of a portrait is far more precious than anything that comes after. I know of no sweeter delight for the critic than to understand and describe a young talent, in all its dewy freshness, all its directness and spontaneity, before acquired, perhaps artificial, elements have found their way into his works. (p. 288)

But if it is important to gain insight into an author at the moment of his first efforts, his first flowering, when he appears fully formed and more than adolescent, when he comes of age, there is also a second moment no less crucial, which must be noted if we are to grasp him as a whole—the moment when he weakens, disintegrates, declines, departs from his own norm. Choose the least shocking, the gentlest words when chronicling this moment, for it is one that comes to almost everyone. (p. 289)

There are never too many ways to go about learning to know a man—man is a complex creature, by no means a pure spirit. What were his religious ideas? How was he affected by the spectacle of nature? How did he behave toward women? What was his attitude toward money? Was he rich, poor? What was his routine, his daily life? Finally, what was his vice or weakness? Every man has one. None of these questions is immaterial when it comes to judging the author of a book or the book itself (unless it is a treatise of pure geometry)—above all, if it is a literary work, for no aspect of human life is alien to literature. (p. 290)

Up to a certain point it is possible also to study talents through their spiritual descendants, their disciples and natural admirers. Affinities may be acknowledged freely or betrayed inadvertently. The genius is a sovereign who creates his own people. Apply this to Lamartine, to Hugo, to Michelet, to Balzac, to Musset. Enthusiastic admirers are a little like accomplices: they worship themselves, with all their own qualities and defects, in their great representative. Tell me who admires and loves you, and I will tell you who you are. However, you must not confuse a writer's genuine public with the throng of vulgar admirers who merely repeat what their neighbors say. (pp. 290-91)

If it is right to judge a talent by his friends and natural followers, it is no less legitimate to verify one's judgment by the enemies he makes without intending to, those who are antipathetic to him or those who instinctively cannot suffer him. Nothing serves better to mark the limits of a talent, to circumscribe his sphere and domain, than to know exactly at what point revolt against him begins. In actual life this can be piquant to watch: in the domain of Letters there are people who detest one another all their lives, without ever having met. Such antagonisms merely reflect unbridgeable differences between intellectual types, differences of blood, of temperament, of early upbringing. (pp. 291-92)

*Charles Augustin Sainte-Beuve, ''On Sainte-Beuve's Method'' (originally published in an expanded form as ''Chateaubriand jugé par un ami intime en 1803,'' in* Le constitutionnel, *July 21-22, 1862), in his* Sainte-Beuve: Selected Essays, *edited by Francis Steegmuller, translated by Norbert Guterman (copyright*

*© 1963 by Doubleday & Company, Inc.; reprinted by permission of the publisher), Doubleday, 1963, pp. 281-92.*

**[F. T. MARZIALS]  (essay date 1866)**

M. Sainte-Beuve is frequently rhetorical; he is seldom, if ever, eloquent. For to be eloquent requires an earnestness, either of passion or conviction, which is not in his nature. He never seems to feel strongly, and does not, therefore, attempt powerful writing. He can, indeed, admire, but his admiration is that of the critic; it never carries him away. He can be angry, but his anger takes the form of sarcastic banter, of neat epigrammatic reproof, not of honest indignation. That this lighter mode of warfare is most effective in literary quarrels is certainly true. M. Sainte-Beuve has furnished a proof of the fact—if any such proof were needed—in his very clever article on M. de Pontmartin, in the third volume of the **'Nouveaux Lundis.'** No sledge-hammer critique, well weighted with hard names, could have dealt that gentleman so shrewd a blow. But as Dr. Johnson liked a good hater, so we confess that we should like to find in M. Sainte-Beuve's writings some passage that proved him capable of real downright scorn and anger. There is, however, another reason besides lack of earnestness, that makes it difficult for him to be eloquent, even if he wished to be so, of which there is no evidence; his habits of mind are too entirely critical, he is too fond of analysing, of seeking for the hidden reasons of things, of discovering delicate shades of difference and affinity. For eloquence delights in large masses of light and shadow, in striking contrasts, in great thoughts and unchecked emotions. It specially abhors those complex feelings and slight frail threads of thought which M. Sainte-Beuve takes pleasure in unravelling. . . . In all his critical inquiries, before studying the author, he first thoroughly studies the man, for in his view of the case, 'as the tree is, so will be the fruit.' (pp. 102-03)

If M. Sainte-Beuve puts himself through [a] severe catechism every time he criticises a man's works—and we see no reason to doubt that he does—we cease to feel astonished at the unrivalled powers of penetration and insight which he displays. Yet there is one danger to which this critical process is exposed, viz., that of attaching too much importance to merely external and accidental influences. A human being is not exactly a chemical compound; and there will always be something in every writer of originality and genius that will escape the most rigid analysis of this kind. It may happen that his education, the society in which he moved, and the thousand little incidents of his daily life, left scarcely any impress on his writings. But apart from such considerations, what we are more concerned in showing is, that M. Sainte-Beuve seems to think he has done enough when he has instituted these searching inquiries. Now, to us it appears that he has only performed half his work. He has indeed *understood*—that is the critic's first duty—but he has not *judged,* which is a duty equally imperative. (pp. 103-04)

[In M. Sainte-Beuve], we see a writer who has at various times come forward as a poet, a novelist, an historian, and a critic; most prominently as a critic. Indeed, as Lord Macaulay, the speaker and historian, was still the essayist, so M. Sainte-Beuve, in whatever character he may appear, is still the critic. His poems . . . are those of a man who has thought much and deeply on the poetical art, rather than of one who sings because nature has filled his soul with music to overflowing. His one novel [**'Volupté'**] is a clever analysis of the character of its hero, and of the three or four persons with whom he is brought into contact, not the spontaneous creation of a little world of living beings. His admirable history of Port Royal is emphatically a critical history, aiming less at narration and description than at the unveiling of the hidden spirit of the Jansenists, and the examination of their literary works. Thus in all his works M. Sainte-Beuve is 'nothing if not critical.' But whereas that expression, as applied by Iago to himself, denoted a mind especially on the alert to discover weak points in everything, it means something essentially different as applied to the French academician. The peculiarity and excellence of his criticism is its disinterestedness, its singular power of appreciating whatever may be good in the most opposite schools, and its wonderful faculty for penetrating into the secrets of the most strangely different natures. And now if we turn from the man's works to the man himself, we see great natural power, a mind originally pliable, subtle, and comprehensive to the very highest degree, curious and penetrative, impartial to a fault. . . . He has been an earnest student, and devoured a mass of reading that might appal the most omnivorous of Germans. And now, after all, what is the result of these natural gifts, of this intercourse with the great and wise, of this life of toil and study—we mean, the result so far as M. Sainte-Beuve himself is concerned? That result is sufficiently apparent in the career we have sketched—the career of one who has kept a large mind open to every variety of influence; who has passed through a most instructive course of experiences, and sipped honey from system after system; who has in the general conflict of opinions made it his constant practice to follow the arguments on every side so far as fully to understand them, but no further; who has on all occasions made light of consistency, and been the most brilliant of literary chameleons; who has scarcely one single fixed opinion on any problem, literary, political, philosophical or religious—in short, of one who has spent his life in fitting his mind to be an elaborate receptacle for well-arranged doubts. (pp. 107-08)

[*F. T. Marzials*], *"M. Sainte-Beuve," in* The Quarterly Review, *Vol. CXIX, No. 237, January, 1866, pp. 80-108.*

## PUTNAM'S MAGAZINE OF LITERATURE, SCIENCE, ART, AND NATIONAL INTERESTS   (essay date 1868)

A literary critic, a genuine one, should carry in his brain an arsenal of opposites. He should combine common sense with tact, integrity with indulgence, breadth with keenness, vigor with delicacy, largeness with subtlety, knowledge with geniality, inflexibility with sinuousness, severity with suavity; and, that all these counter qualities be effective, he will need constant culture and vigilance, besides the union of reason with warmth, of enthusiasm with self-control, of wit with philosophy—but hold: at this rate, in order to fit out the critic, human nature will have to set apart its highest and best. . . .

Long and exacting as is our roll of what is wanted to equip a veritable sure critic, we have yet to add two cardinal qualifications, which by the subject of our present paper are possessed in liberal allotment. The first is, joy in life, from which the pages of M. Sainte-Beuve derive, not a superficial sprightliness merely, but a mellow, radiant geniality. The other, which is of still deeper account, is the capacity of admiration; a virtue,—for so it deserves to be called,—born directly of the nobler sensibilities, those in whose presence only can be recognized and enjoyed the lofty and the profound, the beautiful and the true. (p. 401)

For the perfecting of the literary critic the especial sympathy needed is that with excellence; for high literature is the outcome of the best there is in humanity, the finished expression of healthiest aspirations, of choicest thoughts, the ripened fruit of noble, of refined growths, the perfected fruit, with all the perfume and beauty of the flower upon it. Of this sympathy M. Sainte-Beuve, throughout his many volumes, gives overflowing evidence, in addition to that primary proof of having himself written good poems. Besides the love, he has the instinct, of literature, and this instinct draws him to what is its bloom and fullest manifestation, and his love is the more warm and constant for being discriminative and refined. Through variety of knowledge, with intellectual keenness, he enjoys excellence in the diversified forms that literature assumes. His pages abound in illustrations of his versatility, which is nowhere more strikingly exhibited than in the contrast between two successive papers (both equally admirable) in the very first volume of the *Causeries du Lundi,* the one on Madame Récamier, the other on Napoleon. (p. 402)

Like most writers, of whatever country, M. Sainte-Beuve has formed himself on native models, and the French having no poet of the highest class, no Dante, no Shakespeare, no Goethe, it is a further proof of his breadth and insight that he should so highly value the treasures in the deeper mines opened by these foreigners. Seeing, too, how catholic he is, and liberal towards all other greatness, one even takes pleasure in his occasional exuberance of national complacency. Whenever he speaks of Montaigne or La Fontaine or Molière, his words flame with a tempered enthusiasm. But he throws no dust in his own eyes: his is a healthy rapture, a torch lighted by the feelings, but which the reason holds upright and steady. His native favorites he enjoys as no Englishman or German could, but he does not overrate them. Nor does he overrate Voltaire, whom he calls "the Frenchman par excellence," and of whom he is proud as the literary sovereign of his age. (pp. 404-05)

Out of the severe things occasionally said, the sting is mostly taken by the temper in which they are said, or by the frank recognition of virtues and beauties beside vices and blemishes. In the general tone there is a clear humanity, a seemly gentlemanliness. (p. 406)

A thorough Frenchman, M. Sainte-Beuve delights in French minds, just as a beauty delights in her mirror, which throws back an image of herself. His excellence as a critic is primarily owing to this joy in things French. Through means of it he knows them through and through: they are become transparent; and while his feelings are aglow, his intellect looks calmly right through them, and sees on the other side the shadows cast by the spots and opacities which frustrate more or less the fullest illumination. Freely he exhibits these shadows. Neither Bossuet nor Louis XIV., neither Voltaire nor Béranger, is spared, nor the French character, with its proneness to frivolity and broad jest, its thirst for superficial excitement. Whatever his individual preferences, his mental organization is so large and happy, that he enjoys, and can do equal justice to, Father Lacordaire and M. Michelet, to Madame de Staël and M. Guizot, to Corneille and Goethe, to Fénélon and M. Renan, to Marie Antoinette and Mirabeau.

Have you then for M. Sainte-Beuve, some reader will be impatient to ask, nothing but praise? Not much else. . . . In his mind there is vitality to animate his large acquirement, to make his many chapters buoyant and stimulant. All through his writings is the sparkle of original life.

But let us now cheer the reader who is impatient of much praise, and at the same time perform the negative part of our task.

Well, then, to be bold, as befits a critic of the critic, we beard the lion in his very den. We challenge a definition he gives of the critic. In the seventh volume of the **Causeries,** article **Grimm,** he says: "When Nature has endowed some one with this vivacity of feeling, with this susceptibility to impression, and that the creative imagination be wanting, this some one is a born critic, that is to say, a lover and judge of the creations of others." Why did M. Sainte-Beuve make Goethe sovereign in criticism? Why did he think Milton peculiarly qualified to interpret Homer? From the deep principle of like unto like: only spirit can know spirit. What were the worth of a comment of John Locke on *Paradise Lost,* except to reveal the mental composition of John Locke? The critic should be what Locke was, a thinker, but to be a judge of the highest form of literature, poetry, he must moreover carry within him, inborn, some share of that whereby poetry is fledged, "creative imagination." (pp. 407-08)

Now and then there are betrayals of that predominant French weakness, which the French will persist in cherishing as a virtue,—the love of glory. M. Sainte-Beuve thinks Buffon's passion for glory saved him in his latter years from ennui, from "that languor of the soul which follows the age of the passions." Where are to be found men more the victims of disgust with life than that eminent pair, not more distinguished for literary brilliancy and contemporaneous success than for insatiable greed of glory,—Byron and Chateaubriand? No form of self-seeking is morally more weakening than this quenchless craving, which makes the soul hang its satisfaction on what is utterly beyond its sway, on praise and admiration. . . .

The military glory wherewith Napoleon fed and flattered the French nation for fifteen years, and the astonishing intellectual and animal vigor of the conqueror's mind, dazzle even M. Sainte-Beuve, so that he does not perceive the gaping chasms in Napoleon's moral nature, and the consequent one-sidedness of his intellectual action, nor the unmanning effects of his despotism. The words used to describe the moral side of the Imperial career are as insufficient as would be the strokes of a gray crayon to depict a conflagration or a sunset. (p. 408)

The office of the critic M. Sainte-Beuve administers, not for temporary or personal ends, but with a disinterested sense of its elevation and its responsibilities. Through healthy sympathies and knowledge ample and ripe, through firm sense with artistic flexibility, through largeness of view and subtlety of insight, he enters upon it more than ordinarily empowered for its due discharge. He is at once what the French call *fin* and what the English call "sound." In literary work, in biographical work, in work aesthetical and critical he delights, and he has a wide capacity of appropriation. The spirit of a book, a man, an age, he seizes quickly. With a nice perception of shades he catches the individual color of a mind or a production; and by the same faculty he grasps the determining principles in a character. Delicately, strongly, variously endowed, there is a steady equilibrium among his fine powers. Considering the bulk and vast variety and general excellence of his critical work, is it too much to say of him that he is not only as he has been called, the foremost of living critics, but that he deserves to hold the first place among all critics? No other has done so much so well. Goethe and Coleridge are something more: they are critics incidentally: but M. Sainte-Beuve, with poetical and philosophical qualities that lift him to a high van-

tage-ground, has made criticism his lifework, and through conscientious and symmetrical use of these qualities has done his work well. Besides much else in his many and many-sided volumes, there is to be read in them a full, spirited history of French literature. (p. 410)

"Sainte-Beuve, the Critic," in Putnam's Magazine of Literature, Science, Art, and National Interests, Vol. II, No. X, October, 1868, pp. 401-11.

## A[LFRED] A[USTIN]   (essay date 1878)

[Sainte-Beuve] is the best companion I know; and oral conversation should indeed be good to wean us from his **"Causeries."** He is an unrivalled talker—with his pen. You will say it is monologue, which, as Byron observed speaking of his father-in-law, "old gentlemen mistake for conversation!" But Sainte-Beuve has nothing of the old gentleman about him, in Byron's sense. He is the perfect gentleman of later middle-life, when judgment and manner are at their best, and when experience comes to the aid of good breeding, and weds abundant matter to a courtly air. Neither are Sainte-Beuve's "talks" like the talk of Macaulay or Lord Brougham. He never dogmatises. It is you who are listening, rather than he who is talking; and a man must be amazingly fond of hearing his own voice or expounding his own opinions, who wants to put in his oar when Sainte-Beuve is evenly and equably skimming along, making no ripple, leaving no trail. If I am asked to describe his style, I cannot. He is almost the only good writer I know who has not got one. Good conversation has no style; and neither has Sainte-Beuve. He is, what he describes himself, a talker. . . . I was not thinking of justifying my choice of Sainte-Beuve, as the author I would decide to have on a desert island. I was only trying to describe him as he is. But I perceive I have arrived at an account of him which at any rate explains my preference. On a desert island the most unsociable person would infallibly crave for a companion, and for a companion that would talk. . . . Reading Sainte-Beuve one can never feel alone. More than that. It is not only that he talks to you, the individual reader of the moment; he addresses all intelligent and well-bred people, on subjects that interest intelligent and well-bred people, and in a manner that satisfies intelligent and well-bred people. Reading him on a desert island would be the nearest possible equivalent to moving in the best society.

Such is his manner, his style, if you will, though I just now said that he has none. . . . He is essentially modern, and, using the word in not too literal a sense, homely. He talks about things and people that everybody cares about, in a manner everybody can appreciate. In fact, his manner would escape them, in their attention to what it is he says. Like Wordsworth's perfect woman, he is not too good for daily food, on a desert island or off it. He never gets away into the air, like Ariel, and bids us follow him, if we would hear him singing. He is an honest pedestrian, though not in the current sense of going ever so many miles an hour. (pp. 25-6)

Sainte-Beuve has a **"Causerie"** upon almost every Frenchman or Frenchwoman of eminence in any department of literature or action, since France was properly France, say since the days of Louis XI. What a host of subjects, what a multitude of people are thus given him to discourse about, kings, ministers, poets, soldiers, orators, beauties, great men scarcely yet appreciated, little men who have not even yet found their level, saints, heroes, brilliant impostors, devotees, dramatists, lyrists, satirists, writers of memoirs, memoirs of writers; and there they all are, Monday after Monday, fifty-two of them in every year, for year after year. . . . He is a writer to be read slowly, and one "**Lundi**" ought to be enough for a day. Let us suppose that the whole course was exhausted at the end of five years. Where is the man who could not begin and read them all over again? . . . Sainte-Beuve never sermonizes; and I doubt if a page of his ever sent the dullest reader to sleep. He is always short, never obscure, and ready to finish sooner than you are. My only fear is that, were one wrecked with him on this supposititious island and had one him alone for company for a dozen years, the cry "a sail, a sail!" would come too late; and we should be restored to the tongues of men only to find them vulgar and tiresome.

But what has all this got to do with Sainte-Beuve's critical method? Something, as you would find out, were you left with all his "**Causeries**" on a desert island. For he has, or thinks he has, a critical method, though I confess I never found it out till he told me of it himself. I do not speak of any special confidence. He has described this method in one of the "**Nouveaux Lundis**" [see excerpt above, 1862] and it is abundantly evident that, modest writer as he ostensibly is, he greatly piqued himself on it. (pp. 26-7)

Literary production . . . , according to Sainte-Beuve, is not something distinct or separable from the writer that produces 107and his organisation. One can taste of a work, but it is difficult, if not impossible, to judge it, independently of a knowledge of the man himself. One must say, such a tree produces such fruit. . . .

The man and the work unquestionably are one; just as the man and the fingers, or the man and the eyes, are one. No one would dream of contesting that point. But is it wise, or is it even fair, to judge the work in all, or in part, from the man? . . . Far from being able to allow that it is difficult to judge a book of consequence, "independently of one's acquaintance with the man himself," I should rather be disposed to say that this latter knowledge renders it difficult to judge the work "independently." (p. 28)

Thus, on the threshold, I, who have the privilege of remaining anonymous, or the controversy would seem too arrogant, and, were Sainte-Beuve alive, too unequal, venture to raise an objection. Sainte-Beuve himself was perhaps not insensible to the fact that it might be raised, for he takes care to allow that, where ancient writers are our theme, we are without the means of observation requisite for the employment of his method. That seems to me to be a considerable, not to say a fatal concession. To get hold of the man, he allows, book in hand, is nearly always impossible in the case of the great writers of antiquity, and the utmost our scrutiny can command is a half-broken statue. All that can be done under such circumstances is "to comment on the work, to admire it, and to 'rêver l'auteur et le poète à travers'' [dream of the author and the poet at random] I should have thought that was quite enough, and I confess I hardly seem to be reading Sainte-Beuve, or even a critic at all, but rather—shall I say?—some sonorous, plausible, but shallow word-compeller of the type of M. Victor Hugo, when he passes away from the difficulty with a majestic wave of the hand, and the following pretty phrase: "A mighty river, and rarely fordable, separates us from the great men of old. Let us salute them across the stream!" That is very nice. But had anyone else written it, Sainte-Beuve would have been the first man to observe that it is neither "l'étude littéraire" nor "l'étude morale" [literary study nor moral study] (pp. 28-9)

Sainte-Beuve then goes on to say that he looks forward to the advent of a time when science, having greatly progressed in its career of conquest, there will be formed great families of character, whose principal divisions will be known and determined. In other words, psychology will do for men and women what the conchologist does for shells, though of course not quite so accurately, and subject to greater risks of error; and human society will be one great classified museum, though we presume we shall not be compelled to live in glass cases. Sainte-Beuve, for himself, disclaims any such complete powers of classification; he makes only simple monographs. But he indicates the road, and follows it to the best of his ability. (p. 29)

To know the man himself is, as we have seen, of the utmost importance. But our familiarity with him must not end here, nor, indeed, even begin here. We must first find out, if we can, what is his birthplace, and what his race. . . . (pp. 29-30)

But Sainte-Beuve's critical method has not yet been fully set forth. A distinguished writer must be studied not only in his grandmother, his sisters, or his daughters; we must examine him in his comrades, in his rivals, in his chosen adversaries, in the people he admires or dislikes. Moreover, we must scrutinize him in his dawn, in his full mid-day, and, alas! in his decline. Here we seem to get upon somewhat safer ground, for we are dealing with the man himself and not with his relatives. . . . Upon safer ground, too, we seem to be standing, when Sainte-Beuve tells us that a critic may reap a world of instruction concerning an author by noticing, firstly, whom he imitates; and, secondly, who imitate him. (pp. 31-2)

I wonder if Sainte-Beuve was aware of the important bearing of [his observation that "many a man is hated all his life in the world of letters, without ever having been seen,"] at once so shrewd and so true, upon the principles of his critical method. I will endeavour to show briefly that it seals its condemnation.

"Many a man is hated all his life in the world of letters, without ever having been seen." Quite so. Buy why? For two reasons, it seems to me. Firstly, because the world of letters, like any other world, resents an exhibition of indifference to itself and its existence, and is quick to ascribe what may be only a noble passion for solitude and meditation to a haughty disdain for others. It has been justly observed that you had better do a man a serious injury than wound his vanity. It is with the world, and any particular world, as it is with men. Worlds, and the world of letters in a striking degree, are exceedingly touchy, and will not stand being ignored. For an author of distinction never to be seen is for him to be infected with a host of faults which will always be believed precisely because they cannot be verified. (p. 33)

But I venture to ask if it follows . . . that a man's works can be more fairly estimated when he himself is known and seen? It is perfectly true that a man's poems, or whatever they are, will not be fairly weighed, and will, perhaps, scarcely be weighed at all, so long as he is alive, but refuses to live in the midst of the weighers. They will be fairly weighed, let me add, when he is no longer seen, because he is dead and can no longer be seen, and the vainest and most sensitive of critical circles can no longer be angry because he does not appear before them. But whilst he yet perambulates this egotistical and exacting planet, is it not plain that his daily appearance among his contemporaries will operate as a continual bias, in one direction or the other, upon those who sit in judgment on his works? How often is it that the just judge is found, who, though he detests the author, belauds the work, or loves the writer and damns his book? (pp. 33-4)

I submit, therefore, that the more a man is known as a man and an individual, the less chance is there of his works being fairly measured. The man himself—or what is supposed to be the man himself—is being continually thrust into the page, to discolour its sentiments, to distort its meaning, to obscure its patent drift. If the critic be a friend, he will find each passage heightened in beauty and merit by the recollection of the man who wrote it. If he be other than a friend, each metaphor will become confused, and each simile trite, in the darkening shadow of their objectionable author.

But perhaps the author's grandmothers, sisters, aunts, and nieces can help us here? To put the question is to answer it. They can help in the same sense that all facts help a man who has got a theory, and has not the smallest intention of surrendering it. (p. 34)

"Save me from my friends," is a common observation. "Save me from myself!" would be yet more to the purpose. Happily, Sainte-Beuve saves himself . . . ; Sainte-Beuve, in all, or nearly all, his great critical judgments, ceases to potter among uncles, and aunts, and grandchildren, and goes straight to the author's nearest and truest relatives, his works themselves.

For this, I submit, is the true critical method, and the only sound and secure one. If a critic happens to know anything personal about his author, let him try to forget it. Happy Virgil! Happy Shakespeare! We know nothing about either of your great-grandmothers and precious little more about yourselves. Possibly one was a bit of a courtier, and the other no end of a sad dog. But we don't know; and accordingly we read of the praises of Augustus, and Maecenas, and Marcellus with charmed ears; and we peruse *Romeo and Juliet, Antony and Cleopatra, Venus and Adonis,* and even the *Sonnets* themselves, without turning up the whites of our eyes and wishing it was always Sunday. The best criticism, like the best poetry, is objective. (pp. 34-5)

A[lfred] A[ustin], "Sainte-Beuve's Critical Method," in The Cornhill Magazine (© John Murray 1878), Vol. XXXVIII, No. 223, July, 1878, pp. 24-35.

## ÉMILE ZOLA (essay date 1880)

[*Zola was a foremost author of the French Naturalist movement. While he acknowledges that Sainte-Beuve considered himself a student of contemporary society, he stresses that Sainte-Beuve preferred to study the past. Zola states that Sainte-Beuve experienced a "sort of homesickness" for an earlier era, when writers were esteemed as distinguished men of letters.*]

Sainte-Beuve, whose intelligence is so flexible and so great, and so well able to appreciate modern works, had nevertheless a tender preference for those of the past. He expresses a continual regret, a sort of homesickness, for the dead ages, for the seventeenth century above all; it escapes him, in a page, or in a phrase, on no matter what subject. He acknowledges the present time, he flatters himself that he knows and comprehends all its productions; but his temperament carries him away, and he goes back to the past and lives more at his ease with his melancholy joys and mid his memories as a scholar and a man of letters. He was born two hundred years too late. I have never understood the charm of the literary temperament better, as it was cultivated by old France. Sainte-Beuve was certainly one of the last to feel and weep with this old world,

and its echo vibrates the more strongly in him because he has one foot in each of the two epochs, the past and the present, and because he is more of an actor than a judge. His true confessions were written in his hours of trouble, and they sound like a cry of personal sorrow.

Here is the picture Sainte-Beuve draws of the writer when he turns back to that past about which he dreams. The writer is an erudite and lettered man, who, above all else, needs leisure. He lives in the depths of a library, far from the noise of the street, in a sweet companionship with the Muses. It is a condition of luxury, of spiritual refinement, with just enough mental stimulus, and the soft soothing of one's entire nature. Literature was the pastime of a chosen society, which charmed the poet first, before it contributed to the happiness of a select circle. No hypothesis of forced labor, of prolonged vigils, of work anxiously awaited and accomplished in a hurry; on the contrary, there was a smiling politeness toward inspiration, works were written in favorable hours, in entire ease of heart and mind. . . . Writers were an ornament, a luxury, something lifted out of common life, something that could not be openly bought and sold like other commodities; the great ones alone could pay for this fantasy, as they paid for the privilege of having buffoons and ballet dancers. (pp. 162-64)

In a word, the writer revels in pure letters, in the pleasure of some literary conceit, in discussions about the use of language, in elaborate painting of character, feeling, and passions, not probing them down to their real physiological truth, but setting them forth in tragic tirades and eloquent passages. There is an impassable gulf between the savant who experiments and the writer who describes. (p. 164)

It was the *salons* which called forth the literary instinct and molded it. Books were dear and poorly circulated; the people did not read at all, and the middle class hardly at all; they were far removed from that great current of reading which to-day carries all society with it. It was an exception to come across an impassioned reader devouring all he could find on the booksellers' shelves. And the general mass of readers, what we call public opinion, the universal suffrage, as we might put it, that molds literature to-day, did not then exist; the *salons*, a few rare groups of chosen people, were the only ones to give a decisive judgment. (p. 165)

Naturally the *salons* led up to the academies. It was here that the literary spirit blossomed forth into beautiful rhetoric. Freed from its worldly element, with no more women to humor, it became grammatical and wordy, it plunged into the question of tradition, of rules and formulas. You should hear Sainte-Beuve, this liberal minded man, talking about the Academy with the importance and anger of an honest official who has gone to his office and is discontented with the conduct and work of his colleagues during his absence. (p. 166)

If the true history of the Academy were written, with the letters in which the academicians have confessed the truth, you would have the most extraordinary comic poem about a group of men who had fallen into infantile pride, and into occupations astounding in their uselessness. Sainte-Beuve's writings are very valuable in this connection, for the reason that he gives us some excellent notes on the attitude of the writer in the last *salons* at the commencement of this century. You see the writer feeling very much honored at being received at the houses of the great. He gives them low bows, he is respectful, and shows that he knows his own place and recognizes their superiority. It is an acceptance of the social hierarchy at which he will smile, and skeptically analyze, as soon as his foot has touched the pavement of the street; but in the midst of it, among ladies and hobnobbing with the minister of to-day or to-morrow, he thinks he must bow as if he had still need of that protection, as if he worked only for this class, flattered by its politeness, captivated by the seductions of these aristocratic surroundings, in which letters appeared more noble. It is simply a remnant of court-flattery, a taste for the grace and delightful propriety of good society. Immersed in such reading, Sainte-Beuve seems to forget that it is the presence of the entire nation behind him that gives him his power and his true celebrity. (pp. 167-68)

> *Émile Zola, "The Influence of Money in Literature,"*
> *in his* The Experimental Novel and Other Essays,
> *translated by Belle M. Sherman (translation copy-*
> *right, 1893, by Cassell Publishing Company; origi-*
> *nally published as* Le roman expérimental, *1880),*
> *Cassell, 1893, pp. 161-206.* *

## GEORGE BRANDES (essay date 1882)

[Joseph Delorme, the pseudonymous hero of *Les Poésies de Joseph Delorme,*] is the usual despairing youth of the 1830 period, but there is more of the bourgeois in him than in the heroes of Saint-Beuve's contemporaries; his despair is less magnificent and more true to nature. As regards form, the poems are remarkable for their return to the charming old French metres of Ronsard and Charles d'Orléans, and also for the frequency with which the sonnet . . . recurs. But they interest us chiefly because of the tendency to realism which their author already begins to display, a realism which, though it can sometimes be traced to the influence of the English poets of the Lake School, is yet as a rule, with its daring choice of subjects (in the poem **"Rose"** for example), original and essentially French. The ideal element is represented by the author's ecstatic effusions on the subject of the *Cénacle,* the little fraternal circle of poets and painters into which he had lately been admitted, and the members of which he panegyrises, now collectively, now singly. His admiration of his friends knows no bounds. (pp. 312-13)

*Les Consolations* is dedicated to Victor Hugo in terms of hysterical admiration coupled with expressions of Christian contrition, and Hugo's name occurs frequently in the book; but it was in reality quite as much an offering to Madame Hugo. . . . Of his relations with her he wrote too openly in *Le Livre d'Amour,* a collection of poems which obviously treat of realities. . . . And in the novel *Volupté,* too, we have no difficulty in recognising its author's relations with Victor Hugo and his household in Amaury's relations with the eminent politician, Monsieur de Couaën, and his wife. (p. 313)

In spite of its diffuseness and heaviness, *Volupté* is a delicately profound psychological study. It consists of confessions of the nature of Rousseau's, but recorded in a style which is richer in imagery, more saturated with colour, and more delicately shaded than Rousseau's; the emotionally lyric tone reminds us of Lamartine's *Jocelyn,* a work which treats the same kind of theme more chastely. Sainte-Beuve's book presents us with the life-story of a pleasure-seeking, dissipated youth, interspersed with many a profound, sagacious reflection. It represents the sensual and the tender impulses of the soul as equally destructive of the vigour and energy of youth. It treats mainly of those enervating friendships with young women, especially with young married women, in cultivating which clever young men often squander so much time. The word "squander" seems to me to convey Sainte-Beuve's meaning better than the word

"lose"; for he himself reproaches a gifted writer whose vigorous style is lacking in shades, with having worked too hard and lived too lonely a life, with having injured himself by too seldom seeking the society "which is the best of all, and leads one to lose most time in the pleasantest way, the society of women." (p. 315)

Two things make [*Volupté*] a remarkable [book]—in the first place, the perfect understanding which it displays of the development process and the diseases of the soul, an understanding which speaks of persistent self-examination, and foreshadows the coming critic; in the second place, the insight into feminine character, which reveals the feminine element in Sainte-Beuve's own nature, and prognosticates his unique success in the critical interpretation of the personalities of notable women. (p. 316)

[*Les pensées d'Août*] is the only one of his poetical ventures which was quite unsuccessful, and the poems which the volume contains are certainly his coldest; yet it seems to me, though my opinion is unsupported by any other critic, that it is in this work he first displays marked originality. It is realistic to an extent which is quite unique in the lyric poetry of the Romantic School; no poet had yet ventured to make such free use of the language and the surroundings of daily life. In the North, where a poet even to-day would hardly have the courage to give an omnibus or a railway platform a place in a lyric poem, such a work as *Les Pensées d'Août* would still almost be regarded in the light of a specimen of the poetry of the future.

In it, as in *Les Poésies de Joseph Delorme,* we find several of the characteristics of the English Lake School transplanted to French soil. Sainte-Beuve, like the Englishmen, presents us with simple, sober pictures of real life, and his style, like theirs, is founded upon the conviction that there ought not to be any essential difference between the language of prose and of metrical compositions. But in Sainte-Beuve's poems we have, instead of the strange want of crispness and point of the English poems, a genuinely French dramatic tension. Each of them is a little drama developed within the limits of a short lyric narrative. (pp. 317-18)

[*Port-Royal,*] Sainte-Beuve's longest piece of connected writing, is a unique work of its kind. Disinclination to tread the beaten track, and the Romanticist's sympathy with religious enthusiasm, two characteristics which early distinguished him, influenced him in choosing the history of Jansenism in France as his subject. Jansenism was an enthusiastic, intelligent, intense form of piety, which, though evolved and retained within the pale of Catholicism, was nevertheless distinguished by a personal, that is to say, heretical, passion for truth, which appeals to our understanding by its independence and to our sympathies by its heroically courageous defiance of persecution and coercion. . . .

Sainte-Beuve possessed all the qualifications required of the historian of Jansenism. He was not a believer, but he had been, or believed that he had been one. A man is seldom capable of criticising the views he holds himself, and as seldom of understanding those which he has never held; what we all understand best are the views we once shared, but share no longer. If any one doubts Sainte-Beuve's ability to understand these medieval emotions, that impulse to forsake the world, that strife of the awakened soul with nature, and its repentant, anxious recourse to grace; if any one doubts his comprehension of the real spirit inspiring these sermons and theological pamphlets, of the hearts beating under these nuns' habits, of the devotion, the hopes, and the longings, the mystical ecstasies and the sacred enthusiasm, which flourished on that little spot of holy ground, let that doubter read the first two volumes of **Port-Royal,** as far as the chapter on Pascal, who was easier of comprehension because he was a figure of more magnitude and was already better known. . . . We are frequently reminded of the fact that Sainte-Beuve was originally a novelist. The scenes among the innocent dwellers in that dovecote, the convent, for instance, have all the vividness of well-written fiction. And Sainte-Beuve employs his imagination only in describing; he never invents or misrepresents.

It is a defect in the book that its first parts, though they are much the best reading, are not conceived in the historical style. We are too vividly reminded that the *feuilleton* [newspaper article] has hitherto been their author's vehicle of expression. In [the] earlier volumes Sainte-Beuve simply takes Port-Royal as his starting-point. The old monastery is not much more than his citadel, from which he makes one sortie after another. . . . The later volumes, on the other hand, the style of which is more soberly historical, lack the attraction of these interpolations; and the subject is too much of a special subject to interest long, in spite of the loving care which has been bestowed on it. (pp. 327-28)

Sainte-Beuve has two styles, the youthful and the mature. At the time of his study of sixteenth century literature (from the vocabulary of which he, like the other young Romanticists, adopted various expressions) he got into the habit of picking and choosing his words and polishing and refining his periods to such an extent that he drew down upon himself some justifiably severe criticism. . . .

A style like Sainte-Beuve's second—keen and flexible as a sword-blade—is not easy to characterise. In the first place, it is by no means a striking style. The reader who is not particularly well versed in French literature will not be aware of anything that can be called style. The periods succeed one another unrhythmically; they are not grouped, but proceed carelessly, as Zouaves march; we never come upon a pompous and seldom on a passionate one; occasionally there is an interjection—"O poet!" or the like. The language flows like gently rippling water. But the observant reader is charmed by its noble Atticism. The tone is not assertive, but calmly and quietly sceptic. (p. 329)

Sainte-Beuve made various reforms in the art of criticism. In the first place, he put solid ground beneath its feet, gave it the firm foothold of history and science. The old, so-called philosophic criticism treated the literary document as if it had fallen from the clouds, judged it without taking its author into account at all, and placed it under some particular heading in a historical or aesthetic chart. Sainte-Beuve found the author in his work; behind the paper he discovered the man. (p. 331)

Sainte-Beuve's most marked characteristic was an insatiable thirst for knowledge, a quality which he possessed in the form that may be called scientific inquisitiveness. This directed his life even before it expressed itself in his criticism. At first it is only faintly perceptible in his works, because he began with unlimited praise of his contemporaries, Chateaubriand, Lamartine, Victor Hugo, Alfred de Vigny, and others, a good deal of which he was obliged subsequently to retract—thus progressing in the opposite direction from Théophile Gautier, who began with severity and gradually declined into a nerveless leniency. But it is possible to trace even Sainte-Beuve's first uncritical praise to his critical instincts. Its exaggeratedness

was due to the fact that he stood, as a young man, too near to the personages he criticised; but this circumstance was itself attributable to his curiosity. (pp. 331-32)

And here the critic is confronted by one of his greatest difficulties—he knows the truth only about the living, but may speak it only of the dead. And there is no doubt that it makes a disagreeable impression when the death of an author entirely changes the tone of criticism, as Sainte-Beuve's criticism of Chateaubriand, for example, was altered by the latter's death. His earliest article on Chateaubriand was incense pure and simple. (p. 332)

But when he is at his best, Sainte-Beuve succeeds in finding the golden mean. He does not admire everything and attribute everything to noble motives, but neither does he search for base ones. He neither praises nor depreciates human nature. He understands it. And intercourse with men and women of every description, constant critical observation, French delicacy of perception, and a Parisian training, have given him an extraordinary power of discernment. At his best, the many-sidedness of his mind actually reminds us of Goethe. We are at times tempted to call him "wise"; and few indeed are the critics who tempt us to apply this adjective to them. He very seldom allows himself to be confused or influenced by the popular sentiment connected with a name, no matter whether it is lofty, or pathetic, or depreciatory. . . . With the judicial calm of the scientific investigator, he enumerates his tendencies towards good and his tendencies towards evil, and weighs them in the balance. And by such means he produces a trustworthy portrait—or rather, a series of portraits, each one of which is trustworthy, though some of them contradict each other. For, notable critic as Sainte-Beuve is, he invariably shirks one of the greatest difficulties with which the critic has to contend. A conscientious critic has, as a rule, read the work which he undertakes to interpret and criticise, many times and at various stages of his development; each time he has been struck by something different; and in the end he has seen the work from so many different points of view that it is impossible for him, without doing a sort of inward violence to himself, to maintain one single standpoint, one attitude of feeling. And if he happens to be dealing, not with a single work, but with a highly productive author who has passed through many stages of development, or possibly even with a whole school of literature, the difficulty of making one comprehensive picture out of the many different impressions received under totally different psychical conditions, becomes proportionately greater. . . . This difficulty Sainte-Beuve avoids by constantly producing fresh descriptions and fresh criticisms of the same men and their works, leaving it to the reader to draw his own conclusions. (pp. 333-34)

[The proposition] that every human being whom we judge has altered, has developed steadily, Sainte-Beuve understood better than it had ever been understood before. He not only changes his tone every time he changes his theme, but changes it every time there is a change in the man or woman who is his theme for the time being; his agile talent imitates all the movements of the individual human soul during its development process. Hence his manner is as changeable as his subject. . . . (p. 334)

[Sainte-Beuve's] criticism produces an organism, a life, as poetry does. It does not break up the given material into road-metal and gravel, but erects a building with it. It does not break up the human soul into its component parts, so that we only gain an understanding of it as a piece of dead mechanism, without having any idea what it is like when it is in movement.

No, he shows us the machine at work; we see the fire that drives it and hear the noise it makes, whilst we are learning the secrets of its construction. (p. 336)

> *George Brandes, ''Sainte-Beuve'' and ''Sainte-Beuve and Modern Criticism,'' in his* Main Currents in Nineteenth Century Literature: The Romantic School in France, Vol. V, *translated by Diana White and Mary Morison (originally published as* Hovedstrømninger i det 19de aarhundredes litteratur: Den romantiske Skole i Frankrig, *1882), William Heinemann, l904, pp. 307-20, 327-38.*

**ÉMILE FAGUET**   (essay date 1900)

[*Faguet, a prominent French critic, describes Sainte-Beuve as an outstanding critical thinker and an ''indefatigable investigator of documents concerning mankind.'' Though Faguet terms Sainte-Beuve's verse ''dull and heavy,'' he praises its emotional sincerity. He also admires the honesty of Sainte-Beuve's criticism, which, Faguet maintains, reflects Sainte-Beuve's interest in individuality and his love of truth.*]

From beginning to end of his life Sainte-Beuve was at bottom an observer and an indefatigable investigator of documents concerning mankind. His essential, or at least his most important, quality consisted in an intelligence which never tired of understanding and which sought incessantly new things to understand. (p. 170)

[Sainte-Beuve], the great critic of the nineteenth century was characterized by an indefatigable, intellectual curiosity; a fundamental scepticism, which included curiosity, eagerness, and even sympathy, and lacked only enthusiasm and the anxiety to reach conclusions; a taste for truth, which was only a form of curiosity carried, perhaps, to the farthest possible limits. But these faculties or mental characteristics, excellent on the whole for criticism were spoiled to a certain extent by moral weaknesses, which were not without influence upon his mental health. (pp. 171-72)

In the first place he was not solely a critic. His ambition was twofold: he wanted to be at the same time a critic and a creator. To write verse, to make novels, and to appreciate other people's verse and novels—such was his programme. (p. 172)

[Sainte-Beuve's] poems, sometimes fairly happily conceived, were only occasionally a poet's verses. He had no imagination, although in his time everybody else had too much. He was prosaic, spiritless and cold, not to mention that frequently he was also dull and heavy. Shall I say, also, that he was too sincere? It is almost correct to say so. Rightly convinced that true poetry is the complete expression of our real sentiments, he put himself into his verses with absolute *naïveté.* . . . [In] spite of some fairly brilliant pieces, [*Vie, penseés, et poésies de Joseph Delorme, Les consolations,* and *Pensées d'août*] are, frankly, cold, lifeless and tedious, and only a few pages would be worth including in an anthology.

The most remarkable thing about these verses is their contrast with contemporary poetry. . . . They recall as much as anything the best verses of the Consulat and Empire periods, those of Fontanes and Andrieux, with the inevitable differences arising from their respective dates, and with a richer, or rather fuller, though less clear and less pure, language. And simultaneously Sainte-Beuve, as a critic, was endeavouring to praise the romantic poets, at least Lamartine and Hugo. (pp. 172-73)

His novel, *Voluptuousness* [*Volupté*] . . . , was much more important than his verses. Here, again, he was sincere, he was petty and minute, he was assiduous, and, we are forced to add, he was tedious: but he was more penetrative. Here, again, autobiography preponderates, but it is done, not with greater sincerity, but with a more serious sincerity, so serious that it becomes almost tragic as a consequence. It is a pity that *Voluptuousness* is a novel much less strong and vigorous and done in much less relief than [Stendhal's] *Scarlet and Black:* because, if it had been of about the same literary value, it would be an exact counterpart of *Scarlet and Black.* The latter is a portrait of a young man of 1830, and so is *Voluptuousness.* Sainte-Beuve's [young man] is a weakling, a dreamer, a being without strength of will and with a thousand fancies, full of discordant caprices, charmed in turn and simultaneously with a thousand different purposes, always dominated by an unnerving—that is to say, always passive—sensuality, and, finally, imbued to the very soul with that unhealthy melancholy, a sort of innate tiredness which always precedes action instead of coming after it. He is a son of René, haunted by the memory of Chateaubriand, as the other is haunted by Napoléon. The contrast is curious and instructive.

It gives us, above all, insight into Sainte-Beuve's soul. The hero of *Voluptuousness* ends by retiring from active life into the seclusion of a life of contemplation. Sainte-Beuve would have done just the same if he had been able. He did do so as far as possible. . . . [The] ''dreamy, emotional and excitable languor,'' which is spread through the whole of the novel *Voluptuousness,* was the very basis of Sainte-Beuve's soul, into which he always relapsed after the relaxations of either work or disorder. It was his hidden sore, and he experienced, perhaps, more pleasure in preserving than in healing it. He kept it always.

But, without insisting on these points, it is obvious how important a part Sainte-Beuve's creative works play in the explanation of his critical works. Sainte-Beuve is an ''introspect.'' He likes to watch himself living, slowly, patiently, minutely. The confidences which he gave to the public, and which are rather ridiculous considered as such, are, above all, reports about himself which he wanted to make to himself. (pp. 173-75)

The reasons which led Sainte-Beuve to undertake solely criticism were threefold: first, and without a doubt, the relative failure of his creative works; then, it must be recognized, the exigencies of life; and, thirdly, the great need he felt to discard a ''part of himself,'' which was a burden and, at certain times, a source of considerable sorrow to him. It was a detachment and, like any detachment, a method of purification. (p. 176)

Ordinarily a critic is supported by a certain number of general ideas and guided by a method. Sainte-Beuve had no general ideas and hardly had a method. I have said that he was a sceptic. There is no such thing as an absolute sceptic. People are sceptical in regard to anything which does not concern the matter in which they are interested, and they become very dogmatic in regard to anything concerning that matter. Sainte-Beuve is a sceptic so far as his own religion is concerned, inclusively. The depth of his scepticism is revealed by the names which he gives to it. He lavishes on it ''flattering names.'' He calls it good sense, sense of reality, judicious spirit, spirit of prudence, reason. (p. 177)

Sainte-Beuve aims at the imperceptible diffusion of scepticism among men, as others at the establishment of a single faith and the communion of all men in a single faith. To him it seems that this unanimity, which is the secret desire of humanity, could be best achieved by the complete abandonment of any desire for unanimity, by adopting the conviction that we cannot convince each other, and by the general acceptance of the conclusion that though we can think we cannot reach conclusions. (pp. 177-78)

It is also very interesting to follow Sainte-Beuve in his studies and pictures of the great believers. Then all kinds of sentiments conflict in him. Out of curiosity for what is as far as possible removed from him he has sympathy: for among the greatly curious the very keenness of their curiosity turns into sympathy and even passion. His artistic instinct inspires him to admiration; for in these believers he finds a force, an incredible human power, productive of wonderful effects and of sublime acts. His inner feelings prompt him to resist, to withhold himself, to make reservations. . . . (p. 178)

The whole of his admirable **Port-Royal** is full of . . . inconsistencies, which make it much more interesting than if it were regularly composed, with an artificial or indifferent unity of style. The reader is conscious of the presence of a man with all his different faculties and varied tendencies in play. But beneath the surface, and as a sort of basis, there are two essential instincts: protesting scepticism and the almost quivering joy in understanding. But still the deepest of all these sentiments is certainly scepticism, the sceptical conviction, if I may express it so, this thought which becomes more and more obvious, strengthens itself, asserts itself, affirms itself thorugh insinuation and finally explodes in the conclusion that man is not made to be enveloped in this gloom, or, what is the same thing, in this dazzling light which is too bright for him.

It is relatively easy to be sceptical in regard to former beliefs, or, more correctly, beliefs which are out of fashion. What is more difficult is to break through present beliefs, which we seem to breathe in the air around us. Sainte-Beuve was, perhaps, more free from contemporary convictions than from those of former times; for he mistrusted them more. (pp. 178-79)

[Sainte-Beuve] had scarcely more method than general ideas. It could be said that all the efforts of the nineteenth-century criticism were directed towards its constitution as a science; and Sainte-Beuve reacted vigorously against this very effort. (p. 184)

What he wants is to acquire not only knowledge of, but familiarity with, an author. . . .

And herein lies the reason why Sainte-Beuve has so little liking for general ideas and for a method of criticism which requires, and is made up of, general ideas. What he likes is individuality. A person is never sufficiently individual for him; never made up of features sufficiently marked, in sufficient detail, and sufficiently distinct from those which make up other people's individuality. (p. 185)

Sainte-Beuve did sometimes pretend, either for amusement or perhaps out of condescension to those who are very exacting, to have a method like other people. He repeated several times: "I am making a natural history of minds." By this he meant that, having gathered together the characteristic features of a person, he tried to indicate to what family of minds he seemed to him to belong. He never claimed that there was anything else "scientific" about his criticism. It is little enough. Actually it goes no farther than the devising of ingenious "re-

lationships" between the various fathers of our literature. (pp. 186-87)

In default of a method, or of wanting to have a method, he really did have a critical mind, and he knew excellently in what that consists. To love everything in order to understand; to hate nothing; not only to hate nothing but to disdain nothing; to have a sort of intellectual sympathy, the only sympathy which has no contrary and which does not force one to detest one thing because one loves another. (p. 187)

Above all, he was fond of truth. And just as he liked humanity without respecting it, so he liked truth with the thought at the back of his head that it can never be attained; and he loved it with that very particular passion of a person who does not believe in it. He seemed to say that, if truth escapes us, it is precisely a reason for pursuing it. He did not spare his efforts; he had the last quality, the last "virtue," as he said, of the critic, which consists in an absolute loyalty in his inquiry, his discoveries and his mistakes. . . . Conscience, sympathy, indefatigable and intelligent curiosity, almost refined loyalty, such was the composition of Sainte-Beuve's "critical mind"; thus he made up for lack of method, or perhaps it was because he had qualities which filled its place so well that he paid no heed to method. (p. 188)

> *Émile Faguet, "Sainte-Beuve," in his* Politicians & Moralists of the Nineteenth Century, Vol. 3, *translated by Dorothy Galton (originally published as Politiques et moralistes du dix-neuvième siècle, Société française d'imprimerie et de librarie, Vol. 3, 1900), Ernest Benn Limited, 1928, pp. 165-204.*

### HENRY JAMES   (essay date 1904)

[*A foremost American novelist and critic, James praises Sainte-Beuve for his devotion to literature. To James, Sainte-Beuve embodies the qualities that he most admires in French literature, including moral and intellectual curiosity. In the following review of Sainte-Beuve's correspondence, James analyzes Sainte-Beuve's combined passion for scholarship and life, and describes him as an "observer, a moralist, [and] a psychologist."*]

[Sainte-Beuve] was literary in every pulsation of his being, and he expressed himself totally in his literary life. No character and no career were ever more homogeneous. He had no disturbing, perverting tastes; he suffered no retarding, embarrassing accidents. He lost no time, and he never wasted any. He was not even married; his literary consciousness was never complicated with the sense of an unliterary condition. His mind was never diverted or distracted from its natural exercise—that of looking in literature for illustrations of life, and of looking in life for aids to literature. . . . His career was an intensely laborious one—his time, attention and interest, his imagination and sympathies were unceasingly mortgaged. ["**Correspondance de C. A. Sainte-Beuve (1822-69)**" contains] almost no general letters, pages purely sociable and human. The human and sociable touch is frequent, is perpetual; to use his own inveterate expression, he "slips it in" wherever there is an opening. But his occasions are mostly those of rapid notes dictated by some professional or technical pretext. (pp. 300-01)

[He had] two passions, which are commonly assumed to exclude each other—the passion for scholarship and the passion for life. He was essentially a creature of books, a *literatus;* and yet to his intensely bookish and acquisitive mind nothing human, nothing social or mundane was alien. The simplest way to express his particular felicity is to say that, putting aside the poets and novelists, the purely imaginative and inventive authors, he is the student who has brought into the study the largest element of reflected life. No scholar was ever so much of an observer, of a moralist, a psychologist; and no such regular and beguiled *abonné* to the general spectacle was ever so much of a scholar. He valued life and literature equally for the light they threw upon each other; to his mind one implied the other; he was unable to conceive of them apart. He made use in literature, in an extraordinary manner, of the qualities that are peculiarly social. Some one said of him that he had the organization of a nervous woman and the powers of acquisition of a Benedictine. Sainte-Beuve had nerves assuredly; there is something feminine in his tact, his penetration, his subtlety and pliability, his rapidity of transition, his magical divinations, his sympathies and antipathies, his marvelous art of insinuation, of expressing himself by fine touches and of adding touch to touch. But all this side of the feminine genius was re-enforced by faculties of quite another order—faculties of the masculine stamp; the completeness, the solid sense, the constant reason, the moderation, the copious knowledge, the passion for exactitude and for general considerations. In attempting to appreciate him it is impossible to keep these things apart; they melt into each other like the elements of the atmosphere; there is scarcely a stroke of his pen that does not contain a little of each of them. (pp. 301-02)

He had a very large dose of what the French call "malice"— an element which was the counterpart of his subtlety, his feminine fineness of perception. This subtlety served him not only as a magical clew to valuable results, but it led him sometimes into small deviations that were like the lapses, slightly unholy, of the tempted. It led him to analyze motives with a minuteness which was often fatal to their apparent purity; it led him to slip in—to *glisser,* as he always says—the grain of corrosive censure with the little parcel of amenities. For feats of this kind his art was instinctive; he strikes the reader as more than feminine—as positively feline. It is beyond question that he has at times the feline scratch. The truth is, that his instrument itself—his art of expression—was almost a premium upon the abuse of innuendo. The knowledge that he could leave the impression without having said the thing must frequently have been an intellectual temptation. Besides, it may be said that his scratch was really, on the whole, defensive, or, at the worst, retributive; it was, to my belief, never wanton or aggressive. . . . But he apprehended the personality, the moral physiognomy of the people to whom he turned his attention— Victor Cousin, for instance, Lamartine, Villemain, Balzac, Victor Hugo, Chateaubriand—with an extraordinary clearness and sharpness; he took intellectual possession of it and never relaxed his grasp. . . . He was very apt to remember people's faults in considering their merits. He says in one of his letters that he is more sensitive to certain great faults than to certain great merits. And then, with his passion for detail, for exactitude and completeness, for facts and examples, he thought nothing unimportant. To be vague was the last thing possible to him, and the deformities or misdemeanors of people he had studied remained in his eyes as definite as the numbers of a "sum" in addition or subtraction.

His great justification, however, it seems to me, is, that the cause he upheld was the most important, for it was simply the cause of liberty, in which we are all so much interested. This, in essence, is what I mean by saying that certain of those habits of mind which made many people dislike him were defensive weapons. It was doubtless not always a question of defending

his own character, but it was almost always a question of defending his position as a free observer and appreciator. . . . His instinct, from the beginning of his career, was to mistrust any way of looking at things which should connect the observer with a party pledged to take the point of view most likely to minister to its prosperity. He cared nothing for the prosperity of parties; he cared only for the ascertainment of the reality and for hitting the nail on the head. He only cared to look freely—to look all round. The part he desired to play was that of the vividly intelligent, brightly enlightened mind, acting in the interest of literature, knowledge, taste, and spending itself on everything human and historic. He was frankly and explicitly a critic; he attributed the highest importance to the critical function, and he understood it in so large a way that it gives us a lift to agree with him. The critic, in his conception, was not the narrow lawgiver or the rigid censor that he is often assumed to be; he was the student, the inquirer, the interpreter, the taker of notes, the active, restless commentator, whose constant aim was to arrive at justness of characterization. Sainte-Beuve's own faculty of characterization was of the rarest and most remarkable; he held it himself in the highest esteem; his impression was the thing in the world he most valued. There is something admirable in his gravity, consistency and dignity on this point. (pp. 303-06)

[These] volumes are by no means without testimony to the extreme acuteness with which he could feel irritation and the inimitable neatness and lucidity with which he could express it. (p. 309)

[The] letters of a great critic should contain a great deal of good criticism, and in this respect these volumes will not be found disappointing. They contain a great variety of fragmentary judgments and of characteristic revelations and sidelights. With his great breadth of view, his general intelligence and his love of seeing "juste," Sainte-Beuve was nevertheless a man of strong predispositions, of vigorous natural preferences. He never repudiated the charge of having strong "bents" of taste. This indeed would have been most absurd; for one's taste is an effect, more than a cause, of one's preferences; it is indeed the result of a series of particular tastes. With Sainte-Beuve, as with everyone else, it grew more and more flexible with time; it adapted itself and opened new windows and doors. He achieved in his last years feats that may fairly be called extraordinary in the way of doing justice to writers and works of an intensely "modern" stamp—to Baudelaire and Flaubert, to Feydeau and the brothers Goncourt. There is even in the second of these volumes a letter, on the whole appreciative, to [M. Émile Zola,] the young writer whose vigorous brain, in later years, was to give birth to the monstrous "Assommoir." But originally Sainte-Beuve's was not a mind that appeared likely, even at a late stage of its evolution, to offer hospitality to M. Émile Zola. He was always a man of his time; he played his part in the romantic movement; Joseph Delorme and the novel of "**Volupté**" are creations eminently characteristic of that fermentation of opinion, that newer, younger genius which produced the great modern works of French literature. Sainte-Beuve, in other words, was essentially of the generation of Lamartine and Victor Hugo, of Balzac and George Sand. But he was, if not more weighted, more anchored than some of his companions; he was incapable of moving in a mass; he never was a violent radical. (pp. 313-14)

Sainte-Beuve's was a mind of a thousand sides, and it is possible sometimes to meet it at a disconcerting or displeasing angle. But as regards the whole value I should never for an instant hesitate. If it is a question of taking the critic or leaving him—of being on his "side" or not—I take him, definitely, and on the added evidence of these letters, as the very genius of observation, discretion and taste. (p. 318)

*Henry James, "Sainte-Beuve" (originally published in a different form in* The North American Review, *Vol. CXXX, No. CCLXXVIII, 1880), in* American Literary Criticism, *edited by William Morton Payne, Longmans, Green, and Co., 1904 (and reprinted by Books for Libraries Press, 1968; distributed by Arno Press, Inc.), pp. 299-318.*

### REMY DE GOURMONT   (essay date 1904)

[*Gourmont, known best for his analysis of the French Symbolist movement, defined a critic as a creator of values; to him, Sainte-Beuve was "almost the only critic of the nineteenth century." Gourmont discusses Sainte-Beuve's influence on French literary history, claiming that he "stamped French literature with his own image."*]

The importance of Sainte-Beuve, which is becoming increasingly apparent and unchallenged, affirms the importance of criticism.

Poets and artists create phantoms which sometimes become immortal in the traditions of mankind. The critic, like the philosopher, creates values. The work of art does not conclude. Wherever there is conclusion, there is criticism. Persons of small perspicacity used to ask of Sainte-Beuve: "But what is your conclusion?" "My conclusion," he would reply, "begins with the first line of my study." The critical mind seeks intentions and attributes them necessarily to the very works which are most lacking in them. (p. 205)

Sainte-Beuve was almost the only critic of the nineteenth century, the only creator of values. Although since the Consulate and until the last years of the century, works and pages of criticism have abounded, almost no other critic has had the power to establish durably the image of one of his contemporaries or to bring current opinion to revise old judgments. . . .

What we call a critic today is a former "good student" who has contracted, first from his secondary school and then usually from Ecole Normale [normal school], the taste for wearisome studies. After having been a professor for a time, he passes into journalism, and writes appreciations of new books. He gives his advice, prudently, cites the authorities, ends by insinuating that none of this has any importance. And it is true. Sainte-Beuve, even before he had any inkling of a vocation in criticism, and from the time of his very first essays, seriously interrogated his literary conscience. He had the sense of relationships and relativity. He knew how to dissociate men and works, although his method seemed, on the contrary, to unite them much more closely than anyone—except perhaps the ancients—had ever dared to do before. But he was not unaware that there are men superior to their works, and vice versa. The values that he creates from that moment on are not definitive: he feels and he speaks. But, actually, even if he often has to retouch, he rarely has to erase. (p. 206)

The essential image which we have of Romanticism has been provided by Sainte-Beuve. Writers which he has discussed will always have at least a profile in literary history. We will always have to go to some trouble to make out the lineaments of those about whom he was silent. And this situation will persist, in

spite of all efforts, until such a time as another creator of values comes and revises these paintings. But a parallel with [the French critic and satirist] Boileau could be drawn here: for a long time his authority will probably fare like that of the satirist. It will die down momentarily only to revive again. (p. 207)

During the period following Sainte-Beuve, his authority decreased remarkably, and that in proportion as the years passed. The phenomenon is not unusual and conforms to all that we know of human psychology. It stems from the fact that literary judgments are not purely intellectual—they involve a good deal of sentiment. . . . The result of all this is that the judgments of one generation about the work of following generations often reveal a certain flabbiness. Sainte-Beuve was fond of Baudelaire, but he did not dare to say so. *Madame Bovary* interested him, but he did not know how to distinguish between it and Feydeau's *Fanny*. I think that instead of reproaching Sainte-Beuve for these weaknesses, we would do better to profit from them. (pp. 207-08)

[The] most certain and definitive values that he created were those which found their place between Ronsard and Victor Hugo.

It is he who created Ronsard and the whole Pléiade, and all the excavations that have since been organized into sixteenth century soil.

Today it seems quite natural to love Ronsard and to reread, from time to time, some sonnet from his *Amours*. Before Sainte-Beuve, and outside of a rather narrow circle of inquisitives, Ronsard was esteemed almost to the same extent as Nostradamus. France did not move beyond the singularly erroneous evaluation of this great poet created by Boileau. It is the only judgment of Boileau's that posterity might have cleanly shattered, and it could not do it except with the aid of a Sainte-Beuve. His *Tableau de la poésie française au xvi siècle* seems a bit timorous today, but remember that it was written for the slaves of Boileau. . . . (p. 208)

The second of Sainte-Beuve's creations in the past—we can all name it— is *Port-Royal*. But there he did more than indicate the places where he guessed treasures to be—he himself sank the pickaxe into the burial mound and brought up before astonished eyes a civilization which, while contemporary with *Phèdre* and *Tartuffe*, was also one of catacombs. The discovery of these wild Christians was not without influence on the evolution of religious minds, nor on that of Sainte-Beuve himself. Thus, he knew, in passing from Ronsard to Pascal, the extremes of man's tendencies: he needed no longer be surprised at anything.

To what extent did Sainte-Beuve create the value of Chateaubriand? Such an evaluation would be a delicate matter. There is general agreement in the belief that he intended to disparage Chateaubriand rather than praise him [in *Chateaubriand et son groupe littéraire sous l'empire*]. He appreciated the immense importance of the author of the *Génie*, but he cared little for the man and still less for his tendencies, perhaps because he had submitted to them at the time of his crisis of religiosity. After having first appeared slightly satirical, Sainte-Beuve's portrait of Chateaubriand ended by achieving, in its turn, the perfect resemblance. . . .

Sainte-Beuve fixed the characters of almost all the French writers and some men and women who played an intellectual role from the Renaissance until after the middle of the nineteenth century. The middle ages necessarily escaped him, except for a few figures more historical than literary, and similarly there escaped him, for the reasons that have been given, his contemporaries making the latest news. But everything in between received his mark—he stamped French literature with his own image, and that coinage is still in circulation. (p. 209)

One might say, though with the fear of not being understood, that Chateaubriand and Victor Hugo recreated Gothic architecture. It was dead, it had been scorned for two centuries. Nobody was in the least concerned with it until after the Revolution, when the Consulate suddenly provoked the flowering of a springtime in which everything appeared renewed and rejuvenated. Chateaubriand had portrayed Notre Dame from afar, like a dream-vision. Victor Hugo went inside, made himself at home, rang its bells, and all cathedrals began to resound and revive. Sainte-Beuve, at that very moment, undertaking exactly the work that his century was waiting for, set about remaking French literature. His method, or rather *the* method, for there is only one—was the renewal of motives. . . . [But] for each century the motives for admiration have changed. The one who changes them is the creative critic. In renewing the premises of our judgment, he renews that judgment itself, although it may not vary in its substance, and the work, under this unexpected illumination, appears fresh and almost original. . . . The critical genius of Sainte-Beuve lay in creating gardens and planting trees around chapels which superannuated motives for admiration used to conceal from our own admiration. (p. 210)

> *Remy de Gourmont, ''Sainte-Beuve, Creator of Values'' (originally published in his* Promenades philosophiques, *1904), in his* Selected Writings, *translated and edited by Glenn S. Burne (translation copyright © by The University of Michigan 1966), University of Michigan Press, 1966, pp. 205-10.*

## FERDINAND BRUNETIÈRE  (essay date 1905)

In the eyes of many people Sainte-Beuve's remarkable originality consists in his having transformed criticism from a lifeless analysis of letters to a living biography of men; and nowadays, for many people—too many people—a study of Molière or of Victor Hugo amounts to nothing more than a study of the better-known events of their life. . . . Far be it from me to deny the interest of this kind of knowledge. But Sainte-Beuve was not the man to be blind to the fact that when this tendency is exaggerated the very purpose of criticism is lost. . . . [Before] speaking of men, one must be sure of the value of their work. Psychology, physiology, pathology, and other ''ologies'' certainly are interesting, but it is an interest which cannot but be ancillary. Sainte-Beuve was fully aware of it, and, unless I am very much mistaken, that is what is noticeable in the writings of his second style, the masterpiece of which is his **''Port Royal.''**

No less clearly did he see, though he failed to say so frankly and emphatically enough, what was the fallacy of such biographical criticism and in what way it was misleading. (p. 515)

So true is it that a genuine writer, if only he is inspired with the importance of his subject, forgets himself whilst dealing with it, or, as it is sometimes expressed, subordinates himself to it and puts into it as little of himself as he can, and that involuntarily. That is what Sainte-Beuve, had he not known it already, would have learned at the school of Port Royal. . . .

[I look upon **''Port Royal''**] almost as a model of the way in which literary history should be written, almost, indeed, as the masterpiece of French criticism in the nineteenth century. I do not agree with all its opinions, but I am an enthusiastic admirer of the whole, including the digressions which, with their profusion and diversity, express so well the contingency, mobility and hazard in the sequence of this world's events. Even the style itself does not displease me, with its reticence, its ''repentings'' and all its tangled metaphors, which it is so easy to ridicule for their labored affectation. That extreme precision is never anything more than a means of driving home the analysis of ideas or of completing the delineations of character more scientifically. And if, with the purpose of depicting these characters, or of explaining the minds of the seventeenth century, it sometimes comes about that the author takes the standpoint of his contemporaries, I cannot blame him for it, for it is a way of demonstrating, with a long gradation of shades, the perennity of human nature, and the fact that not only a whole period of our history, but even the whole of psychology may be found within the four walls of one monastery. (p. 517)

In the **''Causeries du Lundi''** the curiosity of the critic is found to be averse to nothing, his powers are equal to any subject of topical interest which current events suggest for his discussion; his case and his adaptability are in no way inferior to his erudition. Mere ordinary monographs, as he called them; and, technically, they are nothing more; but it is difficult to imagine anything more instructive than these monographs; and when read one after another in unbroken succession and without a pause, these monographs give us a glimpse of connections and sequences, as the author himself saw them; and all these ''observations of detail''—the too modest expression is his own—concur and converge in a common end and aim which might be termed ''the natural history of the mind.'' To draw in outline the ''natural history of the mind'' was the purpose of Sainte-Beuve's criticism, a purpose which he was no doubt capable of discovering and adopting for himself—that is clear enough in the **''Causeries''**—but a purpose whose full import was not brought home to him until some time later; in fact—and perhaps it is time to insist on this—not until he came under the influence of those who are considered—and rightly so—his disciples. (pp. 518-19)

[We] scarcely ever mention—if indeed we ever do—the influence of his disciples and his successors; and yet what writer or what artist ever escaped that influence, however small his share in life? There is more Quinault in Corneille than is usually supposed, and in Victor Hugo there is almost as much Leconte de Lisle. In much the same way Taine and Renan are disciples of Sainte-Beuve, but disciples whose principles, nay ideas, Sainte-Beuve did not disdain to adopt, and just as there is some Sainte-Beuve in the ''Etudes d'histoire religieuse'' or in the ''Essais de critique et d'histoire,'' so there is some, and just as much, Taine and Renan in the last volumes of the **''Causeries du Lundi''** and more in the **''Nouveaux Lundis.''** When disciples develop the ideas of a master and carry them to their limits, they bring about two results: in the first place, they set in prominent relief whatever systematic interdependence those ideas may have; secondly, they indicate exactly the boundaries which he will not exceed. For this service Sainte-Beuve is indebted to the Taines and the Renans. Whatever Sainte-Beuve saw of the expression of a reality or of the outlines of a future science in that ''natural history of men's minds''—a nomenclature which may at first have been a mere metaphor to him—he owed it to the novel precision which Renan in his early writings gave to the physiological conception of Race. And Taine's ideas of the ''mutual dependences''—which, according to the theory, unify in one ''order'' Colbert, the gardens at

Versailles, Lebrun's battle scenes, and Racine's tragedies, making them all mere manifestations of the same phase of thought or feeling—all this, as it were, conveyed—if not actually revealed—to Sainte-Beuve the definite expression of what he had instinctively caught glimpses of in his **"Port Royal"** or in his **"Causeries du Lundi."** (pp. 519-20)

I will not attempt to establish a comparison between the **"Nouveaux Lundis"** and the **"Causeries du Lundi"**; I will express no preference; I want to limit myself to one remark. The **"Nouveaux Lundis,"** together with the first of his **"Portraits Contemporains,"** are undoubtedly that portion of his critical work which is most like him. . . . [There] are a dilettantism, a scepticism, and at the same time an optimism, which are the expression of the last phase of Sainte-Beuve's thought; and it is fortunate for him and for us that the excess of it is hidden by his love of literature. If he had ceased to believe in all else (and such a change would not have been a great wrench to him), if he had come to disbelieve even those things which he fancied he believed, he would still have had faith in the power of an apposite word, in the value of a cæsura or a run-on line, in the relative worth of the various styles, in literary glory, in, I am tempted to add, the sacerdotal dignity of criticism; and he was right, for that is what has made his name survive him. (pp. 520-21)

[If] in the history of the nineteenth century (one of its claims to originality is having applied criticism to all things, even where it was not required), the name of Sainte-Beuve is and remains representative of and synonymous with criticism itself, we may feel assured that he owes it to his constant and passionate love of literature. He had not always a full measure of love for literary men, especially if they were his contemporaries; I have not sought to palliate the fact. This is no funeral oration, nor is it an academical panegyric. But I feel bound to say emphatically that he was a true lover of literature; he loved it with intensity and he loved it in all its manifestations. I might even go further and say, that in all the manifestations of the human mind as revealed by word or writing, he looked for literature and found it. (pp. 521-22)

> *Ferdinand Brunetière, "Sainte-Beuve," in* The Living Age *(copyright 1905, by the Living Age Co.), n.s. Vol. XXVII, No. 3177, May 27, 1905, pp. 513-22.*

**ANATOLE FRANCE**   (essay date 1913)

[Sainte-Beuve's biographical preface to *Póesies de Joseph Delorme*] was a fair chance for open confession of self under an assumed name; to show the world all the ideas, passions and feelings fermenting in the headpiece of a young man of decent class, who had vision and understanding for all things, while remaining no one, and living on sixpence a day.

And what is Joseph Delorme, if not young Sainte-Beuve, set forth, studied and adorned with all the lugubrious trappings of the period? (p. 271)

Joseph Delorme is very much like his literary progenitors, [Goethe's Werther, Chateaubriand's René, Constant's Adolphe, and, above all, Sénancour's Obermann]. His whole life was indicated in advance by Sénancour in these few lines: "He had no misfortunes of a striking kind; but, at his entry on this life, he found himself in the ruts of distaste and depression; he stuck in them, he lived in them, grew old in them, before his time, and there he perished."

But Joseph's point of originality was to be frankly middle-class, with no trace of the aristocrat. He is middle-class in birth and in mind; his verse is middle-class even as he is, and is devoted almost exclusively to depicting the average existence. His biography is a small thing handled with much art. Nowadays we are tempted to smile at his recital of sorrows much more imaginary even than himself. (pp. 271-72)

The poems of Joseph Delorme, though mingled of sentiment and inspiration and very diverse in tone, are familiar poems: herein lay their originality. Sainte-Beuve was to some degree an innovator; he proffered pictures of small things, an elegy of detailed incident.

His nature and instinct worked together to make him go as far as possible in the direction of the particular and the precise. His bent is so well determined that when he sings of Italy he invokes no heroic shade. Addressing himself to some fair, humble peasant girl, he will say to her:

> What to me are memories of old time,
> And laurels eternal in which I have no faith!
> But tell me, nor cease to tell,
> O young Neapolitan,
> Harmonious sounding names of woodland trees
> And names whereby you know the hills,
> and every spring,
> And the white houses I see on my horizon.

And he will know a thousand details beyond, a thousand small facts, each nothing in itself, but facts that, put one with another and one after another, make up the whole of life.

He would have domesticated the ode itself, and made into a vehicle of intimacy that which had ever been, whether in celebration of the State or of the Prince, a noble utterance and a sounding pomp: "Quand ton poêle s'éteint" (when your stove goes out), he says in his ***Ode to David the sculptor.***

He was more at home in his use of the elegy, and used every refinement of detail. Not Lamartine, nor Vigny, nor Hugo, nor any other French poet, had tried to do anything like it; Sainte-Beuve went elsewhere for his models. . . . He made himself familiar with Shelley and Wordsworth, and with Crabbe and Cowper, all those true poets, natural and pure, who gave us a poetry suited to man's latest birth, a poetry bearing the delicate impress of modern feeling. (pp. 274-76)

Sainte-Beuve's aspirations are not all purity. . . . Sainte-Beuve's was, elementally, a tortured nature, troubled and harsh. In *Joseph Delorme* is one very odd piece that every reader has scored in his time and whereon I must necessarily pause a moment. You will guess that I am going to speak of the ***Rayons jaunes***—the Yellow Rays. Sainte-Beuve read one day in Mademoiselle Volland's correspondence, a new observation and a fruitful one, such as the magnanimous and talkative Diderot was throwing out all of his life long on every side. This is the passage, as Sainte-Beuve himself was scrupulous to point out:

> A simple physical quality may prove a leading string to the mind which lends itself to it, and guide it to an infinity of different matters. Take a colour, yellow for instance: gold is yellow, silk is yellow, straw is yellow; to how many other threads may this thread not lead? The lunatic does not notice the change; he holds a stalk of shining yellow straw in his hand, and exclaims that he has seized a ray of sunlight.

Hereupon Sainte-Beuve devised a sort of elegy in strophes, in the course of which he gathered together various memories and fancies linked by the yellow thread suggested by Diderot. Starting with a ray from the setting sun, traversing his room, he links up the church where in his childhood he saw the *yellow* lamps and the *yellowed* brow of the old priest, with the *yellow* ivory of the crucifix, and the *yellow* missal which is the believer's solace, then with the *yellow* candles round the deathbed of his old aunt, then with the *yellowed pallium* of the marriage service which never shall be held out over his own head, condemned (he does not say why) to single loneliness, and finally with the rose which shall never *yellow* above his deserted grave. The sequence of ideas is not forced; and it should have a natural effect to give the impression of a random train of thought. It does nothing of the sort, however. The poem lacks naturalness. It is laboured and affected, and the reason is not far to find. We are not led from one idea to another by analogies of form, colour, or scent, except on condition of not perceiving the thread of connection which guides us, or rather leads us astray. As soon as we see it, we break it. Sainte-Beuve, on the contrary, sets himself to show the leading string. As he exerts himself to show how this is yellow and that is yellow, he seems to say to one: "Observe how ingeniously I pass from one yellow to another." But this is not to let the fancies flow, it is the laborious winning of a wager. He would have been better inspired if, in assembling his images of like shade, he had done as the man of whom Diderot speaks, the madman who does not follow his own change of thought; such as each one of us may be, in his hour. (pp. 277-79)

Apart from the English influence, and putting on one side the little poems not wanting in purity and interest, the *Poésies de Joseph Delorme* lack calm, lack serenity. The language is as distorted as the thought. The verse is involved, but, though laboured and distasteful, is not vulgar. This poetry of his goes on a lame foot, but, alternatively, it keeps within bounds. In other words, it is a fermented liquor, rough and sharply-flavoured, but it has its bouquet and savour. (p. 280)

[The *Consolations* breathe] the liveliest and tenderest devotion for Victor Hugo. Sainte-Beuve was tormented . . . with an overweening desire for communion and for marriage. . . . The dedication of the *Consolations* is an ejaculatory prayer the meaning and bearing of which is not to be understood to-day. I imagine that, strongly attached as he was in those days to [Hugo,] the author of *Cromwell,* he found his greatest pleasure in concocting devotional exercises in the style of St. Teresa or St. Catherine of Sienna. The master he so greatly venerated he did not imitate in deed. He never risked the flamboyant, and avoided all cast-off trappings of romantic mediævalism as one would the plague. The *Consolations* are elegies of intimacy; a conversation, a walk, something read, some incident of domesticity, furnish the subject-matter of these little poems, wholesome and sweet of inspiration in spite of certain touches of a sensuous mysticism. They show an affectation of piety altogether different from piety itself. Religion is, for him, a seasoning which lends additional savour to voluptuousness. (pp. 282-83)

There is small aspiration or self-disclosure, and no word of love, in the *Pensées d'août.* The poet no longer pours out his plaint; he says what he has to say. Sainte-Beuve, speaking of his *Pensées d'août,* said jokingly: "I had given them *Joseph Delorme,* and the *Consolations;* I had nothing left but a rat's tail, and I twisted it as I could." Rat's tail or beaver's tail, it is certainly curiously twisted.

*Les Pensées d'août* bordered on prose; Sainte-Beuve, as he said himself, made his verse "simple, at will"; he thought he had discovered a *musa pedestris* [pedestrian muse], a note suited to age and wisdom. . . . The longest of the poems, *Monsieur Jean,* surprised and wounded public susceptibilities.

The *Monsieur Jean* in question is a natural son of Jean-Jacques Rousseau, turned village schoolmaster and remaining simple and brave in his faith and way of life. . . . The poet conceives of it as a Puritan may, and relates it in familiar style. The tale as set out, is grey, and sad and painful. One follows it with that indefinable feeling of weariness and melancholy, attended by a charm of sadness, that we may experience in trudging across an impoverished country-side under a rain-charged sky, along roads deep with ruts. (pp. 286-87)

Sainte-Beuve gave himself scope in [*Pensées d'août*]. He twists his fancies as seems good to him. (p. 288)

[This] has repelled readers, who have not cared to seek out from amidst these unpleasing eccentricities the delicate and charming verse which is there in plenty. (p. 289)

*Joseph Delorme,* the *Consolations,* and the *Pensées d'août* mark the diverse aspects of a single nature. We see Sainte-Beuve in them, always himself, under three different aspects. It is so with all of us. We never rest the same for a moment, and yet we are never other than what we are. We are always in motion, but we never change. Sainte-Beuve, under his three poetical habits, shows himself even as the sensual, troubled, perspicacious man he could not but be, so long as he was Sainte-Beuve. The rest is accidental, and matter of circumstance. We see him in *Joseph Delorme* under the scourge of sharp desire, and still retaining his youthful illusion of unhappiness. It is the last to be got rid of. One believes for long that one is loaded with singular ill-fortune, and dowered with a magnificent gift of sadness. And then we make the discovery one fine day that this is vanity, and that even when we grieve we tread the common path of all. The *Consolations* mark this moment in life. Sainte-Beuve here shows himself as tranquil as it was possible for him to be, almost at peace, satisfied almost; and this is why his emotion is purged and his self-expression softened in tone. But desire, which alone lent beauty to things, dies down with age. (pp. 289-90)

To understand and to explain becomes our sole care. We use words for mere recital, as matter of interest, without feeling or fire, and we come to the *Pensées d'août.*

So, following the poet in his course, we see the whole man. Thus nothing must be overlooked in this poetry in which is depicted for our eyes the most searching, sagacious, and complicated spirit that an ageing civilization has ever produced. (p. 290)

*Anatole France, "Sainte-Beuve, Poet," in his* The Latin Genius, *translated by Wilfrid S. Jackson (translation copyright, 1924, by Dodd, Mead and Company, Inc.; originally published as* Le génie latin, *A. Lemerre, 1913), John Lane/The Bodley Head, 1924, pp. 267-90.*

## MARCEL PROUST (essay date 1919?)

[*In his noted critical work,* Contre Sainte-Beuve, *Proust discusses his view of literature in relation to the concepts of Sainte-Beuve. Proust, in complete opposition to Sainte-Beuve, considers the artist's "personal vision," rather than the superficial facts of the artist's personal life, to be his primary creative source "A book," he states, "is the product of a different self from the self we manifest in our habits, in our social life, in our vices." In the following essay, Proust denounces the heavily biographical critical method that Sainte-Beuve outlined in his 1862 essay (see excerpt above) and ultimately views Sainte-Beuve's poetry as his only worthwhile work.]*

Sainte-Beuve's great work does not go very deep. The celebrated method which . . . made him the peerless master of nineteenth-century criticism, this system which consists of not separating the man and his work, of holding the opinion that in forming a judgment of an author—short of his book being "a treatise on pure geometry"—it is not immaterial to begin by knowing the answers to questions which seem at the furthest remove from his work (How did he conduct himself, etc.), nor to surround oneself with every possible piece of information about a writer, to collate his letters, to pick the brains of those who knew him, talking to them if they were alive, reading whatever they may have written about him if they are dead, this method ignores what a very slight degree of self-acquaintance teaches us: that a book is the product of a different *self* from the self we manifest in our habits, in our social life, in our vices. If we would try to understand that particular self, it is by searching our own bosoms, and trying to reconstruct it there, that we may arrive at it. Nothing can exempt us from this pilgrimage of the heart. . . . (pp. 99-100)

At no time does Sainte-Beuve seem to have understood that there is something special about creative writing and that this makes it different in kind from what busies other men and, at other times, busies writers. He drew no dividing line between the state of being engaged in a piece of writing and the state when in solitude, stopping our ears against those phrases which belong to others as much as to us, and which whenever we are not truly ourselves, even though we may be alone, we make use of in our consideration of things, we confront ourselves and try to catch the true voice of the heart, and to write down that, and not small-talk. (p. 103)

[Sainte-Beuve's] implication that there is something [especially] superficial and empty in a writer's authorship, something deeper and more contemplative in his private life is due to nothing else than the special-pleading metaphor of Necessity. In fact, it is the secretion of one's innermost life, written in solitude and for oneself alone, that one gives to the public. What one bestows on private life—in conversation, that is, however refined it may be . . . or in those drawing-room essays, whittled down to suit a particular circle and scarcely more than conversation in print—is the prouduct of a quite superficial self, not of the innermost self which one can only recover by putting aside the world and the self that frequents the world; that innermost self which has waited while one was in company, which one feels certain is the only real self, and which artist—and they only—end by living for, like a god whom they less and less often depart from, and to whom they have sacrificed a life that has no purpose except to do him honour. Admittedly, from the time Sainte-Beuve began writing the *Lundis,* he did not only change his way of life; he attained to the idea—not a very elevated one—that a life of forced labour, such as he was leading, is inherently more fertile, and, for such characters as are indolent by choice, necessary, since without it they would not yield their fruit. (pp. 104-05)

But Sainte-Beuve remained unable to understand that world apart, shuttered and sealed against all traffic with the outer world, the poet's soul. He believed that it could be counselled, stimulated, repressed, by other people. . . . And so, by failing to see the gulf that separates the writer from the man of the world, by failing to understand that the writer's true self is manifested in his books alone, and that what he shows to men of the world (or even to those of them whom the world knows as writers but who can only resume that character when they put the world behind them) is merely a man of the world like themselves, Sainte-Beuve came to set up that celebrated Method which . . . is his title to fame, and which consists, if you would understand a poet or a writer, in greedily catechising those who knew him, who saw quite a lot of him, who can tell us how he conducted himself in regard to women, etc.—precisely, that is, at every point where the poet's true self is not involved.

His books, especially **Chateubriand et son groupe littéraire,** seem like drawing-rooms opening out of each other, whither the author has invited various conversationalists, who are questioned about the distinguished persons they have known and whose evidence is foredoomed to clash with evidence given by others, and thus to show that in the case of men whom we are wont to praise there is much to be said on both sides, or that those who don't agree must represent a different type of mind.

And there are discrepancies, not betwixt the two sources, but coexisting in the bosom of one visitor. Leaving no stone unturned, Sainte-Beuve remembers an anecdote, goes to find a letter, invokes the witness of some grave eminent person who was philosophically warming his toes, but is more than ready to put in his word or two to prove that a person who has just said one thing meant quite another. (pp. 106-07)

Sainte-Beuve never altered his shallow conception of the creative mind; but his pinchbeck ideal was irrevocably forfeited. Necessity compelled him to renounce his way of life. (p. 107)

At times I wonder if after all Sainte-Beuve's best work is not his poetry. All play of wit is at an end. Things are no longer approached obliquely with a hundred ingenuities and conjuring-tricks. The sorcerer's magic circle is broken. As though the persevering falsehood of his thought had derived from the artificial dexterity of his style, when he leaves off writing prose, he leaves off telling lies. As a student obliged to put his thoughts into Latin is obliged to lay them bare, Sainte-Beuve for the first time comes face to face with reality, and feels straightforwardly about it. There is more honest feeling in the **Rayons Jaunes,** in the **Larmes de Racine,** in any of his poems, than in his prose works. Yet if falsehood forsakes him, all his advantages fly from him too; like some habitual drinker put on a milk diet, along with his artificial vigour, he loses all his strength. . . . Nothing could be more touching than this technical destitution in the great spell-binding critic, practised in all the elegancies, fine shadings, drolleries, all the emotional effects, all the paces and graces of style. All are gone. Out of his vast store of culture, his technical accomplishment, nothing is left to him except the ability to reject anything pompous, stale, or extravagant, and there is an austere refinement in the choice of imagery that in a way recalls the studied perfection of André Chénier's poetry, or that of Anatole France. But all that is an Act of Taste, not his own. He tries to do what he admires in Theocritus, or Cowper, or Racine. Of his own, of what was involuntarily and profoundly his own, almost the only thing is clumsiness. It comes back and back, as if it were a natural tone of voice. But this handful, this charming handful of his poems—charming, and also sincere—this skilful and sometimes successful attempt to express the purity of love, the sadness of dusk in a great city, the spell of memory, the thrill of reading, the woe of unbelieving old age, shows, because one feels it is the only genuine thing about him, the emptiness of the whole of his marvellous, enormous, ebullient work as a critic; since all these marvels come back to this: *Les Lundis,* the outward show; a little poetry, the reality. In the scales of eternity, a critic's verses outweigh all the rest of his works. (pp. 118-19)

> *Marcel Proust, "The Method of Sainte-Beuve" (1919?), in his* Marcel Proust on Art and Literature 1896-1919, *translated by Sylvia Townsend Warner (© 1958 by Meridian Books, Inc.; reprinted by permission of Georges Borchardt, Inc., as agents for the author; in Canada by the Literary Estate of Sylvia Townsend Warner and Chatto & Windus Ltd.; originally published as* Contre Sainte-Beuve, *Librairie Gallimard, 1954), Meridian Books, 1958, pp. 94-119.*

## WILLIAM FREDERICK GIESE (essay date 1931)

[*Giese's study is the first book-length English analysis of Sainte-Beuve's criticism. While Giese acknowledges Sainte-Beuve's naturalistic, classic, and Romantic traits, he does not restrict Sainte-Beuve to any single movement or method. Ultimately, Giese considers Sainte-Beuve's study of literature to be "a document for the study of human nature."*]

Sainte-Beuve's greatest contribution to criticism, aside from his constant revelation that taste and good sense are the soul of it, lay in his use of the historic and biographic elements, and in the large place he gave to character painting. His use of physiology, his naturalism, appears to be, in spite of his own and his critics' emphasis on it, very secondary. It seems less an outcome of his own realism, which did at least as much to restrain as to promote it, than an expression of the spirit of the age. (p. 176)

It was undeniably Sainte-Beuve's own very positive demand for the unadulterated truth that made him find the old rhetorical criticism inadequate. It led him to expand, more than anyone had yet done, the range of criticism by opening so many windows on the past, by multiplying historic sidelights. It was his native talent for seeing life and literature as twin stars, that led him to treat author and book as inseparable. But his naturalism, the moment it assumes a scientific aspect, seems only a half-hearted concession to external influences. If, as he repeatedly acknowleged, the final secret of genius is bound always to elude us, then we can at best hope to see it in outline and no more. The critic can only clarify the outline, he can only supplement the work that embodies the genius, he cannot replace the work. The magic remains with the magician. Physiology, as used by Sainte-Beuve, emits vague conjectures as to the origins of genius, but it never tries to solve the riddle of its nature. (pp. 176-77)

One may be a born naturalist, so to speak, one to whom the very idea of nature, her omnipresent power and majesty, appeal irresistibly, so that she is accepted without question and without protest as the great first cause and the final explanation of all things. That is the way in which the extreme scientific thinker is a naturalist. One may also be a naturalist simply because one's logic is refractory to supernatural explanations, because one is, in Sainte-Beuve's words, "one of those simple-minded folk whom the supernatural always estranges." Sainte-Beuve is a naturalist in this manner. He has nothing of Diderot's intoxication with nature, nothing of Renan's worshipful immersion in the scientific vision of nature. He views her im-

partially and without enthusiasm—and with the normal human aloofness. His acceptance is little more than non-rejection. His understanding only is involved, not his imagination. (pp. 177-78)

Naturalism is his guess, at times even his working hypothesis; it is not his gospel. He may, in the remoter reaches of his thought, land in it; he does not, like Taine, set out from it. He starts from the phenomenon itself, and, in accepting nature, he refuses to impose any system whatever upon it. It is to him a fact, a universe of facts, not a system. (p. 179)

Sainte-Beuve recognized, as all but the most obstinate reactionaries needs must do, that the body influences the spirit. He inclined to think that the physical peculiarities, the sound or depraved health, the temperate or the excessive mode of living of an author are potent in shaping his work, and at times he tried to utilize such considerations in his judgments. That such things profoundly influence men is undeniable, and the critic who could measure as well as affirm the connection would indeed enrich us with invaluable knowledge. We may agree with Sainte-Beuve when he says that if one is to play a great part the body as well as the spirit must be tributary, and that broken health is the explanation of many things. (pp. 180-81)

Sainte-Beuve, in his scientific zeal, now and then gives temporary encouragement to those who fancy that men of letters are classifiable phenomena. He dreams of a time to come when it will be possible, thanks to our accumulated knowledge of detail, to set up classifications and to outline large groups and "families of minds" having common properties. The mysterious dispensations of heredity may also, he hopes, become more apprehensible through study of the ancestry or the immediate kindred of men of genius. Do we, however, find the physiologically significant detail habitually pressed for its meaning by Sainte-Beuve, and do we find these "families of minds" defined and at least tentatively set before us? On the contrary, the physiological detail is usually introduced by him for its picturesque value or its human interest, as a side-thought or an after-thought. It plays no real part. (p. 182)

Everybody who rejects the supernatural is a naturalist—but the vital question is the rigor with which this naturalism is interpreted. Sainte-Beuve had always a sane, a temperate, and a dignified conception of human nature. He did not grub in its animal origins to explain its higher manifestations; he did not paint it revolving in a narrow orbit of inexorable prescription; he views it in its finer avatars with an expectant awe and wonder, concerned at its failures, rejoicing at its achievements, its free and soaring flights, and its sublime potencies. That is the attitude of the humanist. Let us cling to it as long as science will allow. (p. 188)

Sainte-Beuve reads between the lines of his literary documents. He applies his power of divination to extract the truth from the half-truth that is substituted for it, sometimes by the voluntary, oftener still by the involuntary, trickery of human nature, which achieves such consummate skill in deceiving others only because it has perfected this skill by unremitting practice in deceiving itself. We say, and rightly, that for knowing an author there is no source so precious as his correspondence. Yet with what caution we must read it! (p. 216)

Sainte-Beuve has so keen a sense for the particular coloring of a given moment in the past, that he sometimes hints that no amount of posthumous initiation can ever enable us to repeat the lost experience in its virtual integrity. (p. 217)

Sainte-Beuve was . . . of all men the least willing to give up the individual and to reduce him to mere ancient history. In spite of the difficulty, he valiantly attempts, even in dealing with the older authors, to wring from the avaricious hand of time the precious particles of truth that it tries to withhold from posterity. He devotes himself with infinite zeal to piecing together the scattered fragments of personalities long since effaced and to reanimating the *disjecta membra* [pieces tossed about] or lost lives. According to Pascal, the more intelligent a man is, the more he sees of diversity in other men. In this respect, no one was ever more intelligent than Sainte-Beuve. No two men are ever alike for him (despite his faint hope that we may in time learn the science of grouping them into families!). His bent for detecting the special qualities of each man seems almost co-extensive with that of nature in varying them. With what convincing skill he can set up in ten lines a life-sized human figure! (p. 218)

[Anecdotes] are a very large element in Sainte-Beuve's criticism. A whole volume of them might be culled from his work, and a not inconsiderable knowledge of French literature might be derived from such a volume. This device is, of course, nowise new. It is as old as human curiosity, and was perhaps originally practiced in some awkward fashion, by our first parents as they began to grow in experience. (p. 220)

[An anecdote] often fixes indelibly a trait of character; it sums up picturesquely a personality; it conveys indirectly what it might seem ungracious to formulate; it gives us the pleasure, so dear to human nature, of smiling at a weakness in a fellow-mortal. Though not altogether just or ideally true, it gives us lucidity on the most economical terms and in the most lively form. (p. 222)

[Some] anecdotes reveal a single and sometimes gigantic weakness; nothing more. Other anecdotes carry a larger suggestiveness, and afford at least a shrewd hint as to a whole character. (p. 223)

The anecdote also plays a large part in Sainte-Beuve's criticism as a literary ornament, a flower that rises into sudden bloom in the midst of a disquisition, or that pleasantly arrests and reposes the eye at the terminus of some little bypath of his thought. (p. 225)

[The] personal approach to literature through the author, [the] prefixing of his portrait as a frontispiece and a spiritual guide to his work, is so integral a part of Sainte-Beuve's criticism that his method, if he may be said to have a method, is to be found here and not elsewhere. His originality lies in the unique excellence of his practice, in the unexampled diagnostic tact with which he carried on his study of the individual. (pp. 226-27)

Sainte-Beuve is in complete revolt from the old-fashioned criticism which so reverently created the man of genius in the image of his work, which insisted on seeing its splendors and its grandeur reflected in his personality—and on seeing there nothing besides—the criticism typified by the ideal statue or the godlike bust.

There is a very constant danger that the individual shall be exalted into a type, embodying in high relief and idealized falsity some unduly simplified conception of the author as he chose to appear in his work, or as he posed in actual life, or as the public, in need of a hero or an apostle or a harlequin, capriciously chose to pose him. (p. 228)

To sum up in Sainte-Beuve's own words: "Perhaps it is a duty not to tell everything about the great writers, to veil a side that is feeble, petty, useless, human, hostile to the statue. Certainly admiration, that vivifying soul of criticism, which it is so important to transmit, gains by this abstention; the religion of genius is not violated."

Observe that Sainte-Beuve introduces this last statement with a *perhaps*. That is because he has still a last remnant of hesitation. His theory, his method, are not at one with his taste. The main drift of his work is in another direction. . . . If he tends to grant plenary indulgence to a very select few—to no one, assuredly, among his contemporaries, or, I should even say, to no one this side of the seventeenth century—he tends also, in less gracious moods, a little to forget the special dispensation accorded. (p. 232)

[Neither] genius nor works have always been necessary in order to invite the action of Sainte-Beuve's critical faculty. His primary interest was in the individual. An author was not for him a person who wrote (and perhaps lived), but a person who lived—and incidentally grafted some literary fruitage on the tree of life. Literature is at times only his pretext and history his real subject. And in either field he does not demand a great name but only an interesting figure. (p. 235)

In human conduct a long interval separates the act from the motive, and another long interval separates the motive from the personality that entertained it and gave it its individual coloring. We learn the action, we calculate the motive, we conjecture the personality. Herein lies Sainte-Beuve's peculiar art; he restores these lost or hidden connections with such convincingness that the personality which he is studying seems itself restored to life. But in so far as this is accomplished it is accomplished by a rare gift of divination, an instinctive faculty for reading character. (p. 239)

Sainte-Beuve tends to utilize literature as a document for the study of human nature, rather than for its thought and its art. (pp. 239-40)

Many of the questions that Sainte-Beuve puts to an author seem alien to the spirit of literature. Why inquire whether that dry old Jansenist Nicole had or had not let the love of woman mingle with his fear of God? It seems impertinent to ask this, and most critics would but ask the question fruitlessly. Yet Sainte-Beuve is so keenly alive to every sort of literary influence, to every rivulet that winds its way into the stream through the society that lines its banks, that for him such a question at once takes on a literary aspect and significance. He notes a certain dryness in Nicole's style and a corresponding insensitiveness in his taste. (pp. 240-41)

There are, on the other hand, some questions that Sainte-Beuve fails to ask, or presses very lightly when asked. He speaks curiously little of the scholastic education of those of whom he writes, and apparently does not regard this prolonged sojourn in the ante-room of experience as very significant. He emphasizes always the sense for reality which contact with the world imposes on one's thought; he looks to it for that "freedom from what is scholastic, from that purely literary enthusiasm which savors of the class in rhetoric and prolongs it beyond its proper term." What attracts him is the first steps of genius in the world, its earliest affiliations, the group of living and stimulating influences it falls into. (pp. 241-42)

[The] real value of criticism lay for Sainte-Beuve in the total coloring given to a literary judgment or impression by the critic's own mind. He recognized that this is founded on the quick intuitions of taste, which requires to be in its turn fed from rich sources of knowledge—of the appropriate kind, the kind that confers initiation, that corrects, deepens and vivifies the critic's faculties, a many-sided yet intimate knowledge akin to the diagnostic scent of the great physician who, instead of being a specialist in the disorders of some specific organ, has a peculiarly keen sense for whatever in a general way distinguishes disease from health. (p. 245)

There is . . . in Sainte-Beuve's criticism at its best—and no writer is more frequently and more easily at his best—an intensity of life, a harmonious play of the whole concert of faculties operating in unison and at high tension, with a suggestion at the same time of delightful freedom from effort and strain, as though he were born for this special performance. In short, no man of his age shows more palpably the marks of genius absolutely adequate to its task.

He had, beyond all other critics, what may be called multiple consciousness, a quickening intelligence that animated the whole body of his knowledge and seemed to be present at all points at the same time. (pp. 256-57)

His style has a marked unction whenever he speaks of the things of the past which time has spared and consecrated. He dwells with an unforgettable thrill of reminiscent pleasure on any stray remnant of vanishing tradition that he has had the good fortune to gather at first hand from belated representatives of bygone things whom time has suffered to stray into the new age. In their presence he feels—and this is one of the most charming traits of his literary personality—an almost naïve delight; and this delight kindles into a genuine flame of enthusiasm whenever the past comes back to him through the living voice of those who were once a part of it.

This keen sense for what is peculiar to a given moment in the past rendered Sainte-Beuve equally sensitive to what constitutes the individual note or accent of a writer, to that particular intonation which distinguishes his voice, even in a single characteristic utterance, from all other voices. And he distinguishes not less keenly the whole graded gamut of rising or falling notes by which all other writers of the same family are differentiated from the prototype, and echo him each from his respective interval of distance. (pp. 258-59)

Sainte-Beuve is not content to let the dead past bury its dead embalmed in the cold commemoration of conventional eulogy. He has called the necrologies in question, scanned the obituaries, reread the epitaphs, hung a fresh wreath on many a long-neglected grave, and he has recited in the ear of a momentarily attentive public the shrunken titles and honors that appertained to scores of men and women who had dreamed of fame and who had striven for it too feebly to win it, yet with too much charm or too much eloquence to seem deserving of entire forgetfulness. He has interrupted their oblivion and summoned their pale ghosts to walk again in the light of day. But he has gathered so numerous a band of these defunct spirits, and he introduces us to such a bewildering succession of these inarticulate representatives of semi-greatness, that we run much risk of confusing their identities and, from sheer pressure of ghost on ghost, of seeing their momentarily illumined features flash upon us only to fade again into the darkness out of which they were evoked. (p. 260)

The Frenchman, a great master but unhappily also a frequent victim of logic, is never satisfied until he has disposed of a given phenomenon, no matter how complex, by attaching to

it a label that assigns it to some fixed class. The young Sainte-Beuve is labelled *romantic*. The mature Sainte-Beuve is labelled *classic*. In reality, the matter is not quite so simple. The secret of Sainte-Beuve's broad outlook and of his catholic sympathies lay in his freedom from all narrowing and theoretic exclusions, in his openness to the appeal of the most varied inspirations, in the exquisite balance, rare in a Frenchman, that he maintained between nature and culture. In the narrow French sense, he is neither classic nor romantic.

The French classic school stood too much aloof from nature and had too little sense of the mysterious fountainhead of power within the individual from which genius draws its primary substance and its indelible character,

> Wild nature's vigor working at the root.

The great writers of the golden age had a profound sense of order, and of all that it can superadd of lucidity, of fineness, and even of force, to the spontaneous power of native talent; but they tended too readily to confound talent itself with the discipline which purifies and directs it. (p. 264)

The French romanticists, on the contrary, if they had a keener sense of the value of the spontaneous element in genius, failed to understand its nature. They found it almost sufficient in itself. They accepted a quantum, though grudgingly inadequate, of discipline in form; the content of literature remained for them absolutely free and instinctive. The self, which they confounded with genius, was for them sacred, and must suffer no pruning or training. This brought them into violent conflict with taste, with morals, and only too often with common-sense. (p. 265)

Sainte-Beuve was profoundly sensitive to the charm of either classic or romantic inspiration, and . . . the magic of genius counted more with him than did principles and standards even the most rational and irrefragable.

He accepts as final neither the classic over-refinement nor the romantic wildness. He seeks a middle ground. He stands at first very near the romanticists, among them rather than of them for the most part, through constraint of temperament and under protest of taste; later he takes his stand visibly nearer to the classicists, so near as to seem in turn almost identified with them. (p. 274)

Sainte-Beuve is classic in temper more than in theory. He is in his day . . . the one outstanding heritor of the traditional taste, though he applies it with unexampled elasticity. This temper manifests itself in his love for moderation in all things—so much so that his taste seemed timid to most of his contemporaries. His craving was for subdued tints, for *justesse* rather than for telling effect, though the romantic rhetoric, when its flamboyant colors were not too palpably false, often stirred him to profound admiration. But quieter effects pleased him better and held him more permanently. (p. 276)

Sainte-Beuve, in looking back on the period of his romantic enthusiasm, when he forgets the exasperation caused by the faults and the failures of his idols, constantly renews [an] homage to the romantic spirit and reverts with undiminished zest to "that interval of happy and brilliant fantasy, of free imagination, when he had wandered in the gardens of Alcinous."

In truth, he even has along with the romantic impulse a decided touch of the moral relaxation of mood that so commonly goes with it. His point of view is not always masculine enough to be soundly classic, even in his classic moods. This weak spot in his armor appears especially in his dealings with women. He is apt to appear a little too much a woman himself. This helps marvelously toward understanding them, but it is a hindrance in judging them—expecially when they are so exclusively women as to lack certain complementary masculine virtues. . . . Sainte-Beuve shares somewhat the romantic conception of woman, and that conception is ultimately, under all its flowery adornments, Oriental and degrading. (pp. 277-78)

Sainte-Beuve's conception of poetry remains always tinged, not to say deeply dyed, with romantic colors. . . .

Sainte-Beuve even pushes the demand for freedom of inspiration so far as to sanction the romantic irresponsibility which the younger generation in literature is in every age so fond of arrogating, as if self-expression were the sole end as it is the usual source of the literary impulse. (p. 280)

For one so profoundly sensitive to the particular spirit of each successive age, and to what there is of legitimacy in its demand to give expression to its special modes of thought and feeling, to those phases of which this one unique moment and no other in the tide of time is the predestined and responsible representative, for such a one the phenomenon known as the romantic spirit was not a thing to be judged only by its faults of inexperience, by its errors, by its exaggerations, by its insolent rejections, and by its mad precipitancy of affirmation, in a word by its feverish and sickly sides. To class it with epilepsy or with insanity, as the pseudo-classic critic did (not without provocation, it must be admitted), was to fail in the very thing which Sainte-Beuve regarded as the most fundamental condition of sound and useful criticism, namely that the critic should be in intimate contact with the age he lives in. (pp. 281-82)

It is above all as regards style that the opposition of the old and the new tendencies is most fundamental. The sober and chaste restraint bordering on severity, the stern subordination of form to matter, which is the distinction of the classic style, is profoundly hostile to the exuberance, the opulence of color and of imagery, the indulgence of capricious individualism, the complete outpouring of the cornucopia of special gifts without regard to the underlying harmonic theme, that is so characteristic of the romantic genius. (pp. 288-89)

He has so keen a feeling for the presence and the pressure of life itself behind all manifestations of talent that he feels that style is not alone or mainly a matter of study and practice but has its most vital roots in experience, in the variety and intensity of the outer and the inner life. (p. 289)

It is the faults and the eccentricities of the contemporary writers, rather than the modernism of which they are representatives, that Sainte-Beuve dislikes. Herein lies the explanation of the negative note that is so prominent in his judgments of nineteenth century literature. The age had inherited the anarchy created by the eighteenth century revolt from tradition. It had to live amid this anarchy and had to fashion out of its ruins such fragile and temporary refuges for the spirit as it could contrive. As a critic, Sainte-Beuve was pledged to picture these conditions as they really were, and to estimate their questionable fruitage at its true worth. He felt that the romantic age was not one of the great literary epochs and could not furnish genius, however brilliant, with the material and the background for a great literary monument. (pp. 293-94)

*William Frederick Giese, in his* Sainte-Beuve: A Literary Portrait, *Madison, 1931, 367 p.*

NORMAN H. BARLOW   (essay date 1964)

*[Barlow's study focuses on Sainte-Beuve's poetry and its influence on Charles Baudelaire. He identifies Joseph Delorme as a victim of Romanticism's* mal du siècle, *the melancholy that "ravaged the well-being and life itself of many a young romanticist in nineteenth-century France." He also examines the concept of sensuality as depicted in Sainte-Beuve's novel* Volupté.]

The *Vie de Joseph Delorme,* which served as a prologue to the Delorme poems [in *Vie, poésies et pensées de Joseph Delorme*], announced the portrayal of yet another victim of the *mal du siècle* [unease], which had ravaged the well-being and the life itself of many a young romanticist in nineteenth-century France. . . . Except for an obstinately persistent eighteenth-century rationalism peculiar to Sainte-Beuve rather than typical of the *mal du siècle,* the real Joseph Delorme represented, during his poetic period, a true child of the times. (p. 20)

[A] moral portrait [begins] to emerge from the *Poésies de Joseph Delorme* which is completed in the *Consolations.* At this point we are interested in the signs of spiritual consciousness discernible in this portrait; since it is upon such evidence, and on similar indications in the portrait of Sainte-Beuve's Amaury [in *Volupté*], that the validity of a substantial Beuvean legacy rests.

The essence of the Romantic elegy from Delorme's point of view is stated with sober economy in the poem "Le songe." Like the torchbearer of ancient Olympiads, youth carries into the arena of life the flame of its ambition. Destiny appears to smile upon its visions of glory, and it is quickly intoxicated by all that life seems to offer. But the early dreams of resounding action, love, and artistic fulfillment vanish with experience. When the naïve child is awakened from his dream of pure felicity by the harsh light of worldly reality, the torch of his aspiration henceforth illuminates only his defeat and the unending tediousness of his existence. His illusion is dispersed in the tears of his disenchantment. The basis of Delorme's elegiac mood is thus a sense of deprivation: the loss of, or failure to attain, both the worldly and the transcendental treasures of human life; the wasting of energy in striving for ill-chosen objectives; and the worship of false idols. Among these idols, the poet counts love not least, for in its more spiritual form it provides some satisfaction of his need for the ideal. Yet the purity of young love, destined to be lost or perhaps never known, may fall victim to the temptation of a sensual passion that bears its own disenchantment. Thereafter, the orgies of the senses can be halted only by angelic voices, by time, or by death. With the years comes the need for serenity in love or in art, or even for a meaningful life beyond the grave. The phenomenon of the Romantic *mal du siècle* may be visualized, in the case of Sainte-Beuve's hero, as a hopeful upward movement toward fusion in the ideal, countered by an anticlimactic downward curve of disillusionment and despair. The descent from the original high objective imparts the half-tones of a pale irony to many of the loves of Delorme, loves of negation or compensation under the menace of old age and death. (pp. 21-2)

In the verses "A Alfred de M." [a] . . . supernatural voice, communicated through Delorme's moral intelligence, halts him on the very threshold of triumphant desire. The innocence of youth confronts for the first time the sensuous enchantment of carnal forms. The intoxication of desire, be it for woman's flesh or worldly glory, finds all its power in the desiring, nothing but deception in the satisfaction. The freshness of virgin passion is but a fleeting impression, a felicity progressively corroded by mounting experience. This precarious transport and its irrevocable dissolution with time is the source of the young lover's sadness. The moment of meditation is a flash of universal experience, in which the youth regrets the elusive ideal in all human desire. (p. 24)

There comes a stage in [Delorme's] psychological history . . . in which the promises of first love and promiscuity alike have failed. The frustrated poet is driven to new terrain to seek compensation and consolation. His role henceforth will be that of a successor and consoler, forming new liaisons in which both participants accept something less than the attainment of the first lofty ideals. The full ardor has gone out of love, which is now a fragile emotion of compromise, reservation, restriction. (p. 26)

The propitious circumstances have to be found in which, bridging the tempestuous years between adolescence and maturity, two afflicted souls may seek solace in a new happiness together. In the poem **"La contredanse"** Delorme uses the metaphor of two torrents, which, when the turbulence of early passion subsides, discover each other and flow as two calm springs into a lake of harmony. (p. 27)

The elements of compensation and consolation in the autumn season of love represent for Delorme a diminution of the original ideal felicity. They are the only fruits of a search for what Baudelaire later called the "extase de la vie". The frustrations and imperfections encountered by Delorme in his pursuit of earthly happiness focus attention on the other pole of the hero's spiritual duality. . . . Baudelaire again furnished a definition when he named this other pole the "horreur de la vie". This negative postulation of the spirit embraces a disgust with the experiences of this world prompted by the mysterious attraction of the transcendental—the dream of "saintes voluptés" [voluptuous saints]—and a yearning for penetration of the metaphysical mysteries. Like other artists, the poet is particularly susceptible to the messages of celestial voices. The projection of his spirit beyond this world nullifies mundane values for Joseph Delorme and brings about his ennui, the most striking symptom of the Romantic *mal du siècle,* as well as the basic constituent of modern anguish. (pp. 28-9)

In **"Le soir de la jeunesse,"** Delorme congratulates a friend who by calm philosophy has triumphed over the spiritual tyranny imposed by the transports of erotic passion. But he counsels vigilance against the danger of a relapse following such a victory. There are times when the philosoher can drift into a condition of ennui in which the mind's energy and the heart's newly won tranquillity are devoured by an aimless and futile emotionalism founded on a disappointed early love.

Another special state of spleen derives from complete separation from the normal affections and sentiments of human society—absence of family ties or the bonds of warm friendship. This condition produces in **"La veillée"** a particularly heavy atmosphere of gloom. . . . The psychological desolation of **"La veillée"** finds a parallel in the physical dullness of the rural landscape in **"La plaine."** The atmosphere in this poem is one of deprivation, decay, want, exhaustion, and poverty—a complete negation of fruitfulness. (pp. 30-1)

The condition of solitude which produced the depressing tone of **"La veillée"** and **"La plaine"** has other manifestations in different contexts. It may, for example, be a desirable state, a coveted suspension of time's importunate course in which sensuous fantasies can be indulged. It appears in this form in **"Au loisir."** Solitude in the Delorme poems occurs more often,

however, as an adverse circumstance of destiny, which either moves the poet to revolt or is accepted by him with an almost virtuous stoicism. Thus, in **"Rayons jaunes,"** fate has imposed an absence of the joys of normal human affection in family ties. (p. 32)

The anxiety produced by the effect of time on man's life is an important factor contributing to Delorme's feeling of ennui. In the poems of Joseph Delorme, as generally in French elegiac poetry of the Romantic period, the time theme centers upon two phenomena in the psychological and physical existence of every mortal: first, the curve rising from birth through adolescence into the flower of manhood, and finally falling in the decline of old age to ultimate and irrevocable death; second, the endless repetition of nature's cycle of seasons in opposition to the limited duration of any individual mortal span of life. These two cycles contain the possibility of numerous combinations of irony and contrast deriving from the exorbitant compass of man's desires compared with his relatively narrow restriction in time, space, and opportunity. The wave of ascent and decline in man's life is complicated by the fact that individual lives do not blossom, mature, and decline in unison. This circumstance creates a special irony in the contrast between contemporaneous but unequally developed physical and mental lives. The effect of duration on the human body and its faculties is obviously partly physical, but its poetic significance lies in the subjective impression created and active within the individual psyche. The anguish inherent in the consciousness of time is part of the philosophical tragedy of man's alternation between his spiritual and physical natures. (pp. 32-3)

Delorme's inability to accept the horrors of the purely earthly life is strongly influenced by the promptings of supernatural voices. They speak to him primarily as a poet, and it is as the anguish of the artist that the spiritual tragedy of Sainte-Beuve's hero assumes its most acute form. The comprehension of the universal analogy and the penetration of the transcendental mysteries achieved through poetry become the most frequent forms of escape for the hypersensitive soul oppressed by the evil of the world. Poetic expression becomes the only release of a genius yearning for a return to the unity of the Ideal. Agonizingly conscious of the disharmony between himself and his society, the artist-genius heeds the celestial voices and, by his heroic voyage into the unknown of the ethereal spheres, he offers himself as a sacrifice, through the spiritual tortures inherent in penetrating the awesome secrets of the supernatural. (p. 37)

From the haphazardly compiled collection of the Delorme poems, certain categories of psychological experience emerge, which together form the whole climate of anguish in this particular *malade du siècle.* The disorder of composition makes it highly unlikely that Sainte-Beuve intended for this work any formal unity tantamount to a definite aesthetic of anguish. It rather appears that he was merely conscious of expressing certain sentiments or moods which, while related to his personal life, were also characteristic of the young Romantic of his era. Analysis does, in fact, reveal a basic psychological pattern capable of standing as an aesthetic of the *mal du siècle.* This pattern explains Delorme's Romantic agony in terms of the simultaneous postulation of his soul toward the finite and the infinite, with a dual polarity existing between the *extase de la vie* and the *horreur de la vie.* The rising curve of felicity which depends upon the attraction of the *extase* is countered by a decline of disenchantment activated by the ravages of the *horreur.* Torn between the counter-attractions of the finite world and the transcendental Ideal, the spirit falls into a state of inertia. From this paralysis of the soul there are only two apparent issues. First, there is in the present, finite life an intimation, through poetic creation, of the eternal paradise of the Absolute. This is achieved, for an elect band of divinely inspired artists, by the apprehension of the universal analogy in the poetic transformation of the finite world. Second, in the absence of artistic creation, there is in physical death a release of the spirit to a better life beyond the grave. (pp. 43-4)

The *Consolations* can be viewed as a recapitulation of the spiritual dilemma originally described in the "mal de Joseph Delorme," but in this collection of poems the dualism of the soul is stated in specifically Christian terms. The *extase de la vie* has become the aspiration toward God of a contrite Delorme. The *horreur de la vie* is now a condition of spiritual frustration caused by absence from God. Inherent in the *horreur* are the agonies of vices motivated by the essential ennui of separation from the divine. This separation is otherwise defined as sin. From the Christian perspective, the dual polarity of the human soul is seen as sin, or *horreur,* and divine beatitude, or *extase.* Many of the components of man's total psychological experience can be analyzed from one pole or the other. Thus such varying aspects of life as love, death, spleen, artistic genius, pride, and time can all be related to the concept of man's spiritual frustration; similarly, love, humility, peace, and poetic creation can be related to divine inspiration within the *extase* of spiritual fulfillment.

Love, viewed as a feature of the *horreur de la vie,* assumes a carnal nature and becomes, for the Christian, profane. The desires of the flesh and their satisfaction appear in the poem "A M. Viguier" as the aftermath of a fruitless search for absolute truth by the philosophers of pre-Christian Greece. Habitually youth rejects its early childhood nurture in the sacred word of God, seeking wisdom and peace in the delirium of sensual indulgence. (pp. 48-9)

From the Christian point of view, the most serious aspect of the sins of the flesh is that the individual sinner assumes responsibility for leaving his soul in danger of eternal damnation. For example, in the poem 'A mon ami Leroux," the worship of the idol of sensuality is seen not only as an arrogant defiance of the divine, but also—more agonizing in itself—as a wanton sacrifice of the soul. Intoxicated by sensual pleasures, the spirit slowly becomes incapable of honorable passions.

At the pole of the *horreur de la vie,* death, like carnal love, is nothing but spiritual sterility. Instead of the promise of immortal life, there is substituted a senseless and bestial oblivion, "une mort sans reveil" or "une nuit sans jour" sought often by total engulfment in sensuality ("A mon ami Ulric Guttinguer"). But just as the soul in this life yearns for ideal love, so after its worldly exile it craves to blossom in the beatitude of reunion with the divine ("A Fontenay").

Because nothing but the Divine Absolute can satisfy the highest ardor of the human spirit, man's essential dissatisfaction with the profane produces a state of ennui, which he attempts to dissolve by resorting again to the profane distractions. (p. 49)

The Christian tone of the *Consolations* suggests a contrast between the unstable human conception of time and the immutable unity of divine eternity. Such a contrast is indeed presented in the poem "A M. Auguste le Prévost," which is based upon the notion of oblivion. The dead can find little security in the short memories of the living. Permanent trust should rather be reposed by man in his Divine Creator, who is ever forgiving and never forgetful of His most precious creature. The action of time in changing the spiritual attitude of the individual and in steadily eroding the innocent purity of early years may be examined in the verses addressed "A Mademoiselle—." With the passing of the years, the original pure image of the poet can no longer be recognized by the beloved companion of his childhood. It is now a question, for a soul corrupted by the temptations of the world, of rising to partake again of the "voluptés pures." (pp. 50-1)

Sainte-Beuve has shown that poetic creation is active, because of its pains and frustrations, in the negative field of man's spiritual bipolarity. However, he attaches greater importance to the positive activity of such creation, which can be a true *extase.* He sees the poetic art, in the *Consolations,* as an instrument of God designed to develop and enrich man's spiritual life; for the true poet interprets the divine unity through the symbols of the universal analogy. Of all the poems in this collection, that addressed "A mon ami Leroux" examines most extensively the divine qualities of art in general. (pp. 53-4)

*Volupté* in man, according to Sainte-Beuve, possesses a double nature, in that it is a divine gift corrupted by human perversity—a gift which is potentially both the exaltation and the agony of modern youth. . . . (p. 60)

In his portrayal of Amaury, Sainte-Beuve offers a most penetrating analysis of the insidious invasion of vice into man's moral stronghold. . . .

In examining the subtle process of his own moral collapse, Amaury is careful to distinguish between an earlier stage of interior sin and a subsequent overt consummation of desire. (p. 64)

In the case of Sainte-Beuve's hero, spiritual inertia results from a psychological multivalence which tends to resolve itself into a dual polarity of the psyche. From generalizations applicable to a whole young generation, this multivalence is translated into a system depending on the counter-attractions of specific personalities in Amaury's life. At the most potentially fruitful period of his manhood, he finds himself drawn alternately to three women, as if to three towers in the nether region of Limbo. But this perplexity is always without issue, becoming the punishment of an unredeemed abuse of youth's highest promise. (p. 66)

At the end of Sainte-Beuve's novel, the spiritual will of his hero is firmly established in the field of the sublime pole. In a life of Christian piety, Amaury attains to the true *extase de la vie.* Yet the multivalence in his psyche imposes a highly devious route on his progress toward that final destination. The deviations of this complicated itinerary are best explained by the imbalance within his soul of three categories of love: *agape, eros,* and *Venus.* Agape is here intended to define divine love—the source of absolute good—which flows from God to man and, in return, from man both back to God and outward to other men. Eros refers to the lover's desire for, and preoccupation with, the beloved, implying the negation of himself and, if necessary, of his carnal desires. Venus is intended to suggest carnal desire alone—a largely animal phenomenon which can be, but not always is, associated with the more cerebral passion of eros. (pp. 80-1)

*Norman H. Barlow, in his* Sainte-Beuve to Baudelaire: A Poetic Legacy *(reprinted by permission of the Publisher; copyright ©1964 by Duke University Press, Durham, North Carolina), Duke University Press, 1964, 226 p.**

**RENÉ WELLEK** (essay date 1965)

[Sainte-Beuve] should be described as the greatest representative of the historical spirit in France. . . . True historicism is not simply a recognition of historical conditioning, but a recognition of individuality along with and even through historical change. Sainte-Beuve recognizes both things, and at his best he preserves the delicate balance needed to save himself from relativism or overemphasis on external conditions.

Sainte-Beuve's greatest strength is this sense of individuality, his ceaseless striving to define the special tone, the elusive kernel of a personality, whether of a person in real life or the personality emerging from an author's writings. Clearly he is not always a *literary* critic. Frequently—too frequently from our point of view—he is a historian of manners, a psychologist, or a moralist. (pp. 36-7)

[In] much of Sainte-Beuve's practical criticism, literary study becomes subordinate to biography; the poet has to be penetrated, unmasked, discarded in order to reach the man at the bottom. The method, we would feel today, is entirely mistaken. For our literary critic there is no mask to be torn off; there is no "bottom" in the man rather than the work, no question of "sincerity" that can be answered by comparisons with documents from biography. We can merely plead in Sainte-Beuve's behalf that he grew up in the romantic atmosphere in which poets exalted and exhibited their ego and their private lives without apparent disguise. (p. 39)

But Sainte-Beuve is always a jump ahead of his critics. While he is frankly preoccupied with biography, with the psychology of the writer, and the moral problem of sincerity, he knows very well the difference between art and life, the separateness of the world of imagination, and the obliqueness of the relationships between work and man. (pp. 39-40)

It would be a mistake to reduce a discussion of Sainte-Beuve to the question of biography and to contrast him with the historian Taine. Sainte-Beuve cares for both individuality and history. He wrote prolifically not only on the history of thought, the history of sentiment, and social history but also on literary history in a narrow sense. . . . [*Tableau de la poésie française au seizième siècle*] is closest to pure literary history. Sainte-Beuve treats Renaissance literature largely in terms of its poetic and dramatic techniques. He is primarily interested in questions of diction, style, and prosody, and in the differences between the groups and schools of poets. . . . The *Tableau* is an unenthusiastic, cool, and often unperceptive, descriptive account of the Pléiade, fortified with ample quotations. . . .

[*Port Royal*] does not pretend to be literary history. It is primarily the history of the monastery, of the men and women who inhabited it, and of what Sainte-Beuve calls the spirit of Port Royal. Sainte-Beuve is neither expert in theological arguments nor interested in theology, though he obviously sides with the Jansenists against the Jesuits. He is more concerned with a history of religious sentiments, with the depiction of a spiritual type, of a way of life and a form of feeling and thinking. (p. 42)

*Port Royal* discusses incidentally many literary figures and some literary texts. The book has been criticized for artificially dragging in literary subjects that are only remotely connected with Port Royal and for overrating the literary influence of the movement in 17th-century France. But Sainte-Beuve is very well aware that he uses Port Royal as a kind of thread or point of reference and even pretext for literary history. One must rather admire the skill with which he succeeds in enhancing the appeal

of a subject that appears so specialized and remote from imaginative literature. Among the texts and writers discussed, Corneille's *Polyeucte* and Rotrou's *Saint-Genest* are only tenuously related to Port Royal; Guez de Balzac has hardly anything to do with it and serves rather as a foil, as the antitype of the purely literary man; Molière's *Tartuffe* can be brought in only for its anti-Jesuit overtones. But surely Montaigne, though he precedes Port Royal, is needed for the discussion of Pascal, and Racine can be legitimately treated in his relations with the fathers. Sainte-Beuve is necessarily concerned with the ideas of the literary figures, their attitudes toward religion and the issues of the times, and he makes no attempt to give a sense of literary evolution and change. But he manages to convey something of the history of French literary prose—its metaphorical luxuriance in Montaigne, its struggle for classical clarity and composition, its triumph in Pascal—and to elaborate and substantiate his dislike of what today would be described as the "baroque" style of the age of Louis XIII. (pp. 43-4)

The interpretation of the thought of Montaigne and Pascal must attract the student of literature. Montaigne is seen by Sainte-Beuve as the pagan, "the natural man," the tempter of Pascal, as a malicious demon whose "method can be rightly called perfidious." Pascal, in contrast, appears to Sainte-Beuve as the man of faith, "an Archimedes in tears at the foot of the Cross." Sainte-Beuve rejects the attempt of Cousin to transform Pascal into a skeptic and a man of the world who saved himself only by a leap into faith. Sainte-Beuve starts firmly with the assumption that Pascal's "faith precedes his doubt"— that Pascal, like St. John, loved Christ the Saviour with an absorbing devotion. He emphasizes the clarity and sanity of Pascal's mind and style. His deplorable lack of charm and ascetic enmity toward art helped, moreover, to form his sober and bald, metaphorless style. Finally, Sainte-Beuve suggests— somewhat hesitantly embracing the religion of progress and science—that Pascal might finally be disproved not by arguments but by history. The world, Sainte-Beuve hopes, will become a less frightening place and will cease to be a world of exile. To Sainte-Beuve's mind Buffon, biology, and evolution refute or shall refute Pascal. But these limitations of his 19th-century horizon should not conceal the fact that Sainte-Beuve was extraordinarily successful in his task: with complete historical empathy he entered into the mind and feelings of a group of people very alien to the time in which *Port Royal* was written. Whatever minor criticisms may be directed against the inaccuracy of details or even misinterpretations, *Port Royal* remains a triumph of intellectual historiography. In combining history of religious sentiment, historical and biographical narrative, individual psychological portraiture, and forays into literary history, it may seem to constitute a hybrid genre. But what the books lack in purity of method and aim they amply compensate for by local life and by a unifying spirit that is the historical spirit at its best. *Port Royal* reflects Sainte-Beuve's basic convictions: his refusal to suppress the role of chance; his reverence for the mysterious core of human personality; and his distrust of a "philosophy of history" and grandiose schemes. . . . (pp. 44-5)

[*Chateaubriand et son groupe littéraire sous L'Empire*] comes nearer to strict literary history. The **"Opening Discourse"** . . . states quite clearly the case for literary history: "It is not enough to know the men if it is a question of works." While trying to "characterize the production of the mind as an expression of the time and the order of society, one must not neglect to seize on what does not belong to transient life, on what pertains to the immortal and sacred flame, the genius of

Letters itself." Sainte-Beuve approves the task of "reproducing, above all, the movement, the unity and the totality of a literary epoch" and rejects the old, external antiquarianism of classifications and catalogues in favor of a vivid sense of the tradition, a feeling for the true relations, for "what has influenced, for what counts." (p. 45)

It is impossible to establish a neat chronology of Sainte-Beuve's various concepts of criticism. On the whole he seems to move in two directions simultaneously: from an early, more subjective concept of personal expression to far greater objectivity, detachment, and tolerance, and at the same time from a rather uncritical, sympathetic acceptance to an increasing emphasis on the role of judgment, to a definition of taste and the tradition. These two movements of his mind are at cross-purposes. In theory, romantic historicism goes with tolerance, with relativism, but in Sainte-Beuve it is modified and often contradicted by partisanship in the literary battles of the time and by the egotism of a poet seeking for personal expression even in his criticism. The objectivity, the detachment of the later stage models itself rather on the pattern of science. The conversion to a classical taste, however, brings about a reassertion of the judicial function and hence the tone of authority and often of acrimony in Sainte-Beuve's criticism. (pp. 46-7)

In his early stage, Sainte-Beuve thought of criticism as the work of an expositor, even a propagandist of the poets. "After the creation of works of genius there still remains to someone else the worthy task of propagating feeling and admiration for them. Enthusiasm, the Muse of the critic, resides in this." Once he even thought of criticism in this sense as the main and novel function of the time. . . . But now he believes that there is need of a criticism which will "attach itself to the new poets, shame the mediocrities, cry 'Make room!' around the poets, like a herald at arms; march in front of their chariot like a shield-bearer." (pp. 48-9)

Sainte-Beuve usually conceived the role of criticism in . . . objective terms. Its function is primarily and basically judicial. While at certain times he minimized, in theory, the judicial role of criticism, he never ceased judging, and increasingly he affirmed and reaffirmed the role of judgment. The critic, he asserts, must discern with certainty, without any softness, what is good and what will live. . . . The critic has a conservative and corrective function: he "maintains tradition and preserves taste," defends "the degrees of art, the ranks of the spirit." "True criticism consists in studying each being—that is, each author, each talent, according to the conditions of his nature, in giving a vivid and faithful description, but always providing that it classifies him and puts him in his place in the order of art." The critic, Sainte-Beuve believes, has a direct influence upon the trend of literature. (pp. 50-1)

But how is tradition defined? Sainte-Beuve appeals to the central concept of the French critical tradition—the concept of taste. At times, this "taste" means merely "tasting," a form of sheer Epicureanism. . . . Taste "appears always noblest, most perfect, and most genuinely refined and elevated in a saintly moral nature. But it often appears highly developed in very different natures. A certain agreeable corruption (may one confess this?) is not unbecoming and even gives an extreme refinement to some of its rarer modes." But Sainte-Beuve abjures this corrupted taste. His ambition is for the noblest, the most elevated, the most humane taste, a taste which he is willing to define as "the modesty of the mind," which he sees as "the finest and most instinctive" of our organs, as "the

love of the simple, the sensible, the elevated, the great." (pp. 51-2)

Good taste is thus a sense of moderation, of the sensible, the reasonable, combined with a recognition of greatness. It is simply the subjective side of what Sainte-Beuve elsewhere tries to define as the tradition, as the nature of the classical. In two well-known essays, **"What is a Classic?"** [and **"Of Tradition"**] . . . , Sainte-Beuve formulated his views most memorably. The earlier piece elaborates a double point of view: on the one hand, he insists on the Greco-Latin tradition, on a judiciously graduated veneration of the classics; and on the other hand, he recognizes the existence of something transcending this tradition: the works of Homer, Dante, and Shakespeare are classics though they do not conform to the demands of traditional classicism. Sainte-Beuve also sees, of course, that the usual French classicism, with its narrow rules, is a thing of the past, that his time must go beyond it and create a new literature, which will fulfill the demands of the age. . . . A classic is any work, no matter what kind, that has lived up to the standards of beauty and sanity that the critic now demands. Sainte-Beuve is not content to define the classic quality in terms of wisdom, moderation, or reasonableness; it would then include largely writers of the second rank—correct, sensible, elegant writers. The important thing now seems to him to preserve the notion and the cult of the classics and at the same time to widen it. (pp. 52-3)

In the later piece, **"Of Tradition,"** the emphasis on the Latin tradition as it was usually understood is even stronger. . . . He expressly says that a "professor is not a critic"; he need not be aware (as a critic should be) of all novelty. . . . Though Sainte-Beuve thinks that the professor should know the chief new events and should have an opinion, he himself feels at that moment very much like a professor expounding the necessity of preserving tradition. He understands this task of the upholder of tradition as that of a humanist rather than that of an antiquarian. (p. 53)

Sainte-Beuve upholds the tradition that descends from classical antiquity. He appeals to the French as heirs of the Romans: "we have to embrace, to understand, never to desert the inheritance received from those illustrious masters and fathers, an inheritance from Homer down to the latest classic of yesterday, which forms the brightest and most solid portion of our intellectual capital." He grants that, in a way, the poetic faculty is universal in humanity. He wants the French tradition not to be closed and exclusive, but he urges his audience never to abandon atticism, urbanity, the principle of good sense and reason combined with grace. (p. 54)

Sainte-Beuve appeals to Goethe's famous saying: the romantic is the diseased, the classical the healthy. . . . The classic, then, comprises all literature in healthy and happily flourishing condition, literatures in full accord with their times and with their social surroundings. . . . (p. 55)

[In an article entitled **"Les regrets,"** Sainte-Beuve] looks back at romanticism as a sickness of the time. "Hamlet, Werther, Childe Harold, the pure Renés, are sick men of the kind who sing and suffer, who enjoy their malady . . . sickness for sickness' sake." Criticism apparently can and has cured us of such a malady. . . . Sainte-Beuve's criticism has now become definitely social and even moral and, in its implications, absolute in its appeal to some broad but eternal standard. The differences of opinion among critics seem to him to derive simply from differences in perspective. (pp. 55-6)

René Wellek, ''Sainte-Beuve,'' *in his* A History of Modern Criticism, 1750-1950: The Age of Transition, Vol. 3 *(copyright © 1965 by Yale University), Yale University Press, 1965, pp. 34-72.*

## RICHARD M. CHADBOURNE (essay date 1974-75)

[The *Livre d'amour,* which Sainte-Beuve wrote about his affair with Victor Hugo's wife, Adèle,] shares in the ambiguity attached more or less to all love poetry. For whom is such poetry written? To whom does it ''belong''? How can the poet reconcile the two beings within him, the lover with his natural desire for secrecy and intimacy, and the artist with his equally natural desire to translate his private experience into universal terms and to receive some degree of public recognition? (p. 82)

[The *Livre d'amour* is] a ''journal,'' . . . but it is a ''journal *poétique,*'' and that is the essential difference. What matters in reading it is not the literal accuracy of the account of ''what happened,'' but the internal logic and coherence of the interpretation which it provides of a particular experience. (p. 83)

[Sainte-Beuve's] love affair with Adèle Hugo was fertile ground for imaginative projections of what might have been. The most ambitious and the most ennobling of such fictions was *Volupté:* Amaury's love for Madame de Couaën remains platonic; her virtue becomes an instrument of his return to God and his ordination to the priesthood; her death reconciles him with her husband, a tragic figure of failed political ambition. The *Livre d'amour,* though closer to the actual facts of the *roman vécu,* [ ], reshapes and illuminates them in its own manner, providing still another view of its creator, ''tel qu'il aurait voulu être'' [that which he would have liked to be]. (pp. 83-4)

One of the first features to strike the reader about the *Livre d'amour* is that it possesses a unity and a form—an ''architecture,'' one might say today—which were denied to its relatively shapeless companions. It reads, in fact, almost like a novel in verse form.

A kind of ''plot'' allows us to follow, across the 41 numbered poems and the four unnumbered *''Pièces finales,''* the genesis, growth, fulfillment, and decline of their passion, in more or less chronological order but with occasional use, to good psychological effect, of both anticipation and flashback. (pp. 84-5)

As in a novel there are also characters, settings, atmosphere. Basically, as one would expect, the work is a *roman à deux*—the poet and Adèle, ''l'Amie,'' ''la Fiancée,'' ''Elle,'' ''la pauvre captive''—with ''Lui,'' ''le sombre époux,'' ''le jaloux,'' ''le dangereux témoin,'' hovering as a threatening presence in the background. (p. 85)

The cast of characters is small not only because the atmosphere is intimate but also because the lovers had almost no intermediaries and because much of their effort consisted of a search for rendezvous where they might be alone. When secondary characters appear—the other guests at the Hugo home, the philosopher Ballanche intercepting and detaining the poet on his way to a tryst with Adèle . . .—it is usually as unwanted presences, as obstacles to communication between the lovers.

The ''action'' of the work might indeed be summed up as the attempt of two lovers to find suitable meeting places; and these in turn become the characteristic décors of the story. . . .

As for the moral or psychological atmosphere, it is no less well defined and distinctive than the physical. It is marked by frustrations, by separations and long periods of waiting. . . . What

is original about this is not the sense of a frustrated passion that must use all its ingenuity to declare itself, or the sense of secrecy; poets and novelists have traditionally thrived on such handicaps. . . . (p. 86)

A veil of sadness, a shadow, hangs over the work; pleasure and joy, though occasionally real, are short-lived. (p. 87)

[However], strong forces are at work in the *Livre d'amour* which give the concept of love affirmed therein a surprisingly positive quality. These are: the association of love with religion and with the intellectual, quasi-scholarly pursuit which the poet calls ''étude'' . . . , the evocation of various classical and other poetic traditions of love, also a matter of ''study''; and above all, the sifting of experience through the poet's (and to some extent his beloved's) imagination and memory. Much the same forces that operate in *Volupté,* they produce a similar ennobling effect, testifying, as in the novel, to the author's determination to extract from the raw material of his experience some spiritual meaning, some ideal worth striving to attain.

The religious aspiration underlying the work, as Sainte-Beuve recognized, is far from pure. (p. 88)

Adèle Hugo, as the reader of *Les Consolations* knows, attracted Sainte-Beuve in part because her religious faith seemed to promise him support in his own spiritual quest, as well as renewed artistic inspiration after a period of dryness in which it appeared that he might abandon all serious study, all sense of piety and of communication with the Muse. (p. 89)

The lovers' trysts in churches and graveyards were . . . not simply a matter of accident or expediency, but part of their hope of redeeming their adulterous relationship, somehow even of legitimizing it, through acts of piety toward the dead, through ''charité,'' while at the same time avoiding blasphemy. . . .

The linking of love with religion, together with the prospect of aging together and the hope of constancy as time passed, enabled the lovers to cling, even in the midst of adultery, to an ideal of innocence and purity—a paradox that Baudelaire, if not Claudel, would have understood. . . . (p. 90)

The ennobling effect sought by the poet is also enhanced by frequent allusions to classical mythology and to examples of lovers consecrated by tradition. In the [Sonnet beginning ''Si quelque blâme hélas, se glisse à l'origine''] Adèle is cast in the role of Delia, the first love of Tibullus, from whom the epigraph is taken: ''. . . Nos, Delia, amoris / Exemplum cana simus uterqua coma'' (''We shall be love's exemplar even when our hair is white''). Adèle at her *toilette,* at least in the poet's eyes, resembles Hera in the *Iliad* . . . , and the lovers' frustrations are compared with the unhappiness which Penelope, in remarks to Odysseus, attributes to the malevolence of the Gods, ''who could not bear to see us share the joys of youth and reach the threshold of old age together.'' . . . Thus does Sainte-Beuve put two of his favorite classical poets to good use—if one is willing to forgive his somewhat pedantic addiction to footnotes—in the shaping of his own myth of love.

A more significant source of this myth, however, is Petrarch. . . . Petrarch had served to bless the concept of friendship celebrated in *Les Consolations* before being called on to render a similar service to love in the *Livre d'amour.* Petrarch's Laura was another model that Sainte-Beuve had in mind for Adèle. But in the final poem of the epilogue on the theme of the decline of love, he suggests that the role of a more passionate heroine than Laura might have suited her better and that his own circumspect preference for something gentler and subtler than ardent passion may have spoiled their relationship. . . . (p. 91)

Of all the forces at work in the **Livre d'amour** to idealize experience none is so strong as the combined power of imagination and memory, assisted by their auxiliaries, *le cœur* [the heart] and *la rêverie* [the reverie].

Few women in love poetry have been imagined, anticipated, called forth over such a long period of foreshadowing as Adèle, the object of [Sainte-Beuve's] "late love.". . . (p. 92)

All love is a creature of the imagination, but few loves have been so dependent on the imagination as this one.

The poet's knowledge of Adèle is acquired in "the mirror of his heart," and he in turns assumes, as reflected in the mirror of hers, a nobler image than he believed himself to possess in reality. (pp. 92-3)

Memory is inseparable from imagination in [Sainte-Beuve's] creation of a poetic ideal of love. The theme of memory—another characteristically Romantic theme—accounts for some of the finest lines in the **Livre d'amour**. (pp. 93-4)

From the point of view of technique, [the **Livre d'amour**] offers no radical departure from the theory and practice of its companion volumes. It confirms the author's faithfulness to Joseph Delorme's (i.e. his own) motto, *"L'art dans la rêverie et le rêverie dans l'art"* [art in reverie and reverie in art] and to his goal of developing an "Art poétique moderne" [modern poetic art]. He is careful to vary longer poems of the *récit* [narrative] type with shorter forms, especially the sonnet, which stimulated some of his finest efforts. (pp. 94-5)

The **Livre d'amour,** though far from a neglected masterpiece, should be restored to its rightful place in the canon of Sainte-Beuve's poetry. It is unfortunately not free from the notorious defects of the rest of his verse, so often flat, laborious, clumsy. But it contains many isolated *beaux vers* [beautiful poems] that would be the envy of much greater poets, many interestingly conceived though not quite successfully executed poems, and a dozen or so excellent if not great ones. It possesses an impressive thematic unity derived from the *roman vecu* which it recreates. A modest but hardly contemptible score for any poet. . . . (p. 96)

*Richard M. Chadbourne, "Sainte-Beuve's 'Livre d'amour' As Poetry," in* Nineteenth-Century French Studies (© 1975 by T. H. Goetz), Vol. III, Nos. 1 & 2, Fall-Winter, 1974-75, pp. 80-96.

---

## ADDITIONAL BIBLIOGRAPHY

Arnold, Matthew. "Sainte-Beuve." In his *Essays in Criticism, third series*, pp. 137-50. Boston: The Ball Publishing Co., 1910.
    Praises Sainte-Beuve as an outstanding critic in the Naturalist tradition.

Babbitt, Irving. "Sainte-Beuve (before 1848)" and "Sainte-Beuve (after 1848)." In his *The Masters of Modern French Criticism*, pp. 97-188, Boston, New York: Houghton Mifflin Co., 1912.
    Discusses Sainte-Beuve's work as a reflection of the nineteenth-century struggle between tradition and naturalism. Babbitt considers Sainte-Beuve the figure most representative of nineteenth-century intellectual innovations.

Dowden, Edward. "Literary Criticism in France." In his *New Studies in Literature*, pp. 388-418. London: Kegan Paul, Trench, Trubner & Co., 1902.*
    Maintains that Sainte-Beuve's power as a critic lies in his anglicized method of analysis. Dowden states that the general nineteenth-century French method is too systematic, while English criticism seeks only to discover truth without adhering to any rigid critical precepts.

Frye, Prosser Hall. "Sainte-Beuve." In his *Literary Reviews and Criticisms*, pp. 263-90. New York, London: G.P. Putnam's Sons, 1908.
    An appraisal of Sainte-Beuve's critical technique. Frye particularly notes Sainte-Beuve's objective approach to literature.

Harper, George McLean. *Charles-Augustin Sainte-Beuve.* Philadelphia, London: J. B. Lippincott Co., 1909, 388 p.
    A laudatory biographical study which terms Sainte-Beuve France's "most serviceable literary critic."

Lehmann, A. G. *Sainte-Beuve: A Portrait of the Critic, 1804-42.* Oxford: Oxford at the Clarendon Press, 1962, 430 p.
    A biographical and critical analysis of Sainte-Beuve during his early years. Lehmann considers Sainte-Beuve the primary force in the cultural development of nineteenth-century France.

More, Paul Elmer. "The Centenary of Sainte-Beuve." In his *Shelburne Essays, third series,* rev. ed., pp. 54-81. Boston, New York: Houghton Mifflin Co., 1905.
    An appreciative evaluation of Sainte-Beuve.

Mott, Lewis Freeman. *Sainte-Beuve.* New York, London: D. Appleton and Co., 1925, 522 p.
    A historical literary survey which analyzes Sainte-Beuve in relation to the other artists of his day.

Nicolson, Harold. *Sainte-Beuve.* Garden City, N.Y.; Doubleday & Co., 1958, 274 p.
    The definitive biography.

Saintsbury, George. "The Reconstruction of Criticism: Sainte-Beuve." In his *A History of Criticism and Literary Taste in America from the Earliest Texts to the Present Day: Modern Criticism, Vol. III,* pp. 300-29. Edinburgh, London: William Blackwood & Sons, 1935.*
    An analysis of Sainte-Beuve's critical theory that concentrates on the concepts presented in *Port-Royal.*

Thibaudet, Albert. "Part Two: The Generation of 1820, Sainte-Beuve." In his *French Literature from 1795 to Our Era,* translated by Charles Lam Markmann, pp. 248-60. New York: Funk & Wagnalls, 1967.
    Marks *Port-Royal* as the greatest work in the history of literary criticism.

# Richard Brinsley Sheridan

## 1751-1816

(Born Thomas Brinsley Sheridan) Irish dramatist librettist, and poet.

During his brief career as a playwright, Sheridan helped revive the English Restoration comedy of manners, which depicts the amorous intrigues of wealthy society. His best-known comedies, *The Rivals* and *The School for Scandal*, display Sheridan's talent for sparkling dialogue and farce. Like his Restoration predecessors, William Congreve and William Wycherley, Sheridan satirized society, but, unlike them, he injected a gentle morality and sentimentality into his humor. Critics often note a lack of incisiveness and psychological depth beneath the highly-polished surface of Sheridan's plays. However, they are considered by most to be the work of an outstanding theatrical craftsman. Drawing from earlier dramatic conventions, Sheridan created supremely entertaining comedies that continue to attract audiences today.

Sheridan, the son of a prominent actor and a noted authoress, was born in Dublin. When he was eight, the family moved to London, where he attended school. Though he disliked school, he proved to be an excellent student and wrote poetry at an early age. After composing dramatic sketches with friends, Sheridan considered becoming a playwright. His father, however, intended him to study law. When the Sheridans moved to Bath in 1770, Richard met Elizabeth Linley, an outstanding singer and famed beauty. Though she had many suitors, Linley eloped with Sheridan in 1773. Shortly after their marriage, Sheridan abandoned his legal studies in order to devote himself to writing.

The initial performance of his first play, *The Rivals*, failed because of miscasting and the play's excessive length. Undaunted by the poor reception, Sheridan recast several roles, abbreviated sections of the play, and reopened it ten days later to unanimously positive response. The success of *The Rivals* derives from one of comedy's oldest devices: satirizing manners. Its humor is pointed, but never cruel; critics consider *The Rivals* to be the lightest and most innocent of Sheridan's comedies. In the twentieth century, *The Rivals* is noted for its fine characterization. Of special interest is Mrs. Malaprop, a character infamous for her humourously inappropriate word usage, from whose name the word ''malapropism'' is derived.

Sheridan's next work was *The Duenna; or, The Double Elopement*, an opera for which his father-in-law, Thomas Linley, composed the music. While *The Duenna* was initially praised for its humorous libretto and amusing characters, the opera was soon forgotten. Some maintain that Sheridan's satirical talents were simply not suited to musical form. However, *The Duenna*, in addition to *The Rivals* and a minor comedy that was produced soon afterward, *St. Patrick's Day; or, The Scheming Lieutenant*, established Sheridan as a prominent dramatist. When David Garrick retired as owner of the Drury Lane Theatre, Sheridan purchased the theatre and became its manager. In the next two years, he revived a number of Restoration comedies and wrote and produced his most successful comedy, *The School for Scandal*.

*The School for Scandal* is both the most popular of Sheridan's comedies and the most strongly reminiscent of the Restoration period. This attack on a gossip-loving society provides Sheridan's most brilliant display of wit, though its sharp indictment of scandal differs strongly from the gentler tone and approach in *The Rivals*. The play is also noted for its double plot lines, as well as for its superb command of language and its technical refinement. The play's continuous and numerous performances throughout the world attest to its reputation as one of England's best-loved and most enduring comedies.

In 1779 Sheridan produced his last successful work, *The Critic; or, Tragedy Rehearsed*. Strongly influenced by the Duke of Buckingham's *The Rehearsal*, the play provides a satirical look at the theatrical world and is a burlesque of the vanity of artists and critics. Though *The Critic* never achieved the popularity of *The Rivals* or *The School for Scandal*, many sources consider it to be Sheridan's most intellectual work. He later stated that he had hoped to sum up all that previous comic poets had achieved in the satirization of tragedy. His last play was titled *Pizarro*, an adaptation of August von Kotzebue's *Die Spanier in Peru oder Rollas Tod*. A historical drama, *Pizarro* met with popular acclaim but was soon forgotten. Critics today consider it a disappointing conclusion to Sheridan's theatrical career.

In 1780 Sheridan was elected to the House of Commons, where he excelled as an orator. His speeches are considered brilliant; in particular, the four-hour oration denouncing his fellow statesman Warren Hastings is regarded as a masterpiece of persuasion and verbal command. However, Sheridan's interest in politics kept him from his theatrical endeavors and his management of the theater became haphazard. In an attempt to beautify the aging theater, he rebuilt the interior, but it burned down shortly thereafter. Left without resources, Sheridan was unable to finance another Parliamentary campaign. His last years were spent in poverty and disgrace, but shortly before his death, Sheridan regained his reputation as a distinguished statesman and dramatist. When he died in 1816, he was mourned widely and was buried in the Poet's Corner of Westminster Abbey.

While *The Rivals* and *The School for Scandal* have always been popular, some recent critics charge that Sheridan was neither responsible for an English revival of comedy nor particularly innovative. Others fault his refusal to develop emotional subtleties in his characters, and find his dialogue superficially witty, but lacking depth. They contend that the deliberate staginess of his works detracts from their artistic value. Sheridan himself chose to exaggerate and vary the traditional comedy of manners in order to heighten the play's theatricality, an aspect that he maintained intensified the audience's enjoyment. Despite controversy, his works continue to be performed. Alan Downer explained the enduring appeal of Sheridan's plays: "Sheridan is making us laugh at our own dreams, our own small follies. If we can laugh at our dreams, we may be less disappointed when they fail to materialize; if we laugh at our own follies, we may develop a tolerance for the follies of others."

## PRINCIPAL WORKS

*The Duenna; or, The Double Elopement*   (libretto)   1775
*The Rivals*  (drama)  1775
*St. Patrick's Day; or, The Scheming Lieutenant*   (drama)   1775
*The School for Scandal*  (drama)  1777
*A Trip to Scarborough* [adaptor; from the drama *The Relapse* by John Vanbrugh]  (drama)  1777
*The Critic; or, Tragedy Rehearsed*  (drama)  1779
*Pizarro* [adaptor; from the drama *Die Spanier in Peru oder Rollas Tod* by August von Kotzebue]  (drama)  1799
*The Works of the Late Right Honourable Richard Brinsley Sheridan*  (drama)  1821
*The Plays and Poems of Richard Brinsley Sheridan*  (drama and poetry)  1928
*The Letters of Richard Brinsley Sheridan*  (letters)  1966
*The Dramatic Works of Richard Brinsley Sheridan*  (drama)  1973

---

## THE PUBLIC LEDGER   (essay date 1775)

*The Rivals,* as a Comedy, requires much castigation, and the pruning hand of judgment, before it can ever pass on the Town as even a tolerable Piece. In language it is defective to an extreme, in Plot outré and one of the *Characters* is an absolute exotic in the wilds of nature. [Sheridan] seems to have con-

sidered puns, witticisms, similes and metaphors, as admirable substitutes for polished diction; hence they abound in every sentence; and hence it is that instead of the '*Metamorphosis*' of Ovid, one of the characters is made to talk of Ovid's 'Meat-for-Hopes,' a Lady is called the 'Pine Apple of beauty,' the Gentleman in return 'an Orange of perfection.' A Lover describes the sudden change of disposition in his Mistress by saying, that 'she flies off in a tangent born down by the current of disdain'; and a second Tony Lumkin, to describe how fast he rode, compares himself to a 'Comet with a tail of dust at his heels.'

These are shameful absurdities in language, which can suit no character, how widely soever it may depart from common life and common manners.

Whilst thus censure is freely passed, not to say that there are various sentiments in the Piece which demonstrate the Author's no stranger to the finer feelings, would be shameful partiality. . . . (p. 313)

> *A review of "The Rivals," in* The Public Ledger, *January 18, 1775 (and reprinted in* The Major Dramas of Richard Brinsley Sheridan *by Richard Brinsley Sheridan, edited by George Henry Nettleton, Ginn and Company, 1906, pp. 313-14).*

## THE MORNING CHRONICLE   (essay date 1775)

We heartily wish it was a general custom for authors to withdraw their pieces after a first performance, in order to remove the objectionable passages, heighten the favourite characters, and generally amend the play. The author of **The Rivals** has made good use of his time; his comedy is altered much for the better since it was first acted. The cast of it is improved, and all the performers are now perfect, and better acquainted with their several parts. It comes within a reasonable compass as to the time taken up in the representation, and the sentiments thrown into the mouth of Sir Lucius O'Trigger produce a good effect, at the same time that they take away every possible idea of the character's being designed as an insult on our neighbours on the other side of St. George's Channel. In the room of the objectionable and heavy scenes which are cut out, two new ones of a very different turn are introduced, and we remarked more than one judicious alteration in the Prologue.—*The Rivals* will now stand its ground; and although we cannot pronounce it, with all its amendments, a comic chef-d'ouvre it certainly encourages us to hope for a very capital play from the same writer at a future season; he therefore, from motives of candour and encouragement, is entitled to the patronage and favour of a generous public.

> *A review of "The Rivals," in* The Morning Chronicle, *January 30, 1775 (and reprinted in* The Major Dramas of Richard Brinsley Sheridan *by Richard Brinsley Sheridan, edited by George Henry Nettleton, Ginn and Company, 1906, p. 317).*

## RICHARD BRINSLEY SHERIDAN   (essay date 1776)

[*In his preface to* The Rivals, *Sheridan observes that the defects of the first version are due largely to his inexperience as a dramatist. He notes that the audience is a "candid and just critic," while professional reviewers, in contrast, are "puny" and "peevish."*]

There are few writers, I believe, who, even in the fullest consciousness of error, do not wish to palliate the faults which they acknowledge; and, however trifling the performance, to second their confession of its deficiencies, by whatever plea seems least disgraceful to their ability. In the present instance, it cannot be said to amount either to candour or modesty in me, to acknowledge an extreme inexperience and want of judgment on matters, in which, without guidance from practice, or spur from success, a young man should scarcely boast of being an adept. If it be said that under such disadvantages no one should attempt to write a play, I must beg leave to dissent from the position, while the first point of experience that I have gained on the subject is a knowledge of the candour and judgment with which an impartial public distinguishes between the errors of inexperience and incapacity, and the indulgence which it shows even to a disposition to remedy the defects of either.

It were unnecessary to enter into any further extenuation of what was thought exceptionable in [*The Rivals*], but that it has been said, that the managers should have prevented some of the defects before its appearance to the public—and in particular the uncommon length of the piece as represented the first night. It were an ill return for the most liberal and gentlemanly conduct on their side, to suffer any censure to rest where none was deserved. Hurry in writing has long been exploded as an excuse for an author;—however, in the dramatic line, it may happen, that both an author and a manager may wish to fill a chasm in the entertainment of the public with a hastiness not altogether culpable. . . . [Though] I was not uninformed that the acts were still too long, I flattered myself that, after the first trial, I might with safer judgment proceed to remove what should appear to have been most dissatisfactory. Many other errors there were, which might in part have arisen from my being by no means conversant with plays in general, either in reading or at the theatre. Yet I own that, in one respect, I did not regret my ignorance: for as my first wish in attempting a play was to avoid every appearance of plagiary, I thought I should stand a better chance of effecting this from being in a walk which I had not frequented, and where, consequently, the progress of invention was less likely to be interrupted by starts of recollection: for on subjects on which the mind has been much informed, invention is slow of exerting itself. Faded ideas float in the fancy like half-forgotten dreams; and the imagination in its fullest enjoyments becomes suspicious of its offspring, and doubts whether it has created or adopted.

With regard to some particular passages which on the first night's representation seemed generally disliked, I confess that if I felt any emotion of surprise at the disapprobation, it was not that they were disapproved of, but that I had not before perceived that they deserved it. . . . I see no reason why the author of a play should not regard a first night's audience as a candid and judicious friend attending, in behalf of the public, at his last rehearsal. If he can dispense with flattery, he is sure at least of sincerity, and even though the annotation be rude, he may rely upon the justness of the comment. Considered in this light, that audience, whose *fiat* is essential to the poet's claim, whether his object be fame or profit, has surely a right to expect some deference to its opinion, from principles of politeness at least, if not from gratitude.

As for the little puny critics, who scatter their peevish strictures in private circles, and scribble at every author who has the eminence of being unconnected with them, as they are usually spleen-swoln from a vain idea of increasing their consequence, there will always be found a petulance and illiberality in their remarks, which should place them as far beneath the notice of a gentleman as their original dulness had sunk them from the level of the most unsuccessful author.

It is not without pleasure that I catch at an opportunity of justifying myself from the charge of intending any national reflection in the character of Sir Lucius O'Trigger. If any gentlemen opposed the piece from that idea, I thank them sincerely for their opposition; and if the condemnation of this comedy (however misconceived the provocation) could have added one spark to the decaying flame of national attachment to the country supposed to be reflected on, I should have been happy in its fate, and might with truth have boasted that it had done more real service in its failure than the successful morality of a thousand stage-novels will ever effect. (pp. xiv-xvii)

*Richard Brinsley Sheridan, "Preface" (originally published in his* The Rivals, *third edition, John Wilkie, 1776), in his* The Rivals, *edited by Alan S. Downer (copyright 1953 Appleton-Century Crofts, Inc.), Appleton-Century-Crofts, 1953, pp. xiii-xvii.*

### *THE LONDON MAGAZINE; OR, GENTLEMAN'S MONTHLY INTELLIGENCER* (essay date 1777)

Last night a phenomenon in the theatrical world ["**The School for Scandal**"] made its first appearance . . .—that is, a modern comedy, unaided by the deceptions of scenery, or the absurdities of sing-song and pantomime, received by "a brilliant and crouded audience," with the most universal and continued marks of applause. . . .

The piece is an assemblage of wit, sentiment, pointed observation, and improbabilities, unconnected by any grand principle of action. (p. 228)

Besides the plot, and under plots, there is a groupe of figures worked into the body of the piece, which form a kind of club, whose sole delight is in propagating scandal, when they have materials; and when they have none, inventing, adding, and misrepresenting every thing they hear, or their rage, folly, malice, or prolific brains, can suggest. Lady Sneerwell, Mrs. Scandal, Sir Benjamin Backbite, and Crabtree, constitute this valuable society. Joseph, and Lady Teazle, though now and then otherwise engaged, appear to be at least honorary members. It is a pity, that the standing members of the club were not more directly engaged in the business of the piece; but in spite of this objection we do not recollect to have ever heard or read a more just or pointed satire; nor a dialogue fuller of wit than the conversation held up by this very respectable brotherhood and sisterhood of modern mohawks. Besides the general satire, which will hold good as long as the English language is read or understood, the particular application of it to a certain modern daily publication is logically true throughout, and ought to crimson with blushes every cheek which has encouraged such a butchery of male and female reputation. . . .

Few who are capable of judging of this piece will speak the truth. The friends of the author, and other contemporary playwrights, have their prejudices. We labouring under none of these impediments of partiality, rivalship, private pique, or an overflow of wit, we flatter ourselves that we are tolerably enabled to pronounce with critical truth on the merits and demerits of "**The School for Scandal**." The great objects of the satire are detraction and hypocrisy, which, according to character and situation, the author has very artfully blended, sometimes in the same person, and sometimes distinct. The person given to detraction is not always an hypocrite, though he often, nay generally, is one; when it is unaccompanied by hypocrisy it is certainly less noxious; the effects are seldom attended to, and seldomer felt in their consequences; whereas the malignant hypocrite scarcely ever deals in scandal, but to effect some sinister or dark purpose. Scandal is made to answer another very natural and obvious end between the extremes of slander aforethought, and the mere rage for tale-bearing, that of reducing every one to the level of the slanderer. This . . . , as directed to the great end proposed by the author, is one of the keenest and best pointed satires in the English language. (p. 230)

The dialogue abounds in wit throughout; the piece produces new and interesting situations in every scene; sentiments the most natural and elevated arise from those situations. Virtue and principle, operating on conduct, is strongly recommended. Vice is described in its most hideous garb; and yet neither one nor the other are effected in a disgusting sermonic stile. Virtue is judiciously blended with its failings and foibles, and even vice is only rendered hateful on account of its effects on society, and its contradiction to the first uncontaminated principles of our nature. These are a few out of innumerable beauties of a less striking nature, that are thickly strewed in every scene almost, in "The School for Scandal." Let us now perform a very disagreeable part of our duty, that of pointing out some of its leading defects, in which it is almost equally fruitful.

"The School for Scandal" is totally deficient in plot, and of the underplots or incidents, which all ultimately conduce to the *denoument*, and are meant to constitute one complete action, we are still of opinion, that taking the whole business as referable to the end, the plot is still infinitely too complex and overcharged. There is no leading figure on the canvas, no great point seemingly in view. The figures all occupy equal spaces, the incidents equal attention, and the very marriage between the hero and heroine happens as it were by chance. (pp. 230-31)

The means devised by Rowley and Sir Oliver, are too much dwelt and built on; a great part of that business might be well retrenched, which would have a double good effect; that of shortening the piece, and of melting, softening, and qualifying, the means made use of to depretiate Joseph, and raise Charles, in the esteem of his uncle.

To heap coals on poor Joseph's head, for seducing Lady Teazle, is in our opinion very unfair. If there was any seduction at either side, it seemed to arise on that of the lady. . . . On the whole, there is something very improbable in [their] love affair, nor can we at all reconcile Lady Teazle's going to see Joseph's library, to any thing which passed before or after. (p. 231)

Joseph and Charles, in point of character, are the principal figures in the groupe. Joseph, full of morality and sentiment, is always preaching up virtue and feeling; but is at bottom mean, mercenary, malignant, artful, and designing. Charles, on the other hand, is lively, giddy, profligate, and extravagant. His follies and vices are however qualified with openness and generosity; with an unstrung purse; a heart susceptible for others woes; he sympathizes with the unfortunate and miserable. . . . These two are indeed the great characteristic features of human nature, in the early stages of life. Every man under thirty is, in some measure, a Joseph or a Charles. . . . The characters afford no novelty, though they are newly dressed; and we are ready to allow, on the whole, well dressed. But we should have hardly troubled our readers with observations which are on a level with the meanest capacity, were it not to introduce others, of much more importance. What is the tendency of this piece? The author's friends will say; to promote active virtue; to disseminate true sentiment, and distinguish it from the counterfeit; to detect hypocrisy; and to encourage and

deter by punishments and rewards. This may have been his intention, but we will appeal to common sense, to experience, and to a tolerable acquaintance with human nature, whether its incitements to a perseverance in vicious idle habits, and consequential injuries, are not much stronger than to the practice of virtues which cannot be models of imitation to him who does not recognize at least their seeds in his own breast. . . . Charles Surface is rather a dangerous character to be held out to the youth of the present age. . . . Joseph's manners delineate the hypocrite more strongly at this time of day, than the affected prowess of Nol Bluff, the dexterity of Count Basset, or the latitudinary, deistical, pretended principles of Tinsel. . . . [The] character has its use; but when all pretensions to sentiment, as connected with a rule of moral conduct; when every species of morality, arising from incident and situation; when mere animal instinct is preferred to the guidance of reason; when reflexion, comparison, and decision, the leading distinctions between the rational and brute creation, are laughed out of doors, and branded under the general opprobrium of hypocrisy; we rather wish, if it may be presumed that the stage operates on the morals of the people, that the character of Joseph Surface had never been written, at least represented. As on one hand, the fools and rascals may find, without having a genuine spark of Charles's virtue in their frame, a great deal to countenance their follies and vices, in his character, as drawn by the poet; so the brutes in human form, the wolves in sheeps cloathing, by way of keeping clear of the imputation of hypocrisy, sooner than be likened to Joseph Surface, will, in many instances, comence savages in manners, and ruffians in respect of civil society. We shall make no apology to the public, or the author, for saying thus much on the subject. To the first, we can say, it was intended as an act of duty: to the author no apology is necessary; because we think our engagements to the public, so far as we are bound or connected with it, paramount to all other. Secondly, because we are conscious that the singular opinion of an individual will never affect the author in either his profits or his fame, as a first rate dramatic writer. (pp. 231-32)

*A review of "The School for Scandal,"* in The London Magazine; or, Gentleman's Monthly Intelligencer, *Vol. XLVI, May, 1777, pp. 228-32.*

### THE UNIVERSAL MAGAZINE (essay date 1777)

**The School for Scandal** is the production of Mr. Sheridan, and is an additional proof of that gentleman's great abilities as a dramatic writer. The object of the satyre is two-fold—detraction and hypocrisy, which are the prevailing vices of the times; by the first the good are reduced to a level with the worthless, and, by means of the second, the latter assume the appearance of men of virtue and sentiment. Nothing, therefore, could have been more seasonable than this comedy, which, in point of execution, is equal, if not superior, to most of the plays produced for the last twenty years. The characters are drawn with a bold pencil, and coloured with warmth and spirit. (pp. 251-52)

The dialogue of this comedy is easy and witty. It abounds with strokes of pointed satyre, and a rich vein of humour pervades the whole, rendering it equally interesting and entertaining. The fable is well conducted, and the incidents are managed with great judgment. . . . Upon the whole, **The School for Scandal** justifies the very great and cordial reception it met with; it certainly is a good comedy, and we should not at all wonder if it becomes as great a favourite as [Sheridan's] **The**

*Duenna,* to which it is infinitely superior in point of sense, satyre, and moral. (p. 253)

*A review of "The School for Scandal," in* The Universal Magazine, *Vol. LX, No. CCCCXIX, May, 1777, pp. 251-53.*

## THE CRITICAL REVIEW  (essay date 1781)

[*The Critic*] has been seen and admired by every body; and the oftener it is seen, and the oftener it is read, the more it will be applauded. Hypercritical remarks on it would therefore be totally unnecessary. There is, indeed, more true wit and humour crouded into this little performance, than has, perhaps, appeared since the days of Wycherley and Congreve. The impartiality of cool reflection obliges us, at the same time, to condemn that which we cannot but admire. Ridicule is a dangerous and destructive weapon, which . . . destroys every thing before it, without mercy and without distinction. Wantonness of wit, and exuberance of fancy, have carried the ingenious author of *The Critic* beyond the limits of reason, justice, and impartiality. Not content with lashing the false sublime, bombast, and all the stage-trick of modern tragedy, he has attacked tragedy itself, and endeavoured, but too successfully, to render it an object of ridicule and sarcasm. How far it may be consistent with the character of a manager of a theatre to weaken one of its best supports, we leave Mr. Sheridan to determine. Certain however it is, that since the exhibition of *The Critic,* tragedy, which a celebrated writer has declared to be one of the greatest exertions of the human mind, is fallen into contempt; it will be some time at least before she can recover the blow. We hope, notwithstanding, for the credit of a British audience, that they will not be laughed out of their feelings, or suffer themselves to be deprived of that pleasure, not to mention the profit and instruction, which may arise from the exhibition of a good tragedy well performed, for any thing that such a wicked wit as our author can say against it. (p. 331)

*A review of "The Rivals," in* The Critical Review, *November, 1781 (and reprinted in* The Major Dramas of Richard Brinsley Sheridan *by Richard Brinsley Sheridan, edited by George Henry Nettleton, Ginn and Company, 1906, pp. 331-32).*

## GEORGE GORDON NOEL BYRON, LORD BYRON  (journal date 1813)

Lord Holland told me a curious piece of sentimentality in Sheridan. The other night we were all delivering our respective and various opinions on him and other *hommes marquans* [men of note], and mine was this:—'Whatever Sheridan has done or chosen to do has been, *par excellence,* always the *best* of its kind. He has written the *best* comedy (*School for Scandal*), the *best* drama (in my mind, far before that St. Giles's lampoon, the *Beggar's Opera*), the best farce (the *Critic*—it is only too good for a farce), and the best Address (Monologue on Garrick), and, to crown all, delivered the very best Oration (the famous Begum Speech) ever conceived or heard in this country.' Somebody told S. this the next day, and on hearing it he burst into tears!

Poor Brinsley! if they were tears of pleasure, I would rather have said these few, but most sincere, words than have written the Iliad or made his own celebrated Philippic. Nay, his own comedy never gratified me more than to hear that he had derived a moment's gratification from any praise of mine, humble as it must appear to 'my elders and my betters.' (p. 652)

*George Gordon Noel Byron, Lord Byron, in a journal entry of December 17, 1813, in his* Selections from Poetry, Letters & Journals, *edited by Peter Quennell, The Nonesuch Press, 1949, pp. 652-53.*

## [LEIGH HUNT]  (essay date 1816)

Mr. Sheridan's reputation with posterity will arise from what posterity will feel most interested in, and what fortunately constitutes his chief claim upon them,—his dramas. The best of these, the *Rivals,* and the *School for Scandal,* he wrote, as well as the rest, when young; and indeed there is a young sort of feeling in them, though not altogether of the most unsophisticated description. There is something too much of the town about them, and a portion of that bravado spirit in the morality and gallantry, which betrays its time of life by its over-intenseness. . . . [However], Mr. Sheridan's dramas are full of animal spirit; and this, together with a well-educated style, and a great taste for humour and contrast, gives life to their principal excellence, which is rather that of a witty elegance,—a tact for the best of what he found to his hand,— than of originality. He had not even a distinct character enough of his own, personally speaking, to give him the next thing to originality,—perhaps the same thing in its degree, if originals are narrowly analyzed. The newest though not the most entertaining thing in his plays is the character of Falkland in the *Rivals,* which is even said to have been drawn from himself. It is also to very good satirical purpose, aiming at one of those teazing qualities in private life, which after all make up the greatest sum of human disquietude, and which are not sufficiently handled by the assaulters of the social vices, sacred or profane. There has always appeared to us a great comic field almost totally unploughed, in what are called tempers, and in the contradiction between appearances and realities. Yet even Falkland, in one respect, has a forerunner in the old story of the Nut-brown Maid, which was turned into modern verse by Prior in his Henry and Emma. The other characters in Mr. Sheridan's plays,—the gallant Jack Absolute, the would-be gallant Bob Acres, the most absolute and entertaining Sir Anthony, the perversely ingenious Mrs. Malaprop, the Irishman, the Friar, and the Duenna, and the two brothers Charles and Joseph Surface are happy casts from prototypes to be found in hundreds of other Irishmen, Friars, and Duennas, in the gallants, and pretenders, and bullies, of preceding dramatists, and in the Slipslap, Tom Jones, and Blifil, of his precursor Henry Fielding. He seems instead to have had Fielding continually in his mind, or unconsciously in his associations. Even the consistent and retributive Mr. Fag, the footman, who while complaining of his master's injustice kicks the footboy for being troublesome, is traceable to Philosopher Square and Parson Adams. But enough is added, as well as exquisitely kept, to give the author a lasting reputation; and in his operatic songs,—though he had nothing essentially in him to be called poetry,—he has exhibited a very clear and compact vein of after-dinner wit versifying. . . .

Of the moral character of his plays, as affecting society, less need be said, we think, then might be supposed. The effect of the drama upon real life appears to us to be of a very general cast, not a particular one; and to keep alive a certain softness and sociality of spirit, without which, among other helps, a nation might relapse into brutality. We believe we have before expressed our particular admiration of that phrase in Ovid, where he speaks of a taste for the liberal arts—"'haec *sinit* esse feros'—It will not *suffer* men to be barbarous. The extreme of the stage, when there is one, is only an antidote, we conceive, to the extreme of reserve and bigotry. (p. 435)

To sum up the character of Mr. Sheridan,—he was a man of wit, a lively and elegant dramatist, a winning and powerful orator, a sound politician, a lover of real freedom, a careless liver; and Irishman, in short, with much of the worst, and more of the best, of his naturally lighthearted but unfortunate countrymen. His worst can affect but few;—his best will redound to the good of his country, and be the delight of thousands to come. (p. 436)

> [*Leigh Hunt*], "*The Late Mr. Sheridan*," *in* The Examiner, *No. 446, July 14, 1816, pp. 433-36.*

## [GEORGE GORDON NOEL BYRON, LORD BYRON]  (poem date 1816)

[*Byron was an avid admirer of Sheridan. He read the following poem from the stage of the Drury Lane Theatre following Sheridan's death.*]

When the last sunshine of expiring day
In Summer's twilight weeps itself away,
Who hath not felt the softness of the hour
Sink on the heart—as dew along the flower?
Who hath not shar'd that calm, so still and deep,
The voiceless thought, which would not speak, but weep?
A holy concord—and a bright regret,
A glorious sympathy with suns that set—
So feels the fulness of our heart and eyes,
When all of Genius which can perish, dies.
The flash of wit—the bright intelligence—
The beam of song—the blaze of eloquence—
Set with their sun: but still have left behind
The enduring produce of immortal mind;
Fruits of genial morn and glorious noon,
A deathless part of him who died too soon.
From the charm'd council to the festive board,
Of human feelings the enbounded lord;
In whose acclaim the loftiest voices vied,
The prais'd—the proud—who made his praise their pride;—
When the loud cry of trampled Hindestan
Arose to Heaven in her appeal from man,
His was the thunder—his the avenging rod—
The wrath—the delegated voice of God!
Which shook the nations through his lips—and blaz'd,
Till vanquish'd Senates trembled as they prais'd.
And here! On here, where yet all young and warm,
The gay creations of his spirit charm,
The matchless dialogue—the deathless wit
Which knew not what it was to intermit;
The glowing portraits, fresh from life, that bring
Home to our hearts the truth from which they spring;
Here in their first abode to-night you must
Bright with the hues of his Promethean heat—
A Halo of the light of other days,
Which still the splendour of its orb betrays.
But should there be to whom the fatal blight
Of failing wisdom yields a base delight,
Men, who exult, when minds of heavenly tone
Jar in the musick which was born their own;

Still let them pause—Ah! little do they know
That what to them seem'd Vice might be Woe,
Hard is his fate, on whom the public gaze
Is fix'd for ever, to detract or praise.
Repose denies her requiem to his name,
And Folly loves the martyrdom of Fame,
But far from us and from our mimic scene
Such things should be—if such have ever been.
Our's be the gentler wish—the kinder task,—
To give the tribute Glory need not ask.
To weep the vanquish'd beam—and add our mite
Of praise, in payment of a long delight,
Ye Orators! whom yet our councils yield,
Mourn for the veteran Hero of your field,
The worthy Rival of the wondrous *three*,
Whose words were sparks of immorality!
Ye Bards!—to whom the Drama's Muse is dear,
He was your Master! emulate him *here*!—
Ye men of wit and social eloquence!
He was your Brother!—bear his ashes hence!—
While powers of mind, almost of boundless range,
Complete in kind—as various in their change;
While Eloquence—Wit—Poesy—and Mirth,
That humbler Harmonist of Care on earth,
Survive within our souls—while lives our sense
Of pride in merit's proud pre-eminence,
Long shall we seek his likeness—long, in vain,—
And turn to all of him which may remain,
Sighing that Nature form'd but one such man,
And broke the die—in moulding Sheridan.

> [*George Gordon Noel Byron, Lord Byron*], *in extracts from his "A Monody to the Memory of the Late Right Hon. R. B. Sheridan," in* The Gentleman's Magazine and Historical Chronicle, *n.s. Vol. LXXXVI, No. 9, October, 1816, p. 350.*

## WILLIAM HAZLITT  (essay date 1819)

[*Hazlitt, a leading English Romantic critic, included Sheridan in his survey of eighteenth-century comic writers. He describes Sheridan's dramas as "excellent" and praises Sheridan's ability to create characters of substance and depth.*]

Mr. Sheridan has been justly called 'a dramatic star of the first magnitude': and, indeed, among the comic writers of the last century, he 'shines like Hesperus among the lesser lights.' He has left four several dramas behind him, all different or of different kinds, and all excellent in their way;—***The School for Scandal, The Rivals, The Duenna,*** and ***The Critic.*** The attraction of this last piece is, however, less in the mock-tragedy rehearsed, than in the dialogue of the comic scenes, and in the character of Sir Fretful Plagiary, which is supposed to have been intended for Cumberland. If some of the characters in the School for Scandal were contained in Murphy's comedy of Know your own Mind (and certainly some of Dashwoud's detached speeches and satirical sketches are written with quite as firm and masterly a hand as any of those given to the members of the scandalous club, Mrs. Candour or Lady Sneerwell), yet they were buried in it for want of grouping and relief, like the colours of a well drawn picture sunk in the canvass. Sheridan brought them out, and exhibited them in all their glory. If that gem, the character of Joseph Surface, was Murphy's, the splendid and more valuable setting was Sheridan's. He took Murphy's Malvil from his lurking-place in the closet, and 'dragged the struggling monster into day' upon the stage.

That is, he gave interest, life, and action, or, in other words, its dramatic being, to the mere occupation and written specimens of a character. This is the merit of Sheridan's comedies, that every thing in them *tells;* there is no labour in vain. His Comic Muse does not go about prying into obscure corners, or collecting idle curiosities, but shews her laughing face, and points to her rich treasure—the follies of mankind. She is garlanded and crowned with roses and vine-leaves. Her eyes sparkle with delight, and her heart runs over with good-natured malice. Her step is firm and light, and her ornaments consummate! *The School for Scandal* is, if not the most original, perhaps the most finished and faultless comedy which we have. When it is acted, you hear people all around you exclaiming, 'Surely it is impossible for any thing to be cleverer.' . . . Besides the wit and ingenuity of this play, there is a genial spirit of frankness and generosity about it, that relieves the heart as well as clears the lungs. It professes a faith in the natural goodness, as well as habitual depravity of human nature. While it strips off the mask of hypocrisy, it inspires a confidence between man and man. As often as it is acted, it must serve to clear the air of that low, creeping, pestilent fog of cant and mysticism, which threatens to confound every native impulse, or honest conviction, in the nauseous belief of a perpetual lie, and the laudable profession of systematic hypocrisy.—The character of Lady Teazle is not well made out by the author. . . .—*The Rivals* is a play of even more action and incident, but of less wit and satire than *The School for Scandal.* It is as good as a novel in the reading, and has the broadest and most palpable effect on the stage. If Joseph Surface and Charles have a smack of Tom Jones and Blifil in their moral constitution, Sir Anthony Absolute and Mrs. Malaprop remind us of honest Matthew Bramble and his sister Tabitha, in their tempers and dialect. Acres is a distant descendant of Sir Andrew Ague-cheek [from Shakespeare's *Twelfth Night*]. It must be confessed of this author, as Falstaff says of some one, that 'he had damnable iteration in him!' *The Duenna* is a perfect work of art. It has the utmost sweetness and point. The plot, the characters, the dialogue, are all complete in themselves, and they are all his own; and the songs are the best that ever were written, except those in *The Beggar's Opera.* They have a joyous spirit of intoxication in them, and a strain of the most melting tenderness. (pp. 164-65)

Sheridan was not only an excellent dramatic writer, but a first-rate parliamentary speaker. His characteristics as an orator were manly, unperverted good sense, and keen irony. Wit, which has been thought a two-edged weapon, was by him always employed on the same side of the question—I think, on the right one. His set and more laboured speeches, as that on the Begum's affairs, were proportionably abortive and unimpressive: but no one was equal to him in replying, on the spur of the moment, to pompous absurdity, and unravelling the web of flimsy sophistry. (p. 166)

> William Hazlitt, "On the Comic Writers of the Last Century," *in his* Lectures on the English Comic Writers, with Miscellaneous Essays, *J. M. Dent & Sons, Ltd., 1819 (and reprinted by J. M. Dent & Sons, Ltd., 1910), pp. 149-68.*

## THOMAS MOORE    (essay date 1825)

[*Moore, an Irish poet and biographer, wrote the first and, for many, the definitive biography of Sheridan. While some twentieth-century critics find Moore's book to be verbose, they credit Moore with capturing the exuberance of Sheridan's life. The following* excerpt is from the brief critical analysis included in the biography. Moore here discusses the merits and faults of The Rivals and of The School for Scandal.]

[*The Rivals*] exhibits perhaps more humour than *The School for Scandal,* and the dialogue, though by no means so pointed or sparkling, . . . more natural, as coming nearer the current coin of ordinary conversation; whereas, the circulating medium of *The School for Scandal* is diamonds. The characters of *The Rivals,* on the contrary, are *not* such as occur very commonly in the world; and, instead of producing striking effects with natural and obvious materials, which is the great art and difficulty of a painter of human life, [Sheridan] has here overcharged most of his persons with whims and absurdities, for which the circumstances they are engaged in afford but a very disproportionate vent. Accordingly, for our insight into their characters, we are indebted rather to their confessions than their actions. Lydia Languish, in proclaiming the extravagance of her own romantic notions, prepares us for events much more ludicrous and eccentric, than those in which the plot allows her to be concerned; and the young lady herself is scarcely more disappointed than we are, at the tameness with which her amour concludes. Among the various ingredients supposed to be mixed up in the composition of Sir Lucius O'Trigger, his love of fighting is the only one whose flavour is very strongly brought out; and the wayward, captious jealousy of Falkland, though so highly coloured in his own representation of it, is productive of no incident answerable to such an announcement;—the imposture which he practises upon Julia being, perhaps, weakened in its effect, by our recollection of the same device in the Nut-brown Maid and Peregrine Pickle. (pp. 141-42)

Mrs. Malaprop's mistakes, in what she herself calls "orthodoxy," have been often objected to as improbable from a woman in her rank of life; but though some of them, it must be owned, are extravagant and farcical, they are almost all amusing,—and the luckiness of her simile, "as headstrong as an *allegory* on the banks of the Nile," will be acknowledged as long as there are writers to be run away with, by the wilfulness of this truly "headstrong" species of composition. (pp. 142-43)

In reading [John Vanbrugh's comedy *The Relapse,* on which Sheridan based *A Trip to Scarborough*], we are struck with surprise, that Sheridan should ever have hoped to be able to *defecate* such dialogue, and, at the same time, leave any of the wit, whose whole spirit is in the lees, behind. The very life of such characters as Berinthia is their licentiousness, and it is with them, as with objects, that are luminous from putrescence,—to remove their taint is to extinguish their light. If Sheridan, indeed, had substituted some of his own wit for that which he took away, the inanition that followed the operation would have been much less sensibly felt. But to be so liberal of a treasure so precious, and for the enrichment of the work of another, could hardly have been expected from him. Besides, it may be doubted whether the subject had not already yielded its utmost to Vanbrugh, and whether, even in the hands of Sheridan, it could have been brought to bear a second crop of wit. Here and there through the dialogue, there are some touches from his pen—more, however, in the style of his farce than his comedy. For instance, that speech of Lord Foppington, where, directing the hosier not "to thicken the calves of his stockings so much," he says, "You should always remember, Mr. Hosier, that if you make a nobleman's spring legs as robust as his autumnal calves, you commit a monstrous impropriety,

and make no allowance for the fatigues of the winter.''
(pp. 198-99)

It was the fate of Mr. Sheridan, through life,—and, in a great
degree, his policy,—to gain credit for excessive indolence and
carelessness, while few persons, with so much natural brilliancy of talents, ever employed more art and circumspection
in their display. This was the case, remarkably, in the instance
[of *The School for Scandal*]. Notwithstanding the labour which
he bestowed upon this comedy, (or we should rather, perhaps,
say in consequence of that labour) the first representation of
the piece was announced before the whole of the copy was in
the hands of the actors. (p. 241)

The beauties of [*The School for Scandal*] are so universally
known and felt, that criticism may be spared the trouble of
dwelling upon them very minutely. With but little interest in
the plot, with no very profound or ingenious development of
character, and with a group of personages, not one of whom
has any legitimate claims upon either our affection or esteem,
it yet, by the admirable skill with which its materials are managed,—the happy contrivance of the situations, at once both
natural and striking,—the fine feeling of the ridiculous that
smiles throughout, and that perpetual play of wit which never
tires, but seems, like running water, to be kept fresh by its
own flow,—by all this general animation and effect, combined
with a finish of the details almost faultless, it unites the suf-
frages, at once, of the refined and the simple, and is not less
successful in ministering to the natural enjoyment of the latter,
than in satisfying and delighting the most fastidious tastes among
the former. (pp. 245-46)

The defects of *The School for Scandal,* if they can be allowed
to amount to defects, are, in a great measure, traceable to [an]
amalgamation of two distinct plots, out of which . . . the piece
was formed. From this cause,—like an accumulation of wealth
from the union of two rich families,—has devolved that excessive opulence of wit, with which, as some critics think, the
dialogue is overloaded; and which, Mr. Sheridan himself used
often to mention, as a fault of which he was conscious in his
work. That he had no such scruple, however, in writing it,
appears evident from the pains which he took to string upon
his new plot every bright thought and fancy which he had
brought together for the two others; and it is not a little curious,
in turning over his manuscript, to see how the out-standing
jokes are kept in recollection upon the margin, till he can find
some opportunity of funding them to advantage in the text.
The consequence of all this is, that the dialogue, from beginning to end, is a continued sparkling of polish and point: and
the whole of the Dramatis Personae might be comprised under
one common designation of Wits. Even Trip, the servant, is
as pointed and shining as the rest, and has his master's wit,
as he has his birth-day clothes, ''with the gloss on.'' (pp. 246-
47)

Another blemish that hypercriticism has noticed, and which
may likewise be traced to the original conformation of the play,
is the uselessness of some of the characters to the action or
business of it—almost the whole of the ''Scandalous College''
being but, as it were, excrescences, through which none of the
life-blood of the plot circulates. The cause of this is evident:—
Sir Benjamin Backbite, in the first plot to which he belonged,
was a principal personage; but, being transplanted from thence
into one with which he has no connection, not only he, but his
uncle Crabtree, and Mrs. Candour, though contributing abundantly to the animation of the dialogue, have hardly any thing
to do with the advancement of the story; and, like the acces-

sories in a Greek drama, are but as a sort of Chorus of Scandal
throughout. (pp. 248-49)

It has often been remarked as singular, that the lovers, Charles
and Maria, should never be brought in presence of each other
till the last scene; and Mr. Sheridan used to say, that he was
aware, in writing the Comedy, of the apparent want of dramatic
management which such an omission would betray; but that
neither of the actors, for whom he had destined those characters, was such as he could safely trust with a love scene.
There might, perhaps, too, have been, in addition to this motive, a little consciousness, on his own part, of not being exactly
in his element in that tender style of writing, which such a
scene, to make it worthy of the rest, would have required; and
of which the specimens left us in the serious parts of *The Rivals*
are certainly not among his most felicitous efforts. (p. 249)

From the trifling nature of these objections to the dramatic
merits of *The School for Scandal,* it will be seen that . . . they
only show how perfect must be the work in which no greater
faults can be found. But a more serious charge has been brought
against it on the score of morality; and the gay charm thrown
around the irregularities of Charles is pronounced to be dangerous to the interests of honesty and virtue. There is no doubt
that, in this character, only the fairer side of libertinism is
presented,—that the merits of being in debt are rather too
fondly insisted upon, and with a grace and spirit that might
seduce even creditors into admiration. (p. 251)

It should be recollected . . . that, in other respects, the author
applies the lash of moral satire very successfully. The group
of slanderers who, like the Chorus of the Eumenides, go searching about for their prey with ''eyes that drop poison,'' represent
a class of persons in society who richly deserve such ridicule,
and who—like their prototypes in Aeschylus trembling before
the shafts of Apollo—are here made to feel the full force of
the archery of wit. It is a proof of the effect and use of such
satire, that the name of ''Mrs. Candour'' has become one of
those formidable by-words, which have more power in putting
folly and ill-nature out of countenance, than whole volumes
of the wisest remonstrance and reasoning.

The poetical justice exercised upon the Tartuffe of sentiment,
Joseph, is another service to the cause of morals, which should
more than atone for any dangerous embellishment of wrong,
that the portraiture of the younger brother may exhibit. Indeed,
though both these characters are such as the moralist must visit
with his censure, there can be little doubt to which we should,
in real life, give the preference;—the levities and errors of the
one, arising from warmth of heart and of youth, may be merely
like those mists that exhale from summer streams, obscuring
them awhile to the eye, without affecting the native purity of
their waters; while the hypocrisy of the other is like the *mirage*
of the desert, shining with promise on the surface, but all false
and barren beneath. (pp. 251-53)

*Thomas Moore, in his* Memoirs of the Life of the
Right Honourable Richard Brinsley Sheridan, *Vol.
I, third edition, Longman, Rees, Orme, Brown, and
Green, 1825 (and reprinted by Scholarly Press, 1968),
543 p.*

**[EDWIN P. WHIPPLE]**   (essay date 1848)

The design of Sheridan in *The Rivals* was not dramatic excellence, but stage effect. In seeing it performed, we overlook,
in the glitter and point of the dialogue, the absence of the
higher requisites of comedy. The plot is without progress and

development. The characters are overcharged into caricatures, and can hardly be said to be conceived, much less sustained. Each has some oddity stuck upon him, which hardly rises to a peculiarity of character, and the keeping of this oddity is carelessly sacrificed at every temptation from a lucky witticism. The comic personages seem engaged in an emulous struggle to outshine each other. What they are is lost sight of in what they say. Sparkling sentences are bountifully lavished upon all. Fag and David are nearly as sparkling as their masters. The scene in the fourth act, where Acres communicates to David his challenge to Beverley, is little more than a brilliant string of epigrams and repartees, in which the country clown plays the dazzling fence of his wit with all the skill of Sheridan himself. . . . No dramatist whose conception of character was strong would fall into such shining inconsistencies.

The truth is, in this, as in Sheridan's other comedies, we tacitly overlook the keeping of character in the blaze of the wit. Every body laughs at Mrs. Malaprop's mistakes in the use of words, as he would laugh at similar mistakes in an acquaintance, who was exercising his ingenuity instead of exposing his ignorance. They are too felicitously infelicitous to be natural. Her remark to Lydia, that she is ''as headstrong as an allegory on the banks of the Nile,''—her scorn of ''algebra, simony, fluxions, paradoxes, and such inflammatory branches of learning,''—her quotation from Hamlet, in which the royal Dane is gifted with the ''front of Job himself,''—her fear of going into ''hydrostatic fits,''—her pride in the use of ''her oracular tongue and a nice derangement of epitaphs,''—are characteristics, not of a mind flippantly stupid, but curiously acute. (pp. 81-2)

Sir Anthony Absolute is the best character of the piece, and is made up of the elder Sheridan and Smollet's Matthew Bramble. Doubtless Sheridan had many a conversation with his father, of which the first scene between Sir Anthony and Captain Absolute is but a ludicrously heightened description. . . . The fine talk of Falkland and Julia is as unintentionally ludicrous as any comic portion of the play. . . . Indeed, Sheridan's attempts at serious imagery rarely reached beyond capitalizing the names of abstract qualities, or running out commonplace similes into flimsy and feeble allegories. His sentiment, also, is never fresh, generous, and natural, but almost always as tasteless in expression as hollow in meaning. The merit of *The Rivals* is in its fun and farce; and the serious portions, lugged in to make it appear more like a regular comedy, are worse than the attempts of Holcroft, Morton, and Reynolds in the same style.

The farce of *St. Patrick's Day* . . . , though written in evident haste, bears, in a few passages, marks of that elaborate and fanciful wit in which the chief strength of his mind consisted. In the second scene of the first act, the dialogue between Lauretta and her mother, on the relative merits of militia and regular officers, is keen and sparkling. ''Give me,'' says Lauretta, ''the bold, upright youth, who makes love to-day, and has his head shot off to-morrow. Dear! to think how the sweet fellows sleep on the ground and fight in silk stockings and lace ruffles.'' To this animated burst of girlish admiration, Mrs. Bridget contemptuously replies:—''To want a husband that may wed you to-day and be sent the Lord knows where before night; then in a twelve-month, perhaps, to come home like a Colossus, with one leg at New York and the other at Chelsea Hospital!'' This is one of the most startling ludicrous fancies in Sheridan's works. (pp. 82-3)

The diction of *The Duenna,* and the management of its character and incident, evince a marked improvement upon *The*

*Rivals.* The wit, though not so intellectual as that of *The School for Scandal,* is so happily combined with heedless animal spirits, as often to produce the effect of humor. It glitters and plays like heat-lightning through the whole dialogue. Epigram, repartee, and jest sparkle on the lips of every character. The power of permeating every thing with wit and glee—love, rage, cunning, avarice, religion—is displayed to perfection. It touches lightly, but keenly, on that point which admits of ludicrous treatment, and overlooks or blinks the rest. The best of the songs are but epigrams of sentiment. There is a spirit of joyous mischievousness and intrigue pervading the piece, which gives a delicious excitement to the brain. Little Isaac, the cunning, overreaching, and overreached Jew, is the very embodiment of gleeful craft,—''roguish, perhaps, but keen, devilish keen.'' The scene in which he woos the Duenna, and that which succeeds with Don Jerome, are among the most exquisite in the play. The sentiment of the piece is all subordinated to its fun and mischief. The scene in the Priory with the jolly monks is the very theology of mirth. (pp. 83-4)

The wit of *The Duenna* is so diffused through the dialogue as not readily to admit of quotation. It sparkles over the piece like sunshine on the ripples of running water. There are, however, a few sentences which stand apart in isolated brilliancy, displaying that curious interpenetration of fancy and wit, in which Sheridan afterwards excelled. Such is Isaac's description of the proud beauty,—''the very rustling of her silk has a disdainful sound''; and his answer to Don Ferdinand's furious demand to know whither the absconding lovers have gone:—''I will, I will! but people's memories differ; some have a treacherous memory: now mine is a cowardly memory,—it takes to its heels at the sight of a drawn sword, it does i' faith; and I could as soon fight as recollect.'' (p. 84)

*The School for Scandal* [is] a comedy which still occupies the first place on the stage, and which will ever be read with delight for the splendor, condensation, and fertility of its wit, the felicitous contrivance of some scenes and situations, the general brilliancy of its matter, and the tingling truth of its satirical strokes. As a representation of men as they appear, and manners as they are, it has the highest merit. The hypocrisies of life were never more skilfully probed, or its follies exposed to an ordeal of more polished scorn. . . . *The Critic* excels every thing of its kind in the English language, for it is to be compared with Buckingham's *Rehearsal* and Fielding's *Midas,* not with Beaumont's *Knight of the Burning Pestle.* The wit always tells and never tires. (pp. 86-7)

Sheridan's defects as a dramatist answer to the defects of his mind and character. Acute in observing external appearances, and well informed in what rakes and men of fashion call life, he was essentially superficial in mind and heart. A man of great wit and fancy, he was singularly deficient in the deeper powers of humor and imagination. All his plays lack organic life. In plot, character, and incident, they are framed by mechanical, not conceived by vital, processes. They evince no genial enjoyment of mirth, no insight into the deeper springs of the ludicrous. The laughter they provoke is the laughter of antipathy, not of sympathy. It is wit detecting external inconsistencies and oddities, not humor representing them in connection with the inward constitution whence they spring. The great triumphs of comic genius have been in comic creations, conceived through the processes of imagination and sympathy, and instinct with the vital life of mirth. (pp. 87-8)

Now Sheridan's comic personages display none of this life and genial fun. They seem sent upon the stage simply to utter brilliant things, and their wit goes out with their exit. Every thing they say is as good as the original conception of their individuality, and character is therefore lost in the glare of its representation. In truth, Sheridan conceived a character as he conceived a jest. It first flashed upon his mind in an epigrammatic form. In his Memoranda, published by Moore [in his biography of Sheridan], we find the hints of various dramatic personages embodied in smart sayings. Thus, one is indicated in the significant sentence:—"I shall order my valet to shoot me the first thing he does in the morning." Another is sketched us "an old woman endeavouring to put herself back into a girl"; another, as a man "who changes sides in all arguments the moment you agree with him"; and another, as a "pretty woman studying looks, and endeavouring to recollect an ogle, like Lady —, who has learned to play her eyelids like Venetian blinds." In all these we perceive the wit laughing at external peculiarities, and subjecting them to the malicious exaggerations of fancy, but not the dramatist searching for internal qualities, and moulding them into new forms of mirthful being. The character is but one of the many pleasantries it is made to speak. In those instances where Sheridan most nearly produces the effects of humor, it is done by the coöperation of brisk animal spirits with fancy, or by adopting and refining upon the delineations of others.

We would not, in these remarks, be considered as underrating Sheridan's real powers. He is undoubtedly to be placed among the wittiest of writers and speakers. His plays, speeches, and the records of his conversation sparkle with wit of almost all kinds, from the most familiar to the most recondite. Though seldom genial, it is never malignant; and if it barely reaches far beneath the surfaces of things, it plays over them with wonderful brilliancy. No English comic writer, who was not also a great poet, ever approached him in fineness and remoteness of ludicrous analogy. In delicacy of allusion, in exquisite lightness and certainty of touch, in concise felicity and airiness of expression, his wit is almost unmatched. (pp. 88-9)

> [*Edwin P. Whipple*], *"Richard Brinsley Sheridan,"* in The North American Review, *Vol. LXVI, No. CXXXVIII, January, 1848, pp. 72-110.*

## GEORGE GILFILLAN (essay date 1854)

We look upon Sheridan's career and works as, on the whole, the most useless in the history of literature. He said many clever things, made many flashy speeches, has left two or three clever plays, but he has *done* little or nothing; told no new truth, enforced no old one; failed in blasting even "scandal," the only task he set himself in morals to do; and neither helped, nor hindered, by a single inch, the advancement of society. . . .

On the whole, his vein of wit was meagre, nor was it of the subtlest or most refined order. (p. 21)

His plays are his sole title to consideration as an author. The "Rivals" is an uproarious farce rather than a fine play; and, even in its farcical elements, is not so good, we think, as Goldsmith's "Good-natured Man," or "She Stoops to Conquer." It wants Goldsmith's inimitable *bonhommie*. The "School for Scandal" is wearisomely witty; you cry out for a plain scene or a plain sentence as for a pearl of price. The whole of the characters are for ever "talking their best" and doing their worst. The wit, too, is often far-fetched, and the morality is but so-and-so. There is not a spark of humor or true genius.

It is, in short, a display of the utmost length to which mere cleverness can carry an author, and is, perhaps, the best *artificial* comedy in the language. But, when you compare it with even the worst of Shakspeare's plays, what a cold, starched, and heartless affair it seems! The poorest of Shakspeare's comedies is one of nature's flowers—weeds, if you please—but this, the most elaborate of Sheridan's, is a mere gumflower, without scent or savor. "Pizarro" is far worse, and nothing proves more thoroughly that barrenness of imagination we have ascribed to Sheridan. It never rises above a species of convulsive and twisted bombast, worked up as in an agony of ambitious weakness, which we find frequent also in his speeches. His "Duenna" is exceedingly amusing, and pretends to be nothing more. In the "Critic," Sir Fretful Plagiary is capital; and next, perhaps, to Joseph Surface, his deeper and subtler strokes than any character Sheridan has drawn. His other pieces of manufacture for the stage, such as the "Stranger," and the most of his smaller poems, are beneath criticism.

Byron, whose unbounded admiration of Pope and Sheridan is one of the most unaccountable points in all his unaccountable character, says, "that whatever Sheridan seriously attempted was best in its way; he wrote the best opera, the best farce, the best comedy, the best monologue, and made the best speech" [see excerpt above, 1813]. We venture to doubt these *dicta*. The "Duenna" is not equal to the "Beggar's Opera" for originality and spirit, although it is much more elaborate. The "Critic" cannot be compared in rich fun to the "Comedy of Errors." Making the best monologue is but a small achievement. The "School for Scandal," like "Tom Jones," is an admirable piece of art; but like it, too, the materials are vile; it is a palace made of dung, and, even in wit, it is inferior to some of Congreve's. (pp. 21-2)

> *George Gilfillan, "Modern British Orators: R.B. Sheridan," in* The Eclectic Magazine, *Vol. XXXI, No. I, January, 1854, pp. 19-28.*

## W. F. RAE (essay date 1867)

Sheridan wrote, as he lived, for the sake of effect. He aimed at conquering a place in literature as he aimed at becoming the friend of princes and nobles. What other men have done by inspiration he accomplished by energy. Although not a man of great industry, yet he could work with unexampled perseverance till his object was attained. Genius he did not possess. There are no conspicuous failures alternating with successes to be laid to his charge. He had the talent for compassing his ends, and the sense to know the exact measure of his power. . . .

In several respects there is a close resemblance between Dryden and Sheridan. Both were politicians as well as playwrights. Both coveted the title of wits, and both obtained it. As dramatists neither displayed originality, for Dryden copied French, while Sheridan as carefully copied English models. Each succeeded, however, in being recognised as a master of style. Even now there is no better example of easy, idiomatic, and forcible style than that of Dryden, while Sheridan's writings are the best specimens we have of the most expressive words arranged in the most effective order. But in the case of Sheridan far more than in that of Dryden, the culture of the form has been carried to excess. Like the pictures of some pre-Raphaelite artists, his scenes are all foreground. (p. 320)

In his first play [*The Rivals*] the faults are the same as those which characterise his more finished ones. Thomas, a coachman, and Fag, the servant to Captain Absolute, converse in a strain which, however it may have suited the taste of the day, seems to us absurd and artificial. Replying to the inquiry of the former, the latter says, ''Why, then, the cause of all this is love—love, Thomas, who (as you may get read to you) has been a masquerader ever since the days of Jupiter.'' . . . The female characters are as artificial as the male. Mrs. Malaprop, Lydia Languish, and Julia, are women whom we could not find off the stage. Most unnatural of all is the sentimentality of Julia. It has a mawkish flavour which is disgusting. The concluding sentences are as forced and silly as the rant about filial piety in his famous speech. Lydia exclaims, ''Our happiness is now as unalloyed as general.'' Julia adds, ''Then let us study to preserve it so; and while Hope pictures to us a flattering scene of future bliss, let us deny its pencil those colours which are too bright to be lasting. When hearts deserving happiness would unite their fortunes, Virtue would crown them with an unfading garland of modest, hurtless flowers; but ill-judging Passion will force the gaudier rose into the wreath, whose thorn offends them when its leaves are dropped.'' Had there been nothing but this stuff in *The Rivals*, it is doubtful if any audience of the period at which it was produced would have applauded the piece. What gives life to it is the humour of Sir Anthony Absolute, and the broad farce of Acres and Sir Lucius O'Trigger. But it had, as all Sheridan's plays have, the great merit of being a good acting play. He at once caught the knack of writing for the stage. He had an almost intuitive perception of the best way in which to produce effects. (pp. 320-22)

When read, [however,] *The School for Scandal* fatigues by its brilliancy. The effect on the mind resembles that made on the eye by a mirror shown in the International Exhibition of 1862. This mirror was composed of numerous prisms ranged side by side. There is no prettier sight than the rays of light refracted by a prism. But the spectacle, to be appreciated, must be witnessed on a small scale and for a short time. A room lined with huge mirrors formed of clusters of prisms would be unbearable to any one but the Turkish potentate, for whom similar mirrors were designed and manufactured. To those whose tastes are vitiated, the perpetual sparkle of *The School for Scandal* will give unalloyed delight. All whose tastes are natural and acute are soon cloyed with its beauties.

As a whole, *The Critic* is Sheridan's happiest dramatic work. He was essentially a critic, quick to detect imposture, and capable of exposing and punishing it. And in this farce he had full scope for the exercise of his talents. He can claim no credit for originating the plan on which it is framed, as it is modelled on [The Duke of Buckingham's] *The Rehearsal*. The greater is his merit in having succeeded as he has done, because, excepting in the form, *The Critic* differs from any work of the kind ever conceived and executed. The character of Puff is one of the most finished and truthful which Sheridan has created. He is as life-like now as when he first amused the audience of Drury Lane. . . . Puff is as impersonal, yet natural, as Falstaff. He makes us laugh by the absurdity of his comments; still we always feel that his remarks are those which the author of such a tragedy as *The Spanish Armada* [the play within *The School for Scandal*] would have made. It is impossible to believe in Joseph Surface [of *The School for Scandal*], or to regard his luckier brother Charles as a praiseworthy hero. Joseph is too conscious of his villainy: when he says, in reply to Lady Teazle's reproach, ''You are going to be moral, and forget that you are among friends,'' ''Egad, that's true! I'll keep that sentiment till I see Sir Peter,'' we know he is acting a part. Again, when he moralises in this fashion, we feel that is not

the true rogue whom Sheridan would have us take him for, because a genuine rogue dissembles even to himself: ''A curious dilemma, truly, my politics have run me into! I wanted, at first, only to ingratiate myself with Lady Teazle, that she might not be my enemy with Maria; and I have, I don't know how, become her serious lover. Sincerely I begin to wish I had never made such a point of gaining so very good a character, for it has led me into so many cursed rogueries, that I doubt I shall be exposed at last.'' Now, the last thing for which Joseph Surface ought to have professed his dread was ignominious failure. His plausibility is based on self-assurance, and the thought of being exposed would have rendered him incapable of being always prepared for every emergency. A true villain always believes in his ''star.'' Puff, on the other hand, is serenely unconscious of being the object of ridicule. To the hits of Mr. Sneer he has an answer ready which he thinks effective, because he does not perceive that he is being ridiculed. He never doubts that the rubbish uttered by the players is really fine poetry. He is always ready with an ingenious explanation of any alleged mistake. (pp. 322-23)

As literary works, Sheridan's plays no longer seem the paragons of excellence they once did; nevertheless, when well acted, they still charm playgoers as greatly as of old. That they are laboured and artificial is of little consequence: a theatrical audience does not expect natural truth on the stage. What it desires and delights in are smart dialogues and good plots, and these set forth by good performers. A modern English audience also expects sound morality. Joseph Surface, the consummate hypocrite, must be punished. Lady Teazle must be more sinned against than sinning. Wit must be untainted with lewdness. Provided these conditions are fulfilled, the public will applaud the performance. The public of to-day is still the same as that for which Sheridan wrote, a public in which the middle class has the preponderating voice. . . .

This class had begun to frequent the theatre when he wrote. He strove to hit its taste, and he succeeded, because he carefully avoided the style which, had he lived half a century earlier, he might have adopted. Fortunately for his fame as a dramatist, the style which suited his age could only become antiquated when another revolution had taken place in the constitution of theatrical audiences. It may be that the change is in progress, and that even the printed dialogue of Sheridan will fall flat on ears accustomed to verbal absurdities, and that a farce like *The Critic*, wherein character is depicted, will be thought far inferior as a work of art to a burlesque containing masked actors and half-naked actresses. (pp. 323-24)

To the present generation it is important to know whether Sheridan's comedies and speeches are masterly productions, whether they are animated with the vital spark which will render them immortal, whether they will give as much pleasure to those who now or who may hereafter read them as to the audiences which first hailed them with rapturous applause. His place in literature is in the second rank, but in that rank he has no superior. The historian of the English drama will chronicle him as the last great writer of English comedy, and will consider it as foolish to look for the advent of a second Sheridan as of a second Shakespeare. (p. 332)

> *W. F. Rae, ''Richard Brinsley Sheridan,'' in The*
> *Fortnightly Review, n.s. Vol. II, No. IX, September*
> *1, 1867, pp. 310-32.*

### [HENRY JAMES]  (essay date 1874)

[*James, a distinguished novelist and critic, states that* The School for Scandal *has ''hardly a ray of fancy, of the graceful or the ideal, and even its merits—its smartness and smoothness and rapidity—has something hard and metallic.'' James concludes, nonetheless, that the play's ''robustness and smoothness of structure, and its extreme felicity and finish of style . . . sufficiently account for its vitality.''*]

The *School for Scandal* leads off the rather dreary list of the so-called old English comedies, but it stands a head and shoulders higher than its companions. Like most of the better pieces in the English repertory, it is more than a trifle threadbare, and has seen, in its day, no small amount of service. One should speak of it with respect, for, with all its faults, it has played a very useful part. It has often kept a worse play from being acted, and, odd as the fact may appear, it has been almost solely charged, for upwards of a century, with representing intellectual brilliancy on the English stage. There is Shakespeare, of course, but Shakespeare stands apart, and it never occurs to the critic to call him brilliant. We commend him in less familiar phrase. There are the old English comedies just mentioned, which, from Mrs. Inchbald down to London Assurance, are universally acknowledged to be very knowing affairs, and to contain a vast amount of talent, and of that superior sparkle and movement which is independent of the gas-man and the machinery. But for real intellectual effort, the literary atmosphere and the tone of society, there has long been nothing like the *School for Scandal*. . . . It has . . . by this time a certain venerable air; it is an historical relic, an ethnological monument. One might have fancied that it had earned its rest and passed into the province of the archaeologists, but we [often] find it summoned once more to the front and bearing the brunt of the battle. . . . [The ideas of *The School for Scandal*], in so far as it has any, are coarse and prosaic, and its moral atmosphere uncomfortably thin. The main idea is that gossips and backbiters are brought to confusion, that hypocrisy is a nasty vice, and that a fine young fellow who lives freely and sociably and has a kindly word for great and small is likely to turn out better, in the long run, than his elder brother, who is an economist and a ''man of sentiment.'' The types are coarsely depicted, and the morality is all vulgar morality. The play is of course positively none the worse for this latter fact; it is only less imaginative. It has hardly a ray of fancy, of the graceful or the ideal, and even its merit—its smartness and smoothness and rapidity—has something hard and metallic. . . . The distinctively amusing scenes in the *School for Scandal* are those in which Lady Sneerwell's guests assemble to pull their acquaintance to pieces. They are brilliantly clever, but they perhaps best illustrate our charge of coarseness and harshness. Crabtree and Mrs. Candour are absolutely brutal, and the whole circle settles down to its work with the ferocity of vultures and wolves. To measure the difference between small art and great, one should compare the talk of Sheridan's scandal-mongers with that scene in Molière's *Misanthrope* in which the circle at Célimène's house hit off the portraits of their absent friends. In the one case one feels almost ashamed to be listening; in the other it is good society still, even though it be good society in a heartless mood.

And yet there are numerous good reasons why the *School for Scandal* should have had a great popularity. The very fact that its wit is such as all the world can understand, at the same time that it has point enough to make the spectator, who seizes it as it flies, think himself a rather clever fellow; the fact, too, that it hits the average sense of fair play, and does not attempt too fine a discrimination of character; its robustness and smoothness of structure, and its extreme felicity and finish of style,—these things sufficiently account for its continued vitality. (pp. 755-57)

[*Henry James*], in a review of ''School for Scandal,'' in The Atlantic Monthly (*copyright © 1874, by The Atlantic Monthly Company, Boston, Mass.*), Vol. XXXIV, No. CCVI, December, 1874, pp. 754-57.

**J. BRANDER MATTHEWS**   (essay date 1877)

''**The School for Scandal**'' is obviously not a spontaneous improvisation. It is not labored, for its author had the art to conceal art, but its symmetrical smoothness and perfect polish cost great labor. (p. 560)

In ''**The School for Scandal**'' the construction, the ordering of the scenes, the development of the elaborate plot, is much better than in the comedies of any of Sheridan's contemporaries. A play in those days need not reveal a complete and self-contained plot. Great laxity of episode was not only permitted, but almost praised; and that Sheridan, with a subject which lent itself as he did, shows his exact appreciation of the source of dramatic effect. But it must be confessed that the construction of ''**The School for Scandal**,'' when measured by our modern standards, seems a little loose—a little diffuse, perhaps. It shows the welding of the two distinct plots. There can hardly be seen in it the ruling of a dominant idea, subordinating all the parts to the effect of the whole. But, although the two original motives have been united mechanically, although they have not flowed and fused together in the hot spurt of homogeneous inspiration, the joining has been so carefully concealed, and the whole structure has been overlaid with so much wit, that few people after seeing the play would care to complain. The wit is ceaseless; and wit like Sheridan's would cover sins of construction far greater than those of ''**The School for Scandal**.'' It is ''steeped in the very brine of conceit, and sparkles like salt in the fire.''

In his conception of character Sheridan is a wit rather than a humorist. He creates character by a distinctly intellectual process; he does not bring it forth out of the depths, as it were, of his own being. His humor—fine and dry as it is—is the humor of the wit. He has little or none of the rich and juicy, nay, almost oily humor of Falstaff, for instance. His wit is the wit of common-sense, like Jerrold's or Sydney Smith's; it is not wit informed with imagination, like Shakespeare's wit. But this is only to say again that Sheridan is not one of the few world-wide and all-embracing geniuses. . . . [Dramatists] may be divided into three classes: those who can say one thing in one way—these are the great majority; those who can say one thing in many ways—even these are far fewer than they would be generally reckoned; and those who can say many things in many ways—these are the chosen few, the scant half-dozen who hold the highest peak of Parnassus. In the front rank of the second class stands Sheridan. The thing he has to say is wit—and of this in all its forms he is master. His wit in general has a metallic smartness and a crystalline coldness; it rarely lifts us from the real to the ideal; and yet the whole comedy is in one sense, at least, idealized; it bears, in fact, the resemblance to real life that a well-cut diamond has to a drop of water.

Yet, the play is not wholly cold. Sheridan's wit could be genial as well as icy. . . . (pp. 561-62)

The great defect of ''**The School for Scandal**''—the one thing which shows the difference between a comic writer of the type of Sheridan and a great dramatist like Shakespeare—is the unvarying wit of the characters. And not only are the characters all witty, but they all talk alike. Their wit is Sheridan's wit, which is very good wit indeed; but it is Sheridan's own, and not Sir Peter Teazle's, or Backbite's, or Careless's, or Lady

Sneerwell's. It is one man in his time playing many parts. . . . [His] comedy, if a little less artistic in the reading, is far more lively in the acting. It has been said that in Shakespeare we find not the language we would use in the situations, but the language we should wish to use—that we should talk so if we could. We cannot all of us be as witty as the characters of "The School for Scandal," but who of us would not if he could? . . .

"The School for Scandal" was not easy writing then, and it is not hard reading now. Not content with a wealth of wit alone—for he did hold with the old maxim which says that jests, like salt, should be used sparingly; he salted with a lavish hand, and his plays have perhaps been preserved to us by this Attic salt—he sought the utmost refinement of language. An accomplished speaker himself, he smoothed every sentence till it ran trippingly on the tongue. (p. 562)

> *J. Brander Matthews, in a review of "The School for Scandal," in* Appleton's Journal, *n.s. Vol. II, June, 1877, pp. 556-62.*

## MRS. OLIPHANT (essay date 1883)

[*Margaret Oliphant was a prolific Victorian novelist and critic. In her biographical and critical study of Sheridan, from which the following is drawn, she depicts the playwright as a gifted man who squandered his talents. Here she surveys his dramas, which she praises for their lively vigor.*]

Scarcely ever was play so full of liveliness and interest constructed upon a slighter machinery [than in *The Rivals*]. . . . [The] whole action of the piece turns upon a mystification, which affords some delightfully comic scenes, but few of those occasions of suspense and uncertainty which give interest to the drama. This we find in the brisk and delightful movement of the piece, in the broad but most amusing sketches of character, and the unfailing wit and sparkle of the dialogue. (pp. 51-2)

Mrs. Malaprop's ingenious "derangement of epitaphs" is her chief distinction to the popular critic; and even though such a great competitor as Dogberry has occupied the ground before her, these delightful absurdities have never been surpassed [from Shakespeare's *Much Ado about Nothing*]. But justice has hardly been done to the individual character of this admirable if broad sketch of a personage quite familiar in such scenes as that which Bath presented a century ago, the plausible, well-bred woman, with a great deal of vanity, and no small share of good-nature, whose inversion of phrases is quite representative of the blurred realisation she has of surrounding circumstances, and who is quite sincerely puzzled by the discovery that she is not so well qualified to enact the character of Delia as her niece would be. Mrs. Malaprop has none of the harshness of Mrs. Hardcastle, in *She Stoops to Conquer,* and we take it unkind of Captain Absolute to call her "a weatherbeaten she-dragon." The complacent nod of her head, the smirk on her face, her delightful self-satisfaction and confidence in her "parts of speech," have nothing repulsive in them. (pp. 52-3)

The other characters, though full of brilliant talk, cleverness, and folly, have less originality. The country hobbledehoy [Bob Acres], matured into a dandy and braggart by his entrance into the intoxicating excitement of Bath society, is comical in the highest degree; but he is not characteristically human. While Mrs. Malaprop can hold her ground with Dogberry, Bob Acres is not fit to be mentioned in the same breath with the "exquisite

reasons" of that delightful knight, Sir Andrew Aguecheek [from Shakespeare's *Twelfth Night*]. And thus it becomes at once apparent that Sheridan's eye for a situation, and the details that make up a striking combination on the stage, was far more remarkable than his insight into human motives and action. There is no scene on the stage which retains its power of amusing an ordinary audience more brilliantly than that of the proposed duel [between Bob Acres and Sir Lucius]. . . . The two men are little more than symbols of the slightest description, but their dialogue is instinct with wit, and that fun, the most English of qualities, which does not reach the height of humour, yet overwhelms even gravity itself with a laughter in which there is no sting or bitterness. Molière sometimes attains this effect, but rarely, having too much meaning in him; but with Shakspeare it is frequent amongst higher things. And in Sheridan this gift of innocent ridicule and quick embodiment of the ludicrous without malice or *arrière-pensée* reaches to such heights of excellence as have given his nonsense a sort of immortality.

It is, however, difficult to go far in discussion or analysis of a literary production which attempts no deeper investigation into human nature than this. Sheridan's art, from its very beginning, was theatrical, if we may use the word, rather than dramatic. It aimed at strong situations and highly effective scenes rather than at a finely constructed story, or the working out of either plot or passion. . . . The art [of the *Rivals*] is charming, the figures full of vivacity, the touch that sets them before us exquisite: except, indeed, in the Faulkland scenes, probably intended as a foil for the brilliancy of the others, in which Julia's magnificent phrases are too much for us, and make us deeply grateful to Sheridan for the discrimination which kept him . . . from the serious drama. But there are no depths to be sounded, and no suggestions to be carried out. (pp. 53-5)

[The] farce called *St. Patrick's Day; or, the Scheming Lieutenant* [is] a very slight production. . . . (p. 57)

[It] still keeps its ground among Sheridan's works, bound up between the *Rivals* and the *School for Scandal,* a position in which one cannot help feeling it must be much astonished to find itself. (p. 58)

The story of [the *Duenna*] belongs to the same easy, artificial inspiration which dictated the trivial plot of *St. Patrick's Day.* . . . (p. 59)

There is very little character attempted, save in Isaac, who is a sort of rudimentary sketch of a too cunning knave or artful simpleton caught in his own toils; and the dialogue, if sometimes clever enough, never for a moment reaches the sparkle of the *Rivals.* (p. 61)

Posterity, which has so thoroughly carried out the judgment of contemporaries in respect to the *Rivals,* has not extended its favour to the *Duenna.* Perhaps the attempt to conjoin spoken dialogue to any great extent with music is never a very successful attempt: for English opera does not seem to last. (p. 63)

The highly polished diction of the *School for Scandal,* and the high-pressure of its keen and trenchant wit, does not look much like the excited work of the small hours inspired by port; but a man who is fully launched in the tide of society, and sought on all hands to give brilliancy to the parties of his patrons, must needs "steal a few hours from the night." "It was the fate of Sheridan through life," Moore says, "and in a great degree his policy, to gain credit for excessive indolence and carelessness'' [see excerpt above, 1825]. It seems very likely that he has here hit the mark, and furnished an explanation for many of the apparently headlong feats of composition by which many authors are believed to have distinguished themselves. (pp. 74-5)

The *Rivals* sprang into being without much thought, with that instinctive and unerring perception of the right points to rec-ollect and record, which makes observation the unconscious instrument of genius, and is so immensely and indescribably different from mere imitation. But the *School for Scandal*—a more elaborate performance in every way—required a different handling. It seems to have floated in the writer's mind from the moment when he discovered his own powers, stimulating his invention and his memory at once, and prompting half a dozen beginnings before the right path was discovered. Now it is one story, now another, that attracts his fancy. He will enlist those gossiping circles which he feels by instinct to be so serviceable for the stage, to serve the purpose of a scheming woman and separate a pair of lovers. Anon, departing from that idea, he will employ them to bring about the catastrophe of a loveless marriage, in which an old husband and a young wife, the very commonplaces of comedy, shall take a new and original development. Two distinct stories rise in his mind, like two butterflies circling about each other, keeping him for a long time undecided which is the best for his purpose. The first plot is one which the spectator has now a little difficulty in tracing through the brilliant scenes which were originally intended to carry it out, though it is distinctly stated in the first scene, between Lady Sneerwell and Snake, which still opens the comedy. As it now stands this intimation of her ladyship's purpose is far too important for anything that follows, and is apt to mystify the spectator, who finds little in the after scenes to justify it. . . . But while the author is playing with this plot, and designing fragmentary scenes in which to carry it out, the other is tugging at his fancy—an entirely distinct idea, with a group of new and individual characters: the old man and his wife, the two contrasted brothers, one of whom is to have the reputation of being her lover, while the other is the real villain. (pp. 75-7)

How it was that Sheridan was led to amalgamate . . . two plays into one we are left altogether without information. (pp. 81-2)

The scandalous scenes . . . are almost entirely without con-nexion with the plot. They can be detached and enjoyed sep-arately without any sensible loss in the reader's (or even spec-tator's) mind. In themselves the management of all the details is inimitable. The eager interchange takes away our breath; there is no break or possibility of pause in it. The malign suggestion, the candid astonishment, the spite which assails, and the malicious good-nature which excuses, are all balanced to perfection, with a spirit which never flags for a moment. And when the veterans in the art are joined by a brilliant and mischievous recruit in the shape of Lady Teazle, rushing in amongst them in pure *gaité du coeur* [gaiety of heart], the energy of her young onslaught outdoes them all. The talk has never been so brilliant, never so pitiless, as when she joins them. She adds the gift of mimicry to all their malice, and produces a genuine laugh even from those murderers of their neighbours' reputations. This is one of the side-lights, perhaps unintentional, which keen insight throws upon human nature, showing how mere headlong imitation and high spirits, and the determination to do whatever other people do, and a little more, go further than the most mischievous intention. Perhaps

the author falls into his usual fault of giving too much wit and point to the utterances of the young wife, who is not intended to be clever; but her sudden dash into the midst of the dowagers, and unexpected victory over them in their own line, is full of nature. (pp. 83-4)

Apart from these scenes, the construction of the play shows once more Sheridan's astonishing instinct for a striking situ-ation. Two such will immediately occur to the mind of the reader—the great screen scene, and that in which Sir Charles Surface sells his family portraits. The first is incomparably the greater of the two, and one which has rarely been equalled on the stage. The succession of interviews, one after another, has not a word too much; nor could the most impatient audience find any sameness or repetition in the successive arrivals. . . . [The] most matter-of-fact spectator can scarcely repress, even when carried along by the interest of the story, a sensation of admiring wonder at the skill with which all [the] combinations are effected. It is less tragic than Tartuffe, insomuch as Orgon's profound belief, and the darker guilt of the domestic traitor, move us more deeply and it is not terrible, like the unveiling of Iago; but neither is it trivial, as the ordinary discoveries of deceitful wives and friends to which we are accustomed on the stage so generally are; and the fine art with which Sir Peter—something of an old curmudgeon in the earlier scenes—is made unexpectedly to reveal his better nature, and thus prepare the way, unawares, for the re-establishment of his own happiness at the moment when it seems entirely shattered, is worthy of the highest praise. . . . There remains for the comedy of the future (or the tragedy, which, wherever the deeper chords of life are touched, comes to very much the same thing) a still greater achievement—that of inventing an Iago who shall de-ceive the audience as well as the Othello upon whom he plays, and be found out only by us and our hero at the same moment. Probably, could such a thing be done, the effect would be too great, and the indignation and horror of the crowd, thus skil-fully excited, produce a sensation beyond that which is per-missible to fiction. But Sheridan does not deal with any tragical powers. Nothing deeper is within his reach than the momentary touch of real feeling with which Lady Teazle vindicates herself, and proves her capacity for better things. . . . The scene is in itself a succinct drama, quite comprehensible even when de-tached from its context, and of the highest effectiveness. (pp. 84-6)

The other great scene, that in which Charles Surface sells his pictures, has qualities of a different kind. It is less perfect and more suggestive than most of Sheridan's work. We have to accept the favourite type of the stage hero—the reckless, thoughtless, warm-hearted, impressionable spendthrift, as will-ing to give as he is averse to pay, scattering his wild oats by handfuls, wasting his life and his means in riotous living, yet easily touched and full of kind impulses—before we can do justice to it. . . . Charles Surface is the light-hearted prodigal whose easy vices have brought him to the point of destruction. Whatever grave thoughts on the subject he may have within, he is resolute in carrying out his gay career to the end, and ready to laugh in the face of ruin. A more severe taste might consider his light-heartedness swagger and his generosity prod-igality; but we are expected on the stage to consider such characteristics as far more frequently conjoined with a good heart than sobriety and decency. . . . As the prodigal rattles on, with almost too much swing and ''way'' upon him in the tragi-comedy of fate, we are hurried along in the stream of his wild gaiety with sympathy which he has no right to. The au-dience is all on his side from the first word. (pp. 86-8)

It is a curious particular in the excellence of the piece, however, and scarcely a commendation, we fear, in the point of view of art, that these very striking scenes, as well as those in which the scandalmongers hold their amusing conclave, may all be detached from the setting with the greatest ease and without any perceptible loss of interest. Never was there a drama which it was so easy to take to pieces. The screen scene in itself forms, as we have already pointed out, a succinct and brilliant little performance which the simple audience could understand; and though the others might require a word or two of preface, they are each sufficiently perfect in themselves to admit of separation from the context. It says a great deal for the power of the writer that this should be consistent with the general interest of the comedy, and that we are scarcely conscious, in the acting, of the looseness with which it hangs together, or the independence of the different parts. Sheridan, who was not a playwright by science, but rather by accident, did not in all likelihood, in the exuberance of his strength, trouble himself with any study of the laws that regulate dramatic composition. The unities of time and place he preserves, indeed, because it suits him to do so; the incidents of his pieces might all happen in a few hours, for anything we know, and with singularly little change of scene; but the close composition and interweaving of one part with another, which all dramatists ought, but so very few do, study, evidently cost him little thought. He has the quickest eye for a situation, and knows that nothing pleases the playgoing public so much as a strong combination and climax; but he does not take the trouble to rivet the links of his chain or fit them very closely into each other. (pp. 88-9)

*The Critic* is, of all Sheridan's plays, the one which has least claim to originality. Although it is no copy, nor can be accused of plagiarism, it is the climax of a series of attempts descending downwards from the Elizabethan era. . . . But what his predecessors had tried with different degrees of success—or failure—Sheridan accomplished triumphantly. . . . In the *School for Scandal* Sheridan had held his audience in delighted suspense in scene after scene which had merely the faintest link of connexion with the plot of his play, and did little more than interrupt its action. But in [*The Critic*] he held the stage for nearly half the progress of the piece by the mere power of pointed and pungent remarks, the keen interchanges of witty talk, the personality of three or four individuals not sufficiently developed to be considered as impersonations of character, and with nothing to do but to deliver their comments upon matters of literary interest. Rarely has a greater feat been performed on the stage. . . . *The Critic* is as delightful as ever, and we listen to the gentlemen talking with as much relish as our grandfathers did. Nay, the simplest-minded audience, innocent of literature, and perhaps not very sure what it all means, will still answer to the touch and laugh till they cry over the poor author's wounded vanity and the woes of Tilburina. . . . When he has turned the author outside in, and exposed all his little weaknesses (not without a sharper touch here, for it is Mr. Puff, the inventor of the art of advertising as it was in those undeveloped days, and not any better man, who fills the place of the successful dramatist), he turns to the play itself with the same delightful perception of its absurdities. (pp. 95-8)

In *The Critic* [Sheridan] is at the height of his powers; his keen sense of the ridiculous might have, though we do not claim it for him, a moral aim, and be directed to the reformation of the theatre; but his first inspiration came from his own enjoyment of the humours of the stage and perception of its whimsical incongruities. (p. 100)

Sheridan's view of life was not a profound one. It was but a vulgar sort of drama, a problem without any depths—to be solved by plenty of money and wine and pleasure, by youth and high spirits, and an easy lavishness which was called liberality, or even generosity as occasion served. But to Sheridan there was nothing to find out in it, any more than there is anything to find out in the characters of his plays. He had nothing to say further. Lady Teazle's easy penitence, her husband's pardon, achieved by the elegant turn of her head seen through the open door, and the entry of Charles Surface into all the good things of this life, in recompense for an insolent sort of condescending gratitude to his egotistical old uncle, were all he knew on this great subject. And when that was said he had turned round upon the stage, the audience, the actors, and the writers who catered for them, and made fun of them all with the broadest mirth, and easy indifference to what might come after. What was there more for him to say? *The Critic,* so far as the impulse of creative energy, or what, for want of a better word, we call genius, was concerned, was Sheridan's last word. (pp. 107-08)

*Mrs. Oliphant, in her* Sheridan, *Macmillan and Co., 1883 (and reprinted by Harper & Brothers, 1887, 199 p.).*

**BERNARD SHAW** (essay date 1896)

[*A prominent Irish dramatist and critic, Shaw asserts that* The School for Scandal *appears dated not in point of its manners and costume, but in point of its morals, particularly as conveyed by the female characters.*]

*The School for Scandal,* which has got over its first attack [the complaint of being dated] so triumphantly that its obsolete costumes and manners positively heighten its attraction [has] dated very perceptibly . . . in point of morals. Its thesis of the superiority of the good-natured libertine to the ill-natured formalist and hypocrite may pass, though it is only a dramatization of [Henry Fielding's] *Tom Jones,* and hardly demurs to the old morality further than to demonstrate that a bad man is not so bad as a worse. But there is an ancient and fishlike smell about the 'villainy' of Joseph and the ladylikeness of Lady Teazle. If you want to bring *The School for Scandal* up to date, you must make Charles a woman, and Joseph a perfectly sincere moralist. Then you will be in the atmosphere of Ibsen and of *The Greatest of These*—at once. And it is because there is no sort of hint of this now familiar atmosphere—because Joseph's virtue is a pretence instead of a reality, and because the women in the play are set apart and regarded as absolutely outside the region of free judgment in which the men act, that the play, as aforesaid, 'dates.'

Formerly, nothing shocked us in the screen scene except Charles's caddishness in making fun of Sir Peter and his wife under very painful circumstances. But, after all, Charles was not so bad as Hamlet rallying Ophelia at the play or Mercutio chaffing the Nurse. What now jars on us is the caddishness of Lady Teazle, whose conduct for the first time begins to strike us as it would if it were the conduct of a man in the like circumstances. Society forbids a man to compromise a woman; but it also requires him, if he nevertheless does compromise her, to accept as one of the consequences of his action the obligation not to betray her, even if he has to go into the witness-box and swear to her innocence. Suppose Lady Teazle, on being surprised by Sir Peter in Joseph's rooms, had invented a plausible excuse, and had asked Joseph to confirm her. Suppose Joseph had thereupon said, 'No, it is false, every word. My slumbering conscience awakens: and I return to the sacred path of truth and duty. Your wife, Sir Peter, is an abandoned woman who came here to tempt me from the path of honor. But for your arrival I might have fallen; but now I see the blackness of her conduct in all its infamy; and I ask you to pardon me, and to accept the sincerity of my contrition as a pledge for my future good conduct.' Would any extremity of blackballing, cutting, even kicking, be considered too severe for the man who should try to extricate himself at the expense of his accomplice in that straightforward manner? And yet that is exactly what Lady Teazle does without the least misgiving on the part of the dramatist as to the entire approval and sympathy of the audience. In this, as far as I am concerned, the dramatist is mistaken, and the play consequently dates. I cannot for the life of me see why it is less dishonorable for a woman to kiss and tell than a man. . . . At all events, when a married woman comes to a man's rooms with the deliberate intention of enjoying a little gallantry, and, on being caught, pleads for sympathy and forgiveness as an innocent young creature misled and seduced by a villain, she strikes a blow at the very foundations of immorality. (pp. 98-100)

*The School for Scandal* dates on the Woman Question almost as badly as [Shakespeare's] *The Taming of the Shrew*. (p. 101)

> *Bernard Shaw, "The Second Dating of Sheridan" (originally published in* The Saturday Review, London, *Vol. 81, No. 2122, June 27, 1896), in his* Plays & Players: Essays on the Theatre, *edited by A. C. Ward (reprinted by permission of The Society of Authors on behalf of the Bernard Shaw Estate), Oxford University Press, Oxford, 1952, pp. 95-104.*

## WALTER SICHEL (essay date 1909)

[*Sichel's biography of Sheridan analyzes his life and provides a brief study of his plays. In the following excerpt, he notes the longevity of* The School for Scandal *and compares it with the Restoration comedies of William Congreve and Oliver Goldsmith. Sichel considers Sheridan's to be the most supremely amusing and enduring comedies since William Shakespeare.*]

"The School for Scandal" is a phial into which Sheridan distilled the quintessence alike of himself and his time. . . . There is no better instance of improvisation elaborated into art, of the craftsmanship by which art is concealed, or of the terse simplicity into which subtle analysis can be condensed. The play is all champagne, as delicately and carefully made and matured, exhilarating even in the sound as it is uncorked from the smart bottle which promises choiceness, brisk with the same elegance, crisp with the same bouquet, and piquant with the same sparkle. (p. 551)

The most obvious fact about "The School for Scandal" is its life and longevity. No old-English comedy since Shakespeare has worn so well. Whether we reckon it to be a second-rate comedy of the first class, or . . . a first-rate comedy of the second class, or (as some may be allowed to think) a first-rate comedy in the strict sense of that word, nothing will explain its vital power away. This is not due merely to its blaze of wit, still less to its local colour. Something elemental must reside in a work that lasts in differing countries and centuries with undimmed lustre, and persists both as literature and on the stage. Congreve's wit has not so persevered, though there is a freshness about it even when it languishes in his hot-house world. The reason is obvious. Congreve is a spectator, he

stands aloof from his own creations, arranges, criticises, disposes, eyes them like a connoisseur. He is the arbiter of superb elegance, inaccessible to the vulgar; and his wit is an icicle—in his one lurid comedy, "The Double Dealer," an iceberg. On neither side can Sheridan approach him. He was no such intellectual Petronius. He is less classical, less reflective, less chastened. . . . But Sheridan's wit is . . . more salient and infinitely more joyous. The sunshine dances across its facets, and the play of human nature lies, as Sir Henry Irving insisted, at the root of his charm. Sheridan never keeps his characters at a distance; he laughs with and at them. While Congreve sits in state with crown and sceptre, Sheridan jests with his merry court around him; while Congreve never errs, Sheridan heightens his effects by mistakes. Congreve is infallible, but Sheridan is rebellious—the protestant of polished comedy. Compared with Goldsmith, Sheridan is cold; compared with Congreve, he is warm and sociable. His sympathy, no doubt, springs more from the head than the heart; but it is sympathy, and a sympathy which Congreve lacks. The "**School**" is more than a "**Congreve** rocket."

It is customary to think of it merely as a comedy of wit with conventional types for its mouthpiece, as a young man's play, drawn more from books than from men. The assumption is easy, but a little study will soon disprove it. True, its theme is ancient, older than civilisation, as old, indeed, as the sixty-fourth psalm, while the contrasted brothers hark back to Jacob and Esau. . . . But Sheridan was the first to make scandal the sustained motive of a complete play. (pp. 552-53)

Joseph Surface is not the conventional stage hypocrite, nor is he a Tartuffe, the sole monster in the gallery of Molière. Tartuffe is a red-faced, sanctimonious ruffian, cowing a superstitious household beyond the bounds either of his unction or of their credulity. Such was not Sheridan's view or experience of humbugs *in excelsis*. Tartuffe is a savage, Surface is the Iago [from Shakespeare's *Othello*] of comedy, a polished schemer with a persuasive tongue. But he is more than plausible. . . . The rhetoric that conveys his assumed sentimentality has grown into a habit. It has become almost natural, and at the very opening he airs it on the confederate who is obliged to remind him that he is "among friends." Tartuffe is *farouche* and resembles the vulgar fiend of a mystery-play, but the insinuating Joseph is more like a comic version of Milton's Belial. Molière's pietist, like Dickens's Chadband, is satirised only from the outside; Sheridan's casuist is a far subtler conception. Tartuffe, indeed, is the Puritan, Joseph Surface the Jesuit of hypocrisy.

And there is another *trait* which has been overlooked. What Joseph really worships is reputation. He worships it more than the pleasure which it veils, and he worships it so much that he loses sight of character altogether; indeed, he regrets that his character is so good that "he doubts he will be exposed at last." To be thought good is his ideal, but he is unable to be so, and so his spurious respectability goes to pieces through the only bit of unmixed nature about him, his real infatuation for Lady Teazle. (pp. 554-55)

Joseph is a hypocrite in a sentimental suit. The real sentimentalist is Charles Surface—Sheridan, Tom Jones, who you will, at a period when generosity and good intentions were called Benevolence, and Prudence "clinging to the green suckers of youth" like "ivy round a sapling" was held to spoil "the growth of the tree." Saws like "Boys will be boys" and "the reformed rake" would seem to offer but scant pasturage for sentimentalism, but Charles's sentimentality is patent. (p. 556)

If Joseph cants dishonestly from worship of the world's opinion, Charles also cants honestly in his airy bravado. The one pretends to virtue, the other—

> Compounds for sins he has a mind to
> By damning those he's not inclined to.

In one point, however, the critics have wronged the libertine. The man who has "often given grounds of uneasiness" to so many "worthy men" has been called heartless for his bewildered irony when the screen falls. But the circumstances warrant it. (p. 557)

[Lady Teazle] is no mere type of a girl yoked to ridiculous age like the tame Lady Townley in Colman's best comedy, "The Provoked Husband." Marrying to escape her home boredom, she succumbs to the lure of fashion. All along fashion is her temptress. . . . To be thought in the mode, she joins the crew of caballers, though there is no malice in her impulsive composition. Wit, however, does enter into it, and in the war of tongues she holds her own with the best of them. . . . [The] blend in her of art and artlessness, of village hoyden and fine lady, imparts a certain smart simplicity, absent from the Mrs. Pinchwell of Wycherley's "Country Wife"—that shy *ingénue* with a despicable husband. She too longs for the town, but she covets its pleasures and has no pretensions to society; she is farcical—a mere marionette in an interlude of intrigue. Lady Teazle, on the other hand, is not *intrigante* at all. Her archness and freshness are inexhaustible, and in the whole range of comedy there is not a more delightful dialogue than hers with her husband when they "will never, never differ again." She is queen of the frolic stage, winsome even in disgrace. Her very lapses give the impression of scrapes, and her penitence is an April shower. There is no finality about her. (pp. 558-59)

Lady Teazle is no bad emblem of the play itself, so elaborate as to seem artificial yet, really and underneath, naïve—a rustic romp schooled to drop a court curtsey; a piece of eglantine, trained and transplanted into a *parterre*. And their blemishes are the same. The comedy is always just going to touch us and then laughing our emotions away. It plays with the passions which it introduces, and sometimes deafens their appeal by the salvo of its wit. This is owing to its mixed origin, for it started as a sentimental melodrama with witty interludes, while it ended by almost eliminating the part of Maria. None the less it remains a truly human document.

Such lights and shades mitigate the metallic gleam of the play's enamel, and the whole drama is more flexible than it seems—a fresh cause for its permanence. More technical qualities also assist its unfading freshness. Sheridan is a complete master of stage illusion. However improbable some of the situations, as, for instance, the auction-scene and the constant encounters at each other's houses of persons the least likely to meet there; however dazzling the sameness of the wit, a sameness caused by the transference of phrases in the process of composition, and absent, be it noted, from the homely characters of Rowley and Sir Oliver; however inadequate some of the motives, the characterisation is natural as we see it represented. . . . It has been objected that everyone talks, and little happens. But we do not perceive this as we listen. Not only does the subject necessitate the dialogue, but the dialogue *is* the plot—a plot of idea which leads up wonderfully to the three crowning episodes. Sheridan was an adept at stage construction. There are few playwrights who, after the auction and screen scenes, would have ventured on a triple anti-climax—the babble about the supposed duel, the buffeting of Stanley-Premium-Surface, and the final unmasking of "Snake." Yet, so adapted are these to the *finale*, so deftly and humorously handled, that they are not recognisable as anti-climaxes at all. (pp. 560-61)

Sheridan respected the confines of Comedy, disregarded in his day by maudlin pedants, as it has been invaded in ours by a morbid psychology. We have only to read Murphy's sentiments, Colman's fun, and Cumberland's sermons, to feel how flat or torpid comedy had become, and to see that Thalia was almost discrowned. Sheridan restored her reign. He knew that his audience wanted to be amused, and he amused them right royally. (p. 562)

> *Walter Sichel, in his* Sheridan, Vol. I, *Houghton Mifflin Company, 1909, 630 p.*

## GEORGE SAINTSBURY (essay date 1916)

Great as Sheridan's reputation has always been, it may be doubted whether it has been as great as he deserves, when he is considered solely as the author of *The School for Scandal, The Rivals,* and *The Critic.* . . . *Pizarro* is rubbish: and *The Duenna* and *St. Patrick's Day* are not at all worthy of him. But the three masterpieces—all written before he was thirty—are, each in its own way and calibre, masterpieces pure and simple—of higher and lower comedy and of pure or partly pure farce. *The School for Scandal* has roundly and often been pronounced the best comedy in our tongue. These unqualified superlatives are generally rash; and there could hardly be a rasher one than this, because comedy subdivides itself into so many different kinds. It would be as ridiculous to say that *The School for Scandal* is better than [Shakespeare's] *Twelfth Night,* or [Ben Jonson's] *The Alchemist,* or [Congreve's] *Love for Love,* as to say that a perfectly succeeded bottle of Lafite is better than one of Clos Vougeot, or of one of the best vintages of port. (pp. 275-76)

*The School* is perhaps better to see than to read; *The Rivals,* though it can be seen with joy even by persons who do not regard the theatre with extraordinary affection, is even better to read, not merely because you can then skip Falkland and Julia if you choose. That it is quite free from artificiality nobody in his senses would, again, maintain. But Sherican has had the wit to give this artificiality itself that touch of burlesquing sincerer examples of it which saves everything. . . . It must be from lack of the imagination, which can see the presence at once of fairytale and farce, that anybody finds fault with its plot, and fails to discover in it the "brilliancy" allowed *The School for Scandal.* . . . *The Rivals,* is like nothing else—at least nothing that came before it. Malapropism may go back through the recent work of Smollett (associated likewise with Bath), through Swift to Shakespeare; the testy father is as old, even in criticism, as the *Epistle to the Pisos,* and Heaven knows how much older in drama; the comic Irishman, though he only now comes to his own, is, though in another sense, of almost as ancient a house as he could himself claim, and Bob Acres's ancestors were born with the comic drama. But in all the immense bulk and range of our theatre you will find no whole piece of quite the same kind; nor will you, if you extend the search to the houses of Molière or of Calderon. And as Sheridan had here no predecessor in fee, so he has had no exact successor, despite the immense popularity of the thing and the, beyond all doubt numerous, attempts at imitation. His sole heir (as it seems to the present writer, though he puts forward the suggestion humbly and diffidently), and that in a transformed fashion, was the late Sir William Gilbert.

*The Critic,* it has been confessed, is less of an *a-per-se.* . . . Perhaps the most remarkable thing about the play is the way in which the pure farce-burlesque of the close is united to the higher comedy of the Sir Fretful part by the character and deliverances of Puff. There is here, in actual fact, something like the transformation-scene suggested as possible in the case of *The Rivals.*

But still the three plays belong to distinct classes (if in the case of *The Rivals* to a class of one only), and this increases one's admiration of the achievement of their author. . . . (pp. 277-79)

> *George Saintsbury, "The Garden of Minor Verse and the Later Drama—Anstey and Sheridan," in his* The Peace of the Augustans: A Survey of Eighteenth Century Literature As a Place of Rest and Refreshment, *G. Bell and Sons, Ltd., 1916, pp. 270-80.\**

## PROSSER HALL FRYE (essay date 1929)

Sheridan is one of those rare amphibians who live partly in literature, partly in politics; who belong at once to the two elements of imagination and reality. This double *ménage* makes him, like Swift, who is in so far his counterpart, a rather difficult subject of criticism. He is not to be found wholly in his plays or in his speeches—in one sense it is questionable whether he is to be found in both together. He resides in a great measure outside of his professions. He has not a trace of Swift's deadly seriousness. He is at bottom a man of pleasure, to whom these occupations are but expedients—a means to live. (p. 4)

What stood him in the place of principle or even policy, it would sometimes seem, was a desire to strike the imagination. He was, above all, a social creature, the man of an audience. (p. 5)

And yet though Sheridan realizes himself fully neither in literature nor in history, he is always oscillating between these two poles; he is constantly manifesting himself in one or the other of these two worlds—he is either the humorist, the man of fancy and invention, or else the statesman and manager, the man of affairs—ever a little too much of the former, no doubt, to make a complete success of the latter. (pp. 5-6)

To take him too seriously is to falsify his proper impression and effect. In a certain large sense he belongs himself to comedy; and while comedy, too, may be a pretty serious business, its seriousness is not that of politics, irresistibly comic as the latter often appears. At all events, it is the former upon which Sheridan's genius has stamped itself most distinctly.

The French would probably say, as indeed Taine virtually does, that Sheridan, like the rest of his countrymen, has no sense for comedy at all. But we must take our drama as we find it; and Sheridan's is the very best of anything like genuine comedy that we have. (pp. 9-10)

And yet how different is Sheridan himself from Molière, the representative not only of French comedy but of the comic spirit at its fullest and best! It is not merely that he never wholly rid himself of the fatal English sentimentality, that he never completely parted company with the muse of lachrymose comedy against whom he inveighed at his first entrance upon the scene—though that has a good deal to do with it too, and

accounts for his tenderness for Charles Surface, as it does for his lack of the absolute intellectual detachment of perfect comedy, the purely disinterested pleasure in the discernment of character and motive. (pp. 10-11)

[It] is not so much that Molière is greater than Sheridan—or the comparison would be an unfair one—as that he is different. Vastly entertaining as Sheridan is, he belongs with another class—with the wits and the phrase-makers. Like Oscar Wilde he is a producer of smart comedy. (p. 12)

Within these limits, however, Sheridan created the variety. In certain respects the case is much the same with him as with Beaumarchais, whose "Barbier de Séville" came out the same year as "**The Rivals.**" Beaumarchais may have been trying, as he pretends, to naturalize and familiarize the drama; but what strikes us at first is the conventionality of his intrigues—the stock motive, the "literary" commonplace of the plot; it is only later that its perfidiousness becomes evident. And so in his own way with Sheridan. . . . The very quality of his wit is implicated in the manner in which the triteness of the matter is turned against itself. To don a disguise in order to escape discovery by anxious duennas and guardians, is one thing; it is quite another to do it, as Captain Absolute does, to conceal his identity from his mistress herself. To betray a husband out of passion for some one else, and to betray a husband, as Lady Teazle contemplates doing, out of a tenderness for her own reputation, are two very different things. . . . [The] *dénouement* of "**The Rivals**" and "**The School for Scandal**" hinges in both cases on what amounts to a practical joke, the duel in the one and the overthrow of the screen in the other. It is all very English somehow; it is all good fun. And it is this that makes Sheridan so thoroughly enjoyable. And as a natural result in his case the better the joke, the better the play. For this reason "**The Rivals**" is on the whole a more successful effort than "**The School for Scandal**"—just as Mrs. Malaprop is the best of his *dramatis personae*—in spite of the more finished workmanship of the latter piece and its greater significance. The former is more in character, it suited the author better, and it is, if anything, the happier performance. In short, it is more fun, just as Sheridan himself is more fun than Congreve, more fun even than Goldsmith. (pp. 12-14)

> *Prosser Hall Frye, "Sheridan," in his* Visions & Chimeras *(copyright, 1929 by Marshall Jones Company, Inc.), Jones, 1929, pp. 3-19.*

## PADRAIC COLUM (essay date 1935)

[*Colum, an Irish poet and dramatist, here surveys Sheridan's plays, briefly noting their relationship to the works of various other playwrights, including William Congreve, John Synge, and Oscar Wilde.*]

With [Sheridan's] second play, "**The School for Scandal**," the modern drawing-room comedy begins—the comedy of Oscar Wilde and Henry Arthur Jones and Arthur Pinero. Sheridan patterned his upon Congreve's. But neither "**The School for Scandal**" nor the modern comedies that have come from it have inner likeness to such plays as "Love for Love" or "The Way of the World." Congreve's personae are men.

Judged by the standard of "The Way of the World," the greatest of English social comedies, "**The School for Scandal**" is not a first-rate play. The suspense that we feel from the first speeches of Mirabell and Fainall does not come to us in the opening scene of "**The School for Scandal**"; all Congreve's characters are drawn into, all are absorbed by, the action of "The Way of the World," but most of Sheridan's have only a conventional relation to the action—which is the winning of Maria by Charles Surface with the reconciliation of Sir Peter and Lady Teazle through the defeat of Joseph.—Snake, Backbite, Mrs. Candour, are not absorbed by the action; neither, for that matter, is Lady Sneerwell. The current of dramatic interest moves swiftly and steadily in "The Way of the World," but in "**The School for Scandal**" it is neither strong nor steady. Only at the end of the third and the beginning of the fourth act have we any scenes of high comic interest—the scene in which Charles auctions the family portraits to his unrecognized uncle; the renowned screen-scene; the scene in which Joseph Surface so civilly gets out of doing anything for the supposed friend of the family. (p. 262)

But if "**The School for Scandal**" is so loose in structure, so thin in content, as this criticism implies, how has it come to be placed with the great comedies in English? Mainly because the screen-scene is a superb theatrical invention while the scenes before and after are good enough to accompany it. And "**The School for Scandal**" has also the prestige of a classic—it is a classic because it is the first of the modern drawing-room plays.

Those who are impressed by sophistication are likely to put "**The School for Scandal**" before "**The Rivals**." But the earlier play, I consider, has about it much more of the freshness that makes a piece of writing perennial than "**The School for Scandal**" has. There is more Sheridan in "**The Rivals**" than in "**The School for Scandal**." I would mark the distinction by saying that while "**The School for Scandal**" is an English comedy written by an Irishman, "**The Rivals**" is an Irish comedy—an Irish comedy that no other Irish writer has equaled for invention, brilliancy of lines, richness of characterization. The leading character, Captain Absolute, is the type that a much later Irish dramatist [John Synge] was to name "a playboy"—a type that Irish literature is partial to. Another Irish element in "**The Rivals**" is its verbalism—the use of language itself as a comic element. I would distinguish the verbalism of "**The Rivals**" from the superb speech of the great Restoration comedies: as a vehicle of language Sheridan's play does not come near "The Way of the World." . . . What Sheridan displays is not a mastery of speech, but that quality which many Irish writers after him were to show—a virtuosity in speech. Everyone remembers Mrs. Malaprop. But Bob Acres's new fashion in oaths is another instance of the verbalism that has play in "**The Rivals**."

"**The Rivals**" misnames a comedy that has hardly anything to do with rivalry and exists as a study of "humors"—of those eccentricities by which the individual diverges from rational behavior: there is Captain Absolute with his delight in imposture, Sir Anthony with his hastiness and his rages, Lydia Languish with her vaporing romanticism, Faulkland with his moroseness always sapping his present content, Sir Lucius O'Trigger with his fixation on the field of honor, Bob Acres with his seesaw between poltroonery and spirit, Mrs. Malaprop with her unconfined range of language. The characters who do not show such derangement, such divergence from the rational, are purely theatrical types. The lines are rich in comedy and they correspond well with the "humor" that the speaker represents. . . . Certain "humors" are so completely rendered in "**The Rivals**" that they can never be staged again. Mrs. Malaprop can have no successor. And neither can Sir Lucius O'Trigger. These two are not laughing-stocks; there is something of grandeur in them both. If Mrs. Malaprop were merely

a misuser of language, any long acquaintance with her would be intolerable. But we recognize that in her dealing with language there is something creative: she is a woman of genius. And as for Sir Lucius, we can see him as well as hear him— gaunt, solemn, probably shabby, but a gentleman and a man of honor. He speaks literal truth when he says, "I am so poor that I can't afford to do a dirty action."

I have spoken of the "playboy" character in "**The Rivals**"—of the type that behaves in a certain way, that follows a certain course of action, just for the sport of the thing. That type does not appear solely in "**The Rivals**." Properly examined, Joseph Surface [of "**The School for Scandal**"] is a playboy. Not really a hypocrite, not even a fortune-hunter, he is out for humbugging people who are willing to be humbugged and doing it to admiration. We don't want to see Joseph exposed as we want to see Tartuffe exposed: privately we are on his side and we should like to see him hoodwink those two simpletons, his uncle and Sir Peter Teazle. (pp. 262-63)

There is another playboy in "**The Critic**." Puff is no more a literary pretender than Joseph Surface is a social hypocrite: he is in the advertising line and the literary line for the sport of the thing. "**The School for Scandal**" comes between "**The Rivals**" and "**The Critic**," but this last is related to "**The Rivals**" by its high spirits, its holiday mood, its verbalism. "**The Critic**" anticipates Shaw's "Admirable Bashville" in its guying of blank-verse solemnities, and Max Beerbohm's "Savanrolla Browne" in its parody of the medley of characters and incidents that is the amateur's version of the historical drama. The verbalism that was in "**The Rivals**" is versified in "**The Critic**." One wonders how the wit who gave us "**The Critic**" could ever put his hand to "**Pizarro**"—all the highfaluting' senselessness displayed in all the parodied "Spanish Armada" are in this essay in the heroical. (p. 263)

*Padraic Colum, "Revaluing Sheridan," in* Commonweal *(copyright © 1935 Commonweal Publishing Co., Inc.; reprinted by permission of Commonweal Publishing Co., Inc.), Vol. XXII, No. 10, July 5, 1935, pp. 261-63.*

**ROSE SNIDER**  (essay date 1937)

[*Snider identifies the sentimental and satiric aspects of Sheridan's dramas, and discusses his various characters. Throughout the essay, Snider draws comparisons between Sheridan and William Congreve, in addition to other Restoration dramatists.*]

[In his dramas,] Sheridan managed to recapture the spirit of the previous century in his presentation of heartless women, scheming men, and, in general, a cold and worldly-wise society; he tempered this, however, with a genuine warmth of tone decidedly lacking in the more formal plays of Congreve. To satisfy the tastes of an audience not yet recovered from the verbal lashing administered at the close of the previous century by the vehement Jeremy Collier, and to appease his own desire to follow the dictates of society, Sheridan frequently seasoned his comedy with sentimentality, that quality in which Georgians were wont to revel. Aware of the hypocrisy of exaggerated sentimentality, he attacked it through the medium of satire. The fact that comedy was deteriorating through the continued use of this same sentimentality stimulated the young Sheridan to call attention to the regrettable situation. As early as the "**Prologue**" to *The Rivals,* Sheridan's intentions in this direction are indicated, particularly when he laments that "the goddess of the woful countenance—the sentimental Muse'' threatens to displace the Muse of comedy.

Unlike Congreve, who in his five acts found innumerable opportunities for satire, Sheridan lavishly utilized an entire play for satirizing one quality or institution or person. Thus, *The Rivals* is almost entirely given over to an exposé of hypocritical sentimentality; *The School for Scandal* is a thorough-going criticism of malicious scandal-mongering and of sentimentality; and *The Critic* is a final belittling of not only the so-called ''genteel comedy'' but also true comedy with a moral purpose. (p. 42)

In literary wit Congreve is easily the superior of the two, but in simple, infectious gayety Sheridan surpasses his predecessor. Unlike Congreve, Sheridan had but one ambition, that of being a gentleman. Whatever he did was directed toward this end. (p. 43)

The dramatic output of the second half of the eighteenth century was predominantly of the sentimental variety. Though occasionally plays appeared bearing resemblance to the earlier ''manners'' school, such examples were few and far between. . . . By the time Sheridan appeared on the Georgian theatrical scene, the sentimentality of the period was no longer novel; it was taken for granted, not only by those who continued to indulge in it, but by those who criticized it as well. This was a fortunate thing for Sheridan, who chose to be a member of the critical faction.

The words ''sentiment'' and ''sentimentality,'' although they are constantly being confused, are not synonymous. Sentiment is nothing more than the truthful expression of the feelings of a sensitive person; it is sincere and unaffected. Sentimentality is a self-conscious indulgence in feeling, having for its aim either the approval of one's self as a virtuous person (moral sentimentality) or the mere pleasure in the feeling (romantic sentimentality). (pp. 43-4)

In Sheridan's plays the characters most easily remembered for their indulgence in sentimentality are Lydia Languish, Julia, and Faulkland, in *The Rivals;* and Joseph Surface and Maria, in *The School for Scandal.* Faulkland and Surface are obvious satires on the affected, virtuous strain. Julia and Maria, however, must have awed many a female of a generation brought up on that ''genteel comedy'' which Goldsmith derided and sought to remedy. (p. 44)

In dealing first with the romantic aspect of sentimentality, we shall need to glance at one of Sheridan's dramatic devices. In introducing the important characters, Sheridan again and again makes use of that ancient and well-worn device of putting the descriptions into the mouths of minor players. Congreve's technique of introduction, though similar, is not quite so obvious. Since the audience never anticipate the subtler artistry of Congreve, they can the more readily forgive Sheridan's undisguised methods. Sheridan is too much preoccupied with the matter of getting on with the plot to bother with such trivialities, and, accordingly, takes advantage of the easiest method of presentation. Thus, the conversation of the servants introduces us to the first of his satirical characterizations, Lydia Languish (whose surname Sheridan lifted from Congreve's *The Way of the World*). . . . When we actually come face to face with Lydia, we derive an immediate clue to her character from her literary tastes, which incline to such current fiction as *The Delicate Distress, Peregrine Pickle, Humphrey Clinker,* and *A Sentimental Journey*. (pp. 44-5)

Lydia Languish is a lively and likeable person even though she illustrates the eighteenth-century flair for sentimentality carried to the extreme. . . . From her surreptitious reading Lydia has conjured up an impossible world of romance in which she and her loved one are the only inhabitants of any importance. She has given her imagination free rein, and the result is a curious combination of sentiment, vanity, love, and sheer caprice. She has no ulterior motive in carrying on these fanciful notions other than the mere pleasure she derives from doing so. The conventional mode of life is not for her, and in her craving for adventure she is so completely carried away by her romantic ideas that the result is a highly amusing caricature of a young woman of the eighteenth century. (p. 45)

The sentimentality exhibited by Lydia Languish is in keeping with the general taste for the romantic both in character and situation; and in Lydia, then, is to be found Sheridan's criticism of that harmless but ridiculous phase of sentimentality consisting in an excessive reveling in the romantic.

Julia, in the same play, represents the second phase of sentimentality noticed above, a variation consisting of an exaggerated promenading of one's virtues. . . . In Sheridan's hands, [Julia], for all her seriousness of mien, and no doubt because of it, is a subject for caricature, and no one can fail to detect the humor in Sheridan's mock-serious treatment of her. (p. 47)

Had he made the other characters in the play of a piece with Julia, Sheridan might have been warmly embraced by the advocates of the true ''genteel'' comedy, but his disinclination to be in their ranks is shown by his presenting Julia as the sole specimen of her kind in a play possessing a different manner, subject matter, and tempo. This contrast, more than anything else, gives the clue to Sheridan's motive in creating such a character as opposed to others who act and speak more naturally.

As an example of the type of speech considered ''genteel'' by Sheridan's contemporaries, Julia's words to Faulkland, on one of the numerous occasions when he is testing her love for him, are excellent:

> My soul is oppressed with sorrow at the nature
> of your misfortune: had these adverse circum-
> stances arisen from a less fatal cause, I should
> have felt strong comfort in the thought that I
> could now chase from your bosom every doubt
> of the warm sincerity of my love. My heart has
> long known no other guardian—I now entrust
> my person to your honor—we will fly to-
> gether. . . .

Such a speech as the one quoted above may have called forth sympathetic tears from an audience which, because of the change in moral outlook, was taking even its comedy seriously; but, appearing amid the amusing notions of Lydia Languish and the ''ingeniously misapplied'' verbiage of Mrs. Malaprop, it should produce the opposite effect. (pp. 48-9)

Had Sheridan created for Maria a role calling for more than four entrances which almost at once resolve into as many exits, he would have given the audience another Julia. Maria is obviously included as additional satire on the genteel-comedy heroine of the day when it was customary for writers to exhibit the virtues of society rather than its vices. Like Julia, Maria possesses a high sense of duty and loyalty as well as the usual docility and seriousness of purpose. Like all the sentimental ladies, she conveys the impression of having been mistreated.

Her virtues are even more apparent in contrast to the follies of the heterogeneous company in which she finds herself. It is not that Maria is unnecessarily decorous or irreproachable; it is merely that her general make-up is too sensible and restricted for a world where nonsense and carefree actions are in order. Amongst characters whose idiosyncrasies might well have given them a place in a Jonsonian comedy, Maria's sober virtue is noticeably out of place. (p. 49)

In regard to Faulkland, the sentimentality finds expression in a kind of self-torture which, though obviously of serious consequence to himself and the suffering Julia, is ludicrous and contemptible in the eyes of others. . . . He explains to Julia his theory of behavior for lovers as follows:

> For such is my temper, Julia, that I should regard every mirthful moment in your absence as a treason to constancy. The mutual tear that steals down the cheek of parting lovers is a compact, that no smile shall live there till they meet again.

The foregoing, then, is love on the genteel plan which permitted words to speak louder than actions, and catered to false delicacy rather than to sincerity. The drama of sensibility was not an imitation of contemporary life, but a completely artificial set-up, which in turn invited imitation by its observers. True sentiment had given way to sentimentality, and even Sheridan and Goldsmith were not influential enough to restore the comic drama to normality.

Not content with a general satire on the sentimentality prevalent in the contemporary theatre, Sheridan selected the most conspicuous aspect of it—hypocrisy—for further attention. Both audience and playwrights were gradually becoming aware that sentimentality carried to excess was in itself a literary sin. Nothing, however, deserved ridicule so much as this same sentimentality when hypocrisy was its distinguishing feature. Sheridan concentrated upon this particular social fault in the character of his arch-hypocrite, Joseph Surface. (pp. 49-51)

As usual, Sheridan's dramatic technique calls for discussion of a character by those already assembled on the stage before the actual introduction of the character in question. Thus, early in the first act there takes place the following confidential interlude . . . :

> *Lady Sneer.* . . . I know him to be artful, selfish, and malicious—in short, a sentimental knave; while with Sir Peter, and indeed with all his acquaintance, he passes for a youthful miracle of prudence, good sense, and benevolence.
>
> *Snake.* Yes; yet Sir Peter vows he has not his equal in England; and, above all, he praises him as a man of sentiment. . . .

In this way Sheridan invariably informs the audience of the proper attitude to hold in regard to the character introduced. There is no attempt, therefore, to conceal the true nature of Joseph Surface, who is himself so proficient in the art of dissembling that very few of his acquaintances ever suspect it. He is obliged to minimize his duplicity when in the company of Lady Sneerwell since they know each other too well. (pp. 51-2)

There is another rather unexpected aspect to this type of drama, for the more noble, morally, the character considers himself, the more satisfied with himself is he likely to become. In this way egotism links itself up with moralizing, since the individual indulges in it because he approves of himself as being a moral person. . . . In regard to Mr. Surface the satire is rendered greater in proportion to his own duplicity. (pp. 52-3)

Having acquainted the audience with Joseph's character, Sheridan wastes no time in developing the satire. Every moral speech assigned to this character, therefore, is a single pencil-stroke of criticism, as it were, in the outline to be completed at the close of the play. Even when in the company of his back-biting friends, Joseph can not throw off the cloak of genteel respectability which he has found so convenient to don on every other occasion, although his insincerity is so evident that his utterances always reflect the contrary intent of his mind. His winning card is the suave manner in which he poses as the exponent of the attributes of brotherly love. (p. 53)

Lydia Languish, Julia, Maria, Faulkland, and Joseph Surface afforded ample opportunity for Sheridan to develop his satire on the various phases of sentimentality. Although he expended his greatest efforts in this endeavor in *The Rivals,* which he deliberately utilized for this purpose, he introduced satirical bits throughout his dramatic composition.

That notable farce *The Critic,* for example, served more than one purpose. It brought up to date the outmoded line of critical pieces which included such successes as Beaumont and Fletcher's *The Knight of the Burning Pestle,* a satire on the currently popular plays based upon medieval romances; Buckingham's *The Rehearsal,* a burlesque directed at the heroic drama then holding sway; Gay's *The Beggar's Opera,* a farce satirizing contemporary politics and the trend of English opera in imitation of the Italian; and finally Fielding's *Tom Thumb,* a burlesque attacking the stereotyped contemporary tragedies. *The Critic* surpassed all these in its frank criticism of the current fashion in drama. The mock-serious lashing it administered to sentimental literature was one of the most effective single triumphs so far achieved among the various attempts to ameliorate the situation into which the drama, in particular, and all literature, in general, had fallen. The prologue itself is one of the most significant features of the play, and illustrates Sheridan's views on genteel comedy. It is here that his impatience with the affectations of the drama of sensibility is most conspicuous. (p. 55)

As for women, Sheridan did not have Congreve's idealistic conception of woman as a superior creature for whom must be reserved the most beautiful and most eloquent passages. For Sheridan there could be no such partiality. In his plays charming men appear as frequently as do charming women; and the less admirable characters are equally distributed between the sexes. . . . Like Congreve, Sheridan had a first-hand knowledge of women, but he chose to make other use of it. Instead of selecting women whose admirable qualities would attract attention by their rarity and beauty, he preferred more ordinary portraits which would prove attractive in spite of certain less commendable attributes. Indeed, Sheridan seems to have chosen his outstanding female characters more for their idiosyncrasies than for any intrinsically poetic values they might possess.

Female pretensions to education are satirized in Mrs. Malaprop. . . . The good-natured humor underlying each situation occupies the audience so completely that such matters as the frequency or monotony of Mrs. Malaprop's utterances are lightly passed over. Although the contrivance Sheridan employs in presenting Mrs. Malaprop's "select words so ingeniously mis-applied, without being mispronounced" becomes obviously mechanical at times, it does not deserve much criticism on this score. It is merely another instance of Sheridan's insight into the commonplace methods of procuring laughter from the audience. The more sensitive the auditor is to shades of meaning in his vocabulary, the more readily does he respond to each cue offered by Mrs. Malaprop. The resulting laughter is not the intellectual mirth inspired by high comedy; it is closer in spirit to the ready laugh at each turn and tumble of the clown, but is elevated by the use of verbal rather than physical acrobatics.

Mrs. Malaprop exhibits two outstanding foibles: one of these consists in her pretensions to youth; the other, to education. There is nothing in her make-up to suggest the "superannuated frippery" of Congreve's Lady Wishfort, but there are several characteristics shared by the two. Both are conceited women who fancy that theirs has been a superior education, although in reality neither one has much to offer along that line. As *femmes savantes* [knowledgeable women] they rate ridiculously low, but they achieve distinction of a different type by means of their unusual vocabularies. Beside the disreputable language of Lady Wishfort, that of Mrs. Malaprop has an air of refinement. (pp. 56-8)

Sheridan was not merely satirizing the follies represented in Mrs. Malaprop; he was utilizing her as a laugh-provoker as well. . . . Sheridan found much to criticize in contemporary society, but whether or not his criticisms were taken seriously by this society was not to him a matter of vital concern. Above all he liked to please, and if he pleased by the humor of a situation rather than by the satire therein, he was satisfied. In creating the character of Mrs. Malaprop, Sheridan was satirizing all those old women who have a mistaken idea of their own importance and who enjoy upsetting the course of true love. To complete the caricature, Sheridan has her make use of all the verbal blunders he can invent. The inappropriateness of her words contrasts strikingly with her seriousness of mien, and this misuse of words distorts ludicrously each statement she proffers, placing her entirely at the mercy of the audience and the other characters in the play. (pp. 58-9)

Sheridan did not always strive for the clear, cold wit of high comedy, of Congreve or of Molière; he enjoyed the rich, generous laughter awakened by direct humor, whether of character or situation. The profusion of humorless sentimentality had so weakened eighteenth-century comedy that the metallic tinkle produced by the clash of wits in the Congrevean comedy was entirely lacking. Mrs. Malaprop, however, is an indication of the return to true comedy as illustrated in the plays of Goldsmith and Sheridan. (pp. 59-60)

Beneath the general satire there is to be found constantly Sheridan's good-natured humor. The audience is not asked to look upon and despise Mrs. Malaprop for her idiosyncrasies; it is, on the contrary, invited to witness and laugh at her follies. Sheridan was fond of exposing the weaknesses of his characters, but he never designed to rout these foibles; he aimed to please, and found the art of satire most suited to his métier. In only one respect does Sheridan fall short of the prescribed formula for eighteenth-century comedies: there is no happy ending in store for Mrs. Malaprop. . . . [Having] set herself up as an authority on language and love, she is now relegated to a position of minor importance; and there is no indication that she will profit by her experience.

In *The School for Scandal* Sheridan continues his practice of depicting various phases of eighteenth-century society. This play is one of the finest examples there are of the comedy of manners, and as such, it presents a highly realistic picture of the artificial society of that day. Here once again the spirit is that of Molière and Congreve, of *Le Misanthrope* and *The Way of the World*. (pp. 61-2)

Although Lady Sneerwell is obviously the motivating force in the "school for scandal," she is not so adept in the art as Mrs. Candour. The latter best illustrates the type of person who indulges in scandal-mongering for her own amusement. There is no subtlety in her procedure; she merely retails each idle rumor she has heard in her travels about the town and pounces on anything that remotely suggests a scandal. An important feature in Mrs. Candour's reportorial technique is the method of insinuation which contrasts ironically with her affected innocence of intention. The implication of each piece of gossip she relates is exactly the opposite of its accompanying apologetic remark. (p. 62)

Lady Sneerwell, on the other hand, is not so amiable a character. She represents the type who gossip for the sole purpose of defaming others, regardless of whether or not the victims deserve such ill-treatment. . . .

As a third example in this category of female gossips may be included Lady Teazle, the country girl whom Sir Peter married and took back with him to London. She joins the "scandalous college" because it is apparently the fashion of fine society to gossip and she wishes to acquire the mark of sophistication which membership in that society seems to imply. (p. 63)

To assist the "daughters of calumny" in culling and distributing the current bits of slander, Sheridan has provided four males: Joseph Surface, Snake, Sir Benjamin Backbite, and his uncle Crabtree.

The first one may be summarily dismissed. A hypocrite by nature, he can not even be consistent in his attitude to the malicious members of his society. He represents the male counterpart of Lady Sneerwell, for both take part in this slanderous reciprocity primarily for selfish reasons rather than for any light amusement they may derive. He is not a true gossip like Mrs. Candour, whose manner of tale-bearing is so diverting to her observers; he merely contributes to the school by participating in and furthering Lady Sneerwell's projects when there is a chance for individual gain on his part.

Snake is a caricature of the social sycophant. Everything about him suggests exaggeration, even his opinion of himself. His duties as a club-member are menial ones, such as carrying out Lady Sneerwell's orders, forging letters, starting rumors on their way, or perhaps inserting certain paragraphs in the papers. Even Joseph Surface's admonitions do not arouse her suspicions about Snake; and because she believes Snake to be sincere, she entrusts him with her most secret plans. It is not until the close of the play, when Snake sells his services to a higher bidder, that Lady Sneerwell realizes the extent of his perfidy. (pp. 64-5)

The real rivals of Mrs. Candour are two other notable male slanderers, Sir Benajmin Backbite and his uncle Crabtree. They are very much alike, except for the fact that Sir Benjamin poses as a wit and a poet, whereas both men bear greater resemblance to the "wittols" of Congreve than to the true wits. They work as a team, one generally acting as the chorus while the other takes charge of the narration. (p. 65)

Sheridan may have found that his ridicule of the "school for scandal" was of too brief duration for an evening's entertainment at the theatre; he may, also, have desired to follow the practice of earlier and contemporary dramatists in creating intricate plots in which to entangle the characters. Whatever his reason may have been, the complications in this play are on a par with those of almost any of the Restoration comedies of manners, with the exception, perhaps, of *The Way of the World,* a masterpiece of plot complexity. There is, in addition to the portions aimed at the gossips and scandal-mongers which give the play its title, a second plot consisting of a satirical portrait of the old bachelor who takes unto himself a young wife and is not sure he can keep her. The same plot served Wycherley for an entire play, *The Country Wife,* but for Sheridan, who used it in its expurgated form, it merely supplements the "scandal" episodes and introduces some real sentiment into the comedy. Both Sir Peter and Lady Teazle are contributions to the sentimental school of the day, and both have genuine appeal. (p. 67)

Sheridan makes of Sir Peter Teazle a far pleasanter person than the earlier prototypes, Wycherley's Pinchwife and even Congreve's Fondlewife. Although Sir Peter finds himself in a similar predicament, also having married a girl from the country, he reacts in a more gentlemanly fashion than Pinchwife or Fondlewife. Sir Peter is a man of much common sense except in regard to his wife. Like Pinchwife, he was very circumspect in making his marital choice and selected a quiet, unpresuming young lady. (p. 68)

Sheridan frequently employs that made-to-order repartee that was often resorted to by Congreve. It is a kind of wit usually ascribed to the "wittols"; at times, however, even the true wits can not resist making use of it. The audience knows exactly what to expect and yet laughs heartily each time it appears. Sheridan employs this artificial humor in connection with Sir Peter. . . . Sheridan's method of opening the way for wit is all too obvious, but the humor of the situation brings forth the ready response of the audience, nevertheless.

That Sir Peter Teazle is no fool is indicated in his public denunciation of the "school for scandal," in which he maintains that he would have Parliament enact a law against gossip, permitting only "qualified old maids and disappointed widows" to indulge. His protests are of no avail, however, and he becomes a victim of the "school's" persecution. He has his revenge when his wife resigns from the society to become a dutiful and loving wife. (pp. 69-70)

Sheridan's attitude toward the country class was one of tolerant amusement. He satirized them, but did not suggest changes in their mode of life. He portrayed them as he saw them, and he saw them as interesting material for the scrutiny of the artificial London audiences to which he was obliged to cater. . . . Sheridan's country folk . . . are satirized solely for the humor such treatment always imparts to comic drama.

"Fighting Bob" Acres, a minor rival of Captain Absolute for the hand of Lydia Languish [in *The Rivals*], is typical of Sheridan's method in regard to the country fellow and his awkward attempts to cut a fine figure in London society. . . . Acres' delicacy in the choice of oaths is characteristic of the sentimental school, but whether or not it produces the desired effect is doubtful. The reflection upon the language of the genteel comedy is obvious, however; Sheridan could not resist an opportunity which invited comment on this highly affected type of drama. Although Acres' oaths seem to be decidedly lacking

in the vituperative strength generally associated with swearing, they can not be criticized in respect to variety. (pp. 70-1)

Through the character of Acres, also, Sheridan makes sport of that popular eighteenth-century pastime—duelling. Ridicule of this business of maintaining one's honor was certainly not original with our playwright. The Restoration, all too obviously influenced by the French in thought, manners, and costumes, mimicked as well the French gallantry which almost invariably resulted in duelling. . . . Sheridan, not so intent upon improving society as upon deriding the system in general, portrayed the clearly unheroic aspects of the duel by having the cowardly Bob Acres as the challenger and the smug, senile Sir Lucius as the manager who instructs Bob in the fine points of duelling, proving that a duel can be fought on no greater provocation than that of a rival's falling in love with one's own beloved. (pp. 71-2)

Through the character of Bob Acres [Sheridan] has emphasized the impossibility of disguising the earmarks of the country by mere imitation of city fashions; through his treatment of duelling he has held up for ridicule one of the most outstanding foibles of his social class. (pp. 72-3)

> *Rose Snider, "Richard B. Sheridan," in her* Satire in the Comedies of Congreve, Sheridan, Wilde, and Coward, *University of Maine Press, 1937 (and reprinted by Phaeton Press, 1972), pp. 41-73.*

### MARVIN MUDRICK (essay date 1954)

[*Mudrick maintains that Sheridan is a "second-rate and second-hand" dramatist. He criticizes Sheridan's staginess, his stock-comic type characters, his literariness, and the "alarming noises" of his stage machinary.*]

It is by now safe to assert that Sheridan . . . had a passive audience and no cult of manners; that this audience, bottle-fed on sermons and sentimental comedy, refused to recognize entire continents of vitality; that sex was inadmissible and irony incomprehensible; that good nature—which tended to be defined, dramatically, as an incapacity for thought—had replaced good manners; that Sheridan, the presumptive inheritor of the tradition of Congreve, found his inheritance dissipated before he could lay his hands on it, and was in fact writing, not comedies of manners, but—patched out with hasty reconstructions of Jonsonian and Restoration types—good-natured sentimental dramas of comic intrigue and situation, which Fielding had acclimated to fiction, in the guise of anti-sentimentalism, a generation before.

It may be that *The School for Scandal* is a better play than *The Rivals;* but both are miscellanies of stagey, actable situations incorporating sentimental and stock-comic types, and the former is, characteristically, indifferent enough toward motive and design to leave the scandalmongers of the title without function or effect in the play. *The Rivals,* in any case, is not much worse; and it is a more candid and melancholy epitaph on the comedy of manners, indeed on the English comic drama.

The most obvious quality of *The Rivals* is its literariness: its remoteness from live situations seen and live conversations recorded; its dependence on formula, contrivance, tips to the audience, plot summaries, scene-shifting and stage-business, playable circumstances and playable characters at the expense of consistency and subtlety, the comfortable simplifying echo of dead authors' perceptions—all the paraphernalia of the well-made popular play of any age.

Sheridan falls back on formula even while he affects to attack it. The sitting duck of the play is the Julia-Faulkland relationship; but its embarrassing woodenness will exceed the expectations of the most ill-disposed critic. Faulkland is ostensibly a satire on the sentimental hero of the novels Lydia borrows from the lending libraries—all nerves, doubt, sophistry, and remorse. Unluckily, however, he is presented at such length and with such abundant self-justification that Sheridan seems to be soliciting sympathy, or at least fatiguing our attention, on behalf of as windy a bore as any sentimental novel offers. And Julia, whom Sheridan exerts himself to contrast approvingly with her lover, is as smug and dreary a copybook of eighteenth-century posies as might be culled from the collected works of Charlotte Lennox. . . . (pp. 115-16)

Nor is Sheridan more successful when he attempts to manufacture—as a foil to Julia, that sober and responsible heroine—an up-to-date Millamant, her head turned by the reading of novels. The affectation of Congreve's Millamant has a purpose and is subordinated to her wit; the best Sheridan can do by way of expressing Lydia's affectation is to preface her otherwise characterless remarks with a "Heigh-ho!" and to feed the audience on curiously mixed, interminable catalogues of lending-library fiction, in which Smollett is equated with Sterne and both with the true-romance writers of the time—as if Sheridan, acquiescing in the eighteenth-century snobbery toward the novel, is himself incapable of making the distinctions. (One is reduced to looking for signs of the *author's* personality when he gives us no impression of personality, motive, or value in his characters.)

Even Sheridan's theatrical machinery makes alarming noises. In the opening scene [of *The Rivals*] two servants labor, during an implausibly crammed and hearty chat, to identify in detail all the characters and relationships of the play. The audience, as it doubtless deserves, is occasionally treated like an idiot with an ear trumpet: "Ye powers of impudence, befriend me!" says Absolute in an aside, preparing to be impudent, or, preparing to act repentant, "Now for a penitential face." . . . (pp. 117-18)

Conventions are not to be trusted, either. Setting up his recognition scene, in which Lydia looks forward to the prompt exposure of a deception that has in fact been practised only on her, Sheridan has Lydia turn her face from the door and keep it turned away through half the scene, while she wonders why "I han't heard my aunt exclaim yet! . . . perhaps their regimentals are alike, and she is something blind," and later, "How strangely blind my aunt must be!" The suspense is not in the dramatic use of a frankly theatrical device—to throw light, for example, on the cumulative extravagance of self-deception—but simply in waiting for Lydia, whose turning away has made the scene possible if not credible, to turn round and see what is there. (p. 118)

The only figures Sheridan enjoys are his bullies and blusterers: Sir Anthony, the comic-tyrannical father; Acres, the good-natured, swearing country squire with an aversion to dying; Sir Lucius, the obsessed and doctrinaire duelist—"Pray, sir, be easy; the quarrel is a very pretty quarrel as it stands; we should only spoil it by trying to explain it." They are the only characters who speak with an approximation of personality, and they do their amusing vaudeville stunts with a verve that recalls to us, by unhappy contrast, the nullities in the leading rôles.

If Mrs. Malaprop is less consistently amusing (and she does have one Miltonic simile: "as headstrong as an allegory on the

banks of Nile"), it is because her "nice derangement of epitaphs" is an unfunctional, isolated humor, usually a rambling collection of improbable errors interrupted by plain sense whenever Sheridan is anxious to advance the plot, and not at all a determined flood of self-revelation as with her great predecessor, Fielding's Mrs. Slipslop. Again, though, the shattering comparison is with Congreve, with the impressionable virago of an aunt that Sheridan found in *The Way of the World:* Lady Wishfort and her fishwife eloquence. . . . It is not merely that Lady Wishfort . . . [speaks] with a freedom rather indecorous for Sheridan's stage, but that she speaks always as a character involved in the action, and with an energy and particularity of vision beyond Sheridan's powers entirely. (pp. 118-19)

Sheridan—after one has deplored his audience and the sentimental tradition it venerates and imposes—remains a second-rate and second-hand playwright: that there is no great playwright in his time may be the fault of the time, but Sheridan himself will have to bear some of the responsibility for being no better than he is. (p. 120)

*Marvin Mudrick, "Restoration Comedy and Later" (originally an essay presented at the English Institute, Yale University, in 1954), in* English Stage Comedy, *edited by W. K. Winsatt, Jr. (copyright 1955, Columbia University Press, New York; reprinted by permission of the publisher), Columbia University Press, 1955, pp. 98-125.**

## LOUIS KRONENBERGER (essay date 1969)

*The Rivals* is only marginally in the tradition of the comedy of manners; it is with *The School for Scandal* that Sheridan takes his true place there, and displays his true talents. *The School for Scandal* is indeed—whether in public fame or theatrical popularity—the most famous comedy of manners in the language. Here the man of the world in Sheridan fulfills himself, here he indeed restores to the stage the wit and polish of the Restoration. Moreover, as a work for the theater, as something that deftly mingles plot and theme, characterization and background, it offers, I think, a surer hand, a stronger theatrical instinct, than any that the Restoration itself can provide. Equally for verbal polish and theatrical craftsmanship, equally for colloquial ease and theatrical canniness, it deserves its great popular fame. (p. 75)

[The scenes of the scandalmongers] constitute the play's thematic whalebone; they are at once an illustration of manners and a comment on society. They give the play spice; they can also give it a suggestion of glitter. And the theme of scandal does something further: it goes far toward solving a difficulty born of a genteel age. Scandal provides Sheridan with the *sense* of naughtiness, with the atmosphere of sinfulness, which Restoration comedy achieved through sin itself. Of sin itself there is absolutely nothing in the *action* of Sheridan's play; there is only the imputation of sinning. . . . By making scandal the theme of his play, Sheridan could thus brilliantly capitalize on the appearance without the reality. (pp. 76-7)

[But not] for being more strait-laced, is Sheridan's audience any less worldly: it is, if anything, more so, in the sense that hypocrisy is more worldly than frankness.

There is also a kind of aesthetic consideration: Sheridan is writing in an age when "taste" is not a matter of how you deal with things, but rather of what things you may deal with. And just because, in *The School for Scandal,* no one sexually sins, sin now becomes much wickeder and more important than it once was. Restoration comedy is a tedious succession of ladies and gentlemen being thrust behind screens, pushed into closets, hidden under beds, flung down back stairways; such scrambling for cover gets to be as commonplace and routine as closing a window or opening a door. But *here,* in *The School for Scandal,* we have Lady Teazle hiding behind a screen in what, without question, is the most famous scene in all English social comedy, just as the moment when the screen is knocked over constitutes the most climatic moment in all English social comedy. Some of this is clearly due to Sheridan's expertness as a playwright, to his building up the scene to get the utmost from it. But some of it is due to its being, as similar scenes a century earlier never were, so zealously, so breathlessly, scandalous. We are back in an age when sex takes on glamour through being illicit.

Impropriety is thus the very essence of what goes on; except that nothing goes on. The story itself is a good one to the extent that we regard it as merely a story; and it is worked out by someone completely at home in his medium. But, of itself, the story is almost obstreperously fictional: the key point about Sheridan here is not his high comedy but his strong theater sense, the way he can give, even to his scandalmongers, not the sheen of wit alone, but the deviousness of spiders; the way he can plot; the specific way he can unravel, or expose, or turn the tables. There is about it all the conciseness of an adroit theater mind. (pp. 78-9)

We must not undervalue the adroitness of the storytelling and all the graces that go with it—the play has a certain verbal polish and drawing room *ton;* has even a genuine *air* of worldliness. (p. 81)

But when we pass beyond manner to actual substance, we find that sound plotting and brisk movement are only had at a very steep price; that the story belongs wholly to the stage, with no overtones of real life. What I mean by this has nothing to do with surface realism. The comedy of manners has no use for surface realism; being, indeed, concerned with the shams and pretenses of human beings, it has every need of artifice. But since its very orbit is a world of masks, what it must always be moving toward is a general unmasking, so that we see at last the true faces that lurk beneath. . . . [Since] the real dramatis personae of the comedy of manners are the practices of society, the way of the world itself, we see in what fashion they alter and contaminate and corrupt; and though wickedness certainly need not triumph, a sense, at least, of man's dark, divided nature must somehow obtrude. Artifice, when expertly applied, can be a great short cut to truth.

But between artifice and the mere staginess that we encounter at times in *The School for Scandal* there is a crucial difference. Sheridan, we feel, heightens certain of his scenes not in the service of revelation but for the sake of effect. Partly from being too stagy and partly from being too sentimental, his is a real "fiction" plot where, rather than the audience finding out the truth in human nature, the characters find out, for fictional ends, the truth about one another. Even where Sheridan digs a little deeper, as with Lady Teazle's inclination toward sin, we are shown—and expected to believe—that she is now thoroughly sick of social pretense; there is not a hint that this may only be temporary repentance born of sheer fright, and that a month hence this blooming young wife of a man twice her age will be tempted once more. (pp. 82-3)

The trouble with this whole side of the play is not that it is artificial but that it is tame, is not that it snaps its fingers at

realistic truth but that it clicks its heels before conventional morality. . . . What Sheridan . . . wrote in *The School for Scandal* was one of the most brilliant box-office comedies in the language. He too was too worldly in his own calculations to become one of the great delineators of worldliness.

Thus we are in a world of set rewards and punishments, of old-fashioned—or perennial—heroes and heroines, of rich uncles who are won over and wicked brothers who are shown up. As popular theater, there may be nothing wrong with this; but there is something wrong with a man of Sheridan's gifts acquiescing in popular theater. Sheridan satirizes, here, almost nothing that the world in general does not condemn; he nowhere boldly challenges fashionable opinion or assaults fashionable complacency. A Wycherley may not have shocked his own generation, but he can still shock us. A Shaw may not shock us, but he did shock our grandparents. But Sheridan, if at times delightfully impudent, is never at all subversive. Nor, to be fair to the *man,* is this altogether calculating on his part; much of it, I suspect, he half believed in. There was a good deal of the pure romantic in the Sheridan who himself fought duels, himself eloped, himself was overdazzled by the great world. The gentility of his age clearly did him harm, but something beyond conformity enters in; actually, he often did not so much conform as concur. Sheridan's wit always tends to face south and toward the sun; in his portrayal of venom there is nothing personally venomous; he had worldly tastes but not, like Congreve or Molière or La Rochefoucauld, an inviolably worldly mind. His scandalmongers constitute a kind of Greek chorus in a play that Sheridan never really got round to writing on their terms. Their air of iniquity is a false front for the play's essential innocuousness. Indeed, in terms of Sheridan's mastery of his trade, perhaps the most brilliant thing about *The School for Scandal* is not the actual glitter of its dialogue but the seeming wickedness of its plot. (pp. 83-4)

*Louis Kronenberger, "'The School for Scandal',"* in his The Polished Surface: Essays in the Literature of Worldliness *(copyright © 1969 by Louis Kronenberger; reprinted by permission of Alfred A. Knopf, Inc.), Knopf, 1969, pp. 73-84.*

**A. N. KAUL**   (essay date 1970)

[*Kaul asserts that Sheridan is of minimal importance to the history of English comedy. He describes* The School for Scandal *as "a good play . . . in the sense that it is actable and funny and has . . . several well-rounded characters," but as an ultimately trifling drama. Only* The Rivals, *according to Kaul, "can claim a certain amount of significance and limited originality within the larger comic tradition."*]

The place of Sheridan in [the history of English comedy] is not difficult to define. It is not an important place; quite obviously he originates nothing of any importance, and he leads nowhere. Most markedly than Goldsmith, he is a backward-looking dramatist. Even this, however, can suggest an exaggerated importance unless we remember that the comic past was not at this point easily recoverable on the stage. It is conceivable that a greater or more serious dramatist than Sheridan might have succeeded in reanimating the traditions rather than simply and haphazardly borrowing from them, as Sheridan did. But on the whole this would seem to have been very nearly a hopeless task in the given theatrical situation. (pp. 131-32)

With comic energy rehabilitated in the novel, Goldsmith and Sheridan could only lament on the stage the dead hand of sentimentality and write sentimental comedy even as they decried it. At the beginning of *The Rivals* Sheridan, for instance, has his **"Prologue"** point to the figure of Comedy on the stage and exclaim:

> Look on her well—does she seem form'd to teach?
> Should you *expect* to hear this lady preach?
> Is gray experience suited to her youth?
> Do solemn sentiments become that mouth? . . .
> Must we displace her? And instead advance
> The Goddess of the woful countenance—
> The sentimental Muse!

The question raised in these jaunty lines is not only much too hopefully phrased, it is blissfully anachronistic. A Vanbrugh might have addressed it to a Cibber with greater timeliness, even though in Vanbrugh himself . . . the preachy sentimental Muse was already on the point of elbowing out the gay Restoration goddess that Sheridan so plainly wishes to invoke. The question a century later was hardly whether the Muse of Comedy was to be displaced from the stage, since she was in fact virtually defunct there; it was rather whether anything at all could be done to displace the other—the "Goddess of the woful countenance"—who had long usurped the theater as her own exclusive realm. And the very manner in which Sheridan raises the issue shows that, try as he might to brighten her countenance with a jest or two, he has no intention of challenging her authority. (pp. 133-34)

[At first sight, Sheridan's] comedies seem a healthy and realistic comment on the "Virtue Rewarded" formula of sentimental plays. For one thing, he ranged more freely and farther in the past, exerted much greater virtuosity, and no doubt briefly enlivened the jaded stage with a sense of novelty. He also wrote more various kinds of drama. In addition to his three comedies, his two farcical pieces [*St. Patrick's Day* and *The Critic*] exploited the minor strain of what was called "laughing comedy," a type that enjoyed some popularity at the time in reaction against the uniform solemnity and preachiness of genteel comedy. (p. 136)

It was in his comedies that Sheridan went beyond his age and attempted to press into service some of the forgotten themes and traditions of the sixteenth and seventeenth centuries. If we look at these comedies, however, we find again the device of making daring suggestions against the sentimental formula without supporting or even meaning them in the least. Consider, for instance, *A Trip to Scarborough*—an adaptation of an adaptation which provides, because of this very historical background, the clearest test of Sheridan's position on the question of sentimentality. Sheridan's model, [Vanbrugh's] *The Relapse,* though itself a concession to the sentimental view of love, nevertheless shows the "reformed" Loveless entering into a characteristic Restoration intrigue with Berinthia; it thereby disputes Cibber's easy view of reformation and the power of domestic virtue. In reworking *The Relapse,* Sheridan not merely returns to the spirit of the original behind the original but in fact improves on Cibber. While he retains the intrigue with Berinthia, the lovers are now guilty of nothing worse than exchanging a few sly words, and the whole affair becomes ultimately a red herring drawn across the straight path of sentimental love. (pp. 136-37)

The difficulties in *The School for Scandal,* Sheridan's best known comedy, are certainly not smoothed out at one stroke. Nevertheless they are eventually resolved in the approved fashion. *The School for Scandal* is in fact a good play, but only in

the sense that it is actable and funny and has, moreover, several well-rounded characters. But it is also in some ways a remarkably trifling play. "The school for scandal" idea itself is largely ornamental: it has little functional importance, much less the sort of importance one might expect of an idea proclaimed in the title. It is supposed to have been directed at a widespread contemporary vice, but neither this fact nor any amount of cleverness on Sheridan's part can conceal its basic triteness and triviality.

More important, of course, is the play's attack on the sentimental tradition. It is supposed to be a head-on collision, with Sheridan protected by the sturdy old armor of Restoration comedy. Yet the attack turns out to be another red herring, though one much more cleverly manipulated. The center of the attack is Joseph Surface—"a sentimental knave," as Lady Sneerwell calls him—whose grave maxims and virtue conceal what is supposed to be a many-sided villainy. . . . Neatly balanced against him is his brother, Charles, who resembles Goldsmith's Honeywood [in *The Good-Natur'd Man*] and may well have been modeled after that good-natured man. Exactly reversing Joseph's attributes, Charles has the surface appearance of a dissolute rake but is at bottom a perfectly good and generous man. And yet the realities underneath are as unreal and schematic as the surfaces or the masks, so that in the end they cancel each other out equally effectively and leave us with the usual nullity of sentimental comedy. The villainy and the virtue are both discovered and respectively defeated and rewarded. The good Charles, like Goldsmith's Honeywood, even promises to purge himself of his generous little faults in the play's last speech: "Why, as to reforming, Sir Peter, I'll make no promises, and that I take to be a proof that I intend to set about it."

The trickery that characterizes the play is manifest in this speech itself. The good man is really irreproachable, but then he will make no promises to reform himself, reformation being no easy matter, and yet indeed he has already started reforming. This is the sort of attack that Sheridan's play makes on sentimentality, in big matters as well as small. Sheridan might himself have made Lady Sneerwell's admission: "Pshaw!—there's no possibility of being witty without a little ill nature." And indeed very little ill nature enables Sheridan to show his wit as well as his indebtedness to the witty "poets of the last age." This is even true in the case of the arch-villain, Joseph Surface—though we see the virtues and vices of his sentimentality, we see nothing of his amorous knavery. The famous screen scene obviously owes its inspiration to [Wycherley's] *The Country Wife,* yet it should rightly be called the smokescreen scene. . . . Yet to compare this most salacious and daring of Sheridan's scenes with Wycherley's play, or even with the more timely *Tom Jones,* is to see all the more clearly Sheridan's genius for peppering a tale without really spicing it, for raising much dust without allowing any traffic. For, when the screen is removed at last, it proves not merely Lady Teazle but virtually the whole play entirely blameless. (pp. 137-39)

[Sheridan's] plays, while clearly expressing a mild dissatisfaction with the contemporary theater, seem to have gained little other than their reputation from the recourse to older drama. . . . Furthermore, where they appear to diverge from the set formulas of sentimentality in the interests of realism, in a sense they only become more unrealistic—idiosyncratic, unrelated to anything except what they relate, too often dependent on a character or situation that signifies nothing but itself. In other words, the sort of departure they attempt makes them more lively but at the same time more trifling and less relevant.

***The Rivals*** alone can claim a certain amount of significance and limited originality within the larger comic tradition to which it belongs. It also exhibits, more than any other play of Sheridan's, a pastiche of motifs, character patterns, situations, and theatrical devices drawn from various comedies of the preceding two centuries. To the extent to which it is an epitaph on the English comic drama, it is one of those jaunty epitaphs that delight in rehearsing and summarizing the main features and signal achievements of that which has passed from the world. Or, to change the metaphor, the play may be viewed as a sort of archaeologist's surface, an open and remarkably uncomplicated facade showing layer beneath layer of literary history. This side of the play has its own interest and to it we must briefly turn.

To begin with there is the immediate past, or rather the immediate present—the sentimentality of Sheridan's own day and age. "When hearts deserving happiness would unite their fortunes, Virtue would crown them with an unfading garland of modest hurtless flowers." This, one feels, ought to be tongue in cheek, but, being spoken by Julia, one simply cannot be sure. It may be meant quite seriously as the moral of the play. . . . [The] problem of sentimentality looms large within the play, in the shape of Julia and her lover, Faulkland. It is a problem only because here, as in his later plays, Sheridan is not content to offer sentimental love straight but must trifle with it a little. The trifling lies in the character of Faulkland, through whom Sheridan clearly means to ridicule mildly the contemporary notion of the good and sensitive though self-doubting and therefore overly jealous lover. Julia, on the other hand, is presented without question as the epitome of goodness, patience, sense, sensibility, and all the other desirable feminine virtues. (pp. 139-41)

Julia and Faulkland are, of course, important inasmuch as they share the theme of love on almost equal terms with Lydia and Captain Absolute, the real comic heroine and hero of the play. But sentimentality likewise colors certain subsidiary characters and situations of otherwise older ancestry and inspiration. The hero's father, Sir Anthony Absolute, and the heroine's aunt, the famous Mrs. Malaprop, for example, are both character parts in the old tradition of humors. Sir Anthony is parental tyranny or absolute authority. . . . Mrs. Malaprop, whose humor is vanity, goes back in a straight line through Fielding's Mrs. Slipslop to Shakespeare's Dogberry. With Dogberry she shares not merely the habit of malapropism but that unshakable sense of personal worth which is the common source of their aspiring locutions. (pp. 141-42)

With two other peripheral characters Sheridan moves a step closer to Shakespeare. Bob Acres—the country wooer caught in a town world, the pale squire on whom are thrust both the idea of courage and the laws of honor and dueling—is, of course, reminiscent of Sir Andrew Aguecheek. His new domicile being what it is, his gulling becomes an entirely humane affair, and he emerges from the duel not merely without fighting it, but also with the laugh on the other side. The trait of cowardice is in fact transformed into the virtue of good sense; and a major part in the transformtion is played by Acres's servant David, who thus becomes a Falstaffian expounder of common sense against the pretentious claims of honor. (p. 142)

The originality [of ***The Rivals***] lies in the Lydia-Absolute plot, which is the heart of the play. There is no deliberate borrowing

here such as we have seen elsewhere in Sheridan. Yet the story of Lydia and Captain Absolute is not for that reason an idiosyncratic story, unrelated to any other love stories both before or after. On the contrary, its originality lies precisely in its relation to a continuing tradition. It does not imitate older comedies; it shares their critical purpose, and in so doing even foreshadows the point of departure for the later comedy of Jane Austen. (p. 143)

[The] theme marriage for love against marriage for money, although Sheridan suggests it indirectly, is not the comic problem of ***The Rivals***. In Restoration comedy . . . money and marriage on the one hand and love on the other are treated as two separate issues. The problem of Lydia and Captain Absolute is that for them the two happen to be identical. As Absolute pithily summarizes the situation: "My father wants to *force* me to marry the very girl I am plotting to run away with." What, then, keeps the lovers apart—what introduces the element of conflict into their situation—can be seen by comparing them with the other pair of lovers in the play. For in both situations love happens to coincide happily with material advantage and filial duty, so that in each case caprice alone can be said to constitute the lovers' difficulty. The difference, however, is that Faulkland's caprice, self-doubt, is precisely that—a caprice, an idiosyncrasy not unlike the personal idiosyncrasies of the other heroes of Sheridan and Goldsmith, carried here to a still more absurd and tiresome length. Little is needed to subdue it except a turn in the plot at the appropriate moment. By comparison, Lydia's caprice is more in the nature of a comic idea, and something more or less like comic experience is needed to free her from its hold.

Lydia's story is both singular and representative. . . . As we are informed in the first scene, she is "a lady of a very singular taste," a lady who likes her lover "better as a *half-pay ensign* than if she knew he was son and heir to Sir Anthony Absolute, a baronet of three thousand a year." And in the very second scene we know the reason for her singular taste: she is a devourer of romances. Her maid, returning from her errand to the circulating library, reports her failure to procure *The Reward of Constancy, The Fatal Connexion, The Mistakes of the Heart,* and *The Delicate Distress;* nevertheless, she has brought to her mistress an armful of other equally tempting titles along with *Peregrine Pickle, Humphrey Clinker,* and *The Sentimental Journey.* (pp. 145-46)

[What] follows the catalogue of romances shows the extent to which Lydia's sense of reality has faded into the nonsense of her reading. For, as she and Julia bring each other up to date on their respective situations, Lydia constantly filters the facts of both through the haze of romance, making every item coincide with the sort of sentiment expressed in one or the other of the titles mentioned earlier.

The importance of the catalogue, however, is not simply that it expresses confusion by mixing up romances and novels cheek-by-jowl. What the emphasis on books makes clear at the outset is that Lydia is a female Quixote—that, in Sir Anthony's words, "the girl's mad!—her brain's turned by reading." If not mad, she certainly suffers in a mental sense from that imaginary squint whose physical existence or absence provides much laughing matter in various ways at various times in the play. What the interminable catalogue does also is show how little Lydia's "singular taste" is in reality to be considered singular. For, as we learn in the same early scene, not just Lydia but all fashionable ladies are after the same romances and devour them with equal avidity. Lydia's caprice is thus something more than a caprice; it is a fashion, a general squint in the culture of which she is the representative comic heroine.

Lydia's lover, Captain Absolute, is what might be called the positive hero of this culture. He knows what he wants and knows also how to get it all. . . . His solution is not to attempt anything rash or precipitate but instead to "prepare her gradually for the discovery, and make myself necessary to her, before I risk it." This sounds unheroically cool and calculating, and so it is. But within the value-scheme of the play—in contrast, that is, with Lydia's absurd illusions, Julia's vapid sentimentality, and Faulkland's "exquisite nicety"—Absolute becomes the embodiment of manly confidence and good sense. He accepts from the outset the play's thesis that financial interest and filial duty are not opposed to love but are rather its necessary supports and blessings; through his success at the end, Sheridan underlines the same thesis regarding the basic health and harmony of the culture depicted in the play.

In the meantime, Sheridan does his best to protract suspense through the flimsiest theatrical devices and through having Absolute play up to Lydia's fantasies at great length. . . . When the crisis does come at last, it is, of course, not of the expected sort. Discovering that the romantic Beverley and the eligible Absolute are one and the same suitor, Lydia's first reaction is: "So!—there will be no elopement after all!" Later, developing the sentiment, she complains: "when I thought we were coming to the prettiest distress imaginable, to find myself made a mere Smithfield bargain of at last.—There, had I projected one of the most sentimental elopements!—so becoming a disguise!—so amiable a ladder of ropes!—Conscious moon—four horses . . . O, I shall die with disappointment."

What she does, of course, is not die but straighten out her romantic squint and look somewhat within herself and somewhat upon the realities of the world outside. (pp. 147-49)

> *A. N. Kaul, "A Note on Sheridan," in his* The Action of English Comedy: Studies in the Encounter of Abstraction and Experience from Shakespeare to Shaw *(copyright © 1970 by Yale University), Yale University Press, 1970, pp. 131-49.*

## MARK S. AUBURN  (essay date 1977)

[*Auburn surveys Sheridan's lesser-known works:* St. Patrick's Day, The Duenna, A Trip to Scarborough, *and* The Critic. *In summing up Sheridan's achievement, Auburn praises particularly his "complex, fast-moving" plots, "verbal brilliance," and the "careful poise of expectation and surprise in situational comedy."*]

**St. Patrick's Day** revolves around a typical farcical action, the boy-gets-girl-in-spite-of-parents formula. Lieutenant O'Connor wants to wed Lauretta but Justice and Bridget Credulous object to the marriage. . . .

With a line of action so broadly typical, to distinguish Sheridan's exact debt to a farcical tradition is difficult. Many of Samuel Foote's and Charles Macklin's dark satiric farces use this sort of comic frame upon which to build their potent attacks on contemporary society. Garrick's *Miss in Her Teens* and Colman's *Polly Honeycombe*, both of which have been named as sources of *The Rivals*, are as similar to this piece as to Sheridan's first comedy. There is less originality here, in the use of the old device of a disguised lover attempting to circumvent parents, than in *The Rivals*, where Sheridan added the wrinkle of tricking the daughter as well. (p. 62)

Much of the structure and content of *The Rivals* appears to have been in Sheridan's mind when he wrote [*St. Patrick's Day*]. Lauretta, like Lydia, is a spirited girl who can argue amusingly with her equally temperamental mother and who thinks a military man the height of fashion; she is rather more like the harsh Polly Honeycombe than the sprightly Lydia, but she retains an attractiveness necessary to effect the amiable denouement. Dr. Rosy, like Mrs. Malaprop, is characterized largely by a verbal tic—in this case, a propensity to spout three- and four-word moral phrases of the most prosaic kind (anticipatory, perhaps, of the pompously phrased sentiments of Joseph Surface)—and like Mrs. Malaprop's his "humour" has little to do with the conduct of the plot; it exists merely to embellish his playing character. Some of the comic situations arise as they do in *The Rivals* through the careful preparation of mistaken identity and misunderstanding. In both plays, for instance, the opening scenes establish the initial situation through exposition but also characterize peripheral agents in order to set up further local display of them later. . . . The central scene of *The Rivals* occurs when Jack arrives at Mrs. Malaprop's and tricks her into admitting him to see Lydia; in *St. Patrick's Day*, there is a similar scene when O'Connor, disguised as Humphrey Hum, reveals himself to Lauretta. Sheridan again uses the technique of removing the parent (Justice Credulous) from the scene so that the lovers may come to understand one another, then returning him at the crucial moment in order to discomfit them just as success seems at hand. The compressed scope of *St. Patrick's Day* forces the discomfiture to be more immediate than that of *The Rivals*, where Jack does not receive his comeuppance until four scenes later.

As in *The Rivals*, and indeed in all of Sheridan's original dramatic work before *The School for Scandal*, the tone of *St. Patrick's Day* is distinctly amiable. Lieutenant O'Connor is immediately characterized as an essentially honorable fellow. (pp. 63-4)

Little [in *St. Patrick's Day*] points to Sheridan's talent beyond the general compactness of the short piece and a few fine *bon mots*. Among these are Justice Credulous's replies to his wife's preference to follow him to the grave rather than have a quack attempt to cure him ("I'm sensible of your affection, Dearest—and believe me nothing consoles me in my present melancholy situation, so much as the thought of leaving you behind, my Angel" . . . and to her assertion that dying is quick ("Ay, but it leaves a numbness behind, that lasts for a plaguy long time." . . . But there is much in *St. Patrick's Day* that points to a deep and growing familiarity with what will immediately please upon the stage. First, the farce is designed for a hero whose specialty is not comedy. Though his is the title role, Lieutenant O'Connor carries little of the real humor of the piece: a handsome exterior, a slight ability to mimic theatrically obvious types like a country bumpkin or the quasi-Dutch, and the soberness of a straight man to the self-exposures of Dr. Rosy and Serjeant Trounce are all that is necessary for success in the role. Since Clinch [the actor who was to play the role] specialized in tragedy, Sheridan designed for his benefit farce a character that required only enough comic talent to gain success through contrast with his accustomed roles. Second, theatrical coterie jokes abound. Rosy calls O'Connor "my Alexander," setting up a pleasant laugh for the audience which had just seen Clinch perform Alexander the Great in Nathaniel Lee's heroic *The Rival Queens*, his choice for the mainpiece of his benefit night. (pp. 64-5)

Like *The Rivals* and *St. Patrick's Day*, *The Duenna* is both distinctly original and slavishly derivative. Set in the never-

never land that Spain was for eighteenth-century comedy, the plot of *The Duenna* is even more involved than that of *The Rivals*. As in the earlier comedy, *domnées* of character are added to multiple disguises to develop amusing and amiable comedy of situation, complicated and recomplicated, dependent on chance. Where before there was one strict father, now there are two; where before there was one couple whose happiness depended upon circumventing their elders, now there are two; but where before it was character that interested us primarily, now farcical character is subordinated much more completely to plot, so that the tangled imbroglio is constantly before our eyes. As in *The Rivals*, the crusty old father—here, Don Jerome—is hoist with the petard he thought he had so successfully laid; but now all fortifications are blown up together, and the vain Jew Isaac is exploded by his own charge just as Don Jerome's bomb clears the way for Donna Louisa to marry the impecunious Antonio, her jealous brother Ferdinand to marry the slightly sober Donna Clara, and Margaret, the old and ugly duenna who has taken Louisa's place, to make her fortune from her marriage to Isaac.

The action of *The Duenna* has much in common with such mixtures of intrigue and farce popular in Sheridan's time as Susanna Centlivre's *The Wonder: A Woman Keeps a Secret*. (pp. 66-7)

*The Duenna* and *The Wonder* are like one another more in tone than in any specifics of action or character. . . . [In these] pseudo-Iberian comedies, the marks of the intrigue—external obstacles rather than internal flaws, heightened but more artificial concern, frequent reversal of situation, concealed truth producing multilayered comic dramatic irony—combine with an amiability bred of basically good-natured characters and a middle-class moral view to produce comedies typical of the Georgian era.

Analogues to *The Duenna* abound, though no single source leaps forth. A comic plot similar to one principal situation of *The Duenna*—a daughter turned out of doors while the maid passes as the mistress—is found in an Italian comic opera, Carlo Goldoni's *Il Filosopho di Campagna*. (pp. 67-8)

As there are similarities to other plots, so there are to other characters. We can point from the two best playing characters of Sheridan's comic opera—Isaac the Jew and Margaret the ugly duenna—to similar roles already established and long popular on the Georgian stage, and to the actors who created them. One of the most successful comic operas written in the period before *The Duenna* is Isaac Bickerstaff's *The Padlock*. . . . Like *The Duenna*, *The Padlock* combines a farcical Spanish intrigue plot with original songs. (p. 68)

*The Duenna* has a remarkably complicated but compact libretto, . . . is highly amusing, and . . . represents an important step in Sheridan's development.

The plot of *The Duenna* is both the most highly complex and the most highly unified, if not the most probable, of all the plots Sheridan created. The frame, of course, is provided by the four young lovers. Donna Louisa, by virtue of her sprightly grace, impish assurance, and clever trickery, is the most entertaining of these. She is matched with the handsome Antonio, whose artificial introduction with two contrasting love songs at the beginning of the opera may seem absurd and whose love and bravery are assigned, not fully developed, comic characteristics. Contrasted slightly with these two are the sober Clara and the jealous Ferdinand, yet neither is Clara so sober nor Ferdinand so jealous as to lose our interest. Sheridan may have

used as lovers characters very similar to those of *The Rivals*, but he was not about to make again the aesthetic mistakes he made there. . . . [These four lovers] are portrayed as clever enough to get their own ways in spite of strict fathers but are never made particularly witty or given complex personalities with serious internal flaws to be removed. Indeed, only Ferdinand among them has anything like a comic flaw—his jealousy. Interest in the four lovers is important. But the real pleasure in the plot, taken as a whole, comes from the complications provided by three other characters: Don Jerome, Margaret the Duenna, and Isaac the Jew; their physical and psychological idiosyncrasies conflict to create the situations most skillfully designed to evoke laughter. (pp. 72-3)

Of these three idiosyncratic characters, Margaret the Duenna is the least comic. She is an ugly old woman whom Don Jerome has hired to protect his daughter's chastity. . . . Margaret is not funny for her own foibles—she never believes, for instance, when she is pretending to be the young and beautiful Louisa, that she really is young and beautiful—but for her clever manipulation of others to expose their idiosyncrasies. (p. 73)

The most fun of the whole opera is that which is funniest about Margaret—the ongoing sight gag she represents. This technique, common to farce and the basis of a great deal of enjoyment in characters like Bob Acres, sets up a whole series of misunderstood exchanges between Don Jerome and Isaac concerning her beauty. . . .

The tradition out of which Don Jerome springs is clear; he has little to differentiate him from hundreds of other strict fathers, including Sir Anthony Absolute and Justice Credulous. Like most old fathers, he is crusty, testy, and financially motivated. His cynical realism opposes the idealism and love of his children, and of course they eventually turn the tables on him, pitting flexibility against rigidity and asserting the power of clever youth to take over and create the new social order. He is never really a serious threat to the happiness of the young people. . . . Like Sheridan's other old fathers, and like those of late eighteenth-century amiable comedy, even when overreached he proves good-natured. (p. 74)

*The Duenna* is not a comedy of wit, and Don Jerome is not basically a witty character.

The one character around whom this comic opera may be said to revolve is Isaac, the conceited, covetous Jew who seeks to marry Louisa. The audience sees him compounding his egotism and avarice while they know all the while that eventually he will discover his mistakes and receive the come-uppance he so richly deserves. He is a comic villain, but never clever or strong enough to represent a real threat; his faults blind him too completely to allow him to damage the sympathetic characters. (p. 76)

All these characters are somewhat interesting and Isaac especially amusing, but none of them are particularly striking, original, or clever, and none are drawn with sufficient psychological or comic depth to stay in our minds beyond the setting in which they appear. Perhaps not surprisingly in a comic opera, they are primarily types, flat place-holders who provide vehicles for the display of mostly stock comic situations. And the most frequently employed technique of the comic opera is comedy of situation. As it was used in *The Rivals* and *St. Patrick's Day*, this technique of concealing vital information from one or more of the characters is frequently used in *The Duenna*, though never with the same multilayered effect obtained in *The Rivals*. (p. 77)

*The Duenna* is a one-joke comedy. But then, so are many great comedies. Sheridan's brilliant stroke was to exploit this one joke to its fullest possible extent. And his favorite technique here—allowing Isaac multiple asides in which he praises himself and his cleverness, explains his intended actions, weighs his possible alternatives, and never recognizes the cleverness, action, or alternatives as precisely the things which guarantee his downfall—intensifies the comic dramatic irony. (p. 79)

The frivolity of *The Duenna* is matched by the characteristic amiability of the dénouement. But for Sheridan first the frivolity, then to a lesser extent the amiability would disappear, and its disappearance would coincide . . . with Sheridan's own growth. . . . Henceforth, Sheridan would show more concern with carefully structured plot (as he is doing in *The Duenna* in comparison to *The Rivals* and *St. Patrick's Day*), more concern with wit, more concern with satire. However entertaining his later works may be, none of them are merely frivolous. (p. 80)

The changes Sheridan made in *The Relapse* when he adapted it as *A Trip to Scarborough* indicate his awareness of its beauties and of its weaknesses. He simplified [its] Foppington-Fashion plot and redesigned the Amanda-Loveless plot. He invented ties between the two groups of people that make the Amanda-Loveless entrance into the Foppington-Fashion affair probable and necessary, and the entrance of the Foppington-Fashion group into the Amanda-Loveless affair probable, though not necessary. In removing the licentiousness of dialogue and motivation, he destroyed much of the wit, and his redesign of the moral world indicates his own and his time's tastes. In effect, he attempted to make a witty "genteel" comedy of manners with a "low" subplot. (p. 91)

Sheridan makes several other changes in the Foppington-Fashion plot necessary to accommodate the squeamish tastes of his age and typical of the comedies popular in his time. He removes, for instance, the homosexual Coupler and replaces him with the matronly Mrs. Coupler; dramatically she functions identically with her brighter original, but she lacks the spark that every character of a truly great comedy must have, that all the characters of *The Rivals* or *The Duenna* possess. Sheridan also generally cleans up the language and the more blasphemous references. Thus, Foppington refers to his watching the ladies rather than the entertainment at the opera; in *The Relapse* he ogled the women at church. (pp. 93-4)

Another change typical of Sheridan's own style in his original plays is the general emphasis on expectation rather than surprise as the main basis for comedy. . . . [Clearly] as a creator of comic situations Sheridan generally preferred to raise the expectations of the audience for comic conflict rather than surprise them with a totally unexpected reversal. Thus, in *The Relapse*, Foppington's arrival just after Tom had married Hoyden was unexpected; he was not supposed to come down to Tunbelly's for a fortnight, but came early instead on a whim. In *A Trip to Scarborough* he is readying himself to go to his future father-in-law's even when Tom comes to request aid for the second time. Tom does not know that Foppington plans to go so soon, but the audience does, and that knowledge heightens anxiety; Tom's marriage is awaited with the comic analogue of fear. When Tom is finally married, anxiety is allayed, and at the expected arrival of Foppington the emphasis is on the lord's discomfiture. As Sheridan does in *The Rivals* when he announces the identity of Ensign Beverley in the first scene and outlines Sir Anthony's plans for his son in the second, or in *The Duenna* when he makes clear Margaret's imposture and

allows Isaac to disclose all his foolish plans, so here he stresses anticipation of situation and discomfiture of the characters over comic surprise of the auditors. (pp. 94-5)

The integration of the [Foggington-Fashion and Amanda-Loveless plots] alleviated one potentially unsatisfactory element in Vanbrugh's design and made Sheridan's adaptation, if not a more artistic work, certainly a more unified creation. The simplification of the Foppington-Fashion plot removed the difficulties of bigamy and amorality represented in Hoyden's decision to conceal her prior marriage to Fashion and also caused the omission of what some delicate-minded auditors would have found unacceptable criticism of ecclesiastics in the character of the Chaplain. Making Sir Tunbelly into an amiable character instead of the beastly country squire Vanbrugh paints was another result of Sheridan's simplification of the Foppington-Fashion dénouement. (p. 96)

While Sheridan's adaptation of the Foppington-Fashion line of action is typical both of his skills as a dramatist and his acceptance of his period's morality, the most extensive changes to *The Relapse* were in the adaptation of the Amanda-Loveless plot. (pp. 97-8)

No human heart is exposed in [the Amanda-Loveless] plot of *A Trip to Scarborough;* no truth about human nature is revealed through artistic exploration of the soul. In the elegant dance-like structure of the verbal sparring of Loveless and Berinthia in *The Relapse*, the selfishness that is the center of their existence is comically shown. In Sheridan's adaptation there is embarrassment, not comic exposure; mild flirtation, not fully achieved fornication. It is unsatisfying because the stakes are so small; the characters become mildly discomfited, not by their own natures, but by misunderstanding, by situations.

Clearly, the Sheridan who two months later oversaw production of the brilliant screen scene of *The School for Scandal* was capable of utilizing these materials for a comically satisfying and almost licentious effect. But in the Amanda-Loveless plot of *A Trip to Scarborough,* Sheridan was either unwilling or unable to lavish the care necessary to create a masterly or even a tolerably farcical recognition scene, largely because he could not adapt either the intellectual or the moral qualities of Vanbrugh's world to the tastes and suppositions of the Georgian stage and audience. (p. 101)

What Sheridan created in adapting *The Relapse* as *A Trip to Scarborough,* then, was a simplified playing piece, typical of much comedy popular in his time. The more unified action it achieves and the softening of tone make it a complete if rather "genteel" performance. He saw the failure of *The Relapse* to coalesce as a single action, or at least, as two actions mutually dependent on one another in some important way. . . . But he failed to realize that the beauty of Vanbrugh's play lay in its very licentiousness, for that licentiousness was the heart of the comic criticism, its exposure of the selfishness that is in most souls (or at least is seen to be in a time not highly influenced by the doctrine of sentimentalism); and in tidying up the plot, he substituted, for brilliant comic discussion of adultery and virtuous conversions, innocuous situation comedy with little artistic power, mild comic embarrassment for comic revelation of human nature. (p. 103)

Measured against the comic works of Congreve, Vanbrugh, Farquhar, Steele, and Goldsmith, Sheridan's comedies still stand tall in the estimation of audiences, who have supported their frequent revival, and should stand taller in the estimation of critics.

For Sheridan was certainly the finest comic playwright after Congreve and before Shaw. As a writer of theatrical burlesque, Sheridan achieved more than any predecessor or successor in this comic line. As a writer of comedy of manners, his achievement is not so unique but just as enduring. Eschewing the didactic, the melodramatic, the coldly cynical, and the violently satiric, Sheridan charted a middle course dependent upon original characterization, tight construction, and brilliant dialogue. While he never reached the poetic unity or intellectual penetration of Congreve, he wrote in a wider variety of styles, creating a distinctive humane comedy that improved upon the fresh boisterousness of Farquhar while avoiding the cynicism of Vanbrugh, the lachrymosity of the later Steele, and the improbabilities of Goldsmith.

For his subject matter Sheridan turned to his own experience largely; he chose the problems of young love and mature affection, the battle of the sexes, and the natural rebellion of youth against age. What he knew of these subjects and what he learned as he matured are revealed indirectly, not as flashes of insight into distinctly individualized, human characters but as general observations about people in society. Like all comic writers, he was concerned with deception and trickery; but he dealt with self-deception as well, particularly in his later comedies.

He began by structuring his plots according to the bifurcated forms most frequently used by his contemporaries, then moved increasingly toward the fuller unification which achieves most dramatic force in a single comic catastrophe. From first to last he showed extraordinary skill in utilizing for his original work *coups de théâtre:* no one who has seen or read them forgets the letters of *The Rivals, St. Patrick's Day,* and *The Duenna* or the famous scenes of concealment of these and *The School for Scandal.* As he developed in his construction of plot, he became less dependent upon purely physical circumstances—duels and elopements—and more capable of using the full scene for a total theatrical effect dependent upon the movement of the actor's spirit, not upon his legs and arms; an auction scene or a screen scene call for this display of the soul more completely than Jack tricking his father or Margaret imposing upon Isaac. Excepting *The Critic,* the structures of Sheridan's plots move from those which display character for its own sake in his early works to those which enact character for the story's sake in his later comedies.

The forms Sheridan's plots took were always distinctly comic. . . . Beneath all his comic excoriations of folly flows a good-natured tolerance: he fails to be morally serious because he chooses not to scourge vice but rather to expose foibles—a course which will alienate none though it improves few. Despite his insight in his last two major comic works, into what most would call reality—a demonstration that vice is as much a part of human nature as virtue—his evident faith in well-intentioned men and benevolent providence to expel the vicious from society seems unrealistic. He was a sentimentalist.

For his characters Sheridan first chose stage types to which the audience and the actors were long accustomed. Capitalizing upon familiarity from the one and skill from the other, Sheridan molded these type characters into surprisingly original amalgams that live in audiences' minds beyond the frameworks in which they appear. As he became more familiar with his craft and with the actors who gave his plays life, Sheridan ventured to complicate his characters further, but never so far that psychological depth overwhelmed comic effect.

His dialogue was designed primarily to give life to these characters. It was "characteristic," his contemporaries would have said. Only for isolated speeches in the scandal scenes or in *The Critic* would a person reasonably familiar with Sheridan's comedies not be able to identify the speaker. The dialogue is amusing usually because it reveals character and complicates situation, though on occasion it is also manifestly absurd or witty. It is brilliant not because it is especially witty in the epigrammatic manner of a Congreve but because it is so consistently true to character without depending merely upon simple dialect or idiosyncratic tags. When Sheridan did choose to use tags, he created new ones quite beyond the grasp of an ordinary comic playwright—malapropisms, "oaths referential," or Joseph's sentiments. (pp. 178-80)

Throughout his comic work, both manners and burlesque, Sheridan's practice was to take the audience into his confidence, to share with them as much of the events yet to come as would pique their expectations concerning the complex situations unfolding before them. Surprise, when it came, arose from probable consequences joyously anticipated; but neither the expectations nor the surprises were allowed to linger long and thereby lose their force. In this manner, Sheridan managed to invent comedies of situation more delicately balanced between anticipation and astonishment than any of his eighteenth-century contemporaries were capable of creating.

In sum, Sheridan's achievement among writers of English comedy springs from his complex, fast-moving, amiably comic plots peopled by probable yet theatrical characters; from a verbal brilliance dependent not upon wit in the high Restoration comic sense but upon a full consonance of expression to character; and from a careful poise of expectation and surprise in situational comedy. (pp. 180-81)

> *Mark S. Auburn, in his* Sheridan's Comedies: Their Contexts and Achievements *(reprinted by permission of University of Nebraska Press; © 1977 by the University of Nebraska Press), University of Nebraska Press, 1977, 221 p.*

---

## ADDITIONAL BIBLIOGRAPHY

Bingham, Madeleine. *Sheridan: The Track of a Comet.* New York: St. Martin's Press, 1972, 383 p.

> A detailed biography. Bingham maintains that Sheridan, in both his theatrical and political careers, wished to be accepted primarily as a gentleman rather than as an artist or orator.

Brooks, Cleanth, and Heilman, Robert B. "Part Three: Sheridan, *The School for Scandal.*" In their *Understanding Drama: Twelve Plays,* pp. 194-255. New York: Henry Holt and Co., 1945.

> A study guide that interprets *The School for Scandal* as sentimental and melodramatic. Brooks states that "Sheridan comes very close to stating outright that he does not believe in intelligence."

Danziger, Marlies K. *Oliver Goldsmith and Richard Brinsley Sheridan.* New York: Frederick Ungar, 1972, 189 p.*

> A comparison of the two playwrights with commentary on their works. Danziger maintains that their Restoration comedies were written for performance rather than study.

Darlington, William Aubrey. *Sheridan.* New York: The Macmillan Co., 1933, 144 p.

> An objective overview of Sheridan's life with special attention paid to his political career.

Donohue, Joseph W., Jr. "Sheridan's *Pizarro:* Natural Religion and the Artificial Hero." In his *Dramatic Character in the English Romantic Age,* pp. 125-56. Princeton: Princeton University Press, 1970.

Discusses the critical reception of *Pizarro* and examines Sheridan's presentation of Rolla, the protagonist of the drama. Rolla, according to Donohue, is "the epitome of the Romantic man of feeling."

Fitzgerald, Percy. *The Lives of the Sheridans.* 2 vols. London: Richard Bentley and Son, 1886.*

An objective study of Sheridan and his ancestors. While Fitzgerald has little admiration for Sheridan's personal life in his later years, he praises him as a politician and as an author.

Foss, Kenelm. *Here Lies Richard Brinsley Sheridan.* London: Martin Secker, 1939, 390 p.

A detailed biographical study.

Gibbs, Lewis [pseudonym of Joseph Walter Cove]. *Sheridan.* London: J. M. Dent & Sons, 1947, 280 p.

A sympathetic biography. Gibbs denounces reports that Sheridan led a misguided life and claims that he maintained high aesthetic, political, and personal standards throughout his careers as a playwright, theatre manager, and member of Parliament.

Glasgow, Alice. *Sheridan of Drury Lane.* New York: Frederick A. Stokes Co., 1940, 310 p.

A biographical study in the form of a play. Glasgow fictionalizes episodes in Sheridan's life to heighten their dramatic impact.

Hare, Arnold. *Richard Brinsley Sheridan.* Writers and Their Work, edited by Ian Scott-Kilvert. Windsor, England: Profile Books, 1981, 45 p.

An appreciation of Sheridan's plays. Hare places them within the context of eighteenth-century theatrical history, and provides a brief analysis of Sheridan's political career.

Loftis, John. *Sheridan and the Drama of Georgian England.* Cambridge: Harvard University Press, 1977, 174 p.

Maintains that while Sheridan was strongly influenced by his Restoration predecessors, he surpassed them by virtue of his "sensitivity to prose dialogue and . . . his capacity to give familiar dramatic situations intensified force by his mastery of the techniques of burlesque."

Nettleton, George Henry. Introduction to *The Major Dramas of Richard Brinsley Sheridan: "The Rivals," "The School for Scandal," "The Critic,"* by Richard Brinsley Sheridan, edited by George Henry Nettleton, pp. xv-cxvii. Boston: Ginn and Co., 1906.

A discussion of Sheridan's life and his relation to Elizabethan, Restoration, and sentimental drama. Nettleton, a prominent Sheridan scholar, identifies the sources of Sheridan's major plays. He finds Sheridan's strongest influences to be Ben Jonson and William Congreve, but maintains that Sheridan's work is completely original.

Rhodes, R. Crompton. *Harlequin Sheridan: The Man and the Legends.* Oxford: Basil Blackwell, 1933, 322 p.

A biographical study that depicts Sheridan as a politician, playwright, and figure of notoriety.

Sanders, Lloyd C. *Life of Richard Brinsley Sheridan.* New York: Scribner & Welford, 1890, 177 p.

A consideration of Sheridan portraying him as an enigmatic figure. Sanders considers Sheridan's dramatic works to be witty but not poetic, yet concedes that Sheridan's accomplishments "merit him respect and admiration."

Schiller, Andrew. "*The School for Scandal:* The Restoration Unrestored." *PMLA* LXXI, No. 4 (September 1956): 694-704.

Maintains that *The School for Scandal,* though witty and occasionally brilliant, is often labored and didactic.

Sherwin, Oscar. *Uncorking Old Sherry: The Life and Times of Richard Brinsley Sheridan.* New York: Twayne Publishers, 1960, 352 p.

A lengthy biography. According to Sherwin, Sheridan used his literary career as "merely a stepping stone to political reknown."

Sinko, Grzegorz. *Sheridan and Kotzebue: A Comparative Essay.* Wroclaw Society of Science and Letters, series A, no. 27, Wrocław: Skład Główny W Domu Ksiażki, 1949, 32 p.*

An analysis of the two playwrights focusing on *Pizarro,* Sheridan's adaption of Kotzebue's drama.

Sprague, Arthur C. "In Defence of a Masterpiece: *The School for Scandal* Re-examined." In *English Studies Today, third series,* edited by G. I. Duthie, pp. 125-35. Edinburgh: University Press, 1962.

A consideration of *The School for Scandal* as a drama created expressly for its actors.

# Robert Louis Stevenson

## 1850-1894

(Born Robert Lewis Balfour Stevenson) Scottish novelist, short story writer, poet, essayist, dramatist, and prayer writer.

Although critics consider Stevenson an inventive stylist and vivid storyteller, they have, by their emphasis on his life, personality, and fluctuating reputation, created a literary persona that has received more attention than his novels. Several of his works were regarded as classics when first published, and their popular appeal has not diminished. Critics credit the enduring attraction of his romances, including *Treasure Island, Kidnapped: Being Memoirs of the Adventures of David Balfour in the Year 1751,* and *Strange Case of Dr. Jekyll and Mr. Hyde,* to their fast-paced action, strong plots, and well-drawn characters. Stevenson is also noted for his understanding of youth, which is evident both in his early "boys' novels," as they were known, and in his much-loved *A Child's Garden of Verses.* Yet, despite the continuing popularity of Stevenson's work, modern critics no longer accord him the same literary importance offered by their nineteenth-century counterparts.

Stevenson was a sickly, fragile child, and suffered from severe respiratory ailments that frequently interrupted his schooling. His relations with his parents became increasingly difficult as he reached adolescence. His father, a civil engineer, expected him to train for the family profession of lighthouse-building. Stevenson refused, and although he agreed to study law, he rarely attended classes and was never a practicing attorney, preferring the study of literature instead. He decided to teach himself to write by "playing the sedulous ape to Hazlitt, to Lamb, to Wordsworth, to Sir Thomas Browne, to Defoe, to Hawthorne, to Montaigne, to Baudelaire, and to Obermann." Indeed, critics of Stevenson's work often note the influence of these authors, particularly of Defoe and Montaigne, as well as George Meredith.

Motivated by his love for adventure and his need for a climate congenial to his health, Stevenson traveled extensively throughout his life. His journeys to France in the 1870s provided much of the material for his early travel books, *An Inland Voyage* and *Travels with a Donkey in the Cévennes.* In 1876, while in France, Stevenson met Mrs. Fanny Osbourne, an American woman eleven years his senior. When Osbourne returned to California two years later to arrange a divorce, Stevenson followed. The newly-married couple stayed in America for almost a year and then returned to Europe with Lloyd Osbourne, Fanny's son.

In the 1880s, despite his continuing poor health, Stevenson wrote many of his best-known works, including *Treasure Island.* Originally begun as a game for his stepson, the novel was published serially in a children's magazine under the title "The Sea-Cook," and became Stevenson's first popular and critical success. The works that followed, including *A Child's Garden of Verses, Dr. Jekyll and Mr. Hyde,* and *Kidnapped,* strengthened his growing reputation.

In 1887, the Stevensons returned to America. From California, they sailed to Samoa, where Stevenson found the climate congenial to his lung condition. His life on the island consisted of dabbling in local politics, managing his plantation, and writing

*The Granger Collection, New York*

several works, including collaborations with Lloyd Osbourne. He died unexpectedly at forty-four from a cerebral hemorrhage.

Critics frequently praise Stevenson for what Margaret Oliphant called "that fine, transparent, marvellously lucid style." Others challenge this opinion, claiming that Stevenson substituted style for ideas. Most commentators agree that, in their emphasis on exciting plots, rather than analysis or character, Stevenson's fictional works are derived from the tradition of prose romance. His works in genres other than the novel have received mixed reactions. His dramas, written in collaboration with William Ernest Henley, are considered unsuccessful, a judgment attributed to Stevenson's ignorance of dramatic technique and over-reliance on dialogue. His essays and travel sketches have been praised for their humor, perception, grace, and charm. Response to his poetry for adults, in contrast, has been almost uniformly negative. Edmund Gosse criticized the subjectivity of the collection *Underwoods,* noting that Stevenson "enters with great minuteness, and in a very confidential manner, into the theories and moods of the writer himself."

*A Child's Garden of Verses* has enjoyed a far more favorable reception. Although written for children, these poems appeal to adults through their simplicity, tenderness, and ability to entice the reader into the child's world. *Treasure Island* and

*Kidnapped* also reflect his sympathy for and understanding of youth. Both rely heavily on plot to sustain interest, and both contain Stevenson's first credible characters. Yet critics appreciate these books for varying reasons. *Treasure Island* is considered a brilliantly constructed adventure story, while critics praise *Kidnapped* more highly for its authenticity, which strengthens its appeal for adults.

Stevenson's short stories and novels for adults include the works most often cited by modern critics as his best: *The Merry Men and Other Tales and Fables, Island Nights' Entertainments, Dr. Jekyll and Mr. Hyde, The Master of Ballantrae: A Winter's Tale,* and *Weir of Hermiston: An Unfinished Romance.* Unlike his earlier works, these novels and stories examine moral dilemmas presented in an atmosphere imbued with mystery and horror. Modern commentators note certain recurring themes, such as those of the divided self and the nature of evil. His longer narratives are often criticized for their faulty and abrupt endings. *Weir of Hermiston,* the unfinished novel that Stevenson was working on when he died, is considered by many his best work for its forceful style, and psychologically and morally complex characters. Although critics question whether he would have been able to sustain the novel's dramatic interest, *Weir of Hermiston* has fueled conjecture about how Stevenson might have developed artistically had he lived longer.

Explanations vary for the critical fascination with Stevenson's personality rather than his work. His stoic optimism in the face of serious illness, his move to the South Seas, and the personal nature of many of his essays and poems have been much discussed. This fascination resulted in essays, many of them by friends and family, which are now considered eulogistic rather than critical. Although several critics, notably Arthur Symons, have warned readers against this approach, the content of Stevenson criticism did not change until 1914, with the publication of an essay by Frank Swinnerton. Considered by modern critics the most important challenger to the Stevenson myth, Swinnerton rejected the uncritical adoration of early readers and inspired a change in the critical approach to Stevenson, which had previously focused on personal rather than literary aspects. Many commentators underrated Stevenson by assuming that a children's writer has nothing to say to adults. Although critics are still fascinated by his life and reputation, they now respond to his work more often with serious analysis and acclaim. Opinion is still divided over the value of his oeuvre, yet his children's poetry, adventure stories, and adult romances continue to attract readers who appreciate fine writing and exciting adventure.

(See also *Yesterday's Authors of Books for Children,* Vol. 2 and *Dictionary of Literary Biography,* Vol. 18; *Victorian Novelists after 1885.*)

*PRINCIPAL WORKS

*The Pentland Rising: A Page of History, 1666*   (essay) 1866
*An Inland Voyage*   (travel sketches) 1878
*Travels with a Donkey in the Cévennes*   (travel sketches) 1879
*Virginibus Puerisque and Other Papers*   (essays) 1881
*Deacon Brodie; or, The Double Life: A Melodrama Founded on Facts* [with William Ernest Henley]   (drama) 1882
*Familiar Studies of Men and Books*   (essays) 1882
*New Arabian Nights*   (short stories) 1882
*Treasure Island*   (novel) 1883

*A Child's Garden of Verses*   (poetry) 1885
*Macaire* [with William Ernest Henley; first publication] (drama) 1885
*More New Arabian Nights: The Dynamiter* [with Fanny Stevenson]   (short stories) 1885
*Prince Otto*   (novel) 1885
*Kidnapped: Being Memoirs of the Adventures of David Balfour in the Year 1751*   (novel) 1886
*Strange Case of Dr. Jekyll and Mr. Hyde*   (novel) 1886
*Memories and Portraits*   (essays) 1887
*The Merry Men and Other Tales and Fables*   (short stories) 1887
*Underwoods*   (poetry) 1887
*The Black Arrow: A Tale of the Two Roses*   (novel) 1888
*The Master of Ballantrae: A Winter's Tale*   (novel) 1889
*The Wrong Box* [with Lloyd Osbourne]   (novel) 1889
*Admiral Guinea* [with William Ernest Henley]   (drama) 1890
*Ballads*   (poetry) 1890
*Beau Austin* [with William Ernest Henley]   (drama)   1890
*Across the Plains, with Other Memories and Essays* (essays) 1892
*The Wrecker* [with Lloyd Osbourne]   (novel) 1892
*Catriona, a Sequel to "Kidnapped": Being Memoirs of the Further Adventures of David Balfour at Home and Abroad*   (novel) 1893; also published as *David Balfour: Being Memoirs of His Adventures at Home and Abroad,* 1893
*Island Nights' Entertainments*   (short stories) 1893
*The Ebb-Tide: A Trio and Quartette* [with Lloyd Osbourne] (novel) 1894
*The Works of R. L. Stevenson.* 28 vols.   (novels, unfinished novels, short stories, travel sketches, poetry, essays, drama, letters, and prayers) 1894-98
*Weir of Hermiston* (unfinished novel) 1896
**St. Ives: Being the Adventures of a French Prisoner in England*   (novel) 1897
*Poems Hitherto Unpublished.* 2 vols.   (poetry)   1916; also published as *New Poems and Variant Readings,* 1918

*Many of Stevenson's works were originally published in periodicals.

**This work was completed by A. T. Quiller-Couch.

---

[SIDNEY COLVIN]   (essay date 1878)

[*Colvin was Stevenson's close friend, as well as an occasional critic and editor of Stevenson's work. In addition, he acted as Stevenson's literary mentor by introducing him to influential editors and publishers. In his review of* An Inland Voyage, *Colvin praises the "acute self-consciousness of the writer," a quality that many later critics condemn.*]

We have [in *An Inland Voyage*] . . . a traveller whose impressions, and the fancies and reflections with which they are mixed up, are so vivid and so much his own, and whose manner in telling them is in general so happy and taking, that we read and remember his inconsiderable adventures with more pleasure than many others of much greater importance. . . . [This] little volume has about it both in form and matter a touch of the classical and the ideal. It contains passages of feeling, humour, insight, description, expressed with fluency and finish in the best manner of English prose. These descriptions are not in the nature of an inventory of facts; it is a landscape-writing like the landscape-painting of the Japanese, setting down this or that point that happens to have made itself vividly felt, and leaving the rest; so that another traveller might go the same journey and scarcely notice any of the same things. (p. 694)

That acute self-consciousness of the writer, which leads him . . . to unbosom himself now and again in a manner somewhat embarrassing, on the other hand is the secret of his singular gift of realizing and expressing the transitions of physical and intellectual mood through which a traveller passes during such travels as these. . . .

But neither glimpses of scenery, however vivid and poetical, nor moods of the mind and body, however well observed and recorded, are enough of themselves to give substance and variety to a narrative so slight as this. The substance and variety are furnished by two other elements which we naturally look for in such a book—the element of human incident and the element of moralizing reflection. The human incidents and encounters of Mr. Stevenson's voyage are excellent. From the members of the canoeing club at Brussels, whose fraternal enthusiasm compels our own *dilettanti* canoeists to a premature escape, down to the travelling showman and his wife at Précy, we have a series of typical sketches, some simple or tender, and others extremely comical, but all living and genuine, and taken down with a thoroughly quick and sympathetic observation. . . .

In his moralizing, the author has a more uncertain vein. He is wayward and socially rebellious, with a rebelliousness much tempered by humour, but reposing upon one or two positive tenets about which he is plainly in earnest; such as, that men are bound to find out and follow their own real preferences, instead of adopting the preferences ready made and dictated to them by society; and that the "gipsily-inclined among men," if they will but follow their inclinations, will lead lives much more worth living than those who gather grist in "offices"—an "office" being our author's abomination in chief, and his symbol for all intolerable routine and sterile death in life. Paradoxical, according to ordinary standards, in the conclusions, he is often still more paradoxical in the processes of his thinking; as when his own unworkmanlike rashness, in tying the sheet of his sail on the open Scheldt, suggests the reflection how much better and braver we commonly find ourselves when we try than we knew beforehand; or as when the mention of a coarse, semi-English chambermaid at Boom leads on to the praise of the Greek ideal of Artemis the chaste. Paradoxical, then, yet from time to time striking out a flash both new and true—humorously or cordially rebellious, but never sour or puling—material, animal even, in his philosophy, but anon full of fancies the most chivalrous or tender—this brilliant and entertaining writer may at one moment show himself too raw in youth, and at another his words may seem to carry in them an echo of Heine, or at another of Sterne; but we shall acknowledge that he has both gifts and promise, and one inestimable gift in especial—charm. (p. 695)

> [Sidney Colvin], in a review of "An Inland Voyage," in The Athenaeum, No. 2640, June 1, 1878, pp. 694-95.

## SCOTSMAN  (essay date 1879)

It requires some courage . . . in a young author to give to a work on Edinburgh the title of ['**Edinburgh: Picturesque Notes;**']

but in whatever quality Mr Robert Louis Stevenson fails, it is not in what, to borrow a French phrase, may be called the courage of his convictions, one of the most cherished of which is evidently a thorough—and to a large extent just—belief in himself. He sets himself to write picturesquely, and he does it; his air is lofty as his theme; or loftier, for on his native city and all its belongings, its society, its sects, its arts and institutions, he looks down with a sort of divine complacency. The complacency is not without admiration and affection; but these are deeply veiled in the cynical humour which he cultivates. It is not, we believe, 'good form' now-a-days for youths to be earnest or enthusiastic about anything under the sun; yet Mr Stevenson has not so well tutored himself but that some hearty feeling of admiration and warm praise occasionally escapes him. Usually, however, his tone is that of a well-bred lounger, a *flaneur*, not deeply interested in anything, sympathising with well-bred languor in the misery or the welfare of the people he observes and describes, but not much moved by either, or, if moved at all, showing emotion lightly, as becomes a philosopher and a man of the world. . . . [The risk] that professors of cynical humour run is that they are apt to offend every class in its turn, and to this risk Mr Stevenson freely, and at every turn, lays himself open. . . . (pp. 59-60)

Happily Mr Stevenson is yet a young writer, as well as a young man; and if he eschews [the] errors of youth, he may make his mark in letters. The faculty is in him; he has a gift of style; style with a distinct individuality in it, which would be altogether charming if the individuality were less obtrusive. He has great cleverness of phrase; not a little power of observation; and he can light up worn and commonplace topics with very pleasant touches of fancy. The writing of 'picturesque notes' is to a man of his peculiar powers decidedly a snare; that he has not escaped the snare is not wonderful. With a less outworn subject, he would no doubt rise to a more manly and less egotistical treatment; and we trust to see him soon more worthily occupied than he is here in laboriously spinning pretty sentences on his own romantic town. He has it in him even to add to the already grand repute of this most prolific birthplace and dwelling-place of authors. . . . (p. 61)

> An extract from a review of "Edinburgh: Picturesque Notes," in Scotsman, January 21, 1879 (and reprinted in Robert Louis Stevenson: The Critical Heritage, edited by Paul Maixner, Routledge & Kegan Paul, 1981, pp. 59-61).

## FRASER'S MAGAZINE  (essay date 1879)

The expedition of Mr. Stevenson recorded in the charming little book which he has been pleased to call '**Travels with a Donkey,**' is as admirable an example of disgust with the ordinary conditions of pleasure-rambling, as it is of graceful writing, and the original and delicate vein of fancy which this young gentleman has developed. In its key-note, however, we find still something more than the mere fastidious dislike of over-refinement for the pleasures which the rabble share, and desire after a sensation more delicate; in the superiority of that new-fangled old-fashionedness which is the very height of the mode nowadays. The traveller in this case goes a step further. He is a young man of letters, one of those who, standing on the very apex of culture and the nineteenth century, find nothing better to do than to topple over and begin again on the other side; and he is at the same time, we presume, one of those darlings of fortune, who, having no natural hardships of their own, find a piquant gratification in inventing a few artificial ones, that they may know how it feels to be weary, and cold, and footsore, and belated, with the option at any moment of returning to their ordinary life. . . . So Mr. Stevenson turns from life, which is too soft and indulgent, to try how it feels to be a vagabond. It is a caprice like another. . . . 'For my part,' he says, 'I travel not to go anywhere, but to go. The great affair is to move; to feel the needs and hitches of our life more nearly, to come down off this feather-bed of civilisation, and find the globe granite underfoot and strewn with cutting flints.' This is so wonderful a counter-proposition to our innocent assumption that pleasure-travel was an amusement and refreshment for hard-working people, that we cannot but laugh even in the midst of our gasp of surprise. . . . This is the last whim of exquisite youth. The reader can imagine the supreme satisfaction with which the young monarch of civilisation discards it and all its comforts, and contemplates himself in the cunning disguise of a pedlar, exulting vastly in the practical joke which he is playing upon mankind. It is a still more piquant version of the prince travelling incognito, with always an amused wonder that nobody recognises him. (pp. 404-05)

[We] are bound to admit that a prettier book than that which contains the history of this journey we have not met with for a long time. Nothing particular happens to the traveller; he has nothing much to tell us. But he tells us that nothing in detail, hour by hour of his not very long journey, with a happy grace of narrative and lucid flow of musing, which among all the vulgarities and commonplaces of print is singularly refreshing. It is all about himself, but it is not egotistical in the evil meaning of the word. We never feel that we are hearing too much of him, or find his details impertinences—or at least *hardly* ever, to use the guarded language of the popular poet. Though the idea of the expedition is altogether over-fine and superior in its very rudeness, our young author is never priggish. He is perfectly unaffected in his affectation. The innocent vanity of his satisfaction in doing something no one has thought of doing before *is* quite innocent and pleasant, and in no way harms the impression produced on our minds that he is a charming companion, full of good feeling and good taste, as well as of sense and spirit, and with a quite exceptional gift of literary expression. If here and there a passing temptation towards fine writing crosses his mind, it is speedily brushed aside by the natural flow of a style as superior in grace as it is in spontaneousness and ease, to the big mouthings of that talk which we call 'tall' in these days. . . . [Mr. Stevenson's name], in all likelihood, will make itself very well known ere long. We say 'in all likelihood,' with a doubt in our minds as to whether the graceful art of writing about nothing will suffice to build a great and permanent reputation upon. Perhaps it is because we ourselves belong to a more positive age that this doubt affects us. At the present moment it is a delightful gift, and, while our author is young, gives such an air of promise, and of that easy play of nascent power which 'may do anything,' that it is perhaps more attractive than a more solid performance. (pp. 405-06)

> *A review of "Travels with a Donkey," in* Fraser's Magazine, *n.s. Vol. XX, No. CXVII, September, 1879, pp. 404-11.*

### W. E. HENLEY (letter date 1881)

[*Henley was a poet, dramatist, and editor of several periodicals, including* London Magazine, Scots Observer, *and* New Review. *He and Stevenson were introduced to one another by Leslie Stephen in 1875, and they soon became professional partners as well*

*as friends. They collaborated on four plays and often turned to one another for "advice, reproof or praise," as Stevenson remarked in his dedication of* Virginibus Puerisque *to Henley, which Henley acknowledges in the following letter. Relations between the two later became strained, a circumstance reflected in Henley's negative essay on Stevenson in Pall Mall Magazine in 1901 (see additional bibliography).*]

I have read some of the essays [in *Virginibus Puerisque and Other Papers*]. They have made me heartily ashamed of my own style. That's effect number one. Number two is that they are about the best things of their kind I know. I think they'll live: as Charles Lamb lives, if in no other way. Another impression I seem to have is, that I like the style of the new essays better than that of the others—the earlier ones. It is clearer, more sufficient, less foppish or rather less tricksy (not tricky, mind) and more like Style; has more distinction, in fact, and less personality. It's an admirable piece of writing. In Pan ["Pan's Pipes"]—an excellent piece of matter—and the Lamps ["A Plea for Gas Lamps"]—I get wafts of Carlyle. . . . I think, *à la fin des fins* [in the end], that you are a tip-top artist. You have Style, dear lad—the great quality, the distinguishing sign of the Artist, the Amateur's unattainable thing. You are eclectic, reflective, constructive in it: but by God, you've got it. Your writing is—as it seems to me—a creation: an example of that union of the Personal with the Absolute in art which is only to be triggered [?] in the work of the very good men. *Va, mon fils*, I am proud of thee. I used to doubt; but of late I have got wiser, and I doubt no more. I have learned, and I am fresh from my lesson. You are a Writer and you are a Stylist—or, to be more correct, a Master of Style. Little or big, I care not; but a Master certainly. (p. 76)

> *W. E. Henley, in a letter to Robert Louis Stevenson in April, 1881, from the* Stevenson Collection, *No. 4743, The Beinecke Rare Book and Manuscript Library (and reprinted in an extracted form in* Robert Louis Stevenson: The Critical Heritage, *edited by Paul Maixner, Routledge & Kegan Paul, 1981, pp. 75-7).*

### PALL MALL GAZETTE (essay date 1881)

The contents of ['**Virginibus Puerisque and Other Papers**'] furnish evidence of a graver, although not on that account a less brilliant or taking gift than either '**The Inland Voyage**' or '**The Travels with a Donkey**'. They consist for the most part of reflections humorous, didactic, or both at once, on the conduct and issues of life, diversified with side-lights upon literature, art, and travel, and illustrated with an ingenious profusion of images and instances. It is the abundance and coruscation of these which give to Mr. Stevenson's writing its peculiar charm, and which at the same time, but for the soundness of his style and diction, would bring it occasionally within a measurable distance of the faults of affectation and fancifulness. Mr. Stevenson shows himself in the present volume certainly one of the most readable of recent writers, even if he were nothing more. . . . Mr. Stevenson, both in his strong and in his weak points, is nothing if not original, in the sense of having spontaneously and for himself conceived the ideas and experienced the emotions in which he invites us to participate. To accept his invitation will be a refreshment to every one who can enjoy holding conversation on the daily and vital facts of life with a writer who, accepting nothing at second-hand, brings to bear on the facts of experience a gift of singularly luminous and genial insight, and perceptions both poignant and picturesque.

The experiences avowed by Mr. Stevenson include those of sickness and the anticipation of death, but his temper is the reverse of morbid. He is, indeed, equally far removed from pining feebleness and from the opposite and more grotesque condition of the blatantly and affectedly robust. His mood is at once gallant and humorously meditative. His sympathies are all with stirring deeds and hearty sayings. His cherished ideal of life wears a roving, vivid, somewhat gipsy complexion, and he is the sworn opponent of the precepts of elderly prudence, of the apathetic virtues of routine, conformity, and mercantile regularity. He holds a brief on the side of youth and its impulses *versus* age and its calculations. To the pleading of this suit, indeed, his book, as he tells us in its preface, was intended to be entirely addressed. But circumstances, and the slipping away from under the writer of his own vantage-ground of boyish years, have prevented the completion of the plan. Other considerations and other materials have been introduced, so that the volume as it now appears bears a somewhat fragmentary and disconnected character. . . . Where Mr. Stevenson, as it seems to us, best unites in the present volume, the characters of fundamental and formal originality is in one of the divisions of his first essay—that, namely, on **"Truth of Intercourse"**; and in the paper called **"Child's Play"**. The former deals with the difficulties and ambiguities which beset a human creature in the endeavour, upon which so much of his daily happiness depends, to explain to those dearest to him, by means of the imperfect instrument of words, his hourly states and shades of feeling. The latter invites us to extend a more intelligent sympathy than we are commonly capable of to the moods and imaginations of children, and to forbear applying to their visionary narratives the matter-of-fact standard of adult veracity. Both of these essays seem to us as new and just in substance as they are certainly attractive and almost approaching the classical in form. And, indeed, there are few pages in this brilliant volume which are not marked by enough of one or another of these qualities, or of all together, to claim for its author a place of very high promise in contemporary literature. (pp. 77-9)

> *A review of "Virginibus Puerisque and Other Papers," in* Pall Mall Gazette, *Vol. XXXIII, April 16, 1881 (and reprinted in* Robert Louis Stevenson: The Critical Heritage, *edited by Paul Maixner, Routledge & Kegan Paul, 1981, pp. 77-9).*

### E. PURCELL   (essay date 1881)

[*According to the Stevenson scholar, Paul Maixner, Purcell was "one of Stevenson's most humourless and narrowly moralistic critics." In the following discussion of Stevenson's essays, which focuses on* Virginibus Puerisque, *Purcell notes Stevenson's "barrenness of matter" and accuses him of being deficient in morality and originality. Purcell later wrote an appreciative review of* Prince Otto *and* More New Arabian Nights: The Dynamiter (*see excerpt below, 1886*).]

In justice both to Mr. Stevenson and to ourselves, it should be conceded that any estimate of his genius must be perforce a purely individual one. The real question—far more important and interesting than any enquiry as to style or method—is surely this: Are his books in the strict sense genuine?—are they, as they profess to be, the spontaneous, careless pastime of a philosopher, or the studied, artificial, practised work of a man of letters? . . .

But whether he really [experienced the adventures that he describes], or only pretended, or persuaded himself afterwards

that he did so, each reader must judge for himself, according to his own sentimental experiences, his own knowledge of men and books, and still more by noting how far he feels as he reads that undefinable but surely unmistakeable feeling of affectionate *cameraderie,* that strong sense of a personality whom one would like to know in the flesh as well as in the book, and, knowing, would find to be not other than his book, and yet something far better. . . .

Regarding, then, [*Virginibus Puerisque*] as elaborate studies in the literary art—and, after all, Mr. Stevenson may himself view them in no other light—one cannot be deaf to the praises which his refined and flexible style has so fully deserved, and which may here be endorsed without repetition. The many instances of strained metaphor, forced illustration, and obscure extravagance which we might quote are due not to defects of style, but to barrenness of matter. For, cloudy in purpose and confused in execution, these papers were fore-doomed to comparative failure. No hint is now given to remind us of the fact that many of them have already appeared in a magazine; but from the Preface it would seem that they were commenced some years ago as a plea for youth against age, and that, in deference to friendly advice, the title *Life at Twenty-five* has been dropped, and apparently some other things with it. Hence, possibly, the page of orthodox morality which winds up many of the earlier essays, and lends to them so singular an air of vagueness and insincerity. . . .

Yet when he has really anything to say, it is as thoroughly worth saying as it is sure to be well said. The isolated paper on **"Raeburn's Portraits"** shows him at his best, not as a *dilettante* essayist, but as a sympathetic critic skilled alike to read men and their likenesses. Some charming conceits in his **"Plea for Gas-lamps"** are peculiarly timely just now when citizens are going forth nightly to gape at the rival stage-moons. . . . Nor are bright thoughts and wise saws wanting in the first five papers which come under the title *Virginibus Puerisque,* as, for instance, the quaint argument whereby he proves that, "if you wish the pick of men and women, you must take a good bachelor and a good wife." But these, after all, are few, scattered, and isolated, not bound together by any abiding principles of purpose and action firm enough to live by, but embedded in an ooze of platitudes. . . . (p. 21)

It is impossible not to treat the book thus seriously, and so with apparent severity; for nothing can well be more serious than the subjects which it handles with playful dexterity and fantastic wantonness. To complacently ignore its implied claims or its probable influence upon certain readers would be a poor compliment. To them its confident maxims and playful audacity will seem to imply some background of solid opinion. Such, at least, was the inference naturally suggested by Mr. Stevenson's first books. Were his earlier moralisings, so light yet earnest, so fluent yet so inconsistent, but reticent whispers of an uncandid epicureanism, or were they the playful tinkling of some more massive forge whose full ring we must wait to catch? Each succeeding book only proves that they were neither. For if at first the gentle stroke but disguised the latent strength of a self-gained and well-rounded philosophy, right or wrong, it must before now have made itself felt. But what have we here beyond the same clever conceits and ingenious sallies furbished up and re-set in freshly gilt commonplace? In truth, very little. Mr. Stevenson has nurtured his beautiful gifts with rare cultivation. His pen is well worthy—and this praise he at least would feel means much—to describe the heaving tints of a sunset river, or the transient emotions of an artistic soul; but a philosopher or a moralist we cannot allow him to be. And yet at least half of this book consists of moralising upon Death, or, rather, of pathetic mumblings, graceful whimpers, and seductive little shrieks, in which the changes are rung upon every metaphor and simile which ever has been, or ever can be, applied to this new grisly pet of drawing-rooms given over to the infernal amusement of wondering whether life is really worth living. Some of this is merely superior fustian, much of it has been read before, none of it would one desire to read again. This endless fantasia upon the theme of the charnel-house is the more profoundly depressing because it is written in no particular key. Does Mr. Stevenson believe, or does he doubt, or does he reject the doctrine of a future state? Unless he will make this plain he can hardly hope to amuse any man who has himself adopted any one of these alternatives by the ingenuity with which he mingles dirge and carol—one moment sobbing in the procession, the next dancing merrily over the graves. Death is a fashionable subject, but, if one must write for the mere sake of writing, it were more seemly to write of Tar-water. (pp. 21-2)

> E. Purcell, in a review of "Virginibus Puerisque, and Other Papers," in The Academy, Vol. XX, No. 479, July 9, 1881, pp. 21-2.

## W. E. HENLEY (essay date 1882)

[Familiar Studies of Men and Books includes] not a little very admirable work. Mr. Stevenson is not less himself—is not less humorous, perspicuous, original, engaging—when he is critical of character and literature than when he takes to discoursing to bachelors and maids, or playing at travel on Flemish rivers, or trudging, whimsical and adventurous, behind a she-ass in the Cevennes. He has most of, if not all, the qualities that make the critic: an impartial, yet sympathetic, intelligence; a fresh and liberal interest in life and art and man; a student's patience; an artist's fine perceptiveness; a passion for all forms and aspects of truth; a frank, whole-hearted courage; a good method of analysis; rare distinction of style; and singular powers of felicitous and appropriate expression. That this is so the present volume proves abundantly. It is not of equal and unbroken excellence. In places it seems mistaken, and in places it is tedious; it is capable of making you nod, and it is capable of making you swear. But its good matter is good indeed; its bad is only bad in comparison with its best. Its purpose is serious and critical; and it achieves its purpose admirably. But, for all that, it has something of the chief characteristics of its author, it is touched with something of the fresh and happy grace, the bright, humane fancy, the engaging originality, that made such pleasant reading for so many of the *Inland Voyage*, of the *Travels*, and—as I like to think—of the *Virginibus Puerisque*.

The *Studies* are nine in number. They are sufficiently varied in manner and matter. They range from the fifteenth century to the present time, from the France of Villon to the Japan of Yoshida-Torajiro, from Knox at Holyrood to Pepys at Whitehall, from Hugo's novels to the love-letters of Sylvander and Clarinda. It is much the same with the style in which they are written and the spirit of their utterance. Something of the heaviness and sententiousness of John Knox's prelections seems to have crept into Mr. Stevenson's account of them. In his charming note on Charles of Orleans he now and then seems trifling with his subject, much as that subject trifled always with the Muse. The Yoshida-Torajiro is merely a piece of plain storytelling; the principal quality of the **"Gospel According to**

Walt Whitman" is a kind of luminous thoroughness; the manner of the study on Villon is one of picturesque and intelligent contempt, not without hints and suggestions of an acquaintance with Carlyle. In his discourse on Hugo's romances, Mr. Stevenson is young, and as yet not altogether a man of letters; in his essay on Thoreau he carries mere literary skill—mere mastery of diction, phrase, and sentence—to a higher point, I think, than he reaches elsewhere in any one of his works. Variety indeed is a principal attribute of the book. It appears not only in the material and style, but in the temper and tone. Mr. Stevenson's regard for those "qualities of human dealing" with which he has chosen to concern himself is uniformly clear-eyed and independent; in honesty of purpose, in sincerity of insight, he seems incapable of change; he is at all times equable and temperate. But he appropriates his humour to his theme; he alters his tone as he changes his subject. He is scornful with Villon and genial with Pepys; he is happily generous with Whitman as he is sorrowfully just with Burns. He thinks critically and dispassionately; he writes as his thoughts have made him feel. He is solemn, or sententious, or cheerful, just as the study of his author has left him. Each of his essays is the expression of a fitting and peculiar mood of morality and intellect. He reproduces his impressions in effects. He is a critic in method and intelligence, and an advocate in manner and temperament; and he makes you glad or sorry as—with his reflections and conclusions—he has made himself before you. If his criticism were less acute and methodical than it is, the accent and the terms in which it is conveyed would sometimes get it mistaken for an outcome of mere aesthetic emotion. As it is, the critic is equally apparent in it with the man; you can see that the strong feeling has come of clear thinking, and what is purely intellectual is rendered doubly potent and persuasive by the human sentiment with which it is associated. It is possible that this fact will ultimately militate against the success of Mr. Stevenson's *Studies* as criticism; for criticism—a science disguised as Art—is held to be incapable of passion. I cannot but think, however, that it will always count for a great deal in their favour as literature, and that meanwhile it clothes them with uncommon interest and attraction.

> W. E. Henley, in a review of "Familiar Studies of Men and Books," in The Academy, Vol. XXI, No. 517, April 1, 1882, p. 224.

## THE WESTMINSTER REVIEW (essay date 1882)

Mr. Stevenson is beginning to write too much. He has made some very bright and pleasant books, and unfortunately he seems to have become convinced that it is his duty to keep on making bright and pleasant books indefinitely. He has been overpraised by enthusiastic friends and reviewers; he deserved, and still deserves, great praise for his easy literary style and his fresh quaint fancy; but he is young enough to take advice, and let us hope not young enough to consider that he is quite infallible. . . . A volume of essays may be very delightful reading, much for example as Mr. Stevenson's **"Virginibus Puerisque"** was very delightful reading. But [**"Familiar Studies of Men and Books"**] is not quite a volume of essays. It is a volume of magazine articles, each of which is good enough by itself, while the whole set taken together are not particularly valuable. Mr. Stevenson seems to suffer in three ways: First, because he appears to consider that his judgment of most men and most matters is final; secondly, because he entertains the impression that his style is akin to that of Thackeray; thirdly, because he conceives it as his duty to regard everything from some new and startling point of view; to take up one side of every question simply because the other is the more generally accepted. There is an unpleasant affectation of laying down the law running through all these pages, which would make not a few readers inclined to quarrel with him out of sheer weariness at his eternal swagger. . . . [We] must pronounce the volume, as a whole, tiresome and lengthy. Expectations which were inspired by any book bearing the name of the author of the story of **"The Pavilion on the Links"** [published in **"New Arabian Nights"**] have not been gratified here, and we close the book with some pleasure at its being finished, and some regret to find we think so. (pp. 276-77)

*A review of "Familiar Studies of Men and Books," in* The Westminster Review, *n.s. Vol. LXII, No. 1, July, 1882, pp. 276-77.*

## [W. H. POLLOCK]   (essay date 1882)

Since the days of Athos, Count de la Fère, and of the other Count of Monte Cristo, we have not met in fiction a more attractive personage than Prince Florizel of Bohemia, who is the central figure of Mr. Stevenson's *New Arabian Nights.* He combines the dauntless courage and the *grand seigneur* ways and views of life of Athos with the boundless wealth and resource of Monte Cristo, while he has also a princely gaiety and good humour which belonged to neither of the illustrious persons to whom we have compared him. The stories in which he figures . . . are some of the most thrilling and inventive that we have read. They have indeed, and in this we pay their author a very high compliment, not a little of the magnificent extravagance that lent so great a charm to the stories written by the creator of Athos and Monte Cristo [Alexandre Dumas, *père*]. Their faults are faults which are the more irritating because they could have been so easily removed. They lack finish and care. One is annoyed in the middle of an exciting tale to come upon such a slip on the part of the author as his representing a lieutenant in the British army as being introduced and addressed with "Lieutenant" prefixed to his name; or, again, at finding that a person living on one side of a canal has seemingly crossed over to the other side and swum back again with a knife in his mouth, for no other reason than that he may appear dripping wet before the people who are waiting concealed for him. . . . Such slips as these, however, we can forgive far more easily than the curiously ill-judged burlesque ending which Mr. Stevenson has put to the adventures of Prince Florizel and Colonel Geraldine, who corresponds to the Vizier in "The Thousand and One Nights." The reader has followed the fortunes and the amazing and stirring adventures of the Prince with unwavering interest which suffers but little from such pieces of carelessness as are above referred to. He reads anxiously up to the last line of the last adventure, and he might be content to rest there, wishing indeed for more, but thankful for the enjoyment which he has got, and free to form his own conclusions as to the secret of the Prince's mysterious influence and power and as to his future fortunes. Then Mr. Stevenson turns round upon the reader with a statement that "as for the Prince, that sublime person having now served his turn, may go, along with the *Arabian Author,* topsy-turvy into space." This is, at least in the original sense of the word, impertinent enough; not to the purpose, since no reader of intelligence can wish to be reminded that Prince Florizel is merely a device of Mr. Stevenson who has "served his turn." But the statement which follows for the benefit of those imaginary persons who "insist on more specific information" is much worse. Nothing

could well be more inartistic, or more calculated to offend a reader whose admiration for the Prince and for the invention to which he and his delightful adventures are due has been so long aroused, than to suddenly find him disposed of with such a feeble and facetious conclusion as one might expect to find given by an unwise imitator of Mr. Gilbert's style of humour. We could wish indeed that this last paragraph of Mr. Stevenson's first volume could be blacked out like articles supposed to be dangerous in English newspapers sent to Russia. However, until one comes to this last paragraph, there is little but pleasure to be got out of the *New Arabian Nights,* with their striking fertility of invention, their charming touch of a chivalry which is by no means too common either in real life or in fiction, and that other quality of the author's, also by no means too common, of making his readers sup full with horrors and yet putting no offence in it. Even another quality, in itself a fault, that of a seeming disinclination to be at the trouble of unravelling various threads in the stories, is not without its attraction, since it leaves an additional element of mystery for the reader's mind to play with. Yet the author has not shrunk, in the paragraph above referred to, from pulling down the whole fabric of splendour and knightly valour which he has raised for our delight, and suddenly turning the dazzling figure of a hero who in the thick of modern life meets with adventures, and does deeds not less startling than those of the *Mousquetaires,* into the common type of foreign refugee with which we are only too familiar in the pages of many would-be comic writers. However, this unpleasant surprise comes at the very end of the *New Arabian Nights,* and therefore in no way injures the enjoyment of reading the stories through straight on end, as they are certain to be read by any one who once takes the book up. (p. 250)

Of the shorter stories which help to make up the volume, of which the greater part is given to **"The Pavilion on the Links,"** it is difficult, for want of space, to speak adequately. All have originality and, it is hardly too much to say, a touch of genius; in some ways, perhaps, the story of Villon, called **"A Lodging for the Night,"** is the most remarkable. The general effect of the two volumes is to make us wish for more of the same kind, but more carefully finished, from the same pen. (p. 251)

*[W. H. Pollock], in a review of "New Arabian Nights," in* The Saturday Review, *London, Vol. LIV, No. 1399, August 19, 1882, pp. 250-51.*

## ROBERT LOUIS STEVENSON   (essay date 1882)

*[In the following essay, Stevenson defines his conception of the art of fiction, which, he states, must include both riveting plots and ethical outcomes. "In the highest achievements of the art of words," he asserts, "the dramatic and pictorial, the moral and romantic interest, rise and fall together by a common and organic law." Unlike his contemporaries who belittled the fictional romance, Stevenson celebrates the genre for its excitement and realism. He writes: "Some situation, that we have long dallied with in fancy, is realised in the story with enticing and appropriate details. Then we forget the characters; then we push the hero aside; then we plunge into the tale in our own person and bathe in fresh experience; and then, and then only, do we say we have been reading a romance."]*

In anything fit to be called by the name of reading, the process itself should be absorbing and voluptuous; we should gloat over a book, be rapt clean out of ourselves, and rise from the perusal, our mind filled with the busiest, kaleidoscopic dance of images, incapable of sleep or of continuous thought. The words, if the book be eloquent, should run thenceforward in our ears like the noise of breakers, and the story, if it be a story, repeat itself in a thousand coloured pictures to the eye. It was for this last pleasure that we read so closely, and loved our books so dearly, in the bright, troubled period of boyhood. Eloquence and thought, character and conversation, were but obstacles to brush aside as we dug blithely after a certain sort of incident, like a pig for truffles. For my part, I liked a story to begin with an old wayside inn where, ''towards the close of the year 17—,'' several gentlemen in three-cocked hats were playing bowls. . . . Give me a highwayman and I was full to the brim; a Jacobite would do, but the highwayman was my favourite dish. I can still hear that merry clatter of the hoofs along the moonlit lane. . . . [We] read storybooks in childhood, not for eloquence or character or thought, but for some quality of the brute incident. That quality was not mere bloodshed or wonder. Although each of these was welcome in its place, the charm for the sake of which we read depended on something different from either. . . . [All my] early favourites have a common note—they have all a touch of the romantic.

Drama is the poetry of conduct, romance the poetry of circumstance. The pleasure that we take in life is of two sorts— the active and the passive. Now we are conscious of a great command over our destiny; anon we are lifted up by circumstance, as by a breaking wave, and dashed we know not how into the future. Now we are pleased by our conduct, anon merely pleased by our surroundings. It would be hard to say which of these modes of satisfaction is the more effective, but the latter is surely the more constant. Conduct is three parts of life, they say; but I think they put it high. There is a vast deal in life and letters both which is not immoral, but simply a-moral; which either does not regard the human will at all, or deals with it in obvious and healthy relations; where the interest turns, not upon what a man shall choose to do, but on how he manages to do it; not on the passionate slips and hesitations of the conscience, but on the problems of the body and of the practical intelligence, in clean, open-air adventure, the shock of arms or the diplomacy of life. With such material as this it is impossible to build a play, for the serious theatre exists solely on moral grounds, and is a standing proof of the dissemination of the human conscience. But it is possible to build, upon this ground, the most joyous of verses, and the most lively, beautiful, and buoyant tales.

One thing in life calls for another; there is a fitness in events and places. The sight of a pleasant arbour puts it in our mind to sit there. One place suggests work, another idleness, a third early rising and long rambles in the dew. . . . Some places speak distinctly. Certain dank gardens cry aloud for a murder; certain old houses demand to be haunted; certain coasts are set apart for shipwreck. Other spots again seem to abide their destiny, suggestive and impenetrable. . . . The inn at Burford Bridge, with its arbours and green garden and silent, eddying river—though it is known already as the place where Keats wrote some of his *Endymion* and Nelson parted from his Emma— still seems to wait the coming of the appropriate legend. Within these ivied walls, behind these old green shutters, some further business smoulders, waiting for its hour. The old Hawes Inn at the Queen's Ferry makes a similar call upon my fancy. There it stands, apart from the town, beside the pier, in a climate of its own, half inland, half marine—in front, the ferry bubbling with the tide and the guardship swinging to her anchor; behind, the old garden with the trees. Americans seek it already for the sake of Lovel and Oldbuck, who dined there at the beginning of the *Antiquary*. But you need not tell me—that is not

all; there is some story, unrecorded or not yet complete, which must express the meaning of that inn more fully. So it is with names and faces; so it is with incidents that are idle and inconclusive in themselves, and yet seem like the beginning of some quaint romance, which the all-careless author leaves untold. . . . I have lived both at the Hawes and Burford in a perpetual flutter, on the heels, as it seemed, of some adventure that should justify the place; but though the feeling had me to bed at night and called me again at morning in one unbroken round of pleasure and suspense, nothing befell me in either worth remark. The man or the hour had not yet come; but some day, I think, a boat shall put off from the Queen's Ferry, fraught with a dear cargo, and some frosty night a horseman, on a tragic errand, rattle with his whip upon the green shutters of the inn at Burford.

Now, this is one of the natural appetites with which any lively literature has to count. The desire for knowledge, I had almost added the desire for meat, is not more deeply seated than this demand for fit and striking incident. . . . The right kind of thing should fall out in the right kind of place; the right kind of thing should follow; and not only the characters talk aptly and think naturally, but all the circumstances in a tale answer one to another like notes in music. The threads of a story come from time to time together and make a picture in the web; the characters fall from time to time into some attitude to each other or to nature, which stamps the story home like an illustration. Crusoe recoiling from the footprint, Achilles shouting over against the Trojans, Ulysses bending the great bow, Christian running with his fingers in his ears, these are each culminating moments in the legend, and each has been printed on the mind's eye for ever. Other things we may forget; we may forget the words, although they are beautiful; we may forget the author's comment, although perhaps it was ingenious and true; but these epoch-making scenes, which put the last mark of truth upon a story and fill up, at one blow, our capacity for sympathetic pleasure, we so adopt into the very bosom of our mind that neither time nor tide can efface or weaken the impression. This, then, is the plastic part of literature: to embody character, thought, or emotion in some act or attitude that shall be remarkably striking to the mind's eye. . . . Compared with this, all other purposes in literature, except the purely lyrical or the purely philosophic, are bastard in nature, facile of execution, and feeble in result. It is one thing to write about the inn at Burford, or to describe scenery with the word-painters; it is quite another to seize on the heart of the suggestion and make a country famous with a legend. It is one thing to remark and to dissect, with the most cutting logic, the complications of life, and of the human spirit; it is quite another to give them body and blood in the story of Ajax or of Hamlet. The first is literature, but the second is something besides, for it is likewise art. (pp. 229-38)

[Nothing] can more strongly illustrate the necessity for marking incident than to compare the living fame of [Defoe's] *Robinson Crusoe* with the discredit of [Richardson's] *Clarissa Harlowe*. *Clarissa* is a book of a far more startling import, worked out, on a great canvas, with inimitable courage and unflagging art. It contains wit, character, passion, plot, conversations full of spirit and insight, [and] letters sparkling with unstrained humanity. . . . And yet a little story of a shipwrecked sailor, with not a tenth part of the style nor a thousandth part of the wisdom, exploring none of the arcana of humanity and deprived of the perennial interest of love, goes on from edition to edition, ever young, while *Clarissa* lies upon the shelves unread. . . . *Clarissa* has every quality that can be shown in prose, one alone excepted—pictorial or picture-making romance. While *Robinson* depends, for the most part and with the overwhelming majority of its readers, on the charm of circumstance.

In the highest achievements of the art of words, the dramatic and the pictorial, the moral and romantic interest, rise and fall together by a common and organic law. Situation is animated with passion, passion clothed upon with situation. Neither exists for itself, but each inheres indissolubly with the other. This is high art; and not only the highest art possible in words, but the highest art of all, since it combines the greatest mass and diversity of the elements of truth and pleasure. Such are epics, and the few prose tales that have the epic weight. But as from a school of works, aping the creative, incident and romance are ruthlessly discarded, so may character and drama be omitted or subordinated to romance. (pp. 240-42)

True romantic art . . . makes a romance of all things. It reaches into the highest abstraction of the ideal; it does not refuse the most pedestrian realism. *Robinson Crusoe* is as realistic as it is romantic; both qualities are pushed to an extreme, and neither suffers. Nor does romance depend upon the material importance of the incidents. To deal with strong and deadly elements, banditti, pirates, war and murder, is to conjure with great names, and, in the event of failure, to double the disgrace. (pp. 244-45)

[In romance, something] happens as we desire to have it happen to ourselves; some situation, that we have long dallied with in fancy, is realised in the story with enticing and appropriate details. Then we forget the characters; then we push the hero aside; then we plunge into the tale in our own person and bathe in fresh experience; and then, and then only, do we say we have been reading a romance. It is not only pleasurable things that we imagine in our day-dreams; there are lights in which we are willing to contemplate even the idea of our own death; ways in which it seems as if it would amuse us to be cheated, wounded, or calumniated. It is thus possible to construct a story, even of tragic import, in which every incident, detail, and trick of circumstance shall be welcome to the reader's thoughts. Fiction is to the grown man what play is to the child; it is there that he changes the atmosphere and tenor of his life; and when the game so chimes with his fancy that he can join in it with all his heart, when it pleases him with every turn, when he loves to recall it and dwells upon its recollection with entire delight, fiction is called romance. (p. 248)

> *Robert Louis Stevenson, ''A Gossip on Romance'' (originally published in* Longman's Magazine, *Vol. I, No. 1, November, 1882), in his* Memories and Portraits, *Charles Scribner's Sons, 1910, pp. 229-53.*

## [DANIEL CONNOR LATHBURY AND BERTHA LATHBURY] (essay date 1882)

The first thing that strikes the reader of Mr. Stevenson's *New Arabian Nights,* is that he is tasting two pleasures at once. Every great novelist has a style of his own, and we soon learn to think each appropriate to the use to which it is turned. But Mr. Stevenson tells a story in a style so finished and so admirable, that it constitutes a distinct enjoyment in itself. So told, we seem to feel, any story would be worth reading. There is no need to give ourselves this assurance, because the matter of the stories here collected is singularly original and effective. But though original and effective stories are sufficiently uncommon, they are less uncommon than the excellent English

in which these are conveyed. The title properly belongs to the first volume only. In this, the form of the *Arabian Nights* is fairly preserved. The Caliph Haroun Alraschid has his representative in Prince Florizel of Bohemia, and in the first story the very cream tarts of the original are reproduced in the copy. But the resemblance goes no farther. The *New Arabian Nights* deal with adventures, wild enough, indeed, for the farthest East and a distant century, but supposed to take place in London and Paris, amidst the most modern surroundings. The incidents are as strange and startling as in the best of Mr. Wilkie Collins's stories, but improbable or impossible as they are, they do not seem so, because the actors in them behave with perfect consistency. The draft on our credulity is made once for all, and when it has been duly honoured, we are never reminded how large it was in the first instance.

In the first, or Arabian, volume, the most telling story is the **''Suicide Club.''** . . . Various members of the Club are drawn with great spirit, and the excitement attaching to the fatal deal which conveys the signal of death and murder is fully shared by the reader. The succeeding chapters, although complete tales in themselves, link themselves on to the first story; while the adventures of Prince Florizel are brought to a close in another series of tales, called **''The Rajah's Diamond.''** If one or two of these hang fire a little, the interest revives again in **''The House with the Green Blinds;''** and the closing chapter of the volume is a particularly happy specimen of the author's grace of style and expression. When the diamond finds its final resting-place, we can wish for no better conclusion to a series of adventures which have kept our interest alive to the last.

In the second volume, the tales are less distinctive, and in becoming less fanciful they lose, perhaps, a little of their charm. But in one, at least, of them, if the originality is not so striking, the word-painting can hardly be surpassed. The story of a night in the life of Francis Villon is a drama of remarkable power. (pp. 1450-51)

Stories like those which Mr. Stevenson has written naturally suggest the question as to what place such writing holds in literature. They are not novels, and they hardly pretend to describe real life. Strictly speaking, they are grotesque romances, in which the author has allowed himself a considerable licence as to probability of incident. To compare him with another writer of something of the same kind, Mr. Stevenson's treatment of the impossible is bolder than that of Bulwer Lytton, who shelters himself behind the supernatural as soon as probability ceases. He bears more resemblance to the elder Dumas, than to any English author; but in Dumas, the intensity of writing is stronger, and the excitement of the reader far more stimulated, than in the slighter sketches of the *New Arabian Nights.* We can imagine Dumas losing himself in his characters, and believing in his stories, while Mr. Stevenson gives us the impression of being outside both. He is the stage manager skilfully directing his actors, while he never ceases to regard them from the point of view of pure art. He has the advantage, however, of Dumas in the subtle humour which pervades everything he writes. As a collection of grotesque romances, the *New Arabian Nights* are perfect in form and finish; and such an aim is not only legitimate in itself, but constitutes a fresh departure in romance-writing. (pp. 1451-52)

> *[Daniel Connor Lathbury and Bertha Lathbury], ''Mr. Stevenson's Stories,'' in* The Spectator *(© 1882 by* The Spectator*), Vol. LV, No. 2837, November 11, 1882, pp. 1450-52.*

**[H. C. BUNNER]** (essay date 1883)

A few months ago an English book made its appearance in this country, handicapped with the name of '**New Arabian Nights.**' It was, for a time, no more warmly welcomed than might have been the 'New Rabelais,' or 'A Nineteenth Century Nibelungen Lied,' or 'Robinson Crusoe' with all the modern improvements. Then, by and by, one or two of the chorus of indolent reviewers glanced at the first page, read the second, and of a sudden found themselves *bolting* the rest of the book, and finding stomach for it all. . . . For the '**New Arabian Nights**' turned out to be no new 'Arabian Nights' at all; but a very different and surprising something which is much more easily read at full length than described in a few words.

On the face of it, the book is a collection of short stories, each differing from each, every one distinct and singular, yet all linked together by the adventures of one central character, who is half Monte Cristo and half Haroun Al Raschid up to the last page, where in an unexpected fashion he leaves you laughing at him, laughing at yourself, and wondering how long his inventor has been laughing at you both.

This is the book on the face of it. But then, in fact, you cannot speak of the book on the face of it, for under the face is a fascinating depth of subtleties, of ingenuities, of satiric deviltries, of weird and elusive forms of humor, in which the analytic mind loses itself. . . . It would be possible to give an idea of the many delicate touches by which [Prince Florizel] is created and vivified before the reader's very eyes. It would be possible to show how the flavor of the original 'Arabian Nights' is caught and kept by the mere suggestion of an imitation of the style and language. It would not be difficult to show how the "**Story of the Young Man with the Cream Tarts**" leads into the "**Story of the Physician and the Saratoga Trunk**," and that in turn into the "**Adventure of the Hansom Cabs**," the three together introducing us to "**The Suicide Club**" and gratifying us with its complete and final dissolution. . . . (pp. 119-21)

[But were this told], it would give but a vague notion of the characteristic power and charm of the work. . . . Any one who reads the '**Nights**' and the four stories that are bound with them must be struck by the author's versatility, his power of picturesque description, his skill in drawing character with half a touch, and his all-pervading humor.

Yet it seems to us that the qualities we have indicated do not give the key-note of Mr. Stevenson's genius, or whatever one may please to call a faculty one of the most original that we have met since the appearance of Bret Harte. The new author has a power that is strongly akin to the dramatic. He juggles with his readers and with his characters. He dresses up a puppet and tells you it is a man, and you believe it, and hold your breath when the sword is at the puppet's breast. Then he holds up the stripped manikin and smiles maliciously. With him, men and ideas are but literary properties, to be used as he sees fit, for this or that effect. In "**The Pavilion on the Links**" he offers you an ordinary English magazine story of the 'sensation' sort, very well done. . . . "**A Lodging for the Night**" gives an episode in the life of Francois Villon, told with a realism that is at once brutal and poetic; it is the strongest piece of work in the book. It is followed by "**The Sire de Malétroit's Door**,"—another mediaeval French theme, handled, this time, in the pure romantic style. And then there is an odd little conceit ["**Providence and the Guitar**"], where laughter comes near the line of tears, to end one of the brightest, boldest, most

stimulating books that modern fiction has given us. (pp. 121-22)

[*H. C. Bunner*], *in a review of "New Arabian Nights," in* Century Magazine, *Vol. XXV, February, 1883 (and reprinted in* Robert Louis Stevenson: The Critical Heritage, *edited by Paul Maixner, Routledge & Kegan Paul, 1981, pp. 119-22*).

**[ARTHUR JOHN BUTLER]** (essay date 1883)

Mr. Stevenson's genius is not wholly unlike that of Poe, and one might almost suspect that the germ of '**Treasure Island**' is to be found in the 'Gold Beetle,' and especially in its last sentence; but it is Poe strongly impregnated with Capt. Marryat. Yet we doubt if either of those writers ever succeeded in making a reader identify himself with the supposed narrator of a story, as he cannot fail to do in the present case. As we follow the narrative of the boy Jim Hawkins we hold our breath in his dangers, and breathe again at his escapes. The artifice is so well managed that when, for a few chapters, Jim disappears, and the story is taken up by a shrewd doctor, who is never in much danger, the change is felt as a sensible relief. And yet, artistic as the book is, one cannot help feeling that the art is a little too patent. Partly, no doubt, this arises from the fact of the story being laid in the last century. It is given to very few people so to throw themselves into a past age as to avoid all appearance of unreality. In the heroic style this does not matter; but the more real the characters, the more does the difference between the views of one age and another show itself. . . . In the common phrase, a story of this kind is seldom wholly free from the "smell of the lamp." To a reader who can discount this (if one can discount a smell!) it matters little; but it may be doubted whether Mr. Stevenson will succeed as well as inferior artists in pleasing the public whom his story might seem best adapted to reach—the boys. Even if they do not feel the difficulty already indicated, they will demur to his too philosophic rejection of poetical justice in allowing the arch-scoundrel to escape the fate which overtakes all his accomplices. In real life John Silver would hardly have got off; he certainly ought not to do so in fiction.

[*Arthur John Butler*], *in a review of "Treasure Island," in* The Athenaeum, *No. 2927, December 1, 1883, p. 700.*

*PALL MALL GAZETTE* (essay date 1883)

A book for boys which can keep hardened and elderly reviewers in a state of pleasing excitement and attention is evidently no common Christmas book. No one but Mr. Stevenson could have written '**Treasure Island**,' for no one else has his vivid imagination combined with his power of drawing character, his charm of style, and his grave, earnest, perfectly boyish delight in a storm, a shipwreck, a sword combat for two or more. Mr. Stevenson probably wrote '**Treasure Island**' for his diversion; it has the ease and fluency of work that is done in play. Certainly he has contributed more to the diversion of one critic than all the serious and laborious novelists of the year have done. The question may be asked, will '**Treasure Island**' be as popular with boys as it is sure to be with men who retain something of the boy? Our opinion of boys will fall considerably if '**Treasure Island**' is not their perennial favourite. . . . [John Silver] is a perfect hero of crime, and clearly a great favourite of the author's. A cold-blooded murderer, he has yet such excellent manners, is such a clever 'opportunist,' such an ingenious, plausible, agreeable double-dyed traitor, that one can hardly help siding with him in his plots and treasons, and rejoicing when, after all, he escapes clean away from poetical justice. . . . The fight in the rigging between the boy and the wounded pirate holds the reader breathless, as does the scene when the boy is captured by the one-legged man, and is in danger of torture. The skeleton which holds the secret of the treasure is, however, too like an idea of Poe's. The reticence in the matter of 'word-painting' is most praiseworthy, and the description of the island—a horrible, commonplace, foggy, yet haunted island—is eminently original. It is clear that fiction is a field in which Mr. Stevenson is even stronger than in essay and in humorous and sentimental journeying. After this romance for boys he must give us a novel for men and women. (pp. 138-39)

> *A review of "Treasure Island," in* Pall Mall Gazette, *Vol. XXXVIII, December 15, 1883 (and reprinted in* Robert Louis Stevenson: The Critical Heritage, *edited by Paul Maixner, Routledge & Kegan Paul, 1981, pp. 137-39).*

**THE SATURDAY REVIEW, London    (essay date 1885)**

To write good verse for children where children are the only readers written for is no easy feat; to write such children's verse as may delight adults also is more difficult still. Mr. Robert Louis Stevenson, as much of his prose work has shown, is more than commonly well equipped with the qualities which make for success in either of these endeavours; yet we cannot say that in [A Child's Garden of Verses] he has been entirely successful. That simplicity of diction which is essential to such writing he has nearly always at command; the "force of statement"—we can find no less prosaic phrase to describe what we mean—which is characteristic of so much children's talk when it is at once intelligent and unaffected, in this also he is not wanting. Again, he has a quick and vivid fancy, with much power of picturesque description, and he can be humorous and tender, not only by turns, which is common enough, but at the same time. Nor can he be said to have neglected or inexpertly used the various gifts which he possesses. In this volume there is an abundance of graceful fancy, much of it admirably expressed. Some of its lyrics would undoubtedly delight any child old enough to take delight in such things at all; while others, again, will undoubtedly be read with pleasure by its elders. What we look for, however, in a book of this sort, though perhaps it is putting our requirements too high, is the combination of the two kinds of attraction in the same pieces. The highest point attainable in writing of this description is only attained when what may be called the surface-motive of the lyric or the prose-story is sufficient in itself to charm the child, while the adult sense of humour can enjoy the undercurrent of thought or meaning with a relish proportioned to the completeness of its concealment from the younger reader. This point, however, is rarely attained in Mr. Stevenson's verse. He has added to his difficulties—if also to his opportunities—by writing throughout in the person of the child. It is the child's thoughts, fancies, pleasures, ambitions—in short, the child's record of impressions and criticism of life—as given from its own lips; and it is, of course, extremely hard to maintain the requisite tone of *naïveté* in these touches, which are meant to appeal to the appreciation of its elders. The infantile humour or pathos cannot help appearing at times to be too conscious of itself.

*A review of "A Child's Garden of Verses," in* The Saturday Review, *London, Vol. LIX, No. 1534, March 21, 1885, p. 394.*

**[WILLIAM ARCHER]    (essay date 1885)**

[*Archer was a well-known nineteenth-century drama critic. The essay below, which stresses Stevenson's consistently optimistic and one-sided view of life in* A Child's Garden of Verses, *prompted Stevenson to write to Archer, praising the review as "the best criticism I ever had." In a subsequent essay, Archer discusses Stevenson as a narrative writer (see excerpt below, 1885).*]

The child is father to the man, and the Robert Louis Stevenson of to-day clearly takes after his father as figured for us in ['A Child's Garden of Verse']. It is autobiographical rather than dramatic. Mr. Stevenson does not attempt a many-sided view of child life, does not seek to depict varieties of child character, but sets himself to reflect the moods of one particular child, well known to him. He takes an Inland Voyage up the river of Memory, and sketches with his clear, crisp, vivid touch a few of his adventures and experiences. He draws with charming simplicity, yet in the selection of his subjects we trace the irony of self-conscious manhood, and here and there we find a touch in which the artist does not quite conceal his art. This is merely repeating in other words that he does not care to be consistently dramatic. (p. 155)

In **'Virginibus Puerisque'** there is an essay on **"Child's Play"** which should be read as a preface to this booklet. Its first line explains what many readers of the **'Garden'** must find noteworthy, if not absolutely strange, the persistent dwelling on the sunny aspect of childhood, with scarcely a hint of its night side. 'The regret we have for our childhood is not wholly justifiable,' says Mr. Stevenson, assuming as universal a feeling which in many minds is non-existent. He admits further on that 'innocence, no more than philosophy, can protect us from the sting of pain,' but this sting sends no discordant cries through his 'Songs of Innocence.' The child is the very same cheerful stoic whom we admire in the man—a philosopher who does not attempt to bring pain and evil into harmony with any system, but simply disregards and ignores them. (pp. 155-56)

Thoughts of Blake will inevitably intrude themselves upon readers of Mr. Stevenson's verses, but they should at once be banished as impertinent. The two men are on different planes. Their ends are different, their means are different. Blake is a poet who now and then rises to a poignant note beyond Mr. Stevenson's compass as it is above his ambition. Mr. Stevenson is a humourist and an artist in words, a man of alert, open-eyed sanity, unconcerned as to the mystery of childhood, but keenly alive to its human grace and pathos, its fantastic gravity, its logical inconsequence, its exquisite egoism. Moreover, Mr. Stevenson's child, unlike Blake's children, is distinctly an agnostic. He says his prayers, but it is with no 'petitionary vehemence.' He does not seem even to indulge in the fetishism which is the first spiritual experience of so many children. It is the unhappy child who is a metaphysician, and is 'cradled into scepticism by wrong,' or into fetish worship, as the case may be. Mr. Stevenson knows nothing of the fierce rebellions, the agonized doubts as to the existence of justice, human or divine, which mar the music of childhood for so many; or if he realizes their existence, he relegates them to that other life, the life of pain, and terror, and weariness, into which it is part of his philosophy to look as seldom as possible. . . . (pp. 156-57)

[*William Archer*], *in an extract from a review of "A Child's Garden of Verse," in* Pall Mall Gazette, *Vol. XLI, March 24, 1885 (and reprinted in* Robert Louis Stevenson: The Critical Heritage, *edited by Paul Maixner, Routledge & Kegan Paul, 1981, pp. 154-57).*

## H. C. BUNNER  (essay date 1885)

It is rather hard, when once a man's youth has been renewed for him like the eagle's, and he has been led into green pastures such as cows and children only enjoy to the full—it is rather hard to snatch him back by the ear to this dull grown-up world, and to explain to him that it wasn't true after all, that he has only been making believe, under the guidance of an able adult magician—that he is no child, but a dull, mechanic, responsible man, and that he must sit down and write a notice commendatory of the skill of the able magician. . . .

[We] never suspected that [this magician] had the power to unseal the tender springs of childhood's inborn poetry [in *A Child's Garden of Verse*], and set them flowing in the sight of all men to tell to the world that secret which we each one of us, once upon a time, guarded so jealously: the secret of our dear playfellow who could not be seen or heard or felt of with our hands; but only be *thought* and *dreamed;* and whom, since then, we have learned to call Fancy. . . .

But here is this Scotch magician making a child of himself for our benefit. And at first we look on, and smile at his childlike antics and oddities of expression, and say: "How true! very accurate, indeed." And pretty soon we have ceased smiling and commenting, and before long we are children too, doing it all, thinking it all, being it all; and we know that it is true with a truth of which we do not often get glimpses. (p. 103)

We should all be grateful to our magician. But, like all true magicians, he has something more to do than merely to make us laugh and wonder. His art has a stronger hold on nature. Were he only the bright and clever man of talent, who does the bright and clever thing that a man may do with his talent, it would be easy enough to dismiss him with a hatful of thanks and compliments. But we who have read the half dozen books which he has given us must see clearly that we have to deal, not with talent, but with that strange and precious thing which we call genius. If he does no more than he has done—and he gives every sign and promise of doing more—Robert Louis Stevenson is one of these men whom we have to label with the name of genius. And the mission of genius, however it reveal itself, is sad at bottom. There is much in this book that we may teach to the children, at our side; there is much that we may smile over, remembering the childhood from which we grew; but there is also something there that hints of the stifled childhood in us that never grew up; something that touches us with a deep, half-understood, wholly unspeakable grief. (p. 104)

*H. C. Bunner, "Mr. Stevenson's Child's Verses," in* The Book Buyer, *Vol. 11, No. 4, May, 1885, pp. 103-04.*

## WILLIAM ARCHER  (essay date 1885)

[*The following was the first general assessment of Stevenson's work, as well as the first to elucidate several critical points that are repeated throughout Stevenson criticism. While praising his style, Archer charges that Stevenson "is not only philosophically*

*content, but deliberately resolved, that his readers should look first to his manner, and only in the second place to his matter." Archer criticizes Stevenson's "lightness of touch," but finds it adequate to express Stevenson's shallow optimism. Archer states that "Stevenson has no lack of theories to express, but his beliefs are not weighty enough, his truths are not true enough, to demand emphasis." Archer's views in both this and his earlier review of* A Child's Garden of Verses *(see excerpt above, 1885) were disputed by Henry James (see excerpt below, 1887).*]

In the front rank of our new school of stylists, Mr. Robert Louis Stevenson holds an undisputed place. He is a modern of the moderns both in his alert self-consciousness and in the particular artistic ideal which he proposes to himself. He is popular, not, perhaps, with that puff-bred vogue which draws elbowing crowds to Mudie's counters, but with the better popularity which makes his books familiar to the shelves of all who love literature for its own sake. Now, to love literature for its own sake implies a mental habit, which is, perhaps happily, unknown to the many, even to the educated many. To be less concerned about what a man says than how he says it is unutilitarian, unprogressive, not to say reactionary; for the world is not to be regenerated by a nice arrangement of epithets. Mr. Stevenson, however, is not only philosophically content, but deliberately resolved, that his readers shall look first to his manner, and only in the second place to his matter. He has committed himself to the explicit assertion that "there is indeed only one merit worth considering in a man of letters—that he should write well; and only one damning fault—that he should write ill." Shakespeare is not more unconcerned about the advancement of humanity. . . . Mr. Stevenson sometimes inclines to the opinion that an ardent reformer is, as Charles Reade said of a flippant novelist, "impertinent to his Creator." He professes himself an artist in words, and thinks only those thoughts, tells none but those tales, paints those pictures alone, which adapt themselves to his peculiar manner. An impressionist on occasion, he is always an expressionist.

There are fashions in style as in everything else, and, for the moment, we are all agreed that the one great saving grace is "lightness of touch." Of this virtue Mr. Stevenson is the accomplished model. He keeps it always before his eyes, and cultivates in everything a buoyant, staccato, touch-and-go elasticity. In description he jots effects rather than composes pictures. He has a Dickens-like knack of giving life and motion to objects the most inanimate. (pp. 582-83)

In character-drawing, or rather sketching, Mr. Stevenson's effort is the same. Here he forswears analysis as in description he has forsworn synthesis. A few crisp, clean strokes and a wash of transparent colour, and the oddity stands before us as though fresh from the pencil of Mr. Caldecott. For Mr. Stevenson's characters are all oddities. It is to the quaintly abnormal that this method of presentation applies. To draw the normal, to make a revelation of the commonplace, is a task which demands insight quite other than Mr. Stevenson's, labour quite foreign to his scheme. . . . All Mr. Stevenson's personages have hitherto been either wayside silhouettes taken in the course of his wanderings, or figures invented to help out the action of tales whose very essence lies in their unreality. "Long John Silver" is perhaps his most sustained effort in character-drawing, brilliantly successful as far as vividness of presentation is concerned, but conceived outside of all observation, a creature of tradition, a sort of nautical were-wolf. To apply analysis to such a character would merely be to let out the sawdust.

As a narrator Mr. Stevenson marks the reaction against the reigning ethical school. He has somewhere given in his adhesion to a widespread heresy which proclaims narrative to be the consummate literary form, from which all others have been evolved, towards which, in their turn, they all tend. Put it never so speciously, this theory resolves itself in the last analysis into an assertion that incident is more important than character, action than motive, the phenomenon than the underlying cause; yet Mr. Stevenson explains, if he does not justify, the faith that is in him, by proving himself endowed in a high degree with the gift of mere story-telling. Here again the last word of his secret is lightness of touch. He plunges into the midst of things. He is direct, rapid, objective. His characters have always their five senses about them, to record those minutely trivial impressions which, by their very unexpectedness, lend an air of reality to a scene. Who can forget the tap-tap-tap of the blind man's stick on the frosty road, in the opening scene of **"Treasure Island"**? If Mr. Stevenson has a leaning towards the horrible, he presents his horrors frankly, not crudely. As an inventor and interweaver of incidents he has the great advantage of not being over-particular in making them dovetail, but feeling with a just instinct what the reader will demand to know clearly, what he will be content to accept without explanation. His chief efforts in fiction having hitherto been parodies, so to speak, of antiquated narrative forms,—the eastern tale and the romance of piracy—he has been able to throw a veil of light humour over their mere sensationalism, which we miss in such a story as **"The Pavilion on the Links."** (pp. 584-85)

To protest against any fashion not positively vicious is to show a fussy forgetfulness of the flow of time. And indeed lightness of touch is in no sense a fashion to be protested against. It is entirely good so far as it goes; only it may not, perhaps, go quite so far as its modern devotees believe. . . . [But] let us not despise and reject as vices other qualities which have their own due place and function. The current criticism of the day opposes to its one saving grace a deadly sin called "emphasis," conceived as the evil habit of gibbering barbarians without the pale of articulate-speaking culture. Mr. Stevenson confesses how "in a fit of horror at his old excess" he cut out from the first draft of his essay on Whitman "all the big words and emphatic passages.". . . [The] writer who cuts out a true and just emphasis simply because it is emphatic, performs an act, not of wise temperance, but of affectation or cowardice. . . . Mr. Stevenson has no lack of theories to express, but his beliefs are not weighty enough, his truths are not true enough, to demand emphasis. Not that he is sceptical of them or regards them from Pilate's point of view; on the contrary, he gives them forth with great confidence, which may be defined as emphasis without enthusiasm. Occasionally he forgets himself and lets slip an emphatic utterance; and sometimes, be it noted, the emphasis is false. When he calls some page of Thoreau's "the noblest and most useful passage I remember to have read in any modern author," he indulges in a hyperbole. However noble and useful the passage in question, such a sweeping superlative is essentially untenable; unless, indeed, we suppose Mr. Stevenson's memory to be very short, in which case the assertion becomes a mere forcible-feeble circumlocution. But such slips are rare. As a rule, Mr. Stevenson gossips along as lightly as need be. His is healthy human speech, sane and self-contained. We can listen to it long without either irritation or tedium, until suddenly there vibrates across our memory an echo of some other utterance compared with which this light-flowing discourse "is as moonlight unto sunlight, is as water unto wine." Then we reflect that there is a time for everything; a time for lightness and a time for emphasis; a time for speech and a time for song; a time for rippling melody and a time for

rich-woven, deep-toned harmony; and we remember that in English prose there is room for all these different forms of strength and beauty. Lightness of touch is good, but so are power and passion and multitudinous music. The countrymen of Milton need not sneer at majesty of rhetoric; the contemporaries of Ruskin should know that subtlety and splendour may go hand in hand. (pp. 585-86)

> *William Archer, "Robert Louis Stevenson: His Style and His Thought," in* Time, *London, n.s. Vol II, No. 11, November, 1885, pp. 581-91.*

### [W. E. HENLEY]   (essay date 1885)

['**Prince Otto: A Romance**'] is so plainly an essay in pure literature that to the average reader it may be something of a disappointment. It has none of the qualities of an ordinary novel. Means, atmosphere, characters, effects—everything is peculiar. Mr. Stevenson has worked from beginning to end on a convention which is hardly to be paralleled in modern literature. The ordinary material of the novel he throws aside; in half a dozen sentences he gives the results of a whole volume of realism; he goes straight to the quick of things, and concerns himself with none but essentials. That his work is perfectly successful it would be rash to assert. But in some respects—in certain qualities of other than verbal form—it may be taken as a model by anybody with an understanding of art in its severer and more rigid sense, and a desire to excel in the higher ranges of literary achievement. (p. 663)

[The story of Prince Otto and Princess Seraphina] as imagined and set forth by [Mr. Stevenson], is delightful. Dumas would have told it with a more truly human feeling and a more general and taking sympathy than Mr. Stevenson has been able to compass; Alfred de Musset with a rarer note of passion, a touch of humour that would have appealed to a wider public. But neither Musset nor Dumas could have written '**Prince Otto**' as we have it. It is possible that in their several ways they might have proved their case more convincingly; it is probable enough that they would have been a trifle less fantastic, less individual and peculiar, and for that reason in some measure more persuasive. But when all is said, Mr. Stevenson has little or no reason to avoid such a comparison or to dread its results. Here and there—in the turn of his dialogue, the pregnant brevity of his descriptions—he reminds the reader of Mr. George Meredith; here and there he appears to be slightly too personal to be wholly acceptable, a little too histrionic to be quite effective. But his book has a real organic completeness. It lives with its own life, and succeeds by virtue of an inspiration to be found nowhere else. It will scarcely be so popular (it may be) as '**Treasure Island**' or ['**More New Arabian Nights: The Dynamiter**']. But it has been produced as a "classic," so to speak; it may be called the author's diploma piece; and as a "classic," if in no other capacity, it is tolerably certain to endure. Of course, to some extent, it is open to criticism. Otto is, perhaps, a trifle too histrionic, especially in his relations with Madame von Rosen, and Seraphina too priggish and unamiable; it may be that Gondremark—who seems to be a kind of prose sketch of the German Chancellor—requires more energy, a more vigorous humanity than Mr. Stevenson can wield. But, on the other hand, Madame von Rosen is an admirable character in conception and in execution. In the style there are notes of blank verse which afflict the reader with a sense of chill unknown to those who have delighted in the verbal felicity of '**Virginibus Puerisque**' and '**Travels with a Donkey**.' Yet the vocabulary is choice and full, the form varied, the manner elegant and distinguished. The chapter called **"Princess Cinderella"** as a piece of romantic prose will bear comparison with the best work of its kind. This is high praise, no doubt, but no one who reads it will assert that it is too high—perhaps, indeed, it is scarcely high enough. And it is possible to say almost as much of the book considered as a whole. For 'Prince Otto' is a protest against the existence of most of that which is unworthy in the theory and practice of modern literature, and is plainly the work of a man who writes, not for the public of Mudie, but with a constant respect for the principles of art, and an unalterable sense of the excellence of beauty, in life and literature alike. (p. 664)

> [W. E. Henley], *in a review of "Prince Otto: A Romance,"* in The Athenaeum, *No. 3030, November 21, 1885, pp. 663-64.*

### [ANDREW LANG]  (essay date 1886)

Mr. Stevenson's *Prince Otto* was, no doubt, somewhat disappointing to many of his readers. They will be hard to please if they are disappointed in his *Strange Case of Dr. Jekyll and Mr. Hyde.* To adopt a recent definition of some of Mr. Stevenson's tales, this little shilling work is like "Poe with the addition of a moral sense." . . .

Mr. Stevenson's idea, his secret (but a very open secret) is that of the double personality in every man. The mere conception is familiar enough. Poe used it in *William Wilson,* and Gautier in *Le Chevalier Double.* Yet Mr. Stevenson's originality of treatment remains none the less striking and astonishing. The double personality does not in his romance take the form of a personified conscience, the *doppel ganger* of the sinner, a "double" like his own double which Goethe is fabled to have seen. No; the "separable self" in this "strange case" is all unlike that in *William Wilson,* and, with its unlikeness to its master, with its hideous caprices, and appalling vitality, and terrible power of growth and increase, is, to our thinking, a notion as novel as it is terrific. We would welcome a spectre, a ghoul, or even a vampire gladly, rather than meet Mr. Edward Hyde. . . .

It is a proof of Mr. Stevenson's skill that he has chosen the scene for his wild "Tragedy of a Body and a Soul," as it might have been called, in the most ordinary and respectable quarters of London. His heroes (surely *this* is original) are all successful middle-aged professional men. No woman appears in the tale (as in *Treasure Island*), and we incline to think that Mr. Stevenson always does himself most justice in novels without a heroine. It may be regarded by some critics as a drawback to the tale that it inevitably disengages a powerful lesson in conduct. It is not a moral allegory, of course; but you cannot help reading the moral into it, and recognizing that, just as every one of us, according to Mr. Stevenson, travels through life with a donkey (as he himself did in the Cevennes), so every Jekyll among us is haunted by his own Hyde. But it would be most unfair to insist on this, as there is nothing a novel-reader hates more than to be done good to unawares. Nor has Mr. Stevenson, obviously, any didactic purpose. The moral of the tale is its natural soul, and no more separable from it than, in ordinary life, Hyde is separable from Jekyll.

While one is thrilled and possessed by the horror of the central fancy, one may fail, at first reading, to recognize the delicate and restrained skill of the treatment of accessories, details, and character. Mr. Utterson, for example, Jekyll's friend, is an admirable portrait, and might occupy a place unchallenged

among pictures by the best masters of sober fiction. . . . It is fair to add that, while the style of the new romance is usually as plain as any style so full of compressed thought and incident can be, there is at least one passage in the threshold of the book . . . where Mr. Stevenson yields to his old Tempter, "preciousness.". . . It is pleasant to acknowledge [however] that the half-page of "preciousness" stands almost alone in this excellent and horrific and captivating romance, where Mr. Stevenson gives us of his very best and increases that debt of gratitude which we all owe him for so many and such rare pleasures. (p. 55)

> [Andrew Lang], *"Stevenson's New Story,"* in The Saturday Review, *London, Vol. LXI, No. 1576, January 9, 1886, pp. 55-6.*

### THE TIMES, LONDON  (essay date 1886)

> [*According to Longman's & Company, the firm that originally published* Dr. Jekyll and Mr. Hyde, *the following anonymous review sparked reader interest and significantly contributed to the book's popularity.*]

Nothing Mr. Stevenson has written as yet has so strongly impressed us with the versatility of his very original genius as [the **"Strange Case of Dr. Jekyll and Mr. Hyde"**]. . . . Either the story was a flash of intuitive psychological research, dashed off in a burst of inspiration; or else it is the product of the most elaborate forethought, fitting together all the parts of an intricate and inscrutable puzzle. The proof is, that every connoisseur who reads the story once must certainly read it twice. He will read it the first time, passing from surprise to surprise, in a curiosity that keeps growing, because it is never satisfied. For the life of us, we cannot make out how such and such an incident can possibly be explained on grounds that are intelligible or in any way plausible. Yet all the time the seriousness of the tone assures us that explanations are forthcoming. In our impatience we are hurried towards the denouement, which accounts for everything upon strictly scientific grounds, though the science be the science of problematical futurity. Then, having drawn a sigh of relief at having found even a fantastically speculative issue from our embarrassments, we begin reflectively to call to mind how systematically the writer has been working towards it. Never for a moment, in the most startling situations, has he lost his grasp of the grand ground-facts of a wonderful and supernatural problem. Each apparently incredible or insignificant detail has been thoughtfully subordinated to his purpose. And if we say, after all, on a calm retrospect, that the strange case is absurdly and insanely improbable, Mr. Stevenson might answer in the words of Hamlet, that there are more things in heaven and in earth than are dreamed of in our philosophy. . . . Naturally, we compare it with the sombre masterpieces of Poe, and we may say at once that Mr. Stevenson has gone far deeper. . . . Mr. Stevenson evolves the ideas of his story from the world that is unseen, enveloping everything in weird mystery, till at last it pleases him to give us the password. . . .

Nor is it the mere charm of the story, strange as it is, which fascinates and thrills us. Mr. Stevenson is known for a master of style, and never has he shown his resources more remarkably than on this occasion. We do not mean that the book is written in excellent English—that must be a matter of course; but he has weighed his words and turned his sentences so as to sustain and excite throughout the sense of mystery and of horror. The mere artful use of an "it" for a "he" may go far in that respect, and Mr. Stevenson has carefully chosen his language and missed no opportunity. And if his style is good, his motive is better, and shows a higher order of genius. Slight as is the story, and supremely sensational, we remember nothing better since George Eliot's ''Romola'' than this delineation of a feeble but kindly nature steadily and inevitably succumbing to the sinister influences of besetting weaknesses. With no formal preaching and without a touch of Pharisaism, he works out the essential power of Evil, which, with its malignant patience and unwearying perseverance, gains ground with each casual yielding to temptation, till the once well-meaning man may actually become a fiend, or at least wear the reflection of the fiend's image. But we have said enough to show our opinion of the book, which should be read as a finished study in the art of fantastic literature.

> A review of ''Strange Case of Dr. Jekyll and Mr. Hyde,'' in The Times, London (© Times Newspapers Limited 1886), January 25, 1886, p. 13.

## E. PURCELL  (essay date 1886)

I have succeeded in unearthing a number of the *Academy* five years old, in which I rviewed Mr. Stevenson's Essays [see excerpt above, 1881]. . . . He had not then attempted romance; and upon his exquisite little tours and essays some admirers were then trying to build up a claim of original and profound philosophy. Against that claim I protested, perhaps too seriously. He had not—he never will have—any new gospel of life to give us. He has developed precisely as I hoped and prophesied that he would. There still, however, remains that strange mixture of audacious candour and audacious reticence on the great issues of morality which attracted and distressed from the first. On this much might be written interesting to Mr. Stevenson and a few more, but to most others neither acceptable nor helpful. We have no right to demand his scheme of human life; but this is certain, that his puzzling enigmatic ethics, whether they be individual, or whether they are a true reflection of a present transitional state of society, are the real hindrance to his aim of producing a great romance worthy of his genius. In *Prince Otto* he tried, and owns his failure. It seems to me that, if we are to deal at length with men and motives, we must lay a good foundation of ethical principles and repose comfortably upon them. Is not this restful solidity the secret of most works of the imagination of sustained interest? . . . [Unlike Stevenson's, Sir Walter Scott's] mind was quite made up about the right and wrong of most things and persons. He could afford to describe and judge them steadily, without excitement or misgiving; and the reader, soothed and reassured, resigns himself with confidence to the prolonged spell of the great magician. Not that Scott is a greater, or Stevenson a lesser genius for all that. It is but their fate. Equal in imagination, the one is strengthened and disciplined to prolonged flights by his perfect assimilation of conventional principles; the other's course, rapid, erratic, and interrupted, displays far deeper insight, far keener perception, far bolder genius—a genius brilliant but seemingly troubled, because it ventures into a world ignored by Scott, where all is doubt and difficulty.

But in the *New Arabian Nights,* and still more in the *Dynamiter,* the art is phenomenal. [This is] . . . art so carelessly, roguishly exposed, that it charms by its very audacity. The author seems to say: ''Now you need not agitate yourself so much over these horrors—they are only made-up rubbish, and I am laughing at you all the time. I don't mind telling you this, because you know in spite of it, you won't go to bed till you have finished the book.'' Probably there is nothing else quite like this in literature, though it is one of the many aspects of Rabelais. Indeed, no modern English book contains such a profusion and superfluity of talent as this little *Dynamiter*. It is a masterpiece, upon which *Prince Otto* has not improved, and no novelist can read it without gnawing envy. This—on two grounds. One, the insolent prodigality of its invention. . . . Mr. Stevenson flushes a regular three-volume covey of incident, pursues it awhile—for a chapter, a page, a few lines—and then gaily tosses it aside. The novelist must be horrified to see all these valuable plots and promising openings bandied about, instead of being hoarded and doled out to the world in expensive volumes. The *Dynamiter* contains a whole library of possible novels. Its charm lies in this wanton profusion of a spendthrift whose resources seem inexhaustible. The other ground of envy is most interesting, and may not yet have been adequately noticed. . . . [Mr.] Stevenson is a perfect adapter. I have traced so many of his happiest conceptions to other books, that still more might probably be traced by other readers. No one, unless inspired, can evolve ideas and incidents, without some peg of suggestion. It is delightful to notice how Mr. Stevenson hits upon some unlikely material in a book, sees its capabilities, turns it upside down, inside out, transforms it, builds upon it a graceful creation of his own. (p. 140)

[*Prince Otto*] is not a failure at all—it is a success. It is not uninteresting—it is most fascinating. It is confessedly a wild, rambling, nondescript book; but it contains some things of rare beauty and sweetness, and overflows with cleverness and originality. It refines the odours of Auerbach's pine woods and the splendours of Ruskin's skies. But it is disappointing. That is the true verdict. And why? Because we, and the author too, are bent upon his producing something more sustained, more suited to be placed beside, and compared with, and preferred to, other great fictions; and we all expected that *Prince Otto* was to prove the *magnum opus*. Well, we were wrong. It is not even equal to its predecessors; but it still towers above its rivals. (p. 141)

> E. Purcell, in a review of ''Prince Otto: A Romance,'' in The Academy, Vol. XXIX, No. 721, February 27, 1886, pp. 140-41.

## ST. JAMES GAZETTE  (essay date 1886)

Mr. Stevenson is the Defoe of our generation. Since the days when 'Robinson Crusoe' first delighted English readers, no book of adventure has appeared that can pretend to rivalry with the story of 'Treasure Island.' Beside the exquisite prose of Mr. Stevenson, his delightful quaintness of humour and his fertile inventiveness, the romances of Fenimore Cooper seem very poor performances. The simplicity which is the highest art, a mastery of language, and a subtle and sympathetic power of compelling attention, are all at the command of Mr. Stevenson. He is rarely dull, he is often slily humorous, and he is prone to weave into his narrative a fine and brilliant thread of suggestive reflection which is alike characteristic and alluring. The wave of his magician's wand is truly magical; but, while he draws his readers from a too prosaic world to one of aerial fancy, he lets them know in a sort of gravely jesting undertone that it is semblance and not reality. His writings inspire a pleasure which is all the more genuine and refreshing for their innocence; yet their fun, their effectiveness, their brilliancy would be much less striking were they not in part the result of a grave experience and understanding of human life, such as makes every man who is a man desire once more to become as a little child.

It is high praise, therefore, of ['**Kidnapped**'] to say that it is no unworthy companion of '**Treasure Island.**' Its incidents are not so uniformly thrilling; there is no touch of art in it quite equal to the account of the blind sailor's visit to the country inn in the former story; yet '**Kidnapped**' is excellent from end to end. Two characteristics of Mr. Stevenson's last volume are in themselves worthy of notice. The first, that, as in '**Treasure Island,**' he has succeeded in telling a story in which women and feminine influence play positively no part. There is no love-making in '**Kidnapped,**' and, with one exception, no woman takes any share in the action. There are some pretty and touching passages illustrative of the unspoken love of man for man which has been a finer side of human intercourse since the days of David and Jonathan. But of the conventional heroine and the yet more conventional love scene, which are wont to appear even in so-called books for boys, Mr. Stevenson will have none. . . . The second observation is that Mr. Stevenson has boldly and even wisely ventured into the field of Jacobite romance which has already been occupied by the genius of Sir Walter Scott. Different as is the character of his book, we feel that indirectly Mr. Stevenson owes a little of his general idea to the author of 'Rob Roy' and 'Waverley.' But although there is a perceptible parallel between the adventures of David Balfour and those that have immortalized the names of Osbaldistone and Bailie Jarvie, the parallel is too slight to be insisted on. The story of the Jacobite times is an inexhaustible mine for the writer of fiction, and the originality and literary skill of Mr. Stevenson is doubly welcome for this addition to the number of Highland stories. 'Rob Roy' is inimitable; but it says much for Mr. Stevenson's powers that '**Kidnapped**' seems none the less charming for the very reason that it recalls the masterpieces of the greatest story-teller of our century.

Mixed feelings of disappointed curiosity in the present and pleasant hope for the future will contend in the reader's breast when he finds that ['**Kidnapped**'] is not brought to a thorough conclusion, but that several important particulars are left incomplete; with more than a hint that on some other day the further adventures of David Balfour will be related. Of the two personages who play the largest part in these pages, it is hard to say which creates the keener interest: David Balfour, the ostensible hero; or Alan Breck, most pugnacious and attractive of Jacobites, whose views of his duty towards his neighbours and hereditary foes the Campbells are expressed with a humour befitting our English apologists of Irish agrarian outrage. . . . Alan, indeed, is incorrigible on all matters of blood-feuds and fighting, but he is a delightful creature. We shall say nothing of wicked Uncle Ebenezer, or the perils and shipwreck of the brig *Covenant,* or of Mr. Stevenson's wonderfully vivid pictures of physical fatigue and suffering as endured by the Jacobite fugitives who 'took to the heather.' Those who have read Mr. Stevenson know the grace and magic of his pen, and they will need no solicitation to spend a few hours in the delight of '**Kidnapped.**' (pp. 233-35)

> *An extract from a review of "Kidnapped," in* St. James Gazette, *Vol. XIII, July 19, 1886 (and reprinted in* Robert Louis Stevenson: The Critical Heritage, *edited by Paul Maixner, Routledge & Kegan Paul, 1981, pp. 233-35).*

## [R. H. HUTTON]   (essay date 1886)

We question whether Mr. Stevenson will ever again come quite up to the freshness of *Treasure Island,* a book which may be said to have had more charm for boys than even *Robinson Crusoe* itself, though less for men. Indeed, we should be disposed to regard the boys of England who lived before *Robinson Crusoe* was written, as boys without a literature, and the boys who lived between *Robinson Crusoe* and *Treasure Island,* as boys who had only a foretaste of what was in preparation for them; while boys who have lived since *Treasure Island* was published, are boys who have a right to look back on all previous boyhoods with compassion, as boyhoods sunk in comparative darkness, or touched only with the streaks of dawn. *Kidnapped* is not so ideal a story of external adventure as *Treasure Island.* On the other hand, it has more of human interest in it for those who have passed the age of boyhood. It touches the history of Scotland with a vigorous hand. It gives a picture of Highland character worthy of Sir Walter Scott himself. Its description of the scenery of the Highlands in the old, wild times, is as charming as a vivid imagination could make it; and the description of the cowardly old miser who plotted his nephew's death rather than give him up his inheritance, is as vivid as anything which Mr. Stevenson's singular genius has yet invented for us. Nor is there in this delightful tale the least trace of that evil odour which makes *The Strange Story of Dr. Jekyll and Mr. Hyde* so unpleasant a reminiscence, in spite of the originality and eeriness of the inconceivable and illogical marvel on which it is based.

The power of *Kidnapped* consists chiefly in the great vivacity with which the portrait of the Highland chieftain is drawn, and with which the contrast is brought out between the frank vanity of the Highland character and the rooted self-sufficiency of the Lowland character in the relations between the Stewart of Appin and the Lowland hero of the adventures. So far as the mere story goes, though there is plenty of adventure, there is not that rush of danger and enterprise which transfigured *Treasure Island.* The story depends far more for its interest on the realities of history and character than that of the earlier tale. The first striking effect in the book is the description of the hatred in which the uncle of the hero is held by the country-folk in the neighbourhood of his house, the desolation of the old miser's abode, and the struggle in his mind between his horror of his nephew, who may deprive him of his property, and his wish to keep him till some plan of finally ridding himself of the lad occurs. . . . The next great success in the book introduces us to the Highlander, the Stewart chief of Appin, whose character is so skilfully drawn that Scott himself would, we think, have been glad to own the picture. (pp. 990-91)

On the whole, while this book is not quite so unique as *Treasure Island,* it has perhaps even more of the qualities proper to all true literature, and for the lovers of Scotch scenery and Scotch character it is altogether delightful. Mr. Stevenson has, so far as we know, written nothing which is more likely to live, and to be a favourite with readers of all sorts and classes. (p. 991)

> *[R. H. Hutton], in a review of "Kidnapped," in* The Spectator (© 1886 by The Spectator), *Vol. LIX, No. 3030, July 24, 1886, pp. 990-91.*

## [MARGARET OLIPHANT]   (essay date 1887)

[*Unlike Oliphant's later review of* The Master of Ballantrae *(see excerpt below, 1889), the following essay is sharply negative, criticizing Stevenson for mishandling the Scots dialect and for overemphasizing personal information in his volume of poetry,* Underwoods. *Oliphant's closing remarks illustrate a difference between English and American critics. While Americans admired Stevenson's work and welcomed any personal information he was willing to provide, many English critics denounced the preoccupation with the personal, and accused Stevenson of publishing collections such as* Underwoods *to encourage American interest.*]

Mr Stevenson is still young; in his own personality he is exceedingly interesting, we have no manner of doubt, to a large and varied circle. Might we venture to hint, to suggest, that it would be well to be content with that affectionate appreciation, and not allow himself to be deluded into thinking that his house, and his doctors, and his gardeners, and the pretty presents he makes to his friends, are equally absorbing in their interest to a large and already much occupied public? . . . [We] yield to no one in our regard for Mr Henry James. His fine if sometimes hesitating utterances are dear to us. . . . But when we read in ['**Underwoods**'] that the Venetian mirror at Skerryvore, which is not a lighthouse but Mr Stevenson's house at Bournemouth— waits, as the climax of an existence which has seen many pretty things in its native palaces and elsewhere,

> Until the door
> Open, and the Prince of men,
> Henry James, shall come again,

we—well, not to put too fine a point upon it, we laugh. . . . It is not permitted, even to a man of genius, to make his friends, even when they too are men of genius, absurd. The world has nothing to do with these little endearments. . . . Perhaps it rather adds than takes away from the absurdity when they are names which we have heard. The most Christian critic can scarcely refrain from a chuckle of delight when he sees his friend opposite [Mr Henry James] branded as Prince of men. What did the Venetian mirror continue to say when he reflected that bland image? (pp. 709-10)

['**The House Beautiful**'] is very charming and pretty, and sufficiently impersonal to command the general sympathy of all who have houses and live therein, and find their homely roofs glorified with sunrisings and sunsettings every day. . . . [In '**To My Father**'] there is all the honest pride of a good lineage and a personal feeling more justifiable than that which shines through his addresses to contemporary friends. (p. 711)

The second part [of '**Underwoods**'] is taken up with verses— in Scots. Now be it far from us to say that no man is to write in Scots, or what Mr Stevenson calls "Lallan," because Burns has made that language classic; but we do feel that there is a rashness almost blasphemous in the proceeding, when a new rhymester takes up the measure of the "Second Epistle to Davie," and puts some very commonplace sentiments into it, with a little lecture on the pronunciation of vowels before it, and a fear in the middle of it that somebody may take up the book in after-ages—

> May find an' read me, an' be sair
> Perplexed, puir brither! . . .

Does Mr Stevenson really suppose that his address of '**The Maker to Posterity**' will survive to puzzle the antiquaries when the works of that ploughman whose life we are aware he does not approve of, have disappeared into the dust of ages? Does he believe that any man in his senses, or woman either, will find in these poetical exercises anything but faint echoes of

> Him who walked in glory and in joy,
> Following his plough along the mountain-side?

Let us not lose our temper with this rash young man. Much applause has, we fear, turned his head. Having nothing in the world to say in "Lallan" which he could not say better in his

ordinary fine speech (pleasantly breathing a Scotticism here and there, we are glad to say, much more characteristic than the "Scots"), he has framed his verses very nicely, and brought out the different *ow's* and *ou's* and *o's* in a manner which does credit to his breeding. But Mr Stevenson is no rival of Burns, who spoke his natural tongue, and had a great many of the most lovely and delightful things to say in it; and when he speaks of his little pipings as likely to perplex a world which has the works of that great poet before it, he says a very silly thing, quite unworthy of any good sense he may happen to possess, and highly injurious to his unquestionable genius. Let us be done with this foolish self-opinion and disrespect. To be pious about the lighthouse is pretty, to be impious about the fathers of one's tongue and thoughts is detestable. (p. 712)

It is America that is the cause of it all—America which thrusts in her little reputations upon us, and so swears they are of the first rank, that with a gasp, and for the sake of peace, yet with wonderful searchings of heart, we give a feeble assent. A living dog is better—that big continent thinks—than a dead lion; and if Longfellow is as worthy [at] Westminster as Shakespeare himself—or at least as Dryden and Pope and Coleridge—why should not Mr Robert Louis Stevenson be better than Robert Burns? (p. 713)

*[Margaret Oliphant], in a review of "Underwoods," in* Blackwood's Edinburgh Magazine, *Vol. CXLII, No. DCCCLXV, November, 1887, pp. 709-13.*

## HENRY JAMES　(essay date 1887)

[*James was a close friend of Stevenson and a critic and admirer of his work. In the following essay, James refutes William Archer's charge that Stevenson was more concerned with style than subject matter (see excerpts above, 1885), and he identifies the author's major thematic interests as youth and personal heroism. Archer criticized Stevenson's work for its simple philosophy of good health and good spirits, a charge that James refutes by pointing to the difficult circumstances of Stevenson's life, asserting that he had earned the right to cheerful optimism. In addition, James discusses Stevenson's motive for writing, and his contributions to literature: "[Stevenson] would say we ought to make believe that the extraordinary is the best part of life even if it were not, and to do so because the finest feelings—suspense, daring, decision, passion, curiosity, gallantry, eloquence, friendship—are involved in it, and it is of infinite importance that the tradition of these precious things should not perish."*]

There are writers who present themselves before the critic with just the amount of drapery that is necessary for decency; but Mr. Stevenson is not one of these—he makes his appearance in an amplitude of costume. His costume is part of [his] character . . . ; it never occurs to us to ask how he would look without it. Before all things he is a writer with a style—a model with a complexity of curious and picturesque garments. It is by the cut and the colour of this rich and becoming frippery— I use the term endearingly, as a painter might—that he arrests the eye and solicits the brush.

That is, frankly, half the charm he has for us, that he wears a dress and wears it with courage, with a certain cock of the hat and tinkle of the supererogatory sword; or in other words that he is curious of expression and regards the literary form not simply as a code of signals, but as the key-board of a piano, and as so much plastic material. He has that voice deplored, if we mistake not, by Mr. Herbert Spencer, a manner—a manner for manner's sake it may sometimes doubtless be said. He is as different as possible from the sort of writer who regards words as numbers and a page as the mere addition of them; much more, to carry out our image, the dictionary stands for him as a wardrobe, and a proposition as a button for his coat. Mr. William Archer, in an article so gracefully and ingeniously turned that the writer may almost be accused of imitating even while he deprecates [see excerpt above, 1885], speaks of him as a votary of "lightness of touch," at any cost, and remarks that "he is not only philosophically content but deliberately resolved, that his readers shall look first to his manner, and only in the second place to his matter." I shall not attempt to gainsay this; I cite it rather, for the present because it carries out our own sense. Mr. Stevenson delights in a style, and his own has nothing accidental or diffident; it is eminently conscious of its responsibilities, and meets them with a kind of gallantry—as if language were a pretty woman, and a person who proposes to handle it had of necessity to be something of a Don Juan. This bravery of gesture is a noticeable part of his nature, and it is rather odd that at the same time a striking feature of that nature should be an absence of care for things feminine. His books are for the most part books without women, and it is not women who fall most in love with them. But Mr. Stevenson does not need, as we may say, a petticoat to inflame him: a happy collocation of words will serve the purpose, or a singular image, or the bright eye of a passing conceit, and he will carry off a pretty paradox without so much as a scuffle. The tone of letters is in him. . . . (pp. 139-41)

[It is] because he has no speciality that Mr. Stevenson is an individual, and because his curiosity is the only receipt by which he produces. Each of his books is an independent effort—a window opened to a different view. *Doctor Jekyll and Mr. Hyde* is as dissimilar as possible from *Treasure Island; Virginibus Puerisque* has nothing in common with *The New Arabian Nights,* and I should never have supposed *A Child's Garden of Verses* to be from the hand of the author of *Prince Otto.*

Though Mr. Stevenson cares greatly for his phrase, as every writer should who respects himself and his art, it takes no very attentive reading of his volumes to show that it is not what he cares for most, and that he regards an expressive style only, after all, as a means. It seems to me the fault of Mr. Archer's interesting paper, that it suggests too much that the author of these volumes considers the art of expression as an end—an ingenious game of words. He finds that Mr. Stevenson is not serious, that he neglects a whole side of life, that he has no perception, and no consciousness, of suffering, that he speaks as a happy but heartless pagan, living only in his senses (which the critic admits to be exquisitely fine), and that in a world full of heaviness he is not sufficiently aware of the philosophic limitations of mere technical skill. . . . He is not the first reader, and he will not be the last, who shall have been irritated by Mr. Stevenson's jauntiness. That jauntiness is an essential part of his genius; but to my sense it ceases to be irritating—it indeed becomes positively touching and constitutes an appeal to sympathy and even to tenderness—when once one has perceived what lies beneath the dancing-tune to which he mostly moves. Much as he cares for his phrase, he cares more for life, and for a certain transcendently lovable part of it. He feels, as it seems to us, and that is not given to every one. This constitutes a philosophy which Mr. Archer fails to read between his lines—the respectable, desirable moral which many a reader doubtless finds that he neglects to point. He does not feel everything equally, by any manner of means, but his feelings are always his reasons. He regards them, whatever they may be, as sufficiently honourable, does not disguise them in

other names or colours, and looks at whatever he meets in the brilliant candle-light that they shed. (pp. 142-44)

The part of life which he cares for most is youth, and the direct expression of the love of youth is the beginning and the end of his message. His appreciation of this delightful period amounts to a passion, and a passion, in the age in which we live, strikes us on the whole as a sufficient philosophy. . . . Mingled with this almost equal love of a literary surface, it represents a real originality. This combination is the keynote of Mr. Stevenson's faculty and the explanation of his perversities. The feeling of one's teens, and even of an earlier period (for the delights of crawling, and almost of the rattle, are embodied in *A Child's Garden of Verses*), and the feeling for happy turns—these, in the last analysis (and his sense of a happy turn is of the subtlest), are the corresponding halves of his character. . . .

What makes him so [rare] is the singular maturity of the expression that he has given to young sentiments: he judges them, measures them, sees them from the outside, as well as entertains them. He describes credulity with all the resources of experience, and represents a crude stage with infinite ripeness. In a word, he is an artist accomplished even to sophistication, whose constant theme is the unsophisticated. Sometimes, as in *Kidnapped,* the art is so ripe that it lifts even the subject into the general air: the execution is so serious that the idea (the idea of a boy's romantic adventures), becomes a matter of universal relations. What he prizes most in the boy's ideal is the imaginative side of it, the capacity for successful make-believe. The general freshness in which this is a part of the gloss seems to him the divinest thing in life; considerably more divine, for instance, than the passion usually regarded as the supremely tender one. The idea of making believe appeals to him much more than the idea of making love. That delightful little book of rhymes, the *Child's Garden,* commemorates from beginning to end the picturing, personifying, dramatising faculty of infancy—the view of life from the level of the nursery-fender. The volume is a wonder for the extraordinary vividness with which it reproduces early impressions: a child might have written it if a child could see childhood from the outside, for it would seem that only a child is really near enough to the nursery floor. . . . [He] doesn't speak as a parent, or an uncle, or an educator—he speaks as a contemporary absorbed in his own game. That game is almost always a vision of dangers and triumphs, and if emotion, with him, infallibly resolves itself into memory, so memory is an evocation of throbs and thrills and suspense. He has given to the world the romance of boyhood, as others have produced that of the peerage and the police and the medical profession.

This amounts to saying that what he is most curious of in life is heroism—personal gallantry, if need be with a manner, or a banner, though he is also abundantly capable of enjoying it when it is artless. . . . The love of brave words as well as brave deeds . . . is simply Mr. Stevenson's essential love of style. . . . Alan Breck, in *Kidnapped,* is a wonderful picture of the union of courage and swagger; the little Jacobite adventurer, a figure worthy of Scott at his best, and representing the highest point that Mr. Stevenson's talent has reached, shows us that a marked taste for tawdry finery—tarnished and tattered, some of it indeed, by ticklish occasions—is quite compatible with a perfectly high mettle. Alan Breck is at bottom a study of the love of glory, carried out with extreme psychological truth. . . . Mr. Stevenson's kindness for adventurers extends even to the humblest of all, the mountebank and the strolling player, or even the pedlar whom he declares that in his foreign travels he is habitually taken for. . . . The hungry conjurer, the gymnast whose *maillot* is loose, have something of the glamour of the hero, inasmuch as they too pay with their person. ''To be even one of the outskirters of art leaves a fine stamp on a man's countenance. . . . That is the kind of thing that reconciles me to life: a ragged, tippling, incompetent old rogue, with the manners of a gentleman and the vanity of an artist, to keep up his self-respect!'' What reconciles Mr. Stevenson to life is the idea that in the first place it offers the widest field that we know of for odd doings, and that in the second these odd doings are the best of pegs to hang a sketch in three lines or a paradox in three pages.

As it is not odd, but extremely usual, to marry, he deprecates that course in *Virginibus Puerisque,* the collection of short essays which is most a record of his opinions—that is, largely, of his likes and dislikes. It all comes back to his sympathy with the juvenile and that feeling about life which leads him to regard women as so many superfluous girls in a boy's game. They are almost wholly absent from his pages (the main exception is *Prince Otto,* though there is a Clara apiece in *The Rajah's Diamond* and *The Pavilion on the Links*), for they don't like ships and pistols and fights, they encumber the decks and require separate apartments, and, almost worst of all, have not the highest literary standard. Why should a person marry when he might be swinging a cutlass or looking for a buried treasure? Why should he waste at the nuptial altar precious hours in which he might be polishing periods?

(pp. 144-49)

• • • • •

[The] colour of Scotland has entered into [Stevenson] altogether, and though, oddly enough, he has written but little about his native country, his happiest work shows, I think, that she has the best of his ability, the best of his ambition. *Kidnapped* (whose inadequate title I may deplore in passing) breathes in every line the feeling of moor and loch, and is the finest of his longer stories, and *Thrawn Janet,* a masterpiece in thirteen pages (lately republished in the volume of *The Merry Men*), is, among the shorter, the strongest in execution. . . . If it be a good fortune for a genius to have had such a country as Scotland for its primary stuff, this is doubly the case when there has been a certain process of detachment, of extreme secularisation. Mr. Stevenson has been emancipated: he is, as we may say, a Scotchman of the world. (pp. 154-55)

The novelist who leaves the extraordinary out of his account is liable to awkward confrontations, as we are compelled to reflect in this age of newspapers and of universal publicity. . . . Mr. Stevenson leaves so wide a margin for the wonderful—it impinges with easy assurance upon the text—that he escapes the danger of being brought up by cases he has not allowed for. When he allows for Mr. Hyde he allows for everything, and one feels moreover that even if he did not wave so gallantly the flag of the imaginative and contend that the improbable is what has most character, he would still insist that we ought to make believe. He would say we ought to make believe that the extraordinary is the best part of life even if it were not, and to do so because the finest feelings—suspense, daring, decision, passion, curiosity, gallantry, eloquence, friendship—are involved in it, and it is of infinite importance that the tradition of these precious things should not perish. He would prefer, in a word, any day in the week, Alexandre Dumas to Honoré de Balzac, and it is indeed my impression that he prefers the author of *The Three Musketeers* to any novelist except Mr. George Meredith. . . . He makes us say, Let the

tradition live, by all means, since it was delightful; but at the same time he is the cause of our perceiving afresh that a tradition is kept alive only by something being added to it. In this particular case—in *Doctor Jekyll* and *Kidnapped*—Mr. Stevenson has added psychology.

*The New Arabian Nights* offer us, as the title indicates, the wonderful in the frankest, most delectable form. Partly extravagant and partly very specious, they are the result of a very happy idea, that of placing a series of adventures which are pure adventures in the setting of contemporary English life, and relating them in the placidly ingenuous tone of Scheherezade. This device is carried to perfection in *The Dynamiter,* where the manner takes on more of a kind of high-flown serenity in proportion as the incidents are more ''steep.'' In this line *The Suicide Club* is Mr. Stevenson's greatest success. . . . [Mr. Stevenson's most brilliant stroke] is the opening episode of *Treasure Island,* the arrival of the brown old seaman with the sabre-cut at the ''Admiral Benbow,'' and the advent, not long after, of the blind sailor, with a green shade over his eyes, who comes tapping down the road, in quest of him, with his stick. *Treasure Island* is a ''boy's book'' in the sense that it embodies a boy's vision of the extraordinary, but it is unique in this, and calculated to fascinate the weary mind of experience, that what we see in it is not only the ideal fable but, as part and parcel of that, as it were, the young reader himself and his state of mind: we seem to read it over his shoulder, with an arm around his neck. It is all as perfect as a well-played boy's game, and nothing can exceed the spirit and skill, the humour and the open-air feeling with which the thing is kept at the palpitating pitch. It is not only a record of queer chances, but a study of young feelings: there is a moral side in it, and the figures are not puppets with vague faces. If Jim Hawkins illustrates successful daring, he does so with a delightful rosy good-boyishness and a conscious, modest liability to error. His luck is tremendous, but it does not make him proud, and his manner is refreshingly provincial and human. So is that, even more, of the admirable John Silver, one of the most picturesque and indeed in every way most genially presented villains in the whole literature of romance. He has a singularly distinct and expressive countenance, which of course turns out to be a grimacing mask. Never was a mask more knowingly, vividly painted. *Treasure Island* will surely become—it must already have become and will remain—in its way a classic: thanks to this indescribable mixture of the prodigious and the human, of surprising coincidences and familiar feelings. The language in which Mr. Stevenson has chosen to tell his story is an admirable vehicle for these feelings: with its humorous braveries and quaintnesses, its echoes of old ballads and yarns, it touches all kinds of sympathetic chords.

Is *Doctor Jekyll and Mr. Hyde* a work of high philosophic intention, or simply the most ingenious and irresponsible of fictions? It has the stamp of a really imaginative production, that we may take it in different ways; but I suppose it would generally be called the most serious of the author's tales. It deals with the relation of the baser parts of man to his nobler, of the capacity for evil that exists in the most generous natures; and it expresses these things in a fable which is a wonderfully happy invention. The subject is endlessly interesting, and rich in all sorts of provocation, and Mr. Stevenson is to be congratulated on having touched the core of it. I may do him injustice, but it is, however, here, not the profundity of the idea which strikes me so much as the art of the presentation—the extremely successful form. There is a genuine feeling for the perpetual moral question, a fresh sense of the difficulty of being good and the brutishness of being bad; but what there is above all is a singular ability in holding the interest. I confess that that, to my sense, is the most edifying thing in the short, rapid, concentrated story, which is really a masterpiece of concision. There is something almost impertinent in the way, as I have noticed, in which Mr. Stevenson achieves his best effects without the aid of the ladies, and *Doctor Jekyll* is a capital example of his heartless independence. . . . The gruesome tone of the tale is, no doubt, deepened by their absence: it is like the late afternoon light of a foggy winter Sunday, when even inanimate objects have a kind of wicked look. (pp. 165-70)

I have left Mr. Stevenson's best book to the last. . . . [There] are parts of [*Kidnapped*] so fine as to suggest that the author's talent has taken a fresh start, various as have been the impulses in which it had already indulged, and serious the hindrances among which it is condemned to exert itself. There would have been a kind of perverse humility in his keeping up the fiction that a production so literary as *Kidnapped* is addressed to immature minds, and, though it was originally given to the world, I believe, in a "boy's paper," the story embraces every occasion that it meets to satisfy the higher criticism. . . . [The] history stops without ending, as it were; but I think I may add that this accident speaks for itself. Mr. Stevenson has often to lay down his pen for reasons that have nothing to do with the failure of inspiration, and the last page of David Balfour's adventures is an honourable plea for indulgence. The remaining five-sixths of the book deserve to stand by *Henry Esmond* as a fictive autobiography in archaic form. The author's sense of the English idiom of the last century, and still more of the Scotch, has enabled him to give a gallant companion to Thackeray's *tour de force*. The life, the humour, the colour of the central portions of *Kidnapped* have a singular pictorial virtue: these passages read like a series of inspired footnotes on some historic page. . . . There could be no better instance of the author's talent for seeing the familiar in the heroic, and reducing the extravagant to plausible detail, than the description of Alan Breck's defence in the cabin of the ship and the really magnificent chapters of **"The Flight in the Heather."** Mr. Stevenson has in a high degree (and doubtless for good reasons of his own) what may be called the imagination of physical states, and this has enabled him to arrive at a wonderfully exact translation of the miseries of his panting Lowland hero, dragged for days and nights over hill and dale, through bog and thicket, without meat or drink or rest, at the tail of an Homeric Highlander. The great superiority of the book resides to my mind, however, in the fact that it puts two characters on their feet with admirable rectitude. I have paid my tribute to Alan Breck, and I can only repeat that he is a masterpiece. It is interesting to observe that though the man is extravagant, the author's touch exaggerates nothing: it is throughout of the most truthful, genial, ironical kind; full of penetration, but with none of the grossness of moralising satire. The figure is a genuine study, and nothing can be more charming than the way Mr. Stevenson both sees through it and admires it. Shall I say that he sees through David Balfour? This would be perhaps to underestimate the density of that medium. Beautiful, at any rate, is the expression which this unfortunate though circumspect youth gives to those qualities which combine to excite our respect and our objurgation in the Scottish character. Such a scene as the episode of the quarrel of the two men on the mountainside is a real stroke of genius, and has the very logic and rhythm of life: a quarrel which we feel to be inevitable, though it is about nothing, or almost nothing, and which springs from exasperated nerves and the simple shock of temperaments. The

author's vision of it has a profundity which goes deeper, I think, than *Doctor Jekyll*. I know of few better examples of the way genius has ever a surprise in its pocket—keeps an ace, as it were, up its sleeve. And in this case it endears itself to us by making us reflect that such a passage as the one I speak of is in fact a signal proof of what the novel can do at its best, and what nothing else can do so well. In the presence of this sort of success we perceive its immense value. It is capable of a rare transparency—it can illustrate human affairs in cases so delicate and complicated that any other vehicle would be clumsy. To those who love the art that Mr. Stevenson practises he will appear, in pointing this incidental moral, not only to have won a particular triumph, but to have given a delightful pledge. (pp. 171-74)

> *Henry James, "Robert Louis Stevenson" (1887; originally published in* The Century Magazine, *Vol. XXXV, No. 6, April, 1888), in his* Partial Portraits *(© 1888 by Henry James), Macmillan and Co., 1888, pp. 137-74.*

**GAVIN OGILVIE [Pseudonym of J. M. BARRIE]** (essay date 1888)

Some men of letters, not necessarily the greatest, have an indescribable charm to which we give our hearts. . . . Of living authors, none perhaps bewitches the reader more than Mr. Stevenson, who plays upon words as if they were a musical instrument. To follow the music is less difficult than to place the musician. . . . Mr. Stevenson puzzles the critics, fascinating them until they are willing to judge him by the great work he is to write by and by when the little books are finished. Over **"Treasure Island"** I let my fire die in winter without knowing that I was freezing. But the creator of Alan Breck has now published nearly twenty volumes. It is so much easier to finish the little works than to begin the great one, for which we are all taking notes.

Mr. Stevenson is not to be labelled novelist. He wanders the byways of literature without any fixed address. Too much of a truant to be classified with the other boys, he is only a writer of fiction in the sense that he was once an Edinburgh University student because now and again he looked in at his classes when he happened to be that way. A literary man without a fixed occupation amazes Mr. Henry James [see excerpt above, 1887]. . . . That **"Dr. Jekyll and Mr. Hyde"** should be the author of **"Treasure Island," "Virginibus Puerisque"** by the author of **"The New Arabian Nights," "A Child's Garden of Verses"** by the author of **"Prince Otto,"** are to him the three degrees of comparison of wonder, though for my own part I marvel more that the author of "Daisy Miller" should be Mr. Stevenson's eulogist. One conceives Mr. James a boy in velveteens looking fearfully at Stevenson playing at pirates.

There is nothing in Mr. Stevenson's sometimes writing essays, sometimes romances, and anon poems to mark him versatile beyond other authors. One dreads his continuing to do so, with so many books at his back, lest it means weakness rather than strength. He experiments too long; he is still a boy wondering what he is going to be. With Cowley's candor he tells us that he wants to write something by which he may be forever known. His attempts in this direction have been in the nature of trying different ways, and he always starts off whistling. Having gone so far without losing himself, he turns back to try another road. Does his heart fail him, despite his jaunty bearing, or is it because there is no hurry? Though all his books are obviously by the same hand, no living writer has come so near fame from so many different sides. Where is the man among us who could write another "**Virginibus Puerisque**," the most delightful volume for the hammock ever sung in prose? The poems are as exquisite as they are artificial. "**Jekyll and Hyde**" is the greatest triumph extant in Christmas literature of the morbid kind. The donkey on the Cevennes (how Mr. Stevenson belabored him!) only stands second to the "**Inland Voyage**." "**Kidnapped**" is the outstanding boy's book of its generation. "**The Black Arrow**" alone, to my thinking, is second class. We shall all be doleful if a marksman who can pepper his target with inners does not reach the bull's-eye. But it is quite time the great work was begun. The sun sinks while the climber walks round his mountain, looking for the best way up. (pp. 119-20)

The key-note of all Mr. Stevenson's writings is his indifference, so far as his books are concerned, to the affairs of life and death on which their minds are chiefly set. Whether man has an immortal soul interests him as an artist not a whit: what is to come of man troubles him as little as where man came from. He is a warm, genial writer, yet this is so strange as to seem inhuman. His philosophy is that we are but as the lighthearted birds. This is our moment of being; let us play the intoxicating game of life beautifully, artistically, before we fall dead from the tree. We all know it is only in his books that Mr. Stevenson can live this life. . . . A common theory is that Mr. Stevenson dreams an ideal life to escape from his own sufferings. This sentimental plea suits very well. The noticeable thing, however, is that the grotesque, the uncanny, holds his soul; his brain will only follow a colored clew. The result is that he is chiefly picturesque, and, to those who want more than art for art's sake, never satisfying. Fascinating as his verses are, artless in the perfection of art, they take no reader a step forward. The children of whom he sings so sweetly are cherubs without souls. It is not in poetry that Mr. Stevenson will give the great book to the world, nor will it, I think, be in the form of essays. Of late he has done nothing quite so fine as "**Virginibus Puerisque**," though most of his essays are gardens in which grow few weeds. Quaint in matter as in treatment, they are the best strictly literary essays of the day, and their mixture of tenderness with humor suggests Charles Lamb. (pp. 123-25)

The great work, if we are not to be disappointed, will be fiction. . . . Critics have said enthusiastically—for it is difficult to write of Mr. Stevenson without enthusiasm—that Allan Breck is as good as anything in Scott. Alan Breck is certainly a masterpiece, quite worthy of the greatest of all story-tellers, who, nevertheless, it should be remembered, created these rich side characters by the score, another before dinner-time. English critics have taken Alan to their hearts, and appreciate him thoroughly, the reason, no doubt, being that he is the character whom England acknowledges as the Scottish type. . . . [Though] Mr. Stevenson's best romance is Scottish, that is only, I think, because of his extraordinary aptitude for the picturesque. Give him any period in any country that is romantic, and he will soon steep himself in the kind of knowledge he can best turn to account. Adventures suit him best, the ladies being left behind; and so long as he is in fettle it matters little whether the scene be Scotland or Spain. The great thing is that he should now give to one ambitious book the time in which he has hitherto written half a dozen small ones. He will have to take existence a little more seriously—to weave broadcloth instead of lace. (pp. 126-28)

> *Gavin Ogilvie [pseudonym of J. M. Barrie], "Robert Louis Stevenson" (originally published in* British Weekly, *November 2, 1888), in his* An Edinburgh

Eleven: Pencil Portraits from College Life, *Lovell, Coryell & Company, 1888, pp. 115-28.*

### GEORGE MOORE   (essay date 1888)

I will state frankly that Mr. R. L. Stevenson never wrote a line that failed to delight me; but he never wrote a book. You arrive at a strangely just estimate of a writer's worth by the mere question: 'What is he the author of?' for every writer whose work is destined to live is the author of one book that outshines the other, and, in popular imagination, epitomises his talent and position. What is Shakespeare the author of? What is Milton the author of? What is Fielding the author of? . . . Mr. Stevenson is the author of shall I say, '**Treasure Island**,' or what?

I think of Mr. Stevenson as a consumptive youth weaving garlands of sad flowers with pale, weak hands, or leaning to a large plate-glass window, and scratching thereon exquisite profiles with a diamond pencil.

I do not care to speak of great ideas, for I am unable to see how an idea can exist, at all events can be great out of language; an allusion to Mr. Stevenson's verbal expression will perhaps make my meaning clear. His periods are fresh and bright, rhythmical in sound, and perfect realizations of their sense; in reading you often think that never before was such definiteness united to such poetry of expression; every page and every sentence rings of its individuality. Mr. Stevenson's style is over smart, well-dressed, shall I say, like a young man walking in the Burlington Arcade? Yes; I will say so, but, I will add, the most gentlemanly young man that ever walked in the Burlington. Mr. Stevenson is competent to understand any thought that might be presented to him, but if he were to use it, it would instantly become neat, sharp, ornamental, light, and graceful; and it would lose all its original richness and harmony. It is not Mr. Stevenson's brain that prevents him from being a thinker, but his style. (pp. 328-29)

> *George Moore, in an extract from his* Confessions of a Young Man, *Swan Sonnenschein, Lowrey & Co., 1888 (and reprinted in* Robert Louis Stevenson: The Critical Heritage, *edited by Paul Maixner, Routledge & Kegan Paul, 1981, pp. 328-30).*

### [MARGARET OLIPHANT]   (essay date 1889)

[It is] inappropriate to use the word joyful in any connection with the '**Master of Ballantrae**'; for a tale of more unmitigated gloom, with less admixture of any consolation human or divine, it has seldom been our lot to read. That it should have held the careless reader, who loves adventure it is true, but still more loves sunshine and cheerfulness and a happy ending, through the hard ordeal of serial publication, is a testimony to the power of sheer genius and literary force such as we have never known the like of. (p. 696)

Mr Stevenson can never be the founder, or even leader, of a new school. There is nothing in his art which can confer a new impulse. He may be copied, it is true; but as the chief thing in him to be copied is genius, and that is a thing incommunicable, we doubt whether his imitators will ever attain any importance. It is not that we should not all be the better of studying that fine, transparent, and marvellously lucid style which once was full of all manner of exquisite caprices and mannerisms, as is the fashion of youth, but now has settled down to its work as an incomparable medium for the telling of a terrible story, self-corrected of all the prettinesses which were becoming to lighter subjects, but would be totally out of place in such as this—but only that no mere style could commend the astonishingly painful fables in which Mr Stevenson is most strong, without that grip of power which must exist in the hand which exercises it, and which no training can confer. . . . Mr Stevenson may teach his contemporaries an old but never worn-out lesson, that there are more things in heaven and earth than have been yet dreamt of by any philosophy, and may lead them to search over again for themselves into the endless complications of human relationship when stripped of all the glosses of conventional representation, and even of natural feeling; which will be partly good and partly bad, as most human impulses are. (p. 697)

[The **'Master of Ballantrae'**] is a story of the relationship between two brothers, kept with great austerity of purpose wholly within the lines of its selected ground, but without any contrasting group of beings more happily inspired to relieve the readers mind—a characteristic which increases the intensity of the tale. The brothers themselves are indeed contrasted in a remarkable way, especially in the beginning of the story; but . . . [no character makes] us aware that hatred is not the rule of family life, or that relentings of the heart may still come in, however desperate may be the impulse of fraternal opposition. From beginning to end the two brothers of Durrisdeer hate each other with boundless and unchangeable animosity. There is no relenting on either side,—even less perhaps on that of the virtuous and otherwise tender-hearted brother [Henry] than on that of the reprobate [James]. We are made indeed to feel that his utter odiousness, falsehood, and selfishness have been revealed with such pitiless distinctness, that Henry hates the incarnation of every evil quality in James, whereas the other only hates his brother's person and the advantages of position which are in his eyes stolen from himself. . . . We are not, indeed, even when most carried on by the stream of events and excited by the sombre occurrences and wonderful pictures of the story, allowed at any time fully to approve, much less to entertain a thorough sympathy for the virtuous brother. No one in the group, indeed, except perhaps the teller of the tale, the subdued yet distinct personality of Ephraim Mackellar, the steward, secretary, and *doer* of the house, attracts our sympathy. The old lord is a pathetic figure, and the unfortunate lady who stands between the two brothers has traces of sense and spirit did it suit the narrator to keep her less determinedly in the background, but we can fix no affection on either. And the servants in the house, the country people, the dim society in the background, gentlemen and clowns, are all alike detestable. There is no generosity or kindness among them. Not one, until there comes into the house the keen-sighted spectator Mackellar, whose wits are marvellously sharpened (as always occurs in fiction) by the fact that he is bound to see through and record everything, does justice to Henry. He is always pushed aside by his own family, slandered outside, his every act misconstrued. This is perhaps one reason why the atmosphere of the book is so gloomy. There are abundance of beautiful sketches of Durrisdeer and the surrounding country. But in the story itself the sun never shines, the air is lowering and ominous, a constant consciousness of calamity, of wrong and injustice, brooding over the house.

In the midst of this gloom, however, the two prominent figures revealed to us are masterly. . . . The elder brother [James, Master of Ballantrae], . . . is the rebel not from any chivalrous principle nor faith in the Jacobite cause (for which neither of them would seem to have cared the least), but for vanity and restless ambition which prompted him to run the risk—great as it was—with a hope of self-aggrandisement not to be obtained in any other way. The very keynote is thus struck in a sordid tone. . . . We have had many gay prodigals before who injured and swindled all their belongings, yet never lost the power of charming and deceiving. It is indeed quite a common character in fiction. But there is something in the Master's charm which is original, as is his depravity. It deceives nobody, for he becomes odious and the most intolerable of burdens even to the father who spoilt him, and the woman who loved him; but, on the other hand, the good Mackellar who detests him cordially, finds a variety and companionableness in the fellow-traveller whom he is forced to accompany which almost makes up to him for the horror of a wintry voyage. This paradox has in it a strange humanity which raises it infinitely above the usual haunting spectre of the wicked son.

We are compelled to doubt, however, whether anything so odious as the Master could have retained in his downfall and deterioration any such reality of original brightness—and this not by an effort or for a purpose of evil: for he captivates Mackellar when it is entirely useless to do so, not with the object of making a tool of him, but in mere—to use such a word—wantonness of good-nature and pleasure in pleasing. ''You could not have been so bad a man if you had not had all the machinery of a good one,'' says Ephraim, not with Mr Stevenson's usual felicity of phrase; but the mixture of this curious fascination and of a strain of never quite extirpated nobleness in what is, taking it altogether, the most odious character in modern fiction, is one of the most remarkable conceptions of a ruined angel which has ever been given to the world.

Henry, the good brother, is scarcely less remarkable in his way, though he is less attractive. He is, to start with, ''a good solid lad,'' . . . but so self-restrained in his Scotch *dourness*, and so little apt to show his better side, that not even those who are most deeply indebted to him recognise his worth. . . . We think Mr Stevenson errs in making Henry so completely misunderstood. He despises the commonalty too much to give them a chance of showing how the race, sooner or later, always does recognise a good man. . . . [Henry is] unspeakably *dour*. He is magnanimous in every act, but in feeling never relents, always regarding his brother with remorseless antipathy. The shock of disappointment which is his only feeling when he ascertains that he has not killed him in the wild, sudden duel . . . is utterly unlike anything which we remember in fiction. It may be true to nature in such exceptional circumstances, though stubborn prejudice insists in our bosom that he should have been in some degree relieved as well as disappointed by his failure. Hatred, however, grows between the two by every meeting, along with, on the side of the innocent, a certain horror of belief in the wicked Master as in a man who walks the world protected by his infamy,—a man whom nothing can kill, in diabolical armour, sustained by all the powers of darkness. Henry's deterioration under this fixed idea, the madness produced in him by his brother's persecution, the horrible way in which his imagination and every thought are chained to the movements of his enemy, is deeply tragic, though so painful that we would fain struggle against it, and declare it to be impossible and untrue. In this respect Mr Stevenson must bear the brunt of his own singular tragical power,—for our heart revolts at the remorseless purpose which enfolds the good man in a web of such despair. (pp. 699-701)

[Some critics] cannot disabuse themselves of the idea that Mr Stevenson's book must be a book more or less for boys. We trust that this sombre tragedy will for ever do away with that delusion. It is very strong meat for men,—too strong, we fear, for many gentle readers. . . . Here all is uncompromising, tragic, and terrible, a deadly struggle all through, ending in a scene which for impressive horror has few equals in anything we know. Mr Stevenson scarcely unbends enough to permit his fascinated reader here and there a laugh. Humour is subdued, and fun is not in this winter's tale. He does not intend to cheer our hearts, but to congeal our blood. (p. 702)

*[Margaret Oliphant], in a review of "The Master of Ballantrae: A Winter's Tale," in* Blackwood's Edinburgh Magazine, *Vol. CXLVI, No. DCCLXXXIX, November, 1889, pp. 696-702.*

## GEORGE MOORE (essay date 1889)

So unanimous have been the journals of culture in their praise of Mr. Stevenson's genius, especially as manifested in [**'The Master of Ballantrae'**]. . . that I am almost constrained to apologise for the unseemliness of a perverse taste which refuses to accept even as excellent that which others are agreed to praise as sublime. My difficulty is certainly not inconsiderable; a man, not to say a critic, may very well write himself down an ass before he well knows where he is; and yet it seems sure when one considers it that all cannot be right with a book of adventure in which no very decided story is told. . . . In making this suggestion, I feel like the child in Hans Andersen's tale of the lying weavers who persuaded the King and his court that they were supplying them with garments of magical lightness when they had only persuaded them to walk about naked. When the child said: 'No father, the King and his court are walking about naked,' everybody recognised the truth and the weavers were stoned out of the town.

As naked of story as the King and his court were of clothes, **'The Master of Ballantrae'** seems in my eyes. No doubt diligent searching would reveal the workings of the plot . . . but it does not strike me as being any part of my critical duty to follow up the various zigzag lights which flickered across the pages. Suffice it to say for the condemnation of the book, that the story—if there is a story—is involved in many disjointed narratives. The author fails to set forth his scheme as he did in **'Treasure Island,'** as Defoe did in 'Robinson Crusoe,' as did, indeed, every writer who has written a book of adventures that has outlasted a generation. I have read all but the last thirty or forty pages—these the very strictest sense of critical duty could not induce me to toil through—without receiving one distinct impression concerning either 'The Master of Ballantrae,' his sons, the steward, Mr. MacKellar, their aims, or their achievements. Never does Mr. Stevenson grasp his story and do his will of it. His claim upon it is that of a white, languid hand, dreamily laid, and fitfully attempting to detain a gallant who would escape; ineffectively the hand is laid on the lappet and on the sleeve. (pp. 354-55)

Some three or four scenes, however, fix themselves upon my mind. I remember the pirate vessel and its captain, and this captain Mr. Stevenson has characterised very skilfully, but merely from the outside. It is a clever 'make-up': just such a one as a clever actor would invent; and the life on board is also excellently well invented. But nowhere any breath of design, nor are we held under spell of any imaginative impulse, creative or descriptive. We float on a painted ocean in a painted boat, among a little wretchedness of cardboard and tinsel. (p. 355)

As soon as we are quit of the pirate vessel the story is taken up by another person, and we drift into a mist of vapidities, we wade through dry deserts of barren artificialities, until at last we fall in with an oasis in the shape of a duel between two brothers. And upon my word the scene is very nicely done. Yes; it is very nice in the modern and in the original sense of the word. So nice is it, so beguiling is the art that there are times when it seems that Mr. Stevenson is rising to the situation, and is really investing his subject with some passion and dignity. But hardly has the impression entered the mind than it is destroyed by some more than usually irritating trick of phrase.

Again the story becomes a doll, and the author a dollmaker; an eyelash is added, and a touch of carmine is laid on the corner of the lips.

The duel done with, we drift again into vain seas of speech where windless sails of narrative hang helpless and death-like, and vague shapes, impersonal as unimagined hosts, people the gloom; and through the sepulchral weariness, the self-conscious style sounds like a fog horn. (pp. 355-56)

Mr. Stevenson's book is representative of the little morbid hankering after taste so prevalent is these days. It is as pretty as a drawing-room that has been recently re-decorated and arranged, according to the latest canons of fashion. I say recently decorated, because the style seems to me to betray the writer who does not think as he writes; but who elaborately translates what he has first written out in very common language into an artificial little tongue which he takes to be gentle; and through the emendations we often read the original text, as happens in inadequate translation from a foreign language. . . . In his desire for elegance, Mr. Stevenson, seems to have here strained grammar not a little: 'All would *redound* against poor Henry.' 'And sometimes repenting my *immixture* in affairs so private.' 'But we decided at last to *escalade* a garden wall.' 'The thought of a man's death—of his *deletion* from the world.' (p. 358)

These seem to me merely calculated niceties of phrase, and not sentences born of the context, as are those of the great masters . . . . **'The Master of Ballantrae'** is the weakest piece of writing of Mr. Stevenson's with which I am acquainted. The best is [**"A Lodging for the Night: A Story of François Villon"** from **'New Arabian Nights'**]. In this story, for the space of some ten or twelve pages he is strong, picturesque, and, what he never is elsewhere, original. In all his other work he suggests to me a sort of gracious attendant to Edgar Poe— a Ganymede limned by some eighteenth century artist in the pseudo classic draperies of that century. (pp. 358-59)

Contemporaneous criticism, whether it be made of praise or blame, is poor stuff indeed; all is unstable except genius, and genius is not immediately recognizable even by the most capable and best intentioned; its attributes have always remained undefinable. Yet there is a sin which the future pardons less easily than any other—vacuousness and affectation—for the sincere is the kingdom of the future, and it seems to me impossible to deny that **'The Master of Ballantrae'** is in exceeding degree vacuous and insincere. (p. 359)

*George Moore, in a review of "The Master of Ballantrae," in* Hawk: A Smart Paper for Smart People, *Vol. IV, November 5, 1889 (and reprinted in* Robert Louis Stevenson: The Critical Heritage, *edited by Paul Maixner, Routledge & Kegan Paul, 1981, pp. 354-59).*

## WILLIAM ERNEST HENLEY (poem date 1889)

*[The following poem recounts Henley's reaction to meeting Stevenson and illustrates the tendency of Stevenson's friends and critics to focus attention on his character and personality.]*

Thin-legged, thin-chested, slight unspeakably,
Neat-footed and weak-fingered: in his face—
Lean, large-boned, curved of beak, and touched with
    race,
Bold-lipped, rich-tinted, mutable as the sea,
The brown eyes radiant with vivacity—
There shines a brilliant and romantic grace,
A spirit intense and rare, with trace on trace
Of passion, impudence, and energy.
Valiant in velvet, light in ragged luck,
Most vain, most generous, sternly critical,
Buffoon and poet, lover and sensualist:
A deal of Ariel, just a streak of Puck,
Much Antony, of Hamlet most of all,
And something of the Shorter-Catechist.

> *William Ernest Henley, "Apparition," in his* A Book of Verses, *second edition, Scribner & Welford, 1889, p. 41.*

## A. CONAN DOYLE (essay date 1890)

Somewhere, I think that it is in the preface to **"Prince Otto,"** Mr. Stevenson remarks in his playful, half-earnest way, "I still purpose, by hook or crook, this book or the next, to launch a masterpiece." There are many who, on reading his last book, **"The Master of Ballantrae,"** may be inclined to think that he has carried out his promise. If a strong story, strongly told, full of human interest, and absolutely original in its situations, makes a masterpiece, then this may lay claim to the title. (p. 417)

Bearing the extreme fallibility of contemporary criticism before our minds, . . . we must weigh our words carefully before we speak of masterpieces. Yet, if the intense inward conviction of a sympathetic reader may count for anything, Mr. Stevenson had at the very time when he penned those words already given to the world one piece of work so complete in itself, and so symmetrically good, that it is hardly conceivable that it should ever be allowed to drop out of the very first line of English literature. **"The Pavilion on the Links"** marks the high-water mark of his genius, and is enough in itself, without another line, to give a man a permanent place among the great story-tellers of the race. Mr. Stevenson's style is always most pure, and his imagination is usually vivid, but in this one tale the very happiest use of words is wedded to the most thrilling, most concentrated interest. It would be difficult to name any tale of equal length in which four characters . . . stand out so strongly and so clearly—the more Titanic for the lurid background against which they move. (p. 418)

Yet if **"The Pavilion on the Links"** has claims to be considered a masterpiece, and may confidently hope to stand the merciless test of time, the same must also be conceded to **"Dr. Jekyl."** In fact, of the two, **"Dr. Jekyl,"** though slightly inferior as a work of art, has the greater certainty of longevity. The allegory within it would lengthen its days, even should new methods and changes of taste take the charm from the story. As long as man remains a dual being, as long as he is in danger of being conquered by his worse self, and, with every defeat, finds it the more difficult to make a stand, so long **"Dr. Jekyl"**

will have a personal and most vital meaning to every poor, struggling human being. . . . So craftily is the parable worked out that it never obtrudes itself upon the reader or clogs the action of the splendid story. It is only on looking back, after he has closed the book, that he sees how close is the analogy and how direct the application. On the whole, it can hardly be doubted that, whatever may become of his longer books, Mr. Stevenson's aspiration has been doubly realized, and that he has already produced not one, but two pieces of work which, test them as you will, still make good their claim to the title of masterpiece.

One cannot speak of **"Dr. Jekyl"** and of **"The Pavilion on the Links"** without alluding to the other short stories in the three series of **"The New Arabian Nights,"** **"The Merry Men,"** and **"The Dynamiter."** It must be confessed that they are very unequal. Were they all up to the standard of the two already discussed, or even up to the less exacting level of the first episode of **"The Suicide Club"** or of **"The Sire De Maletroit's Door,"** they might lay a claim to the highest place among such collections. Many of the tales, however, are slight and inconsequent to an exasperating extent. The brilliancy and vigor of the style will always carry the reader along, but the exiguous story leaves an empty and dissatisfied feeling behind it. It jars upon one to see so perfect an instrument applied to so inconclusive a purpose. Yet even when the tale, as a whole, misses its mark, there will always remain some strange, telling phrase, some new, vivid conception, so apt or so striking, that it is not to be dismissed from the memory. For example, the Mormon story in **"The Dynamiter"** might fade away as a connected tale, but how are we to forget the lonely fire in the valley, the white figure which dances and screams among the snow, or the horrid ravine in which the caravan is starved. It is just these sudden flashes of extraordinary lucidity and vigor which make it so very difficult to assess the value of such tales or to weigh them against others which may preserve a higher average, although they are never capable of rising to such extreme brilliancy. (pp. 418-19)

[Mr. Stevenson] can claim to have mastered the whole gamut of fiction. His short stories are good, and his long ones are good. On the whole, however, the short ones are the more characteristic, and the more certain to retain their position in English literature. The shorter effort suits his genius. With some choice authors, as with some rare vintages, a sip gives the real flavor better than a draught. It is eminently so with Mr. Stevenson. His novels have all conspicuous virtues, but they have usually some flaw, some drawback, which may weaken their permanent value. In the tales, or at least in the best of the tales, the virtues are as conspicuous as ever, but the flaws have disappeared. The merits of his short stories are more readily assessed too as his serious rivals in that field are few indeed. Poe, Nathaniel Hawthorne, Stevenson; those are the three, put them in what order you will, who are the greatest exponents of the short story in our language. . . .

**"Prince Otto"** is chronologically the first of Stevenson's longer works of fiction, and there is internal evidence that it was written at the time when he was most strongly under the influence of George Meredith. No one can read the German chapters of "Harry Richmond" and then turn to **"Prince Otto"** without feeling that the one has, in a distant and perfectly legitimate way, inspired the other. There is the same petty and formal court situated in some vague Teutonic cloudland, the same fine, diplomatic flavor about it, the same unreal and yet charming Dresden-china characters with their cross purposes, their quick wits, and their polished talk. In Meredith's book, however, we are on good terms with the inimitable Roy Richmond, before he brings us to this no-man's-land, and we have therefore one tangible person whom we know, and who furnishes us with some sort of a standard by which we may measure the others. We miss this in Stevenson's. For a time we cling to the English traveller, Sir John, as one person who is well within our own personal knowledge, and at first he justifies our trust; but, alas, Sir John becomes corrupted by the manners of Grunewald, and plunges off into aphorism and shadowdom. Even Gordon, the Scotch soldier of fortune, cannot bear up against the prevailing tone, but becomes as introspective and didactic as his sovereign lord. Hence it comes that there is a mist—iridescent, if you will, but none the less a mist—which hangs over the whole business and separates it from the work-a-day world, as we know it. The people are not human. They are bright, witty, perverse, wise, but they are not human. We do not see any of them clearly. We cannot take much personal interest in their fortunes, in their loves, or in their hates. (p. 419)

A very singular mental reaction took Mr. Stevenson from one pole to the other of imaginative work, from the subtle, dainty lines of **"Prince Otto"** to the direct, matter-of-fact, eminently practical and Defoe-like narratives of **"Treasure Island"** and of **"Kidnapped."** Both are admirable pieces of English, well conceived, well told, striking the reader at every turn with some novel situation, some new combination of words which just fits the sense as a cap fits a nipple. **"Treasure Island"** is perhaps the better story, while **"Kidnapped"** may have the longer lease of life as being an excellent and graphic sketch of the state of the Highlands after the last Jacobite insurrection. Each contains one novel and admirable character. Alan Breck in the one, and Long John in the other. Surely John Silver, with his face the size of a ham, and his little gleaming eyes like crumbs of glass in the centre of it, is the king of all seafaring desperadoes. Observe how the strong effect is produced in his case, seldom by direct assertion on the part of the story-teller, but usually by comparison, innuendo, or indirect reference. . . . John himself says, "There was some that was feared of Pew, and some that was feared of Flint; but Flint his own self was feared of me. Feared he was and proud. They was the roughest crew afloat was Flint's. The devil himself would have been feared to go to sea with them. Well, now, I tell you, I'm not a boasting man, and you seen yourself how easy I keep company; but when I was quartermaster, *lambs* wasn't the word for Flint's old buccaneers." So by a touch here and a hint there, there grows upon us the individuality of this smooth-tongued, ruthless, masterful, one-legged devil. He is to us not a creation of fiction, but an organic living reality with whom we have come into contact; such is the effect of the fine suggestive strokes with which he is drawn. And the buccaneers themselves, how simple and yet how effective are the little touches which indicate their ways of thinking and of acting. (p. 420)

There is still a touch of the Meredithian manner in these [adventure] books, different as they are in general scope from anything which he has attempted. There is the apt use of an occasional archaic or unusual word, the short, strong descriptions, the striking metaphors, the somewhat staccato fashion of speech. Yet in spite of this flavor, they have quite individuality enough to constitute a school of their own. Their faults, or rather perhaps their limitations, lie never in the execution, but entirely in the original conception. They picture only one side of life, and that a strange and exceptional one. There is

no female interest. We feel that it is an apotheosis of the boy's story—the penny number of our youth *in excelsis*. But it is all so good, so fresh, so picturesque, that, however limited its scope, it still retains a definite and well-assured place in literature. (pp. 420-21)

**"The Black Arrow"** can hardly rank with the books already mentioned. Whether it is that the telling of the story in the third person does not suit Mr. Stevenson's method so well as the personal narrative or whether it may be that the mediaeval atmosphere is uncongenial to him, the result is certainly very far below his usual level. In most of his writing, he appears to produce an effect without striving for it. Here, on the contrary, he strives continually, but never quite attains it. There is none of that air of precision and reality which marked its predecessors, nor is it worthy in any way to be compared to them. Here, however, as in his weaker tales, there are occasional vivid flashes which go far to leaven the whole. The picture of the unhappy man who runs down the glade amidst the laughter and the arrows of the concealed archers, is as good as it could be, and so is the sketch of the tumultuous flight, thundering down the road, and of the pursuer who hacks about with a broken sword, "cursing the while in a voice which was scarce human." In these touches we see the great writer, while what falls below may be well put down to stress of travel and fluctuation of health. The same may be said of **"The Wrong Box."** Fear, horror, surprise, are emotions on which he can work as few have ever done, but humor or its twin brother pathos have never yet shown themselves to be prominent among his gifts. Least of all is broad humor adapted to his genius. Besides, in this particular instance, there is a somewhat grim and repellant basis to the joke, which makes it just a little incongruous and ghastly. (p. 421)

**"The Master of Ballantrae,"** however, is a bird of another feather. It aims high, and falls very little short of the point aimed at. It may, perhaps, be less graphic than **"Kidnapped,"** and lack the continuous stir of **"Treasure Island,"** but it is broader in its scope, and freer in its handling than either of its predecessors. It contains one carefully elaborated and delicately drawn female figure in Alison Graeme, whose whole character, in its strength and in its perversity, is admirably natural and original. The male characters, too, are a stronger group than he has ever before brought together. . . . The minor characters are all good, from the pragmatical Mackellar, and the faithful Secundra Dass, down to the objectionable, piratical gentleman who burns sulphur, and shrieks "Hell! hell!" in his cabin. We do not seem to see the Sarah and her crew quite as plainly as we did the old Walrus, nor is there a Long John upon her ship's books. The whole story centres, however, round the diabolical master, and it is upon his cold, methodical, black-hearted villainy that it must chiefly depend for its effect. A more utterly ruthless scoundrel has never been depicted. (pp. 421-22)

Mr. Stevenson, like one of his own characters, has an excellent gift of silence. He invariably sticks to his story, and is not to be diverted off to discourse upon views of life or theories of the universe. A story-teller's business is to tell his story. If he wishes to air his views upon other matters he can embody them in small independent works, as Mr. Stevenson has done. Where a character gives vent to opinions which throw a light upon his own individuality that is a different thing, but it is surely intolerable that an author should stop the action of his story to give his own private views upon things in general. . . . Mr. Stevenson is too true an artist to fall into this error, with the result that he never loses his hold upon his reader's attention.

He has shown that a man may be terse and plain, and yet free himself from all suspicion of being shallow and superficial. No man has a more marked individuality, and yet no man effaces himself more completely when he sets himself to tell a tale. (p. 422)

> *A. Conan Doyle, "Mr. Stevenson's Methods in Fiction," in* The National Review, *London, Vol. XIV, No. 83, January, 1890, pp. 646-57.*

## [R. H. HUTTON]   (essay date 1891)

There is something wanting in Mr. Stevenson's work as a poet and we believe it to be that idealising gleam of insight which gives wholeness of effect, and especially satisfying finish of effect, to the subjects treated. There is not one of these ballads [in *Ballads*] which does not leave the reader with a sense of disappointment, or even of want. And yet now and then Mr. Stevenson seems to pass from the mere vivid narrator of life and action into the poet. Only he never sustains the poetic glow for long together; and, what is more, he never binds the whole ballad together by the significance (romantic or otherwise) which he gives to its whole drift and the impression it leaves behind. For example, in "**The Song of Rahéro: a Legend of Tahiti**," which is the first ballad in the book, there is plenty of vigour, plenty of movement, plenty of keen external vision but there is no wholeness uniting the separate parts. . . . Perhaps the finest and most truly poetical passage in this little volume of ballads is that in which the mood of Támatéa's mother changes from that of despair at her son's murder to that of thirst for vengeance. . . . For the most part, Mr. Stevenson is content with the outward adventure he describes, and passes over the motives and passions of men so lightly, that there is no wholeness, no singleness of conception, in his ballads. "**The Feast of Famine**" is very inferior even to "**The Song of Rahéro**," not only in this but in all other respects. The tale is not so lucidly told, and the close of it is feeble and ineffective. (p. 17)

[On] the whole, Mr. Stevenson's ballads have disappointed us. He does not give any poetical integrity to his subjects. The action, when action is described, is vigorously and vividly described; but the adventure overpowers the motive, and the resulting effect is one of adventure pieced together in verse. And seeing how high Mr. Stevenson can rise into the region of poetry when he has mused sufficiently on his theme, this is necessarily a disappointment to the reader. (p. 18)

> [*R. H. Hutton*], *"Mr. Stevenson's 'Ballads'," in* The Spectator (© *1891 by The Spectator), Vol. LXVI, No. 3262, January 3, 1891, pp. 17-18.*

## RICHARD LE GALLIENNE   (essay date 1892)

Mr. Stevenson's final fame will be that of an essayist, nearest and dearest fame of the prose-writer. Nearest and dearest, because the largest amount of selfish pleasure enters into the writing of essays, approaching, as it does, as nearly as possible to writing merely for writing's sake—as the lyric-poet just sings for singing's sake: the joy in the mere exercise of a faculty. . . . [The essayist] builds not, but he pitches his tent, lights his fire of sticks, and invites you to smoke a pipe with him over their crackling. While he dreamily chats, now here now there, of his discursive way of life; the sun has gone down, and you begin to feel the sweet influences of Pleiades.

At least, so it is with Mr. Stevenson, the Stevenson we care for most. And it seems certain that it is so he would be re-

membered of us; for this new volume of essays [*Across the Plains*] abounds in continual allusions to the joyous practice of the literary craft, plainly confiding to us that the pleasure of the reader and the writer in their "Stevenson" is mutual. (p. 462)

The business of real art [is, according to Stevenson,] "to give life to abstractions and significance and charm to facts." The latter half of this simple and suggestive statement is especially applicable to Mr. Stevenson's work, particularly in the case of such books as the *Travels with a Donkey,* and *The Inland Voyage.* Nothing could be more commonplace than the "adventures" which supply the theme, nothing less so than Mr. Stevenson's account of them. Looking ahead, sometimes, the road seems straight and uninteresting enough. Nothing in sight promises anything. So we are often inclined to feel when, slowly but surely, some well-worn fact, which we had ignored as quite unpromising, begins opening out beneath the eye of Mr. Stevenson's meditative imagination like a morning flower. He sees everything as if it had never been looked on before. Nothing has, so to say, gone cold for him. For him there is no such thing as merely *hard* fact. Each fact is a sensitive centre of infinite interest. And he makes us aware of this with a simplicity so natural that we are apt to forget that his record is anything more than a record of actual fact, that it is, as Mr. Pater would say, "the transcript of his sense of fact rather than the fact" itself. The expression which his themes thus take on is not that of mystery or wizardry, as in Coleridge or Miss Christina Rossetti; it is rather, to use a phrase of Mr. Stevenson's own, that of a "solemn freshness" born, I should say, of a constant habit—a co-operation between the philosophic and the poetic instincts—of relating particulars to generals. . . .

Of the essay, pure and simple, where the talk pursues its wayward round about a given theme, there are three or four examples in [*Across the Plains*] worthy to rank with anything in *Virginibus Puerisque.* Of these "**The Lantern-Bearers**" and "**Pulvis et Umbra**" are the most striking.

Mr. Stevenson has never touched a home-spun theme to finer issues than in "**The Lantern-Bearers**" [from *Virginibus Puerisque*]. His power, referred to above, of transfiguring facts into symbols, is here seen in its triumph. The strange passion of small boys for a bull's-eye is the humble text for a large and literally illuminative discourse on that poetry—more difficult than anything in Browning—other people's poetry; and on the true realism, which "always and everywhere is that of the poets." (p. 463)

The strong reminiscence of the style of Sir Thomas Browne in . . . ["**Pulvis et Umbra**"] . . . is appropriate to the quaint vision which is its theme, and is blent with Mr. Stevenson's own individual style no less successfully than Lamb used to blend such rich old colours in his own wonderful writing. [In] these two essays, and in similar essays in *Virginibus Puerisque,* Mr. Stevenson reminds us of the old prose masters in another quality than their Latinisation. He has the same high solemnity of accent, stirring one's heart by groups of simple words, wherein one seeks in vain for the secret of the magic. We have no writer of nobler English than Mr. Stevenson at present among us. Occasionally, one admits, the art peeps out a little, but it serves to remind us that we are in the hands of a writer who will not willingly give us less than his highest.

And then the all-pervading manliness, blowing like the breath of pinewoods through all Mr. Stevenson writes, the real feeling of *camaraderie* set up between him and his reader, and the still untroubled sanity of his simple philosophy of life. These are the root-qualities beneath all his charm of expression. (p. 464)

> *Richard Le Gallienne, in a review of "Across the Plains, with Other Memories and Essays" (reprinted by permission of The Society of Authors as the Literary Representatives of The Estate of Richard Le Gallienne), in* The Academy, *Vol. XLI, No. 1045, May 14, 1892, pp. 462-64.*

## [J. ST. LOE STRACHEY]  (essay date 1892)

[*The Wrecker*] is a tale of the sea, full of shipwreck, murder, and sudden death; but interwoven with this narrative of the strange and fateful things that happen "to the suthard of the line"—that region of romance where the rules that govern this work-a-day and prosaic world of ours are over-ridden and set at naught—are a series of studies of men and manners in Paris, in Edinburgh, and in San Francisco. In these studies, Mr. Stevenson shows a power of humorous and didactic delineation which, though very different in style and manner from that of Dickens, is yet, by its freshness, its bonhomie, and its ability to hold the reader spellbound over the most prosaic details, suggestive of Charles Dickens. Many of the characters and the incidents described are, we fully believe, destined to make an impression on the English-speaking world comparable to that produced by the creator of Mr. Micawber. Especially is this true of Pinkerton. Mr. Stevenson has drawn in him a "type" which is characteristically American,—the pushing businessman, whose heart is as true and his nature as generous, as his mercantile transactions are shady, and who joins an intense love of his country, and an eager desire for culture, with a willingness to do almost anything but hurt a woman or injure a friend, in order to further a bogus speculation or to advertise a worthless "product.". . . [The] alert, eager, boisterous [American] spirit has been caught and transferred to his pages by Mr. Stevenson with an art that is beyond admiration. Without losing a point of humour, he has contrived to paint a picture which cannot be said to be exaggerated, and which is throughout sympathetic and attractive. Even when Pinkerton is engaged in his most objectionable speculations, and is practising his worst barbarisms and vulgarities, our hearts warm to him. . . . (p. 132)

Judged, however, as a whole [*The Wrecker*] is not altogether satisfactory. The character-drawing and the impressions of American and French life are excellent; but the sensational story on which they are somewhat inartistically superimposed, though good enough as a piece of sensationalism, somehow seems out of place. Here, too, we must make a protest against the shambles business in the last chapter. It is quite unnecessarily brutal. Still, in spite of any and every defect that can be urged against it, the book is in the fullest sense a delightful one. . . . (p. 133)

> [*J. St. Loe Strachey*], *"Mr. Stevenson's New Story," in* The Spectator (© 1892 by The Spectator), *Vol. LXIX, No. 3343, July 23, 1892, pp. 132-33.*

## LIONEL JOHNSON  (essay date 1893)

No better plays have been written in prose than ["**Deacon Brodie**," "**Beau Austin**," and "**Admiral Guinea**"] since Sheridan wrote. I do not say in the proprieties of the stage, scenic convention, histrionic technicality, but in dramatic spirit, the force and life of dramatic literature. The conceptions are strongly simple; the style is neat, moving, natural; the characters are expressed by creatures of flesh and blood. Here is the stir of action, the business and reality of the world; here is romance, that touch of strangeness and delightful wonder which animates all the work of these authors. . . .

[These] plays are played out *somewhere;* most plays seem to be played out *anywhere.* Apart from the characters and the actions, we live a definite life while we read these plays. However tame the plots might have been, however weak the characters, our authors would still have given us this comfortable sense of being in a real place of a certain character. Here we are indebted to the sympathetic imagination, helped by historical insight, of the storyteller and the poet. A phrase here, a phrase there, conveys us to Georgian times, Edinburgh magnates, Tunbridge "quality": phrases pointed, speaking, charged with a positive genius of propriety. Further, each play has its internal greatness of interest, each deals with the fortunes of a soul, the life of a conscience—not, of course, with the magical concentration of Browning's art upon this single interest, but rather letting a lively train of incident go forward till some sudden collision of motives, or collapse of pretences, or flash of light, takes place. . . .

["**Deacon Brodie**"], which is of some length, with plenty of admirable characters and bustling scenes, is finely melodramatic—if by that word we may mean a bold presentation, to eye and ear, of moving incident and speech. The thing is not dainty, delicate, but forcible and emphatic. Thieves' slang, sometimes of a very modern sound, exciting collisions and situations, infinite movement and animation, help to make the piece lively; you feel the external air of adventure and desperate attempts, and, beneath it all, the drama of moral sentiment and spiritual strife. But these are not obtruded.

"**Beau Austin**" is dainty and delicate. Everything about it is modish, of an exquisite mannerism. . . . The piece half makes itself. But its authors have displayed the neatest, brightest fancy; the familiar figures are alive once more, neither in Dresden nor in Chelsea, but in flesh and blood. The story is a version of Richardson's masterpiece; we have a splendid Lovelace and a divine Clarissa. . . .

The whole piece goes delightfully; every character, great or small, is in keeping with the time and place. . . . It is full of grace and wit, flowing on and flashing out, freshening and kindling the whole play. It is with Beau Austin himself that doubts begin and end; is he quite so natural as one would like to think him? Lovelace is acceptable, because Richardson chose to give him genius; a man so brilliant in accomplishments of mind, no less than in external graces, stands outside the common ranks. But Beau Austin is less of a Lovelace than of a Beau Brummel; we do not perfectly acquiesce in his sudden yielding to Fenwick's appeal. (p. 277)

Pope was wont to protest that you could not tell a writer by his style. But, apart from the appearance of old Pew, and the buccaneer element, the smell of the sea, and the clash of cutlasses, it is hard not to trace the hand of Mr. Stevenson dominant in "**Admiral Guinea**." . . .

Admiral Guinea, Captain Gaunt, once slave-dealer, now "sinner saved," . . . is a powerful character. Hard to the world, because to himself; haunted by the thought of his past villainies, which killed his loved wife; agonised with care and fear for his child Arethusa; a romantic, passionate heart under the outward harshness and austerity. Old Pew has no less of the blackguard about him than before. . . .

These are three enchanting pieces, worthy of their authors and of the stage. (p. 278)

Lionel Johnson, in a review of "Three Plays," in The Academy, n.s. Vol. XLIII, No. 1091, April 1, 1893, pp. 277-78.

## LIONEL JOHNSON (essay date 1893)

Of no living man, and of no lately dead man, can we say that he is classic: simply because the judgment of other ages, and often of other races, has not been passed upon him. But some living men are probationary classics, classics on approval: such is Mr. Stevenson. In him I find a modern Addison, with the old graces and the old humours. True, he is definitely "romantic": he loves the stir of adventure, the whole business of the whole world: he is an ardent enthusiast for tasting many kinds of life. But he has no fierce, feverish brilliance and rapidity; not like those vague persons who have been called "unattached Christians," he is full of attachment to humanity, and is not satisfied with making hasty, clever, soulless sketches of mankind. Wherever he goes, he learns to know and love the heart, the soul, the true and active nature, of the country and the country men. . . . Mr. Stevenson shall we say that he is all cordiality, all sympathy, all comprehension? It is hard to find the exact expression for that power of reaching through the externals to the interior of things: of discerning in and by the outward aspects and manners of men their very selves and natures. Mr. Stevenson so wins upon us by his minutely appropriate style, that we cannot fail to see what he would be at; what it is in these peoples and places—Scotch be they, or Samoan—that touches him, rouses his human interest and concern. . . . Mr. Stevenson is full of the movement, the animation of life. With no forced phrases, no calculated recklessness or brutality of speech, he takes us, not into the landscape and setting of men's lives, but into their secret. He writes, to outward view, with no eye but for his own pure personal pleasure: not with an eye to an astonished or shocked or captivated public.

In these *Island Nights' Entertainments* he moves among South Sea traders, natives, missionaries, among the unhomely wonders of nature, among the ways, superstitions, aspects, employments, of a strange world, yet easily and quietly: his creatures, native or European, in their various stations, are vicious or virtuous, or both, honourable or dishonourable, pleasant or unpleasant, just as men are in Edinburgh or London. . . . The passions of love and hate, and greed and cruelty and spite—universal things—move us upon the beach of Falesá [in the story **"The Beach of Falesá"**] as upon the plain of Troy; I never met Wiltshire, or Uma, or Tarleton the missionary, or Case their enemy, but I have no difficulty in accepting them. But the enchantments and prodigies of the other stories, even when mingled, as in **"The Bottle Imp,"** with plenty of common human feeling, perplex and confound me. Native superstitions and beliefs are one thing, but these magical affairs are another. Unless you slip into the writer's humour, and are willing to believe in them while you read them, they simply fail to have any stuff and substance. To most readers the seas and islands and people in themselves are strange and enchanting: the chiefs, the women, the native ways, delight us; to bring magic bottles and all manner of wizardry into scenes already wonderful is something of a bathos. . . . This is not to say that Mr. Stevenson's two fantastic stories are not happily told. They are told with singular felicity. But **"The Beach of Falesá"** gives its true value to the book. This, told in the forcible words of

a trader, direct, clear, unhesitating, is a piece of the most admirable narrative: it has two or three of the best dramatic scenes that Mr. Stevenson has ever written. It is a somewhat bloody and breezy narrative; but, without weakening its vigour, Mr. Stevenson prevents it from being brutal, by touches of that unique style with which, as it were, he brings the ugliest and coarsest things into the pale of beauty, and gives to all the rough lives and places of the world the consecration, not of a brutal or of a silly sentiment, but of an honest and sincere humanity. (pp. 473-74)

Lionel Johnson, in a review of "Island Nights' Entertainments," in The Academy, Vol. XLIII, No. 1100, June 3, 1893, pp. 473-74.

## RICHARD LE GALLIENNE (essay date 1894)

A loyal admiration may occasionally, I trust, permit itself a loyal fault-finding. Messrs. Stevenson and Osbourne's new romance, *The Ebb-Tide,* demands loyalty in both directions. Part I. seems to me good, sound adventure. It holds us with the true Stevensonian spell, a tale 'of marvellous oceans swept by fateful wings.' But when we turn from it, in breathless expectation, to Part II., the change is abrupt and painful. The spell seems suddenly to have failed, and the more we read of the insufferable, impossible Attwater, prig and pearl-fisher, university man and evangelist, expert alike with his Bible and his Winchester, the unreality increases. Even the three men whose fortunes had fascinated us in Part I. seem to lose their humanity so soon as the *Farallone* glides into the still waters of the coral-island lagoon. . . . In the self-conscious atmosphere of this fairy island none of the men, who up till now have borne themselves with a certain vigour and individuality, seem any longer able to be themselves. The little Cockney [Huish] alone preserves something of his original character. . . . It is difficult to understand Mr. Stevenson's intention in [making this change in Part II]. Did he get a little tired of his story, and determine, in a whimsical mood, to wind it up in a spirit of pure farce—just as once, the reader may remember, he mischievously let the sawdust out of his Prince Florizel of Bohemia?

I have other faults to find with *The Ebb-Tide*: the extreme self-consciousness of some of the writing, and the stilted style of some of the conversations. These latter are mainly in the mouths of Robert Herrick, another university man fallen on evil days and harbouring with strange bedfellows, and, of course, Attwater, who always talks like a book—one of Mr. Meredith's. (pp. 146-47)

Apart from Herrick's occasionally stilted talk, and particularly Attwater's—who, however, is so unnatural as a whole that, so to say, it would be still more unnatural if his talk were not so too—Mr. Stevenson himself is a little too consciously the literary artist here and there in this new book. If the book were anything but a book of adventure, one would not mind. I am far from missing the charm of a certain air of literary self-consciousness in its right place; but in dealing with rough seamen and perils upon the high seas this literary daintiness strikes a somewhat incongruous note. . . . (p. 148)

However, the first part of *The Ebb-Tide* is as thrilling a piece of narrative as Mr. Stevenson has written; and one or two of the situations—such as that where Huish and the captain drink champagne all day long in the cabin, and leave the ship to look after itself; or the moment when the fraud in the champagne cargo is discovered—are as dramatic as anything Mr. Stevenson has done. (p. 149)

Richard Le Gallienne, "R. L. Stevenson" (1894), in his Retrospective Reviews: A Literary Log, 1893-1895, Vol. II (reprinted by permission of Dodd, Mead & Company, Inc.), Dodd, Mead, 1896, pp. 215-20.

## ARTHUR SYMONS (essay date 1894)

[*Symons was one of the first commentators to caution critics regarding the negative repercussions of overpraising Stevenson. The following, written at the height of Stevenson's fame, calls on critics to judge Stevenson objectively. In attempting to present a fair estimation of his importance, Symons ranks Stevenson with Henry David Thoreau and George Borrow among "the men of secondary order in literature."*]

Within a few days after the news of [Stevenson's] death reached England, English newspapers vied with each other in comparing him with Montaigne, with Lamb, with Scott, with Defoe; and he has been not merely compared, but preferred. Uncritical praise is the most unfriendly service a man can render to his friend; but here, where so much praise is due, may one not try to examine a little closely just what those qualities are which call for praise, and just what measure of praise they seem to call for?

Stevenson somewhere describes certain of his own essays as being "but the readings of a literary vagrant." And, in truth, he was always that, a literary vagrant; it is the secret of much of his charm, and of much of his weakness. He wandered, a literary vagrant, over the world, across life, and across literature, an adventurous figure, with all the irresponsible and irresistible charm of the vagabond. To read him is to be for ever setting out on a fresh journey, along a white, beckoning road, on a blithe spring morning. Anything may happen, or nothing; the air is full of the gaiety of possible chances. And in this exhilaration of the blood, unreasoning, unreasonable, as it is, all the philosophies merge themselves into those two narrow lines which the **"Child's Garden of Verses"** piously encloses for us:

> The world is so full of a number of things,
> I am sure we should all be as happy as kings.

It is the holiday mood of life that Stevenson expresses, and no one has ever expressed it with a happier abandonment to the charm of natural things. In its exquisite exaggeration, it is the optimism of the invalid, due to his painful consciousness that health, and the delights of health, are what really matter in life. (pp. 77-8)

His art, in all those essays and extravagant tales into which he put his real self, is a romantic art, alike in the essay on **"Walking Tours"** [from **"Virginibus Puerisque"**] and in the **"Story of the Young Man with the Cream Tarts."** Stevenson was passionately interested in people; but there was something a trifle elvish and uncanny about him, as of a bewitched being who was not actually human, had not actually a human soul, and whose keen interest in the fortunes of his fellows was really a vivid curiosity, from one not quite of the same nature as those about him. He saw life as the most absorbing, the most amusing, game; or, as a masquerade, in which he liked to glance behind a mask, now and again, on the winding and coloured way he made for himself through the midst of the pageant. It was only in his latest period that he came to think about truth to human nature; and even then it was with the picturesqueness of character, with its adaptability to the humorous freaks of incident, that he was chiefly concerned.

He was never really himself except when he was in some fantastic disguise. From **"The Pavilion on the Links"** to **"Dr Jekyll and Mr Hyde,"** he played with men and women as a child plays with a kaleidoscope; using them freakishly, wantonly, as colours, sometimes as symbols. In some wonderful, artificial way, like a wizard who raises, not living men from the dead, but the shadows of men who had once died, he calls up certain terrifying, but not ungracious, phantoms, who frisk it among the mere beings of flesh and blood, bringing with them the strangest "airs from heaven or blasts from hell." No; in the phrase of Beddoes, Stevenson was "tired of being merely human." Thus there are no women in his books, no lovers; only the lure of hidden treasures and the passion of adventure. It was for the accidents and curiosities of life that he cared, for life as a strange picture, for its fortunate confusions, its whimsical distresses, its unlikely strokes of luck, its cruelties, sometimes, and the touch of madness that comes into it at moments. For reality, for the endeavour to see things as they are, to represent them as they are, he had an impatient disregard. These matters did not interest him.

But it is by style, largely, we are told, that Stevenson is to live, and the names of Lamb and of Montaigne are called up on equal terms. Style, with Stevenson, was certainly a constant preoccupation. . . . He was resolved from the first to reject the ready-made in language, to combine words for himself, as if no one had ever used them before; and, with labour and luck, he formed for his use a singularly engaging manner of writing, full of charm, freshness, and flexibility, and with a certain human warmth in the words. . . . But, in comparing him with the great names of literature, we cannot but feel all the difference, and all the meaning of the difference, between a great intellect and a bright intelligence. The lofty and familiar homeliness of Montaigne, the subtle and tragic humour of Lamb, are both on a far higher plane than the gentle and attractive and whimsical confidences of Stevenson. And, underlying what may seem trifling in both, there is a large intellectual force, a breadth of wisdom, which makes these two charming writers not merely charming, but great. Stevenson remains charming; his personality, individual and exquisite as it was, had not the strength and depth of greatness. And, such as it was, it gave itself to us completely; there was no sense, as there is with the really great writers, of reserve power, of infinite riches to draw upon. Quite by himself in a certain seductiveness of manner, he ranks, really, with Borrow and Thoreau, with the men of secondary order in literature, who appeal to us with more instinctive fascination than the very greatest; as a certain wayward and gipsy grace in a woman thrills to the blood, often enough, more intimately and immediately than the august perfection of classic beauty. He is one of those writers who speak to us on easy terms, with whom we may exchange affections. . . . Stevenson awakens something of the eternal romance in the bosom even of the conventional. It is a surprising, a marvellous thing to have done; and to afford such delights, to call forth such responsive emotions, is a boon that we accept with warmer rejoicing than many more solid gifts. But to be wine and song to us for a festive evening is, after all, not the highest form of service or the noblest ministration of joy. . . . Stevenson captivates the heart: that is why he is in such danger of being wronged by indiscriminate eulogy. Let us do him justice; he would have wished only for justice. It is a dishonour to the dead if we strive to honour their memory with anything less absolute than truth. (pp. 78-82)

Arthur Symons, "Robert Louis Stevenson" (1894), in his Studies in Prose and Verse (reprinted by permission of the Literary Estate of Arthur Symons), Dutton, 1904, pp. 77-82.

## RICHARD LE GALLIENNE   (essay date 1895)

No writer had ever a firmer hold on the realities of human nature and human conduct [than Stevenson in *The Amateur Emigrant*]. Describing [one] of his fellow-travellers, a certain Mackay, full of utilitarian social ideals and cheap 'schoolbook materialism,' he says: 'He could see nothing in the world but money and steam-engines. He did not know what you meant by the word happiness. He had forgotten the simple emotions of childhood, and perhaps never encountered the delights of youth. He believed in production, that useful figment of economy, as if it had been real, like laughter.' *As if it had been real, like laughter!* There, in a sentence, is Stevenson's view of life. The spiritual good of his books, apart from their literary charm, is in his robust insistence on the realities of the simple human emotions. No writer ever loved a 'man,' or, for that matter, a woman, more whole-heartedly, wherever he found them; and no writer had less to say to the sham society puppetry that usurp those noble descriptions. Children and mothers, pretty young women and brave men, he was always on the look-out for these—with, might one say his 'wild, accommodating eye,' though the eye belongs to a strapping young Irishwoman, in whose casual kindness to a handsome, but ragged, young stowaway, Stevenson, as usual, sees a whole heart-moving history. (pp. 218-19)

This *Amateur Emigrant,* indeed, is inferior to none of Mr. Stevenson's writings in its *verve,* its whim, its humanity, and general charm. To my thinking, it is even better than the samples of it already published in *Across the Plains,* and it is quite rich in patches of the true Stevensonian purple. . . . (p. 219)

[Stevenson] will only be forgotten when Hazlitt and Lamb have fallen beneath the poppy of oblivion; and some of us dare to think, without irreverence, that there is that in his writing which comes nearer to 'the great heart of man' he loved so well than the writing of his great forerunners; for sometimes it seems that he deals with weightier matters in no less winning and masterly a fashion. (p. 220)

Richard Le Gallienne, "R. L. Stevenson" (1895), in his Retrospective Reviews: A Literary Log, 1893-1895, Vol. II (reprinted by permission of Dodd, Mead & Company, Inc.), Dodd, Mead, 1896, pp. 215-20.

## WALTER RALEIGH   (essay date 1895)

Stevenson is best where he shows most restraint, and his peculiarly rich fancy, which ran riot at the suggestion of every passing whim, gave him, what many a modern writer sadly lacks, plenty to restrain, an exuberant field for self-denial. Here was an opportunity for art and labour; the luxuriance of the virgin forests of the West may be clipped and pruned for a lifetime with no fear of reducing them to the trim similitude of a Dutch garden. His bountiful and generous nature could profit by a spell of training that would emaciate a poorer stock. (p. 17)

To a man with Stevenson's live and searching imagination, every work of human hands became vocal with possible associations. Buildings positively chattered to him; the little inn at Queensferry, which even for Scott had meant only mutton and currant jelly, with cranberries 'vera weel preserved,' gave him the cardinal incident of *Kidnapped.* How should the world ever seem dull or sordid to one whom a railway-station would take into its confidence, to whom the very flagstones of the pavement told their story, in whose mind 'the effect of night, of any flowing water, of lighted cities, of the peep of day, of ships, of the open ocean,' called up 'an army of anonymous desires and pleasures?' To have the 'golden-tongued Romance with serene lute' for a mistress and familiar is to be fortified against the assaults of tedium.

His attitude towards the surprising and momentous gifts of life was one prolonged passion of praise and joy. There is none of his books that reads like the meditations of an invalid. He has the readiest sympathy for all exhibitions of impulsive energy; his heart goes out to a sailor, and leaps into ecstasy over a generous adventurer or buccaneer. . . . A high and simple courage shines through all his writings. (pp. 21-4)

Stevenson's life was a grave devotion to the education of himself in the art of writing. (p. 31)

[The artist in words] must have two things: a fine sense, in the first place, of the sound, value, meaning, and associations of individual words, and next, a sense of harmony, proportion, and effect in their combination. (pp. 33-4)

Stevenson had both these sensitive capabilities in a very high degree. His careful choice of epithet and name have even been criticised as lending to some of his narrative-writing an excessive air of deliberation. His daintiness of diction is best seen in his earlier work; thereafter his writing became more vigorous and direct, fitter for its later uses, but never unillumined by felicities that cause a thrill of pleasure to the reader. Of the value of words he had the acutest appreciation. *Virginibus Puerisque,* his first book of essays, is crowded with happy hits and subtle implications conveyed in a single word. (pp. 34-5)

His loving regard for words bears good fruit in his later and more stirring works. He has a quick ear and appreciation for live phrases on the lips of tramps, beachcombers, or Americans. (p. 36)

[The] praise of Stevenson's style cannot be exhausted in a description of his use of individual words or his memory of individual phrases. His mastery of syntax, the orderly and emphatic arrangement of words in sentences, a branch of art so seldom mastered, was even greater. And here he could owe no great debt to his romantic predecessors in prose. . . . Stevenson harked further back [than Dumas and Scott] for his models, and fed his style on the most vigorous of the prose writers of the seventeenth and early eighteenth centuries, the golden age of English prose. (pp. 38-9)

It was from writers of Harrington's time and later that Stevenson learned something of his craft. Bunyan and Defoe should be particularly mentioned, and that later excellent worthy, Captain Charles Johnson, who compiled the ever-memorable *Lives of Pirates and Highwaymen.* Mr. George Meredith is the chief of those very few modern writers whose influence may be detected in his style. (pp. 39-40)

Those touches of archaism that are so frequent with him, the slightly unusual phrasing, or unexpected inversion of the order of words, show a mind alert in its expression, and give the sting of novelty even to the commonplaces of narrative or conversation. A nimble literary tact will work its will on the phrases of current small-talk, remoulding them nearer to the heart's desire, transforming them to its own stamp. This was what Stevenson did, and the very conversations that pass between his characters have an air of distinction that is all his own. His books are full of brilliant talk—talk real and convincing enough in its purport and setting, but purged of the languors and fatuities of actual commonplace conversation. It is an enjoyment like that to be obtained from a brilliant exhibition of fencing, clean and dexterous, to assist at the talking bouts of David Balfour and Miss Grant, Captain Nares and Mr. Dodd, Alexander Mackellar and the Master of Ballantrae, Prince Otto and Sir John Crabtree, or those wholly admirable pieces of special pleading to be found in *A Lodging for the Night* and *The Sire de Malétroit's Door* [in *New Arabian Nights*]. (pp. 40-2)

[The highest note of Stevenson's] stories is not drama, nor character, but romance. In one of his essays he defines the highest achievement of romance to be the embodiment 'of character, thought, or emotion in some act or attitude that shall be remarkably striking to the mind's eye.' His essay on Victor Hugo [*Victor Hugo's Romances* in *Familiar Studies of Men and Books*] shows how keenly conscious he was that narrative romance can catch and embody emotions and effects that are for ever out of the reach of the drama proper, and of the essay or homily, just as they are out of the reach of sculpture and painting. (p. 46)

Stevenson's work is a gallery of romantic effects that haunt the memory. Some of these are directly pictorial: the fight in the round-house on board the brig *Covenant;* the duel between the two brothers of Ballantrae in the island of light thrown up by the candles from that abyss of windless night; the flight of the Princess Seraphina through the dark mazes of the wood,—all these, although they carry with them subtleties beyond the painter's art, yet have something of picture in them. But others make entrance to the corridors of the mind by blind and secret ways, and there awaken the echoes of primaeval fear. The cry of the parrot—'Pieces of eight'—the tapping of the stick of the blind pirate Pew as he draws near the inn-parlour, and the similar effects of inexplicable terror wrought by the introduction of the blind catechist in *Kidnapped,* and of the disguise of a blind leper in *The Black Arrow,* are beyond the reach of any but the literary form of romantic art. (pp. 54-5)

The animating principle or idea of Stevenson's longer stories is never to be found in their plot, which is generally built carelessly and disjointedly enough around the central romantic situation or conception. The main situation in *The Wrecker* is a splendid product of romantic aspiration, but the structure of the story is incoherent and ineffective, so that some of the best passages in the book—the scenes in Paris, for instance—have no business there at all. The story in *Kidnapped* and *Catriona* wanders on in a single thread, like the pageant of a dream, and the reader feels and sympathises with the author's obvious difficulty in leading it back to the scene of the trial and execution of James Stewart. *The Master of Ballantrae* is stamped with a magnificent unity of conception, but the story illuminates that conception by a series of scattered episodes. That lurid embodiment of fascinating evil [James, Master of Ballantrae], part vampire, part Mephistopheles, whose grand manner and heroic abilities might have made him a great and good man but for 'the malady of not wanting,' is the light and meaning of the whole book. . . . Stevenson never came nearer than in this character to the sublime of power.

But an informing principle of unity is more readily to be apprehended in the shorter stories, and it is a unity not so much of plot as of impression and atmosphere. His islands, whether situated in the Pacific or off the coast of Scotland, have each of them a climate of its own, and the character of the place seems to impose itself on the incidents that occur, dictating subordination or contrast. The events that happen within the limits of one of these magic isles could in every case be cut off from the rest of the story and framed as a separate work of art. The long starvation of David Balfour on the island of Earraid, the sharks of crime and monsters of blasphemy that break the peace of the shining tropical lagoons in *Treasure Island* and *The Ebb Tide* . . .—these imaginations are plainly generated by the scenery against which they are thrown; each is in some sort the genius of the place it inhabits.

In his search for the treasures of romance, Stevenson adventured freely enough into the realm of the supernatural. When he is handling the superstitions of the Scottish people, he allows his humorous enjoyment of their extravagance to peep out from behind the solemn dialect in which they are dressed. . . . *The Strange Case of Dr. Jekyll and Mr. Hyde* and the story of *The Bottle Imp* are manufactured bogeys, that work on the nerves and not on the heart, whatever may be said by those who insist on seeing allegory in what is only dream-fantasy. The supernatural must be rooted deeper than these in life and experience if it is to reach an imposing stature: the true ghost is the shadow of a man. And Stevenson shows a sense of this in two of his very finest stories, the exquisite idyll of *Will o' the Mill* and the grim history of *Markheim* [from *The Merry Men and Other Tales and Fables*]. Each of these stories is the work of a poet, by no means of a goblin-fancier. (pp. 55-60)

His genius, like the genius of Nathaniel Hawthorne, was doubly rich in the spirit of romance and in a wise and beautiful morality. But the irresponsible caprices of his narrative fancy prevented his tales from being the appropriate vehicles of his morality. He has left no work—unless the two short stories mentioned above be regarded as exceptions—in which romance and morality are welded into a single perfect whole, nothing that can be put beside *The Scarlet Letter* or *The Marble Faun* for deep insight and magic fancy joined in one. (p. 62)

For the appreciation of morality in [a wide] sense high gifts of imagination are necessary. Shakespeare could never have drawn Macbeth, and thereby made apparent the awfulness of murder, without some sympathy for the murderer—the sympathy of intelligence. These gifts of imagination and sympathy belong to Stevenson in a very high degree; in all his romances there are gleams from time to time of wise and subtle reflection upon life, from the eternal side of things, which shine the more luminously that they spring from the events and situations with no suspicion of homily. (p. 64)

The wide outlook on humanity that expresses itself in [many] passages . . . is combined in Stevenson with a vivid interest in, and quick appreciation of, character. The variety of the characters that he has essayed to draw is enormous, and his successes, for the purposes of his stories, are many. Yet with all this, the number of lifelike portraits, true to a hair, that are to be found in his works is very small indeed. In the golden glow of romance, character is always subject to be idealised; it is the effect of character seen at particular angles and in special lights, natural or artificial, that Stevenson paints; he does not attempt to analyse the complexity of its elements, but boldly projects into it certain principles, and works from those. It has often been said of Scott that he could not draw a lady who was young and beautiful; the glamour of chivalry blinded him, he lowered his eyes and described his emotions and aspirations. Something of the same disability afflicted Stevenson in the presence of a ruffian. He loved heroic vice only less than he loved heroic virtue, and was always ready to idealise his villains, to make of them men who, like the Master of Ballantrae, 'lived for an idea.' (pp. 66-8)

One character must never be passed over in an estimate of Stevenson's work. The hero of his longest work is not David Balfour, in whom the pawky Lowland lad, proud and precise, but 'a very pretty gentleman,' is transfigured at times by traits that he catches, as narrator of the story, from its author himself. But Alan Breck Stewart is a greater creation, and a fine instance of that wider morality that can seize by sympathy the soul of a wild Highland clansman. 'Impetuous, insolent, unquenchable,' . . . Alan Breck is one of the most lovable characters in all literature; and his penetration . . . blossoms into the most delightful reflections upon men and things. (pp. 71-2)

A great part of Stevenson's subtle wisdom of life finds its readiest outlet in his essays. In these, whatever their occasion, he shows himself the clearest-eyed critic of human life, never the dupe of the phrases and pretences, the theories and conventions, that distort the vision of most writers and thinkers. He has an unerring instinct for realities, and brushes aside all else with rapid grace. (pp. 72-3)

[His] sense of the realities of the world,—laughter, happiness, the simple emotions of childhood, and others,—makes Stevenson an admirable critic of those social pretences that ape the native qualities of the heart. (p. 74)

[A profound] sense of the realities of life and death gives the force of a natural law to the pathos of *Old Mortality* [from *Memories and Portraits*]. . . . The whole description, down to the marvellous quotation from Bunyan that closes it, is one of the sovereign passages of modern literature; the pathos of it is pure and elemental. . . . (p. 76)

[Lastly], Stevenson excels at what is perhaps the most delicate of literary tasks and the utmost test, where it is successfully encountered, of nobility,—the practice, namely, of self-revelation and self-delineation. To talk much about oneself with detail, composure, and ease, with no shadow of hypocrisy and no whiff or taint of indecent familiarity, no puling and no posing,—the shores of the sea of literature are strewn with the wrecks and forlorn properties of those who have adventured on this dangerous attempt. But a criticism of Stevenson is happy in this, that from the writer it can pass with perfect trust and perfect fluency to the man. He shares with Goldsmith and Montaigne, his own favourite, the happy privilege of making lovers among his readers. (pp. 77-8)

*Walter Raleigh, in his* Robert Louis Stevenson, *Edward Arnold, 1895, 79 p.*

### [JOSEPH JACOBS]    (essay date 1896)

Stevenson's **'Weir of Hermiston'** certainly promised to be the best of his novels; yet it is impossible to tell how the promise would have been carried out. . . .

The fact is that the development of the story does not reach a point at which Stevenson would have competed with the great masters of romance. His theme was to have been that of Brutus condemning his son, the Brutus in this particular instance being the hanging Lord Braxfield, known in Scotch gossip. This was

to have been led up to by a tale of seduction and murder, and followed by the breaking of the gaol in which the condemned hero was confined. As the story at present exists it breaks off before seduction or murder, condemnation or rescue. Under these circumstances it is impossible to say what increase of mastery Stevenson had obtained during the last weeks of life in the delineation of the acuter phases of human passion.

Of the hanging judge, however, we see enough to feel confident that he would have proved a masterpiece. The coarse dignity and power of the man are brought out sufficiently well in the prologue to make one feel confident that the scene of the trial, if it could have been given some show of *vraisemblance* [verisimilitude], would have been effective. But could it? Such a violation of the decencies of justice as the condemnation of a son by his own father would no more have been possible in Scotland than anywhere else in modern times. Stevenson was aware of this difficulty, and was casting about for a mode of overcoming it. . . .

The weakness of the book consists in its villain, "the young fool advocate," who was to have seduced the heroine and to have been slain by the younger Hermiston. But he is too facile and flimsy a rogue to impart tragic intensity to any part of the plot hinging on him. It would have taxed all Stevenson's ingenuity to have preserved our respect for his heroine if she had become the victim of such a plaster Mephistopheles.

It would, indeed, have been the heroine that would have taxed Stevenson's powers to the utmost. He had evidently braced himself up to prove to the world that he could draw a woman. But the very elaborateness of the effect arouses our doubts. Nearly fifty pages—about one fifth of the whole fragment—are devoted to the first glances and meeting of the lovers. This does not look like mastery. A greater artist would have produced his effects with fewer lines. Indeed, the whole book promised to be of unusual length for Stevenson if it had been carried out on the same scale as the preliminaries. Greater power is shown, however, in the few touches which make the heroine's mother stand out for us and live. Another female portrait almost equally successful is that of the elder Kirstie, the heroine's aunt and the hero's retainer, who is attached to him with a devotion the complex elements of which are indicated with masterly skill. Yes, Stevenson could draw a woman, but it was only when the fires of her womanhood had burnt down. To him woman remained throughout the eternal puzzle. The very last page of the book before us contains the sentence, "He saw for the first time the ambiguous face of woman as she is." The words might apply to Stevenson as much as to his hero. But the great masters of romance know something more of woman than that. . . .

Stevenson has been scarcely so successful with the "Four Black Brothers of the Cauldstaneslap," who were to have become the deities of the machinery of the tale. So far as we have them, none of them lives except Dandie the poet. The story of their ride after their father's murderers is largely spoilt for us by the mixture of Scots and English in which it is written. Indeed, the whole book carries the licence of the "kailyard" to an extreme. We can scarcely have half the book before us, yet already the glossary, which is eminently necessary, deals with over a couple of hundred words. Lord Hermiston objects to "palmering about in bauchles." He talks a little "sculduddery" after dinner. We have "ettercaps" and "carlines," scraps of Scots "ballants," and, in short, the book is not for the Southron.

But it is perhaps unreasonable to judge this fragment as if it had been presented to us in what would have been its final form. There can be little doubt that Stevenson, with his fine literary tact, would have reduced the dialect and shortened some of the preliminaries if he had had time to complete the book. But Stevenson's friends have made such exaggerated claims for it that one is called upon to judge it from the standpoint of the highest, and to indicate its failings when so judged. That it indicates a further stage towards maturity in Stevenson's art can be willingly granted. That the handling of character is as firm as in any other part of his work is equally obvious. **'Weir of Hermiston'** intensifies our regret at the early loss of its author. It promised to be—it might have been—his masterpiece. Even as it is, it is a masterly torso.

> [*Joseph Jacobs*], *in a review of "Weir of Hermiston," in* The Athenaeum, *No. 3578, May 23, 1896, p. 673.*

## JOHN JAY CHAPMAN  (letter date 1896)

Stevenson's manner of writing is the last form of whipped up literary froth, very well done. It's the last charge of *ces messieurs* [these men]. The content is, can be expressed only, with four decimals of chemical formulas. It can't be seen, only surmised. Stevenson is a bad influence because he's so highly artificial. He struts and grimaces and moralizes and palavers and throws in tid bits of local color, fine feeling, graceful ornament, O my, ain't he clever—the rogue—hits you in the mid-riff—don't he—so beautiful—did you catch that—how smartly he led up to that anecdote—how well he lays in his Scotch pathos—his British patriotism—his nautical knowledge—and such light diet! I swear I am hungry for something to read every time I lay down Stevenson—give me rye bread, give me notes to Dante, give me a book about the world. I say I can read Wordsworth's poems and find them full of exciting reality and honesty of talent, after an hour or two of this fictitious fellow Stevenson. It's sham literature. It's all of it sham. The romances all sham romances, the essays are sham essays, the poems are sham poems. I have read **'Treasure Island'** many times and the first time or two enjoyed it. **'Kidnapped'** which always seemed to me the best of them—those I had read—(for some I stuck on) is a remarkable work of art. What talent— what talent, but sham! (pp. 115-16)

> *John Jay Chapman, in an extract from a letter to Mrs. C. Grant LaFarge (Florence Lockwood) on August 11, 1896, in* John Jay Chapman and His Letters, *edited by M. A. DeWolfe Howe (Copyright, 1937 by M. A. DeWolfe Howe. Copyright © renewed 1964 by Quincey Howe, Helen Howe Allen, Mark DeWolfe Howe. Reprinted by permission of Houghton Mifflin Company), Houghton Mifflin, 1937, pp. 115-16.*

## GEORGE SAINTSBURY  (essay date 1896)

Mr. Stevenson has been praised by some of his contemporaries and juniors with an uncritical fervour which has naturally provoked depreciation from others; and the charm of his personality was so great that it is extremely difficult for any one who knew him to hold the scales quite even. As the most brilliant and interesting by far, however, of those English writers whose life was comprised in the last half of the century he absolutely demands critical treatment here, and it so happens that his method and results were extremely typical of the literary move-

ment and character of our time. . . . Adopting to the full, and something more than the full, the modern doctrine of the all-importance of art, of manner, of style in literature, Mr. Stevenson early made the most elaborate studies in imitative composition. There is no doubt that he at last succeeded in acquiring a style which was quite his own; but it was complained, and with justice, that even to the last he never attained complete ease in this style; that its mannerism was not only excessive, but bore, as even excessive mannerism by no means always does, the marks of distinct and obvious effort. This was perhaps most noticeable in his essays, which were further marred by the fact that much of them was occupied by criticism, for which, though his taste was original and delicate, Stevenson's knowledge was not quite solid enough, and his range of sympathies a little deficient in width. In his stories, on the other hand, the devil's advocate detected certain weak points, the chief of them being an incapacity to finish, and either a distaste or an incapacity for introducing women. This last charge was finally refuted by **Catriona**, not merely in the heroine, but in the much more charming and lifelike figure of Barbara Grant; but the other was something of a true bill to the last. It was Stevenson's weakness (as by the way it also was Scott's) to huddle up his stories rather than to wind them off to an orderly conclusion.

But against this allowance—a just but an ample one—for defects, must be set to Stevenson's credit such a combination of literary and story-telling charm as perhaps no writer except Mérimée has ever equalled; while, if the literary side of him had not the golden perfection, the accomplished ease of the Frenchman, his romance has a more genial, a fresher, a more natural quality. Generally, as in the famous examples of Scott, of Dumas, and of Balzac, the great story-tellers have been a little deficient in mere style; the fault in Stevenson, if it could be called a fault, was that the style was in excess. But this only set off and enhanced, it did not account for, the magic of his scene and character, from John Silver to Barbara Grant, from **"The Suicide Club"** to the escapes of Alan Breck. Very early, when most of his critical friends were urging him to cultivate the essay mainly, others discerned the supremacy of his story-telling faculty, and, years before the public fell in love with **Treasure Island**, bade him cultivate that. Fortunately he did so; and his too short life has left a fairly ample store of work, not always quite equal, seldom quite without a flaw, but charming, stimulating, distinguished as few things in this last quarter of a century have been. (pp. 339-41)

> *George Saintsbury, "The Novel Since 1850," in his* A History of Nineteenth Century Literature: 1780-1895 *(copyright, 1896, by Macmillan and Co.), Macmillan, 1896, pp. 317-41.* *

## GEORGE MOORE  (essay date 1897)

> [*In a review of William Butler Yeats's* The Secret Rose, *Moore compares Stevenson and Yeats. He disparages Stevenson's style as "trickery", finding that "his whole art consisted in substituting rare words and new turns of phrase for old and familiar epithets." But Moore primarily denigrates Stevenson's influence on the course of the fictional romance, a form which he believes emphasizes action and excludes the inner life. He states that "the time has come to remind the world that great literature cannot be composed from narratives of perilous adventures. The narratives of the ancient writers were declarations of their philosophical faiths. Stevenson is the leader of those countless writers who perceive nothing but the visible world. . . ." Moore's view was disputed by Arthur Quiller-Couch (see excerpt below, 1897).*]

Yeat's 'The Secret Rose'] teaches many things. Its first lesson is that Stevenson is not the only man who ever lived who wrote English prose; and at the present time a more welcome truth could hardly be whispered in the world's ear, for many are surely tired of the lapwing cry, 'Stevenson and So-and-so and So-and-so and Stevenson.' . . .

About ten years ago I read a story by Stevenson. I forget which, nor does it matter—it was in a volume entitled **'The Merry Men.'** I was struck by the unexpectedness of every epithet; but while admiring the extraordinary epithet, I remembered the ordinary one, and was much exercised by the ingenuity with which the latter had been avoided, and what still further increased my wonderment was that in every instance the extraordinary epithet and turn of phrase was an improvement upon the ordinary. Every sentence held a fresh surprise, and my admiration waxed until I happened upon a man who stopped a clock with an 'interjected finger' [from **"Markheim"**. At this I cried, 'Halt.' Now I see, I said, that this man's style is but a conjuror's trick—a marvellous trick, but a trick. He spins one plate, two plates, three plates; he goes on throwing up plates until a dozen are whirling in the air. He throws up the thirteenth, and, lo! one comes down crashing. . . . 'This man,' I said, 'is saying the ordinary things in very neat language; but ordinary thoughts are better expressed in ordinary language. . . . He translates. . . . . He picks the common words out and sticks in rare words.' . . . (p. 476)

All Stevenson is in that unfortunate 'interjected finger'; he imagined no human soul, and he invented no story that anyone will remember; his whole art consisted in substituting rare words and new turns of phrase for old and familiar epithets and locutions. . . .

'The Secret Rose' teaches truths still more essential than that Stevenson wrote with the brain of a boy and the imagination and perceptions of the meticulous eighteenth century. It teaches a lesson sadly needed at the present moment—that romance comes from within and not from without. Murder is deemed romantic, and reviewers recommend So-and-so's last romance because 'the sword is rarely if ever sheathed during the long course of the narrative.' Since the days of Stevenson massacre has succeeded massacre, and always in the name of romance, and writers have been found to follow popular taste with the meekness of mummers. Stevenson's conception of life has been mixed with bog-water and kneaded by the literary agent, but, at best, it was a trivial conception; it was never higher than that of a blithe noble-hearted boy, a boy who prefers a raft to a boat, and hopes to be one day a pirate captain on the Spanish Main. To such superficial conception of life Stevenson brought his talent for literary marquetry, and a public, jaded by the unromantic moralities of positivism, accepted eagerly books that were at least free from geological theology. To this was added the fascinating theory that books might be beautifully written, though they contained no more thought than might be swallowed by an urchin of six. The public was at once interested, the public always is interested in tricks—tricks are fertile, and tricks may be learnt. A man stops a clock with an inserted finger. Open the Thesaurus, look out 'inserted,' and among the equivalents you will find 'interjected.' (pp. 476-77)

[It] is my belief that the time has come to remind the world that great literature cannot be composed from narratives of perilous adventures. The narratives of the ancient writers were declarations of their philosophical faiths. Stevenson is the leader of those countless writers who perceive nothing but the visible

world; and these are antagonistic to the great literature, of which Mr. Yeats's 'Secret Rose' is a survival or a renaissance. . . . (p. 477)

> *George Moore, in an extract from a review of "The Secret Rose," in* Daily Chronicle, *April 24, 1897 (and reprinted in* Robert Louis Stevenson: The Critical Heritage, *edited by Paul Maixner, Routledge & Kegan Paul, 1981, pp. 475-77).*

### A. T. QUILLER-COUCH    (essay date 1897)

[*Quiller-Couch, an English critic, editor, and novelist, completed Stevenson's novel* St. Ives *after Stevenson's death. In the following essay, he refutes George Moore's charges against Stevenson (see excerpt above, 1897) by praising his style and documenting his use of moral ideas.*]

For the moment Mr. Moore has allowed his intellect and his affections to be captivated by the beauty of the 'moral idea' in fiction. . . . I trust that Mr. Moore will not allow [this idea] to grow into a monomania: for my present purpose is to show . . . that to deny 'moral ideas' to Stevenson is to betray either a limited acquaintance with his writings or a lack of sympathy so profound as to nullify any attempt to grasp his intentions. (p. 478)

That Stevenson had tricks of style all must allow: that the inexperienced might be led to value him by these tricks and grace-notes, may also be granted. But I think I state no singular case in saying that while I have grown to admire these tricks less and less, I have grown to like Stevenson more and more. Marry, for why? Well, for several reasons, and among them because his writings, taken as a whole, are filled with a sound and honest philosophy of life. This is precisely what Mr. Moore denies. (p. 479)

I feel obliged to suggest that Mr. Moore might with profit resume and extend his study of Stevenson. To save trouble he might begin with the volume he dropped, **'The Merry Men.'** It contains two stories (at least) which I fancy he must have overlooked—**"Will of the Mill"** and **"Markheim."** . . . [Will of the mill] lives and vegetates; but there is one adventure, one voyage, that no man may shirk. There arrives at length a passenger who tells him this, and that the time has come. The passenger's name is Death; and with him at length Will of the Mill sets forth upon his travels. Call this an allegory, a mystery, what you will; I ask, does it not contain a 'moral idea'? Is it not built upon the moral idea that excess of cautious wisdom is a disease of the soul, paralysing manhood? Take **"Markheim"** in which a man, red-handed from a murder, reviews his past, interrogates his 'other self' in a vision, and so, having a way of escape from the law but no way of escape from himself, surrenders to the police. (pp. 479-80)

You may call this a straining of the moral insight, if you choose; but only in wantonness of depreciation can you talk of it as the writing of a man 'who perceived nothing but the visible world.' Take **'The Master of Ballantrae'**; here you have a longer story broad-based upon a moral idea. For the tragedy of that book does not of course reside in the Master and his wickedness, but in the gradual (and to my thinking, most subtly revealed) deterioration of the honest brother whom he persecutes. Take **'Dr. Jekyll and Mr. Hyde'**: it is the downright deliberate allegorising of a moral idea—the idea of two natures contending in a man. Remove that idea, and the story crumbles into a heap of nonsense. Again, is there no moral idea in the study of 'Kirstie' in **'Weir of Hermiston'**?—no moral idea in the over-darkened 'Ebb-Tide,' that tale of varied depravity and its varied rewards?—no moral idea in **"The Bottle Imp?"**—if not, there is no moral idea in the story of Alcestis. These tales stand, I admit, at various removes from life, as we observe life. But each has its informing lesson, and the lesson of each is sought in the heart of man.

At the same time, we must admit that Stevenson's fancy was capricious; and often enough he told a story out of sheer caprice, and left morality behind him. But his Essays redress the balance, and his Poems. (p. 480)

The majority of Stevenson's poems and practically the whole body of his Essays depend upon moral insight for their origin and their justification. It is from the sum total of his work that we deduce his philosophy; and finding it, as we think, a full one, we have surely some reason to complain of a critic who on a confessedly imperfect acquaintance with his writings assures the world that the man had no moral insight at all. Should Mr. Moore retain his opinion after a perusal of **'Across the Plains'** and **'Songs of Travel'**; and should he still cling to his admired phrase, 'The best-dressed young man that ever walked the Burlington Arcade' [see excerpt above, 1888]; well—I shall be sorry, but at least we shall have a little more ground on which to build a compromise. (p. 481)

> *A. T. Quiller-Couch, "The Moral Idea" (reprinted by permission of the Literary Estate of A. T. Quiller-Couch), in* The Speaker, *Vol. XV, May 1, 1897 (and reprinted in* Robert Louis Stevenson: The Critical Heritage, *edited by Paul Maixner, Routledge & Kegan Paul, 1981, pp. 478-82).*

## [JOSEPH JACOBS] (essay date 1897)

['**St Ives: Being the Adventure of a French Prisoner in England**'] is a rattling, touch-and-go tale of adventure of a somewhat ordinary type, yet relieved by some fine but slight studies in characterization. That it will not add to Stevenson's reputation is clear from this description, as well as from his own doubts about the book. . . . Perhaps the most remarkable (and significant) thing about the book is the skill with which Mr. Quiller Couch has supplied the last six chapters, which both in style and briskness of treatment bear an astonishing resemblance to the preceding thirty. It was a dangerous and difficult task that Mr. Quiller Couch undertook, and to some it might seem of disputable taste. But he has come out of the ordeal triumphantly, and for once a patch has proved to be not altogether a botch. (p. 518)

The fact is, this book bears the mark of a fagged mind on almost every page of it. It is largely reminiscent of other works of the same writer. . . . [The] majority of incidents recall similar passages in Stevenson's earlier books, and prove that while he was occupied in writing '**St. Ives**' his mind had lost its power of fresh combination. That the loss was only temporary that vigorous fragment '**Weir of Hermiston**' is more than sufficient proof.

Little fresh as are the incidents, they are even less well considered and connected. The story is practically of an escaped military prisoner who travels from Edinburgh to his uncle's place in the south, and then returns to the northern capital. The motive for the return is supposed to be an invincible desire to see the loved one, but the coxcomb tone in which the fair one is wooed does not make this return at risk of death any the more probable. Stevenson may possibly have felt this, as he props up the motive with a somewhat trumpery charge of

assault in which others might be implicated for the hero's sake. . . . Altogether the book, regarded from the point of view of plot, is a panorama of improbabilities.

Nor on the character side is there much to attract. . . . [There is, for example,] the unconvincing nature of the hero's position as an Anglo-Scotch Frenchman. The heroine is somewhat of a lay figure. More care has been taken with the villain, but he is after all merely a lath that is not even painted to look like iron; and in the relations of the hero, either to heroine or villain, there is nothing inevitable, nothing that could not be otherwise.

Yet unsatisfactory as the book is, both in construction and characterization, it has an interest of its own to the student of Stevenson's art. Previous to this book, his studies in characterization were somewhat forced, and he had clearly to content himself with but a few figures on the stage. He characterized "with deeficulty." But here at last he began to show himself a compeer of the masters in that quality in which they specially proved their mastery. What distinguishes Fielding, Scott, Dickens, Thackeray, and even Charles Reade to a certain extent, is the ease and fecundity with which they create minor characters. It is possible they crowd their canvases too much, but the total result is to produce that effect of bustling life which it is the peculiar function of the novelist to reproduce. Here in '**St. Ives**' Stevenson for the first time came to his own in this respect; it is crowded with subordinate figures, the majority of them alive and some of them uproariously kicking. . . . [Whether] they are portrayed in few or in many lines—almost every character introduced has the tang of individuality. . . .

[There are] some anachronisms of fact and tone. . . . These discrepancies would doubtless have been removed if Stevenson had lived to revise the proofs, but no amount of revision could have made up for the want of cohesion in the plot, the inefficient colouring of the chief characters.

It is needless to say that in speaking in these somewhat slighting terms of '**St. Ives**' we are judging it by a high standard. Whether destined to be classic or no, there is no doubt that Stevenson's work stands out markedly from the ruck of machine-made fiction, and this very book with all its faults shows that he was slowly maturing to a mastery of his art which might have raised him to an equality with the greatest of the past. (p. 519)

> *[Joseph Jacobs], in a review of "St. Ives: Being the Adventures of a French Prisoner in England," in* The Athenaeum, *No. 3651, October 16, 1897, pp. 518-19.*

## JOHN JAY CHAPMAN (essay date 1898)

In the early eighties, and in an epoch when the ideals of George Eliot were still controlling, the figure of Stevenson rose with a sort of radiance as a writer whose sole object was to entertain. Most of the great novelists were then dead, and the scientific school was in the ascendant. Fiction was entering upon its death grapple with sociology. Stevenson came, with his tales of adventure and intrigue, out-of-door life and old-time romance, and he recalled to every reader his boyhood and the delights of his earliest reading. We had forgotten that novels could be amusing.

Hence it is that the great public not only loves Stevenson as a writer, but regards him with a certain personal gratitude. There was, moreover, in everything he wrote an engaging humourous touch which made friends for him everywhere, and excited an interest in his fragile and somewhat elusive personality supplementary to the appreciation of his books as literature. (p. 217)

[In] whatever key he plays,—and he seems to have taken delight in showing mastery in many,—the reader feels safe in his hands, and knows that no false note will be struck. His work makes no demands upon the attention. It is food so thoroughly peptonized that it is digested as soon as swallowed and leaves us exhilarated rather than fed.

Writing was to him an art, and almost everything that he has written has a little the air of being a *tour de force*. Stevenson's books and essays were generally brilliant imitations of established things, done somewhat in the spirit of an expert in billiards. In short, Stevenson is the most extraordinary mimic that has ever appeared in literature. (pp. 220-21)

He became a remarkable, if not a unique phenomenon,—for he never grew up. Whether or not there was some obscure connection between his bodily troubles and the arrest of his intellectual development, it is certain that Stevenson remained a boy till the day of his death. (p. 223)

To a boy, the great artists of the world are a lot of necromancers, whose enchantments can perhaps be stolen and used again. To a man, they are a lot of human beings, and their works are parts of them. . . . But Stevenson was not a man, he was a boy; or, to speak more accurately, the attitude of his mind towards his work remained unaltered from boyhood till death, though his practice and experiment gave him, as he grew older, a greater mastery over his materials. It is in this attitude of Stevenson's mind toward his own work that we must search for the heart of his mystery.

He conceived of himself as ''an artist,'' and of his writings as performances. As a consequence, there is an undertone of insincerity in almost everything which he has written. His attention is never wholly absorbed in his work, but is greatly taken up with the notion of how each stroke of it is going to appear. (pp. 224-25)

Ultimately speaking, the vice of Stevenson's theories about art is that they call for a self-surrender by the artist of his own mind to the pleasure of others, for a subordination of himself to the production of this ''effect'' in the mind of another. They degrade and belittle him. Let Stevenson speak for himself; the thought contained in the following passage [from **''Letter to a Young Gentleman''**], is found in a hundred places in his writings and dominated his artistic life.

> The French have a romantic evasion for one employment, and call its practitioners the Daughters of Joy. The artist is of the same family, he is of the Sons of Joy, chose his trade to please himself, gains his livelihood by pleasing others, and has parted with something of the sterner dignity of men.

(pp. 226-27)

The reason why Stevenson represents a backward movement in literature, is that literature lives by the pouring into it of new words from speech, and new thoughts from life, and Stevenson used all his powers to exclude both from his works. He lived and wrote in the past. That this Scotchman should appear at the end of what has been a very great period of English literature, and summarize the whole of it in his two hours' traffic on the stage, gives him a strange place in the history of that literature. He is the Improvisatore, and nothing more. It is impossible to assign him rank in any line of writing.

If you shut your eyes to try and place him, you find that you cannot do it. The effect he produces while we are reading him vanishes as we lay down the book, and we can recall nothing but a succession of flavors. It is not to be expected that posterity will take much interest in him, for his point and meaning are impressional. He is ephemeral, a shadow, a reflection. He is the mistletoe of English literature whose roots are not in the soil but in the tree. (p. 243)

And what kind of a man was Stevenson? Whatever may be said about his imitativeness, his good spirits were real. They are at the bottom of his success, the strong note in his work. They account for all that is paradoxical in his effect. He often displays a sentimentalism which has not the ring of reality. And yet we do not reproach him. He has by stating his artistic doctrines in their frankest form revealed the scepticism inherent in them. And yet we know that he was not a sceptic; on the contrary, we like him, and he was regarded by his friends as little lower than the angels.

Why is it that we refuse to judge him by his own utterances? The reason is that all of his writing is playful, and we know it. The instinct at the bottom of all mimicry is self-concealment. Hence the illusive and questionable personality of Stevenson. Hence our blind struggle to bind this Proteus who turns into bright fire and then into running water under our hands. The truth is that as a literary force, there was no such man as Stevenson; and after we have racked our brains to find out the mechanism which has been vanquishing the chess players of Europe, there emerges out of the Box of Maelzel a pale boy.

But the courage of this boy, the heroism of his life, illumine all his works with a personal interest. (pp. 246-47)

This courage and the lovable nature of Stevenson won the world's heart. He was regarded with a peculiar tenderness such as is usually given only to the young. Honor, and admiration mingled with affection followed him to his grave. Whatever his artistic doctrines, he revealed his spiritual nature in his work. It was this nature which made him thus beloved. (p. 247)

> *John Jay Chapman, ''Robert Louis Stevenson,'' in his* Emerson and Other Essays *(copyright, 1898, by Charles Scribner's Sons), Charles Scribner's Sons, 1898, pp. 217-47.*

**ARTHUR WING PINERO**   (lecture date 1903)

[*Pinero, a dramatist and admirer of Stevenson's work, examines his plays in light of the principles Pinero considers necessary to good drama. He attributes their ''inadequate success'' to Stevenson's imitation of outdated models, his failure to focus his dramatic talent, his ignorance of modern dramatic technique, and his mistaken belief that rhetoric alone will ensure a drama's success.*]

Why should Stevenson the dramatist take such a back seat, if you will pardon the expression, in comparison with Stevenson the novelist, the essayist, the poet? (p. 27)

Stevenson, with all his genius, failed to realize that the art of drama is not stationary, but progressive. By this I do not mean that it is always improving; but what I do mean is that its conditions are always changing, and that every dramatist whose ambition it is to produce live plays is absolutely bound to study carefully, and I may even add respectfully—at any rate not contemptuously—the conditions that hold good for his own age and generation. This Stevenson did not—would not—do. We shall find, I think, that in all his plays he was deliberately imitating outworn models, and doing it, too, in a sportive, half-disdainful spirit, as who should say, ''The stage is a realm of absurdities—come, let us be cleverly absurd!'' In that spirit, ladies and gentlemen, success never was and never will be attained. (pp. 29-30)

No one can doubt that he had in him the ingredients of a dramatist. What is dramatic talent? Is it not the power to project characters, and to cause them to tell an interesting story through the medium of dialogue? This is *dramatic* talent; and dramatic talent, if I may so express it, is the raw material of theatrical talent. . . . Now, dramatic talent Stevenson undoubtedly possessed in abundance; and I am convinced that theatrical talent was well within his reach, if only he had put himself to the pains of evolving it. (pp. 31-2)

[Let] me revive in your memory [one] of Stevenson's essays which throws a curious light upon his mental attitude towards the theater. I refer to that delightful essay in **'Memories and Portraits'** called **'A Penny Plain and Twopence Colored.'** It describes . . . his juvenile delight in those sheets of toy-theater characters, which, even when he wrote, had ''become, for the most part, a memory'' and are now, I believe, almost extinct. . . . [Unfortunately,] even to his dying day he continued to regard the actual theater as only an enlarged form of the toy theaters which had fascinated his childhood—he continued to use in his dramatic coloring the crimson lake and Prussian blue of transpontine romance—he considered his function as a dramatist very little more serious than that child's-play with paintbox and pasteboard on which his memory dwelt so fondly. He played at being a playwright; and, ladies and gentlemen, he was fundamentally in error in regarding the drama as a matter of child's-play.

Observe, too, that these dramas of the toy theater were, before they reached the toy theater, designed for almost the lowest class of theatrical audiences. They were stark and staring melodramas. (pp. 39-41)

[For his first attempt at drama, **'Deacon Brodie or the Double Life'**], what is the theme he chooses? A story of crime, a story of housebreaking, of dark lanterns, jimmies, center-bits, masks, detectives, boozing-kens—in short a melodrama of the deepest dye, exactly after . . . the toy-theater type. It evidently pleased him to think that he could put fresh life into this old and puerile form, as he had put, or was soon to put, fresh life into the boy's tale of adventure. And he did, indeed, write a good deal of vivacious dialog—the literary quality of the play, though poor in comparison with Stevenson's best work, is of course incomparably better than that of the models on which he was founding. But unfortunately it shows no glimmer of their stagecraft. . . . [One] would have thought that the future author of **'Dr. Jekyll and Mr. Hyde'** was precisely the man to get its full effect out of the ''double life'' of his burglar hero. But not a bit of it. From sheer lack of stagecraft, the effect of the ''double life'' is wholly lost. Brodie is a patent, almost undisguised scoundrel thruout. There is no contrast between the respectable and the criminal sides to his life, no gradual unmasking of his depravity, no piling up, atom by atom, of evidence against him. Our wonder from the first is that anyone should ever have regarded him as anything else than the poor, blustering, blundering villain he is. From the total ineffectiveness of the character, one cannot but imagine that Stevenson was hampered by the idea of representing strictly the historical personage. In this, for aught I know, he may have succeeded; but he has certainly not succeeded in making his protagonist

interesting in the theater, or in telling the story so as to extract one tithe of its possibilities of dramatic effect. (pp. 44-6)

[**'Deacon Brodie'**] is chiefly interesting as exemplifying the boyish spirit of gleeful bravado in which Stevenson approached the stage. (p. 47)

In **'Admiral Guinea'**—a much better drama—the influence of his penny-plain-two-pence-colored studies is, if possible, still more apparent. . . . [In] writing this play his effort was constantly, and one may almost say confessedly, to reproduce the atmosphere of conventional nautical melodrama—to re-handle its material while replacing its bald language with dialog of high literary merit. (pp. 47-9)

[If] beautiful speeches, and even beautiful passages of dialog, made a good drama, **'Admiral Guinea'** would indeed be a great success. But what chiefly strikes one after seeing or reading the play is that Stevenson's idea of dramatic writing was that fine speeches, and fine speeches alone, would carry everything before them. . . . **'Admiral Guinea'** is mainly rhetoric, beautifully done but with no blood in it. (pp. 57-8)

In **'Beau Austin'** we have certainly Stevenson's nearest approach to an effective drama. In spite of its inacceptable theme, it is a charming play and really interesting on the stage. A little more careful handling of the last act might have rendered it wholly successful. But still we see traces of the old crudity of technic of the toy-theater, and still the author evidently conceived that the essence of the drama resides in rhetoric, in fine speeches. (pp. 58-9)

[While there is much in **'Beau Austin'**] that is beautiful, much that is true and subtle, there is very little that is truly and subtly expressed. The beauty the authors aimed at was, I believe you will agree with me, the absolute beauty of words, such beauty as Ruskin or Pater or Newman might achieve in an eloquent passage, not the beauty of dramatic fitness to the character and the situation. (p. 63)

[The] dramatist is bound to select his particular form of technic, master, and stick to it. He must not jumble up two styles and jump from one to the other. That is what the authors of **'Beau Austin'** [Stevenson and William Ernest Henley] have not realized. Their technic is neither ancient nor modern; their language is neither poetry nor prose—the prose, that is to say, of conceivable human life. . . . [Even] in **'Beau Austin,'** far superior tho it be to his other plays, Stevenson shows that he had not studied and realized the conditions of the problem he was handling—the problem of how to tell a dramatic story truly, convincingly and effectively on the modern stage—the problem of disclosing the workings of the human heart by methods which shall not destroy the illusion which a modern audience expects to enjoy in the modern theater. (pp. 64-5)

**'Deacon Brodie'** and **'Admiral Guinea'** are what I may perhaps describe as stage-coach plays—deliberate attempts to revive an antiquated form. But **'Beau Austin'** is not even that. It is a costume play, I admit; but its methods are fundamentally and essentially modern. The misfortune is that the authors had not studied and mastered the formula they were attempting to use, but were for ever falling back, without knowing it, upon a bygone formula, wholly incongruous with the matter of their play and the manner in which alone it could be presented in the theater of their day. (p. 66)

When Stevenson says: ''The theater is the gold mine,'' and when [his biographer] Mr. Graham Balfour tells us that Stevenson felt that ''the prizes of the dramatist are out of all proportion to the payment of the man of letters'' [see additional bibliography], the implication obviously is that the gold mine can be easily worked, that the prizes are disproportionate to the small amount of pains necessary in order to grasp them. That was evidently the belief of these two men of distinguished talent; and that was precisely where they made the mistake. . . . Stevenson's novels were not ordinary, and I do not for a moment imply that the amount of mental effort which produced, say, the '**Master of Ballantrae,**' might not, if well directed, have produced a play of equal value. But Stevenson was never at the trouble of learning how to direct it well. On the contrary, he wholly ignored the necessity for so doing. What attracted him to the drama was precisely the belief that he could turn out a good play with far less mental effort than it cost him to write a good novel; and here he was radically, woefully in error. And the inadequate success of his plays, instead of bringing his mistake home to him, merely led him, I am afraid, to condemn the artistic medium which he had failed to acquire. (pp. 68-9)

Stevenson, with all his genius, made the mistake of approaching the theater as a toy to be played with. The facts of the case were against him, for the theater is not a toy; and facts being stubborn things, he ran his head against them in vain. Had he only studied the conditions, or in other words got into a proper relation to the facts, with what joy should we have acclaimed him among the masters of the modern stage! (pp. 71-2)

> *Arthur Wing Pinero, in his* Robert Louis Stevenson As a Dramatist *(originally a lecture delivered at the Music Hall in Edinburgh on February 24, 1903; copyright 1914 by Dramatic Museum of Columbia University),* Dramatic Museum of Columbia University, *1914, 78 p.*

### LAFCADIO HEARN   (lecture date 1903?)

The greatest romantic writer, almost of the century,—if we except Sir Walter Scott—was a man who lived and died in our own time, contemporary with us, representing both in his thought and sentiment the best that the Later Victorian Period had to give. I mean Robert Louis Stevenson. (pp. 782-83)

[You] must not think, even in the case of Stevenson, that popularity is a test of the best work. It is the least known work of Stevenson that should especially interest the literary student; and [**"Island Nights' Entertainments"**] is an example. The best of the stories, I think, is **"The Beach of Falesa."** It is a tale of Polynesian witchcraft,—so wonderfully told that it has all the terror of reality. The most striking page in it is perhaps that of the transformation, when the victim in the story finds himself alone upon the Sea of the Dead, in a small boat, with the wizard, whose body begins to grow larger and larger until the boat bursts. There is no finer page of weird writing in modern literature. (p. 787)

It is not surprising that [Stevenson] should have produced the best boys' book of adventure ever written, **"Treasure Island."** Certainly the mere story here would not give the book the unequalled merit which it has. The plan of the story reminds us a little of various tales by Washington Irving. But not even Irving could have written with such wonderful style and realistic colour. You read Irving or Maryatt, and remember the story—that is all. But when you read Stevenson you remember the very words: sentences and paragraphs remain in imagination as if they had been burnt into it. That is what the difference of style means. (p. 788)

I should put **"The Wrecker"** at the head of all Stevenson's modern stories. Every character in it lives with extraordinary life, and every one is typical as well as human. The tale is the wildest of romances—yet you can not say that anything in it is impossible. Romantic as the story is, the characters are intensely realistic. And for this reason I think that the book best represents Stevenson's effect upon English literature. For the great power of him lay just in this method of combining romance and realism. Nobody did the same thing in exactly the same way before—nobody ever thought it possible. To make a purely romantic plot, which, however improbable, could not be considered impossible; and to make all the characters of the story purely human, everyday types—so real in all their words and acts that we can touch them and feel them and hear them—that was an extraordinary feat. . . . (pp. 789-90)

> *Lafcadio Hearn, "The Victorian Era: R. L. Stevenson" (1903?), in his* A History of English Literature in a Series of Lectures, Vol. II, *edited by R. Tanabe and T. Ochiai, The Hokuseido Press, 1927, pp. 782-91.*

### SIDNEY COLVIN   (essay date 1911)

[*The following is taken from Colvin's introduction to the second edition of* The Letters of Robert Louis Stevenson, *which he edited. Critics faulted his editorial work on both this and the first edition, charging that he omitted letters that would have disturbed the public's image of Stevenson as an innocent yet adventurous invalid, and thus created a one-sided portrait which contributed to the precipitous rise and fall of his reputation. Colvin's introduction includes a defense of his own editorial technique, which he states is necessarily discreet to protect people still living. As his essay demonstrates, Colvin was one of many of Stevenson's admirers who found his conversation more witty and original than his writing; his warm portrait of Stevenson attempts to bring that charming conversationalist to life.*]

No reader of [*The Letters of Robert Louis Stevenson*] will close it, I am sure, without feeling that he has been throughout in the company of a spirit various indeed and many-mooded, but profoundly sincere and real. (p. xxi)

[In these letters], Stevenson the deliberate artist is scarcely forthcoming at all. He does not care a fig for order or logical sequence or congruity, or for striking a key of expression and keeping it, but becomes simply the most spontaneous and unstudied of human beings. He has at his command the whole vocabularies of the English and Scottish languages, classical and slang, with good stores of the French, and tosses and tumbles them about irresponsibly to convey the impression or affection, the mood or freak of the moment; pouring himself out in all manner of rhapsodical confessions and speculations, grave or gay, notes of observation and criticism, snatches of remembrance and autobiography, moralisings on matters uppermost for the hour in his mind, comments on his own work or other people's, or mere idle fun and foolery.

By this medley of moods and manners, Stevenson's letters at their best come nearer than anything else to the full-blooded charm and variety of his conversation. Nearer, yet not quite near; for it was in company only that this genial spirit rose to his very best. Few men probably have had in them such a richness and variety of human nature; and few can ever have been better gifted than he was to express the play of being that was in him by means of the apt, expressive word. . . . (p. xxxi)

[In] the best of these letters of Stevenson's you have some echo, far away indeed, but yet the nearest, of his talk—talk which could not possibly be taken down, and of which nothing remains save in the memory of his friends an impression magical and never to be effaced. (p. xli)

> *Sidney Colvin, in an introduction to* The Letters of Robert Louis Stevenson: 1868-1880, Scotland—France—California, Vol. I, *edited by Sidney Colvin (copyright, 1899, 1907, 1911, by Charles Scribner's Sons), revised edition, Charles Scribner's Sons, 1911, pp. xv-xli.*

### FRANK SWINNERTON (essay date 1915)

[*Swinnerton's study is one of the most important and frequently discussed works on Stevenson in the twentieth century. As the first major attack on Stevenson, it has had a significant impact on his reputation, and from the time of its publication, fewer critics have defined Stevenson as a major writer. Swinnerton avoided discussing Stevenson's personality and attempted to evaluate his work using objective critical methods. He charged that Stevenson's romances were merely a series of picturesque and exciting incidents that lacked unifying themes or realistic characters, elements which Swinnerton considers vital to the romance. While acknowledging the clarity of his style and the value of his books for children, Swinnerton rates Stevenson as "a writer of the second class."*]

[Stevenson's] writing is very clear. It is a model in its freedom from ambiguities. If clarity is a virtue in writing, as I believe it to be, then Stevenson deserves praise for most admirable clarity. There is no difficulty of style. It is easy to read, because it has so much grace; but it is also easy to understand, because it is in a high degree explicit. It is essentially a prose style; as I think Stevenson was essentially a prose-writer. His poems have this same clearness (though surely he was never a master of poetic form to the extent to which he was a master of prose), and clearness in poetry is a less notable virtue than clearness in prose. . . . Even in [poetry], however, his clearness has its virtue; because the mark of the ostentatiously minor poet is obscurity of diction. Stevenson was not obscure in diction, and he was not obscure in thought, as so many writers with little to say are obscure. He went, in fact, to the other extreme. His poems are too explicit to be good poems. They are the poems of a man with all his wits about him; they are the poems of a man who always had his wits about him. (pp. 189-90)

If Stevenson's habitual attitude of mind be then examined it will prove to be directly opposed to the habit of mind of the poet. He was about as poetic as a robin. But his habit of mind (unlike that of the robin) was moral as well as practical. It was not philosophical; nor would one willingly use in this connection the word spiritual. It was moral and practical; it was fundamentally a prose habit of mind. The highest and the lowest were alike strange to Stevenson's mind; it had excellent equipoise, an admirable sanity. It had not, normally, a very wide range of sympathy or interest. (p. 190)

He was essentially technical in his attitude to style and to art in general. He did not regard writing as a means of expressing truths; he seems to have regarded it as an end in itself. He does not seem to consider the notion of writing to express an idea; his impulse is to gather together as many incidents as will make a book. . . . I cannot help remarking how entirely absent from any declaration by Stevenson is the sense of an artist's profound disinterested imagining. So far from being profoundly disinterested, he seems to have followed here the

custom he admits following in childhood, that of reading and watching everything for the sake of wrinkles subsequently to be used in play. It seems as though he took imaginative writing at its lowest valuation, as so much "fake," as so much invention very ingeniously contrived but never really, in the last resort, perfectly believed by the creator—as, in fact, something "pretended." Now Stevenson's practice, in that case, is better than his theory. Scenes in his romances, and some of his short stories in bulk, are the work of an artist who was working at the bidding of his inspiration. Stevenson did, at these times, believe as an artist in the work he was making. I can give no account of the artist's state of mind; but it is quite certain that Stevenson did not "pretend" his best work, and that no artist "pretends" his best work. An artist can distinguish between that part of his work which is the result of intense belief and that part which is agnostic. Stevenson seems not to have been so sure; for his aims, whether they are at "vitality" or at the death of the optic nerve and the adjective, suggest that he invariably adopted the attitude of the craftsman, the professional writer of novels for popular consumption. Even so, he is to be applauded for his freedom from artistic cant. If he is too intent upon rattling the bones, at least that is more candid than the habit of playing the priest.

From this question of Stevenson's conviction, however (the question of the inevitable as opposed to the practicable), arises a further question. . . . [In] the case of a work of art there is left with the reader some abiding emotion, an evocation, as it were, of emotion distinct from all incidental emotions, excitements, dreads, or anxieties aroused in the course of the book. In that pervading and prevailing emotion, it seems to me, lies the particular quality which distinguishes a work of art from a work of merely consummate craft. If I question whether such abiding emotion is evoked by the longer stories of Stevenson, I am bound to answer that these do not arouse in me any emotion greater than that of interest, the consequence of a succession of pleasant excitements. The romances as a whole have great ingenuity, many scenes to which all readers must look back with recollected enjoyment. In no case does the book reappear as a whole. The recollection is a recollection of "plums." That they are good plums does not affect the validity of the argument. . . . (pp. 192-95)

[All] good novels, of whatever kind, whether modern or historical, must be based upon idea and upon character. To Stevenson, character was incidental. To Stevenson incident, picturesque or exciting, and the employment of an atmosphere, or appropriate "style," were the most important things in romance. That was perhaps the grave mistake which made his romances what they are, and which has very considerably affected the romantic novels published since Stevenson's time and written in accordance with his conventions. The use of conventional characters, easily-recognisable romantic types, has for twenty years and more been accepted by English romantic novelists as a legitimate evasion of the need for creating character. . . . If Stevenson's romances had enjoyed the strength of definite themes, and if they had been based upon character, the whole position of the romantic novel in England at the present day might have been different. As it is, the romantic novel is a survival. The freshness of Stevenson's manipulated convention is stale, and the imitators of Stevenson have forsaken romance for the writing of detective mystery stories. They still have popularity; but they have no status.

But it may be urged that Stevenson saved his ideas for that more direct appeal to readers which is the special privilege of the essay. Now the point in this case is to be reached by the inquiry as to what ideas Stevenson expressed in his essays. They are very simple. Stevenson's essays are either fanciful treatments of pleasant, or attractive, or ingenious notions; or they are frankly homiletic. Stevenson loved courage, and he thought that courage should have trappings. To his mind the bravest actions were the better for a bit of purple. But when we penetrate beyond this crust of happy truism there is little that will reward us for the search. There is no thought, and little enough feeling in the essays: their charm lies in the fact that they dress prettily, and sometimes beautifully, the rather obvious philosophical small-change which most people cherish as their private wisdom. The essays flatter the reader by mirroring his own mind and giving it an odd twist of grace. They are shrewd mother-wit, dressed for a fairing. That is what causes the popularity of the essays—that and the air they have of "looking on the bright side of things." They do look on the bright side; they are homely, cheerful, charming; they will continue to adorn the bookshelf with a pretty, pale, bedside cheerfulness which will delight all whose culture exceeds their originality. But I believe that they have ceased to be regarded (it has almost become ridiculous that they should ever have been regarded) as comparable with the essays of Montaigne, or Hazlitt, or Lamb; because their day is sinking and their fragility is seen already to indicate a want of robustness rather than a delicacy of perception. By this I do not mean to suggest that already the essays are out of date: they are only out of date in some instances, and even if they were completely out of date that fact would not have much ultimate critical significance. What is, however, very significant, is that they have ceased to stand as essays, and have become goods for the monger of phrases. Their "aptness," which of old was the charm that dignified the trite moralism, has recoiled upon them: they are seen to be mere aggregations of "happy thoughts," fit to be culled and calendared for suburban households. . . . [The] teaching of the essays is one of compromise, not of enlarged ideals; it is the doctrine of "that state of life" which finally ends in a good-natured passivity not unlike the happy innocence of the domesticated cat. Thus, for all his powerful desire to preach, Stevenson taught nothing but a bland acquiescence; for the field of battle to which he likened marriage as well as life was a field in which there was no headstrong conflict of ideal and practice, but a mere accommodation which a phrase could embody.

There seems to be a general tendency to protest against such opinions, not because the opinions are adequately countered, but because in most readers Stevenson produces a vague doting which is entirely uncritical. Stevenson in such warm hearts is incomparable; and a question is a perceptible rebuff to their confidingness. The prevailing feeling appears to be one of affectionate admiration, a matter of personal attraction rather than of critical esteem. . . . Stevenson says, "We are all mighty fine fellows; and life is a field of battle; but it is better to be a fool than to be dead; and the true success is to labour''; and the reader feels that Stevenson is One of Us! He is not, that is to say, austere; he does not ask uncomfortable questions; he makes no claim upon his readers' judgment, but only upon their self-esteem and their gratified assent. He even tells them about himself. He says, "I knew a little boy''; and his readers say: "It's himself!" They read with enormous satisfaction.

Well, all that is delightful; but in its way it is a red-herring. It does not help us to assay the literary value of Stevenson's work. It is simply a wide illustration of the fascination which Stevenson had for his friends. It is an extension of that rare

thing, personal charm. We may say that it ought not to influence readers; and no doubt it influences some too-critical readers adversely (criticism being understood by all admirers of Stevenson as the merest corrosion); but the fact is that it cannot be ignored by anyone who seeks to account for Stevenson's continued, and even now barely declining, popularity. Another very good reason is that Stevenson had extraordinarily good friends. I think it probable that no writer ever had friends more loyal and affectionate. They criticised his work privately to its great improvement, and then sold his work when it was completed, acting as counsellors and agents. And this was done with the same affectionate admiration which readers of his work still feel. . . . I can only assume that a slight air of sentimentalism which runs through [his] essays and romances alike, and over into such short stories as *Will o' the Mill* and *Markheim,* combines with the thin optimism of the essays and the picturesque variety of incident of the romances to give body to [his personal] charm. . . . [The merits of his romances] include occasional pieces of distinguished imagination, a frequent exuberance of fancy, and a great freshness of incident which conceals lack of central or unifying idea and poverty of imagined character. Intrinsically, although their literary quality is much higher, the romances—with the possible exception of *Kidnapped*—are inferior to the work of Captain Marryat.

Finally, the fact which all must recognise in connection with Stevenson's work is the versatility of talent which is displayed. From essays personal to essays critical; from short-stories picturesque to short-stories metaphysical, and stories of bogles to fairy stories of princes and magic bottles and wondrous enchanted isles; from tales of treasure to the politics of a principality, from Scottish history to tales of the South Seas; from travel books to poems for men and children . . .—that is a dazzling record. Quite obviously one cannot contemplate it without great admiration. When it is remembered also that it is the product of a man who was very frequently (though not, as is generally supposed, continuously) an invalid, the amount of it, and the variety, seems to be impossible. Yet it is possible, and this fact is which finally explains our attitude to Stevenson. We think it marvellous that he should have been able to write at all, forgetting, as we do, that "writing his best was very life to him." . . . He is known chiefly in these days as a writer; and in the future he will be still more clearly seen as a writer. The weaknesses of his work will be realised; to some extent his writing will fall in popular esteem; but he will be less the brave soul travelling hopefully and labouring to arrive, and more the deliberate writer. . . . He will go down into literary history as the man who became a professional writer, who cared greatly about the form and forms of expression. . . . [At] the end of his life Stevenson was at last to be found basing his work upon principles, really and consciously grasped, from which the incidental outcome was of less importance than the main realisation. Where he had hitherto been shuttlecocked by his impulses, and tethered by his moralism, he became capable of appreciating ideas as of more importance than their expression. If he had been less prolific, less versatile, less of a virtuoso, Stevenson might have been a greater man. He would have been less popular. He would have been less generally admired and loved. But with all his writing he took the road of least resistance, the road of limited horizons; because with all his desire for romance, his desire for the splendour of the great life of action, he was by physical delicacy made intellectually timid and spiritually cautious. . . . In the versatility of Stevenson we may observe his restlessness, the nervous fluttering of the mind which has no physical health to nourish it. In that, at least, and the charming and not at all objectionable inclination to pose. He was a poseur because if he had not pretended he would have died. . . . We shall do ill to pity Stevenson, because pity is the obverse of envy, and is as much a vice. Let us rather praise Stevenson for his real determination and for that work of his which we can approve as well as love. To love uncritically is to love ill. To discriminate with mercy is very humbly to justify one's privilege as a reader.

It is sufficient here to maintain that Stevenson's literary reputation, as distinct from the humanitarian aspect of his fortitude, is seriously impaired. It is no longer possible for a serious critic to place him among the great writers, because in no department of letters—excepting the boy's book and the short-story—has he written work of first-class importance. His plays, his poems, his essays, his romances—all are seen nowadays to be consumptive. What remains to us, apart from a fragment, a handful of tales, and two boy's books (for *Kidnapped*, although finely romantic, was addressed to boys, and still appeals to the boy in us) is a series of fine scenes—what I have called "plums"—and the charm of Stevenson's personality. Charm as an adjunct is very well; charm as an asset is of less significance. We find that Stevenson, reviving the never-very-prosperous romance of England, created a school which has brought romance to be the sweepings of an old costume-chest. I am afraid we must admit that Stevenson has become admittedly a writer of the second class, because his ideals have been superseded by other ideals and shown to be the ideals of a day, a season, and not the ideals of an age. In fact, we may even question whether his ideals were those of a day, whether they were not merely treated by everybody as so much pastime; whether the revival of the pernicious notion that literature is only a pastime is not due to his influence. We may question whether Stevenson did not make the novel a toy when George Eliot had finished making it a treatise. . . . Stevenson seems very decidedly to have betrayed the romantics by inducing them to enter a *cul-de-sac;* for romantic literature in England at the present time seems to show no inner light, but only a suspicious phosphorescence. And that fact we may quite clearly trace back to Stevenson, who galvanised romance into life after Charles Reade had volubly betrayed it to the over-zealous compositor.

Stevenson, that is to say, was not an innovator. We can find his originals in Wilkie Collins, in Scott, in Mayne Reid, in Montaigne, Hazlitt, Defoe, Sterne, and in many others. No need for him to admit it: the fact is patent. "It is the grown people who make the nursery stories; all the children do, is jealously to preserve the text." That is what Stevenson was doing; that is what Stevenson's imitators have been doing ever since. And if romance rests upon no better base than this, if romance is to be conventional in a double sense, if it spring not from a personal vision of life, but is only a tedious virtuosity, a pretence, a conscious toy, romance as an art is dead. . . . And if it is dead, Stevenson killed it. (pp. 195-209)

> *Frank Swinnerton, in his* R. L. Stevenson: A Critical Study *(reprinted by permission of the Literary Estate of Frank Swinnerton), Mitchell Kennerley, 1915, 216 p.*

## LEONARD WOOLF   (essay date 1924)

There has never been a more headlong fall in a writer's reputation than there was in Stevenson's after his death. The consumptive Scotsman who walked down Bond Street in a black shirt, a red tie, a velvet jacket, and a smoking-cap, and who finally retired to live and die on a coral island in the South

Seas, was just the man to captivate the taste of the romantic 'nineties. (p. 39)

The climax of the legend was that Stevenson not only wore a velvet coat, had flashing eyes, and was a brilliant talker, but was also a great writer, a great novelist, a great essayist, a great thinker, and a consummate artist in words. That romantic age in which Andrew Lang, Mr. Gosse, Henley, and Sir Sidney Colvin were prophets swallowed the legend whole, asked for more, and got it. Stevenson seemed to have been permanently placed in a very high niche among the greatest of writers when the younger generation began to read [George Bernard Shaw's] *Plays Pleasant and Unpleasant*. The effect was appalling: the velvet coat suddenly lost its romance; the name "Tusitala" roused no more emotions than did such monosyllables as "Shaw" or "Wells"; and ill-mannered young men began to say that the rhythm of Stevenson's great passages was spoiled for them because they could always hear the machinery grinding out the tune. (pp. 39-40)

If Stevenson is not the great writer whom they thought him to be thirty years ago, . . . he is better than his present reputation among "highbrows" would lead one to suppose. The worst thing about him is his literary style. . . . As an essayist Stevenson is already dead, and I do not believe that anyone will ever be able to resurrect him in the essay. The reason is that in that form of writing a false literary style tells most fatally against a writer, particularly when, as with Stevenson, he has nothing original to say. It is astonishing how drearily thin and artificial the famous "**Aes Triplex**" [from *Virginibus Puerisque*] and "**Pulvis et Umbra**," for instance, are when one reads them again. Stevenson had no style of his own; as he said himself, he played the "sedulous ape" to great prose writers, and the consequence is that his essays have the same flavour as those which brilliant undergraduates send in for University prizes. (p. 41)

Stevenson was quite a good imitator of great writers, but he was not a great writer or artist himself. His ear for verbal music was not fine, and his phrases are rather laboured. He is, indeed, at his best where he is sufficiently interested in his subject to forget about his style. He can then write good, plain, honest English which makes no pretensions to be great literature. This is the case in *Treasure Island* and in some of his other stories. I must have read *Treasure Island* many times, but, when I read it again [recently]. . . , it still carried me along with it, and was thoroughly entertaining. It is preeminently a day-dream type of story, and Stevenson always remained a typical day-dream writer. He appeals to the child or to the primitively childish in grown men and women. There is nothing against him in that; a good story is rare, and personally I hope that I shall never grow too old to enjoy one. *Treasure Island, Kidnapped, The Master of Ballantrae* are all good stories, and the more Stevenson forgets himself and his style in them and becomes absorbed in telling the tale, the better they are. And there is one other form of writing in which occasionally the same thing happens to him. He wrote one really good essay, the essay on Samuel Pepys in his *Familiar Studies of Men and Books*. There again the character and story of Pepys caught his attention, and he forgot to think about his words and periods: the result is a vigorous, subtle study of an extremely interesting person. (pp. 42-3)

> *Leonard Woolf, "The Fall of Stevenson" (originally published in* The Nation and the Athenaeum, *Vol. XXXIV, No. 14, January 5, 1924), in his* Essays on Literature, History, Politics, Etc. *(reprinted by per-*

mission of the author's Literary Estate and The Ho-garth Press), L. and Virginia Woolf, 1927, pp. 39-43.

## ARTHUR QUILLER-COUCH  (essay date 1924)

*Kidnapped* (as everyone knows) is a capital tale, though imperfect; and [its sequel] *Catriona* (as the critics began to point out, the day after its issue) a capital tale with an awkward fissure midway in it. (p. 88)

Put *Kidnapped* and *Catriona* together within the same covers, with one title-page, one dedication (here will be the severest loss), and one table of contents, in which the chapters are numbered straight away from I to LX: and—this above all things—read the tale right through from David's setting forth from the garden gate at Essendean to his homeward voyage, by Catriona's side, on the Low Country ship. And having done this, be so good as to perceive how paltry are the objections you raised against the two volumes when you took them separately. Let me raise again one or two of them.

(1) *Catriona* is just two stories loosely hitched together—the one of David's vain attempt to save James Stewart, the other of the loves of David and Catriona and in case the critic should be too stupid to detect this, Mr. Stevenson has been at the pains to divide his book into Part I and Part II. Now this, which is a real fault in a book called *Catriona*, is no fault at all in *The Memoirs of David Balfour*, which, by its very title, claims to be constructed loosely. In an Odyssey the road taken by the wanderer is all the nexus required; and the continuity of his presence (if the author know his business) is warrant enough for the continuity of our interest in his adventures. (pp. 88-9)

(2) In *Catriona* more than a few of the characters are suffered to drop out of sight just as we have begun to take an interest in them. There is Mr. Rankeillor, for instance, whose company in the concluding chapter of *Kidnapped* was too good to be spared very easily; and there is Lady Allardyce—a wonderfully clever portrait; and Captain Hoseason—we tread for a moment on the verge of re-acquaintance, but are disappointed; and Balfour of Pilrig; and at the end of Part I away into darkness goes the Lord Advocate Prestongrange, with his charming womenkind.

Well, if this be an objection to the tale, it is one urged pretty often against life itself—that we scarce see enough of the men and women we like. And here again that which may be a fault in *Catriona* is no fault at all in *The Memoirs of David Balfour*. Though novelists may profess in everything they write to hold a mirror up to life, the reflection must needs be more artificial in a small book than in a large. In the one, for very clearness, they must isolate a few human beings and cut off the currents (so to speak) bearing upon them from the outside world: in the other, with a larger canvas, they are able to deal with life more frankly. . . . [As] it is, Barbara Grant must go her way at the end of Chapter XX; and the pang we feel at parting with her is anything rather than a reproach against the author.

(3) It is very certain, as the book stands, that the reader must experience some shock of disappointment when, after 200 pages of the most heroical endeavouring, David fails in the end to save James Stewart of the Glens. Were the book concerned wholly with James Stewart's fate, the cheat would be intolerable; and, since a great deal more than half of *Catriona* points and trembles towards his fate like a magnetic needle, the cheat is pretty bad if we take *Catriona* alone. But once more, if we are dealing with *The Memoirs of David Balfour*—if we bear steadily in mind that David Balfour is our concern—not James Stewart—the disappointment is far more easily forgiven. Then, and then only, we get the right perspective of David's attempt, and recognise how inevitable was the issue when this stripling engaged to turn back the great forces of history.

It is more than a lustre . . . since David Balfour, at the end of the last chapter of *Kidnapped,* was left to kick his heels in the British Linen Company's office. Five years have a knack of making people five years older; and the wordy, politic intrigue of *Catriona* is at least five years older than the rough-and-tumble intrigue of *Kidnapped;* of the fashion of the *Vicomte de Bargelonne* rather than of the *Three Musketeers*. But this is as it should be; for older and astuter heads are now mixed up in the business, and Prestongrange is a graduate in a very much higher school of diplomacy than was Ebenezer Balfour. And if no word was said in *Kidnapped* of the love of women, we know now that this matter was held over until the time came for it to take its due place in David Balfour's experience. Everyone knew that Mr. Stevenson would draw a woman beautifully as soon as he was minded. Catriona and her situation have their foreshadowing in *The Pavilion on the Links*. But, for all that, she is a surprise. She begins to be a surprise—a beautiful surprise—when in Chapter X she kisses David's hand "with a higher passion than the common kind of clay has any sense of"; and she is a beautiful surprise to the end of the book. The loves of these two make a moving story—old, yet not old: and I pity the heart that is not tender for Catriona when she and David take their last walk together in Leyden, and "the knocking of her little shoes upon the way sounded extraordinarily pretty and sad." (pp. 89-91)

> *Arthur Quiller-Couch, in an extract from "Robert Louis Stevenson" (originally published in a slightly different form as "First Thoughts on 'Catriona'," in* The Speaker, *Vol. VIII, September 9, 1893), in his* Adventures in Criticism *(copyright, 1924 by Arthur Quiller-Couch; copyright renewed © 1953 by Foy F. Quiller-Couch), Cambridge at the University Press, 1924, pp. 83-106.*

## JOHN GALSWORTHY  (lecture date 1928)

[Tchehov] is just as emphatically an author from whom we turn away when our sands run low, as the Scotsman Stevenson is *the* writer whose books we take up if we have influenza. . . . If he had been gifted with good health Stevenson might have been a great tragic writer; as it was, he was simply had to be light-hearted. He escaped into ink, and was never so happy as with a drawn pen in his hand. The older I get, the more I appreciate him. Which some would say is a sign of dotage. I used to say it myself in the days of my youth. For at that time I was so given to sitting in the French and Russian draughts that were blowing in the then rather stuffy room of English fiction, and so, as they say, 'fed-up' with the undiscriminating Stevensonian chorus of that period, that I used to look on him as an 'agreeable rattle' rather mannered and incurably romantic. I know better now. True! He is not a main-stream *novelist;* he had not health enough to spare for any great philosophic urge or any very robust curiosity. He lived, too, in the moment, and to the full—not of the type which psychologises and worries about whys and wherefores. But he is a main-stream *writer*, and what I used to take for acquired 'manner' I now feel to be the natural expression of an intensely vivid, sensitised and adventurous spirit. His style, with its unexpectedness of diction, in almost every sentence, must be acquitted of exoticism or the smell of the lamp. It expressed a curiously glancing nature, a continually stimulated interest, and it was munitioned quite naturally by startling powers of observation and a superb memory. (pp. 258-60)

I doubt if any other British writer has used the unexpected with more apt spontaneity. Whatever commentators may say on this point, that has become my conviction from re-reading him; and it is an attribute so priceless as to make up for multitudinous deficiencies. Unlike many stylists so-called, Stevenson is very easy to read, sentence by sentence; the unexpected words call no halt, and the grammar is clear as good spring water—no heavy-footed rounding-up, no violent ellipses, no attempts to get effect by vain and damnable iteration.

Stevenson, like Dumas, was a romanticist; absorbed in telling a tale rather than revealing human types and phases of human life. In **'Kidnapped'** and **'Catriona,'** truly, he was not far off being absorbed equally in tale and character, which is the happy mean; and, again, at the end of his life he was trying for realism in **'The Ebb Tide'** and **'Weir of Hermiston.'** But in the round he was a romanticist. . . . [Stevenson's] chief fault, as novelist, was taking themes scarcely worthy of his powers. Where, as in **'Dr. Jekyll and Mr. Hyde,'** his subject is deep, he shies at it, and the result is somewhat lurid. In **'The Ebb Tide'** he is almost alarmed by his own lack of compromise in handling what our critics are so fond of calling the 'sordid' side of life. How he would have ended **'Weir of Hermiston'** it is difficult to say—but he would probably have run away from the tragic story planned, although, if you remember, his lovers were to end happily, or, rather, in America.

As a teller of a tale, though in a slighter way, he is the equal of Dumas and Dickens; and he is their superior in dexterity and swiftness. There are no *longueurs* in Stevenson. He had but one main theme, that essential theme of romance, the struggle between the good and the bad, of hero against villian, and often with the heroine absent, or merely looking over the wall. (pp. 260-62)

Stevenson was so vivid and attractive as a person, so picturesque in his travels and his ways of life, so copious and entrancing in his essays and his letters, and so pleasing as a poet, that his general self overshadows him as novelist. But compare with his novels all the romantic novels written since, even those heavenly twins 'The Prisoner of Zenda,' and 'Rupert of Hentzau' [by Anthony Hope], and you will see how high he stands. In fact, next to Dumas, he is the best of all the romantic novelists, certainly the best British romanticist, and I shall be extremely astonished if at this time of day he is ever deposed from that position. For though the world is not yet too old to read and enjoy romance, it grows less and less capable, I think, of producing writers with the bloom that Stevenson had on his spirit, and the spring he had in the heels of his fancy. . . . Machines have crept into the writing of romance, and when machines clatter in the brain, we hear no longer the piping on the hills. And so, I think, we shall not see Stevenson dethroned. And I am fairly certain that, of British nineteenth century writers, he will live longer than any except Dickens. (pp. 263-64)

*John Galsworthy, "Four More Novelists in Profile" (originally an address given in 1928), in his* Candelabra: Selected Essays and Addresses *(copyright, 1932, by John Galsworthy; copyright renewed © 1960 by A.J.P. Sellar & R. H. Sauter; reprinted by permission of Charles Scribner's Sons),* W. Heine-mann, Ltd., 1932 (and reprinted by Charles Scribner's Sons, 1933, pp. 249-69).*

## H. W. GARROD   (essay date 1929)

There may seem . . . to be something of perversity in directing attention from a great novelist and essayist to a minor poet. A great novelist I think Stevenson was; and if there were anywhere in the world minor poets, I suppose he would be among them. (p. 180)

He wrote a great deal of verse which is not poetry at all; how much we have only recently learned [with the publication of *New Poems*]. . . . There is about the office of a father always some element of blind fanaticism; along every street there are pushed brats who would not have been preserved save that some one begat them. That for these two hundred and eighteen children [the two hundred and eighteen poems published in *New Poems*], begotten under grudging stars, Stevenson did not mean to make some provision, I cannot certainly affirm. . . . But that a poet who published so little while he lived should wish to publish so much when he was dead; that an artist who, in life, cared so much for the decencies of craftsmanship should be willing, in dying, to expose the disorder of his workshop, his stop-gaps and subterfuges; that this cautious earth-keeping genius should hope to reach heaven by stacking his lumber—all this I find it hard to believe. . . . Of course, the *New Poems* were bound to be interesting. Many of them are intimate and personal; and I should be sorry if we might not express unblamed the curiosity which we properly feel about that best part of a book, the writer of it. Many of them are interesting, again, for the manner in which they illustrate the influences under which Stevenson's poetical talent developed itself. I am not sure that I knew before—though I might have guessed from his Letters—how much Stevenson's verse owes to Latin verse and to French verse. I had not before marked so plainly the influence of Matthew Arnold. I had not suspected the degree to which Stevenson was interested in metrical experiment. Some of the best pieces of the *New Poems* are experiments in classical metres. Yet again, one or two of the poems give, or hint, the first version of something done better at a later date. There is a first version, for example, of the famous *Requiem*—'Under the wide and starry sky'; yet a version so much inferior to that which we know that I could wish it away, interesting as it is. (pp. 181-82)

Most of us write bad poetry because we cannot help it. From the *New Poems* I learned, what I had long suspected from the old ones, that Stevenson wrote bad poetry on purpose. And not only that. It was because he did so that his best poetry is as good as it is. I speak darkly; and it is time to be obliged to lighten my darkness. But in fact what makes the poetry of Stevenson interesting, what makes the best of it as good as it is, proceeds from his unremitting effort to escape from art into nature. . . . [The balance of art and nature], that inspired adjustment, Stevenson never quite finds in his prose—in his essays he comes nowhere near it; he comes near to it in his later novels. Whether he brought to verse less conscience, or more, I am never quite certain. (p. 183)

It is this effort to recapture natural notes that so often makes him write the kind of verse of which all his books contain some and the *New Poems* a great deal: verse in which the studied avoidance of art conducts, not to nature, but to prose. We shall be just to this kind of verse if we conceive it as written, not to exercise Stevenson in an art, but to exercise him out of it.

He is bullying himself out of that too much art which was, in fact, a disease of the mind with him—so much a disease of the mind that, if you read his Prayers, you discover that he can only *pray artistically*. That even in his best poetry he is successful in recapturing natural notes, I should not like to say. (pp. 183-84)

A good many people, I know, are offended, in his poetry, by nothing so much as by what they feel to be its *pretended* naturalness. I think them stupid; but I so far follow them that I recognize the degree to which a particular kind of make-believe colours all Stevenson's poetry. I am not thinking merely of the *Child's Garden of Verses*. No doubt, a Child's Garden of Verses would be best made by children, if children could make as good verses as grown-up people. But they cannot; and the pretended naturalness of the *Child's Garden* has no greater element of pretence than accompanies any other attempt at communication between grown-ups and children. This genre Stevenson created; whether a valid and enduring one, I am not sure. At least he is as successful in it as his imitators. The *Child's Garden of Verses* was his first book of verse; and here at least his genius for make-believe exercises itself without offence. But I have the suspicion that the book could have been written only by some one who had first learned to be a child late in life; that in it Stevenson is, in fact, trying to recapture a nature from which [illness] had excluded him. . . . Loving [all naturally healthy life] intensely, he can recapture it only by indulging the same kind of make-believe speech and sentiment as he employs to recapture childhood in the *Child's Garden*. The world of all his poetry becomes something of a garden-world, accordingly, and is to that extent, and in that sense, a sham world. . . . A sham optimist he was; and it is only one of a number of shams. He shammed happy; he shammed well; he shammed young and piratical; he shammed the natural man. But it is all the shamming of a heroical invalidism; and as such gains, perhaps, in poetry, as much as it loses, by being found out. In all this pretended naturalness there is more of nature than in some of the robuster sincerities with which it contrasts. (pp. 184-85)

Among his shams was the sham of not being a poet. (p. 185)

Of the *Ballads* I will not say more than that, firstly, you cannot keep a Scot from this kind; secondly, that, without being especially readable, they can be read, and that, in *Rahero*, the talk between Rahero and Tamatea has character; but thirdly, that two lyric quatrains of it are worth all the rest of the book— the one Rahero's song:

> House of mine, in your walls, strong sounds the sea,
> Of all sounds on earth dearest sound to me.
> I have heard the applause of men, I have heard it arise
>     and die:
> Sweeter now in my house I hear the trade-wind cry.

There is nothing in it; but the ring of it stays; and of Rua's song in the *Feast of Famine* the same is true:

> Night, night it is, night upon the palms,
> Night, night it is, the land-wind has blown.
> Starry, starry night, over deep and height;
> Love, love in the valley, love all alone.

At the same time that he was writing the *Ballads* Stevenson wrote most of the *Songs of Travel*—and this is . . . far and away his best book of verse. I do not know that, in comparison with *Underwoods*, it brings anything new in kind. As far as kind goes, it repeats the successes of *Underwoods*. But the

percentage of failures is far smaller—there are not many pieces which you could reasonably wish away, and of the best there is enough, I think, taken with the best of *Underwoods*, to make it proper to think of Stevenson as more certainly a poet than any writer whose fame was founded in the same period or in a later period. In both the kinds in which he is successful in *Underwoods*, the late Victorian lyric preluding the Georgian, and the blank verse lyric, he shows, in *Songs of Travel*, both more power and more ease. The improved ease is most notable in the lyrics proper. There is more of music in them, more of that bright hurry of notes proper to lyric. . . . [Even] in the *Songs of Travel*, it is in the graver lyric, in those poems where he weds ethical reflection to lyrical expression, that Stevenson attains his purest felicity. One or two pieces in this order, the lines, for example, to S. R. Crockett, and the stanzas beginning 'In the highlands, in the country places . . .' have found their way into the anthologies. For myself, I like better, and think more like Stevenson, a poem which I have not seen in any anthology, the poem entitled '**Youth and Love**'. . . . (pp. 189-91)

A dozen of other pieces I could mention where, in this book, Stevenson achieves individual expression; some of them executed in measures of a strangely haunting quality—I am thinking, when I say that, especially of the '**Wandering Willie**' verses, which I have not time to quote. I do not know whether any one has made a 'Fifty Best Poems of Stevenson'. I should like to see a book of just that compass, disengaging from the too great weight of inferior work the work of pure and noble quality. (p. 191)

> H. W. Garrod, "The Poetry of R. L. Stevenson," in his The Profession of Poetry and Other Lectures (reprinted by permission of Oxford University Press), Oxford University Press, Oxford, 1929, pp. 179-93.

### V. S. PRITCHETT   (essay date 1946)

To the hardworking British reader of the late 19th century, bent on his practical purposes, Stevenson proposed an opposite ideal. He spoke of the rewards of idleness and art, of the Bohemian and vagrant life which has freed itself of middle-class convention and has replaced this by the sensible notion of doing as one pleases. Or rather of doing what one pleases with an air. The attack upon the standards of the commercial middle class had proceeded since the early years of middle-class power after the French Revolution. . . . Stevenson brought his own moral, practical, genteel and very Scottish contribution to this general movement. He was not prepared in fact to say with Rabelais, "Do what you will." He was not prepared to preach the unthinking sensuality of Burns, the vagrant brotherhood of Whitman or the hard-living, passionate, criminal and medieval vagrancy of Villon. The dualism and caution of his Calvinist heritage soon extinguished the impulse of real rebellion in Stevenson. What he did propose was the safe, respectable and harmless indulgence of having the Bohemian air, if not the Bohemian heart. He proposed a form of personal dandyism which would relieve the drabness of commercial life. He established an egoism, a declaration of personal independence from established religions, creeds and codes which unconsciously reflected the self-regarding, not to say swashbuckling, philosophy of economic life. He proposed to dress up. (pp. vii-viii)

[In Stevenson, preacher] and actor change clothes. By temperament he has the virtues and defects of youth. He is a writer of brilliant beginnings. He catches the sensation of being athletically alive, which is especially the gift of youth. In *Treasure Island* and in *Kidnapped* this sense of physical action is wonderful and youth's dominant preoccupation with its own fear and courage plays naturally upon it. The timidity, the pride, the caution, the heady excitement of youth, its day dreams and admirations, are wonderfully rendered by Stevenson in these two books. They have been dismissed as boys' books; but *Kidnapped* is far more than a boy's book. It is about the hunter and the hunted in man, and it is criss-crossed by the comedy of youthful vanity. When we complain of Stevenson's mannerisms and of his artificiality, we ought to distinguish between the purely mannered, and that ingrained love of the devious and elaborate which comes naturally from the rich and compressed scruples of the Scottish character and from the tribal ironies of Scottish religious history. The Scottish character in all its tribal varieties is an onion with many skins; it is given to strife, to infinitely drawn-out arguments; it cultivates evasion; it jumps from the wanton to the secretive. A consuming conceit is relieved by a fantastic and racy vanity. The vanity of Alan Breck and the conceit of David Balfour in *Kidnapped* issue from the deeper places of Scottish character; and so does the acuteness with which they see through each other. But the story of their relationship contains a universal statement about the loyalties and uncertainties of youth.

In *Kidnapped* we see Stevenson writing within his range. He knows youth. He knows fear. He knows courage. And, to clinch his judgment, he writes of the Scottish scene. It can be said without any doubt at all that Stevenson is at his best only when he sticks to the scene he knew from his childhood. *The Master of Ballantrae* is a second argument for this view and once more Stevenson is writing out of his very bones. This book has been criticised for two undoubtedly serious defects. The woman in the story is a complete failure. The story turns on her behaviour and, because she is wooden, it never turns, but simply lengthens. The second criticism seems far less serious now than it did to the critics who looked for an exciting last act to the dramatic story. The Master wilts at the end. But neither of these criticisms affects the fine indigenous quality of the story which is well-rooted in a peculiar and important layer of the Scottish mind—I mean the Calvinist conscience and in that part of it that plays with the conception of pure evil. . . . Can we imagine a character formed by the doctrine of Predestination, that is to say, a man absolutely evil and certainly damned? This theme of the damned soul is one to which Stevenson often returns. The Master is precisely such a character. His graceful and inexhaustively wicked figure breaks through the mannered cloak and dagger convention in which the story is written. He is an evil spirit but not a romantic one. One feels he is some animal atom of elemental energy. There is nothing more frightening than his courage, frightening because it is not selfless courage; but courage with a brain to restrain it at the last minute but one. He is a master mind driving others to the wicked or fatal act. He is thinking of the last trick, not the last stand; and when he dies, Stevenson thinks of a brilliant twist of fate for him. He dies not because of his defiance, but because of a miscalculation.

This story contains a theme recurrent in Stevenson's work. It appears in *Jekyll and Hyde,* in an earlier story called *Markheim* on a similar theme; in a story called *Olalla* [in *The Merry Men and Other Tales and Fables*]; I am not referring to the theme of pure evil or the division of good and evil in a single nature; but to a more personal theme that lies inside it. Stevenson was intensely preoccupied with cruelty and especially with the re-

lation of torturer and tortured. He was a puritan who saw his problems in black and white. He saw the fulfilled man oppressing the frustrated, the graceful man oppressing the graceless, the man of wilful energy punishing the stoic. We can imagine that as an invalid Stevenson was far more preoccupied with the unheroic, the degrading and injurious power of pain than he usually cared to admit among the brave gestures of his essays. . . . And so in *The Master of Ballantrae* we see in the portrait of the Master's unjustly treated brother, an unsparing condemnation of the weak. Too much injustice, too much suffering, too much submission to a bad fate and of what cannot be cured poisons his character. Robbed, he becomes a miser, betrayed in his love, he eats his heart out until he has no heart, outraged he is enslaved by the desire for revenge. It is one of the masterly psychological perceptions of this story that the persecuted character is enfeebled when he acts against his own nature and puts his vengeance into action. Our sympathies change. We begin to admire the devil of the story. To the end he is in full possession of his diabolical faculties and refreshingly free from Calvinist introspection.

Stevenson presented this tale of persecution and disloyalty with the spaciousness and ingenuity of the great and measured storyteller. The scenes are precise. The incident of the duel by candlelight and the removal of the body by smugglers, has vivid physical life. The choice of detail is in our highest dramatic tradition. Long after putting the book down we see Alison's hand fly open when by accident she touches the blood on the sword. We still see that scene in the American wilderness when the Master, failing to trick the men hired to murder him, turns over on his side by the camp fire. They can stab him now his back is turned, but neither fear nor recklessness has made him turn. He turns with the hopelessness that the intellectual man feels when he finds that he has got to start his brain working it all out again with painful cunning once more. Stevenson was a subtle and mature psychologist in these narrow dramas of calculation and conscience. The dreams of the Master's brother are what the modern psychoanalyst would predict. Stevenson's intuitions in the province of illness and self-inflicted pain are never off the mark. (pp. viii-xi)

*Weir of Hermiston* has all the air of being the complete, the unanswerably great Scottish novel. Could Stevenson have sustained the quality of those sixty thousand words? With him, the brilliant beginner, the question must always be doubtful; but in *Weir* he at last wrote a book in which he throws off the coat of a youthfulness grown threadbare and merely professional and enters upon maturity. One thing we notice at once. His marriage has at last taught Stevenson one thing: it has taught him to draw a woman. The character of the younger Kirstie in *Weir of Hermiston* suggests that Stevenson's instinct has become warm and normal. He is no longer frozen by what he has so often called "the ambiguity" of female nature. The younger Kirstie is the beginning of a real woman, coquettish, variable, passionate, unabashed by her sexual instincts, powerful in her feeling and undisturbed by her quite conscious desire for power which, we are told by Chaucer, is the chief wish of her sex. And the young Kirstie is matched by old Kirstie, her aunt, who is a woman in the mould of Juliet's nurse. How far both these women are from the wooden heroines of the early novels.

I suppose that within his artificial conventions, Stevenson's distinctive quality is his sense of space. A man so preoccupied with attitude has an eye for placing attitude where it can be most effectively seen, and so he places his scenes at a fitting distance from each other, with an unflurried order and particularity, so that we do not blunder into them but are quietly brought to the point where the view is best. This leisurely expertness of direction makes him a master of narrative, and we are always engaged at once by it. We enjoy it as we enjoy the performance, the clean, cunningly varied speeds and trained movements of an athlete on a long run. In *Weir of Hermiston* Stevenson has extended the application of this sense of space to character. In the portrait of the appalling hanging judge, the Lord Justice Clerk, full to the neck with port, bubbling obscenities, pursuing the wretches in the dock with inhuman witticisms, and sitting up all night on his cases, Stevenson drew one of those three-dimensional and majestic figures which reconcile us to the shocking exigencies of human nature. There is more than a hint of Sheridan Le Fanu's Mr. Justice Harbottle in this portrait, and remarkable as Le Fanu's story is, we must grant that Stevenson's is greater. For if Lord Hermiston is soaked in port and brutality he is also transfigured by authority. He is a good deal more like Justice than the detached and insipid lady with the scales. . . . [*Weir of Hermiston*] has come out of the roots of Stevenson's life, and though the Lord Justice Clerk is a grotesque and heightened creation of the romantic mind, we can hear the accent of Stevenson's own father, in Hermiston's bitter words to his son: "Na, there's no room for splairgers (people who splash about) under the fower quarters of John Calvin."

Stevenson has stopped "splairging"; he has reached the richest moment of life, the moment of power and judgment. He has ceased to act or to romance away from Calvinism. (pp. xii-xiii)

If we ask whether Stevenson could have sustained the imposing architectural plan of *Weir* we are obliged to admit to ourselves that the answer is in doubt. His versatility stands against him. His addiction to words for their own sake has not gone. *Weir*, like *The Master of Ballantrae*, is a mannered book; one can only say that *Weir* has a better manner. And then we cannot forget the narrowness of his range. With Stevenson it is either all youth, or all conscience. His unmistakable contribution to the English novel is a small one, though, when he was writing, it was very important. I repeat, it is his gift of narrative. That is a quality which his plainer successors in our time especially value. His men with a conscience or an air are the fathers of those modern heroes, the tough or the Byronic, who are all air and no conscience. His *Letters,* so many of which were written with one eye on the reading public, are filled with small, exciting examples of the narrator's art and throughout his work he uses the first person singular with a flexibility which our contemporaries must admire. His "I" is something more than the reporter's "I," that is to say, it is not neutral, timeless and uttered in a void, but has some ascertainable human complexity in it. It is an "I" with a background, with a past as well as a present. It has the seductive art of impersonation. (p. xiv)

*V. S. Pritchett, "Introduction" (copyright © 1946 by V. S. Pritchett; reprinted by permission of Literistic, Ltd.), to* Novels & Stories *by Robert Louis Stevenson, edited by V. S. Pritchett, The Pilot Press, Inc., 1946, pp. vii-xv.*

## DAVID DAICHES   (essay date 1947)

[*The following essay, as well as Daiches's 1951 study (see excerpt below), sparked a renewed interest in Stevenson after the relative critical neglect following the appearance of Frank Swinnerton's study in 1915 (see excerpt above). Daiches defends Stevenson by* tracing his artistic development from a writer of romance, with its picturesque description, convincing atmosphere, and adventurous incidents, to an author of dramatic novels, which incorporate elements of the romance as well as portraying moral dilemmas and psychologically complex characters. Daiches believes that Stevenson was able to integrate both of these forms only in his last novel, *Weir of Hermiston.]*

The peculiar qualities of the Stevensonian romance are perhaps best studied by taking a general view of Stevenson's short stories. For—if we except *Treasure Island* and that piece of "tushery" *The Black Arrow*—in his longer works the pure vein of romance is never to be found alone; other intentions are intermingled; the claims of psychology, history, topography and autobiography assert themselves, and the adventure story changes as it proceeds, to become something more complicated and sometimes less adequately integrated. It is not, of course, true, that Stevenson was simply or even essentially a romancer; to diagnose his artistic character thus would be to ignore not only his preoccupations with style, but also certain less definable but extremely important aspects of his art which emerge in the first part of *The Master of Ballantrae* and, triumphantly, in the unfinished *Weir of Hermiston.* But romance, in the simple old-fashioned sense of "a rattling good yarn," was certainly one important element in Stevenson's literary character and ambitions. The exciting world of make-believe had been one . . . of the factors responsible for his choosing the career of author: ever since he had discovered . . . the contrast between physical inaction and the adventurous world of the imagination, one of the main functions of literature had always been for him the escapist and compensatory one of presenting a thrilling, exciting, yet essentially moral life to writer and reader. (pp. 3-4)

It is this combination of romantic adventure with optimistic morality that we see so clearly in Stevenson's short stories. As these stories are admittedly intended as pleasing wish-fulfilments and substitutes for actual inactivity, there can be no suggestion of the triumph of evil, or of death finally overtaking the hero, in such works. The morality is of the breeziest kind: people are punished and rewarded according to their intentions rather than their acts: it is, indeed, the morality of Fielding and Robert Burns and the sentimental Deists of the eighteenth century. The good heart is all. (pp. 4-5)

It may help to explain why Stevenson was at the same time so fond of the pipe-and-carpet-slippers interior and of the single horseman, cloaked and booted, pursuing his lonely way across the common. (pp. 6-7)

[Stevenson] was essentially a moralist at heart. . . . His quarrel with conventional Edinburgh morality was not that it was moral but that it was pessimistic and narrow. Stevenson makes this quite clear in his essay, **"A Gossip on a Novel of Dumas's"** [in *Memories and Portraits*], where he praises *Le Vicomte de Bragelonne* for its "unstrained and wholesome morality" and, remarking that "there is no quite good book without a good morality," proceeds to distinguish between "puritan morality" and the broader morality with which fiction should concern itself. (p. 10)

The optimistic morality underlying Stevenson's writing is seen with particular clarity in *The Dynamiter*, where a serious moral problem is presented through a series of adventure stories, and when the stories are finally resolved satisfactorily with a "happy ending," the moral problem disappears. Indeed, it might be said without unfairness that Stevenson uses the technique of the adventure story to make morality more amenable to optimism. A resolution on the physical level is presented as at the same time a moral solution: if the Dynamiter's victims escape and everyone, or nearly everyone, is brought together happily at the end, then the evil which originally produced the Dynamiter is finally exorcised. The device—the presentation of an optimistic morality through the adventure story—is not of course original with Stevenson. It is the very basis of nineteenth century melodrama. But Stevenson uses it with far greater subtlety than the writers of melodrama ever did, and he adds a pinch of irony sufficient to insure him against any charge of naiveté or hypocrisy. On the few occasions where Stevenson omits the touch of irony altogether—as in *The Black Arrow*—the work is, in his own phrase, "tushery."

The element of childhood reminiscence that plays so important a part in Stevenson's work is continually modified by a quite different adult strain which manifests itself sometimes by irony and sometimes in purely stylistic devices. The adult strain is more consistently visible in his short stories than in his novels. *Treasure Island* and *The Black Arrow* were written primarily for boys, and the main tone derives from his recollection of what had appealed most to his imagination as a boy. In his short stories he is largely concerned with the studied turn of phrase, the well cadenced paragraph, the mannered style. *The New Arabian Nights* is an adult work in which the adventures appropriate to a boy's imagination are cleverly embedded in an atmosphere of irony, and the author, while sacrificing none of the exciting properties of the adventure story, manages to parade himself, a knowing and worldly figure, before the sophisticated reader.

But not all Stevenson's short stories are careful combinations of the adolescent and the sophisticated. Often they are pure allegories, where the action is strictly subordinated to the allegorical intention and is of little interest in itself. This is true of *Will o' the Mill,* in which the generalised nature of the allegory gives Stevenson a certain latitude to indulge in careful picturesque description as the story moves slowly forward. A remarkable sense of atmosphere is achieved in this story, but it is an uneconomical achievement in that its contribution to the allegory is, if not superfluous, at least ambiguous. The charm of the situation interested Stevenson as much as its meaning, with the result that the picture of rustic living is filled out in idyllic detail until the shape of the allegory is almost lost.

Stevenson was always interested in the presentation of atmosphere, but it took him a long time before he could put his gift for creating atmosphere to its most effective literary purpose. *Thrawn Janet,* for example, a short story which has been much overpraised, possesses an atmosphere disproportionate, in its nature and intensity, to the action, which is simple and even mechanical, in the conventional supernatural tradition. *The Pavilion on the Links* and *The Merry Men* are stories written to illustrate Stevenson's feeling about the atmosphere of certain parts of the Scottish coast: this is particularly true of the latter, where the action is almost purely symbolic: in the former there is a not altogether successful attempt to use a flamboyant and melodramatic episode as a means of suggesting the quality of the Scottish east coast near North Berwick. As a result, the effective handling of realistic detail in the first part of the *Pavilion* loses part of its force in the face of an action which is on a wholly different level of probability. (pp. 10-13)

That Stevenson sometimes used the short story form to try out his hand simply at the creation of atmosphere is made clear by *A Lodging for the Night,* an attempt to give substance to his impressions of the background of Villon. Like its companion piece *The Sire de Malétroit's Door,* but more effectively, it reads like a sketch for a scene in a novel: indeed, a great deal of Stevenson's essays and short stories which have for their primary function the building up of atmosphere read like lost chapters from novels—backgrounds lacking an appropriate foreground. It was not until he came to write the early part of *The Master of Ballantrae* that Stevenson showed that he could use "organically" his gift for creating atmosphere; and in the unfinished *Weir of Hermiston* he demonstrated conclusively that he had learned how to use both description and narrative to their best mutual advantage.

The three short stories which must head any list of Stevenson's work in this field are *Thrawn Janet,* the *Pavilion on the Links* and *The Beach of Falesa.* In the first two, magnificent though they are in parts, the relation of action to background and atmosphere is disproportionate. *The Beach of Falesa* is the one short story in which Stevenson is wholly successful in plotting an action that follows easily and naturally the line laid down by the atmosphere. It is the best integrated of all Stevenson's short stories. The atmosphere of shabby intrigue spiced with danger, that is so much a part of trading life in the islands of the South Seas, is not only perfectly comprehended and recorded: the action at every point at once illustrates and makes inevitable the mood suggested by all the background description. The adventure story is here refined to a high degree of social and psychological subtlety without losing its quality as adventure story, a feat which, of Stevenson's contemporaries, only Conrad could emulate and surpass. *The Beach of Falesa* stands with *Weir of Hermiston* as a sign showing the way Stevenson could have developed had he lived: he was moving towards the final reconciliation of the two major strains which had run through all his work, the adolescent and the adult, action and atmosphere, adventure story and essay. This reconciliation had been attempted earlier in other ways—notably through the mixture of adventure and irony in *The New Arabian Nights*—but it was with the final solution that Stevenson found his real stature as a writer.

When Stevenson tried romance without irony in a short story he made a bad mess of it: *Olalla,* with its cardboard Spanish setting and preposterously artificial action, humorless, wooden and conventional is a complete failure, and shows very clearly what happened when Stevenson took a theme from the schoolboy side of his talent and inflated it with an eye on an adult audience. Stevenson as a pure romancer, the Stevenson of *Treasure Island,* did best when writing in terms of a young audience, just as Stevenson the stylist and ironist could only operate in a "pure" state when writing essays for adults. The romancer could only sublimate his narrative talents if he combined them with the products of the other side of his genius—his sense of character and atmosphere, of "local colour" and history, which eventually was to become senior partner in the curious literary firm of Robert Louis Stevenson and Son. (pp. 14-16)

[Stevenson] was aware of the necessity of grounding an adventure story if not in "what every schoolboy knows" at least in what every schoolboy would like to know. The adventure story is the bridge which transforms childhood incidents from what they were to what in a romantic age they might have been. "His stories," says Stevenson of the ideal writer, "may be nourished with the realities of life, but their true mark is to satisfy the nameless longings of the reader, and to obey the ideal laws of the daydream." (pp. 24-5)

The difference between Stevenson's adventure stories and the wish-fulfilment stories of the pulp magazines is that while the latter represent formulas calculated to satisfy the frustrated ambitions of millions of dull and conventional citizens, the former are highly finished and well-patterned arrangements of incidents in which the emphasis of the hero's lot is on excitement rather than on good fortune. Further, the ''I'' of the stories—Jim Hawkins or David Balfour—is not gifted with any unusual qualities or exceptional abilities; he simply *happens* to become involved in picturesque adventures appropriate to the setting in which they are enacted. And the difference between Stevenson's stories and a modern ''mystery'' is that Stevenson is more interested in the appropriately picturesque rather than in the thrilling or exciting as such. His eye is always on the locale, the environment, and though of course he does enjoy exciting incident for its own sake, the incident is always chosen in the first place because of its relation to the setting— the Hawes Inn, Rannoch Moor, the Island of Earraid. (p. 26)

Stevenson made a distinction between the romantic and the dramatic. ''Drama is the poetry of conduct, romance the poetry of circumstance,'' he wrote. In his romantic novels, therefore, the ''probability'' does not lie in the relation between character and event but in the relation between incidents and setting. Character drawing in the romantic novel is therefore to be done in large, broad strokes, with none of the psychological delicacy demanded of the dramatic novel. There is no inevitability in the decisions taken by the characters, and no moral implication. Even Dr. Jekyll is not shown as taking his fateful decision to experiment in disassociation as a result of any characteristic weakness of character: his motives are indicated with the utmost brevity; the interest lies in the action only, and not in its relation to character. (p. 27)

One can see how the emphasis on style is in no way contradictory to the insistence on excitement and picturesque adventure; for the background in the light of which the adventures become appropriate and therefore, in Stevenson's sense of the term, romantic, must be painted in with the utmost effectiveness if the sense of that appropriateness is to be communicated to the reader. Further, romance does not consist in adventure, but in the appropriate arrangement of adventure with reference both to the setting and to the reader; the romantic novelist must combine the art of the oral story teller with the ability to suggest physical background that one associates with a more sophisticated type of art. (pp. 27-8)

If romance deals with fortuitous happenings, which are at the same time perfectly appropriate to the setting, while the dramatic novel deals with events arising out of the internal compulsions of character, it is clear that Stevenson's career moved slowly from the romantic to the dramatic phase as he developed. Yet he never left the romantic phase behind: there is nothing in Stevenson's view of the relation of action to environment that makes such a relation incompatible with dramatic writing. In other words, dramatic writing can include many of the qualities of the romantic and become not worse but better as a result. *Weir of Hermiston,* which marks Stevenson's final transition from the romantic to the dramatic novel, nevertheless retains all those qualities of appropriate picturesqueness which constituted the *raison d'être* of his earlier novels. Only here these qualities are not the *raison d'être* of the novel; they are enriching qualities, which give background and depth to what is essentially a study of character. (p. 28)

Stevenson was working towards a type of novel in which, while his sense of the picturesque could have full scope, his sense of the genuinely dramatic could also operate. . . . Stevenson's success is complete: the romantic elements in the novel add tremendously to the effectiveness of the essentially dramatic story without postulating a conflicting kind of probability. (p. 29)

When one considers how early Stevenson dedicated himself to literature and how hard he worked at his craft, it is perhaps surprising that he arrived so late at the discovery of the kind of writing in which alone real greatness lies. . . . He came to literature with too many words and too few insights, and it took time for his insights to catch up with his technique. In this sense he was a classical rather than a romantic writer, for one meaning of these two overworked terms is that the classical writer is one whose apparatus exceeds his insights while the romantic writer tends to have a vision much grander than the tools he has to express it with. The greatness of either kind of writer lies in his ability to find a vision that will do justice to his technique or to develop a technique that will be adequate to give full expression to his vision. Stevenson wholly achieved this balance only in his last, unfinished work. (pp. 30-1)

> *David Daiches, in his* Robert Louis Stevenson *(copyright 1947 by New Directions; copyright renewed © 1975 by David Daiches; reprinted by permission of David Higham Associates Limited, as literary agents for David Daiches), New Directions Books, 1947, 196 p.*

**DAVID DAICHES**   (lecture date 1951)

Preoccupation with the problem of craftsmanship did not prevent Stevenson from developing a view of the novel as a profound interpretation of an aspect of the human dilemma. Though in his earlier years he was pretty much just sharpening his tools, he never lacked ideas, and his ideas tended to be concerned with the larger human problems. A year before his death Stevenson, in a letter to James, expressed his dislike of Anatole France because he merely ''writes very prettily.'' He might not have been so suspicious of merely ''pretty'' writing earlier in his career, but the fact remains that even when he was castigating those who liked Shakespeare for his moral sentiments rather than for his ability to hew out a dramatic design, he was aware that design is important because it illuminates a human situation and that craftsmanship is a means to an end. When he finally brought his tools and his insights together— when, that is, he was mature enough to use the most fitting means to the highest end—he was absolutely unbeatable. The first part of *The Master of Ballantrae* is as good as anything in the language, and *Weir of Hermiston,* that glorious fragment, is the work of a true master of the art of tragic narrative, a work of full genius which can hold its own with any novel written.

All of Stevenson's novels have a highly sensitive moral pattern. By this I do not mean that they are didactic, or edifying, or orthodox in point of view; I mean simply that the design of the narrative, and the interplay of character which carries on the narrative, is keyed to some profound moral problem, or it might be better to say moral dilemma—for Stevenson shares with the great writers of tragedy the knowledge that there are no permanent solutions to the real human problems.

Consider even *Treasure Island,* that admirable adventure story, with its breath-taking opening, its clearly etched incidents, its magnificent movement, and its fine sense of *participation.* . . . [Even] in this boy's adventure story there is a carefully worked out moral pattern, and one which presents a dilemma rather than solves a problem. One has only to put the book beside, say, R. M. Ballantine's *Coral Island* to see this at once. In Stevenson heroic endeavor is not automatically linked to obvious moral goodness; what we admire is not always what we approve of; energy of personality belongs to Long John Silver and not to any conventional hero; and the virtuous are saved in the end almost contemptuously by Lady Luck and an irresponsible boy who does not quite know what he is doing. That Stevenson was here consciously exploring the desperate ambiguity of man as a moral animal is perhaps too much to say; but it is interesting that he should have arranged his adventure story in this way and that the moral pattern of the work so completely transcends anything we might expect of this kind of novel. The author of *Dr. Jekyll and Mr. Hyde,* so clearly at work in *The Master of Ballantrae,* can be discerned, however dimly, even in *Treasure Island.* (pp. 8-10)

That *Treasure Island* is a magnificent adventure story I should be the last to deny; but one must also affirm that its craftsmanship is well-nigh miraculous, the texture of its narrative rich and suggestive, and the moral ideas implicit in its action effectively disturbing. (p. 10)

One might perhaps say that the difference between a popular (in the bad sense of the word) novelist and a serious novelist is that the former pushes his situations into what might be called clichés of plot, which make it appear that no situations are presented in the book which cannot be adequately taken care of by the author. Thus in such books all problems posed by love between the sexes are finally and permanently solved by marriage; villains are either killed off or converted; and adventure is made conventionally worth while by linking it to some simple pattern of good and evil. How different from all this is *Treasure Island*! The characters for whom our sympathies are enlisted go off after hidden treasure out of casual greed, and when their adventure is over have really achieved very little except a modicum of self-knowledge. And Silver, magnificent and evil, disappears into the unknown, the moral ambiguities of his character presented but unexplained. Is this the work of a velvet-coated aesthete who enjoyed playing with words?

Stevenson could have blocked off overtones as well as any popular hack writer if he had wished to do so. But the fact is that even in his immature and imitative work we can see this desire to ring in the human implication through style and allusion which is the mark of a major writer. He may not have lived to fulfill all his promise as a novelist, and he was certainly moving towards an impressive new phase when he died, but from the beginning he gave indications of where he was going. I do not share the admiration of some critics for *Prince Otto,* but I would say that its faults derive in part from his attempt to put too much into it, to achieve a deliberate ambiguity of suggestion larger than the narrative will bear. It is certainly not bad because it is simply "precious": it is, I suggest, defective because Stevenson tries to put in by means of style levels of meaning which are blocked by the plot. He had difficulty, in his earlier work, in coming to terms with his insights and his skills, in knowing how to distribute the burden of meaning between the direction of the narrative line and the actual fabric and quality of the line itself, as it were. The fault is not lack of substance, but unevenness of texture. And, contrary to what is often thought, it is not the fault of a man with nothing to say and lots of fancy ways of saying it, but of a man with more to say than he quite knows how to handle. Stevenson was a thoughtful and intelligent man, much con-

cerned throughout his life with the tragic ambiguity of the human animal: further, he had (or eventually developed) the clear-eyed pragmatic cheerfulness of the true pessimist. Read his novels and stories with these facts in mind and you will see them more clearly for what they are: tragedies either fully developed as such (as in *The Master of Ballantrae* and *Weir of Hermiston*) or made into comedies by wry manipulation or a kind of shrugging pragmatism. The latter is true, in a sense, even of *New Arabian Nights.* It is quite certainly true of *Kidnapped.* Henry James censured the business towards the beginning of *Kidnapped* with the parsimonious uncle: "The tricks," he says, "he plays upon his ingenuous nephew are a little like those of country conjurors." James is right, but the uncle is in the book to provide an opening and a closing which could move potential tragedy (and is not the story of Alan Breck and James of the Glens and David's implication in their fate potential tragedy?) into hard comedy: he is a pair of wry parentheses which enclose the disturbing meanings of the main part of the story. (pp. 10-12)

There is both a subtlety and a richness of implication in the way *Kidnapped* is unfolded, which presents the human situation as beyond all neat solutions and simplifications. The characters of Alan, both noble and ridiculous, and of David, both prudential and heroic, are drawn with a wise and cunning pen— even Captain Hoseason has his challenging moral ambiguities—and it is only when we come back to the miserly old uncle at the end and see David enter his rightful inheritance that a coarser moral pattern is, almost ironically, presented. (p. 13)

This richness of implication is, of course, present in even greater degree in *The Master of Ballantrae,* perhaps the first novel in which Stevenson fully demonstrated the nature of his tragic vision. The very idea of the novel is evidence of a fine invention and a profound sense of the moral implications of character. (p. 14)

No writer was so clearly aware of the qualities and defects of his own work as Stevenson, and his synopses of his own novels, written to friends when he was in the midst of composition, are invaluable as presenting us with his own view of what he was doing and what the basic design of the work was. However, in the summary of *The Master of Ballantrae* which he sent to James he did not comment on the deliberate moral ambiguity of the situation, which is the novel's most impressive single quality. The elder brother, evil but thoroughly attractive, is another of those fascinating experiments in the ambivalence of character which Stevenson projected most explicitly in *Dr. Jekyll and Mr. Hyde* but which runs through all his work in some degree. The whole texture of the narrative, which revolves so significantly round the projection of character, is shot through with tragic awareness of the paradox of human relations, and if he brings the story to an end with a trick conclusion it is for much the same reason that he begins and ends *Kidnapped* with the parsimonious old uncle—to force a solution to a situation which is in fact insoluble. He had delved too deeply into character and destiny to be able to come easily again to the surface.

This, indeed, remains an important weakness in Stevenson's mature work. His imagination tended to carry him to areas from which he could not easily return, and he more than once drew on artful but not organically appropriate devices in order to help him back. It is probable that this would have been true of *Weir of Hermiston* too, for what we know of how the story was to conclude suggests that he was prepared to surrender to a contrived ending to rescue his hero and heroine. (p. 15)

It seems that always in the last analysis Stevenson shied away from the full implications of his tragic vision. It is true that in **The Beach of Falesá** he produced a story so carefully wrought in its essentially tragic texture that plot became almost irrelevant—I personally consider this story superior even to **Thrawn Janet** and **The Pavilion on the Links,** in both of which texture and mood are likewise more important than the deployment of incident—but in a novel of any length, where the narrative line had to carry the surface interest to the end, he tended to bend the line towards its conclusion with an almost ironic shrug, which corresponded, on the level of art, to what superficial observers considered to be his optimism on the level of life. Just as his optimism represented a quietly wry acceptance of the inevitable, thus masking a profound pessimism, so even his apparently light-hearted works often represent a shrugging off of the tragic vision. If this is an exaggeration—and, like all generalizations about writers, of course it is an exaggeration—it is I think a suggestive and a justifiable one, and points to a more central truth about Stevenson both as man and as artist than the traditional view of the happy invalid would suggest. (p. 16)

[I consider **Weir of Hermiston**] the fine flower of Stevenson's fictional art. On casting my mind back on the book again some years after I last read it with analytic care, what strikes me most of all, perhaps, is its perfectly handled emotional rhythm, and the place of dialogue in establishing that rhythm. Perhaps a non-Scottish reader has not as sensitive an ear for dialogue in Scots as someone brought up in Stevenson's native Edinburgh, but I must confess that I always find Stevenson's dialogue most convincing and most firmly wrought into the fabric of the novel when he is handling the Scots tongue. The careful balance between Archie's English speech and his father's almost belligerent doric sets a ground swell going throughout the work, and it is the rise and fall of this swell which carries the whole emotional burden. It is all done with a perfect ear, a fine gearing of vocabulary to character, and a profoundly dramatic use of language. (p. 17)

No writer in the English language was more seriously and profitably concerned with the art of fiction: [Stevenson] thought about it, argued about it, wrote about it, and produced it. Here is no man to be patronised or pitied: he was a notable practitioner of "the art of fictitious narrative in prose" who produced some of the most memorable fiction in our language and who, both by his theory and by his practice, extended the frontiers of art, leaving for the enjoyment of later generations a store of good reading and a life to wonder at. Few men have done more. (p. 22)

> *David Daiches, in his* Stevenson and the Art of Fiction *(originally a lecture delivered at Yale University on May 18, 1951; copyright, 1951, by David Daiches; reprinted by permission of David Higham Associates Limited, as literary agents for David Daiches), 1951, 22 p.*

## LESLIE A. FIEDLER   (essay date 1954)

[*Fiedler, a noted American literary critic, identifies the realm of myth and archetype as the source of "clues to the meaning and unity of Stevenson's work." Unlike Frank Swinnerton, who charges that Stevenson's works lack a "unifying idea" (see excerpt above, 1915), Fiedler identifies a consistent myth in several of Stevenson's novels, noting that "the organizing mythic concept might*

*be called the Beloved Scoundrel or the Devil as Angel, and the books make a series of variations of the theme of the beauty of evil—and conversely the unloveliness of good."*]

Is a liking for **Treasure Island** a literary enthusiasm or a minor subliterary vice, like reading detective stories? The enthusiasm of the first generation of Stevensonians found a critical approach to what seemed to them all charm and magic impertinent; but today we are inclined to be suspicious of the easy triumphs of the R.L.S. style; and the genre of Romance to which Stevenson's reputation is tied has been relegated among us to the shelves of the circulating library. (p. 77)

The characters of Stevenson seem to have an objective existence, a being prior to and independent of any particular formal realization. They are, in short, not merely literary creations, but also embodiments of archetypal themes—and it is in the realm of myth, which sometimes overlaps but is not identical with literature, that we must look for clues to the meaning and unity of Stevenson's work. (p. 78)

[When] we have come to see Stevenson's development as a writer of fiction in terms of a struggle to exploit ever more deeply the universal meanings of his fables, with the least possible surrender of their structure and appeal as "howling good tales," we shall be able to understand, perhaps better than their author ever did, certain contradictions of tone and intent in the later books.

Over and over again since his reputation was first questioned, critics have asked: Is there in Stevenson's work a single motivating force, beyond the obvious desire to be charming, to please, to exact admiration—that seems to us now a little shallow and more than a little coquettish? Frank Swinnerton, who led the first reaction against the uncritical adulation of R.L.S. found in only one book, **Jekyll and Hyde,** a "unifying idea" [see excerpt above, 1915]. But "idea" is a misleading word; a single felt myth gives coherence, individually and as a group, to several of Stevenson's long fictions—and it is the very myth explicitly stated in **Jekyll and Hyde.** The books besides the latter are **Treasure Island, Kidnapped, The Master of Ballantrae** and the **Weir of Hermiston;** the organizing mythic concept might be called the Beloved Scoundrel or the Devil as Angel, and the books make a series of variations of the theme of the beauty of evil—and conversely the unloveliness of good. The Beloved Scoundrel makes his debut as Long John Silver in **Treasure Island.** (p. 79)

Long John Silver is described through a boy's eye, the first of those fictional first-person-singulars who are a detached aspect of the author. It is Jim Hawkins who is the chief narrator of the tale, as it is Jim who saves the Sea-Cook from the gallows. For the boy, the scoundrel par excellence is the Pirate: an elemental ferocity belonging to the unfamiliar sea and uncharted islands hiding bloodstained gold. And yet there is an astonishing innocence about it all—a world without sex and without business—where the source of wealth is buried treasure, clean gold in sand, for which only murder has been done, but which implies no grimy sweat in offices, no manipulating of stock, none of the quiet betrayals of capitalist competition. The very embodiment of this world, vain, cruel, but astonishingly courageous and immune to self-deprecation, able to compel respect, obedience—and even love—is John Silver; and set against him for a foil is Captain Smollett, in whom virtue is joined to a certain dourness, an immediate unattractiveness. Not only Jim, but Stevenson, too, finds the Pirate more lovable than the good Captain. (pp. 80-1)

*Kidnapped,* like *Treasure Island,* was written for a boys' magazine, and in both all important relationships are between males.
In *Kidnapped,* however, the relation of the Boy and the Scoundrel, treated as a flirtation in the earlier book, becomes almost
a full-fledged love affair, a pre-sexual romance; the antagonists
fall into lovers' quarrels and make up, swear to part forever,
and remain together. The Rogue this time is Alan Breck Stewart, a rebel, a deserter, perhaps a murderer, certainly vain
beyond forgiveness and without a shred of Christian morality.
The narrator and the foil in this book (certainly, technically
the most economical—perhaps, in that respect, the best of
Stevenson) are one: David Balfour is Jim Hawkins and Captain
Smollett fused into a single person. David must measure the
Scoundrel against himself, and the more unwillingly comes to
love that of which he must disapprove. Here good and evil are
more subtly defined, more ambiguous: pious Presbyterian and
irreverent Catholic, solid defender of the status quo and fantastic dreamer of the Restoration—in short, Highlander and
Lowlander, Scotland divided against itself. It is the Lowlander
that Stevenson *was* who looks longingly and disapprovingly at
the alien dash, the Highland fecklessness of Alan through the
eyes of David . . . , but it is the Highlander he *dreamed* himself
. . . that looks back. The somber good man and the glittering
rascal are both two and one; they war within Stevenson's single
country and in his single soul.

In *Dr. Jekyll and Mr. Hyde,* which Stevenson himself called a
*"fable"*—that is, a dream allegorized into a morality—the
point is made explicit: "I saw that of the two natures that
contended in the field of my consciousness, even if I could
rightly be said to be either, it was only because I was radically
both." . . . *Jekyll and Hyde* is a tragedy, one of the only two
tragedies that Stevenson ever wrote; but its allegory is too
schematic, too slightly realized in terms of fiction and character, and too obviously colored with easy terror to be completely convincing; while its explicit morality demands that
evil be portrayed finally as an obvious monster.

In *The Master of Ballantrae,* Stevenson once more splits in two
for dramatic purposes what is in life one: unlovely good and
lovely evil, restoring to the latter the glitter and allure proper
to his first vision. *The Master* is a splendid book, Stevenson's
only truly embodied tragedy—and the wittiest of his works, in
its device of placing the narration of the tragic action in the
mouths of comic characters, a story told turn and turn about
by the comic alter ego of the graceless good man and that of
the winning scoundrel, the burlesque Scotsman and the burlesque Irishman, Mackellar and the Chevalier Burke—comic
both of them, it is worth noticing, by virtue of their cowardice.
To Stevenson, as to all small boys, cowardice is the laughable
vice—as courage is the unimpeachable virtue. And yet for this
book, the boys' scoundrel, one-legged Pirate or Kilted Highland Rebel will not do; there must be an adult villain, though
he must live and die in terms of a "howling good tale." That
villain is James Durrisdeer, the Master of Ballantrae.

He is, like John Silver or Alan Breck, absolutely brave and
immediately lovable, though unscrupulous and without mercy,
two-faced and treacherous, inordinately proud and selfish. But
he is all these conventionally villainous things in an absolute
sense; he is the very maturity, the quintessence of evil. He is
for a time like Long John a Pirate, like Alan a Rebel (and like
the later Frank Innes a Seducer), but these are for him mere
shadowy forms of what he is ideally. . . . Beside ultimate
villainy, the Pirate and the Highland Rebel seem scarcely adult;
theirs is the rascality of the nursery, laughable rather than

terrible—and they serve at last only to define the Master's
"deadly, causeless duplicity," that final malevolence which
must be called "beautiful," the "nobility of hell." (pp. 81-
3)

One of the happiest strokes of invention in *The Master* is the
presentation of elemental good and evil as brothers: Esau and
Jacob in their early contention, Cain and Abel in their bloody
ending. It is an apt metaphor of their singleness and division.

Henry, the younger brother of the Master, James, is patient,
loyal, kind though not generous, at first more than reasonably
pious and humble. He has, however, the essential flaw of
Stevenson's virtuous men. . . . Henry does not compel love,
not his father's nor that of Alison, the woman who marries
him believing that her real beloved, his malefic brother, is
dead. He feels his lack of appeal as a kind of guilt. . . . (p. 83)

The Master *is* evil, that imagined ultimate evil which the student Stevenson naïvely sought in the taverns and brothels of
Edinburgh, another Mackellar, his notebook in hand! It is the
quality that, Stevenson found, women and unlettered people
instinctively love—the dandiacal splendor of damnation that
even a Mackellar must call at one point "beautiful!" The study
of such double feeling is not common in the nineteenth century,
which preferred melodrama to ambivalence; and it is the special
merit of Stevenson to have dealt with a mode of feeling so out
of the main stream of his time. (p. 84)

It is Stevenson's difficult task . . . to contain in a single tale
the eternally re-enacted myth and the human story, the historical event—and to do it in "Mackellarese"! Small wonder if
he felt his problem almost impossible, and if, to some degree,
he failed. I do not think he understood the precise nature of
his difficulty ever (there is a price to pay for choosing to be a
child), but he sensed its presence. "My novel is a tragedy
. . . ," he wrote to Henry James. "Five parts of it are bound
[sound?], human tragedy; the last one or two, I regret to say,
not so soundly designed; I almost hesitate to write them; they
are very picturesque, but they are fantastic; they shame, perhaps degrade, the beginning. I wish I knew; that was how the
tale came to me however. . . . Then the devil and Saranac
suggested this *dénouement,* and I joined the two ends in a day
or two of feverish thought, and began to write. And now—I
wonder if I have not gone too far with the fantastic? . . . the
third supposed death and the manner of the third re-appearance
is steep; steep, sir. It is even very steep, and I fear it shames
the honest stuff so far. . . ."

The "honest stuff," the "sound, human tragedy" is the story
of the hatred of two brothers and its genesis: the love of Alison
for the Master; his supposed death at Culloden; her marriage
to Henry, who has all the while loved her; and the Master's
reappearance. . . . This aspect of his novel Stevenson has handled with great psychological accuracy: the Master's reappearance causing the disconcerting transformation of what had
been a touching loyalty to the dead into a living infidelity; the
Master's two faces, graceful charm for Alison and his father,
careless scorn for Henry and the Steward; the timid rage of
Mackellar mounting toward the climactic moment at sea when
he discovers he is not quite the coward—or the Christian—he
has thought himself. . . . (pp. 85-6)

But the "steep" denouement that joined itself to the soundly
human story, one freezing night at Saranac, impelled the original material toward allegory, in the direction of the mythical.
In that remote place, Stevenson had remembered a story told
him by an uncle many years before: a tall tale of an Indian

fakir who could, by swallowing his tongue, put himself into a state of suspended animation that would permit his being buried alive and later exhumed without any permanent ill effects. The last presumed death of the Master was to be such a deliberate East Indian sham, translated to the Province of Albany. To justify so "fantastic" a conclusion in terms other than the merely picturesque, Stevenson would have had frankly to abandon ordinary standards of credibility, to make the Master *really* a devil, and to risk the absurdity of a myth of the deathlessness of evil. But that would have impugned the *human* tragedy he had already blocked out, and he dared be in the end only fantastic enough for a yarn; that is to say—far from too fantastic—not fantastic enough. (p. 86)

Stevenson will have the fabulous, but he will have it rationally explicable too. The Master must be provided with an Indian servant, must indeed have been in India himself; and there must even be an interpolated narrative to give us a glimpse of him there. The voice which frankly terms him supernatural, which asserts, "He's not of this world. . . . He was never canny!" must be that of a man nearly mad. If *The Master* seems to pull apart a little at the seams, it is this timidity on the part of its author that is the cause. . . . Perhaps the real trouble was that Stevenson, unlike his characters, did not really believe in Hell.

And yet the ending is effective all the same. The Master, who had seemed to die at Culloden, and had turned up again only to be apparently killed in a duel with his younger brother, is carried off by smugglers, healed, and returns once more to pursue his brother on two continents; but Henry, finally tormented out of humility and reason, turns on James, who, at last trapped by the cutthroats his younger brother has hired to kill him, "dies" and is buried in the midwinter American wilderness. Dug up by his Hindu servant under the eyes of his brother, the Master revives for a moment, just long enough to cause the death by heart failure of the onlooking Henry, and to ensure their burial under a single marker in that remote waste.

The point is the point of *Jekyll:* evil will not die until it has corrupted the good to its own image and brought it down by its side to a common grave. (p. 87)

[*The Master*] is precisely a pleasurable story, a work of real wit: a tragedy seen through the eyes of a comic character. Much more just seems to us the comment of Henry James, written out of his first enthusiasm: "A pure hard crystal, my boy, a work of ineffable and exquisite art." The word "crystal" is peculiarly apt; it is a winter's tale throughout, crystalline as frost, both in scene, from the wintry Scottish uplands to the icy, Indian-haunted Albanian forest; and in style the dry, cold elegance of "Old Squaretoes"—preserved in a subzero piety in which nothing melts. The quality of the writing alone—the sustained tour de force of "Mackellarese," that merciless parody of the old maid at the heart of all goodness and of Stevenson himself, which makes style and theme astonishingly one in this book—is the greatest triumph of Stevenson's art. (p. 88)

                    *Leslie A. Fiedler, "Introduction" (reprinted by permission of the author), in* The Master of Ballantrae *by Robert Louis Stevenson, Holt, Rinehart and Winston, 1954 (and reprinted in* No! in Thunder: Essays on Myth and Literature *by Leslie A. Fiedler, Beacon Press, 1960, pp. 77-91).*

## ROBERT KIELY (essay date 1964)

[*The following discussion of* Treasure Island, Kidnapped *and* David Balfour *forms part of Kiely's book-length study of Stevenson's*

*adventure fiction. In his introduction, Kiely states that the object of his critical study is to prove that "as a writer—particularly as a writer of fiction—[Stevenson] has a value for the mature reader which transcends the entertaining accidents of his life and the virtuosity of his prose style." Kiely's work also includes an insightful essay on the history of Stevenson's literary reputation.]*

*Treasure Island* is one of the most satisfying adventure stories ever told primarily because it is the most unhampered. The great pleasure in reading the first few chapters depends not only on the gathering mystery, but on the exhilarating sense of *casting off* which Stevenson gives us. I mean casting off both in the nautical sense of leaving port and in the conventional sense of throwing off encumbrances. It is the perennial thrill of the schoolboy tossing away his books on the last day of the term or the youth flinging off his sticky clothes for the first swim of the season. What this amounts to is a temporary change of roles, a peeling down to what seems for the moment our least complicated and perhaps our most essential self.

Stevenson begins the process in *Treasure Island* with shameless dispatch by getting rid first of geographical place and time present and all the demands that go with them. (pp. 68-9)

Before the *Hispaniola* can sail in search of the treasure, the characters must all shed their old selves, determined up until then only by the faintly vocational fact that one is an innkeeper's boy, one a doctor, one a squire, and so forth, and assume the new roles required by the nature of the adventure. . . . [The] characters of *Treasure Island* are assigned roles which best fit their previously if sketchily established selves. (p. 70)

Perhaps a corollary to the dismissal from the novel of historically measurable time and the complexity of human personality is Stevenson's cavalier casting off of the serious consequences of mortality. It is not that people do not die in *Treasure Island*. They drop on all sides throughout most of the book. There are, of course, the expected casualties among the pirates and the loyal but minor members of the crew, once the fighting gets under way on the island. But the fatalities before that are rather different and particularly indicative of the efficient purpose death serves in the story. (p. 71)

Death in *Treasure Island* is quick, clean, and above all, efficient for the rapid advancement of the plot. It never provokes a sense of real pathos even in the case of Jim's father, and it is not an impediment in the lives of the surviving characters. On the contrary, especially in the early part of the book, removal of characters by natural or "accidental" means is another step in the process of casting off the potential obstacles to free movement in the adventure to come. (p. 74)

Long John Silver is the kind of character critics like to give hyphenated names to: villain-as-hero, devil-as-angel, and so forth. Certainly the duplicity of the man justifies these labels even if it does not seem adequately explained by the clichés they have become. Silver appears to be physically weak because of the loss of one of his legs, yet Jim repeatedly notes what a husky man he is and how well he maneuvers even aboard ship. He is capable of being generous, kind, and reasonable, as he demonstrates both on the voyage out and at the end of the story when his position on the island is weakened. But he is also capable of uncomplicated cruelty. In both moods he holds a kind of parental sway over Jim. (pp. 74-5)

Silver is a player with two faces, that of the blustering buccaneer with a good heart (like Bones) and that of the cripple with a vicious heart and almost superhuman strength (like Pew).

For us to ask which is the "real" Silver, to push aside the whiskers and try to see which of the two roles is better suited to the countenance behind is unfair, irrelevant to the spirit of the novel, and not worth the trouble because it is impossible to do. It is also unconvincing to attempt integrating Bones and Pew in order to show Silver's double nature as springing from a single psychological source. The contradictory tendencies are not presented as part of a complex personality fraught with tension and paradox. Such a union of traits is not impossible for a novelist to achieve in a sea dog. Melville and Conrad both accomplish it. But Stevenson does not do it in *Treasure Island.* (pp. 76-7)

One of the pleasures in reading *Treasure Island* is in observing Long John Silver making his repeated "quick-changes," alternating rather than growing or developing, bounding back and forth between "Bones" and "Pew." Stevenson again and again allows him to assume his most Pew-like part, unctuous and perfidious, only to be defied and shattered by a verbal barrage from a loyal member of the crew which transforms him into "Bones," a roaring but impotent husk. (p. 77)

There is no basic personality from which [Silver] may derive strength when challenged or to which the reader may assign responsibility when [he] is doing the threatening. He is a weed that flourishes in ideal conditions but shrivels almost without resistance at the first sign of opposition. The point of the story as well as the pleasure in reading it is in the active conflict, not in its cause or even its final result. To try to speak seriously of good or evil in *Treasure Island* is almost as irrelevant as attempting to assign moral value in a baseball game, even though a presumable requisite to enjoying the contest involves a temporary if arbitrary preference for one side or the other. (p. 78)

Later on, most obviously in *Dr. Jekyll and Mr. Hyde* and in *The Master of Ballantrae,* Stevenson returns to the theme of the double personality and tries with varying success to raise in the midst of melodrama serious moral and psychological questions. But it is important to see that his first impulse is to play a game and to teach us nothing more or less than how to play it with him. *Treasure Island* belongs not in the ironic mold of *Huckleberry Finn,* in which the adult world is seen through the eyes of a boy for what it really is. Without the transcendental overtones, it follows more closely in the tradition of Blake's *Songs of Innocence* and Wordsworth's "We Are Seven." The child is isolated from the adult world, protected from it by his own lack of experience, and does not really see it at all except in imperfect and distorted glimpses. We learn precious little about the psychology of evil from Long John Silver and nothing of real consequence about nineteenth-century morality from reading *Treasure Island.* (pp. 79-80)

[*Kidnapped* and its sequel *David Balfour,* or *Catriona*] are usually taken as though they belonged in an altogether different category from *Treasure Island.* Both novels admit details of geographical locale and historical time which are obviously missing from the earlier book, in which chronology is presented through the highly omissive mind of a child and an island is a place where treasure is buried, not an actual piece of land a given number of miles off the coast of England. There is also the difference in the ages of the heroes. Jim Hawkins is only a boy (though Stevenson, in keeping with his avoidance of particulars in *Treasure Island,* does not give his precise age) whereas David Balfour, we are informed on page three of *Kidnapped,* is a youth of seventeen when he first sets out on his adventures.

But in spite of these admittedly important differences, the basic impulse evident in the two later books, their primary value and interest to the reader, as well as Stevenson's apparent pleasure in writing them, places them with *Treasure Island* in the category of adventure fiction as boy's dream. At the center of the two books lies not psychology, or morality, or politics, or patriotism, or history, or geography, or romantic love, but "the problems of the body and of the practical intelligence, in clean, open-air adventure." Both *Kidnapped* and *David Balfour* are essentially amoral novels, aimless, hectic, and almost totally devoid of characters complex enough to experience the pleasures or pains of maturity.

*Kidnapped,* like *Treasure Island,* begins with the death of the young hero's father, and his departure from the familiar comforts and limitations of home to sections of Scotland previously unknown to him. . . . David, like Jim Hawkins, is not plunged immediately into the unfamiliar world of buccaneers and Highland outlaws, but is given a hint of it by the eccentric and treacherous ways of parsimonious Uncle Ebenezer, his closest living kinsman, to whom he goes to claim a rightful inheritance. But Ebenezer, for all his wickedness . . . , is physically vulnerable, like Blind Pew, the apoplectic Captain Flint, and one-legged John Silver. (pp. 81-2)

[Neither] in *Kidnapped* nor in *Treasure Island* is physical weakness necessarily an outer sign of inner moral decay as we often find it to be in Hawthorne and Melville. Nor does Stevenson, for all his borrowings from the Gothic, use physical deformity as Poe does, primarily as a macabre sign of insane depravity. Though the abnormalities of Pew, Silver, and Ebenezer obviously have in them elements of the grotesque, Stevenson generally insists upon employing them in their least symbolic and most literal sense. If an unnatural appearance frightens the boy-hero, it also gives him evidence of physical frailty in his enemy. In a genre which turns on "the problems of the body and the practical intelligence," that is a grave disadvantage indeed.

The weakness of the villain—or, more accurately, would-be villain since the skulduggery is rarely if ever carried out successfully—prevents evil from taking a permanent hold in the book. It should be remembered that in spite of the unexpected reserves of strength possessed by Pew and Silver their disabilities finally do them in. . . . Nor does Stevenson really humanize his villains in making them vulnerable. It is simply his way of dissipating the threat of wickedness, of nipping evil in the bud, by reducing its physical power. Ebenezer Balfour is a bogie-man like Bones and Pew and Silver, who can be depended upon to fall with a half-comic, half-pathetic, but very loud thud at the appropriate moment.

Uncle Ebenezer has sufficient strength and treachery, however, to have his nephew shanghaied by a disreputable crew of slave-traders under the leadership of the next potential "badman" of the story, Captain Elias Hoseason. (pp. 82-3)

[In Captain Hoseason], as in the case of John Silver, we have a character ready to play two roles, shedding one and assuming the other as the situation requires. Stevenson does not use the dual nature as an excuse to raise a subtle question of morality or to complicate the conscience of the captain, but rather as a way of neutralizing his character and side-stepping moral judgment of it altogether. (p. 84)

*Kidnapped,* we soon come to realize, is . . . not so very different in spirit from *Treasure Island.* As in all games, at least two sides are required, though neither has a profound moral advantage over the other. We are, of course, expected to root for David and his Highland companion, Alan; we hear the story told from their point of view, and as a result, they seem to be friendlier company than Ebenezer, Hoseason, and the redcoats. But we are often reminded that the members of the opposition have their better sides along with their weaknesses, and although for the duration we agree to notice only their meanness, there is always the possibility that in some future skirmish they might make fairly respectable allies. (p. 86)

One reason *Kidnapped* has been taken more seriously than *Treasure Island* is that the alignment of opponents is more complex than in the earlier book. We begin with David Balfour alone against Uncle Ebenezer; then David, who is a Whig Lowlander, and Alan Breck, a Tory Highlander, are against Hoseason and his pirates; then David and Alan flee through the Highlands from the wrathful Campbells and the King's redcoats. The infiltration into the game of ancient rivalry between Highland and Lowland Scots and the historical enmity between Jacobite and Whig give the novel more weight than *Treasure Island,* and a point beyond the immediate conflict of characters engaged in tricking, battling, and escaping one another. (pp. 86-7)

*Kidnapped* has an authenticity which could not be claimed for *Treasure Island,* but when that authenticity threatens to intrude on the relatively carefree adventure with serious ethical and political questions, Stevenson withdraws from it. (p. 87)

The surface of *Kidnapped* reveals an attempt by Stevenson to move away from the self-contained world of *Treasure Island,* but the internal logic of the narrative discloses again and again his compelling need to prolong that inconsequential dream. (p. 89)

In many ways [*David Balfour*] is a more sophisticated novel than either *Treasure Island* or *Kidnapped,* and, although it is avowedly a sequel to the latter book, critics have been hesitant for a variety of reasons to consider the two together. *David Balfour,* like *Kidnapped,* is narrated in the first person by the young hero, but in parts it comes closer to being a "domestic and usual novel" than anything else Stevenson wrote because it deals with Barbara Grant's attempts at turning David into a gentleman and with the love affair between David and Catriona Drummond. It differs from *Kidnapped,* too, in its comparative paucity of visual imagery. Whereas *Kidnapped,* with a much simpler plot, seems visually a cluttered book, full of gloomy lairs, somber estates, complicated moorland topography, tartans and plaids and significant silver buttons, *David Balfour,* with a more intricate plot, becomes barer and barer as the story progresses. (pp. 89-90)

Still, notwithstanding these differences, *David Balfour* provides an interesting and fitting conclusion to a study of Stevenson's adventure fiction as youthful dream. Like *Treasure Island* and *Kidnapped,* its basic impulse is play. Its incidents are without serious moral implications, its characters without psyches, its politics without issue, and its history without consequence. There is a tone in the book which suggests that Stevenson was at last beginning to find the game stale, was becoming disillusioned with the efficacy of dream, but for all that, it does represent one last fling, even during a time when his imagination was probing other and more serious prospects of adventure.

*David Balfour* is the closest Stevenson ever came to writing an eighteenth-century novel. Other books, *Treasure Island* and *Kidnapped* included, were set in that century, but in no other work does he contribute, along with Scott, Dickens, and Thackeray, to that body of nineteenth-century fiction deliberately imitative of the style and spirit of the preceding era. The note he strikes is a modified English picaresque in the tradition of Fielding and Smollett, only without the humor. The hero and heroine are generalized types whose even features and open expressions reflect pure spirits and essentially good natures. Their faces, like their personalities, undergo no development in the course of the narrative, but are caught in an attitude early in the book which is statically maintained throughout. David's first glimpse of Catriona fixes her mask in the mind of the reader as it does in his own, and whether she pouts, weeps, or shouts invective, the basic expression somehow never changes. (pp. 90-1)

*David Balfour* bears other earmarks of eighteenth-century romance. There is the pretense, especially suggestive of Defoe, that what is being related is historically true. But although names, places, and incidents are borrowed from Scottish history, and the intricacies of political intrigue are probed at some length, Stevenson makes an attempt, in the proper spirit of neoclassicism, to avoid particularization of character and locale. . . .

Despite its impressive and authentic touches of the eighteenth century, *David Balfour* remains an unmistakably Victorian novel. It is not a lusty story, and David, for all his youthfulness, is not a lusty hero. The most obvious, though certainly not the single sign of this, is Stevenson's treatment of David's relationship with Catriona. One does not expect the breezy sexuality of *Moll Flanders* or *Tom Jones,* which is typical of only one kind of eighteenth-century romance in any case, but there is an almost bleak solemnity in the love affair between David and Catriona which appears peculiarly Stevensonian and Victorian. (p. 93)

[Although] Catriona is the weak female supposedly under the protection of the sturdy hero, she gains power over David until she is able alternately to entice and mortify him, acting with a duplicity not altogether unlike that of Silver and Hoseason. Stevenson manages to turn even love into a contest which depends much more heavily on an assumed position within a rigid framework than on the unruly responses of the human heart to another creature imperfectly understood. (pp. 94-5)

Catriona's dream is an avowed case of sex envy, the female desiring to play the male role, which she eventually does as David's querulous partner in adventure. David's inability to use the sword, insofar as it too may be taken as a sign of underdeveloped masculinity, corresponds symbolically with his immature treatment of Catriona as sister, mother, fellow-adventurer, and only rarely and timidly as lover. The usefulness of this interpretation is in what it tells us of Stevenson's apparently unconscious desire to keep the story in the realm of boy's adventure in spite of the presence of a grown heroine and a hero past puberty. It is Stevenson, who, once he has her in the book, seems to wish Catriona were "a man child" and finally treats her almost as though she were; and it is Stevenson who provides his young hero with a mistress and then makes him behave like a little boy before her.

In this adolescent game of adventure, Stevenson does with the love affair what in *Treasure Island* and *Kidnapped* he had done with history, time, and morals: he sacrifices it to the cause of action and conflict for their own sake. (pp. 96-7)

Catriona's best reason for existing in the novel is not so that David can make love to her (which he hardly ever gets a chance to do), but so that all this excitement may occur. Stevenson's original impulse to include a heroine in his book may have been a sign of growing pains, but the use to which he finally puts her shows him reverting incorrigibly to old tricks. ''Pure dispassionate'' adventure is still his mill. . . . (pp. 97-8)

For all the intrigue, kidnapping, border-crossing, spying, and sword-play, David Balfour, without being Shandean, is an impotent hero, and without being Quixotic, is one of the most inactive and inept heroes in the noncomic literature of adventure. While excitement and peril rage around him, he spends most of the novel *not* being able to do what he wants to. (p. 98)

There is action enough in [*David Balfour*], and there may be the illusion that David is in the midst of it, whereas in fact he is rarely the initiator of or an active participant in any of it. If he is in the middle at all, he stands in the eye of the storm, inactive, observant, relatively undisturbed. In *Treasure Island* the contrary is true of Jim Hawkins. . . . (pp. 98-9)

*Treasure Island* is Jim's story in every way. He responds resourcefully to trouble throughout the adventure and is actively embroiled in dangerous exploits from beginning to end. How is it that little Jim Hawkins, an innkeeper's son, is deft with two pistols against Israel Hands and can sail a schooner by himself while his fictional big brother cannot duel in the park because his schoolmaster father never taught him the principles of fencing? It would seem that the boy's dream is breaking up, being intruded upon by the consciousness of the limitations of the world in which training, physique, age, and balance of odds have direct bearing on the possibilities of active heroism. The process of casting off, so airily begun in *Treasure Island,* has become less easy for Stevenson to accomplish and less convincing to himself when he tries it. (p. 99)

In the boyish adventures following *Treasure Island* we find only a Jim Hawkins in decline—a hero with all the vulnerability and most of the limitations of youth without its protective and audacious fancy. If Jim is the perfect image of the dream hero in a child's game, capable of everything, and David in *David Balfour* is an adolescent plagued by his own inadequacy, David in *Kidnapped,* one year younger, is an interesting cross between the two. He is less inept than his later self but there are signs even in *Kidnapped* that the hero is not dauntless. Although at times he is energetic and active, he also has a way of falling dazed or unconscious at moments of crisis requiring physical resistance or endurance. (p. 100)

Unlike Stevenson's sickly villains, the ailing hero is neither cowardly nor ultimately ineffectual, but becomes rather an effective innocent, a peacemaker, a potential martyr. Although he may be physically incapable of defending himself, he still *thinks* and *talks* like a hero—is loyal to friends, unwilling to yield on a point of honor, unafraid to die. When heroic action is called for, the protagonist's flesh sometimes proves weak, but his spirit is usually willing. Stevenson turns David's frailty to his advantage in *Kidnapped* just as in *David Balfour* he makes his lack of skill and inability to act, in love and war, inverse signs of honor and heroism.

What happens between *Treasure Island* and *David Balfour,* then, resembles in miniature what happened between Homer and Tennyson: the idea of bravery has been separated from the act. (p. 101)

The curious thing about Stevenson is that although, by the time he wrote *David Balfour,* he seemed to be growing more conscious of the inadequacy of child's play as a way of art and

of the ultimate self-deception inherent in daydreaming as a way of life, he continues to treat his protagonists without irony. *Treasure Island, Kidnapped,* and *David Balfour* are not tragic or comic books because in them there is no moral or philosophical ideal . . . reached. And that, of course, is because in narrative terms there is none implied. Taken together, however, as part of a creative experiment, there is in the three books an artistic ideal attempted: the reintegration through fiction of mind and body into heroic action. (p. 102)

> *Robert Kiely, in his* Robert Louis Stevenson and the Fiction of Adventure *(copyright © 1964 by the President and Fellows of Harvard College; excerpted by permission), Cambridge, Mass.: Harvard University Press, 1964, 285 p.*

---

## ADDITIONAL BIBLIOGRAPHY

Aldington, Richard. *Portrait of a Rebel: The Life and Work of Robert Louis Stevenson.* London: Evans Brothers, 1957, 245 p.
  An intimate portrait of Stevenson that combines biographical information with reasoned conjecture about his inner life supported by quotations from his letters. Aldington represents Stevenson's life as a continual revolt against his parents, his family's Scotch Calvinist religious dogma and social mores, and his never-ending illness. Almost defensive in tone, this book betrays a strong prejudice against anyone who stood in Stevenson's way, including at various times his parents, his wife, and virtually all of his friends.

Balfour, Graham. *The Life of Robert Louis Stevenson.* Rev. ed. New York: Charles Scribner's Sons, 1915, 364 p.
  The official, family-approved biography, first published in 1901. Immediately following Stevenson's death, many of his family and friends tried to eliminate any faults from his public image by depicting him as an innocent and brave invalid. Critics now consider this biography one such attempt, and believe that Balfour's idealized portrait of Stevenson contributed to the negative backlash evident in many twentieth-century critical and biographical works.

Beerbohm, Max. ''A Puzzle in Literary Drama.'' In his *Around Theatres,* pp. 146-51. London: W. Heinemann, 1924. Reprint. New York: Simon and Schuster, 1954.*
  Analyzes *Macaire* and *Beau Austin* to identify the contributions of the two authors, Stevenson and W. E. Henley. After determining that the characters, stagecraft, and dialogue of both dramas are exactly what one would expect of Stevenson, Beerbohm states that Henley ''was so affected by the fascinating personality of his companion that he lost his own identity, and became Stevenson, thought like Stevenson, imagined like Stevenson. . . .''

Booth, Bradford A. ''The Vailima Letters of Robert Louis Stevenson.'' *Harvard Library Bulletin* XV, No. 2 (April 1967): 117-28.
  A preview of a new edition of Stevenson's letters that Booth did not live to complete or publish. These letters were originally edited by Stevenson's friend, mentor, and critic, Sidney Colvin [see excerpts above, 1878 and 1911]. While acknowledging the difficulties in handling references to, in Colvin's phrase, ''the intimate affairs of private persons,'' Booth characterizes Colvin's editorial procedures as excessively censorious. In this essay, Booth briefly chronicles the history and nature of the friendship between Colvin and Stevenson and comments that the ''letters to Colvin from the South Pacific are, in effect, Stevenson's journal for these years. They are enormously long, . . . and they detail both his literary life and his daily activities with a fullness which every biographer has appreciated.''

Chesterton, G. K. *Robert Louis Stevenson.* New York: Dodd, Mead & Co., 1928, 211 p.
  A critical biography that defends Stevenson against earlier hostile commentaries. After denouncing critics' preoccupation with the

author's life, Chesterton summarizes his critical approach to Stevenson: "I propose on the present occasion to be so perverse as to interest myself in literature when dealing with a literary man; and to be especially interested not only in the literature left by the man but in the philosophy inhering in the literature. And I am especially interested in a certain story, which was indeed the story of his life, but not exactly the story in his biography. It was an internal and spiritual story; and the stages of it are to be found rather in his stories than in his external acts."

Egan, Joseph J. "From History to Myth: A Symbolic Reading of *The Master of Ballantrae.*" *Studies in English Literature* VIII, No. 4 (Autumn 1968): 699-710.
    A modern, technical reading of *The Master of Ballantrae* that explores the conflicting natures of the Durie brothers.

Egan, Joseph J. "Dark in the Poet's Corner: Stevenson's 'A Lodging for the Night'." *Studies in Short Fiction* VII, No. 3 (Summer 1970): 402-08.
    A symbolic reading of Stevenson's representation of the poet François Villon in his short story "A Lodging for the Night."

Eigner, Edwin. *Robert Louis Stevenson and Romantic Tradition.* Princeton: Princeton University Press, 1966, 258 p.
    Finds Stevenson's fiction "closely related to . . . the nineteenth century prose romance." Eigner defines that tradition, as well as Stevenson's place within it, through comparisons with other works.

Furnas, J. C. *Voyage to Windward: The Life of Robert Louis Stevenson.* New York: William Sloane Associates, 1951, 566 p.
    Considered the most balanced and authoritative biography on Stevenson. Furnas's access to previously unavailable material, his diligent research, and his graceful prose style render this a reliable and readable account of the author's life. The work includes an extensive bibliography of works published on Stevenson between 1885 and 1950, and an appendix that recounts the rise and fall of Stevenson's reputation.

Gosse, Edmund. "Robert Louis Stevenson." In his *Critical Kit-Kats,* pp. 273-302. 1913. Reprint. St. Clair Shores, Mich.: Scholarly Press, 1971.
    Gosse's personal recollection of Stevenson, whom he considered "the most inspiring, the most fascinating human being that I have ever known."

Gwynn, Stephen. *Robert Louis Stevenson.* London: Macmillan and Co., 1939, 267 p.
    An introduction to Stevenson's life and work. Gwynn describes his work as "a biography only in so far as it follows out facts and events which influenced or determined the special development of Stevenson's literary gift, and of his contemporary fame."

Hammerton, J. A., ed. *Stevensoniana.* London: Grant Richards, 1903, 350 p.
    A collection of late nineteenth-century biographical and critical essays.

Hannah, Barbara. "Robert Louis Stevenson." In her *Striving Towards Wholeness,* pp. 38-71. New York: G. P. Putnam's Sons, 1971.
    A Jungian analysis of Stevenson's fiction that explores the role of the unconscious in the act of creation. Hannah finds that Stevenson's work demonstrates his belief in the "dual nature of man" and the individual's desire for integration.

Hart, Francis Russell. "Stevenson, Munro, and Buchan." In his *The Scottish Novel: From Smollett to Spark,* pp. 154-81. Cambridge: Harvard University Press, 1978.*
    Traces the development of Stevenson's views on romance from his theoretical essays "A Gossip on Romance" and "A Humble Remonstrance" through his late novels.

Hellman, George S. *The True Stevenson: A Study in Clarification.* Boston: Little, Brown, and Co., 1925, 253 p.
    An early biography that attempts to debunk the popular myth of Stevenson as a saint by focusing on his egoism and on his sexual relationships.

Henley, W. E. "R.L.S." *The Pall Mall Magazine* XXV, No. 104 (December 1901): 505-14.
    A review of the official biography by Graham Balfour (see entry above). Henley compares Balfour's portrait of Stevenson as a moralist in Samoa with the friend he remembers: "the unmarried and irresponsible Lewis: the friend, the comrade, the *charmeur.*" Henley's now-famous reference to Balfour's portrait of Stevenson as "this Seraph in Chocolate, this barley-sugar effigy of a real man" marks the first widely-publicized reaction against the Stevenson myth.

Hicks, Granville. "The Code of the Empire Builders." In his *Figures of Transition: A Study of British Literature at the End of the Nineteenth Century,* pp. 261-315. New York: The Macmillan Co., 1939.*
    A historical survey that discusses Stevenson as one of a group of late nineteenth-century English writers who form a link between Victorian and modern literature.

James, Henry. "The Letters of Robert Louis Stevenson." *The North American Review* 170, No. 1 (January 1900): 61-77.
    A review of *The Letters of Robert Louis Stevenson to His Family and Friends.* James discusses Stevenson's correspondence in an attempt to understand his personality and his fiction. He praises Stevenson's novels and letters as the narrative of his life story: "he never fails of the thing that we most love letters for, the full expression of the moment and the mood, the actual good or bad or middling, the thing in his head, his heart or his house."

Lascelles, Mary. *The Story-Teller Retrieves the Past: Historical Fiction and Fictitious History in the Art of Scott, Stevenson, Kipling, and Some Others.* Oxford: Clarendon Press, 1980, 167 p.*
    A thematically-arranged assessment of the use of historical settings, events, and personages in the works of Stevenson and other authors. Lascelles's aim is to understand "the working of the imagination . . . in the story-teller and in those on whom he casts his spell. . . . I wanted to know how the past challenged the imagination of both."

Lucas, E. V. *The Colvins and Their Friends.* London: Methuen & Co., 1928, 365 p.*
    A record of the friendships of Sir Sidney Colvin and Lady Colvin, the former Mrs. Frances Sitwell, presented primarily through letters. Both the Colvins were close friends of Stevenson throughout his life, and Sidney Colvin was also a critic and editor of much of his work. This volume contains portions of the correspondence between Stevenson and Colvin, as well as selected letters of Lady Colvin, Mrs. Stevenson, George Moore, W. E. Henley, and other friends and contemporaries.

Maixner, Paul, ed. *Robert Louis Stevenson.* The Critical Heritage Series, edited by B. C. Southam. London: Routledge & Kegan Paul, 1981, 532 p.
    A compilation which includes extensive excerpts from primarily nineteenth-century critical writings about Stevenson, including material from letters, obscure periodicals, and other hard-to-obtain sources. In addition, annotations which summarize the importance of the critics and their relationships to Stevenson are included for many of the excerpts. Maixner's introductory essay provides the newcomer to Stevenson with a comprehensive and straightforward account of his career, his reception by his contemporaries, his fluctuating reputation, and his critical standing today.

Masson, Rosaline, ed. *I Can Remember Robert Louis Stevenson.* New York: Frederick A. Stokes Co., 1923, 369 p.
    An anthology of personal reminiscences and tributes to Stevenson that form a biographical overview of his life.

Nabokov, Vladimir. "Robert Louis Stevenson: *The Strange Case of Dr. Jekyll and Mr. Hyde.*" In his *Lectures on Literature,* edited by Fredson Bowers, pp. 179-206. New York and London: Harcourt Brace Jovanovich, 1980.
    A compilation of Nabokov's notes from lectures delivered at Wellesley College and Cornell University from 1941 to 1958, organized here in essay form by the editor, Fredson Bowers.

Nabokov discusses *The Strange Case of Dr. Jekyll and Mr. Hyde*, which he considers Stevenson's "most wonderful book."

Noyes, Alfred. "Stevenson." In his *Some Aspects of Modern Poetry*, pp. 96-117. London: Hodder and Stoughton, 1924.
An appreciative essay on the poetic quality of Stevenson's work. Noyes believes that this quality is not limited to his verse; he states that Stevenson's writing arose "from the deep inner well-springs of poetry," and therefore discusses both his prose and verse.

Osbourne, Lloyd. *An Intimate Portrait of R.L.S.* New York: Charles Scribner's Sons, 1924, 155 p.
A personal account of Stevenson's family life by his stepson. This biography maintains the adulatory regard in which Osbourne held Stevenson from the time he was first captivated by the author's charm when he was eight years old.

Pope Hennessy, James. *Robert Louis Stevenson*. London: Jonathan Cape, 1974, 277 p.
A balanced, modern biography that avoids taking sides in the controversy over the Stevenson myth.

Quiller-Couch, Sir Arthur. "Robert Louis Stevenson: Dec. 22, 1894." In his *Adventures in Criticism*, pp. 96-100. New York: G. P. Putnam's Sons, 1925.
An obituary first published in *The Speaker* in 1894, soon after news of Stevenson's death reached England. Critics deride this article for its adulatory tone best characterized by Quiller-Couch's declaration: "Put away books and paper and pen. Stevenson is dead. Stevenson is dead, and now there is nobody left to write for."

Smith, Janet Adam, ed. *Henry James and Robert Louis Stevenson: A Record of Friendship and Criticism*. London: Rupert Hart-Davis, 1948, 284 p.*

An account of the relationship between Stevenson and Henry James, who were close friends from their first meeting in 1885 until Stevenson's death. This work, which includes critical essays by the two authors as well as their correspondence, chronicles their friendship, their views on their craft, and their technical criticism of each other's work.

Saposnik, Irving S. *Robert Louis Stevenson*. New York: Twayne Publishers, 1974, 164 p.
A brief survey, arranged by genre, that discusses the whole of Stevenson's work.

Stephen, Leslie. "Robert Louis Stevenson." In his *Studies of a Biographer, Vol. IV*. New York, London: G. P. Putnam's Sons, 1907, pp. 191-229.
A biographical essay that examines Stevenson's beliefs rather than his life to provide the basis for an appreciation of his work. Stephen was one of the author's first supporters and the editor of *The Cornhill Magazine*, to which Stevenson contributed many of his early essays.

Steuart, J. A. *Robert Louis Stevenson: Man and Writer*. London: Sampson Low, Marston & Co., 1924, 655 p.
A rebuttal of Graham Balfour's portrait of Stevenson that attempts to dispel the myth surrounding Stevenson's life and to "make him out a living, breathing human being."

Ward, Hayden W. "'The Pleasure of Your Heart': *Treasure Island* and the Appeal of Boys' Adventure Fiction." *Studies in the Novel* VI, No. 3 (Fall 1974): 304-17.
Analyzes the continuing appeal of *Treasure Island*. Ward recalls that the novel was written to entertain Stevenson's stepson Lloyd Osbourne, and finds that, because it provides "imaginative stimulation without intellectual pressure," it continues to appeal to both children and adults.

# William Makepeace Thackeray

## 1811-1863

(Also wrote under the pseudonyms of Michael Angelo Titmarsh, Samuel Titmarsh, George Savage Fitz-boodle, Mr. Snob, Yellowplush, Ikey Solomons, The Fat Contributor, and Jeames de la Pluche, among others) English novelist, essayist, short story, fairy tale, and sketch writer, poet, critic, and editor.

Thackeray is best known for his satiric sketches and novels of upper- and middle-class English life and is credited with bringing a simpler style and greater realism to the English novel. *Vanity Fair: A Novel without a Hero*, a panorama of early nineteenth-century English upper-middle class society, is generally regarded as Thackeray's masterpiece. This satiric novel comprises the most comprehensive treatment of the concerns central to all of Thackeray's works: the divisive effects of greed, class, and social ambition. Although *Vanity Fair* has received more critical attention than any of his other works, many regard *The History of Henry Esmond, Esq., a Colonel in the Service of Her Majesty Q. Anne*, a historical novel set in early eighteenth-century England, as his most well planned and carefully executed work. Still others feel that his miscellaneous sketches and essays, particularly *The Yellowplush Correspondence* and the *Roundabout Papers*, are the fullest expression of his genius.

Born in Calcutta, Thackeray was sent to England at the age of six following the death of his father. His mother, who remarried and remained in India, did not return to England for four years. During these years Thackeray attended several boarding schools where he was extremely unhappy. He later attended the prestigious Charterhouse School and then Trinity College, which he left before finishing his degree. After reading law for a short time he moved to Paris where he studied art. Although he eventually abandoned the idea of making his living as a painter, Thackeray continued to sketch and paint throughout his life and illustrated many of his own works. While studying in Paris he married a young Irishwoman named Isabella Shawe, and shortly after their marriage they returned to London where Thackeray began writing professionally, contributing to *Fraser's Magazine*, *The New Monthly Magazine*, and later to *Punch*. In 1839 the Thackerays' second daughter died in infancy, and the next year, shortly after the birth of their third daughter, Isabella went mad, never regaining her sanity. Because she outlived him, Thackeray was unable to remarry and was thus deprived of the family life he so desired. Nevertheless, he remained devoted to his two daughters throughout his life.

During the years before the success of *Vanity Fair*, Thackeray wrote numerous reviews, essays, comic sketches, and burlesques under more than a dozen comic pseudonyms. Among the best-known of these early pieces is *The Yellowplush Correspondence*, a series of satiric sketches written in the guise of a cockney footman's memoirs. The most successful of the early burlesques is *Catherine*, a parody of the crime story popular in Thackeray's day. This work is the strongest expression of Thackeray's contempt, discernible throughout his other works, for the prevalent literary convention of glorifying criminals. *The Luck of Barry Lyndon*, his first lengthy novel, was strongly influenced by Henry Fielding's *Jonathan Wild* and demon-

strates his keen interest in eighteenth-century literary forms. This work, which first revealed Thackeray's skill at depicting the language and manners of an earlier age, was also his first serious attack on social pretension. His increasing scorn for the shallow acquisitiveness of Victorian society is obvious in *The Book of Snobs*, a collection of satiric character sketches which first appeared as *The Snobs of England, by One of Themselves* in *Punch*. This series denounces the snobbery and greed bred by the changes in social attitudes and relationships brought about by the Industrial Revolution and the resulting redistribution of wealth and power.

For *Vanity Fair*, his first signed work, Thackeray adopted the publication form of monthly periodical installments already made popular by Charles Dickens. This comprehensive satire of corruption in upper- and middle-class English society is set during the Waterloo crisis and revolves around the lives of two characters, the passive Amelia Sedley and the ambitious, conniving Becky Sharp. Thackeray's treatment of these characters has sparked endless debate, for although Becky is ostensibly the negative character, it is she who actively engages the reader's interest and sympathy, while Amelia, though good-hearted, appears in the final analysis to be dull and ineffectual. Becky Sharp is often praised, in fact, as one of the most memorable anti-heroines of the nineteenth century. The other major and minor characters are also noted for their lifelike complexity. The themes central to Thackeray's earlier writings are clarified and fully developed in *Vanity Fair,* in which he delivers his most scathing attack on the heartless pretension prevalent in nineteenth-century English life. He also successfully demonstrates his pessimistic conclusion that self-interest is at the heart of human motivation. In addition, Thackeray first uses in *Vanity Fair* the narrative technique employed throughout his subsequent novels: the omniscient, didactic narrator who comments freely upon the motives and actions of the characters.

Finally successful and well-known, Thackeray went on to write *The History of Pendennis: His Fortunes and Misfortunes, His Friends and His Greatest Enemy,* the first of three related novels based on his own experiences. *The History of Pendennis* chronicles the early life of Arthur Pendennis, who takes the role of the narrator in the sequels, which are titled *The Newcomes: Memoirs of a Most Respectable Family* and *The Adventures of Philip on His Way through the World.* All three novels are set in contemporary London and are narrated in the manner, according to Thackeray, of "a sort of confidential talk." Although their narrative technique is often considered diffuse and overly didactic, these novels are praised for their convincing characterization and vivid depiction of Victorian society.

*Henry Esmond* is Thackeray's only novel completely written before publication and issued in book form without first being serialized. Critics often cite these circumstances when praising the novel's careful organization and elegant style. Set during the reign of Queen Anne, *Henry Esmond* is written in imitation of early eighteenth-century English prose. Although it offended some readers due to the incestuous overtones of Henry Esmond's marriage to Lady Castlewood, it is now regarded as one of the greatest nineteenth-century English historical novels. Its sequel, *The Virginians: A Tale of the Last Century,* is generally considered to be inferior.

In 1859 Thackeray became the first editor of and chief contributor to *Cornhill Magazine.* During his last years he contributed numerous essays and several novels to the journal, including *The Adventures of Philip* and *Lovel the Widower.* The essays collected in the *Roundabout Papers,* however, are probably the most highly valued of these contributions. In these nostalgic, rambling pieces Thackeray wistfully recounts his childhood experiences, travels, and his impressions of Victorian literature, politics, and social issues. He was in the midst of publishing *Denis Duval* in *Cornhill Magazine* when he died suddenly on Christmas Eve, 1863.

Criticism of Thackeray's works primarily revolves around several issues, including his narrative technique and his use of satiric irony. Many early critics were particularly disturbed by Thackeray's cynicism. Others claimed that his satiric depiction of self-interested rogues served a useful moral purpose and was sufficiently balanced with sensitivity and compassion. In contrast, his twentieth-century detractors have been far more critical of the sentimentality which often creeps into his works. Thackeray's omniscient narrative technique continues, however, to be the most controversial element in his fiction. While many claim that the authorial commentary is intrusive and interferes with dramatic unity, others believe that this method enhances Thackeray's work by creating a deliberate moral ambiguity that actively involves readers by forcing them to render their own judgments. Another area of interest for both critics and biographers is the possible autobiographical sources for Thackeray's works. Numerous studies have been

published which examine the parallels between his private relationships and experiences and the characters and plots of his works. Critics often maintain that Thackeray's intense emotional involvement with characters based closely upon real-life models severely limited his artistic achievement.

During his life Thackeray's work was regarded as the great upper-class counterpart to Dickens's panorama of lower-class Victorian society; however, his reputation declined at the turn of the century. Early twentieth-century critics often found his vision of society limited and his characterization impeded by his deference to Victorian conventions. More recently there has been a resurgence of interest in Thackeray and numerous studies have appeared which afford his works a more sympathetic treatment. Thus, although Thackeray no longer ranks as an equal of Dickens, his works continue to inspire a diverse body of critical interpretation, and he is generally recognized as one of the major writers of the mid-Victorian era.

(See also *Something about the Author,* Vol. 23, and *Dictionary of Literary Biography,* Vol. 21: *Victorian Novelists Before 1885.*)

## PRINCIPAL WORKS

*The Yellowplush Correspondence* [as Yellowplush] (sketches) 1838
*Catherine* [as Ikey Solomons, Esq., Junior] (novel) 1839-40; published in journal *Fraser's Magazine*
*The Paris Sketch Book* [as Mr. Titmarsh] (travel sketches) 1840
*A Shabby Genteel Story* (novel) 1840; published in journal *Fraser's Magazine*
*The History of Samuel Titmarsh and the Great Hoggarty Diamond* [as Samuel Titmarsh] (novel) 1841; published in journal *Fraser's Magazine;* also published as *The Great Hoggarty Diamond,* 1848
*The Irish Sketch Book* [as M. A. Titmarsh] (travel sketches) 1843
*The Luck of Barry Lyndon* [as Fitz-Boodle] (novel) 1844; published in journal *Fraser's Magazine;* also published as *The Luck of Barry Lyndon: A Romance of the Last Century,* 1852
*The Book of Snobs* (sketches) 1848
*Vanity Fair: A Novel without a Hero* (novel) 1848
*The History of Pendennis: His Fortunes and Misfortunes, His Friends and His Greatest Enemy.* 2 vols. (novel) 1849-50
*The History of Henry Esmond, Esq., a Colonel in the Service of Her Majesty Q. Anne* (novel) 1852
*The English Humourists of the Eighteenth Century* (lectures) 1853
*The Newcomes: Memoirs of a Most Respectable Family.* 2 vols. (novel) 1854-55
*Miscellanies: Prose and Verse.* 4 vols. (essays, sketches, short stories, and poetry) 1855-57
*The Virginians: A Tale of the Last Century.* 2 vols. (novel) 1858-59
*Lovel the Widower* (novel) 1861
*The Adventures of Philip on His Way through the World* (novel) 1862
*Roundabout Papers* (essays) 1863
*Denis Duval* (unfinished novel) 1864
*The Complete Works of William Makepeace Thackeray.* 30 vols. (novels, short stories, sketches, poetry, essays, travel sketches, letters, and lectures) 1904

*The Letters and Private Papers of William Makepeace
     Thackeray. 4 vols.   (letters and journals)   1945-46*

---

**THE SPECTATOR**   (essay date 1840)

[The **Paris Sketch Book** consists] of sketches and stories descriptive of Parisian life and character, with discursive remarks on French novels, dramas, and pictures. The flippant touch-and-go style of magazine-writing, where commonplace labours to appear dashing and brilliant, is not fit, however, for continuous reading: hence it may be that the sarcastic humour of this writer appears occasionally forced, and his descriptions exaggerated. This broad caricature style is suitable to the characteristics of demireps and gamblers, amongst whom he is most at home. His vein of humour is essentially satirical; it is too severe and biting to be pleasant. His etchings are masterly, and distinguished by grotesque drollery, of a caustic kind, that is shown to advantage in hitting off the expression of villains and their dupes.

*A review of ''The Paris Sketch Book,'' in* The Spectator *(© 1840 by* The Spectator*), Vol. XIII, No. 629, July 18, 1840, p. 689.*

**ATLAS**   (essay date 1841)

There is some good sense very roughly delivered in [**Comic Tales and Sketches,** which includes the **Yellowplush Papers**]. The author is a humourist, but, unhappily, his humour lies on the ill-natured side of things, and he can hardly ever say a funny thing without blending it with a sarcasm. We need not describe the inevitable consequences of this original defect of taste. It lowers the tone of his pleasantry, changes the sparkling relish to a bitter flavour, infuses an essential vulgarity into the whole work, and deprives it not only of the applause to which the writer's merits under more auspicious circumstances would entitle him, but of all chance of being generally read. The personalities of this work are not merely gross in themselves, but they are gratuitous. *Mr. Yellowplush,* who thinks as well as writes like a footman, goes out of his way to fling dirt at people he happens to dislike; but it is a thousand to one whether he does not offend the bulk of his readers by such proceedings, even more than the objects of his gutter abuse.

Mr. Titmarsh ought to seek subjects better suited to his talents than such topics as these. He has a vein of vigorous whim in him that will not fail him, if he tries a higher flight. Mere personalities—or, still worse, naked and shallow national prejudices—are beneath contempt. The utmost they can achieve for a writer, is to surround him for a moment with a little notoriety, which dies out as fast as a flash of fireworks, and leaves him in his former darkness. It is the business of a philosophical satirist to abandon the paths of personal malice, and generalize the attributes of society. If he cannot do this, but is still compelled from narrowness of intellect, or poverty of heart to hang upon the skirts of scandal, then there is no hope for him. This is not so with Michael Angelo Titmarsh. Why then does he not do something worthy of himself? (pp. 18-19)

*A review of ''Comic Tales and Sketches,'' in* Atlas, *June 19, 1841 (and reprinted in* Thackeray: The Critical Heritage, *edited by Geoffrey Tillotson and Don-*

ald Hawes, Routledge & Kegan Paul, 1968, pp. 18-19).

**[ABRAHAM HAYWARD]**   (essay date 1848)

[*Finding* Vanity Fair *superior to all of Thackeray's previous works, Hayward praises the novel for its ''entire freedom from mannerism and affectation both in style and sentiment.'' Although he acknowledges the satiric element in* Vanity Fair, *Hayward claims that Thackeray has actually ''given us a plain old-fashioned love story.'' Hayward also states that Thackeray depicts women more accurately than any other male writer except Honoré de Balzac. In contrast, subsequent critics are highly critical of Thackeray's treatment of women. Finally, Hayward maintains that Thackeray's ''range of subjects is not limited to class.'' Some later critics, particularly Georg Lukács (1937) and Mario Praz (1952), maintain that Thackeray's vision of life is severely limited precisely because he writes only of the upper- and middle-classes.*]

In forming our general estimate of [Mr. Thackeray], we wish to be understood as referring principally, if not exclusively, to '**Vanity Fair**' (a novel in monthly parts), though still unfinished; so immeasurably superior, in our opinion, is this to every other known production of his pen. The great charm of this work is its entire freedom from mannerism and affectation both in style and sentiment,—the confiding frankness with which the reader is addressed,—the thoroughbred carelessness with which the author permits the thoughts and feelings suggested by the situations to flow in their natural channel, as if conscious that nothing mean or unworthy, nothing requiring to be shaded, gilded, or dressed up in company attire, could fall from him. In a word, the book is the work of a gentleman, which is one great merit; and not the work of a fine (or would-be fine) gentleman, which is another. Then, again, he never exhausts, elaborates, or insists too much upon anything; he drops his finest remarks and happiest illustrations as Buckingham dropped his pearls, and leaves them to be picked up and appreciated as chance may bring a discriminating observer to the spot. His effects are uniformly the effects of sound wholesome legitimate art; and we need hardly add that we are never harrowed up with physical horrors of the Eugene Sue school in his writings, or that there are no melodramatic villains to be found in them. One touch of nature makes the whole world kin, and here are touches of nature by the dozen. His pathos (though not so deep as Mr. Dickens') is exquisite; the more so, perhaps, because he seems to struggle against it, and to be half ashamed of being caught in the melting mood: but the attempt to be caustic, satirical, ironical, or philosophical, on such occasions, is uniformly vain; and again and again have we found reason to admire how an originally fine and kind nature remains essentially free from worldliness, and, in the highest pride of intellect, pays homage to the heart.

'**Vanity Fair**' was certainly meant for a satire: the follies, foibles and weaknesses (if not vices) of the world we live in, were to be shown up in it, and we can hardly be expected to learn philanthropy from the contemplation of them. Yet the author's real creed is evidently expressed in these few short sentences:

> The world is a looking-glass, and gives forth to every man the reflection of his own face. Frown at it, and it will in turn look sourly upon you; laugh at it and with it, and it is a jolly kind companion; and so let all young persons take their choice.

But this theory of life does not lead Mr. Thackeray to the conclusion that virtue is invariably its own reward, nor prevent him from thinking that the relative positions held by great and small, prosperous and unprosperous, in social estimation, might sometimes be advantageously reversed. (pp. 50-1)

Still the balance is fairly held. There are good people of quality as well as bad in his pages,—pretty much as we find them in the world; and the work is certainly not written with the view of proving the want of re-organisation in society, nor indeed of proving any thing else, which to us is a great relief. (p. 52)

[We] heartily rejoice that Mr. Thackeray has kept his science and political economy (if he has any) for some other emergency, and given us a plain old-fashioned love-story, which any genuine novel reader of the old school may honestly, plentifully, and conscientiously cry over. (p. 53)

The interest, however, is too much divided to be deep; and what strikes us most in the conduct of the narrative is, the apparent ease with which such a number and variety of characters are brought upon the stage without crossing or jostling. Numerous, too, and varied as they are, almost every one of them is obviously a copy from the life. . . . Mr. Thackeray's familiarity with foreign manners and modes of thinking, adds greatly to the reader's confidence; and we believe lady readers are pretty generally agreed that he has penetrated farther below the surface of their hearts than any other male writer; with perhaps the exception of Balzac, whose knowledge is confined to French women. Yet, though uniformly disposed to exalt the good qualities, he never glosses over the weaknesses, of the sex. (pp. 60-1)

We have said, with reference to **'Vanity Fair,'** that Mr. Thackeray never exhausts, elaborates, or insists too much upon anything; but we cannot repeat the compliment with reference to **'The Snob Papers,'** in 'Punch.' The original notion of these was not a bad one, but it is literally worked thread-bare; and the author appears at last to have lost sight entirely of the true meaning of the term. According to him, every man who does a mean or dirty action (for example, an earl who haggles with or cheats a tradesman) is a *snob*. To give a precise definition of the word would puzzle the best of living etymologists; but we may safely say, that, in popular acceptation . . . it implies both pretension and vulgarity. (p. 63)

We have another fault to find with his minor works, particularly discernible in that clever and amusing production of his entitled **'Mrs. Perkins' Ball.'** Why are the middle classes to be satirised if they venture to give parties without the means and appliances of wealth? Why are young ladies and gentlemen to be prevented dancing except to Weippert's music, or supping except under Mr. Gunter's presidency? . . . [The] petty miseries entailed on the Perkins' family by their hospitality and good-nature, were fraught, to us, with more melancholy than mirth. The worst of setting up for a satirist is, that when food for satire is no longer to be found in sufficient quantity, it must be manufactured, or discovered by dint of a minute scrutiny into the allowable shifts and pardonable weaknesses of mankind or womankind. (pp. 64-5)

A writer with such a pen and pencil as Mr. Thackeray's is an acquisition of real and high value to our literature, and we have not the slightest fear that he will either fall off, or write himself out; for, we repeat, he is not a mannerist, and his range of subjects is not limited to a class. High life, middle life, and low life, are (or very soon will be) pretty nearly the same to him: he has fancy as well as feeling; he can either laugh or

cry without grimacing; he can skim the surface, and he can penetrate to the core. Let the public give him encouragement, and let him give himself time, and we fearlessly prophesy that he will soon become one of the acknowledged heads of his own peculiar walk of literature. (p. 67)

[Abraham Hayward], "Thackeray's Writings," in The Edinburgh Review, *Vol. LXXXVII, No. CLXXV, January, 1848, pp. 46-67.*

### [GEORGE HENRY LEWES] (essay date 1848)

[*Lewes was a prominent Victorian journalist and author who founded the periodical the* Leader *and later served as the first editor of the* Fortnightly Review. *Sounding a note that recurs throughout the criticism of Thackeray's works, Lewes maintains that Thackeray's skepticism in* Vanity Fair *is excessive, and that he forgets the noble aspects of human nature while "trampling on cant, while exposing what is base and mean, and despicable." Yet Lewes praises Thackeray for his humor, "the strong sense of reality pervading his writing," and for his excellent satire in* The Book of Snobs.]

[Thackeray's] style of writing is so singularly winning, so easy, masculine, felicitous, humourous and pleasant, that unless to very obtuse perceptions, one sees not how he could fail of being attractive. He has no asperities; he presents no rough points against which the reader's mind is thrust with pain; his manner is unobtrusive, his mannerism is not obvious. He offends no one by the vehemence of his opinions, nor by dogmatism of manner. His wit is delicate, his pathos simple, and rather indicated than dwelt upon. He indulges in no false sentiment; disturbs you by no ambitious bursts of rhetoric. There is no fustian in him, no glare from the footlights is thrown upon exaggerated distortions of human nature. Trusting to truth and humour, he is the quietest perhaps of all contemporary writers.

Thackeray is not a man to create partizans. He espouses no 'cause;' has no party. The applause he seeks is the legitimate applause bestowed on an artist: and he excites, therefore, admiration rather than passionate attachment. (pp. 44-5)

We, for our own part, cannot but applaud this. The artist, unfettered by political or social theories, is better enabled to represent human nature in its truth, and his works thus leave a more permanent and satisfactory impression. (p. 45)

[While] applauding him for his admirable judgment in steering clear of party questions, and didactic purposes, we must not let slip the occasion of remonstrance on two points—the only two—in which he seems to us reprehensible.

As a satirist, it is his business to tear away the mask from life, but as an artist and a teacher he grievously errs when he shows us *everywhere* corruption underneath the mask. His scepticism is pushed too far. While trampling on cant, while exposing what is base and mean, and despicable, he is not attentive enough to honour, and to paint what is high, and generous, and noble in human nature. Let us not be understood to say that he *fails* to honour the finer portion of our nature; but he does not honour it enough. He uses the good more as a condiment to relieve the exhausted palate. Touches here and there, exquisite though brief, show us that his heart responds to what is noble, and that his soul conceives it distinctly. But he almost seems ashamed of it, as if it were an unmanly weakness; and he turns it off with a laugh, like a man caught in tears at the theatre. In **Vanity Fair,** his greatest work, how little is there to love! The people are all scamps, scoundrels, or humbugs. The only persons who show paternal affection are Rawdon Crawley and old Osborne. Beautifully is it done, with exquisite truth and feeling; but by what bitter irony are this foolish blackleg and this coarse brutal old wretch selected as the sole exhibitors of such an affection! Dobbin, whose heart is so noble—the only one in the book—is made ridiculous. We are perfectly aware of the *truth* of these portraits; we admit the use of contrasts in art; but we still think that in thus making the exception stand for the rule he has erred both against art and nature. (p. 46)

Whether carelessness or scepticism we know not, but the moral of his books is that every one—reader and author included—is no more than a puny, miserable pretender; that most of our virtues are pretences, and when not pretences are only kept up because removed from temptation.

And this brings us by a natural transition to the second count in our charge against him. We refer to a detestable passage in **Vanity Fair,** wherein, after allowing Becky, with dramatic propriety, to sophisticate with herself, to the effect that it is only her poverty which makes her vicious, he adds from himself this remark:—'And who knows but Rebecca was right in her speculations, and that it was only a question of money and fortune which made the difference between her and an honest woman? If you take temptations into account, who is to say that he is better than his neighbour? A comfortable career of prosperity, if it does not make men honest, at least keeps them so. An alderman coming from a turtle feast, will not step out of his carriage to steal a leg of mutton; *but put him to starve, and see if he will not purloin a loaf.'* . . . Was it carelessness, or deep misanthropy, distorting that otherwise clear judgment, which allowed such a remark to fall? What, in the face of starving thousands, men who literally die for want of bread, yet who prefer death to stealing, shall it be said that honesty is only the virtue of abundance! (p. 47)

To quit this tone of serious remonstrance for one of more congenial admiration, let us notice how peculiarly his own is Thackeray's humour. It steals upon you in the quietest unpretending way, so that you seem to co-operate with him in producing the joke. He never frames and glazes his ideas. He never calls upon you to admire them by any trick of phrase or oddity of language. He does not insist upon your admiration—he wins it. The simplest words, and in the simplest manner, are used to bring out his meaning; and wit of the finest quality, as well as hearty humour, seem to spring from him without an effort. The ease of his writing is little less than marvellous. . . . (pp. 47-8)

Another peculiarity in Thackeray, which he has in common with all the great writers, and which distinguishes him from almost all his contemporaries, is the strong sense of reality pervading his writing—a reality never lost sight of even in his most extravagant bursts of humour. . . . Life, not the phantasmagoria of the stage and circulating library, is the storehouse from whence he draws. . . . [There is] nothing theatrical in his manner; the same must be said of his people; they are all individuals . . . , having the unmistakeable characteristics of men, and not being abstract ideas nor traditional conceptions of character. While reading Thackeray you feel that he is painting 'after nature;' not that he is inventing figments, nor drawing from the *repertoire* of a worthless stage.

In [**The Book of Snobs**], what a variety of characters, and how unmistakeable! *Snobs* perhaps they are not all; but are they not

all real? And yet what a tempting subject to seduce a writer into farcical impossibilities—mere fancy pieces humorously drawn!

The impartiality with which he has laid on the lash, is one of the most amusing things in the book; he does not content himself with sneering at the rich and titled snobs, but turns round with equal severity upon the poor and envious snob. . . . The reader laughing at some ludicrous picture of sycophantic snobbishness, is suddenly turned upon by this terrible satirist, and made to confess that he, the laughing reader, in spite of his scorn of all this snobbishness, would do the very same thing were he in the same place. We believe Thackeray stands alone in the art with which he achieves this. Other satirists flatter their readers, by implication at least,—but he ruthlessly arrests the complacent chuckle, and turns the laugh against the laugher.

There never was a humourist of high excellence without an accompanying power of pathos. In Thackeray we find repeated touches as exquisite as Sterne or Jean Paul; but they are seldom more than touches. He seems averse to grief, and dwells not on the 'luxury of woe.' (pp. 48-9)

But if we venture into details we shall never conclude. To use the consecrated phrase—'Thackeray's writings will repay perusal'—and reperusal! (p. 49)

> [*George Henry Lewes*], *in a review of "The Book of Snobs," in* Morning Chronicle, *March 6, 1848 (and reprinted in* Thackeray: The Critical Heritage, *edited by Geoffrey Tillotson and Donald Hawes, Routledge & Kegan Paul, 1968, pp. 44-9).*

### CHARLOTTE BRONTË  (letter date 1848)

> [*Brontë, the English novelist and poet, dedicated her novel* Jane Eyre *to Thackeray. In the following two letters, she praises him as "the first of modern masters" and "a purely original mind."*]

The more I read Thackeray's works the more certain I am that he stands alone—alone in his sagacity, alone in his truth, alone in his feeling (his feeling, though he makes no noise about it, is about the most genuine that ever lived on a printed page), alone in his power, alone in his simplicity, alone in his self-control. Thackeray is a Titan, so strong that he can afford to perform with calm the most herculean feats; there is the charm and majesty of repose in his greatest efforts; *he* borrows nothing from fever, his is never the energy of delirium—his energy is sane energy, deliberate energy, thoughtful energy. The last number of **'Vanity Fair'** proves this peculiarly. Forcible, exciting in its force, still more impressive than exciting, carrying on the interest of the narrative in a flow, deep, full, resistless, it is still quiet—as quiet as reflection, as quiet as memory; and to me there are parts of it that sound as solemn as an oracle. Thackeray is never borne away by his own ardour—he has it under control. His genius obeys him—it is his servant, it works no fantastic changes at its own wild will, it must still achieve the task which reason and sense assign it, and none other. Thackeray is unique.

> *Charlotte Brontë, in an extract from a letter to W. S. Williams on March 29, 1848, in* The Brontës: Their Lives, Friendships, and Correspondence, 1844-1849, *Vol. II,* Thomas James Wise, M. A. Oxon, John Alexander Symington, eds., Basil Blackwell, 1932 (and reprinted in Thackeray: The Critical Heritage, *edited by Geoffrey Tillotson and Donald Hawes, Routledge & Kegan Paul, 1968, p. 51).*

## CHARLOTTE BRONTË   (letter date 1848)

I regard Mr Thackeray as the first of modern masters, and as the legitimate high priest of Truth; I study him accordingly with reverence. He, I see, keeps the mermaid's tail below water, and only hints at the dead men's bones and noxious slime amidst which it wriggles, *but,* his hint is more vivid than other men's elaborate explanations, and never is his satire whetted to so keen an edge as when with quiet mocking irony he modestly recommends to the approbation of the public his own exemplary discretion and forbearance. . . . His mind seems to me a fabric as simple and unpretending as it is deep-founded and enduring—there is no meretricious ornament to attract or fix a superficial glance; his great distinction of the genuine is one that can only be fully appreciated with time. There is something, a sort of 'still profound,' revealed in the concluding part of *Vanity Fair* which the discernment of one generation will not suffice to fathom. A hundred years hence, if he only lives to do justice to himself, he will be better known than he is now. A hundred years hence, some thoughtful critic, standing and looking down on the deep waters, will see shining through them the pearl without price of a purely original mind. . . .

> *Charlotte Brontë, in an extract from a letter to W. S. Williams on August 14, 1848, in* The Brontës: Their Lives, Friendships, and Correspondence, 1844-1849, Vol. II, *Thomas James Wise, M. A. Oxon, John Alexander Symington, eds., Basil Blackwell, 1932 (and reprinted in* Thackeray: The Critical Heritage, *edited by Geoffrey Tillotson and Donald Hawes, Routledge & Kegan Paul, 1968, p. 52).*

## [ROBERT BELL]   (essay date 1848)

> [*Bell was one of the first critics to identify the bourgeois focus of* Vanity Fair, *stating that Thackeray depicts "the Vanity Fair of the vulgar great." Rather than as a work with a defined plot and identifiable hero,* Vanity Fair *is interpreted by Bell as a vast depiction of the vices of a whole segment of society. While Bell faults Thackeray for his one-sided interpretation, claiming that he "does not shew us the whole truth" about human nature and society, he maintains that beneath the cynicism of* Vanity Fair *there is an important moral, and that Thackeray exposes the vices of the world "for the benefit of mankind." He concludes that few writers have displayed "more fertility of invention, or a more accurate knowledge of life."*]

The same characteristics [found in the *Yellow-Plush Correspondence*] may be traced throughout [*Vanity Fair*]; the same quality of subtle observation, penetrating rarely below the epidermis, but taking up all the small vessels with microscopic vision; the same grotesque exaggeration, with truth at the bottom; the same constitutional instinct for seizing on the ridiculous aspect of things, for turning the 'seamy side' of society outwards, and for exposing false pretensions and the genteel ambition of *parvenus.* The task to which the natural bent of Michael Angelo's genius leads him is a disagreeable one, and often distressingly painful; but he never seems to be aware of that fact. He dissects his victims with a smile; and performs the cruellest of operations on their self-love with a pleasantry which looks provokingly very like good-nature. The peculiarities and eccentricities of matter and manner with which he started are here as trenchant as ever. No author ever advanced so far in reputation without advancing further in novelty of enterprise. He has never gone out of himself from the beginning, or out of the subjects over which he possesses so complete a mastery. He has never broken new pastures, but only taken

a wider and more thoughtful survey of the old. Yet such are the inexhaustible resources of the soil, and such the skill with which he works them, that we are never conscious of the slightest sense of monotony. All is fresh, versatile, and original.

The follies, vices, and meannesses of society are the game hunted down by Mr. Thackeray. He keeps almost exclusively amongst the middle-classes; not the fashionable circles, but the people who ape them. The distinction is important, since it gives him a larger scope with less restriction. It is by this standard he must be tested. We must always keep in mind that his *Vanity Fair* is not the Vanity Fair of the upper ranks, where a certain equanimity of breeding absorbs all crudenesses and angularities of character, but the Vanity Fair of the vulgar great, who have no breeding at all. Into this picture all sorts of portraits are freely admissible. There is nothing too base or too low to be huddled up in a corner of the canvass. (p. 320)

The people who fill up the motley scenes of *Vanity Fair,* with two or three exceptions, are as vicious and odious as a clever condensation of the vilest qualities can make them. The women are especially detestable. Cunning, low pride, selfishness, envy, malice, and all uncharitableness, are scattered amongst them with impartial liberality. It does not enter into the design of *Vanity Fair* to qualify these bitter ingredients with a little sweetness now and then to shew the close neighbourhood of the vices and the virtues as it lies on the map of the human heart, that mixture of good and evil, of weakness and strength, which, in infinitely varied proportions, constitutes the compound individual. The parts here are all patented for set functions, and no lapse into their opposites ever compromises the integrity of the *rôle.* There is some reason in this. The special section of society painted in this book resembles, in more particulars than mere debauchery of life, the conduct of a masquerade where a character is put on as a disguise, and played out with the best skill of the actor, until drunkenness or the death-bed betrays his secret. It is a lie from first to last; and no class of people in the world stand in such need of consistency as liars. . . . *Vanity Fair* is a movable wardrobe, without hearts or understandings beneath. But there still remains the question—important to all Art that addresses itself to the laudable business of scourging the foibles and criminalities of mankind—Is there any den of vice so utterly depraved, any round of intercourse so utterly hollow and deceitful, that there is not some redeeming feature lurking somewhere, under rags or tinsel?

This revolting reflex of society is literally true enough. But it does not shew us the whole truth. Are there not women, even in *Vanity Fair,* capable of nobler things than are here set down for them? (pp. 320-21)

We touch upon this obvious defect in this remarkable work because it lies upon the surface, and must not only challenge general observation, but is not unlikely to draw down in some quarters indiscriminating censure. Over-good people will be apt to shudder at a story so full of petty vices and grovelling passions. . . . But this sort of apprehension, natural enough in its way, is manifestly founded upon a false and superficial estimate of the tendency of the work. Beneath the sneers and cynicism of *Vanity Fair* there is an important moral. . . . The vices painted in this book lie about us as 'thick as leaves in Vallambrosa.' We tread amongst them every day of our lives. Mr. Thackeray exposes them for the benefit of mankind. He shews them plainly in all their hideousness. He warns us off the infected spots. . . . [He] produces upon the whole such a view of the egotism, faithlessness, and low depravities of the society he depicts, as to force us to look into the depths of a loathsome truth which the best of us are willing enough to evade, if we can. (p. 321)

The defect is not in the moral of *Vanity Fair*, but in the artistical management of the subject. More light and air would have rendered it more agreeable and more healthy. The author's genius takes him off too much in the direction of satire. He has so quick an instinct for the ridiculous, that he finds it out even in the most pathetic passages. He cannot call up a tear without dashing it off with a sarcasm. Yet his power of creating emotion is equal to his wit, although he seems to have less confidence in it, or to have an inferior relish for the use of it. Hence the book, with a great capacity for tenderer and graver things, excels in keen ridicule, and grotesque caricature, and irresistible exaggerations of all sorts of social follies and delinquencies. . . . [His] heads are portraits, not passions; he describes less the philosophy of human action than the contrasts and collisions of a conventional world; and he seizes upon the small details which make up the whole business of the kind of life he paints with a minuteness, precision, and certainty, and throws them out with a sharpness of outline and depth of colour rarely if ever equalled. (p. 322)

Looking back upon this story, we are struck more than ever by the simplicity of its conduct. It is not constructed upon a legitimate principle, or upon any principle at all. It is a novel without a plan, as without a hero. There are two distinct narratives running through it, which not only never interfere with each other, but frequently help each other on. Shoals of characters are drafted through its pages, but they never crowd or jostle each other, or produce the slightest confusion of action or obscurity of incident. . . . The established usages of novels are entirely set aside. . . . [The interest is not] kept up by factitious means. There are no extraneous sources opened as we go along—no episodes to relieve the route—no superfluous characters to strew it with variety. The interest is progressive and complete to the end.

There is another merit in this story. It is free from over-refinement or elaboration. All is direct, palpable, and close. The touches exhibit the decisive hand of a true artist. (p. 332)

[Although] we should be unwilling to lose a page of *Vanity Fair*, we may advise the author to keep within narrower limits in future. It is a gigantic undertaking to get through this massive volume. . . . [Yet], large as this octavo is, we put it down with reluctance. The originality of the treatment, the freshness and fluency of the style, and the absence of peculiarities in the diction or terms of expression, inspire it with the charm of perpetual variety. No writer was ever less of a mannerist, and few writers have displayed within the compass of a single story more fertility of invention, or a more accurate knowledge of life. (pp. 332-33)

> [*Robert Bell*], in a review of "Vanity Fair," in Fraser's Magazine, *Vol. XXXVIII, No. CCXXV, September, 1848, pp. 320-33.*

### [ELIZABETH RIGBY]   (essay date 1848)

['**Vanity Fair**,'] much as we were entitled to expect from its author's pen, has fairly taken us by surprise. We were perfectly aware that Mr. Thackeray had of old assumed the jester's habit, in order the more unrestrainedly to indulge the privilege of speaking the truth . . . but still we were little prepared for the keen observation, the deep wisdom, and the consummate art

which he has interwoven in the slight texture and whimsical pattern of '**Vanity Fair**.' . . . With all [its] unpretending materials it is one of the most amusing, but also one of the most distressing books we have read for many a long year. We almost long for a little exaggeration and improbability to relieve us of that sense of dead truthfulness which weighs down our hearts, not for the Amelias and Georges of the story, but for poor kindred human nature. In one light this truthfulness is even an objection. With few exceptions the personages are too like our every-day selves and neighbours to draw any distinct moral from. We cannot see our way clearly. Palliations of the bad and disappointments in the good are perpetually obstructing our judgment, by bringing what should decide it too close to that common standard of experience in which our only rule of opinion is charity. For it is only in fictitious characters which are highly coloured for one definite object, or in notorious personages viewed from a distance, that the course of the true moral can be seen to run straight—once bring the individual with his life and circumstances closely before you, and it is lost to the mental eye in the thousand pleas and witnesses, unseen and unheard before, which rise up to overshadow it. And what are all these personages in '**Vanity Fair**' but feigned names for our own beloved friends and acquaintances, seen under such a puzzling crosslight of good in evil, and evil in good, of sins and sinnings against, of little to be praised virtues, and much to be excused vices, that we cannot presume to moralise upon them—not even to judge them,—content to exclaim sorrowfully with the old prophet, 'Alas! my brother!' Every actor on the crowded stage of '**Vanity Fair**' represents some type of that perverse mixture of humanity in which there is ever something not wholly to approve or to condemn. (p. 83)

But if these performers give us pain, we are not ashamed to own, as we are speaking openly, that the chief actress herself gives us none at all. For there is of course a principal pilgrim in '**Vanity Fair**,' as much as in its emblematical original. Bunyan's 'Progress;' only unfortunately this one is travelling the wrong way. And we say 'unfortunately' merely by way of courtesy, for in reality we care little about the matter. No, Becky—our hearts neither bleed for you, nor cry out against you. . . . People who allow their feelings to be lacerated by such a character and career as yours, are doing both you and themselves great injustice. No author could have openly introduced a near connection of Satan's into the best London society, nor would the moral end intended have been answered by it; but really and honestly, considering Becky in her human character, we know of none which so thoroughly satisfies our highest *beau idéal* of feminine wickedness, with so slight a shock to our feelings and proprieties. (p. 84)

Upon the whole, we are not afraid to own that we rather enjoy her *ignis fatuus* course, dragging the weak and the vain and the selfish, through mud and mire, after her, and acting all parts, from the modest rushlight to the gracious star, just as it suits her. Clever little imp that she is! What exquisite tact she shows!—what unflagging good humour!—what ready self-possession! Becky never disappoints us; she never even makes us tremble. We know that her answer will come exactly suiting her one particular object, and frequently three or four more in prospect. What respect, too, she has for those decencies which more virtuous, but more stupid humanity, often disdains! What detection of all that is false and mean! What instinct for all that is true and great! She is her master's true pupil in that: she knows what is really divine as well as he, and bows before it. . . .

We are not sure . . . whether we are justified in calling her 'le mauvais coeur' [an evil heart]. Becky does not pursue any one vindictively; she never does gratuitous mischief. The fountain is more dry than poisoned. She is even generous—when she can afford it. . . .

In short, the only respect in which Becky's course gives us pain is when it locks itself into that of another, and more genuine child of this earth. No one can regret those being entangled in her nets whose vanity and meanness of spirit alone led them into its meshes—such are rightly served; but we do grudge her that real sacred thing called *love,* even of a Rawdon Crawley, who has more of that self-forgetting, all-purifying feeling for his little evil spirit than many a better man has for a good woman. We do grudge Becky *a heart,* though it belong only to a swindler. (p. 85)

**'Vanity Fair'** is pre-eminently a novel of the day—not in the vulgar sense, of which there are too many, but as a literal photograph of the manners and habits of the nineteenth century, thrown on to paper by the light of a powerful mind; and one also of the most artistic effect. Mr. Thackeray has a peculiar adroitness in leading on the fancy, or rather memory of his reader from one set of circumstances to another by the seeming chances and coincidences of common life, as an artist leads the spectator's eye through the subject of his picture by a skilful repetition of colour. . . . There is that mutual dependence in his characters which is the first requisite in painting every-day life; no one is stuck on a separate pedestal—no one is sitting for his portrait. There may be one exception; we mean Sir Pitt Crawley, senior: it is possible, nay, we hardly doubt, that this baronet was closer drawn from individual life than anybody else in the book. . . . The whole course of the work may be viewed as the *Wander-Jahre* of a far cleverer female *Wilhelm Meister* [of Johann von Goethe's novel *Wilhelm Meisters Wanderjahre*]. We have watched her in the ups-and-downs of life— among the humble, the fashionable, the great, and the pious— and found her ever new; yet ever the same. . . . (pp. 86-7)

> [*Elizabeth Rigby*], *in a review of "Vanity Fair: A Novel without a Hero," in* The London Quarterly Review, *Vol. LXXXIV, No. CLXVII, December, 1848, pp. 83-7.*

## [DAVID MASSON]  (essay date 1851)

Both [Mr. Dickens and Mr. Thackeray] seem to be easy penmen, and to have language very readily at their command; both also seem to convey their meaning as simply as they can, and to be careful, according to their notions of verbal accuracy; but in Mr. Dickens's sentences there is a leafiness, a tendency to words and images, for their own sake; whereas in Mr. Thackeray's one sees the stem and outline of the thought better. . . . On the whole, if we had to choose passages at random, to be set before young scholars as examples of easy and vigorous English composition, we would take them rather from Thackeray than from Dickens. There is a Horatian strictness, a racy strength, in Mr. Thackeray's expressions, even in his more level and tame passages, which we miss in the corresponding passages in Mr. Dickens's writings. (pp. 61-2)

On the whole it may be said that, while there are few things that Mr. Thackeray can do in the way of description which Mr. Dickens could not also do, there is a large region of objects and appearances familiar to the artistic activity of Mr. Dickens, where Mr. Thackeray would not find himself at home. And as Mr. Dickens's artistic range is thus wider than that of Mr.

Thackeray, so also his style of art is the more elevated. Thackeray is essentially an artist of the real school; he belongs to what, in painting, would be called the school of low art. All that he portrays—scenes as well as characters—is within the limits, and rigidly true to the features, of real existence. In this lies his particular merit. . . . Dickens, on the other hand, works more in the ideal. . . . Seizing the notion of some oddity as seen in the real world, Mr. Dickens has run away with it into a kind of outer or ideal region, there to play with it and work it out at leisure as extravagantly as he might choose, without the least impediment from any facts except those of his own story. One result of this method is, that his characters do not present the mixture of good and bad in the same proportions as we find in nature. Some of his characters are thoroughly and ideally perfect; others are thoroughly and ideally detestable; and even in those where he has intended a mingled impression, vice and virtue are blended in a purely ideal manner. It is different with Mr. Thackeray. The last words of his **"Pendennis"** are a petition for the charity of his readers in behalf of the principal personage of the story, on the ground that not having meant to represent him as a hero, but "only as a man and a brother," he has exposed his foibles rather too freely. So, also, in almost all his other characters his study seems to be to give the good and the bad together, in very nearly the same proportions that the cunning apothecary, Nature herself, uses. Now, while, according to Mr. Thackeray's style of art, this is perfectly proper, it does not follow that Mr. Dickens's method is wrong. . . . Art is called Art, says Goethe, precisely because it is *not* Nature; and even such a department of art as the modern novel is entitled to the benefit of this maxim. (pp. 74-5)

But, while Mr. Dickens is both more extensive in the range, and more poetic in the style of his art than Mr. Thackeray, the latter is, perhaps, within his own range and in his own style, the more careful artist. His stroke is truer and surer, and his attention to finish greater. This may be, in part, owing to the fact that Mr. Thackeray can handle the pencil as well as the pen. Being the illustrator of his own works, and accustomed, therefore, to reduce his fancies to visible form and outline, he attains, in the result, greater clearness and precision, than one who works only in language, or who has to get his fancies made visible to himself by the pencil of another. Apart, however, from the real talent with which Mr. Thackeray illustrates his pages, it may be cited as a proof of the distinctness with which he conceives what he writes, that the names of his characters are almost always excellent. Mr. Dickens has always been thought particularly happy in this respect; we are not sure, however, that Mr. Thackeray does not sometimes surpass him. Dr. Slocum, Miss Mactoddy, the Scotch surgeon Glowry, Jeames the footman—these and such-like names, which Mr. Thackeray seems to throw off with such ease, that he lavishes them even on his incidental and minor characters—are, in themselves, positive bits of humour. (p. 76)

Why is Mr. Dickens, on the whole, genial, kindly, and romantic, and Mr. Thackeray, on the whole, caustic, shrewd, and satirical in his fictions? Clearly, the difference must arise from some radical difference in their ways of looking at the world, and in their conclusions as to the business and destinies of men in it. (p. 81)

Mr. Thackeray being . . . less dogmatic in his habits of writing than Mr. Dickens, less given to state and argue maxims in a propositional form, it is not so easy to obtain passages from his writings explaining his general views in the first person.

On the whole, however, judging from little indications, from the general tone of his writings, and from literary analogy, we should say that he differs from Mr. Dickens in this, that, instead of clinging to any positive doctrine, from the neighbourhood of which he might survey nature and life, he holds his mind in a general state of negation and scepticism. There is in **"Pendennis"** a very interesting chapter, entitled *"The Way of the World,"* . . . in which Mr. Thackeray falls into a more serious strain than usual. A long, and almost religious, dialogue takes place between Pen, then in a low moral state, and professing himself a sceptic . . . , and his elder friend Warrington, who retorts his arguments, denounces his conclusions, and tries to rekindle in him faith and enthusiasm. (p. 83)

Mr. Thackeray does not only report Pen's opinions, he also comments on these opinions very gravely in his own name, and he combats them through the medium of Warrington. . . . Accordingly, it seems to us, that in this antinomy between Pen and Warrington, we may, without any injustice, discern the main features of the author's own philosophy of life. In other words, it seems to us that there are many parts of Mr. Thackeray's writings in which the spirit of the Pendennis theory may be assumed to predominate; but that, ever and anon, traces of the Warrington spirit are also to be found in them. (p. 85)

On the whole, we should say that Mr. Thackeray has nowhere exhibited this serious spirit so conspicuously as in the second volume of his **"Pendennis;"** and remarking this, and how good the effect is, we must admit, without any prejudice to our previous observation regarding the necessity of Mr. Thackeray's keeping obstinately to his own style of art, that we should like to see him in future diminish the Pen a little and develop the Warrington. (p. 87)

> [*David Masson*], *"'Pendennis' and 'Copperfield': Thackeray and Dickens," in* The North British Review, *Vol. XV, No. XXIX, May, 1851, pp. 57-89.\**

## [GEORGE BRIMLEY]   (essay date 1852)

*Esmond* is an autobiographical memoir of the first five-and-thirty years of the life of an English gentleman of family, written in his old age after his retirement to Virginia. . . .

The book has the great charm of reality. The framework is . . . historical: men with well-known names, political, literary, military, pass and repass; their sayings and doings are interwoven with the sayings and doings of the fictitious characters; and all reads like a genuine memoir of the time. . . .

Mr. Thackeray's humour does not mainly consist in the creation of oddities of manner, habit, or feeling; but in so representing actual men and women as to excite a sense of incongruity in the reader's mind—a feeling that the follies and vices described are deviations from an ideal of humanity always present to the writer. The real is described vividly, with that perception of individuality which constitutes the artist; but the description implies and suggests a standard higher than itself, not by any direct assertion of such a standard, but by an unmistakeable irony. The moral antithesis of actual and ideal is the root from which springs the peculiar charm of Mr. Thackeray's writings; that mixture of gayety and seriousness, of sarcasm and tenderness, of enjoyment and cynicism, which reflects so well the contradictory consciousness of man as a being with senses and passions and limited knowledge, yet with a conscience and a reason speaking to him of eternal laws and a moral order of the universe. It is this that makes Mr. Thackeray a profound

moralist, just as Hogarth showed his knowledge of perspective by drawing a landscape throughout in violation of its rules. So, in Mr. Thackeray's picture of society as it is, society as it ought to be is implied. He could not have painted Vanity Fair as he has, unless Eden had been shining brightly in his inner eyes. The historian of "snobs" indicates in every touch his fine sense of a gentleman or a lady. No one could be simply amused with Mr. Thackeray's descriptions or his dialogues. A shame at one's own defects, at the defects of the world in which one was living, was irresistibly aroused along with the reception of the particular portraiture. But while he was dealing with his own age, his keen perceptive faculty prevailed, and the actual predominates in his pictures of modern society. His fine appreciation of high character has hitherto been chiefly shown (though with bright exceptions) by his definition of its contrary. But, getting quite out of the region of his personal experiences, he has shown his true nature without this mark of satire and irony. The ideal is no longer implied, but realized, in the two leading characters of *Esmond*. The medal is reversed, and what appeared as scorn of baseness is revealed as love of goodness and nobleness—what appeared as cynicism is presented as a heart-worship of what is pure, affectionate, and unselfish. (p. 1066)

*Esmond* will, we think, rank higher as a work of art than either *Vanity Fair* or *Pendennis:* because the characters are of a higher type, and drawn with greater finish, and the book is more of a complete whole. . . .

[The style] is manly, clear, terse, and vigorous, reflecting every mood—pathetic, grave, or sarcastic—of the writer: and the writing has these qualities because the writer knows what he means to say, and does not give the public thoughts half-worked-out, or thoughts on matters where clear thinking is impossible. (p. 1067)

> [*George Brimley*], *"Thackeray's 'Esmond'," in* The Spectator (© 1852 by The Spectator), *Vol. 25, No. 1271, November 6, 1852, pp. 1066-67.*

## [JOHN FORSTER]   (essay date 1852)

We have at once to express, in the warmest terms of praise, our appreciation of the skill and taste with which *Esmond* is written. Mr. Thackeray has caught the true tone of the writers of Queen Anne's time, and has sprinkled with a duly sparing hand the few peculiarities of grammar proper to them, imitating at the same time their more numerous peculiarities of diction, and throwing in here and there little marks of an elegant, yet what we now should call somewhat of a pedantic, display of classical quotation, with consummate tact. There is no excess, no strain after effect. . . . [He] has not so much imitated any single writer, as he has carried his own pen back into Queen Anne's time; they are his own characteristic trains of thought with which his pages are informed, his own touches of humour with which they are enlivened. The story of the novel, too, is sufficiently ingenious, and although faulty in several respects, is very elegantly constructed, and carried onward through ingenious windings, gratifying constant curiosity until the end. . . . Whether by its style, or by the treatment of its subject, in short, the book thoroughly occupies our minds with a sense of strength on the part of the writer, of which the manifestation is made always gracefully. (p. 723)

*Esmond*, though by no means equal to *Vanity Fair* in interest, excels even that well-written work as a display of literary power; and we are glad also to see that many of its passages show a better and healthier tone of social feeling. We wish it were possible for us to say more than this, and to add that Mr. Thackeray, before writing *Esmond,* has quite conquered what we hold to the defect in his mind which obstructs the free development of his genius, and appears hitherto to have rendered it impossible for him to present pictures of life that we can regard as true copies. If Mr. Thackeray could but have faith in the hidden spark of the divinity which few men or women lose out of their hearts, if he could see his neighbours really as they are and so describe them, if he could be brought to feel that there is fairer play in finding the good that is in evil things than in dragging out the evil that is in good things,—his hold upon a true fame, still for the present doubtful, would be assured and strong. As he now sees life, and paints it, he is wasting the genius and resources of an admirable colourist on pictures false in drawing and perspective.

Should this continue to be so? Is it matter of necessity that so radical a defect in the works of an author who abounds in ready wit, tact, and genius, should run uncorrected through his writings to the last? We cannot think it. It seems to us that Mr. Thackeray has already suffered himself partially to correct his crude way of viewing human nature, and that to some such sense we are indebted for genial and graceful passages that occur not unfrequently in *Esmond.* But the old vice still remains; and the consequence of a false method of treatment founded upon it is, that, with all our admiration for the writing of *Esmond,* we read it from the first page to the last without receiving in our minds, from any character or scene depicted in it, a distinct impression of vitality. We cannot persuade ourselves that there is a single character described at any length in this history which could belong to any being made of flesh and blood. (pp. 723-24)

The truth is that Mr. Thackeray hangs over the fictitious people on his paper too much as their creator and their judge. He does not think his own way in among them, and talk of them as a man should talk of men. If they be men and women, he must be the God who judges them; if he be a man, they must be puppets. In every case they lie without him and beneath him. There is not a character in *Esmond,* not the most spotless, over which we do not constantly feel that Mr. Thackeray is bending with a smile of pity; turning up now and then the prettiest coat, to show some dirt upon the lining; exhibiting to us something adorable, that he may aggravate our perception in it of something detestable; laying down for us such consolatory doctrine as that kindness and meanness are both manly; producing for his own satisfaction, in a word, mere distortions and unnatural defects,—all because the wires are held by him, and it is his sovereign will and pleasure to show the working of his men and women thoroughly. . . .

[We] too often find in Mr. Thackeray's works dream figures only, almost always brilliant or grotesque, almost always impossible. Even Becky Sharp, remembered as she is among the figures of English fiction likely to endure, too often verges on the unreal; and one of the leading characters in [*Esmond*], Beatrix,—a readjustment, with some change of the materials, of Becky Sharp,—is a being perfectly impossible. (p. 724)

All educated readers, we are sure, will enjoy *Esmond* heartily. . . . It is the work, in many respects, of a master's hand; yet it incurs the risk of perishing, because the genius and labour in it are spent upon ill-chosen material. Worse writing on a better ground would have the chance of lasting longer; and we cannot refrain from stating our belief that Mr. Thackeray is to

a great extent writing upon sand while he is founding books upon his present notions of society. (p. 726)

> [John Forster], in a review of "Esmond: A Story of Queen Anne's Reign," in The Examiner, No. 2337, November 13, 1852, pp. 723-26.

## [THEODORE MARTIN]   (essay date 1853)

Not many years ago, when reputations which are now effete were at their zenith, a pen was busy in our periodical literature, in which the presence of a power was felt by those who watched that literature, which seemed only to want happier circumstances to develop into forms worthy of a permanent place among English classics. . . . In Mr. Thackeray's lucubrations under all [his various] pseudonyms, there was a freshness and force, a truthfulness of touch, a shrewdness of perception, and a freedom from conventionalism, whether in thought or expression, which argued in their originator something more akin to genius than to mere talent. Here was a man who looked below the surface of things, taking nothing for granted, and shrinking from no scrutiny of human motives, however painful; who saw clearly and felt deeply, and who spoke out his thought manfully and well. In an age of pretence, he had the courage to be simple. To strip sentimentalism of its frippery, pretension of its tinsel, vanity of its masks, and humbug literary and social of its disguises, appeared to be the vocation of this graphic satirist. . . . He claimed no superiority, arrogated for himself no peculiar exemption from the vices and follies he satirized; he had his own mind to clear of cant as well as his neighbours', and professed to know their weak side only through a consciousness of his own. Just as he proclaimed himself as Mr. Snob, *par excellence,* when writing of the universal snobbishness of society at a later date, so in the **"Confessions of Fitzboodle,"** or **"The Yellowplush Papers,"** he made no parade of being one whit wiser, purer, or more disinterested than other people. Relentless to foppery, falsehood, and rascality, however ingeniously smoothed over or concealed, he was not prone to sneer at frailty, where it laid no claim to strength, or folly where it made no pretence of wisdom. The vices of our modern social life were the standing marks for the shafts of his ridicule, but here and there, across his pages, there shot gleams of a more pleasing light, which showed how eagerly the lynx-eyed observer hailed the presence of goodness, and candour, and generosity, whenever they crossed his path. (pp. 364-65)

[Just] as there are many things in life which it is best not to know, so in [Mr. Thackeray's] pictures of tainted humanity there is much to startle the faith, and to disquiet the fancy, without being atoned for by any commensurate advantage. . . . There is no vulgar daubing in the portraiture of all [his characters];—the lines are all true as life itself, and bitten into the pages as it were with vitriol. Every touch bears the traces of a master's hand, and yet what man ever cared to return to the book, what woman ever got through it without a sensation of humiliation and disgust? Both would wish to believe the writer untrue to nature, if they could; both would willingly forego the exhibition of what, under the aspect in which it is here shown, is truly "that hideous sight, a naked human heart."

Of all Mr. Thackeray's books [the **"Yellowplush Papers"**] is, perhaps, the most open to the charge of sneering cynicism, and yet even here glimpses of that stern but deep pathos are to be found, of which Mr. Thackeray has since proved himself so great a master. We can even now remember the mingled sensation of shuddering pity and horror, with which the conclusion of this story years ago impressed us. (pp. 365-66)

["**Luck of Barry Lyndon**"] was a little relieved by brighter aspects of humanity, but so little, that it can never be referred to with pleasure, despite the sparkling brilliancy of the narrative, and abundant traces of the most delightful humour. (p. 368)

[A] vein of delicate sarcasm runs throughout the tale, where every page is marked by that matchless expressiveness and ease of style for which Mr. Thackeray is the envy of his contemporaries. . . . For a time the reader is carried along, with a smiling admiration of the author's humour, and quiet way of bringing into view the seamy side of a number of respectable shams; but when he finds that he is passed along from rake to swindler, from gambler to ruffian,—that the men lie, cheat, and cog the dice, and that the women intrigue, or drink brandy in their tea, or are fatuous fools, the atmosphere becomes oppressive, and even the brilliancy of the wit begins to pall. Yet there are passages in this story, and sketches of character, which Mr. Thackeray has never surpassed. Had these been only mingled with some pictures of people not either hateful for wickedness or despicable for weakness, and in whom we could have felt a cordial interest, the tale might have won for its author much of the popularity which he must have seen, with no small chagrin, carried off by men altogether unfit to cope with him in originality or power.

There is always apparent in Mr. Thackeray's works, so much natural kindliness, so true a sympathy with goodness, that only some bitter and unfortunate experiences can explain, as it seems to us, the tendency of his mind at this period to present human nature in its least ennobling aspects. Whenever the man himself speaks out in the first person, as in his pleasant books of travel,—his "**Irish Sketch Book**," and his "**Journey from Cornhill to Cairo**,"—he shows so little of the cynic, or the melancholy Jaques—finds so hearty a delight in the contemplation of all simple pleasures, and so cordially recognises all social worth and all elevation of character, as to create surprise that he should have taken so little pains in his fictions to delineate good or lofty natures. (pp. 368-69)

The salutary influence of Dickens's spirit may . . . be traced in the writings of Mr. Thackeray about this period, tempering the bitterness of his sarcasm, and suggesting more pleasing views of human nature. The genius of the men is, however, as diverse as can well be conceived. The mind of the one is as hopeful as it is loving. That of the other, not less loving, though less expansive in its love, is constitutionally unhopeful. . . . Dickens's serious characters, for the most part, relish of melodramatic extravagance; there is no mistake about Thackeray's being from the life. Dickens's sentiment, which, when good, is good in the first class, is frequently far-fetched and pitched in an unnatural key—his pathos elaborated by the artifices of the practised writer. Thackeray's sentiment, rarely indulged, is never otherwise than genuine; his pathos is unforced, and goes to the roots of the heart. . . . [Thackeray's style] has always been manly and transparent, presenting his idea in the very fittest garb. . . . [There] is no want of heart in Thackeray, but its utterances are timorous and few, and held in check by the predominance of intellectual energy and the habit of reflection. Thackeray keeps the realities of life always before his eyes. . . . The mirth which Thackeray moves rarely passes beyond a smile, and his pathos, while it leaves the eye unmoistened, too often makes the heart sad to the core, and leaves it so. Both are satirists of the vices of the social system;

but the one would rally us into amendment, the other takes us straight up to the flaw, and compels us to admit it. Our fancy merely is amused by Dickens, and this often when he means to satirize some grave vice of character or the defects of a tyrannous system. It is never so with Thackeray: he forces the mind to acknowledge the truth of his picture; and to take the lesson home. Dickens seeks to amend the heart by depicting virtue; Thackeray seeks to achieve the same end by exposing vice. Both are great moralists; but it is absurd to class them as belonging to one school. (pp. 370-71)

It cannot be denied that Mr. Thackeray's ideas of excellence, as they appear in his books, are low, and that there is little in them to elevate the imagination, or to fire the heart with noble impulses. His vocation does not lie peculiarly in this direction; and he would have been false to himself had he simulated an exaltation of sentiment which was foreign to his nature. It has always seemed to us, however, that he has scarcely done himself justice in this particular. Traces may be seen in his writings of a latent enthusiasm, and a fervent admiration for beauty and worth, overlaid by a crust of cold distrustfulness, which we hope to see give way before happier experiences, and a more extended range of observation. (pp. 371-72)

The unpretending character of Mr. Thackeray's fictions has no doubt arisen in a great degree from a desire to avoid the vices into which the great throng of recent novelists had fallen. While professing to depict the manners and events of every-day life, their works were, for the most part, essentially untrue to nature. . . .

Their characters were either paragons of excellence, or monsters of iniquity—grotesque caricatures, or impossible contradictions; and the laws of nature, and the courses of heaven, were turned aside to enable the authors to round off their tales according to their own low standard of morality or ambition, and narrow conceptions of the working of God's providence. In criticism and in parody, Mr. Thackeray did his utmost to demolish this vicious state of things. The main object of his "**Luck of Barry Lyndon**," and his "**Catharine Hayes**," was to show in their true colours the class of rogues, ruffians, and demireps, towards whom the sympathies of the public had been directed by Bulwer, Ainsworth, and Dickens. . . . Never was antidote more required; and the instinct of truth, which uniformly guides Mr. Thackeray's pen, stamped his pictures with the hues of ghastly reality. (pp. 372-73)

[It] was natural that in his first work of magnitude, "**Vanity Fair**," Mr. Thackeray should strike out a course which might well startle those who had been accustomed to the old routine of caterers for the circulating libraries. . . . He plainly had no ambition to go on feeding the public complacency with pictures of life, from which nothing was to be learned. . . . To place before us the men and women who compose the sum of that life in the midst of which we are moving,—to show them to us in such situations as we might see them in any day of our lives,—to probe the principles upon which the framework of society in the nineteenth century is based,—to bring his characters to the test of trial and temptation, such as all may experience,—to force us to recognise goodness and worth, however unattractive the guise in which they may appear,—in a word, to paint life as it is, coloured as little as may be with the hues of the imagination, and to teach wholesome truths for every-day necessities, was the higher task to which Mr. Thackeray now addressed himself. (pp. 373-74)

That Mr. Thackeray may have pushed his views to excess, we do not deny. He might, we think, have accomplished his object quite as effectually by letting in a little more sunshine on his picture, and by lightening the shadows in some of his characters. Without any compromise of truth, he might have given us somebody to admire and esteem, without qualifications or humiliating reserves. That no human being is exempt from frailties, we need not be reminded. . . . It is a sorry morality which evermore places the death's-head among the flowers and garlands of the banquet. In "**Vanity Fair**," Mr. Thackeray has frequently fallen into this error; and he has further marred it by wilfully injuring our interest in the only characters which he puts forward for our regard. Anxious to avoid the propensity of novelists to make Apollos of their heroes, and paragons of their heroines, he has run into the opposite extreme and made Dobbin,—the only thoroughly excellent and loveable character in the book,—so ungainly as to be all but objectionable, and his pet heroine, Amelia, so foolishly weak as to wear out our patience.

This is all the more vexatious, seeing that the love of Dobbin for Amelia is the finest delineation of pure and unselfish devotion within the whole range of fiction. Such love in woman has often been depicted, but Mr. Thackeray is the first who has had the courage to essay, and the delicacy of touch to perfect, a portraiture of this lifelong devotion in the opposite sex. (pp. 374-75)

His writings abound in passages of tenderness, which bespeak a heart gentle as a woman's, a sensitiveness only less fine;—a depth of pity and charity, which writers of more pretence to these qualities never approach. "The still, sad music of humanity" reverberates through all his writings. He has painted so much of the bad qualities of mankind, and painted them so well, that this power has been very generally mistaken for that delight in the contemplation of wickedness or frailty, and that distrust of human goodness, which constitute the cynic. But this is to judge him unfairly. If his pen be most graphic in such characters as Becky Sharp, the Marquis of Steyne, Miss Crawley, or Major Pendennis, it is so because such characters present stronger lines than the quiet charities or homely chivalry in which alone it is possible for excellence to express itself in the kind of life with which his writings deal. Such men and women strike the eye more than the Dobbins, the Helen Pendennises, and Warringtons of society. These must be followed with a loving heart and open understanding, before their worth will blossom into view; and it is, to our mind, one of Mr. Thackeray's finest characteristics, that he makes personages of this class so subordinate as he does to the wickedly amusing and amusingly wicked characters which crowd his pages. This, indeed, is one of those features which help to give to his pictures the air of reality in which lies their peculiar charm, and make us feel while we read them as though we were moving among the experiences of our own very life. Here and there amid the struggle, and swagger, and hypocrisy, and time-serving, and vanity, and falsehood of the world, we come upon some true soul, some trait of shrinking goodness, of brave endurance, of noble sacrifice. So is it in Mr. Thackeray's books. In the midst of his most brilliant satire, or his most crowded scenes, some simple suggestion of love and goodness occurs, some sweet touch of pathos, that reveals to us how kind is the nature, how loving and simple the soul, from which they spring.

It is not cynicism, we believe, but a constitutional proneness to a melancholy view of life, which gives that unpleasing colour to many of Mr. Thackeray's books which most readers resent. . . . He insists on dashing his brightest fancies with need-

less shadows, and will not let us be comfortable, after he has done his best to make us so. There is a perversity in this, which Mr. Thackeray, in justice to himself and kindness to his readers, should subdue. Let him not diminish his efforts to make them honester, and simpler, and wiser; but let him feed them more with cheerful images, and the contemplation of beauty without its flaws and worth without its drawbacks. No writer of the day has the same power of doing this, if he pleases. (pp. 376-77)

[A] selection of Mr. Thackeray's best essays would, in our opinion, eclipse the united splendour of the whole British Essayists, both for absolute value in thought, and for purity and force of style. Had he never written anything of this kind but "**The Book of Snobs**," he would have taken first honours. What a book is this, so teeming with humour, character, and wisdom! (p. 380)

What wonder Mr. Thackeray should be so often condemned, when the foibles and vices which he paints are just those which, more or less, infect the whole body of society. Some way or other, he hits the weakness or sore point of us all. Nothing escapes his eye; and with an instinct almost Shakspearian he probes the secrets of a character at one venture. . . . Despite the carping of critics, his teaching has found its way to men's hearts and minds, and helped to make them more simple, more humble, more sincere, and altogether more genuine than they would have been but for "**Vanity Fair**," "**Pendennis**," and "**The Book of Snobs**." (pp. 383-84)

Minor incongruities and anachronisms are unquestionably to be found [in "**Esmond**"]; but the characters are never inconsistent, and the events follow in easy succession to a natural close. The canvas is unusually crowded, still there is no confusion in the grouping, nor want of proportion in the figures. As they are in substance unlike the novels of any other writer, so do they seem, in point of construction, to be entirely in harmony with their purpose. We therefore feared that in a novel removed both in subject and in style from our own times, we should miss something of the living reality of Mr. Thackeray's former works, and of their delightful frankness of expression, without gaining anything more artistic in form. The result has, we think, confirmed these fears.

"**Esmond**" is admirable as a literary feat. In point of style, it is equal to anything in English literature; and it will be read for this quality when the interest of its story is disregarded. The imitation of the manner of the writers of the period is as nearly as possible perfect, except that while not less racy, the language is perhaps more grammatically correct. Never did any man write with more ease under self-imposed fetters than Mr. Thackeray has done; but while we admire his skill, the question constantly recurs, why impose them upon himself at all? He has not the power—who has?—of reviving the tone as well as the manner of the time; and, disguise his characters as he will, in wigs, ruffles, hair powder, and sacs, we cannot help feeling it is but a disguise, and that the forms of passion and of thought are essentially modern—the judgments those of the historian, not the contemporary.

It is, moreover, a great mistake for a novelist to introduce into his story, as Mr. Thackeray has done, personages of either literary or political eminence, for he thereby needlessly hampers his own imagination, and places his readers in an attitude of criticism unfavourable to the success of his story. . . . The novelist cannot, moreover, keep within the limits of the biographer, but must heighten or tone down features of character for the purposes of his story. This he cannot do without violating that rigorous truth which ought uniformly to be preserved, wherever the character or conduct of eminent men is concerned. (pp. 384-85)

Mr. Thackeray is, we believe, no favourite with women generally. Yet he ought to be so; for, despite his sarcasms on their foibles, no writer has enforced their virtues more earnestly, or represented with equal energy the wrongs they suffer daily and hourly in their hearts and homes from the selfishness and sensualism of men. There are passages in this book for which they may well say of him, as that woman said of Dickens for his "Christmas Carol," "God bless him!" They do not forgive him, however, for the unnatural relation in which he has placed his hero and Lady Castlewood. . . . (pp. 387-88)

Mr. Thackeray will write better books than this, for his powers are ripening with every fresh emanation from his pen; his wisdom is more searching, his pathos sweeter, his humour of a more delicate flavour. . . . [He is] the only satirist who mingles loving-kindness with his sarcasm, and charity and humility with his gravest rebuke. (p. 388)

> [*Theodore Martin*], *"Thackeray's Works," in* The Westminster Review, *n.s. Vol. III, No. II, April 1, 1853, pp. 363-88.*

### [MARGARET OLIPHANT] (essay date 1855)

[The] *Rose and the Ring* is not a political satire, though one of its princes is of Crim Tartary; and we are afraid that those who look for one of Mr. Thackeray's wicked and witty comments upon the world in general, will be disappointed in this book. He is not in the vein of teaching either; his Christmas carol does not treat of a magical dream and a wonderful transformation, like some other Christmas carols of our acquaintance. Thanks to Mr. Thackeray, this fairy tale is a pure flash of mirth and laughter, and knows no moral. . . . [We] have no doubt that everybody who has not read the *Rose and the Ring,* will be satisfied to know that Mr. Thackeray dispenses poetic justice with an unfaltering hand. . . . (p. 88)

Mr. Titmarsh has never before produced so pleasant a picture-book, nor one whose pictures were so worthy of the text. These illustrations are greatly superior to all their predecessors by the same hand; they are so good that the artist is fairly entitled to rank with the author in this pleasant production; and altogether. . . , we are glad that we have to thank Mr. Thackeray for the honest laugh which is not at any one's expense.

Mr. Thackeray, in his own proper person, has not made less progress in kindness and good humor than has his *alter ego,* if we trace his course from *Vanity Fair* to the *Newcomes.* Everybody praises Becky Sharp, and the history in which she fills so important a place. Does everybody like that clever, unbelieving, disagreeable book? But there is nothing to be said on the subject of *Vanity Fair,* which has not been said already— that all its rogues are clever and amusing, and all its good characters fools—that Amelia is a greater libel upon womankind than Becky herself, and that there is a heated, crowded atmosphere in the story which has scarcely any relief, seeing that the good people are by no means a match for the bad, and cannot even pretend to balance the heavy scale of evil. . . . There are many admirable things in [*Vanity Fair,* however]— a great sparkle of sayings and happy turns of expression; and the scenes are cut sharp and clear in their outline, and dullness is not within these pages. Nevertheless, we carry but one personage with us in real kindness when we close the volume. Of all its men and women, only Major Dobbin is worth the least morsel of love. (p. 89)

[In *Pendennis*] we find a little more to commend. There is Warrington, who has no splay feet; there is sweet Mrs. Pendennis, whom we consent to accept as an angel. It is a sad thing to think of Warrington, such a man as he is, spending his life in those chambers in Lamb Court, with nothing to do but to write articles, the fate of which he cares nothing for. . . . Few can paint a wasted life, and great powers wearing down with the continual dropping of every day, better than Mr. Thackeray; but we are glad to think that he has still the means of rescue for this character in the exhaustless resources of fiction. . . . Pendennis himself, though he is good-looking and fashionable, and writes a successful novel, is but a very poor fellow after all—not only falling far short of an ideal hero, but not much to brag of for a very ordinary man. Mr. Thackeray avowedly scorns the loftiness of common romance, and will not have an exalted personage for the principal figure on his canvass; but Mr. Arthur Pendennis does not possess a single feature of the heroic. (pp. 89-90)

[There] is much more satisfaction in meeting with Harry Foker, who is Mr. Thackeray's special property, the type of a class which our novelist has brought out of the shadows into the clearest and kindliest illumination. . . . Not a refined gentleman by any means, it is only genius that can commend this brave good-hearted simpleton to all our affections. A lesser artist might have been afraid of a character so little intellectual, and felt its defective points a reproach to his invention; but Mr. Thackeray has been able to seize upon the genuine sparkle of this uncut jewel, upon the reverence for goodness, the humble self-estimation, the tender-heartedness, and the unsuspected pathos which lie in its depths. It is strange, when he has proved himself so capable of its exercise, that Mr. Thackeray should so much overlook this true alchemy of genius. . . . [Mr. Thackeray] does better service when Harry Foker and Jack Belsize, and even Rawdon Crawley, show their honest hearts to us, than when he produces Mr. Pendennis, with all his gifts, as a specimen of modern education, and the civilization of the nineteenth century. . . .

Only in one respect does *Pendennis* sin more grossly than *Vanity Fair.* Blanche Amory is more detestable, because she is less clever than Becky. How much does Mr. Thackeray owe to the world of womankind, by way of reparation for foisting into their ranks such a creation as this! . . .

And here we touch upon our author's greatest imperfection. Mr. Thackeray does not seem acquainted with anything feminine between a nursery maid and a fine lady—an indiscriminate idolater of little children, and an angler for a rich husband. The "perfect woman, nobly planned," has no place in the sphere of Mr. Thackeray's fancy. (p. 90)

Though we have serious fault to find with the story of Esmond, we are constrained to admit, at the outset, that the execution of this story is exquisite. In comparison with this, almost every other historical work we are acquainted with, except the romances of Scott, is a mere piece of masquerade. The age is not a great age, we confess, in spite of its Blenheim and its Ramilies, its Steele and its Addison; but such as it is, we have it here, a picture which is not merely paint, but is about the best example of absolute reproduction which our literature possesses. . . . The picture is perfect in its truth to nature, which is universal, and to manners, which are limited and transitory.

Harry Esmond is not a boy of Queen Victoria's time, in the little cavalier's suit proper to Queen Anne's . . . . We never find ourselves deceived in him through all his history—the mask does not slip aside for a moment to show a modern face underneath. This book is a marvellous historical picture; in this point of view it is an unrivalled performance, and worthy of all the plaudits which a work, attended by so many difficulties, has a right to claim.

Nevertheless, with so much in its favour, this admirable production carries failure in it as a story, as a piece of human life represented for the sympathy of all humanity—our most sacred sentiments are outraged, and our best prejudices shocked by the leading feature of this tale. It is not only that Lady Castlewood is the confidant of the hero's passionate love for her daughter, yet compensates his disappointment in that quarter with her own hand—but it is the intolerable idea that this woman, who is pure as an angel, and as severe in her judgment of the backsliding as a pure woman may be—a wife—and, still more, a mother, defended by the spotless love of little children—nevertheless cherishes for years a secret attachment to the boy to whom she gives the protection of her roof! This error is monstrous and unredeemable. If we do not count it among the affronts which Mr. Thackeray puts upon his countrywomen, it is because it is too gross an error to look like truth; but it is not less disagreeable on this score. Mr. Thackeray has spent all his pains to make this character a loveable and womanly one, and Rachel, Lady Castlewood, is a very "sweet" person we confess, and would be worthy the idolatry of her historian but for this unaccountable blunder. (pp. 91-2)

The hero himself is a hero in the proper acceptation of the word. It is not the faulty modern young gentleman any longer, but the antique ideal which Mr. Thackeray has resorted to, in consent, perhaps reluctant, but certainly complete, to the old canons of his art. Harry Esmond has all the generosity, all the unselfishness, all the unrewarded and unappreciated virtues of genuine romance. (p. 92)

There is no book of Mr. Thackeray which is so worthy of a great reputation as [the] uncompleted story [of the *Newcomes*]. As full of character as its predecessors, it redeems their errors gallantly; and we could almost fancy that, in the scorn of genius for that accusation which pronounced him unable to manage the ideal, Mr. Thackeray has showered a glory of manliness and goodness upon the inhabitants of this little world. There has never been a nobler sketch than that of the Colonel. The innocent heart and simple honour of this old man, and his horror of all falsehood and impurity, are enough to cover a multitude of Mr. Thackeray's sins. (p. 93)

There is no mist in this book; every one is an individual, pleasant or otherwise, and detaches himself or herself clearly from the background. The story is not in very good order, broken up as it is by retrospections and anticipations; and it is not good taste of Mr. Pendennis to appear so frequently before the curtain, and remind us unpleasantly that it is fiction we are attending to, and not reality; but we think the great mass of his readers will bear us out in our opinion, that the *Newcomes* is not only the most agreeable story, but the cleverest book which Mr. Thackeray has yet contributed for the amusement and edification of the admiring public.

When all this is said, there still remains a great deal to say which is less complimentary to our novelist. It is not, perhaps, the most agreeable information in the world to understand that our innocent schoolboys must plunge into a very unequivocal

abyss of "pleasure," before they can come forth purged and renovated like Lord Kew. . . . We cannot acknowledge that between the innocence of youth and the goodness of matured life, there lies a land of darkness through which every man must pass; nor do we perceive the advantage of convincing Mr. Thackeray's youthful audience that this is a necessity. . . . [It] is not to be disputed that his stronghold is among those whose portraits he draws so truthfully, and whose life he describes with so much zest. Now here is scope and verge enough for any amount of genius; but surely it is not advisable that our teacher should lead his pupils to great harm on the way to great good. Is not that the loftiest purity which does not find it needful to fall? (pp. 94-5)

We are not sure how far the English language will be benefited by the dialogues of Mr. Thackeray; they are very clever, very entertaining, and their slang is admirable; but it is very doubtful if it will be an advantage to make these Islands no better than a broad margin for the witticisms and the dialect of Cockaigne. . . . Mr. Thackeray's narrative is so pure and vigorous in its language, and his colloquial freedoms are so lively and entertaining, that there are no real exceptions to be taken to him; but every Thackeray and every Dickens has a host of imitators, and it is not an agreeable prospect to contemplate the English of Shakespeare and Bacon overwhelmed with a flood of Cockneyism—a consummation which seems to approach more nearly every day.

Mr. Thackeray is no poet; for one of the highest of the poet's vocations, and perhaps the noblest work of which genius is capable, is to embody the purest ideal soul in the most lifelike human garments; and this is an effort which our author has not yet attempted. Perhaps the title which Mr. Thackeray would rather choose for himself would be that of an historian of human nature. In his sphere he is so eminently. Human nature in its company dress, and with all its foibles on, is the subject he delights to treat of; but Mr. Thackeray is not great in home scenes, where the conventional dress is off, and the good that is in a man expands under the cheerful glow of the domestic fire. Mr. Thackeray does not drape his hero in the purple, or make pictures of him as he walks loftily among suffering men; but takes him to pieces with wicked mirth, calling upon all men to laugh with him at the idol's demolition. (pp. 95-6)

> [Margaret Oliphant], "Mr. Thackeray and His Novels," in Blackwood's Edinburgh Magazine, Vol. LXXVII, No. CCCCLXXI, January, 1855, pp. 86-96.

### [WHITWELL ELWIN]  (essay date 1855)

> [Elwin was one of the first critics to discuss Thackeray's narrative technique of commenting freely on the characters and the progress of the action in his novels. In praise of this method, he states that "these disquisitions would be blemishes if they were not signal beauties." Elwin also recognizes the similarities between Thackeray and Henry Fielding, which are often mentioned by subsequent critics. In addition, Elwin views the lack of a well-defined plot in Thackeray's novels not as a defect, but as evidence that "the true and the probable are his domain."]

[*The Newcomes*] is Mr. Thackeray's masterpiece, as it is undoubtedly one of the masterpieces of English fiction, if fiction is the proper term to apply to the most minute and faithful transcript of actual life which is anywhere to be found. . . . Mr. Thackeray looks at life under its ordinary aspects, and copies it with a fidelity and artistic skill which are surprising. . . . Truth is never sacrificed to piquancy. The characters in *The Newcomes* are not more witty, wise, or farcical than their prototypes; the dull, the insipid, and the foolish, speak according to their own fashion and not with the tongue of the author; the events which befall them are nowhere made exciting at the expense of probability. (pp. 230-31)

For all the exactness with which Mr. Thackeray follows life, it will be found that each character is usually in its aggregate an original conception. The range is unusually wide, and from the most noble the Marquis of Farintosh down to little Miss Cann, the humble governess who gives lessons by the hour, the many persons of every degree who compose the miscellaneous group are marked by traits as distinctive as the features of their faces. . . .

It is indeed a marvellous perception of truth of character which can thus keep every member of the crowd so continuously faithful to his own nature, a rare tact which, without the least exaggeration, can impart interest to so much which in society is wearying and commonplace as well as to that which is intrinsically winning. (p. 232)

Mr. Thackeray has nobly redeemed in *The Newcomes* the defect alleged against his former novels—that they were more employed in satirising evil than in setting forth excellence. His present production gains by the change. The larger infusion of benevolence, honour, and disinterestedness into the story makes it pleasanter to read, and gives, we think, a juster notion of the world. . . . Altogether the charge of cynicism, so often urged against him, was always exaggerated, and is now become an anachronism. (p. 234)

[No] writer of fiction has surpassed Mr. Thackeray in the force with which he sets forth the beauty of pure hearts, and the contempt which he casts upon everything evil, however gilded by success. . . . With all his tendency, in fact, to satire, Mr. Thackeray has nowhere employed it in his novels upon improper objects. . . . Calamity, physical and mental, is safe from his lash. . . . False pretension and imposture, the affectations and the hypocrisies, the duperies and the greediness of life, are his chosen and legitimate prey. . . . (pp. 235-36)

Mr. Thackeray, beyond all other novelists, loves to comment upon his own text—to stop in his story, indulge in reflections, analyse the motives of his characters, and cross-examine his readers upon their individual propensities. His book is in many parts a discourse upon human nature illustrated by examples. These disquisitions would be blemishes if they were not signal beauties; but the skill with which he unravels the complex windings of the heart, the art with which specious and conventional malpractices are shown under their proper aspects, the pensive tenderness of the sentiments, the charm of the composition, has won general admiration for passages which, were they less perfect, would cumber the tale. As it is, there is nothing which could so little be spared. (pp. 236-37)

Many of these moralisings and reflections are pervaded by a mild and tranquil melancholy, which give them a strong hold upon the heart. Mr. Thackeray has shown himself in a hundred passages of his story a consummate master of genuine pathos. . . . By a line, or an allusion, he recalls a train of tender recollections, and stirs up sleeping sadness into life. So delicate is the touch by which he awakens sorrowful emotions, that we are apt to imagine that we alone have entered into his meaning until we learn how many have been affected by the same passage in the same way. In the longer scenes of misfortune and grief his tact never forsakes him; there is a chasteness of de-

scription, a skilful and sparing selection of details, a manliness of tone which it would be difficult to overpraise. He knows what to relate, and what simply to indicate; he understands the sacredness of sorrow, and never rends away the veil from weeping faces.

Mr. Thackeray is a humourist, as every writer of fiction must be who takes an extended view of human nature. . . . It is a peculiar charm of the light and pleasant wit which sparkles through [*The Newcomes*] that it never has the air of being studied. It shines forth in a name, an epithet, a parenthesis, in numberless undefinable ways, and always as if it sprung out of the subject, and had not been introduced for the sake of being facetious.

The exception of the work is not below the conception. . . . There is no appearance of effort, no studied artifice of composition, but neither is there any approach to baldness in the simplicity of his phraseology, or to carelessness in the freedom of his style. The narrative runs on in a rich abundance of strong, idiomatic, sterling English, often applied in a novel and felicitous manner, and sufficiently adorned by occasional metaphors of the same masculine stamp. [Mr. Thackeray] even manages to give additional raciness by the not unfrequent use of colloquial vulgarisms, which if they were introduced with less skill would debase his style. It is with reluctance we confess that he has turned language to good account which in all other hands has hitherto revolted every person of cultivated mind, for we fear the evil effects of his example, and are sorry the black patches should heighten the beauty. (pp. 237-39)

In *The Newcomes* we have 'the form and pressure of the very age and body of the time' as regards huge masses of society; and the author not having been forestalled by contemporaries, is safe from the rivalry of predecessors. But more than this, he is, in the whole construction of his story, in his style, in his sentiments, unlike any other novelist; there is not one of whom it is truer to assert that he is a voice and not an echo. Fielding is the genius whom he most nearly resembles—for there is the same manliness, the same fidelity to nature, the same deep and precise knowledge of the mixed motives which influence mankind; but there is little similarity in the application of these qualities, which, if a comparison were instituted, would be found to have produced rather a contrast than a parallel. (p. 239)

There are not many defects in [*The Newcomes*] to set against its merits. Rapidity of movement, a throng of incidents, is never a characteristic of Mr. Thackeray's stories; and such is the interest he excites by the development of his characters, that we do not usually desire that he should quicken his pace. Sometimes, however, he lingers too long, and we are only surprised that in a copious novel . . . there should not be more than two or three scenes which have been unduly drawn out to fill their ample frames. (pp. 240-41)

That there is little plot, in the strict sense of the word, and that little of no very exciting kind, is not to be numbered, in our opinion, among the defects of the tale. To be hurried on in breathless suspense distracts the attention from the merits of style, sentiment, and character, and appeals chiefly to minds which are incapable of appreciating more sterling qualities. Mr. Thackeray has simply been faithful to the instincts of his genius. The true and the probable are his domain, and he intuitively casts aside whatever offends against his theory of his art. (pp. 241-42)

'What a wonderful art!' so we may suppose some future critic of the English humourists to say—'what an admirable gift of nature was it by which the author of these tales was endowed, and which enabled him to fix our interest, to waken our sympathy, to seize upon our credulity, so that we believe in his people, speculate gravely upon their faults or their excellences, and talk about them as if we had breakfasted with them this morning in their actual drawing-rooms, or should meet them this afternoon in the Park! What a genius!—what a vigour!—what a bright-eyed intelligence and observation!—what a wholesome hatred for meanness and knavery! What a vast sympathy!—what a cheerfulness!—what a manly relish of life!—what a love of human kind! What a poet is here!—watching, meditating, brooding, creating! What multitudes of truths has that man left behind him! What generations he has taught to laugh wisely and fairly! What scholars he has formed and accustomed to the exercise of thoughtful humour, and the manly play of wit!' Such is Mr. Thackeray's character of Fielding [taken from his lecture on Hogarth, Smollett, and Fielding in *The English Humourists*]—such to the letter is the character, as a novelist, of the author of *The Newcomes*. (pp. 251-52)

> [Whitwell Elwin], in an extract from a review of ''The Newcomes,'' in Quarterly Review, *Vol. XCVII, September, 1855 (and reprinted in* Thackeray: A Critical Heritage, *edited by Geoffrey Tillotson and Donald Hawes, Routledge & Kegan Paul, 1968, pp. 230-52).*

## [W. C. ROSCOE]   (essay date 1856)

As an Artist, [Mr. Thackeray] is probably the greatest painter of manners that ever lived. He has an unapproachable quickness, fineness, and width of observation on social habits and characteristics, a memory the most delicate, and a perfectly amazing power of vividly reproducing his experience. It is customary to compare him with Addison and Fielding. He has perhaps not quite such a fine stroke as the former; but the *Spectator* is thin and meagre compared with *Vanity Fair*. Fielding has breadth and vigour incomparably greater; but two of his main excellencies, richness of accessory life and variety of character, fly to the beam when weighed against the same qualities in Thackeray. (p. 178)

The social human heart, man in relation to his kind—that is [Mr. Thackeray's] subject. His actors are distinct and individual,—truthfully, vigorously, felicitously drawn; masterpieces in their way; but the personal character of each is not the supreme object of interest with the author. It is only a contribution to a larger and more abstract subject of contemplation. Man is his study; but man the social animal, man considered with reference to the experiences, the aims, the affections, that find their field in his intercourse with his fellow-men: never man the individual soul. He never penetrates into the interior, secret, *real* life that every man leads in isolation from his fellows, that chamber of being open only upwards to heaven and downwards to hell. He is wise to abstain; he does well to hold the ground where his pre-eminence is unapproached,—to be true to his own genius. But this genius is of a lower order than the other. The faculty that deals with and represents the individual soul in its complete relations is higher than that which we have ascribed to Mr. Thackeray. . . . [In] the plot and conduct of his story Mr. Thackeray does not exhibit more than a very high power of grouping his figures and arranging his incidents; but his best characters are certainly creations, living breathing beings, characteristic not only by certain traits, but by that atmosphere of individuality which only genius can impart. Their distinctive feature and their defect . . . is this,

that not one of them is complete; each is only so much of an individual as is embraced in a certain abstract whole. We never know any one of them completely, in the way we know ourselves, in the way we imagine others. We know just so much of them as we can gather by an intercourse in society. Mr. Thackeray does not penetrate further. . . . (pp. 179-80)

Thackeray leaves the reader to his own imagination. He gives no clues to his character, as such; he is not leading to an image of his own. . . . He is interested more in the external exhibitions of character and the feelings than in character itself; his aim is not to reproduce any single nature, but the image that the whole phenomenon of social life has left impressed on his mind. (pp. 180-81)

If Mr. Thackeray's genius is not of the very highest order, it is the very highest of its kind. The vividness, the accuracy of his delineation goes far to compensate for a certain want of deeper insight. . . . [His] figures are to Shakespeare's what Madame Tussaud's waxworks are to the Elgin Marbles—they are exact figures from modern life, and the resemblance is effected somewhat too much by the aid of externals; but there is a matchless sharpness, an elaborateness and finish of detail and circumstantiality about his creations. He has an art peculiarly his own of reproducing every-day language with just enough additional sparkle or humour or pathos of his own to make it piquant and entertaining without losing vraisemblance. His handling of his subject, his execution, are so skilful and masterly, that they for ever hold the attention alive. . . . He is master of the dramatic method which has of late preponderated so much over the narrative. Perhaps the greatest attraction of his writings consists in the wonderful appropriateness of the language and sentiments he puts into the mouths of his various characters; and he not only makes them express themselves, but he manages, without any loss of dramatic propriety, to heighten the tone so as to give some charm or other to what every one says; and not only this, but with an ease which veils consummate dexterity, he makes these dramatic speeches carry on the action and even convey the author's private inuendo. (p. 182)

If the power of producing the impression of reality were the test of the highest creative power, Thackeray would perhaps rank higher than any one who has ever lived,—higher than Defoe. But Thackeray's mode of creating an impression of reality is more complicated than Defoe's. It is not that simple act of force by which the latter identifies himself with his hero. It arises in great measure from his way of knitting his narrative on at every point to some link of our every-day experience. His fiction is like a net, every mesh of which has a connecting knot with actual life. Many novelists have a world of their own they inhabit. Thackeray thrusts his characters in among the moving every-day world in which we live. We don't say they are life-like characters; they are mere people. We feel them to be near us, and that we may meet them any day. . . . All artists have an ultimate aim which shapes their working. . . . Thackeray only desires to be a mirror, to give a true but a brilliant reflection; his vision is warped, no doubt, by peculiarities of his own; but his aim is to reproduce the world as he sees it.

His conception of a story is, like his conception of a character, incomplete. There is no reason why he should begin where he does, no reason why he should end at all. He cuts a square out of life, just as much as he wants. . . . This, however, is little more than a technical shortcoming, and certainly does not much affect the reader, to whom skill in the conduct of the story is infinitely more important. And in the conduct of his story, in the management of his narrative, in the interlinking of incident, the way in which one character is made to elucidate another, in which every speech and every entrance carries on the action, in the ease, the grace, the hidden skill with which the intricate complication of interests and events are handled and developed, Mr. Thackeray justly claims our highest admiration. In all that belongs to execution he shows a mastery that almost makes us think he has some secret peculiar power, so effortless is his brilliancy, so easy his touch. His tale is like a landscape growing under the instinctive rather than conscious hand of a master. (pp. 183-84)

There is one direction, however, in which Mr. Thackeray's resources have always been remarkably limited. It is curious how independent he is of thought; how he manages to exist so entirely on the surface of things. Perhaps he is the better observer of manners because he never cares to penetrate below them. He never refers to a principle, or elucidates a rule of action. But this latter is a characteristic which belongs rather to his character as a moralist than an artist. What we are now concerned with is the absence from his books of what we are accustomed to call ideas. In this respect Thackeray is as inferior to Fielding, as in some others we cannot help thinking him superior. . . . The force of Thackeray's writings is derived from the strength of his feelings; great genius he has, and general vigour of mind, but not the *intellectus cogitabundus*. . . . Thackeray never reasons, he never gains one step by deduction; he relies on his instincts, he appeals to the witness within us; he makes his statement, and leaves it to find its own way to the conviction of his readers; either it approves itself to you, and you accept it, or it does not, and you leave it. The highest moral truths have been thus enunciated, perhaps can only be thus enunciated; but Mr. Thackeray does not enunciate great truths. The most he does is to generalise on his social observation. He is not absolutely destitute of some of those distilled results of a wide knowledge of men which properly come under the head of wisdom; but they are very disproportioned to the extent and penetration of his perception. He occupies a good deal of space in half-meditative, half-emotional harangues on the phenomena of life. . . . It is with the feelings and the affections that Mr. Thackeray is at home. They supply with him the place of reasoning-power. Hence he penetrates deeper into the characters of women than of men. He has never drawn, nor can he ever draw, a man of strong convictions or thoughtful mind; and even in women he deals almost exclusively with the instinctive and emotional side of their nature. This feature gives a certain thinness and superficiality to Mr. Thackeray's works. He nowhere leaves the mark of a thinker. Even his insight is keen and delicate rather than profound. But his deep and tender feeling makes him sensitive to those suggestions which occupy the boundary-land between the affections and the intellect, the country of vain regrets and tender memories, of chastened hopes and softened sadness, the harvest-field in every human soul of love and death. The voice of Mr. Thackeray's tenderness is at once sweet and manly; and when he will allow us to feel sure he is not sneering at himself, its tone is not unworthy to speak to the most sacred recesses of the heart. (pp. 185-86)

Mr. Thackeray's pathos is good; but his humour is better, more original, more searching. He never rests in the simply ludicrous or absurd. Irony is the essence of his wit. His books are one strain of it. He plays with his own characters. In the simplest things they say the author himself gets a quiet backstroke at them. It is not enough for him to depict a man ridiculous, he makes him himself expose his own absurdities, and gathers a

zest from the unconsciousness with which he does so. He treats his *dramatis personae* as if he were playing off real men. His wit is not a plaything, but a weapon, and must cut something whenever it falls; it may be a goodnatured blow, but it must touch some one. . . . In general he is grave, composed, even sad, but he is never uninterested in the personal adventures he is engaged in narrating; his sympathies are always keenly alive, though often he prefers to conceal how they are enlisted. At bottom he has a warm, almost a passionate interest in his own creations. They are realities to him as to the rest of the world. (p. 187)

His sense of beauty is warm and lively. If he had as much of the negative sense of good taste which discards the ugly and jarring elements as he has of the positive sense which detects and appreciates the beautiful, his works would be far pleasanter reading. He sees beauty every where; his love of it mingles with the affectionateness of his nature, and throws a softening grace over his pages, relieving a bitterness which without it would sometimes be scarcely sufferable. . . .

Of his bad taste his works furnish only too abundant evidence. It was a happy idea to look at society from the footman's point of view; but a very little of that sort of fun suffices. (p. 191)

The advantage of using such a mouthpiece, if it be an advantage, is this, that it gives an opportunity of saying things more vulgar, biting, and personal, than a man's self-respect or shame would allow him to say out of his own mouth. It is a *quasi* shifting of the responsibility. But if we give Sheridan credit for his wit, we must give Thackeray credit for his vulgarity. This feature greatly disfigures his works, and shows itself not only in the gusto and ease with which he enters into the soul of a footman, but in a love of searching out and bringing into prominent view the more petty and ignoble sides of all things. We don't quarrel with a humorist for exposing the vulgar element in a vulgar man, and in taking all the fun he can out of it. . . . What we quarrel with is vulgarity in the tone of the work. . . . (pp. 191-92)

Not from false taste, but from something deeper,—a warp in the very substance of his genius,—arises another unwelcome characteristic. *Vanity Fair* is the name, not of one, but of all Mr. Thackeray's books. The disappointment that waits upon human desires, whether in their fulfilment or their destruction, the emptiness of worldly things, the frailty of the affections, the sternness of fate, the hopelessness of endeavour, *vanitas vanitatum* [vanity of vanity],—these are his themes. The impression left by his books is that of weariness; the stimulants uphold you while you read; and then comes just such a reaction as if you had really mingled closely in the great world with no hopes or ambitions outside it; you feel the dust in your throat, the din and the babbling echo in your ears. . . . [To] drop the curtain and leave the mind jaded with small discontents, perplexed with unsolved difficulties, and saddened with the shortcomings of fruition,—this is to be false to the high and soothing influences of art, and to misuse the power she gives. (pp. 192-93)

As a Moralist, his philosophy might be called a religious stoicism rooted in fatalism. The stoicism is patient and manly; kindly though melancholy. It is not a hardened endurance of adverse fate, so much as an unexamining inactive submission to the divine will. (p. 193)

His fatalism is connected with a strong sense of the powerlessness of the human will. He is a profound sceptic. Not a sceptic in religious conviction, or one who ignores devotional feeling,—far from it; but a sceptic of principles, of human will, of the power in man to ascertain his duties or direct his aims. He believes in God *out of the world*. He loves to represent man as tossing on the wild sea, driven to and fro by wind and waves, landing now on some shining fortunate isle, where the affections find happy rest, and now driven forth again into the night and storm. . . . He speaks to you as one fellow-subject to another of the Prince of this world. He has no call to set things right, no prompting to examine into the remedy. His vocation is to show the time as it is, and especially where it is out of joint. His philosophy is to accept men and things as they are. . . .

With a very strong sense of the obligation of moral truthfulness, and the profoundest respect for, and sympathy with, simplicity and straightforwardness of character, he has no interest in intellectual conclusions. He would never have felt sufficient interest to ask with Pilate, "What is truth?" Always occupied with moral symptoms, intently observing men, and deeply interested in their various modes of meeting the perplexities of life, he never attempts to decide a moral question. He rarely discusses one at all; and when he does so, he is studiously careful to avoid throwing his weight into either scale. (p. 194)

From this form of mind springs, in great measure, that scepticism to which we have alluded. A writer can scarcely help being sceptical who sees all sides of a question, but has gathered no principles to help him to choose among them; who has no guiding rules to which to refer, and whose instincts alone prevent the field of his conscience from being an absolute chaos. Only by these instincts he tests the characters of men and the propriety of actions; and wherever they alone can serve as guides, they do so faithfully, for in him they are honest and noble. (p. 195)

He professes to paint human life; and he who does so, and who does not base his conception on that religious substructure which alone makes it other than shreds of flying dreams, is an incomplete artist and a false moralist. (p. 201)

Some of Mr. Thackeray's lesser works are infused throughout with a genial kindly spirit; such are the *History of Mr. Samuel Titmarsh and the Great Hoggarty Diamond* (which it is pleasant to hear is a favourite with the author), and the *Kickleburys on the Rhine, Dr. Birch's School, &c.* In these, foibles are pleasantly touched with cheerful happy raillery, and a light, gay, yet searching tone of ridicule, and a tender pleasing pathos, pervade the story: "the air nimbly and sweetly recommends itself;" the wit plays freshly and brightly, like the sun glittering through the green leaves on the wood-paths. But in the mass of his works the tendencies we have before spoken of give a dark and unpleasing ground to the whole picture; and on it he draws in strong black and white. His general view of English society is a very low and unrelieved one. It is a true but a strictly one-sided representation, selected partly for its amusing elements, partly from an unhappy idiosyncrasy of the author. (pp. 205-06)

As a set-off against these unpleasing elements in Mr. Thackeray's writings, there is one whole side of his genius which casts a pure and pleasant sunshine over his pages. He has a heart as deep and kind as ever wrote itself in fiction. His feelings are warm and impetuous, his nature honest, truthful, honourable. . . . Whatever his defects,—and they are great,—he must always take his stand as one of the masters of English fiction; inferior to Fielding, because he wants his breadth and range, the freeness of his air, and the soundness of his moral

healthfulness; but his rival in accuracy of insight and vigour of imagination; and perhaps, as we have before said, more than his rival in fertility. And since Fielding's time, though characters have been drawn more complete than any one of Mr. Thackeray's, no fiction has been written in the school to which his imagination belongs which can bear a moment's comparison with **Vanity Fair**. This is hitherto his masterpiece, and will probably always remain so. There is a *vis* in it greater than in any of his other works—the lines are more sharply, deeply cut, the whole more marked with the signs of special and peculiar genius. Our pleasure in it alternates vividly with dislike— almost repulsion; but our admiration is compelled by all parts of it, and our eagerest sympathy by some. Dobbin and Amelia will always remain living inmates of the English mind. . . . Thackeray's genius is in many respects not unlike that of Goethe; and such another woman as Amelia has not been drawn since Margaret in *Faust*.

Of his other great works, **Pendennis** is the richest in character and incident, and the least pleasing; the **Newcomes** the most humane, but less vigorous and concentrated than any of the others; **Esmond**—the later parts at least—by far the best and noblest. . . . He is freed from his devotion to the petty satire of modern conventions, and has fewer calls for the exercise of small contempts. The main characters, Esmond, his mistress, and Beatrix, are the ablest he has drawn; they are not less vivid than his others, and more complete. Esmond is strong, vigorous, noble, finely executed as well as conceived. . . . Beatrix is perhaps the finest picture of splendid, lustrous, physical beauty ever given to the world. . . . And both her character and that of her mother are master-pieces of poetical insight; the latter blemished, however, here and there with the author's unconquerable hankering to lay his finger on a blot. He must search it out, and give it at least its due blackness. (pp. 210-12)

In the **Newcomes** "the elements are kindlier mixed" than in any of the other fictions; there is a great softening of tone, a larger predominance is given to feeling over sarcasm. As before, the book is a transcript from life; but the life is more pleasantly selected, and the baser ingredients not scattered with so lavish a hand. . . . [However, there] is the same want of ballasting thought, the same see-saw between cynicism and sentiment, the same suspension of moral judgment. The indignant impulse prompts the lash, and the hand at once delivers it; while the mind hangs back, doubts its justice, and sums up after execution with an appeal to our charity on the score of the undecipherable motives of human action, the heart's universal power of self-deception, and the urgency of fate and circumstance. (pp. 212-13)

> [W. C. Roscoe], "W. M. Thackeray, Artist and Moralist," in The National Review, *London, Vol. II, No. III, January, 1856, pp. 177-213.*

**[JAMES FITZJAMES STEPHEN]** (essay date 1856)

In some respects, [**Barry Lyndon**] appears to us the most characteristic and best executed of Mr. Thackeray's novels, though it is far less known, and is likely, we think, to be less popular than the rest. **Barry Lyndon** is the history of a scoundrel from his own point of view, and combines the habitual freshness of Fielding with a large measure of the grave irony of *Jonathan Wild*. To be able, with perfect decency and propriety, to take us his abode in the very heart of a most unmitigated blackguard and scoundrel, and to show how, as a matter of course, and without any kind of denial or concealment, he *bonâ fide* considers himself one of the best and greatest of men, is surely one of the hardest tasks which could be imposed on an author; yet Mr. Thackeray has undertaken and executed it with perfect success. (p. 783)

[The] genius of the novelist not only makes us feel that his hero would naturally look upon himself as a wronged and virtuous man—"the victim," as he is made to say on his title-page, "of many cruel persecutions, conspiracies, and slanders,"—but also that even in this wretched kind of existence all was not bad—that wheat as well as tares grow in the most unkindly and ill-cultivated soil. The ability with which this is managed is quite wonderful. . . .

The parenthesis which marks the point at which Mr. Barry has succeeded in convincing himself that his profession is, on the whole, highly honourable and noble, though a few mean interlopers may disgrace it, is inconceivably ludicrous, and shows a depth of humour almost sublime. . . . To show how Mr. Barry contrives to look upon himself as an ill-used man through the whole of his eventful life, would require little less than an abstract of the entire book. We may mention more particularly, however, his wonderful account of his relations to his wife, in which, after detailing with a high moral tone the measures which he thought necessary to bring her to a sense of her conjugal duties—consisting in a long series of the most brutal acts of tyranny and violence—he describes with a sort of contemptuous pity her low spirits, nervousness, bad health, and general dulness, and concludes by the quiet remark—"My company from this fancied I was a tyrant over her; whereas I was only a severe and careful guardian over a silly, bad-tempered, and weak-minded lady." We have not the slightest doubt that such a man would seriously and *bonâ fide* take exactly that view of such conduct. . . .

The conception of Barry Lyndon's character involves, however, some grains of good. Indeed, their absence in any man whatever would have been conclusive evidence that the book in which he was depicted was not written by Mr. Thackeray. His courage is genuine courage. He really is a very brave man; and although he knows it, and is inordinately vain of it, we think the picture is true to nature. (p. 784)

Artistically considered, we should almost be inclined to place **Barry Lyndon** at the head of the list of Mr. Thackeray's books. It has an immense advantage over his better known works in being far shorter—for which reason the plot is clearer, simpler, and more connected than it is in **Vanity Fair, Pendennis,** or the **Newcomes.** Every page carries the story on, and with the exception of Barry's meeting with his uncle at Berlin, and of a rather melodramatic episode which takes place at a small German court, the story is as natural and easy as if it were true. . . . In most of Mr. Thackeray's more elaborate performances, his own views of the world appear to us to be insisted on too openly and too often; but there is nothing of this in **Barry Lyndon.** It is neither a melancholy nor a cheerful book, but a fair and wonderfully skilful portrait of a man whom we feel as if we had known personally. The accessories are described in as life-like and vigorous a manner as the main subject. We do not think that Mr. Thackeray's extraordinary power of description was ever more strongly illustrated than in the sketches which this volume contains of the wild, mad Irish life of Dublin and the provinces in the last century—of the horrible mechanism of man-stealing and espionage by which Frederick II. maintained his power—of the strange career (half-highwayman, half-*grand seigneur*) of a professional gambler—or

of the petty Courts in which, before the French Revolution, so many sham sovereigns played at kings and queens, with human beings for their counters. All these, and many other subjects of the same kind, are sketched off rapidly, easily, and with a life and distinctness altogether marvellous. . . . (pp. 784-85)

[*James Fitzjames Stephen*], *in a review of "Barry Lyndon," in* The Saturday Review, *London, Vol. 2, No. 61, December 27, 1856, pp. 783-85.*

**[GOLDWIN SMITH]**   (essay date 1859)

The grand objection to revivifying the social era depicted in **'The Virginians,'** is that it has never died; it has been perpetuated for us by immortal artists. . . . Fielding, Smollett, Richardson, Hogarth, have already done that which the author of **'The Virginians'** undertakes to do; and they have done it with a truth, breadth, freedom, on which morality and decency forbid their imitator to venture in our age. Mr. Thackeray's hand is perpetually checked by moral considerations, and his picture is therefore timid and incomplete. He does not venture to introduce, but only to allude to, the gallantries which play so great a part in Fielding and Smollett, as they did in the evil life of those times. He has a hundred ingenious devices for denoting without actually expressing the blasphemies with which the fine gentlemen he is describing gave point and force to their conversation. That he should feel this necessary does honour to his sense of morality and religion and to that of the public for which he writes, but it spoils him as a novelist of the last century. (p. 444)

Of the plot of **'The Virginians'** we have only to say what the topographer said of the snakes in Iceland. There is none. There is only a string of incidents woven together, serving for the delineation of character and the expression of sentiment. . . . We know Mr. Thackeray does this habitually and on principle; and we do not wish to be guilty of the ungracious platitude of quarrelling with one good thing for not being another. But it must be owned that a well-conducted plot is a pleasant thing; and that a story without a story wants a principal element of itself. It is the plot that prevents us from being too conscious of the art exercised in the delineation of characters, or exerting our critical faculties too keenly on the characters delineated. By the absence of a plot, the whole weight is thrown on the character-painting, and our critical acumen is always kept awake to observe whether the painting is correct. (p. 445)

Besides [the] imaginary characters . . . , a number of historical personages are introduced in **'The Virginians.'** Almost all the persons of note of the time, royal, political, ecclesiastical, social, and literary, are made to pass over the stage, and some take a considerable part in the action and dialogue. This use of real characters in fiction seems to us . . . rather a questionable habit. It can scarcely fail to taint history, which, it should be remembered, is not only a repository of facts but a school of right sympathies, and which for both purposes requires absolute adherence to the truth and nothing but the truth. (p. 449)

[Moreover], the juxtaposition of real with imaginary characters is injurious to the object of the novelist's art. A novel, while we are reading it, is to us neither a *reality* nor a *fiction,* but an *illusion*—an allusion of which we are half conscious, unless we have the good fortune to be very young or very imaginative, but to which we surrender ourselves more or less completely in proportion to the skill with which the novel is written. The intrusion of realities obviously tends to dispel this illusion. . . .

The reintroduction of characters from previous novels also breaks the illusion in another way. We know beforehand, and have it fixed in our minds, that these characters are fictitious, so that about *them* there can be no illusion any more. To give the action of a novel a background of real history, as is done in **'Vanity Fair,'** the background of part of which is Brussels in the campaign of 1815, is a different thing, it will be observed, from mixing up historical with imaginary personages in the action; it perverts no history, excites no criticism, and rather tends to make the illusion more complete by making the fiction more circumstantial. (pp. 449-50)

The historical scenes . . . show Mr. Thackeray's descriptive powers, though there is no subject for their exercise here equal to the battles of Marlborough in **'Esmond.'** In the details of manners, habits, and costume we have observed no flaw; and indeed it would be presumptuous to pretend to find flaws in a painter who is so thoroughly master of his subjects as Mr. Thackeray is of the social life of the last century. . . . [Yet, each] century, each generation, has its own phase of thought and feeling, the result of all that has gone before as well as of all that exists, of which a writer can no more divest himself by any effort of intellect or imagination than he can put off the form of his own body or the peculiarities of his own mind. **'Vanity Fair,' 'Pendennis,'** and **'The Newcomes,'** in which Mr. Thackeray has portrayed the living manners of his own age, as Fielding and his contemporaries did theirs, most nearly correspond, of all the works of our day, to 'Tom Jones' and 'Roderick Random;' and they bear a truer and deeper resemblance to their prototypes of the eighteenth century than is or can be borne by any artificial reproduction.

There is one point in which Fielding is a model for all times, and in which Mr. Thackeray is his worthy disciple, and we venture to think, perfectly his equal. That point is, style and beauty of composition. The last century was certainly more studious, generally speaking, of form than ours. You may open any page of Fielding at random, and read it with pleasure, without reference to the story or context, merely as a piece of exquisite writing. The same may be said of Mr. Thackeray. (pp. 451-52)

The philosophy of life embodied in **'The Virginians,'** as in Mr. Thackeray's other novels, is sound and sensible rather than deep. Its ideal character, the young, good-looking, good-natured, high-spirited Harry Warrington, is a fair measure of its profundity. Deeper character can only be displayed in more serious action, and the more serious actions of life, excepting war, are repudiated by Mr. Thackeray as subjects for fiction, in a passage of this work, in which he seems to us rather to confound together the *serious* and the *prosaic*. We cannot accuse **'The Virginians'** of cynicism, if by cynicism is meant either want of geniality of sentiment, or a sour view of human nature. . . . It must be allowed, however, that whether from something amiss in his own spectacles, or from using those of Fielding too often, he sometimes exaggerates the number of people in the world who wear a mask. 'Daily in life,' he says, 'I watch men whose every smile is an artifice, and every wink is an hypocrisy.' With deference to the opinion of so great an observer of character, we doubt whether many men are even capable of sustaining such lifelong efforts of dissimulation; and suspect that Mr. Thackeray has put too harsh a construction on that ordinary social hypocrisy which springs partly from the mere desire to please, and which, though ignoble, does not go very deep into the heart. (p. 453)

[*Goldwin Smith*], in a review of *"The Virginians,"* in The Edinburgh Review, *Vol. CX, No. CCXXIV, October, 1859, pp. 438-53.*

## H. A. TAINE   (essay date 1863-64)

[*One of the most influential French literary critics and historians of the nineteenth century, Taine here maintains that Thackeray's satire is calculated and permeated by hatred. He strenuously objects to Thackeray's moral polemics, arguing that they interfere with his art and reduce his characters to mere puppets. Taine states that* Henry Esmond *is Thackeray's one great work because it lacks moral intent, and he laments the fact that Thackeray's excessive didacticism has prevented him from producing more works of its caliber.*]

Of all satirists, Thackeray, after Swift, is the most gloomy. . . . Indignation, grief, scorn, disgust, are his ordinary sentiments. When he digresses, and imagines tender souls, he exaggerates their sensibility, in order to render their oppression more odious. The selfishness which wounds them appears horrible, and their resigned sweetness is a mortal insult to their tyrants: it is the same hatred which has calculated the kindliness of the victims and the harshness of the persecutors. (pp. 176-77)

It is clear that the author is not carried away by passing indignation or pity. He has mastered himself before speaking. He has often weighed the rascality which he is about to describe. He is in possession of the motives, species, results, as a naturalist is of his classifications. He is sure of his judgment, and has matured it. He punishes like a man convinced, who has before him a heap of proofs, who advances nothing without a document or an argument, who has foreseen all objections and refuted all excuses, who will never pardon, who is right in being inflexible, who is conscious of his justice, and who rests his sentence and his vengeance on all the powers of meditation and equity. The effect of this justified and contained hatred is overwhelming. . . . When we have read to the end of Thackeray, we feel the shudder of a stranger brought before a mattress in the operating-room of an hospital on the day when cautery is applied or a limb is taken off.

In such a case the most natural weapon is serious irony, because it bears witness to concentrated hatred: he who employs it suppresses his first feeling; he feigns to be speaking against himself, and constrains himself to take the part of his adversary. On the other hand, this painful and voluntary attitude is the sign of excessive scorn; the protection which apparently is afforded to an enemy is the worst of insults. . . . Thus the more serious the irony, the stronger it is; the more you take care to defend your adversary, the more you degrade him; the more you seem to aid him, the more you crush him. (pp. 177-78)

If we only consider [human passions] as virtuous or vicious, our lost illusions will enchain us in gloomy thoughts, and we will find in man only weakness and ugliness. This is why Thackeray depreciates our whole nature. He does as a novelist what Hobbes does as a philosopher. Almost everywhere, when he describes fine sentiments, he derives them from an ugly source. Tenderness, kindness, love, are in his characters the effect of the nerves, of instinct, or of a moral disease. (p. 188)

In literature as well as in politics, we cannot have everything. . . . To transform the novel is to deform it: he who, like Thackeray, gives to the novel satire for its object, ceases to give it art for its rule, and the complete strength of the satirist is the weakness of the novelist.

What is a novelist? In my opinion he is a psychologist, who naturally and involuntarily sets psychology at work; he is nothing else, nor more. He loves to picture feelings, to perceive their connections, their precedents, their consequences; and he indulges in this pleasure. In his eyes they are forces, having various directions and magnitudes. About their justice or injustice he troubles himself little. (p. 205)

All is changed by the intervention of satire; and more particularly, the part of the author. When in an ordinary novel he speaks in his own name, it is to explain a sentiment or mark the cause of a faculty; in a satirical novel it is to give us moral advice. . . . Thackeray subjects us [to many lessons]. That they are good ones no one disputes; but at least they take the place of useful explanations. A third of a volume, being occupied by warnings, is lost to art. Summoned to reflect on our faults, we know the character less. The author designedly neglects a hundred delicate shades which he might have discovered and shown to us. The character, less complete, is less lifelike; the interest, less concentrated, is less lively. Turned away from it instead of brought back to it, our eyes wander and forget it; instead of being absorbed, we are absent in mind. And, what is worse, we end by experiencing some degree of weariness. (pp. 206-07)

This regular presence of a moral intention spoils the novel as well as the novelist. It must be confessed, a volume of Thackeray has the cruel misfortune of recalling the novels of Miss Edgeworth or the stories of Canon Schmidt. (p. 207)

Let us console ourselves: the characters suffer as much as we; the author spoils them in preaching to us; they, like us, are sacrificed to satire. He does not animate beings, he lets puppets act. He only combines their actions to make them ridiculous, odious, or disappointing. . . . [We] soon see that we are before the foot-lights, in front of bedizened actors, whose words are written for them, and their gestures arranged. (pp. 208-09)

Suppose that a happy chance lays aside these causes of weakness, and keeps open [the] sources of [Thackeray's] talent. Amongst all [his] transformed novels appears a single genuine one, elevated, touching, simple, original, the history of Henry Esmond. Thackeray has not written a less popular nor a more beautiful story. (p. 214)

Esmond speaks; and the necessity of adapting the tone to the character suppresses the satirical style, the reiterated irony, the bitter sarcasm, the scenes contrived to ridicule folly, the events combined to crush vice. Thenceforth we enter the real world; we let illusion guide us, we rejoice in a varied spectacle, easily unfolded, without moral intention. We are no more harassed by personal advice; we remain in our place, calm, sure, no actor's finger pointed at us to warn us at an interesting moment that the piece is played on our account, and to do us good. At the same time, and unconsciously, we are at ease. Quitting bitter satire, pure narration charms us; we take rest from hating. (pp. 214-15)

On the other hand, the long reflections, which seem vulgar and out of place under the pen of the writer, become natural and interesting in the mouth of the chief character in this novel. (p. 215)

With the reflections we endure the details. Elsewhere, the minute descriptions appear frequently puerile; we blamed the author for dwelling, with the preciseness of an English painter, on school adventures, coach scenes, inn episodes; we thought that this intense studiousness, unable to grasp lofty themes of art, was compelled to stoop to microscopical observations and photographic details. Here everything is changed. A writer of memoirs has a right to record his childish impressions. . . . We forget the author, we listen to the old Colonel, we find ourselves carried back a hundred years, and we have the extreme pleasure, so uncommon, of believing in what we read.

Whilst the subject obviates the faults, or turns them into virtues, it offers for these virtues the very finest theme. A powerful reflection has decomposed and reproduced the manners of the time with a most astonishing fidelity. . . . This perfect imitation is not limited to a few select scenes, but pervades the whole volume. Colonel Esmond writes as people wrote in the year 1700. . . . The style of *Esmond* has the calmness, the exactness, the simplicity, the solidity of the classics. Our modern temerities, our prodigal imagery, our jostled figures, our habit of gesticulation, our striving for effect, all our bad literary customs have disappeared. Thackeray must have gone back to the primitive sense of words, discovered their forgotten shades of meaning, recomposed an obliterated state of intellect and a lost species of ideas, to make his copy approach so closely to the original. The imagination of Dickens himself would have failed in this. To attempt and accomplish this, needed all the sagacity, calmness, and power of knowledge and meditation.

But the masterpiece of the work is the character of Esmond. Thackeray has endowed him with that tender kindliness, almost feminine, which he everywhere extols above all other human virtues, and that self-mastery which is the effect of habitual reflection. These are the finest qualities of his psychological armoury; each by its contrast increases the value of the other. We see a hero, but original and new, English in his cool resolution, modern by the delicacy and sensibility of his heart. (pp. 215-17)

[It] is to be remembered that Thackeray has produced no other; we regret that moral intentions have perverted these fine literary faculties; and we deplore that satire has robbed art of such talent. (p. 223)

A character is a force, like gravity, or steam, capable, as it may happen, of pernicious or profitable effects, and which must be defined otherwise than by the amount of the weight it can lift or the havoc it can cause. It is therefore to ignore man, to reduce him, as Thackeray and English literature generally do, to an aggregate of virtues and vices; it is to lose sight in him of all but the exterior and social side; it is to neglect the inner and natural element. (pp. 225-26)

*H. A. Taine, "The Novel Continued—Thackeray," in his* History of the English Literature, Vol. IV, Part I, *translated by H. Van Laun (originally published as* Histoire de la littérature anglaise, *L. Hachette et cie, 1863-64), Chatto & Windus, 1880, pp. 165-226.*

## CHARLES DICKENS   (essay date 1864)

*[Dickens and Thackeray are considered by many to be the two most prominent English novelists of the mid-Victorian era. Though the two never became close friends, they were well-acquainted and somewhat begrudgingly admired each other's works. In the late 1850s, however, a friend of Dickens's named Edmund Yates published a sarcastic review of* The Four Georges *which highly offended Thackeray. Dickens's subsequent involvement in the fight over the article caused a rift in his relationship with Thackeray and the two were reconciled only days before Thackeray's death. In the following obituary tribute to Thackeray, though he hints that perhaps Thackeray's "satirical pen" had "gone astray or done amiss," Dickens nevertheless praises Thackeray for his*

characterization, his *"subtle acquaintance with the weaknesses
of human nature,"* and his *"mastery over the English language."*
He also describes Denis Duval *as "much the best of all his
works."*]

If, in the reckless vivacity of his youth, his satirical pen had
ever gone astray or done amiss, [Mr. Thackeray] had caused
it to prefer its own petition for forgiveness, long before:

> I've writ the foolish fancy of his brain;
> The aimless jest that, striking, hath caused pain;
> The idle word that he'd wish back again.

In no pages should I take it upon myself at this time to discourse
of his books, of his refined knowledge of character, of his
subtle acquaintance with the weaknesses of human nature, of
his delightful playfulness as an essayist, of his quaint and
touching ballads, of his mastery over the English language.
(pp. 130-31)

But, on the table before me, there lies all that he had written
of his latest and last story [*Denis Duval*]. That it would be very
sad to any one—that it is inexpressibly so to a writer—in its
evidences of matured designs never to be accomplished, of
intentions begun to be executed and destined never to be completed, of careful preparation for long roads of thought that he
was never to traverse, and for shining goals that he was never
to reach, will be readily believed. The pain, however, that I
have felt in perusing it, has not been deeper than the conviction
that he was in the healthiest vigour of his powers when he
wrought on this last labour. In respect of earnest feeling, far-
seeing purpose, character, incident, and a certain loving picturesqueness blending the whole, I believe it to be much the
best of all his works. That he fully meant it to be so, that he
had become strongly attached to it, and that he bestowed great
pains upon it, I trace in almost every page. It contains one
picture which must have cost him extreme distress, and which
is a masterpiece. There are two children in it, touched with a
hand as loving and tender as ever a father caressed his little
child with. There is some young love, as pure and innocent
and pretty as the truth. And it is very remarkable that, by
reason of the singular construction of the story, more than one
main incident usually belonging to the end of such a fiction is
anticipated in the beginning, and thus there is an approach to
completeness in the fragment, as to the satisfaction of the
reader's mind concerning the most interesting persons, which
could hardly have been better attained if the writer's breaking-
off had been foreseen. (p. 131)

> *Charles Dickens, "In Memoriam," in* The Cornhill
> Magazine *(© John Murray 1864), Vol. IX, No. 50,
> February, 1864, pp. 129-32.*

## WALTER BAGEHOT  (essay date 1864)

Thackeray, like Sterne, looked at everything—at nature, at life,
at art—from a *sensitive* aspect. His mind was, to some considerable extent, like a woman's mind. It could comprehend
abstractions when they were unrolled and explained before it,
but it never naturally created them; never of itself, and without
external obligation, devoted itself to them. The visible scene
of life—the streets, the servants, the clubs, the gossip, the
West End—fastened on his brain. These were to him reality.
They burnt in upon his brain; they pained his nerves; their
influence reached him through many avenues, which ordinary
men do not feel much, or to which they are altogether imper-
vious. He had distinct and rather painful sensations where most
men have but confused and blurred ones. . . . He could not

help seeing everything, and what he saw made so near and
keen an impression upon him, that he could not again exclude
it from his understanding; it stayed there, and disturbed his
thoughts. (pp. 350-51)

A painfulness certainly clings like an atmosphere round Mr.
Thackeray's writings, in consequence of his inseparable and
ever-present realism. We hardly know where it is, yet we are
all conscious of it less or more. A free and bold writer, like
Sir Walter Scott, throws himself far away into fictitious worlds,
and soars there without effort, without pain, and with unceasing
enjoyment. You see as it were between the lines of Mr. Thackeray's writings, that his thoughts were never long away from
the close proximate scene. His writings might be better if it
had been otherwise; but they would have been less peculiar,
less individual; they would have wanted their character, their
flavour, if he had been able while writing them to forget for
many moments the ever-attending, the ever-painful sense of
himself.

Hence have arisen most of the censures upon him, both as he
seemed to be in society and as he was in his writings. He was
certainly uneasy in the common and general world, and it was
natural that he should be so. The world poured in upon him,
and *inflicted* upon his delicate sensibility a number of petty
pains and impressions which others do not feel at all, or which
they feel but very indistinctly. As he sat he seemed to read off
the passing thoughts—the base, common, ordinary impressions—of every one else. (pp. 351-52)

He could not emancipate himself from such impressions even
in a case where most men hardly feel them. Many people
have—it is not difficult to have—some vague sensitive perception of what is passing in the minds of the guests, of the
ideas of such as sit at meat; but who remembers that there are
also nervous apprehensions, also a latent mental life among
those who 'stand and wait'—among the floating figures which
pass and carve? But there was no impression to which Mr.
Thackeray was more constantly alive, or which he was more
apt in his writings to express. (p. 352)

Nothing in itself could be more admirable than this instinctive
sympathy with humble persons; not many things are rarer than
this nervous apprehension of what humble persons think.
Nevertheless it cannot, we think, be effectually denied that it
coloured Mr. Thackeray's writings and the more superficial
part of his character—that part which was most obvious in
common and current society—with very considerable defects.
The pervading idea of the **'Snob Papers'** is too frequent, too
recurring, too often insisted on, even in his highest writings. . . . (p. 353)

He lacerates 'snobs' in his books as if they had committed an
unpardonable outrage and inexpiable crime. That man, he says,
is anxious 'to know lords; and he pretends to know more of
lords than he really does know. What a villain! what a disgrace
to our common nature! what an irreparable reproach to human
reason!' Not at all; it is a fault which satirists should laugh at,
and which moralists condemn and disapprove, but which yet
does not destroy the whole vital excellence of him who possesses it. . . . (p. 355)

In transient society it is possible, we think, that Mr. Thackeray
thought too much of social inequalities. They belonged to that
common, plain, perceptible world which filled his mind, and
which left him at times, and at casual moments, no room for
a purely intellectual and just estimate of men as they really are
in themselves, and apart from social perfection or defect. He

could gauge a man's reality as well as any observer, and far better than most: his attainments were great, his perception of men instinctive, his knowledge of casual matters enormous; but he had a greater difficulty than other men in relying only upon his own judgment. . . . By the constitution of his mind he thought much of social distinctions; and yet he was in his writings too severe on those who, in cruder and baser ways, showed that they also were thinking much.

Those who perceive that this irritable sensibility was the basis of Thackeray's artistic character, that it gave him his materials, his implanted knowledge of things and men, and gave him also that keen and precise style which hit in description the nice edges of all objects,—those who trace these great qualities back to their real source in a somewhat painful organisation, must have been vexed or amused, according to their temperament, at the common criticism which associates him with Fielding. Fielding's essence was the very reverse; it was a bold spirit of bounding happiness. No just observer could talk to Mr. Thackeray, or look at him, without seeing that he had deeply felt many sorrows—perhaps that he was a man *likely* to feel sorrows—that he was of an anxious temperament. Fielding was a reckless enjoyer. He saw the world—wealth and glory, the best dinner and the worst dinner, the gilded *salon* and the low sponging-house—and he saw that they were good. Down every line of his characteristic writings there runs this elemental energy of keen delight. There is no trace of such a thing in Thackeray. A musing fancifulness is far more characteristic of him than a joyful energy.

Sterne had all this sensibility also, but—and this is the cardinal discrepancy—it did not make him irritable. . . . Thackeray was pained by things, and exaggerated their imperfections; Sterne brooded over things with joy or sorrow, and he idealised their sentiment—their pathetic or joyful characteristics. This is why the old lady said, 'Mr. Thackeray was an uncomfortable writer,'—and an uncomfortable writer he is. (pp. 355-56)

There is a tinge—a mitigated, but perceptible tinge—of Swift's philosophy in Thackeray. 'Why is all this? Surely this is very strange? Am I right in sympathising with such stupid feelings, such petty sensations? Why are these things? Am I not a fool to care about or think of them? The world is dark, and the great curtain hides from us all.' This is not a steady or an habitual feeling, but it is never quite absent for many pages. It was inevitable, perhaps, that in a sceptical and inquisitive age like this, some vestiges of puzzle and perplexity should pass into the writings of our great sentimentalist. He would not have fairly represented the moods of his time if he omitted that pervading one. (pp. 356-57)

*Walter Bagehot, "Sterne and Thackeray," in* The National Review, *London, Vol. XVIII, April, 1864 (and reprinted in* Thackeray: A Critical Heritage, *edited by Geoffrey Tillotson and Donald Hawes, Routledge & Kegan Paul, 1968, pp. 350-57).*

## ANTHONY TROLLOPE (essay date 1879)

[*Trollope's* Thackeray *is one of the earliest book-length critical studies of Thackeray's works. Trollope's assessment is largely positive and he praises highly Thackeray's realism, characterization, and exquisite style. Yet he adds that Thackeray's style is flawed by "a certain affected familiarity." Trollope argues that Thackeray's narrative structure often robs his works of their integrity by creating a sense of detachment and lack of dignity that Trollope finds inappropriate to the novel. He regrets that Thackeray was preoccupied to such a great extent with the negative,*

*but conjectures that Thackeray was so intent upon bettering the world through his denunciations of social evil that he often neglected to depict the positive aspects of life.*]

[Regarding] the realism of Thackeray, I must rather appeal to my readers than attempt to prove it by quotation. Whoever it is that speaks in his pages, does it not seem that such a person would certainly have used such words on such an occasion? If there be need of examination to learn whether it be so or not, let the reader study all that falls from the mouth of Lady Castlewood through the novel called *Esmond,* or all that falls from the mouth of Beatrix. They are persons peculiarly situated,—noble women, but who have still lived much out of the world. The former is always conscious of a sorrow; the latter is always striving after an effect;—and both on this account are difficult of management. A period for the story has been chosen which is strange and unknown to us, and which has required a peculiar language. One would have said beforehand that whatever might be the charms of the book, it would not be natural. And yet the ear is never wounded by a tone that is false. . . . Thackeray never disappoints. Whether it be a great duke, such as he who was to have married Beatrix, or a mean chaplain, such as Tusher, or Captain Steele the humorist, they talk,—not as they would have talked probably, of which I am no judge,—but as we feel that they might have talked. We find ourselves willing to take it as proved because it is there, which is the strongest possible evidence of the realistic capacity of the writer. (pp. 187-88)

[In another] division of pure fiction,—the burlesque, as it is commonly called, or the ludicrous,—Thackeray is quite as much at home as in the realistic, though, the vehicle being less powerful, he has achieved smaller results by it. Manifest as are the objects in his view when he wrote *The Hoggarty Diamond* or *The Legend of the Rhine,* they were less important and less evidently effected than those attempted by *Vanity Fair* and *Pendennis.* Captain Shindy, the Snob, does not tell us so plainly what is not a gentleman as does Colonel Newcome what is. Nevertheless the ludicrous has, with Thackeray, been very powerful, and very delightful. (p. 191)

No writer ever had a stronger proclivity towards parody than Thackeray; and we may, I think, confess that there is no form of literary drollery more dangerous. The parody will often mar the gem of which it coarsely reproduces the outward semblance. . . . But it must be acknowledged of Thackeray that, fond as he is of this branch of humour, he has done little or no injury by his parodies. They run over with fun, but are so contrived that they do not lessen the flavour of the original. . . . [He] has been grotesque without being severely critical, and has been very like, without making ugly or distasteful that which he has imitated. . . . The ludicrous alone is but poor fun; but when the ludicrous has a meaning, it can be very effective in the hands of such a master as this. (pp. 194-96)

Whatever Thackeray says, the reader cannot fail to understand; and whatever Thackeray attempts to communicate, he succeeds in conveying.

That he is grammatical I must leave to my readers' judgment, with a simple assertion in his favour. . . . He quarrels with none of the laws [of grammar]. As the lady who is most attentive to conventional propriety may still have her own fashion of dress and her own mode of speech, so had Thackeray very manifestly his own style; but it is one the correctness of which has never been impugned. (pp. 199-200)

I am inclined to think that his most besetting sin in style,—the little earmark by which he is most conspicuous,—is a certain affected familiarity. He indulges too frequently in little confidences with individual readers, in which pretended allusions to himself are frequent. "What would you do? what would you say now, if you were in such a position?" he asks. . . . In the short contributions to periodicals on which he tried his 'prentice hand, such addresses and conversations were natural and efficacious; but in a larger work of fiction they cause an absence of that dignity to which even a novel may aspire. You feel that each morsel as you read it is a detached bit, and that it has all been written in detachments. The book is robbed of its integrity by a certain good-humoured geniality of language, which causes the reader to be almost too much at home with his author. There is a saying that familiarity breeds contempt, and I have been sometimes inclined to think that our author has sometimes failed to stand up for himself with sufficiency of "personal deportment."

In other respects Thackeray's style is excellent. . . . [The] reader always understands his words without an effort, and receives all that the author has to give. (p. 201)

Now let the reader ask himself what are the lessons which Thackeray has taught. Let him send his memory running back over all [his] characters . . . , and ask himself whether any girl has been taught to be immodest, or any man unmanly, by what Thackeray has written. A novelist has two modes of teaching,—by good example or bad. It is not to be supposed that because the person treated of be evil, therefore the precept will be evil. . . . [Thackeray's examples] have all been efficacious in their teaching on the side of modesty and manliness, truth and simplicity. (pp. 204-05)

There remains for us only this question,—whether the nature of Thackeray's works entitle him to be called a cynic. The word is one which is always used in a bad sense. . . . [They] who have called him a cynic have spoken of him merely as a writer,—and as writer he has certainly taken upon himself the special task of barking at the vices and follies of the world around him. Any satirist might in the same way be called a cynic in so far as his satire goes. . . . But that is not all that the word implies. It intends to go back beyond the work of the man, and to describe his heart. It says of any satirist so described that he has given himself up to satire, not because things have been evil, but because he himself has been evil. Hamlet is a satirist, whereas Thersites is a cynic. If Thackeray be judged after this fashion, the word is as inappropriate to the writer as to the man.

But it has to be confessed that Thackeray did allow his intellect to be too thoroughly saturated with the aspect of the ill side of things. We can trace the operation of his mind from his earliest days, when he commenced his parodies at school; when he brought out *The Snob* at Cambridge, when he sent *Yellowplush* out upon the world as a satirist on the doings of gentlemen generally; when he wrote his *Catherine,* to show the vileness of the taste for what he would have called Newgate literature; and *The Hoggarty Diamond,* to attack bubble companies; and *Barry Lyndon,* to expose the pride which a rascal may take in his rascality. Becky Sharp, Major Pendennis, Beatrix, both as a young and as an old woman, were written with the same purpose. There is a touch of satire in every drawing that he made. A jeer is needed for something that is ridiculous, scorn has to be thrown on something that is vile. (pp. 206-08)

He was "crying his sermon," hoping, if it might be so, to do something towards lessening the evils he saw around him. We all preach our sermon, but not always with the same earnest-

ness. He had become so urgent in the cause, so loud in his denunciations, that he did not stop often to speak of the good things around him. Now and again he paused and blessed amid the torrent of his anathemas. There are Dobbin, and Esmond, and Colonel Newcome. But his anathemas are the loudest. It has been so I think nearly always with the eloquent preachers. (p. 208)

> *Anthony Trollope, in his* Thackeray *(1879), Macmillan and Co., Limited, 1906 (and reprinted by Gale Research Company, 1968), 216 p.*

## W. C. BROWNELL (essay date 1901)

[*Brownell, unlike critics such as H. A. Taine (1863-64), Charles Whibley (1903), and J.Y.T. Greig (1950), argues that Thackeray's subjective narrative technique enhances the realism of his novels. He maintains that "the reality of his 'happy, harmless fable-land' is wonderfully enhanced by the atmosphere with which his moralizing enfolds it, and at the same time the magic quality of this medium itself enforces our sense that it is fable-land, and enables us to savor* as *illusion the illusion of its art."*]

[Thackeray] is already a classic. He is the representative English man of letters of his time, and one of the few great novelists of the world. . . . [And yet], with the increase of his vogue, Thackeray has inevitably become to an appreciable extent, during the past few years, the prey of critical pedantry. . . . [Fiction] having become a "finer art" since Thackeray's day, owing to the vigorous filing and sandpapering no doubt which it has received in the course of our critics' and craftsmen's culture evolution, the artistic vulnerability of Thackeray as an old practitioner is logically deduced. (pp. 3-5)

[The] gospel of art for art's sake is reduced to absurdity when it is applied to the novel. . . . To force the note of "art" in the novel is to circumscribe its area of interest and limit its range of expression. It is a sacrifice to formalism that is at once needless and useless. . . . Why is there such a sense of life in **"The Newcomes,"** compared with Turgenieff's "Virgin Soil," that the story of the latter seems by comparison to vibrate idly *in vacuo*? Because Thackeray enwraps and embroiders his story with his personal philosophy, charges it with his personal feeling, draws out, with inexhaustible personal zest, its typical suggestiveness, and deals with his material directly instead of dispassionately and disinterestedly, after the manner of the Russian master. (pp. 5-7)

When Thackeray is reproached with "bad art" for intruding upon his scene, the reproach is chiefly the recommendation of a different technic. . . . [For] the novel on a large scale, the novel as Thackeray understood and produced it, Thackeray's technic has certain clear advantages. In order to deal with life powerfully, persuasively, and successfully, the direct method is in some respects superior to the detached. . . . [Thackeray] never lost sight of relations and atmosphere, and for these—in which the sense of reality resides—a freer technic is salutary. (pp. 7-8)

If Thackeray's "subjectivity" destroyed illusion it would indeed be inartistic. The notable thing about it is that it deepens illusion. The reality of his "happy, harmless fable-land" is wonderfully enhanced by the atmosphere with which his moralizing enfolds it, and at the same time the magic quality of this medium itself enforces our sense that it *is* fable-land, and enables us to savor *as* illusion the illusion of its art. (p. 9)

And it is to be observed that this atmosphere, which exists to such serviceable artistic ends in Thackeray's fiction, exists invariably *as* atmosphere. . . . The reticulation of personal comment that rests so lightly and decoratively on the fabric of his story, all the imaginative connotation, so to say, philosophical and sentimental, of his novels, has but an auxiliary function and plays no structural part. It is not used to fill out the substance and round the outlines of his personages, who exist quite independently of it. It serves, on the contrary, to detach them from the background, to detach them from their creator himself. It is absolutely true that Thackeray's "subjectivity" in this way subtly increases the objectivity of his creations. They are in this way definitely "exteriorized." In this way we get the most vivid, the most realizing sense of them as independent existences; and in this way we get Thackeray too. (p. 10)

[Anyone] but a pedant more interested in the rules than in the result of novel-writing can see that [his] familiar commentary not only attests but greatly enhances the sense of reality, of life, in the characters that furnish its text. Even technically considered, it is in this respect the acme of art. In Thackeray's hands it does not distract the attention, but concentrates it upon the representative, the typical, the vital traits of his personages. (pp. 12-13)

When personal expression is so easy, so admirable, and so successful as Thackeray's, when, as with him, it is a faculty clearly to be exercised instead of repressed, the temptation to rely upon it, to overwork it, to give it a free rein, is very great. Even in the unique **"Roundabout Papers,"** which are its expression *par excellence,* there are instances of this excess. **"Philip"** is a notable instance. . . . It is, indeed, a *tour de force* in prolixity. The proportion of Thackeray to Philip is prodigious. The story is decidedly thin; there is next to no plot, and the incidents are few and of the same family. The first hundred pages are astonishing variations on the single theme of Philip's antagonism to his father. A great deal of the book is pure "copy." . . . [However, the] characters save the story from mediocrity—and triumphantly. They are drawn with the true Thackerayan firmness and distinction. Where, indeed, is there a weak line in any portrait of his populous gallery? (pp. 13-15)

How he thinks and feels in the presence of the drama they are enacting immensely extends the range of our interest. Conceive **"The Newcomes"** without the presence of Thackeray upon the stage—minus the view it gives us of the working of its author's mind, the glimpses of his philosophy, the touches of his feeling. (pp. 16-17)

In a more definite and apposite way, therefore, than is true of a personality that produces works of a more impersonal order, Thackeray's own nature becomes the most interesting and important subject to consider in connection with his works. (p. 17)

Of all prose writers of the first rank he is the most purely instinctive. His high spirits are astonishing. They are the source of the infectiousness of his humor as well as responsible for its occasional triviality. (p. 20)

Such a nature is too ample to be distinctly critical, and Thackeray's had its prejudices, searching as was the mind that governed it. His body of doctrine was traditional, and he devoted little thought to what Carlyle calls "verifying one's ready-reckoner." His genius is rather that of the born novelist. . . . [Yet] it appears as unmistakably in his essays, his burlesques, his sketches, his literary criticism, as in his novels themselves.

No writer whose fame rests, as Thackeray's larger fame does, on notable works of fiction, has written miscellaneous literature of such distinction. (pp. 20-1)

[His poetry] is of the kind that is accurately called "verses," but it is as plainly his own as his prose; and some of it will always be read, probably, for its feeling and its felicity. It is the verse mainly but not merely of the improvisatore. It never oversteps the modesty becoming the native gift that expresses itself in it. . . . Metrically and in substance the **"Ballads"** are excellent balladry. They never rise to Scott's level of heroic *bravura,* and though the contemplative ones are deeper in feeling than any of Scott's, they are poetically more summary and have less sweep; one hardly thinks of the pinions of song at all in connection with them. Prose was distinctly Thackeray's medium more exclusively than it was Scott's. (p. 22)

Nowhere is the special quality of his genius more apparent than in the admirable series of **"Lectures on the English Humourists of the Eighteenth Century,"** which is literary criticism of a high order, but distinctly the criticism of the novelist rather than of the critic. It occupies, for this reason, a place by itself. . . . It quite neglects the element of literary evolution, is unconscious of the historical or any other method, does not discuss the poetic weakness of an age of prose, and is not based on minute and studious textual examination of its subject but on saturation with it. . . . From the point of view of literary criticism, at least of the scientific literary criticism of the present day, the work may certainly be said to have been lightly undertaken. . . . The characters of the writers are the real subject of the series, which is an unequalled gallery of literary portraits. Each one is all there. The painter may have treated the detail indifferently here and there, over-emphasized an expression, missed the full value of some features, but they stand out with the same vivid distinctness that belongs to the characters of his fiction. He has visualized them in the same way. . . . He was, in a word, by temperament and faculty, first and last a novelist.

For this reason his world is an extremely concrete world. His people are the people we meet or might meet; his characters are types, not variants and exceptions, and, accordingly, they have a human and social rather than a psychological interest. . . . [They] are delineated rather than dissected; they are not explored clinically. They are not studied and scrutinized in the spirit of the scientist or the philosopher. (pp. 23-5)

[In Thackeray's] view character is spectacle, significant spectacle, to be sure, and its significance often copiously insisted upon, but essentially spectacle, and not the illustrative incarnation of interesting traits and tendencies. (p. 27)

The idea underlying the world Thackeray constructed is the intricate moral complexity of character—an idea illustrated with a completeness and relief not perhaps to be met with elsewhere outside of Shakespeare and Molière. . . . Thackeray's absorption in the moral interest of character is, on the other hand, naturally limiting. . . . [In] confining himself in the main to character not merely in its elemental traits, but in its morally significant ones as well—a realist like Thackeray renounces a field so large and interesting as justly to have his neglect of it accounted to him as a limitation. The colorless characters . . . , such as Dickens's Jingles and Swivellers, have few fellows in his fiction, from which the seriousness of his satiric strain excludes whatever is not significant as well as whatever is purely particular. The loss is very great, considering his world as a *comédie humaine* [human comedy]. It involves more than the elimination of psychology—it diminishes the number of types; and all types are interesting, whether morally important or not.

But in Thackeray's case it has two great compensations. In the first place, the greater concentration it involves notably defines and emphasizes the net impression of his works. It unifies their effect; and sharply crystallizes the message to mankind. . . . In the second place, it is his concentration upon the morally significant that places him at the head of the novelists of manners. It is the moral and social qualities, of course, that unite men in society, and make it something other than the sum of the individuals composing it. Thackeray's personages are never portrayed in isolation. They are a part of the *milieu* in which they exist, and which has itself therefore much more distinction and relief than an environment which is merely a framework. How they regard each other, how they feel toward and what they think of each other, the mutuality of their very numerous and vital relations, furnishes an important strand in the texture of the story in which they figure. . . . So far as it goes, therefore,—and it would be easy to exaggerate its limitations, which are trivial in comparison,—Thackeray's picture of society is the most vivid, as it is incontestably the most real, in prose fiction. . . . And in addition to the high place in literature won for him by his insight into character, Thackeray's social picture has given him a distinction that is perhaps unique.

Furthermore, compared with the moral interest of character, that of its purely psychological peculiarities is distinctly less vital and permanent. . . . Character, indeed, *means* moral character. . . . And I have never heard it suggested that Thackeray's personages, morally considered as they are, lacked psychological definition. . . . The moral element in their portrayal adds reality and relief, as well as importance. Its complexity, at any rate, is Thackeray's theme, and he, at least, found it inexhaustible. With him no passion is simple, no motive unmixed. (pp. 27-30)

Nowhere is this to be so plainly noted as in his women. . . . Thackeray triumphs with equal distinction in the analysis that discovers the sound alloy in base metal and in that which finds dross in the most refined. Rachel Castlewood and her brilliant daughter, Ethel Newcome and Rebecca, are equally complicated. (pp. 30-1)

Taken as a whole, it is true, Thackeray's human comedy is less comprehensive than Balzac's, with which alone it is to be compared in the world of prose fiction. Taken as a whole, it lacks that appearance of vastness and variety which Balzac's has, and perhaps the appearance in such a matter answers as well as the reality. Considered, that is to say, purely as a world of the imagination, Thackeray's is the more circumscribed. But it is born of less travail; it is constructed with the effortless ease of greater spontaneity; its preliminary simplification has been carried farther; and, if less complicated and ingenious, less speculative and suggestive, it is far more real. Its philosophy is more human, more winning, more attaching, and in a very deep sense more profound. The note of artificiality, the fly in Balzac's ointment, the weak point in his superb equipment, never appears in Thackeray. His charm is infinitely greater. His power is rendered at least equivalent by its conjunction with the simplicity that Balzac lacks. And his narrower range is perhaps to be ascribed to his lesser absorption, perhaps to the less varied and more conventional world that he had to depict. At any rate, it proceeds from no inferiority to his great contemporary and compeer in native equipment and vital force for the specific work of the novelist—the portrayal of the play

of human forces, inspired and directed by searching scrutiny of the human heart. (pp. 36-7)

It is true that [Thackeray] had no talent for abstract thinking, for abstruse philosophy. But to assume that he has no philosophy would be to ignore the significance of one of the most definite and complete syntheses of human phenomena that have ever been made, and a synthesis, moreover, incomparably buttressed by the acutest analysis and the most copious illustration. He does not stimulate thought, in the sense of speculation, so much as he arouses reflection. His ideas are moral ideas rather than metaphysical—the ideas for which Voltaire eulogized English poetry. And he deals with them powerfully, cogently, winningly, rather than refining upon them and following out their evolution as a disinterested exercise of the mind. . . . The concrete illustration of ideas in character is what interests Thackeray and what he interests us with. But in this his interest and his power of interesting us are hardly to be measured. . . . There is no missing the tenor of his gospel, which is that character is the one thing of importance in life; that it is tremendously complex, and the easiest thing in the world to misconceive both in ourselves and in others; that truth is the one instrument of its perfecting, and the one subject worthy of pursuit; and that the study of truth discloses littlenesses and futilities in it at its best for which the only cloak is charity, and the only consolation and atonement the cultivation of the affections. (pp. 37-9)

Thackeray is undoubtedly to be classed with the world's elegant writers—the writers of whom Virgil may stand as the type and exemplar, the writers who demand and require cultivation in the reader in order to be understood and enjoyed. (pp. 42-3)

The variety and range of his style, which are extraordinary, answer exactly to the range and variety of his own thought and feeling and share his extraordinary vitality and interest in all sides of every subject. No one has so light a touch and no one can stir us so deeply, leaving the nerves unassailed. . . . And not only is he himself the source of the color of his style: he is the source also of its sustained quality. His style is adapted to the largest as well as to cabinet canvases because it is the natural expression of his own largeness of view and depth of feeling, instead of being the result of some rhetorical penchant, or the anxious education of illustrating some idea of energy, clearness, cogency, or whatnot. . . . Like his art and like the world of his imagination, it is an outgrowth of the most interesting personality, perhaps, that has expressed itself in prose. (pp. 45-6)

> *W. C. Brownell, "Thackeray," in his* Victorian Prose Masters, *Charles Scribner's Sons, 1901, pp. 3-46.*

## CHARLES WHIBLEY (essay date 1903)

[*Whibley's study is indicative of the general decline in Thackeray's critical reputation around the turn of the century. He criticizes Thackeray's obsession with snobbery, maintaining that it distorts his outlook on life and adversely affects most of his works. Regarding Thackeray's didactic narrative technique, Whibley states that Thackeray "plays the same part in his books as is played in Greek tragedy by a chorus of tiresome elders." Although he criticizes Thackeray for his lack of "a controlling hand, a settled purpose" in regard to style, he admits that Thackeray's writing is often eloquent. He also praises his versatility, but concludes that a fundamental, irreconcilable conflict exists in Thackeray between "the sentimental moralist . . . and the keen-eyed ironist. . . ."*]

With much of Thackeray's satire it is easy to sympathise. All honest men hate tuft-hunting as they hate an assumption of gentility. . . . But [in *The Book of Snobs*] Thackeray does not stay his hand at legitimate denunciation. He worries his point, until he himself becomes the mouthpiece of mean thoughts. He seems to be haunted by a species of self-consciousness; he is surprised that he is where he is; he knows that somebody is above or below him; but he cannot take his place in the world (or anybody else's place) for granted. (p. 84)

In truth, there is a touch of wounded pride in every page of this *Book of Snobs*, which Thackeray should never have betrayed. (pp. 84-5)

*The Snob Papers* betray a lack of humour, an inability to look at things in their right proportion, which it is not easy to condone. Thackeray was persuaded that all things are barbarous which are not of practical utility. . . . He hated tradition, and denounced in set terms "the brutal, unchristian, blundering Feudal system." But to denounce is not to abolish. As we are born of the past, so we cannot, by a mere act of will, rid ourselves of our ancestry and its influence. The Feudal system may be all that a hostile fancy paints it, but it shaped the world we live in, the only world we shall ever live in. Nor would Thackeray's argument be sound, unless he re-created the human race, and let it fight out its battles *in vacuo*. (p. 86)

But if *The Book of Snobs* is based upon a confusion of thought, it none the less has conspicuous merits. The style, though now and again forced to a witticism, is often as lucid and supple as Thackeray's best; the sketches of character scattered up and down the book are admirably fresh and truthful, nor does the fact that he afterwards drew them on a larger scale impair their interest and veracity. . . . *The Book of Snobs* touched the popular fancy, and made Thackeray famous. It achieved more than this: it profoundly influenced its author. . . . [He] never shook himself free from its bondage. Henceforth he was, more often than not, a chronicler of snobs, and it was only when his imagination carried him back to the eighteenth century that he forgot the twisted standard of life he had himself set up. It is not uncommon, this spectacle of an author enslaved by his own book; but the slavery dimmed Thackeray's outlook upon the world. . . . (pp. 87-8)

[Thackeray] called [*Vanity Fair*] "a novel without a hero"; he might have called it a novel without a plan. He confesses himself that the moral crept in of itself, and that he "wasn't going to write in this way when he began." In other words, the story grew as it chose, from month to month, and dragged its author after it. And this explains its failure to stop when it should. (pp. 91-2)

[The] book has not a plan or motive in the sense that Balzac and the moderns have understood it. For Thackeray, although he might . . . have studied the *Comédie Humaine*, remained old-fashioned to the end, and let his personages wander up and down as they listed, content if only he could now and again slip in a sentiment, or castigate a favourite vice on his own account. But the charge commonly brought against *Vanity Fair* that it is heartless and cynical cannot be sustained for a moment. A novel of manners does not exhaust the whole of human life, and Thackeray had a perfect right to choose such puppets for his shows as aroused his keenest interest. Nor is the book merely a novel of manners; it is a satire as well. The author does not ask his readers to profess sympathy with his ruffians. He demands no more than an appreciation of a witty presentment and of deft draughtsmanship. If he had suppressed the

sentiment, which ever rose up in his heart, *Vanity Fair* might have been as un-moral as [William Congreve's] *The Way of the World,* and what a masterpiece it would have been! Even Amelia, a very Niobe of tears, is drawn with a cold contempt, and I am not certain that she is not as savage a piece of satire as Becky herself.

But Thackeray, though he loved to masquerade as a man of the world, could not help looking even at his own creations with an eye of pity or dislike. He plays the same part in his books as is played in Greek tragedy by a chorus of tiresome elders, and it is this constant intrusion which gives certain passages in *Vanity Fair* a rakish, almost a battered, air. The reader would never dream of taking such persons as Rawdon and his Aunt seriously, were he not told to do so by the author of their being. . . . [Thackeray] forgets the impartiality of the artist, and goes about babbling with his own puppets.

These excesses of sentiment are plain for all to see. They interrupt the progress of the story with irritating frequency. They put a needless accent upon what is called the "cynicism" of Thackeray, and confuse the very simple method of the book. (pp. 92-4)

[Thackeray] is so closely set upon disquisition that he cannot refrain the hand of sentiment even from the character of Rawdon Crawley, whose rough, amiable brutality might have been pictured without a flaw. . . . A story which needs annotation fails of its main purpose, and the reader may justly feel irritated who is not left to form his own conclusions.

It is especially in satire that sermonising has no place, for satire is of itself a method of reproof. Though Aristophanes at times laid aside the lash for the lyre, he knew the limits of his *genre* too well to lapse into moral discourses. But Thackeray acts the sheep-dog to his own characters. . . . And when he is angry with them, he scolds them with almost a shrewish tongue. But, despite this concession to his own and the popular taste, Thackeray—with *Vanity Fair*—well deserved the place which he won in the literature of his age. Its style, peculiarly simple and straightforward, was free both from rhetoric and ornament. It suppressed all the tricks of the novelist, and threw what discredit it could upon fine writing. At the same time, it was various enough to express the diverse persons and changing emotions which are the material of the book. The characters are as distinguished as the style. Seldom in the history of English romance had a more genteel company been gathered together, and even when it is disreputable, it is still the best of bad company. (pp. 94-6)

Thackeray possessed in a greater measure than any other English writer the *style coulant* [fluent style] which Baudelaire ascribed in dispraise to George Sand. His words flow like snow-water upon the moutain-side. He could no more restrain the current of his prose than a gentle slope could turn a rivulet back upon its course. His sentences dash one over the other in an often aimless succession, as though impelled by a force independent of their author. The style, as employed by Thackeray, has its obvious qualities and defects. It is so easy that it may be followed by the idlest reader, who willingly applies to literature the test of conversation. The thread of argument or of character is so loosely held that it need not elude a half-awakened attention. On the other hand, the style must needs be at times inaccurate and undistinguished. The solecisms of which he is guilty, and they are not few, may readily be forgiven. It is more difficult to pardon the frequent lack of distinction, especially as in *Esmond* Thackeray proved that he could write, if he would, with perfect artistry. But the method of his more familiar books seems the result less of artifice than of temperament. He seldom gives you the impression that he has studied to produce a certain effect. An effect is there, of course, facile and various, but beyond his management. He is so little conscious of his craft that he rarely arrives at the right phrase, thus presenting an obvious contrast to Disraeli, who, often careless in composition, yet sowed his pages with pearls of speech which time cannot dim. But how little do we take away from the most of Thackeray beyond a general impression of gentlemanly ease!

From this it follows that he possessed no economy of speech. He never used one word, if a page and a half could adequately express the meaning; and at all save his high moments you miss a controlling hand, a settled purpose. (pp. 243-44)

While Thackeray left the words to look after themselves, he confesses himself the humble slave of his own characters. "Once created," said he, "they lead me, and I follow where they direct." He devised his actors as by instinct, and without realising the full meaning of the drama in which they played their part. . . . It is not strange, therefore, that he regarded the personages in his own dramas as quite outside himself. . . . And it was precisely this externality which linked Thackeray and his characters in the bonds of acquaintance. Had they been the deliberate and conscious creations of his brain, they would have been at once more and less familiar to him. He would have remembered precisely where the strings lay which pulled the figures; but he could not have said, "I know the people utterly—I know the sound of their voices." . . . We may be quite sure that he never encountered Sir Francis or Beatrix Esmond, for these he made himself; but the majority of his characters grew without his knowledge, and even against his will. (pp. 245-46)

It was this fatality, this frank obedience to his own puppets and his own pen, which explains the frequent formlessness of Thackeray's work. But though he permitted most of his books to write themselves, it must not be thought that his style was uniformly hazardous. Despite its occasional inaccuracy, despite its loose texture, it has many shining qualities. It is graphic, various, and at times eloquent. It is easy to recall a hundred passages which would entitle Thackeray to a high place among the writers of English. The Waterloo chapters of *Vanity Fair,* much of *Esmond,* Harry Warrington's first visit to England, Denis Duval's journey to London,—these, to name but a few, are touched by the hand of a master, who need fear comparison with none. Even where Thackeray's prose is least under control, it inspires no more than his own regret that he did not write "a completely good book." For it is always the prose of a man of letters. (p. 246)

In nothing did he show himself a man of letters more clearly than in his versatility. He could bend his mind to more than one kind of literature. For him the English language was an instrument upon which he could play many measures. In his hands it was apt for satire or reflection, for fiction or criticism. Though he was often careless of his own style, he had a quick perception of style in others, as is proved by his imitations of the novelists, the very perfection of criticism. . . . And he could turn easily from a full-length novel to the exquisite fooling of a tale written for children. His *Christmas Books,* though written in conformity with a prevailing custom, are by no means the worst of his works, and he seldom surpassed the amiable drollery and good humour which keep *The Rose and the Ring* ever fresh.

Once upon a time he aspired to be a painter . . . ; and it is therefore the more remarkable that he is seldom deliberately "picturesque." He does not, like the novelists of our own day, ladle his local colour out from a full bucket. He may weary the reader with tedious sermons; he never tries his patience with purple passages of irrelevant description. Indeed, he so sternly suppresses the external world that when you recall his novels, you have but a faint impression of the scene on which the drama is played. The few landscapes which he sketches produce, from their very rarity, an astonishing effect. . . . Thackeray is more deeply interested in his characters than in their environment; and though his reticence is vastly preferable to the ill-considered picturesqueness nowadays so popular, we would gladly have exchanged a hundred of his sermons for one deft sketch of an English countryside or foreign watering-place. (pp. 249-51)

[There] were always two men in Thackeray, the sentimental moralist, whose obvious "lessons" were long since forgotten, and the keen-eyed ironist, for whom life was an amusing game, whose rules were independent of virtue, and in which the scoundrel was most often victorious. It is this twofold character which explains why most of Thackeray's work was marred by a kind of uncertainty, and justifies Carlyle's admirable comment,—"a beautiful vein of genius lay struggling about in him." The genius never overcame the struggle. When the ironist was disposed to take a large view, the moralist interrupted his vision, and the moralist was so tight bound to the superstitions of his age, that he will probably never appear as great as he did to some of his contemporaries. (pp. 252-53)

> *Charles Whibley, in his* William Makepeace Thackeray, *William Blackwood and Sons, 1903, 262 p.*

## GEORGE SAINTSBURY (essay date 1908)

[*Saintsbury is considered one of the most influential English critics and literary historians of the early twentieth century. His* A Consideration of Thackeray *is a collection of his introductions to the Oxford editions of Thackeray's works. In these introductions, which together cover all of Thackeray's writings, Saintsbury concentrates primarily on his humor, characterization, and style. Though he maintains that* Barry Lyndon *fails in interest, he calls* Vanity Fair *"a prodigal of delights." Saintsbury also considers the subtle blend of historical depiction and modern viewpoint in* Henry Esmond *masterful, stating: "A greater novel than* Henry Esmond *I do not know. . . ."*]

[In his early writings Thackeray] showed, almost from the first and in ever-increasing measure and with less alloy, qualities of the very rarest kind. The most unmistakable—or what ought to have been the most unmistakable—of these was the omnipresence of a peculiar humour, or wit and humour mingled, unlike that of any previous writer as a whole but bearing most resemblance to Fielding and Shakespeare—a humour casual, unpremeditated, or at least never laboriously led up to, *parenthetic* as one may almost call it—rising, like bubbles in sparkling wine, independently of the substance of the narrative or discussion, but giving life to it. The second, more slowly developed, and perhaps hidden from careless or obtuse observers by the caricature and the dialect of such things as *The Yellowplush Papers,* was an especially remarkable command of character, sometimes revealed by only a very few strokes, but those of such a vivifying character as we must once more go to Shakespeare to equal. The third was a quite marvellous style. . . . [His style] may again owe something to Fielding, but it is in its essence almost wholly original. It is more like the result of thinking aloud than the style of any other writer. But it is also more than this. The writer thinks for himself *and* for 'the other fellow'—for an imaginary interlocutor who makes objections, spies the ludicrous side of what has been said, and so forth. Thus, the body of his critical and miscellaneous writings, and the framework of his novels, consists of a sort of fused dialogue or conversation, lighted up constantly by the humour and wit above mentioned, and vignetting the character-sketches, the descriptions, and the rest. This sort of thing could not be perfected at once, but it may be discovered in pieces which he wrote when he was not more than six-and-twenty, such as *The Professor.* (pp. 18-19)

[*Catherine*] is a very odd book—the oddest in all Thackeray's work, and the most difficult to 'place' satisfactorily. . . . For myself I prefer it to *Barry Lyndon,* though it is more immature. . . . It could hardly have been made more disgusting (in fact a good deal of repulsive detail was actually removed in the reprint) without becoming a mere study of horror and grime in itself and for its own sake. . . . On the other hand, if the object was what it holds itself out to be—the satire by parody of books like [Dickens's] *Jack Sheppard,* with something more than a glance backward at *Eugene Aram,* and something of a glance sideways at *Oliver Twist,* then one may question, first, whether it is not a little too disgusting as it is, and secondly, whether in any true sense it 'gets at' any of the originals. It is neither melodramatic enough, nor romantic enough, nor sentimental enough to do this: nor does it caricature any of these features sufficiently. On the other hand, as a piece of *Jonathan Wild* irony, though quite admirable in parts, it is not sustained enough: the author either cannot or will not keep on the grimace and gesture of the half-Mephistophelian, half-angelic mentor; and is constantly telling a plain tale, by no means disagreeable except for the unusual sordidness of the characters. . . . In short the author never knows quite what hare he is hunting: and the reader is perpetually puzzled and vexed at the way in which the dogs change scent and course. (pp. 51-3)

[Yet] *Catherine* is Thackeray's first considerable and substantial *story.* Most of the things he had done in this kind had been slight sketches. . . . *Catherine* is a complete novel; there is beginning, middle, and end; not yet perfect but very well advanced character, sustained in different cases and personages throughout the book; good conversation and description; as well as no small manifestation of the author's peculiar fashion of showmanship; still more of his idiosyncrasy of style; and not a little of his predilection for a special subject and period— the manners, customs, speech, and folk of the eighteenth century. The opening chapters of *Catherine,* despite the company to which we are introduced, are absolutely of the best novel-romance kind. . . . There is a curious saturation with history and literature which betrays itself, not in digression or padding, but by constant allusion and suggestion; a light, current, apparently facile, sketching of scene and character which suddenly plunges (as a great phrase of Walt Whitman's has it) to 'the accepted hells beneath', but recovers itself at once and goes placidly on; above all, a shower of original and memorable phrases, never paraded, never dwelt upon too long, but more absolutely startling in their unique felicity than the most laboured conceits of mere phrasemongers.

It is of course true that before long, the want of thorough *digestion* in the scheme begins to betray itself; and the rather worse than picaresque degradation of the characters begins to be irksome. . . . Moreover, Thackeray has overloaded his story with incident in proportion to its length, and has made leaps

and bounds of omission which, possible in a chronicle-drama, are dangerous in a novel. . . . [As] for 'Cat' herself, she is, like her history, that most dangerous thing, a failure of a masterpiece. And so it happens that though the excellences of the thing are plentifully provided up to the very close, ghastly as it is, the faulty disposition of these excellences and the company in which they find themselves make the book almost impossible to *enjoy.* (pp. 53-5)

[If *Hoggarty Diamond*] has less power than parts of *Catherine,* it is far less unequal; if it has not the wilder humour of *Yellowplush* and *Gahagan,* it tries more difficult strings and does not fail in the trial. And that extraordinary fullness and variety of living presentation which was to be—which was already— Thackeray's great and almost unique attribute appears here marvellously to those who have eyes. . . . The pathos of the whole need not annoy any sensible person: it is not dashed and brewed to mawkishness in the fashion of some writers, and it certainly sets off the comic and satiric parts legitimately enough. The richness and variety of these and of the characters that work them out are quite astonishing. . . . (pp. 67-8)

It may possibly be owing to natural perversity; but I confess that I like *Barry Lyndon* less than any other book of Thackeray's, less even than *Catherine,* which is much inferior in art, and very much less than *Philip,* which may be said to be inferior in art likewise. (p. 93)

Parts of [*Barry Lyndon*] are equal to almost anything that even he ever did. The opening Irish chapters are quite admirable; they show his marvellous powers of improving experience capitally. . . . Lady Lyndon's first husband and the elder Chevalier de Balibari—but especially the former—are creations of the author's best; no other living man could have drawn, with such few and such powerful strokes, a character, if only a minor character, so complete and so original as Sir Charles. Her Ladyship, though not quite so good as she would have been a few years later, is still excellent. Of the seasonings of eighteenth-century manners and so on the same may be said; while everywhere and all over the book there is abundance of the incomparable Thackerayan incident, situation, phrase, insinuation, suggestion, aside—as well as direct narrative and exposition. . . . [It] may be more than conceded—cheerfully and vigorously asserted—that the general style shows to the very full [an] advance in dignity, success without trick, flexibility, [and] general artistic achievement. . . . And yet—! To begin the devil's advocate part, Thackeray does not seem to me either to have conceived clearly, or to have maintained steadily, his own attitude towards the story. There can be no doubt—in fact it is agreed—that he took *Jonathan Wild* in no slavish sense as a model. But in doing this he hampered himself enormously by making it an autobiography. You *can* make a man represent himself as a scoundrel or a fool or both: . . . Thackeray himself has done it here with great success in parts. But it is a frightful strain: and it is a great question whether it can possibly be done on a very large scale without 'incompossibility'. . . . [Has] not Thackeray forgotten that he is Barry rather too often? . . . [Was] Mr. Barry Lyndon, either as Redmond Barry, as the Chevalier, or in his glory, exactly the person to moralize on the Seven Year's War, as he or his creator does in chapter iv? I have no objection to moralizing if 'de morals is goot'. Thackeray's sermons never bore me when they are his, or Mr. Pendennis's, or those of anybody *congruous.* But that Barry should preach me I own surprises me.

There is, moreover, another point in which the autobiographical scheme, not necessarily of course, but as a matter of fact and by likelihood beforehand, had hampered and clogged the narrative and exposition. We get too many things recounted and too few acted, with the effect of something like the *récits* in conventional French tragedy. (pp. 94-6)

In short, to make a clean breast of it, *Barry Lyndon* fails—to me—in interest. . . . (p. 96)

[The] advances and advantages in respect of all his former work are immense and unmistakable [in *Vanity Fair*]. In the first place he has at last given himself—or has been given—proper scope and scale. . . . As for construction, *Vanity Fair* is nearly the best of all its author's works—in fact it is almost the only one in which any attention is paid to construction at all. In scheme, as apart from details, it is difficult to remember any other author, except perhaps Defoe, who, having written so long and so much, suddenly made such a new and such an ambitious 'entry' in literary competition, and not merely in the particular department of novel-writing.

In that department, however, the novelty, if not so absolute as that of *Robinson Crusoe,* was of a higher strain. (pp. 165-66)

Only perhaps in his very earliest period and in his immature work is he guilty—if even there—of [the] 'lowest imitation',— [the] mere carrying off of whole figures from the pageant of life, and botching them into the tapestry of literature. That a very large number of his traits, incidents, individual details are taken from, or suggested by, actuality, there need be no doubt— it is in fact the secret and reason of his unsurpassed truth to life itself. But these things are all passed through the alembic or the loom of art—redistilled or rewoven into original and independent composition. . . . There are the books which depend for their interest on the fact that their characters *have been* live men and women; and those which depend for it on the fact that they *are* live men and women. Thackeray's books belong to the second.

Those other vivifying arts of his which have been many times sketched in general, appear to the full in *Vanity Fair.* Thackeray does not 'set' his scenes and situations with the minute touches of detail as to furniture and the like. . . . But he has a setting of his own which places things and persons quite firmly in the reader's conception: and he employs it here from the Academy for young ladies in Chiswick Mall to his final (or almost final) scenes at Pumpernickel. It is, however, perhaps not in actual description of any kind that his life-giving and individualizing touch most fully consists. It is in queer nondescript devices— though 'device' is a bad word for things that come so naturally—tricks of names, humorous or fantastic asides—indescribable confidences as it were between himself and his reader, which establish intimate relations. (pp. 171-72)

It is with these subtle condiments of humour and suggestion that the author seasons his whole book. Whether it has, or has not, 'the best story' as he himself thought, he was quite right as to the excellence of the title. In the steady maintenance of the point of view of that title—so admirably defined and described in the Preface—its greatest merit as a book, from the severe old critical standpoint, perhaps consists. Its greatest claim to admiration, with some at least, is in the lavish and masterly presentation of character—too uniformly sombre-tinted it may be, but faultlessly drawn—from the triumph of Becky downwards. But its greatest attraction of all is in the constant procession-pageant of scenes and incidents which serve to bring out these characters, and in the wonderful dexterity and variety of presentation and style . . . [The] Devil's Advocate may say, with some truth, that in the opening or ante-Waterloo part,

which occupies half the book, the action somewhat drags, and that, though the Amelia and Becky stories are ingeniously enough intertwisted, the transitions from one to the other, and even some of the scenes themselves, do not 'go off trippingly' as Captain Clutterbuck says. Still, once more, the manner saves everything; and so it does in the latest division of the book which succeeds the discovery of Becky's misdoings.

But there is another part where, though the manner is more triumphant than ever, the matter partakes the triumph and is fully worthy of its less unequal partner. From the beginning of chapter xliv, when Sir Pitt *fils* comes to stay in Curzon Street, to the great catastrophe itself, the artist is thoroughly inspired, the rider has settled to the race, and is getting every possible effort out of the horse. Not merely is it all good, but there is in it that steady *crescendo* of expectation and satisfaction which only occurs at the supreme moments of life and of literature. The catastrophe itself is simply beyond praise— it is one of the greatest things in English: but it is perfectly led up to. For, as in other uncertain and accidental matrimonies, when matter and manner do go thoroughly together, then all is indeed well. In these hundred pages . . . there is not a line, not a phrase that is weak or wrong. There is nothing like them anywhere. . . . The variety, the intensity, the cool equal command, are not only unmatched, they are unmatchable in novel-literature: and the circumstances preclude their being matched in any other. . . . [The] manner plays up in unfailing provision of style and atmosphere, of satire, and pathos, and humour, and 'criticism of life'. (pp. 173-75)

[One] finds a curious unanimity among qualified and well-affected judges that *Pendennis* is, perhaps, the most *delightful* of Thackeray's novels. (p. 178)

The book is a long one, but from first to last it is prodigal of delights. . . . The remnant of self-distrust which threw the action of *Vanity Fair* back for half a generation has vanished entirely, and the society is practically contemporary. Almost every kind of life comes in, and the parts in these kinds are played by almost every sort of character. Much more trouble is taken with scene and setting. There is hardly anything in *Vanity Fair* (except the grim arch between the two staircases) which gives us the *décor* as a hundred things do in *Pendennis*, from Fairoaks and the country about it to Shepherd's Inn. If, as has been admitted, the texture of the story is very loose— if it is a chronicle-play rather than a drama of the Unities— there is the consolation (very much more than a compensation for some folk) that the scenes of which it is combined or strung together never flag or drag for one moment. (pp. 178-79)

Of scenes and incidents you may, they say, weary. I doubt it, but I think it possible. The play of character may become so familiar that the enjoyment of it is, at least, palled; but there is in *phrase*—in certain peculiar collocations of the written word—a charm like that of Cleopatra. It never wearies, because it is never quite the same. Imbedded as it is to a certain extent in its context, you may miss it wholly on one re-reading, and so it comes to you all the fresher at the next. Even if this does not happen, it has, if it is of the first water, a quality at once of the opal and of the diamond which is absolutely infinite and inexhaustible. (p. 186)

A greater novel than *Esmond* I do not know; and I do not know many greater books. It may be 'melancholy', and none the worse for that: it *is* 'grand'.

For though there may not be much humour of the potato throwing sort in *Esmond*, it will, perhaps, be found that in no book of Thackeray's, or of any one else's, is that deeper and higher humour which takes all life for its province—which is the humour of humanity—more absolutely pervading. And it may be found likewise, at least by some, that in no book is there to be found such a constant intertwist of the passion which, in all humanity's higher representatives, goes with humour hand in hand—a loving yet a mutually critical pair. Of the extraordinarily difficult form of autobiography I do not know such another masterly presentment. . . . The success is, in fact, the result of that curious 'doubleness'—amounting, in fact, here to something like *triplicity*—which distinguishes Thackeray's attitude and handling. Thus Henry Esmond, who is on the whole, I should say, the most like him of all his characters (though of course 'romanced' a little), is himself and 'the other fellow', and also, as it were, human criticism of both. At times we have a tolerably unsophisticated account of his actions, or it may be even his thoughts; at another his thoughts and actions as they present themselves, or might present themselves, to another mind: and yet at other times a reasoned view of them, as it were that of an impartial historian. The mixed form of narrative and mono-drama lends itself to this as nothing else could: and so does the author's well-known, much discussed, and sometimes heartily abused habit of *parabasis* or soliloquy to the audience. . . . But its efficacy in this peculiar kind of double or treble handling is almost indisputable, even by those who may dispute its legitimacy as a constantly applied method. (pp. 193-94)

If the champions of 'Unity' were wise, they would take *Esmond* as a battle-horse, for it is certain that, great as are its parts, the whole is gerater than almost any one of them—which is certainly not the case with *Pendennis*. And it is further certain that, of these parts, the personages of the hero and the heroine stand out commandingly, which is certainly not the case with *Pendennis*, again. The unity, however, is of a peculiar kind, and differs from the ordinary non-classical 'Unity of Interest' which Thackeray almost invariably exhibits. It is rather a Unity of *Temper*, which is also present (as the all-pervading motto *Vanitas Vanitatum* almost necessitates) in all the books, but here reaches a transcendence not elsewhere attained. The brooding spirit of *Ecclesiastes* here covers, as it were, with the shadow of one of its wings, the joys and sorrows, the failures and successes of a private family and their friends, with the other fates of England and Europe; the fortunes of Marlborough and of Swift on their way from dictatorship, in each case, to dotage and death; the big wars and the notable literary triumphs as well as the hopeless passions or acquiescent losses. It is thus an instance—and the greatest—of that revival of the historical novel which was taking place. . . . (p. 197)

[Nothing] has yet been said of one of the most salient characteristics of *Esmond*. . . . This is, of course, the attempt, certainly a very audacious one, at once to give the very form and pressure of the time of the story—sometimes in actual diction—and yet to suffuse it with a modern thought and colour which most certainly were *not* of the time. The boldness and the peril of this attempt are both quite indisputable. . . . (p. 198)

So far from there being anything illegitimate in this attempt to bring one period before the eyes of another in its habit as it lived, and speaking as it spoke, but to allow those eyes themselves to move as they move and see as they see—it is merely the triumph and the justification of the whole method of prose fiction in general, and of the historical novel in particular. . . . That a man should have the faculty of reproducing contemporary or general life is wonderful; that he should have the

faculty of reproducing past life is wonderful still more. But that he should thus revive the past and preserve the present—command and provide at once theatre and company, audience and performance—this is the highest wizardry of all. And this, as it seems to me, is what Thackeray had attempted, and more, what he has done, in the *History of Henry Esmond.* (p. 200)

[With *The Newcomes,* once] more we have the abounding wealth and ease—the *copia*—of *Pendennis* without that certain disorderliness which has been admitted in the case of the elder masterpiece. . . . In a certain sense, too, the story is not merely more definite and coherent than that of *Pendennis,* but it is of a higher strain—the strands are not only more deftly twisted, but they are more various and of choicer quality. If there are no such unique presentations of special sides of life as those of the Oxbridge and Fleet Street parts of *Pendennis,* life itself at large is treated much more fully, freely, and variously. The higher society which had been partly anticipated in *Vanity Fair,* wholly so in *Esmond,* and slightly touched in *Pendennis,* is here grappled with and subdued to the purposes of art in the most fearless and triumphant fashion. It is infinitely more real in handling than Balzac's, and superior in artistic powers to any one else's attempts in the same kind. The mere variety, subordinated as it is to a fairly general scheme, is a wonderful thing, as is the way in which the great length of the book permits itself absolutely no *longueurs* of episode or padding. Above all, perhaps, there is no book in which Thackeray has attained to such a Shakespearian pitch of pure tragi-comedy: that is to say, not tragedy with a happy ending, not comedy turned to tragic conclusions, but both blended and contrasted, grave and gay mixed, in the special English fashion of dramatic presentation. (pp. 209-10)

[Perhaps] in no book is Thackeray's peculiar fashion of 'address to the reader' more happily managed. The abundance of incident, character, and conversation possibly carries this off better than is the case in books where the story is less skilfully managed, or, at any rate, rather less abundantly provided. . . . [Here] its application is uninterruptedly felicitous, from the Fable before the beginning to the disposition of the characters after the end. (p. 220)

Many things in [*Philip*] are of his absolutely best: it has a sort of *bonus* of autobiographic interest—not intruded, but generously offered for those who like to take or leave—which is not equalled by any of the books except *Pendennis*. It is full of delightful scene, character, incident, talk. But still the warrior has gone into battle with his armour rather carelessly laced and braced; the builder has not looked in all cases to the tempering of his mortar. (p. 236)

The present writer is not ashamed to confess that he reads *Philip* as often as any of the books—that his objections as a critic do not interfere in the least with his enjoyment as a reader. But that is probably an unnatural state of things, begotten of long practice in separating personal likes from artistic appreciation. As a critic, though he certainly will not throw *Philip* to the wolves, he is bound to say that it is not the prettiest nor the best behaved of the children of its family. (p. 242)

Philip and Charlotte are quite real persons—. . . they exist, and behave themselves as they ought to do in accordance with the laws of their existence. But, in this one instance, Thackeray's experiments in the true realism may be thought to have brought him near that false realism of which we have since seen and are still seeing so much. It is true that, in the novel, to secure the highest artistic effect, and at the same time the greatest satisfaction to the reader, the characters must be real, and their actions must be probable in themselves, or made so. But it is not true that this is sufficient. They must be made in some way or other *agreeable;* and if they are made disagreeable they will not and ought not to succeed. . . . Philip—Charlotte is rather null than anything else, she does not hinder, if she does not help—is not agreeable in any way. . . . [One] takes no interest in him; does not even passively enjoy his company; does not want to see him again. With the vast majority of Thackeray's characters you want to see them again very much. (pp. 242-43)

Thackeray is in this respect inferior to Shakespeare—that he either cannot, or does not choose to, leave his characters with the universal humanity which is of no special age at all; though he ransoms this to some extent by his unmatched faculty of giving them the character of their own age. . . . [With] his oddly mixed indifference to chronology and sense of actuality he has striven to give the newer *nuance* to Philip, to make him a young man not of the late 'thirties but of the early 'sixties. And I think the effect is rather one of 'confusion of kinds'. (p. 244)

Life and Abundance—these are the two things that are to be found in [Thackeray], to be found in him everywhere; and to be found out of him, in the same degree and to the same extent, nowhere, as I believe, in the English or in any novel. (p. 249)

[From Hunt, Lamb, and Hazlitt] came all the essayists and all the Essays of the English nineteenth century. Among these essayists I do not know a greater than Thackeray: among the collections of these essays I do not know one so great as the *Roundabout Papers.* (p. 255)

To me the *Roundabout Papers* are almost as much a whole, a microcosm, as many celebrated books of great writers composed nominally on a single theme: but of course they are individual wholes as well. And their individuality and, so to speak, 'promiscuousness' prevented that appearance of the desultory which, though it far exceeds the reality, is charged against his larger single works. (p. 256)

[Quick] changes and many-faceted presentations of thought had always been natural to Thackeray; and now at last he was at liberty to indulge them as he liked, and yet under the control of his own judgement. (pp. 256-57)

One very remarkable feature of this crop of the 'last of life for which the first was made' is to be found in the large number of passages which it contains directly consisting of, or indirectly conveying, literary criticism. . . . [In] earlier days this was Thackeray's very weakest point (except politics which here hardly figure at all); that, with occasional *aperçus* of surprising acuteness and truth, he was at the mercy of all sorts of gusts, not exactly of caprice, but of irrelevant and extraneous influence. Here the 'calmed and calming *mens adepta*' remedies all this in the most satisfactory fashion. (pp. 260-61)

[There] is perceptible, not a mere acceptance of what had previously been rejected or questioned, because the critic's powers of discrimination are blunted and his interests cloyed, but a true mellowing of perception and a determination to hold fast to that which is good. . . . You will not find Thackeray praising rubbish anywhere, and in these *Roundabouts* least of all. But you will find him no longer inclined to harp and carp on trifles; and not in the least ready to be blown away by some gust of doctrine (or ignorance) in regard to his subjects. In fact, these *Roundabout Papers* exhibit their author in a state

only to be described by one of the stock adjectives of criticism, and one which has been even more abused than most of these hardly treated vocables. They are thoroughly *ripe.* . . . The abundance of matter and the perfection of handling match each other constantly: and over all and above all and through all there is perpetual suffusion of that unforced and inimitable style and phrase which makes subject almost indifferent and constitutes treatment of itself. Over all too there rules the true *Phantasus*—the principle of that part or side of the poetic quality which belongs equally to poetry and to prose, which Thackeray shows in both, and which goes hand in hand with his unerring truth to nature and reality. (pp. 262-63)

> *George Saintsbury, in his* A Consideration of Thackeray *(originally published as introductions to* The Oxford Thackeray, *edited by George Saintsbury, Oxford University Press, Oxford, 1908), Oxford University Press, London, 1931, 273 p.*

## PERCY LUBBOCK   (essay date 1921)

[*Lubbock, an English author whose literary criticism was greatly influenced by Henry James, considered dramatic presentation, rather than authorial narration and description, the most effective means of narrative expression. He characterizes Thackeray as "a painter of life, a novelist whose matter is all blended and harmonized together . . . in a long retrospective vision." Although he regards Thackeray as a master of panoramic depiction, he ultimately finds his narrative method deficient because he repeatedly fails in his depiction of the small dramatic moment.*]

Thackeray saw [his novels] as broad expanses, stretches of territory, to be surveyed from edge to edge with a sweeping glance; he saw them as great general, typical impressions of life, populated by a swarm of people whose manners and adventures crowded into his memory. The landscape lay before him, his imagination wandered freely across it, backwards and forwards. The whole of it was in view at once, a single prospect, out of which the story of Becky or Pendennis emerged and grew distinct while he watched. He wrote his novel with a mind full of a surge and wash of memories, the tenor of which was somehow to be conveyed in the outward form of a narrative. And though his novel complies with that form more or less, and a number of events are marshalled in order, yet its constant tendency is to escape and evade the restrictions of a scenic method, and to present the story in a continuous flow of leisurely, contemplative reminiscence.

And that is evidently the right way for the kind of story that Thackeray means to create. For what is the point and purpose of *Vanity Fair,* where is the centre from which it grows? Can it be described as a "plot," a situation, an entanglement, something that raises a question of the issue? Of plots in this sense there are plenty in *Vanity Fair,* at least there are two; Becky dominates one, Amelia smiles and weeps in the other. They join hands occasionally, but really they have very little to exchange. . . . Side by side they exist, and for Thackeray's purpose neither is more important than the other, neither is in the middle of the book as it stands. Becky seems to be in the middle, certainly, as we think of her; but that is not where Thackeray placed her. He meant Amelia to be no less appealing than Becky is striking; and if Amelia fails and drops into the background, it is not because she plays a subordinate part, but only because she plays it with so much less than Becky's vivid conviction. . . . [The] book as a whole turns upon nothing that happens, not even upon the catastrophe of Curzon Street; that scene in Becky's drawing-room disposes of *her*, it leaves the rest of the book quite untouched.

Not in any complication of incident, therefore, nor in any single strife of will, is the subject of *Vanity Fair* to be discerned. It is not here but in the impression of a world, a society, a time—certain manners of life within a few square miles of London, a hundred years ago. Thackeray flings together a crowd of the people he knows so well, and it matters not at all if the tie that holds them to each other is of the slightest. . . . The light link is enough for the unity of his tale, for that unity does not depend on an intricately woven intrigue. It depends in truth upon one fact only, the fact that all his throng of men and women are strongly, picturesquely typical of the world from which they are taken—that all in their different ways can add to the force of its effect. The book is not the story of any of them, it is the story which they unite to tell, a chapter in the notorious career of well-to-do London. Exactly how the various "plots" evolve is not the main matter; behind them is the presence and the pressure of a greater interest, the mass of life which Thackeray packs into his novel. And if that is the meaning of *Vanity Fair,* to give the succession of incident a hard, particular, dramatic relief would be to obscure it. Becky's valiant struggle in the world of her ambition might easily be isolated and turned into a play—no doubt it has been; but consider how her look, her value, would in that case be changed. Her story would become a mere personal affair of her own, the mischance of a certain woman's enterprise. Given in Thackeray's way, summarized in his masterly perspective, it is part of an impression of manners.

Such, I take it, is Thackeray's difference, his peculiar mark, the distinction of his genius. He is a painter of life, a novelist whose matter is all blended and harmonized together—people, action, background—in a long retrospective vision. Not for him, on the whole, is the detached action, the rounded figure, the scenic rendering of a story; . . . Thackeray preferred the manner of musing expatiation, where scene melts into scene, impressions are foreshortened by distance, and the backward-ranging thought can linger and brood as it will. Every novel of his takes the general form of a discursive soliloquy, in which he gradually gathers up the long train of experience that he has in mind. The early chapters of *Esmond* or *Pendennis,* the whole fragment of *Denis Duval* are perfect examples of Thackeray's way when he is most himself, and when he is least to be approached by any other writer of fiction. All that he has to describe, so it seems, is present to him in the hour of recollection. . . . But still, though the fullness of memory is directed into a consecutive tale, it is not the narrative, not its order and movement, that chiefly holds either Thackeray's attention or ours who read; the narrative is steeped in the suffusion of the general tone, the sensation of the place and the life that he is recalling, and it is out of this effect, insensibly changing and developing, that the novel is created.

For a nearer sight of it I go back to *Vanity Fair.* The chapters that are concerned with Becky's determined siege of London—"How to live well on nothing a year"—are exactly to the point; the wonderful things that Thackeray could do, the odd lapse of his power when he had to go beyond his particular province, both are here written large. . . . Her campaign and its untimely end are to be pictured; it is an interlude to be filled with stir and glitter, with the sense of the passage of a certain time, above all with intimations of insecurity and precarious fortune; and it is to lead (this it must do) to a scene of final and decisive climax. . . . An impression is to be created, grow-

ing and growing; and it can well be created in the loose panoramic style which is Thackeray's paramount aim. A general view, once more, a summary of Becky's course of action, a long look at her conditions, a participation in her gathering difficulties—that is the nature and the task of these chapters, that is what Thackeray proceeds to give us.

He sets about it with a beautiful ease of assurance. From his height he looks forth, takes in the effect with his sweeping vision, possesses himself of the gradation of its tone; then, stooping nearer, he seizes the detail that renders it. But the sense of the broad survey is first in his thought. . . . Briefly, to all appearance quite casually, the little incident shows itself and vanishes; there is a pause to watch and listen, and then the stream sets forward again, by so much enriched and reinforced. (pp. 93-100)

That foreshortening and generalizing, that fusion of detail, that subordination of the instance and the occasion to the broad effect, are the elements of the pictorial art in which Thackeray is so great a master. So long as it is a matter of sketching a train of life in broad free strokes, the poise and swing of his style are beyond praise. And its perfection is all the more notable that it stands in such contrast with the curious drop and uncertainty of his skill, so soon as there is something more, something different to be done. For Becky's dubious adventure has its climax, it tends towards a conclusion, and the final scene cannot be recalled and summarized in his indirect, reminiscential manner. It must be placed immediately before us, the collapse of Becky's plotting and scheming must be enacted in full view, if it is to have its proper emphasis and rightly round off her career. . . . Does Becky fail in the end? After all that we have heard of her struggle it has become the great question, and the force of the answer will be impaired if it is not given with the best possible warrant. The best possible, better even than Thackeray's wonderful account of her, will be the plain and immediate *performance* of the answer, its embodiment in a scene that shall pass directly in front of us. The method that was not demanded by the preceding phases of the tale is here absolutely prescribed. Becky, Rawdon, Steyne, must now take the matter into their own hands and show themselves without any other intervention. Hitherto, practically throughout, they have been the creatures of Thackeray's thought, they have been openly and confessedly the figures of *his* vision. Now they must come forward, declare themselves, and be seen for what they are.

And accordingly they do come forward and are seen in a famous passage. Rawdon makes his unexpected return home from prison, and Becky's unfortunate disaster overtakes her, so to say, in our very presence. Perhaps I may seem to exaggerate the change of method which I note at this point; but does it not appear to any one, glancing back at his recollection of the book, that this particular scene is defined and relieved and lighted differently, somehow, from the stream of impressions in which it is set? A space is cleared for it, the stage is swept. This is now no retrospective vision, shared with Thackeray; it is a piece of present action with which we are confronted. It is strictly dramatic, and I suppose it is good drama of its kind. But there is more to be said of it than this—more to be said, even when it has been admitted to be drama of rather a high-pitched, theatrical strain. The foot-lights, it is probably agreed, seem suddenly to flare before Becky and Rawdon, after the clear daylight that reigned in Thackeray's description of them; they appear upon the scene, as they should, but it must be owned that the scene has an artificial look, by comparison with the flowing spontaneity of all that has gone before. And this it is exactly that shows how and where Thackeray's skill betrays him. He is not (like Dickens) naturally inclined to the theatre, the melodramatic has no fatal attraction for him; so that if he is theatrical here, it is not because he inevitably would be, given his chance. It is rather because he must, at all costs, make this climax of his story conclusively *tell;* and in order to do so he is forced to use devices of some crudity—for him they are crude—because his climax, his *scène à faire* [necessary scene], has been insufficiently prepared for. Becky, Rawdon, Steyne, in all this matter that has been leading up to the scene, have scarcely before been rendered in these immediate terms; and now that they appear on their own account they can only make a sure and pronounced effect by perceptibly forcing their note. A little too much is expected of them, and they must make an unnatural effort to meet it. (pp. 100-03)

I am not trying, of course, to criticize *Vanity Fair;* I am looking for certain details of method, and the small instance is surely illuminating. It shows how little Thackeray's fashion of handling a novel allowed for the big dramatic scene, when at length it had to be faced—how he neglected it in advance, how he refused it till the last possible moment. It is as though he never quite trusted his men and women when he had to place things entirely in their care, standing aside to let them act; he wanted to intervene continually, he hesitated to leave them alone save for a brief and belated half-hour. It was perverse of him, because the men and women would have acquitted themselves so strikingly with a better chance; he gave them life and vigour enough for much more independence than they ever enjoyed. The culmination of Becky's adventure offered a clear opening for full dramatic effect, if he had chosen to take advantage of it. . . . It is incredible that he should let the opportunity slip. There was a chance of a straight, unhampered view of the whole meaning of his matter; nothing was needed but to allow the scene to show itself, fairly and squarely. (pp. 103-04)

Yet the chance is missed, the triumphal evening passes in a confused haze that leaves the situation exactly where it was before. The episode is only a repetition of the kind of thing that has happened already. There are echoes of festive sound and a rumour of Becky's brilliance; but the significant look that the actual facts might have worn and must have betrayed, the look that by this time Thackeray has so fully instructed his reader to catch—this is not disclosed after all. There is still nothing here but Thackeray's amusing, irrepressible conversation *about* the scene; he cannot make up his mind to clear a space before it and give the situation the free field it cries out for. (p. 104)

Right and left in the novels of Thackeray one may gather instances of the same kind—the piercing and momentary shaft of direct vision, the big scene approached and then refused. (p. 105)

In all [his] well-remembered books Thackeray, in an expansive mood, opens his mind and talks it out on the subject of some big, loosely-knit company of men and women. He remembers, as we all remember, with a strong sense of the tone and air of an old experience, and a sharp recollection of moments that happened for some reason to be salient, significant, peculiarly keen or curious. . . . Thackeray has these flashes in profusion; they break out unforgettably as we think of his books. . . . We no longer listen to a story, no longer see the past in a sympathetic imagination; this is a higher power of intensity, a fragment of the past made present and actual. But with Thack-

eray it is always a fragment, never to any real purpose a deliberate and continuous enactment.

For continuity he always recurs to his pictorial summary. . . . Thackeray roams to and fro in his narrative, caring little for the connected order of events if he can give the sensation of time, deep and soft and abundant, by delaying and returning at ease over this tract of the past. (pp. 107-09)

In Maupassant's drama we are close to the facts, against them and amongst them. . . . Certainly he is "telling" us things. . . . But the *effect* is that he is not there at all, because he is doing nothing that ostensibly requires any judgement, nothing that reminds us of his presence. (p. 113)

But Thackeray—in *his* story we need him all the time and can never forget him. He it is who must assemble and arrange his large chronicle, piecing it together out of his experience. Becky's mode of life, in his story, is a matter of many details picked up on many occasions, and the power that collects them, the mind that contains them, is always and openly Thackeray's; it could not be otherwise. It is no question, for most of the time, of watching a scene at close quarters, where the simple, literal detail, such as anybody might see for himself, would be sufficient. A stretch of time is to be shown in perspective, at a distance; the story-teller must be at hand to work it into a single impression. And thus the general panorama, such as Thackeray displays, becomes the representative of the author's experience, and the author becomes a personal entity, about whom we may begin to ask questions. Thackeray *cannot* be the nameless abstraction that the dramatist (whether in the drama of the stage or in that of the novel) is naturally. I know that Thackeray, so far from trying to conceal himself, comes forward and attracts attention and nudges the reader a great deal more than he need; he likes the personal relation with the reader and insists on it. But do what he might to disguise it, so long as he is ranging over his story at a height, chronicling, summarizing, foreshortening, he *must* be present to the reader as a narrator and a showman. It is only when he descends and approaches a certain occasion and sets a scene with due circumspection—rarely and a trifle awkwardly . . .—that he can for the time being efface the thought of his active part in the affair. (pp. 113-15)

Confronted with a scene—like Becky's great scene, once more—we forget that other mind; but as soon as the story goes off again into narrative a question at once arises. *Who* is disposing the scattered facts, whose is this new point of view? It is the omniscient author, and the point of view is his—such would be the common answer, and it is the answer we get in *Vanity Fair.* By convention the author is allowed his universal knowledge of the story and the people in it. But still it is a convention, and a prudent novelist does not strain it unnecessarily. Thackeray in *Vanity Fair* is not at all prudent; his method, so seldom strictly dramatic, is one that of its nature is apt to force this question of the narrator's authority, and he goes out of his way to emphasize the question still further. He flourishes the fact that the point of view is his own, not to be confounded with that of anybody in the book. And so his book, as one may say, is not complete in itself, not really self-contained; it does not meet and satisfy all the issues it suggests. Over the whole of one side of it there is an inconclusive look, something that draws the eye away from the book itself, into space. It is the question of the narrator's relation to the story. (p. 115)

[In] all his later work he refused to remain the unaccountable seer from without. He did not carry the dramatizing process very far, indeed, and it may be thought that the change in his method does not amount to much. In *The Newcomes* and its successors the old Thackerayan display seems essentially the same as ever, still the familiar, easy-going, intimate outpouring, with all the well-known inflexions of Thackeray's voice and the humours of his temperament; certainly Pendennis and Esmond and George Warrington and Thackeray have all of them exactly the same conception of the art of story-telling, they all command the same perfection of luminous style. . . . [Thackeray] uses the device of the narrator "in character" very loosely and casually, as soon as it might be troublesome to use it with care. (pp. 125-26)

Esmond tells [his] story quite as Thackeray would; it all comes streaming out as a pictorial evocation of old times; there is just as little that is strictly dramatic in it as there is in *Vanity Fair*. Rarely, very rarely indeed, is there anything that could be called a scene; there is a long impression that creeps forward and forward, as Esmond retraces his life, with those piercing moments of vision which we remember so well. But to the other people in the book it makes all the difference that the narrator is among them. Now, when Beatrix appears, we know who it is that so sees her, and we know where the seer is placed; his line of sight, striking across the book, from him the seer to her the seen, is measurable, its angle is shown; it gives to Beatrix a new dimension and a sharper relief. Can you remember any moment in *Vanity Fair* when you beheld Becky as again and again you behold Beatrix, catching the very slant of the light on her face? Becky never suddenly flowered out against her background in that way; some want of solidity and of objectivity there still is in Becky, and there must be, because she is regarded from anywhere, from nowhere, from somewhere in the surrounding void. Thackeray's language about her does not carry the same weight as Esmond's about Beatrix, because nobody knows where Thackeray is, or what his relation may be to Becky. (pp. 126-27)

When we are shown what Esmond sees, and nothing else, there is first of all the comfortable assurance of the point of view, and then there is the personal colour which he throws over his account, so that it gains another kind of distinction. It does not matter that Esmond's tone in his story is remarkably like Thackeray's in the stories that *he* tells; in Esmond's case the tone has a meaning in the story, is part of it, whereas in the other case it is related only to Thackeray, and Thackeray is in the void. When Esmond ruminates and reflects, his manner is the expression of a human being there present, to whom it can be referred; when Thackeray does the same, there is no such compactness, and the manner trails away where we cannot follow it. Dramatically it seems clear that the method of *Esmond* has the advantage over the method of *Vanity Fair*. (p. 128)

> *Percy Lubbock, in his* The Craft of Fiction (*reprinted by permission of Jonathan Cape Ltd, on behalf of the Estate of Percy Lubbock), Cape, 1921 (and reprinted by Charles Scribner's Sons, 1955), 276 p.**

### JOSEPH WARREN BEACH (essay date 1932)

[It] is worth while—leaving out of account the shining merits of Thackeray in other directions—to consider some of the disadvantages under which he labors from his neglect of the dramatic principle. (p. 164)

In Thackeray there is no such thing as dramatic continuity; we are perpetually passing from one place to another, from one character to another. Thus in the culminating scenes of "**Vanity Fair**," the most dramatic in the book—beginning with Becky's triumph at Lord Steyne's party, and ending with the break-up of her ménage with Rawdon—we are part of the time with Rawdon, part with Becky, part with Rawdon again; we pass continually from one place to another; there is a whole chapter inserted at the height of the action which goes back to an earlier period and brings the story up to the time of the party. Altogether this climax of the book is handled in as undramatic a manner as possible.

The want of a steady center of interest is naturally still more to be felt in those passages—the staple of the book—in which there is no development of any scene or group of scenes beyond a very few pages. In order to get the greatest effect from a steady center of interest, more is necessary than to refrain from shifting from one person to another. It is necessary to have characters strong enough so that we recognize them as constituting centers of interest, persons who take strong hold on our feelings or imagination, and whose rôle is important enough to make them major characters. Of such there are in "**Vanity Fair**" but two, Becky Sharp and Amelia, with the possible addition of Major Dobbin and Rawdon Crawley, admitted to the rank of major characters more on account of their rôle in the story than because of their intrinsic interest.

If, then, these four persons were followed steadily through the story, if some one or other of them were invariably present, so that the action came to us as part and parcel of their personal experience, "**Vanity Fair**" would more nearly meet the conditions of dramatic narrative. But this is very far from being the case. There is a large number of minor characters, less important in the plot, to whom the author gives his attention from time to time. They are more or less interesting in one way or another, but not interesting enough to stand by themselves, and yet their histories are given in fairly regular alternation with that of principals. (pp. 165-67)

Toward all these characters Thackeray seems to feel an equal responsibility; since they are in his chronicle, he will tell us what there is to be told of them; and he will tell it at the point where it comes in most naturally, which is generally in the midst of what he is saying about his major characters. We find them amusing; we recognize their importance as social exhibits; we regard them as acquaintances and are glad to know what happens to them. But there is nothing important about them, nothing that we cannot wait until to-morrow to learn. And it is figures such as these, who interest us as gossip interests, for whom the principals are constantly being asked to give way.

Not that there is anything so very urgent about the principals. These are not figures of tragedy, creatures of destiny. . . . There is no mystery to be solved, but merely the mild question of what next. So that the reader suffers no great hardship when he is asked to postpone his interest in Becky or Amelia in favor of Mrs. Bute Crawley or old Mr. Osborne. (p. 167)

Thackeray's novel gives . . . the impression of a mere series of sketches loosely strung along on a tenuous thread of plot. And we are reminded that Thackeray started as an essayist and illustrator, and was a long time coming to the novel form.

That the essayist was still dominant in Thackeray's technique is indicated by the very large proportion in his novels of summary narrative where the born story-teller (say Dickens) would have given us drama. . . . As to formal characterization, distinct from exposition, there is extremely little. Here is an author, famous for the vivid reality of his characters, who very seldom thinks it necessary to halt his story for two minutes in order to tell us what these people are like. (p. 168)

There is in Thackeray an enormous amount of small change. His **"Vanity Fair"** is an entire composition of little happenings illustrative of greed, snobbishness, social climbing. There are so many of these little happenings that not a quarter of them could be properly presented scenically, and Thackeray does not seem willing to leave any of them out. (p. 170)

It often seems as if Thackeray were overwhelmed by the sheer bulk of the multiple history about which he feels called on to keep us informed. He loses himself in the items without making anything of them as story. He can neither reconcile himself to leaving them out, nor find the energy or time to show them to us properly. It is as if his spirit flagged, as if he were overcome with sheer laziness. (p. 171)

At times we feel as if Thackeray were simply incapable of selection. He follows his characters from day to day as if he felt it necessary to account for every moment of their time. . . . Each minor division of the story must be concluded, like the whole story at the end, by telling what happened to everybody.

This author seems at times to be carried along on the stream of his story instead of himself directing the story in a carefully marked channel. He is like a traveler conscientiously recording from day to day the progress of the journey and the occupations of his fellow-voyagers. The story carries his characters to Belgium. But you can't get to Belgium without crossing the Channel, and you can't cross the Channel without going down the river, and you can't go down the river without first embarking on transports. . . . And so Thackerary proceeds to record the fact that his characters engage in sight-seeing and the pursuit of pleasure. This is what makes slow reading of so much of Thackeray.

It is true that, even in such generalized narrative, Thackeray can sometimes be entertaining. This applies particularly, in **"Vanity Fair,"** to whatever concerns Becky Sharp. He is so genuinely interested in this plucky and unscrupulous adventuress, and in the means by which she manages to make her way in the world, that even an outline statement of her methods has its savor. . . . Above all the irony of Thackeray is forever vividly aware of the slight and as it were merely technical differences between the ways of good society and of Bohemia, and the most cursory statement of some of Becky's experiences is pleasantly spiced with this irony. (pp. 172-73)

**"Vanity Fair"** is like a great sheet of drawing-paper filled from rim to rim, from corner to corner, with charcoal sketches of human figures, crowded close together for economy of space. They are exercises in drawing and have this much in common that they are all in illustration of a common theme. But the lover of pictures cries out for spacing, for grouping, for subordination and perspective, for some organic principle of composition. (pp. 173-74)

There appears to be no planning at all in Thackeray's writing of his chapters. He does not seem to consider in advance what scene is to be the culminating point and just what is necessary in preparation for this scene; which details are to be subordinated and which may be eliminated altogether. He does not seem to be concerned to bring down the curtain effectively at the end of the act. He has so much material to cover, or so much copy to turn out, for this instalment. He seems to live from hand to mouth. He ambles along pleasantly, taking his

time, plucking here a flower and there a wholesome herb. (p. 175)

The net result of his method is that we have in Thackeray a minimum sense of that dramatic present that makes the reading of a novel swift and exciting.

The dramatic novelist, whose concern is for the scenes where we have this sense of the here and now, wishes to reduce so far as possible the element of exposition. . . . With the non-dramatic writer, the exposition is the very body of the story, which is one long tissue of summary chronicle. The scenes give the impression of being anecdotes illustrative of the chronicle. They may be, and in Thackeray they frequently are, the cream of the book, but they give the impression of being merely incidental. (p. 176)

*Joseph Warren Beach, "Dramatic Present: Thackeray, Tolstoy," in his* The Twentieth Century Novel: Studies in Technique *(© 1932, renewed 1960; excerpted by permission of Prentice-Hall, Inc., Englewood Cliffs, NJ 07632), Appleton-Century-Crofts, Inc., 1932, pp. 164-76.**

## DAVID CECIL    (essay date 1934)

[*Though Cecil maintains that Thackeray's works lack the timeless quality of Dickens's, he still considers Thackeray "a great novelist, and a very original one." He argues that Thackeray was the first novelist to do what Leo Tolstoy and Marcel Proust would later do more extensively: "use the novel to express a conscious, considered criticism of life." Cecil praises the structural schemes and eloquent style of Thackeray's major novels, particularly* Vanity Fair; *yet Cecil claims that he is not the most successful Victorian novelist because his imaginative vision does not match his power of execution. Cecil concludes that despite his "technical brilliance" and originality, Thackeray is "ultimately . . . dissatisfying," because his deference to Victorian convention caused him to be untrue to his genuine creative inspiration.*]

The dust lies thicker on Thackeray than on Dickens. . . . [If] one dips at random into, say, *Pendennis,* one can quite understand the reason. No gale of vitality, fresh and strong as on the day of its birth, blows into our lungs as from the briefest paragraph of *David Copperfield.* An effluence does arise from the pages, but it is faint and a little musty, a waft as from long-closed rooms, out-moded dresses laid up in lavender, the sallowed leaves of ancient periodicals. The world that meets us in them was once the great humming, bustling, contemporary world, we feel: but it is so no longer. Its hum is dwindled to a murmur, soon it will have subsided into final silence.

Of course, this is only a superficial impression. Ten minutes' steady reading is enough to teach one that Thackeray's novels are living works of art, not dead period pieces. But they have not the triumphant independence of time which characterises those of Dickens. They are more occupied with the ephemeral customs and concerns of the age in which they were written. . . . (pp. 77-8)

[It] is a pity, for we should enjoy him. Thackeray is a great novelist, and a very original one. In his own time he was always being compared to Dickens, and he has been ever since. But no comparison could be more inept; they belong to two entirely different species of writer. (p. 78)

Not that they wrote about different people. Thackeray's characters are contemporary English people: and though they are higher in the social scale than Dickens', they are predominantly middle-class. But they are regarded from a different angle.

Dickens is interested in individuality. . . . Thackeray is interested not in the variety, but in the species; not in men, but in man.

This does not mean his range is larger than that of Dickens or Scott; in some ways, indeed, it is more limited. But it is not limited as theirs is to types of human character, but to certain aspects of human character as a whole. Certain motives and qualities universally present in man stir Thackeray's imagination; it is in so far as it deals with these qualities and motives that his writing is creative. (pp. 78-9)

[His] range is hard to define completely in a phrase. The shortest way of doing it is to say it covers all the aspects of human nature implied in the titles of his two most characteristic books, *Vanity Fair* and *The Book of Snobs*. That sounds a hostile view of human nature: but it is not so. Thackeray liked people, and for the most part he thought them well-intentioned. But he also saw very clearly that they were all in some degree weak and vain, self-absorbed and self-deceived. And he had a power unparalleled among novelists for detecting these qualities in their various degrees and manifestations. His out-and-out climbers and snobs and egotists are the most profoundly-studied in English literature. . . . [Yet, his] is not a comfortable talent. At moments the reader feels as if he can hardly bear to look, as one victim after another is laid on the operating-table, one after another petty shame, petty arrogance, petty subterfuge, is exposed to the light of day by Thackeray's neat unrelenting scalpel. All the same it is the fountain of his achievement, the instrument of his creative imagination; it is by its means that he makes his characters alive. (pp. 79-80)

In itself it merely shows he was an acute observer. And observation, however imaginative, is not enough to create that self-dependent, self-consistent world which is the special mark of the great novelist. How far he can do this depends on the use he makes of his observation.

Now its ignorances and vanities, its self-deceptions and self-absorptions, are far from making up the whole of human nature. But they are, it must be repeated, universal to it. . . . [And it] is Thackeray's first and characteristic achievement that by isolating and exhibiting these motives in all their ubiquitous and tortuous manifestations through the labyrinth of human conduct, he imposes a new unity and order on that chaotic human life which is the material of his art. This is the way his creative imagination expresses itself; this is how he makes his world. (pp. 83-4)

Thackeray is the first novelist to do what Tolstoy and Proust were to do more elaborately—use the novel to express a conscious, considered criticism of life. He has generalised from the particular instances of his observation to present his reader with a systematic philosophy of human nature.

It was a great innovation—his unique precious contribution to the development of the novel. And of course it gives his books a force unshared by any, however full of genius, that deal merely with particulars. It may be a narrow view—Thackeray's was—but even a narrow view of so big a subject is something pretty big; only a creative imagination of a high power could work on so large a scale; choose for its ground so huge an area of experience, assimilate to its own colour so different and varied a mass of facts. And the impression it makes on the reader is proportionately formidable. (p. 86)

The effects of time . . . are the occasion of some of Thackeray's most characteristic triumphs. He had a special sensibility to

the relics of the past. . . . Indeed, Thackeray's books are like memories, memories of an old man looking back, disillusioned but not embittered by experience, in the calm summer twilight of his days.

Finally, his vision enabled him to impose an organic unity on the chaos of the large-scale English novel. Outwardly his stories seem just like Fielding's or Dickens', a heterogeneous mass of people and incidents artificially united by their association with a central figure. . . . But in Thackeray the variety is the subject; for all its manifestations are different illustrations of those laws of human conduct which it is his object to portray. Pendennis or Clive Newcome is there, to give the particular point of vantage through which we survey these laws at work, and in consequence Thackeray's books suffer from none of that irrelevancy and division of interest which we find in everything Dickens or Scott ever wrote. His best characters do not play secondary rôles in the story . . . : each has its necessary contribution to make towards the total impression. (pp. 87-9)

[Thackeray] was a conscious artist, with a turn for technical experiment. Even in *Esmond, Pendennis, The Newcomes,* which adhere in their main outline to the broad conventions that had ruled the English novel since its inception, hero, villain, final marriage and the rest of it, this turn shows itself. The old conventions are used, but not for the old purpose. And in his masterpiece, *Vanity Fair,* he breaks with the convention altogether. This is Thackeray's second great claim to fame. For his new matter, he did in *Vanity Fair* invent a new and absolutely original form, a form supremely adapted to suit his intricate subject. His contemporaries hardly seemed to realise this; nor has it been completely realised since. There are enough of the old formulas left in *Vanity Fair* to make people speak of it as if it were a Victorian novel of the orthodox type. . . . But a glance at Thackeray's title should have shown them they were wrong. For one thing it is not called 'Amelia Sedley', but *Vanity Fair*; the centre of the book, that is, is not to be found in any one figure. And secondly it is called a 'Novel without a Hero'. Now this does not just mean that it has a heroine instead; it means that there is no character through whose eyes we are supposed to survey the rest of the story and with whose point of view we are meant wholly to sympathise. For here, that panorama of life which is the subject of all Thackeray's books is openly the subject; here, writing about Vanity Fair, he calls his book *Vanity Fair*. And it is the salient fact about *Vanity Fair,* in Thackeray's view, that it admits no heroes. To be heroic is to dominate circumstance; in the Vanity Fair of Thackeray's imagination everyone is the slave of circumstance. To exhibit this he has devised his original structure; a structure that so far from being loose and illogical is of an almost operatic symmetry. (pp. 89-90)

The structural scheme of *Vanity Fair* is Thackeray's greatest technical achievement: and the structural originality which conceived it his greatest technical talent. . . . No one has ever been better at manipulating a huge mass of material. He can make his effects so quickly: indicate a situation, draw a scene in few words; he had that unteachable gift for dialogue which can make a character reveal itself in its lightest phrase. (pp. 93-4)

Over the surface of the whole book is spread equally the tone of Thackeray's personality. However varied the vicissitudes through which the story moves, it is told us by the same voice, with the same tricks of speech; however different the characters and scenes he is drawing, they bear the signature of Thackeray's style of draughtsmanship.

And it is a highly individual style. Thackeray's creative imagination is most impressively apparent in the moral order he imposes on experience, but it shows itself in another way too, in his way of presenting his story. His actual method of describing scene and character is, to steal a phrase from the art critics, a 'stylised' method. Unlike Dickens his achievement lies in its truth to recognisable reality, but like Dickens he is not a realist. He does not attempt to reproduce with a photographic accuracy all the facts, important and unimportant, that make up the surface of any scene—like Zola, say. He sedulously selects from them those he thinks the most significant. And even these he does not present with the unemphasised plainness of Trollope. In the visible as much as in the moral world he accentuates the traits which in his view give his model its individuality, heightens the lights, darkens the shadows. (pp. 95-6)

[Another] distinguishing mark of Thackeray's method of presentation is the mood in which he writes. Told as they are openly in his person, the scenes of the story are inevitably steeped in the mood with which he regarded life in general and them in particular. . . . And in consequence we are conscious of a double emotion, that of its actors and, more predominantly, that of Thackeray observing them. (pp. 98-9)

[Irony] is the keynote of Thackeray's attitude. Indeed no other was possible to one watching the little victims of 'Vanity Fair' at play all heedless of their fate: Thackeray can be dramatic and pathetic and comic and didactic: but pathos, drama, comedy and preaching alike are streaked with the same irony. (p. 99)

His very choice of words is dictated by it. And this brings us to his last distinguishing talent, his style. Thackeray's style is of a piece with the rest of his work. It seems negligent enough, full of colloquialisms and digressions and exclamations and abrupt transitions. But in reality it is a highly conscious affair—with its negligence beautifully adapted to express his prevailing slippered reminiscent mood. Its most colloquial expressions are picked, its easiest rhythms calculated, every chapter, every paragraph works up from a chosen and effective opening to a final telling sentence. And it reaps the reward of its conscientiousness. Its apparent ease makes it flexible enough to cover without awkwardness all the vast variety of mood and incident which Thackeray's subject-matter entails, and to pass naturally from one to the other. The writing never, as in the novels of many conscious artists, gets between us and the subject. . . . Thackeray can soar and drop and brood and perorate and weep and laugh with equal ease. (p. 100)

For [his style] is eloquent. It has the precision and felicity of the real stylist, the vigilant sense of words that makes the most trifling page living and significant and pleasing. . . . And it is style that enables him to do what Trollope could never do, rise to an effect of beauty. . . . (pp. 100-01)

Yet for all his accomplishment Thackeray is not the most successful Victorian novelist. . . . For one thing he is among the writers, like Tennyson, whose executive talent was on a greater scale than his creative inspiration. He can conceive huge structural schemes, but only muster up a sparse band of ideas for them to carry. He can manipulate masses of material, but the masses are all masses of the same thing. Further, though man's vanity and helplessness reveal themselves in every aspect of his life, they are far from being the only things that reveal themselves. And Thackeray thought they were. Nothing can appear on his pages without it has been sifted through the sieve of his moral canon: and some of the largest chunks of human experience do not get through such a sieve at all. . . . Even as a moral canon, Thackeray's is a limited one. As we have seen, it admits of no heroic characters; it has no bearing on those larger, subtler problems that face the characters of George Eliot. . . . [The] order Thackeray imposed so lucidly on life gave no room for such problems. His plots turn on the struggle between selfishness, worldly, self-indulgent or vain, and instinctive honesty, kindness and humility. And they turn on nothing else at all.

Nor is his world so big as it appears at first sight. One is apt to get an impression that a writer who uses a large and crowded canvas commands a greater variety of characters than one who paints on a small scale. But this is not necessarily true. . . . Thackeray, concerned again and again with the same situation and the same motives, repeats his characters again and again. . . . Thackeray's army is a stage army; only put up your opera-glasses and—shadowed by different helmets, led under different banners—you meet the same faces.

Thackeray, too, like all Victorian novelists is a very uncertain craftsman. In spite of his virtuosity, there were some branches of his craft he never fully mastered or was too lazy to trouble about if he did. In his more conventionally-ordered books his hold on structure is very slack; he does not bother to weave the different strands of his theme together, loose ends dangle in the air; no careful revision has cut out the tufts of unnecessary material that have accumulated during the hurry of first writing. And he is almost always too long. . . . Thackeray's armchair method brings with its advantages some terrible dangers; he cannot mention that a character is cheated of twopence without stepping forward and explaining to us that things are not always what they seem, that many apparent sheep are really wolves in sheep's clothing, that the love of money is a great temptation, and a hundred other such unheard-of and astonishing truisms; and he repeats them again and again and again. Dickens can be cheap, Trollope can be flat: Thackeray can be worse, Thackeray can be a bore.

It is a distressing fault, but not a fatal one. . . . The grave accusation that can be brought against Thackeray is that he sometimes errs in conception; and that, where his genius should have shown itself most triumphant, in his conception of character. That insight into human infirmity which is the actuating impulse of his imagination sometimes fails him, that moral order which it was his brilliant achievement to impose on experience, suddenly breaks down. This happens especially when the plot of his story brings him up against an incident involving the delicate question of sexual irregularity. (pp. 102-06)

But it is not only when he ought to be dealing with their sexual weaknesses that Thackeray's grasp on his characters slackens. It can be as surprisingly uncertain when describing characters with no sexual weaknesses at all, his respectable people, above all his respectable women. (p. 106)

[His] inconsistencies in character are Thackeray's most serious fault. But one can understand why he committed them. They are due to the influence of the age in which he lived. The militant moral views that ruled every aspect of Victorian life with so tyrannical a sway, were not ultimately consistent with that moral order whose creation is the centre of Thackeray's artistic achievement. And he modified his order to suit the age. (p. 109)

His view of human nature was essentially inconsistent with the typical Victorian one, yet he himself was a Victorian, educated in the Victorian atmosphere; so that all the unselfconscious part of his outlook, his prejudices, his emotional responses, were Victorian through and through. Nor did he ever re-model his sentiment to fit what he felt to be the truth. (p. 112)

The truth is—and it is the first truth to be realised in arriving at any estimate of Thackeray's achievement—that he was born in the wrong period. He is the only important Victorian novelist who was. . . . [For] the development of imaginative force no age could have provided more favourable conditions than the Victorian. Thackeray's strength, on the other hand, lies not in imaginative force, but in his power of construction and his insight into the processes of human nature. Morever, it needs for its full expression an atmosphere of moral tolerance. His genius, in fact, and his age, were always pulling him different ways. And he yielded to the age.

He can hardly be blamed. . . . Thackeray's was eminently a sociable genius. None the less, his weakness was disastrous to him. For it meant that he fell into the greatest fault to which an artist is liable, he was false to his central creative inspiration. (pp. 114-15)

Thackeray never does . . . fulfil himself. Deliberate artist as he was, he never wrote outside his range: but at its very centre, in his keenest penetration of human infirmity, his hand, hampered by the pressure of his period, will sometimes falter, fumble, swerve aside. With the consequence that his achievement, in spite of all its originality, all its technical brilliance, is ultimately—and judged by the very highest standards—dissatisfying. In the midst of Thackeray's subtlest melody, his richest passage of orchestration, there jars on our ears, faintly, a false note. (pp. 115-16)

> *David Cecil, "William Makepeace Thackeray," in his* Early Victorian Novelists: Essays in Revaluation *(copyright 1935 by The Bobbs-Merrill Company, Inc.; copyright renewed © 1962 by David Cecil; used by permission of the publisher, The Bobbs-Merrill Company, Inc.; in Canada by Constable & Company Limited), Constable, 1934 (and reprinted by Bobbs-Merrill, 1935, pp. 77-116).*

### GEORG LUKÁCS (essay date 1937)

[*A Hungarian literary critic and philosopher, Lukács is considered one of the leading Marxist literary critics. He asserts that Thackeray's primary intent in* Henry Esmond *is to expose false heroism "in order to strip history of its periwig." Although he considers the memoir form appropriate for this purpose, he maintains that its subjectivism ultimately distorts historical objectivity and degrades the historical figures depicted in the novel. This trivialization reveals the fundamental error in "the making private of history. . . ."*]

Thackeray is an outstanding critical realist. He has deep ties with the best traditions of English literature, with the great social canvases of the eighteenth century, which he treated at length in several interesting critical studies. Consciously, he has no interest in separating the historical from the social-critical novel, that is in turning the historical novel into a genre of its own, which was generally the objective result of this development. However, he does not base himself on the classical form of the historical novel, that is on Scott; instead, he attempts to apply the traditions of the eighteenth century social novel to a new type of historical novel. . . . [Eighteenth] cen-

tury historical events were included in the English realist novel particularly in Fielding and Smollett, however only insofar as they came into direct contact with the personal lives of the heroes; thus from the standpoint of the general conception and artistic tendencies of this period, only episodically and never really affecting the chief problems of the novels.

Thackeray, then, consciously takes over this manner of portrayal in his historical novels, but his outlook and artistic aim are quite different from those of the eighteenth century realists. *The approach of the latter towards historicism* grew in a natural way out of their social-critical, realist tendencies. It was one of the many steps towards that realistic conception of history, of social and natural life, which reached its apex in Scott or Pushkin. In the case of Thackeray this *return* to the style and structure of the novels of the eighteenth century stems from a quite different ideological cause, from a deep and bitter disillusionment with the nature of politics, with the relations between social and political life in his own time. This disillusionment expresses itself satirically. By resuming the style of the eighteenth century Thackeray wishes to expose contemporary apologetics.

He, therefore, sees the dilemma in the portrayal of historical events as a choice between public pathos and private manners, the glorification of the one or the realistic depiction of the other. Thus when his hero, Henry Esmond, telling his own story—at the turn of the seventeenth to eighteenth centuries—polemically counters the official histories with the novels of Fielding, when in a discussion with Addison he defends the rights of realism in describing war against poetic embellishment, his language—the language of the memoir—captures the tone of the period beautifully, yet at the same time it expresses Thackeray's own artistic convictions. The basis of this style is the exposure of false heroism, in particular the reputed heroism fostered by historical legend. . . . Thackeray requires this exposure in order to strip history of its periwig, in order to deny that English and French history took place only at the courts of Windsor and Versailles.

Of course, . . . the novel is not meant to be an objective picture of the time, but simply the hero's autobiography. But apart from the fact that this relationship between private manners and historical events is very similar, say, to that in *Vanity Fair*, with a writer as important and conscious as Thackeray the composition of *Henry Esmond* cannot be accidental. The memoir is an appropriate form for Thackeray's exposure of pseudo-greatness. Everything can be seen from the proximity of everyday private life and, shown in this microscopic way, the false pathos of the artificial, self-imagined hero collapses. And this is what is intended. . . . [When] every great man swindle of history has been exposed, there remains just the honesty of simply, slightly above average men capable of real sacrifice like the hero himself.

This picture is remarkably consistent. But is it a real picture of the time, as Thackeray intended? (pp. 201-03)

[Thackeray] does not see the people. He reduces his story to the intrigues of the upper classes. Of course, he knows perfectly well that these trivialities are confined to the class he describes and tell us nothing of the real historical process. (p. 203)

But he thereby dispels historical objectivity, and the more compellingly he motivates his characters psychologically, the subtler this private psychology, the more haphazard it all appears in an historical perspective. The psychology is not wrong, on the contrary it very subtly shows the accidental nature of the political standpoints of the characters. But this accidentality can only appear truly false, if placed within an objective class context where it becomes a factor of historical necessity. Scott's *Waverley* also joins the Stuart Rebellion by accident; but he is simply there as a foil to those for whom the revolt is a social-historical necessity. The perspective in which Thackeray shows Marlborough, however, is purely private. His hero, he says, has become a bitter enemy rather than an enthusiastic follower of Marlborough simply because of bad treatment at a levée. The resulting caricature is such that Thackeray himself feels compelled to counter his own subjectivism with supplementary corrections and notes to his memoirs. But these corrections lessen the one-sidedness only theoretically, they cannot give the figure of Marlborough any objective-historical relief.

This subjectivism degrades all the historical figures who appear in the novel. We see only the "all-too-human" side of Swift, so that we should have to regard him as a petty intriguer and careerist, if we did not have a different picture of him from *his own* works. But even characters whom Esmond describes with obvious sympathy, such as Steele and Addison, the well-known writers of the epoch, are objectively degraded, because their personalities reveal no more than the normal, sociable habits of everyday private life. What made them into important representatives of the epoch, into ideologists of big social changes is excluded from the story by Thackeray's general conception. . . . *The Spectator* turns up in **Henry Esmond**, too; the hero uses his personal friendship with the editors in order to ridicule the frivolous coquetry of the woman with whom he is in love and so exert a beneficial moral influence upon her. No doubt such articles did appear in the journal. But to reduce its historical role to private episodes of this kind means, objectively, the distortion of history, its degradation to the level of the trivial and the private.

Thackeray undoubtedly suffered as a result of this discrepancy. In another historical novel (*The Virginians*) he gives voice to his dissatisfaction. He argues that it is not possible for the present-day writer to show his characters in the context of their professional lives, their actual work etc. The writer has to confine himself to the passions—love or jealousy—on the one hand and to outward forms of social life (in the superficial "worldly" sense) on the other. Thackeray herewith states very tersely the decisive failing of the period of the nascent decline of realism—though without understanding the real social causes and their artistic consequences. He does not see this failing as the result of a narrowed-down and one-sided conception of man, of the fact that characters have come adrift from the main currents of popular life and hence from the really important problems and forces of the age. (pp. 203-05)

Thackeray is too conscious a realist, too strongly tied to the traditions of true realism for him to take [the] naturalist way out. Hence he escapes back beyond the classical and for him unattainable form of the historical novel to an artificial renewal of the style of the English Enlightenment. This archaism, however, can only led to problematic results, as it does elsewhere. The quest for a style leads to stylization, bringing the weaknesses in Thackeray's general conception of social life garishly to the surface, stressing them much more strongly than he would consciously intend. His only wish is to expose false greatness, pseudo-heroism, yet the effect of his stylization . . . is to show every historical figure, whatever his importance, in a disparaging and sometimes thoroughly destructive light. He wishes to counter this with the genuine, inner nobility of simple morality, but his stylization turns his positive charcters into

tedious, insufferable paragons of virtue. True, the literary traditions of the eighteenth century lend cohesion to his works and this has a beneficial effect at a time when naturalism is beginning to break up narrative form. Still, this cohesion is only a stylistic one, it does not touch the depths of the portrayal; hence at most it can only cover up the "problematic" which arises from the making private of history, but not solve it. (pp. 205-06)

> *Georg Lukács, "The Historical Novel and the Crisis of Bourgeois Realism" (1937), in his* The Historical Novel, *translated by Hannah Mitchell and Stanley Mitchell (English translation copyright © 1962 by Merlin Press Ltd), Merlin Press, 1962, pp. 171-250.\**

## JOHN W. DODDS (essay date 1941)

[*Dodds's* Thackeray: A Critical Portrait *is a biographical and critical interpretation that traces the development of Thackeray's ability to blend "his instinctive play of the comic spirit and his aptitude for the probing of human weaknesses . . .". Dodd maintains that* Pendennis *is Thackeray's "most intimate revelation of himself" and that* Henry Esmond *is his greatest work of art. He also praises the* Roundabout Papers, *which he considers "the logical fruit of that reflective retrospective tone which is so strong in the novels."*]

[The stories of **The Yellowplush Papers** and the **Yellowplush Correspondence**] are well told, in the lucid style and with some of the strength if not the subtlety of characterization which Thackeray was to show later. But their total impression is unsatisfying, and it comes, I think, from their author's failure to recognize that he is trying to blend two incompatible themes, the humorous and the cruelly realistic. The result of this attempt, one might suppose, would be the grotesque. It fails to reach that, however. . . .

Thackeray had still much to learn about his art. His somewhat fumbling efforts to blend his instinctive play of the comic spirit and his aptitude for the probing of human weakness are one of the signs of his artistic immaturity. (p. 39)

The development of Thackeray's narrative art is the gradual coalescing and purification of two divergent points of view which, in his earlier work, can be studied almost independently. Their stratification is distinct even though he baffles us by attempting to superimpose them. On the one hand there is the professional funny man with a true and native sense of the ludicrous and the grotesque, and with a nice feeling for bathos. On the other hand, is the man with a clinical interest in blackguards, searching among the seams of the social fabric for the *pediculi* which infest them; never cheaply cynical or misanthropic, but focusing his vision with a painful intensity upon shabby and vulgar motives, ferreting out meanness and cruelty, and isolating without pity, in its chemically pure form, not heroic sin but scurvy and malignant rascality. To this end his gallery of Deuceaces, Earls of Crabs, Mrs. Shums, Captain Rooks, Stubbses, Catherines, Gorgons, and Scullys. These are the more painful because they are not melodramatic Dickensian villains smelling of grease paint and false whiskers. They are brutally real.

Knowing Thackeray, we know him capable of a supreme tenderness, and we are aware that he came to show for the human race not only a lacerated pity but also a pervasive relish and enjoyment. Even his sordidness has a prophylactic purpose. His concern is to strip the pretence from life and, without sneering at frailty, to scrutinize human motives wherever they might lead him. The mistake in art, in [his] early years, was not merely in his tortured preoccupation with cynical sinners—even that could be creative—but in his frequent attempts to immerse them in a bath of burlesque. Far from tempering the satire, this makes it seem more than a little hideous. Thackeray retained always his gift for probing beneath the surface and exposing sham; he retained, too, his essentially humorous appreciation of men and events. But as he grew in wisdom both of these fused into a new molecular combination; out of the lion came forth sweetness. He could always take the button off the foil when it seemed necessary, yet for the most part sympathy blended with satire to make the irony which is the most striking quality of his best work.

In the unfinished *Shabby Genteel Story,* which was to be continued years later, with a difference, in *Philip,* he is still fascinated by the spectacle of fools and knaves. He is a bit gentler with the fools, however, if no less severe on the knaves. (pp. 44-5)

In perspective against Thackeray's other narratives, *A Shabby Genteel Story* is mildly transitional in nature. The stuff of the story itself is still refractory, but it shows Thackeray strengthening his hand in characterization and approaching in narrowing circles the goal of the comico-satirico-sympathetic upon which he was to lay his distinctive mark. (p. 46)

[*The Great Hoggarty Diamond*] marks a distinct advance in every way over *A Shabby Genteel Story.* The satire is softened; the humour is unobtrusive if no less keen; and the sense of integrated characterization is very clear. Thackeray is shaping his materials here with a firm hand and his chief actors have a three-dimensional tangibility. (p. 59)

The whole story has unity, strength, and the careful documentation of an infinitude of amusing and realistic touches. The most noticeable advance is not in the conscious pathos, which, understandable though it is in the light of Thackeray's personal troubles at the time, skirts closely at some points the shoals of dangerous sentiment; but rather in the close-packed variety of character and situation, and in the understanding sympathy by means of which Thackeray gives his story humanity and charm. (p. 60)

As might be expected, the *Irish Sketch Book* is above all else an honest travel-book. If it is more monotonous than the later *Cornhill to Cairo,* it is perhaps through the repetition of much the same kind of scene in the various towns and counties. Although Thackeray is as quick as ever to catch the humorous and the picturesque in both scenery and people, his tone is somewhat constrained. . . . For us here, [this work] is important in so far as it reveals Thackeray labouring with and not quite overcoming his prejudices. He is revolted by much that he sees, yet he is sympathetic in his desire to understand it. (pp. 65-6)

In general he succeeds in giving an impression of dreariness and dirt, particularly in his descriptions of Dublin and southern Ireland. (p. 66)

*Cornhill to Cairo* still holds a worthy place among travel books—by the supreme felicity of its style, often lighted by flashes of amusement, for Thackeray could catch the grotesque and the ridiculous as well as the picturesque; by its lively and shrewdly observant descriptions, catching in its net a wide variety of manners and people and scenery; and by its complete honesty.

It is admirably good humoured from the very beginning. . . . (pp. 69-70)

The book is that refreshing thing among travel-books: completely a record of its author's own reactions. Thackeray is no whit disturbed that it reveals his limitations as well as his ability to appreciate keenly. When Thackeray travels, he is an Englishman, and an honest Englishman. (p. 70)

[*Barry Lyndon*] has all the verve and the rounded perfection of style that one expects of Thackeray at his best. With *Barry Lyndon* he leaves his apprenticeship behind. (p. 72)

*Barry Lyndon* is the consummation of that revolt against the sentimental treatment of crime in popular fiction which [is found] . . . in Thackeray's literary reviews and in his *Catherine.* Here, however, he forgets to be didactic and becomes fertilely creative. Barry is no lay figure but a creature of flesh and blood, and his career is turned into absorbing narrative. . . . Thackeray does not attempt the double-edged satire of *Jonathan Wild,* where Fielding's concern is to show that the great men of all ages have succeeded through the exercise of the same qualities of greatness as Wild's: that is, cruelty and fraud. Thackeray attempts and achieves something subtler and more artistic—the damning of a rogue out of his own mouth. Barry tells his own story. (p. 73)

Thackeray was to find broader and more engaging themes, but never was his control of his materials firmer, his artistic intuition keener, than in this story of the slow decay of a bragging scoundrel.

In spite of its subject, *Barry Lyndon* is not depressing and never tedious. The completely ironic point of view makes Barry's exposure infinitely amusing. (pp. 73-4)

Here, then, is Thackeray's first unqualified artistic success in the art of the novel. There is enough fused intellect in it for half a dozen stories; never before or after did he give more deftly the very anatomy of baseness. And yet by the persuasiveness of his style and the brilliance of his sustained point of view, this seeming *tour de force* becomes narrative art of a high order. (p. 75)

Much of the typical Thackerayan quality of *Vanity Fair* had been foreshadowed . . . in the earlier miscellaneous work. Thackeray had not come with one leap into artistic maturity; he was Titmarsh still. Many of the characters who crowd the pages of the novel have family resemblances to earlier creations. The view of life is essentially the same, too: clear, cool, astringent, eyeing the grotesqueries and hypocrisies and inanities of life's battles with a shrewd appraising glance. Yet Thackeray combines with the acidulous an infiltration of love and pity. . . . The paradoxes and the brilliant achievements of *Vanity Fair* are the paradoxes and the brilliance of the man. (pp. 108-09)

What is it that gives one, as he lays down *Vanity Fair,* such a sense of life lived? What is the special quality of Thackeray's creative imagination and how does it work itself out into character? If we can answer these questions we shall be close to his secret. (p. 109)

Thackeray was in the main line of the English novel of character. . . . [The] characters *are* the plot, or at least the plot springs easily and unostentatiously from the relationships in which the characters stand to one another. This casualness and steady avoidance of manipulated drama yields that lack of scenic tension which is basic to Thackeray's method.

Part of this method stems from his own awareness of his limitations as well as his instinctive recognition that 'big scenes' are the more powerful if they are few. (p. 110)

Join an antiseptic hatred for cruelty and insincerity to a corollary affection for gentleness and honesty; add to that a quality of subtle observation and a nice sense for just the right amount of artistic distortion, and you have the ironist of *Vanity Fair.* Some critics, misled by Thackeray's 'I have no head above my eyes. I describe what I see,' have brought heavy guns to bear on what they call his lack of a philosophy or even of an adequate equipment of ideas. It is true that Thackeray had small talent for abstract thinking; and his generalizations are not infrequently comfortably conventional. Nevertheless he did bring the scenes of the Fair within the framework of a conception of life which had point and penetration and which conveyed a moral concept of human nature, in its large sense. His thinking is fused thought, concrete, objectified in action and speech, but to the careful reader unmistakable. It is always expressed through character and exists, in the great novels, on several planes of realism, from near-caricature to the subtlest and most acute revelation of personality.

The clue to Thackeray's art in the novels, then, is not its occasional devastating satire, or its wit, or its amiable moralizing digressions, or its occasional bursts of sentiment controlled and tempered by a quizzical humour. . . . The clue to his art is the complete and covering irony through which his view of life is filtered. It is an irony softened by a sad and wistful humanity, sharpened at times by an indignation against cant and affectation, but warmed also by the gentle melancholy that comes with the ironist's perception of the gap between man's aspiration and achievement. (pp. 117-18)

Connected with [the] large ironic treatment is the point of view from which Thackeray tells the story. It is not as easy to identify and fix here as it is in the later novels. Sometimes he seems to be the omniscient novelist, sharing the inmost thoughts and feelings of his characters; sometimes the spectator *ab extra* [from outside], pretending to be unable to know the minds of his people, even going out of his way to validate their independent existence. (pp. 119-20)

The method is of course the seemingly casual, chatty soliloquizing of a man sitting in his arm-chair by the fireside and telling a story. It is of all narrative manners the most flexible, but also the one most likely to lead into windy digression. Thackeray keeps the digressions under reasonably good control in *Vanity Fair,* although his approach allows for a variety of moods and comments. Typically it permits him to pluck the reader by the sleeve and draw him off into a corner, there to comment familiarly upon the passing scene. (p. 120)

[He] has come in for a good deal of abuse because of this habit. The test ought to be: does it help the story or get in the way? Does it make it seem more or less real? Does it add to or detract from our enjoyment? (p. 121)

It seems to me that Thackeray's interpolations add, in the long run, to the illusion of reality, certainly to our enjoyment of the story. In the dramatic novel they would be quite out of place, but in the discursive novel of manners they indicate the mood of the story and intensify the mellow, introspective manner which is the very tissue of a Thackeray novel. . . . One distinction needs to be made, however. When he is adding an ironic or a whimsical note to the margin of the action he can be completely felicitous. Yet occasionally the moralist defeats the artist and upon the characters are poured the vials of Thackeray's ethical indignation. Still worse are the places where, in a fervour of sentimental adoration, Thackeray releases a flood of sensibility about some character who, on his own showing, is not worth the emotion. (pp. 121-22)

It has been said that Thackeray's men and women are static characters, that they do not develop or deteriorate in the course of the book, and that what we get is a progressive revelation or unfolding of people whose dominant tendencies are fixed when they first appear. Within certain limits this is true, as indeed it must be in the character novel of broad range, where the interest comes not so much from the inner growth or decay of the individual as from the interplay between individuals and groups. Nevertheless the sense of time lies heavy upon *Vanity Fair.* It is not merely that the action covers almost two decades, but rather that time, under Thackeray's hand, becomes a thing almost palpable. He evokes, through his retrospective, brooding manner and the wide slow movement of his narrative, a sense of hours and years slipping past. His characters, therefore, live in time as well as in space, and the mutation of character as it goes through the furnace of the years approximates, if it does not actually constitute, development. (pp. 124-25)

The case of Amelia is of great critical importance, for it carries us into the heart of the contradiction which sometimes disturbed the balance of Thackeray's art. (p. 127)

The conflict in Thackeray seems to have been between a deeply set worship of womanhood as an ideal, and a critical inability to see things except as they are. All things gentle and soft and honourable appealed to him; yet he knew that lovely woman can stoop to the most banal follies. And so he defends Amelia against herself and writes in the margin comments with which to soften the stern reality of his reporting. Amelia is patently not worth the sentiment he lavishes on her. This inconsistency, a conflict of head and heart, extends . . . into the other novels. . . . (p. 129)

For Thackeray [Becky Sharp] became, whether he would or no, the dominating character of the book, giving a unity to its heterogeneous action and pulling into one framework its several families. More than that, she acts as a catalytic agent upon the others. Jos, Sir Pitt, George, Rawdon, Steyne—all capitulate, in their various ways, to her charm. She releases in them qualities which are not always pleasant but which are very revealing, and so she becomes the touchstone for their characters. (p. 131)

*Pendennis,* though not Thackeray's best novel, is in some ways his most intimate revelation of himself. It, rather than *Vanity Fair,* reads like a first novel, for it is confessedly autobiographical. Like all such stories it furnishes fruitful but dangerous material for the biographer, for Arthur Pendennis is both more and less than Thackeray; no one can be sure just where the fictional and the creative is superimposed upon the reminiscent. (p. 144)

Thackeray did not always avoid the dangers of diffuseness and redundancy; *Pendennis* could have been shortened to its artistic improvement. Yet the redundancies are the redundancies of life itself, and here again Thackeray gains that cumulative effect which informs his best novels. Although the story bores us at times, at the end we come away with the feeling that we have lived with these people and that we know them as we know our own friends. Thackeray keeps firm hold of the one thread which could lead him successfully through such a labyrinth of a thousand pages: the sustained projection of character. (p. 146)

In addition to its autobiographical interest [*Pendennis*] is important because it shows Thackeray entering fully into the mood of mellow reminiscence which had already become his characteristic manner. As in all his work, its blemishes and its triumphs lie close together and it is frequently hard to disentangle them. But one thing is clear even to the casual reader: there are enough good things in *Pendennis,* and sufficient creative energy, to cut up into half a dozen stories for lesser novelists. (p. 159)

[If] *Esmond* is not Thackeray's greatest novel it is his greatest work of art and certainly one of the best of all historical novels. He attempted a rare and difficult feat and he accomplished it triumphantly. (pp. 160-61)

[In] spite of the fact that the events in *Esmond* are more than customarily dashing and exciting, the ground swell of the novel is sombre and its effect one of mitigated tragedy. . . . Yet the story is so full of good things, of crowded life and action and brilliant historical colouring, and the sadness is set off by such a counterpoint of lively intrigue that the reader remembers the action longer than the mood of melancholy. (p. 161)

Thackeray's sensitiveness to the past reaches its full fruition in this novel; his love for the historical eighteenth century fuses with his other love for the personal and retrospective method of telling a story. (p. 163)

[No] style could seem less conscious of itself than Thackeray's. Like all great narrative styles it is simple in vocabulary and structure. The right word is always there, set plainly into its context without tortured effort or puzzle-headedness. The sentences slip along with an almost colloquial ease, flowing into every curve of the author's thought—idiomatic, strong, and sure. For all its subtlety of rhythm and its hint of distant harmonies it is sinewy and clean. No extravagant words, a minimum of set rhetorical device, and yet a sense of happy abundance—the lucid outpouring of a mind in which word and idea are one. (pp. 173-74)

Thackeray's is an intensely personal style—in the best sense of that word. It is urbane and civilized, but its good breeding is not colourless nor its simplicity monotonous, and its colour is that of Thackeray's own rich and varied personality. . . . As has often been pointed out, the kinship of Thackeray's style is with the eighteenth century—with Fielding's fine free strength and still more with the meditative, genial, ruminating eloquence of the essayists, with Addison particularly. From these come, perhaps, the haunting musical cadences which play through the lines of both his novels and his essays—for Thackeray is as much the essayist turned novelist as he is the novelist who diverges into the essay.

It is a remarkably even style. If there are few purple patches there are few stylistically monotonous ones. . . . Thackeray never writes merely to exercise his pen, although his habit of chatty, confidential familiarity sometimes makes him garrulous. Occasionally we wish to prune him because he goes into unnecessarily long-winded detail, but never because he is in the slightest degree artificial or affected.

In spite of this embroidery of comment, however, Thackeray often approximates the naked purity of Swift. . . . This simplicity of Thackeray's is capable, however, of a wide range of effects. It can be trenchant as well as meditative, hilarious as well as pensive. It bends metaphor to its will. At its best it

has a homely felicity shot through, as often as not, with a familiar humour which builds a paragraph to a climax and then guides it down to a smooth conclusion. (pp. 175-76)

[It] is surprising to find how little the style of *Esmond* differs in arrangement and substance from Thackeray's normal style and how completely, at the same time, he seems to have identified himself with a memoir-writer of the eighteenth century. (p. 177)

[For] the most part the sentence texture, the broad rhythm of thought in *Esmond* is not consciously or closely imitative at all; it is soaked so thoroughly in the atmosphere of a period that it becomes a sort of re-creation, even to the extent of obscuring to the average reader the many places, both in conversation and in disquisition, where Thackeray expresses ideas that are not of the eighteenth century in tones that are modern. Over the whole book, however, eighteenth century or not, lies a heavy brooding sense of time past. . . . (pp. 177-78)

[*The Newcomes*] is in many ways the richest of all [Thackeray's] novels, the complete realization of his talent for seizing upon a whole society and fixing it in words. As time went on Thackeray was inclined to repeat his characters and situations; none knew that better than he. In some ways even *The Newcomes* is just a better *Pendennis,* but it is so much better that it stands, in its scope and variety, with *Vanity Fair* at the head of all the novels. Never had Thackeray's grasp of character been firmer, his observation shrewder, his satire sharper, or his humanity deeper. There is in *The Newcomes* a balance of all that is best in Thackeray and least of that with which it has been necessary for us to find fault. (p. 193)

One of the criticisms brought against *The Newcomes* is that Thackeray is unable here, indeed is unable in any of his work, to enunciate great truths; . . . in short, that he lacks *ideas* in the larger sense. The charge is serious enough to merit close consideration. Certainly Thackeray's approach was not patently intellectual or philosophical in the sense that Charlotte Brontë's or George Eliot's or Meredith's was. . . . To be sure, Thackeray does rely more on his intuition than on his reasoning power to approach truth, and his best ideas are expressed concretely through character rather than through exhortation. Profundity, however, is a matter of relative definition, and Thackeray's deep and sensitive intuitions coupled with his microscopic observation give him a grasp of those borderline suggestions of character which are not pure idea, or yet pure feeling, but which probe and illuminate facets of human nature sometimes hidden from the philosopher. (pp. 199-200)

It is difficult to compare *Vanity Fair* and *The Newcomes.* Each is great in its own way, for similar and for different qualities. Thackeray never went higher than the former, nor deeper than the latter. Together they stand at the head of his performance. (p. 210)

[*Philip*] comes naturally into comparison with *Pendennis* and *The Newcomes,* for like them it is a picture of mid-nineteenth-century English society. . . . To say that it is less good than either of the others is to indicate that the thread of Thackeray's narrative invention was becoming more and more tenuous. His own criticism of the book was that it 'had not enough story.' Never greatly concerned with plot, he was coming more and more to depend upon prolixity rather than creation. (pp. 221-22)

Like *Pendennis* and *The Newcomes, Philip* is penetrated by the reminiscent vein which came so easily to Thackeray. . . . The manner is once again that of the mellow old gentleman telling the tale from his armchair. At its best this quality of ruminating retrospection had given a certain personal richness to Thackeray's novels; in *Philip* the excess of this quality is more apparent. (p. 223)

This much must be said in criticism of the tissue of the narrative as a whole, its structural amorphousness, its repetitiousness, its reiterative musings. That it is still a solid and considerable book—better in some ways than *The Virginians*—is testimony that Thackeray's eye and hand had by no means lost all their cunning. Buttressing the weaknesses are many pungent and a few brilliant scenes. . . . It is impressively clear that the decline of Thackeray's narrative power brought with it little weakening of his amazing ability to catch in words that abundant sense of reality in characterization which is his great contribution to fiction. These are for the most part people seized firmly in a great creative imagination and given there an independent life. (pp. 223-24)

The *Roundabout Papers* are the distillation of those moods and attitudes which give the clue, not to Thackeray as a novelist *per se*—that is, as a creator of scene and character—but to that individuality of manner and treatment and way of thinking which is almost as much a part of the novels as their plots or their people. If behind the novels there is a quality of mind Thackerayan as distinct, say, from Dickensian or Trollopian, that quality is beautifully fixed in the essays. They are the logical fruit of that reflective retrospective tone which is so strong in the novels. Here he is freed from the necessity of feeding his reflections into the interstices of a novel, free to be as discursive as he chooses and as frankly egoistic as a good familiar essayist must be. Here he can turn easily from subject to subject and let his vastly allusive mind play freely over both the contemporary scene and the past, bathing each in the warm afternoon glow of his rich personality. Whim, fancy, jocularity, sympathy, respect for goodness and simplicity and honesty, occasional reproof for meanness and injustice—all and more are here. He is still perceptibly the satirist of Vanity Fair and the moralist of the week-day sermons; but he is the satirist softened and the moralist mellowed. Benignity envelops him without dulling the edge of his humour. To be sure, the actual stuff of which the essays are made is of uneven excellence. He sometimes seizes upon material which not all his powers of fancy or imagination can refine. But in no similar number of pages is his personality so characteristically displayed. When he does get hold of a felicitous topic he adorns it not only with his gracious chatty fireside manner but also with his canny insight into motive and with his wide sympathy with human weakness and frailty—including his own frailty! (p. 236)

The *Roundabouts* are in the great tradition of the familiar essay, from Montaigne down through Addison and Steele and Goldsmith to Leigh Hunt, Lamb, and Hazlitt. At their best they are perhaps closer to Elia than to any of the others. Thackeray's direct simplicity kept him away from the conscious old-world quaintness which Lamb delighted in. Yet there is in both much of the same love of the fantastic, the same frank admission of prejudices and weaknesses, the same rich allusiveness, literary and otherwise, and the same delicate embroidery of a whim or elaboration of an idea which unfolds into manifold connotations, beginning with almost nothing and proceeding like a train of Greek fire round a whole periphery of related suggestions. But when one gets through with a *Roundabout* he realizes that Thackeray, like Lamb, has made a central point neatly and that there is a unity to the thing after all. Thackeray also

wraps his ideas in the humour which is perhaps the central quality of the best of such writing, sometimes a little wistful or rueful, but just as likely to be extravagant or robust—a humour saltier and more worldly than Lamb's. (p. 237)

[The *Roundabouts*] are as original and amusing as they are honest. What brings it all home, of course, is the style, which never was more nearly right than in these essays. It has that sense of abundance and effortless ease which gives validity to this kind of writing. Unrhetorical, loose in structure, it can be eloquent, and is always precise in its effects. What language can do in the way of fusing word and idea, thought and feeling, Thackeray makes it do in the prose of the *Roundabouts*. It is as transparent and clean as it is subtle in its seemingly uncalculated rhythms. (p. 242)

Thackeray's verses are to poetry much as his illustrations are to art. What they can do they do well. For what they do not pretend to do they cannot be criticized. The 'ballads,' as he called his rhymes, vary greatly in quality. At their infrequent worst they are compounded of rather sterile sentiment in the 'Keepsake' manner, or of unlicked humour. At their best they bubble with a sprightly and buoyant gaiety crossed, however, by frequent touches of pathos. Typically they combine sentiment and humour—and sometimes indignation—in a merry-sad brew of Thackeray's own peculiar tap. (pp. 242-43)

With a few exceptions the ballads are on a poetically low level, *vers de société* [society verse] or mere humorous doggerel. He does not attempt the higher flights; his muse was a homely one and he recognized it for such. His emotion is tender and warm rather than ecstatic or inspired. At the same time one can learn from his more serious verse something about his philosophy of life. In *The Pen and the Album,* for example, he shows us how he liked to think of himself as the jester with the tragic face behind the mask. (p. 244)

His best effects, however, are humorous ones. He can turn an amusing verse with neat skill, the rhymes—including the ingenious double and triple ones—falling exactly right, the whole tone bright and glancing. (p. 246)

Although Thackeray's ballads are among the best of their kind, no one would pretend that their kind was the best. Nevertheless they are of a piece with his other work, warmed by the same sunshine and darkened by the same shadows. In his rhymes as in his novels and essays he is the hater of shams and affectations, literary or social; the brisk, tolerant sceptic with a tear in his eye; the lover of laughter and the wistful observer of evanescent happiness. (p. 248)

*John W. Dodds, in his* Thackeray: A Critical Portrait *(copyright © 1941 by Oxford University Press; copyright renewed © 1968 by John Wendall Dodds; reprinted by permission of the author), Oxford University Press, New York, 1941 (and reprinted by Russell & Russell, Inc, 1963), 257 p.*

**EDMUND WILSON** (essay dates 1945, 1947)

The appearance of [*The Letters and Private Papers of William Makepeace Thackeray*] is, of course, an event of the first importance. However tepidly one may admire Thackeray, it is impossible not to be fascinated by the extraordinary document they constitute on the London literary world, nineteenth-century society in both London and Paris . . . , and Victorian family life. . . . I am not sure that a comparable record exists for any Victorian Englishman. (p. 292)

If Thackeray today lacks readers, I believe that it is due to his defects as a novelist, and that, though *Vanity Fair* will remain, the rest of his work is not likely ever much to be read again. Nor can I imagine that this record of his life will create a "Thackeray legend." Interesting though the record is and good though some of his letters are (he is to be seen at his most entertaining in his correspondence with Mrs. Brookfield), we find in them the same weaknesses that prevented him from ever becoming a really top-flight novelist. . . . Beside the great Englishmen of the Victorian era, Thackeray reveals himself here, even more clearly than in his published writings, rather a shallow commentator on life, and whereever we run into a letter by Dickens or by Edward FitzGerald, we get the impression of a soundness and dignity that contrasts with Thackeray's chatter. (p. 295)

Here, also, the falsity that one feels in his novels appears to much worse advantage, because here the human relations are real. Edmund Yates infuriated Thackeray in his later years by calling him a *"faux bonhomme"* [false good-natured man], but the derogatory descriptions of Thackeray always tend to strike that note, and one is made rather uneasy, in these letters, by his professions of geniality and affection. . . . One decides that, though a very demonstrative, he was rather a cold man. . . . The sentimentality that mars his novels was an element of his daily life. In the very act of recognizing it and castigating it, he is unable to shake it off. . . . He is strongest when he is seeing through people and giving a shabby account of the world, but the bitter view he takes of human motives itself implies the sentimental vision, because what he is being bitter about is the fact that human behavior does not live up to this. He can never study motives coolly, as Stendhal or Tolstoy could, and, beside their journals and memoirs, these self-revelations of Thackeray's seem hopelessly second-rate. (pp. 295-97)

•  •  •  •  •

[To] go back to Thackeray, in one's later years, when one no longer takes great writers on faith, is to be made more aware of his weaknesses without discovering much that is new. Of course, his vein at its best was excellent; but it is so much merely a vein that is always running thin or insipid. One cannot count on him to do anything solid, and even *Henry Esmond*, though carefully built, has always seemed to me rather flimsy. One falls back on the conclusion, borne out by these letters, that Thackeray had in his day and for a certain length of time thereafter a kind of social value that made him seem a greater writer than he was. He was the chronicler of a middle-class world which, though sometimes humiliated by poverty, always pretended to education and gentility. . . . The ups and downs of this world and the assertion of its fundamental dignity, as well as a certain dissatisfaction with its methods, aims and rewards, really constitutes Thackeray's whole subject, and he never gets outside that subject. He cannot see society as a whole as Dickens was able to do, with all the paradoxes involved in its structure and the dislocations caused by its growth. He is unable to interest himself in personalities or relations for their own sake, as Henry James or Jane Austen did—in such a way as to use them for materials in composing a work of art. His situations and characters are sketches on a somewhat higher plane, to be sure, than the drawings he dashed off in his letters, but more or less the same sort of thing. (pp. 356-57)

*Edmund Wilson, "Thackeray's Letters: A Victorian Document" (1945) and "An Old Friend of the Fam-*

*ily: Thackeray" (1947), in his* Classics and Commercials: A Literary Chronicle of the Forties *(reprinted by permission of Farrar, Straus and Giroux, Inc.; copyright 1950 by Edmund Wilson; copyright renewed © 1978 by Elena Wilson), Farrar, Straus and Giroux, 1950, pp. 291-97, 348-58.*

### J.Y.T. GREIG   (essay date 1950)

[*Grieg's* Thackeray: A Reconsideration *is one of the harshest assessments of the author. He maintains that Thackeray lacks "a stable and undeviating mind" and, in refutation of David Cecil (see excerpt above, 1934), states that Thackeray did not have "a systematic philosophy of human nature to present." In direct opposition to George Saintsbury and John W. Dodds (see excerpts above, 1908 and 1941), Grieg condemns Thackeray for his subjective narrative style. He maintains, in addition, that Thackeray's chief weakness as a novelist is his heavy reliance upon real-life models which, he argues, have a disastrous effect upon his fiction. Despite his strongly negative opinions given here, Grieg states in his later essay, "Thackeray: A Novelist by Accident," that he counts himself among Thackeray's admirers (see additional bibliography).*]

What [Thackeray] lacked was a stable and undeviating mind.

It is this mutability, perhaps more than any other quality of the man, which serves, on the one hand, to mark him off from the bulk of his contemporaries, and, on the other, to account for his declining fame in the present century. To the men of his own day he was enigmatic and disturbing; to the men of ours he appears hesitant, irritating in his vacillations, even poor-spirited. (p. 2)

No man since the late George Saintsbury [see excerpt above, 1908] has written on Thackeray with more understanding and sympathy than Lord David Cecil in *Early Victorian Novelists* [see excerpt above, 1934]; but even he seems to shoot wide of the mark when he speaks of the author of *Vanity Fair, Pendennis,* and *Esmond*—the only works in the canon comparable with, let us say, *David Copperfield, The Return of the Native, The Idiot,* and *Anna Karenina*—as 'imposing a moral order on experience.' It is surely an overstatement to say that 'Thackeray is the first novelist to do what Tolstoy and Proust were to do more elaborately—use the novel to express a conscious, considered criticism of life . . . to present the reader with a systematic philosophy of human nature'. . . . [This] implies that Thackeray resembled Fielding, Tolstoy, and Proust in having a systematic philosophy of human nature to present. This implication is false. No doubt Thackeray wished to have one. At times also he thought he had. But a systematic philosophy was beyond his powers. He had no sooner stated a conviction than he wanted to insert a question-mark; no sooner taken up an attitude than he wondered if he wasn't being insincere, foolish, or extravagant; no sooner underlined a moral than he cocked a snook at it. Greatly as he admired Fielding, he had little of Fielding's stability of purpose; and in the end all that was left to him was the paralysing thought, 'Vanity of vanities, all is vanity'. Even this moral he had too little resolution to maintain without evasions. (pp. 4-5)

['The Snobs of England', afterwards republished as *The Book of Snobs*] is rather tiresome. Though sometimes entertaining, it is much too long, too full of repetitions; its humour is often forced, and its wit flat. Considered as a fact in the life of Thackeray, however, it is most important. (pp. 90-1)

The 'Snob' papers may . . . be regarded as a sort of catchment-area in the development of Thackeray as a writer. Turbulent streams from a great many of his earlier works flow into them, settle, then pour out again, purified, less turbulent, and less turbid, into later novels. After this series in *Punch* it is always the mature Thackeray that we encounter in print. For better, for worse, he is what he is. Though he may still develop and improve his technical skills, yet the substance of his work, his prevailing interests, themes, types of character, and opinions on life—these will change very little in the seventeen years still remaining to him. His mind and habits of thinking were formed by the time he completed 'The Snobs of England.' (p. 91)

[The] trouble with him was that he had no relatively firm social theory to control his pen. He had no standards, except the vague ones of a 'gentleman', by which he could measure social aberrations. Like many another social physician, he could only name the disease, and attack its symptoms. To get down to ultimate causes would have needed more systematic thinking than his untrained and inconstant mind was capable of undertaking. (pp. 92-3)

He had no effective cure for the 'sickness of an acquisitive society.' He delivered his blows so impulsively and indiscriminately that they fell almost as often on the innocent as on the guilty. His values were confused and variable; and the final impression after a reading of *The Book of Snobs* is one of exasperation. If everybody is a snob (including Mr. Snob, the author), and if nearly every human action is an example of snobbery, both terms are meaningless. (p. 93)

Lacking a coherent, integrated social theory, [Thackeray] grew timid and unsure, like a sniper who decamps when the battle grows warm. His avowed doctrine, 'Fun is good, truth better, love best of all', though it sounded well, did not seem to bear directly on his practice as novelist or critic. He lacked the jaunty optimism of Dickens. . . . Dickens's work was buoyed up by his genuine belief in the goodness of man, and in the power of charity to reform the world. That was excellent; it was individualism moralized and justified. Thackeray, on the contrary, presented human society as Vanity Fair—'not a moral place certainly; nor a merry one, though very noisy.' . . . Nor could he find any more comfortable words with which to end his first full-length novel than: 'Ah! *Vanitas Vanitatum* [Vanity of Vanities]! which of us is happy in this world? Which of us has his desire? or, having it, is satisfied?—Come, children let us shut up the box and the puppets, for our play is played out'.

To appeal to the Victorian middle classes in a tone so *morne* [gloomy] was extraordinary, irritating, and in the end ineffectual. . . . Dickens with his gusto, and despite much cheap jollity and still cheaper pathos, did more to shake the Victorians' complacency than his saturnine, disjointed rival. Dickens hung together. Thackeray did not. (pp. 100-01)

'Discursive' is the epithet that he applies to his Muse. It is aptly chosen. What he enjoys doing and can do extremely well is panoramic narrative. Chapter XXXVIII of *Vanity Fair* offers a good example. He entitles it 'A Family in a very small Way', and uses it to give a summary account, unhurried but economical, of the Sedleys after their downfall. An even better example is the long discursive tale of Becky's social ascent, leading up to the triumphs at Gaunt House, and so to the crisis in her life. Nothing finer of its kind is to be found in Thackeray, and, indeed, not many passages of sustained narrative in the whole range of English literature surpass it. (p. 116)

As a 'dramatic' writer, presenting what Henry James calls 'the discriminated occasion', Thackeray varies in power. He lacked the dramatic gift of sustaining an occasion at a high pitch, and when he tried to do this, often tumbled into melodrama, fustian, or cant. On the other hand, when he kept the occasion brief, he could often make it memorable. In *Vanity Fair* Becky is concerned in all the best of the discriminated occasions, and, apart from the crisis, Thackeray has pitched every one of them on the level of high comedy. As for the crisis itself—when Rawdon returns from the spunging-house and finds Becky alone with Lord Steyne—this is one of Thackeray's undoubted triumphs. . . . [Yet] he strikes two false notes—one when he bestows a 'horrid' smile on Becky, and one when he allows the noble marquis to 'grind' his teeth. Otherwise the performance, quick and sure-fingered, is without a flaw.

But, this discriminated occasion over, in sidles Thackeray the preacher to exploit it. . . . (pp. 116-17)

To the reader of to-day . . . , Thackeray's question, 'Was she guilty?', is astounding. Even more so is his care not to answer it. It is true that he was thinking of his prudish readers, but this is not the whole truth. He was squeamish himself. Sex to him was a dangerous volcano, and now, as always, he refused to approach too near. he could only skirt round and round the crater with his nerves a-jangle. (p. 117)

If *Pendennis* is taken piece by piece (for a whole the novel is not), it will be found to contain a greater proportion of Thackeray's best writing than any other book. The first section of it, from the memorable opening with the Major at breakfast in his club to the conversation, so quiet, quintessential, and perfect in tone, between Pen and Bows on the bridge at Chatteris, is as good as anything else of its kind in the whole range of English fiction: it is virtually a long-short story, complete in itself, beautifully balanced, continuously interesting, remarkably free from digressions and almost entirely free from sermons, and written throughout in Thackeray's current, sinewy, well-bred prose. . . . [The second section, Pen at Oxbridge,] is nearly equal to the first. Then the trouble starts: the novel begins to vary in quality from the very good to the very bad. Thackeray can still write with something like the brilliance he maintained throughout the first section; but only for a chapter or two at a time; and there is no telling when he will. He has become erratic and uncertain. Strange to say, he has also lost his skill in the art of panoramic narrative, the very art in which he excelled in *Vanity Fair,* and in which, happily, he was to excel again in later novels. (p. 119)

What the critical reader recalls from this novel, when he looks back upon it, is a quite unusual number of discriminated occasions, some short, some long, some very good, some very bad. It is almost as if Thackeray, in his now conscious rivalry with Dickens, had resolved to surpass Dickens in his own field—the dramatic. He could, so long as he kept within the bounds of high comedy. The tense scene, the pathetic scene, were for the present beyond him. (pp. 119-20)

Structurally, there is little good to be said of *Pendennis*. As I have already pointed out, it tends to fall into sections, related to one another only by the presence of the hero and perhaps a few other characters; and although, as in his previous novel, Thackeray ultimately works in both a love-story and a plot of intrigue, neither is of much account. . . . (p. 120)

Despite its faults (which are grievous), *Pendennis* comes nearest of all Thackeray's books to revealing the essential novelist—if by this is meant a writer who can present his readers with immediately 'knowable' human beings. Of the principals in *Pendennis,* only Laura is an out-and-out failure. Pen will serve; he is better, at all events, than the bulk of so-called heroes. The treatment of Helen is infuriating; but if we prune away all the sentimentalizing, agonizing, and sermonizing with which Thackeray tries to choke the life out of her, we discover, a little to our surprise, that she is not only central to the book, but also credible and veracious to the last detail. Blanche and the Major are the greatest triumphs. (p. 125)

For a study of Thackeray's methods . . . , the most interesting characters in this novel are the Fotheringay and George Warrington. The first is a remarkable achievement; one of the most remarkable in English fiction. For she is a character without a character—a Galatea. She is little more than a statue which has been trained to declaim speeches. Yet somehow the statue lives. The reader believes in her, 'knows' her, though the amount that he can 'know about' her is negligible. Anyone can fill a void with something tangible; but to leave a void empty, and yet compel the reader to a sense of some living presence there, is something of a triumph in the art of the novelist.

George Warrington is composite, and not quite there. One is apt to think he is there, but in this one is deceived. He can talk well. Nevertheless the voice is nine parts Thackeray's. Warrington, indeed, during most of the book, is a second incarnation of the author—Thackeray some ten years older, wiser, less romantic and impulsive than the young Pendennis. This becomes a trick of Thackeray's: he repeated it in *The Newcomes* and *Philip*, though in these novels it is Pendennis who is the older incarnation, and Clive and Philip the younger ones. In *Esmond* he achieves something like the same effect by turning the book into memoirs, the memoirs of a mature Harry looking back upon his younger self; and part of his dissatisfaction with *The Virginians* was very likely due to his not being able to do the same sort of thing there. (p. 126)

*Esmond* is more steadfast and inexorable than any of his other works. Many good judges have disliked it, but few who have been willing to surrender themselves to it have failed to get the sense of its inevitability. All the events recorded *must* have happened just so; the characters are not puppets being manipulated by the author's supple fingers and discoursed upon in weekday sermons; like the sun shining on their heads and the waters of the Thames flowing past their homes, they appear actual, inerrably known. (pp. 154-55)

[The] book has been called 'picturesque.' The adjective needs qualification. *Esmond* is full of what seem like pictures, sharply visualized and beautifully composed; it is fuller of these, undoubtedly, than the other novels. The discriminated occasions that we recall from *Esmond* are more often immobile or 'posed' than the ones that we recall from *Vanity Fair* or *Pendennis*; they are tableaux rather than scenes of action. (p. 155)

In spite of occasional lapses into theatricality and rant, to which Thackeray was always liable, *Esmond* reaches and sustains a level of style unique in his work. . . . [He] was cultivating a style, a special style. As the book purported to be the memoirs of a man born in the late seventeenth century, . . . it was necessary that his style should correspond. But to say that Thackeray imitated or affected the Augustans is to suggest that the style of *Esmond* is unnatural—a collection of antiques out of Wardour Street. It is not. The marvel of it is that it always reads like Thackeray, and yet, simultaneously, like someone who had died a century before him—not Steele or Addison or Swift or Pope or Bolingbroke, but someone unidentified who *might* have been a close friend and admirer of all of them.

Very rarely do we catch the author at his tricks. He has not only assimilated the political and social history of the time but also acquired the very tone of voice of a man who lived then. (pp. 158-59)

It has become a commonplace of criticism to say that Thackeray has the air of a man remembering. . . .

Thackeray avows the method himself, several times. 'I believe a man forgets nothing', says Barry Lyndon on revisiting his old home; and although the book in which this remark occurs is an early one, written before Thackeray had learned by experiment and failure that peculiar reminiscential manner which so well expresses his withdrawn, hesitant, sceptical, yet sensitive and at times sentimental attitude of mind, the remark might be chosen as a motto for his work. (p. 180)

He filled his books with people, places, and episodes that he took from his own private and personal experience. (p. 184)

Thackeray very often did 'brook dictation from his sitters.' That was his chief infirmity, and it is for that reason, more than for any other, that we cannot rank him among 'the greatest novelists.' Saintsbury is almost certainly right about them. They take hints from experience; they reproduce the quality of it; they re-fashion the details. They are masters of their experience. They shape it into something rich and strange. Thackeray could do the same—sometimes. He re-shaped his experience of the various models—two, three, it does not matter how many there were—that he used for Becky Sharp, so that the woman in the novel became a new creation, unhampered by the accidents of real life. But this he was incapable of doing when his relationship to the living original of a character in fiction was predominantly emotional: The principal witness in support of this charge is his mother. The effect she produced upon his fiction—direct when he chose to portray her as Helen Pendennis; indirect, though little less powerful, when he touched, even lightly, on the Mother-Child theme—was disastrous. Disastrous, too, in varying degrees, were his other obsessions with people. . . . (pp. 185-86)

Thackeray was above all a novelist who remembered. He would certainly have proved a better one had he learned to forget as well. (p. 186)

> *J.Y.T. Greig, in his* Thackeray: A Reconsideration *(reprinted by permission of Oxford University Press), Oxford University Press, London, 1950 (and reprinted by Archon Books, Hamden, CT, 1967), 216 p.*

## MARIO PRAZ (essay date 1952)

Thackeray, to put it briefly, was an ironist through repressed romanticism. . . . [He] was solidly anchored to the predominant bourgeois ethics of his time, and derived material for caricature from his moralistic abhorrence of all excess. (p. 189)

Like those medieval artists who sometimes portrayed a putrid corpse at the back with a splendid, sumptuous, youthful figure in front, Thackeray never ceases to evoke the repulsive moral skeleton side by side with the rosy outward appearance. (p. 201)

Thackeray is indeed bitter and harsh, but he remains always a gentleman, he remains, that is, within the framework of Victorian society; he is a cynic in yellow gloves, respectful, when all is said and done, of the conventions. He does not truly see life as it is, but with a caricature-like distortion which is conditioned by the exigencies of morality, and it is thanks to this moralizing tendency that his criticism is acceptable to an extremely moral society; he does not depict vice either under alluring forms, as the French did, or under forms so totally repugnant that they shock the moral sense, but rather as it is depicted by a preacher, so that it remains always in the world of logic and argument and never descends to the point of direct, emotional contact. The thrill of intuitive, electrical contact is lacking in Thackeray: his appeal is to the mind of his reader rather than to his emotional experience. (p. 207)

[In] contrast to Carlyle who exalts the hero, whom he puts forward as a combined reproof and pattern to an anti-heroic, bourgeois age, Thackeray sets himself up as deliberately anti-heroic, even to the title of his most famous novel—*Vanity Fair, a Novel without a Hero*. The virtuous, in his novels, are intellectually inferior to the wicked, and all claim to superhuman or heroic qualities is excluded, even from virtue, to a point when the reader begins to wonder whether virtue and imbecility are not the same thing. Christian humility? This quality, certainly, has been observed in Thackeray, and corresponds perfectly to one of the aspects of Biedermeier, that of the revival of Christian meekness and resignation. (p. 213)

The very conception that Thackeray formed of the superior man is an anti-heroic conception. The hero, for Thackeray, is not an exceptional man; he is, rather, a man just like other men who only 'in the presence of the great occasion' is capable of showing his superiority over other men; when the critical moment is over, he falls back into normality, into mediocrity. Thackeray's conception of the hero, therefore, is relative, not absolute. His ideal is not so much an individual, as a rule of conduct—the gentleman. . . . (pp. 224-25)

The tone of Thackeray's sentimentalism is naturally, when it displays itself, elegiac. Elegiac, too, and not cruel (as they would be, were the novelist perfectly logical) are the endings of Thackeray's novels. . . .

Elegiac and melancholy, also, is Thackeray's attitude towards modern progress. In this he is a bourgeois of the Lamb type, not of the Macaulay type which hails the latest scientific discoveries with delight. The eyes of Thackeray are turned towards the past. (p. 240)

That is the reason why Thackeray's novels are by perference set in the past, and that is why the most successful parts of them are always the descriptions of the protagonists' youth—Pendennis, Clive, Warrington, Philip. It is romantic, this idolizing of the past; but romantic in a calm, middle-class, Biedermeier manner. . . . [The 'disenchanted' Thackeray] reserved his sense of wonder and enchantment for the past. He too projected himself into a form of exoticism. And he wrote *Esmond* in the language of the past. Of the past, it was chiefly the private life, the family atmosphere, that he saw; not the great political events, the social and economic currents. . . . Thackeray, then, sees the past in the light of a dream; and he sees the past as an environment, as an atmosphere, not in the form of great historical figures. It is a curious contradiction in him that, on the one hand, he demolishes the epic point of view, on the other, he yearns nostalgically towards the past; this is his fundamental ambiguity—to be anti-romantic but not satisfied with the present. (p. 243)

[He] avoids strong scenes; he prefers psychological analysis to description of feelings, or rather he replaces both effect and emotion by a corresponding logical thread, and prefers a picture to a dramatic scene; that is, instead of identifying himself with his characters, he stops to contemplate them, and, as he does

so, their voices die in their throats, as if the sound apparatus of a film came suddenly to a halt. (p. 254)

[Just] as the modesty of Thackeray is the modesty of Jane Austen, but without magic, so is his style the style of Addison, but again without magic. Here, in fact, is the eighteenth century turned bourgeois, gone flat. . . . [The] ideal at which Thackeray aimed [was] simplicity and precision. And evidently he thought he had attained to it. . . . [Yet simplicity], to be a virtue, must be 'essential' . . . : a precise style with a fascination that might be described as geometrical, a style made for communication rather than for magical persuasiveness. Now in Thackeray simplicity is not 'essential': he is familiar, he is verbose; pages of his essays might with advantage be condensed; or rather, as one reads them, one is tempted to skip entire sentences which are mere sequences of *clichés*, paraphrases, and commonplaces. . . . Thackeray often says things that were not worth saying, and in a form that does not even confer a memorable accent upon commonplaces, as happens, for example, in Pope. (pp. 257-59)

A poet, a great artist, Thackeray is not; but within the compass of an honest, genuine, bourgeois *sermo pedestris* [plain conversation] he attains an excellence of his own; he is, as he himself said, *vin ordinaire* [ordinary wine], but from a good cask, 'from the right tap.' . . . Flaubert, who did not worry about being a gentleman, gives a complete portrait of Madame Bovary, pitilessly showing up every corner of her soul. But a modest gentleman like Thackeray could not do the same with Becky Sharp. Charlotte Brontë, taking up one of Thackeray's metaphors, wrote: 'He, I see, keeps the mermaid's tail below water, and only hints at the dead men's bones and noxious slime amidst which it wriggles.' And we seem to see him, this faultlessly dressed gentleman, holding down the mermaid in her pool, with a grappling-hook—for fear the splashes should soil his clothes: and, to tell the truth, we believe in the mermaid's tail only because the placard informs us of it; actually all that we see is a young lady of respectable appearance. So much, and no more, could be done to provide Victorian eyes with a representation of Evil. Imagine the stir that a *Madame Bovary* would have caused in that world, and compare the picturesque, sentimental-romance superficialities of *Pendennis* with the bitter experience of *L'Éducation sentimentale!* (p. 260)

*Mario Praz, "William Makepeace Thackeray," in his* The Hero in Eclipse in Victorian Fiction, *translated by Angus Davidson (© Oxford University Press 1956; reprinted by permission of Oxford University Press; originally published as* La crisi dell'eroe nel romanzo vittoriano, *G. C. Sansoni, 1952), Oxford University Press, London, 1956, pp. 189-260.*

**JOHN A. LESTER, JR.**  (essay date 1954)

[*Lester's analysis of Thackeray's narrative method is one of the most important studies of his literary technique. Lester discusses in detail Thackeray's device of chronological redoubling, found throughout the novels. He maintains that the memoir form in which nearly all Thackeray's novels are written provides him with the perfect temporal relationship to his story, and give him a "view of all events spread out at once before him." Responding to critics such as Percy Lubbock (1926) who maintain that Thackeray fails in his depiction of the dramatic moment, Lester argues that Thackeray consciously employed the method of redoubling in order to catch "the enduring response which is remembered for a lifetime."*]

Students of Thackeray have long observed in his novels a singular attitude toward time. He looks with an Olympian view on his characters and events, and sees the course of his story laid out as it were in panorama before him. Over this panorama he can look before and after, moving backwards and forwards freely in time, selecting detailed scenes here or there as he chooses. . . .

Using this freedom of motion, Thackeray characteristically doubles backwards and forwards in the course of telling his story. The redoublings are there in his first substantial work of fiction (*Catherine* . . .), and they remain a major narrative device in his final and incomplete novel, *Denis Duval*. . . . (p. 393)

These characteristic redoublings may be ascribed in part to a natural bent, the Thackerayan "roundabout manner." In his non-fictional prose he often proceeds in the same back-and-forth fashion, not only in the *Roundabout Papers* but in *English Humourists* and *The Four Georges* as well. The great majority of the redoublings in his fiction, however, stem from a deeper cause than this, and reveal Thackeray's subtle motives as a craftsman. A survey of the whole range of his reversals in chronology suggests two main types of motivation which may lie behind them. The first includes those redoublings which Thackeray employs in order to solve specific technical problems in telling his story; the second includes motives of thought and temperament of which one suspects Thackeray himself was not always fully aware. (p. 394)

Many of Thackeray's redoublings result from his instinct to plunge "into the midst of things." A dramatic scene, drawn from the full course of the action, brings the reader at once into the story. It stakes a strong claim on his interest. But at the same time it raises questions: who are these characters? what are their motives? The plunge in medias res brings as its inevitable consequence the doubling back, the recapitulation of what has gone before.

The best illustrations of Thackeray's use of this device are found in the opening chapters of his novels. . . . [He] has thoroughly mastered the device of starting his novel in the midst of things, and of doubling back to gather up the background explanations later. (pp. 394-95)

Continually, as he proceeds, Thackeray stores up events and developments to be related later. (p. 395)

One cannot long examine the chronological pattern of Thackeray's novels without becoming aware of a second technical problem which confronted him—the necessity of adapting his narrative for publication in instalments or separate parts. . . . There can be no doubt that this method of publication directly influenced the form and narrative technique of his fiction. From the time of his first extensive narrative published in instalments (*Catherine* . . .), Thackeray was aware that his story had to be shaped accordingly.

Very frequently Thackeray's method is to end an instalment or part with a sudden new turn of plot. It may be a leap forward to a scene well in the future, requiring in the next instalment an explanation-retrospect of the sort we have considered. It may be simply a dramatic episode. . . . The essence is that the number end on a note of suspense, a promise of events to be explained and characters' reactions to be studied. (pp. 395-96)

A final technical motive behind Thackeray's chronological redoublings lies in the nature of his subject-matter, in his desire to present a panoramic picture of society. . . . The doublings back to pick up different threads of the story, new scenes from the pageant of society, are by no means confined to *Vanity Fair*. More reversals in chronological sequence in the major novels can be attributed to this motive than to any other single cause. These findings point to the truth of Lord David Cecil's view that in all Thackeray's novels the panorama of life is the real subject [see excerpt above, 1934]. . . . Every Thackeray novel is in some degree a novel without a hero; in all of them the chief protagonist is society itself. Characters from his other novels enter and depart. They bring a sense that each story is selected from a large society which lives on outside the novels and independent of them. Thackeray is never happier than when in the midst of a large and varied number of characters, diverse incidents, and numerous interwoven plots, all clamoring to be told and commented on. (pp. 397-98)

The total of all the redoublings which can thus be ascribed to motives of technique accounts for rather more than half of the redoublings in Thackeray's fiction. They can be counted as technical devices, part of his strategy to keep the narrative alive and moving on from one installment to the next.

There remains a substantial number of redoublings in Thackeray's work where the motive is not primarily technical and where the search for a cause leads us deeper into the mind and quality of Thackeray as an artist. (p. 398)

Thackeray is more interested in his characters' reactions to events than he is in the events themselves. Many of his strongest effects—and not a few of his weaknesses—can be traced directly to this deep predisposition of his art. Around any dramatic incident in his narrative Thackeray will search tirelessly to explore its repercussions in the minds and sentiments of his characters. The action as such may seem to get buried beneath the comments of Thackeray and the characters upon it. (p. 399)

From Thackeray's work as a whole one may derive this generally valid formula: the more explosive and unexpected the scene, the more eager Thackeray is to explore different characters' reactions to it. That is to say . . . , the more explosive the scene, the more redoublings are set in motion as a result of it. . . . Wherever a turn of the plot closely affects the hearts and ambitions of his characters, Thackeray will follow its ramifications wherever they lead. (pp. 399-400)

Every reader of Thackeray has noticed what may be called the retrospective vision in his work, the fondness for looking backward, the glowing effects of nostalgic memory which he can command. The sources of this mood of retrospect are subtle and deeply imbedded in Thackeray's temperament. . . .

The "reminiscential manner" has direct effect on Thackeray's handling of chronological sequence in his narrative. Among his important novels, all but *Pendennis* are written to some degree as "memoirs" and told by a narrator in later years, after all the events of the narrative are past. This memoir pose gives Thackeray precisely the time relationship to his story which he desired to maintain—the view of all events spread out at once in a panorama before him. We see him in his first eager and extensive exploitation of this vantage-point in *Barry Lyndon,* where the recurring glances from present prosperity to future despair provide much of the delightfully ironic self-revelation of the tale. In his last novel, *Denis Duval,* he acknowledges explicitly the technique which has served him so well: "Why do I make zigzag journeys? 'Tis the privilege of old age to be garrulous, and its happiness to remember early days." . . . The writer of memoirs has freedom to move back and forth over the whole range of events, following any theme where it leads him.

Using this freedom, Thackeray gains new strength in his rôle as "social preacher." He sees human virtues and vanities in the long result of time. (p. 400)

[He] can view his characters now in the press of present action, now in the mature and deliberate retrospect of after life. (p. 401)

Coincident with Thackeray's doublings backward and forward in time as he tells the story is another characteristic narrative device—his variation between the method of telling the story personally, in his own words, and that of presenting it in dramatic scenes. It soon proves futile to survey simply these two poles of author-presentation and dramatic enactment. A Thackeray novel displays not only the two poles but every shade and variety of narrative presentation in between. The varieties of intermediate "semi-scenes" which he invents for his narrative shed new light on his purpose as a novelist.

It can be said to begin with that one's general impression in reading Thackeray is correct—he is reluctant to embark on a direct, dramatic scene. He makes little deliberate effort to prepare for a scene, and when one does arrive, he reserves at all times the liberty to intrude and interject comments of his own. (p. 402)

Many detailed observations of Thackeray's handling of the scene go to support this general conclusion. He very rarely gives us, for example, a scene which in its sheer drama or "theater" is felt to be presented for its own sake. His most memorable moments . . . are remembered not for the action that takes place, but for the vivid development and re-alignment of character which they suddenly announce. There are a few Thackeray scenes where the unfolding of dramatic action is the author's main concern. . . . But usually Thackeray will circumvent the *scène à faire* [necessary scene] entirely. (pp. 402-03)

Another trait of Thackeray's narrative which reveals his lack of concern for the dramatic scene as such is his vagueness in locating scenes in time and place. Often as the first character speaks we do not know where or when the episode is taking place, or to whom the lines are spoken. Voices are heard first in a Thackeray scene; the fixing of the conversation in time and place, even the identification of all the characters present, are left till later on, if indeed they are revealed at all. . . . In most of Thackeray's scenes traces of this vagueness can be found; they are scenes often without time or setting, conversations from that Fable-land from which Thackeray assures us his characters have come.

Between the direct author-narration in Thackeray's novels and the rare dramatic scenes lies a host of varied and hybrid "semi-scenes." They are infinite in variety; they defy systematic description or classification. (pp. 403-04)

The most common and revealing type of semi-scene in Thackeray presents scene and dialogue not as of a specific time and place, but as a sample of the habitual speech and action of the characters. The habitual scene is usually clearly marked by the "Clive would say" or the "Captain Rawdon often said" which introduces it. The habitual verb may be simply a method of approaching the scene; from the "would say" of the introduction the scene moves quickly into sharper and more specific focus. (p. 404)

Moving across the broad expanse of his imagined history, Thackeray developed an extraordinary art of "hedgehopping," jumping from one incident to another yet somehow fusing the fragmentary intermittent impressions into a whole scenic sequence. The result can be a chaos of disjointed detail, but it rarely is. By virtue of his peculiar detachment, the timeless wisdom of his comment on events and character, Thackeray can touch the intermittent scene with magic. It becomes a delicate balance of scene and summary, of the voices and actions of people plus an acceleration of tempo which reveals their meaning and consequence. (pp. 404-05)

The intermittent scene sacrifices much of the actuality of the dramatic scene fully prepared for and performed, but it gains something which was apparently more important to Thackeray: a coalescence of characteristic speech and action with the long-range moral perspective of the social preacher. . . . In all of Thackeray's novels there are scattered bits of speech and dialogue, flung out in the course of author-narration as being somehow typical of the accent and manner of a character being referred to. Only rarely is the interjected quote accompanied by any gesture or visualized action; hardly ever does it conjure up a sense of specific scene. (p. 405)

[Yet the] interjected quotation lends a vitality to Thackeray's long blocks of commentary; not the vitality of an actual dramatic scene, but of the spoken voice suddenly heard through the author's narration, clear, with its distinctive accent. There are abundant examples of the interjected quotation in Thackeray's fiction, from first to last. It is admirably suited to his bent as a novelist, for it allows him freedom to reminisce over his narrative at will, yet always be able to call on his characters to speak their own words and confirm the point he is making.

The types of semi-scene which Thackeray resorts to could be enumerated almost indefinitely. There are purely allegorical scenes . . . connected only by implication with the action of the story, imagined scenes, where Thackeray confesses that he does not know precisely what took place, but he "fancies" it "must have been" something like this, reported scenes, in which the characters' direct discourse is paradoxically rendered indirectly; there are even times when Thackeray invites the reader to look to his own experience and compose his own scene as he pleases. There is seemingly no end to Thackeray's invention of semidramatic scenes.

Faced with such a bewildering array of devices for avoiding dramatic enactment of the story, one is forced to seek the governing motive behind them. Thackeray's invention of scenes midway between author-narration and dramatic presentation is always resourceful and usually effective. But what leads him to apply his inventiveness in this direction in the first place?

From the evidence of the scenes alone we can derive a portion of the answer. There is one quality which is shared in common by all these types of semi-scene—they are all in some degree *illustrative*. They are all offered as being significant because, beyond their artistic value as discriminated occasions, they illustrate a truth of character or human behavior which Thackeray means to convey. It goes without saying that his allegorical scenes exist primarily to illustrate a general moral truth. It is nearly as obvious that his habitual scenes do the same; they convey enduring, recurrent traits of character rather than momentary or chance reactions under the stress of an actual scene. Again, the onset of a scene in Thackeray is very commonly heralded by a generalized comment. . . .The scene then follows to illustrate this general truth. In Thackeray's early work the illustrative character of his scenes is occasionally explicit; certain scenes in *Catherine, The Ravenswing,* and *Barry Lyndon* are introduced by a ''for example,'' or ''for instance.'' In his mature fiction the illustrative quality of the scene is less deliberately pointed, but it remains a distinctive characteristic of his scenic method. It reveals an essential quality of Thackeray's orientation to the craft of fiction. (pp. 406-07)

It is clear that fidelity to a particular moment in time, or to systematic chronological sequence, is not essential to his creative art. He is most at ease when he has ample freedom to roam backwards and forwards ''timelessly.'' It is equally plain that his creative energy is most active when it is not confined to the time and setting of a specific scene to be acted out; he moves most freely when he can bob in and out of the action, select, synthesize, and comment.

We have evidence for one further delimitation of Thackeray's artistic range: he is not primarily interested in the portrayal of individualized, self-operative fictional characters. There is some familiar evidence which would seem to suggest such a conclusion—Thackeray's forgetfulness of the names of his characters, his recurrent reference to them as puppets, his selection of stereotype names for minor characters . . . ; but all of these may be accounted for by traits of mind and temper quite peripheral to Thackeray's creative genius. More pertinent would be the evidence suggested by Lord David Cecil that there is patent inconsistency in some of Thackeray's major characterizations, though it is difficult to feel that such inconsistencies have been conclusively demonstrated.

What is provided by a survey of Thackeray's narrative technique is a wealth of other evidence, woven deeply and consistently through all of Thackeray's fiction, which points in essentially the same direction. In Thackeray's doublings away from the specific time of an action, his lightning switches from a characterization now to a characterization ''in after years,'' there is implied an urge to catch not the eccentricity or special vividness of the moment, but the enduring response which is remembered for a lifetime. In his withdrawals from the actual to the habitual scene there is the same motive at work. What is true of characters at any one moment is not so important to Thackeray as what is true of them in the long run and in retrospect, when they are seen under the glance of eternity, and interpreted in the light of timeless moral comment. In the occasional scenes which are referred to the reader's own experience for confirmation there is the clearest evidence that it is the lasting truth of human nature, rather than the random truth of diverse individuals, that lies closest to the heart of Thackeray's creation. To embrace the enduring emotions and experience of his characters, the author's own chorus of comment is heard persistently, echoing the worldly wisdom of a lifetime. . . . (pp. 407-09)

It is what his characters represent that is the sure and stable center in Thackeray's work. The timeless and enduring traits of human nature are what he seeks to evoke, and to this purpose his entire narrative technique has been shaped and modified. . . . His concern is not so much with the scene vividly realized as with the worldly wisdom and truth that may be abstracted from it. He devoted all his craftsmanship to the task of sifting out that wisdom from the pageant that moved before him in his novels. He invented an entire range of narrative devices with which he could discriminate and reflect the essence of the characters and events he was portraying. To have evolved for this special purpose a distinctive style, an original management of time, and countless new shades of scenic pre-

sentation is more than to have developed a ''Thackerayan manner''; it is the mark of genius. (p. 409)

*John A. Lester, Jr., ''Thackeray's Narrative Technique,'' in PMLA, 69 (copyright © 1954 by the Modern Language Association of America; reprinted by permission of the Modern Language Association of America), Vol. LXIX, No. 3, June, 1954, pp. 392-409.*

## KATHLEEN TILLOTSON (essay date 1954)

*Vanity Fair,* more than any later novel save *Esmond,* bears the marks of what Trollope called 'forethought . . . the elbow-grease of the novelist'; and more than any, it has at the same time the buoyant improvisation in detail arising from the practised skill of the journalist. (p. 225)

By choosing as his field 'the debatable land between the middle classes and the aristocracy' [see excerpt above by W. C. Roscoe, 1856] he takes a social area which, though less extensive than Dickens's gives him considerable vertical range. (pp. 235-36)

There is less scope for oddity than in Dickens's world, for Vanity Fair is a world in which it is important to conform. Those who give up the pretence of conforming, like Sir Pitt Crawley or Lord Steyne, show that Thackeray can provide his own grotesques with only the monstrosity which actual life provides. Specific comparison with Dickens illustrates Thackeray's different attitude to reality: the observed reality is often the same, but Thackeray mines into it, where Dickens makes it a springboard into fantasy. Even in his names Thackeray wishes 'to convey the sentiment of reality'. Dickens's may be actual, but they are chosen for their oddity and comic appropriateness, while Thackeray masks his satire in plausibility, preferring a subtle suggestiveness; as in 'Steyne', with its pun and its relation to Regency Brighton; or the contrast, rich in association, of the liquid and romantic 'Amelia Sedley' with the hinted racial astuteness of 'Rebecca Sharp'.

Thackeray's characters exist in a denser context than perhaps any characters in fiction. (p. 236)

[They] are so mixed, so often on a moral borderland, so subject to time, and also so gradually unfolded—often with unpredictable detail—that they do not give the impression of being static. But they are not shown as evolving, nor do they undergo much inward conflict; and so the unity given to a novel by dominating or developing characters is not found. Only one of Thackeray's novels—*Pendennis*—is even formally built upon the fortunes of a single character; and Arthur Pendennis is less an interesting individual than a nineteenth-century variant of Everyman.

Without recourse to obvious devices, without a hero or heroine or any single central figure, without any 'inward' study of development in character, Thackeray nevertheless makes us feel *Vanity Fair* a unity. This has sometimes been underestimated, and the novel apologized for as loose, rambling, and casual, though admitted to be rich and comprehensive: the apology may even lay the blame on the serial form. But the serial novel, serially written, is . . . really the less likely to be loose and rambling; only some degree of forethought makes such writing even possible. . . . (pp. 239-40)

The clear and obvious line of progression in the novel is surely also, when closely considered, the chief of its unities: that is, the converging and diverging, parallel and contrasting fortunes of the two girls, Rebecca Sharp and Amelia Sedley. In narrative terms, the basis of the contrast is simple (the moral contrast, on the other hand, is ironic and complex); it is that Rebecca attempts actively to shape her own fortunes, while Amelia passively accepts hers. (pp. 240-41)

If Thackeray has an ideal [of womanhood] in mind, then Amelia and Becky are both far (though not equally far) removed from it; of the disproportion between heart and brain possible to the feminine character they provide extreme instances. Some readers may be more legitimately misled by the necessary difference in treatment. The active Becky can be displayed, where the suffering, yielding Amelia must be described. The tone of the description is deliberately ambiguous, seeming often sentimentally protective, but with enough impatience breaking through to show that the author wishes to confuse and make fun of the sentimental reader. It is not necessary to attribute confusion to Thackeray himself; there is room with such a character for genuine indulgence as well as impatience. Besides, he has an ulterior, 'literary' motive in Amelia: Becky is a wholly new kind of heroine, Amelia the old kind ironically exposed. . . . Becky is one of those characters—like Chaucer's Pardoner—who can fully engage our aesthetic sympathies while defying most of our moral ones; Thackeray is not less a moralist for allowing us to enjoy her as a spectacle, for his judgement of her is firm. (pp. 245-46)

There is a moral comment in the fact that Becky's downfall comes through the relations that she most despised; it is the innocent and stupid who confound her. She calculates brilliantly, but, like Iago, not quite brilliantly enough. . . . Contempt for other people is necessary to successful villainy; but within it lie the seeds of its own defeat. The walls of egoism rise, in the end, too high. By suggesting all this, Thackeray does more than condemn Becky; he gives a less pessimistic moral direction to his story. Goodness is not wholly ineffectual.

These, then, are some of the ways in which Thackeray gives shape and purpose to his great pictorial mass; but the most important way has been often undervalued by later readers, because misunderstood. The whole is 'brilliantly illuminated by the author's own candles'; Thackeray is constantly present, commenting on the action. . . . [He] is frankly the manufacturer of the narrative ('there are some terrific chapters coming presently'); he is the 'producer' of particular characters (especially of Amelia, who can do so little for herself); he is by turns the responsible, omniscient narrator ('for novelists have the privilege of knowing everything'), the irresponsible, baffled spectator ('Was she guilty or not?'), even the mere reporter. . . . The atmosphere of his personality—not his private, but his artistic personality—envelops the story. (pp. 250-52)

His commentary is in part a bridge between past and present, suggesting what time changes, what it leaves unchanged; putting past and present alike in a longer perspective. And it is a moral perspective. . . . Without Thackeray's own voice, the melancholy and the compassion of his attitude to Vanity Fair might escape us. It is needed merely as relief, from a spectacle that might otherwise be unbearably painful. And not only morally painful, but mentally impoverished. The characters, the best as well as the worst, are almost without ideas; the intellectual atmosphere of the novel is provided by the commentary. (p. 253)

Thackeray does not escape into commentary from any weakness in presentation; *Vanity Fair* is particularly rich in single scenes which reveal his power of presenting characters and

action without comment, through dialogue, grouping, and gesture. Nor is he impulsively allowing his stored reflections to overflow; the effect of casualness in the commentary is as calculated as in Sterne. The commentary is itself art, selective and economical. Thackeray never tells everything; he leaves much to be read between the lines; the tone of intimate confidence often masks a real reserve. He knows when not to comment directly at all. (p. 254)

The commentary springs also from Thackeray's wish to 'convey the sentiment of reality'. Through it he openly admits, as no modern novelist dare, *all* the relations of the novelist to his story. . . . The great picture is not the less great from our final awareness that we and the author stand outside its frame. The words are a recall to life and individual responsibility as the preacher lays his cap and bells aside. (pp. 255-56)

> *Kathleen Tillotson, "Four Novels: 'Vanity Fair',"*
> *in her* Novels of the Eighteen-Forties *(reprinted by permission of Oxford University Press), Oxford University Press, Oxford, 1954, pp. 224-56.*

## A. E. DYSON (essay date 1964)

[*Dyson's essay on* Vanity Fair *is regarded as one of the best considerations of Thackeray's social criticism. Through a detailed discussion of Amelia Sedley and Beckey Sharp, he explores the effect that society, or Vanity Fair, has on morality. Dyson concludes that it is Thackeray's considerable capacity for compassion that makes* Vanity Fair *an enduring work of art.*]

Thackeray claims, as a novelist, the right to be a total realist, and that realism meant, for him, coming to terms with a radically unheroic world. . . .

*Vanity Fair* is surely one of the world's most devious novels, devious in its characterisation, its irony, its explicit moralising, its exuberance, its tone. Few novels demand more continuing alertness from the reader, or offer more intellectual and moral stimulation in return. (p. 12)

[Thackeray] said of himself on one occasion that he was created with 'a sense of the ugly, the odd, of the meanly false, of the desperately wicked'. The intensity with which he always responded to the human comedy pushed him towards a more radical criticism of society than perhaps he intended. . . . One sees how readily his temperamental restlessness responded to the restlessness of Vanity Fair itself—to its noise and bustle, its surface gaiety, its instinctive cruelty, its truthlessness and faithlessness, its occasional courage and resilience, its desolating lack of heart's ease.

Such considerations lead us very naturally towards Thackeray's pervasive ambivalence of tone. Where does he stand in relationship to his characters, and to their world? Does he come to them chiefly as friend or foe? The explicit indications of attitude, which are numerous enough, and to some readers offensive, do not take us very far. In the opening pages—beautifully and hauntingly written, like so much that is to follow them—he presents himself as a puppet-master, the sole creator of his characters, and their destiny. . . . [Yet] *Vanity Fair* turns out to be a novel where the puppet-master is, after all, bound by the iron discipline of his own greatness. The characters come alive, and their creator cannot blacken or praise them superficially without his readers detecting and resenting the lie; they come alive in the real world of human morality, where every complexity of sensitive response must be allowed for, where the creator fully approves of such complexity or not. . . . [Becky Sharp] defies any rule of characterisation that simple logic might prescribe, and becomes as familiar and unpredictable as if we had known her all our lives. Thackeray, of course, knew when his characters came alive as well as we do, and his rôle of puppet-master is only one of the various *personae* he adopts. Sometimes, he claims the puppet-master's privilege of knowing his characters' secret thoughts, and telling us what these are. But at other times he is reticent, as one would be in life. . . . (pp. 12-13)

The reader of *Vanity Fair* soon finds other evidence to belie the notion that artifice and contrivance are all. To an unusual degree we have the sense of a real world going on all round the main characters, full of diversity and colour, full of characters who appear and disappear, enacting at the edge of our consciousness the same patterns of sin and anxiety which hold the centre of the stage. This use of surrounding detail and seeming irrelevance to reinforce the main structure of the book reminds us of Sterne; as, to a lesser extent, does the fluidity of the time-scale that Thackeray adopts. Though there is nothing as obviously eccentric as the digressions and flash-backs of *Tristram Shandy*, we find that Thackeray's narrative does shift backwards and forwards in time in a way not always easy to chart. The effect is of a 'real world' into which the novelist's memory dips rather than of an artificial world which he creates as he goes along. Later in the novel, Thackeray represents himself as a man who learns of all the main events by hearsay. The omniscient narrator, the preacher in cap-and-bells, gives way to this further *persona,* middle-aged, curious and detached.

To learn caution about Thackeray's role as puppet-master is to learn caution about the explicit moral judgments of which the novel is full. Some modern critics have blamed Thackeray for saying too much, but this is surely a naive misunderstanding of his technique. The tradition of commenting upon characters goes back at least to Fielding, but even in *Tom Jones* we are kept continuously on the alert. . . . Fielding adopts the pose of a conventional moralist as a challenge, forcing us to match our personal wits and sense of values against his own. In *Vanity Fair* Thackeray pursues a similar strategy, with ironic overtones even subtler in their range. We are reminded of Fielding's influence in the knowing, man-of-the-world asides; in the ferocity, the gusto almost, with which various kinds of hypocrisy are exposed. There is even something of Sterne in Thackeray's willingness to act the fool, to claim the cap-and-bells as his own. But the prevailing tone of *Vanity Fair* is very different from Fielding's, and *a fortiori* [all the more] from Sterne's. There is a lack of warmth about it in certain moods. . . . For though Thackeray's iconoclasm is in part exuberant, it also has a tinge of bitterness; it is nearer than Fielding and Sterne ever are to despair. Very readily the teasing and flamboyance give way, at moments of strain, to the tone of the preacher, no longer in cap-and-bells, but solemn and prophetic now in his own right. The title of the novel is taken from Bunyan, and though Thackeray has nothing of Bunyan's clear-cut doctrine to depend upon, he shares the occasional mood of a Wisdom writer; religious judgments are inescapably present, though not directly expressed. In the introductory note **"Before the Curtain"**, we are warned of the melancholy induced by Vanity Fair—a melancholy which gives rise to, and shades into, compassion for the suffering and transience of man. Behind the ostensible warmth of tone, which we can never rely on, there is warmth of a deeper and costlier kind. We are involved in the fate of the characters we laugh at, not distanced from them;

it really matters to us to know what happens to them in the end.

Obviously Thackeray's tone is a complex affair, where local nuances relate to the strategy of the whole. We are always left wondering what to make of it, whether it really is as simple, or as moderately simple, as it is dressed out to seem. There is the rather arch playfulness, for instance, which surrounds both Becky and Amelia: is this simply a sentimental evasiveness on Thackeray's part, or does it serve some more devious end? On the surface, the archness is tender towards Amelia, sharp (like her name) towards Becky; yet its eventual effect is to diminish Amelia, whilst making Becky appear interesting, and even great. Around Amelia Thackeray deliberately creates a cloying tone, apparently in order to confirm the complacency of his readers, yet really to create in them a growing unease: what *are* these virtues we are being so cosily invited to admire? How *can* we respond with this degree of whimsy to an adult? Around Becky, however, the same tone plays with very different effect. Throughout the novel, she is referred to as 'our little schemer', very much as one might speak of a naughty but not wholly unsympathetic child. (pp. 13-15)

In the contrast between Becky and Amelia, the moral characters of the two girls are always involved. At a very deep level, Thackeray was critical of them both. The notion that his attitude to either can be taken at face value can survive only for a reader of the most superficial kind. . . .

On the face of it, Amelia is the virtuous girl of the two, sweet and gentle, though with a helplessness that soon begins to cloy. . . . As the novel progresses, her future is increasingly overshadowed by fears, and we sense that she is destined to be a casualty in the battle of life.

Her virtues also turn out to be more tainted than they at first appear. Her great claim to virtue is the passiveness of self-sacrifice, yet is self-sacrifice, as she practises it, not an insidious self-indulgence in disguise? (p. 17)

Becky, in contrast, is ostensibly bad, yet her heroic qualities shine out against Amelia's faults. She is sparkling, clever and resilient; from her earliest years she has had to live by her wits, and if the world is against her, is this not mainly because she inherited neither status nor wealth? (p. 18)

[It] is clear that Thackeray overstates the conventional case against Becky knowingly and deliberately, as the case against Tom Jones was overstated by Fielding. When we ask how we come to detect this, and in any way at all to be on Becky's side, the answer takes us nearer to the heart of the book. At one level, it may be simply that Becky's courage and resilience are admirable in themselves, whether they are applied for good or ill; in this familiar sense Thackeray may be of his heroine's party without knowing it, or more likely, knowing it slightly better than he would wish. Another possibility is that our sympathy with Becky is sentimental or indulgent and little more. Some critics, indeed, have written as though this were true of Thackeray himself. His 'sentimentality' can be dissociated, they suggest, from his 'irony', and regarded as a balance on the other side: when bitter censoriousness has brought Becky down, good-natured sentimentality brings her up again. Tears and laughter alternate like April weather, and the author is simply a creature of his moods. Such a view is . . . extremely superficial, but where Becky is concerned there may be a particular reason why it appeals. Criminals always *are* easier to sympathise with from a distance, in literature as in life; Becky is undeniably a character more easy to forgive when she is safely contained in the pages of a book. (pp. 18-19)

The fact is that she *belongs* to Vanity Fair, both as its true reflection, and as its victim; for both of which reasons, she very resoundingly serves it right. Like Jonson's Volpone, she is a fitting scourge for the world which created her—fitting aesthetically, in the way of poetic justice, and fittingly moral, in that much of her evil is effective only against those who share her taint. Dobbin is largely immune to her, since he is neither a trifler, a hypocrite nor a snob. The other characters are all vulnerable in one or other of these ways, and we notice that those who judge her most harshly are frequently the ones who have least earned such a right.

The right to judge is, of course, the crux, for Vanity Fair is a social place, and no critique of individual characters can be conducted in a void. What Thackeray comes near to suggesting, like Bunyan before him, is that a society based upon privilege and money is rotten in some fundamental sense. The very concepts of Christian morality become, in such a context, an evasion; an attempt to visit upon the underprivileged and the unprotected sins which more properly belong to society at large. . . . Almost every sin in Vanity Fair can be traced, beyond personal weakness, to the fundamental laws of money and class; to fawn upon the rich and kick the poor is a Christian law of the land. . . . The poor have more than their chains to lose in Vanity Fair; they have their opportunities for hurting one another as well. If Thackeray went less far than the Marxists in political analysis, it may have been (to give him the benefit of the doubt) because his view of human nature was correspondingly gloomier than theirs.

The whole institution of marriage is bound up with these attitudes, as Thackeray is also concerned to bring home. . . . He was reticent about physical love, as all Victorians were, but in *Vanity Fair* there are franknesses that can shock us even now. Becky, for instance, is not a sensual woman at all; given wealth and social position, she would have managed without sexual adventures fairly well. She is willing to marry Joseph Sedley for all his absurdity; and our very revulsion from this, if we experience revulsion, may be only a sentimental lack of realism about marriage of our own. In Vanity Fair, as Thackeray depicts it, sex is as little reverenced or respected as anything else. On the one hand, it is a subject for endless gossip and malice. . . . And on the other hand, it is a powerful asset to a mother looking round for a good catch for her daughter. Though the weaklings of the world like Amelia may think only of love, a mother will think rather of physical attractiveness and charm. These are the true assets she has to trade with in the marriage market—assets almost as substantial as the dowry itself, though who doubts that money speaks a little louder in the end?

In all such matters Thackeray reports faithfully and even ferociously what the world is like, with a directness that speaks very strikingly across a hundred years of sexual emancipation to ourselves. (pp. 19-21)

Our sympathy with Becky, to return to this, is so closely connected with as to be almost inseparable from the context of Thackeray's social realism. Even while conventional judgments are being made against her, a social background is movingly, if less noisily, sketched. . . . In a society using Christian values almost wholly perversely, resilience and energy are forced to know themselves, in a Becky, as conventional sins. For this reason too we forgive her, for we see how little right society

has to judge her as it does. She is indeed its reflection, and interesting to us largely because she has the courage and energy, though so heavily handicapped, to play its game. We notice that though she employs hypocrisy, she is never taken in by it herself; she does not make her sin a virtue, and is to this degree preferable to those who do. She is never revengeful or consciously hard-hearted; she is able (a really saving grace) to laugh at herself exactly as though she were someone else.

Reflecting upon this, we see the deeper purposes Thackeray must have in mind. To a much larger extent than we would expect, Becky's judgements on people are the novelist's own. . . . Because she sees the standards by which the world actually lives in such sharp contrast with the standards by which it professes to live, she can judge as well as exploit it in its chosen terms. For, indeed, she belongs to Vanity Fair herself, and reform, whether for herself or for it, is very far from her thought. She glories in the world's game with all the superior energy and intelligence that she can command. It may even be fair, if one thinks in these terms, that the comparatively innocent should have to suffer along with the rest. (pp. 21-2)

Becky's character rises in our esteem as that of her victims sinks. How could her gaiety and courage have expressed themselves in any more worthy way? Had she been born to position or power, she would have risen nobly to the rôle. . . . She could have been a Queen, we are told, if she had been born to it; and it is apparent enough that she could.

Lacking, however, these natural advantages, Becky knows that the appearance of respectability and wealth must be sought for instead. And since Vanity Fair is as much pleased with the appearance as the reality, until such time as the discrepancy is seen through and the hunt can begin, Becky has all her intuitive understanding of its values on her side. (p. 22)

Again and again Thackeray reminds us that we, too, belong to Vanity Fair. To condemn Becky easily is *a fortiori* to condemn ourselves; how are we to make any judgment without resorting to hypocrisies deeper and more shameful than her own? The imaginative power of Thackeray's vision forces the reality of this dilemma upon us; some further dimension must be sought before we can be sure that we have the right. Should it be the religious dimension, perhaps, to which the word 'vanity' directs us? Or the political one, to which the whole analysis of class and money appears to point? (p. 23)

[We] can by no means be sure how far Thackeray would have committed himself in such ways. . . . Most of his explicit comments reinforce the notion that he is criticising human individuals rather than the structure of society as a whole, yet the novel's pattern, I have tried to show, prevents us from leaving the matter comfortably at this.

Perhaps Thackeray never did decide how far the poison at work in Vanity Fair is a social sin, which decisive social action might remove, and how far it is a personal flaw, an ineradicable vanity in the heart of man. The lack of a clear-cut answer may account in part for his restlessness, which we always sense behind the apparently easy elegance of the style. Religious and political solutions can, however, be a form of glibness themselves. Can we expect Thackeray to offer a clearer answer to such problems than we have worked out for ourselves? For at least a hundred years now the western mind has been discovering enigmas and doubts. In extending our understanding and compassion, Thackeray does the work a novelist is chiefly concerned to do.

This brings us to the novel's true greatness, to its claim to be one of the undoubtedly major novels that we have. . . . We sense the capacity for [compassion] in Thackeray's great sonorous phrases about vanity: 'Yes, this is Vanity Fair; not a moral place certainly; nor a merry one, though very noisy'; we sense it in the sympathy we are made to feel for nearly all of the characters, even when—and perhaps especially when— we have also seen them at their worst. (pp. 23-4)

The most remarkable example of Thackeray's compassion . . . is surely to be found in his dealings with Amelia. The strategy of her characterisation is at least as subtle as Becky's, though there are somewhat different ends in view. . . . [The] main intention of Thackeray's irony . . . [is] to trap us into an easy and arch indulgence towards her in order to shatter this, later, with a very damaging moral critique. But this is half the story only, and not the half that matters most. It is in keeping with the subtlety we expect from a major novelist that our disillusionment with Amelia should contain a further trap of its own. The swing from simple indulgence to simple censure is easy to make; too easy if morality is to be much more serious than a game. By shifting the tone of his irony in various puzzling ways, Thackeray invites us not only to see the causes of judgment, but to probe their validity. With Amelia as with Becky, in fact, we are made to look beyond conventional judgments to that true situation—more costly to contemplate—which we so often miss. When Thackeray rebukes our easy sentimentality towards Amelia, he is clearing the way not for cynicism, but for pity of a truer kind. Cynicism indeed is not the opposite to sentimentality but its twin, another kind of shallowness which we too easily swing towards when rebuked. We discover that though sentimental indulgence is a travesty of compassion, clear-sighted judgment ought to be simply a stepping-stone on the way. What Thackeray makes us see is that Amelia is an incurably neurotic woman, destined to unhappiness whether things go well with her or ill. The contrast between herself and Becky is to some degree a contrast between robust mental health and mental defeat. Becky survives even the gravest hardships and rebuffs, Amelia remains fearful even when she achieves, or seems to achieve, her heart's desire. (pp. 24-5)

We rush too easily into censoriousness when reading novels, as Thackeray well knew; the luxury of catching fictional characters out in errors can be very readily mistaken for unusual moral maturity in ourselves. Compassion is better than censure, in literature as in life; by involving us as he does with his characters, Thackeray makes this more than usually plain. It is just when we want to judge most harshly that he allows his stress to fall another way—on the perversity of circumstances and the shortness of time, on the need for forgiveness which embraces us all. The most memorable moments in the novel are those when this insight comes to the surface, and the deep currents of feeling crystallise in phrases we are never likely to forget. The tormented striving, the enigma, the restlessness give way to a grander sense of human solitude and need. Things go wrong for this character or that beyond any deserving, and we see him confronting the world bewildered and alone. . . . To all of us in Vanity Fair, the weak and the strong, the proud and the humble, the good and the bad, there come such moments, when after the bustle and gaiety, the hoping and working, the striving and fearing, we find ourselves downcast and alone. At such moments, in Thackeray's depiction of them, all the irony and cynicism, the hatred of worldliness and scorn of fools, give way to [a] note of a deeper compassion. . . . (pp. 26-7)

*A. E. Dyson, "'Vanity Fair': An Irony Against Heroes," in* Critical Quarterly *(reprinted by permission of Manchester University Press), Vol. 6, No. 1, Spring, 1964, pp. 11-31.*

## JOHN LOOFBOUROW   (essay date 1964)

[*Loofbourow's* Thackeray and the Form of Fiction *is primarily an exploration of Thackeray's development as a parodist. Loofbourow, who considers Thackeray an influential novelist, claims that "the most important source of narrative content in Thackeray's prose is the satirical allusion to typical literary conventions." Finding most of these literary modes present in* Vanity Fair, *including the "fashionable" chivalric romance, the pastoral, and the mock-epic, he praises Thackeray's ability to skillfully blend these diverse literary forms in a unified narrative.*]

Style is a vital element in Thackeray's fiction—it is an instrument upon which he develops an almost entirely new range of effects. Subtleties of language have been less associated with mid-Victorian writers than with more recent novelists, and this fact has tended to obscure the full meaning of Thackeray's narrative method. But, like the novels of Henry James, Thackeray's fiction depends as much upon its expressive as upon its dramatic elements. . . . (p. v)

Thackeray's work must be read like witty poetry—a poetry expressed in delicate conceits and sustained allusions rather than in the traditional narrative rhetoric of his own time. Nevertheless, style in Thackeray is seldom pure sound effect. Readers who crave the subtle harmonies of words can find endless delight in his novels; but Thackeray's harmonies are as significant as they are delightful, and his most sonorous sequences are never without the counterpoint of suggestive meanings. (pp. v-vi)

The changes that transformed the eighteenth-century convention into the modern novel were, of course, diffuse and various; many years of experimentation separate Fielding's work from E. M. Forster's. But halfway through the nineteenth century there was a shorter period of intense activity—similar to the slight but irreversible diversion, by a genetic mutation, of a continuous process of evolution—and Thackeray's writing is a major factor in this crucial development.

Despite the tendency to associate Thackeray with a familiar tradition, his important novels represent a new kind of writing. The significance of his work has been obscured by its apparently conventional elements; whereas many of Thackeray's conventions were used for unprecedented artistic purposes, for instance, when he adopts the mannerisms of popular fiction to represent the compulsive emotional drives that animate his characters. In developing such creative methods, Thackeray fundamentally altered the accepted relationships between words and content, style and form. Subject and expression are unified in his novels as they had not been before; and in this achievement, his use of language is the critical element. (pp. 3-4)

Thackeray was the first English novelist to create a narrative medium in which form and content are derived from the expressive patterns of the language itself. For example, he can produce an emotional climax by means of allusive verbal effects where there is literally no "plot" climax in the narrative action. Earlier English novelists set forth a preconceived incident in language designed primarily for communication. In Thackeray, intense, suggestive images give to literal event a further dimension, or even discredit appearance and create a divergent imaginative reality of their own. (p. 4)

The new relationship between matter and language is a continuous theme in Thackeray's artistic development. His first literary pieces were parodic or derivative. From successive interactions of parody and imitation, he gradually developed a suggestive, allusive prose that included in its own resources the elements of form and content; and, even so early as *Vanity Fair,* his language has the complex participation in narrative event that we have come to expect in the modern novel. No earlier novelist attained such verbal richness, and later novelists, from George Eliot to Vladimir Nabokov, are indebted to Thackeray's experimentation. (p. 5)

The most important source of narrative content in Thackeray's prose is the satirical allusion to typical literary conventions. Even when these conventions are modified by Thackeray's personal manner, they retain their suggestive force and summon up meaningful, familiar images. But the significance of the allusions must be recognized before their effect can be appreciated. Such literary images—sentimental idealisms, chivalric codes, neoclassical mannerisms—may mirror states of mind or represent emotional events; they may be satiric fantasies or poetic insights; and their purpose must be understood in the narrative context. This recognition is helpful in reading *Vanity Fair,* where Thackeray first integrates and purposefully controls his allusive sequences; it is essential for *Henry Esmond,* where the expressive patterns are subtler and more significant. (pp. 5-6)

In analyzing *Vanity Fair,* it is important to discriminate basic prose "textures"—sentiment, romance, pastoral, mock-epic. A word like "textures" is needed to indicate the quality of these modes; for Thackeray's allusive conventions are not discrete "styles" but aspects of an expressive unity. (p. 6)

In *Henry Esmond, Vanity Fair*'s expressive experiment is given new artistic value. Verbal patterns in *Vanity Fair* seem to create effective form *ex nihilo* and its literal "plot" is a vestigial convention. In *Esmond,* both literal and imaginative form are effective, the one a counterpoint to the other. The verbal textures of Thackeray's previous work interact in *Esmond* with literal elements of historical event and objective plot structure. And *Esmond*'s biographical-historical modes are used in a new way. They are part of a serious attempt to write a novel that will fulfill the epic function—epic not in an impressionistic but in a definable sense, and in a way not attempted by earlier writers. (p. 7)

*Esmond*'s epic purpose is indicated not by literal parallels with Homer and Virgil but by a sequence of classical allusions characterizing the hero's role and initiating climaxes that mirror heroic events in creative metaphor. As in [James Joyce's] *Ulysses* and [Marcel Proust's] *Remembrance of Things Past,* echoes of familiar literary conventions in *Esmond* simulate the hero's personal assimilation of the artistic traditions of his culture. Esmond's experience is characteristically subjective and is typically conveyed by the textures of the prose itself; the novel's irreducible elements of historical event and temporal structure combine with its expressive textures as objective fact is correlated with subjective experience. (p. 8)

Most of Thackeray's major literary modes are present in *Vanity Fair.* First, there is "fashionable" fiction—partly because it became popular at nearly the same time that Thackeray began writing, and partly because this impressionistic medium is fundamental to Thackeray's prose, acting as a common denominator between his novels and the fiction of his time. As recent as the romantics, it is the recurrent butt of Thackeray's early

parodies; transmuted and assimilated, it is a major theme in *Vanity Fair.* Next, there is chivalric romance. . . . Romance runs through *Vanity Fair* like a counterpoint to the "fashionable" manner and is essential to the coloring of character and the creation of structure. Finally, one finds the eighteenth-century genres of pastoral and mock-epic, reflecting Thackeray's affinity for neoclassical satire; in *Vanity Fair,* although polished and pointed beyond the scope of his early parodies, they are static interludes, but in his later novels they are creatively assimilated. (pp. 8-9)

Thackeray's first novels were *Catherine* . . . and *Barry Lyndon.* . . . *Barry Lyndon* is an imitation of Fielding's *Jonathan Wild;* it offered little scope for originality, but it gave Thackeray practice in controlling dramatic narrative and permitted him to experiment *in extenso* with eighteenth-century satirical conventions. *Catherine,* however, is unmistakably part of Thackeray's artistic development. In this earlier novel, textures of "fashionable" prose—the sentimental convention and its variant, the romance of crime—are elaborately exploited, and pastoral is ironically introduced in the climactic scenes. Although *Catherine*'s expressive textures often fail to integrate with the narrative, they are forced to work together, and if their conjunction is sometimes constrained, it is always fruitful. (p. 11)

[*Vanity Fair,*] Thackeray's first major novel, is the immediate result of his satiric apprenticeship, and it is very possibly his greatest work. It is not his subtlest, not his finest artistically, not his most profound; but it continues to soar, like an imperfect and successful balloon, delighting observers who are not concerned with more specialized phases of performance and purpose. Here, for the first time, the varied materials of the early burlesques are woven together in an extended, progressive pattern. Sentimental parody provides the substance of Amelia's point of view and of her love for George; romance furnishes satirical metaphors for Rawdon and for the relation between George and Dobbin. Pastoral and classical myth suggest Becky's motives and comment on her devious intrigues.

But Thackeray's development does not end with *Vanity Fair.* His expressive resources are further extended in each of his later novels as well as in *Henry Esmond.* In *Pendennis* . . . , the pastoral tradition—an isolated metaphor in *Vanity Fair*—becomes a sustained and integral theme. In *The Newcomes* . . . , mock-epic—equally restricted in *Vanity Fair*—is combined with serious classical allusion to form a fundamental, organic narrative mode; and, in this novel, a new expressive resource appears: the fairy tale motif that had acquired its now-familiar romantic quality in the nineteenth century and was a source of significant allusion for Henry James.

The most important aspect of *Vanity Fair,* however, is not the simple presence of expressive conventions, but their synthesis in a continuous fiction. . . . [Before] Thackeray, most novelists followed some one controlling mode—romance with Scott, manners with Austen, burlesque with Fielding. In *Vanity Fair,* for the first time, multiple expressive traditions are assimilated in a sustained narrative, familiar conventions are integrated into a single, more intricate entity.

The major modes of *Vanity Fair*—textures of "fashionable" fiction and chivalric romance—are elements of organic form rather than ornamental elaborations. Satirical echoes of "fashionable" convention begin and conclude the novel, control its shape, and are diffused through the narrative; sentimental and melodramatic variants differentiate the pseudo-heroines, Amelia and Rebecca. Romance motifs create a contrasting sequence that inscribes sharp tangents of dramatic structure upon the diffused, continuous ground of the "fashionable" mode. The two conventions are both opposed and complementary; together they determine the effective form of *Vanity Fair.* (pp. 11-13)

> *John Loofbourow, in his* Thackeray and the Form of Fiction *(copyright © 1964 by Princeton University Press; excerpts reprinted by permission of Princeton University Press), Princeton University Press, 1964, 236 p.*

## EDWIN MUIR   (essay date 1965)

*Vanity Fair* and *Madame Bovary* both attempted something new. Flaubert planted himself outside society, as a judge. Thackeray discarded the conventional framework of fiction as it had been known, and pleased or shocked his readers by showing his characters moving about as they did in the actual world; something which was not done again, on a greater scale, until Tolstoy. . . . [*Vanity Fair*] is filled with genius, and is the chief picture of Victorian life painted by a man of discriminating intelligence as well as of imagination. Thackeray saw the main lines of Victorian society, for he conformed to them and disliked them.

Flaubert's vision of society is as clear as Thackeray's but it is more full and exact. Both men are alike in their critical view of society; they are unlike in every other way. Thackeray is a gregarious writer; Flaubert, a solitary writer. Thackeray speaks from the very middle of society; he is conscious of it in the same way that the eighteenth-century novelists were; that is to say, he is aware not only of the characters he is describing but of a circle of educated readers who are critically weighing his words, so that he falls naturally into a conversational tone. (pp. 185-86)

Flaubert confessed that Emma was himself. Becky is not Thackeray in the same complete sense; yet she is like him in an important respect: that, while herself a snob, she sees through snobbery. The difference between them is that while Thackeray exposes snobbery, Rebecca uses it to advance her aims; she is what Thackeray might have been if he had not had a heart and a conscience. She is in the secret, like himself, and he has more respect for her than for old Osborne, the perfect believing snob, or his son George, though they are honest, and she is not honest at all. For she is honest to herself, though dishonest to every one else. She is the only character in the story who could understand what Thackeray is saying, and he treats her with the wry intimacy of one who knows too much. Yet he was not able to draw her completely; the conventions of the age and his own mixture of timidity and snobbery prevented him from dealing with her with the frankness of a Fielding. . . . Thackeray shows Becky consorting with the worst international riff-raff, spongers and cheats and bullies. But what she was doing in their company is only to be guessed at; and half of her is left to our imaginations. The silence about this side of her life gives her the appearance of taking everything and giving nothing, and makes her more repulsive than she would have been if Thackeray had dealt frankly with her. She becomes an image of moral corruption, without a heart.

Thackeray makes Becky all head, and her counterpart, Amelia Sedley, all heart. Amelia changes in the course of the story, but Becky does not. . . . (pp. 188-89)

Being all head, one might have expected Becky to achieve social success. Instead she is a failure. . . . Yet she was a pretty young woman, with unusual intelligence and no scruples, and she was resolved to succeed. . . . She stands outside society . . . , belongs to no class, and carries out a raid on society by means which society was not supposed to use. Her progress is a sort of pilgrim's progress conducting her to the semblance of respectability as a completely bogus yet not unrespected member of the aristocracy. One feels that we can read in her the great fable of the Victorian age. (p. 190)

> *Edwin Muir, "Emma Bovary and Becky Sharp," in his* Essays on Literature and Society *(copyright © Edwin Muir 1949 and The Hogarth Press Ltd. 1965; excerpted by permission of the President and Fellows of Harvard College), revised edition, Cambridge, Mass.: Harvard University Press, 1965, pp. 182-94.\**

## JULIET McMASTER   (essay date 1971)

[*In contrast to critics such as J.Y.T. Grieg (see excerpt above, 1950), McMaster finds that Thackeray's subjective narrative technique is essential to the success of his fiction. She maintains that Thackeray is deliberately ambiguous in order to "sharpen our moral perception and to evoke the complexity of experience itself," and that* Vanity Fair *is a great novel mainly because of the authorial presence which provides both its immediacy and universality.*]

Thackeray is a consummate artist very much in control of what he is doing, whose major novels are works of thematic coherence and aesthetic integrity; and . . . he is also a highly sophisticated ironist, exploiting to the full the potential of the various personae he adopts, and introducing ambiguity deliberately, to sharpen our moral perception and to evoke the complexity of experience itself. (p. vii)

Against the contention that Thackeray was a dilettante, too careless as an artist to mind whether his reader believed in the imaginative reality of his creation or not, I suggest that he was as conscious and painstaking in his art in his way, and as successful, as Keats or Sterne or James were in theirs, and that his commentary, his infamous 'lyric leak,' has its positive uses in involving the reader and so subtly increasing the 'sentiment of reality' of the novel. (p. viii)

[It] was Thackeray's achievement so to interweave his fiction with our lives that we draw on our memories of his novels almost as we draw on the material of our own past experience.

How is it done? To a large extent, I would suggest, by the presence of one character whom, if the reader has not been too much imbued with post-Jamesian criticism, he will perhaps have remembered and enjoyed as much as any of the others— Thackeray himself: or at least those facets of himself that he chooses to show us. And here we come, of course, as we were bound to, to the question of the authorial commentary. . . . Thackeray's novels are great works of art for various reasons, but not the least of them is the author's presence: they live because of his commentary, not in spite of it. Sounding through those great organisms, *Vanity Fair, Pendennis,* and *The Newcomes,* like the heartbeat in the body, is the unifying tone of the narrator, a regular and reassuring reminder of the life and harmony of the whole. For the life of the novels comes not just from the vitality of the characters and action depicted in them, but from the tone and reactions of the man who tells the story; and more—from the reader's own personal responses, elicited, though not determined, by his. (pp. 1-2)

[In] Thackeray's novels we have the sense that we are being told the story by a fellow human being: he is informative, though not usually analytical, about the characters and the context in which they act, and sympathetic in his relation of its relevance to his and our own lives, if often questionable in his preferences and values. (pp. 5-6)

In his fiction, of course, Thackeray was to make manifold use of this participation. His novels are certainly about Amelia, Becky, Arthur Pendennis, Clive Newcome, and the rest; but they are also *about,* and in no superficial way, our response to these characters and to the world they live in. His authorial presence is his strategy to elicit this response. And the moral experience of the novel is largely a matter of the reader's decision as to where he wants to place himself among the various attitudes dramatized for him in the author's commentary.

A standard objection to what has come to be known as 'authorial intrusion' is that it consists of *telling,* whereas it is the author's business to *show,* and the reader's to make up his own mind. To refute this charge one need only repeat that the commentator in Thackeray's novels is no ultimate authority. The commentary does not constitute the 'moral' of *Vanity Fair* or of any of the other novels, though it certainly is part of the moral experience of reading them. The reader has to be prepared to make his own independent judgments just as much in the passages of commentary as in the passages of direct scenic presentation, and frequently more so, because of the deceptive plausibility of the commentator's arguments. (pp. 8-9)

The passages of commentary are not directives on what to think. Each is at best only one way of looking at the matter; and the next may be a different way, or emphatically the wrong one. 'What Thackeray is saying' about the characters is to be found in the facts of the narrative, and only fragmentarily and often misleadingly in the commentary. The reaction of those readers of Thackeray who wish that he would stop *talking* and get on with his subject is thus misguided, for the talk, with the attitudes expressed in it, is itself part of the subject. (p. 11)

In generalizing about the nature of the authorial presence in Thackeray's novels, one inevitably becomes involved in a series of qualifications; for it is a lambent light, playing on the fictional world sometimes brilliantly, but sometimes like an ultraviolet ray, invisible but still effective. None of the various names we use for this presence—Thackeray, the narrator, the persona, the implied author, the omniscient author—fully defines its nature, though they have their local applications. There are the various roles that the author chooses to play within the world of his characters. . . . [And the] range of interlocked roles extends continuously from the fiction to the history, from the imagined world to the actual world. Thackeray may infringe the rules of consistency, but in the process he can connect the novel's world with his reader's, and involve us personally in the lives of his characters.

In this context it is useful to examine the prologue to *Vanity Fair,* 'Before the Curtain.' Critics have traditionally denounced Thackeray's puppet metaphor as a derogation of the artist's duty to create life and to convince us of the imaginative reality of the world he presents. . . . Nevertheless, the prologue, far from being a piece of artistic irresponsibility, seems to me to be a study, as carefully wrought as one of Keats' odes, of the nature of the artist's relation to his artifice, and of both to the perceiver, the man to whom the artist's vision is to be communicated. (pp. 12-13)

It is in its way a kind of epitome of the whole novel: a concentrated statement of the content as well as the technique, proceeding not by descriptive analysis but, like a poem, by a series of images. (p. 13)

[Part] of Thackeray's achievement in **'Before the Curtain,'** and in *Vanity Fair* as well [is] to see his own identity with the meanest figure of his creation. . . . This humility, as well as the godlike confidence of the puppeteer, is embodied in *Vanity Fair* as in its prologue. (pp. 18-19)

It is a marvellous piece of work, that prologue—a kind of distilled essence of the novel, without being in any crude way an explanation or an apology or a synopsis. It not only gives a preview of the content of the novel . . . ; it gives also a foretaste of the method, offering a series of metaphors for that varying presence of the artist in his work, and preparing us for the tone and changing moods of the narrative and for the part that we, as spectators and evaluators, are to play ourselves.

So I do not defend Thackeray from the charge of exposing his own illusion. He certainly does assert his liberty to juggle with his characters, not just in calling them puppets (which, by the way, is a matter of almost literal truth—the writer *is* the omnipotent being who proposes and disposes of his characters; Thackeray differs from other authors only in admitting it), but in various other ways in all his novels. For instance, in *The Virginians* he reassures us about the fate of Harry Warrington when he is knocked unconscious by telling us that he has no intention of squandering his hero so early in the novel . . . , and in *The Newcomes* confesses that it was a matter of expediency that he eliminated Lady Kew when he did. . . . (pp. 21-2)

It was part of both his moral and artistic purpose to force the reader, during the act of reading, to make comparisons from one world to the other, to bring to bear his knowledge of one on the evaluation of the other; in fact, to break down, or at least as far as possible to overlook, that barrier between illusion and reality. (p. 23)

[Thackeray] does not try for this kind of intensity. He persuades us to live not *through* his characters but, in our own identities, *with* them, and makes us feel that our lives unfold together. (p. 24)

Another means by which Thackeray cements the relationship between himself and the reader, which to so large an extent sustains his created illusion, is his use of burlesque. It is characteristic of the novelist who depends on irony and an intimate communication with his readers, like Fielding, Sterne, Jane Austen, and Thackeray, that parody is an initial creative impulse. (p. 29)

But for the most part Thackeray gave up direct parody in his novels for a light texture of burlesque supported by a sophisticated pattern of allusion, and frequent remarks on how 'I disdain, for the most part, the tricks and surprises of the novelist's art' . . . , and on his determination to write about men and women, not heroes and heroines, about the everyday occurrences of ordinary life, not the wild coincidences and providential resolutions of romance, and so on. His principle of realism, of course, prompted him in his reaction from romance, just as it has prompted similar remarks in most novelists who, as a matter of tradition, deny heroic status to their protagonists. . . . But Thackeray makes thematic use of his reaction. *Vanity Fair* deserves its subtitle of **'A Novel without a Hero,'** because the specifically unheroic nature of man—and of woman too, for all the ironic claims for that title alternately for Amelia and Becky—is his subject. Literary, as well as social, pretension is to be Thackeray's satirical butt. It is to be the reader's business in *Vanity Fair,* as it is Catherine Morland's in [Jane Austen's] *Northanger Abbey,* to distinguish between the true and the false, both in life and in literature. . . . [Thackeray] allows the reader to retain his own location and his own identity, but makes him experience the novel's delusions and enlightenments for himslef. (pp. 30-1)

[The] emphasis on the incongruity between romance and reality, or between the pose and the truth, is both subject and technique in *Vanity Fair.* Frequently the reader is ironically invited to see the sordid facts of the lustful and rapacious world through the rose-coloured spectacles of the novel of sentiment. (p. 32)

Because Thackeray speaks personally, the reader reacts personally, and is often provoked to take issue with the narrator on his judgments and allegiances among the characters. Such a reaction must be based on the supposition that somehow we know more of the characters and surrounding circumstances than he tells us—that is, that these are autonomous beings—people—whose faults and virtues may be speculated on, but not finally assessed. It is an unobtrusive process by which we are made to react in this way, for the comments to which we react are often diffused through the whole narrative, and take the form not only of passages of explicit evaluation but of brief interpolated phrases and adverbs, which may be from the narrator's personal viewpoint, or from that of some character in the action, or of some hypothetical reader. (p. 39)

The novelist can speak as the final authority on the actions and the motives of the characters he creates, whereas the raconteur who is telling us an anecdote of people he knows, and that we may know too, will frequently, as a matter of honesty or in deference to our feelings, admit to a limitation in his knowledge. Now Thackeray often makes such an admission: '*I think* [Amelia] was more frightened than even the people most concerned,' he says, with an air of uncertainty. '*Perhaps* [Becky] just looked first into the bouquet, to see whether there was a *billet-doux* hidden among the flowers.' The narrator's professed ignorance, not just on minor matters like these, but also in matters of substance, is one more of Thackeray's devices for endowing his narrative with something like the quality of life. We cannot know *all* about his characters, as we cannot know all about a person. Much of his writing seems to assume, and so helps us to assume, the existence of his literary creations outside the limits of his volume. And besides this, his professed uncertainty is an invitation for the reader's participation. (p. 42)

In declaring, as it were, open season on his characters by discussing them with us himself, he has given them the stature and ambiguity of real people. (p. 44)

And so, intricately, the reader is lured into the world of Vanity Fair, and made to recognize it as his world, and to think of the characters, to whom he has been introduced by his friend the author, and about whose domestic lives he has heard some piquante gossip, as his acquaintances. Such a proceeding may be a sort of heresy to the reader or the critic trained in the Jamesian scheme, who may exclaim angrily about 'aesthetic distance,' and the 'closed precinct' that a novel ought to be. But Thackeray simply does not believe in aesthetic distance, at least in any strict applicaiton of the phrase. For him a close and personal relation with the reader, albeit a varied one, and a confidential intercourse with him about his novel and his

characters, and the rights and wrongs of their actions in a fallen world that author, reader, and characters equally inhabit, and the concerns they have in common—all this is the life blood of the illusion he creates. *Vanity Fair* is a great novel not in spite of that authorial presence but becuase of it, for it is what gives the novel its peculiar immediacy of appeal as well as its universality of application. (p. 48)

Qualification is necessary. Commentary, involving this rather dangerous process of breaking the illusion of reality, is not good in itself, but only when done well. . . . Thackeray himself, of course, was not always successful: *The Virginians* breaks down under the weight of the commentary, which there becomes turgid and lacks the sparkle and bite of the earlier novels. But he *could* do it well; and at its best it is not only entertaining and thematically relevant, but it works as a sort of magic to build a bridge between us and the characters, from the actual world around us to the imaginary world of Vanity Fair. (p. 49)

'First the world was made: then, as a matter of course, Snobs.' This is Thackeray's version of Genesis in *The Book of Snobs,* the work which established him as virtually the world authority on the subject. Through his career that initial vision of snobbery as the human condition expands into the greater concept of the world of Vanity Fair, and is carried on through the quest for the true gentleman in *Pendennis,* to the study of respectability in all its forms in *The Newcomes.* (p. 127)

Of course snobbery is not all that Thackeray's novels are about: they are far more than just lively studies of middle-class manners. His minutely realized social milieu is the context for individual dramas which have implications far beyond the business of mere status-seeking. But it is in this area, in his portrayal of the social universe, that much of the comedy and page-to-page vitality of his novels reside. . . . And though Thackeray's chosen setting is always that World, 'wherever there is a competition and a squeeze,' the effect is not repetitive, for he manages to make every snob also an individual. (pp. 127-28)

And, behind all his vivid dramatization of social climbing, inside all his incarnated snobs, there is a solid structure of ideas. Thackeray is a shrewd social commentator, even if, writing in the hungry forties, he did not choose manufacturers and factory operatives for his characters. (p. 128)

'It is among the RESPECTABLE classes of this vast and happy empire that the greatest profusion of Snobs is to be found' . . . , Thackeray declares. And so it is the vicissitudes of middle-class existence that he chronicles. He can range above and below this world that he knows so well, with some insight into the aristocracy. . . . But for the most part his lords are seen in relation not so much to each other as to the middle-class society which adulates them; and his lower orders are usually of the servant class. (pp. 128-29)

The middle-class world that Thackeray chose to write about is representative enough, we understand, of the rest of the world. He suggests the same struggles and status-seeking going on upwards in the higher levels of the aristocracy and downwards among the servants. (p. 129)

Thackeray was preoccupied with class as he saw the world around him was preoccupied with it. If a character's position on the social ladder does not always determine what he is, it is at least always relevant. Relations are constantly seen in terms of class gradations, so that even a short novel like *Lovel the Widower,* which has the old Cinderella plot of the low-born maid's marrying the master, becomes a little social history. (pp. 129-30)

A Snob is *'he who meanly admires mean things'*. . . *:* it is this inversion of values that Thackeray the social historian portrays, and Thackeray the satirist and moralist exposes. He depicts that elaborate confusion between status and function, between appearance and essence, with a show of being an impartial chronicler, often with the explicit assumption that these things are as they must and should be. But his irony is constantly implying the essential values that society has debased, and showing up the sham that has come to be accepted as the reality. (pp. 130-31)

There are various reasons why *The Newcomes* has always lagged so far behind *Vanity Fair* in popularity and critical attention. It is not as lively, the characters are less vividly animated, the incident and commentary are not as piquante. *Vanity Fair* contains more of the sparkling exaggerations of satire—showing, in effect, one Dobbin in a world of cheats and humbugs—and its satirical vision makes its theme more obvious, and more immediately interesting. The ratio of good to bad is perhaps more realistic in *The Newcomes,* which shows a number of characters who, if not good, are concerned with the problem of how to live according to conscience in a fallen world. But its scope is in certain ways the larger for this increased realism: its emotional appeal is greater, for ultimately we care less for the sirens and parasites like Becky and Amelia than for decent people like Clive, Ethel, and Colonel Newcome.

It is also slow to get going, and never achieves the pace of Thackeray's first novel. He takes his time to describe the various branches of the family, and to define the world in which Colonel Newcome is to grow old and his son is to grow up. Structurally, too, it does not hold together as tightly as *Vanity Fair.* With its vast number of characters, three of whom are rival claimants for the central position, and its spread of time and place, and its accumulation of detail, it is a novel that one easily gets lost in. . . . Nevertheless, it is not only endowed with life, but also thematically and artistically coherent, though its range and complexity tend to make its effect cumulative rather than immediate. (p. 153)

*The Newcomes* is the 'Memoirs of a Most Respectable Family,' and their claim to respectability rests as much on their money as on their solid Quaker background and their three generations of virtuous apprentices. And Thackeray's subject is that complex union of, or confusion between, financial and moral values, good and goods, which constitutes 'respectability.'

Money, as a determinant of respectability, is a central principle that holds together at once the Newcome family and the novel, permeating language and imagery and dominating character and action. . . . Through the novel people are judged by the size of their balance, relationships progress in terms of who opens and who closes how large an account, battles are fought in which the manoeuvres are transferring an account or bouncing a cheque.

As mercenary transactions dominate the action, so financial terminology pervades the language, giving a distinctive texture to the novel. Love, morality, art, and faith are all discussed in financial terms. (pp. 155-56)

The marriage market itself is of course a central image in the novel, and the repetition of the mercenary marriage and its outcome between various couples is a unifying structural principle. . . . According to the philosophy of Society, marriage

'is but a question of money on one side and the other.'. . . But those who hold this tenet, however substantial their actual bank balance, find through the course of the novel that there are multiple debts accruing in trust and affection. (p. 157)

It is part of the intricate structure of the novel that the great world which it depicts in such painstaking detail is reflected in miniature in numerous little microcosms through the book. Each little community or institution, each gathering of people, even a single object like the coconut tree, has the quality of being complete in itself, with its own centre of gravity and its own set of revolving satellites within the major system. (p. 162)

Learning how to live, at once with the world and with one's own consciousness, is one of the main subjects of the novel. This is the task before Ethel, who is a product of her environment and at the same time manages eventually to assert herself against it. 'You belong to your belongings, my dear,' Lady Kew tells her . . . ; but Ethel has to develop in moral consciousness to the point where her belongings belong to her. In the first part of the novel she is gaining money, prestige, or suitors; but by the end she has learned how to give them away.

Ethel Newcome is Thackeray's best heroine; indeed she compares favorably with any heroine of the nineteenth-century novel. Besides being both vivid and likable, she has a dynamism which most of Thackeray's major females lack: she learns about herself, and changes as a result of her knowledge. She has a full and complex moral life and development. She has Becky's strong character, without Becky's siren's tail. She is like Beatrix in many ways . . . but, where Beatrix is finally tainted by her ambition and selfishness, Ethel is redeemed, and convincingly so.

*The Newcomes* is slow to get going because Thackeray takes the necessary time to build up the world in which his individual dramas are to be enacted. The effect is the more powerful for being cumulative; and by the time Clive, Ethel, and the rest reach their moments of decision, we have a full awareness of the complex pressures to which they are subject. (pp. 163-64)

'To push on in the crowd, every male or female . . . must use his shoulders. If a better place than yours presents itself just beyond your neighbour, elbow him and take it.'. . . This is what *The Newcomes* is about, rather than how 'the fox is caught in his trap, the lamb is rescued from the wolf, and so forth.' In the Newcome world, your vices are your assets. . . .

The animal imagery that is a connecting motif of the novel works in two ways. Much of it connects with the moral fables of the opening and closing pages; the beasts with which the human characters are compared are anthropomorphic and humorous, and evoke a moral response. . . . [The] images present an ordered moral universe, in which behaviour can be classified as good or bad, wise or foolish.

But the animal imagery also suggests an amoral universe, and the topical view of nature as red in tooth and claw, a predatory struggle for survival. These animals—and birds and snakes predominate here—are drawn not from La Fontaine or the bestiaries but from natural history, and they are divided not into good and bad but into predators and victims. (p. 173)

And yet an exposition of *The Newcomes* suggesting that Thackeray presented English society as a savage and predatory struggle for survival needs some qualification. His faculty for seeing every side of a question prevented him from writing a *roman à thèse* in the manner of Zola and the naturalists. He is exposing the tendency of the middle classes to disguise their concern for making money as the concern for saving their souls, and to gush about romance while practising self-interest. But romance and the veneration for true goodness are not laughed out of court in the process. As Barnes Newcome represents the refined savagery of a greedily self-seeking society, so the artist J. J. Ridley stands for the truth of human ideals. He can conceive of beauty, love, and heroism in his imagination, and realize them in his art. . . . (p. 174)

[*The Newcomes*] is not just a sprawling narrative that contains some amusing characters and some graphic description of manners in mid-Victorian society. It is a carefully organized novel in which style and imagery, as well as character and action, contribute to a unifying theme, and in which the length is adapted to the complexity of the content. The action takes place, and the characters find their moral being, in a minutely realized milieu in which 'respectability' is the dominant operative standard. In relating his story in language that elevates 'fumbling in a greasy till' to heroism and reduces love and faith to mere commodities, Thackeray conveys society's confusion of values by stylistic means. And that counterpoint between style and matter does more than illuminate a contemporary vice: it reflects some of the contradictions of human existence. As the animal imagery suggests both the ordered moral universe of fable and the savage jungle of popular Darwinism, so the pattern of contrasts between illusion and reality, fantasy and hard fact, aspiration and achievement, conveys how far human practice falls short of human ideals. (p. 176)

Thackeray is, after all, an acknowledged master of the novel of manners, but his novels are also subtle and intense studies of human psychology. So far, I have considered his characters as animals in a social jungle, and as human beings for whom this society is a context for moral choice; but of course they exist at a level that is deeper than either of these, with motives that cannot be fully explained by social or moral aspirations, though they may be influenced by them.

It is curious to what an extent the active and often furious or agonized psychic life of Thackeray's characters has been overlooked. . . . There is a usual assumption, which is indeed part of the truth, that Thackeray depicts a superficial society, typified by superficial characters, tenth-rate people always trying to prove they are ninth-rate, uninterested in each other except as they are higher or lower in the pecking order, and operating according to a consistent if unpleasant rationale. (p. 177)

Extended analysis of a character or a relationship, of course, Thackeray does not give us. He does not enter the mind and describe its workings in detail in the manner of George Eliot, or chronicle the minute fluctuations of a relationship like James. What we know of his characters we must gather for the most part from speech and gesture, external manifestations. From these and from occasional supplementary comments the reader must do the work of the psychiatrist himself. But there is plenty of material to work on; for in the packed incident and among the crowds of characters there is always more going on than meets the eye. In an image or an apparently insignificant scene, in a word, a kiss, a blush, the reader has glimpses of depths of motive and ambivalence of emotion of which the characters themselves are often unaware.

The conflict of conscious and unconscious motivation is a strong force in all of Thackeray's work. This is why his characters so often escape close examination, for they themselves often rationalize in social terms the motives that have a deeper origin. (p. 178)

It is particularly the ambiguity in the relations between the generations that interests Thackeray. The love of two young people of marriageable age, which he is so ready to dismiss as just another instance of the same old inevitable attraction, becomes tense and absorbing when seen in relation to the love and demands of the parents' generation. Mothers and sons, daughters and fathers! (pp. 178-79)

The central emotional relationships in the novels repeatedly take the form of a triangle of which parent and child, either as lovers or as sexual rivals, are two of the corners. In a Victorian novel such a situation must necessarily be suggested rather than analysed in detail, but it was perennially interesting to Thackeray. (p. 180)

The mother-daughter-lover triangle is only one of the various possiblities of allegiances and rivalries between the generations that Thackeray explores. Such ambivalent relationships are not only the focus of emotional interest in the novels, but their recurrence and variation constitute a structural pattern which often has as much force as the formal plot. (p. 187)

In applying Freudian psychology to an interpretation of Thackeray's novels, there is a danger of being too solemn and so forgetting the air of amused ironic detachment that often plays about his depiction of these primal situations. And to reduce all his characters to Oedipuses and Electras is to rob them of both their humour and their individuality. Of course the novels are far from being just a set of textbook variations on [Freud's] *Totem and Taboo*. But, again, it is a question of emphasis. I assert only that Thackeray concerned himself, consciously and repeatedly, with that aspect of human relationships that Freud has best analysed, and this is one reason that his novels have subtlety and intensity. And not only subtlety and intensity, but humour too. (p. 221)

'If Fun is good, Truth is still better, and Love is best of all' . . . : it is Thackeray's familiar maxim. But a study of the triangle relationships between the generations involves yet another qualification to his moral of 'the vanity of success and of all but Love and Goodness'; for the more carefully we read the novels the more we can see that love is no more the *summum bonum* than is goodness. We are shown love that 'beareth all things, believeth all things, hopeth all things, endureth all things.' But we are also shown love that demands all things, grasps all things, and devours all things.

Indeed, in his best work Thackeray has in effect revised that scale of values he outlined in *The Book of Snobs*. Fun he never abandoned, though his fun is tinged with the sadness that made him think a 'jaundiced livery' best suited his part numbers, for all the jester's antics they contained. But love, and goodness too, he had examined so intently in all their operations in this fallen world of Vanity Fair that his reservations about them matched his veneration. It is truth, finally, that he values highest. . . . He will not shirk the disagreeable matter that he finds so intricately involved with the agreeable. For his vision is one that recognizes primarily the contradicitons of existence. Whether we examine his personal standpoints, his social, moral, or psychological preoccupations, we find him showing how the quest for social eminence becomes snobbery, how the aspiration to sainthood becomes moral tyranny, how tenderness fosters aggression and an embrace turns into a stranglehold, and how truth itself includes a measure of illusion.

He will not let his reader shirk the business of assessment, either. We are to know the Beckys of this world for what they are; but his ironic stances, tempting us to align ourselves with the sentimental or the worldly-wise, undercut any glib judgments, for they make us know too the precarious moral bases from which we judge. (pp. 222-23)

His very technique of maintaining a confidential relation with his reader is determined by his desire to be honest, to look his audience straight in the eye, and so avoid as far as possible the posturing which he finds so easily to himself and to all who take it upon themselves to address a listening public. (p. 223)

In his major work at least, I believe Thackeray satisfies us, not only that he can tell the truth, but that the breadth of his vision, the truth he has to tell, is worth our listening to. His alternate poses as sentimental novel-reader, pillar of respectability, and detached cynic add up not to successive retreats but to a brave attempt to know all round a character or situation, from various viewpoints. The shifts of sympathy in which he involves us are not an evasion of judgment, but an inducement to us to judge responsibly. And his probing into the sensitive spot in the most hardened snob, and explorations of the ulterior motives and secret agonies that underlie the humdrum lives of ordinary individuals, are part of a deeply perceptive vision of humanity. His irony is a means of knowing. (p. 224)

*Juliet McMaster, in her* Thackeray: The Major Novels *(© University of Toronto Press 1971), University of Toronto Press, 1971, 230 p.*

## BARBARA HARDY   (essay date 1972)

Coming to the study of Thackeray from George Eliot and Dickens, two other great Victorian novelists, I was at first struck by apparently unrelated things: his comic self-consciousness as an artist, very much closer to the eighteenth- than to the nineteenth-century novelist, and his explicit refusal to use fiction for high moral triumphs. The self-consciousness and the lack of moral optimism, I now believe, are closely related to each other as aspects of his radical thinking and caring about humanity. Thackeray has frequently been accused of cynicism and pessimism, probably less because he is so critical of society, than because he offers neither the humane meliorism of George Eliot, nor the quasi-Christian optimism of Dickens, nor the tragic sublimities of Thomas Hardy. (p. 11)

What Thackeray wanted to do, he explained apropos the decidedly muted ending of *Vanity Fair,* was to make us dissatisfied. Dissatisfaction is far from a tragic response, and Thackeray's pessimism is nothing like as heartening as Hardy's, or even Gissing's. With the exception of *Henry Esmond*, the novel of 'cut-throat melancholy', his novels are comic novels, and he is an uncomfortable writer, apparently believing in neither stoicism or baptisms of suffering, and, while not dissenting from Christianity, offering no religious solutions. (p. 12)

If occasionally he shows a Helen or Laura Pendennis possessed of a religious faith and piety that awe the average sensual hero like Arthur Pendennis, such characters draw attention to the absence of embodied religious feeling in the novels. The religious moments in Thackeray either have a veil drawn over them, which has the effect of a neutral reticence rather than a sacred awe, or are handled rather sanctimoniously, as with the last days of Colonel Newcome in Charterhouse. What Thackeray's beliefs were, and what he implied in such reticence or excess, is less important than the existence of a social criticism and moral action in art which seems to depend no more than

George Eliot's morality on any conception of 'what is not human'.

Thackeray is, then, neither a comforting Christian, nor an agnostic optimist, nor a strongly humane pessimist. (pp. 12-13)

Thackeray is a highly rational and realistic artist, and his excessive rationality may have led him to avoid visionary suggestions or symbols of love and creativity. His hopes are pitched very low, but their presence is immensely important, acting as assurance of his warmth and generosity (despite the satirist's and the joker's stance) and as a sign of the fierce and feeling heart at the centre of his social analysis. (p. 14)

[His] acute and precise presentation of the dense details of social surfaces, institutions, appearances, customs, objects, all graded, classed, placed, timed and priced, makes his novels much more socially informative than the work of more profound artists like Dickens and George Eliot. They *are* more profound, mining depths of the human mind and heart, and showing agonies, joys and creativity which hardly ever come into the world of Thackeray. I say 'hardly ever' because Henry Esmond's insight into the process of creative self-discovery in expression, whether of the artist or the imaginative man, with the closely related insight into the processes of feeling and memory, shows Thackeray's imagination sensitively active in ways not represented in his three great social novels, *Vanity Fair, Pendennis* and *The Newcomes.* But these insights and explorations are exceptions in Thackeray, and one would not go to his social novels for revelations about passion, endurance, joy, creation, faith, imagination. However, his usual limitation has its special virtue. His brilliant understanding of the surface, and his abstention from systematic criticism and voiced social ethic, allow society to show itself, astounding, mad, hollow, frightening.

He does not make a passive record. He is a critic, a clown, a satirist, a preacher, but his actual preaching and his eloquent irony about society, seen magnificently in such set-pieces as the analysis of Sir Pitt Crawley, or the two chapters in *Vanity Fair,* 'How to Live Well on Nothing A-Year', while incisive, are accompanied by a portrait that is far more eloquent, dramatized and indirect. Society's excessive and loveless occasions and ceremonies, its artificiality and shams, its pursuit of profit, its transformation of life into traffic and commodity, all reveal themselves unmistakably in a detached and eloquent self-exposure. The humour, tolerance and ease of Thackeray's comments on his social and personal experience in his letters, are replaced in his fiction by a shaped exposure of a cruel, cold, mad world.

There are a few things to notice about the forms of this social 'self-exposure'. It contains but also moves beyond Thackeray's explicit moral commentary, and it is often much more strongly emotional than the commentary itself. Thackeray as preacher in motley, one of his favourite authorial roles, is usually ironic, amused, affectionate, rational, well balanced. Thackeray as dramatist, showing rather than telling, or showing as well as telling, creates scenes which appeal to the sense of justice, the sense of moderation, the sense of generosity, even the sense of restrained pleasure. But his fierceness of attack on injustice and indeed his sense of the values of love and justice emerge through the collection of social facts and surfaces. Feasts, ostentatious displays, ceremonies, costumes, objects, cosmetics, masks, acts, strokes of wit go far beyond his rational appeals, analysis and commentary, to move us, dazzle us, disgust us, horrify us. . . . He creates a social surface which is an encrustation on human life, falsifying, enclosing, hardening, and destroying. (pp. 16-18)

The contrast between the natural and the studied, the sincere and the plagiarized or performed existence, is made very explicit. But it is in the local scenes that the radicalism of argument is found. Every part of human life, every emotional act, is seen as tarnished or stemming twistedly from the greed (even in Amelia and Dobbin), the competition (even in Laura, Helen and Rachel) and the pursuit of goods and profits (even in Colonel Newcome). What emerges is the disgust or ironic pointing of sheer excess, dishonesty and lovelessness.

Thackeray does not always support drama with commentary, and he also frequently avoids the appeals and arguments of contrast. Riches, gain and snobbishness make their way in the novels, and make themselves felt by over-exposure and accumulation. . . . Although Thackeray uses the central contrast of Becky and Amelia in *Vanity Fair,* it turns out to be a very sly one, making us see resemblances where we had begun to expect only differences. It is, moreover, the only major contrast of this kind that he makes. His method is unlike that of the other Victorian novelists—George Eliot, Dickens, Trollope, Meredith, Henry James—who make extreme use of the polarity, the antithesis, the sheep-and-goat division. Thackeray does not divide human nature in this way, and it may well be that he used the grand comparative method for the first and last time in *Vanity Fair,* perhaps discovering through and in the writing that what was clearer than the opposition between vice and virtue was a generalized, common pressure from society. Idolatry links even Amelia with the false gods of Vanity Fair, and even Dobbin has his vanities. But whatever the reason, Thackeray exhausted the device of contrast in this novel, and in the later ones it is absent. (pp. 18-19)

[Although Thackeray possessed] an exceptionally rational imagination, he did of course, like all great artists, reveal more than he consciously set out to reveal, perhaps indeed more than he knew or more than he knew he knew. Although he was a most conservative liberal, his novels work through report, locally imagined individual case, and accreted unity, to make what is to my mind one of the most revolutionary statements in the Victorian novel. I should make it clear that by 'revolutionary' I do not refer to doctrines or programmes of political revolt, but to revolutionary feeling. When Thackeray shows the polite and cultivated circle, we are as far as we could possibly be from Virginia Woolf's Mrs Ramsay and her dinner-party with the *Boeuf en Daube.* . . . The feast, the object, and the delight compel a radical disgust, rejection or despair. His art emerges as most rational when least conscious. It is also most sane when what it displays is most absurd.

Thackeray's symbolism is frequently what I want to call a *literal* or *external* symbolism. It consists of symbols which already exist as facts of life: the meal, the house, the party, the polite address, the present, the entertainment, the song, the dance and the play. Thackeray is a most careful and intricate artist and his symbolic structure reflects his care and intricacy, but I believe that his symbols are most effectively eloquent of radical feeling when they are not inventions of art but reports on life. Thackeray is the great sociologist of nineteenth-century fiction, the great accumulator of social symbols of class and money. To read him is to read a fictional form of Veblen's *The Theory of the Leisure Class,* or Marcel Mauss's *Essai sur le Don,* or Galbraith's *The Affluent Society.* Like these eloquent social scientists, he is not merely reporting or describing. Certain facts, if gathered together, unified, and shown in vivid

particularity, create a statement of horror, disgust, incredulity. This is what Thackeray's portrait of conspicuous consumption, mercenary marriage and self-indulgence creates. But unlike the sociologist, he works through particularity. He is a great psychologist too, and the social particularities—vivid sensuous and visual pictures of drawing-rooms, dining-rooms, meals, clothes, houses, streets, servants—are shown as the environment which creates, moulds, corrupts and restricts people and their relationships. As a critic of society, if we take him only at the face value of his explicit attacks, and of his conspicuous jokes, we will find him fervent, witty, sharp, but limited in range and depth. But if we attend to his implicit, as well as his explicit, analysis, we see his full range and depth of attack. And we see more. He shows what society is doing to people, perverting, crippling, and killing their capacity for love. He is radical in the way of his great ancestors in moral satire, Juvenal, Bunyan, Swift, Johnson, and in his most profound and central themes he reveals and criticizes the profound and central corruptions of Victorian society. (pp. 19-21)

> *Barbara Hardy, in her* The Exposure of Luxury: Radical Themes in Thackeray *(© 1972 Barbara Hardy), Peter Owen, 1972, 190 p.*

### WINSLOW ROGERS   (essay date 1975)

Thackeray was obsessed with the question of how to know and trust his own feelings. . . . In conceiving of his novels as "a sort of confidential talk between writer and reader," he denies himself a comfortable distance between his life and his writings. The danger is that of being overwhelmed by his private thoughts and feelings and of not being able to give them artistic shape. (pp. 149-50)

Self-consciousness in Thackeray means more than his notorious habit of breaking the fictional illusion. He nervously turns against all of the fictional devices and conventions that are his stock in trade. Sometimes he explicitly draws attention to the artificiality of his writing: "I know that the tune I am piping is a very mild one . . ." Sometimes he undermines his own effects, by not allowing them to have the impact he presumably intended. He denies even modest expectations of suspense. . . . He openly chides himself for his cynical and digressive habits: "Be quiet. Don't pursue your snarling, cynical remarks, but go on with your story." He wavers between contradictory attitudes toward the world his characters inhabit, sometimes castigating it fiercely, sometimes acquiescing in its materialism. . . . The effect of these shifts and juxtapositions is often not a balancing of opposed perspectives, not a creative irony, but rather a nervous retreat, closing off a discussion that has got out of hand. . . . (pp. 150-51)

As a result Thackeray cannot develop larger structural ironies. No event in a Thackeray novel can have a stable meaning; no character can be finally known. For all its energy, *Vanity Fair* . . . tends to become an endless spiral of reflections and reverberations, mirrors and echoes. Though the narrative perspective is more fully controlled in *The History of Henry Esmond* . . . , this novel is a sort of optical illusion, facing now one way, now the other. (p. 151)

Of Thackeray's four major novels, *Pendennis* and *The Newcomes* are most useful in exploring some of the consequences of Thackeray's self-consciousness. . . . [In] them we can see Thackeray's narrative personality given its fullest embodiment. The personality revealed is that of the "implied author" of these novels.

What is the meaning of the implied author's presence in and behind the fictional world of *Pendennis*? One of the first problems we are aware of is Thackeray's uneasy relationship to his characters. He is overwhelmed by surfaces, appearances, gestures, and roles and has a deep uncertainty about human identity. At times he feels that the inner life of any other person is sacred and unknowable, but he is just as ready to assume that what cannot be known does not exist and that his characters are merely painted puppets. (p. 154)

Thackeray's particular conception of human character is most fully expressed in chapter 59 of *Pendennis,* where he says that "we alter very little," much less than we like to think, and that "circumstance only brings out the latent defect or quality, and does not create it." This is a limited conception of human character, an odd basis for a novel portraying in detail the growth of an artist. *Pendennis* reads like a *Bildungsroman* [novel portraying the youthful development of a major character] without a *Bildung* [formation; i.e., development]. It takes all of Thackeray's ingenuity to maintain our interest over this long novel in a protagonist who merely goes on revealing his essential nature over and over in different situations. (pp. 154-55)

[There] is a deviousness in Thackeray's relationship to Pen and to his readers. More than anything else, his deceptiveness is what raises and then holds our interest in *Pendennis*. (p. 155)

He is less interested in moral growth than in the human weaknesses and self-deceptions that make a character (or a reader) think it has taken place. By pretending to show growth, and then revealing that Pen is subject to the same self-deceptions hundreds of pages later, Thackeray makes us share as well as criticize Pen's limitations. The narrator's undependability and the alertness it demands of us partially make up for the lack in *Pendennis* of the teeming social world of *Vanity Fair*, in which a different kind of richness is achieved by the juxtaposition of so many different forms of selfish striving. In *Pendennis* Thackeray is trying to encompass in his own narration the richness of response that can give life to the portrayal of a static character.

A similar deviousness rescues the portrait of Helen Pendennis from sentimentality. . . . The incompatibility between Helen as a saintly figure and Helen as the earthly jealous mother remains. Throughout the novel Thackeray continues to give partial and unreconciled glimpses of Helen Pendennis; this is an unusual but effective method of characterization. (pp. 155-56)

The ending of the novel is . . . weak because Thackeray cannot maintain his deviousness. He wants to show Pen essentially unchanged, but at the end he cannot help implying that Pen is worthy of marrying Laura Bell. He tries to keep up a duality of response, suggesting that Pen is still playing a part (though a more attractive one) and that he is lucky to come off so well. But the impression persists that by choosing Laura over Blanche Amory he has achieved a self-mastery beyond the limitations of a static character. In *Pendennis* (unlike *The Newcomes*) Thackeray is still too dependent on the conventional Victorian happy ending. The problem is not self-consciousness, but a lack of complete confidence in his self-conscious narrative method.

*The Newcomes* is a far more successful novel than *Pendennis*. . . . In it Thackeray's self-consciousness shows itself best in his creative use of temporal perspectives. (pp. 156-57)

Just as Thackeray will often hold contradictory opinions about a character without reconciling them, he often expresses inconsistent attitudes about the past and the passage of time. We expect the greatest historical fiction to achieve a temporary resolution, enabling us to assent to both the remoteness of the past and its essential closeness. In Thackeray's novels the two feelings appear side by side but usually remain distinct. Either the past is all quaint trappings and queer ceremonies or it is indistinguishable from the present. The fictional world being created is either a remote fable-land or an everyday world just around the corner from our own.

The reader first senses the passage of time in *The Newcomes* through the agonizing slow pace of the novel. . . . The reader senses various patterns, such as the ongoing counterpoint between the language of financial materialism and the language of romance, but it is difficult to see why the counterpoint should be so unemphatic and repetitive. The vague and inconsistent chronology is another source of perplexity. Thackeray too often contradicts himself about the passage of years or the age of a character.

More significant and more bewildering is the variety of temporal perspectives through which the story is filtered. (pp. 157-58)

Yet the discrepancies . . . are essential to his achievement in conveying the feel of human memory. Just as he thinks that "we alter very little," he thinks that we rarely in our own lives transcend our confused everyday attitudes about the past. Most of the time we hold contradictory notions in our minds without being aware of the conflict—responding now to the unchanging and permanent aspects of human affairs, now to the ever-changing flux of experience. His art is an attempt to find a way to go on expressing this inconsistency in our memories, not to transcend it as so many other artists have tried to do. He is trying neither to recapture the past nor to find one satisfying image of it, but rather to render the texture of our feelings about that past. (pp. 159-60)

Thackeray had no interest in autonomous literary structures, and he knew he was not at his best when trying to carry his readers away from themselves into an independent fictional world. He was aware of himself as a man and as a storyteller, and he self-consciously made that awareness part of the story he was telling. The best of his novels justify themselves by the energy with which he gives voice to so many different impulses and intentions in continuous conflict, those of author and reader as well as those of characters. The illusion is created that every possible human perspective will be taken up, that even the meanest character or reader will have things seen his way for a moment. Though his personal strivings will be ultimately seen as vanity, they will be noticed and be given momentary dignity and plausibility.

This is not to say that Thackeray belongs with Sterne, Joyce, and Nabokov, novelists whose interest in characters and events is an excuse to explore the secondary fictional world of the novelist's relationship to his writing and to his readers. . . . Thackeray belongs in no one else's camp. The successes he achieves come from an unusual conception of himself as a writer. He refuses to take himself seriously as an artist, refuses to create impersonal, independently existing fictions. That refusal was caused by an inability to make disciplined demands on himself. The result is fortunate, as his mind is most interesting when most free and unforced, when his reflections can follow one another according to his momentary inclinations.

But this method makes its own demands: constant nervous energy to keep up a flexibility of response and a continuing readiness to turn on one's own formulations and assert the contrary.

Behind Thackeray's decline is an impatience with this kind of storytelling, combined with an inability to avoid it and work out for himself some other conception of his art. The late novels are spoiled not by self-consciousness but by his refusal to be as thoroughly self-conscious as he had been earlier. In his late years he lost patience with human diversity and complexity and grew unable to continue doing justice to its endless ramifications. He more and more tended to fall back on one particular sentimental voice as the last word. At his best he created fictional works of great power because of the self-conscious awareness that no person, not even the omniscient author, deserves that final word. (pp. 161-63)

> *Winslow Rogers, "Thackeray's Self-Consciousness," in* The Worlds of Victorian Fiction, *edited by Jerome H. Buckley (copyright © 1975 by the President and Fellows of Harvard College; excerpted by permission), Cambridge, Mass.: Harvard University Press, 1975, pp. 149-63.*

## JOHN CAREY   (essay date 1977)

Thackeray was a born sketcher. . . .

The immediacy of the sketch, its certainty and speed of line, and its seeming carelessness, as well as its power of ridicule, appealed to Thackeray's deepest preconceptions about art. . . . He had a brilliant gift for the impromptu in words as well as in drawing. Plenty of his thrown-off things survive, mostly bawdy—like his reaction to an unusually well-developed specimen of female portraiture, "'Tis true 'tis titty, titty 'tis, 'tis true'. . . . (p. 34)

Words were his job, and he strove to give them the immediacy of life. A start towards this was inventing new, onomatopoeic ones for noises which the old noise-words failed to distinguish between. 'Cloop', for the special noise of a wine-cork being drawn, proved handy, in view of Thackeray's subject matter. . . . 'Plapping' does for bears and water, too. The zoo's white bears in the **Roundabout Papers** 'winked their pink eyes as they plapped up and down by their pool', and Barnes Newcome's eloquence goes 'plapping on like water from a cistern'. (pp. 38-9)

Missiles and impacts, even without special words for them, are used to force vividness into Thackeray's writing. No one forgets Becky flinging Johnson's Dictionary into Miss Pinkerton's front garden at the start of **Vanity Fair,** or Rawdon tossing his son up in his arms and bumping his head against the ceiling, and frantically begging him not to cry lest he should wake Mama. . . .

But Thackeray's normal subject matter did not allow books or children to be thrown about much. What he developed was a style that, even in unviolent moments, works in flashes or spurts that relay a lot of information and suggestion very fast, so that the reader, as in life, sees more rapidly than he understands. (p. 39)

This deft suggestiveness happens all over Thackeray. Selecting examples is like picking grains from a beach. The contexts, of course, do not need to be quick or bright themselves. At sea off Algiers he notes 'gloomy purple lines of African shore, with fires smoking in the mountains'. There it is the sense of

brooding, unknown watchers that the glimpse of smoke supplies. But the thing is observed almost cursorily, while Thackeray's attention is sweeping on to the next bit of landscape, just as in a sketch it might be caught in a couple of pencillings. His metaphors and similes are put in with the same masterful carelessness—brief, unelaborate—like someone switching a light on and off to glance round an empty room. . . .

In the comic work the simile or metaphor has to illuminate and demolish the target at one go, while still remaining perfectly succinct and natural. Thus in **A Shabby Genteel Story** the curls of the Misses Gann are, we are informed, arranged on their shining foreheads 'damp and black as leeches'. The extreme, if oily, care the girls have taken over their coiffure, and their profound unwholesomeness, drop on the reader in one short, fat word. . . .

When Thackeray is being ironic (and he is among the greatest of English ironists), the casual air becomes vital. The tone has to be refrigerated, the detonating words craftily muted, so that the reader is almost out on the other side of them before their ridicule bursts around him. (p. 40)

To maintain the negligence and bravura Thackeray had to get his effects with the simplest words. They had to look easy and spontaneous. . . . But though the words had to be just common bits of currency, they had to be capable of linking into subtle compositions. Compare, as an illustration, the way Thackeray uses an ordinary word like 'hard' in describing two different facial expressions. First, the Earl of Crabs. In **Yellowplush** we see him looking 'hard and kind' at nurserymaids in the park. Here the two words tend to contradict each other. 'Hard' conveys the lustful glare; 'kind', the smiles with which the old lecher tries to mask it. The combination is quick and masterly— and looks easy because the words are so mundane. . . . The second 'hard' is used to depict little Rawdon's look in the head-bumping episode. He looked, we're told, 'in a very hard and piteous way at his father', and strove to obey his terrified injunction not to cry lest he wake Mama. Here 'hard' operates quite differently. It registers the boy's clenched effort to keep back his tears. It also suggests his startled realization that his father is afraid. He has good reason to look hard: he has just learnt something new about his parents' relationship. This power to make ordinary words do subtle things very quickly is a hallmark of Thackeray's style. . . . (p. 41)

[Thackeray] loved light, and was endlessly intrigued by its vagaries and coruscations. In the Mediterranean he kept trying to find words for the effects of 'astonishing brightness' —the palm trees in Rhodes 'with a sort of halo of light round about them'; Lisbon 'hot and shaky', as if there were an earthquake in the air. . . . How people or objects restricted or reflected light was the first, and often the only characteristic he noticed about them—the hulking London footman making a darkness in the cabin as he stoops through it in **The Kickleburys on the Rhine;** or the silver stubble on Major Pendennis's chin 'like an elderly morning dew'. . . . (p. 42)

Watching light meant documenting things which might not, to the unpainterly, seem very gripping—like the Paris gutters, which Thackeray apologized for dwelling on, but found irresistible. Buttons come into this category. It can safely be said that Thackeray is the leading describer of buttons among English novelists. They are frequently a great deal more important to him than either the clothes they fasten or their wearers. (pp. 43-4)

On the lookout for highlights, Thackeray's eye also relished objects that had just come out of someone's mouth—pipes, cigars, bits of barley-sugar—which, being still covered with saliva, shone. . . . The peculiar intimacy of something just taken out of the mouth gave it an erotic as well as a luminous potential for Thackeray. The bewitching Minna Löwe in ***The Fitzboodle Papers*** lights Fitzboodle's pipe for him, sucking the amber mouthpiece seductively, and tossing her head back to blow the smoke out, until Fitzboodle grows faint with desire, and hurries home to mumble the amber mouthpiece between his lips 'like a bit of barley-sugar'. (pp. 45-6)

This association of glistening amber-colour with sex ties in, of course, with Thackeray's fixation about girls with blonde or auburn or red hair. He found them both disturbing—even repellent—and irresistible, and often tries in the early works to resolve the quandary with jocular references to 'carrotty' locks, and so forth. . . .

Arms, though, not hair, were the part of the female anatomy that aroused Thackeray most. Their paleness and mobility satisfied his craving for reflected light. . . . (p. 46)

These gleaming, shoulder-mounted antennae which Thackeray's women are fitted out with are not sexually attractive in any simple sense. They carry a feeling of threat and hardness—arms for arming—which complicates their allure. . . . The feats of hypocrisy and meanness of which women are uniquely capable often occupy his pen. The shining arms they carry in his stories are not just light-effects, but express a particular view of the world (as, indeed, all light-effects must: Thackeray's buttons, for instance, draw attention to the cultural gulfs that lurk within minutiae—like eating peas with a knife). The separateness of women, and their need to fight or exploit men in order to survive, much impressed him. Becky and Amelia, in their different ways, both illustrate this—as do all his worthwhile females. (p. 47)

Another type of display-cabinet, incidentally, that occurs so frequently in Thackeray's work that it gets to seem like a nervous tic is the bow-window of a London club with a row of faces behind it. The details vary. . . . But basically the thing remains the same, and has the starkness of an emblem: a bulge of glass, with faces peering through it at the world beyond clubland. In its repetitiveness it provides an instance of the way in which Thackeray's art simplifies and schematizes life—as any art must—while appearing to represent its complexity. And it again shows that Thackeray's light-effects entail an interpretation of the world. The gleaming pane of glass represents his acknowledgement of a social barrier, and the faces beyond, comfortable, yet faintly comic, reflect his inclination to be ironic about social barriers and uphold them at the same time. Like bare arms, club windows are an expression of his divided feelings.

Bare shoulders which with their bony points of shoulder-blade and collar-bone make more efficient light-reflectors than bare arms, usually indicate moral unsoundness in Thackeray's women. . . . They are consequently less common than arms, but Thackeray uses them brilliantly as a focus in ***Going to See a Man Hanged***—an eye-witness account of the execution of the murderer François Benjamin Courvoisier, which was published in *Fraser's* in August 1840.

A masterpiece of impressionistic reporting, this work draws together a mesh of light-effects (growing more garish as the sun rises), and of intensely relished physical images, so that the vividness of life stands out clamorously against the darkness into which Courvoisier is to be plunged. That he is to be, as it were, blacked-out—hooded and dropped into a dark hole

from which the executioner's hands reach up to pull his legs and strangle him—is the aspect of his fate that seems most horrific to Thackeray. . . . The group which most excites his contempt comprises several tipsy, dissolute-looking young people, with one man 'lolling over the sunshiny tiles, with a fierce sodden face', while the women of the party:

> were giggling, drinking and romping, as is the wont of these delicate creatures; sprawling here and there, and falling upon the knees of one or other of the males. Their scarves were off their shoulders, and you saw the sun shining down upon the bare white flesh, and the shoulder-points glittering like burning glasses.

Thackeray's objection is not precisely moral. A young thief's mistress in the crowd, who swaps ribaldry with the standers-by, behaves quite as disreputably as the roof-top group, yet he feels attracted to her and her 'devil-may-care candour'. The harshly-lit women perched on the roof repel him because they create a cruel, raucous light-effect with their bare shoulders, besides being immodest. His sensitivity to light and his morals are intertwined. (pp. 48-50)

Thackeray's response to light was too various for it to have any regular association with moral repulsion, as in this glimpse of glittering Jezebels above the gallows. But when the lights start to dazzle and cluster around women in his writing it often spells danger, as if the gleam of their jewels or flesh, or simply of pieces of metal they are holding, were an unwholesome energy darting out of them. (p. 50)

[In] the later Thackeray, the light-effects deteriorate. They tend to become stagey. Gems and various kinds of lighting-equipment are accumulated in a mechanical way when a big scene has got to be written, and anyone used to reading Thackeray will be able to tell beforehand that significant action is afoot, simply by the amount of candle-power about. (pp. 50-1)

Young Thackeray, on the other hand, found himself swept into fantasy by light. . . . Light takes the commonness out of common objects in the early writing—a barley-sugar stick, a woman's shoulders 'like burning glasses', or the Bluecoat boy he notices in *Beulah Spa*—'His yellow stockings glittered like buttercups on the sunshiny grass'. . . . In these examples the light is chance and quick, and caught by Thackeray in quick, seemingly spontaneous images. The light-sources are vulgar, not gems or Embassy Balls, and they are important in themselves, poetically, not as flares for some dramatic event which the narrative is about to unroll. (p. 51)

What Thackeray's streamlined palette evinces is rigorous control.

The colours he usually limited himself to, in order to get the most resplendent effect most succinctly, were red and white. Red intrigued him. . . . Red's capacity to startle is exploited by Thackeray in, for instance, ***The Paris Sketch-Book,*** where he recounts how he unfortunately turned up too late for the guillotining of Lacenaire, and found, when he got to the place, only some ragamuffins dancing on a puddle of red ice. Less gruesomely, the winter sun, 'hung like a red-hot warming-pan' in the 'lilac haze' over Dulwich ponds (from the ***Roundabout Papers),*** shows redness lighting up Thackeray's style even late in life. (pp. 52-3)

As against red's warmth, white, used alone, was sinister for Thackeray. In the béguinage at Ghent, for instance, he saw 'a couple of old ladies in white hoods tugging and swaying about at two bell ropes', while five hundred others, in white veils, sat mutely contemplating, and it struck him as frightful—'white, and ghastly. Like an army of tombstones by moonlight'. Nuns, or any species approaching them, always upset him—enforcing that apprehension of woman's separateness and armedness that glinting white arms and shoulders also aroused. (p. 54)

But red and white flagrantly juxtaposed constitute the standard Thackerayan colour-combination, as much a mark of his style as club-windows or buttons, and there with the same eye-rinsing intent. As you follow the reds and whites through his career, you notice, as with other light-effects, a tendency towards the mechanical. Where before there had been an eager response to garishness and odd angles and low life, you find yourself landed with a sort of candy-striped routine. (p. 55)

Thackeray's manipulation of light and colour falls off, then. Slovenly formulas replace the quick, bright perceptions. It affects the very bones of his writing. For it would, as I have suggested, be over-simple to regard light and colour as optional extras, unconnected with meaning. To a large extent they determine what meanings can be purveyed. The importance, for Thackeray, of the arresting light-effects that people make with their clothes and bodies, for instance, relates both to a watchfulness and to a detachment from them, as people, that permit irony to operate. Similarly, the definiteness of his colouring, with its hard contrasts and unqualified tones, is of a piece with the peremptoriness and certitude that irony roots in. More tolerant, concessive or involved meanings could not co-exist with light and colour as Thackeray apprehends them. (pp. 56-7)

> *John Carey, in his* Thackeray: Prodigal Genius *(©1977 by John Carey; reprinted by permission of Faber and Faber Ltd), Faber and Faber, 1977, 208 p.*

---

## ADDITIONAL BIBLIOGRAPHY

Auchincloss, Louis. "The Two Ages of Thackeray." In his *Reflections of a Jacobite*, pp. 29-41. Boston: Houghton Mifflin Co., 1961.
    Argues that although Thackeray, "as he grew older, became an increasingly complacent Victorian novelist, he became also the greatest of them." Auchincloss maintains, however, that Thackeray differs from the Victorians in his theory of human motivation, and concludes that his "perception of self-interest is the ABC of modern psychology."

Chesterton, G. K. Introduction to *Masters of Literature: Thackeray*, edited by G. K. Chesterton, pp. ix-xxxii. London: George Bell and Sons, 1909.
    A general overview of Thackeray's major works. Chesterton concludes that "Thackeray represents, in that gigantic parody called genius, the spirit of the Englishman in repose."

Craig, G. Armour. "On the Style of *Vanity Fair*." In *Style in Prose Fiction*, edited by Harold C. Martin, pp. 87-113. English Institute Essays, 1958. New York: Columbia University Press, 1959.
    A consideration of the style of *Vanity Fair* based on the close analysis of several of the novel's key scenes.

Ennis, Lambert. *Thackeray: The Sentimental Cynic*. Evanston, Ill.: Northwestern University Press, 1950, 233 p.
    A biography which explores the development of Thackeray's attitudes toward life and society and the extent to which these attitudes shaped his works.

Flamm, Dudley. *Thackeray's Critics: An Annotated Bibliography of British and American Criticism, 1836-1901*. Chapel Hill: The University of North Carolina Press, 1967, 184 p.

A thorough, well-annotated bibliography of nineteenth-century criticism of Thackeray's works.

Fraser, Russell A. "Sentimentality in Thackeray's *The Newcomes*." *Nineteenth-Century Fiction* 4, No. 3 (December 1949): 187-96.
    A discussion of sentimentality in *The Newcomes* illustrated by lengthy excerpts from several of the novel's most important scenes.

Grieg, J.Y.T. "Thackeray: A Novelist by Accident." In *From Jane Austen to Conrad: Essays Collected in Memory of James T. Hillhouse*, edited by Robert C. Rathburn and Martin Steinmann, Jr., pp. 72-81. Minneapolis: University of Minnesota Press, 1958.
    Proposes that Thackeray "took to prose fiction as an afterthought" and therefore never achieved a fully satisfying technique in art. Grieg's earlier study, *Thackeray: A Reconsideration* presented a harsher assessment (see excerpt above, 1950).

Hannay, James. *Studies on Thackeray*. 1868. Reprint. Port Washington, N.Y., London: Kennikat Press, 1970, 107 p.
    The first book-length critical survey of Thackeray's works.

Harden, Edgar F. *The Emergence of Thackeray's Serial Fiction*. Athens: The University of Georgia Press, 1979, 385 p.
    A detailed analysis of "the compositional processes that resulted in the month-by-month appearance of [Thackeray's] serial fiction." Through the close examination of manuscripts and proof-sheets for the monthly installments of Thackeray's major novels, Harden refutes the common view of Thackeray as a careless and hasty writer.

Hubbell, Jay B. *"The Virginians* of William Makepeace Thackeray." In his *South and Southwest: Literary Essays and Reminiscences*, pp. 153-74. Durham, N.C.: Duke University Press, 1965.
    An account of Thackeray's two lecture tours of the United States and how they inspired and influenced *The Virginians*. Hubbell also considers the accuracy of Thackeray's depictions of George Washington and eighteenth-century Virginia society and calls *The Virginians* "one of the first and best of Anglo-American international novels."

Jackson, Holbrook. "William Makepeace Thackeray." In his *Great English Novelists*, pp. 255-80. London: Grant Richards, 1908.
    A general critical introduction to Thackeray's works which includes a brief account of his life.

Kiely, Robert. "Victorian Harlequin: The Function of Humor in Thackeray's Critical and Miscellaneous Prose." In *Veins of Humor*, edited by Harry Levin, pp. 147-66. Cambridge: Harvard University Press, 1972.
    An examination of Thackeray's use of humor in such works as *The Irish Sketch Book* and *The English Humourists*.

Kronenberger, Louis. "*Vanity Fair*." In his *The Polished Surface: Essays in the Literature of Worldliness*, pp. 201-16. New York: Alfred A. Knopf, 1969.
    Finds *Vanity Fair* "the prime instance, the perfect example of worldliness in the long and, on the whole, constantly worldly English tradition."

Lord, Walter Frewen. "The Apostle of Mediocrity." *The Nineteenth Century and After*, No. 301 (March 1902): 396-410.
    Maintains that Thackeray refused to acknowledge excellence, preferring, rather, to depict only the ludicrous and the discreditable in his works.

Lyall, Sir Alfred C. "Thackeray." In his *Studies in Literature and History*, pp. 76-120. 1915. Reprint. Freeport, N.Y.: Books for Libraries Press, 1968.
    A basic introductory discussion of Thackeray's major novels. Lyall estimates that Thackeray will always stand in the front rank of Victorian novelists.

O'Connor, Frank. "Thackeray: *Vanity Fair*." In his *The Mirror in the Roadway: A Study of the Modern Novel*, pp. 111-24. New York: Alfred A. Knopf, 1956.
    Demonstrates that Thackeray "is unique among Victorian novelists in having no romanticism in him."

Olmsted, John Charles. *Thackeray and His Twentieth-Century Critics: An Annotated Bibliography, 1900-1975*. New York, London: Garland Publishing, 1977, 249 p.

An indispensable source on twentieth-century Thackeray scholarship.

Phillipps, K. C. *The Language of Thackeray*. The Language Library, edited by Eric Partridge. London: Andre Deutsch, 1978, 205 p.

A detailed study of Thackeray's style, grammar, use of proper names, and modes of address. Phillipps also considers the effectiveness of Thackeray's imitation of eighteenth-century English in *Henry Esmond*.

Quennell, Peter. "*Vanity Fair*." In his *Casanova in London*, pp. 97-110. New York: Stein and Day, 1971.

A general discussion of *Vanity Fair*. Quennell concludes that "it is from Thackeray's response to reality, rather than from his criticism of mankind, that his tale derives its epic character."

Ray, Gordon N. *The Buried Life: A Study of the Relation Between Thackeray's Fiction and His Personal History*. London: Oxford University Press, 1952, 148 p.

Demonstrates the great extent to which Thackeray modeled the characters and plots of his major novels on acquaintances, family members, and personal experiences.

Ray, Gordon N. *Thackeray: The Uses of Adversity, 1811-1846*. Vol. I; *Thackeray: The Age of Wisdom, 1847-1863*. Vol. II. New York: McGraw-Hill Book Co., 1955, 1958.

The definitive biography.

Sedgwick, Henry Dwight. "Some Aspects of Thackeray." In his *Essays on Great Writers*, pp. 309-54. 1903. Reprint. Freeport, N.Y.: Books for Libraries Press, 1968.

Maintains that although Thackeray's style is excellent, his artistic vision is ultimately false.

Stevenson, Lionel. *The Showman of "Vanity Fair": The Life of William Makepeace Thackeray*. New York: Charles Scribner's Sons, 1947, 405 p.

A lively, well-written general biography.

Stewart, David H. "Thackeray's Modern Detractors." In *Papers of the Michigan Academy of Science, Arts, and Letters, Vol. XLVIII*, edited by Hubert M. English, Jr., pp. 629-38. Ann Arbor: The University of Michigan Press, 1963.

Explores the sources of negative twentieth-century criticism of Thackeray's works. Stewart divides Thackeray's detractors into four general groups: "the aristocrats, the psychologists, the Victorian repudiators, and the critical formalists."

Sutherland, J. A. *Thackeray at Work*. London: The Athlone Press, 1974, 165 p.

An examination of Thackeray's process of revision. Sutherland illustrates, through Thackeray's correspondence and a close analysis of extant manuscripts of his major novels, "Thackeray's general manner of going about his work."

Swinnerton, Frank. "William Makepeace Thackeray: 1811-1863." In *The Great Victorians*, edited by H. J. Massingham and Hugh Massingham, pp. 471-81. Garden City, N.Y.: Doubleday, Doran & Co., 1932.

Maintains that Thackeray was the most "typically Victorian" of the Victorian novelists and that his gentility was a handicap that seriously restricted his themes.

Tillotson, Geoffrey. *Thackeray the Novelist*. Cambridge: Cambridge University Press, 1954, 312 p.

Demonstrates that the unification devices found throughout his fiction indicate that Thackeray intended for his numerous works to form a whole. Illustrating his argument with lengthy excerpts from the major novels, Tillotson shows how Thackeray used structure, recurring characters, imagery, the authorial "I," and a pervasive underlying philosophy to create a continuity between his major works.

Van Ghent, Dorothy. "On *Vanity Fair*." In her *The English Novel: Form and Function*, pp. 139-52. New York: Holt, Rinehart and Winston, 1953.

An exploration of *Vanity Fair*'s narrative technique.

Wagenknecht, Edward. "Counter-Blast: W. M. Thackeray." In his *Cavalcade of the English Novel*, pp. 268-85. New York: Henry Holt and Co., 1954.

A good introductory discussion of Thackeray's life, major works, literary techniques, and point of view.

Wells, Chauncey W. "Thackeray and the Victorian Compromise." In *Essays in Criticism*. University of California Publications in English, edited by W. H. Durham, M. J. Flaherty, and C. W. Wells, Vol. I, pp. 179-99. Berkeley: University of California Press, 1929.

Claims that the true history of the Victorian Age can only be read in the works of Thackeray. Wells maintains that Thackeray is the only writer who fully treats the "Victorian compromise" between the rich bourgeoisie and the landed aristocracy, who kept the English lower classes in their subservient position.

Weygandt, Cornelius. "Thackeray." In his *A Century of the English Novel*, pp. 83-101. New York: The Century Co., 1925.

Maintains that Thackeray is the greatest master of English prose.

Wheatley, James H. *Patterns in Thackeray's Fiction*. Cambridge, Mass., London: The M.I.T. Press, 1969, 157 p.

Examines Thackeray's uses of parody, structural patterns, and realism. Wheatley argues that parody "is both conceptually and biographically fundamental to Thackeray's career as a novelist."

# (Johann) Ludwig Tieck

## 1773-1853

(Also wrote under the pseudonym of Peter Lebrecht) German novella writer, novelist, dramatist, poet, translator, essayist, critic, and editor.

Tieck was one of the most diverse, prolific, and influential of the German Romantic writers. His *Marchen*, novellas based on fairy tales, embody many Romantic elements: satiric irony, innovative form, psychological exploration of human motives, and a belief in the primacy of the imagination. These works are considered his greatest achievement.

Tieck was born in Berlin. Early in life, he developed an interest in acting, but his father persuaded him to continue his education. While still in school, he demonstrated considerable writing talent and worked as a ghost writer for a schoolmaster who wrote pulp novels. In 1792, Tieck began his university studies, attending Halle, Göttingen, and Erlangen; his major fields of study included theology, philosophy, philology, and literature. At Göttingen, he began writing *Geschichte des Herrn William Lovell*, a novel influenced by the works of Johann Wolfgang von Goethe and Samuel Richardson. At the university, he also became close friends with Wilhelm Heinrich Wackenroder, whom he had known at the Friedrich Werder Gymnasium. Wackenroder, one of the founders of German Romanticism, became a major influence on Tieck's later work. In 1793, the two traveled throughout southern Germany and together discovered the cultural wealth of the medieval era. *Franz Sternbalds Wanderungen*, on which they collaborated, is based on their journey and is one of the first *Künstlerromane*, or novels about artists. Following his travels, Tieck went to Berlin, where he worked as a hack writer from 1794 to 1797, composing serious fiction in his spare time. During this period, he published *Volksmärchen*, a collection of novellas and dramas based on German folk stories, which brought him immediate recognition. Novels, plays, poetry, and more novellas quickly followed.

Already an established author in 1798, Tieck moved to Jena where he came under the influence of Friedrich and August Wilhelm von Schlegel and other members of their circle—Goethe, Friedrich von Schiller, and Novalis. During this formative period, Tieck also became interested in the works of William Shakespeare and Miguel de Cervantes. August Wilhelm von Schlegel involved Tieck in translating Shakespeare's plays, a project which consumed much of his energy for the next thirty years, and which strengthened his interest in Elizabethan drama. He traveled to England in 1817 to further his research, and eventually completed numerous editions of English drama in German translation, in addition to several collections of critical essays and a biographical novel about Shakespeare. Tieck also prepared editions of then little-known German authors such as Heinrich von Kleist, wrote a biography of Cervantes, and translated *Don Quixote* into German. Beginning in 1800, Tieck became increasingly crippled by rheumatic fever, and his daughter Dorothea assumed many of his duties on Schlegel's project. In 1819, Tieck was named official *Dramaturg*, or dramatic consultant, to the Dresden city theater, and from 1841 until his death he lived as writer-in-residence at the court of King Frederick William IV of Prussia.

Tieck's long literary career can be divided into two major periods. The early, romantic period includes *Abdallah*, a gothic novel; *Peter Leberecht, eine Geschichte ohne Abeuteuerlichheiten*, *Geschichte des Herrn William Lovell*, and *Franz Sternbalds Wanderungen*, novels which treat the theme of an individual's search for self-knowledge; and *Volksmärchen*, a group of imaginative novellas and dramas. In *Volksmärchen*, Tieck explores the relationship between reality and the imagination. Using a dense, poetic style, Tieck creates an atmosphere which enables his readers to accept improbable occurrences as possible, even inevitable. Tieck is often praised for his masterful depiction of the supernatural. He is also praised for his integration of numerous themes, such as the loss of innocence, dualism in nature, guilt, fatalism, and the destructive power of love. His plays *Der gestiefelte Kater (Puss in Boots)*, *Ritter Blaubart (Bluebeard the Knight)*, *Die verkehrte Welt (The Land of Upside Down)*, and *Prinz Zerbino, oder Die Reise nach dem guten Geschmack*, reflect his experiments in dramatic irony. By allowing his characters to comment on themselves, the action, stage techniques, and the audience, Tieck intentionally destroys the artistic illusion of his plays in order to satirize conventional values.

By contrast, the second phase of Tieck's career is marked by growing artistic and personal conservatism, an interest in mysticism, and, especially in the later novellas, a bitter attack on the Young Germans—a group of younger poets who rejected German Romanticism and Idealism, and advocated political, religious, and sexual reform. Major works of Tieck's second period include the dramas *Leben und Tod der heiligen Genoveva, Kaiser Octavianus, Fortunat,* and the novel *Vittoria Accorombona (The Roman Matron).* More political and less ironic and poetic than his earlier endeavors, these later works were unfavorably received.

Early in his career, August Wilhelm Schlegel, Johann Fichte, and many others had judged Tieck to be the artistic equal of Goethe. He had produced *Puss in Boots,* a satiric masterpiece, and had been among the first writers to employ the principles of German Romanticism formulated by the Schlegels. However, in his later years, younger writers such as Heinrich Heine labeled him a decadent conservative. There is still considerable debate over Tieck's achievement. While some critics believe that Tieck's works are marred by a lack of internal unity, others praise his ability to depict in his fiction the chaos which he perceived in life.

Tieck's work has influenced writers as diverse as Heine, E.T.A. Hoffmann, Nikolai Gogol, Paul Verlaine, Edward Bulwer-Lytton, Samuel Taylor Coleridge, and Nathaniel Hawthorne. For introducing English and Spanish literature into the German canon, for developing the novella form, and for experimenting with dramatic irony, Tieck is considered a key figure among the German Romantic writers.

## PRINCIPAL WORKS

*Abdallah* (novel) 1795

*Geschichte des Herrn William Lovell.* 3 vols. (epistolary novel) 1795-96

*Peter Leberecht, eine Geschichte ohne Abeuteuerlichheiten* (novel) 1795

*Der gestiefelte Kater* [first publication] (drama) 1797 [*Puss in Boots,* 1974]

*Ritter Blaubart* [first publication] (drama) 1797 [*Bluebeard the Knight,* 1844]

*Volksmärchen (novellas and drama) 1797

*Franz Sternbalds Wanderungen* [with Wilhelm Heinrich Wackenroder] (novel) 1798

*Prinz Zerbino; oder, Die Reise nach dem guten Geschmack* [first publication] (drama) 1799

*Die verkherte Welt* [first publication] (drama) 1799 [*The Land of Upside Down,* 1978]

*Kaiser Octavianus* [first publication] (drama) 1804

*Leben und Tod der heiligen Genoveva* [first publication] (drama) 1804

*Fortunat* [first publication] (drama) 1816

*Gedichte.* 3 vols. (poetry) 1821-23

*Novellen.* 7 vols. (novellas) 1823-28

*The Pictures. The Betrothing* (novellas) 1825

*Der Anfruhr in den Cevennen* (novella) 1826 [*The Rebellion in the Cévennes,* 1845]

*Love Magic. The Faithful Eckhart and the Tannenhauser. Auburn Egbert* (novellas) 1826

*Ludwig Tiecks Schriften.* 28 vols. (novels, novellas, drama, poetry, and essays) 1828-54

*The Old Man of the Mountain, The Love Charm, and Pietro of Abano* (novellas) 1831

*Des Lebens Überfluss* (novella) 1839

*Vittoria Accorombona* (novel) 1840 [*The Roman Matron,* 1845]

*The Mysterious Cup. The Runenberg* (novellas) 1843

*Letters of Ludwig Tieck, Hitherto Unpublished: 1792-1853* (letters) 1937

**Five Dramas of Ludwig Tieck Hitherto Unpublished (drama) 1959

*This collection includes the novella *Der blonde Eckbert.*

**This collection includes the dramas *Medea, Meiners, Gotthold, Siward,* and *Braddeck.*

---

## THOMAS DE QUINCEY (essay date 1825)

There was in Tieck's early works the promise, and far more than the promise, of the greatest dramatic poet whom Europe had seen since the days of Calderon: there was a rich, elastic, buoyant, comic spirit, not like the analytical reflection, keen biting wit, of Molière and Congreve and other comic writers of the satirical school, but like the living merriment, the uncontrollable, exuberant joyousness, the humour arising from *good* humour, not, as it often does, from *ill* humour,—the incarnation, so to say, of the principle of mirth,—in Shakespeare, and Cervantes, and Aristophanes; and, as a wreath of flowers to crown the whole, there was the heavenly purity and starlike loveliness of his *Genoveva.* Had the rest of Tieck's life kept pace with the fertility of the six years from 1798 to 1804, he must have been beyond all rivalry the second of German poets; and, as Aeschylus in the *Frogs* shares his supremacy with Sophocles, so would Goethe have invited Tieck to sit beside him on his throne. Unfortunately for those who would have feasted upon his fruits, the poet, during the last twenty years, has been so weighed down by almost unintermitting ill health that he has published but little. . . . Latterly, [however,] Tieck's genius has taken a new spring, in a somewhat different direction from that of his youth. He has written half a dozen novels. . . . [And not] many people, even in this country, possess a more extensive and accurate acquaintance with our ancient drama than Tieck; no one has entered more fully into the spirit of its great poets than Tieck has shown himself to have done in the prefaces to his *Old English Theatre* and his *Shakespeare's Vorschule;* few have ever bestowed such attention on the history of the stage in all countries, or have so studied the principles of dramatic composition and the nature of dramatic effect; hardly any one, I may say no one, ever learnt so much from Shakespeare: no one, therefore, can have more to teach us about him; and . . . no one was ever so able to trace out the most secret workings of the great master's mind, or to retain his full, calm self-possession when following him in his highest flights; no one ever united in such perfection the great critic with the great poet. One may look forward, therefore, with confidence to the greatest work in aesthetical criticism that even Germany will ever have produced. (pp. 464-65)

[In my translation of Tieck's tale **The Love-Charm,** grievously I] must have failed if any reader with a feeling for poetry does not perceive and enjoy the beauty of the descriptions, especially of the two eventful scenes, the power and passion of the wild dithyramb, the admirable delineation of the characters in proportion to their relative importance, and the poetical harmony and perfect *keeping* of the whole. Nothing can be more delicate than the way of softening the horror that might be felt for the bride. She has not even a name, that there may be no distinct object for our disgust to fasten on; she is only spoken of under titles of a pleasurable meaning; her beauty, like Helen's on the walls of Troy, is manifested by its effect; the young men are astonished at it; her air of deep melancholy impresses even the gayest and most thoughtless, and is thus more powerful than if pages had been employed in giving utterance to her remorse. . . . The poet has . . . wisely kept all his power of characteristic delineation for the two chief persons in the tale; and rarely have any characters been brought out so distinctly within a work of such dimensions. The contrast between them runs through every feature, yet each is the necessary complement to the other; the abuse which they vent in the ball-room each against his dearest friend, and in the ears of almost a stranger, is in the true style of our frail affections, veering before the slightest puff of self-will; nor is there a circumstance mentioned about either which tends not to complete the picture and is not all but indispensable. On some occasions a whole life and character are revealed by a single touch; as, for instance, when Emilius exclaims, *No bread! Can such things be?* No other man could have been so ignorant of what goes on in the world as to marvel at such a common occurrence. . . . [The] whole scene of the peasant's marriage,—which at first sight may appear like a somewhat idle digression, brought in for no better reason than amusement,—is absolutely necessary to the tale as a work of art. It not only shows the character of Emilius in a fresh and important point of view, not only supplies him with fuel, so that he is ready to burn at the approach of the first spark . . . : the peasant's wedding is necessary as a contrast, as a complement, and as a relief to the other marriage; nor can that calm and masterly irony which is among the first elements in the mind of a great poet be more clearly manifested than it is here, where the pomp and rejoicing of the great and wealthy are suddenly turned ''into sorrow and lamentation and dismay,'' while the poor and the abashed and the despised are enabled to pass their days in what to them is comfort, and to obtain the enjoyment of a day ''unto which in after-times they may look back with delight.'' (pp. 465-66)

> *Thomas De Quincey, '' 'The Love-Charm' : A Translation from Tieck'' (originally published in* Knight's Quarterly Magazine, *No. 7, Autumn, 1825), in his* The Collected Writings of Thomas De Quincey, Vol. XII, *edited by David Masson, A. & C. Black, 1897, pp. 434-67.*

## JOHANN WOLFGANG VON GOETHE   (essay date 1826)

My mind has been stimulated in many ways by [Tieck's] noteworthy book [*Dramaturgic Fragments*].

As a dramatic poet, as a writer who by extensive travels and by personal observation and study of foreign theatres has qualified himself as a critic of insight and knowledge in connection with our native theatre, and as one who by scholarly study has fitted himself to be a historian of past and present times, the author has an assured position with the German public, which is here especially evident and notable. In him, criticism rests upon pleasure, pleasure upon knowledge, and these criteria, which are usually thought of as distinct, are here fused into a satisfying whole.

His reverence for Kleist is highly praiseworthy. As far as I am personally concerned, in spite of the sincerest desire to appreciate him justly, Kleist always arouses in me horror and aversion, as of a body intended by nature to be beautiful, but seized by an incurable illness. Tieck is the very reverse; he dwells rather upon the good that has been left by nature; the deformity

he puts aside, excusing much more than he blames. For, after all, this man of genius deserves only our pity; on this point we do reach agreement.

I also agree with him willingly when, as champion for the unity, indivisibility and inviolability of Shakespeare's plays, he wants to have them put on the stage without revision or modification from beginning to end. (pp. 126-27)

Though in these respects I completely approve of the valuable efforts of my old co-worker, I must confess that I differ from him in some of his utterances; as, for instance, that ''Lady Macbeth is a tender, loving soul, and as such should be played.'' I do not consider such remarks to be really the author's opinion, but rather paradoxes, which in view of the weighty authority of our author can only work great harm.

It is in the nature of the case, and Tieck himself has presented significant illustrations of the fact, that an actor who does not feel himself to be quite in agreement with the conventional portrayal, may in clever fashion modify and adjust it to himself and his own nature, and fit the new interpretation so well as to provide, as it were, a new and brilliant creation, and indemnify us for the clever fiction with unexpected and delightful new grounds of comparison and contrast.

This we must admit as valid; but we cannot approve the case where the theorist makes certain intimations to the actor, whereby the latter is led astray to portray the rôle in a new manner and style against the obvious intention of the poet. (pp. 127-28)

An important paper is Tieck's explanation of the *Piccolomini* and the *Wallenstein* [both by Friedrich Schiller]. I saw these plays develop from beginning to end, and I am filled with admiration at the degree of penetration which he shows in treating a work which, although one of the most excellent not only on the German stage but on all stages, yet in itself is unequal, and for that reason often fails to satisfy the critic, although the crowd, which does not take the separate parts with such strictness, is necessarily charmed with it as a whole. (p. 128)

> *Johann Wolfgang von Goethe, ''Ludwig Tieck's 'Dramaturgic Fragments','' translated by Randolph S. Bourne (1826), in his* Goethe's Literary Essays, *edited by J. E. Spingarn, Harcourt, Brace and Company, 1921 (and reprinted by Books for Libraries Press, 1967; distributed by Arno Press, Inc.), pp. 126-29.*

## FRASER'S MAGAZINE   (essay date 1831)

[The tales in *The Old Man of the Mountain, the Love Charm, and Pietro of Abano: Tales from the German of Tieck*] are short, but then they possess a grace, an ease, a deep meaning and philosophy, which, after enchanting the reader, will somewhat tax his powers of reflection, although his labour will be rewarded with the precious fruit of moral conviction, if he be zealous and right-minded, and a seeker after the truths of life. We have unfolded throughout the flowing narrative the lofty aspirations of a susceptible and ingenuous mind, and a beautiful development of true poetic feeling; while superior powers of reflection and judgment have laid open some of the mysteries of existence, which, for the most part, lie deeply hidden in the breast of man, making him the blind instrument, though an accountable one, of excitement and passion. Even in the simple guise of these tales the most important of subjects is partially unravelled—that man is, generally speaking, the framer of his own destiny—that he is born a free agent, to all purposes—that he has the golden talent of life committed to his custody—and that, according to his careful or careless guardianship of the same, will his after-reckoning elevate him to denizenship amid celestial spirits, or depress him to the dismal condition of everlasting and unrelenting agony.

This is high praise, but not higher than the volume deserves. . . . (p. 446)

The novels of Tieck are chiefly ironical. Many, like *The Pictures* and *The Betrothed,* are occasional, and even polemical, in their origin; and if they had not a value quite independent of their temporary interest, would pass with it. But the things against which their irony is levelled are identified with human nature. Enthusiasm is continually misdirected, being propagated rather by imitation than originally excited, in the individual who feels it, by the conscious development of his own powers and energies, in the contemplation of a particular subject. Tieck's tales, besides, are almost perfect models of composition, and in a kind nearly new to English literature, and which we should like to see naturalised in it. . . . [The] compression of the elements which compose them within the smallest possible compass, constitute the peculiar charm and character of such novels, which differ from longer tales in something else than quantity. They must not be confounded, either, with the *novelas* and *novelle* of Spanish or Italian literature, which are in general only circumstantial anecdotes. None of their component parts must be left undeveloped, none dilated to an arbitrary extent. The characters must be various and original, such as if introduced under any circumstances would be remarkable; but, as finding room to act freely and shew themselves fully in so small a space, shall excite peculiar surprise and delight. Such are the especial qualities which impart so much interest to the novels of Tieck, and entitle him to universal commendation. (p. 460)

*"Tales from Tieck,"* in Fraser's Magazine, *Vol. IV, No. XXII, November, 1831, pp. 446-60.*

## [GEORGE MOIR]   (essay date 1833)

[Tieck] seems to have perceived that [Bluebeard] was not an ordinary being, but he evidently wanted that knowledge of human nature which was necessary to understand the anomalies he presented [in this character in *Bluebeard*]. His plummet was too short to fathom so profound a character. (p. 207)

In Tieck's view, the marvellous of the Nursery Tale was to be reduced as nearly as possible to the standard, of common life no longer to remain the moving principle of the story, but only occasionally to manifest itself in fitful glimpses, sufficient to remind the reader or spectator, that an invisible agency, like a thread of silver tissue, pervaded and ran through the whole web of human existence. The main interest was to rest on human passions, crimes, or follies, and the ever-springing changes which the ordinary courses of real life exhibits. The difficulty, therefore, was in such a case to find a subject which should possess the airy charm of a Nursery Tale, and yet the human interest should not be entirely merged in the allegorical or the marvellous. . . .

The great aim of Tieck throughout is evidently to keep down the marvellous as much as possible, as so even to render it doubtful whether there be any marvel in the case after all; to pitch every thing on a subdued and natural key, and to produce

his catastrophes by motives and incidents arising naturally out of the contrast characters of his piece. (p. 209)

The subsidiary characters are grouped about [Bluebeard] with much diversity of feature and situation. Even the characters of the sisters . . . are discriminated by light, yet decided touches. The brothers, too, are ably drawn, and the peculiarities of their characters are made to exercise a natural and important influence on the progress of the drama. (p. 210)

The wit, such as it is, is too obviously prepared, and the characters too palpably opposed to each other, on a principle of absolute contrast. Had *Bluebeard* been written in three Acts instead of five, and the action confined to the single idea of the punishment of curiosity, it would have been an admirably effective acting play. The whole of the last Act is dramatic, and agitating in the highest degree. As it is, however, we scarcely wonder that, as yet, *Bluebeard*, though printed in 1797, and read, admired, and lauded by every German critic, since Schlegel led the way in the *Jena Literatur Zeitung*, has found no manager enterprising enough to bring it upon the stage. (p. 223)

[George Moir], *"Tieck's 'Bluebeard',"* in Blackwood's Edinburgh Magazine, *Vol. XXXIII, No. CCIV, February, 1833, pp. 206-23.*

## HEINRICH HEINE   (essay date 1835)

[*In his later works, Tieck criticized the ideals and work of the writers associated with the Young Germany movement. Their contempt for German Romanticism and political conservatism made them natural enemies to Tieck. In the excerpt below, Heine, who sympathized with many of the beliefs of the Young Germans, evaluates Tieck's achievement. Although he states that Tieck "is always a great poet, for he can create living forms, and words burst from his heart which can move our own," he finds his works ultimately derivative and asserts that "a fainted-heartedness, something undecided and uncertain, or a certain feeble-mindedness, is, and ever was, to be observed in him."*]

After the Schlegels, Ludwig Tieck was the most effective author of the Romantic school. For it he fought, thought, and sang. . . . He was, like the Delphian god, intoxicated with lyrical fire and critical cruelty. And when, like him too, he had pitilessly flayed alive some literary Marsyas he merrily grasped with bloody fingers the golden chords of his lyre and sang a sweet song of love.

The poetical polemic which Tieck waged in dramatic form against the adversaries of the school belongs to the most remarkable curiosities of our literature. They are satirical plays, which are generally compared with the comedies of Aristophanes. Yet they differ from the latter almost as much as a tragedy by Sophocles differs from one by Shakespeare. If the ancient comedies had the same cut and style, the strictly drilled step, and the exquisitely metrical language of ancient tragedies, so that they might pass for parodies, so are the dramatic satires of Tieck cut in as original and strange a manner, just as Anglicanly irregular and as metrically capricious as the tragedies of Shakespeare. (pp. 341-42)

[Tieck is] the best novelist in Germany. Yet all his works are not of equal worth or of the same kind. We can distinguish in him, as in painters, many manners. (p. 346)

The works which Tieck wrote in his first style, mostly tales and long novels, among which **"William Lovell"** is the best, are very insignificant and without poetry. It would seem as if the rich poetic nature of this man was frugal or stinted in his youth, and that he saved up all his spiritual wealth for a later time. Or was Tieck himself ignorant of the treasure which was in him, and were the Schlegels needed to discover it with their divining-rod? For as soon as he came into touch with them, all the riches of his imagination, his deep feeling and his wit, at once showed themselves. Diamonds gleamed, the purest pearls rolled out in streams, and over all flashed the ruby, the fabulous carbuncle gem of which romantic poets have often said and sung. . . . His best [dramatic] productions [written in his second style] are **"The Emperor Octavian," "The Holy Genofeva,"** and **"Fortunatus."** . . . (pp. 347-48)

Far more precious than those dramas [however] are the novels which Tieck wrote in this, his second manner. These too are mostly taken from old popular legends. The best are **"The Blonde Eckbert"** and **"The Runenberg."** In these compositions we feel a mysterious depth of meaning, a marvellous union with Nature, especially with the realm of plants and stones. (p. 348)

But now a strange change takes place in Tieck, which is shown in his third manner. Having been silent for a long time after the fall of the Schlegels, he again appeared in public, and that in a manner which was little expected of him. The former enthusiast, who had once in visionary zeal thrown himself on the breast of the Roman Catholic Church, who had fought enlightenment and Protestantism with such power, who breathed nothing but feudality and the Middle Age, and who only loved art in naïve outpourings of the heart, now appeared as the foe of what was visionary, as a depicter of modern middle-class life, as an artist who required in art the clearest self-consciousness—in short, as a reasonable man. Thus has he shown himself in a series of recent novels. . . . A deep study of Goethe is visible in them, and it is specially this Goetheism which characterises his third style. There is the same artistic clearness, cheerfulness, repose, and irony. (pp. 349-50)

Tieck is always a great poet, for he can create living forms, and words burst from his heart which move our own. But a faint-heartedness, something undecided and uncertain, or a certain feeble-mindedness, is, and ever was, to be observed in him. This want of decision is only too perceptible in all that he did or wrote. Certainly there is no independent character in his works. His first manner shows him as a mere nothing, his second as a true and trusty squire of the Schlegels, his third as an imitator of Goethe. His theatrical criticisms, which he published under the title of **"Dramaturgic Pages,"** constitute his most original work; but they are theatrical criticisms. (p. 352)

Tieck never troubled himself with serious studies; his work of this kind was limited to modern languages and the older documents of German poetry. As a true Romanticist he was always a stranger to classic studies; nor did he ever busy himself with philosophy, which seems to have been altogether repugnant to him. From the fields of philosophy Tieck gathered only flowers and switches—the first for the noses of his friends, and the latter for the backs of his foes. With serious culture or scientific agriculture he had naught to do. His writings are bouquets and bundles of rods, but never a sheaf with ears of corn. (p. 353)

*Heinrich Heine, in a chapter in his* The Works of Heinrich Heine, Vol. V, *translated by Charles Godfrey Leland (translation copyright, 1892; originally published as his* De l'Allemagne, 1835*), William Heinemann, 1892, pp. 341-58.*

*THE FOREIGN QUARTERLY REVIEW* (essay date 1839)

The *Novellen* of Tieck . . . furnish a striking proof of the facility with which the public mind in Germany is led astray, and of the numerous false directions in which it has wandered within the last fifteen years. Most, if not all of these works, are written to correct some erroneous tendency of the time, to exhibit some popular fallacy in its true colours, to show as in a mirror their folly to the gaping multitude, and thus warn them back to reason.

They throw also much valuable light on the radical defects of the German character, as well as on the nature of the absurdities in which our Trans-Rhenane cousins have of late years indulged. (p. 359)

We would here observe that the tales of Tieck may still further be recommended to the English reader for the simplicity, purity, and beauty of their style, and for their uniformly unobjectionable character and tendency. Whether the author's object be to depict Catholic bigotry, as in his masterly story, *Der Hexen-Sabbath;* or puritanical hypocrisy, as in that sweet and simple tale, *Die Verlobung;* or wild passions and the workings of fanaticism, as in *Des Dichters Leben (Erster Theil),* and in *Der Aufruhr in den Cevennen;* or venial eccentricities and the comicalities of German provincial life, as in the exquisite *Novelle, Der Jahrmarkt;* he is always easy and natural, and never shows the slightest disposition to recur to the meretricious colouring of late years in such great demand amongst German novel-writers, as with the notorious wallowers in that fetid slough yclept the French romantic school. His principal defect indeed is, not straining after excitement, but too studiously avoiding it. Some of his tales principally consist of conversations and, though admirably penned, do not furnish the kind of matter which the English reader is accustomed to seek in works of fiction. Tieck should in fact always be read in a contemplative mood: he will certainly disappoint those who take up a story for mere temporary amusement, and remain passive in expectation of startling incidents, or a romantic denouement: his works on the contrary are sources of instruction, not directly conveyed, but to be extracted by mental exertion on the part of the reader himself. (p. 360)

Whether a nation in the book of history is infected by political fever, or a German town in one of Tieck's stories suffers under masonic delusion—the moral is the same. The more men wander from the old, beaten track, the nearer they esteem themselves to the goal to which that track alone can lead them. The wilder their speculations, the more confident they feel of their certain and rapidly-approaching realization. The more transitory and fantastic their dreams, the more assured are they of their reality, and that they have risen to stand for ever. Towards illustrating human delusion therefore, truth always has been, and always will be stronger than fiction. Man cannot imagine himself so weak and credulous as he really is.

That singular self-complacency which prompts the deluded to be superfluously confident, and to indulge luxuriously in daydreams of peace and security, whilst danger is evidently imminent; that smile with which man is led by fate to the slaughter,—has been graphically delineated by Tieck, and frequently imparts at once the simplest and deepest tragic interest to his descriptive scenes. (pp. 368-69)

[With] respect to purity of style, moral tendency, and philosophic truth, no more estimable works can be found in the whole range of German literature than the *Novellen* of Tieck. (p. 380)

*"Tieck's Collected Tales," in* The Foreign Quarterly
Review, *Vol. XXIII, No. XLVI, July, 1839, pp. 358-
80.*

## THOMAS CARLYLE   (essay date 1839)

[Tieck's literary life began with] the publication of three Novels, following each other in quick succession: *Abdallah, William Lovell* and *Peter Leberrecht.* These works found small patronage at their first appearance, and are still regarded as immature products of his genius; the opening of a cloudy as well as fervid dawn; betokening a day of strong heat, and perhaps at last of serene brightness. A gloomy tragic spirit is said to reign throughout all of them; the image of a high passionate mind, scorning the base and the false, rather than accomplishing the good and the true; in rapt earnestness 'interrogating Fate,' and receiving no answer, but the echo of its own questions reverberated from the dead walls of its vast and lone imprisonment.

In this stage of spiritual progress, [however,] . . . it was not Tieck's ill fortune to continue too long. His *Popular Tales,* published in 1797 as an appendage to his last Novel, under the title of *Peter Leberrechts Volksmährchen,* already indicate that he had worked his way through these baleful shades into a calmer and sunnier elevation; from which, and happily without looking at the world through a painted glass of any sort, he had begun to see that there were things to be believed, as well as things to be denied; things to be loved and forwarded, as well as things to be hated and trodden under foot. The active and positive of Goodness was displacing the barren and tormenting negative; and worthy feelings were now to be translated into their only proper language, worthy actions. In Tieck's mind, all Goodness, all that was noble or excellent in Nature, seems to have combined itself under the image of Poetic Beauty; to the service and defence of which he has ever since unweariedly devoted his gifts and his days.

These *Volksmährchen* are of the most varied nature: sombre, pathetic, fantastic, satirical; but all pervaded by a warm genial soul, which accommodates itself with equal aptitude to the gravest or the gayest form. A soft abundance, a simple and kindly but often solemn majesty is in them: wondrous shapes, full of meaning, move over the scene, true modern denizens of the old Fairyland; low tones of plaintiveness or awe flit round us; or a starry splendour twinkles down from the immeasurable depths of Night. (p. 244)

A very slight power of observation will suffice to convince us that Tieck is no ordinary man; but a true Poet, a Poet *born* as well as *made.* Of a nature at once susceptible and strong, he has looked over the circle of human interests with a far-sighted and piercing eye, and partaken deeply of its joy and woe; and these impressions on his heart or his mind have been like seed sown on fertile ground, ripening under the skyey influences into rich and varied luxuriance. He is no mere observer and compiler; rendering back to us, with additions or subtractions, the Beauty which existing things have of themselves presented to him; but a true Maker, to whom the actual and external is but the *excitement* for ideal creations, representing and ennobling its effects. His feeling or knowledge, his love or scorn, his gay humour or solemn earnestness, all the riches of his inward world, are pervaded and mastered by the living energy of the soul which possesses them; and their finer essence is wafted to us in his poetry, like Arabian odours on the wings of the wind.

But this may be said of all true poets; and each is distinguished from all by his individual characteristics. Among Tieck's, one of the most remarkable is his combination of so many gifts in such full and simple harmony. His ridicule does not obstruct his adoration; his gay Southern fancy lives in union with a Northern heart. With the moods of a longing and impassioned spirit he seems deeply conversant; and a still imagination, in the highest sense of that word, reigns over all his poetic world. Perhaps, on the whole, this is his distinguishing faculty; an imagination, not of the intellect, but of the character, not so much vague and gigantic as altogether void and boundless. A feeling as of desert vastness steals over us in what appeared to be a common scene; or in high passages, a fire as of a furnace glows in one small spot, under the infinitude of darkness: Immensity and Eternity seem to rest over the bounded and quickly-fading.

His mind we should call well cultivated; for no part of it seems stunted in its growth, and it acts in soft unimpeded union. His heart seems chastened in the school of experience; fervid, yet meek and humble, heedful of good in mean forms, and looking for its satisfaction not in passive, but in active enjoyments. His poetical taste seems no less polished and pure: with all his mental riches and excursiveness, he merits in the highest degree the praise of chaste simplicity, both in conception and style. No man ever rejected more carefully the aid of exaggeration in word and thought, or produced more result by humbler means. Who could have supposed that a tragedy, no mock-heroic, but a real tragedy, calculated to affect and excite us, could have been erected on the groundwork of a nursery tale? Yet let any one read *Blaubart* in the *Phantasus,* and say whether this is not accomplished. Nor is Tieck's history of our old friend *Bluebeard* any Fairyland *George Barnwell* [a play by George Lillo]; but a genuine play, with comic as well as tragic life in it; 'a group of earnest figures, painted on a laughing ground,' and surprising us with poetical delight, where we looked for anything sooner.

In his literary life, Tieck has essayed many provinces, both of the imaginative and the intellectual world; but his own peculiar province seems to be that of the *Mährchen;* a word which, for want of a proper synonym, we are forced to translate by the imperfect periphrase of Popular Traditionary Tale. Here, by the consent of all his critics, including even the collectors of real *Mährchen,* he reigns without any rival. The true tone of that ancient time, when man was in his childhood, when the universe within was divided by no wall of adamant from the universe without, and the forms of the Spirit mingled and dwelt in trustful sisterhood with the forms of the Sense, was not easy to seize and adapt with any fitness of application to the feelings of modern minds. It was to penetrate into the inmost shrines of Imagination, where human passion and action are reflected in dim and fitful but deeply significant resemblances, and to copy these with the guileless humble graces which alone can become them. Such tales ought to be poetical, because they spring from the very fountains of natural feeling; they ought to be moral, not as exemplifying some current apophthegm, but as imaging forth in shadowy emblems the universal tendencies and destinies of man. That Tieck has succeeded thus far in his Tales is not asserted by his warmest admirers; but only that he now and then approaches such success, and throughout approaches it more closely than any of his rivals. (pp. 248-49)

*Thomas Carlyle, "Preface and Introductions to the Book Called German Romance," in his* Critical and Miscellaneous Essays, Vol. I, J. Munroe and Com-*

pany, 1839 (and reprinted in his Critical and Miscellaneous Essays: Collected and Republished, Vol. I, Scribner, Welford, and Company, 1872, pp. 228-84.*

### MONTHLY REVIEW   (essay date 1841)

Entertaining as we do no little esteem for Herr Tieck's literary character, we cannot but regret that the current of his fame has hitherto run so smoothly: we fear it is destined to encounter a rude re-action, and that his genius from being extravagantly overrated will, according to the world's laudable custom in such cases, be punished by unjust depreciation and neglect. Tieck has long maintained a high place amongst the foremost spirits of his nation, and now stands confessedly at the head of its living authors, the death of Goëthe having left him in undisputed possession of the literary sovereignty of Germany. . . . [Notwithstanding] this, or rather exactly because of . . . this, we are convinced that disappointment must be the predominant feeling of the English reader on perusing the tales of this first of modern German authors. In [the tales collected in *Gesammelte Novellen*], regarded as models in Germany, the Englishman will frequently be struck by the absence of qualities he has been accustomed to consider the most essential in fictions purporting to treat of real life. He will find in them indeed wit, humour, fancy, subtlety of thought, felicity of language, and, pervading them all, rather dimly felt than practically impressed, a kindly spirit of moderation in judgment and feeling, that were it less obscurely transcendental,—would it but more invest itself in the forms of palpable reality,—would win from us the gracious names of common sense and charity. But this high praise is marred by the want of living interest in the narrative. Tieck holds up to nature no mirror reflecting with life-like accuracy the forms, the actions, and the passions of this busy world; he neither unlocks the deep fountain of our tears, nor agitates us with fear and hope, nor startles us from the repose of our easy chair with the earthquake of inextinguishable laughter. We read his tales with pleasure, alloyed it may be now and then with a sense of tediousness, and we insensibly acquire for their author as we proceed the esteem and regard that is due to a kindly, honourable, and discerning nature; but we never as we read forget the book, ourselves, and all surrounding objects, to be borne away in the spirit into other scenes, and to live, and feel, and suffer, and enjoy in the persons of other men: we never lose our consciousness of our own locality, nor for a moment forget its topographical distinctness from Thebes or Athens. The truth is, the story is with Tieck for the most part a matter of minor consideration; what wonder is it then if it should be of still less importance for the reader? Its principal use is to serve as a vehicle for light sketches of character, and witty sallies, and above all for discussions and dissertations on philosophy, literature, and art. Such a form it is obvious can have few intrinsic charms; it imposes on the author difficulties to be overcome, rather than it rids him, in attracting the reader's attention: and herein lies the peculiar triumph of Tieck's genius that he does throw a grace over this unpromising form, and by the influence of a style in the highest degree clear, and racy, and tinged with the warm colouring of a poetic fancy, engage and long sustain the reader's interest. To this may perhaps in some measure be attributed the excessive praise bestowed by some English critics on Herr Tieck's latter tales. Our admiration of them is somewhat akin to what we accord to the clever performances of the Italian fantoccini: the actors are but puppets; in the language they are supposed to utter, we recognise throughout the voice of the man in the box, under all the disguises it assumes, and our admiration of the skill evinced in making the most of such imperfect mechanism induces us to overvalue the intrinsic merit of the exhibition. The Germans indeed seem to consider the action of the puppets as more natural than nature itself;—according to them truth abides alone in the conceptions of the poet's mind, and the phenomena of actual life are but its travestie. Thus [the German critic] Sternberg exalts Tieck far above Sir Walter Scott, because the latter forsooth displays but the lower artistic power of setting before us the very flesh and blood of humanity, treading a soil every feature of which we behold as in actual vision, while Tieck, disdaining such mere journeywork, imparts to us the sublimities of a more ethereal poetry. We own we are not sufficiently German to be penetrated by the force of this criticism. (pp. 608-10)

> "Tieck's German Novels," in Monthly Review (copyright © 1841), n.s. Vol. I, No. IV, April, 1841, pp. 608-20.

### THE SOUTHERN QUARTERLY REVIEW   (essay date 1846)

There is an ever living freshness and beauty, especially in the best German writers who have passed, or are passing, off the stage, which leads us frequently to turn to their pages for pleasure or consolation, and, of these, we admire none more than Ludwig Tieck, the rival of the celebrated Göethe, as a critic, and, as is admitted on all hands, one of the finest minds and rarest scholars, that his country, so fruitful in genius, has produced. We are now, however, more particularly concerned with his **"Gestiefelle Kater."**

Years elapsed before the merits of this production were fully acknowledged. The young and thoughtless laughed at, while they delighted in its bold strokes, and the great conservative mass shrugged their shoulders in contempt—yet, still, it made its silent way, and at the present day, ranks among the finest of the poet's dramatic works. Many of its scenes are replete with keen wit and satire, and most unsparingly does the author apply the lash to reigning, arbitrary error. (pp. 237-38)

The author must have felt very confidently the intrinsic worth of his piece, to venture so often to destroy its illusion, as he does in its several acts, where his pit performers freely vent their jests on the play itself; yet we find examples of the same in Aristophanes; and even Shakspeare himself, in some of his tragedies, at one minute, allows his drama to appear as truth, and in the next, utters some speech, which casts ridicule on the allusion. (p. 238)

Had Ludwig Tieck been assured of the public representation of this, his early jeu d'esprit, he would have probably thrown far more dramatic effect into his third act which, as it now stands, is little more than a dressing up of the old story, and replete with caustic wit as, for instance the description of the journey to the magician's palace, is only humorous, not dramatic. In fact, the failure visible in the concluding action of the piece, as viewed in juxta-position with the stirring machinery of the foregoing scenes, casts a shadow on that discriminating taste, which otherwise so well conceived and executed its part. (pp. 242-43)

> "Tieck's 'Gestiefelle Kater'," in The Southern Quarterly Review, Vol. IX, No. XVII, January, 1846, pp. 237-43.

**FRASER'S MAGAZINE**   (essay date 1847)

Tieck is an author of such universal celebrity, his reputation is so firmly established, and his name so widely spread throughout the literary world, that to dwell upon his merits as a writer would be altogether superfluous. The versatility of his genius is very remarkable, and in every thing he has attempted his success has been unquestionably beyond the ordinary standard. The peculiarity of his humour, the brilliancy of his wit, the richness of his imagination, justly class him among poets of a high order. Tieck, though a disciple of Goethe, is not an imitator even of so great an original. His ideas, his style, his opinions, are all peculiar to himself; he relies, and with reason, upon his own powers. . . .

*Vittoria Accorombona* is a remarkable work; it constitutes, we think, the single species of its class. Tieck styles it a romance; but it is rather a poetical biography of the celebrated woman whose name it bears. The freshness of mind and warmth of feeling displayed throughout these pages are surprising, especially if the author's advanced age be taken into consideration. It is a historical romance. . . . (p. 567)

*Vittoria Accorombona* is no imitation; it is an original medal struck for the occasion. . . .

Tieck undertook a difficult task when he selected for his heroine a woman whose superiority of intellect places her above and beyond all ordinary rules. It is not easy to invest such a character with interest. . . . The consciousness of her superiority is too apt to tempt her to transgress the limits of female propriety. No genius, however splendid, can compensate for this. . . .

Tieck and Madame de Staël are, as far as we can recollect, the only authors of modern times who have ventured to represent women of genius moving in the ordinary relations of life. (p. 568)

The most striking feature of the work before us is, that it transplants us at once, and without effort, into another age. Like the Seven Sleepers, we wake to manners and opinions wholly different to our own. The great marvel, however, is, that we ourselves become, as if by magic, suddenly imbued with them. We are thus prepared not to judge of men and events according to our preconceived views of morality, but we see with the eyes and hear with the ears of the sixteenth century. (p. 573)

*"Tieck's 'Vittoria Accorombona',"* in Fraser's Magazine, *Vol. XXXVI, No. CCXV, November, 1847, pp. 567-75.*

**THE BRITISH QUARTERLY REVIEW**   (essay date 1853)

*William Lovell* is a novel in the form of letters interchanged between its various characters, and by this epistolary method (if method it may be called), the story is made to bound like an india-rubber ball from hand to hand, till readers of but moderate perseverance are well nigh driven to despair. . . . The remembrance of the book is like that of some passionately wild Adagio, and the key-note, through every modulation, is, 'he who perfectly knows himself will hold mankind for monsters.' . . . It is a chaos of sentiments, many of them characteristic of the Romanticists generally, showing how Tieck had come under the influence of their modes of thought, and had adopted their views of life. At the same time, however,

in the character of Lovell he censures indirectly some of their wilder extremes. (pp. 357-58)

[*Abdallah*], like *William Lovell,* is obviously the production of an undeveloped period, distracted with unanswered questions, social and moral. But, like the first novels of Goethe, it told with force upon the contemporary waste of common-place. (p. 358)

[*The Wanderings of Franz Sternbald*] is certainly one of the most excellent novels in the German language. The beauty of the characters, the poetry of the style, the conversations upon painting, all add their charms to an harmonious picture of the sunny side of life in the Middle Ages. (p. 359)

The reader will have remarked . . . that admixture of flame and cloud, of beauty and of nonsense, of genuine feeling and inane extravagance, which is so distinctive of the Romantic School. The aim in this work . . . is the glorification of art. (p. 360)

The story of *The Fair Egbert* is one of the most beautiful [of the tales in *Phantasus*], but marred by the excess of that fatalistic gloom which is the skeleton almost ever present at the brightest feasts of the Romanticists. The only blemish of the *Runenberg* is an error in the same direction. (p. 361)

The tales of Tieck are everywhere illustrative of the Romanticist principles, of the peculiar effort made by that school to combine the real and the ideal. . . . Accordingly, Tieck mingles with his most fanciful creations the discussion of everyday topics, and intersperses the wonders of fairy-land with satirical side-thrusts at the prosaic absurdities of literary coteries or fashionable affectation, and above all, at the expiring follies of that decrepit state which was about to vanish down its own trapdoors. Minor incidents, such as happen unnoticed every day, suddenly appear, fraught with deep instruction and unlooked-for beauty, showing to us hand in hand the sisters Poetry and Truth. (pp. 361-62)

In this walk, Tieck is the very king of story, and under his footsteps sprang, with fresh life, a tender shoot of historic poetry, which is struggling now towards manhood. (p. 362)

It is against . . . stage evils and . . . public ignorance that the satire of [*The World Topsy-turvy*] is mainly directed.

The poem of *Prince Zerbino in Search of Good Taste* is somewhat in the same style, though with almost less regard to any rules of form. It contains very much of what appears upon the surface to be pure nonsense; but how often it happens that the jester proves wiser than the sage. (p. 365)

[It has] been advanced, concerning these dramatic tales, that with all their irony there is nothing in them. This is, in fact, true to a certain extent. The material of the pieces was the author's last solicitude. His great endeavour was the emancipation of form from the strict bondage of rule and custom by which it had so long been hampered. It is the material by itself against which he is for ever crusading. In *Puss in Boots,* he brings all the force of his sharp-shooting to bear against the ignorance and conceit which compose the subject of certain sentimental didactic plays. *The Dwarf* is a satire on the false imitation of the antique, and *Bluebeard* upon the solemn absurdities of the popular chivalrous romances. The life and spirit of the plays is to be found in the untrammelled capricious form, which bends the subject to its will, defying all rule, and satirizing its own achievements. . . . However much of justice there may be in the censure which has fallen upon Tieck . . . , it is but fair to remember what we have to throw into the other scale—his labours to root out the weeds which were growing up apace and destroying the vitality of the drama; his anxiety to see in the place of these a natural growth, deriving its nourishment from the national history, its vigour and success from a healthy national taste. (pp. 374-75)

> *"Ludwig Tieck," in* The British Quarterly Review, *Vol. XVIII, No. XXXVI, November 1, 1853, pp. 355-80.*

### GEORGE BRANDES   (essay date 1873)

An apprehensive disposition, predisposing to hallucinations, congenital melancholy, at times verging on insanity, a clear, sober judgment, ever inclined to uphold the claims of reason, and a very unusual capacity for living in and producing emotional moods—such were the principal characteristics of Ludwig Tieck. He was the most productive author of the Romantic School, and, after its disruption, he wrote a long series of excellent novels, depicting past and present more realistically than Romantic writers were in the habit of doing. (p. 59)

Tieck's first work of any importance is **William Lovell**. . . . In it, when treating of art, he already occasionally touched the strings upon which the Romantic School subsequently played. (p. 60)

[There] is no book which reveals to us more distinctly the foundations on which the Romantic movement rests. . . . [Yet] *Lovell* is an extremely tedious book to read now-a-days; the style is tiresomely diffuse, the characters are as if lost in mist. Some of the subordinate figures, the devoted old man-servant, for instance, are weak imitations of Richardson—there is not a trenchant trait nor a dramatic situation in the whole book. Its merit, which is as German as are its defects, lies in its psychology. The hero is a youth who is led, slowly and surely, to do away, as far as he himself is concerned, with all authority, to disregard every one of the traditional, accepted rules of life, until at last he is leading the life, not only of a confirmed egotist, but of a criminal. (p. 61)

Tieck had perceived what were to be the characteristics of the new school, in personal lawlessness, and the glorification of this lawlessness, under the name of imagination, as the source of life and art. Lovell is an extravagant personification of these characteristics. . . . [He] is one of this period's many variations of the Don Juan-Faust type, with a touch of Schiller's Franz Moor. Satiety of self-contemplation has, in his case, led to a boundless contempt for mankind, to a ruthless sweeping away of all illusions; the one and only consolation being that thus hypocrisy is unveiled and the ugly truth seen. . . . [Lovell] is as cold as ice, as cold as Kierkegaard's shadow of a seducer, whom he in this particular anticipates. He does not commit his excesses with his flesh and blood, but with his fantastically excited brain. He is a purely intellectual being, a North German of the purest water. And there is one particular in which he is, in anticipation, astonishingly Romantic. When he has, so to speak, burned himself out, when every spark of conviction is extinguished in his mind, and all his feelings lie ''slain and dead'' around him, he seeks refuge in the supernatural and places his trust in mystic revelations, of which an old impostor has held out the prospect. (pp. 63-4)

The personality here is so hollow, weighs so light in its own estimation, that the impression it produces on itself is that it is both real and unreal; it has become unfamiliar to itself, and

has as little confidence in itself as in any exterior power. It stands outside its own experiences, and when it acts, feels as if it were playing a part. (p. 64)

[In] this one man's habit of mind we have all that, which, transferred to art, became the notorious irony of Romanticism. Here, in the character, is the undisguised egotism which looks upon life as a rôle; there, in art, the misconception and exaggeration of Schiller's idea that artistic activity is ''a game,'' a play, *i.e.* an activity without any outward aim—in short, the belief that true art is that which perpetually shatters its own edifice, renders illusion impossible, and ends, like Tieck's comedies, in self-parody. There is the very closest resemblance between the manner in which the hero acts and the manner in which the comedy is written. The irony is one and the same; it may all be traced back to the same egotism and unreality. (p. 65)

> *George Brandes, "Tieck and Jean Paul," in his* Main Currents in Nineteenth Century Literature: The Romantic School in Germany, *Vol. II, translated by Diana White and Mary Morison (originally published as* Hovedstrømninger i det 19de aarhundredes litteratur: Den romantiske Skole i Tydakland, *1873), William Heinemann, 1902, pp. 59-68.\**

### GEORGE HENRY DANTON   (essay date 1907)

[*The following is taken from the earliest book-length study in English of Tieck. Danton concentrates on the progression of Tieck's treatment of nature throughout his career from "the voluptuous pictures in natural setting of the early works to the gloomy and sensual demonism" of his later works. Danton concludes that Tieck's "distinct contribution is a vivid spiritualization, not merely of the forces of nature but of nature itself."*]

Tieck was not interested in life. The main elements of his work are poetry and art. He felt the indefinite pains of an unreal existence, and had a certain blindness toward the great problems of the world and something of that Don Quixote who meant so much to him. He dealt too much with abstractions even for Germans, among whom abstractions have a value not understood by more practical foreigners. (p. 1)

One feels that he does not know life, that he has not observed closely and that he cannot characterize it. His personages run together; they become lay-figures upon which to drape costumes, or they suggest dummies in the hands of a ventriloquist. (p. 2)

Both in philosophical receptivity and in religious fervor, Tieck was of the impressionable type, and as he came under various influences at different periods of his career, so the result tends to become an undigested mass of ideas from many sources, with a consequent shifting of attitude. The most important factors in his cultural sum are plainly Goethe, Jacob Boehme and Shakespere, but Fichte, Ben Johnson, Cervantes, the Romanticists, Schiller and Solger, not to mention many others, exert a more or less transitory influence on him.

It was under the influence of Fichte's philosophy, as well as from a natural predilection for such ideas, that Tieck early came to believe that the whole outside world was only a reflex of himself, and that whatever was there, was projected there by his own ego. In **"Abdallah"** and **"Lovell"** this philosophy led to an ideal of life which made pleasure its aim. . . . (p. 33)

This idea runs through Tieck's works in several forms; in one of the **"Lebenselemente,"** self-observation is identified with observation of nature. In "**Das alte Buch**" the reaction of man upon nature is very strongly expressed in the words "Ohne Stimmung ist keine Natur da" [Without atmosphere there is little nature], while in "**Die Vogelscheuche**," the idea has degenerated into a statement almost therapeutic in value, where the astronomer Heinzmann expatiates on the influence of the spiritual body on the material. . . .

Yet though the poet in these and other passages may believe this world to be only a reflex of himself, he cannot help but indicate that the world of observable objects, interacts upon him in a way that makes it possible for the critic to speak of nature-influence. Nature-analysis cannot always mean mere self-analysis; the poet in so far as he is a poet and a creator of plastic forms, must have an objective attitude toward nature, and Tieck in his most transcendental period does live outside of himself and not in a world purely ideal. Nature is ever present before one's eyes, as he himself makes the stranger tell the drunken miner in "**Der Alte vom Berge;**" it is this nature that he emphasizes, in which he sees bonds of sympathy with man, and whose cult is a continual source of happiness. (p. 35)

Probably nowhere more than in "**Die Vogelscheuche**," that novel in which Tieck almost more than in any other work loosed the bonds of his fancy, gave free rein to his imagination and wove truth and unreality so madly together that it is impossible to disengage the one from the other in the ludicrous tapestry, is found the sense of the minute in nature. Here the real world, the sober every-day world of Philistinism, is visited by the maddest and most fantastic of elves, elves who have a real existence in this world and are a part of its daily doings. . . . The variety of fantastic impressions grows with each word, in spite of the fact that the whole is a vehicle for Tieck's satire and for an expression of his dislike of certain schools and creeds, for he betrays besides this tendentiousness a fine sense of attention to and feeling for the great mass of creeping and budding things that man does not usually notice. His sympathy with the bee and bird and his insight into the life of the smallest living creature are almost unrivaled. (p. 46)

[But] Tieck neither emphasises nor develops to any very great extent the direct education of nature as such. (p. 54)

Dark, desolate or terrible nature is a background for man's actions. Prospero worrying over the absence of his son in "**Das Reh**," finds all the world in a tumult; the sun has fled, the air moans, the storm is unchained, and never before has the sky been so heavy over the kingdom. Quite in accord with this are the restless days of "**Peter Lebrecht**," though they are satirically meant. (p. 64)

Thus Tieck progresses from the voluptuous pictures in natural setting of the early works to the gloomy and sensual demonism of his version of the Tannhäuser saga and to distortions of fancy such as are found in "**Das Donauweib**" and in "**Der greichische Kaiser**," where all nature is represented as offering a series of voluptuous forms to the intoxicated eye of the sensualist. On the other hand, in "**Octavianus**," the delicate interlacing of the two elements is wrought out with infinite skill and with great luxuriousness of language and imagery, so that one feels that here are signs of power and life. (pp. 80-1)

There seems to be in Tieck a titanic wrestling with nature, not as Jacob wrestled with God for a blessing, or even with the discouraged horror of one like Antenor struggling with a monster whose strength is renewed at every fall to the earth, but with a savage rebellion at the mystery, and with a feeling of the hopelessness of a strife against one's own most intimate

terrors. Here at least it may be said that Tieck rises to the level of a great poet, since in a feeling for and in an expression of the psychology of mystery he is unsurpassed. (p. 81)

Nothing shows more clearly the intensity of Tieck's feeling for the life of the world about him and his sense of being surrounded by a nature animated and anthropomorphic than the many passages which assign to nature eyes and sight. The externally impinging lowers and lurks at every turn, and man seems never able to escape the fixed and watchful eye of the universe. (p. 83)

[Nature] is endowed with mental as well as physical attributes. The trees shake their heads with an inner joy, and nod as if pious; the oak-tree is delighted or solemn. Solemnity also characterizes the advancing night and the stars. In "**Das Reh**," when heaven is threatening no blade of grass dares to raise its head. (p. 84)

Even the highest human attributes, such as will and memory, are assigned to natural objects. . . .

It is perfectly natural that the relation of [natural] objects to man should be both friendly and hostile. . . . (p. 85)

The hostility of nature is expressed for example, in its anger. . . . [The] grass can raise itself against man and the trees can scold. . . . Even in so banal a story as "**Ulrich der Empfindsame**," the idea crops out with an element of satire; ". . . even inanimate nature rebels against me, flint, tinder, fuel, waist-coat and satin stockings," while in "**Klage und Trost**" the very road is faithless and leads the lover from his mistress. This enmity can become so strong that Lovell under the influence of terror can feel that the world itself holds him fast and that all nature points at him in scorn. (p. 86)

It is only because Tieck was so at home in such a nature that it did not rouse in him more of that abject terror that might be expected from one who presented it on this side so constantly. Conventionalities like the enigma of the moonlight, the terror of the dark that the daylight drives away, or of woods and ruins, fade into insignificance before the reality of the interpretation of the Tannhäuser saga, or before the demonism of "**Der blonde Eckbert**" and of "**Der Runenberg**." This is the subtle power of such novels as "**Der Wassermensch**," "**Der Mondsüchtige**," and "**Waldeinsamkeit**," and is of importance in understanding "**Karl von Berneck**." The love ravings of Golo as expressed in that song around which the whole drama was written, "Dicht von Felsen eingeschlossen," convey a sense of abandon to these forces which amounts, in the words of Hettner, to pure nature fatalism.

It may in general be said that Tieck's attitude shows him to be in a transition stage. He is not absolutely on the plane of the moderns, for he lays too much stress on the traditional phases of the lighter and happier sides of nature, and the mood of Richard Jefferies, "Nature is beautiful always," is in the main foreign to him; he is, however, distinctly modern in his antagonism to mere utilitarianism in nature, since he wished its beauty to be enjoyed for its own sake. His distinct contribution is a vivid spiritualization, not merely of the forces of nature but of nature itself. (p. 87)

*George Henry Danton, in his* The Nature Sense in the Writings of Ludwig Tieck *(copyright 1907, Columbia University Press; reprinted by permission of the publisher), Columbia University Press, 1907 (and reprinted by AMS Press, Inc., 1966), 98 p.*

EDWIN H. ZEYDEL   (essay date 1931)

[*Despite his considerable success as a critic and translator, Tieck is most often discussed as a novella writer, poet, and dramatist. In one of the earliest considerations in English of Tieck's translations and studies of Elizabethan literature, Zeydel discusses the importance of Tieck's criticism to contemporary German theater, and asserts that one of his greatest contributions was his insistence that Shakespeare's plays be staged as they were in Shakespeare's time.*]

What is the significance, from the German viewpoint, of [Tieck's] studies in [Elizabethan literature]? The five fragments of his **Buch über Shakespeare** point at first to a purely rationalistic approach and an interest in practical questions of stagecraft. This attitude toward Shakespeare was new to Germany. In their later sections the fragments advocate a more theoretical point of view and a concern for the dramas as works of literature and of art. . . . The early essay **Über die Kupferstiche** shows Tieck's intuitive appreciation of Shakespeare's native power and an ability to sense the most dramatic situations in his plays. The paper **Shakespeares Behandlung des Wunderbaren,** written quite in Lessing's manner, reveals a clear recognition of the distinction between Shakespeare's technique in tragedy and that which he employs in comedy.

By making dramas of Ben Jonson accessible for the first time to German readers, Tieck performed a distinct service. His critical studies of this author are profound and significant.

In the three collections of translations, **Altenglisches Theater, Shakespeares Vorschule** and **Vier Schauspiele von Shakespeare,** sixteen Elizabethan plays now not ascribed to Shakespeare were rendered accessible to German readers. Thus Germans were enabled not only to judge the nature of these dramas, but also, by means of comparison, to form conclusions as to Shakespeare's preeminent position as an Elizabethan. The effect of **Altenglisches Theater** and **Vier Schauspiele,** to be sure, Tieck impaired by calling all the ten plays early works of Shakespeare. This penchant for blindly assigning doubtful plays to Shakespeare was one of Tieck's greatest weaknesses as a Shakespearean critic. Other faults were his general tendency to jump at conclusions which suited his preconceived romantic notions; his inadequate knowledge of the English language; and his condescending attitude toward the English critics, which grew out of a crotchet that he alone understood and appreciated Shakespeare. There is a peculiar dualism in Tieck, worthy of serious attention. In his imaginative works he constantly strove to banish all subjectivism. In his critical work, however, he was subjective to a fault.

In **Shakespeares Vorschule** Tieck proved more cautious, for here he gave [the English dramatists] Greene, Heywood, Rowley and Massinger full recognition.

The **Dramaturgische Blätter** and **Der junge Tischlermeister** offered helpful criticism of the acting and staging of Shakespeare's plays in Germany at the time. In this and in his constant endeavor to have the plays staged as they were staged in Shakespeare's day—with absolute fidelity to the texts—lies one of Tieck's most important services. Though his ideas concerning the Shakespearean stage were only partially correct, they anticipated many of the reforms introduced later in the nineteenth century. . . . And had it not been for Tieck, the Schlegel translation of Shakespeare would hardly have been completed. This redounds to Tieck's credit, whatever may be the defects of the continuation sponsored by him. Moreover, the very fact that he revived the Schlegel project prompted others to compete

with him in the task of turning Shakespeare into German. Thus he paved the way for the modern eclectic editions of which Germany may well be proud. Tieck was also the first German writer to call attention to Shakespeare's merits as a sonneteer and to attempt a German rendering of one of his sonnets. . . . Finally, in **Dichterleben** he contributed a poet's attempt, considered successful at the time but now regarded as a failure, to recreate the early life of Shakespeare.

We may conclude then that Tieck was a bold pioneer who pointed the way to the new era of Cohn, Creizenach and the modern critics, and who through his very misconceptions challenged later scholars to take up the gauntlet; that he made no systematic exploration of Shakespeare but rather a series of useful forays; that he was the first German to take Shakespeare's contemporaries seriously and to study Shakespeare not as an isolated phenomenon but against the background of his times; that Shakespeare's popularity on the German stage is due mainly to the example which he set; and that because of his insistence upon the romantic point of view his critical studies, though extensive and searching, were largely futile from the point of view of philological research. (pp. 33-5)

Both Tieck and Lamb praise the magic of Shakespeare's poetic imagery yet find fault with details. In his own country each is a pioneer laboring for a better understanding of Shakespeare. Both critics laud Shakespeare's gentleness and sweetness and his renaissance qualities. But Tieck is better read, more sympathetic and more intuitive than Lamb; in this respect he resembles Coleridge and Hazlitt. His criticism is, however, not typical of German critical scholarship in general as opposed to English. For while the average German critic is perhaps more cautious and objective than the English critic in appraising and disposing individual facts, Tieck is bold and individualistic. This explains why his general sweeping statements are of more interest today than his numerous specific hypotheses, long since exploded.

Usually Tieck shows good sense, keen feeling and imagination, a wide reading and independence of judgment free from cant. While he grasps the essentially dramatic as opposed to the theatrical, yet he does not miss the important lyrical element in Shakespeare. On the whole he is anti-classical and applauds Shakespeare's magnificent abandon and his insouciance of the unities.

On the other hand, it should be emphasized that he carried his intuitive method too far. (pp. 35-6)

*Edwin H. Zeydel, in his* Ludwig Tieck and England: A Study in the Literary Relations of Germany and England During the Early Nineteenth Century *(copyright © 1931 by Princeton University Press), Princeton University Press, 1931, 264 p.*

ALFRED EDWIN LUSSKY   (essay date 1932)

In full agreement with the practice of Cervantes, Sterne, and Goethe in *Wilhelm Meister,* Tieck destroys the objectivity of his own literary work by intentional subjective and personal thrusts, first, at himself as author and at his own literary creations, especially his characters, including the hero; second, at his reader; and, third, at the banal popular literary output of his day. (p. 163)

Nowhere in his works probably is this . . . brought out more plainly than in his prose tale **Peter Lebrecht.** Tieck seeks to justify his method of procedure by commenting upon the circumstance that the author stands just like a porter, as it were, with bent back at the entrance portals of his story, while the readers pass by. . . . (p. 165)

One of the methods by which Tieck attempts to show his sovereign control over his literary material, although thereby sacrificing the objectivity of the latter, consists in his ready reference to the devices of literary or dramatic craftsmanship. (p. 195)

[Nearly] all of the tricks of the dramatic craft, all the props which the ordinary playwright is at great pains to keep from the view of the audience, are thrown into bold relief by the glaring searchlight of Tieck's type of romantic irony. . . .

Tieck [also] upon occasion destroys the objectivity of his work, just as do Cervantes, Sterne, and Goethe, by frequent reference to the work itself or parts of it. (p. 196)

Finally, one might make mention, too, of the allusion by Tieck or his characters to works of his, other than the ones in which the allusion occurs. Nestor, for example, speaks in *Prinz Zerbino* with gentle irony of one of Tieck's other works, *Franz Sternbalds Wanderungen*. . . . (p. 197)

[The] so-called romantic irony displayed by Goethe and Tieck—and for that matter by all the great host of writers who before and after them revealed a similar tendency—is fundamentally of quite a different character from that originally pointed out in the works of Shakespeare by Schlegel in elucidation of his doctrine. The romantic irony of Goethe and Tieck—for critics also give the name of romantic irony to this secondary kind—is far removed from depending, as does the original kind, upon the preservation of the objectivity of the literary work which it pervades, for it actually *requires a destruction of the objectivity wherever it manifests itself*. In fact, it follows as a natural consequence from Friedrich Schlegel's theory that in all those places in Shakespeare where there is the greatest amount of romantic irony there is also the *greatest degree of objectivity;* but where in Goethe and Tieck there is the greatest amount of their kind of romantic irony (the secondary kind) there is the *least degree of objectivity*. (pp. 240-41)

To speak still more plainly, what is called romantic irony in such works as *Don Quixote, Tristram Shandy, Wilhelm Meister, Godwi,* **Peter Lebrecht,** and *Der gestiefelte Kater, is not romantic irony at all in Friedrich Schlegel's meaning of the term,* for it lacks objectivity, the indispensable element for the display of the true kind of romantic irony. The writers of these works indulge rather in a plain and ordinary kind of irony at the expense of their own selves, their works, their readers, and their literary contemporaries. (pp. 241-42)

> *Alfred Edwin Lussky, in his* Tieck's Romantic Irony: With Special Emphasis upon the Influence of Cervantes, Sterne, and Goethe *(copyright, 1932, by The University of North Carolina Press), University of North Carolina Press, 1932, 274 p.*

## E. K. BENNETT (essay date 1934)

The Romantic writers beginning with Tieck had considerably enlarged the scope of the Novelle both in regard to its subject matter and its content. . . . In the works of Tieck and Hoffmann the 'marvellous' spreading from the critical point of the story comes to be the characteristic of the whole story, and the Novelle so completely changes its character that far from being an account of everyday events which are just distinguished from the everyday, by an unexpected twist given to them, it

is, with the Romantics, an account of events, of which the most striking characteristic is that they do not belong to the ordinary world. (p. 77)

In a general estimate of Tieck's later Novellen it can be said that only those works have taken a permanent place in the development of the genre which are, on the whole, free from Tendenz: the Künstler and historical Novellen, and both types have their origin in the works of earlier writers (Kleist and Hoffmann). In the historical Novellen Tieck definitely contributed something to the development of a special form, which reaches its summit in the works of Conrad Ferdinand Meyer. The Novellen, however, which are essentially presentations of prevailing social and literary conditions with satirical intention—the Tendenznovellen—have long since ceased to be of interest, as they are in essence alien to the form of the Novelle. It may indeed be maintained with some justification that Tieck's literary and poetical gifts were peculiarly unsuited to the Novelle as a genre. Tieck was a facile writer, and, as with most facile writers, he possessed a mind of no great profundity. What he has to say, he says with great ease, with a specious poeticalness and unfailing loquacity. Further, he was by nature as well as under the influence of Romantic theories regardless of the purity of form. All these things are characteristic of his early works—*Franz Sternbald's Wanderungen, Kaiser Oktavian, Genoveva, Prinz Zerbino*—works which are wearisome by reason of their length, the shallowness of their poetical quality, and the continual oscillation between epic, dramatic and lyric form: they are the antithesis of those qualities which are demanded of the writer who practises the severe artistry of the Novelle. Again, though a certain amount of reflection may be conceded as a permissible element in the Novelle, it is only tolerable when it is the reflection of a mind of originality or profundity such as Cervantes. Tieck had considerable critical ability and his *aperçus* on art and poetry and the art of life are often marked by real acumen and artistic perception, but his reflections upon questions other than aesthetic ones are not the outcome of a deeply philosophic mind. The result is that the action of his Novellen is overlaid and suffocated with reflections of negligible importance. Nor is the action itself, when unearthed, of such interest as to hold the attention of the reader.

Tieck brought the Novelle back from the exoticism of the later Romantic writers into the circle of contemporary subject matter. He set it to deal with the world of actuality, with social, literary and political conditions but in a form which was unsuited to its specific nature, and his treatment of the genre had no real or lasting influence upon its development, except in so far as it revealed to the Jung Deutschland [Young Germany] writers the possibility of using the Novelle form for their own tendencious purposes. (pp. 92-4)

> *E. K. Bennett, "The Discursive Novelle," in his* A History of the German "Novelle": From Goethe to Thomas Mann, *Cambridge at the University Press, 1934, pp. 77-105.\**

## RAYMOND M. IMMERWAHR (essay date 1953)

*Der Blaubart* differs markedly both from the extreme, programmatic exemplification of romantic drama later furnished by Tieck in *Kaiser Octavianus* and from the fantastic comedy of *Der gestiefelte Kater* in that it has a coherent plot with considerable dramatic suspense, follows realistic principles in the portrayal of serious and comic characters alike, and employs the traditional comic situations of realistic comedy.

The one stylistic device of *Blaubart* suggesting fantastic comedy is its deliberate anachronism: Fairy-tale characters in a medieval setting refer to esthetic and psychological principles of eighteenth-century rationalism. . . . The incongruity involved in these anachronisms is sometimes comical, but in more serious scenes it has an ironic effect. There is pronounced irony in the solipsistic skepticism of the character Simon, the attitude to which Tieck gave fullest expression in his novel *William Lovell.* (pp. 47-8)

In addition to . . . strictly fantastic elements, Tieck's comedies contain instances of gross exaggeration, bizarre incongruity, and horseplay, which are highly implausible but do not directly contradict laws of nature or logic. (p. 49)

[His] attack upon contemporary cultural and literary tendencies [in *Der gestiefelte Kater*], though seriously motivated, leaves the impression more of playful fun than of earnest polemics, for the obvious enjoyment which Tieck derives from his own fantastic caricatures prevents us from feeling any resentment or indignation toward their prototypes. In the last analysis, Tieck's satire is but a vehicle for comedy. . . .

The comic technique of *Der gestiefelte Kater* is . . . related to that of popular farce and that of Aristophanic comedy. However, since its fantasy is always intended to be comical and its comedy is all either fantastic or farcical, it has little kinship with that fantastic comedy of Shakespeare which evokes a fantastic world primarily for its poetic beauty and presents comic episodes and characters which, for the most part, are not fantastic or incredible. (p. 52)

[*Der gestiefelte Kater*] affords genuine amusement and incites frequent spontaneous laughter but fails to sustain its mirth throughout. The whimsical fantasy with which it plays upon the childhood world of fairy tale, the one brilliant characterization, the usually rapid pace of jest and play, and the fresh colloquial speech (unfortunately lost in translation) are at times overclouded with the bookish dust from excessive allusions to intellectual and journalistic fashions and *belles-lettres;* the jokes at the expense of theatrical representation—really amusing at first—begin to wear thin with constant repetition and strained elaboration. But these defects of *Der gestiefelte Kater* as farcical comedy are less serious than its shortcomings as satire. Tieck's essential satiric purpose was to assert the claims of poetic fantasy against a prosaic, unimaginative rationalism. Had he concentrated upon this worthy objective and found universally valid terms for it, *Der gestiefelte Kater* might still have been a major contribution to modern European comedy. But much of Tieck's satire was wasted on ephemeral intellectual and belletristic fads, and his extreme, narrowly antirationalistic point of view could not awaken a response outside of his immediate literary circle.

Tieck's second fantastic comedy [*Die verkehrte Welt*] is at once a much bolder and a much less successful venture into the comic and satiric territories explored by the first one. Intended to develop and intensify the fantastic-comic style of *Der gestiefelte Kater,* it falls far short of its goal and at times becomes lost upon entirely extraneous paths. (p. 62)

[The] brilliantly conceived unity of mock plot, irrational comedy, and satire is highly ludicrous in its broad outlines but fails dismally throughout most of its execution. Scaramuccio, the Muses, and one or two other characters are mirth-provoking for a time, and a few short scenes are hilariously funny, but otherwise that tedium which was just beginning to creep into *Der gestiefelte Kater* holds unbroken sway here. Again and again promising comic devices stale with endless repetition. The most pedantic verbosity takes the place of the economy of language and pace of movement which are indispensable to comedy. It is indeed difficult to understand how the lively dialogue of *Der gestiefelte Kater* and these tiresome exercises in the logic of irrationality could stem from the same author. Finally, the satire of *Die verkehrte Welt,* though it has more universal bearing than that of the earlier comedy, is seldom comical; left as an end in itself, it becomes sheer polemics. (p. 64)

The emphasis on irrationality of situation in this comedy carries with it the deliberate elimination of individualized character portrayal. The Spectators and several other figures are exaggerated even beyond the point of caricature into mere abstractions of stupidity; some are like fleeting apparitions in a weird dream. Their speeches are not so much instances of ludicrous stupidity as studied experiments in the meaningless. (p. 66)

The struggle between the forces of utilitarian rationalism and poetic fantasy, upon which most of the episodes in *Die verkehrte Welt* focus, affords possibilities of dramatic suspense and economy, but these are left unexploited. Furthermore, *Die verkehrte Welt* fails to communicate that unifying spirit of hilarity which can justify a willfully devious and circuitous path in fantastic comedy. (p. 67)

> Raymond M. Immerwahr, *in his* The Esthetic Intent of Tieck's Fantastic Comedy *(copyright 1953 by the Committee on Publications Washington University), Washington University Studies, 1953, 150 p.*

**RALPH TYMMS**    (essay date 1955)

*[Tymms believes that Tieck "was most successful in evoking in his* Märchen *the atmosphere of mystery and terror," and that he best achieves that atmosphere when "he strays from the original" folktales he used as models. When Tieck abandons the tale of terror for excursions into satire or drama, Tymms adds, "he fails to achieve his best results." Like Raymond M. Immerwahr (see excerpt above, 1953), Tymms considers Tieck's manipulation of dramatic conventions somewhat contrived, and concludes that "Tieck was a successful writer, a pioneer, but only in [the* Marchen*]."]*

The renewal of the *Märchen* was the distinctive romantic contribution to modern German literature (together with the renewal of the folk-song), and it was Ludwig Tieck who first made this contribution acceptable to a wider reading public, even before Friedrich Schlegel devised his theoretical justification of the genre in his aesthetic *Athenäum Fragmente.* Tieck was in fact one of the earliest and most influential, and for a time the most popular, of the writers associated with the *Athenäum* doctrines of romanticism. He was most successful in evoking in his *Märchen* the atmosphere of mystery and terror. . . . Perhaps the essential feature of Tieck as a writer is that he seems to have no heart, or at any rate to be inadequate in his emotional reactions to anything but blatant horrors. . . . Nor is he concerned, essentially, with the motives of human behaviour, in any co-ordinated total conception of the mind's processes, though isolated bizarre incidents attract his attention; he prefers to leave it to Hoffmann to probe into the mind in a more systematic way, using careful observation instead of erratically picking on individual peculiarities in isolation. Predominantly then he was less the born writer, concerned with presenting a more or less plausible account of the motives for human action, than the showman, who relies on his knack of seizing upon, and exploiting, sensational incidents and features; above all, of devising situations in which a sense of horror may be evoked. . . . [Yet, though] he is best at evoking horror, he occasionally succeeds in cracking what appears to be a spontaneous joke, but too often his sense of fun is painfully contrived, and even his satire (which has an edge to it) is usually wasted on insignificant objects. (pp. 52-3)

Usually he relies on existing plots for his *Märchen* and culls them from the old chap-books in which medieval tales and legends were crudely recounted for unsophisticated readers or audiences in the fifteenth and sixteenth centuries. As his own contribution he reshapes them to his own purposes when he wishes, especially by intensifying any horrific atmosphere there may be: for, like most of the romantics who followed him, he has a proprietary attitude to the old literature, and no feeling of piety to historical authenticity holds him back from radical adaptation. But his main innovation is, in some notable instances, to pay lip-service to the medieval setting by means of occasional stylistic archaisms, while, at the same time, he is blatantly unfaithful to the spirit of the old tales, attributing to the extrovert, uncomplicated figures of the chap-book the self-awareness of a modern man, his capacity for self-observation and for recording his own reactions to the impact of the supernatural on his life. It is this which makes Tieck's tales, at their best, more than an imitation of the old folk-tales; his are artificial, introvert versions of the old simple, unsubtle themes. It is precisely this distinctive contribution of his own, historically quite out of character, which makes his stories so remarkable to-day: the farther he strays from the original, the better the result, to our taste—and best of all when he invents the whole story himself, as in *Der blonde Eckbert* and *Der Runenberg* (unfortunately there are few other instances). . . . Tieck's characters are not even remotely in keeping with their often vaguely medieval costume and setting; their uneasy, complicated, self-conscious minds do not begin to match the spurious artlessness of the narrative style: there could hardly be more anachronistic denizens for the traditional world of the *Märchen*. Tieck was trying to get the best of both worlds when he joined, and even led, the escapist return to a fairytale vision of the Middle Ages, at the same time offering his readers very up-to-date eccentric psychological motives for the external action. (pp. 55-6)

Of [his early works], *Almansur* is a particularly anaemic yet effusive production, eloquent from the first of precocious misanthropy. . . . (p. 57)

*Abdallah* is a longer, and more ferocious story: once again Tieck dallies with a fairy-tale orientalism, before turning to the vague medievalism which is characteristic of many of his romantic *Märchen*. (p. 58)

*Karl von Berneck* is really another experiment in *Märchen*-like gruesomeness, though it is written in a pretentious dramatic form as a *Ritterdrama*, or 'chivalric' play. Wackenroder described it, ridiculously enough, as a 'medieval *Orestes*' ('Orestes in Ritterzeiten'), but it would be more appropriate to call it a 'Gothick' Hamlet, if it has to be related to any drama of consequence. But Tieck lacks the art of bringing this Hamlet to life, or even half-life, and Karl remains a pasteboard figure to which is attributed dialogue which at times implies quasi-Shakespearean subtleties of characterization—awareness of guilt and morbid irresolution. To some extent this cardboard Hamlet puts the blame for his own inadequacy on to an outside fate which then makes an appearance in the form of an ancestral wraith, a bogy man in which neither Tieck nor anyone else could possibly believe. . . . [The] horrific atmosphere he tries

to evoke has something of the unintentionally burlesque about it, rather than a serious attempt to recreate a mood of numinous awe. Nor does he even unambiguously represent the ghost as something in which he professes to believe himself: he leaves the question open (and so he does in *Abdallah*) as to whether the supernatural visitation is the product of the hero's subjective hallucination, or is meant to be an objectively perceptible phenomenon. But whichever it is, the ghost is not a success. . . . (pp. 58-9)

Tieck was repetitive: favourite motifs recur throughout his work, and Abdallah's progressive corruption and disillusionment is a theme which is lovingly repeated in *William Lovell* at great length. (p. 59)

In spite of the combination of the extravagant and the tedious in this phase of adolescent gloom in Tieck's literary career, *Almansur, Abdallah, Berneck* and *Lovell* arouse at least a rather specious interest from their semi-autobiographical evocation of mood, though it is melodramatically handled: and at times they give a slight foretaste of his future adept handling of the horrific *Märchen*. (p. 61)

[In his later romantic] phase, Tieck wrote predominantly satirical comedies, often round an existing fairy-tale, as well as usually gruesome, or at least serious, narrative *Märchen* in the mood of *Abdallah* and *William Lovell*. The two categories of comedy and sombre *Märchen* frequently overlap, as in the case of *Ritter Blaubart*. . . . It is not satirical, but it is in part funny and yet also partly horrific. On the other hand, the *Leben und Tod des kleinen Rothkäppchens* . . . has an atmosphere of false naïveté that is comic, and even the tragic outcome is not treated quite seriously. . . . In *Die verkehrte Welt* there is still another combination of satire, comedy and *Märchen*-components; for it is comic, the satirical component is predominant, and yet it is not based on a fairy-tale theme. The narrative *Märchen*, for their part, though untouched by humour, have frequently sardonic implications of their author's misanthropy, as in *Die Freunde* and *Der blonde Eckbert*.

*Ritter Blaubart*—to return to that—is a curious example of the mixed genre, a fairy-tale play with a happy ending, yet unsatirical and for the most part horrific. It seems to be a hybrid, combining the declamatory hysteria of *Karl von Berneck* (Tieck's adolescent *Ritterstück*) and the facetiousness of his full-blown *Märchen*-plays. The comic effects are few and laboured. . . . (pp. 61-2)

[In *Der gestiefelte Kater*] Tieck took refuge in satire, instead of indulging in melancholy: gloom is exorcized. The result is a fairy-tale extravaganza, what might be termed a multiple pantomime, because it is on the lines of the old play-within-a-play, with a great deal of confusion wilfully caused by the introduction of extraneous personages. It is loaded with gibes against literary critics and writers in the Berlin of Tieck's own day; but almost without exception they are ephemeral figures, unworthy of serious hostility, and this robs the satire of its point. (p. 63)

Tieck's main comic gambit in . . . his *Märchen*-comedies is what was called 'romantic irony'—in his usage the repeated surrender of the dramatic illusion by making the characters spectators in their own play, aware of their ambivalent role, and sometimes aware even of their awareness; it is as if they see themselves proliferated in the panels of a mirror-cabinet, or in the simultaneous participation and spectatorship of the dreaming mind. The systematic—painfully systematic!—sabotage of the dramatic conventions starts off in the opening scenes of *Der gestiefelte Kater* when the preliminary surmises of the audience about the entertainment to be provided are presented as part of the dialogue of the play, a sort of arabesque framework round the play and one which encroaches on the play itself. . . . The trouble with this heavy-handed exposure of the main theme as a fiction from the start is that there is no dramatic illusion left to demolish later on, though this does not deter Tieck from trying to do so through the course of all three plays. (pp. 64-5)

In much the same way as he attributes in his serious *Märchen* modern complicated emotional reactions to conventional fairy-tale personages, Tieck reinterprets in these *Märchen*-comedies the stereotyped fairy-tale situation, or something resembling it, in an anachronistic and burlesque spirit: on occasion the result is quite happy, in a harmless way. (p. 65)

[For *Die verkehrte Welt,* as] usual, Tieck borrowed his main themes—even his title—from existing works; and, as in *Der gestiefelte Kater,* such dramatic action as there is in *Die verkehrte Welt* is interrupted by a cross-fire of mock-naïve comments from the audience, which is once again included within the embrace of the play-within-a-play, extended and proliferated to a tedious degree. (p. 67)

There is harmless satire—almost wholly literary—in *Die verkehrte Welt,* but with fewer malicious personalities than in *Der gestiefelte Kater.* The main theme is itself satirical in a burlesque, entirely unsubtle sense. . . . (p. 68)

Both *Der gestiefelte Kater* and *Die verkehrte Welt* were written with great speed, but years elapsed between the beginning and the completion of *Prinz Zerbino;* as a result it is even more unspontaneous and heavy than *Die verkehrte Welt,* and much more so than *Der gestiefelte Kater.* Its literary satire is often so obscure that for the revised version published in the *Schriften* in 1828 Tieck introduces it with a lengthy gloss. . . . (p. 71)

Tieck's main preoccupation seems to be to devise interconnecting vortices of unreality: alternatively, critics have been reminded of Chinese carved ivory hollow balls or cubes, contained one inside the other. That is all there is to *Zerbino*—it is ingenious but trivial, laboriously devised, only to be demolished by the author himself, as a main part of the entertainment. The climax of this process of disintegration comes when Zerbino, despairing of finding the spring of good taste, threatens to tear the play apart, scene by scene, in case the elusive quarry has slipped his notice and is still lurking somewhere inside: and he is described as pushing the play backwards, as if it is a machine in reverse motion, so that the preceding scenes now come back into view! (p. 73)

Tieck's *Märchen*-comedies can be seen . . . to consist of what are often very slight variations on two constant themes, the first being the anachronistic treatment of traditional fairy-tale motifs, and the second the interruption and destruction of the dramatic illusion, chiefly by multiplying the play-within-a-play gambit of the Elizabethan drama. . . . [His characters] are puppets, and he treats them as roughly and unsympathetically as a petulant child might treat his toys. . . . This convention of puppet-characters, to whom are attributed (incongruously) pathologically bizarre emotional reactions, is part of Tieck's bequest to romantic fiction. . . . (p. 74)

Tieck continues his assault on reality, and his reversal of the usually accepted evaluation of dream and actuality, and his exposure of love and friendship as insubstantial figments of the imagination—or of magic—in his masterpiece, the prose

*Märchen* of *Der blonde Eckbert.* . . . It was *Der blonde Eckbert* which justly established his reputation as the pioneer of the romantic *Märchen* as a serious form of modern literature, and later romantic story-tellers—from Brentano and Arnim to Hoffmann and Heine—accepted it as a model. It is one of the very few stories in which Tieck invented the plot himself, although the narrative technique is (superficially at least) *Märchen*-like, and there are component incidents which were either culled from existing fairy-tales, or might have been; and it is so effective as a terror-*Märchen* that one can only regret that Tieck did not invent his own plots more often instead of almost always borrowing from elsewhere.

Though *Der blonde Eckbert* has a vaguely medieval, fairy-tale setting, there are none of the semi-parodistic stylistic archaisms which Tieck sometimes uses—only a studied simplicity, which sets off all the more effectively the nightmarish complication of the doomful tale he tells; with a positively sinister show of detachment he describes the impingement of the supernatural, in an aggressive, malignant, vengeful form, upon human existence. (p. 81)

The degradation of the individual to puppet-status fits in with Tieck's *Märchen*-treatment of character and of personal motives for action, but it is the reverse to Fichte's and Novalis's glorification of the Ego as the all-powerful creator of all outside itself. Tieck wants the best of both worlds—to deny his characters human rights of self-determination and yet, simultaneously, to imply the romantic author's almost boundless arbitrary powers. It is of course one more of his inconsistencies that he should combine these contrasting attitudes, viewing his characters as the preordained victims of a malignant fate at the same time as he premises his own artistic irresponsibility. (p. 88)

[*Der Runenberg*] is yet another of Tieck's *Märchen* on the theme of the dangerous lures of Fairyland, which enslave a man's mind and blur his sense of reality and ethical responsibility; next to *Der blonde Eckbert* it is probably the best of Tieck's stories—the most urgent and effective in communicating the horrific atmosphere of man's enslavement to hostile elemental forces outside himself. Once again, . . . the implication is that this subordination to supernatural external forces is imagined, that it is the result of another attempt—doubtless a subconscious one—to pass on the blame for one's own inner inadequacy and irresolution to some imaginary tyrant. (pp. 91-2)

Tieck's handling of obsessive ideas which are supposed by the victim to be produced by 'possession' by an outside power, has evident affinities with later psychological tenets, especially with those of the semi-intuitive Freudian variety, which postulate the existence of complexes—'bundles' of psychic energy which may express themselves through the emotions, and even take over control of the mind. This link between Freudian psychology and the German romantic conception of the Other Self (a secondary personality which may assume control at the expense of the first, habitual self) shows once more that Tieck could, in his desultory way, come upon isolated psychological phenomena of great interest and strangeness. . . . Tieck on the one hand points forward (rather by chance, it would seem) in the *Runenberg* to future developments in psychological interpretation when he stumbles on these curious aspects of the subconscious or semi-conscious mind; but on the other hand he is very much bound up with his old story-books and Böhme, and looks back nostalgically to age-old, often alchemical, fancies about metals and mining. (p. 94)

Whenever Tieck strays from the tale of terror—even when he indulges in satire—he fails to achieve his best effects. This is evident in the *Grossdramen,* the so-called 'grand dramas', which are in fact inflated versions of such earlier verse-*Märchen* as *Magelone.* . . . Indeed of all Tieck's bogus medieval products the *Grossdramen* [*Genoveva, Kaiser Octavianus,* and *Fortunat*] are the most pretentious and the least seductive in their romantic enchantments; at best they may recapture for some modern readers a sense of 'period'—of the romantic masquerade of Gothicism, together with a certain amount of the ferocious gloom and the isolated comic lines which the author handles well. (p. 100)

The only consoling feature about the puppetry of the *Gross-dramen* is that their author devises their mock-Gothic absurdities with such blatant disbelief that it is evident that he is determined that we shall realize with relief that he is not as great and credulous a fool as he seems at first sight, for he makes it practically impossible in the *Grossdramen* for the reader to accept his medieval masquerades as being anything more than the half-burlesque deception they are. . . . (p. 102)

Far from being a world-in-little, or microcosm, the Tieckian *Grossdrama* is universal only in the inadmissible sense that it is a hotch-potch of scraps or samples: there is certainly no sign of a true synthesis of the components. And by degrading the drama, as he did in effect in the *Grossdrama,* to the status of an overgrown *Märchen* in dialogue form, Tieck was denying his writing the validity of real life as it is lived by adult people who are neither stock characters from the pantomime, puppet-play or chap-book, nor so caught up in the romantic mood that they prefer to live a dream. For all its pretensions the *Gross-drama* is a showy hoax, the most insincere of all Tieck's literary insincerities; the myriad facets of this supposed romantic gem may be seen on closer inspection to be merely like the little bits of coloured glass in a child's kaleidoscope. (p. 104)

Whenever Tieck strays from the *Märchen* he becomes ineffectual—during his long romantic phase at least—and the *Grossdramen* are instances of this. So are his novels. The brooding gloom which is powerfully conveyed in some of his *Märchen,* most signally in *Der blonde Eckbert* and *Der Runenberg,* is a most dreary feature of his first novel, *William Lovell,* if only because it is conveyed with empty, rhetorical swagger and at excessive length. The same is true of the picturesque romantic-Gothic décor, the cheerfully unhistorical back-cloth of crenellated castles and fairy-tale forests, which is such an attractive feature of several of the *Märchen,* but becomes merely tiresome in his second novel, *Franz Sternbalds Wan-derungen.* . . . (p. 106)

As writers of the tale of terror, Brentano has more poetic invention, Hoffmann a greater, almost instinctive, insight into underlying strata of consciousness, and a much more realistic attitude to the possibility of 'possession' by an outside spiritual force than Tieck shows; and both Brentano and Hoffmann probably believed in at least some part of the marvels they relate. Tieck gives the impression, whether it is a just one or not, of not believing in his own magic, though there was an incongruous vein of superstition running through his predominantly sceptical temperament, and he was supposed to suffer from hallucinations at intervals during his life; perhaps he had a greater apprehension of the supernatural than his stories would suggest—for in them there is a curious ring of insincerity and sardonic detachment which seems to disavow belief in what he tells. In [the] late phase of his life, Tieck also had as a contemporary an innovator in the tale of terror—Edgar Allan

Poe. . . . Poe's *Ligeia,* a story of the supernatural resuscitation of a dead woman's body by the spirit of another, already dead, appeared in the same year as *Pietro.* In contrast to Poe's emphatic, intensely emotional and declamatory presentation of the weird and grotesque, Tieck's stagy tableaux and . . . curiously detached narrative style make a faded, devitalized impression. (p. 118)

In effect, *Pietro* is an epilogue to Tieck's *Märchen*-technique, an ultimate *Bravourstück* which recapitulates the triumphs and weaknesses of the whole tradition he had initiated forty-odd years before. It betrays the pretentiousness, probably the plagiarism, and certainly the insincerity, which he combines with the adeptness of an assured master of narrative, and (so strangely) with what seems to be a genuine apprehension of ferocious elemental forces which confront man. . . . Tieck was a successful writer, and a pioneer, but only in [the *Märchen,*] an inconsiderable literary medium which to-day appeals or impresses on account of its romantic 'period' quaintness, and by the savage vehemence which it sometimes reveals, incongruously. Otherwise his tales are little more than a curious commentary on cults and wilful eccentricities which have long since lost their magic—fanciful medieval reminiscence and half make-believe apprehension of supernatural 'possession'. What raises Tieck's *Märchen* above these trivialities are—apart from the undoubted narrative gifts—the isolated and (as it seems) almost absent-minded flashes of psychological intuition which may penetrate, though they do not light up, the darkest corners of the subconscious mind, none the less effectively because the prevailing atmosphere is that of the elaborate hoax, the bogus fairy-tale. (pp. 119-20)

*Ralph Tymms, ''Ludwig Tieck,'' in his* German Romantic Literature *(reprinted by permission of Methuen & Co. Ltd),* Methuen, 1955, pp. 52-120.

### RENÉ WELLEK    (essay date 1955)

[*Wellek's* A History of Modern Criticism *is a major, comprehensive study of the literary critics of the last three centuries. In his consideration of Tieck as a critic and literary scholar, Wellek concludes that Tieck ''contributed importantly to a description and criticism of the romantic artist,'' although his work ''is now hopelessly obsolete.''*]

Ludwig Tieck is usually considered the head of the German romantic school. As critic he cannot, however, be ranked with the Schlegels. His mind was too loose, too incoherent to contribute to a theory of literature; his taste, though well-defined, was rarely expounded in arguments substantial enough to make him a good practical critic. His work as a literary scholar, however meritorious at its time and place, is now hopelessly obsolete. It would be easy to dismiss him on all three counts. Yet something can be said for Tieck as a critic.

Tieck is an eclectic who reflects the influences of his time and of his friends. He passed through several fairly distinct stages: an early preparatory period which reflects his reading in English aesthetics and in Herder; a period (mainly between 1797-99) in which he adopts his friend Wackenroder's religion of art; a later period (mainly between 1800-03) which shows the influence of the Schlegels; and then, after a pause, a new period (after about 1810) when he accepts the guidance of his friend F. W. Solger. We can trace all the key concepts of the time in Tieck's writings, though they are used uncertainly and shiftingly. For example, he oscillates disconcertingly between a conception of ''genius'' as pure inspiration and a Schlegelian stress on the share of consciousness in creation. So "irony," which Tieck employed profusely and originally in his satirical comedies, is used in his critical writings sparingly and vaguely. Only much later, under the influence of Solger, does Tieck arrive at distinctions between "lower" and "higher," and "positive" and "negative" irony. He then condemns "vulgar" irony and accepts an interpretation which makes it identical with objectivity, with the poet's power over his material. Tieck did much to popularize the term "romantic," but he himself used it quite loosely, in the old sense of anything marvelous or medieval. Late in life he insisted that all poetry since antiquity is "romantic" and that it is impossible to draw a distinction between the "romantic" and the "poetic." Clearly, not much in the way of theory can be learned from Tieck.

In Tieck's many writings we can find, of course, a mass of literary opinions. . . . [But little] is elaborated and substantiated, analyzed and argued. It is merely stated, for Tieck wants criticism to convey an immediate feeling of his personality.

The mass of editorial labors, translations from Elizabethan dramatists, the translation of *Don Quixote,* the collaboration and supervision of the German Shakespeare, after August Wilhelm Schlegel had given it up—all this has only historical interest today. Research has shown that Tieck's translations and revisions are often grossly inaccurate. Today we would have no sympathy for his enthusiasm for the Shakespearean *apocrypha.* (pp. 93-4)

Of his published papers on Shakespeare the earliest one, written when he was only twenty, **"Shakespeare's Treatment of the Marvelous"** . . . , is critically the most interesting. It is an excellent exercise in psychological criticism in the English manner. . . . The paper shows traces of 18th-century rationalistic misconceptions: Shakespeare's handling of the marvelous is thought to be an attempt at hiding the lack of rules, at making us forget the laws of aesthetics. Hamlet seeing the ghost in the closet scene or Macbeth seeing Banquo's ghost at the banquet is action supposedly capable of natural explanation, of an allegorical sense. Yet on the whole the piece is full of sensitive observations and is surely superior to earlier discussions of the same topic by Mrs. Montagu and Joseph Warton. Compared with it, Tieck's next published piece, **"Letters on Shakespeare"** . . . , is rambling and diffuse. (pp. 94-5)

Tieck's failure as a Shakespeare critic seems most clearly demonstrated by the novel **Dichterleben** . . . , in which Shakespeare, Greene, Marlowe, Nashe, Florio, the Earl of Southampton, the Dark Lady of the Sonnets, etc. appear as fictional figures. The book is curious for being one of the earliest novelistic treatments of the death of Marlowe and of the triangle between Shakespeare, Southampton, and the Dark Lady. As a picture of Elizabethan England, however, it is incredibly sentimental and false. It has no historical accuracy or atmosphere and little narrative interest. (pp. 95-6)

Likewise, Tieck's interest in Spanish literature leaves us with a similar sense of disappointment. There is hardly any criticism of Cervantes in Tieck's writings. . . . Only his defense of the insertion of the novella "El Curioso Impertinente" [into *Don Quixote*] may be quoted as an illustration of the Schlegelian method of finding organic unity in a great work at all costs. . . .

Tieck was the first German deeply interested in Calderón, and was the first to imitate his meters and devices in German drama. He infected August Wilhelm Schlegel with his enthusiasm. . . . (p. 96)

Tieck also played a certain role in the revival of older German literature. In 1803 he brought out a badly modernized collection of *Minnelieder.* Its introduction proved very influential. Jakob Grimm tells us that he caught his enthusiasm for the study of German antiquities from it. It is, however, no monument of erudition, but rather a popular rehearsal of some of the Schlegels' opinions. (pp. 96-7)

But all these activities are completely overshadowed, in critical importance, by Tieck's editions of Lenz, Novalis, and Heinrich von Kleist, and by his discussions of Goethe, in which a coherent and original taste emerges. Tieck has a strong feeling in favor of the German Storm and Stress and the early Goethe. . . . To him Goethe is the problematic artist, not unlike Goethe's own Tasso or Goethe's friend Lenz or Kleist, in their revolt against society and in their nearness to madness and suicide. . . . To modern Kleist enthusiasts the introductory essay on Kleist will appear vague in its biographical information and excessively cool in its appreciation of the works. Tieck's interest is clearly psychological and personal. He is attracted by the "dark force" inside Kleist which destroyed him. . . . (pp. 97-8)

Later in his life Tieck tried to forget his romantic past. . . . He judged his own younger contemporaries severely and unsympathetically. . . . Tieck also had no use for Young Germany, whose political radicalism went against his grain. In speaking of Heine he gave vent to his anti-Semitism; but he also thought him only a poor imitator of Goethe and complained of his impertinence, vulgar irony, and monotony.

In all of Tieck's criticism the discussions of Goethe, Lenz, and Kleist have the most personal tone. They suggest that Tieck was profoundly involved in the problem of the artist in society, in the danger of poetry to a poet's mental health. Personally Tieck had escaped the danger and could interpret his own evolution as one toward sanity and truth. At the same time he preserved an interest and sympathy for the artist "at the brink" of the abyss, since as a young man he had experienced this feeling on his own pulses. (p. 98)

Tieck himself escaped into historical realism and irony. But he preserved a taste for the problematical, broken, and antisocial artist, which is only imperfectly overlaid with admiration for the versatility, sanity, and impersonality of Shakespeare. Tieck was no metaphysician like Friedrich Schlegel, no mystic like Novalis, no theorist like August Wilhelm Schlegel. But he contributed importantly to a description and criticism of the romantic artist. (p. 100)

*René Wellek, "The Early Romantics in Germany: Wackenroder and Tieck," in his* A History of Modern Criticism, 1750-1950: The Romantic Age, *Vol. 2 (copyright, 1955, by Yale University Press), Yale University Press, 1955, pp. 88-100.**

**JAMES TRAINER** (essay date 1964)

Tieck's objective [as a Gothic Novelist] was at once more indefinite and more complex [than Mrs. Radcliffe's], and consequently his method demanded a deeper understanding of the literary potentialities of the material at his disposal, as well as greater skill in marshalling it to his purposes. He differed primarily from Mrs. Radcliffe in that the existence of supernatural powers and even the fact of their intervention in human affairs were no longer mere artistic embellishments to a story but an essential presupposition to a philosophy of the universe. . . . (p. 52)

Tieck's interest in the non-physical world extended throughout his entire adult lifetime, and his youthful occupation with the horrific novel resulted, in his earliest works, in a colourless imitation of the supernatural techniques of these models. This influence is immediately obvious in *Abdallah*, in *William Lovell* [and] in *Karl von Berneck*. . . . *Abdallah* [is] an accumulation of mental tortures, ghastly visions and nightmares of unbroken horrific content, in which every available means of suggestion and connotation was applied to deepen the mood. The monstrous, supranatural figures of Mondal and Omar were descendants not of any Shakespearean progenitor, but simply more imaginative versions of the grotesque apparitions so beloved of the poetasters. It was only after a close study of the works of Shakespeare that Tieck began to formulate his own supernatural method, based on the observation that the necessary illusion must be created before the action involving the marvellous ever begins. In this way there is no abrupt hiatus between mortal and supramortal, the boundary between the two is not even distinguishable and the reader's tendency to rationalise is overcome before it can begin to operate. . . . The fact that Tieck genuinely accepted the existence of phenomena classifiable as supernatural contributed greatly to their convincing portrayal, since the principle of universal demonism which represented every object as "possessed", was eminently suited to the building up of the necessary illusion. Once that is established, we have reached not only an understanding of one of his literary procedures, but also the crux of his philosophy of the supernatural. This consisted in replacing the subjective distinction between the real and the marvellous with the belief that the two differ only in the degree of frequency, that any event normally accepted as supernatural would with constant repetition come to be regarded as everyday, and an equal belief in the converse, that most things which we consider everyday are in fact miracles stripped of their deeper mystery by their recurrence. This runs completely contrary to the objectives of Mrs. Radcliffe whose rejection of a higher order served to lay stress on this material world of reality as the only true one, a strong distinction being drawn between the religious and the superstitious with which she equated the supernatural. Tieck's romantic demonism was aimed rather at establishing through the medium of the empiric natural world the existence of a preternatural system. To the man who is conscious of the presence of this force in his daily surroundings its appearance in less usual forms will not entail any loss of logical sequence. This theme . . . runs through the whole of Tieck's mature work. . . . Tieck never made it clear, as R. Tymms has pointed out [see excerpt above, 1955], whether the hallucination was a subjective phenomenon in the mind of the beholder, or whether it was meant to be generally perceptible. But the fundamental issue is that for the victim of the apparition it was a reality in the same sense as any other object; if what he sees at this moment is not real, then for him there can be no reality, in other words, the natural and the marvellous fall together, for they are one and the same. From earliest childhood we accept the facts of creation, birth and death, the tenets of a Christian faith embracing resurrection and a world beyond, the wonders of nature and countless similar mysteries which make a fairy-tale of life itself and defy all attempts to reduce the universe to a material automaton. It was on this argument that Tieck based the incoherent world of his *Märchen* where it is equally vain to ask after the *whence* or the *whither*. Not that the results of this method were uniformly successful. The tales of *Phantasus* are still celebrated as Tieck's most satisfactory prose compositions because the realms of the marvellous and the everyday are there literally indistinguishable; but often the

achievement was far inferior to the intention. Most noticeably in the analysis of the psychological impact of the supernatural on man's mind, Tieck found himself unable to go much beyond Mrs. Radcliffe in her somewhat automatic registration of certain emotions to suit certain situations. (pp. 67-71)

[In *Abdallah*] the still-dormant qualities of Tieck are to be found buried beneath much that can be described only as bombast and pretension. Unordered thoughts and partly-digested ideas are thrown together in the attempt to portray a psychological clash of character. Yet if one must concede that the psychological progression in the story is automatic and not very compelling, its very presence does represent the author's desire not to be satisfied with the outward action alone. In this he would perhaps have been well advised to use the medium of the drama, for the tendency is already very strong in the preference given to dialogue, and the technique of prefacing long stretches of direct speech simply with the speaker's name, as is customary in a formal drama. Doubtless such a discipline would still have been beyond the powers of Tieck, as even *Abdallah,* despite its weaknesses, stands considerably above his earliest crude dramas. And it must be placed to Tieck's credit that the characters of this story are much more individually convincing in delineation than those of the usual horror story. His tyrant ruler, while every inch a tyrant, is nonetheless perfectly credible within the framework of this tale, just as Selim is a fairly consistent blend of fatherly love and severity. Tieck has succeeded in animating his figures, even the lesser participants such as Abubeker and Raschid, so that each has a distinctive personality which raises him above the customary "type". . . . The love scenes between Abdallah and Zulma possess a certain lyrical quality which well conveys the rapture the hero finds alone in the presence of his love. And if the verses themselves are artificial and construed, the failure in execution should not obscure the good intention of relieving the basic harshness with occasional, softer tones. . . . (pp. 97-8)

*Abdallah*'s place among the works of Tieck is not a high one, but the work was nevertheless of great importance in the literary progress of its writer. . . .

Its weaknesses became quickly as apparent to Tieck as they are to us today, but the work had to be written. And it is as integral a part of Tieck's creation as *Franz Sternbalds Wanderungen* which, without *Abdallah*, could never have been written. (p. 98)

*Franz Sternbalds Wanderungen* represents Tieck's major contribution to German Romantic prose, being the first important work written in imitation of Goethe's *Wilhelm Meister* and having itself provided inspiration for Novalis' *Heinrich von Ofterdingen*. In time *Sternbald* followed very closely upon *William Lovell* . . . which, in its turn, had originated in the same period of personal storm and stress as *Abdallah*. Yet in atmosphere and intention the two are worlds apart, the violence and extravagance of the earlier story having by now given way to a mellower and more moderate tone in which the hero, no longer exposed to the rigours of dialectic argumentation, can surrender himself to the impressions of light, colour and music. (p. 99)

Like Abdallah [Franz] sets out on his venture in innocence and simplicity of mind, but unlike Abdallah he remains indifferent to the pernicious influence of exploiters and philistines—although it is unfortunate that the novel breaks off at a point where Franz too seems to have failed in his mission and to have become the victim of his baser desires. One cannot press the comparison with *Abdallah* very far without discovering the magnitude of the gulf which separates the two, for in *Sternbald* the narrative is conducted on a plane which is both loftier in feeling and more profound in thought. The inquisitiveness of imagination has grown into the enquiry of intellect. Frequently, it is true, Tieck uses Franz as a mouthpiece to air many of his own views upon the plastic arts, upon the interrelation of the various art media and the merits of specific painters and schools. But if it were merely an apotheosis of painting, the novel would have much less claim to our interest. Its importance lay in the evocation of that particular elusive mood which was to determine the course of the nascent Romantic movement. Franz is engaged in a life of *seeking*, trying to establish his own identity within a fluid and often hostile world where only utility and practicality are understood. The rewards, he knows, will not be his as of right, but only in so far as he can show himself to be worthy of them. (p. 101)

Sternbald possesses further a psychological dimension which had hitherto been lacking in Tieck's demonic heroes. Lovell, like Sternbald, had been receptive to outside influences, but his scale of feelings was one that contained only extremes whether of joy or sorrow, between the ecstasy of delight and the misery of grief there were none of those intermediate degrees at which the majority of men do in fact lead their lives. Franz is not oblivious of the advantages which financial security would mean in terms of material comfort, but it would be death to his art: he can appreciate that for his fellow men the married state is something desirable, but for the painter, as for the Romantic artist in general, it implied unwanted responsibility, respectability and commitment to a life of orthodoxy. One facet of the progress of Tieck's Romantic impulse is revealed in the reversal of Abdallah's longing for marriage with Zulma into Franz' resolution to remain independent of family ties.

The pseudo-mediaeval world of Sternbald is one of colour, sound and latent mystery in which the narrative is often punctuated by involved and sometimes confusing interpolations which bear little obvious connection with the central thread of the story. It is in treatment rather than structure that Tieck's progress as a craftsman can be seen, for if many of the constituent elements which went to make up *Abdallah* were still present here, they had by now been subjected to a refinement which replaced the stereotype reactions, epithets and descriptions by a language more precisely cultivated to suit the spirit of the subject matter. (pp. 102-03)

[Franz'] free will is of no avail against the greater natural forces which confront him. This is the predicament of the Romantic existence, for here is a named individual living at a specific time in a given geographical area who is virtually an anonymous, lost soul typical of the human condition in any time or place. It is chiefly in this respect that *Sternbald* advances far beyond *William Lovell* or *Abdallah*. At most *Abdallah* had presented a distorted reflection of the author's own dilemma at a particularly despondent moment in his life; only with *Sternbald* did Tieck approach a form of *Universalpoesie*, the depiction of man in the universe, prepared to stand or fall by his belief in the supremacy of artistic expression over all other human enterprise. It is this change in the view of man to emphasise his spiritual potential that distinguishes the Romantic hero from the earlier versions. He is a complex and confused being, striving towards a fuller form of existence that cannot be obtained without effort and self-discipline. And alongside the increasing awareness of his own powers and the discovery of new faculties which enrich his personality, there emerges a feeling of humility in the face of such cosmic grandeur—every nerve conveys unknown sensations, a wealth of fresh experiences engulfs him in rapid succession, man's capacity seems infinite. (pp. 107-08)

The means of transformation from a literature intent only on creating an atmosphere of physical suspense to one which had as its object the portrayal of the mood of hopeful but unavailing search for an unattainable earthly satisfaction lay through the highly intellectual process of abstraction. By proceeding along the line through *The Mysteries of Udolpho* [by Ann Radcliffe], *Abdallah* and *William Lovell* to *Franz Sternbalds Wanderungen* we are aware of this gradual refinement, but even that is less striking than the further single step from *Sternbald* to [Novalis's] *Heinrich von Ofterdingen*. Tieck's creative instinct had brought him to the highest point of which his talent was capable, and it was for others to produce the masterpieces. (p. 109)

*James Trainer, in his* Ludwig Tieck: From Gothic to Romantic (© *copyright Mouton & Co., Publishers, The Hague; reprinted by permission of the author*), *Mouton & Co., 1964, 113 p.*

### ROBERT M. WERNAER (essay date 1966)

We can easily distinguish a number of stages in [Tieck's] literary development. When he first met Wackenroder, there was something in him of his friend's childlike naiveté and simplicity, evidenced by his earliest writings, especially *Die Sommernacht*. This trait was the sympathetic bond which united these two men. Soon, however, Tieck's peculiar constitution of mind came to the surface, and clung to him throughout his romantic period, nor did it ever leave him entirely, not even in his later, more realistic period of literary activity. It appeared, almost from the beginning, in *Abdallah* [and in *Das Grüne Band*]. . . . It is not easy to give a name to it since it is a rather complex phenomenon. We may call it an unrestrained, undisciplined imagination or fancy. A rich imagination is the gift of all true poets; yet in order that it may serve its natural function in the production of truly beautiful works, it must pass through severe training. Such a training was foreign to Tieck's nature. At certain periods of his life, he allowed himself to be wholly dominated by the whims of his imagination, to which he surrendered himself *ad libitum*,—images, ideas, emotions flowing unrestrained and without co-ordination from a too ready, untutored pen. (p. 61)

[Tieck] gives us everywhere "a glimpse of beauty," but rarely ever "beauty in its full perfection." He preferred to be butterfly rather than bee, to live in the sunshine and sport rather than to gather honey, to play with poetic moods and images, to enjoy the pranks of his own wonderful gift of imaging states of feeling rather than to produce, by patient labor, an artistic work. Therefore, much of what he wrote during his romantic period lacked in certitude and earnestness of purpose, and, consequently, in humanistic value.

However, through Wackenroder's influence, these playful tendencies in Tieck's mental make-up were checked to a considerable degree. We find him at work imitating Wackenroder's own style and Wackenroder's personal romanticism. We can trace this in Tieck's contributions to Wackenroder's *Herzensergiessungen*, in his *Phantasieen,* and his novel *Sternbald*. Tieck's romanticism was, therefore, to a considerable degree, molded by that of Wackenroder. Meanwhile he did not remain within his friend's narrow circle, but enlarged it, added new material, and, ultimately, went into entirely independent lines. Other influences began to play upon him. Wackenroder's individualism became, under his hands, more individual, his emotionalism more emotional, his religion less naive, his symbolism more allegorical, the mystery in his poetry more marvelous, the border lines separating one art from another less distinct, music a more intricate part of the romantic style. He adds the element of love, a more intimate, personal association with nature, a larger patriotism centering in the Middle Ages, and the elements of irony, satire, and humor. Important is the presence of a rationalistic strain in Tieck's mental make-up. This was not in Wackenroder. It increases the difficulty of analyzing the complexity of Tieck's nature, and leads us back again to his chief defect. . . . Tieck was a romanticist of the emotional kind; yet at the beginning of his romantic career he wrote, in a satirical vein, a number of realistic stories almost totally free from romanticism, and, besides, gave himself up to criticism of a perfectly rational kind; and again, at the end of his romantic career, we find him writing realistic stories and criticism. So voluminous and so important are these later products of his realistic period, that it would seem almost as though Tieck's true mission was not that of a romanticist, but rather that of a realistic novelist, as indeed he has been called the father of modern German realistic fiction. (pp. 62-3)

Tieck was a *Stimmungspoet* [mood poet]. Some of his lyrical compositions and some portions of his imaginative prose, written under the sway of poetic *Stimmung,* rank high as literary products and insure for him a permanent place in German literature. All the same, only small portions of his poetry are ideally perfect, for ideas, feelings, and images rarely harmoniously blend, intellect, emotion, imagination but rarely unite to serve one great artistic end. Too often, in the course of his romantic writings, he is dominated by a blind genius in which intellect is not allowed its due share.

One of Tieck's most brilliant accomplishments was an extraordinary power of mimicry. . . . This power of mimicry was one of his most fundamental traits, and explains many of the inconsistencies of his literary career. It appears, in full play, in his satirical dramas, [*Der gestiefelte Kater, Die verkehrte Welt,* and *Prinz Zerbino*] . . . , and lurks behind most of his literary products. Tieck *acts* his writings, playing their parts for the sake of the play. Indeed, he sometimes acts serious rôles, as in his Märchen, *Der blonde Eckbert* . . . , [*Der Runenberg*], and in scenes of his dramas *Genoveva* . . . , [and *Kaiser Octavianus*]; indeed he sometimes presents wonderful scenes, picturing before us a dream life of extraordinary beauty, but, for the most part, it is the beauty of the fleeting, momentary, playful mood, which has not in it the aspirations after high human ideals; indeed he sometimes forgets himself, and then his acting seems as if it were real life, but it is, after all, only his own individual life, not the life of the great world in which the individual has blended into the lasting, permanent qualities of humanity. Tieck lacked in seriousness. Later on he himself became suspicious of the unsubstantial note of his works. (pp. 63-4)

> Robert M. Wernaer, "Romantic Leaders," in his
> Romanticism and the Romantic School in Germany,
> *Haskell House, 1966, pp. 55-82.**

## JOHN M. ELLIS   (essay date 1974)

[*Der blonde Eckbert has received much attention from critics interested in its psychological emphasis. Ellis's reading of the*

*novella is the most complete and sustained analysis of* Der blonde Eckbert *as a "paranoid fantasy."*]

In **Der blonde Eckbert** a pattern of events occurs with great frequency: there is an opposition of isolation, loneliness, restriction and narrowness on the one hand, and expansion, escape, freedom and openness on the other. There is movement between the two constantly: expansion is always followed by a process of restriction, which then again turns towards its opposite. This appears to me to be the most important abstraction which can be made from all that happens in the tale. The pattern occurs equally in physical settings and in the characters' personal experiences of their relationships or lack of them. (p. 82)

Both the main characters . . . gravitate towards lives which are physically and personally isolated, but try to escape from the restriction which comes with protection and safety, personally by searching for a spouse, friend, or child, physically by leaving the safe little home. But each time, the attempted escape or expansion fails, or it becomes an even greater restriction. . . . The pattern of escape into a protected but restricted life, followed by the development of feelings that this state is insufficient and even unprotected, which then lead to a further escape: this is a recurring cycle which dominates the story. (pp. 84-5)

[The] basis of the whole pattern . . . is paranoia: the cycle of seeking security in an escape into isolation, which itself then becomes threatening and oppressive. This is the common factor in Bertha's constant running to a protective retreat, only to find it inadequate and run again, and Eckbert's self-defeating attempts to make friends to relieve his isolation and to find allies against the hostile world surrounding him. But the paradox of the paranoid's attempts to find new security is that they must result in new dangers and so increase the paranoia. For only *total* allegiance is adequate, and this inevitably develops a view of the world as being composed of two camps and two only, that which is hostile and that which is friendly. In **Der blonde Eckbert,** as in real life cases of paranoia, this division is always exceedingly clear and well-articulated, and no one is allowed to escape it; a newcomer to the situation is first greeted as a ray of hope and potential ally, and given a complete account of the paranoid's obsessive problems, which itself constitutes a demand for them to be shared. And so Eckbert exposes himself completely to Walther and Hugo. . . . The impulse of a paranoid to confess everything to everyone is part of his obsession with his own problems, his demand for security, but so repels everyone that his paranoia comes to seem more justified; and this is exactly the function of Eckbert's confessions in the story. The confessions are also part of the general paradox of the alternation of attempts to expand his world and its becoming increasingly narrow; his demand for complete friendship is what destroys his friendships. (pp. 86-7)

**Der blonde Eckbert** is best regarded as a paranoid fantasy; it contains a fully developed 'conspiracy' against its central figure. It is not just that several apparently unrelated figures were secretly united against him, for there are two further points which make the conspiracy even more threatening. The first is that it is precisely his closest friends who are involved—a horrifying projection of paranoid fear and suspicion. The second is that this is not just an alliance: involved is one ever-present person, another projection of the paranoid's reduction of the reality of the world to two people: himself and his enemy. At the same time, all of nature seems involved in the conspiracy. . . . And yet another aspect of the theme of paranoia lies in Eckbert's struggles to escape merely getting him deeper into trouble and bringing him finally to the place of his punishment. (p. 88)

[Bertha] adds to the story the theme of guilt and inevitable punishment, and the overt projection of what is only implicit in Eckbert, that the paranoid brings punishment upon himself. It is Bertha who also contributes to the thematic structure of the story that concomitant of all paranoid fears, the fantasy of a life with no problems, the world of riches and ideal marriage. In the same vein is the fantasy of childish innocence, an unproblematic life shattered by her growing up, which inevitably brings sin, and invokes the forces which threaten her. The degree of the intertwining of the characters of Eckbert and Bertha is evidenced by the fact that we naturally accept Eckbert's becoming heir to his sister/wife's sins, and finally going to the old woman's cottage to pay for them. (p. 90)

Eckbert arrives at the centre of the wood, where he finds the old woman and hears the song of the dead bird and the barking of the dead dog. Here occur the last two developments of the paranoid fantasy: the completion of the pattern of his persecution, and the total loss of contact with reality. The helplessness of Eckbert is stressed by the inevitability of his fate, as the theme of 'Erbsünde' [original sin] appears: it is his father's sin that started the process. Yet the contrary motif appears too: his fate was *both* the ultimate result of things beyond his control, *and* exacerbated by his own action, and that of Bertha, in their offending the old woman.

Throughout the story an air of unreality and of indistinctness has prevailed, and a large part in the creation of this effect was played by the reporting of sounds and avoidance of visual descriptions of situations. . . . And now, at the end of the story, Eckbert's experiences are almost totally aural, no visual experience being reported at all. . . . [The] physical world has no clear orientation points for him any more. Tieck's use of . . . sounds in the final words of the story to suggest the final slipping away of all contact with the outside world from Eckbert is remarkable. . . . (pp. 91-2)

All of the monotony of paranoia is here in the tedious repetition of the same sounds; and there is a final loss of any ability to take in the shapes of the outside world, or the distinctions present there, as even Eckbert's final impressions, the three sounds, begin to blur and to grow remote. The ultimate state of loneliness and being cut-off from everything has at last come. Relating to anything outside oneself involves seeing its distinctive quality and responding to the distinctions which exist in reality; this blurring of everything, the loss of all distinctions between one thing and another, in short, the complete loss of any contact with reality, is the logical outcome of the process beginning with Eckbert's seeking in his friends only what was in himself, and ignoring their real existence as themselves.

Tieck's exploitation of the narrative convention of the *Märchen* affords an interesting illumination of the possibilities of that convention; and conversely, the meaning of his story is illuminated by the manner of its use of those possibilities. In a realistic convention, any element of fantasy would have to be clearly marked as the imaginings of one of the characters of the story; but in the convention of the *Märchen* narrator, a complete paranoid fantasy is possible in which the conspiracy against Eckbert *does* exist, and his friend really can be his enemy in disguise. We can, in fact, scarcely talk of the unreality of any one part of the text within its context in the story. . . .

The point is that illusion and reality are in a different relationship to each other in the *Märchen;* only the whole story can be an illusion, as though it were a nightmarish dream embodying a fantasy of paranoia. In such a fantasy 'objective' evidence of the existence of the global danger . . . cannot be contrasted with unreal imaginings; for the distinction between imaginings and what is real exists as little in the *Märchen* as it does in the dream. Because *Der blonde Eckbert* is a *Märchen*, imaginings take on a life of their own, and the paranoid fear of Eckbert that the world is closing in on him can—with terrifying effect—come true. (pp. 92-3)

*John M. Ellis, "Tieck: 'Der blonde Eckbert'," in his* Narration in the German Novelle: Theory and Interpretation *(© Cambridge University Press 1974), Cambridge University Press, 1974, pp. 77-93.*

## OSCAR MANDEL (essay date 1978)

[*In his introduction to the first English translation of* The Land of Upside Down, *Mandel argues that* Prinz Zerbino, Puss in Boots, *and* The Land of Upside Down *represent "a bolder and more radical manipulation of structure than anything that was to be attempted before the twentieth century." Mandel maintains that Tieck "should be recognized as one of the great humorists of his age," and that his comic dramas rather than his novellas are his true masterpieces.*]

Among the novels, tales, poems, critical essays, translations and dramatic works that Ludwig Tieck was producing at a rapid pace in his mid-twenties, we find three ambitious plays proposing a bolder and more radical manipulation of structure than anything that was to be attempted before the twentieth century. . . .

One of these plays is an enormously long, occasionally brilliant, but over-literary and finally stifling work entitled *Prinz Zerbino, oder die Reise nach dem guten Geschmack (Prince Zerbino, or the Journey to Good Taste)*. . . . The other two, however . . . , are in my opinion Tieck's twin masterpieces, and superior as works of art to the far better known and more influential *Märchen* he composed.

The first of these two theatrical jests is *Der gestiefelte Kater* . . . , and this *Puss in Boots* is established, in the German world at any rate, as a minor classic. (p. 7)

The other experimental comedy is *Die verkehrte Welt* . . . , given its first translation here as *The Land of Upside Down.* (p. 8)

It is no accident that Tieck's best work is also his most apparently formless. Both before and after writing these anarchical pieces, Tieck tried hard to become a fascinating storyteller. . . . But when all is said and done, Tieck must be rated an ineffectual narrator. He is hasty, careless, unable to concentrate, lackadaisical, lacking in moral passion and fervor . . . , and ultimately unscrupulous. He meanders when we want him to come to the point, blurs what ought to be sharp, holds out promises he does not keep, forgets what he should have remembered, and cheats for effect.

These several sins against orderly and convincing narration turned into virtues as soon as the aesthetic and thematic purpose became to overturn narration. Where desultory rambling was obviously more important and charming than any destination, where moral shilly-shallying (so harmful to his serious works) could raise no eyebrows, and where digression could be accepted as substance rather than unwelcome intrusion—there

Tieck's brand of irresponsible and chameleonic genius was at home.

For Tieck—who should be recognized as one of the great humorists of his age—belongs to that considerable band of wool-gathering comic writers, lazy or apparently lazy, careless or apparently careless, among whom we name his favorites, Cervantes and Sterne, and, in his own lifetime, Byron and Musset. (pp. 10-11)

[In his drama, Tieck] demonstrates that the logical, commonsensical, "bourgeois," or "Enlightened" laws of theater-making can be and should be transmuted by Poetry. As the playwright sets out to write a parable in which the Imagination is struggling against Dull Routine, it occurs to him that the act of telling a story is itself Dull Routine. He then sabotages his own story, saves only as much of the original straightforward parable as he needs, and proceeds to play delicious havoc with the rest. How deeply the innovators of our century would have been indebted to Tieck—if they had known him. (p. 19)

A natural (though by no means inevitable) consequence of Romantic transcendence—the urge to *break through the frame*—is a tendency to dissolve into formlessness. . . . [Yet] *The Land of Upside Down* is formless only at first blush, and it does not take us long to realize that Tieck seldom if ever deserts his chosen theme as he dances from vignette to vignette and, while seeming to pay no attention, gradually gathers together the strands of the rebellion against Scaramuccio.

Tieck's failures, when he does fail, are of a simpler kind. The vignettes do not always shine. We detect signs of haste. Here and there Tieck strains to be comical and fails. Foxberry, Starberry, and the Fat Woman are not very amusing; the Greenfeather-Lisette romance is lame; and something better could have been managed with the illumination and masquerade episode, and with the animals, and with Mopsa and Phyllis. (p. 23)

Tieck amuses us . . . with his mixture of styles, his mad non-sequiturs, his visual inventiveness, and his anticlimaxes which, as in the case of Admetus and Alcestis' farewell and Lofty's soulful speech, sometimes fuse with his theatrical games. Noteworthy too is the mischievous courtliness of the dialogue, reminiscent of Cervantes' tone . . . , and the quaint originality of many of his expressions. . . . (p. 24)

[The] plays of Tieck, like those of Byron, Musset, and others remind us that a cultural phenomenon new to Western civilization was born in the Romantic Age. For the first time in our history a number of serious dramatists are writing plays for which there is no theater. Consciously separated from the primarily bourgeois audience they despise, they address themselves to an elite on paper, and if they tend to lose as a result some of the useful commonsense that comes of having to satisfy a paying public, they gain a new liberty of scenic and thematic conceptions, conceptions independent of the practical exigencies of performance. (p. 26)

> *Oscar Mandel, in his introduction to* The Land of Upside Down *by Ludwig Tieck, translated by Oscar Mandel with Maria Kelsen Feder (© 1978 by Associated University Presses, Inc.), Associated University Presses, 1978, pp. 7-26.*

**GLYN TEGAI HUGHES** (essay date 1979)

At first sight it appears that most of what is specifically Romantic in Tieck is concentrated between the years 1797 and 1803, but this is to disregard the persistence of his sense of imbalance between the world and self. What is more to the point about Tieck is that total commitment almost always leads to scepticism; all his significant works are self-questioning. Uncertainty of intention is allied to an ultimate mistrust of apocalyptic. Hot for certainties he finds only compromises.

Often he declines to search and we have the mass of occasional verse and ephemeral stories. Sometimes a literary historical interest attaches even to these; and sometimes Tieck's momentary enthusiasms or brooding uncertainties raise him above himself in works that still speak to us.

*Franz Sternbalds Wanderungen* combines historical impact with a continuingly attractive limpidity of vision. It is perhaps difficult to look back to its appearance in 1798 without remembering later Romantic novels exploiting similar motifs; yet, for contemporaries, it marked the birth of a new kind of novel. . . . The novel is unfinished, and the two existing parts do not, at first sight, appear to be adequately related. . . . What the novel does, however, is to suggest, even in its unresolved state, an equilibrium ultimately attainable through the natural world, whose mystery and perils do not exhaust its significance. It is also revelation, a hieroglyph of the divine, an inkling of wholeness. Schelling's world-soul moves in it, but the concept is not a wholly abstract one; Tieck creates valid pictures, even if the subjective interlacing of emotion and the external world is sometimes facile and formulaic. (pp. 30-2)

Florestan represents the extreme of subjectivism and rootlessness, the open-ended approach to the world, and his influence certainly dominates sections of the novel. Thus an air of improvidence and dilettantism pervades much of the central core of the work, giving perhaps too much stress to vague aspirations and diaphanous uncertainties. Yet the overriding impression left by the novel is of a commitment to the natural world that, in spite of criticism levelled at Tieck as a lightweight, is of a different order of intensity from the normal eighteenth-century enthusiasm. There may indeed, as contemporary critics suggested, be too many morning or evening scenes; but they created a new mode of vision. . . .

Tieck's other major achievement of this period is the Märchen *Der blonde Eckbert*. . . . (p. 32)

Somehow [his supernatural interest, his folk memories, his knowledge of Shakespeare], and more, fused in *Eckbert* to a new synthesis that would be imitated, but seldom achieved, by succeeding Romantic writers and by Tieck himself. What is presented here is the equivocal nature of reality, and the instability of viewpoint, reflected in the narrative technique, causes the whole Märchen to proceed on a knife edge. There are symbols, certainly: the dog and the bird are aspects of reality and illusion, of nature and wish-fulfilment. But the symbols, too, are insubstantial and elusive; all is relative, all uncertain, dreamlike, perhaps even dreamt. Eckbert's own psychological state seems to make him confuse reality and illusion; his persecution mania blurs all the edges of experience. (p. 33)

*Der blonde Eckbert* calls normality in question. The senses present us with unreliable data; memory and temporal awareness play tricks; . . . all interpretations are elusive. The general atmosphere of the work reinforces the hallucinatory effect. The style is uncomplicated and the limitations of the Märchen form are accepted, though themes and levels of narrative awareness are interwoven. Descriptions are inconclusive and dreamlike. . . . Every now and again Tieck catches his breath at the abyss of life, and *Eckbert* is the finest expression of this.

It would be easy to go on from here to justify Tieck's use of irony as a protective device against such unnerving consciousness; but this would be to make Tieck more reflective and less intuitive than he is. The Romantic Irony of the plays is, and seems, more literary than metaphysical. (pp. 33-4)

In *Der gestiefelte Kater* Tieck takes Perrault's Puss in Boots fairytale and makes of it a statement about aesthetic illusion, a satire on contemporary literary, moral and political attitudes and an elegantly amusing amalgam of comedy and farce. (p. 34)

The satire on rationalism and sentimentality, against classicistic good taste and the lumpishly prosaic nature of contemporary criticism, is in the first place directed against the audience, against the real contemporary audience through the fictive one; but it also includes a good deal of ephemeral criticism of figures from the underworld of the Enlightenment. (pp. 34-5)

What interests us more now, and this is true of *Die verkehrte Welt* . . . and of *Zerbino,* is the significance of the breaking of the dramatic illusion; though in *Zerbino* this occurs mainly towards the end of the play and is overlaid with other effects in a general and laboured attempt at uniting a variety of experiences, a Romantic 'universal' experiment. (p. 35)

Tieck certainly uses the interplay of dramatic illusion and disillusion to point the inadequacy of a rationalist, common-sense approach to theatre, to a play. He plays with the play, he allows the alogical free rein, he balances poetry between fantasy and buffoonery. (pp. 35-6)

It is very odd that nearly all Tieck's dramas should be unplayable. *Der gestiefelte Kater* has had the occasional successful performance, particularly of late with the renewed interest in anti-illusionist theatre. It is, in other words, precisely because it plays with the concept of unplayability, because its theatrical world is called in question, that the *Kater* can still appeal. . . .

*Genoveva* was an attempt to recreate the mood of the childlike piety of the Crusade period. It is a sprawling, sentimental piece with much virtuosity in the metrical patterns and with some lyrical scenes of considerable beauty. . . . For later readers, however, the artificiality of Tieck's re-creation, the sterile longing, the *longueurs* of the psychological analyses, the over-explicit parade of belief, the almost total lack of dramatic tension, all these seem to disqualify it from serious consideration. (p. 36)

[In *Kaiser Octavianus* the] story line is no more than an excuse for a bewildering succession of scenes, reflective, comic, narrative, fantastic, realistic, sentimental, ironic, idealized, parodistic. . . . The work is certainly full of mood-pictures, drenched with imagery, often synaesthetic, and its recent admirers may well be right in claiming that it should not be judged by conventional standards of dramatic tension. Yet the overwhelming impression it leaves, is, unhappily, one of a not very significant jumble. (pp. 36-7)

The Tieck of . . . later years retains an ironical view, even if overlaid at times with the fashionably sentimental. His best-known Novelle, *Des Lebens Überfluß* . . . , is characteristic both of the irony and the sentiment. . . . It fits the theory of the Novelle very well, with its turning-point, its not too obtrusive symbols . . . , its intrusion of the extraordinary into the everyday. Like most of Tieck's Novellen it is carried along by conversation, with diary extracts and reminiscences here providing flashbacks; and, fairly artificially, the wheels always come full circle. As everyday life is reduced to, or below, the barest essentials, the direct criticism of contemporary society

so often seen elsewhere in Tieck's later Novellen yields here to oblique indications of the fear of revolution, the breakdown of social order—for better or for worse, the undue sway of materialism. The Novelle is a hymn to married love and to the power of imagination, an attempt to portray an Eden that is urban and contemporary but at the same time abstract, shut off from reality, which is not even visible through the windows. The reduction to the purified essence of existence is, however, achieved by wild improbability and by such stupefyingly inattentive ingenuousness on the part of the wife, that Tieck's attempted irony is drowned in mawkishness. (pp. 38-9)

Scant justice has been . . . done to [the novel *Vittoria Accorombona*] or to *Der junge Tischlermeister*. . . . This long Novelle, circling around the problems of marriage and of a social structure in upheaval, places the worlds of appearance and reality, the question of the role we have to play, against a background of detailed discussion of stage performances. Tieck, in his own way, is challenging Weimar. He has survived and is now arbiter and reconciler. Through him Romanticism flows into Biedermeier and Poetic Realism. (p. 40)

*Glyn Tegai Hughes, "New Ways of Feeling: Wackenroder, Tieck and 'The Night Watches'," in his* Romantic German Literature *(© Glyn Tegai Hughes 1979; reprinted by permission of Holmes & Meier Publishers, Inc., New York; in Canada by Edward Arnold (Publishers) Ltd), Holmes & Meier, 1979, Arnold, 1979, pp. 21-40.\**

---

## ADDITIONAL BIBLIOGRAPHY

Birrell, Gordon. *The Boundless Present: Space and Time in the Literary Fairy Tales of Novalis and Tieck.* University of North Carolina Studies in the Germanic Languages and Literatures, edited by Siegfried Mews, no. 95. Chapel Hill: The University of North Carolina Press, 1979, 160 p.\*

Includes a close reading of *Der Blonde Eckbert* and *Der Runenberg.* Birrell devotes special attention to Tieck's use of space and time motifs, and compares his technique with that of Novalis.

Corkhill, Alan. *The Motif of "Fate" in the Works of Ludwig Tieck.* Stuttgarter Arbeiten Zur Germanistik, edited by Ulrich Müller, Franz Hundsnurscher, and Cornelius Sommer, no. 38. Stuttgart: Akademischer Verlag Hans-Dieter Heinz, 1978, 238 p.

Traces the motif of fate in *Abdallah, Die Geschichte des Herrn William Lovell, Der Blonde Eckbert,* and *Leben und Tod der heiligen Genoveva.* Corkhill links Tieck's treatment of fate with his interest in mysticism, his preoccupation with the existence of evil, and his awareness of the shifting nature of reality.

Ewton, Ralph W., Jr. "Childhood Without End: Tieck's *Der Blonde Eckbert.*" *The German Quarterly* XLVI, No. 3 (May 1973): 410-27.

A careful examination of *Der Blonde Eckbert.* Ewton concludes that the central theme of the novella is a desire to escape reality and return to the protected, magical world of childhood.

Hewett-Thayer, Harvey W. "Tieck's Novellen and Contemporary Journalistic Criticism." *The Germanic Review* III, No. 4 (October 1928): 328-60.

A survey of contemporary German critical response to Tieck's writings. Hewett-Thayer traces the shifting assessments of Tieck's work up to the 1840s and analyzes the elements which determined various attitudes toward his work.

Kimpel, Richard W. "Nature, Quest, and Reality in Tieck's *Der Blonde Eckbert* and *Der Runenberg.*" *Studies in Romanticism* IX, No. 3 (Summer 1970): 176-92.

A comparison of Tieck's treatment of nature, quest, and reality in *Der Blonde Eckbert* and *Der Runenberg*. In both novellas nature aids the passage from ordinary to supernatural experience, Kimpel finds, but in *Der Runenberg* the theme of nature is developed more fully and systematically.

Lillyman, W[illiam] J. "Ludwig Tieck's *Der Runenberg*: The Dimensions of Reality." *Monatshefte* 62, No. 3 (1970): 231-44.

Examines the theme of ambiguity in Tieck's *Der Runenberg*. Because the narrator is neutral and does not judge each character's perception of reality, Lillyman finds Tieck's characterization and delineation of point of view particularly successful in conveying the ambiguous nature of reality.

Lillyman, William J. *Reality's Dark Dream: The Narrative Fiction of Ludwig Tieck*. Berlin, New York: Walter de Gruyter, 1979, 159 p.

An analysis of Tieck's narrative technique. Lillyman praises Tieck's experiments with perspective, but finds his characterization deficient.

Matenko, Percy. *Ludwig Tieck and America*. University of North Carolina Studies in Germanic Languages and Literatures, no. 12. Chapel Hill: The University of North Carolina Press, 1954, 120 p.

An account of Tieck's interactions with American visitors in Germany, his critical reception in America, and his influence on American authors.

Paulin, Roger. "The Early Ludwig Tieck and the Idyllic Tradition." *The Modern Language Review* 70, No. 1 (January 1975): 110-24.

A study of the influence of eighteenth-century sentimental literature on the early works of Ludwig Tieck. Paulin asserts that though Tieck incorporated some idyllic elements into his early work, he was in his later works faithful to a more realistic tradition.

Trainer, James. "The Märchen." In *The Romantic Period in Germany: Essays by Members of the London University Institute of Germanic Studies*, edited by Siegbert Prawer, pp. 97-120. London: Weidenfeld and Nicolson, 1970.*

A discussion of the philosophy implicit in Tieck's novellas. Trainer comments on the juxtaposition of reality and the imagination, and the importance of the role of nature.

Zeydel, Edwin H. *Ludwig Tieck, the German Romanticist: A Critical Study*. Princeton: Princeton University Press, 1935, 406 p.

A useful introduction to Tieck which includes a chronological account of his life and career, as well as general critical commentary on his works.

# Henrik Arnold Wergeland

## 1808-1845

(Also wrote under the pseudonym of Siful Sifadda) Norwegian poet, dramatist, journalist, essayist, and translator.

As a champion of Norwegian nationalism and as a lyric poet, Wergeland is considered one of the most important of Norway's writers. He profoundly influenced his country's intellectual and cultural life during the crucial decades following Norwegian independence in 1814.

Wergeland was born in Kristiansand and grew up in Eidsvoll. His father, a pastor and high school teacher, participated in the writing of the Norwegian Constitution in 1814. A man of lofty spiritual and political ideals, Nicolai Wergeland educated his son in accordance with the principles of Jean Jacques Rousseau, and instilled in him a love of freedom and nature. Wergeland attended the university in Kristiania (now Oslo) from 1825 to 1829 and received a degree in theology. Though he tried repeatedly to obtain a ministerial post, his radical politics thwarted his attempts. Wergeland publicly professed his staunch opposition to the Danish hegemony in Norway, arguing that, although the Norwegian Constitution had mitigated the political power that Denmark exercised over Norway, Denmark's cultural dominance in Norway still threatened her true independence. Wergeland advocated democracy, widespread educational reform to provide schooling for the common citizen, and the purging of Danish linguistic elements from the Norwegian language in order to restore it to its original purity.

Nowhere was Wergeland's patriotic stand expressed more fully than in his ongoing feud with J. S. Welhaven. Welhaven, a Norwegian poet and critic, believed that terse, formalistic poetry, as sanctioned by Danish universities and intelligentsia, represented the artistic ideal. He censured Wergeland's poetry for its nationalistic and romantic excesses, while Wergeland countered with charges that Welhaven was a traitor to Norway. Their dialogue, published in various newspapers, is significant to Norwegian cultural history; the two poets presented aesthetic alternatives for the developing Norwegian literature. As G. M. Gathorne-Hardy notes, Welhaven's theory tended toward formalism, while Wergeland promoted a lyrical freedom for the advancement of nationalism.

Wergeland's brashness, the sensuality of his poetry, and his unconventional personal life prevented him from securing a government position. However, in 1839, King Charles XIV John of Sweden-Norway appointed Wergeland keeper of the State Archives. A generous annuity accompanied the post and Wergeland, for the first time, achieved a measure of financial security. But his critics, led chiefly by Welhaven, denounced Wergeland's acceptance of the stipend as a betrayal of his own democratic ideal.

Wergeland made his first appearance as a published author with a group of political farces written under the pseudonym of Siful Sifadda. These plays, of which *Ah!* is the most representative, enjoyed considerable success because of their topicality and satiric wit. Wergeland's second group of dramas evinces his interest in the works of Shakespeare, and includes the tragedy *Sinclars død*, as well as *Irreparabile tempus,* a dramatic farce modeled after Shakespeare. But it was not until the publication of *Digte, første ring,* his first volume of poetry,

that Wergeland was acknowledged as one of Norway's leading poets. This collection of love poetry, which is addressed to "Stella," the fictional composite of Wergeland's ideal woman, has been called one of Wergeland's most beautiful poetic achievements.

Critics generally agree that *Skabelsen, mennesket og messias,* the epic poem which followed *Digte, første ring,* is Wergeland's most important accomplishment. Influenced by the works of Lord Byron and John Milton, the poem received wide acclaim for its sumptuous imagery, primitive energy, and pantheistic celebration of nature. Wergeland based the 750-page poem, which he completed in a few weeks, on the Old and the New Testaments, dividing it into three parts: Creation, Aberration, and Salvation. Some critics fault the poem for excessive imagery and a lack of direction, but others praise Wergeland's originality and ambition. The ideas that Wergeland discussed in the epic are essentially those of the Age of Enlightenment: the spiritual perfectability of the individual, intellectual enlightenment, and the possibility of discovering God through an understanding of the universe. Therefore, while Wergeland's exploration of poetic form, love of nature, and vivid imagery link him with the Romantic school, his themes reflect the neoclassical aspects of his education. Near the end of his life, Wergeland revised *Skabelsen, mennesket og messias.* The new version, which is more concise and restrained than the original, is titled simply *Mennesket,* to reflect the enlarged treatment of the role of humanity in the creation myth.

Wergeland's later poetry shows development of his lyrical ability. Many critics argue that his later work, though more subdued and less innovative than the early poetry, represents Wergeland at his peak. Some, however, cite its calmer tone as a negative trait.

Wergeland was politically active throughout his life, and edited four proletarian periodicals. As his career progressed, his political and social consciousness became an increasingly significant force in his writing. He wrote numerous pamphlets and tracts and a history of the Norwegian Constitution entitled the *Norges konstitutions historie,* as well as *Jøden* and *Jødinen* ("The Jewess"), poems urging the Norwegian government to allow the immigration of displaced Jews, who were then prohibited from settling in Norway. "My life must be a faithful comment on my poetry," he wrote, and the admiration that the Norwegian people lavished upon him, both as a patriot and as a writer, indicated that he lived up to his goal. His last works include *Hassel-nødder,* a collection of autobiographical short stories, regarded by many as his best prose writing.

Critics concur that Wergeland's poetry represents his greatest achievement. However, they debate whether Wergeland's early or late poetry deserves more praise: some commentators consider *Skabelsen, mennesket og messias* unsurpassed among Wergeland's works, while others maintain that only his last poetry, especially *Jan van Huysums blomsterstykke* ("Jan van Huysum's Flower-Piece") and *Den engelske lods,* will endure. While Wergeland is a legendary figure in Norway, elsewhere he is virtually unknown. Critics question whether Wergeland has been elevated by the people of Norway because of his nationalism, or whether his artistic merits alone warrant his excellent reputation in his homeland.

Wergeland contributed significantly to the cultural growth of Norway by helping to nurture a revolutionary spirit in Norwegian poetry. In doing so, he reflected the movement toward Romanticism in Europe.

## PRINCIPAL WORKS

*Ah!* [first publication] (drama) 1827
*Irreparabile tempus* [first publication] (drama) 1828
*Sinclars død* [first publication] (drama) 1828
*Digte, første ring* (poetry) 1829
*Skabelsen, mennesket og messias* (poetry) 1830; also
     published as *Mennesket* [revised edition], 1845
*Digte, anden ring* (poetry) 1833
*Spaniolen* (poetry) 1833
*Poesier* (poetry) 1838
*Jan van Huysums blomsterstykke* (poetry) 1840
     ["Jan van Huysum's Flower-Piece" published in *Poems,*
     1929]
*Norges konstitutions historie* (history) 1841-43
*Svalen* (poetry) 1841
*Jøden* (poetry) 1842
*Venetianerne* [first publication] (drama) 1843
*Den engelske lods* (poetry) 1844
*Jødinen* (poetry) 1844
     ["The Jewess" published in *Anthology of Norwegian
     Lyrics,* 1942]
*Hassel-nødder* (short stories) 1845
*Henrik Wergeland's samlede skrifter.* 9 vols. (drama,
     poetry, and prose) 1852-57

*Samlede skrifter, trykt og utrykt.* 23 vols. (poetry and
     prose) 1918-40
*Poems* (poetry) 1929
*\*Anthology of Norwegian Lyrics* (poetry) 1942

\*This work includes translations of eleven poems by Wergeland.

---

### J. S. WELHAVEN (poem date 1830)

[*The following poem initiated the long critical dispute between Wergeland and Welhaven. Here Welhaven attacks Wergeland for "cutting reason's cable" and for the incomprehensibility of his poetry.*]

How long will you indulge in senseless raving,
     In crazy brandishing of Quixote's spear?
See how, for all your airy wings a-waving,
     Straight for a bottomless morass you steer!
The sun you seek is wildfire of the bog,
A crawling eft the Pegasus you flog!

Then murmur not that none of us is able
     To judge a genius soaring past our sight:
Where is the art in cutting reason's cable
     To drift about in realms of cloudy night?
Your place assured a thousand votes will fix,
The place the Muse reserves for—lunatics.

> *J. S. Welhaven, " 'To Henrik Wergeland' " (originally published as an unsigned poem in* Morgenbladet, *August 15, 1830), in* Poems *by Henrik Wergeland, translated by G. M. Gathorne-Hardy, Jethro Bithell, and I. Grøndahl, Gyldendal Norsk Forlag, 1929 (and reprinted by Greenwood Press, Publishers, 1970), p. xxix.*

### EDMUND W. GOSSE (essay date 1872)

[*The following excerpt is from the first serious study in English of Wergeland's works. Though Gosse presents the patriotic fervor of Wergeland's early poetry as a negative trait, he praises Wergeland's* Skabelsen, mennesket og messias *for having "revolutionised the literature of Norway." The critic's opinion that "only his deathbed poems . . . will be read in future times" remained unchanged and is stated more harshly in Gosse's later evaluation of Wergeland (see excerpt below, 1925). Gosse concludes that Welhaven's criticism had a beneficial effect upon Wergeland's poetry—an estimation that Gathorne-Hardy disputed (see excerpt below, 1929).*]

[Wergeland's] genius, slowly developing out of the chaotic elements around it, took form, and colour, and majesty, till it lifted its possessor to a level with the noblest spirits of his time. (p. 437)

[His] ideal love for 'Stella' woke the seeds of poetry in him; he began to versify, and soon, forgetting Stella, worshipped a still less tangible but more important mistress, the Muse Thalia herself.

The first work published by the afterwards eminent poet was *Ah!* a farce. It is usual with his admirers to pass over this and his other boyish productions in silence, but it is undoubtedly a fact that after the appearance of *Ah!* . . . he wrote a great number of farces in quick succession. . . . That Wergeland himself did not prize these trifles very highly would seem from his publishing them under an Arabic pseudonym—*Siful Si-*

*fadda*. Those who have read them speak of them as not altogether devoid of fun, but founded principally on passing events, that have lost all interest now. . . . [The lyrical poems of *Digte, Forste Ring*] showed he had distinct and worthy aims in art. These poems had an immense success; they were brimful of tasteless affectations and outrages of rhythm as well as reason, but they were full, too, of Syttendemai [May 17, 1814, the Norwegian independence day] enthusiasm, and they spread through the country like wild fire. . . . There are real and great merits about these early poems; they show some true knowledge of nature, some lyrical loveliness; but it was not for these, it was rather for the defiance of all laws of authorship, that the people of Christiania adored him. . . . *Skabelsen, Mennesket og Messias* (**'The Creation, Man and the Messiah'**) [is] a drama of elephantine proportions. This portentous poem caused great diversion among the poet's enemies, and was the actual cause of [Welhaven's] attack upon him, which ultimately divided the nation into two camps, and revolutionised the literature of Norway. (p. 438)

*Spaniolen,* a charming little poem . . . shows a great improvement in style, and proves the beneficial effect of the criticism brought to bear on him. (p. 439)

The last five years of his life saw his genius scatter all the clouds and vapours that enwrapped it.

The first of these swan-songs was *Jan van Huysums Blomsterstykke* (**'J. van Huysum's Flower-piece'**), a series of lyrics with prose interjaculations. This is by far the most beautiful of his political poems—for such it must be called, being thoroughly interpenetrated by his fiery republicanism. No poet has decked the bare shell of politics with brighter wreaths than Wergeland; and it must be remembered that while in the mouth of an English poet these principles are dreamy and Utopian, to a Norwegian of that time they were matter of practical hope. . . . In *Jan van Huysums Blomsterstykke* the poet takes a flower-piece of [the painter van Huysum's] cunning workmanship, and gazes at it till it seems to start into life, and the whole mass—flowers, insects, and the porcelain jar itself—becomes a symbol of passionate humanity to him. The blossoms are souls longing for a happier world; here the poppies cry for vengeance like bubbles of blood from the torn throat of some martyr for liberty; here the tulips flame out of their pale-green sheaths like men who burst their bonds and would be free; roses, columbines, narcissi, each suggest some brilliant human parallel to the poet, and all is moulded into verse that is melody itself. One rises from reading the poem as from studying some exquisite piece of majolica, or a page of elaborate arabesques; one feels it never can be as true to one's own faith as it was to the writer's, but one regards it as a lovely piece of art, shapely and well proportioned. (pp. 440-41)

*Svalen* (**'The Swallow'**) [is] a poem suggested by the bereavement of the poet's excellent sister Augusta. It was 'a midsummer morning story for mothers who have lost their children,' and was sent to cheer the downcast heart of his sister. It is one of the most ethereal poems ever written; a lyrical rhapsody of faith in God and triumph over death. . . .

A few months before the end [of Wergeland's life] his last and greatest poem appeared—*Den engelske Lods* (**'The English Pilot'**)—in which all his early life of travel and excitement seems to have passed before his eyes and to have been photographed in verse. There is no trace of depression or weakness; it is not the sort of book a man writes upon his death-bed; it is lively and full of incident, humorous and yet pathetic. The groundwork of the piece is a reminiscence of the poet's own visit to

England many years before. Kent, Brighton, the Isle of Wight, and the 'Hampshire-Fjord' are drawn in rose-colour by an only too enthusiastic pen, and the idyllic story that gives title to the whole—namely, the loves of Johnny Johnson and Mary Ann—is interwoven skilfully enough. The only drawback is that the poet, whose English was defective, must needs preserve the local colouring by hauling bits of our language, or what he supposed it to be, bodily into his verse. Such a passage as this, coming in the middle of an excited address to Liberty in England, breaks down one's gravity altogether:

> Ho! Johnny, ho! how do you do?
> Sing, Sailor, oh!
> Well! toddy is the sorrows' foe!
> Sing, Sailor, oh!

It should be a solemn warning to those who travel and then write a book not to quote in the language of the country. (pp. 441-42)

[Wergeland] had much of the flabby mental texture of Coleridge—a soft woollen fabric shot through with gold threads. . . . Of all the voluminous writings of Wergeland, only his deathbed poems (forming the latter half of the third volume of his collected works) will be read in future times. . . . (p. 442)

*Edmund W. Gosse, "Norwegian Poetry Since 1814," in* Fraser's Magazine, *Vol. VI, No. XXXIV, October, 1872, pp. 435-49.\**

## C. F. KEARY (essay date 1892)

[The literature of Norse independence] attained its zenith in the writings of a poet of much higher inspiration than the others, Peter [*sic*] Wergeland by name, the father, as he is generally reckoned, of modern Norse poetry. Wergeland's writing is distinguished by the sort of graceful and facile optimism which is most popular with the half educated. . . . To compare Wergeland to Longfellow will perhaps give the English reader the best notion of what I mean by the facile and graceful, but it must be also added rather cheap and conventional poetry of this author. The best known of Wergeland's poems is '**Den Engilske Lods,**' '**The English Pilot.**' It gives a series of travel-pictures very largely of English coast scenery in graceful and agreeable verse. (p. 360)

*C. F. Keary, "Literature," in his* Norway and the Norwegians, *Charles Scribner's Sons, 1892, pp. 359-73.\**

## THE NATION (essay date 1908)

Even in its revised form, the epic [**"Creation, Man, and the Messiah"**] is in many respects as chaotic as the newborn world, the creation of which we witness in the opening stanzas. It contains lyric gems of singular beauty, but they have to be laboriously dug from a mass of débris. Through the entire poem, however, Wergeland breathes the message of love and of faith in the ultimate redemption of mankind, in progress, in evolution from baseness to nobility, and in the final assimilation of man with God.

"**Man**" is Byronic in its conception and execution; and indeed many of Wergeland's poetical writings recall Byron's manner. There is, however, this difference. Byron, the skeptical, critical, dissatisfied spirit remains chained to earth. Wergeland, on the other hand, is always in conscious flight toward the ether. Byron expressed the disappointment of his age; Wergeland voices the aspiration of a nation born in the dark hours of Europe's travail, but full of hope and virility. Moreover, Wergeland was through and through a democrat, not only in theory, but in his understanding of the common people, in his self-sacrificing labor for their physical and spiritual welfare, in his faith in their ability to rise. Indeed, in this respect, he somewhat reminds one of our own Walt Whitman, although of the two, Wergeland was by far the more active and practical. Wergeland took hold and did things, where the other contented himself with mere preaching. (p. 529)

The intensity of Wergeland's spirit of nationality is perhaps one reason why his name is hardly known beyond the borders of his own country; but in that country and in the hearts of his own people, it strikes a sympathetic chord whenever mentioned; it stands for all that tends towards growth on national lines, for every endeavor to elevate and ennoble existence. (p. 530)

> J., ''The Wergeland Centenary,'' in The Nation (copyright 1908 The Nation magazine, The Nation Associates, Inc.), Vol. LXXXVI, No. 2241, June 11, 1908, pp. 529-30.

## AGNES MATHILDE WERGELAND  (essay date 1916)

[The editors of NCLC are unable to determine whether Wergeland was a relative of Agnes Mathilde Wergeland. In the following essay, she singles out Wergeland's desire to foster a Norwegian national literature as an important aspect of his achievement as a writer, a view that opposes that of Edmund Gosse (see excerpt above, 1872). She finds Wergeland's initial efforts at nationalism ''exaggerated and tumultuous,'' but believes that ''the later preëminence of Norwegian literature has fully justified his zeal.'']

[As a young man, Wergeland] was already known as a poet of indisputable originality, turbid and turgid, but with extraordinary luxuriance and primitiveness. (p. 39)

The Congress of 1814 had brought to Norway independence as a nation. But the liberty granted by the new constitution had now to be made real and practical by growth in the inner mental life of the people itself. . . . The national instinct now demanded manifestations in literature, language, art, science, and in enlightened public opinion, which should justify the nation's claims to recognition from other nations. (p. 40)

[Wergeland's poetry of the 1830s] possesses the same restlessness and stormy character as the popular feeling expressed. It sprang from a sense of new power, not quite conscious of itself or certain of its aim. That he was right later events have fully proved. The background of his conception of nationality was not dreamy sentiment. Though poetical, it was not mystical, but was the thought of natural progress and was an ideally rational aim such as both nations and individuals must hold. (pp. 42-3)

His enthusiasm for a national literature was indeed exaggerated and tumultuous, but it was necessary and found its response in national pride and national ambition. The later preëminence of Norwegian literature has fully justified his zeal. His adversaries, however, would not grant its value and significance even for the time. To them it seemed evident that Norway could not change her condition. Even the language they thought too barbarous for poetical expression and far inferior in melody to the Danish. This also Wergeland combated, and pointed out the superior right of Norwegian words, both because they were Norwegian and sounded true and familiar to people of Norway, and because they had a more suggestive fullness of volume

and thus approached the strong resonant tone of the old original language. (p. 49)

A glance at the literary activity of Wergeland from 1830 to 1840 shows that he understood better than anybody the historical justification of the political turmoil because he saw the ideal meaning hidden under the noisy quarrel. Himself pushing along and exciting the popular feeling and being in turn excited by it, he was in the happiest sympathy with his people; that kind of sympathy which is the surest footing for any poet, however vague and obscure the sympathy may be on the part of the nation at large. His poems, from the epos of humanity down to songs for the seventeenth of May (the day of independence), mirror the thoughts and feelings of the time. His farces, too, were political and polemical. And besides being incessantly active as a poet, he was an indefatigable journalist. His newspaper articles were innumerable, mostly anonymous, but in a style easily recognized. Scarcely a subject that roused the interest of the day escaped his active pen. Destined only for the moment, scratched down on sudden impulses, most of the articles cannot be properly judged if torn from their connection. They are chiefly an expression of that constant watchfulness with which he threw a hint here and a hint there, thus giving what the infant democracy needed—direction and guidance. They helped to keep the people in a constant vibration, conscious of how much was yet to be done, how many demands had yet to be satisfied. The articles were in style epigrammatic, often careless; but they contained so much positive and practical information, they had so much power to agitate and to illumine subjects of general importance that at the time they were of great value. (pp. 49-50)

Nothing gives better evidence of [Wergeland's] enthusiastic interest in the [Jewish] cause than [**The Jew, Nine Blooming Branches from a Thornbush** and **The Jewess, Eleven Blooming Branches**]. They are political in a way, but the political element is united and fused with the most delicate, noble poetry. We cannot read **The Three** without being won by the grace with which tolerance is preached, and by the beauty and truthful coloring of the oriental life depicted, at once brilliant and naive. Who can help being inspired by the sad yet mild indignation of **The Wreck**? Or of **Moses on the Mountain**? And **Christmas Eve** surpasses them all in majesty and touching beauty. (p. 57)

When one comes to speak of Wergeland just as a poet, one is tempted to say first of all that the place to think of him and approach him is not in a room, within walls that shut off our view, but out in the open air under the tent above and the traveling clouds—those ''wonderlands of the sun''—whose praise he sang and to which his poetry may be likened: out among the woods and the meadows he loved and where he felt at home. For walls and doors do not suggest that spirit of freedom, that true human expansion, whose apostle he was. Beyond the expression of patriotic devotion—of which so much has here been said—and beyond the expression of general brotherhood and of human love, his poetry is above all a celebration of nature. The sun, the earth, the universe are to him constant sources of inspiration. His is a poetry whose richness of color and beauty of imagery can be equalled by few and surpassed by still fewer. To English-speaking people Shakespeare represents the acme of enthusiastic language, the highest reach of splendor in glowing expression. And the same symphonic beauty of style, the same profusion of imagery and color are characteristic of Henrik Wergeland;—with the difference that his power is lyric rather than dramatic, and he applies his art to describe the world, the cosmos, rather than man, the microcosmos. Compared with his robust, many-colored sensuousness, the seraphic brilliancy of Shelley often grows pale and the ecstatic contemplation of Wordsworth didactic. The romantic age fostered such poets, worshippers of Nature, in which their souls were at liberty to ramble, ejaculating dithyrambs at every shrine, intoxicated with the magnificence of the great Vesture of Spirit. Wergeland, too, lies at the feet of Nature, yet not in a speculative or femininely sensitive or mystical attitude. He worships with the feeling of pure, jubilant youth, with enthusiasm glowing warm, and with a note of virility that most romanticists lack.

It is a sad fact for Norwegians that Wergeland's true position among the great poets of the world is not and perhaps cannot be generally understood: that we have to sing his praise to people incredulous because they have no means of knowing the facts or are too foreign to our national spirit to appreciate the character of his production. To put his work into translation would be as difficult as to translate the word-music of Swinburne and the spiritual suggestiveness of Tennyson. (pp. 58-9)

The huge epic of his youth, **Creation, Man, and Messias,** has never been much read, yet its ideas underlie everything Wergeland wrote later. . . . The poem is full of exalted poetry and sentiment, and its ideas are those which for several generations had been leaving their impress upon European culture. In fact, it is the deism of the eighteenth century that finds expression in this account of universal history. The striving thought of that period in every direction is recognizable—Christianity seen as the gospel of the rights of man, philanthropy, liberalism tending toward republican government, hatred of oppressors and usurpers, socialistic utopias—all these are here expressed in positive poetical form. Yet the poet does not slip either into a pagan or a narrow Christian direction or into scepticism. Indeed, it is not too much to say that in this work is presented the best poetical summary in any literature of that eventful deistic movement in European thought. . . . Its basic idea was the constant inspiration of [Wergeland's] whole life and activity. This idea is that the germ of perfection is present in the human race from the beginning, and though it may seem hidden or dormant for long periods, it is certain to revive, grow, and become triumphantly victorious in the end. But that idea is the basis of many shorter poems also, poems less philosophical and ambitious and more truly successful. It is on these that his fame and influence rest.

His finest political poem is **The Spaniard,** in which the cowardly policy of Ferdinand VII in the July revolution is arraigned and the final victory of liberty warmly prophesied. There are magnificent lines in this poem and such description of the highlands of Norway as are found nowhere else in our literature.

A strange and characteristic work is **Jan van Huysum's Flowerpiece.** In this is the most complete expression of his mythmaking tendency, his poet's habit of seeing the bee and the rose not merely as an insect and a flower but as endowed with souls like his own soul and able to enter into joyous communion with him.

His greatest, most magnificent poem, and one of his latest, is **The English Pilot.** . . . [His] impressions of the North Sea, the channel, and the luxuriant English nature are lived over again with a freshness and intensity of imagination fairly overwhelming. Such lavish splendor of natural scenery as Wergeland here produces no Norse poet has ever produced—not even he himself. Everything glitters and sparkles. It is not nature, but nature raised to its highest potency by a rich, glorious, poetical imagination. Within this wonderful wealth of natural scenery the

story of the pilot is enclosed. We are shown the busy life of a powerful nation and historical memories attaching to that, civilization in its greatness and its corruption, the fresh life of the sailor at home and out in the world, the patriarchal happiness of homelife, nature in her grandeur and her innocence— all these elements are gathered and shaped in one supreme finished mould. Nowhere else did his poetical gifts find so broad a playground or reveal themselves thus in their fullness and variety.

The period from 1830 to 1845 is most significant in the history of [Norwegian] literature. . . . But the most prominent figure was and is Henrik Wergeland. He held this leading position not only because of his poetical genius but because in him was united all that moved the young Norway of the time. . . . (pp. 60-3)

> *Agnes Mathilde Wergeland, ''Henrik Wergeland,'' in her* Leaders in Norway and Other Essays, *edited by Katharine Merrill, George Banta Publishing Company, 1916 (and reprinted by Books for Libraries Press, 1966; distributed by Arno Press, Inc.), pp. 38-63.*

### EDMUND GOSSE   (essay date 1925)

The beauty of some of Wergeland's imagery and the melody of certain of his verses were little appreciated, and it was its violence, obscurity, and over-emphasis which made his writing popular. He was tempted to resign himself more and more to mere eccentricity. Some of his pieces of the 1828-1832 period exceed in grotesque tastelessness what can well be imagined. Fortunately, at that date, his career was checked by the arrival of an antagonist [Welhaven] who exposed with extreme severity what was absurd in Wergeland's conception of art. (p. 143)

The effect upon Wergeland was remarkable. Though his admirers foamed with rage, he himself refrained from counterattack, and laid the strictures of Welhaven to heart. . . . [He] published **Poesier,** a cycle of fourteen love-poems, in which his rapture took varied and beautiful forms of fancy, and where a technical advance over what he had hitherto published was marked. There was still too much oddity and emphasis, but these were expressed with an abundance of rich and vivid imagery. The extravagance of Wergeland's form was still further subdued in the long poems which he now began to issue with startling rapidity, **Jan van Huysum's Flower-Piece** . . . , **The Jew** . . . , **The Jewess** . . . , and **The English Pilot** . . . . (pp. 143-44)

On his death-bed he wrote **The Wallflower,** one of the simplest and most original lyrics in the language; he was always at his best in expressing his discriminating love of flowers.

After the death of Wergeland, his genius fell into desuetude, and the reproach of want of art was constantly repeated. The Danish critics of authority called him a *Udigter,* a poetaster. Of late years his fame has enjoyed revival and the importance of his writings has been even overrated in Norway, where the extreme politicians have taken him as a precursor, and have asserted his importance. Foreign opinion cannot acquiesce in a patriotic fallacy which greets Wergeland as a singer of equal magnitude with Goethe, Shelley, and Victor Hugo. He most nearly resembles the last-mentioned, but on an altogether lower level. Without perfection of form, no poetry reaches the highest grade, and Wergeland, with all his volubility and amplitude, and in spite of his frequent and even dazzling felicities, scarcely ever approaches perfection. He represents the burning desire of a new country to prove itself independent of the literature of an old country which has long practised and polished an identical language. (pp. 144-45)

Edmund Gosse, "The Poetry of Norway," in The Oxford Book of Scandinavian Verse: XVIIth Century—XXth Century, *edited by Edmund Gosse and W. A. Craigie, Oxford University Press, Oxford, 1925, pp. 141-98.\**

## FRANCIS BULL   (essay date 1929)

Though neither vague nor obscure, [Wergeland] is certainly involved and intricate—his images succeed each other in such number and with such rapidity, that the ordinary mortal is left breathless. This almost Shakespearian exuberance of imagery is especially characteristic of Wergeland's juvenile poetry. . . .

If one had to distinguish between earthly and heavenly poets, one would unhesitatingly place Henrik Wergeland among the latter; or, perhaps, to borrow a phrase of his own coining, among the "poetic poets". With flowers and butterflies, with a tree or a rabbit, he talks as if he were one of themselves, and he is in his element in the fairyland of the clouds or among the stars of the Milky Way. But men and women and everyday realities he cannot quite understand. For the miserable, destitute and outcast his heart yearns, and he is consumed with a passionate love of his people and mankind; but the human figures in his poetic works are apt to become types and mouthpieces for his ideas, rather than actual persons. (p. viii)

Wergeland once said that he could climb to Heaven on a gossamer, and his readers will admit the truth of his words. His poetry starts on earth, but it rises straight to the skies. Reality cannot hold him, he soon soars to the freer realm of ideas. He does not depend upon concrete instances to symbolize his thoughts; the idea emerges directly in the poem, though it is always richly clad in imagery, decked with "lyrical ivy". And his imagery is not sculptured in the calm beauty of classical form, but created by visual fancy charged with feeling. Every picture is painted with such warmth and intensity that it moves the heart as much as it pleases the inward eye. . . .

Wergeland was not without philosophical power and insight; but his poetry is distinguished, above all, by the spontaneous originality of his genius. He responds immediately to every impression; his poems are not the fruit of meditation, they are conceived and born in a moment, under stress and strain. His feelings are as violent as a child's, his thoughts and visions turn into myths, as they do in the minds of primitive people. Directness rather than polish being the chief quality of his verse, he appeals to our simple feelings, to the child in us. (p. ix)

Wergeland was something more than a local Norwegian singer . . . , in fact, his place is among the great poets who have created values for all peoples and all times. (p. xi)

Francis Bull, in a preface to Poems by Henrik Wergeland, *translated by G. M. Gathorne-Hardy, Jethro Bithell, and I. Grøndahl, Gyldendal Norsk Forlag, 1929 (and reprinted by Greenwood Press, Publishers, 1970), pp. vii-xi.*

## G. M. GATHORNE-HARDY   (essay date 1929)

[*Gathorne-Hardy praises Wergeland's early poetry as "not the best" but "most arresting" of his work. Contradicting Edmund Gosse (see excerpt above, 1872), Gathorne-Hardy states that Wergeland "never showed any sign of acquiescence in Welhav-en's critical standards," and he views the Welhaven-Wergeland feud in the context of the opposition between formalism and freedom in the nineteenth century. Since Wergeland saw himself as a prophet of liberty and spiritual unity with nature, Gathorne-Hardy finds him representative of his age, and comparable in some respects with Byron, William Blake, William Wordsworth, and Percy Bysshe Shelley.*]

[A] new and strikingly impressive literary personality is even more evident in the poetry of **"Digte, første Ring"** than in the more restrained and mature verse of Wergeland's later development. For all its wild eccentricity and crude lack of taste, it is marked by a richness of imagery and an originality of form which makes it, though not the best, perhaps the most arresting work of Wergeland's whole career. The form may easily be taken, at a first glance, for formlessness, so great is the departure from the conventional models of the time; yet the metrical discipline is seen on a closer examination to be generally strict and severe, based apparently upon the rules of Latin prosody, though never conforming exactly to any actual classical model. These dactylic metres, employed for the most part in unrhymed verse, give a passionate swing to these poems which succeeds in expressing, to a very remarkable degree, the fiery eagerness of the young poet's character. Blemishes and absurdities are indeed both frequent and conspicuous, but they are manifestly due either to a youthful innocence which is incapable of distinguishing good from bad, or to the defects of qualities inherently poetic,—a turbulent imagination which presents ideas in so swift and fluent a sequence as to give no time for discrimination, and a passionate love of freedom which sets even the most salutary conventions at defiance. . . . But in the midst of all this temperamental effervescence we can constantly discern the "disjecti membra poetae" [disjointed limbs of the poet], and sometimes, as in . . . ["**My little Rabbit**"], he rises, even at this early stage, to heights which he never surpassed.

In ["**My little Rabbit**"], his grasp of the idea of an evolutionary and continuous creation seems far in advance of his age, though something of the same conception may be traced in the Prophetic Books of William Blake. This theme, to which Wergeland frequently recurred, e.g. in the opening words of his cantata, **"Vord Lys!"** (**Let there be Light** . . .), is the connecting thread which runs through his great dramatic epic, **"Skabelsen, Mennesket og Messias"** (**Creation, Humanity and Messiah**). . . . In the conception of a gradual advance towards human perfection, which is embodied in this work, he owes perhaps some debt to the Norwegian philosopher, Niels Treschow, though we know that in his earlier poem, **"Napoleon,"** he had arrived independently at some of Treschow's conclusions, before he had ever studied his works. . . . [His] influence upon Wergeland was, in fact, rather confirmatory than educational; placing the seal of scientific philosophy upon ideas due in the first instance to poetic intuition. An influence more directly traceable in **"Skabelsen, Mennesket og Messias,"** and even in the revised version, **"Mennesket,"** which Wergeland brought out immediately before his death, is that of Byron. The spirit character, Phun-Abiriel, a compound of intellectual scepticism and energetic action, is a typically Byronic figure, though the sympathies of Wergeland are clearly opposed to the doubts expressed by this being. The style as well as the thought of the poem shows marked Byronic influences; this becomes very evident on comparing it with passages in [Byron's] "Cain" and "Heaven and Earth"—e.g. Scene III of the latter. In fact, Wergeland would hardly have denied these resemblances: originally he intended to borrow for his poem the title, "Heaven and Earth," and though he succeeded in ridding himself, at a comparatively early stage, from the incubus of doubt with which his study of the English poet had afflicted him, he still retained an admiration for Byron's genius sufficient to lead him, rather extravagantly, to couple his name with that of Plato in the verses **"Til en Gran"**. . . . Yet the Norwegian's imperfect knowledge of the English language protected him from any lasting temptation to imitate the style of Byron, once he had definitely shaken off the spell of his ideas.

The existence of other influences is more open to question. In spite of Wergeland's expressed admiration for Shakespeare, we must remember that it was Shakespeare at second hand, in a Danish translation, who could indeed divert his energy to unwise attempts at drama, but could hardly affect his literary style. For Henrik Steffens, the Germanicized Norwegian romantic who certainly inspired the Danish poet, Oehlenschläger, Wergeland no doubt felt an intellectual sympathy, as is shown in the dedication of **"Skabelsen, Mennesket og Messias."** Some of Steffens' work shows affinities with the pantheistic views expressed by Wergeland, but, as will be made clear later, Wergeland definitely rejected the backward-looking romanticism for which Steffens stood, after one very early and never repeated experiment.

It was in fact Wergeland's marked originality which exposed him at this stage, with **"Digte første Ring"** and **"Skabelsen"** to his credit, to the hostile criticism of a rival, and more conventional, school of thought. (pp. xxv-xxix)

The nature of [the critical controversy between Wergeland and Welhaven (see excerpt above, 1830)] is often completely misunderstood, and it is, indeed, doubtful whether the real issue was even grasped by the protagonists. It is usual to state that Wergeland represented the crude nationalistic standpoint; Welhaven the more cultured cosmopolitan. It would be almost more correct to assert the exact opposite. It is true that Wergeland regarded himself, and was regarded, as above all else a national poet and prophet, and that he rejected the canons of criticism which his antagonist imported from Denmark. But in relying upon Denmark, through which literary fashions penetrated but slowly, Welhaven only succeeded in keeping steadily behind the times. Wergeland's nationalism, on the other hand, was tempered by an interest in contemporary movements, literary and political, which was really cosmopolitan, and he consequently takes his place naturally in the great poetic revolution or renaissance of his age. The issue between the poet and his critic was therefore, in reality, merely a phase of the dispute which we can trace about this time all over Europe and the British Isles, between the advocates of a cramping formalism and the apostles of a new freedom—between the ideas of versification as craftsmanship and poetry as the vehicle of a quasi-religious message and as a political force.

For the revolution which affected poetry towards the end of the eighteenth and the beginning of the nineteenth century had as its key-note liberty. . . . The new liberty which was being claimed for the poet gave, as Wergeland saw, plenty of scope for an inspiration derived from more practical matters. In its aspiration towards freedom from the tyranny of rules which fettered the verse of the preceding age, it found and felt a common ground with the political and religious movements of the same period. Reaction against a cramping authoritarianism was, in fact, in the air, and all aspects of life were affected by it. Until the advent of Wergeland, poetry—so called—had been in Norway a genteel accomplishment for comfortably placed officials to practise in their spare time. In his hands, and in those of men similarly inspired all over Europe, it became the articulate expression of the whole spirit of the age,

a force potent for the direction of national destinies and the aspirations of mankind. (pp. xxx-xxxiii)

I find myself quite unable to agree with the late Sir Edmund Gosse, who . . . states that Wergeland "laid the strictures of Welhaven to heart" [see excerpt above, 1925]. Certainly it is not true that, as the same author asserts, "he himself refrained from counter-attack." On the contrary, the two poets were engaged for some time in a constant exchange of satirical rhymes. . . . It was quite natural that, as he grew older, Wergeland should have purged his style of some of its youthful crudities. But he never showed any sign of acquiescence in Welhaven's critical standards, and . . . the strife was still raging in 1838, the year in which Sir Edmund detects a marked improvement. The fact is ignored that the poems published in 1833, **"Caesaris,"** **"Spaniolen,"** and most of the verses of **"Digte, Anden Ring,"** have precisely the same characteristics as those which Welhaven made the object of his attack. Wergeland himself gives the year 1834 as the date when he first was able to distinguish good from bad, but there is no indication anywhere that this development was in any way due to the criticisms of his rival. (p. xxxiv)

In order to appreciate [Wergeland], we must understand and sympathise with his conception of the poet's call,—a dedication of his special talent to the service of his nation and of mankind. . . . His aim was not so much decorative as prophetic. To the pure artist it matters supremely if, by the inclusion of some irrelevant detail he disturbs the balance of his work; to the orator or the prophet it is of little consequence if some passage of his utterance falls below the highest level, provided he can awaken eyes to see and ears to hear. And in a country as poverty-stricken and unenlightened as he felt the contemporary Norway to be, there was so much to be said and done, and so little time for the gigantic task before him. We need not wonder, then, at the superficial faults which provide the critic with a facile excuse for a depreciatory verdict,—the chaotic flood of imagery and the desperate and frequently disastrous efforts of the poet to cram a dozen different pictures into the frame of a single sentence. Of such defects Wergeland himself was perfectly conscious. With a smile he confesses that

> By parentheses unnumbered
> The reader is encumbered;
> But also for the author they are horns
> Entangling him like Abram's ram in thorns,
> Ever more hopelessly, in sorry trim,
> Where he won't get his thought,
>     but the critic will get him.

(pp. xlii-xlv)

Wergeland is too much himself to be an easy subject for comparisons. . . . No one who opened **"Digte, første Ring"** could have felt for an instant that he was reading the work of [any other Norwegian writer]. . . . The outstanding feature was a complete and unmistakeable break with all national tradition.

Owing perhaps to his rejection of the mediaevalism which so strongly influenced Teutonic literature, he seems more akin to some of our British poets than to those of his own country or lands adjacent to it. The temporary influence of Byron has been touched on already: in his youth, indeed, Wergeland was often spoken of as a Norwegian Byron, but the resemblance . . . was never very close, and in later years was imperceptible. As a democrat and a poet of the people, he clearly felt a kinship with Burns, many of whose songs he translated; but, except in so far as he followed the Scottish poet in basing many of his verses on popular folk-tunes, his sympathy with the man did not result in any marked community of style or thought. Probably his imperfect grasp of the language hindered any closer affinity; there are at least three definite mistranslations in his version of "Mary Morison," and we can see from **"the English Pilot"** that he never really mastered English—to say nothing of Scotch!

The resemblances which strike one most are often to poets whose work, in all probability, he had never read. Not infrequently we are vividly reminded of Blake, but Wergeland, in spite of Welhaven's assertion, was eminently sane and even practical in his writings; in spite of some suggestions of mystic experience, as in **"Svalen,"** there was little of the mystic temperament about him, and for all his love of imagery he eschewed symbolism. In Wordsworth we find the essence of Wergeland's nature-gospel expressed in such [poems as] . . . "Tintern Abbey." . . . (pp. xlv-xlvii)

But while [Wordsworth's] deeper nature-philosophy is evidently shared by Wergeland, his habitual reaction to the beauties of the world about him is something far more direct and simple. He retains to the last that unquestioning joy in the mere outward appearance of such things which in Wordsworth faded with the passing years. The delight which impelled him to song in

> The scarlet on an insect's wing

had in it all the unreasoning pleasure of a child. . . . It is even extremely doubtful whether Wordsworth's poetry would have appealed to Wergeland: certainly he would have repudiated the English poet's dictum—which is exactly in the spirit of Welhaven—that "poetry takes its origin from emotion recollected in tranquillity;" his fiery and uncontrollable Muse responded rather to the stimulus of a present emotion at boiling point. Tranquillity is the last quality which anyone would dream of attributing to Wergeland. Even where he expresses himself as having found peace, as in **"I det Grønne"** and **"Paa Sygeleiet,"** the reader cannot fail to notice how full his mind is of the disturbing emotions which he affects to have overcome. Like his spiritual successor, Bjørnson, he was a born fighter, full of the joy of battle; as he somewhere remarks, "A fighting existence is delightful when one has a beak!" (pp. xlvii-xlviii)

In Shelley, as in Wordsworth, we find the Wergelandian idea of the spiritual unity in Nature. . . . The political views of Shelley are also remarkably akin to those of the Norwegian poet: both men shared a burning hatred of tyranny, and sympathised with all their souls in the contemporary aspiration towards liberty of every kind. But here again, there is no reason for suspecting any direct influence: such thoughts were in the air. The differences between the work of Shelley and Wergeland are no less striking than the resemblances. In spite of the troubles which beset his life, there was a robust light-heartedness, a humorous pluck, and an unconquerable hopefulness about Wergeland. . . . [He] declares that the heart is strengthened by suffering, as the arm is by fighting, and as the voice is raised in the storm. But really, one feels on reflection, between the cultured and ethereal flow of Shelley and the peaks and abysses of Wergeland's unregulated inspiration there can be few points of contact to invite comparison. (pp. xlviii-xlix)

After all, we must conclude, Wergeland was first and foremost an original character: the merits and defects of his art both arise from its spontaneity. There was no perceptible line between the poet and the man. . . . [His] poetry is a natural expression of his mind. It is characteristic of him that he so often interposes prose passages in his poems, or begins, as in

**"Kaadt Ukrudt,"** in a conversational style that may be verse, but can hardly be called poetry. He is just talking—and then he gets excited, and sings. As the emotion rises, inspiration descends on him in a flood, till he can hardly get out what he wants to say. (p. l)

It may not always be first-rate poetry, but it is perfect self-expression. It is like the torrent in spate, necessarily turbid, and carrying along with it a lot of miscellaneous rubbish, but after all the mountain burn has beauties which we miss in the pellucid waters of a sluice-controlled chalk-stream. Of course, too, there were other and milder moods which found their natural expression in his poetry and on such occasions he is perhaps at his best. But he is always himself, meaning intensely every word he says. Much poetry that we read gives us the impression of a work of art as detached from its creator as a painting or a sculpture; Wergeland always conveys the illusion of the spoken voice,—he seems to be talking to us. That is perhaps the great secret of his continued influence;—"He being dead yet speaketh." (p. li)

> *G. M. Gathorne-Hardy, in an introduction to* Poems
> *by Henrik Wergeland, translated by G. M. Gathorne-*
> *Hardy, Jethro Bithell, and I. Grøndahl, Gyldendal*
> *Norsk Forlag, 1929 (and reprinted by Greenwood*
> *Press, Publishers, 1970), pp. xiii-liii.*

### SIGMUND SKARD (essay date 1944)

[*The first critic to argue that Wergeland's early poetry was his greatest accomplishment, Skard praises Wergeland's "unbridled imagination of genius" and his "primitive spontaneity." Skard believes that in Wergeland's later, more mature, and technically more proficient poems, "something of the seraphic splendor is lost," though his work does gain a "new stamp of reality."*]

[The] most amazing thing about [**Creation, Man, and Messiah**] is not its lack of clarity and moderation, but the grandeur of the ideas and the power with which the youthful author has made the subject serve them. . . . Through the centuries of prehistory and history Wergeland follows the slow development of individuals and nations toward real liberty, their fight against kings and clergy and their struggle to understand themselves and realize their common ideals of freedom, truth, and love as symbolized in the Saviour. In this immense historical pageant, filled out by his contemporary poems, he musters his allies in past and present, from the prophets, Socrates, Plato, and Christ to Washington, Kosciusko, Lafayette, and Bolivar; from North America, "where the seed of my own liberty grew in the shelter of the sycamore," to France, "the land of life," and the white cliffs of Great Britain, "freedom's stronghold mid the ocean." But all of it converges into a program for his own work. Poets are no articles of luxury, but servants of their nation. . . . (pp. 198-99)

The final aim of [Wergeland's] work was a general liberation of the mind. (p. 205)

His practical activity outlines his human maturation. His poetry reveals the sources and the deep unity behind it.

He had violent forces to cope with; his first poems show the battle. Hardly in any literature is there a poetry of comparable volume and quality in which the unbridled imagination of genius breaks forth with such an overwhelming, almost terrifying might. His myth-making fancy moves in leaps of association through all times and worlds with sovereign arbitrariness. The violent rhythms burst with ideas and images; everything is high-strung, swelling, and luxuriant, like "the thought of demented angels.'' He himself felt as if he were in the hands of the powers when his visions came, whirled away ''like a mote among motes.'' Nothing could be farther from the main line of Norse literary tradition, not making exception for the most bizarre skaldic verse.

But this difficult poetry has a unique charm: seldom in literature has the primitive spontaneity of genius been so nakedly revealed. Sometimes the reader has the feeling of being present at some majestic event in nature. And in every feature there is what Wergeland himself called ''the wildborn dignity'' of his mind—a mixture of spirituality and concretion, of earthbound sensuality and dizzy seraphic flight which soon left his stimulator, Shakespeare, behind and is wholly his own. The wide plains of romantic feeling are opened to Norwegian poetry in his verse, never to be closed again.

Through the struggling confusion, moreover, there is from the very beginning a fight for clarity, in idea and form; the teaching of Holberg had not been lost on his pupil. Wergeland's thoughts are not soddy and muddled, there are just too many of them as yet. Here is no trace of that weakish vagueness which he ridiculed in many romanticists; everything is power and energy. Through the drifting clouds of formlessness there are sudden flashes of blinding lucidity, which are not unknown in Norse tradition, and a patient toil for mastery of the unruly verse. And the struggle for form is the expression of a moral fight: Wergeland's painful liberation from that bitter and misanthropic Byronism which for years darkened his youth. These poems show how hard he had to work for his own personal liberty, and how dearly he paid for the optimism which was to carry his humanitarian work.

In the creation of his maturity these forces of counterpoise gradually won the upper hand. It cost him long and patient self-education, which for years made his poetic writing shrink to a trickle; but he emerged as a different man. He always remained a ''romantic'' poet; his basic experience was always that of universal sympathy, conceived in a realm of his own where colors and proportions were not of this world and mute things spoke in celestial voices. But more and more the spontaneous act of conception involved the form and the law. Something of the tropical exuberance was lost; but other things came instead. It is the testimony of an almost incredible perfectibility that the lucid and simple nursery rhymes of the 1840's were written by the man who one decade before had indulged in the *Creation*.

Still deeper goes the ripening of his feeling; the universal sympathy comes down from the universe and goes into the huts of men. Again something of the seraphic splendor is lost. There is a new depth instead, and a new stamp of reality. Some of these efforts are pathetic. He struggled to become a folk poet, and the obstacles often were insurmountable; too long had he lived among the stars. But nobody would wish away from his works all these songs for the common man, ditties for miners and chanteys for sailors, ''ballads,'' and versified commandments. Again they testify to the unity of his endeavor: no simple task was too simple, if only it had to do with the fundamental things. In recompense, things came closer to him; the feeling of fellowship broke the barriers. In the social poems of his later years the romanticist is already close to realism, not that of the eyes, but of the heart. In his series of commemorative poems, ranging from the leaders of the country and the world

to the ruined genius found dead at the roadside, the individualization is not too sharp; but the hidden kernel of nobility and grandeur is brought out with the force of the sculptor.

His most intimate expression remained the soliloquy with nature: a tree, a flower, a child. The filmlike motley of his youth has disappeared. The absorption is complete: he is engulfed in a depth of goodness revealed to him alone. But this isolating concentration is just momentary; around him are the whispering voices of life's active, daily community, without which he could not exist. Often he connects the two worlds himself, or they insensibly mingle: he is talking about the same things. The rain quenches the thirst of the tree, the dew from the leaves bathes the drying shrub, and the hind with her fawn kneels in the grass, licking the full drops in a hazy understanding of this miracle of love. Should man have less of love toward his fellow-beings? (pp. 207-10)

The keystone of . . . [his last] year was his remodeling of the **Creation**, ''to show them my real intentions.'' There was much to correct in the form, nothing in the basic ideas; he had always believed in them. But in a new concluding canto he returned to the great views of his youth, telling the world about the future he dreamed for it. Looking into coming millenniums, his visionary eye saw a community of happy republics, only divided by hedges of roses, where war was abolished and prisons turned into granaries, where religion was a common good and race differences forgotten, where the workers lived as happily in their cleanly quarters as wealth in its palaces, and men, women, and children equally shared the rights of life, guided by the goodness of the human heart. (p. 212)

*Sigmund Skard, ''The Genius of the Heart: Henrik Wergeland,'' in* The Voice of Norway *by Halvdan Koht and Sigmund Skard (copyright 1944, copyright renewed © 1972, Columbia University Press, New York; reprinted by permission of the publisher), Columbia University Press, 1944, pp. 193-214.*

---

## ADDITIONAL BIBLIOGRAPHY

Blegen, Theodore C., and Ruud, Martin B. ''Songs from Henrik Wergeland's Last Play.'' In *Norwegian Emigrant Songs and Ballads,* edited and translated by Theodore C. Blegen and Martin B. Ruud, pp. 75-98. Minneapolis: The University of Minnesota Press, 1936.

A discussion of Wergeland's attitude toward Norwegian emigration. The chapter includes lyrics and, in four cases, musical annotations for seven songs from *The Mountain Hut,* Wergeland's last play, which treats the subject of emigration.

Falnes, Oscar J. *National Romanticism in Norway.* Studies in History, Economics and Public Law, edited by the Faculty of Political Science of Columbia University, no. 386. New York: Columbia University Press, 1933, 398 p.*

Examines Wergeland's role in the Norwegian nationalism movement. Falnes concludes that Wergeland acted as ''a storm center in public life'' because his poetry drew its popular appeal from his hatred of the Danish hegemony in Norway.

Jorgenson, Theodore. ''Wergeland and Welhaven.'' In his *History of Norwegian Literature,* pp. 181-202. New York: The Macmillan Co., 1933.

Documents the controversy between Wergeland and Welhaven as representative of the struggle between a neo-classical and a romantic aesthetic in Norway.

# John Wilson

## 1785-1854

(Also wrote under the pseudonym of Christopher North) Scottish critic, essayist, short story writer, novelist, and poet.

For his contributions to *Blackwood's Edinburgh Magazine*, Wilson is often ranked with the great essayists of the nineteenth century. Though not the journal's editor, he was its primary contributor, under the pseudonym Christopher North, for over a quarter of a century. His vigor, eloquence, rollicking humor, and devil-may-care attitude captured the attention of the public and gave the Tory "Maga" a competitive edge over the popular Whig journal, *The Edinburgh Review*. Wilson changed the tone of periodical literature in Scotland with his *Noctes Ambrosianae*, a series of witty dialogues originally published in *Blackwood's*, in which contemporary issues and personalities are treated with levity, gravity, and pungent satire. For his rendering of Scottish dialect in the *Noctes* he has been compared with Sir Walter Scott and Robert Burns.

The son of a wealthy gauze manufacturer, Wilson was born in Paisley, Scotland and was educated at a small parish school in the Highlands. The influence of his early religious education is obvious in Wilson's poems and stories, most of which extol the healing powers of quiet resignation and piety in the face of hardship. Wilson reveled in the beautiful mountains and hills of the Highlands and spent his free time swimming, sailing, and hiking in the countryside. He later studied at the Universities of Glasgow and Oxford, where he became increasingly interested in athletics. A wrestler, boxer, fisherman, runner, and mountain climber, Wilson excelled in many sports. Despite his desultory study habits, he graduated from Oxford with high honors and was awarded the Newdigate Prize for poetry in 1806. Wilson's love of nature and his fondness for sport inspired many of his *Blackwood's* essays, particularly those collected in *The Recreations of Christopher North*.

After graduating from college in 1807, Wilson purchased Elleray, an estate on Lake Windermere in the English Lake District, where he met Thomas De Quincey, Samuel Taylor Coleridge, Robert Southey, and William Wordsworth. Wilson had long admired Wordsworth, and his first volume of poetry, *The Isle of Palms, and Other Poems*, with its simple diction and emphasis on nature, immediately identified him as a disciple of the Lake School. *The City of the Plague, and Other Poems*, though more popular with the public, was, like the earlier volume, criticized for its repetition, diffuseness, ornamentation, and sentimentality. Some critics did note, however, that the indulgent and generous spirit of Wilson's poetry represented a healthy departure from the Lakist presumption of exclusive taste and judgment. Most later critics believe that Wilson's verse, because of its insipid sentimentality, deserves to be ignored.

In 1815, Wilson's uncle embezzled most of the fortune left him by his father. Shortly after, Wilson moved with his wife and family to Edinburgh, where he was admitted to the bar, but never practiced law. In October, 1817, Wilson contributed his first notable article to *Blackwood's*, the notorious "Translation from an Ancient Chaldee Manuscript." Written by Wilson, James Hogg, and John Gibson Lockhart, the composition is

a parody of prominent Whig figures written in scriptural language, and it created such a stir that it had to be suppressed. Nevertheless, it succeeded in bringing notoriety to the new magazine. In the ensuing years, Wilson composed hundreds of articles for *Blackwood's*, most of which have been included in the various editions of his collected works.

With the support of Sir Walter Scott and other influential Tories, Wilson in 1820 was elected Professor of Moral Philosophy at the University of Edinburgh, a post he held for thirty years. Although he was not qualified for the position, his oratorical power and his voluminous literary output earned him the respect of his students and colleagues. During the 1820s, in addition to his work for *Blackwood's*, Wilson published a collection of short stories, *Lights and Shadows of Scottish Life: A Selection from the Papers of the Late Arthur Austin*, and two novels, *The Trials of Margaret Lyndsay* and *The Foresters*. Written in a prose style that many consider to be overly embellished, these works are generally regarded as uncontrolled, sentimentalized visions of pastoral life which bear little resemblance to reality.

Critics generally agree that the *Noctes Ambrosianae* are the best expression of Wilson's talent. These imaginary conversations, which appeared in *Blackwood's* from 1822 to 1835, feature the characters Christopher North, the Ettrick Shepherd, and Timothy Tickler, who were based on, respectively, Wilson, Hogg, and Wilson's uncle, Robert Sym. Originally the joint productions of Wilson, Lockhart, William Maginn, Hogg, and others, by 1825 they were written primarily by Wilson. Commentators consistently praise the *Noctes* for their originality, variety, humor, and exuberance. Many critics attribute the power of the *Noctes* to the intermingling of contradictory elements. Philosophical discussion, literary criticism, and political commentary are laced with poetry, satire, and bacchanalian humor in what Robert Chambers describes as a "lavish effusion of brilliant verbiage." While twentieth-century critics note that the freshness of the *Noctes* has diminished because of their topical interest, most agree that the character of the Ettrick Shepherd in particular remains a superb creation.

Wilson is not recognized as a great critic. His criticism, which was frequently written in haste, is often deficient in sagacity, analysis, and finish. He could be severe and stinging, and he reserved his harshest words for gifted young writers whom he sincerely wanted to help by objectively analyzing their work. His other critical opinions are largely regarded as the projections of his varying moods; his conflicting assessments of Wordsworth's poetry, for instance, are often cited as evidence of his subjectivity. Indiscriminate benevolence, on the other hand, led him to equate such authors as Joanna Baillie and William Shakespeare.

Critics are virtually unanimous in the belief that Wilson's reputation rests upon his contributions to *Blackwood's*, especially the *Noctes Ambrosianae* and his out-of-door papers describing sport and scenery. As Christopher North, Wilson escaped the moralizing sentimentality of his poetry and fiction, and became, in the words of Maginn, the "Duke of Humbug, of Quiz, Puffery, Cutup, and Slashandhackaway; . . . Baron of Balaam and Blarney; and Knight of the most stinging Order of the Nettle."

## PRINCIPAL WORKS

*The Isle of Palms, and Other Poems*  (poetry)  1812
*The City of the Plague, and Other Poems*  (poetry)  1816
*Lights and Shadows of Scottish Life: A Selection from the
    Papers of the Late Arthur Austin*  (short stories)  1822
*The Trials of Margaret Lyndsay*  (novel)  1823
*The Foresters*  (novel)  1825
*Critical and Miscellaneous Essays.* 3 vols.  (essays)  1842
*The Recreations of Christopher North.* 3 vols.  (essays)
    1842
*The Noctes Ambrosianae of "Blackwood."* 4 vols.  (essays)
    1843
*Noctes Ambrosianae.* 5 vols. [with William Maginn, John
    Gibson Lockhart, James Hogg, et al.]  (essays)  1854
*The Works of Professor Wilson of the University of
    Edinburgh.* 12 vols.  (essays, short stories, and poetry)
    1855-58

---

## [FRANCIS JEFFREY]  (essay date 1812)

[*Editor of the* Edinburgh Review *from 1803 to 1829, Jeffrey is notorious for his unsparing criticism of the Lake Poets. While noting that Wilson's poetry displayed many of the characteristics of the Lake School, such as simple, childish diction and a "predilection . . . for engrafting powerful emotions on ordinary occurrences," Jeffrey commends Wilson for his "warm unaffected philanthropy" and hails him as a new and superior member of the Lake School.*]

[Mr Wilson] is a new recruit to the company of lake poets;—and one who, from his present bearing [in *The Isle of Palms, and Other Poems*] promises, we think, not only to do them good service, and to rise to high honours in the corps; but to raise its name, and advance its interests even among the tribes of the unbelievers. Though he wears openly the badge of their peculiarities, and professes the most humble devotion to their great captain, Mr Wordsworth, we think he has kept clear of several of the faults that may be imputed to his preceptors; and assumed, upon the whole, a more attractive and conciliating air, than the leaders he has chosen to follow. He has the same predilection, indeed, for engrafting powerful emotions on ordinary occurrences; and the same tendency to push his emotions a great deal too far—the same disdain of all worldly enjoyments and pursuits—and the same occasional mistakes, as to energy and simplicity of diction, which characterize the works of his predecessors. But he differs from them in this very important particular, that though he does generally endeavour to raise a train of lofty and pathetic sensations upon very trifling incidents and familiar objects, and frequently pursues them to a great height of extravagance and exaggeration, he is scarcely ever guilty of the offence of building them upon a foundation that is ludicrous or purely fantastic. He makes more, to be sure, of a sleeping child, or a lonely cataract—and flies into greater raptures about female purity and moonlight landscapes, and fine dreams, and flowers, and singing-birds—than most other poets permit themselves to do,—though it is of the very essence of poetry to be enraptured with such things:—But he does not break out into any ecstacies about spades or sparrows' eggs—or men gathering leeches—or women in duffle cloaks—or plates and porringers—or washing tubs—or any of those baser themes which poetry was always permitted to disdain, without any impeachment of her affability, till Mr Wordsworth thought fit to force her into an acquaintance with them.

Though Mr Wilson may be extravagant, therefore, he is not perverse; and though the more sober part of his readers may not be able to follow him to the summit of his sublimer sympathies, they cannot be offended at the invitation, or even refuse to grant him their company to a certain distance on the journey. The objects for which he seeks to interest them, are all objects of natural interest; and the emotions which he connects with them, are, in some degree, associated with them in all reflecting minds. (pp. 373-74)

Mr Wilson is not free from some of the faults of diction, which we think belong to his school. He is occasionally mystical, and not seldom childish: But he has less of these peculiarities than most of his associates: and there is one more important fault from which, we think, he has escaped altogether. We allude now to the offensive assumption of exclusive taste, judgment and morality which pervades most of the writings of this tuneful brotherhood. There is a tone of tragic, keen and intolerant reprobation in all the censures they bestow, that is not a little alarming to ordinary sinners. . . . Mr Wilson, however, does not seem to believe in the necessity of this extraordinary monopoly; but speaks with a tone of indulgent and open sociality, which is as engaging as the jealous and assuming manner of some of his models is offensive. The most striking characteristics, indeed, as well as the great charm, of the volume before us, is the spirit of warm and unaffected philanthropy which breathes over every page of it—that delighted tenderness with which the writer dwells on the bliss of childhood, and the dignity of female innocence—and that young enthusiasm which leads him to luxuriate in the description of beautiful nature and joys of a life of retirement. (pp. 375-76)

The most considerable of these [poems] is **'The Isle of Palms,'** which, though it engrosses the whole title-page, fills considerably less than half the volume,—and perhaps not the most attractive half. . . . [Never], certainly, was there a poem, pretending to have a story, in which there was so little narrative; and in which the descriptions and reflections bore such a monstrous proportion to the facts and incidents out of which they arise. This piece is in irregular rhymed verse, like the best parts of Mr Southey's 'Kehama'; to which, indeed, it bears a pretty close resemblance, both in the luxuriance of the descriptions, the tenderness of the thoughts, the copiousness of the diction, and the occasional harmony of the versification,—though it is perhaps still more diffuse and redundant. (p. 376)

To those who delight in wit, sarcasm, and antithesis, the greater part of [**'The Isle of Palms'**] will appear mere raving and absurdity;—to such as have an appetite chiefly for crowded incidents and complicated adventures, it will seem diffuse and empty;—and even by those who seek in poetry for the delineation of human feelings and affections, it will frequently be felt as too ornate and ostentatious. The truth is, that it has by far too much of the dreaminess and intoxication of the fancy about it, and is by far too much expanded; and though it will afford great delight to those who are most capable and most worthy of being delighted, there are none whom it will not sometimes dazzle with its glare, and sometimes weary with its repetitions.

The next poem in the volume [**'The Angler's Tent'**] is perhaps of a still more hazardous description. . . . It is one of the boldest experiments we have lately met with, of the possibility of maintaining the interest of a long poem without any extraordinary incident, or any systematic discussion; and, for our own parts, we are inclined to think that it is a successful one. There are few things, at least, which we have lately read, that have pleased or engaged us more than the picture of simple innocence and artless delight which is here drawn, with a truth and modesty of colouring far more attractive, in our apprehension, than the visionary splendours of **'The Isle of Palms.'** (pp. 383-84)

[Though *The Isle of Palms, and Other Poems*] has many faults, it has a redeeming spirit, both of fancy and of kindness, about it, which will not let them be numbered. It has, moreover, the charm of appearing to be written less from ambition of praise, than from the direct and genuine impulse of the feelings which it expresses; and though we cannot undertake to defend it from the scorn of the learned, or the ridicule of the witty, we are very much mistaken if it does not afford a great deal of pleasure to many persons almost as well worth pleasing. (p. 388)

> [*Francis Jeffrey*], *in a review of "The Isle of Palms, and Other Poems," in* The Edinburgh Review, *Vol. XIX, No. XXXVIII, February, 1812, pp. 373-88.*

### THE MONTHLY REVIEW   (essay date 1812)

As far as we can discover Mr. Wilson's meaning amid the labyrinth of his digressions [in the **'Isle of Palms'**], his Heroine seems to be a lady voyaging on a connubial speculation on board the Honorable East India Company's ship *Hope*, and his

Hero to be a guinea-pig in the same vessel. Such a hero and such a heroine would, in the better days of poetry, have been regarded as unworthy of a line. . . . [We] shall not be surprised if Mr. Wilson's next poem, instead of celebrating a speculating Miss and a guinea-pig, should carry some mysterious Chelsea-pensioner down the Thames in a coal-barge, to cultivate a love-adventure in the Isle of Dogs.

The story, in which the lady and gentleman before us play their parts, is slender to an excess. (pp. 34-5)

[The reader] will never be able to conceive how so long a poem as the present could be manufactured from such scanty materials:—but Mr. Wilson has a talent in this way. Nothing with him moves straight forwards, but all is circuitous. If he wished to inform us that his heroine tumbled down stairs, he would begin by describing how she went up them, and inquiring whether she fell out of the window. (p. 35)

This prolixity of detail is not the only fault which we must lay to Mr. Wilson's charge: he seems, in the progress of his tale, to scatter about little miscellaneous defects, collected for the purpose, from every author that has fallen within his reach. In imitation of Mr. Scott, the poem is chiefly written in lines of eight syllables, the measure exactly most unfit for a composition of any length; and, after the example of Mr. Southey, this measure is rendered still worse by occasionally introducing long lines and short lines of every species and denomination. (pp. 35-6)

These faults are the less excusable in the present author, because they will drag with them into oblivion beauties which ought to be remembered:—for in spite of his affectation, his prolixity, and his metre, we can always perceive a delicacy of feeling, an enthusiastic fondness for the beauties of nature, and poetical abilities worthy of more noble and more prosperous endeavours. Better models, and more caution in composing, might perhaps raise Mr. Wilson's name to a rank little inferior to that of the most popular poets of the day; while, writing as he has written in the **'Isle of Palms,'** his errors are so flagrant, and his beauties are so outshone by their surrounding tinsel, that we cannot flatter him with the slightest prospect of success. Yet we think that the author . . . will be acknowledged as a poet of no common ability. (p. 36)

As to the smaller pieces in [*The Isle of Palms, and Other Poems*], we may observe that they generally partake of the same character with the larger Poem. The best are, perhaps, **'Lines to Melrose Abbey'** and **'the Picture of a Blind Man.'** . . . We [advise Mr. Wilson] to burn all his present models,—to apply himself to Dryden, Pope, and Johnson, and to change his jig-measure-metre for our natural couplet or for the Spenser stanza; we may then fairly argue, that, provided he thinks before he writes, and corrects carefully afterward,—he may produce a poem which men of sound judgment will receive with pleasure, and which may be remembered with honor to him when he is no more. (p. 38)

> *A review of "The Isle of Palms, and Other Poems," in* The Monthly Review, *London, Vol. LXVIII, May, 1812, pp. 34-8.*

### THE ECLECTIC REVIEW   (essay date 1813)

We had hoped, from the fate of Mr. Wordsworth's last volumes, that the breathings and sensibilities of a certain school of poets were at an end. . . . We had not read three pages of

['The Isle of Palms, and Other Poems'], before we found ourselves undeceived.

Before we state what Mr. Wilson has done, we cannot but
indulge ourselves a moment in the thought of what he might
have done. With a warm heart, with the most amiable benevolence, with a devout love of nature, with an exquisite feeling
of moral beauty, with a great command of diction;—with all
this, had but his sensibilities been judiciously restrained, and
his taste properly formed, he might certainly have become a
lasting favourite with the public. As it is, we fear—but we
will not anticipate the judgement of our readers.

We shall speak, in order, of his sensibility and his taste. The
former is chiefly awakened by natural beauties. . . . (p. 22)

It seems . . . that it would be the wisdom of the poet, either
to give his landscape, and let his readers people it with what
fancies they may severally choose,—or to hint at the general
effect produced upon the mind, and leave every one to please
himself in the tracing out of that effect. . . .

How does Mr. Wilson manage the matter? Why, after a long
account of the moonlight sea, he gives us his own sensibilities
on the occasion with a scrupulous minuteness. (p. 23)

[We] cannot but look upon [Mr. Wilson's taste] as a very
vitiated one. There is a certain flimsy tawdriness that runs
through the whole. The 'Isle of Palms' is a like a French
palace—all gilding and cornice, and looking-glass. The reader
cannot view this volume without impinging upon sun-light,
and star-light, and the 'deep place of moon-beams,' and 'winged
glory,' and 'gladsome glide,' and 'halcyon glow,' and 'blos-
somy gems,' and 'clustring bloom,' and 'bird like fluttering,'
and 'fairy forms.' Mr. W., disgusted with the drawing-room-
dress in which the muses have sometimes appeared, their hoops
and furbelows, and embroidered satins, has carried them off
to the solitudes of the lakes, but he has drest them in such a
profusion of wild-wood flowers, and peacock's plumes, as is
almost equally displeasing. (p. 27)

[The] extreme diffusion of Mr. W.'s style has scattered [the
'Isle of Palms'] over four cantos. And four cantos of verse so
finical and tawdry require no ordinary degree of patience.

Then Mr. W. is not content with the old narrative style: he
hears and sees every thing; and by his 'lists' and 'los' would
have his readers do so too. The poem moreover is conducted
in the style of question and answer. 'Is she a vision wild and
bright?' 'Is no one on the silent deck?' &c. These are artifices
which should never frequently occur, and which indeed have
been long ago so hackneyed that we do not care how little we
see of them for the future.

Yet the poem bears indisputable marks of genius; the very
faults are not the faults of dullness; and we could certainly
exhibit some passages from it which are strikingly beautiful. . . .

Undoubtedly there is to be found in [the smaller poems in 'The
Isle of Palms'] much of the same sickliness of sentiment, and
glare of ornament which we have already noticed, and delivered
in the same diffusive and wandering carelessness of style. (p.
28)

[The] most pleasing pieces in the volume are those in blank
verse. Here the reader will meet with fancy and feeling most
happily combined, and with tenderness and benevolence with
which he cannot fail to be delighted, the whole delivered in
verse of a most soothing and delicate harmony. (p. 30)

*A review of "The Isle of Palms, and Other Poems,"
in* The Eclectic Review, *Vol. IX, January, 1813, pp.
22-34.*

[FRANCIS JEFFREY]   (essay date 1816)

[There] is something extremely amiable . . . in the character
of Mr. Wilson's genius:—a constant glow of kind and of pure
affection—a great sensibility to the charms of external nature,
and the delights of a private, innocent, and contemplative life—
a fancy richly stored with images of natural beauty and simple
enjoyments—great tenderness and pathos in the representation
of sufferings and sorrow, though almost always calmed, and
even brightened, by the healing influences of pitying love,
confiding piety, and conscious innocence. Almost the only
passions with which his poetry is conversant, are the gentler
sympathies of our nature—tender compassion—confiding affection, and guiltless sorrow. From all this there results, along
with a most touching and tranquilizing sweetness, a certain
monotony and languor, which, to those who read poetry for
amusement merely, will be apt to appear like dullness, and
must be felt as a defect by all who have been used to the
variety, rapidity, and energy of the more popular poetry of the
day. The poetry [in *The City of the Plague, and Other
Poems*] . . . , is almost entirely contemplative or descriptive.
There is little incident, and no conflict of passion or opposition
of character.—The interest is that of love or of pity alone: there
is no entanglement of situation, no opposition of interests—
no struggle of discordant feelings. There is not even any delineation of guilt, or any scene of vengeance, resentment, or
other stormy passion. The effect of the piece, at least, never
depends upon such elements. The author seems to have written
just to embody the scenes and characters on which he had most
pleasure in dwelling—and his chief art consists in fixing his
eye intently upon them—and drawing them with the truth, the
force, the fondness and the fullness of complete portraits of
beloved objects. In pursuing this pleasing occupation, he was
not likely to become so soon wearied as the comparatively
indifferent spectators in whose eye he was working;—and from
this has resulted another fault—the excessive diffuseness and
oppressive fulness of most of his pictures and details—which
has inevitably led to occasional weakness in the diction, and
a want of brilliancy and effect in the colouring of the style.
Still, however, there is a charm about the work, to which it
would be unfortunate, we think, to be insensible—a certain
pastoral purity, joined with deeper feelings, and more solemn
and impressive images than belong to pastoral—and reflecting,
if not the more agitated and deeply shaded scenes of adventurous life, an enchanting image of peace, purity, and tenderness, which, we hope, is not more unlike the ordinary tenor
of actual existence.

The most important piece in [this] volume, is a dramatic poem
entitled, 'The City of the Plague,'—by which is meant London,
during the great sickness of 1666. . . . A great part of Mr.
Wilson's materials, and indeed most of the ground colour of
his poem, are derived from [De Foe's history of the calam-
ity];—and there is not much complication or invention in the
particular incidents he has imagined for bringing them into
connexion. Though the nature of the subject, and the uniformity
of sadness to which it inevitably led, rendered it eminently
unfit for actual representation, and not very suitable for a dramatic form, we think there are many dramatic beauties in the
poem before us, and a very great number of passages that are
both pathetic and poetical in a very high degree. (pp. 460-62)

The Fourth Scene [of the First Act] is rather an unsuccessful attempt to represent one of those seemingly unnatural orgies,—those frantic displays of wild and daring revelry, to which the desperation of the time naturally gave rise. . . . [Mr. Wilson] has not in any one instance caught the true tone of profligacy, or even of convivial gaiety. It seems as if he had not the heart to represent human creatures as thoroughly reprobate or unamiable. Accordingly, they all give signs of penitence and good feeling. Even the prostitutes are gentle-hearted, delicate and interesting beings; and the master of those unseemly revels, turns out to be graced with almost every virtue under heaven. However creditable it may be to his philanthropy, this faint-heartedness in conceiving profligacy, is a great defect in an author who deals in effect. (p. 465)

There is another dramatic fragment, entitled—'**The Convict,**' which we think has extraordinary merit.—The subject is the conviction and deliverance, at the place of execution, of an innocent country man, upon whom accidental circumstances had fastened irresistible suspicions of murder. The topics may seem low and ignoble, but the interest excited is prodigious, and of a true tragic character,—while the piety of the unhappy victim, the innocent simplicity of his wife and children, and the rustic images belonging to his condition, serve to redeem the horror of the main incidents, and lend a certain elegance and dignity to what might otherwise appear but a dreadful or an edifying story. The great merit of the piece, however, consists in the fine dissection and leisurely display of all the terrible emotions that belong to such an occurrence, and in forcing the reader to contemplate it steadily and fixedly, till all the powerful emotions with which it is pregnant are developed, and find their way to the heart. (p. 472)

[Mr. Wilson] has undoubtedly both the heart and the fancy of a poet; and, with these great requisites, is almost sure of attaining the higher honours of his art, if he continue to cultivate it with the docility and diligence of which he has already given proof. Though his style is still too diffuse, and his range too limited, the present volume is greatly less objectionable on these grounds than [*The Isle of Palms, and Other Poems*]. It has also less of the peculiarities of the Lake School; and, in particular, is honourably distinguished from the productions of its founders, by being quite free from the paltry spite and fanatical reprobation with which, like other fierce and narrow-minded sectaries, they think it necessary to abuse all whose tastes or opinions are not exactly conformable to their own. There is no shadow of this ludicrous insolence in the work before us; in consequence of which, we think it extremely likely, that he will be execrated and reviled, on the first good opportunity, by his late kind masters. (pp. 475-76)

> [*Francis Jeffrey*], in a review of *"The City of the Plague, and Other Poems,"* in The Edinburgh Review, *Vol. XXVI, No. LII, June, 1816, pp. 458-76.*

### THE LONDON LITERARY GAZETTE   (essay date 1822)

[The twenty-four tales in *Lights and Shadows of Scottish Life*] deserve to be called excellent in conception, composition, power and pathos. As pictures of society, and portraits of a race of beings fast, we fear, wearing away, if not already as if they had never been, in the villages and the wilds of Scotland, they appeal most touchingly to the heart; and we will venture to predict that many a rugged nature will melt before the simple and affecting annals of these humble actors in the sad dramas of life in which they are raised to—no, not to fret and strut—

but to endure their hour in patient suffering and pious resignation. Such is the tenor of the author's way. Sadness, and even gloom, seem congenial to his moods of mind; he is the Heraclitus of the lonely and rural retreat, though without the austerity of the philosopher. Perhaps the religious cast of his opinions is rather more strong than we admire in productions of mere fiction. The name of God is so frequently invoked, as sometimes, we think, to be almost taken in vain; and even in the most solemn imaginings of human misery, we are loth to have the sacred and blessed names of the Saviour too commonly or irreverently introduced. We are convinced that no irreverence is meant, and that, on the contrary, this blemish proceeds from the intensity of an opposite feeling; but still we deem it a duty to enter our protest against the habit here carried to an excess. (p. 304)

> A review of *"Lights and Shadows of Scottish Life: A Selection from the Papers of the Late Arthur Austin,"* in The London Literary Gazette, *No. 278, May 18, 1822, pp. 304-06.*

### BLACKWOOD'S EDINBURGH MAGAZINE   (essay date 1823)

[The] author of [the *Trials of Margaret Lyndsay*] has most undoubtedly kept up the interest of it with extraordinary power, and yet he has not assumed the merit of a skilfully-arranged story, or artificial development of plot, which has often failed even with some highly celebrated and most popular novelists. He has shewn his heroine, Margaret Lyndsay, most amiable, virtuous, and pious, through a variety of trials from her childhood upwards, not in adventures at all uncommon or complex, but amidst privation and distresses which reach the poor and the lowly in ordinary life, and call forth those qualities and dispositions, whether good or evil, which such situations exhibit, attended with their customary effects, and attended with their customary joys or sorrows,—joys never buoyant with violent rapture, sorrows not often sunk in deep despair, and neither the one nor the other expressed in the vehemence of impassioned language, and but rarely productive of dramatic incidents, such as strike or overpower the feelings of the reader; rarely, we say, for a few such do occur, and their effect is, no doubt, the more overwhelming, on account of the sparingness with which the author has put forth this particular branch of his powers.

This is certainly a useful species of composition: if it can extend the empire of virtue and religion, and bring their excellencies into contact with the humble ranks of society, traced through scenes with which the higher classes of mankind are often but little, too little, familiar, it may profit both. "Take physic," (says the tempest-beaten Lear,)

> Take physic, Pomp;
> Expose thyself to feel what wretches feel,
> That you may cast the superflux to them,
> And shew the heavens more just.

Such may reasonably be expected to be the effect of such biography as that of Margaret Lyndsay, and as such we would earnestly recommend it to the perusal of the gay and the happy, whose youth has been lapped in the indulgences of wealth, or reposed amidst the indolent privileges of high birth or elevated rank. They need be in no apprehension of encountering tedium or ennui in the perusal; for, true to nature, and to humble nature, as the work is, there is also a deep tinge of poetry and passion thrown over it, which, without diminishing the fidelity of the picture of lowly life, exalts the character of the composition, and preserves sure and undoubted the position of its author. . . . [*Lights and Shadows of Scottish Life*] is still valued, as exhibiting a beautiful union of the spirit of poetry with that of the most ordinary human life; and, in spite of occasional exaggerations both of language and sentiment, . . . making perpetual appeals to the best, and purest, and simplest emotions of the human bosom. In the [*Trials of Margaret Lyndsay*], the reader will, on the whole, recognize much of the same general character, both as to excellencies and defects. He will find, indeed, the same tendency to exuberance of ornament, but he will find it less indulged. He will find, perhaps, less of fancy, less of ideal beauty, less of pure imagination; but then he will find, unless we be greatly mistaken, a stronger mastery over the affections, and a deeper insight into the affairs of that humble, but often agitated, world, with which this author's moral contemplations are so familiar, and in which they seem to take so much melancholy pleasure. It appears to us, that there is more of earnestness and fervour in some of the quiet homely descriptions in this tale, than in the more brilliant expositions of mingled fancy and feeling in the former volume. There are single phrases,—images,—circumstances, scattered everywhere, which have all the power of pathos, and yet seem as if they had fallen involuntarily from the pen. There is more of the poet's power, and less of poetical embellishment; and great as the writer's popularity is, we are sure it would be much increased if he would carry this matter still further, and, without sacrificing any part of his inspiration, which is, and always must be, essentially poetic, labour to subdue his expression still more nearly to the ordinary level of prose composition. (pp. 549-50)

In the delineation of character, there is perhaps some want of individual feature, the amiable as well as the unamiable traits being of a general kind. The principal character, Margaret Lyndsay, is every thing that is lovely in person and excellent in mind; but we seldom see, in her sentiments or conduct, those sudden, abrupt, unforeseen outbreakings of soul, which strike deep on our feelings, or impress themselves strongly on our memory. But perhaps the object of this writer is better answered by this level tone, as it might be called, of character, which suits the rank and condition of the persons of this drama, than it would have been by more vehement ebullitions of passion, which are shewn amidst the storms of more exalted life, amidst scenes of higher and more public interest. The same answer may be made to a defect which some critics, who require strongly impressive qualities in fictitious writing, may object to this work, that there is too little of *relief* in the delineations of character, and in the circumstances of the persons introduced into it. But the author may reply, that Nature, in the simple forms in which this tale is meant to exhibit her, does not deal in extremes, and is best represented in those middle tints which belong to the world as it is. He may rely on it, that his taste has not deceived him; and that there is a charm about the purity, innocence, and loving nature of his heroine, quite sufficient to make anything that befals her intensely interesting.

The general style of the work is of a piece with this picture of ordinary life. It does not rise into eloquence of an ardent or impassioned sort; but its language has a quiet elegance and refinement, which flows in an even tenor of proper and carefully chosen expression, discriminating sufficiently the personal appearances, as well as the moral attributes, of the persons, and the graphic description of the scenery, in the midst of which they are placed, morally speaking. . . . The style sometimes approaches perhaps too near to poetry, in the redundance of epithets,—epithets occasionally of a compound

sort. . . . [And] yet we allow, that, in the finer and more minute attributes of mind, it is difficult to express the almost imperceptible gradations to which these are subject without a compound expression. . . . [Surely] that person must be of a strange mind, who would run the risk of weakening a writer of great and acknowledged genius, by pressing upon him too closely the consideration of a few mere superficial peculiarities, which in no way whatever affect the general tone of his intellect, but, in removing which, he might perhaps chance to remove something well worth all the triumphs that ever mere criticism could achieve. (pp. 552-53)

[It is] one of the excellencies of this little work, that it everywhere inculcates the purest morality and the most sincere piety in every situation and circumstance, whether of good or ill fortune, the good which it enhances, the ill which it supports. . . .

Such histories as this of the *Trials of Margaret Lyndsay,* which "come home to the business and bosoms" of the lower classes, are well calculated to form the manners and character of that great body of the people, on whom depend the peace, the security, and the happiness, of the social state. We have read no work indicative of such talents for stories of this kind as this book, and the *Lights and Shadows of Scottish Life.* . . . (p. 557)

> *A review of "The Trials of Margaret Lyndsay," in* Blackwood's Edinburgh Magazine, *Vol. XIII, No. LXXVI, May, 1823, pp. 548-57.*

**[FRANCIS JEFFREY]   (essay date 1823)**

['*Lights and Shadows of Scottish Life*' is] an affected, or at least too poetical a title,—and, standing before a book, not very natural, but bright with the lights of poetry. It is a collection . . . characteristic of Scottish scenery and manners—mostly pathetic, and mostly too favourable to the country to which they relate. They are, on the whole, we think, very beautifully and sweetly written, and in a soft spirit of humanity and gentleness. But the style is too elaborate and uniform;—there is occasionally a good deal of weakness and commonplace in the passages that are most emphatically expressed,—and the poetical heightenings are often introduced where they hurt both the truth and the simplicity of the picture. Still, however, they are founded in a fine sense of the peculiarities of our national character and scenery, and a deep feeling of their excellence and beauty—and, though not executed according to the dictates of a severe or correct taste, not calculated to make much impression on those who have studied men and books 'with a learned spirit of observation,' are yet well fitted to minister delight to less fastidious spirits,—and to revive, in many world-wearied hearts, those illusions which had only been succeeded by illusions less innocent and attractive, and those affections in which alone there is neither illusion nor disappointment. (pp. 180-81)

['**The Trials of Margaret Lindsay**'] is too pathetic and full of sorrow for us to say much of it. It is very beautiful and tender; but something cloying, perhaps, in the uniformity of its beauty, and exceedingly oppressive in the unremitting weight of the pity with which it presses on our souls. Nothing was ever imagined more lovely than the beauty, the innocence, and the sweetness of Margaret Lindsay, in the earlier part of her trials; and nothing, we believe, is more true, than the comfortable lesson which her tale is meant to inculcate,—that a gentle and affectionate nature is never inconsolable nor permanently unhappy, but easily proceeds from submission to new enjoyment. But the tale of her trials, the accumulation of suffering on the heads of the humblest and most innocent of God's creatures, is too painful to be voluntarily recalled. . . . (p. 189)

> [*Francis Jeffrey*], in a review of *''Lights and Shadows of Scottish Life''* and *''The Trials of Margaret Lindsay,''* in The Edinburgh Review, *Vol. XXXIX, No. LXXVII, October, 1823, pp. 158-96.*

### THE BRITISH CRITIC (essay date 1826)

The brilliant example of the Great Unknown [Sir Walter Scott] has raised such a host of Scottish romancers, that the critics have been fairly thrown out in the chase. . . . [Here] we have overtaken a gentleman who stands accountable for three closely printed octavos [**"Lights and Shadows of Scottish Life," "Trials of Margaret Lyndsay,"** and **"Foresters"**]. His pretensions are considerable, his merits and success not inconsiderable, and he dedicates to Sir Walter Scott; yet we are bound to declare that, if indeed of the Waverley blood, he is but a cousin very many times removed. His tales are mere poetical visions, and ought to have been in rhyme, for there is nothing of prose about them either in the thoughts or diction. The restraints of metre would have retrenched many unpleasing superfluities of ornament which now encumber his style, and he might have successfully rivalled the pathetic stories of Barry Cornwall— He seems, however, to have a higher aim than merely to please as a poet; . . . the title of his first work and the subject-matter of them all profess to exhibit traits of national character, a very difficult task to execute well at any time, but undertaken under peculiar disadvantage when [Scott and John Galt] have both exhausted their varied powers upon Scottish subjects.

However, we should be sorry to condemn any one for following such high examples. . . . But we are afraid that our present author is not one of those from whom we may look for any addition to our knowledge of living manners. He paints the romance of life, and not the reality. He seems to be a man of warm feelings, and some eloquence, but either he has never studied living men, or he has not the heart to represent them as they are. In the warmth of his imagination he wings his way back to the golden age, shuts his eyes upon sad reality, and transforms the Land of Cakes into an Arcadian Vale. . . . [If] our author had merely published his sketches as imaginary studies, without pretending to have drawn them from nature, we should have dismissed him without censure as an elegant trifler. (pp. 149-50)

The **"Lights and Shadows"** consist of twenty-four pastoral stories or sketches, after the manner of Geoffry Crayon [Washington Irving], but far below him in every quality of merit. There is no variety, no humour, no nice discrimination of character. The author draws entirely upon his fancy. He borrows no aid from history or tradition, or even from the legendary lore of a land of poetical superstitions. He never refers to books, or real men, dead or living; but he dreams a dream, and straightway commits it to paper in language flowery as the meadows of May, and sweet as murmuring zephyrs. (p. 151)

He selects a few romantic incidents, generally simple, but seldom very natural, interlards them with much trite and trashy sentiment, and pours over the whole a flood of smooth and glittering, but inflated and fantastic, diction. (p. 153)

[The stories] are all of the same cast—tales of love or sorrow— of elegant joys and sentimental distress. The author's range is

very limited, but his pathos would often be exceedingly effective, if his inordinate love of fine writing did not betray him perpetually to the very verge of burlesque. His sentimentality, though very tiresome, is in general inoffensive enough; yet now and then we do meet with a notion both singular and false. (p. 155)

[The **"Trials of Margaret Lindsay"** is] as doleful a ditty as ever was chanted by tragic bard; nevertheless, it does not falsify the remark we made in the beginning, that Scottish life, in the hands of this author, is upon the whole very bright and happy; for the reader will find . . . that, though "heaviness may endure for a night, joy cometh in the morning." . . .

The story is very inartificial in its construction, being little more than a rambling collection of melo-dramatic incidents, devised for stage effect, and the introduction of rivers of sentiment. Violent excitements of passion, exaggerated distresses, sudden alternations of grief and joy, angelic resignation, and heroic constancy, are the vulgar materials of romance which the author works up in every scene. But even the most slight and trivial incidents of the story are sufficient to set his lack-a-daisical muse a-going; and page after page of rapid sensibility and puling pastoral affectation so utterly exhausts our patience, that after closing the volume we can hardly criticize with due politeness. (p. 156)

[The] mere plan of the fable leads us to remark, that the author has fallen into the common error of sentimental writers in taking his subject from low life. . . . [Nothing] can be more unsentimental than the simple annals of the poor. . . . The unsophisticated manners of shepherds and mechanics may furnish an important field of study to the philosopher, and some interesting subjects to the skilful dramatist; but when the sentimentalist comes upon the same ground, he produces immediately such unnatural combinations of rusticity and refinement as we every where meet with in the volumes before us. (p. 159)

There is another error of design yet more important, which we have observed in the tale now under review. The moral which the author seems labouring from beginning to end to inculcate, is that piety and prudence, however beset by the snares of the world, will yet always be triumphant, and sure of happiness even on this side the grave. A pious fraud perchance is here intended. But all frauds are dangerous; although in this the delusion is very palpable; yet once attach a man to the pleasing theory of impartial justice upon earth, and every instance occurring to the contrary will be as likely to shake his trust in Providence, as to correct the error of his philosophy.

Of the various characters introduced into this tale, the greater part are very insipid in themselves, and depend for their effect almost entirely upon the exciting situations in which they are placed. There are some sweet touches in the picture of the idiot girl: but the only approach to spirit and force is in Hannah Blantyre. (p. 160)

There runs throughout these volumes a very warm vein of piety—but, like the author's morality, it is far too sentimental and obtrusive. (p. 161)

[We] could exhibit a choice collection of exotic, vulgar, fantastic, and nonsensical phrases, but . . . we shall content ourselves with observing that the author's diction stands in need of the pruning-hook almost as much as his fancy. . . .

[The **"Foresters"**] exhibits the very same merits and defects which we have found in the two preceding works; the same harmony, feeling, and pathos, impaired by the same sickly sensibility and quaint affectation. . . . [The author] is neither an accurate delineator of manners, like Fielding; nor a profound master of the passions, like Shakspeare, nor yet, like the same great bard, a sublime magician. We could willingly forgive him for soaring into the clouds, if he would now and then introduce us to a Prospero, or an Ariel, an awful Ghost, or a Fairy Queen. But unfortunately he is just poetical enough to substitute fancy for observation, without venturing once within the enchanted circle. His men and women are neither quite what they are, nor quite what they should be; but a kind of imaginary beings taken from that insipid midway region between the visible and the invisible world in which we lose the warm reality of the one, but meet not yet with the mystic shadows and aerial music of the other. (p. 162)

[With] all our objections to the romantic delusions which abound in these tales, we must confess that if some of them could be realized, the world would be a much pleasanter place than it is. We meet every now and then, in turning over the pages, with visions of purity and happiness which are very charming, though altogether imaginary. A poetic mantle is thrown, as if in mockery, over the prosaic realities and sordid details of human life. (p. 163)

We now take leave of our author in the spirit of charity, assuring him that what we have said, we have not said in petulance or envy, but from a sincere persuasion that he is misusing his own genius, and ministering to a false and sickly taste but too prevalent among readers of fiction. That he means well we cannot doubt. He is every where pious, moral, and humane, but sentiment is the ruin of him. He aspires to the dignity of a moral teacher, without having soberly studied the passions of the human heart. The consequence is that he gives the reins to a warm imagination, and instead of communicating solid instruction for the conduct of life, he exhibits pleasing, but delusive pictures of the world, drawn from fancy, and tending to make men indolent and romantic, and unfit for the vulgar affairs of mortality. (p. 164)

> "Scotch Novels," in The British Critic, Vol. I, No. II, January, 1826, pp. 149-64.

## SAMUEL TAYLOR COLERIDGE  (conversation date 1833)

[Coleridge, a leading English Romantic poet and critic, asserts that Wilson's close association with Blackwood's Magazine was a "reckless spending" of talent. This is the first expression of the opinion, often echoed by later critics, that if Wilson had focused his energies in a different direction, he could have become a far greater writer. Coleridge's assessment of Wilson's talent is disputed by Thomas De Quincey and George Saintsbury (see excerpts below, 1850 and 1886) but affirmed by George Gilfillan (see excerpt below, 1854) and other later critics.]

Professor Wilson's character of Charles Lamb in the last Blackwood, "Twaddle on Tweedside," is very sweet indeed, and gratified me much. It does honour to Wilson, to his head and his heart.

How can I wish that Wilson should cease to write what so often soothes and suspends my bodily miseries, and my mental conflicts! Yet what a waste, what a reckless spending, of talent, ay, and of genius, too, in his I know not how many years' management of Blackwood! . . . Two or three volumes collected out of the magazine by himself would be very delightful. But he must not leave it for others to do; for some recasting and much condensation would be required; and literary exec-

utors make sad work in general with their testators' brains. (pp. 220-21)

> Samuel Taylor Coleridge, in a conversation with Henry Nelson Coleridge on May 14, 1833, in his Specimens of the Table Talk of Samuel Taylor Coleridge, edited by Henry Nelson Coleridge, Harper & Brothers, 1835 (and reprinted in The Table Talk and Omniana of Samuel Taylor Coleridge by Samuel Taylor Coleridge, edited by T. Ashe, George Bell and Sons, 1884, pp. 220-21).

## ALLAN CUNNINGHAM  (essay date 1834)

[Wilson] courted public attention, first, in his poem of 'The Isle of Palms:' it exhibits scenes of enchanting beauty, a prodigality of loveliness united to uncommon sweetness and tranquil grace. 'The City of the Plague' succeeded: a noble and deeply pathetic poem. . . . It possesses great dramatic interest, and displays picture after picture of private suffering and public misery: the darkness is relieved by such flashes of light as few bards have at command; in the abodes of despair there are rays of hope let in—on the brink of the grave flowers of beauty are scattered; nor do we tread the floor of the charnelhouse but in joy mingled with fear. His most dolorous scenes are redeemed back to our sympathy by inimitable touches of nature; and we rise from the spell of perusal sobered and elevated.

His poetical powers are very varied: that is, he can handle any subject in its own peculiar spirit. His 'Edith and Nora' is one of those fairy-fictions of which he once promised a volume; there is a wondrous beauty shed over the landscape on which he brings out his spiritual folk to sport and play, and do good deeds to men: nor has he wasted all his sweetness on the not insensible earth; he has endowed his fairies with charms from a hundred traditions, assigned them poetic and moral tasks, and poured inspiration into their speech. Another fine poem of his is 'An Address to a Wild Deer:' for bounding elasticity of language, hurrying thoughts, and crowding imagery, it is without a parallel. Indeed, throughout all his smaller poems there is a deep feeling for nature; an intimate knowledge of the workings of the heart, and a liquid fluency of language almost lyrical. He is distinguished, in all his compositions, for splendour of imagination, for loftiness of thought, for sympathy with all that is grand or honourable in man, for transitions surprising and unexpected, but never forced, and for situations such as appear to an eye which sees through all nature. He may be accused sometimes of an overflow of enthusiasm about his subject; nor has he escaped from the charge of sometimes overflooding sentiments with words. . . . [Yet, he] is a foe to all affectation, either in dress or verse, and mauls the fop of the toilet and the fop in poetry with equal wit and mercilessness. (pp. 90-2)

> Allan Cunningham, "Wilson," in his Biographical and Critical History of the British Literature of the Last Fifty Years, Baudry's Foreign Library, 1834, pp. 89-92.

## GRAHAM'S MAGAZINE  (essay date 1842)

No man of [Professor Wilson's] age has shown greater versatility of talent, and few, of any age, richer powers of imagination. His literary influence has far exceeded that of any Englishman who ever existed. His scholarship, if not profound, is excursive; his criticism, if not always honest, is analytical, enthusiastic, and original in manner. His wit is vigorous, his humor great, his sarcasm bitter. His high animal spirits give a dashing, free, hearty and devil-may-care tone to all his compositions—a tone which has done more towards establishing his literary popularity and *dominion* than any single quality for which he is remarkable. The faults of Professor Wilson, as might be supposed from the traits of his merits, are many and great. He is frequently led into gross injustice through personal feeling—this is his chief sin. His tone is often *flippant.* His scholarship is questionable as regards extent and accuracy. His style is apt to degenerate, or rather *rush,* into a species of bombastic *periphrasis* and *apostrophe.* . . . His analysis, although true in principle (as is always the case with the idealist) and often profound, is nevertheless deficient in that calm breadth and massive deliberateness which are the features of such intellects as that of Verülam [Francis Bacon]. In short, the *opinions* of Professor Wilson can never be safely adopted without examination.

> A review of *"Critical and Miscellaneous Essays,"* in Graham's Magazine, *Vol. XX, No. 1, January, 1842, p. 72.*

## THE EDINBURGH REVIEW   (essay date 1843)

['**The Recreations of Christopher North**' is] in every way remarkable . . . , whether regarded as illustrative of the character of the writer, or of the tendencies of the criticism of the time, to which his influence and example have given so general and decided a direction. It is not indeed easy to say, whether the interest which [the] perusal [of these volumes] excites is chiefly to be referred to the very singular combination of moral and mental powers implied in their composition—where qualities which are generally deemed incompatible are found to be united in harmony—or to the strong feeling of the influence which this combination, expressing itself in forms of such originality and power as to arrest the attention of literary men, and at the same time, to appeal to the ordinary tastes and sympathies of the public, by the use of instruments at once familiar and powerful, must have exercised upon the taste of the time, and the whole tone and spirit of our criticism, as well as its form. . . .

[Such] are the vivacity and picturesque truth with which [North's] sayings and doings have been here depicted, that few creatures of the imagination have succeeded in impressing their image on the public with more distinctness of portraiture, or a stronger sense of reality. Few indeed find any difficulty in calling up before the mind's eye, with nearly the same vividness as that of an ordinary acquaintance, the image of this venerable *eidolon*—who unites the fire of youth with the wisdom of age, retains an equal interest in poetry, philosophy, pugilism, and political economy—in short, in all the on-goings of the world around him, in which either matter or spirit have a part; and who passes from a fit of the gout to a feat of gymnastics, and carries his crutch obviously less for purposes of use than of intimidation. (p. 72)

Considerable changes, we perceive, have taken place on these Essays since they first appeared in a periodical form. . . . [Yet] in all, essentially—and wisely we think—they retain their original character. For, unquestionably, not a little of their peculiar charm was derived from the contrast between the occasional nature of their origin, and the depth and permanent importance of the views which many of them embodied;—from observing how frequently it happened that slight hints, caught up as if by accident, and handled in a spirit of sportive dalliance, were made by some secret and cunning alchymy to change their

nature and to expand into speculations of deep and wide significance, connected with human nature, or the principles of poetry and art; and how, from a foundation that seemed at first slender and unsubstantial, if not mean and misplaced, a stately fabric of philosophic truth, studded with imagery and stored with wisdom, rose before us like a bright and noiseless exhalation. . . .

From [the] perpetual interchange of humour and earnestness, playful trifling and sound philosophy, these volumes stimulate the feeling of curiosity in a high degree. We soon feel that we have resigned ourselves into the hands of a companion and guide, the eccentricities of whose course it is impossible to calculate. The line of curves by which Sterne illustrates the no-progress of Tristram Shandy is its only parallel. Start with him from what latitude you may, no one can foresee in what zone the excursion is to terminate, or through what strange scenes or devious wanderings we shall be led. The title of the essay, or the nature of the subject, throws but the feeblest light upon the probabilities of its treatment. . . . Indeed, in the perusal of the '**Recreations,**' we can scarcely say we are reasonably assured of any one thing beforehand; except that in all probability every mood of mind in which the subject can be viewed will be run through, and in quick succession: the note of mirth suddenly passing into the mournful, and again, by delicate resolution, modulating back into the key of cheerfulness. Experience soon teaches us that the presiding influence under which these volumes were composed is Mutability; and 'that nothing here long standeth in one sway.' (p. 74)

There are some classes of minds to which these rapid changes of scale, and this blending of different elements within the same composition, may appear illegitimate and barbarous;—particularly the department of literary criticism. (p. 75)

But surely, in any view, that *principle must be erroneous* which would exclude from the criticism of poetry and art—or from those views and observations on life, and character, and morals, which are generally, though rather vaguely, classified under the term Essays—a wide field of humour, an extensive range of excursive fancy, and a union of the comic and serious elements, such as meet us daily in every scene of life itself. (p. 76)

[The objection] lies rather to its application; that on the one hand, the test of the ludicrous, as applied to the criticism of literature, is too systematically employed, and urged beyond its due bounds; and, on the other, that the opposite feeling of admiration and reverence which great works awaken in the minds of poetical spirits, though vivifying the composition with the eloquence of conviction, is apt to overpower the judgment, and to result in vague eulogy rather than discriminating criticism. Either would be a formidable objection if it existed. . . . [It] appears very plain that [in the '**Recreations**'] the two charges in a great measure neutralize each other—that they are, in fact, inconsistent in their nature; and that in neither case does there exist any substantial ground of objection.

If, indeed, the writer of these volumes had applied his power of presenting what he pleases in the most irresistibly comic light, to things which, either in nature or art, should be exempt from ridicule, we should be the last to vindicate such a perversion of talent. But from this charge he is completely free. Those feelings which the human heart consecrate as holy, are sacred to him. Religion, love, honour, self-devotion—all the charities of the soul—are cherished and embalmed by him in words of music. In no instance, so far as we are aware, is that which is truly good or great presented by him under a ludicrous point of view. Even in dealing with the great creations of art, the same feeling of veneration is perceptible. When he seeks to fathom their spirit, or explain their structure, the reverence of his words denotes his consciousness that a certain sacredness resides within. (pp. 78-9)

[We] would ask with confidence . . . whether the author's almost unequalled command of the humorous and the ludicrous has tended in any degree to impair his sensibility to what is really elevated or poetical? or, whether the consciousness of his power of ridicule has led him to use it tyrannously or like a giant? Has its tendency been to convert the writer into a critical Dragon, treating the field of literature as a province bound to supply him with an annual contingent of youthful victims?

On the contrary, towards true poetry, or even the very germs and indications of poetry . . . , there never, perhaps, was criticism so indulgent and encouraging. Justly is he entitled to the praise he claims for himself, of 'guarding from mildew the laurels on the brow of the Muses' sons.' If, amidst the noisy Babel of ephemeral strains which assails his ear, he catches the melody of the simplest verse that embodies in truthful words a true emotion, he does not willingly let it die. It is to him a labour of love to preserve it, to prolong its echo into the world; to find for it, by graceful and kindly introduction, 'fit audience, and that not few.' (pp. 80-1)

The absence of another element which is too apt to trouble our views of literature, is remarkable in these volumes. . . . [There] is not only nothing harsh or unkind towards those of opposite [political] sentiments; but, we might more truly say, an absolute negation of the very feeling of political difference. Genius is revered and embraced as of no party; for the domain of poetry is here regarded as a peaceful and hallowed ground . . . [where] contending parties may lower and fold their banners as if beneath the roof of a common sanctuary, or above some honoured and lamented grave. (pp. 81-2)

[There is] little foundation . . . [for the] supposition that the criticism [in the 'Recreations'] is exaggerated in its praise or censure, unaccompanied with definite reasons, or leading to no sufficiently tangible result. Indeed, as regards the contents of these volumes, and generally all the *later* criticism of the same writer, the supposition would be eminently inapplicable. In the paper entitled, '**An hour's talk on Poetry**,' the manner in which the works of the great poets of the present age are dealt with, in considering the question whether any of them have produced a work entitled to be called a *great poem,* sufficiently shows with what discrimination of good and bad— of performance and failure—the claims of contemporary genius are estimated. But above all, the manner in which the critic deals with Wordsworth, is in itself a sufficient refutation of the idea of the indiscriminating style of criticism which can see no blemish in a favourite, as it can recognize no merit in an opponent. No one has laboured so assiduously as the author of these '**Recreations**' in the task of conversion of the public mind, first to tolerate, and at last to admire, Wordsworth. His earliest efforts were directed to open the eyes of his countrymen to the deep meaning of his poetry, avoiding as it did all the ordinary and popular means of excitement, and to attune their ears to its solemn and soothing harmonies. He states no more than the simple truth, when he says, with a just pride in having achieved what he believes to be a high and useful end, that he has been the means of diffusing Wordsworth's poetry not only over this island, but the furthest dependencies of the British

empire, and throughout the states of America. . . . But as it was the labour of his earlier years to teach the public to understand and admire this great poet, so it becomes the duty of his maturer age to take care that the admiration which he has thus been the main cause of instilling into the public mind, shall prove not a blind idolatry, but a discriminating devotion. Accordingly, with the respect due to great ability employed in the cause of virtue for upwards of half a century, yet with the candour and dignified sincerity with which one man of genius ought to deal with another, he points out, in the course of these volumes, not a few defects of omission and commission in the works of this great artist. . . . (pp. 82-3)

[We should] say that the character of the criticism contained in these volumes . . . is mainly distinguished from the greater part of the popular criticism of the day, by its combination of analyses of parts, often very detailed, with general views as to the plan and spirit of the work reviewed. Indeed its minute dissection of particular passages, both as to thought and diction, carries us back to the school of Johnson and Addison, rather than to our own time. (p. 86)

[To the] system of general blame and praise, unaccompanied by a due application of critical particulars, the practice of the writer of these '**Recreations**' stands completely opposed. (p. 87)

The homeliness of some of the illustrations and expressions in [these volumes] will enable the reader to form some idea of the very singular style of these '**Recreations**'—illustrating the grandest objects by the most familiar, and, by its homeliness, perplexing critics. This *imbroglio* appears of course still more conspicuous and even startling, in those papers where the writer abandons himself with less restraint to the comic vein. Side by side with the most fancifully beautiful illustrations, or following close on some passage of poetic and musical diction, comes some picture most prosaically ludicrous—some slang phrase of the day—some quotation, how changed from its original application!—or some Scotch expression, tempting to the writer by its graphic force and the comic associations with which it is connected. The result is a strange composite, blending all orders of architecture, and employing all materials, from porphyry and lapis lazuli down to the commonest brick and mortar. It reminds us of St Mark's at Venice, in which Saracenic domes are strangely imposed upon Gothic nave, and blocks of Egyptian granite are fantastically mingled with Italian marble and mosaic: yet all blended into a marvellous arabesque, and possessing a strange unity and originality of character.

With all this, however, we must own that we would not regret if the contrasts were somewhat less violent, and if here and there an obtrusive epithet or image were eliminated. We do not know that to any of them the term *coarseness* can be justly applied. But if the line of division between the sublime and the ridiculous be slender, still more so is that which separates the familiar from the vulgar: and were there no other reason for erring on the side of caution, it should be sufficient that this style, seductive as it always must be from its variety and apparent ease, would soon become intolerable in imitation. The transitions from the most elevated views to the most ludicrous—and from the most select and ornate expression to the most homely vernacular, may be harmonized; and are, no doubt, to a great extent harmonized in this case by the dexterous workmanship of genius. . . . [But unless] redeemed by the highest talent, this style of writing is one of the most dangerous and offensive that can be attempted: and . . . , highly as we appreciate the generous spirit which the author of these volumes has carried into criticism, and the benefits which may be derived from the application of humour as well as imagination and judgment to the estimate of literature, we almost doubt whether the benefit has not been practically balanced by the injury arising from the prevalence of a system of criticism, founded, as is generally the case, rather on an imitation of his manner than his spirit; and which has preserved and exaggerated his faults, without approaching his excellences. (pp. 90-1)

> *A review of "The Recreations of Christopher North," in* The Edinburgh Review, *Vol. LXXVII, No. CLV, February, 1843, pp. 72-104.*

## CHARLES KNIGHT  (essay date 1848)

[John Wilson's] permanent reputation will, we think, rest upon his prose writings. His contributions to "Blackwood's Magazine" raised the whole tone and character of periodical literature. The keenest wit, the most playful fancy, the most genial criticism, the deepest pathos, were lavished year after year with a profusion almost miraculous. Some of the finest of these productions have been collected as **"The Recreations of Christopher North."** It would be difficult to point to three volumes of our own times that have an equal chance of becoming immortal. (pp. 343-44)

> *Charles Knight, in a prefatory note to "Highland Snow Storm," in* Half-Hours with the Best Authors, *Vol. II, edited by Charles Knight, Porter & Coates, 1848, pp. 343-44.*

## THOMAS DE QUINCEY  (essay date 1850)

[*De Quincey, who occasionally appeared in the* Noctes Ambrosianae *as the Opium Eater, was one of Wilson's closest friends. De Quincey differs with Coleridge, Gilfillan (see excerpts above, 1833; and below, 1854), and the majority of Wilson's critics in his belief that Wilson's essays are ample expression of his genius.*]

Out of [his] magazine articles has been drawn the occasion of a grave reproach to Professor Wilson. Had he, it is said, thrown the same weight of energy and the same fiery genius into a less desultory shape, it is hard to compute how enormous and systematic a book he might have written. . . . [The] whole doctrine from which exhales this charge against the Professor of misapplied powers calls for revision. Wise was that old Grecian who said . . . Big book, big nuisance! (p. 294)

[There is] a philosophy of human nature, like the philosophy of Shakspere, and of Jeremy Taylor, and of Edmund Burke, which is scattered through the miscellaneous papers of Professor Wilson. Such philosophy by its very nature is of a far higher and more aspiring nature than any which lingers upon mere scholastic conundrums. It is a philosophy that cannot be presented in *abstract* forms, but hides itself as an *incarnation* in voluminous mazes of eloquence and poetic feeling. Look for this amongst the *critical* essays of Professor Wilson; which, for continual glimpses and revelations of hidden truth, are perhaps absolutely unmatched. By such philosophy his various courses of lectures—we speak on the authority of many of his highest students—are throughout distinguished; and more especially those numerous disquisitions on Man's Moral Being, his Passions, his Affections, and his Imagination, in which Professor Wilson displays his own genius, its originality and power.

[Of] one who walks in the van of men the most memorable and original that have adorned our memorable and original age,

we conclude by saying, in a spirit of simplicity and fidelity to the truth, that from Professor Wilson's papers in *Blackwood,* but above all from his meditative examinations of great poets, Greek and English, may be formed a *florilegium* of thoughts the most profound and the most gorgeously illustrated that exist in human composition. (p. 301)

> *Thomas De Quincey, "Professor Wilson—Sketch in 1850" (originally published in* Hogg's Instructor, *1850), in his* The Collected Writings of Thomas De Quincey, *Vol. V, edited by David Masson, A. & C. Black, 1897, pp. 289-302.*

## GEORGE GILFILLAN  (essay date 1854)

[*Expanding on the idea, first expressed by Samuel Taylor Coleridge (see excerpt above, 1833), that* Blackwood's Magazine *was not an adequate outlet for Wilson's genius, Gilfillan laments that Wilson, by not fully developing any of his various talents, left a body of work incommensurate with his abilities. Despite these reservations, however, Gilfillan concludes by stating that Wilson was "Scotland's brightest son . . . ; and he, [Walter] Scott, and [Robert] Burns, must rank everlastingly as the first three of her men of genius."*]

[Wordsworth's poetry] made a deep and permanent impression upon [Wilson's] mind. . . . It determined his bias toward subjective instead of objective song; materially, as we think, to his disadvantage. Wilson was by nature fitted to be, as a poet, a great compound of the subjective, and the subjective with the objective somewhat preponderating, but the influence of Wordsworth, counteracted only in part by that of Scott, made the subjective predominate unduly in his verse; and he who might have been almost a Shakspere, had he followed his native tendency, became, in poetry, only a secondary member of the Lake School. (p. 26)

[*City of the Plague*] had beautiful passages, but, as a whole, was "dull, somehow dull." It aspired to be both a great drama and a great poem—and was neither. Two or three pages of it are still remembered, but the poem itself has gone down, or, rather, never rose. (p. 28)

[The *Noctes Ambrosianae*] intoxicated the world. They resembled the marvels of genius, of the stage, and of ventriloquism united to produce one bewitching and bewildering whole. The author seemed a diffused Shakspere, or Shakspere in a hurry, and with a printer's "devil" waiting at his door. Falstaff was for a season eclipsed by the "Shepherd," and Mercutio and Hamlet together had their glories darkened by the blended wit and wisdom, pathos and fancy, of Christopher North. The power of these dialogues lay in the admirable combination, interchange, and harmonious play of the most numerous, diverse, and contradictory elements and characters. Passages of the richest and most poetical eloquence were intermixed with philosophical discussion, with political invectives, with literary criticism, with uproarious fun and nonsense, with the floating gossip of the day, and with the sharpest of small talk. The Tragedy, the Comedy, and the Farce were all there, and the farce was no *after-piece*, but intermingled with the entire body of the play. . . . Each dialogue is in fact a miniature "Don Juan," jerking you down at every point from the highest to the lowest reaches of feeling and thought; and driving remorselessly through its own finest passages, in order to secure the effects of a burlesque oddity, compounded of the grave and the ludicrous, the lofty and the low. Each number in the series may be compared to a witch's caldron, crowded and heaving with all strange substances, the very order of which is disorganisation, but with the weird light of imagination glimmering over the chaos, and giving it a sort of unearthly unity. Verily, they are Walpurgis Nights, these **Noctes Ambrosianae.** The English language contains nothing so grotesque as some of their ludicrous descriptions, nothing so graphic, so intense, so terrible, as some of their serious pictures; no dialogue more elastic, no criticism more subtle, no gossip more delightful, no such fine diffusion, like the broad eagle wing, and no such vigorous compression, like the keen eagle talon; but when we remember, besides, that the **Noctes** contain *all* these merits combined into a wild and wondrous whole, our admiration of the powers displayed in them is intensified to astonishment, and, if not to the pitch of saying, "Surely a greater than Shakspere is here," certainly to that of admitting a mind of cognate and scarce inferior genius. (pp. 29-30)

[Wilson] had, contrary to common opinion, much metaphysical subtlety, which had not indeed been subjected, any more than some of his other faculties, to careful cultivation. But none can read some of his articles, or could have listened to many of his lectures, without the conviction that the metaphysical power was strong within him, and that, had he not by instinct been taught to despise metaphysics, he might have become a metaphysician, as universally wise, as elaborately ingenious, as captiously critical, as wilfully novel, and as plausibly and profoundly wrong, as any of the same class that ever lived. But he *did* despise this science of pretensions, and used to call it "dry as the dust of summer." Of his imagination we need not speak. It was large, rich, ungovernable, fond alike of the beautiful and the sublime, of the pathetic and the terrible. His wit was less remarkable than his humour, which was one of the most lavish and piquant of his faculties. Add to this, great memory, keen, sharp intellect, wide sympathies, strong passion, and a boundless command of a somewhat loose, but musical and energetic diction, and you have the outline of his gifts and endowments. He was deficient only in that plodding, painstaking sagacity which enables many commonplace men to excel in the physical sciences. (p. 37)

His powers have never, we think, found an adequate development. It is only the bust of Wilson we have before us. Yet let us not, because he has not done mightier things, call his achievements small; they are not only very considerable in themselves, but of a very diversified character. . . . And, first, as a critic, criticism with him was not an art or an attainment: it was an insight and an enthusiasm. He loved everything that was beautiful in literature, and abhorred all that was false and affected, and pitied all that was weak and dull; and his criticism was just the frank, fearless, and eloquent expression of that love, that abhorrence, and that pity. Hence his was a catholic criticism; hence his canons were not artificial; hence he abhorred the formal, the mystical, and the pseudo-philosophic schools of criticism; hence the reasons he gave for his verdicts were drawn, not from arbitrary rules, but directly from the great principles of human nature. With what joyous gusto did he approach a favourite author! His praise fell on books like autumn sunshine, and whatever it touched it gilded and glorified. And when, on the other hand, he was disgusted or offended, with what vehement sincerity, with what a noble rage, with what withering sarcasm, or with what tumultuous invective, did he express his wrath. His criticisms are sometimes rambling, sometimes rhapsodical, sometimes overdone in praise or in blame; often you are compelled to differ from his opinions, and sometimes to doubt if they are fully formed in his own mind, and in polish, precision, and depth, they are inferior to a few others; but, in heartiness, eloquence, variety, consum-

mate ease of motion, native insight, and sincerity, they stand alone.

We have alluded to his extraordinary gift of humour. It was not masked and subtle, like Lamb's; it was broad, rich, bordering on farce, and strongly impregnated with imagination. It was this last characteristic which gave it its peculiar power. . . . (pp. 37-8)

[Although] many of his tales are fine, they are so principally from the poetry of the descriptions which are sprinkled through them. He does not tell a story well, and this because he is not calm enough. . . . Scott *says* his stories, and Wilson *sings* them. Hence, while Wilson in passages is equal to Scott, as a whole, his works of fiction are greatly less interesting, and seem less natural. Wilson is a northern Scald, not so much narrating as pouring out passionate poetic rhapsodies, thinly threaded with incident. . . . Even in description he is not, in general, equal to Scott, and that for a similar reason. Wilson, when describing, rises out of the sphere of prose into a kind of poetic rhythm; Scott never goes beyond the line which separates the style of lofty prose from that of absolute poetry. Wilson is too Ossianic in his style of narration and description; and had he attempted a novel in three or four volumes, it had been absolutely illegible. Even **Margaret Lindsay,** his longest tale, rather tires before the close through its sameness of eloquence and monotony of pathos; only very short letters should be *all* written in tears and blood. And his alternations of gay and grave are not so well managed in his tales as in his **Noctes.** Yet nothing can be finer than some of his individual scenes and pictures. . . . In no modern, not even Scott, do we find prose passages so gorgeous, so filled with the intensest spirit of poetry, and rising so finely into its language and rhythm. . . . (pp. 38-9)

We have of late frequently applied, to apparently fine prose writing, the test of reading it aloud, and have judged accordingly of its rhythm, as well as of its earnestness and power. Few authors, indeed, can stand this. . . . All the better passages . . . of Hall, Chalmers, Foster, Scott, Croly, De Quincey, and, we add, of Macaulay, triumphantly pass the ordeal; and so, too, the descriptions in the **Lights and Shadows of Scottish Life.** (p. 39)

His poetry proper has been generally thought inferior to his prose, and beneath the level of his powers. Yet, if we admire it less, we at times love it more. It is not great, or intense, or highly impassioned, but it is true, tender, and pastoral. . . . As a poet, however, Wilson was deficient, far more than as a prose writer, in objective interest, as well as in concentration of purpose. His poetry has neither that reflective depth which causes you to recur so frequently to the poetry of Wordsworth, nor that dazzling lightness and brilliance of movement which fascinates you in Scott. It is far, too, from being a full reflection of his multifarious and powerful nature; it represents only a little quiet nook in his heart, a small sweet vein in his genius, as though a lion were to carry somewhere within his broad breast a little bag of honey, like that of the bee. It does not discover him as he is, but as he would wish to have been. His poetry is the Sabbath of his soul. And there are moods of mind—quiet, peaceful, autumnal moments—in which you enjoy it better than the poetry of any one else, and find a metaphor for its calm and holy charm in the words of Coleridge—

The moonbeams *steep'd in silentness,*
The *steady weather-cock.*

The revolving, impatient wheel, the boundless versatility of Wilson's genius, quieted and at rest, as we see it in his poetry, could not be better represented than in these lines. (pp. 41-2)

In his periodical writings alone [however] do we find anything like an adequate display of his varied powers. You saw only the half-man in the professor's chair, and only the quarter-man in his poetry; but in the *Noctes,* and the satirico-serious papers he scattered over *Blackwood,* you saw the whole Wilson—the Cyclops now at play, and now manufacturing thunderbolts for Jove; now cachinnating in his cave, now throwing rocks and mountains at his enemies, and now pouring out awful complaints, and asking strange, yet reverent queries in the ear of the gods.

Wilson's relation to his age has been, like Byron's, somewhat uncertain and vacillating. He has been, on the whole, a ''lost leader.'' He has, properly speaking, belonged neither to the old nor new, neither to the conservative nor to the movement, neither to the infidel nor the evangelical sides. Indeed, our grand quarrel with him is, that he was not sufficiently in earnest; that he did not with his might what his hand found to do; that he hid his *ten* talents in a napkin; that he trifled with his inestimable powers, and had not a sufficiently strong sense of stewardship on his conscience. . . . Splendid passages and inestimable thoughts, of course, abound in all that Wilson wrote, but the want of pervasive purpose, of genuine artistic instinct, of condensation, and of finish, has denied true unity, and perhaps permanent power, to his writings. He will probably be best remembered for his *Lights and Shadows*—a book which, although not a full discovery of his powers, lies in portable compass, and embalms that fine nationality which so peculiarly distinguished his genius. (pp. 42-3)

Wilson had every inducement to have done more than he did. . . . [His] uncertainty should not have paralysed and emasculated a man of his gigantic proportions. If beset by doubts and demons, he ought to have tried at least to fight his way through them, as many a resolute spirit has done before him. . . . Although not a writer for bread, much of his writing arose to the tune of the knock of the printer's ''devil;'' and his efforts for the advancement of the race, although we believe really sincere, were to the last degree fluctuating, irregular, and uncertain.

It is a proof, we think, of Wilson's weakness, as well as of his power, that he has been claimed as a possible prize on so many and such diverse sides. He might have been, says one, the greatest preacher of the age. He might have been, says another, the greatest actor of the day. He might have been, says a third, the greatest dramatist, next to Shakspere, that ever lived. He might have been, says a fourth, a powerful parliamentary orator. He might have been, says a fifth, a traveller superior to Bruce or Park. Now, while this proves the estimation in which men hold his vast versatility, it proves also, that there was something wrong and shattered in the structure of a mind which, while presenting so many angles to so many objects, never fully embraced any of them, and while displaying powers so universal, has left results so comparatively slender.

Nevertheless, after all these deductions, where shall we look for his like again? A more generous, a more wide-minded, a more courteous, and a more gifted man, probably never lived. By nature he was Scotland's brightest son, not, perhaps, even excepting Burns; and he, Scott, and Burns, must rank everlastingly together as the first Three of her men of genius. (pp. 43-4)

George Gilfillan, ''Professor Wilson,'' in his A Third Gallery of Literary Portraits, *1854 (and reprinted in his* A Gallery of Literary Portraits, *J. M. Dent & Co., 1909, pp. 22-45).*

### JAMES FREDERICK FERRIER   (essay date 1855)

[*Ferrier, who was Wilson's son-in-law, edited* The Works of Professor Wilson of the University of Edinburgh. *In his preface to the* Noctes Ambrosianae, *he lauds the conversations for their humor and dramatic power, and he ranks Wilson above both Sir Walter Scott and Robert Burns as a master of the Scottish dialect. Ferrier's views are disputed by George Douglas (see excerpt below, 1897).*]

[The dialogues of Professor Wilson's *Noctes Ambrosianae*] are sustained to the end with a dramatic propriety,—with a force and variety of thought,—with a fervour of feeling,—with an exuberance of humour,—with an affluence of poetical imagery, and with a freedom and elasticity of language which are certainly unparalleled in the species of composition to which they belong. (p. viii)

The Ettrick Shepherd of the *Noctes Ambrosianae* is one of the finest and most finished creations which dramatic genius ever called into existence. . . . Bearing in mind that these dialogues are conversations on men and manners, life and literature, we may confidently affirm that nowhere within the compass of that species of composition is there to be found a character at all comparable to this one in richness and readiness of resource. In wisdom the Shepherd equals the Socrates of Plato; in humour he surpasses the Falstaff of Shakespeare. Clear and prompt, he might have stood up against Dr Johnson in close and peremptory argument; fertile and copious, he might have rivalled Burke in amplitude of declamation; while his opulent imagination and powers of comical description invest all that he utters either with a picturesque vividness, or a graphic quaintness peculiarly his own. Be the theme what it may, tragical or comical, solemn or satirical, playful or pathetic, high or low, he is always equal to the occasion. In his most grotesque delineations, his good sense never deserts him; in his most festive abandonment his morality is never at fault. He is intensely individual, and also essentially national. Hence he is real— hence he is universal. His sentiments are broad and catholic, because, careless whom he may conciliate or whom he may offend, he pours them forth without restraint—the irrepressible effusions of a strong humorous soul, which sees only with its own eyes, and feels only with its own heart. . . . [He] is always the same inimitable original—the same self-consistent Shepherd, ever buoyant amid the shifting eddies of the discourse— ever ready to hunt down a humbug, or to shower the spray of an inexhaustible fancy over the realities of life, until their truthfulness becomes more evidently true. His periods have all the ease and idiom of living speech, as distinguished from the stiffness of what may be termed spoken language, and this to an extent which is not always to be met with even in dramatic compositions of the highest order.

In another respect, the dialect of the Shepherd is peculiar; it is thoroughly Scottish, and it could not be Anglicised without losing its raciness and spoiling entirely the dramatic propriety of his character. Let it not be supposed, however, that it is in any degree *provincial,* or that it is a departure from English speech in the sense in which the dialects of Cockneydom and of certain English counties are violations of the language of England. Although now nearly obsolete, it ranks as a sister-tongue to that of England. It is a dialect consecrated by the genius of Burns, and by the usage of Scott; and now confirmed as classical by its last, and in some respects its greatest, master. This dialect was Burns's natural tongue; it was one of Sir Walter's most effective instruments; but the author of the *Noctes Ambrosianae* wields it with a copiousness, flexibility, and splendour which never have been, and probably never will be, equalled. (pp. xvii-xix)

*James Frederick Ferrier, in a preface to* The Works of Professor Wilson: "Noctes Ambrosianae," *Vol. I by John Wilson, edited by James Frederick Ferrier, William Blackwood and Sons, 1855, pp. v-xx.*

### THE NATIONAL REVIEW, LONDON (essay date 1856)

Wilson in supplying [the] demands [of *Blackwood's Edinburgh Magazine* and his professorship] gave exercise to faculties and broke into depths of his genius which he might have gone on versifying for ever, so far as appears from any competence he possessed in that line, without so much as disturbing or even finding out. He wrote tales for the magazine, in which, while his imagination had as free scope as it had in verse, his constitutional Scotticism, his shrewd observation of Scottish humours, his sensibility to the woes of real life, and his powers of eloquent description and delineation of character, had a still freer and more minute range. . . . [He wrote] subtle philosophical disquisitions, not very connected or systematic perhaps, but gleaming with brilliant ideas, and tinged throughout with that rich and highly-coloured mode of metaphysics which Coleridge was diffusing through England. . . . [Careless] of the formality and sedateness conventionally identified with the gown of a Scotch Professor . . . , he wrote papers for the magazine, in which he was seen throwing the gown off and making a football of it, . . . commenting on men and manners, on life and literature, from the point of view of an inspired king of the gypsies, or from amid the uproarious conditions of a city orgie. (pp. 177-78)

Wilson's *Isle of Palms,* and his other early poems, are far enough from exhibiting any savage or barbaric vigour. They might very well have been written by some lily-handed young gentleman. . . . A languid and monotonous sweetness is their chief characteristic; and for strength or sinew, or any kind of true human interest, not to speak of excellence even in their own kind, they are not to be compared for a moment with the weakest poems of Wordsworth. . . . [Had] Wilson stopped here, he could have been remembered only as the most feminine of the Lakists. But *Blackwood* and the Professorship came to his rescue, and he found his true element in prose. Here, while he could be soft and pathetic and Lakist when he chose, he could also break out in all directions to the full extent of his constitutional endowments. He could satirise, he could rave, he could philosophise, he could rollick in humour and phantasy, without any sense of restriction; he could deport himself altogether as a man, not only able to leap, and wrestle, and swim, and drive gigs, as well as write, but whose very peculiarity it was that he was bent on introducing the spirit of leaping, and wrestling, and swimming, and gig-driving, into literature. And, certainly, in his *Noctes,* above all, he showed what could be done in this way. It was a fresh and truly original mode of writing. . . . (pp. 182-83)

Wilson, though in the *Noctes* he brought a fulness and breadth of humanity into periodical writing which was not to be found in the contemporary periodical literature of Cockneydom, or in that of Edinburgh Whiggism, was yet not free from blame in respect of certain habits which he brought along with his merits. (p. 185)

[The] *Noctes* are full of passages showing a . . . want of fastidiousness or even of ordinary sense of conventional decorum. Olfactory allusions, and allusions to the secretions and the digestive process, abound to an extent reminding one of the ancient reputation of Edinburgh, or the still more ancient reputation of Shoreditch or Billingsgate. Were we to collect instances, we could fill a page with mere adjectives and substantives, in the use of which Wilson revels, while the majority of writers regard them as belonging to that part of the English language which is necessary for the completeness of the dictionary as a register of terms for all objects and sensations known to exist, rather than for current service in speech or polite literature. . . . [It] is evident that the habit in question was one form of Wilson's audacity, and that, looking with contempt on what he would have called "squeamishness," as part and parcel of the enervated constitution of a Whig-and-Cockney generation, he regarded an exhibition of the reverse as a sign of sound health and manly Toryism. But in any case he went too far. . . . A man is not less of a man surely for hesitating to draw images from the sewer when he can at all avoid it, any more than he would be less of a man for hesitating personally to enter a sewer when there was no special reason why he should. (pp. 185-86)

Distinct from this fault . . . was Wilson's habit of ferocious personality. . . . [Here] also, we think, he transgressed the customary bounds. And whether he transgressed the customary bounds or not, he transgressed the bounds of right and reason. . . . Where the controversy is one between obvious right and obvious wrong, between obvious wisdom and obvious idiotcy, a strong and rather direct style of personal reprobation is readily forgiven. When Wilson himself, for example, in describing the execution of the murderer Burke, lauds the multitude for their execrations of him on the scaffold, and even dwells on the picture of the murderer in the torments of hell,— the ferocity of the personality, if so it may be called, will be justified to most by the decided conviction that Wilson was in the right in *that* debate. . . . But the personalities in the *Noctes* which most attract notice were in the interest of no more vital controversy than that between Whiggism and Toryism. . . . [Wilson] rioted in Toryism as he did in every thing else; and though, all the while, he was laughing with himself at his own fury, and quite as conscious as any one could be that his hatred of Whiggism was a kind of literary simulation to promote the public fun and keep the ball incessantly going, yet often he was betrayed by the excess of his simulation into real acts of malevolence and rancour. (pp. 186-88)

[Yet this] is the mere recklessness of an acquired habit of strong speech, and no man could, on occasion, be more generous to political opponents than Wilson. "The animosities are mortal," was his own magnificent saying; "but the humanities live for ever." Accordingly, at the very time when he was mauling some of the Whigs . . . , he was paying tributes of unstinted praise to the genius of others; while even of those who were the objects of his invectives in these *Noctes,* many lived to know the man more closely, and to understand the spirit of sheer waywardness in which the invectives were uttered. This very rhetorical levity in the habit of abuse, however, made it the less excusable as a literary fault. (p. 189)

[The] Shepherd is a glorious personation. He deserves to stand as one more in the series of great comic creations bequeathed to the world by such men as Aristophanes, and Plautus, and

Rabelais, and Shakespeare, and Cervantes, and Scott. In the very conception of him there was something audacious. (p. 191)

A considerable proportion of the effect of the dialogue [of the *Noctes*] arises from the quantity of miscellaneous disquisitional matter imbedded in it, in the shape either of shrewd opinion, or of subtle philosophical doctrine, or of keen literary criticism. (p. 192)

[The] grand peculiarity of the *Noctes,* that which distinguishes them from the bulk of British prose-literature past and present, consists . . . in their being a splendid example on a large scale of what may be called prose-poetry or prose-phantasy. . . . [In prose-poetry] Wilson was certainly one of our greatest masters. He had the theory of prose-poetry; and he certainly was a far greater poet in his prose than in his verse. Even in the select company of those who might be enumerated as our prose-poets he has a peculiar place—not only as having practised the mode of literature under notice on so large a scale, but also as having practised an almost unique fashion of it. As a specimen, for instance, of what may be called the savage-sublime in literature, the *Noctes* are all but unparalleled. They are prose-poetry of the Teutonic order, as distinct from the classical. (pp. 193-94)

[All] the highest work of the *Noctes* falls to the Shepherd. And this leads us to note, as one other peculiarity about these compositions in their present form as a substantial addition to our permanent literature, the circumstance that they are a new specimen—and perhaps the last specimen on a large scale that the world can expect—of the use of the Scottish dialect for literary purposes. The Scotch of Wilson, as put into the mouth of the Ettrick Shepherd, is quite as genuine and natural and rich as that of either Burns or Scott, and possesses qualities of its own, showing that even these great masters of the national dialect had not fathomed all its resources. The fact that it was in this dialect, so uncouth to the English ear, that Wilson, Oxford man and practised English writer as he was, achieved his highest literary successes, is not unworthy of remark. It proves a certain deep congeniality between his whole intellectual mode and nature and the forms of phraseology which the Scottish language provided. It is as if, associated with the Scottish language and bound up with its very being, there were a certain traditional cast of thought incapable of being efficiently maintained in any other *ensemble* of linguistic conditions, and as if in this cast of thought Wilson was most at home. What that cast of thought is, it might be difficult to define. To a great extent its speciality seems to consist in a vein of self-irony—an incessant tendency to the humorous in the midst of the serious. (p. 198)

We have dilated sufficiently on the merits of the volumes before us to convey our impression that in virtue of them alone, apart from his other numerous writings, Wilson deserves the place which has been generally accorded to him as a man of true genius and one of the greatest British writers of the present century. Were we again, in conclusion, to revert to the negative side, we should have to point out how that frequent coarseness of speech and that exaggerated license of personal invective which marred the real worth of the *Noctes* even on their first appearance, detract still more from their literary perfection as writings destined for a longer existence. . . . [These] were perhaps only forms of what may be noted in conclusion as the prevailing defect not only of the *Noctes,* but of Wilson's whole literary life—his tendency to expatiate and luxuriantly effloresce rather than to concentrate, compress, and elaborate. It was Goethe who used to insist on a certain habit, which he

called *specification.* . . . In this habit of specification, concentration, or whatever we may call it, Wilson was certainly deficient. He rioted and luxuriated in the use of his powers; but prescribed for them no distinct succession of definite tasks, and submitted them to no rigorous discipline. Hence, in his speculative thinking, with all its subtlety, a want of that iron tenacity, the result of thought coherently prosecuted, often attained by inferior men; and hence, even in his splendid descriptions and phantasies, a frequent excess of what he himself would have called mere *sugh,* and a frequent want of that closeness, finish, and intense keenness of effect, which, with the same imagery for the material, a severer artist could have aimed at. The truth is, those who knew Wilson unanimously feel that, as relics of such a magnificent human being as he was, all the writings that he has left behind him are less than adequate. What we have as Wilson's works in 1856, including even these glorious *Noctes,* is less than Scott and others who knew the Wilson of 1816 might have expected, and did expect, from such a soul lodged in such a physique. And so, after all, the moral is, that in literature as in war, one may often back the dark-skinned little Roman, drilled and disciplined, against the large succulent Goth, with eyes azure as the heavens and locks like golden sunbeams, whose first appearance terrifies him. . . . Only, the Shepherd is certainly right in recommending open-air exercise; and every one must admit, that if the Goth were disciplined, the Roman, unless he too were of the same huge stature, would have a poor chance. (pp. 199-200)

> "The 'Noctes Ambrosianae'," *in* The National Review, *London, Vol. III, No. V, July, 1856, pp. 175-200.*

### *SOUTHERN LITERARY MESSENGER* (essay date 1859)

In [Christopher North] true merit ever found a faithful friend; but alas! for the charlatan that fell in his way. Upon such he had no mercy. He tormented them with sneers; he tortured them with sarcasm; he withered them with laughter, and annihilated them with wit. A word from him argued immediate success, while one stroke from his lash was almost certain literary death. Wilson was wanting in that keen perception and wonderful power of analysis that distinguished Lord Jeffrey, and in that research and profoundness of thought which has made Macaulay the best reviewer that ever lived. How-much-so-ever we admire Wilson, candour compels us to attribute to him a very limited knowledge of human nature. With certain phases he was as familiar as he was with the birds, flowers, skies, clouds, moors, hills and dales; but there were others with which he seemed only partially acquainted. As a proof, we need only to refer to his prose stories. In them exist no deeply laid schemes, no portrayal of human nature in its profundity, no insight into those mysterious depths of the soul, such as we find in Bulwer and Dickens. It is true he knew Sir Walter Scott, Allan Cunningham and James Hogg; William Maginn, Robert Sym and John G. Lockhart. These men he fully comprehended, because they were his friends. Wilson was too much of a Scotchman in thought, feeling and purpose, to be a strictly impartial critic. He loved England; but he adored Scotland. . . . He admired an Englishman, but he loved a Scotchman—and this partiality frequently exhibited itself in his criticisms. To him Byron was a clever poet; but how dear was James Hogg! He sympathized with the poor the world over; but it was the peasantry of his own dear mountains that awakened his interest, and claimed his tears and prayers. Though this feeling did not cause him to act with downright injustice, yet it cast a dampness upon his usual vigour, and checked the ardour of his enthusiasm. In criticising an American, Dana or Willis, for instance, he was candid, liberal, courteous and generous; but in speaking of Burns or Scott or Hogg, he mingled with that candour, liberality and generosity, so much poetry of thought, so much enthusiastic praise, and so much geniality of feeling, that one cannot fail to identify him as a son of Scotia. (pp. 407-08)

[When North speaks of Scott, we] are at a loss to know which to admire most, the criticised or the critic. In writing of Byron he viewed with the calmness of a surgeon, and summed up his conclusions with the accuracy of a great mathematician. In writing of Scott his soul burned with love for the man; all the heroes he had depicted stalked before him, and the pride which he felt in beholding Scotland towering in learning and literature, filled him with delight—even rapture. (pp. 408-09)

That some of his criticisms were severe we do not deny; but we do contend that he was generally just and generous. . . . If Wilson admired a work for its intrinsic merit, with what brilliancy could he invest the book! . . .

If he had written no other book, [*The Lights and Shadows of Scottish Life*] would have fixed his fame. It is a prose poem, breathing forth in the sweetest and most elevated strain the feelings and sentiments of a great mind; and painting scenes which awakened a sympathy in the breasts of the humble as well as in the hearts of the high-born. **"The Lilly of Liddesdale"** is a story fraught with the finest feelings of our humanity. It glows with all the gorgeous hues of a refined and brilliant imagination; it touches all the tenderest chords which bind man to man. . . .

*The Lights and Shadows* is a book of sparkling pearls. . . . None but a man whose heart was full of sympathy and love for his fellow-man could have written it. (p. 409)

[*The Trials of Margaret Lyndsay*] is the best of Wilson's stories. . . .

[It] is the most pathetic story ever penned. Like all of Wilson's stories, it teaches a lesson of morality and religion, and is mingled with a deep sadness that sometimes becomes oppressive. He loved and sympathized with the poor—hence he delighted to portray their trials—their sufferings—their meekness, and their firm and unshaken reliance on the promises of the Bible. But Wilson was not a great novelist; his characters too nearly resemble each other, and they are too good—too pure and too perfect for our sinful world. There is, also, too much sameness in style—in imagery—in comparison, and in incident. After reading one or two of his stories, the reader can always guess, with tolerable accuracy, at the main incidents of the rest. . . .

Notwithstanding these minor objections, *Margaret Lyndsay* is full of beauty and will be loved and wept over by the Scottish maidens as long as the heather blooms upon the sunny hillsides, or the Highland is the home of the humble laird. (p. 410)

Margaret Lyndsay will accomplish more in the great battle for morality, virtue and religion than a thousand ranting hypocrites will ever do. . . . As long as there are those who love the true and beautiful—the power of religion—the brilliancy of morning—the calm hush of evening, and the quiet Sabbath day, so long will Margaret Lyndsay exert a beneficial influence over the heart of sinful man, and be remembered with delight. . . .

In the *Foresters* there is not so much oppressive sadness, and it is, perhaps, more true to nature, and more interesting in incidents than the former, but taken as a whole, it is inferior to *Margaret Lyndsay*. (p. 411)

Wilson is in his native element [in *The Recreations of Christopher North*]. In these articles he appears in the full strength of his genius, and displays a power of analysis, a beauty of diction and a world of wealth that is wonderful. . . . [Christopher North is a] genial, generous and noble being, who from the fulness and freshness of his great mind, is ever ready to help the weak—to cheer the broken in spirit, and to lift up the oppressed. (pp. 411-12)

**"An Hour's Talk About Poetry,"** is the most *perfect* criticism in the English language. It is a sparkling gem in the literature of the age. In it are seen to perfection all those characteristics that made Wilson the most brilliant man of the nineteenth century. . . .

For variety [the *Noctes Ambrosianae*] have never been surpassed. . . . Amid such a profusion of pearls and diamonds, the reader never grows weary. . . . We can easily imagine a man of high culture and extensive information writing one of these articles, but we are lost in wonder and astonishment, when we know that for thirteen years they appeared regularly like the beautiful stars of night. (p. 412)

To pronounce the work a noble production is feeble praise. It is a garden, blooming with blushing roses—a kaleidoscope, reflecting an infinite variety of beauties and perfections—a peristrephic panorama, representing scenes of greatness and grandeur. Abounding in philosophy, metaphysics, politics, poetry, wit, humour, pathos and criticism, the *Noctes* present to the reader a "feast of fat things." . . . All that a refined taste can claim,—that an extensive reading can command,—that a brilliant imagination can offer,—that a glowing fancy can portray,—that a poet's soul can breathe, may here be found. (p. 413)

Ages will pass away before we will see the counterpart of John Wilson. In body and mind he was a perfect man. . . . His labours will long be remembered—and his name covered with glory, will descend to posterity an inheritance which will gladden, beautify and adorn the literature of every age. (pp. 413-14)

> *"Professor John Wilson,"* in Southern Literary Messenger, *Vol. XXVIII, June, 1859, pp. 401-14.*

**GEORGE SAINTSBURY**    (essay date 1886)

[*Saintsbury, a renowned English literary critic and historian, dismisses Wilson's poetry, fiction, and criticism, but praises the* Noctes Ambrosianae *and Wilson's miscellaneous essays describing sport and scenery for their energy, variety, and veracity. Saintsbury disputes the common notion (see excerpts above by Samuel Coleridge, 1833, and George Gilfillan, 1854) that Wilson was a "monument of wasted energies and half-developed faculty." Saintsbury expresses doubt that "there was anything in him much better than he actually did, or that he could have polished and sand-papered the faults out of his work."*]

Wilson has written [in the words of Thomas Carlyle] "intrinsically nothing that can endure," if it be judged by any severe test. An English Diderot, he must bear a harder version of the judgment on Diderot, that he had written good pages but no good book. Only very rarely has he even written good pages, in the sense of pages good throughout. The almost inconceivable haste with which he wrote . . . would not of itself account for the puerilities, the touches of bad taste, the false pathos, the tedious burlesque, the more tedious jactation which disfigure his work. A man writing against time may be driven to dulness, or commonplace, or inelegance of style; but he need never commit any of the faults just noticed. They were due beyond doubt, in Wilson's case, to a natural idiosyncrasy, the great characteristic of which Carlyle has happily hit off in the phrase, ''want of a tie-beam.'' . . . The least attractive point about Wilson's work is undoubtedly what [Carlyle] elsewhere describes as his habit of ''giving a kick'' to many men and things. There is no more unpleasant feature of the *Noctes* than the apparent inability of the writer to refrain from sly ''kicks'' even at the objects of his greatest veneration. A kind of mania of detraction seizes him at times. . . . The most disgraceful, perhaps the only really disgraceful, instance of this is the carping and offensive criticism of Scott's *Demonology,* written and published at a time when Sir Walter's known state of health and fortunes might have protected him even from an enemy, much more from a friend, and a deeply obliged friend such as Wilson. Nor is this the only fling at Scott. Wordsworth, much more vulnerable, is also much more frequently assailed; and even Shakespeare does not come off scot-free when Wilson is in his ugly moods.

It need hardly be said that I have no intention of saying that Scott or Wordsworth or Shakespeare may not be criticised. It is the way in which the criticism is done which is the crime; and for these acts of literary high treason, or at least leasing-making, as well as for all Wilson's other faults, nothing seems to me so much responsible as the want of bottom which Carlyle notes. I do not think that Wilson had any solid fund of principles, putting morals and religion aside, either in politics or in literature. He liked and he hated much and strongly, and being a healthy creature he on the whole liked the right things and hated the wrong ones; but it was for the most part a merely instinctive liking and hatred, quite un-coördinated, and by no means unlikely to pass the next moment into hatred or liking as the case might be.

These are grave faults. But for the purpose of providing that pleasure which is to be got from literature . . . , Wilson stands very high, indeed so high that he can be ranked only below the highest. . . . When Wilson begins to talk fine, when he begins to wax pathetic, and when he gets into many others of his numerous altitudes, it will behove the reader, according to his own tastes, to skip with discretion and vigour. (pp. 271-74)

His poems are now matters of interest to very few mortals. It is not that they are bad, for they are not; but that they are almost wholly without distinction. He came just late enough to have got the seed of the great romantic revival; and his verse work is rarely more than the work of a clever man who has partly learnt and partly divined the manner of Burns, Scott, Campbell, Coleridge, Wordsworth, Byron, and the rest. Nor, to my fancy, are his prose tales of much more value. (p. 277)

[If a] reader is of the modern cutlet-and-cup-of-coffee school of feeding, he will no doubt find the *Noctes* most grossly and palpably gluttonous. (p. 285)

But any one . . . who can enter into the spirit of days merrier, more leisurely, and if not less straitlaced than our own, yet lacing their laces in a different fashion, will find the *Noctes* very delightful indeed. The mere high jinks, when the secret of being in the vein with them has been mastered, are seldom unamusing, and sometimes . . . are quite admirable fooling.

No one who has an eye for the literary-dramatic can help, after a few *Noctes* have been read, admiring the skill with which the characters are at once typified and individualised, the substance which they acquire in the reader's mind, the personal interest in them which is excited. And to all this, peculiarly suited for an alterative in these solemn days, has to be added the abundance of scattered and incomplete but remarkable gems of expression and thought that come at every few pages, sometimes at every page, of the series.

Some of the burlesque narratives . . . are inimitably good, though they are too often spoilt by Wilson's great faults of prolixity and uncertainty of touch. The criticisms, of which there are many, are also extremely unequal, but not a few very fine passages may be found among them. The politics, it must be owned, are not good for much, even from the Tory point of view. But the greatest attraction of the whole, next to its sunshiny heartiness and humour, is to be found in innumerable and indescribable bits, phrases, sentences, short paragraphs, which have, more than anything out of the dialogues of the very best novels, the character and charm of actual conversation. To read a *Noctes* has . . . not much less than the effect of actually taking part in one. . . . (pp. 287-88)

This peculiar charm is of necessity wanting to the rest of Wilson's works, and in so far they are inferior to the *Noctes;* but they have compensatory merits of their own, while, considered merely as literature, there are better things in them than anything that is to be found in the colloquies of those men of great gormandising abilities—Christopher North, James Hogg, and Timothy Tickler. Of the four volumes of *Essays Critical and Imaginative,* the fourth, on Homer and his translators, with an unfinished companion piece on the Greek drama, stands by itself. . . . [It] may, I think, be put almost first in its own division of the art, though whether that division of the art is a high or low one is another question. I should not myself rank it very high. With Wilson, criticism, at least here, is little more than the eloquent expression of likes and dislikes. . . . He can preach (though with too great volubility, and with occasional faults of taste) delightful sermons about what he likes at the moment—for it is by no means always the same; and he can make formidable onslaughts with various weapons on what he dislikes at the moment—which again is not always the same. But a man so certain to go off at score whenever his likes or dislikes are excited, and so absolutely unable to check himself whenever he feels tempted thus to go off, lacks the very first qualifications of the critic. . . . His most famous sentence ''The Animosities are mortal, but the Humanities live for ever'' is certainly noble. But it would have been better if the Humanities had oftener choked the Animosities at their birth. (pp. 288-90)

[In Wilson's essays on Wordsworth, most written prior to 1822,] it is evident that he is ambitiously groping after a more systematic style of criticism than he found in practice to be possible for him. Although he elsewhere scoffs at definitions, he tries to formulate very precisely the genius of Scott, of Byron, and of Wordsworth; he does his best to connect his individual judgments with these formulas; he shuns mere verbal criticism, and (to some extent) mere exaltation or depreciation of particular passages. But it is quite evident that he is ill at ease; and I do not think that any one now reading [his earliest essay on Wordsworth] can call it a successful one, or can attempt to rank it with those which, from different points of view, Hazlitt and De Quincey . . . wrote about Wordsworth. Indeed, Hazlitt is the most valuable of all examples for a critical comparison with Wilson; both being violent partisans and crotcheteers, both being animated with the truest love of poetry, but the one possessing and the other lacking the "tie-beam" of a consistent critical theory.

A dozen years later Wilson had cast his slough, and had become the autocratic, freespoken, self-constituted dictator, Christopher North. He was confronted with the very difficult problem of Mr. Tennyson's poems. . . . [They] seemed to him to be the work of a "cockney" . . . , and he was irritated by some silly praise which had been given to them. So he set to work, and perpetrated the queerest jumble of sound and unsound criticism that exists in the archives of that art. . . . [To] borrow one of his own favourite words, he simply "plouters"—splashes and flounders about without any guidance of critical theory. . . . If he does not exactly blunder right (and he sometimes does that), he constantly blunders wrong—goes wrong, that is to say, without any excuse of theory or general view. That is not criticism.

We shall not find matters much mended from the strictly critical point of view, when we come, ten years later, to the article on [Macaulay's] "Lays." . . . [He] goes appallingly wrong all through on general critical points.

Yet, according to his own perverse fashion, he never goes wrong without going right. Throughout his critical work there are scattered the most intelligent ideas, the neatest phrases, the most appreciative judgments. (pp. 291-94)

Wilson's renown as an athlete, a sportsman, and a lover of nature, who had a singular gift in expressing his love, has not yet died; and there is an ample audience now for men who can write about athletics, about sport, and about scenery. Nor is it questionable that on these subjects he is seen, on the whole, at his best. True, his faults pursue him even here, and are aggravated by a sort of fashion of the time which made him elaborately digress into politics, into literature, even (God rest his soul!) into a kind of quasi-professional and professorial sermonising on morals and theology, in the midst of his sporting articles. But the metal more attractive of the main subject would probably recommend these papers widely, if they were not scattered pell-mell about the *Essays Critical and Imaginative,* and the *Recreations of Christopher North.* . . . Of the scenery of loch or lake, of hill or mountain, he was at once an ardent lover and a describer who has never been equalled. His accustomed exaggeration and false emphasis are nowhere so little perceptible as [in these papers]. . . . The progress of the sportsman has never been better given than in **"Christopher North in his Sporting Jacket."** In **"The Moors"** the actual sporting part is perhaps a little spoilt by the affectation of infallibility, qualified it is true by an aside or two, which so often mars the Christopherian utterances. But Wilson's description has never been bettered. (pp. 295-98)

I do not think he was a good reviewer, even after making allowance for the prejudices and partisanships of the time. . . . He is too prone to the besetting sins of reviewing—the right hand defections and left hand fallings off, which, being interpreted, consist first in expressing agreement or disagreement with the author's views, and secondly in digressing into personal statements of one's own views of things connected with them instead of expounding more or less clearly what the book is, and addressing oneself to the great question, Is it a good or a bad piece of work according to the standard which the author himself strove to reach? I have said that I do not think he was on the whole a good critic. . . . That he was neither a great, nor even a very good poet or taleteller, I have no doubt

whatever. But this leaves untouched the attraction of his miscellaneous work, and its suitableness for the purpose of recreation. For that purpose I think it to be among the very best work in all literature. Its unfailing life and vigour, its vast variety, the healthy and inspiriting character of the subjects with which in the main it deals, are the characteristics which make its volumes easy-chair books of the best order. Its beauty no doubt is irregular, faulty, engaging rather than exquisite, attractive rather than artistically or scientifically perfect. I do not know that there is even any reason to join in the general lament over Wilson as being a gigantic failure, a monument of wasted energies and half-developed faculty. I do not at all think that there was anything in him much better than he actually did, or that he ever could have polished and sand-papered the faults out of his work. It would pretty certainly have lost freshness and vigour; it would quite certainly have been less in bulk, and bulk is a very important point in literature that is to serve as recreation. It is to me not much less certain that it never would have attained the first rank in symmetry and order. I am quite content with it as it is, and I only wish that still more of it were easily accessible. (pp. 301-03)

*George Saintsbury, "Christopher North," in* Macmillan's Magazine, *Vol. LIV, July, 1886 (and reprinted as "Wilson," in his* Essays in English Literature: 1780-1860, *Percival and Co., 1890, pp. 270-303).*

## HENRY A. BEERS   (essay date 1893)

The glee, the abandon, with which Wilson and Lockhart and Maginn poured out ridicule on a cockney or a Whig, their uproarious contempt, the names that they called him, the blackguardly epithets that they applied to him, the personalities of their attack—these are luxuries that no reputable review can now afford. And yet "Christopher North" was not an unkindly man. . . . The first age of the great modern reviews and magazines was an age of kicks and rough horse-play. . . . Libel suits and challenges rained upon magazine editors. . . .

It would not be fair to hold Wilson responsible for all this, but he was largely contributory to it. It was a generation of fighters, and Christopher loved a fight almost as much as he loved trout-fishing, or deer-stalking, or a leaping-match, or a cocking-main, or a drinking-bout. . . . There was no malice in the "veiled editor" of "Blackwood." His hatred of Whigs was official. The **"Chaldee Manuscript"** was conceived in a spirit of noisy fun. The same spirit inspired the roistering and convivial Toryism of the **"Noctes Ambrosianae,"** and the roaring choruses that accompanied the clink of glasses in Ambrose's snuggery. The criticism in "Blackwood's," the roasting of Hazlitt and Moore, the sneers at Hunt's "Rimini," were simply other expressions of Wilson's love of fighting, his wild fun and high animal spirits. (p. 361)

Like Charles Kingsley, of whom [Wilson] constantly reminds one, he was always a good deal of a boy. . . . They were alike . . . in the eager, impulsive, uneven way in which they poured themselves out upon paper; in a certain illogical cast of mind. . . . Wilson's Toryism was an affair of instinct and temperament rather than of reasoned convictions. Indeed, he was a man of no opinions, in the strict sense of that word. Prejudices he had, tastes, whims, likes, and dislikes, but, properly speaking, no opinions. (pp. 361-62)

Christopher was a great creature, and there is imperishable stuff in the **"Noctes."** That famous series has not the even excellence—the close grain—of Holmes's "Breakfast-Table" papers. There is too much of it, and it should be read with judicious skipping. A large part of the dialogue is concerned with matters of temporary interest. The bacchanalian note in it becomes at times rather forced, and the reader wearies of the incessant consumption of powldoodies, porter, and Welsh rabbits. But the Ettrick Shepherd is a dramatic creation of a high order, and the vehicle of wit, eloquence, and poetry always racy, if not always fine. The same exuberance, for good and for bad, characterizes the **"Recreations"** and the other miscellaneous papers, which place their author high, though not among the highest, in the line of British essayists. Christopher was, after all, most at home in his sporting-jacket, and his outdoor papers are the best—**"The Moors," "The Stroll to Grasmere,"** and the rest. His literary criticism, though interesting as the utterance of a rich personality, is seldom wise or sure. (p. 362)

> *Henry A. Beers, "'Crusty Christopher' (John Wilson)," in* The Century *(copyright, 1893, by The Century Co.), Vol. 45, No. 3, January, 1893, pp. 361-62.*

## GEORGE DOUGLAS   (essay date 1897)

[*Douglas's* The Blackwood Group *is an important study of the literary circle involved with* Blackwood's Magazine. *Douglas finds that the* Noctes Ambrosianae, *"though they may still be dipped into with pleasure, will scarcely stand critical examination nowadays." He maintains that Wilson's "injudicious critics," particularly James Frederick Ferrier (see excerpt above, 1855) have done him an injustice by judging the* Noctes *as permanent literary contributions when they were never intended by the author to be more than hastily written essays "concerned with topics and persons of long since exhausted interest." Douglas defends the lack of polish in Wilson's writing by asserting that quantity, rather than quality, was the distinguishing characteristic of Wilson's genius.*]

Of course [the *Isle of Palms*] irresistibly recalls Bernardin's masterpiece [*Paul et Virginie*], and, judging between the two, it must be acknowledged that in originality and artistic perfection the Frenchman's prose has greatly the advantage. But it is noticeable and must be counted to Wilson's credit that, whilst profoundly influenced by pre-Revolutionary thought, he never, even at this early period of his life, allows himself to be led away from the paths prescribed by virtue and religion. His healthy instinct, fortified by excellent training, sufficed to show him that anarchy in the moral world is no more a part of nature's scheme than is habitual excess; and thus the worship of Liberty and the State of Nature, which afterwards led to such questionable results in the cases of Byron and of Shelley, left him entirely unharmed. (pp. 16-17)

[*The City of the Plague*] forms a startling contrast to the *Isle of Palms,* for, in place of nature at its softest and sentiment sweet to the point of cloying, we are now presented with the gloomiest and ghastliest of studies in the charnel-house style. Several of the scenes depicting the madness of the London streets at the period of the great pestilential visitation are by no means without a certain power, which, however, inclines to degenerate into violence. Two young sailors—certainly most unlike to all preconceived notions of the seamen of the age of Blake—help to supply the necessary relief and 'sentiment,' of which there is no lack. But, from beginning to end, there is little or nothing truly poetical in the tragedy. The movement of its blank verse is most frequently harsh and jolting, and

serves to confirm one in the opinion that the author was well-inspired when he abandoned poetry. . . . Nor do the minor poems which make up the remainder of the volume show cause for altering this judgment. Certainly they abound, even to excess, in evidence of the love of nature; but that alone never yet made a poet. (p. 19)

[The] real significance of [*Blackwood's Magazine*] in its early days consists, not in stories of challenges sent or damages paid, but in the fact that it afforded to John Wilson a first opportunity of giving full and free play to his talents. The characteristic of his genius was not so much *fineness* as abundance, and thus we may believe that his gain from the new stimulus to constant and rapid production more than balanced his loss from absence of opportunities of polishing his work. Certainly from the time of his active and regular employment, he began to throw off those tendencies to affectation and philandering which had characterised his early efforts in the 'Lake' school, and though he never quite lost the habit of as the French say 'caressing his phrase,' he became from henceforth more virile, more himself. (p. 23)

[Wilson's novels and stories] consist uniformly of tales of pastoral or humble life, and the author has recorded that his object in writing them was to speak of the 'elementary feelings of the human soul in isolation, under the light of a veil of poetry.' The impression which they produce upon a reader of the present day is that this programme has been but too systematically adhered to. The stories themselves do not lack interest, and their motives are at all times human; but they are deliberately localized in some other world than ours, and if there thence ensues a certain aesthetic gain, it is accompanied by a more than proportionate loss in vraisemblance and in moral force. To speak more plainly, if the world of Wilson's tales is a better world than ours, it yet remains an artificial one, his stories develope in accordance with the rules of a preconceived ideal, and a weakening of their interest is the result. For though many a writer has seen life in a way of his own, Wilson seems to have deliberately set himself to see it in a way belonging to somebody else. In fact, throughout [his novels and tales], he aspires to appear in the character of a prose Wordsworth; but he is a Wordsworth who has lost the noble plainness of his original, and though his actual style is less marred by floridness and redundancy here than elsewhere, still the vices of prettiness, self-consciousness, artificiality, and sentiment suffice to stamp his work as an imitation, decadent from the lofty source of its inspiration. (pp. 29-30)

The tone of [*The Foresters*] is peaceful and soothing; it inculcates cheerfulness and resignation, and holds up for our edification a picture of that contentment which springs from the practice of virtue. A group of faultless creatures—for none but the subordinate characters have any faults—pursue the tenor of their lives amid fair scenes of nature, and, when sorrow or misfortune falls to their lot, meet it with an inspiring fortitude. To scoff at such a book were to supply proof of incompetence in criticism—of which the very soul consists in sympathy with all that is sincere in spirit and not inadequate in execution. . . .

[The *Trials of Margaret Lyndsay*] is that which most forcibly conveys the lessons common to all—the teaching of Wordsworth, that is to say, as made plain by a sympathetic disciple. (p. 31)

[From] trial to trial do we follow [Margaret Lyndsay] until at last she is left in possession of a very modest share of felicity, whilst from her story we learn the lesson of the duties of courage and cheerfulness, the consolations of virtue, and the healing power of nature. (p. 32)

Scattered over the pages of the *Noctes,* there are no doubt some shrewd and pregnant observations upon writers and upon literature. But these sparse grains of salt are not enough to preserve the general fabric from decay; whilst the more numerous errors of judgment in which his work abounds require no pointing out. As a reviewer North was not lacking in discrimination, as may be seen in the historical though generally misconceived essay on Tennyson; and, granted a really good opportunity . . . , no man knew better how to avail himself of it. The pages signed by him also afford abundant evidence of the gentleness, generosity, and enthusiasm of his spirit. But when so much has been said, what remains to be added? Of stimulus to the reader, of conspicuous insight into the subject discussed, we find but little.

Turning to the essays, collected under the title of **'Recreations of Christopher North,'** we sometimes see the author to better advantage, as, for instance, when he dons his 'Sporting Jacket,' and recounts in mock-heroic style the Sportsman's Progress. The subject was one which keenly appealed to him, rousing all the enthusiasm of his perfervid nature, and some very bright and characteristic pages are the result. (pp. 40-1)

[The] far-famed *Noctes Ambrosianae,* by much the most celebrated of Wilson's writings, though they may still be dipped into with pleasure, will scarcely stand critical examination nowadays. Of course, from their very nature, they have come to labour under the disadvantage of being largely concerned with topics and persons of long since exhausted interest. And, again, their convivial setting, which pleased in its own day, is now probably by many looked upon askance, and that, it must be confessed, not without some show of excuse. If this were all, it would be well. . . . [But] Wilson wrote his dialogues hastily and presumably wrote them for the moment, so that to judge them as permanent contributions to literature is to judge them by a standard contemplated not by the author, but by his injudicious critics. Amongst these, Professor Ferrier . . . most confidently claims that they possess solid and lasting qualities, and in the front rank of these qualities he places humour and dramatic power. Now to us, except in outward form, the *Noctes* appear almost anything rather than dramatic; they are even less dramatic than the conversation-pieces of Thomas Love Peacock. It is true that of the two principal talkers one speaks Scotch and the other English; but in every other respect they might exchange almost any of their longest and most important speeches without the smallest loss to characterisation. The same authority (I use the word in a purely empirical sense) enthusiastically lauds the creation of The Shepherd; and upon him it is true that, by dint of insistence on two or three superficial mannerisms, a certain shadowy individuality has been conferred. But surely it is needless to point out that a label is not a personality, and that this sort of thing is something quite apart from dramatic creation. The critic then goes on to say that 'in wisdom the Shepherd equals the Socrates of Plato; in humour he surpasses the Falstaff of Shakespeare.' The last part of the sentence strikes us as even more surprising than the first, for had our opinion of the imaginary revellers at Ambrose's been asked we should have had to confess that, though they possess high spirits in abundance and a certain sense of the ludicrous, of humour in the true sense— of the humour, I won't say of a Sterne, but of a Michael Scott— all are alike entirely destitute. And one may even add that with persons of equally high spirits such is almost always the case.

Well then, it may be asked, if they lack both humour and dramatic power, in what qualities, pray, do these world-famed dialogues excel? The answer is, of course, that in brilliant intellectual and rhetorical display the *Noctes* are supreme. Yet here, also, there is often about them something too much of deliberate and self-conscious fine-writing. And yet, even today, when tastes have changed and fashions altered, the exuberance of their eloquence is hard to withstand, and in reading them we sometimes almost believe that we are touched when in reality we are merely dazzled. This dazzling quality is not one of the highest in literature: with the single possible exception of Victor Hugo, the greatest writers have always been without it. But it pervades, floods, overwhelms the *Noctes.* It is a somewhat barren, and unendearing quality at best; yet, after all, it is an undoubted manifestation of intellectual power; and whatever it may be worth, let us give Wilson full credit for having excelled in it. (pp. 43-5)

[If] Wilson himself, as apart from his writings, be indeed, as we believe him to be, an immortal figure, by releasing him from the burden of ill-judged praise which like a mill-stone hangs about his neck, and by setting him in his true light, we shall have done him no disservice. On the poetic imagination, then, he looms as one heroically proportioned; whilst more practical thinkers will cherish his memory as that of a most brilliant contributor to the periodical literature of his day, a great inspirer of youth, and a standard and pattern to his countrymen of physical and intellectual manhood. (pp. 45-6)

> *George Douglas, "John Wilson," in his* The "Blackwood" Group, *Charles Scribner's Sons, 1897, pp. 9-46.*

**ARTHUR CECIL HILLIER**   (essay date 1899)

There is possibly no one of whom it can be said one half so truly as of Wilson, the famous "Christopher North," that he became in the end the victim of his own eloquence. Once there was hardly any influence so puissant as his, hardly any name so authoritative, hardly any figure so commanding. . . . He had something in him that was well-nigh epic, a supreme and noble carelessness, the dash and eagerness of a mediaeval Norseman. . . . Yet it must be confessed that he was but too frequently run away with by this Berserkir impetuosity of his. . . . Wilson never knew when to stop.

The worst of it is, too, that although the charm of this reckless, magnificent personality is by no means altogether lost to us, not very much of it can really be said to have escaped into his writings, effusive and frequently splendid as they are. (p. 64)

Wilson's manifestations of himself are imperfect and incomplete, and what cast a spell over men, his coevals, has evaporated largely with the inevitable lapse of time. The glamour has gone; the prepossession has vanished; the magic is no more; and his literary work must conquer by the mere might of his pen, or not at all. That work, unquestionably most unequal and yet magnificent at its best, falls conveniently into three divisions.

There are the famous **'Noctes Ambrosianae,'** compact of boisterous fun and eloquence, and blending paradoxes with potations and the most peremptory and dogmatic philosophy with an almost Brobdingnagian delight of meat and drink. . . . Next in order of merit, come **'The Recreations of Christopher North'** and **'The Imaginative Essays,'** the best of which treat of sport, wild scenery and wild animal life. And then there are **'The**

**Critical Essays,'** which are rather defective in subtlety, but which were a great power in their own day. His verse and his novels need hardly be ranked as a fresh division of his work; they may be thrown rather into a kind of mental appendix, although the novels and tales—his verse is merely nugatory—exhibit certain of his weaknesses, such as his pleasure in elegiac, lachrymose sentiment, far more unguardedly than anything else that is his.

The **'Noctes'** are by no means perfect themselves, but for the chief defect in them Wilson was not in any sense responsible. They were not written to reappear as a substantive collection, and . . . [they] are unusually bulky for a work that has no sort of inner growth or evolution, no natural climax and no inevitable dissolution. Nevertheless this becomes a kind of merit in its way, for the perpetual discursiveness of the **'Noctes'** and their continuous discontinuity render them one of the best of bedside books. The entirely casual and opportunist and vagabond nature of the inspiration makes it possible to read in these dialogues at any moment, with no necessary acquaintance with what has gone before, and not the least anticipation of what is likely to follow; and, accordingly, few serial nondescript publications have so entirely the charm of variety and surprise as these same miscellaneous and multifarious entertainments. (p. 65)

At all events the **'Noctes'** were an ideal medium for Wilson, because the clash of argument and the necessary alternations of dialogue placed a curb upon an incorrigible diffuseness of style which elsewhere is his very worst failing. . . . (p. 66)

James Hogg, the Ettrick Shepherd, is Wilson's supreme triumph, although the portrait was glorified, idealised and transfigured as all admit who knew much of the original. . . .

The finest flights at [the] hilarious, glorified, uproarious meetings [of Christopher North, the Ettrick Shepherd, and Timothy Tickler] are almost invariably [the Shepherd's]. . . . He is perhaps too eloquent in this literary presentment of him; but, at the same time, it does convey the idea of a man rapt away and borne along by some genius or demon within, and this is heightened by his rusticity in a way that is singularly piquant and arresting. (pp. 67-8)

[With De Quincey,] the opium-eater, Wilson is not entirely successful, and, after a couple of evenings, he suddenly vanishes in a thoroughly De Quinceyan fashion, which is perhaps the most characteristic thing in the portrait. Better, at all events, than anything put into De Quincey's mouth is the shepherd's description of the Opium-Eater's abiding sense of sublimity. . . . (p. 68)

[For] the sake of such outpourings and the really genuine fun that is sometimes in the **'Noctes,'** it is more or less easy to pardon a somewhat obstreperous humour, never vapid, but sinning in the more old-fashioned and perhaps excusable extreme of being plethoric and quite unequivocally farcical. . . . Never has one read before of any conviviality so vehement, occasionally so spirited in its stupendous exaggeration, and so obstinately carnivorous.

Moreover, it is seldom Wilson's criticism of literature or his largeness of speculation that is in the main attractive. In matters of censorship, in the analysis of genius based on patient or fine sympathy, he is too impulsive and perhaps too prejudiced to succeed. He knew what was bad and could do terrible execution upon literary pretenders. He did not always know what was good or how good it was, and one never expects from him the

delicate discrimination of Lamb, the mastery of Hazlitt, or those jets of light that De Quincey will turn quite suddenly upon any theme at the last despairing moment when he seems to have lost himself too hopelessly.

But for spirit and a certain demoniac energy, for rapid, vivid, impassioned descriptions of sport and scenery, and for pictures dashed off with a large and sweeping brush, Wilson has hardly a rival that he needs to fear, if he has one at all. (pp. 68-9)

Connected closely with Wilson's love of scenery is his passion for sport, and he is too honest to conceal its cruelty. He was by nature a kindly man. Yet he has at times a touch of something savage and primitive as though he had wildfire in his blood, and morally reprehensible as it may be, a note of barbaric, exultant joy in devastation gives extraordinary effectiveness to his too frequent and not wholly Christian apotheosis of slaughter. This does not prevent him from having the most intimate sympathy with wild animal life. In **'Christopher in his Aviary'** he displays a passionate power of identifying himself with the keen, rending delight of the hawking bird nesting in a coign of vantage amid sterile, fissured cliffs, and if he seldom achieves the more delicate felicities of style, the more quiet and crepuscular effects, there is none like him for rendering the acrid smell of the lair or the eyrie. The two unsurpassable things in the **'Noctes'** are the Shepherd's adventure among the crags when attempting to rifle an eagle's nest, and the reminiscence, mainly humorous, that he professes to have of ante-natal experiences as a lion's whelp.

Perhaps the passage about the eagles is in some respects the finer from its grim reality, and the high, shrill and fierce note maintained in it throughout. (pp. 69-70)

To Wilson's purely critical writings one would not turn for fine appreciation, though it would be ungrateful not to remember that he did inestimable service in his day by championing the poetry of Wordsworth, Coleridge, and even Shelley, with all the popular and stimulating resources of his powerful rhetoric, and yet more by the influence which his name and reputation could not fail to insure. . . .

The most notorious of Wilson's critical performances, however, was the famous article [published in *Blackwood's* in May, 1832] in which he reviews Tennyson's early volume of 1830 [*Poems, Chiefly Lyrical*]. Yet the review was not unjust. Some of the things singled out for ridicule deserved it, and were suppressed or altered in later editions; others were more or less nugatory; and, perhaps, the only very gross blunder was to hold up to obloquy the lovely lines known as 'The Dying Swan.' (p. 71)

Nevertheless, this review is one more sample of the old bad style of criticism. Christopher poses as the literary chief of an older generation who is justified in taking up a spoilt and petted young poet, shaking him as a dog does a rat, and setting him down in his proper place. He is full of praise indeed for such triumphs as 'Mariana,' and 'The Recollections of the Arabian Nights,' but he forgets that a man capable already of such work, was deserving of respect even in his failures, and though not exempt from the finer kinds of irony, ought certainly to have been attacked, if at all, with a rapier rather than a battle-axe, to say nothing of a bludgeon. (pp. 71-2)

But impulsiveness was the true cause of all Wilson's mistakes, and Professor Hertford is possibly right when he hints that it was geniality and expansiveness, in other words licentious good-nature, which induced him to rank Moore above Burns, and place Joanna Baillie on a level with Æschylus and Shakespeare. The same effusive good-nature it is which induces him not merely to condone the errors of Burns, but to enter into an elaborate comparison between this poet and, of all people in the world, Doctor Johnson! (p. 72)

Yet the final word about Wilson's criticism must always be that it was upon the whole beneficently exercised, and that he did work which critics infinitely more gifted, such as Lamb and Hazlitt, were unable to do in regard to the great outside public; because they had not the authority.

Of his own poetry there is nothing to be said. The authentic vibration of the line is not in it, nor the true heart-beat of verse. Nor are his **'Tales'** and his novels really successful. Indeed, for a writer of his thrilling powers he is singularly tame in fiction; and one of his short stories, **'The Lily of Liddisdale,'** might be an exquisite, a miraculously clever, burlesque upon all the others, if it were not too obviously offered in the most implicit good faith and put in the most conspicuous place in the volume. It is not too much to say, in fact, that **'The Lily'** is the extreme example of the length to which a man of genius may go without knowing that he is absurd. (pp. 72-3)

['**The Lily'**] seems to have just sincerity enough to render the satire on the short story of the age most exquisitely poignant. But nothing could be more inauspicious as the initial effort of narrative in a volume of serious tales. It must be admitted, however, that Wilson's other stories can be taken gravely; only, after making every allowance for inevitable differences of style and technique, they do not display any real capacity for fiction. (pp. 73-4)

[In] fiction the fault of Wilson is that he is so conventional, even where his plots are strewn with the ruins of the seventh commandment. Nevertheless, there are still advocates to be found for the better of his two longer novels, **'The Trials of Margaret Lyndsay.'** This has indeed real pathos, although a reader should hardly approach it expecting to receive such keen emotion as he may have experienced in reading 'Sylvia's Lovers' or almost any of the stories of Mrs. Gaskell.

Taking his work as a whole, however, he has wonderful sweep of wing, and he always brings with him the atmosphere of the moors, the sense of bleak, shrewd mountain air, richened with the scent of peat and heather. But his manner, as a rule, is rather energetic than fine; at least it is so where he is not dealing with external nature, and it is a certain want of fineness that distinguishes him from the three or four contemporary masters of prose who stand beyond cavil upon a higher plane. He was not, for example, a man of such a rare and exquisite spirit as Lamb. . . . There is no single place of which Wilson can give the whole genius as Lamb seems to give the soul of old London. . . . (p. 74)

Neither has he like Hazlitt a completely sustained and overmastering style, terse, mordant, cutting, closely woven in texture, and so full of the marrow of idiom and the rude glow of life, that his panegyrics are flushed with the freshest colour and his denunciations written in vitriol and sulphuric acid.

Nor is he like De Quincey the master of a rich, dim, dreamy rhetoric, a processional pomp of clauses, subdued and mellowed to the very finest musical pitch, an emblazoned but not garish pageantry of phrase; although he has certainly not De Quincey's gossiping irresponsibility of temperament. And . . . he has—in mere authorship, for it is not a question of social attraction—none of the imperious personality of Lan-

dor writing upon tablets of granite and of marble and assiduously burying them in the sands of the desert.

He is not to be named with these: he has not often their consummate felicities and finalities of expression; he does not mint his paragraphs with an unmistakable individuality, nor make an image of himself in language as undeniable and less perishable than his bodily form. One knows instinctively that a misplaced comma or an omitted colon would have caused De Quincey sleepless nights, because it would have defaced the character of a sentence. But, as often as not, a paragraph in Wilson will be punctuated by a flight of ardent dashes, although where it is good his prose is singularly easy and dignified in movement notwithstanding its fervour.

Above all, Wilson has not the solidity of any of these great writers. He is altogether more unsound and unsafe, and can be merely featureless and fatiguing. His best work is rarely so delicate as theirs and there is far less of it. (pp. 74-5)

Still for rapid, daring, vehement, electrifying bursts of straightforward rushing eloquence, as a matter of course defective in the very best kinds of chiselled or intricate beauty, but full of splendour, he is, where really inspired, unrivalled in his own generation; and the last impressions of him left on a reader's mind are those of amazing energy and fire. (p. 75)

> *Arthur Cecil Hillier, "'Christopher North'," in* Temple Bar, *Vol. CXVI, No. 458, January, 1899, pp. 64-75.*

**JOHN S. FLORY**   (essay date 1904)

Always impressionable and responsive, [Wilson] possessed the faculty also of distinguishing the true from the false in any subject. This ability, coupled with his remarkable ease and fluency of expression, at once qualified him eminently for success in the broad field of literature. (p. 448)

While he is always interesting, fresh, and original, it is his critical work chiefly that ranks him with the greater essayists of the nineteenth century, and gives him a permanent place in literature.

In several ways Wilson was eminently endowed with critical powers. His remarkably sympathetic nature brought him into such a spiritual rapport with an author and his work as few men could have experienced. In a less independent character than Wilson's, this quality would have produced a mere eulogist, wholly unfitted as a critic. By his power of insight he was intellectually quick to distinguish between what was profound and what was mere fog in the mind of the writer. His hatred of all kinds of sham and insincerity made him apt to detect any false sentiment and tricks of thought or expression, which were sure to bring down with emphasis the cudgel of his condemnation.

It must be admitted that at times the very wealth of his faculties led him into extravagances and inconsistencies, for which it is not easy to excuse him. Yet it should be remembered that those were intense times, and wars of words were common. Although his harsh critical strictures frequently raised a storm of anger against him, he did not find pleasure in "whipping" simply for its own sake. All sorts of cant and artificiality he heartily despised, and his one aim as a critic was to cultivate a taste for that which is true, direct, and manly in literature, as in life. It may be possible that he was sometimes over-harsh in his methods of lashing or shaming a young author out of a false position; but if the chastisement was severe, it was so because of his sincere desire to turn youthful genius into right paths.

The case of Tennyson may be cited as a concrete example of Wilson's method, and of his influence as a critic. Tennyson's first volume of poems that attracted notice was that of 1830. . . . In all his censure, the critic assumed a paternal attitude toward the poet, spoke to him in terms of authority, and admonished him with the loving interest of a father.

In commendation of Tennyson's merits, Wilson was fully as enthusiastic as he had been severe in the censure of his faults. He perceived, in the better verses, the promise of a great poet. Sincerity, individuality, and simplicity, he pointed out as the impulses for the young poet to follow. And he was not slack in predicting the poet's future greatness, if he would but develop his powers in a natural way. It says much for the critical ability of Wilson that he discerned in Tennyson, at this early date, the future laureate, and foretold the time when, with proper development, millions would join him in proclaiming that "Alfred Tennyson is a poet." (pp. 452-53)

A service not very different from that done for Tennyson, Wilson performed also for our American poet, Bryant. . . . Up to the time of Wilson's review, it was generally held that the American poet's treatment of nature was in every way original, and, since the poems were short, therefore condensed. Wilson showed that in both of these respects the judgment was wrong. (p. 454)

Wilson bestowed upon Bryant the richest praise for his sincerity and the simplicity of his manner. He showed that the introduction of the American background into poetry is Bryant's peculiar work. The poet's independence in seeing nature with his own eyes and portraying it as he saw it deserves high praise, and Wilson was not loath to bestow it. So clearly did he define Bryant's position as poet, both historically and essentially, that many mooted questions as to his work were cleared up once for all.

It must not be inferred, from what has been said, that Wilson's critical judgments were never mistaken. Neither should it be assumed that as an essayist he was without faults. Indeed, with all his merits, he had one or two faults of a flagrant sort. His too great severity has already been referred to. While his stinging criticisms generally were just and helpful, it is also unfortunately true that there are instances when his assaults were coarse beyond extenuation, and from which beneficial results were not to be expected.

As an artist in literature, the worst thing that can be said about Wilson is, that his work lacks literary form. His paragraphing is sometimes far from good, and his sentences frequently leave the impression of carelessness and haste. These faults are not to be wondered at, however, when we consider the rapidity with which nearly all of his work was produced. But when all has been said for and against his work, the fact remains that Professor Wilson was one of the most remarkable men of his time. Had he written nothing but **"Noctes Ambrosianae,"** he would be ranked among the wits of the nineteenth century. Had he applied himself to poetry, he might have become a formidable rival of Scott in his own territory. If he had confined himself to practical politics, he could have become, if his published essays may serve as a basis of judgment, an authority on jurisprudence and political relations. In the world of imagination, he suggests De Quincey in the fantasies and vagaries of the dream world of unreality. Had he produced nothing

except those discriminating and stimulating criticisms, he would unquestionably be one of the noteworthy and, to us, one of the best beloved of English critics. Should it so have happened that he had not written at all, Professor Wilson would still be remembered as a popular and inspiring lecturer who filled a chair in the University of Edinburgh. And I may yet add that, had he neither written nor lectured on philosophy, the world would not yet have forgotten him as one of the great conversationalists and engaging personalities which the first half of the nineteenth century produced. A man that could perform so many things and do them all well is not to be quarreled with because he did not do everything in a faultless manner. (pp. 454-55)

*John S. Flory, "John Wilson As an Essayist," in*
The Sewanee Review *(reprinted by permission of the editor; published 1904 by The University of the South),*
*Vol. XII, No. 4, October, 1904, pp. 448-55.*

## C. T. WINCHESTER (essay date 1910)

If we would estimate the literary work of Wilson, we must credit him, first of all, with having found out how to edit a magazine. For the instant success of *Blackwood's,* as well as its continued prosperity for more than twenty years, was due more largely to Wilson than to Lockhart. There is doubtless more finish in Lockhart's work; his keen and caustic satire is cruelly effective, and he was, I think, an abler critic than Wilson. But Wilson had a more intimate sympathy with his readers, a quicker sense of what would interest or amuse them at the moment; and above all he had an exuberant vitality, an immense volume of good spirits that seemed to pervade the magazine. He may almost be said to have introduced a new style into English periodical writing; he shocked the proprieties hardly more by his matter than by his manner. His style is colloquial to the last degree; it is the man himself. The personal note is dominant, to be sure, in all the essayists of the period; but the others, Hazlitt, Lamb, De Quincey, . . . recognized literary standards, admired and imitated certain literary models. Wilson, on the other hand, simply let himself go. He is sentimental, or abusive, or hilarious, as the mood takes him; but he is always rhetorical, profuse, careless of decorum. Of course in such writing you will not expect nicety of judgment, chasteness or precision of phrase. Wilson writes as the traditional Irishman played the violin, "by main strength." But there is great personal force in such a manner; it is big John Wilson talking, declaiming, jesting, shouting from the page. The unpardonable sin in the columns of a magazine is dulness; and Wilson is never dull.

As to the permanent literary value of his work, that is another matter. For one thing it was usually done in too much haste to be lasting. . . . The very qualities that gave its buoyancy to this writing at the time are peculiarly liable to evaporate in the course of a century. The effervescent humor has lost its bubble now, and tastes a little flat on the palate. A style so highly exhilarated doesn't keep well. And what is worse, this exaggerated animation suggests something factitious; we suspect it to be got up to order, like the devotional moods some pious people induce by rubbing their hands together. The man, we say, makes too much fuss over expression, and although going at full speed, doesn't seem to get on. Nor is it only his form that suffers; his opinions are often ill-considered, his critical verdicts hasty and sometimes contradictory, his rough-and-ready censure of men and measures rash and indiscriminate. His energy has too little intellectual quality; it often seems nothing but the expression of a full and healthy physical life. We shall have to admit that in all respects Wilson was a good deal of a Philistine. (pp. 179-82)

But the most serious discount from the permanent value of Wilson's work is the lack of any central purpose. . . . Wilson, so far as I can discover, had no message. He had to keep the printer's devil in copy, and he took care that what he furnished should not be dull; but it is vivacity rather than earnestness that his writing shows. As leading editor of a pronounced Tory magazine, he was bound to observe a journalist's consistency; but while we need not question the sincerity of his views, the eagerness of his political writing seems to proceed rather from partisan feeling than from any profound conviction. He loved the stir and warmth of controversy, and with his cocksure opinions and his command of imaginative epithet, controversy was certain to be both spirited and picturesque; but he cannot be called the consistent and resolute advocate of any cause. In his miscellaneous, discursive papers, like the *Noctes,* he touches a wide variety of topics without special personal interest in any, or seeming to feel a call to convince or persuade us of anything. There is no real urgency in the man. Even in his critical verdicts it is difficult to trace any consistent principles. As a result, his taste was never sure. In his own writing he never quite perceived the difference between the humorous and the hilarious, between comedy and buffoonery, between pathos and bathos. He records his impressions of men and books in lively, often in very emphatic, language; but they are capricious and sometimes conflicting. When in his moods he is liable to damn his most favorite idol. (pp. 183-85)

[*The Isle of Palms*] is interesting as being, at least in conception, an early specimen of the romantic school of poetry. It was probably suggested by some of Southey's big romances; the metre, at all events, is clearly reminiscent of Southey. It is an odd mixture of wildly improbable incident and very sweet sentiment. . . . [It] is hardly exaggeration to say that Wilson never wrote a line of genuine poetry. He lacked the gift of compression and the gift of melody, and uniformly diluted his passion into a gush of lukewarm sentiment.

Nor are the *Tales* much better. They are stories of humble life, and most of them are meant to be very pathetic. Their subjects are not cheerful. . . . [They] average almost exactly two and one-half deaths to each tale—which is depressing. Besides this high mortality there is a large assortment of childless widows, broken hearts, forsaken maidens, family Bibles, churchyards, and deserted cottages. When Wilson makes an attempt upon our sensibilities he is not to be satisfied with any halfway effects. The obverse of any healthy pathos is usually humor; but Wilson seems afraid of mixing them, and there is hardly a gleam of humor in these *Tales.* It is to be feared, however, that to see this boisterous sentimentalist grow willowy and lachrymose sometimes does provoke from the irreverent reader a smile. His style, too, is not realistic or natural, but rhetorical and melodramatic. (pp. 186-88)

Among the miscellaneous writings are several papers of a purely critical character, of which the most important are those on Burns, on Coleridge, on Wordsworth . . . , on Macaulay's *Lays of Ancient Rome,* and the once famous—or notorious— review of Tennyson's first volume. None of these can be given a very high place in the body of English critical literature. Wilson's opinions . . . depended greatly on his moods, and we never can be quite sure that the verdict of to-day is not to be contradicted by the verdict of to-morrow. His criticism is based on no defined principles, and of necessity, therefore, is

often arbitrary and capricious. Indeed, he seldom makes any attempt at systematic and reasoned estimate of the work under examination; he simply sets down—usually in very pronounced fashion—his own impulsive feeling about his author. His criticism is the record of John Wilson's likes and dislikes. Hence it is likely to be very exaggerated and very diffuse. . . . Everywhere he gossips and comments, rather than interprets. But, at all events, his criticism, though sometimes wrongheaded, is sincere and hearty. It is never the dry, technical jargon of the professional critic. Wilson's appreciation was certainly limited. He liked sentiment and action in their pronounced forms; he disliked weakness, prettiness, over-refinement. It was inevitable that this big-chested critic with a voice like a megaphone, who admired Macaulay's drum-and-trumpet *Lays,* should think little of John Keats, and should deride the owls and mermen, and "airy, fairy Lillians" of young Mr. Alfred Tennyson. Yet within his limits, if we will make allowance for occasional personal prejudice, Wilson's appreciations and aversions are quite intelligible, and command our interest if not always our agreement. When he heartily enjoys a book, his comments are sure to be stimulating, and are sometimes really incisive. And even when he has a mind to scourge, so long as he is only recounting his own genuine feeling, and not feeding some personal or political spite, he seldom goes far wrong. . . . In a word, Wilson is a pleasant commentator, but not a great critic. His spontaneous judgments are usually well enough; he is not always wise when he attempts to justify them. Indeed, much of his best literary criticism is to be found in the brief, incidental comment and opinion scattered through his miscellaneous writings. There are many of these excellent *obiter dicta* in the *Noctes.*

Far better than the tales or the criticism are the out-of-door papers. In them Wilson is nearly at his very best. To be sure, here as everywhere, Christopher seems in a state of over-exhilaration. His fancy is too flamboyant, and his manner vagarious to the last degree. . . . Yet in these papers there is nothing factitious; the enthusiasm is not forced. They are full of space and breeziness. Christopher is in the open, where he was born to be, and the fresh air goes to his head. Mr. Saintsbury pronounces Wilson's descriptions of scenery better than anything of the kind in English prose; but I think he must have forgotten a good deal to say that [see excerpt above, 1886]. I should rather say that Wilson had not in any high degree the gift of description proper. There are, to be sure, many vivid and beautiful glimpses in his pages; but, as a rule, he does not set the landscape before you. What he can do is to make you feel his own joy in it. In reality he is not describing the scene, he is relating his own experience. . . . In all these outdoor papers Wilson's animation is contagious. (pp. 189-94)

But it is in the *Noctes* that we must look for the fullest display of Wilson's powers. Here his imagination, his wisdom, his satire, his pathos, his exuberant humor, are all seen at their best. Nothing else so well shows his almost marvellous affluence and volubility. (p. 194)

Certainly a manner so discursive and rambling as Wilson's found in the *Noctes* the best possible form of expression. Impulsive, sentimental, he had little power of connected thinking, and could rarely keep himself to one theme for ten minutes together. (pp. 196-97)

[The dialogue] in the *Noctes* is by no means the talk of half-befuddled men, whose god is their belly and who mind earthly things. It is mostly very good talk indeed, playing over all sorts of subjects with quick intelligence, and glowing with fun and fancy. There are bits of excellent criticism in it, not quite dissolved in a wide welter of words. In fact, . . . Wilson's literary criticism is often at its best in these incidental comments struck out in the heat of conversation. . . . [Books,] new or old, are praised and damned without any nice qualifications of sentence. Moreover, the plan of the *Noctes* serves to disguise Wilson's frequent inconsistencies; for on such jovial occasions the opinions of the critics will naturally vary with their moods, and Wilson as Christopher must inevitably often disagree with Wilson as the Shepherd. But, taken together, the papers afford an interesting conspectus of literary news and criticism for some ten years. And there is a deal of sound sense—of a rather high Tory sort—on a great variety of other matters. . . . The great charm of the *Noctes* is the buoyant, ebullient life that pulses all through them. (pp. 198-99)

The Shepherd, in particular, is delightful. In his talk you get Wilson's humor, sentiment, and imagination in their superlative forms. The humor cannot be called quiet or delicate; yet the Shepherd has store of neat quips and jests, and now and then strikes out a vivid portrait in few words. . . . Some of his satiric hits are very good. . . . The Shepherd's anger, too, sometimes inspires passages of hearty Scottish malediction that are animating reading. But best of all are his passages of flamboyant, full-length description or narrative. The Shepherd's imagination, like his humor, is very profuse; it revels in details and lavishes adjectives. Yet the resulting picture is always real and glowing. . . . [Certain passages] will occur to all lovers of the *Noctes* as striking examples of the union of effusive sentiment or humor with vivid and realistic detail. They are better than the similar rhetorical fantasies and elaborate pathetic passages in Wilson's other works, because they seem more spontaneous. And, although his characteristic manner fairly runs riot in them, the Scottish dialect gives them a homely naturalness and keeps their sentiment from getting mawkish.

On the whole, we may admit that Wilson could not add much to the world's knowledge, and that he did little to champion any reform or advance. His prejudices were obstinate, his judgments often capricious or perverse. He lacked fixed and reasoned convictions; he lacked steadfast earnestness of resolve. We distrust the sanity of his opinions and the consistency of his conduct. Moreover, his mind would not work steadily at low pressure. As a result, his writing has no repose, no quiet certainty of manner; he is liable to fatigue us, after a little, by the very noise of his enthusiasm. . . . [Yet few] writers of his generation contributed more to the literature of cheer than Wilson. . . . His humor, to be sure, is not of the gentle variety that enlivens five o'clock tea, but it is never merely bacchanalian—which makes the dreariest of all writing. Even in the most exhilarated passages . . . there is far more of cheer than of inebriation. . . . In the merciless winnowing of time all of his verse, all the *Tales*, and most of the criticism will doubtless fall into oblivion—nay, have already descended thither. But the wholesome Out-of-Door Papers and the *Noctes* ought to live at least another century as part of the literature of invigoration. In them Christopher and the Shepherd are too much alive soon to die out of the memory of men who love good fellowship and hearty cheer. (pp. 200-03)

> *C. T. Winchester, "John Wilson," in his* A Group of English Essayists of the Early Nineteenth Century, *The Macmillan Company, 1910 (and reprinted by Books for Libraries Press, 1967; distributed by Arno Press, Inc.), pp. 166-203.*

## MAURICE HEWLETT   (essay date 1920)

Bad buffoonery as much of [the *Noctes Ambrosianae*] is and full to the throttle of the warm-watery optimism induced by whisky, yet as fighting literature it is incalculably better than its modern substitute in *Blackwood*. . . . Christopher North and his co-mates must have had the stomachs of ostriches. The guzzling and swilling which were the staple of the *Noctes* were remarked upon at the time as incredible as well as disgusting; but it is to be presumed that they wouldn't have been there if, to the majority at least, they had not been a counsel of perfection. (p. 147)

When the *Noctes* can stand away from Politics and Literature . . . they can wile away a winter evening very pleasantly. Christopher North had an eye for character, a sense of humour, and knew and loved the country. . . . He is at his best when he combines his loves, as he does in the person of the Shepherd. Keep the Shepherd off *(a)* girls, *(b)* nursing mothers, *(c)* the Sabbath, *(d)* eating, *(e)* drinking, *(f)* his own poetry, and he is good reading. . . . Edward FitzGerald [the English editor and translator] could have made a good book out of the *Noctes*, cutting it down to one volume out of four. As it is mainly, it will stand or fall by its high spirits. The really funny character in it is Gurney, the shorthand writer, who is kept in a cupboard, and at the end of the last uproarious chapter, when the coast is cleared of the horseplaying protagonists, "comes out like a mouse, and begins to nibble cheese." That is imagination. (p. 148)

> *Maurice Hewlett, " 'Noctes Ambrosianae'," in his* In a Green Shade: A Country Commentary, *G. Bell and Sons, 1920 (and reprinted by Books for Libraries Press, 1969; distributed by Arno Press, Inc.), pp. 147-50.*

## MALCOLM ELWIN   (essay date 1934)

[Wilson had] a delicate ear for the melody of language and a rare responsiveness to the beauties of nature. *The Angler's Tent* . . . , *Lines Written in a Burial-Ground, The Magic Mirror,* and *The Children's Dance* contain lines and images of exceptional beauty, though admittedly these are too often mingled with convenient catch-phrases and trite expedients. . . . The 'O sinless babe' sort of apostrophe occurs so often for the sake of complement to verse and thought, as to suggest limitation of fancy and hasty composition. The latter fault, in the light of his later career, was bound to have prevented Wilson from ever reaching the front poetical rank; he wrote always in haste, and having flung it off, paused never to polish or revise, but rose in relief from his chair, glad that the job was done, like a boy out of school. (pp. 42-3)

[*Lights and Shadows of Scottish Life, The Trials of Margaret Lyndsay,* and *The Foresters* all] contain isolated scenes of impressive power, inspired passages of almost lyrical rhapsody, and uniformly glorious descriptive prose. But [Wilson] lacked the knack of narrative; his story moves slowly, with little incident and much digression, the habit of the essayist to start a hare and follow it leading him astray from his main business. Possessed of an equally eloquent descriptive style, he had Scott's vices as a novelist without his virtues. We are tempted to skip Scott's long descriptions, however brilliant or beautiful, in pursuit of his plot; if we succumb to the temptation with Wilson, we cease to read him, for his plots are negligible. Nobody, except De Quincey, wrote more lovely and melodious prose, but it is better enjoyed in the critical and imaginative essays of Christopher North . . . than in the novels of John Wilson. (p. 71)

Necessarily the *Noctes,* as a topical commentary, contains much of ephemeral interest. Nothing assumes the air of tiresome archaism so quickly as the discussion of contemporary politics. But apart from the politics, the *Noctes* marvellously withstand the test of time, a fact which pays the highest tribute to Wilson's character as a critic. He had the fine catholic taste which comes from genuine culture, enabling him always, in spite of journalistic bias and occasionally hasty judgment, to lay an unerring finger on the essential features of a work of art and to discuss them with sympathy and sense. (pp. 72-3)

The inequality of Wilson's work is the inequality of a prolific journalist. At his worst, he is a professional word-spinner intent on filling his prescribed space, capable of crudity, vulgarity, petty trifling, and conscious sensationalism, ranting rhetoric and coarse buffoonery; at his best, he ranks with Hazlitt, Lamb, and Thackeray in the first flight of periodical essayists, sensitive, sympathetic, shrewd and inspiring, a discriminating and constructive critic, possessed of contagious enthusiasm, a gargantuan sense of humour, a picturesque imagination, and exquisite eloquence.

As a stylist, he has never received due recognition. Though no more than a minor poet, he learned his lesson from the Lake School, and fulfilled his literary destiny. He was the pioneer of the romantic movement in prose as Coleridge and Wordsworth were pioneers in poetry. Instead of the classical correctness and elaborate pomposity of the later eighteenth-century stylists, like Gibbon, he introduced a style of colourful melody and flexible grace, vibrant with nervous emotion and spirited vigour. In his essays on *Christopher at the Lakes, Christopher on Colonsay,* Coleridge, and *On the Punishment of Death* are evident the same wonderful harmony and colour of style as in De Quincey's *Confessions of an English Opium-Eater.*

Similarly and correlatively, he was a pioneer in journalism. He revived the traditions of periodical literature, left languishing since the days of Addison, Steele, the *Spectator* and *Tatler.* . . . Jeffrey and the *Edinburgh Review* had opened a new era of the periodical, but as highbrow pundits, sober, severe, and academic, appealing only to the serious and intellectual. Wilson, Lockhart, Maginn, Lamb, and Hazlitt revolutionized the popular periodical, lifting literary journalism from the hands of Grub Street hacks and developing its functions on the lines of Steele and Addison. Wilson led the van; in his own day, he was recognized as the leader. Lamb and Hazlitt have come into their own, and the time for Wilson's recognition is long overdue. (pp. 74-5)

> *Malcolm Elwin, "Wallflower the First: 'Christopher North'," in his* Victorian Wallflowers: A Panoramic Survey of the Popular Literary Periodicals *(reprinted by permission of the Estate of Malcolm Elwin), Jonathan Cape, 1934, pp. 25-84.\**

### DAVID DAICHES   (broadcast date 1954)

[A] combination of gush and energy is the clue to [Wilson's] character and career. The moral earnestness of the early Romantic Movement worked on his native tendency to emotional self-indulgence to develop a taste for lachrymose sentimentalities of the most embarrassing kind; but at the same time his enormous vitality, his relish of sensation and of physical exertion, gave him a gusto that often enabled him to carry off his emotional debauches with dash and even splendour. In

another age he might have written Rabelaisian stories or been a revivalist or run a one-man radio show. As it was, he became a journalist and a professor of moral philosophy. The journalist was Christopher North, the fluent, lively, unpredictable, reckless, self-contradictory, flamboyant, mischievous and wholly preposterous contributor to *Blackwood's Magazine;* the professor held the Chair of Moral Philosophy at Edinburgh from 1820 until 1851, an absolute impostor, dependent for his lectures on material supplied to him regularly by a friend, a fraud, a windbag, who declaimed high sounding platitudes in a magnificent voice to cheering students. (pp. 122-23)

[His poetry] showed a certain emotional and verbal facility and a taste for a melodramatic plot. Wilson is now very properly forgotten as a poet. . . .

[His] vigour and his ability to write about anything in a tone of exalted conviction made him just the man for [*Blackwood's Magazine*]. *Blackwood's* made Wilson and Wilson made *Blackwood's.* (p. 123)

[He] was an utterly irresponsible critic, liable to be carried away by his own verve and gusto and precipitated into saying the most outrageous things. Yet by the same token his critical essays for 'Maga' had a splendid energy, especially after he had assumed the character of Christopher North. . . .

To write as Christopher North seemed to precipitate the extrovert side of his nature and to eliminate, at least for long periods, the moralizing sentimentalist. This is particularly true of the series called *Noctes Ambrosianae.* . . . (p. 126)

[Wilson's] ultra-sentimental tales of Scottish village life anticipate the worst of the Kailyard school; his poetry is facile and derivative; his criticism is unprincipled and erratic. But at his best Christopher North had the kind of brilliance that comes from sheer energy. The *Noctes Ambrosianae,* self-consciously picturesque, exaggerated, preposterous, as they often are, nevertheless are above all *living:* they project the man's own image of himself with brilliant clarity, as well as with a boisterous kind of wit that is like nothing else in English—or Scottish—literature. He played up to his own notion of romanticism, and produced a unique brand of it. (p. 131)

> *David Daiches, "Christopher North" (originally a radio broadcast in the Third Programme of the BBC on August 8, 1954; reprinted by permission of the British Broadcasting Corporation), in his* Literary Essays, *Philosophical Library Publishers, 1957, pp. 122-31.*

### IAN JACK   (essay date 1963)

One of Wilson's oddest and most unamiable habits was his practice of praising and censuring the same writer at the same time. At one moment he stands out as one of the first reviewers to appreciate the genius of Wordsworth, at the next he rounds on him for 'ludicrously' over-rating his own powers, and calls *The Excursion* 'the worst poem of any character in the English language'. At times it is difficult to believe that Wilson was wholly sane. After attacking him on numerous occasions he had the assurance to ask Wordsworth for a testimonial; and although Wordsworth complied with this request we again find Wilson planning to attack him in the *Quarterly,* after his death, as 'a fat ugly cur'. His motives are hard to understand, but much must be laid to the account of vanity and envy. He was pathologically touchy, incapable of tolerating any criticism of his own writings or character; and for all his physical prowess he was an abject moral coward. Although he was capable of generosity, as we see in his treatment of De Quincey, he had an innate love of hurting people, even if they had been kind to him. 'Though averse to being cut up myself', he once wrote, without a trace of irony, 'I like to abuse my friends.' But the thought that he himself might be exposed filled him with horror. (p. 336)

The popularity of [*Noctes Ambrosianae*] . . . reminds us of the popularity of some inferior radio or television serial today: the quality of the material is low, and it is difficult now to read more than a few pages with any enjoyment. The popularity of the *Noctes* in America is not difficult to explain: they appealed to the nostalgia of exiled Scots. The series is an example of that coarsening and cheapening of Scotland and its way of life which still proves so popular with tourists. It is easy to see why this sort of dialogue suited Wilson: he was able to attribute some sentimental outburst to the Shepherd and then make Christopher North interrupt with a sarcastic comment: rather as Byron so often turns on himself with a witty couplet at the end of an octave stanza. Throughout the series Wilson was in the position that he relished: that of the man to whom all the credit is due, but who stands safe from censure or imputed responsibility. (p. 337)

> Ian Jack, "Miscellaneous Prose," in his English Literature: 1815-1832 (© Oxford University Press 1963; reprinted by permission of Oxford University Press), Oxford University Press, Oxford, 1963, pp. 312-50.*

## FRANCIS RUSSELL HART   (essay date 1978)

[John Wilson] is not impressive as a novelist, but his unimportance in the origins of the Scottish novel is not simply a problem of art. It can be argued that he preferred the short sketch—the nineteenth-century prose idyll, with blank verse counterparts in Wordsworth and Tennyson—to the novel. Wilson's fiction began with *Lights and Shadows of Scottish Life* . . . , [and] as "Christopher North" [he] later flourished as "editor" of Lowland idylls. These idylls anticipate the development of a major Scottish Victorian form, generally ignored now: the parochial idyll and its curious kin, the domesticated *kunstmärchen*, "scenes," "legends," and "sketches" of regional life and tradition. . . . (p. 80)

Wilson's novels are two: *Margaret Lyndsay* and *The Foresters*. Wilson's mode combines ornate sentimentality and presbyterian severity in a pastoral setting. . . . Like Lockhart, [he] derives his ideas of pastoral simplicity and tragedy from his understanding of Wordsworth. Wilson's characters seem occasionally to have stepped out of *The Excursion*, free of Wordsworth's kind of transcendentalism, and much given to "feminine" intensities of affection, to the pieties of home and parish, and to deathbed repentances worthy of Dickens. The narrator invariably views his humble subjects with a mixture of solemn respect and generalizing condescension—"the simple dwellers," "the children of labour and poverty." His social perspective is generically Scottish, and in humble and intelligent respectability he professes to find "the native character of the race." But his intention is to show in such character the "human heart."

Minor characters are recognizable originals of Scottish parochial manners. (pp. 80-1)

The truth Wilson propounds is the same embraced by Lockhart and Ferrier. Man without the light of faith is a blind, infatuated

worldling. But a gloomy and fanatical Calvinism, such as that held by the "severe and gloomy preacher" that casts Margaret [Lyndsay's] blind sister into deep melancholy, is as mistaken as complacent worldliness. Thoughtful intelligence ennobles the Scottish lowly, but feverish intellectuality without the peace and assurance of faith is worse than ignorance. Wilson's ideal is the intelligent, pious peasant, Michael Forester, who, blinded by lightning, becomes a patriarchal Job figure. His theme is Michael Forester's rejoinder to the condescending, class-conscious father of Lucy [Forester's] suitor: "Do you think, Mr. Ellis, that in poor men's huts the best natural affections do not reside in as great force and purity as in the dwellings of the rich or noble?" . . . Wilson's dream of cultural conciliation and fulfillment is projected in the final marriage of Lucy Forester. She marries the son of a Westmoreland vicar, who takes her home to the Lakes, with the comfortable proviso that the families will visit annually back and forth.

Margaret Lyndsay's destiny is more varied and catastrophic. . . . For Margaret, successive and innumerable trials lead to an earthly paradise, an innocent pastoral home, which is only the final stage on the way to a loftier inheritance. (pp. 82-3)

Lucy Forester is a character of a different kind. Seemingly an echo of Wordsworth's Lucy Gray, she is not just a part of innocent nature but a part of locality. . . . Lucy's affections are confined to her idyllic Clydesdale parish. . . . But her affections must be chastened and shifted, and the spirit of the Scottish hut finds a new love and a home elsewhere, in a greener vale.

Margaret Lyndsay's fortunes are remote from such mawkish idyllicism. Still, like the great character Chris Guthrie in Gibbon's *A Scots Quair*, she is Scotland in archetype, the suffering daughter and wandering orphan, undergoing successive exiles in search of some true Scottish home. . . . [In] dark city streets, the innocent is tightly bound to some dear green place, some remembered idyll. But in this severely pious book, such a place has an ambiguous quality—of childhood innocence, but also of pagan indulgence. (pp. 83-4)

With such patterns and place-archetypes in Wilson, we are clearly in the borderland between novel and romance. We are also on the verge of Scottish Victorianism. (p. 84)

> Francis Russell Hart, "The Other Blackwoodians," in his The Scottish Novel: From Smollett to Spark (copyright ©1978 by Francis Russell Hart; excerpted by permission of the President and Fellows of Harvard College), Cambridge, Mass.: Harvard University Press, 1978, pp. 53-84.*

---

## ADDITIONAL BIBLIOGRAPHY

De Quincey, Thomas. "Sketch of Professor Wilson." In his *The Uncollected Writings of Thomas De Quincey, Vol. I*, pp. 225-64. New York: Scribner and Welford; London: Swan Sonnenschein & Co., 1890.
   A character sketch based on personal reminiscences by one of Wilson's closest friends.

Gordon, [Mary]. *"Christopher North": A Memoir of John Wilson, Late Professor of Moral Philosophy in the University of Edinburgh.* New York: The H. W. Hagemann Publishing Co., 1894, 484 p.

A "simple domestic memoir" by one of Wilson's daughters. Gordon relies heavily upon her father's correspondence with his family and with his contemporaries.

Lounsbury, Thomas R. "Christopher North's Review" and "Christopher North's Later Attacks on Tennyson." In his *The Life and Times of Tennyson: From 1809 to 1850*, pp. 227-44, pp. 465-96. New York: Russell & Russell, 1962.

Explores the motives behind Wilson's critical essays on Alfred, Lord Tennyson's poetry. Lounsbury contends that Wilson's review of Tennyson's first volume of poetry was a reasonable estimate of the poet's talent and that Wilson's harshest comments were directed more toward Tennyson's adulators than Tennyson himself. Tennyson's unprovoked retort, according to Lounsbury, embittered Wilson and caused him to deliberately castigate Tennyson in a series of articles beginning in 1836.

Oliphant, [Margaret]. *Annals of a Publishing House: William Blackwood and His Sons, Their Magazine and Friends.* 2 vols. New York: Charles Scribner's Sons, 1897.*

A behind-the-scenes account of Wilson's involvement with *Blackwood's Magazine* including correspondence between Wilson and his editors. Volume I contains a complete chapter describing Wilson's early association with *Blackwood's* and his years as principal contributor. Volume II includes frequent references to Wilson's services to the magazine after William Blackwood's death in 1834.

Strout, Alan Lang. "Purple Patches in the *Noctes Ambrosianae*." *ELH: A Journal of English Literary History* 2, No. 4 (December 1935): 327-3!.

Defends the originality of Wilson's criticism by exploring the origins of a few select passages in the *Noctes Ambrosianae*. In order to discredit the claim made by Elsie Swann in her biography of Wilson (see annotation below) that Wilson relied on his friend Alexander Blair for the bulk of his ideas, Strout explains how Wilson developed the ideas for three of the finest scenes in the *Noctes*.

Strout, Alan Lang. "'Christopher North' on Tennyson." *The Review of English Studies* XIX, No. 56 (October 1938): 428-39.*

Refutes Thomas R. Lounsbury's analysis of the poet-critic relationship between Alfred, Lord Tennyson and Wilson (see annotation above). Strout maintains that Wilson was never intentionally unfair to Tennyson, nor were his essays on Tennyson's poetry motivated by Tennyson's retaliatory squib on "crusty Christopher," which was written in response to Wilson's May, 1832 review of his first volume of poetry.

Strout, Alan Lang. "A Study in Periodical Patchwork: John Wilson's *Recreations of Christopher North*, 1842." *The Modern Language Review* XXXVIII, No. 1 (January 1943): 88-105.

A study of the essays in *The Recreations of Christopher North* in relation to their originals, which first appeared in *Blackwood's Magazine*. Strout discusses the merits and defects of the various omissions and additions and attempts to show Wilson's inconsistency as a critic by tracing his treatment of Wordsworth's poetry.

Swann, Elsie. *Christopher North (John Wilson).* Edinburgh, London: Oliver and Boyd, 1934, 255 p.

A biography which emphasizes Wilson's dependence, as a critic and a philosopher, on his friend Alexander Blair. Swann asserts that "Wilson was not to be trusted when he followed his own devices and did not refer to Blair."

# Appendix

The Academy
Appleton's Journal
The Athenaeum
The Atlantic Monthly
Atlas
Blackwood's Edinburgh Magazine
The Book Buyer
The Bookman, *New York*
The British Quarterly Review
British Weekly
The Broadway Journal
Brownson's Quarterly Review
Bulletin of The John Rylands Library
The Century Magazine
The Christian Examiner and Religious
  Miscellany
CLA Journal
College English
Commonweal
The Cornhill Magazine
The Critic, *New York*
Critical Quarterly
The Critical Review
Criticism
Daily Chronicle
The Eclectic Magazine
The Eclectic Review
The Edinburgh Review
Encounter
Essays in Criticism
Essex Gazette
The Examiner
The Foreign Quarterly Review
The Fortnightly Review
Fraser's Magazine
French Studies

Galaxy
The Gentleman's Magazine and Historical
  Chronicle
German Life and Letters
Godey's Lady Book
Graham's Magazine
Harper's New Monthly Magazine
Hawk: A Smart Paper for Smart People
Hogg's Instructor
The Independent
Indiana Slavic Studies
The International Monthly Magazine
Knight's Quarterly Magazine
The Leader
The Literary Digest International
The Literary World
The Living Age
The London Literary Gazette
The London Magazine; or, Gentleman's
  Monthly
The London Quarterly Review Intelligencer
Longman's Magazine
Macmillan's Magazine
Monthly Review
The Monthly Review, *London*
The Morning Chronicle
The Nation
The National Review
The National Review, *London*
The Nation and the Athenaeum
New German Studies
The New Monthly Magazine
The New Quarterly Review
Nineteenth-Century French Studies
The North American Review
The North British Review

Nottingham French Studies
Pall Mall Gazette
PMLA
Poetry
The Public Ledger
Putnam's Magazine of Literature, Science,
  Art, and National Interests
Putnam's Monthly: A Magazine of
  Literature, Science and Art
The Quarterly Review
Quarterly Review of Literature
The Review of English Literature
The Romantic Review
Russell's Magazine
Russian Literature Triquarterly
Russian Review
Russky Invalid Literary Supplement
The Saturday Review, *London*
Scotsman
The Sewanee Review
Slavic and East European Journal
The Southern Literary Messenger
The Southern Quarterly Review
The Speaker
The Spectator
St. James Gazette
Temple Bar
Time, *London*
The Times, *London*
The Universal Magazine
The Virginia Magazine of History and
  Biography
The Westminster and Foreign Quarterly
  Review
The Westminster Review

571

**THE EXCERPTS IN NCLC, VOLUME 5, WERE REPRINTED FROM THE FOLLOWING BOOKS:**

*Allen, Margaret Vanderhaar*. The Achievement of Margaret Fuller. *The Pennsylvania State University Press, 1979.*

*Annenkov, P. V.* The Extraordinary Decade. *Edited by Arthur P. Mendel. Translated by Irwin R. Titunik. University of Michigan Press, 1968.*

*Auburn, Mark S.* Sheridan's Comedies: Their Contexts and Achievements. *University of Nebraska Press, 1977.*

*Bald, Marjory A.* Women-Writers of the Nineteenth Century. *Cambridge at the University Press, 1923.*

*Balzac, Honoré de*. The Wild Ass's Skin (La peau de chagrin). *Translated by Ellen Marriage. J. M. Dent and Co., 1895.*

*Balzac, Honoré de*. Letters of Honoré de Balzac to Madame Hanska: 1833-1846. *Translated by Katherine Prescott Wormeley. Hardy, Pratt and Co., 1900, Little, Brown, and Company, 1911.*

*Balzac, Honoré de*. The Works of Honoré de Balzac. The Magic Skin, The Quest of the Absolute and Other Stories, Vol. I-II. *Edited by William P. Trent. Translated by Ellen Marriage. Thomas Y. Crowell Co., Inc., 1900.*

*Barlow, Norman H.* Sainte-Beuve to Baudelaire: A Poetic Legacy. *Duke University Press, 1964.*

*Baudelaire, Charles.* Baudelaire As a Literary Critic. *Translated by Lois Boe Hyslop and Francis E. Hyslop, Jr. The Pennsylvania State University Press, 1964.*

*Beach, Joseph Warren.* The Twentieth Century Novel: Studies in Technique. *Appleton-Century-Crofts, Inc., 1932.*

*Beaty, John O.* John Esten Cooke, Virginian. *Columbia University Press, 1922, Kennikat Press, 1965.*

*Beebe, Maurice.* Ivory Towers and Sacred Founts: The Artist As Hero in Fiction from Goethe to Joyce. *New York University Press, 1964.*

*Belinsky, V. G.* Selected Philosophical Works. *Foreign Languages Publishing House, 1948.*

*Bell, Bernard W.* American Literature, 1764-1789: The Revolutionary Years. *Edited by Everett Emerson. The University of Wisconsin Press, 1977.*

*Bennett, E. K.* A History of the German "Novelle": From Goethe to Thomas Mann. *Cambridge at the University Press, 1934.*

*Berlin, Isaiah.* Russian Thinkers. *Edited by Henry Hardy and Aileen Kelly. The Viking Press, 1978, Penguin Books, 1979.*

*Besser, Gretchen R.* Balzac's Concept of Genius: The Theme of Superiority in the "Comédie humaine." *Librairie Droz, 1969.*

*Bowman, Herbert E.* Vissarion Belinski, 1811-1848: A Study in the Origins of Social Criticism in Russia. *Harvard University Press, 1954.*

*Bowra, C. M.* Inspiration and Poetry. *Macmillan, 1955.*

*Brandes, George.* Main Currents in Nineteenth Century Literature: The Romantic School in Germany, Vol. II. *Translated by Diana White and Mary Morison. William Heinemann Ltd., 1902, Boni & Liveright, 1923.*

*Brandes, George.* Main Currents in Nineteenth Century Literature: The Romantic School in France, Vol. V. *Translated by Diana White and Mary Morison. William Heinemann, 1904.*

*Brontë, Charlotte; Brontë, Emily; and Brontë, Anne.* The Brontës: Life and Letters, Vol. II. *Edited by Clement Shorter. Hodder and Stoughton, 1908.*

*Brownell, W. C.* Victorian Prose Masters. *Charles Scribner's Sons, 1901.*

*Browning, Elizabeth Barrett.* The Letters of Elizabeth Barrett Browning, Vol. II. *Edited by Frederic G. Kenyon. Smith, Elder, & Co., 1897.*

*Brückner, A.* A Literary History of Russia. *Edited by Ellis H. Minns. Translated by H. Havelock. T. Fisher Unwin, 1908.*

*Brunetière, Ferdinand.* Honoré de Balzac. *Translated by Robert Louis Sanderson. Lippincott, 1906.*

*Buckley, Jerome H., ed.* The Worlds of Victorian Fiction. *Harvard University Press, 1975.*

*Bull, Francis. Preface to* Poems, *by Henrik Wergeland. Translated by G. M. Gathorne-Hardy, Jethro Bithell, and I. Grondahl. Gyldendal Norsk Forlag, 1929, Greenwood Press, Publishers, 1970.*

*Byron, George Gordon Noel, Lord Byron.* Selections from Poetry, Letters & Journals. *Edited by Peter Quennell. The Nonesuch Press, 1949.*

*Carey, John.* Thackeray: Prodigal Genius. *Faber and Faber, 1977.*

*Carlyle, Thomas.* Critical and Miscellaneous Essays, Vol. I. *J. Munroe and Company, 1839.*

*Carlyle, Thomas.* Critical and Miscellaneous Essays: Collected and Republished, Vol. I. *Scribner, Welford, and Company, 1872.*

*Carrère, Jean.* Degeneration in the Great French Masters: Rousseau—Chateaubriand—Balzac—Stendhal—Sand—Musset—Baudelaire—Flaubert—Verlaine—Zola. *Translated by Joseph McCabe. T. Fisher Unwin, Limited, 1922.*

*Cecil, David.* Early Victorian Novelists: Essays in Revaluation. *Constable, 1934, Bobbs-Merrill, 1935.*

*Chapman, John Jay.* Emerson and Other Essays. *Charles Scribner's Sons, 1898.*

*Chapman, John Jay.* John Jay Chapman and His Letters. *Edited by M. A. De Wolfe Howe. Houghton Mifflin, 1937.*

*Cobbett, William.* Porcupine's Works: Containing Various Writings and Selections, Exhibiting a Faithful Picture of the United States of America, Vol. II. *Cobbett and Morgan, 1801.*

*Coleridge, Samuel Taylor.* Specimens of the Table Talk of Samuel Taylor Coleridge. *Edited by Henry Nelson Coleridge. Harper & Brothers, 1835.*

*Coleridge, Samuel Taylor.* The Table Talk and Omniana of Samuel Taylor Coleridge. *Edited by T. Ashe. George Bell and Sons, 1884.*

*Collie, Michael.* Laforgue. *Oliver and Boyd, 1963.*

*Collie, Michael, and L'Heureux, J. M. Critical Notes to* Dernier vers, *by Jules Laforgue. Edited by Michael Collie and J. M. L'Heureux. University of Toronto Press, 1965.*

*Colvin, Sidney. Introduction to* The Letters of Robert Louis Stevenson: 1868-1880, Scotland—France—California, Vol. 1, *by Robert Louis Stevenson. Edited by Sidney Colvin. Charles Scribner's Sons, 1911.*

*Cornillon, Susan Koppelman, ed.* Images of Women in Fiction: Feminist Perspectives. *Rev. ed. Bowling Green University Popular Press, 1973.*

*Cowie, Alexander.* The Rise of the American Novel. *American Book Company, 1951.*

*Croce, Benedetto.* European Literature in the Nineteenth Century. *Translated by Douglas Ainslie. Alfred A. Knopf, 1924.*

*Cunningham, Allan.* Biographical and Critical History of the British Literature of the Last Fifty Years. *Baudry's Foreign Library, 1834.*

*Daiches, David.* Robert Louis Stevenson. *New Directions Books, 1947.*

*Daiches, David.* Stevenson and the Art of Fiction. *Yale University Press, 1951.*

*Daiches, David.* Literary Essays. *Philosophical Library Publishers, 1957.*

*Danton, George Henry.* The Nature Sense in the Writings of Ludwig Tieck. *Columbia University Press, 1907, AMS Press, Inc., 1966.*

*Davidson, James Wood.* The Living Writers of the South. *Carleton, 1869.*

*Davie, Donald, ed.* Russian Literature and Modern English Fiction: A Collection of Critical Essays. *The University of Chicago Press, 1965.*

*De Quincey, Thomas.* The Collected Writings of Thomas De Quincey, Vol. V. *Edited by David Masson. A. & C. Black, 1897.*

*De Quincey, Thomas.* The Collected Writings of Thomas De Quincey, Vol. XII. *Edited by David Masson. A. & C. Black, 1897.*

Dobrolyubov, N. A. Selected Philosophical Essays. *Edited by M. Yovchuk. Translated by J. Fineberg. Foreign Languages Publishing House, 1956.*

Dodds, John W. Thackeray: A Critical Portrait. *Oxford University Press, 1941, Russell & Russell, Inc., 1963.*

Dostoievsky, F. M. The Diary of a Writer, Vol. I. *Edited and translated by Boris Brasol. Charles Scribner's Sons, 1949, George Braziller, 1954.*

Douglas, Ann. The Feminization of American Culture. *Knopf, 1977, Avon Books, 1978.*

Douglas, George. The ''Blackwood'' Group. *Charles Scribner's Sons, 1897.*

Duthie, Enid L. The Themes of Elizabeth Gaskell. *Rowman and Littlefield, 1980.*

Eliot, George. George Eliot's Life As Relayed in Her Letters. *Edited by J. W. Cross. William Blackwood and Sons, 1885.*

Eliot, George. The George Eliot Letters: 1852-1858, Vol. II. *Edited by Gordon Haight. Yale University Press, 1954.*

Ellis, John M. Narration in the German Novelle: Theory and Interpretation. *Cambridge University Press, 1974.*

Elwin, Malcolm. Victorian Wallflowers: A Panoramic Survey of the Popular Literary Periodicals. *Jonathan Cape, 1934.*

Faguet, Émile. Politicians & Moralists of the Nineteenth Century, Vol. 3. *Translated by Dorothy Galton. Ernest Benn Limited, 1928.*

Fanger, Donald. The Creation of Nikolai Gogol. *Belknap Press, 1979.*

Ferrier, James Frederick. Preface to The Works of Professor Wilson: ''Noctes Ambrosianae,'' Vol. I, *by John Wilson. Edited by James Frederick Ferrier. William Blackwood and Sons, 1855.*

Fiedler, Leslie A. Introduction to The Master of Ballantrae, *by Robert Louis Stevenson. Holt, Rinehart and Winston, 1954.*

Fiedler, Leslie A. No! in Thunder: Essays on Myth and Literature. *Beacon Press, 1960.*

Fiedler, Leslie A. Love and Death in the American Novel. *Rev. ed. Stein and Day, 1966.*

Field, Andrew, ed. The Complection of Russian Literature: A Cento. *Atheneum, 1971.*

Fontenot, Chester J., Jr. Writing about Black Literature. *Nebraska Curriculum Development Center, 1976.*

France, Anatole. The Latin Genius. *Translated by Wilfrid S. Jackson. John Lane/The Bodley Head, 1924.*

Freeborn, Richard. The Rise of the Russian Novel: Studies in the Russian Novel from ''Eugene Onegin'' to ''War and Peace.'' *Cambridge at the University Press, 1973.*

Frye, Prosser Hall. Visions & Chimeras. *Jones, 1929.*

Galsworthy, John. Candelabra: Selected Essays and Addresses. *W. Heinemann, Ltd., 1932, Charles Scribner's Sons, 1933.*

Garrod, H. W. The Profession of Poetry and Other Lectures. *Oxford University Press, 1929.*

Gaskell, Elizabeth Cleghorn. Mary Barton and Other Tales. *Chapman and Hall, 1848.*

Gaskell, Elizabeth Cleghorn. The Works of Mrs. Gaskell: Mary Barton and Other Tales, Vol. I. *Edited by A. W. Ward. Smith, Elder & Co., 1906.*

Gathorne-Hardy, G. M. Introduction to Poems, *by Henrik Wergeland. Translated by G. M. Gathorne-Hardy, Jethro Bithell, and I. Grøndahl. Gyldendal Norsk Forlag, 1929, Greenwood Press, Publishers, 1970.*

Gautier, Theophile, & others. Famous French Authors: Biographical Portraits of Distinguished French Writers. *Worthington, 1879.*

Giese, William Frederick. Sainte-Beuve: A Literary Portrait. *Madison, 1931.*

Gifford, Henry. The Hero of His Time: A Theme in Russian Literature. *Edward Arnold & Co., 1950.*

*Gilfillan, George.* A Gallery of Literary Portraits. *J. M. Dent & Co., 1909.*

*Goethe, Johann Wolfgang von.* Goethe's Literary Essays. *Edited by J. E. Spingarn. Harcourt, Brace and Company, 1921, Books for Libraries Press, 1967.*

*Gogol, Nikolai.* Letters of Nikolai Gogol. *Edited by Carl R. Proffer. Translated by Carl R. Proffer with Vera Krivoshein. University of Michigan Press, 1967.*

*Gogol, Nikolai.* Selected Passages from Correspondence with Friends. *Translated by Jesse Zeldin. Vanderbilt University Press, 1969.*

*Gosse, Edmund, and Craigie, W. A., eds.* The Oxford Book of Scandinavian Verse: XVIIth Century—XXth Century. *Oxford University Press, 1925.*

*Gourmont, Remy de.* The Book of Masks. *Translated by Jack Lewis. J. W. Luce and Company, 1921, Books for Libraries Press, 1967.*

*Gourmont, Remy de.* Selected Writings. *Translated and edited by Glenn S. Burne. University of Michigan Press, 1966.*

*Green, F. C.* French Novelists: From the Revolution to Proust. *J. M. Dent & Sons Ltd., 1931.*

*Grieg, J.Y.T.* Thackeray: A Reconsideration. *Oxford University Press, 1950, Archon Books, 1967.*

*Griswold, Rufus Wilmot.* The Prose Writers of America: With A Survey of the Intellectual History, Condition, and Prospects of the Country. *Rev. ed. A. Hart, 1852, Garrett Press, Inc., Publishers, 1969.*

*Hardy, Barbara.* The Exposure of Luxury: Radical Themes in Thackeray. *Peter Owen, 1972.*

*Hart, Francis Russell.* The Scottish Novel: From Smollett to Spark. *Harvard University Press, 1978.*

*Hazlitt, William.* Lectures on the English Comic Writers, with Miscellaneous Essays. *J. M. Dent & Sons, Ltd., 1910.*

*Hearn, Lafcadio.* A History of English Literature in a Series of Lectures, Vol. II. *Edited by R. Tanabe and T. Ochiai. The Hokuseido Press, 1927.*

*Heine, Heinrich.* The Works of Heinrich Heine, Vol. V. *Translated by Charles Godfrey Leland. William Heinemann, 1892.*

*Hemmings, F.W.J.* Balzac: An Interpretation of ''La comédie humaine.'' *Random House, 1967.*

*Henley, William Ernest.* A Book of Verses. *2d ed. Scribner & Welford, 1889.*

*Hewlett, Maurice.* In a Green Shade: A Country Commentary. *G. Bell and Sons, 1920, Books for Libraries Press, 1969.*

*Holliday, Carl.* A History of Southern Literature. *The Neale Publishing Company, 1906, Kennikat Press, 1969.*

*Howells, W. D.* Criticism and Fiction. *Harper & Row, 1891.*

*Hubbell, Jay B.* The South in American Literature: 1607-1900. *Duke University Press, 1954.*

*Hughes, Glyn Tegai.* Romantic German Literature. *Holmes & Meier, 1979, Arnold, 1979.*

*Huneker, James.* Essays by James Huneker. *Charles Scribner's Sons, 1929.*

*Hunt, Herbert J.* Balzac's ''Comédie humaine.'' *The Athlone Press, 1959.*

*Immerwahr, Raymond M.* The Esthetic Intent of Tieck's Fantastic Comedy. *Washington University Studies, 1953.*

*Jack, Ian.* English Literature: 1815-1832. *Oxford University Press, 1963.*

*James, Henry.* Partial Portraits. *Macmillan and Co., 1888.*

*Kaul, A. N.* The Action of English Comedy: Studies in the Encounter of Abstraction and Experience from Shakespeare to Shaw. *Yale University Press, 1970.*

*Kayser, Wolfgang.* The Grotesque in Art and Literature. *Translated by Ulrich Weisstein. Indiana University Press, 1963, McGraw-Hill Book Company, 1966.*

*Keary, C. F.* Norway and the Norwegians. *Charles Scribner's Sons, 1892.*

*Kent, Leonard J.* The Subconscious in Gogol and Dostoevskij, and Its Antecedents. *Mouton, 1969.*

*Kiely, Robert.* Robert Louis Stevenson and the Fiction of Adventure. *Harvard University Press, 1964.*

*Kingsley, Charles.* Charles Kingsley: His Letters and Memories of His Life. *Edited by F. E. Kingsley. Charles Scribner's Sons, 1877.*

*Knight, Charles.* Prefatory Note to Half-Hours with the Best Authors. *Edited by Charles Knight. Porter & Coates, 1848.*

*Koht, Halvdan, and Skard, Sigmund.* The Voice of Norway. *Columbia University Press, 1944.*

*Kronenberger, Louis.* The Polished Surface: Essays in the Literature of Worldliness. *Knopf, 1969.*

*Kropotkin, P.* Russian Literature. *McClure, Phillips & Co., 1905, Benjamin Blom, 1967.*

*Laforgue, Jules.* Selected Writings of Jules Laforgue. *Edited and translated by William Jay Smith. Grove Press, 1956.*

*Lampert, E.* Studies in Rebellion. *Routledge and Kegan Paul, 1957.*

*Le Gallienne, Richard.* Retrospective Reviews: A Literary Log, 1893-1895, Vol. II. *Dodd, Mead, 1896.*

*Legters, Lyman H., ed.* Russia: Essays in History and Literature. *Brill, 1972.*

*Lehmann, A. G.* Sainte-Beuve: A Portrait of the Critic, 1804-1842. *Oxford at the Clarendon Press, 1962.*

*Lermontov, Mikhail.* The Demon and Other Poems. *Translated by Eugene M. Kayden. The Antioch Press, 1965.*

*Lermontov, M. Yu.* A Hero of Our Time. *Translated by Paul Foote. Penguin Books, 1966.*

*Liedke, Herbert R.* Literary Criticism and Romantic Theory in the Work of Achim von Arnim. *Columbia University Press, 1937.*

*Lock, Peter W.* Balzac: "Le père Goriot." *Edward Arnold (Publishers) Ltd., 1967.*

*Loggins, Vernon.* The Negro Author: His Development in America to 1900. *Columbia University Press, 1931, Kennikat Press, Inc., 1964.*

*Loofbourow, John.* Thackeray and the Form of Fiction. *Princeton University Press, 1964.*

*Loshe, Lillie Deming.* The Early American Novel. *Columbia University Press, 1907.*

*Lowell, James Russell.* A Fable for Critics: Or, Better, a Glance at a Few of Our Literary Progenies from the Tub of Diogenes. *Putnam's, 1848.*

*Lubbock, Percy.* The Craft of Fiction. *Cape, 1921, Charles Scribner's Sons, 1955.*

*Lukács, George.* Studies in European Realism: A Sociological Survey of the Writings of Balzac, Stendhal, Zola, Tolstoy, Gorki, and Others. *Translated by Edith Bone. Hillway Publishing Co., 1950.*

*Lukács, Georg.* The Historical Novel. *Translated by Hannah Mitchell and Stanley Mitchell. Merlin Press, 1962.*

*Lussky, Alfred Edwin.* Tieck's Romantic Irony: With Special Emphasis upon the Influence of Cervantes, Sterne, and Goethe. *University of North Carolina Press, 1932.*

*Maguire, Robert A., ed.* Gogol from the Twentieth Century: Eleven Essays. *Princeton University Press, 1974.*

*Maixner, Paul, ed.* Robert Louis Stevenson: The Critical Heritage. *Routledge & Kegan Paul, 1981.*

*Mandel, Oscar.* Introduction to The Land of Upside Down, *by Ludwig Tieck. Translated by Oscar Mandel with Maria Kelsen Feder. Associated University Presses, 1978.*

*Masaryk, Thomas Garrigue.* The Spirit of Russia: Studies in History, Literature and Philosophy, Vol. I. *George Allen & Unwin, 1919, Allen & Unwin, 1967.*

*Mathewson, Rufus W.* The Positive Hero in Russian Literature. *Columbia University Press, 1958, Stanford University Press, 1975.*

*Matlaw, Ralph E., ed.* Belinsky, Chernyshevsky, and Dobrolyubov: Selected Criticism. *Dutton, 1962.*

*McMaster, Juliet.* Thackeray: The Major Novels. *University of Toronto Press, 1971.*

*Mersereau, John, Jr.* Mikhail Lermontov. *Southern Illinois University Press, 1962.*

*Mirsky, D. S.* A History of Russian Literature from Earliest Times to the Death of Dostoyevsky. *Alfred A. Knopf, Inc., 1927.*

*Mirsky, D. S.* A History of Russian Literature from Its Beginnings to 1900. *Edited by Francis J. Whitfield. Vintage Books, 1958.*

*Moore, George.* Conversations in Ebury Street. *William Heinemann, 1924, Chatto & Windus, 1969.*

*Moore, Thomas.* Memoirs of the Life of the Right Honourable Richard Brinsley Sheridan, Vol. I. *3d ed. Longman, Rees, Orme, Brown, and Green, 1825, Scholarly Press, 1968.*

*More, Paul Elmer.* Shelburne Essays, fifth series. *G. P. Putnam's Sons, 1908.*

*Muir, Edwin.* Essays on Literature and Society. *Rev. ed. Harvard University Press, 1965.*

*Nabokov, Vladimir.* Nikolai Gogol. *New Directions, 1961.*

*Nason, Elias.* A Memoir of Mrs. Susanna Rowson, with Elegant and Illustrative Extracts from Her Writings in Prose and Poetry. *Joel Munsell, 1870.*

*O'Connor, Frank.* The Mirror in the Roadway: A Study of the Modern Novel. *Alfred A. Knopf, 1956.*

*Ogilvie, Gavin [pseudonym of J. M. Barrie].* An Edinburgh Eleven: Pencil Portraits from College Life. *Lovell, Coryell & Company, 1888.*

*Olgin, Moissaye J., ed.* A Guide to Russian Literature. *Harcourt Brace Jovanovich, 1920.*

*Oliphant, Mrs.* Sheridan. *Macmillan, 1883, Harper & Brothers, 1887.*

*Oliphant, Mrs.; Linton, Mrs. Lynn; Alexander, Mrs.; & others.* Women Novelists of Queen Victoria's Reign: A Book of Appreciations. *Hurst & Blackett, Limited, 1897.*

*Oliver, E. J.* Balzac, the European. *Sheed and Ward, Inc., 1960.*

*Ossoli, Margaret Fuller.* Memoirs of Margaret Fuller Ossoli. *Rev. ed. Edited by Arthur B. Fuller & others. The Tribune Association, 1869.*

*Parrington, Vernon Louis.* Main Currents in American Thought, an Interpretation of American Literature from the Beginnings to 1920: The Romantic Revolution in America, 1800-1860, Vol. 2. *Harcourt Brace Jovanovich, 1958.*

*Payne, William Morton, ed.* American Literary Criticism. *Longmans, Green, and Co., 1904, Books for Libraries Press, 1968.*

*Petter, Henri.* The Early American Novel. *Ohio State University Press, 1971.*

*Pinero, Arthur Wing.* Robert Louis Stevenson As a Dramatist. *Dramatic Museum of Columbia University, 1914.*

*Poggioli, Renato.* The Poets of Russia: 1890-1930. *Harvard University Press, 1960.*

*Pollard, Arthur.* Mrs. Gaskell: Novelist and Biographer. *Harvard University Press, 1966.*

*Pound, Ezra.* Literary Essays of Ezra Pound. *Edited by T. S. Eliot. New Directions, 1954.*

*Prawer, Siegfried, ed.* The Romantic Period in Germany. *Weidenfeld and Nicolson, 1970.*

*Praz, Mario.* The Hero in Eclipse in Victorian Fiction. *Translated by Angus Davidson. Oxford University Press, 1956.*

*Pritchett, V. S. Introduction to* Novels & Stories, *by Robert Louis Stevenson. Edited by V. S. Pritchett. The Pilot Press, Inc., 1946.*

*Pritchett, V. S.* The Living Novel & Later Appreciations. *Rev. ed. Random House, 1964.*

*Proctor, Thelwall.* Dostoevskij and the Belinskij School of Literary Criticism. *Mouton Publishers, 1969.*

*Proust, Marcel.* Marcel Proust on Art and Literature 1896-1919. *Translated by Sylvia Townsend Warner. Meridian Books, 1958.*

*Pushkin, Alexander.* Pushkin on Literature. *Edited and translated by Tatiana Wolff. Methuen & Co. Ltd., 1971.*

*Quennell, Peter.* The Singular Preference: Portraits & Essays. *Collins, 1952.*

*Quennell, Peter.* Baudelaire and the Symbolists. *Rev. ed. Weidenfeld and Nicolson, 1954.*

*Quiller-Couch, Arthur.* Adventures in Criticism. *Cambridge at the University Press, 1924.*

*Quinn, Arthur Hobson.* American Fiction: An Historical and Critical Survey. *D. Appleton-Century Company, Inc., 1936.*

*Rahv, Philip.* Image and Idea: Fourteen Essays on Literary Themes. *New Directions, 1949.*

*Raleigh, Walter.* Robert Louis Stevenson. *Edward Arnold, 1895.*

*Ramsey, Warren, ed.* Jules Laforgue: Essays on a Poet's Life and Work. *Southern Illinois University Press, 1969.*

*Redding, J. Saunders.* To Make a Poet Black. *University of North Carolina Press, 1939.*

*Richardson, Charles F.* American Literature, 1607-1885: American Poetry and Fiction, Vol. II. *G. P. Putnam's Sons, 1889.*

*Rogers, Samuel.* Balzac & the Novel. *The University of Wisconsin Press, 1953.*

*Rourke, Constance.* The Roots of American Culture and Other Essays. *Edited by Van Wyck Brooks. Harcourt Brace Jovanovich, 1942.*

*Sainte-Beuve, Charles.* Sainte-Beuve: Selected Essays. *Edited by Francis Steegmuller. Translated by Norbert Guterman. Doubleday, 1963.*

*Saintsbury, George.* Essays in English Literature: 1780-1860. *Percival and Co., 1890.*

*Saintsbury, George.* A History of Nineteenth Century Literature: 1780-1895. *Macmillan, 1896.*

*Saintsbury, George. Introductions to* The Oxford Thackeray. *Edited by George Saintsbury. Oxford University Press, 1908.*

*Saintsbury, George.* The Peace of the Augustans: A Survey of Eighteenth Century Literature As a Place of Rest and Refreshment. *G. Bell and Sons, Ltd., 1916.*

*Saintsbury, George.* A History of the French Novel (to the Close of the 19th Century): From 1800 to 1900, Vol. II. *Macmillan and Co., Limited, 1917.*

*Saintsbury, George.* A Consideration of Thackeray. *Oxford University Press, 1931.*

*Seduro, Vladimir.* Dostoyevski in Russian Literary Criticism: 1846-1956. *Columbia University Press, 1957.*

*Setchkarev, Vsevolod.* Gogol: His Life and Works. *Translated by Robert Kramer. New York University Press, 1965.*

*Shaw, Bernard.* Plays & Players: Essays on the Theatre. *Edited by A. C. Ward. Oxford University Press, 1952.*

*Sheridan, Richard Brinsley.* The Rivals. *3d ed. John Wilkie, 1776.*

*Sheridan, Richard Brinsley.* The Major Dramas of Richard Brinsley Sheridan. *Edited by George Henry Nettleton. Ginn and Company, 1906.*

*Sheridan, Richard Brinsley.* The Rivals. *Edited by Alan S. Downer. Appleton-Century-Crofts, 1953.*

*Sichel, Walter.* Sheridan, Vol. I. *Houghton Mifflin Company, 1909.*

*Silz, Walter*. Realism and Reality: Studies in the German Novelle of Poetic Realism. *University of North Carolina Press, 1954.*

*Simmons, Ernest J*. Introduction to Russian Realism. *Indiana University Press, 1965.*

*Slonim, Marc*. The Epic of Russian Literature: From Its Origins through Tolstoy. *Oxford University Press, 1950.*

*Snider, Rose*. Satire in the Comedies of Congreve, Sheridan, Wilde, and Coward. *University of Maine Press, 1937, Phaeton Press, 1972.*

*Stacy, R. H*. Russian Literary Criticism: A Short History. *Syracuse University Press, 1974.*

*Stevenson, Robert Louis*. Memories and Portraits. *Charles Scribner's Sons, 1910.*

*Swinnerton, Frank*. R. L. Stevenson: A Critical Study. *Mitchell Kennerley, 1915.*

*Symons, Arthur*. Studies in Prose and Verse. *Dutton, 1904.*

*Symons, Arthur*. The Symbolist Movement in Literature. *Rev. ed. Dutton, 1908.*

*Taine, H. A*. History of the English Literature, Vol. IV, Part I. *Translated by H. Van Laun. Chatto & Windus, 1880.*

*Taine, Hippolyte Adolphe*. Balzac: A Critical Study. *Funk & Wagnalls Company, 1906, Haskell House Publishers Ltd., 1973.*

*Terras, Victor*. Belinskij and Russian Literary Criticism: The Heritage of Organic Aesthetics. *The University of Wisconsin Press, 1974.*

*Thibaudet, Albert*. French Literature from 1795 to Our Era. *Translated by Charles Lam Markmann. Stock, 1936, Funk & Wagnalls, 1968.*

*Tillotson, Geoffrey, and Hawes, Donald, eds*. Thackeray: The Critical Heritage. *Routledge & Kegan Paul, 1968.*

*Tillotson, Kathleen*. Novels of the Eighteen-Forties. *Oxford University Press, 1954.*

*Trainer, James*. Ludwig Tieck: From Gothic to Romantic. *Mouton & Co., 1964.*

*Trollope, Anthony*. Thackeray. *Macmillan and Co., Limited, 1906, Gale Research Company, 1968.*

*Trotsky, Leon*. Literature and Revolution. *Translated by Rose Strunsky. International, 1925.*

*Tuell, Anne Kimball*. A Victorian at Bay. *Marshall Jones Company, Inc., 1932.*

*Turgenev, Ivan*. Literary Reminiscences and Autobiographical Fragments. *Translated by David Magarshack. Farrar, Straus and Cudahy, Inc., 1958, Faber and Faber, 1959.*

*Turnell, Martin*. The Novel in France: Mme de LaFayette, Laclos, Constant, Stendhal, Balzac, Flaubert, Proust. *Hamish Hamilton, 1950.*

*Tymms, Ralph*. German Romantic Literature. *Methuen, 1955.*

*Urbanski, Marie Mitchell Olesen*. Margaret Fuller's ''Woman in the Nineteenth Century'': A Literary Study of Form and Content, of Sources and Influence. *Greenwood Press, 1980.*

*Van Doren, Carl*. The American Novel. *Macmillan, 1921.*

*Wagner, Jean*. Black Poets of the United States: From Paul Laurence Dunbar to Langston Hughes. *Translated by Kenneth Douglas. University of Illinois Press, 1973.*

*Watts, Emily Stipes*. The Poetry of American Women from 1632 to 1945. *University of Texas Press, 1977.*

*Wegelin, Oscar*. Jupiter Hammon, American Negro Poet: Selections from His Writings and a Bibliography. *C. F. Heartman, 1915, Books for Libraries Press, 1969.*

*Weil, Dorothy*. In Defense of Women: Susanna Rowson (1792-1824). *The Pennsylvania State University Press, 1976.*

*Wellek, René*. Continuity and Change in Russian and Soviet Thought. *Edited by Ernest J. Simmons. Harvard University Press, 1955.*

*Wellek, René*. A History of Modern Criticism, 1750-1950: The Romantic Age, Vol. 2. *Yale University Press, 1955.*

*Wellek, René.* A History of Modern Criticism, 1750-1950: The Age of Transition, Vol. 3. *Yale University Press, 1965.*

*Wergeland, Agnes Mathilde.* Leaders in Norway and Other Essays. *Edited by Katharine Merrill. George Banta Publishing Company, 1916, Books for Libraries Press, 1966.*

*Wergeland, Henrik.* Poems. *Translated by G. M. Gathorne-Hardy, Jethro Bithell, and I. Grøndahl. Gyldendal Norsk Forlag, 1929, Greenwood Press, Publishers, 1970.*

*Wernaer, Robert M.* Romanticism and the Romantic School in Germany. *Haskell House, 1966.*

*Whibley, Charles.* William Makepeace Thackeray. *William Blackwood and Sons, 1903.*

*Whittier, John Greenleaf.* Whittier on Writers and Writing: The Uncollected Critical Writings of John Greenleaf Whittier. *Edited by Edwin Harrison Cady and Harry Hayden Clark. Syracuse University Press, 1950.*

*Williams, Kenny J.* They Also Spoke: An Essay on Negro Literature in America, 1787-1930. *Townsend Press, 1970.*

*Wilson, Edmund.* Axel's Castle: A Study in the Imaginative Literature of 1870-1930. *Charles Scribner's Sons, 1931.*

*Wilson, Edmund.* Classics and Commercials: A Literary Chronicle of the Forties. *Farrar, Straus and Giroux, 1950.*

*Wilson, Edmund.* A Window on Russia: For the Use of Foreign Readers. *Farrar, Straus and Giroux, 1972.*

*Winchester, C. T.* A Group of English Essayists of the Early Nineteenth Century. *The Macmillan Company, 1910, Books for Libraries Press, 1967.*

*Winsatt, W. K., Jr., ed.* English Stage Comedy. *Columbia University Press, 1955.*

*Wise, Thomas James; Oxon, M. A.; and Symington, John Alexander, eds.* The Brontë's: Their Lives, Friendships, and Correspondence, 1844-1849, Vol. II. *Basil Blackwell, 1932.*

*Woolf, Leonard.* Essays on Literature, History, Politics, Etc. *The Hogarth Press, 1927.*

*Wright, Edgar.* Mrs. Gaskell: The Basis for Reassessment. *Oxford University Press, 1965.*

*Zeydel, Edwin H.* Ludwig Tieck and England: A Study in the Literary Relations of Germany and England During the Early Nineteenth Century. *Princeton University Press, 1931.*

*Zola, Émile.* The Experimental Novel and Other Essays. *Translated by Belle M. Sherman. Cassell, 1893.*

*Zweig, Stefan.* Master Builders: A Typology of the Spirit. *Translated by Eden Paul and Cedar Paul. Viking Penguin Inc., 1939.*

ISBN 0-8103-5805-0

90000>

9 780810 358058